Fodor's

SOUTH AFRICA

4th Edition

Where to Stay and Eat
for All Budgets

Must-See Sights
and Local Secrets

Ratings You Can Trust

Fodor's Travel Publications   New York, Toronto, London, Sydney, Auckland
www.fodors.com

FODOR'S SOUTH AFRICA

Editors: Alexis C. Kelly (lead editor), Deborah Kaufman

Editorial Production: Linda Schmidt

Editorial Contributors: Brian Berkman, Sanja Cloete-Jones, Karena du Plessis, Debra A. Klein, Jennifer Stern, Kate Turkington, Tara Turkington

Maps & Illustrations: David Lindroth, *cartographer*; Bob Blake and Rebecca Baer, *map editors*

Design: Fabrizio LaRocca, *creative director*; Guido Caroti, Siobhan O'Hare, *art directors*; Melanie Marin, *senior picture editor;* Moon Sun Kim, *cover designer*

Cover Photo (Kokerboom trees): Russell Burden/Index Stock Imagery

Production/Manufacturing: Angela L. McLean

COPYRIGHT

Copyright © by Fodor's Travel, a division of Random House, Inc.

Fodor's is a registered trademark of Random House, Inc.

All rights reserved. Published in the United States by Fodor's Travel, a division of Random House, Inc., and simultaneously in Canada by Random House of Canada, Limited, Toronto. Distributed by Random House, Inc., New York.

No maps, illustrations, or other portions of this book may be reproduced in any form without written permission from the publisher.

Fourth Edition

ISBN 978–1–4000–1799–7

ISSN 1091–4757

SPECIAL SALES

This book is available at special discounts for bulk purchases for sales promotions or premiums. Special editions, including personalized covers, excerpts of existing books, and corporate imprints, can be created in large quantities for special needs. For more information, write to Special Markets/Premium Sales, 1745 Broadway, MD 6-2, New York, New York 10019, or e-mail specialmarkets@randomhouse.com.

AN IMPORTANT TIP & AN INVITATION

Although all prices, opening times, and other details in this book are based on information supplied to us at press time, changes occur all the time in the travel world, and Fodor's cannot accept responsibility for facts that become outdated or for inadvertent errors or omissions. So **always confirm information when it matters,** especially if you're making a detour to visit a specific place. Your experiences—positive and negative— matter to us. If we have missed or misstated something, **please write to us.** We follow up on all suggestions. Contact the South Africa editor at editors@fodors.com or c/o Fodor's at 1745 Broadway, New York, NY 10019.

PRINTED IN THE UNITED STATES OF AMERICA

10 9 8 7 6 5 4 3 2

Be a Fodor's Correspondent

Your opinion matters. It matters to us. It matters to your fellow Fodor's travelers, too. And we'd like to hear it. In fact, we need to hear it.

When you share your experiences and opinions, you become an active member of the Fodor's community. That means we'll not only use your feedback to make our books better, but we'll publish your names and comments whenever possible. Throughout our guides, look for "Word of Mouth," excerpts of your unvarnished feedback.

Here's how you can help improve Fodor's for all of us.

Tell us when we're right. We rely on local writers to give you an insider's perspective. But our writers and staff editors—who are the best in the business—depend on you. Your positive feedback is a vote to renew our recommendations for the next edition.

Tell us when we're wrong. We're proud that we update most of our guides every year. But we're not perfect. Things change. Hotels cut services. Museums change hours. Charming cafés lose charm. If our writer didn't quite capture the essence of a place, tell us how you'd do it differently. If any of our descriptions are inaccurate or inadequate, we'll incorporate your changes in the next edition and will correct factual errors at fodors.com immediately.

Tell us what to include. You probably have had fantastic travel experiences that aren't yet in Fodor's. Why not share them with a community of like-minded travelers? Maybe you chanced upon a beach or bistro or B&B that you don't want to keep to yourself. Tell us why we should include it. And share your discoveries and experiences with everyone directly at fodors.com. Your input may lead us to add a new listing or highlight a place we cover with a "Highly Recommended" star or with our highest rating, "Fodor's Choice."

Give us your opinion instantly at our feedback center at www.fodors.com/feedback. You may also e-mail editors@fodors.com with the subject line "South Africa Editor." Or send your nominations, comments, and complaints by mail to South Africa Editor, Fodor's, 1745 Broadway, New York, NY 10019.

You and travelers like you are the heart of the Fodor's community. Make our community richer by sharing your experiences. Be a Fodor's correspondent.

Happy traveling!

Tim Jarrell, Publisher

CONTENTS

MAPS

CLOSE UPS

CONTENTS

ABOUT
THIS BOOK

Our Ratings

Sometimes you find terrific travel experiences and sometimes they just find you. But usually it's up to you to select the right combination of experiences. That's where our ratings come in.

As travelers we've all discovered a place so wonderful that its worthiness is obvious. And sometimes that place is so experiential that superlatives don't do it justice: you just have to be there to know. These sights, properties, and experiences get our highest rating, **Fodor's Choice,** indicated by orange stars throughout this book.

Black stars highlight sights and properties we deem **Highly Recommended,** places that our writers, editors, and readers praise again and again for consistency and excellence.

By default, there's another category: any place we include in this book is by definition worth your time, unless we say otherwise. And we will.

Disagree with any of our choices? Care to nominate a place or suggest that we rate one more highly? Visit our feedback center at www.fodors.com/feedback.

Budget Well

Hotel and restaurant price categories from ¢ to $$$$ are defined in the opening pages of each chapter. For attractions, we always give standard adult admission fees; reductions are usually available for children, students, and senior citizens. Want to pay with plastic? **AE, DC, MC, V** following restaurant and hotel listings indicate if American Express, Diner's Club, MasterCard, and Visa are accepted.

Restaurants

Unless we state otherwise, restaurants are open for lunch and dinner daily. We mention dress only when there's a specific requirement and reservations only when they're essential or not accepted—it's always best to book ahead.

Hotels

Hotels have private bath, phone, TV, and air-conditioning and operate on the European Plan (a.k.a. EP, meaning without meals), unless we specify that they use the Continental Plan (CP, with a Continental breakfast), Breakfast Plan (BP, with a full breakfast), or Modified American Plan (MAP, with breakfast and dinner), or are all-inclusive (AI, including all meals and most activities). We always

list facilities but not whether you'll be charged an extra fee to use them, so when pricing accommodations, find out what's included.

Many Listings	
★	Fodor's Choice
★	Highly recommended
✉	Physical address
♦	Directions
⌂	Mailing address
☎	Telephone
🖷	Fax
⊕	On the Web
✍	E-mail
🖾	Admission fee
☉	Open/closed times
Ⓜ	Metro stations
🖃	Credit cards
Hotels & Restaurants	
🏠	Hotel
⇖	Number of rooms
☖	Facilities
🍴	Meal plans
✕	Restaurant
⬠	Reservations
↘	Smoking
🍸	BYOB
✕🏠	Hotel with restaurant that warrants a visit
Outdoors	
🏌	Golf
⚑	Camping
Other	
♨	Family-friendly
⇨	See also
✉	Branch address
☞	Take note

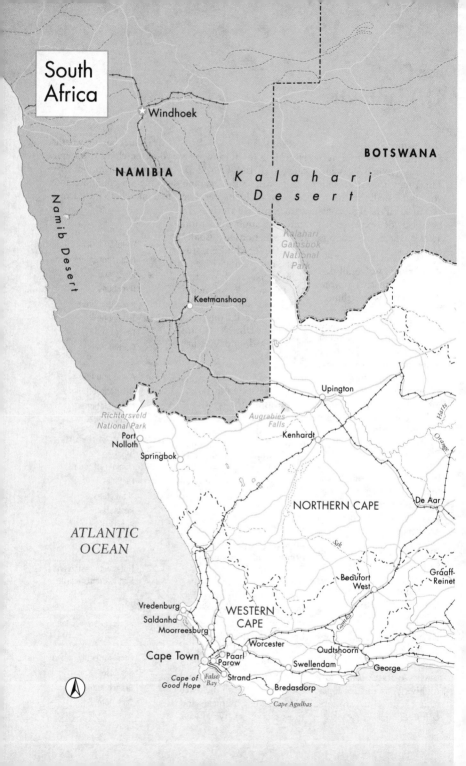

South Africa

Windhoek

NAMIBIA

BOTSWANA

Kalahari Desert

Namib Desert

Kalahari
Gemsbok
National
Park

Keetmanshoop

Upington

Harts

Richtersveld
National Park

Augrabies
Falls

Kenhardt

Orange

Port
Nolloth

Springbok

NORTHERN CAPE

De Aar

ATLANTIC
OCEAN

Sak

Beaufort
West

Graaff-
Reinet

Vredenburg

Saldanha

Moorreesburg

WESTERN
CAPE

Gamka

Worcester

Oudtshoorn

Cape Town

Paarl
Parow

Swellendam

George

Cape of
Good Hope

False
Bay

Strand

Bredasdorp

Cape Agulhas

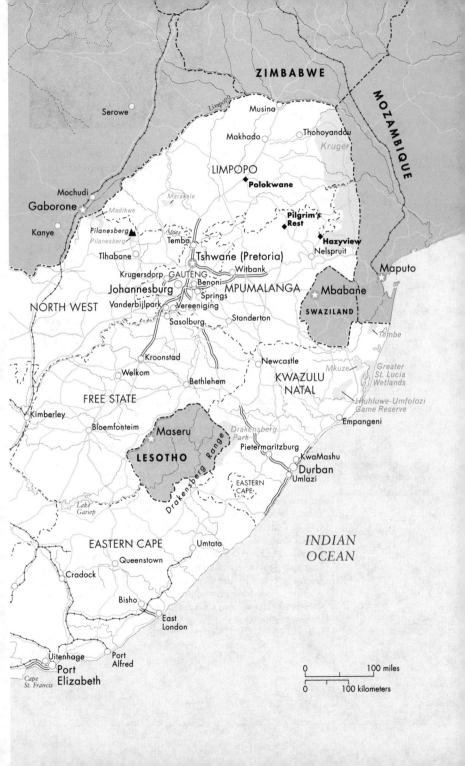

WHAT'S WHERE

CAPE TOWN & THE PENINSULA 	Capetonians tend to pity those who don't have the good fortune to live in their Eden. Their attitude is understandable—Cape Town is indeed one of the world's fairest cities. Backed by Table Mountain, the city anchors a stunning coastline: mountains cascading into the sea, miles of beaches, and inland enclaves where giant oaks shade 17th-century wineries. Despite cutting-edge dining and high-tech hotels, the city's charm is revealed in the many 18th-century buildings and the Cape Malay architecture that highlight its past as the sea link between Europe and the East.
WINELANDS & BEACHES: THE WESTERN CAPE 	The jewel of the province might be the Cape Winelands, where jagged mountains are the backdrop for centuries-old Cape Dutch estates that produce some of the world's finest wines. Stellenbosch, Paarl, and Franschoek make popular day trips from Cape Town. Overnighters continue down to the coast to the Overberg region's tranquil farms and popular beach resorts. Hermanus, once a tiny fishing village, is now one of the world's best land-based whale-watching sites. It's a short drive from Cape Agulhas, the southernmost tip of Africa. The long, lonely coastline's beaches and towering dunes framed by sheer, rocky mountains create the West Coast's feeling of desolation in places. Inland, the Cederberg Mountains offer fantastic scenery and exercise.
THE GARDEN ROUTE & THE LITTLE KAROO 	The aptly named Garden Route stretches 208 km (130 mi) through some of South Africa's most inspiring scenery: forest-cloaked mountains, myriad rivers and streams, and Indian Ocean beaches backed by thick, indigenous bush. On the way to Tsitsikamma National Park, stop into some of South Africa's most popular resorts, including Plettenberg Bay, and Knysna, a charming town set behind dramatic sandstone cliffs that guard an oyster-rich lagoon. The Little Karoo, separated from the coast by the Outeniqua Mountains, is a semiarid region famous for its ostrich farms, turn-of-the-20th-century "feather palaces," and Cango Caves, one of the world's most impressive networks of underground caverns.

 	The Eastern Cape is one of South Africa's most populated and diverse provinces, home to seaside family getaway cities, like Port Elizabeth and East London, as well as hundreds of bird species and the nation's premiere elephant sanctuary, Addo Elephant National Park. The Wild Coast's long deserted beaches, the Great Karoo's vast open spaces, and looming mountain wildernesses once formed the backdrop to the country's fiercest conflicts, and contain some of the oldest fossils in the world. The Eastern Cape probably has the most interesting cultural heritage of any South African province, with a long history of resistance to colonialism and apartheid. It was here that the British colonialists, the Dutch settlers, and the Xhosa tribespeople all clashed and then compromised to create a tapestry of heritages in this historically rich region.
DURBAN & KWAZULU-NATAL 	Steamy heat, the heady aroma of spices, and a polyglot of English, Hindi, and Zulu give the bustling port city of Durban a tropical feel. Some of the country's most popular swimming beaches extend north and south of the city; inland you can tour the battlefields where Boer, Briton, and Zulu struggled for control of the country. The Drakensberg is a breathtaking sanctuary of soaring beauty, crisp air, and some of the country's best hiking. In the far north Hluhluwe-Umfolozi and several private reserves have wildlife rivaling that of Kruger Park. Bird-watchers will want to head north to spot some of the 500 species that pass through the salt- and freshwater marshes, coral reefs, and coastal plains of the Greater St. Lucia Wetland Park, South Africa's first natural World Heritage Site.
JOHANNESBURG & ENVIRONS 	The corridor between Johannesburg and Pretoria, now called Tshwane, contains the satellite suburbs of Sandton, Rosebank, and the township Soweto. Downtown's skyscrapers are largely empty, although a new energy is revitalizing some quarters of the city, with a Museum of Apartheid and the refurbished Market Theater complex. Johannesburg, nicknamed Egoli, "place of gold," is rich in ancient history. Nearby Sterkfontein is home to the Cradle of Humankind archaeological site and some of the world's oldest human fossils. More recent history, such as the struggle for black equality, played out in the black townships ringing the city. A tour of Soweto and the city center will give you a feel for the new South Africa.

WHAT'S WHERE

MPUMALANGA & KRUGER NATIONAL PARK

Classic Africa—the Africa of heat, thorn trees, and big game—sprawls through the scrub and plains in Mpumalanga and the Limpopo Province on the Mozambique border. The great allure here is game-viewing, either in famed Kruger National Park or in an exclusive private reserve. But the area has much more to offer than animals. The Drakensberg (Afrikaans for "Dragon Mountains") divides the subtropical lowveld from the high interior plateau. Some of the country's most luxurious lodges are tucked away in these mountains of mists, forests, waterfalls.

VICTORIA FALLS

Its Makololo name, Mosi-oa-Tunya (literally, "the Smoke that Thunders") doesn't undersell this amazing natural wonder—the world's largest curtain of water (but not the tallest falls). Wending its way through the heart of several African countries, the Zambezi River gains power and strength on its last miles, joining Botswana's Chobe River to form the vast plunge between Zambia and Zimbabwe. Two towns share its flow of visitors: Livingstone (named for the 19th-century explorer), in Zambia, and the even more aptly named Victoria Falls, in Zimbabwe. The former has recently transformed itself into an adrenaline junkie's paradise, with heart-thumping micro-light flights, abseiling, bungee jumping, and white-water rafting activities in, above, and around the famous gorge's churning flow.

BOTSWANA & NAMIBIA'S BEST SAFARI DESTINATIONS

Botswana's pristine Okavango Delta's trademark game numbers and variety come at a price. The trade-off is unsurpassed boutique wildlife viewing, teeming herds, and silent nights. Chobe National Park is best known for elephant herds and more budget-friendly digs, and the Central Kalahari Game Reserve is the second-largest conservation area in the world. The spectacular Moremi Wildlife Reserve lies along the northern section of the Delta, and the Liyanti Reserve, known for its varied habitats, borders Chobe's western borders.

Few countries have landscapes as spectacular as Namibia's. The 12.1 million-acre Namib Naukluft National Park is home to the highest sand dunes in the world, as well as eerie desertscapes and canyons filled with plants. The numerous water holes at Etosha National Park draw lions, rhinos, antelope, zebras, and wildebeests. And the starkly beautiful, aptly named Skeleton Coast has rugged cliffs, treacherous winds and currents, crashing seas, and the ghosts of shipwrecks in the shifting sands.

WHEN TO GO

South Africa's seasons are opposite to those in the northern hemisphere, but temperatures rarely reach North American lows and it rarely snows.

Peak tourist season is from November through March, when hotel prices rise dramatically and space fills up. The situation is worse during South Africa's summer vacation, December 1–January 15, and during major school holidays: the two weeks surrounding Easter and a month in July or August.

Although the most popular time to visit Cape Town is November through January, the best weather is between February and March; even the shoulder months of October and April can be a great time to escape crowds. Cape winters (May–August) are unpredictable. This "secret season" finds cold, windy, rainy days interspersed with glorious sun. Stay for a week or more, and you're bound to have at least a few gorgeous days (with bargain rates to boot).

Hot summer months are the worst for game-viewing. With abundant water, animals have no reason to congregate at watering holes, and new long grasses make it difficult to see anything. Game-viewing improves once the rains end in late March or April. By October, there is usually very little standing water or vegetation cover, making game-viewing excellent, although the humid weather can be a bit uncomfortable.

Johannesburg enjoys hot sunny summers broken by afternoon thunderstorms. Winter days are generally mild and sunny, but nights can be decidedly frosty. Rain, sleet, and even a little snow are possible.

Climate

The following are average daily maximum and minimum temperatures for some major cities in southern Africa.

Forecasts Weather Channel (⊕ www.weather.com) **South African Weather Service** (☎ 082/233-9000 ⊕ www.weathersa.co.za)

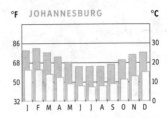

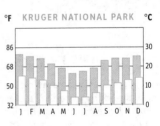

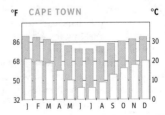

QUINTESSENTIAL SOUTH AFRICA

The Old Man (or Young Woman) and the Sea

The Southern Coast is a great place to explore water-bound wildlife. You can swim with the penguins at Boulders Beach on the Cape Peninsula or cage dive alongside great white sharks if you're feeling brave. Landlubbers can still go whale-watching. From July to November the coast is alive with the annual procession of whales, first the Southern Right whales and later the humpbacks, which frolic and remain with their calves until December or early January. From the cliff-top walkways of Hermanus look straight down on these graceful behemoths, or get a closer view from a boat in Plettenberg Bay. Bottlenose dolphins live in these waters all year.

Winelands

Spend lazy afternoons watching the sun pull shadows across peaks that look like they belong on wine labels, and nights sampling savory African, French, or Indian fare. Or slip away to a spa ringed by vineyards growing some of the world's tastiest whites and varietals. Go for a half-day of cheese tasting to clear your palate, or a bike ride to clear your head. Classic Cape Dutch buildings provide the backdrop for historical walking tours in South Africa's oldest university town, Stellenbosch, or make afternoons quaffing crisp sauvignon blanc at outdoor cafés seem educational. Some of the country's plushest inns and spectacular, award-winning vineyards make this a very easy place to relax.

Bush Dinners

The drums beat, the hyenas trill, and the flames flicker as you enter the dirt-floored boma, a traditional African space open to the night skies, which is an essential safari treat. Urbanites can play it safe in restaurants like Johannesburg's Moyo, which brings the outdoors in with dramatic entertainment. Traditionalists should sign up ahead of time for one of the organized Kruger Park evenings, where only a mere wall of thatch separates you from the lions and elephants you feared hours earlier in broad daylight.

Exploring Apartheid

The legacy of apartheid is hard to avoid in South Africa, but learning a bit about the history will help you comprehend what you see. A good place to start is Cape Town's Robben Island, the prison colony where Nelson Mandela and other political prisoners lived a harsh existence. Visitors can speak with former inmates about their time here. Back on shore, the District Six Museum demonstrates apartheid's effects on one local Cape Town community. In Johannesburg, visit the Apartheid Museum, where visitors are given a pass card—a replica of the document all black South Africans were required to carry during apartheid—that is used for entry to the museum whose multimedia exhibits will haunt you long after you've left. Also worth visiting are the Mandela Family Museum, the Hector Pieterson Memorial and Museum, and the Regina Mundi Church in Soweto.

IF YOU LIKE

Beaches

South Africa's coastline stretches from tiny towns to desolate windswept acres, and most beach lovers can find exactly what they're after, be it a private cove or an endless stretch of sand. Surfers can hang ten on some of the most challenging waves in the world, while great white sharks patrol the waters, along with seasonal whales and playful penguins.

Atlantic beaches are rough and cold, but dramatic, while the False Bay beaches gently lap warm water near tide pools and small seafront cafés. Some of the best combine nature and activities, but don't be afraid to pull the car over and discover your own sliver of sand.

Boulders Beach, Simon's Town. The sparkling coves ringed by dramatic boulders are also home to a colony of African penguins. Share your spot in the sand with these curious creatures, but a warning: they can be quite loud.

Camps Bay. A broad Atlantic beach backed by looming Table Mountain, and a street full of umbrella-shaded cafés. The perfect place to watch a sunset, or to stroll.

Diaz Beach, Cape Point. Many consider this secluded spot, reachable only on foot via a short trail, the Cape's most beautiful beach. Unfortunately the currents are pretty strong and swimming is not advised.

St. James. Just south of Kalk Bay's shops, St. James's colorful changing cabanas are photo icons. The gentle surf and tidal pool on False Bay are perfect for kids.

Game-Viewing

Kruger Park may well be the granddaddy of game viewing in South Africa, but smaller reserves attract visitors seeking boutique accommodation, a special sense of place, or a particular type of game. And, if you're game to explore outside South Africa, Botswana and Namibia offer world-class game viewing, as well as luxury accommodations.

Eagles Cragg, Shamwari Game Reserve. Conservation-minded Shamwari's best accommodation is this sleek lodge.

Ecca Lodge, Kwandwe Private Game Reserve. Clean, modern lines take the place of animal skins and trophies in this game reserve in the Karoo scrub near Grahamstown.

Mala Mala, Mpumalanga. Retaining that genuine bushveld feel of bygone days, Mala Mala, which adjoins Kruger National Park, is the largest privately owned Big Five game area in South Africa. The animal viewing is unbeatable.

Duba Plains, Okavango Delta, Botswana. This small, intimate camp puts you in the middle of wall-to-wall game in the heart of the delta.

Serra Cafema, Namibia. Along the Skeleton Coast near the border with Angola, this remote camp amid the dunes feels like an oasis.

Shopping & Strolling

From exotic African crafts to trendy modern designs, South Africa's cities and suburbs offer a variety of ways to stalk souvenirs and handicrafts.

Long Street, Cape Town. Shop for curios and stop in for tapas beneath the intricate latticework of the Victorians that line this popular street. Side streets are chock-full of cafés and shops selling Africana and modern housewares.

Melville, Johannesburg. It's just one long block, but the cute shops and cafés of 7th Street from 1st to 5th avenues make Melville a must-do for a warm South African afternoon. Stop for wine or coffee anywhere, while drinking in local crafts and high-end designers in this youthful Johannesburg neighborhood.

Kalk Bay, Cape Peninsula. A seaside fishing village with just enough local crafts and cafés set on a strip of colorful storefronts across from a working harbor. It makes a great lunch stop on the drive down to Cape Point.

Rosebank, Johannesburg. Home to shopping malls, restaurants, hotels, art galleries, designer shops, and craft markets, this area is the ultimate destination for well-to-do locals and tourists alike. Make sure to visit the Rosebank Rooftop market, open every Sunday, and the African Craft Market.

Playing Like a Local

South Africa's rich cultural offerings run from the rhythms of Soweto to the jazz riffs of Cape Town's clubs. Drama and dance combine to form the rich cultural mosaic of South Africa, where native beats mingle with European traditions. Step out like a local and soak it in.

Jazzart Dance Theatre, Cape Town. The country's oldest modern dance company has a range of programs, and teaches in disadvantaged communities.

Jazz Tours, Cape Town. Join like-eared aficionados for a tour that will show you the roots of jazz and expose you to some local ear candy.

Kirtsenbosch National Botanical Gardens, Cape Town. The 1,304 acres feature indigenous southern African plants that captivate even the locals. Come for lawn picnics in the shadow of Table Mountain and stay to listen to Winter Concert Series.

Market Theatre, Johannesburg. One of the country's renowned venues showcasing new works, with a rich legacy. During the era of apartheid it was one of South Africa's only venues where all races could watch together.

ON THE CALENDAR

LATE SUMMER January	The multiday **Cape Minstrel Carnival** ushers in the New Year, as thousands of South Africans dressed in bright costumes take to the streets of Cape Town to sing and dance, accompanied by marching bands.
FALL February	The **Cape Town Pride Festival** is one of Africa's largest gay events and features floats and elaborate costumes. **South Africa's FNB Dance Umbrella** is a monthlong series of international dance at several Johannesburg venues.
March	The **Argus Cycle Tour,** in Cape Town, is the largest individually timed race in the world, with about 40,000 competitors riding a scenic 108-km (67-mi) course. Original South African music, comedy, and public art come together for the three-week-long **Cape Town Festival** spreading across The Company Gardens and featuring performances on the African Summer Stage. The **Cape Town International Jazz Festival** draws thousands to Cape Town for three days.
March or April	The **Klein Karoo Nasionale Kunstefees,** in Oudtshoorn, is one of the most popular performing- and visual-arts events of the season, but much of it may go over your head if you don't speak Afrikaans. The annual **Nederburg Auction** is *the* event of the wine community, when South Africa's finest old and new wines go under the hammer. The **Two Oceans Marathon** draws 8,000 runners for a grueling 56-km (35-mi) course that circumnavigates part of the Cape Peninsula.
April	**Splashy Fen,** in KwaZulu-Natal, is one of the most popular music festivals in South Africa. Originally concentrating on folk music, it's rapidly becoming more contemporary. Try your endurance on the new 160-km (100-mi) and 80-km (50-mi) **Addo Elephant Trail Run,** an extreme marathon that combines skills, will, and the ability to overcome the sheer terror of bumping into wildlife as you race through the national park.
WINTER May	The **MIAGI Festival,** formerly the International Classical Music Festival, runs in several major cities, with performances over the course of several days in May. The **Pink Loerie Festival,** in the pretty coastal town of Knysna, is a celebration of gay pride and culture.
June	When winter storms hit Cape Town, surfers from all around the world gather to compete at Dungeons in **Big Wave Afri-**

	ca. Freezing water and 20-foot-plus bone-crunching waves make this a really tough one.
June to July	The **National Arts Festival** has been a Grahamstown tradition since the 1970s, and features more than 1,500 performances of every conceivable visual- and performing-art form, from many cultures and languages over the course of the 10-day event. The late-June through early-July **Durban International Film Festival** is South Africa's longest-running festival of its kind; it started in 1979. Screenings include films from South Africa and from international directors. Every June and July, millions of silvery sardines make the journey up the southern cape for the warm waters of the Wild Coast and the KZN's South Coast. Called the annual **Sardine Run,** it has been described as one of the greatest marine spectacles on earth.
July	Quickly becoming an annual tradition, the **Stellenbosch International Chamber Music Festival** takes place on the grounds South Africa's oldest university in the country's second-oldest town, both named Stellenbosch. The **Knysna Oyster Festival** has road races, mountain-bike races, cookouts, and—of course—oysters, oysters, and oysters.
SPRING August	The **Imana Wild Coast Challenge**, a mountain-bike ride of about 199 km (124 mi), traverses some of the most spectacular scenery in South Africa; it skirts the beaches and cliffs of the Wild Coast and occasionally heads inland. In early August the hills around Tshwane ring with music, as some of South Africa's best bands, and best partygoers, assemble for the annual **Oppikoppi Music Festival.**
August to October	Wind down the weekend in Paarl at the **Nederburg Concert Series,** sipping wine and listening to Sunday classical concerts at the Nederburg Wine Estate.
September	It's really just a big party with a bit of hectic consumerism with a whale motif, but the **Hermanus Whale Festival** is fun nevertheless. The **Cape Town International Comedy Festival** provides three weeks of laughs from a roster of up-and-coming comedians in several unique venues. Johannesburg's month-long **Arts Alive Festival** turns ordinary places such as the V&A Waterfront into performance spaces for world-class perform-

	ers and exciting culturally relevant events, like best-dressed "Swenka" contests and raucous traditional dances.
October	Look out for the purple **jacaranda blossoms** that blanket South Africa's capital city, Tshwane, giving it its nickname "Jacaranda City."
	The **Good Food and Wine Festival**, in Gauteng, is a celebration of all the good things in life.
SUMMER November	The **94.7 Challenge**, named after a local radio station, is Johannesburg's biggest cycling race. It's—surprise— 94.7 km (just under 60 mi), which is not that far, but it's pretty hilly.
	The **Nedbank Golf Challenge,** held at Sun City, is one of the richest in the world, with a purse worth more than $4 million.
	November is film month in Cape Town, with a whole lot of film festivals all orbiting around the **Cape Town World Cinema Festival.**
Mid-November to Mid-March	The **Spier Arts Summer Festival** welcomes internationally known musicians to its outdoor festival stage on the winery's estate in Stellenbosch.
	Table Mountain is the backdrop for romantic summer nights at the **Kirstenbosch Summer Concert Series** beneath the stars.
	Turtle-Spotting Season in St. Lucia, KwaZulu-Natal is the time to find Volkswagon-sized leatherbacks hauling themselves ashore to lay eggs.
December to January	December's **Wavescapes Film Festival** starts off with a free giant screening on Clifton's Fourth Beach, then rides a wave of surf-themed local and international flicks.
	The Swazi king blesses the harvest during the **Ncwala, or First Fruits Ceremony,** common to many African Nguni tribes in Swaziland and KwaZulu-Natal.

WORLD CUP 411

Held since 1958, the FIFA World Cup is truly a worldwide event; more than 40 billion fans in more than 200 countries tuned in for the 2006 World Cup in Germany. The 2010 World Cup, June 11 through July 11, expects to have an even larger audience, and South Africa is hard at work getting the country ready for its moment to shine. Throughout the country, airports are getting makeovers, neighborhoods are being revamped, and municipalities are scrambling to perfect the 10 venues that will host the 64 matches and team practices. Some stadiums are being built from scratch, while others are being remodeled and expanded.

Around 3 million tickets, which should go on sale in 2008, are expected to be sold for the 2010 World Cup. A million will be saved for South African fans, another million will be used for international visitors, and the remaining will go for FIFA purposes. As in Germany, there will be large public-viewing areas for those who can't get tickets.

The official logo, which has been called a "symbol of hope" by some, was inspired by Khoi-San rock paintings and pictures a soccer player over the shape of Africa.

WHO IS PLAYING?

Thirty-two teams compete in the World Cup, with allocations made geographically. Europe will enter 13 teams; the Americas, eight; Africa, six, including the one automatically allotted to the host nation. Asia will have four teams, and a fifth slot will go to the winner of a playoff with the Oceania region. Worldwide qualifying matches started in 2007.

WHERE ARE THE GAMES?

Matches will be spread across the country, in 10 different stadiums in nine cities.

Soccer City

Located near Soweto, Soccer City is set to be the main venue for the tournament. Construction should be completed by 2009, and the old FNB Stadium will have all the modern conveniences. When lit at night the stadium will create the image of a traditional African cooking pot, making it a new landmark for Johannesburg.
Hosting: Opening and closing matches, as well as first- and second-round, and quarter-final play
Location: Johannesburg
Capacity: 94,000

Ellis Park

A short 15-minute walk makes this is the closest facility to the Johannesburg city center. It was originally constructed as a rugby venue, and was the site of the 1995 Rugby World Cup final when South Africa bested New Zealand. The arena is getting new upper tiers at either goal post.
Hosting: First- and second-round, and quarter-final play.
Location: Johannesburg
Capacity: 61,000

Green Point Stadium

Planted snugly between Cape Town's V&A Waterfront and Signal Hill, Greenpoint will be part of what's being termed an "African Renaissance Complex," with a retractable dome, just in case the "Cape Doctor" comes to call. (That's the local nickname for the unpredictable Cape weather conditions, which can be particularly chilly and even wet in June and July.)
Hosting: Semifinal play
Location: Cape Town
Capacity: 70,000

Moses Mabhida Stadium

Upgrades to this stadium near Durban's Golden Mile include new roofed upper

WORLD CUP 411

tiers. Plans also call for a slatted facade that will protect against the elements, but still allow views to the outside and a dramatic arch across the stadium's rooftop. As for the stadium's name, at press time it was causing a bit of controversy and a debate was raging over whether or not to change it.
Hosting: first- and second-round and semifinal play
Location: Durban
Capacity: 70,000

Nelson Mandela Bay Stadium
Soccer teams will trade kicks and passes in this modern stadium, which is being built specifically for the games.
Hosting: First- and second-round and semifinal play
Location: Port Elizabeth
Capacity: 50,000

Loftus Versfeld Stadium
Located in the Embassy Row vicinity in South Africa's executive capital, this stadium is home to Sundowns, a South African soccer club.
Hosting: First- and second-round play
Location: Tshwane (Pretoria)
Capacity: 50,000

Royal Bafokeng Stadium
Only minor renovations will bring the relatively new stadium up to FIFA standards, including updating scoreboards. Soccer fans should keep in mind that the stadium's location, just 90 minutes outside Johannesburg, means that you can gamble in Sun City between matches.
Hosting: First- and second-round play
Location: Rustenburg, North West Province
Capacity: 42,000

Peter Mokaba Stadium
Located in the capital of the Limpopo province, which was previously known as Pietersburg, the stadium is named after the activist Peter Mokaba, a native of the area. The arena, which was scheduled to get a major face-lift, has since been torn down. At press time, no official plans for the brand new stadium, other than its capacity and name, had been released.
Hosting: First-round play
Location: Polokwane, Limpopo Province
Capacity: 46,000

Mattafin Stadium
This brand-new stadium, also known as Mbombela Stadium, was built specifically for the games. It's close to the city center, local airport, and game parks for those who need even more action.
Hosting: First-round play
Location: Nelspruit, Mpumalanga Province
Capacity: 46,000

Vodacom Park
Also known as Free State Stadium, this arena is getting some new additions including a second tier that is being added to the main grandstand. There will also be a new electronic scoreboard and sound system—perfect for hearing the announcer over the din of the crowd.
Hosting: First- and second-round play
Location: Bloemfontein, Free State Province
Capacity: 48,000

HOW CAN I GET TICKETS?

Tickets are expected to go on sale in 2008. It's a good idea to check the FIFA Web site ⊕ www.fifa.com or the South Africa's official World Cup Web site ⊕ www.sa2010. gov.za for official tournament, ticket, and schedule information as the dates draw near. Several tourism and soccer Web sites (⊕ www.southafrica.info/2010 ⊕ www. southafrica2010.org) are also tracking World Cup 2010 details and are good sources of information to keep an eye on.

Cape Town & Environs

WORD OF MOUTH

"The Cape of Good Hope was beautiful. We saw ostrich and stopped at Boulder's Beach to see the penguins (I could have spent all day there). From Hermanus, we drove back through the mountains to the winelands. We stopped at Spier Vineyard and also went to Saxenburg Vineyard—it's very small, but the wines were fantastic. We ended our trip with a ride up the cable cars to the top of Table Mountain. The views are spectacular."

—swtravelbug

Updated by
Karena du
Plessis and
Brian Berkman

IF YOU VISIT ONLY ONE place in South Africa, make it Cape Town. Elegant Cape Dutch buildings, characterized by big whitewashed gables, often a thatch roof, and shuttered windows, abut imposing monuments to Britain's imperial legacy. In the Bo-Kaap neighborhood the call to prayer echoes from minarets while the sweet tang of Malay curry wafts through the cobbled streets. And everywhere, whether you're eating outdoors at one of the country's best restaurants or sipping wine atop Table Mountain, you sense—correctly—that this is South Africa's most urbane, civilized city.

As impressive as all this is, though, what you will ultimately recall about Cape Town is the sheer grandeur of its setting—Table Mountain rising above the city, the sweep of the bay, and mountains cascading into the sea. You will likely spend more time marveling at the views than anything else. Francis Drake wasn't exaggerating when he said this was "the fairest Cape we saw in the whole circumference of the earth," and he would have little cause to change his opinion today. You could spend a week exploring just the city and peninsula—and a lifetime discovering the nearby wonders of the Western Cape, including the Winelands, one of the great highlights of a trip to South Africa.

ORIENTATION & PLANNING

ORIENTATION

Cape Town lies at the northern end of the Cape Peninsula, a 75-km (47-mi) tail of mountains that hangs down from the tip of Africa, ending at the Cape of Good Hope. Drive 15 minutes out of town, and you may lose yourself in a stunning landscape of 18th-century Cape Dutch manors, historic wineries, and white-sand beaches backed by sheer mountains.

The area between Table Mountain and Table Bay, including Cape Town central and the nearby areas of Gardens, Oranjezicht, Tamboerskloof, and Bo-Kaap, is known as the City Bowl. An orderly street grid and the constant view of Table Mountain make it almost impossible to get lost. Major arteries running toward the mountain from the sea are Adderley, Loop, and Long streets; among the major cross streets are Strand, Longmarket, and Wale, which, be warned, is alternately written as WALE ST. (the English version) and WAALST (in Afrikaans) on signs. The heart of the historic city—where you'll find many of the museums and major buildings—is Government Avenue, a pedestrian mall at the top of Adderley Street. St. George's Mall, another major pedestrian thoroughfare, runs the length of commercial Cape Town.

Once you leave the city center, orienting yourself becomes trickier. As you face Table Mountain from the city, the distinctive triangular-shape mountain on your left is Devil's Peak; on the right are Signal Hill and Lion's Head. Signal Hill takes its name from a gun fired there every day at noon. If you look carefully, you will see that Signal Hill forms the rump of a reclining lion, and the maned Lion's Head looks south past Table Mountain (this is best seen from the N1 as you drive in to town). On the other side of Signal Hill and Lion's Head lies the fashionable Atlantic Seaboard. This stretch of coast, also known as Millionaire's Row, is made up of the cosmopolitan Granger Bay, Green Point, and Sea Point through to the exclusive suburbs of Clifton, Camps Bay, and Llandudno. Heading the other way, around Devil's Peak, you come to Cape Town's Southern Suburbs—Rondebosch, Newlands, Claremont, and the

> ### A WORD OF EXPLANATION
>
> Street signs in Cape Town will be alternately in English or Afrikaans. For example, *Wale* is English and *Waal* is Afrikaans, but they mean the same thing. In Afrikaans you don't put a space between the name and the street, circle, close, road or lane. So an address could be Orange Street or Oranjestraat, for example.

classy Constantia. The vibrant Waterfront lies north of the City Bowl on the other side of the freeways that separate the docks from downtown, and the nearby Waterkant is another fashionable enclave. But there's a lot more to the city than these predominantly white suburbs. The infamous Cape Flats stretch over what used to be sandy flat areas (hence the name) between the city center and the northern suburbs of Panorama, Tygerberg, and Durbanville. The sprawling townships of Khayelitsha, Nyanga, Langa, and Gugulethu are also an integral part of Cape Town, and each year these informal settlements continue to grow as immigrants move from the countryside, and the rest of the continent, looking for work.

The Cape Peninsula, much of which is included in Table Mountain National Park (TMNP), extends for around 40 km (25 mi) from the city through to Cape Point. The park comprises Table Mountain, most of the high-lying land in the mountain chain that runs down the center of the peninsula, the Cape of Good Hope nature reserve, and Boulders Beach. The steep mountain slopes leave little room for settlement in the narrow shelf next to the sea. On the east side the peninsula is washed by the waters of False Bay. Here, connected by a coastal road and railway line, lie the suburbs of Muizenberg, St. James, Kalk Bay, and Fish Hoek, as well as the naval base at historic Simon's Town. The western shores of the peninsula are wilder and emptier, pounded by huge Atlantic swells. In addition to the hamlets of Scarborough, Kommetjie, Noordhoek, and Llandudno, you'll find the fishing port of Hout Bay.

TABLE MOUNTAIN

Often likened to San Francisco, Cape Town has something that the City by the Bay doesn't—Table Mountain. The mountain, or tabletop, is vital to Cape Town's identity. It dominates the city in a way that's difficult to comprehend until you visit. In the afternoon, when creeping fingers of clouds spill over Table Mountain and reach toward the city, the whole town seems to shiver and hold its breath. Depending on which side of the mountain you live on, it even dictates when the sun will rise and set.

CITY CENTER

The center of Cape Town is fairly small and very easy to find your way around. There's an interesting mix of old and new architecture, and it's not difficult to imagine what the settlement would have been like when it was first established as a refreshment station for passing ships. Cape Town, as the city center is usually called, comes alive each morning as white-collar workers and street traders head into town for work. There are shopping malls, department stalls, open-air markets, and plenty of restaurants and coffee shops where you can take a break.

VICTORIA & ALFRED WATERFRONT

Once a seedy harbor, the Victoria & Alfred Waterfront, also referred to as the V&A Waterfront or simply the Waterfront, has been transformed into one of South Africa's premier destinations. Each year millions of locals and visitors flock to this area sandwiched between Robben Island and Table Mountain to shop, eat at one of the many outdoor restaurants and bars, go to the movies, or just stroll about while watching the passing crowds. It's still a working harbor, which only adds character, but now expensive hotels and plush apartments line the water's edge, and enthusiastic buskers perform in the walkways and public squares.

THE PENINSULA

The Cape Peninsula is a crooked finger of land that juts out into both the Atlantic and Indian oceans. This rugged outcrop, which has been described as the gateway to Africa, starts with the majestic Table Mountain and ends at Cape Point. The mountain range not only shapes the city and the beaches, but also gives Cape Town its unique character: it's impossible to ignore the contrast between urban sophistication and the looming wilderness on the city's doorstep. Cape Point, right at the end of the peninsula, may not quite be the southernmost tip of Africa, but its breathtaking and rugged beauty is well worth a visit.

BEACHES

Cape Town beaches are as varied as the people who live here, and everybody has a favorite. There are wild expanses of sand, sea, and sky; family beaches popular with moms and their children; and sophisticated hangouts where Cape Town's slinky set strips down to minuscule thongs and struts its stuff. Be warned, however, that the beaches on the Atlantic Ocean side, including Clifton, Camps Bay, and Llandudno, might be some of the most beautiful in the world, but the water is excruciatingly cold. False Bay beaches like Fish Hoek, Muizenberg, and Boulders don't have the cachet of the Atlantic Ocean beaches, but the water is a lot warmer.

PLANNING

Whatever activities you hope to accomplish in Cape Town, head up Table Mountain as soon as the wind isn't blowing. Cape Town wind is notorious, and the mountain can be shut for days on end when there are gales. Summer (October–March) is the windiest time of the year, and during December winds can reach 60 km (37 mi) an hour.

TOP REASONS TO VISIT

City Sophistication Cape Town is a cosmopolitan city with a rich heritage that it's proud to display. It might be more laid-back than Johannesburg, but it has shaken off its sleepy, parochial air and now bristles with world-class shops and restaurants and cutting-edge art and design.

Lofty Aspirations Fantastic Table Mountain towers over Cape Town and dominates the whole peninsula. Exploring the mountain is a must; you can either take the cable car to the top or hike up various routes.

Nature's Playground Capetonians are proud of their city's stylish good looks and make the most of the mountain and beaches. You can take advantage of the area's natural beauty and follow their lead. In summer you'll find lots of profes-

sionals shrugging off their suits as they head for the beach after work with their surfboards, picnics, and sundowners. In winter they bundle up against the cold and go walking, mountain biking, or running in one of the city's many green spaces.

To Market, To Market Cape Town's markets are the best in the country—informal, creative, artistic, and with a good selection of both tacky and splendid African curios.

Historical Heritage Cape Town is saturated with an extremely rich and fascinating history. At Robben Island you can stand in Mandela's old cell and learn about political and social banishment during apartheid, while the District Six Museum tells the poignant tale of the destruction of one of the country's most vibrant inner-city neighborhoods.

The southeaster winds can also bring Portuguese men-of war, or "blue bottles"—stinging, jellyfishlike creatures—which means swimming is out of the question at these times for all but the robust. One of the best months to visit is April, when the heat and wind have abated and the Cape is bathed in warm autumnal hues. The rains in winter can put off visitors, but this time of the year holds its own charm: the countryside is a brilliant green, and come early spring you have the whales and wildflowers to look forward to.

TAKE IT ALL IN

3 Days: With three days you can manage to see many of the city's major sights—including Company's Gardens, Castle of Good Hope, District Six Museum, and the Bo-Kaap—on your own or with a tour. Weather permitting, try to also work in a Robben Island tour, which will take around 3½ hours, and lunch at one of the outdoor restaurants at the V&A Waterfront, where you can eat while watching working tugboats maneuver past sleek million-dollar yachts. The cable-car ride to the summit of Table Mountain is a must; go in the morning, and in the afternoon, drive out to Camps Bay, where you can kick off your shoes to stroll along the beach. To round out the evening, find a sophisticated sea-facing bar for a drink before going on to dinner. On another evening, discover the rhythm of Africa by heading to the Green Dolphin at the V&A Waterfront, where you can listen to terrific jazz. Or for a

CLOSE UP

Cape History at a Glance

It is said that Cape Town owes its very existence to Table Mountain. The freshwater streams running off its slopes were what first prompted early explorers to anchor here. In 1652 Jan van Riebeeck and 90 Dutch settlers established a refreshment station for ships of the Dutch East India Company (VOC) on the long voyage east. The settlement represented the first European toehold in South Africa, and Cape Town is still sometimes called the Mother City.

Those first Dutch settlers soon ventured into the interior to establish their own farms, and 140 years later the settlement supported a population of 20,000 whites and 25,000 slaves brought from distant lands like Java, Madagascar, and Guinea. Its position on the strategic cusp of Africa, however, meant that the colony never enjoyed any real stability. The British occupied the Cape twice, first in 1795 and then more permanently in 1806, bringing with them additional slaves from Ceylon, India, and the Philippines. Destroyed or assimilated in this colonial expansion were the indigenous Khoekhoen (previously called Khoikhoi and Hottentots), who once herded their cattle here and foraged along the coast.

Though South Africa's more recent history is better known, it's worth remembering that between 1889 and 1902 the British and the Boers (Afrikaans for "farmers") also fought bitterly and that the conflicts that have shaped and scarred the country haven't always been between black and white. The wounds of the 20th century are largely attributable to apartheid, however. In 1948 the National Party (the Nats) was voted into power and apartheid machinery

set in motion. Black education was accepted as inferior, whole communities were moved, and the majority of South Africans were unable to vote. Fortunately, however, exceptional men and women—Nelson Mandela being the most famous and best-loved— were determined to change the status quo. In fact, the antiapartheid struggle began as soon as the Nats came to power. While F. W. de Klerk was president, in late 1989, negotiations began, Mandela was released from prison, and the first democratic election was held in 1994. For their efforts, de Klerk and Mandela received the Nobel peace prize for an achievement others thought impossible.

More than a decade since apartheid's demise, South Africa *is* a different country, but poverty and unemployment are still huge problems. Some changes are beginning in such areas as free basic health care, education, and services such as potable water and sanitation, though 2006 and 2007 saw a lot of protest action about the lack of delivery. The new struggle being fought in South Africa, and the rest of the continent, is the battle against HIV/AIDS. At the beginning of 2007 it was estimated that there were 1,500 new HIV/AIDS infections every day.

Legacies of apartheid still fester, and although the city is made up of many nationalities that mingle happily, it is still divided along racial and economic lines. As you drive into town along the N2 from the airport, you can't miss the shacks built on shifting dunes as far as the eye can see—a sobering contrast to the luxury of the city center. A tour of these areas offers a glimpse of the old South Africa.

real taste of contemporary African music, go to Mama Africa for pulsing marimba music.

5 or More Days: With at least five days, you can enjoy all the sights listed above as well as a trip to the Winelands in Constantia, Stellenbosch, Franschhoek, and Paarl. From the harbor you can take a cruise to Seal Island or, for a more adventurous activity, admire the sunset from the back of a horse at Noordhoek. Wend your way along the False Bay coast to Boulders Beach, in Table Mountain National Park, where you'll find African penguins in profusion. From here, follow the road to the Cape of Good Hope and Cape Point. You can take the steep walk to the point or take the funicular. It looks as if this is where the Indian and Atlantic oceans meet—sometimes there is even a line of foam stretching out to sea—but of course it's not. (That happens at Cape Agulhas, on the Cape's southern coast.) For a late lunch make your way back to the pretty fishing village of Kalk Bay, where the streets are lined with antiques shops and there are plenty of excellent restaurants to relax in. However you spend your time, on your last night back in Cape Town have a drink at the Bascule bar at the Cape Grace (at the V&A Waterfront) and watch the gulls wheel overhead against a backdrop of Table Mountain. Chances are, you won't want to leave.

HEALTH & SAFETY

There's no reason for paranoia in Cape Town, but there are a few things to look out for. Avoid the city center at night and on Saturday afternoons and Sundays, when it is very quiet. Street kids and roving teens are blamed for much of the petty crime, but sophisticated crime syndicates are often involved, and many of Cape Town's fraudsters are smartly dressed. Cell phones can be snatched from car seats through open windows and even out of people's hands while in use. Watch your pockets at busy transportation interchanges and on trains. Pick a crowded car; if you suddenly find yourself alone, move to another one. Public transportation collapses after dark. Unless you're at the Waterfront or are in a large group, use metered taxis. Better still, rent a car, but don't leave valuables visible and don't park in isolated areas. Poor signage is an issue in Cape Town, especially in the black townships, where most streets still have numbers rather than names and many streets are not signed at all. Carry a good map, and visit township attractions only as part of an organized tour with a reputable operator. Women and couples are strongly advised not to walk in isolated places after dark. If you want to walk somewhere in the evening, make sure you do so in a large group, and stay vigilant at all times.

As in other major cities, drug use is a problem in Cape Town. IV-drug use carries a high risk of HIV transmission, as does the sex trade (which also carries the risk of other sexually transmitted diseases). AIDS is a huge problem in South Africa, so exercise appropriate caution. The drug of choice for children on the street is glue. You will undoubtedly come across many people begging in Cape Town, including kids, but you are encouraged not to give cash directly to children, as this often supports either a glue habit or adults lurking in the background. If you are concerned and wish to contribute, consider supporting people who sell *The Big Issue* magazine (associated with a worthy organization of the same name), or giving food instead of money.

DISCOUNTS

For one fee, the **Cape Town Pass** (⊕*www.capetownpass.co.za*) provides admission to 50 Cape Town–area attractions, including Kirstenbosch, selected museums, and the Two Oceans Aquarium. The pass, which comes with its own guide to the attractions, costs R275 for one day, R425 for two days, R495 for three days, and R750 for six days. You can buy the pass online or from tourism offices, guesthouses and hotels, and travel agents. If you're keen to explore South Africa's many wilderness areas, consider buying a **SANParks Wild Card** (⊕*www.sanparks. org*), but be sure to read all the fine print. There are several types of passes covering different clusters of parks for individuals, couples, and families; an individual pass to all the parks costs R795.

OUT ON THE TOWN

Cape etc. is a great bimonthly roundup of entertainment in Cape Town; at this writing there was talk of making this a monthly publication. For weekly updates try "Friday," the entertainment supplement of the *Mail & Guardian,* or the "Top of the Times" in Friday's *Cape Times.* Both are informed, opinionated, and up-to-date. The *Argus* newspaper's "Tonight" section gives you a complete daily listing of what's on, plus contact numbers. Tickets for almost every cultural and sporting event in the country (including movies) can be purchased through **Computicket** (☎*083/915–8000* ⊕*www.computicket.co.za*); the problem is that you need a credit card with a South African address. Cape Town is a very gay-friendly city. For information on the gay scene, contact **Africa Outing** (☎*021/671–4028 or 083/273–8422* ⊕*www.afouting. com*). Geared toward gay and lesbian travelers, **Gay Net Cape Town** (⊕*www.gaynetcapetown.co.za*) provides information on events and venues in Cape Town.

AT THE BEACH

Cape Town's beaches on both the Atlantic and False Bay sides are legendary. The beaches at Milnerton, Blouberg, and Long Beach (in Noordhoek) stretch endlessly, and you can walk for miles without seeing a fast-food outlet or drink stand. But you will see seagulls, dolphins, penguins, and whales (in season). Forget about swimming in the Atlantic, though; even a quick dip will freeze your toes. The "in" crowd flocks to Clifton, a must for sunbathers. If it's swimming you're into, head to the warmer waters of St. James, Kalk Bay, Fish Hoek, and Simon's Town, where the warm Benguela current sweeps along the False Bay side of the peninsula. The beaches are dotted with tidal pools, which make swimming even more comfortable, and are safe for kids. Windsurfers congregate at Blouberg, where several competitions are held. At Boulders or Seaforth you can sunbathe and snorkel in the coves and pools, sheltered by huge granite rocks. Cape Town's surfing community appreciates Muizenberg, Kommetjie, Fish Hoek, Hout Bay, and Blouberg. For kite surfing, Strandfontein and Sunrise beaches are the places to try or to watch. Don't be tempted to try kite surfing for the first time when the wind is pumping, however—it's far too dangerous.

VISITOR INFORMATION

Cape Town Tourism (⊠ *The Pinnacle, Burg and Castle Sts., Cape Town Central* 🖂 *Box 1403, 8000* ☎ *021/487–6800* ⊠ *Clock Tower Centre, South Arm Rd., Waterfront* ☎ *021/405–4500* ⊕ *www.tourismcapetown.co.za*) is the city's official tourist body, providing information on tours, hotels, restaurants, rental cars, and shops. It has a coffee shop, wineshop, and Internet café. The staff also makes hotel, tour, and travel reservations. The office at Burg and Castle streets is open weekdays 8–6, Saturday 8:30–1, and Sunday 9–1. The Waterfront branch is open daily 9–9.

EXPLORING CAPE TOWN

Cape Town has grown as a city in a way that few others in the world have. Take a good look at the street names. Strand and Waterkant streets (meaning "beach" and "waterside," respectively) are now far from the sea. However, when they were named they were right on the beach. An enormous program of dumping rubble into the ocean extended the city by a good few square miles (this can, no doubt, be attributed to the Dutch obsession with reclaiming land from the sea). Almost all the city on the seaward side of Strand and Waterkant is part of the reclaimed area of the city known as the Foreshore. If you look at old paintings of the city, you will see that originally waves lapped at the very walls of the castle, now more than half a mile from the ocean.

TABLE MOUNTAIN

Along with Victoria Falls on the border of Zimbabwe and Zambia, Table Mountain is one of southern Africa's most beautiful and impressive natural wonders. The views from its summit are awe-inspiring. The mountain rises more than 3,500 feet above the city, and its distinctive flat top is visible to sailors 65 km (40 mi) out to sea. In summer, when the southeaster blows, moist air from False Bay funnels over the tabletop, condensing in the colder, higher air to form a tablecloth of cloud. Legend attributes this low-lying cloud to a pipe-smoking contest between the devil and Jan van Hunks, a pirate who settled on Devil's Peak. The devil lost, and the cloud serves to remind him of his defeat.

Climbing will take two to three hours, depending on your fitness level. There is no water along the route; you *must* take at least 2 liters (½ gallon) of water per person. Table Mountain can be dangerous if you're not familiar with the terrain. Many paths that look like good routes down the mountain end at treacherous cliffs. ■**TIP→ Do not underestimate this mountain.** It may be in the middle of a city, but it is not a genteel town park. Wear sturdy shoes or hiking boots; always take warm clothes, such as a windbreaker, and a mobile phone; and let someone know of your plans. The mountain is safe if you stick to known paths, but, although the paths are marked, it is easy to become disoriented, especially when there is heavy cloud cover. Look for the Table Mountain map by Peter Slingsby at most major outdoor stores

The Wilds of Table Mountain

Despite being virtually surrounded by the city, Table Mountain is a remarkably unspoiled wilderness. Most of the Cape Peninsula's 2,200 species of flora—about as many plant species as there are in all of North America and Europe combined—are found on the mountain. This includes magnificent examples of Cape Town's wild indigenous flowers known as *fynbos*, Afrikaans for "fine bush," a reference to the tiny leaves characteristic of these heathlike plants. The best time to see the mountain in bloom is between September and March, although you're sure to find some flowers throughout the year.

Long gone are the days when Cape lions, zebras, and hyenas roamed the mountain, but you can still glimpse *grysboks* (small antelopes), baboons, and rabbitlike *dassies* (rhymes with "fussy"). Although these creatures, also called rock hyraxes, look like oversize guinea pigs, this is where the similarities end; the dassie's closest relative is the elephant. They congregate in large numbers near the Upper Cable Station, where they've learned to beg for food. Over the years a diet of junk food has seriously compromised their health. ■ TIP→ **Visitors are encouraged not to feed them tidbits—no matter how endearing they look.**

or the shop at the Lower Cable Station. If you are on the mountain and the weather changes dramatically (heavy rain, mist) and you can't tell where you are, just sit tight and call Wilderness Search and Rescue (⇨ *Emergencies in Cape Town Essentials, below*) to let them know you're in trouble. You will be rescued as soon as the weather permits. Walking around in the mist is very dangerous. Also be aware that in light of occasional muggings here, it's unwise to walk alone on the mountain. It's recommended that you travel in a group or, better yet, with a guide.

Atop the mountain, well-marked trails offering 10- to 40-minute jaunts crisscross the western Table near the Upper Cable Station. Many other trails lead to the other side of Platteklip Gorge and into the mountain's catchment area, where you'll find reservoirs, hidden streams, and incredible views. Feeling adventurous? Try a rappel from the top—it's only about 350 feet, but you're hanging out over 3,300 feet of air (⇨ *Rappelling in Sports & the Outdoors, below*). A shop at the top of the mountain, appropriately called the Shop at the Top, sells gifts and curios.

One really great way to get acquainted with this majestic mountain and all its moods is to hike part of the **Hoerikwaggo Trail** (☎ *021/465–8515* ⊕ *www.sanparks.org*), which opened in 2006. This is an ambitious initiative, the details of which are still being finalized. The plan is that eventually you will be able to hike from the Lower Cable Station at the top of town to the Cape Point lighthouse along the spine of mountains that runs the length of the peninsula. "Hoerikwaggo Trail" is actually a misnomer, as it's more of a "bouquet" of trails of different lengths and destinations. The three-day trail aimed at international tourists

1

A Good Ride

Fodor's Choice The **Table Mountain Aerial Cableway** is a slick operation. Two large, wheelchair-friendly revolving cars, which provide spectacular views, take three to five minutes to reach the summit. Operating times vary from month to month according to season, daylight hours, and weather. To avoid disappointment, phone ahead for exact times. You can't prebook for the cable car, but the longest you'll have to wait is about a half hour and then only in peak season (December 15–January 15). Several tour operators include a trip up the mountain in their schedules.

The Lower Cable Station lies on the slope of Table Mountain near its western end. It's a long way from the city on foot, and you're better off traveling by car, taxi, or *rikki* (a small, low-tech minibus). To get there from the City Bowl, take Buitengracht Street toward the mountain. Once you cross Camp Street, Buitengracht becomes Kloof Nek Road. Follow Kloof Nek Road through the residential neighborhood of Gardens to a traffic circle; turn left on Tafelberg Road and follow signs to the Table Mountain Aerial Cableway. Taxis from the city center to the Lower Cable Station (one way) cost about R60, and rikkis (which start running at 7 AM weekdays and 8 AM weekends) cost R20 per person. ⊠ *Tafelberg Rd.* ☎ *021/424–8181* ⊕ *www.tablemountain.net* ☞ *R120 round-trip, R60 one way* ⊙ *Hrs vary so it's best to check when you arrive, but usually daily 8:30–7:30.*

starts at the Waterfront and ends at Kirstenbosch. It's guided, fully catered, and accommodation (in tents, cottages, and huts) is top-notch. Expect to pay around R1,900 or R1,500 with a SANParks Wild Card (⇨ *Discounts in Planning, above*).

NEED A BREAK?

During the warm summer months Capetonians are fond of taking picnic baskets up the mountain. The best time to picnic is after 5, as some say sipping a glass of chilled Cape wine while watching the sun set from Table Mountain is one of life's great joys. The large self-service restaurant called, quite simply, **The Restaurant** (☎ *021/424–8181*) serves great hot breakfasts, light meals, sandwiches, and local wine, and has a good salad bar. **The Cocktail Bar** (☎ *021/424–8181*) dishes up a spectacular view along with cocktails and bar snacks from 2 until the last cable car. As you might expect, the place has a good wine list, with local labels predominating.

CITY CENTER

In Cape Town's city center, glistening glass-and-steel office blocks soar over street vendors selling everything from seasonal fruit and flowers to clothes and cigarettes. Sandwiched in between these modern high-rises are historic buildings dating to the 1600s. There's also an impressive collection of art-deco buildings undergoing restoration here. Don't try to navigate the center of Cape Town by car. It's small enough to walk, and this way you'll be able to explore the many galleries, coffee shops, and markets that appear on every corner.

TIMING & PRECAUTIONS
If you are pressed for time, you can explore the city in a day, getting the lay of the land and a feel for the people of Cape Town while visit-

Flowers have been sold in Trafalgar Place, near Adderley Street, for the last 100 years.

ing or skipping sights as your interests dictate. However, if you'd like to linger in various museums and galleries, you could easily fill two days. Start at about 9, when most workers have finished their commute, and then stop for a long, leisurely lunch during the hottest part of the day, finishing the tour in the late afternoon. If you have to head out of town on either the N1 or N2, be sure to finish before 4, when rush-hour congestion takes over and you can sit in traffic for a couple of hours at a stretch.

Except for the top end of Long Street and around Heritage Square, where there are lots of bars and cafés, the city center dies at night, and you are advised not to wander the streets after most Capetonians have left for home. The last commuters leave around 6 (note that the city center can also be deserted on weekends). The biggest threat is groups of street children, who might mug you for your cell phone, jewelry, or money. This situation is slowly changing, though it still has a long way to go. Many of the old office blocks that have been abandoned by businesses are being converted into upscale apartments, and people are once again making the city center their home. The opening of the Mandela Rhodes Place complex has also brought more people into the city center after hours.

WHAT TO SEE

CAPE TOWN
CENTRAL
❷

Adderley Street. Originally named Heerengracht after a canal that once ran the length of the avenue, this street has always been Cape Town's principal thoroughfare. It was once the favored address of the city's leading families, and its oak-shaded sidewalks served as a promenade for those who wanted to see and be seen. By the mid-19th century the oaks had all been chopped down and the canal covered, as Adderley became the main commercial street. By 1908 it had become so busy that the city planners paved it with wooden blocks in an attempt to dampen the noise of countless wagons, carts, and hooves. In recent years Adderley Street has lost most of its charm. Although there are a couple of beautiful old buildings dating to the early 1900s, they are mostly crowded out by uninspiring office buildings, and the sidewalks are packed with street hawkers selling everything from fruits and vegetables to cell-phone covers and tea towels. City management is trying to halt the urban decay, however, and there's plenty of evidence of regeneration. A lot of old office buildings are now being converted to upscale apartments, and beautiful old art-deco buildings are getting the spit and polish they so desperately need. ⊠ *Cape Town Central.*

❶ **Cape Town Tourism Information Office.** One of the best information offices in South Africa, Cape Town Tourism is filled with helpful and knowledgeable people. It has a currency-exchange office, a wineshop with tastings, an Internet café, a coffee shop, and loads of information, including a National Parks and Cape Nature Conservation desk and an accommodations desk. ✉ *The Pinnacle, Burg and Castle Sts., Cape Town Central* ✆ *Box 1403, 8000* ☎ *021/487–6800* ⊕ *www. tourismcapetown.co.za* ✉ *Free* ☉ *Weekdays 8–6, Sat. 8:30–1, Sun. and public holidays 9–1.*

★ ❸ **Castle of Good Hope.** Despite its name, the castle isn't one of those fairytale fantasies you find perched on a cliff. It's a squat fortress that hunkers into the ground as if to avoid shellfire. Built between 1665 and 1676 by the Dutch East India Company (VOC) to replace an earthen fort constructed in 1652 by Jan van Riebeeck, the Dutch commander who settled Cape Town, it's the oldest building in the country. Its pentagonal plan, with a diamond-shape bastion at each corner, is typical of the Old Netherlands defense system adopted in the early 17th century. The design was intended to allow covering fire for every portion of the castle. As added protection, the whole fortification was surrounded by a moat, and the sea nearly washed up against its walls. The castle served as both the VOC headquarters and the official governor's residence, and still houses the regional headquarters of the National Defence Force. Despite the bellicose origins of the castle, no shot has ever been fired from its ramparts, except ceremonially.

You can wander around on your own or join one of the guided tours at no extra cost. Also worth seeing is the excellent William Fehr Collection. Housed in the governor's residence, it consists of antiques, artifacts, and paintings of early Cape Town and South African history. Upstairs, John Thomas Baine's *The Greatest Hunt in Africa,* celebrates a "hunt" in honor of Prince Alfred, when nearly 30,000 animals were driven together and slaughtered. ✉ *1 Buitenkant St., Cape Town Central* ☎ *021/787–1200* ⊕ *www.castleofgoodhope.co.za* ✉ *R20* ☉ *Mon.–Sat. 9–3:30; tours at 11, noon, and 2.*

NEED A BREAK?
De Goewerneur Restaurant (✉ *1 Buitenkant St., Cape Town Central* ☎ *021/787–1202*), in the central courtyard of the Castle of Good Hope, serves both lunch and dinner. Expect traditional South African food such as *waterblommetjie bredie* (a rich tomato stew made with small water plants only found in the Cape), *bobotie* (a lighty spiced, baked mince dish), and the usual light meals and teas. From the veranda you get a pleasing view of the lawn and the buildings beyond.

❷❹ **Church Street.** The center of Cape Town's art and antiques business, the section between Burg and Long streets is a pedestrian mall filled with art galleries, antiques dealers, and small cafés. This is the site of a daily antiques and flea market. ✉ *Cape Town Central.*

❺ **City Hall.** Though this attractive Edwardian building constructed in 1905 is in need of sprucing up, it's still a commanding presence overlooking the Grand Parade. What was the seat of local administration is now home to the Cape Town Philharmonic Orchestra (the acoustics in

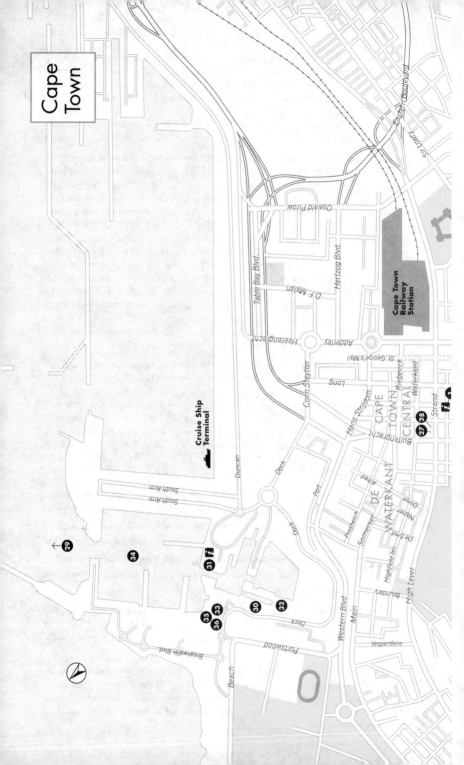

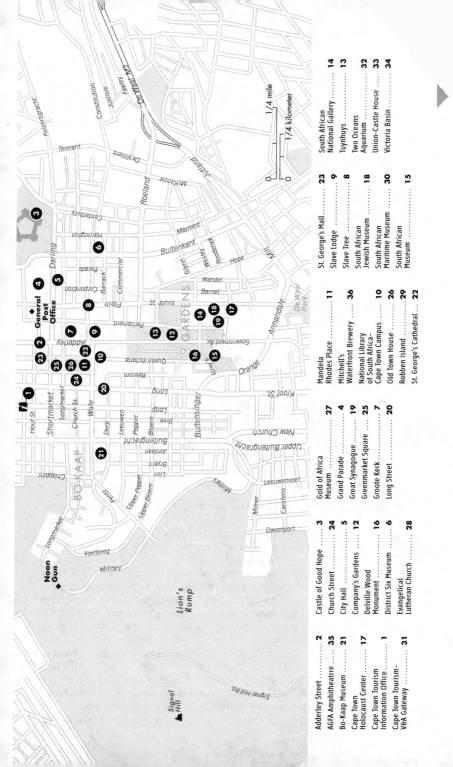

GARDENS

BO-KAAP

Noon
Gun

Lion's
Rump

Signal
Hill

Signal Hill Rd.

General
Post
Office

0   1/4 mile

0   1/4 kilometer

e main hall are phenomenal) and City Library. Some of the building's
ne was imported from Bath, England, and the clock is a scaled-down
lica of Big Ben. You can ask at security to visit the clock tower. From
alcony overlooking Darling Street, Nelson Mandela gave his historic
speech upon his release from prison in 1990. ⊠*Darling St., Cape Town
Central* 🕾*021/467–1567 library* 🖃*Free* ⊙*Library Mon. and Wed.
10–5:30, Tues. 1–5:30, Thurs. and Fri. 10–2, Sat. 9–2.*

★ ⑫ **Company's Gardens.** These are all that remain of a 43-acre garden laid
out by Jan van Riebeeck in April 1652 to supply fresh vegetables to
ships on their way to the Dutch East Indies. By 1700 free burghers were
cultivating plenty of crops on their own land, and in time the VOC
vegetable patch was transformed into a botanic garden. It remains a
delightful haven in the city center, graced by fountains, exotic trees,
rose gardens, aviaries, and a pleasant outdoor café. At the bottom of
the gardens, close to Government Avenue, look for an **old well** that
used to provide water for the town's residents and the garden. The
old water pump, engraved with the maker's name and the date 1842,
has been overtaken by an oak tree and now juts out of the tree's trunk
some 6 feet above the ground. A huge **statue of Cecil Rhodes,** the
Cape's prime minister in the late 19th century, looms over the path that
runs through the center of the gardens. He points to the north, and an
inscription reads, YOUR HINTERLAND IS THERE, a reference to Rhodes's
dream of extending the British Empire from the Cape to Cairo. ⊠*Between Government Ave. and Queen Victoria St., Cape Town Central*
🖃*Free* ⊙*Daily 6–6.*

⑯ **Delville Wood Monument.** The monument honors South Africans who
died in the fight for Delville Wood during the great Somme offensive
of 1916. Of the 121 officers and 3,032 soldiers who participated in
the three-day World War I battle, only five officers and 750 soldiers
survived unhurt. Facing the memorial is a **statue of Brigadier General
Lukin,** who commanded the South African infantry brigade during
World War I. ⊠*Company's Gardens, Cape Town Central.*

★ ➏ **District Six Museum.** Housed in the Buitenkant Methodist Church, this
museum preserves the memory of one of Cape Town's most vibrant
multicultural neighborhoods, and of the district's destruction in one of
the cruelest acts of the apartheid-era Nationalist government. District
Six was proclaimed a white area in 1966, and existing residents were
evicted from their homes, which were razed to make way for a white
suburb. The people were forced to resettle in bleak outlying areas on
the Cape Flats, and by the 1970s all the buildings here, except churches
and mosques, had been demolished. Huge controversy accompanied
the proposed redevelopment of the area, and only a small housing
component, Zonnebloem, and the campus of the Cape Technicon have
been built, leaving much of the ground still bare—a grim reminder of
the past. There are plans to bring former residents back into the area
and reestablish the suburb; however, the old swinging District Six can
never be re-created. The museum consists of street signs, photographs,
life stories of the people who lived there, and a huge map, where former
residents can identify the sites of their homes and record their names.

This map is being used to help sort out land claims in advance for a two-hour walking tour of the dist amount. Directly opposite the museum is the notoric police station, where many antiapartheid activists died from mysterious causes. ✉ *25 Buitenkant St. tral* 🕾 *021/466-7200* ⊕ *www.districtsix.co.za* ✉ *Tues.–Sat. 9–4, Sun. by appointment.*

㉘ **Evangelical Lutheran Church Complex.** Established as an act of defiance against the Dutch in 1779, this is the oldest church in South Africa. Not only did the Dutch East India Company exert commercial control over early Cape Town, but it also had a stranglehold on religion. The VOC recognized only the Dutch Reformed Church, and other faiths were banned. The Lutherans were not content to put up with this religious bullying, however, so in 1774, when Martin Melck, a wealthy land-owner, donated a barn and land in town, they started worshipping. Five years later the VOC relented slightly, and once religious freedom was granted, German sculptor Anton Anreith was commissioned to convert the barn into a church. This was also the first church that welcomed slaves to its services, as long as they occupied the designated slave pews running down either side. ✉ *98 Strand St., Cape Town Central* 🕾 *021/421-5854* ✉ *Free* ☉ *Weekdays 10–2; service Sun. at 10.*

★ ㉗ **Gold of Africa Museum.** This museum in the historic Martin Melck House chronicles the history and artistry of African gold and houses arguably one of the best collections in the world. The exquisite exhibition upstairs, cleverly displayed in a darkened room, may leave you gasping—artisans from Mali, Senegal, Ghana, and the Ivory Coast certainly knew how to transform this precious metal. Downstairs is a workshop where you can watch jewelers busy at their craft. When you've taken in all the opulence you can, you can escape to the great coffee shop in a secluded courtyard and forget that you're in the center of a busy city. Book ahead for a Pangolin Night Tour (R35; four-person minimum), which includes a guided flashlighted tour of the collection and a glass of wine with gold flakes. ✉ *96 Strand St., Cape Town Central* 🕾 *021/405–1540* ⊕ *www.goldofafrica.com* ✉ *R20* ☉ *Mon.–Sat. 9:30–5.*

❹ **Grand Parade.** Once a military parade ground, this is now just a bleak parking lot. A statue of Edward VII serves as a parking attendant and seagull resting post. It was here, on his release on February 11, 1990, after 27 years in prison, that Nelson Mandela addressed an adoring crowd of more than 100,000 supporters from the balcony at City Hall. Today this is the site of South Africa's oldest flea market, which has been held on Wednesday and Saturday mornings for decades. It's not tourist oriented, but it is the best place to see some of the "real" Cape Town. Pop into one of the informal food stalls for a *gatsby* (a sandwich on a long roll filled with french fries, lettuce, tomato, and a choice of fresh or pickled fish, curry, or steak) or a *salomie* (roti, a soft round bread, wrapped around a curry filling) for a cheap lunch. Finish it off with some delicious *koeksusters* (sweet, braided, lightly spiced, deep-fried pastries). Watch out for pickpockets, and don't wear flashy jewelry, as you might leave the area without it. ⊠*Darling, Lower Plein, and Buitenkant Sts., Cape Town Central.*

★ ㉕ **Greenmarket Square.** For more than a century this cobbled square served as a forum for public announcements, including the 1834 declaration abolishing slavery, which was read from the balcony of the Old Town House, overlooking the square. In the 19th century the square became a vegetable market as well as a popular watering hole, and you can still enjoy a drink at an open-air restaurant or hotel veranda while watching the crowds go by. Today the square has a fun outdoor market *(⇨Shopping, below)*, and is flanked by some of the best examples of art-deco architecture in South Africa. ⊠*Longmarket, Burg, and Shortmarket Sts., Cape Town Central.*

❼ **Groote Kerk** *(Great Church)*. One of the most famous churches in South Africa, the Groote Kerk was built in 1841 on the site of an earlier Dutch Reformed church dating from 1704. The adjoining clock tower is all that remains of that earlier building. Among the building's interesting features are the enclosed pews, each with its own door. Prominent families would buy their own pews—and lock the doors—so they wouldn't have to pray with the great unwashed. The enormous pulpit is the joint work of famous sculptor Anton Anreith and carpenter Jan Jacob Graaff. The lions supporting it are carved from local stinkwood; the upper portion is Burmese teak. The organ, with nearly 6,000 pipes, is the largest in the southern hemisphere. Approximately 200 people are buried beneath the Batavian soapstone floor, including eight governors. There are free guided tours on request. ⊠*43 Adderley St. (enter on Parliament St.), Cape Town Central* ☏*021/422–0569* ▨*Free* ⊙ *Weekdays 10–2; services Sun. at 10 and 7.*

❷⓪ **Long Street.** The section of Long between Orange and Wale streets is lined with magnificently restored Georgian and Victorian buildings. Wrought-iron balconies and fancy curlicues on these colorful houses evoke the French Quarter in New Orleans. In the 1960s Long Street played host to bars, prostitutes, and sleazy hotels, but today antiques dealers, secondhand bookstores (Clarke's is a must), pawnshops, the Pan-African Market, and funky clothing outlets make this the best browsing street in the city. Lodgings here range from backpackers' digs to the more exclusive Metropole. At the mountain end is Long Street Baths, an indoor swimming pool and old Turkish *hammam* (steam bath). ⊠*Cape Town Central.*

❶❶ **Mandela Rhodes Place.** This is the first of many inner-city renovations that are set to transform Cape Town and bring people back into the city center at the end of the work day. Developers bought three beautiful old buildings in the heart of historic Cape Town and combined them into a 21st-century showpiece. The impressive complex—named for two very different personalities who helped shape South Africa, Cecil Rhodes and Nelson Mandela—contains a hotel, apartments, restaurants, and coffee shops. Also here is the city's only winery, which stocks bottles from small independent vintners who are producing wine from grapes grown on inner-city and suburban plots. ⊠*At Burg St., Church*

St., Wale St., and St. George's Mall, Cape Town Central ☎*No phone* ⊕*www.mandelarhodesplace.co.za.*

⑩ National Library of South Africa–Cape Town Campus. Launched as the National Library in 1999, with the amalgamation of the State Library in what was then Pretoria and the South African Library here, this library owes its existence to Lord Charles Somerset, governor of the Cape Colony. In 1818 he imposed a wine tax to fund the creation of a library that would "place the means of knowledge within the reach of the youth of this remote corner of the Globe." In 1860 the library moved into its current home, a neoclassical building modeled after the Fitzwilliam Museum in Cambridge, England. The library has an extensive collection of Africana, including the works of many 18th- and 19th-century explorers, and an impressive map collection that attracts worldwide attention. At last count the enormous post-card collection numbered more than 10,000 pieces. ✉*5 Queen Victoria St. (enter through Company's Gardens), Cape Town Central* ☎*021/424–6320* ⊕*www.nlsa.ac.za* 🎫*Free* ⊗*Mon., Tues., Thurs., and Fri. 9–5, Wed. 10–5.*

㉖ Old Town House. For 150 years this was the most important civic building in Cape Town. Built in 1755 as a guardhouse, it also saw duty as a meeting place for the burgher senate, a police station, and from 1840 to 1905 as Cape Town's city hall. All road distances to and from Cape Town are measured from this building, which is a beautiful example of urban Cape Dutch architecture, with thick whitewashed walls, green-and-white shutters, and small-paned windows. Today it's home to the extensive **Michaelis Collection** of 17th-century Dutch paintings, including evocative etchings by Rembrandt, as well as changing exhibits. ✉*Greenmarket Sq., Cape Town Central* ☎*021/481–3933* ⊕*www. iziko.org.za/michaelis* 🎫*Free* ⊗*Weekdays 10–5, Sat. 10–4.*

NEED A BREAK? The Ivy Garden (✉*Greenmarket Sq., Cape Town Central* ☎*021/423–2360*), in the courtyard of the Old Town House, serves light lunches and teas in a leafy, green setting, and is a good place to escape the hustle and bustle of Greenmarket Square.

㉒ St. George's Cathedral. This cathedral was once the religious seat of one of the most recognizable faces—and voices—in the fight against apartheid, Archbishop Desmond Tutu. In his position as the first black archbishop of Cape Town (he was elected in 1986), he vociferously denounced apartheid and relentlessly pressed for a democratic government. It was from these steps that he led a demonstration of more than 30,000 people and coined the phrase the Rainbow People to describe South Africans in all their glorious diversity. The Anglican cathedral was designed by Sir Herbert Baker in the Gothic Revival style; construction began in 1901, using sandstone from Table Mountain. The structure contains the largest stained-glass window in the country, some beautiful examples of late-Victorian stained glass, and a 1,000-year-old Coptic cross. If you want to hear the magnificent organ, go to the choral evensong at 7 on Sunday evening, the 9:15 AM or 7 PM mass on Sunday, or the 11 AM mass on the last Sunday of every month. ⊠*5 Wale St., Cape Town Central* ☎*021/424–7360* ✎*Free* ☉*Daily 8–5; services weekdays at 7:15 AM and 1:15 PM, Sat. at 8 AM, Sun. at 7:15 AM, 8 AM, 9:15 AM, 7 PM (and 11 AM last Sun. of month).*

WHO'S THAT?

The imposing statue with his back turned toward the Slave Lodge is of Jan Smuts, a statesman, soldier, naturalist, and philosopher. In the mid-20th century he was also the leader of the United Party, which believed in a unified South Africa. Had he not been defeated by the National Party in 1948, South African history would have taken a very different turn.

❷❸ **St. George's Mall.** This promenade stretches almost all the way to the Foreshore. Shops and cafés line the mall, and street vendors hawk everything from T-shirts to African arts and crafts. Street performers and dancers gather daily to entertain crowds of locals and visitors, who rub shoulders on their way to and from work or while sightseeing. ⊠*Cape Town Central.*

❾ **Slave Lodge.** Previously known as the South African Cultural History Museum, this beautiful building has a dark past. It was built in 1679 by the Dutch East India Company to house slaves, convicts, and lunatics, and from 1815 to 1914 the building housed the supreme court. Today it's a museum, which is in the process of being redeveloped to more accurately represent the diverse cultures of all South Africans, not just white settlers. As such, it hasn't yet found its place among Cape Town's top museums. Though it does have an excellent collection of colonial furniture, letters, coins, paintings, and clothes, they are not on permanent display. The museum's temporary exhibits are usually hardhitting and evocative looks at apartheid and racism and are well worth the visit. ⊠*49 Wale St., Cape Town Central* ☎*021/460–8242* ⊕*www. iziko.org.za/slavelodge* ✎*R10* ☉*Weekdays 10–4:30, Sat. 10–1.*

❽ **Slave Tree.** An inconspicuous concrete plaque marks the spot where slaves are purported to have been auctioned under an enormous Canadian pine tree that once stood here. Slavery began in the Cape Colony in 1658, when free burghers petitioned the government for farmhands. The first group of 400 slaves arrived from Guinea, Angola, Batavia (modern-day Java), and Madagascar. During the first British occupation of the Cape (1795–1803), 17,000 slaves were brought from India, Ceylon, and the Philippines, swelling the total slave population to 30,000. Slavery was abolished by the British in 1834, an act that served as the final impetus for one of South Africa's great historical events, the Great Trek, when thousands of outraged Afrikaners set off in their covered wagons to establish a new state in the hinterland where they would be free from British taxation and laws. A section of the tree is on display at the District Six Museum. ⊠*Spin St., Cape Town Central*

☻ ❶❺ **South African Museum.** This museum has some excellent examples of rock art that will give you insight into the ancient Khoisan culture. The museum also has an interesting section on the fossil remains of prehistoric reptiles and other animals, and the spectacular Whale

Well, where musical recitals are often held under suspended life-size casts of enormous marine mammals. Shark World thrills children with exhibits on the sharks that ply the oceans. The adjoining planetarium stages a variety of shows throughout the week, some of which are specifically designed for children as young as five. ⊠*25 Queen Victoria St., Cape Town Central* ☎*021/481–3800* ⊕*www.iziko.org.za/sam* ⊠*Museum R10, planetarium R20* ☉*Museum daily 10–5; planetarium shows weekdays at 2, plus Tues. at 8 PM, and weekends at noon, 1, and 2:30.*

⓭ Tuynhuys *(Town House).* Parts of the Tuynhuys date from the late 17th and early 18th centuries. In the early 1700s foreign dignitaries were no longer being entertained at the castle for fear that state secrets would fall into the wrong hands, so the then Governor's Pleasure House was converted to accommodate them. (The British royal family even stayed here in 1947.) The elegant building with its classical columns now contains the offices of the state president and is not open to the public. ⊠*Government Ave., Cape Town Central.*

BO-KAAP   You'll know you're in the Bo-Kaap (Afrikaans for "on top of the Cape")
★   when you catch the heady smell wafting from Atlas Trading Co., which is often packed with housewives stocking up on fresh spices, or when you hear the call of the muezzin from one of the many mosques in the area. You might even have to sidestep lights, cameras, and film stars, since the district is an oft-used setting for movies and magazine shoots—the brightly colored houses make a stunning backdrop. Bo-Kaap is the historic home of the city's Muslim population, brought from the East as slaves in the late 17th and early 18th centuries. So it's no surprise that it's also home to the Auwal Mosque, the oldest mosque in South Africa. Today the area remains strongly Muslim, and it's fascinating to wander the narrow cobbled lanes past mosques and colorful flat-roof houses. Here you'll find the largest collection of pre-1840 architecture in South Africa, with many homes combining elements of Cape Dutch and British styles. The Bo-Kaap is also known as the Malay quarter, even though its inhabitants originated from all over, including the Indonesian archipelago, India, Turkey, and Madagascar. To experience all that the area has to offer and because there have been a few muggings in the Bo-Kaap, we recommend that you take a guided tour (⇨ *Tours in Cape Town Essentials, below)* or stick to Buitengracht, Dorp, Rose, and Shortmarket streets.

NEED A
BREAK?   **Noon Gun Tearoom and Restaurant** (⊠ *273 Longmarket St., Bo-Kaap* ☎*021/424–0529*) on the slopes of Signal Hill is a good place to stop for a breather and some traditional, home-cooked Malay food. Your entertaining hostess, Miriam Misbach, cooks up a mean curry and *biryani* (a spicy rice-based dished). And her samosas are to die for. The menu is limited, but Miriam's repertoire is anything but; she's chatty and engaging.

㉑ Bo-Kaap Museum. Built in the 18th century, this museum was originally the home of Abu Bakr Effendi, a well-known Turkish scholar and prominent leader in the Muslim community. He was brought here in the mid-19th century to help quell feuding between Muslim factions and is believed to have written one of the first books in Afrikaans. The house has been furnished to re-create the lifestyle of a typical Malay family in the 19th century. (Since the exhibits aren't labeled, you might do better to visit the museum as part of a guided tour of the Malay quarter.) Look for works by artist Gregoire Boonzaire, who is famous for capturing both the chaos and charm of neighborhoods such as the Bo-Kaap and District Six. ☒*71 Wale St., Bo-Kaap* ☎*021/481–3939* ⊕*www.iziko.org.za/bokaap* ☒*R5* ⊙*Mon.–Sat. 9–4.*

GARDENS **Cape Town Holocaust Centre.** This museum is both a memorial to the 6
★ ⑰ million Jews and other victims of Nazism who were killed during the Holocaust and an education center whose aim is to create a caring and just society in which human rights and diversity are valued. The permanent exhibit is excellent and very moving. A multimedia display, comprising photo panels, text, film footage, and music, creates a chilling reminder of the dangers of prejudice, racism, and discrimination. ☒*88 Hatfield St., Gardens* ☎*021/462–5553* ⊕*www.ctholocaust. co.za* ☒*Free* ⊙*Sun.–Thurs. 10–5, Fri. 10–1.*

NEED A
BREAK?
Government Avenue ends opposite the impressive gateway to the Mount Nelson Hotel (☒*76 Orange St., Gardens* ☎*021/483–1000* ⊕*www. mountnelson.co.za*)**, complete with two pith-helmeted gatekeepers. The Nellie, as it's known, was erected in 1899 to welcome the Prince of Wales on his visit to the Cape and today is one of Cape Town's most fashionable and genteel social venues. Come for the terrific high tea. The pastry selection can tempt even the most jaded palate.**

⑲ **Great Synagogue.** Built in 1905 in the baroque style, this synagogue, known as South Africa's mother synagogue, has notable twin towers and a dome, and was apparently inspired by Florentine architecture. The Aron Kodesh, the closet in which the Torah scrolls are stored, is flanked by two beautiful mosaic panels, and light filters through an impressive stained-glass window. The synagogue is the center of a Jewish complex that includes the South African Jewish Museum, the Jacob Gitlin Library, and the Cape Town Holocaust Centre, which is housed in the Albow Centre, next door. A volunteer can lead you on a tour of the synagogue Sunday–Thursday; it's best to call ahead to arrange a time. ☒*88 Hatfield St., Gardens* ☎*021/465–1405* ⊕*www.gardens-shul.org* ⊙*Hrs vary; no tours Fri. or Sat.*

⑱ **South African Jewish Museum.** Spanning 150 years, this museum captures the story of South African Jewry from its beginnings. The Themes of Memories (immigrant experiences), Reality (integration into South Africa), and Dreams (visions) exhibits are dynamically portrayed with high-tech multimedia and interactive displays, reconstructed sets, models, and Judaica artifacts. Also here are a computerized Discovery Center with a roots bank, a temporary gallery for changing exhibits, a museum restaurant and shop, and an auditorium. The museum also screens an exclusive 20-minute documentary on Mandela throughout

IT'S ALL BELLS, WHISTLES — & UMBREL

One of the greatest celebrations in Cape Town is the annual Cape Coon New Year Carnival, also known as the Cape Town Minstrel Carnival or, more simply, as the Coon Carnival (although the term "coon" does rankle some South Africans, it's more accepted in Cape lingo than it would be in the United States or Great Britain, and hence remains the popular name of the festival). The origins of this January festival date to the early colonial period, when slaves were given time off to celebrate New Year's Day. The tradition continue even after the emancipation of slavery and is the most visible reminder of a way of life that saw its finest flowering in District Six. Today thousands of wild celebrants take to the streets in vibrant costumes—complete with matching umbrellas—to sing *moppies* (pronounced a somewhat guttural *more peas,* they're vaudeville-style songs), accompanied by banjos, drums, and whistles. The celebration lasts one or two days.

the day. ✉ *88 Hatfield St., Gardens* ☎ *021/465–1546* ⊕ *www.sajew-ishmuseum.co.za* 💲 *R35* ◷ *Sun.–Thurs. 10–5, Fri. 10–2.*

⓮ **South African National Gallery.** This museum houses a good collection of
Fodor'sChoice 19th- and 20th-century European art, but its most interesting exhibits
★ are the South African works, many of which reflect the country's traumatic history. An excellent example of contemporary South African art is the ghoulish sculpture *The Butcher Boys,* by Jane Alexander. Walk around these three sitting figures with an air of foreboding and menace about them, and you'll be shocked to discover their exposed spines. This is the stuff of nightmares, recalling the torture activists suffered at the hands of the security police during the height of apartheid. The gallery owns an enormous body of work, so exhibitions change regularly, but there's always something provocative—whether it's documentary photographs or a multimedia exhibit chronicling South Africa's struggles with HIV and AIDS. The director, Marilyn Martin, is known for innovative, brave, and sometimes controversial exhibitions and her outspoken stance on art policy and development. Free guided tours on Tuesday and Thursday take about an hour. ✉ *Government Ave., Gardens* ☎ *021/467–4660* ⊕ *www.museums.org.za/sang* 💲 *R10* ◷ *Tues.–Sun. 10–5; tours Tues. and Thurs. at 11 and 1.*

VICTORIA & ALFRED WATERFRONT

The Victoria & Alfred Waterfront is the culmination of a long-term project undertaken to breathe new life into the historical dockland of the city. It is one of Cape Town's most vibrant and exciting attractions, and construction is ongoing. Expensive apartments are being built at the marina, and hundreds of shops, movie theaters, restaurants, and bars share quarters in restored warehouses and dock buildings, all connected by pedestrian plazas and promenades. It's clean, it's safe, and it's car-free.

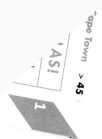
PRECAUTIONS

see the area's major sights in half a day, but that won't give time for shopping, coffee stops, or lunch, or for all that the has to offer. A more leisurely approach would be to set aside day, at the end of which you could find a waterside restaurant d enjoy a cold glass of wine or a sophisticated cocktail.

crowds of people, security cameras, and guards, this is one of st places to shop and hang out in the city. That said, you should still keep an eye on your belongings and be aware of pickpockets.

WHAT TO SEE

35 AGFA Amphitheatre. This popular outdoor space mounts performances ranging from concerts by the Cape Town Philharmonic Orchestra to gigs by jazz and rock bands. (Check with the Waterfront's Cape Town Tourism office for a schedule of events.) The amphitheater stands on the site where, in 1860, a teenage Prince Alfred inaugurated the construction of a breakwater to protect ships in the harbor from devastating northwesterly winds. ⊠*Near Market Sq., Waterfront* ☎*021/408–7600 for schedule* ⊕*www.waterfront.co.za.*

31 Cape Town Tourism—V&A Gateway. The Waterfront branch of the tourism office has the lowdown on everything happening in the area, including upcoming events and shows. Here you can arrange walking tours of the Waterfront, book accommodations, and get information about the whole Western Cape. ⊠*Clock Tower Centre, South Arm Rd., Waterfront* ☎*021/405–4500* ⊕*www.tourismcapetown.co.za* ⊠*Free* ☽*Daily 9–9.*

36 Mitchell's Waterfront Brewery. One of a handful of microbreweries in South Africa, Mitchell's produces four beers: Forester's Draught Lager, Bosun's Bitter, Ravenstout, and Ferrymans Ale. (Forester's Draught Lager, regarded as a "healthful" beer, contains no preservatives and has a fairly light taste.) Tours, for which reservations are essential, include beer tasting and a look at the fermentation tanks. ⊠*E. Pier Rd., Waterfront* ☎*021/419–5074* ⊠*R20* ☽*Weekdays 7–5.*

NEED A BREAK?

After a visit to the brewery next door, you won't want to wait long for a nice cool one at **Ferryman's Tavern** (⊠ *E. Pier Rd., Waterfront* ☎ *021/419-7748*), and you won't have to. In addition to Mitchell's brews, you can sample other South African beers. Constructed in 1877 of bluestone and Table Mountain sandstone, Ferryman's is one of the oldest buildings in the harbor. Before 1912 the temperance movement in Cape Town had managed to force a ban on the sale of alcohol within the docks. As a result, a host of pubs sprang up just outside the dock gates, particularly along Dock Road.

29 Robben Island. Made famous by its most illustrious inhabitant, Nelson Mandela, this island, whose name is Dutch for "seals," has a long and sad history. At various times a prison, leper colony, mental institution, and military base, it is finally filling a positive, enlightening, and empowering role in its latest incarnation as a museum. Robert Sobukwe and Walter Sisulu were also imprisoned here for their role

Fodor's Choice ★

in opposing apartheid. For many years the African National Cc
secretary-general, Sisulu died in 2003 in his early nineties and
given a hero's burial. Sobukwe, founding president of the Pan Africa.
ist Congress, proved to be such a thorn in the government's side that he
was imprisoned in the 1960s under the special Sobukwe Clause, which
had to be renewed every year to keep him in jail. John Voster, then the
country's minister, said of Sobukwe, "He is a man with magnetic personality, great organizing ability, and a divine sense of mission," and it
was these very qualities that made him such a threat. He was treated
slightly better than other prisoners but was kept completely isolated
from them—an especially terrible punishment for a man with such a
strong sense of community. In addition to these more recent prisoners,
there have been some fascinating (and reluctant) inhabitants of this
at once formidable and beautiful place. One of the first prisoners was
Autshumato, known to the early Dutch settlers as Harry the Hottentot.
He was one of the main interpreters for Jan van Riebeeck in the mid-
17th century, and was imprisoned for opposing British colonial rule,
as was his niece Krotoa. In 1820 the British thought they could solve
some of the problems they were having on the Eastern Cape frontier by
banishing Xhosa leader Makhanda to the island. Both Autshumato and
Makhanda (also spelled Makana) escaped by rowboat, but Makhanda
didn't make it.

Declared a World Heritage site on December 1, 1997, Robben Island
has become a symbol of the triumph of the human spirit. In 1997
around 90,000 made the pilgrimage; in 2006 more than 300,000
crossed the water to see where some of the greatest South Africans
spent much of their lives. Visiting the island is a sobering experience,
which begins at the modern Nelson Mandela Gateway to Robben
Island, an impressive embarkation center that doubles as a conference
center. Interactive exhibits display historic photos of prison life. Next
make the journey across the water. Boats leave on the hour, and the
crossing takes 30 minutes.

Tours are organized by the Robben Island Museum. (Other operators advertise Robben Island tours but just take visitors on a boat
trip *around* the island.) As a result of the reconciliation process, most
tour guides are former political prisoners. During the 2½-hour tour
you walk through the prison and see the cells where Mandela and
other leaders were imprisoned. You also tour the lime quarry, where
Mandela spent so many years pounding rocks; in summer the reflection off the rock is blinding, and Mandela's eyesight—but thank-
fully not his insight—was irreparably damaged by the glare. The tour
also takes you past Robert Sobukwe's house and the leper church.
Many of the prison buildings have been renovated, but there are also
plans to upgrade unoccupied houses where the wardens used to live,
extend the harbor, and make the island more wheelchair-friendly. It
can get pretty crowded, so reserve in advance, and take sunglasses
and a hat in summer. ■ TIP→ **You are advised to tip your guide only
if you feel that the tour has been informative.** ☎ *021/413–4220 or
021/413–4221 for information, 021/413–4209, 021/413–4210, or*

13–4211 for reservations, 021/413–4217 or 021/413–4219 for sales ⊕www.robben-island.org.za ⌨R150 ⊙Summer, daily 9; winter, daily 7:30–6; last boat generally leaves island at 8 in ner and 5 in winter (opening times and boat departures can vary, one ahead to check).

African Maritime Museum. As this museum demonstrates, Cape history is tied to the sea. Among the exhibits about the ships of Table Bay are models of the mail ships that used to ply the oceans. A fascinating model of Cape Town harbor as it appeared in 1885 was built by some convicts and wardens with an excellent eye for detail, as is evident in the intricate rigging on the sailing ships. The museum also has photographs and negatives of the more than 9,000 ships that called at Cape Town during the 20th century. ⊠*Union-Castle Building, Dock Rd., Waterfront* ☎*021/405–2880* ⊕*www.iziko.org.za/maritime* ⌨*Free* ⊙*Daily 10–5.*

☾ **③②** **Two Oceans Aquarium.** This aquarium is considered one of the finest Fodor'sChoice in the world. Stunning displays reveal the marine life of the warm ★ Indian Ocean and the icy Atlantic. It's a hands-on place, with a touch pool for children and opportunities for certified divers to explore the vast, five-story kelp forest or the predator tank, where you share the water with a couple of large ragged-tooth sharks (*Carcharias taurus*) and get a legal adrenaline rush (R450, R350 with own gear). For something completely different, try a copper-helmet dive with antique dive equipment in the predator tank (R650). If you don't fancy getting wet, you can still watch the feeding in the predator tank every day at 3. But there's more to the aquarium than just snapping jaws. Look for the endangered African penguins, also known as jackass penguins because of the awkward braying noise they make; pulsating moon jellies and spider crabs; and, if you're lucky, the strange and elusive sunfish. ⊠*Dock Rd., Waterfront* ☎*021/418–3823* ⊕*www.aquarium.co.za* ⌨*R70* ⊙*Daily 9:30–6.*

③③ **Union-Castle House.** Designed in 1919 by famed British architect Sir Herbert Baker, this house was headquarters for the famous Union-Castle shipping line. Before World War II many English-speaking South Africans looked upon England as home, even if they had never been there. The emotional link between the two countries was symbolized most strongly by the mail steamers, carrying both mail and passengers, that sailed weekly between South Africa and England. In 1977, amid much pomp and ceremony, the last Union-Castle mail ship, the *Windsor Castle*, made its final passage to England. Even today older South Africans like to wax lyrical about the joys of a voyage on one of those steamers. Union-Castle House is now home to several banks and small businesses. Inside Standard Bank you can still see the iron rings in the ceiling from which mailbags were hung. ⊠*Quay 4, Waterfront.*

③④ **Victoria Basin.** The basin was constructed between 1870 and 1905 to accommodate the huge increase in shipping following the discovery of diamonds at Kimberley and gold on the Witwatersrand. The South Arm was used as a debarkation point for British troops, horses, and matériel during the Second South African War (1899–1902), also called the Boer War. Much of the fodder for the British horses was shipped in from Argentina and was catastrophically infested with rats and fleas. As a result, bubonic plague broke out in Cape Town in February 1901, causing wholesale panic and hundreds of deaths. The basin today is nothing like its grim past, however. The gorgeous Cape Grace hotel presides at the water's edge, as do privately owned penthouses and another luxury hotel currently under construction. ⊠ *Waterfront*

THE PENINSULA

The Peninsula is a treat for any visitor to Cape Town, and a round-trip drive that takes in both the False Bay coastline and the Atlantic Ocean is a memorable experience. Among the highlights of the False Bay coast are the quaint fishing village of Kalk Bay and Boulders Beach, with its African penguin colony. Cape Point and the Cape of Good Hope nature reserve are at the tip of the peninsula, and few fail to fall in love with the fynbos and windswept beauty of the area. Heading home via Noordhoek, Chapman's Peak, and Hout Bay will give you plenty to ooh and aah about—the coastal drive is one of the most spectacular in the world.

TIMING & PRECAUTIONS

Distances on the peninsula are not that great, so it's certainly possible to drive the loop in a day, visiting a few sights of interest to you. It's equally possible, however, to spend three days here, either moving slowly around the peninsula and staying in a different guesthouse each night or returning to a central spot in the Southern Suburbs at the end of each day. Just remember, however, that during peak season (generally mid-November–mid-January) and holidays, traffic can keep you gridlocked for many frustrating hours. If you don't have time for the Winelands but still want to experience the Cape's excellent wines, work in a visit to Constantia's excellent estates. Although touring the peninsula poses no obvious danger, you are advised not to park or walk alone in isolated areas. And watch out for baboons at Cape Point. If you're carrying food, they invite themselves to lunch.

WHAT TO SEE

⟲ ★ ㊻ **Boulders Beach.** This series of small coves lies among giant boulders on the outskirts of Simon's Town. Part of Table Mountain National Park, the beach is best known for its resident colony of African penguins. You must stay out of the fenced-off breeding beach, but don't be surprised if a wandering bird comes waddling up to you to take a look. Penguin-viewing platforms, accessible from either the Boulders Beach or Seaforth side, provide close-up looks at these comical birds. When you've had enough penguin peering, you can stroll back to Boulders Beach for some excellent swimming in the quiet coves. This beach is great for children because it is so protected, and the sea is warm and calm. It can get crowded in summer, though, so go early. Without traffic, it takes about 45 minutes to get here from town, less from the Southern Suburbs. ⊠ *Follow signs from Bellvue Rd., Simon's Town* ☎ *021/786–*

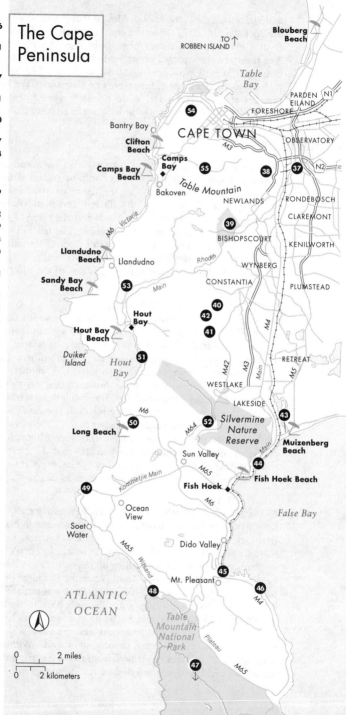

The Cape Peninsula

2329 ⊕ *www.sanparks.org* ☞ *R25* ⊙ *Daily 8–6:30.*

NEED A BREAK?

Serving a hearty breakfast, light lunch, tea, dinner, and drinks, **Boulders Beach Lodge and Restaurant** (⊠ *Boulders Beach parking lot* ☎ *021/786–1758*) has a huge veranda that's great for gazing out over False Bay and watching the sun set. Even though you're facing east, False Bay sunsets are still spectacular. Consisting mostly of reflected light, they are pastel pink, pale blue, lavender, and gold.

As comical as the African penguin may seem, the future doesn't look too bright for these pied birds, which are regarded as an endangered species. Newspaper reports in early 2007 suggested that the African penguin (*Spheniscus demersus*) population had taken a hammering as a result of declining anchovy and sardine stocks. Up to 50,000 birds were lost in just two years. This is bad news for the African penguins, who call Boulders Beach and Stony Point near Betty's Bay (⇨ *Chapter 2*) in the Overberg home. Penguins mate for life and have been known to return to the same nesting site for up to 15 years.

🔸 **Buitenverwachting.** Once part of Dutch governor Simon van der Stel's original Constantia farm, Buitenverwachting (which means "beyond expectation" and is roughly pronounced "Bait-in-fur-wagh-ting") has an absolutely gorgeous setting. An oak-lined avenue leads past the Cape Dutch homestead to the modern cellar. Acres of vines spread up hillsides flanked by more towering oaks and the rocky crags of the Constantiaberg mountain. Buitenverwachting's wine is just as good as the view. The largest seller is the slightly dry Buiten Blanc, an easy-drinking blend of a few varietals. The best red is Christine, a blend of mostly cabernet sauvignon and merlot. The winery's eponymous restaurant is also worth a visit. ⊠ *Off Klein Constantia Rd.* ☎ *021/794–5190* ☞ *Tastings free* ⊙ *Weekdays 9–5, Sat. 9–1.*

NEED A BREAK?

Buitenverwachting (⊠ *Off Klein Constantia Rd.* ☎ *021/794–1012*) serves great picnic lunches during the summer months (November–April) under the oaks on the estate's lawns. It's an idyllic setting and a most civilized way to cap a morning of wine tasting. Each picnic basket is packed with a selection of breads, chicken and other meat, pâtés, and cheeses. You can buy a bottle of estate wine as an accompaniment. The picnic costs R95 per person, and reservations are essential.

🔸 **Cape Point and the Cape of Good Hope.** Once a nature reserve on its own, this section of Table Mountain National Park covers more than 19,000 acres. Much of the park consists of rolling hills covered with fynbos and laced with miles of walking trails, for which maps are available at the park entrance. It also has beautiful deserted beaches (you can swim at some of these beaches, but note that there are no amenities or lifeguards). Eland, baboon, ostrich, and bontebok (a colorful antelope that was hunted to near extinction in the early 20th century) are among the animals that roam the park. A paved road runs 12½ km (8 mi) to

Fodor's Choice ★

the tip of the peninsula, and a turnoff leads to the Cape of Good Hope, a rocky cape that is the southwesternmost point of the continent. A plaque marks the spot—otherwise you would never know you're standing on a site of such significance.

The opposite is true of Cape Point, a dramatic knife's edge of rock that slices into the Atlantic. Looking out to sea from the viewing platform, you feel you're at the tip of Africa, even though that honor officially belongs to Cape Agulhas, about 160 km (100 mi) to the southeast. From Cape Point the views of False Bay and the Hottentots Holland Mountains are astonishing. The walk up to the viewing platform and the old lighthouse is very steep; a funicular (R31 round-trip, R21 one-way) makes the run every three or four minutes. Take a jacket or sweater—the wind can take your breath away. It took six years, from 1913 to 1919, to build the old lighthouse, 816 feet above the high-water mark. On a clear day the old lighthouse was a great navigational mark, but when the mists rolled in it was useless, so a new and much lower lighthouse (286 feet) was built at Dias Lookout Point. The newer, revolving lighthouse, the most powerful on the South African coast, emits a group of three flashes every 30 seconds. It has prevented a number of ships from ending up on Bellows or Albatross Rock below. You can't go into the lighthouses, but the views from their bases are spectacular.

The park has some excellent land-based whale-watching spots. About June–November, whales return to these waters to calve. You're most likely to see the Southern Right whale in False Bay, but the occasional humpback and Bryde's whale also show up. When the water is calm you may even be lucky enough to see a school of dolphins looping their way past. The Rooikrans parking lot is good for whale-watching, but there are any number of lookout points. It's just a matter of driving around until you see the characteristic spray or a shiny black fluke.

The mast you see on the western slopes of Cape Point near the lighthouse belongs to the Global Atmosphere Watch Station (GAW). The South African Weather Bureau, together with the Fraunhofer Institute in Garmisch, Germany, maintains a research laboratory here to monitor long-term changes in the chemistry of the earth's atmosphere, which may impact climate. This is one of 20 GAWs throughout the world, chosen because the air at Cape Point is considered particularly pure most of the time.

A large sit-down restaurant has better views than food (but that is saying a lot). Also here are a kiosk selling snacks and three gift shops. During peak season (December–January), visit Cape Point as early in the day as you can; otherwise you'll be swamped by horrendous numbers of tour buses and their occupants. Fun alternatives include an escorted bike trip to the point with private companies such as BazBus and Daytrippers (⇨ Tours in Cape Town Essentials, below), and an overnight hike with comfortable basic accommodations and incredible views, which is booked through South African National Parks. ⚠ Be wary of baboons in the parking lot; they have been known to steal

1

food and can be dangerous if provoked. Do not feed them. Unfortunately the indigenous chacma baboons are increasingly under threat, and in 2006 it was estimated that only 375 (148 females, 43 males, and 184 infants in 10 troops) remain in the Cape Peninsula. ⊠*Off the M65 (Plateau Rd.)* ☎*021/780–9526 or 021/780–9204* ⊕*www.sanparks. org* ☎*R55* ☉*Apr.–Sept., daily 7–5; Oct.–Mar., daily 6–6; last exit 1 hr after closing.*

★ ❺ **Chapman's Peak Drive.** After being closed for several years in the early 2000s due to rock slides and unstable cliff faces, this fantastically scenic drive reopened after a major reconstruction that involved state-of-the-art engineering techniques, some of which had never been used on South African roads. But that wasn't the first engineering feat for this road that clings to the mountainside. Work began on the drive in 1910, when it was considered an impossibility. Charl Marais, a mining surveyor, wasn't deterred by the task and set about surveying a route by sending a worker ahead of him to chop out footholds and create rudimentary platforms for his theodolite. There are stories of him hanging on to the side of the cliff by ropes and nearly losing his life on a number of occasions. His tenacity paid off, and with the help of 700 convicts a road was chipped and blasted out of the rock. Chapman's Peak Drive officially opened in 1922. A reporter from a local newspaper waxed lyrical, writing that the road was much like a woman, "always changing, luring, and at moments giving you a quick sense of danger." You can access the drive from both Noordhoek and Hout Bay.

★ ❹ **Groot Constantia.** The town of Constantia takes its name from the wine estate established here in 1685 by Simon van der Stel, one of the first Dutch governors of the Cape. After his death in 1712 the land was subdivided, with the heart of the estate preserved at Groot Constantia. The enormous complex enjoys the status of a national monument and is by far the most commercial and touristy of the wineries. Van der Stel's magnificent homestead, the oldest in the Cape, lies at the center of Groot Constantia. It's built in traditional Cape Dutch style, with thick, whitewashed walls, a thatch roof, small-paned windows, and ornate gables. The house is a museum furnished with exquisite period pieces. The old wine cellar sits behind the manor house. Built in 1791, it is most famous for its own ornate gable, which contains a sculpture designed by Anton Anreith. The sculpture, depicting fertility, is regarded as one of the most important in the country. The cellar houses a wine museum with displays on wine-drinking and storage vessels dating to antiquity.

In the 19th century the sweet wines of Groot Constantia were highly regarded in Europe, but today Groot Constantia is known for its splendid red wines. The best is the excellent Bordeaux-style Gouverneurs Reserve, made mostly from cabernet sauvignon grapes with smaller amounts of merlot and cabernet franc. The pinotage is consistently good, too, reaching its velvety prime in about five years. The estate operates two restaurants: the elegant Jonkershuis and Simon's, which serves sophisticated meals in a spectacular setting. You can also bring your own picnic—or buy a picnic from Jonkershuis for R110 per person—and relax on the lawns behind the wine cellar. ☒ *Off Constantia Rd., Constantia* ☎ *021/794–5128 winery, 021/795–5140 museum, 021/794–6255 Jonkershuis, 021/794–1143 Simon's* ☎ *Museum R10, tastings R20, cellar tour with tastings R25* ☉ *Museum daily 10–5. Winery May–Sept., daily 9–5; Oct.–Apr., daily 9–6. Tours 7 times per day starting at 10.*

㊲ Irma Stern Museum. This museum is dedicated to the works and art collection of Irma Stern (1894–1966), one of South Africa's greatest painters. The museum is administered by the University of Cape Town and occupies the Firs, the artist's home for 38 years. She is best known for African studies, particularly her paintings of indigenous people inspired by trips to the Congo and Zanzibar. Her collection of African artifacts, including priceless Congolese stools and carvings, is superb. ☒ *Cecil Rd., Rosebank* ☎ *021/685–5686* ⊕ *www.irmastern.co.za* ☒ *R10* ☉ *Tues.–Sat. 10–5.*

☪ ★ ㊹ Kalk Bay. This small, fascinating harbor, which shelters a weathered fishing fleet, takes its name from the seashells that were once baked in large kilns near the shore to produce lime (*kalk*). Tiny cottages crowd the narrow cobbled streets, clinging to the mountain, and funky clothing shops, galleries, antiques shops, and cozy bistros can fill a whole day of rambling. Here gnarled fisherfolk rub shoulders with artists, writers, surfers, yuppies, New Age trendies, and genteel ladies with blue hair rinses. During whale seasons the gentle giants rub up against the harbor wall, and if you time your visit right you can almost touch them. You can also walk up any of the steep stairways to Boyes Drive and from there up the mountain, or relax and down a few beers in the sun at the Brass Bell while local surfers strut their stuff on Kalk Bay Reef. Other possibilities on your to-do list might include dropping your own line off the pier (fishing supplies are available from the small supermarket on the Main Road) or watching the harbor seals that loll around waiting for fishy discards when the boats come in. The lives of the fisherfolk are changing rapidly due to declining fish stocks, and many are now shorebound without an income due, in part, to the controversial requirement for fishing permits.

NEED A BREAK?

Kalky's (☒ *Kalk Bay Harbour, Kalk Bay* ☎ *021/788–1726*), right on the harbor, is a great place to get generous portions of fish-and-chips. The seagulls will fight for any of your leftover scraps, as will Robby, the resident seal. The **Olympia Caféé and Deli** (☒ *Bottom of St. John's Rd., Kalk Bay* ☎ *021/788–6396*), a Mediterranean café, is one of the best places to eat in Cape Town and is usually packed to capacity, especially weekends. At the affiliated bakery just around the corner, you can buy take-away cappuccinos, melt-in-your-mouth croissants, and pasties filled with springbok and sometimes even rabbit. Pop in, elbow your way through the locals who won't start their day without something from "The Deli" (as it's fondly known), and take whatever you've bought to the harbor wall (just a two-minute walk away), where eat and watch the seals gambol in front of you.

🄲 ㊴ Kirstenbosch National Botanic Gardens. Spectacular in each se
Fodor'sChoice world-famous gardens showcase stunning South African
★ magnificent setting, extending up the eastern slopes of Ta
tain and overlooking the sprawling city and the distant
Holland Mountains. No wonder the gardens are photographed from
every angle. They aren't just enjoyed by out-of-town visitors, however;
on weekends Capetonians flock here with their families to lie on the
lawns and read their newspapers while the kids run riot. Walking trails
meander through the gardens, and grassy banks are ideal for a picnic
or afternoon nap. The plantings are limited to species indigenous to
southern Africa, including fynbos—hardy, thin-leaved plants that proliferate in the Cape. Among these are proteas, including silver trees and
king proteas; ericas; and *restios* (reeds). Magnificent sculptures from
Zimbabwe are displayed around the gardens, too.

Garden highlights include a large cycad garden, the Bird Bath (a beautiful stone pool built around a crystal-clear spring), and the fragrance
garden, which is wheelchair-friendly and has a tapping rail and Braille
interpretive boards. Those who have difficulty walking can take a comprehensive tour lasting 45 minutes to an hour (R25; hourly 9–3) in
six-person (including the driver) golf carts. Another wheelchair trail
leads from the main paths into the wilder section of the park, getting
close to the feel of the mountain walks. Concerts featuring the best of
South African entertainment—from classical music to township jazz
to rock and roll—are held on summer Sundays starting an hour before
sunset, but get there early, as the space fills up quickly with picnicking
music lovers. A visitor center by the conservatory houses a restaurant,
bookstore, and coffee shop. Unfortunately, muggings have become
increasingly more common in the gardens' isolated areas, and women
are advised not to walk alone in the upper reaches of the park far from
general activity. ⊠ *Rhodes Ave., Newlands* ☎ *021/799–8783* ⊕ *www.
nbi.ac.za* ⊠ *R30* ☉ *Apr.–Aug., daily 8–6; Sept.–Mar., daily 8–7.*

㊷ Klein Constantia. *Klein* (rhymes with "stain") means "small" in Afrikaans
and indicates the relative size of this portion of Simon van der Stel's
original 17th-century Constantia estate. The winery has an impressive
modern cellar, and its Cape Dutch homestead, visible as you drive in,
was built in the late 18th century. This estate produces wines of superb
quality, as awards displayed in the tasting area attest. The excellent
sauvignon blanc is used as a point of reference by many South African
connoisseurs and vintners. The closest you'll come to the famous Constantia wine of the 18th century is the Vin de Constance, a sweet wine
made from predominantly muscat de Frontignan grapes. The cabernet
sauvignon is one of the best produced in the Cape—a collector's wine
that will develop wonderfully over time. ⊠ *Klein Constantia Rd., Constantia* ☎ *021/794–5188* ⊕ *www.kleinconstantia.com* ⊠ *Tastings free*
☉ *Weekdays 9–5, Sat. 9–1; cellar tours weekdays by appointment.*

🄲 ㊾ Kommetjie. A pleasant, somewhat isolated suburb, Kommetjie has a
scenic 45-minute walk down Long Beach that leads to the wreck of
the *Kakapo,* a steamship that ran aground on her maiden voyage in
1900. This is a surfer's paradise, with some really big waves and a

few gentler breaks. Because of a series of attacks on Long Beach, you are advised to walk here only in a group. If you don't have security in numbers, walk instead to the Kommetjie lighthouse, the tallest cast-iron tower on South Africa's coast, at Slangkoppunt, almost exactly midway between Robben Island and Cape Point. The lighthouse has a 5-million-candlepower light and a range of 30 nautical miles, with four flashes every 30 seconds. Nearby **Imhoff Farm** (⊠*Kommetjie Rd.* ☎*021/783–4545*) is a good stop if you're traveling with children, as there are camel and horseback rides, a rather scruffy petting zoo, crafts shops, and a coffee shop.

㊸ If you're visiting the beach community of Muizenberg, there are two sights worth seeing. **Het Post Huys** (⊠ *Main Rd.* ☎*021/788–7972* 🖾*Free*), one of the oldest buildings in the country still standing, was constructed in 1673 as a lookout post and signal station. It also served as an early toll station in precolonial times but now houses an exhibition on the Battle of Muizenberg (1795) as well as more recent photos chronicling the town's heyday. The opening hours depend on the availability of volunteers, so call ahead or else take a chance and drop by. **Rhodes Cottage Museum** (⊠*246 Main Rd.* ☎*021/788–1816* 🖾*Free* ☉*Daily 9–5*) was the seaside home of Cecil John Rhodes (1853–1902). Considering the power wielded by Rhodes, his cottage was surprisingly humble and spare, and yet this is where he chose to spend his last days in 1902, preferring the cool sea air of Muizenberg to the stifling opulence of his home at Groote Schuur. The cottage, including the bedroom where he died, has been completely restored. Other rooms display photos documenting Rhodes's life.

㊿ **Noordhoek.** This popular beach community has stunning white sands that stretch forever. The small bordering village has become a retreat for the arts-and-crafts community and has a couple of galleries and boutiques. You can walk all the way to Kommetjie on the aptly named Long Beach. It's also very popular with horseback riders and surfers, but don't walk alone or when the beach is deserted, as beach attacks are not uncommon.

NEED A BREAK? The **Red Herring Restaurant** (⊠*Noordhoek* ☎*021/789–1783*) is a favorite local hangout for surfers and dogs (yes, dogs; lots of people bring their canine friends here). Skabenga's, the upstairs bar, has a fantastic view. The pizzas are good, and the beer is always cold, but the service is a bit erratic.

★ **㊡** **Ou Kaapse Weg** (*Old Cape Road*). The shortest route between Noordhoek and Constantia is also the most scenic, with lovely flowers and distant vistas of False Bay in the east and the Atlantic in the west. Heading toward the city over Ou Kaapse Weg you get an excellent view of the sprawling Pollsmoor Prison next door to the exclusive Steenberg wine farm and golf estate—a stark illustration of the contradictions that continue to plague South Africa.

★ **㊳** **Rhodes Memorial.** Rhodes served as prime minister of the Cape from 1890 to 1896. He made his fortune in the diamond rush at Kimberley, but his greatest dream was to forge a Cape–Cairo railway, a tangible symbol of British dominion in Africa. The classical-style granite memorial sits high on the slopes of Devil's Peak, on part of Rhodes's old estate, Groote Schuur. A mounted rider symbolizing energy faces north toward the continent for which Rhodes felt such passion. A bust of Rhodes dominates the temple—ironically, he's leaning on one hand as if he's about to nod off. ⊠ *Off Rhodes Dr., Rondebosch* 🎟*Free.*

NEED A BREAK? The **Rhodes Memorial Restaurant** (⊠ *Off Rhodes Dr., Rondebosch* 🖀 *021/689-9151*), tucked under towering pines behind the memorial, is a pleasant spot that serves breakfast, tea, and a light lunch.

48 Scarborough. This tiny vacation community has one of the best beaches on the peninsula. Scarborough is becoming popular with artists and craftspeople, and you'll find their offerings exhibited at informal galleries. From Scarborough to Kommetjie the M65 hugs the shoreline, snaking between the mountains and the crashing surf. This part of the shore is considered unsafe for swimming, but experienced surfers and windsurfers revel in the wind and waves.

54 Signal Hill. Where Signal Hill Road swings around the shoulder of Lion's Head and runs along the flank of Signal Hill, the views of Table Mountain and the city below are superb. The road ends at a parking lot overlooking Sea Point and all of Table Bay. Be careful around here, especially if it's deserted. There have been incidents of violent crime.

★ **45 Simon's Town.** Picturesque Simon's Town has many lovely old buildings and is close to what are possibly the peninsula's best swimming beaches, Seaforth and Boulders. The town has had a long association with the Royal Navy. British troops landed here in 1795 before defeating the Dutch at the Battle of Muizenberg, and the town served as a base for the Royal Navy from 1814 to 1957, when it was handed over to the South African navy. Today you are bound to see plenty of men and women decked out in crisp white uniforms.

Jubilee Square, a dockside plaza that serves as the de facto town center, is just off the main road (St. George's Road). Next to the dock wall stands a **statue of Just Nuisance**, a Great Dane adopted as a mascot by the Royal Navy during World War II. Just Nuisance apparently liked his pint of beer, and would accompany sailors on the train into Cape Town. He had the endearing habit of leading drunken sailors—and only sailors—that he found in the city back to the station in time to catch the last train. The navy went so far as to induct him into the service as an able seaman attached to the HMS *Afrikander.* He died at the age of seven in April 1944 and was given a military funeral. Just below Jubilee Square is the popular Simon's Town Waterfront, with numerous shops and restaurants; a toy museum; a nearby gemstone factory; and Bear Basics, where you can buy any number of cute teddy bears and even trendier gear for them to wear, including outfits made out of traditional South African fabrics. Day cruises and deep-sea fishing trips also leave from the harbor.

NEED A BREAK? **At Just Sushi Bar & Restaurant** (✉ *Simon's Town Waterfront, Simon's Town* ☎ *021/786–4340*) the sushi is fresh, the atmosphere is friendly and unpretentious, and the prices are welcoming.

55 **Tafelberg Road.** This road crosses the northern side of Table Mountain before ending at Devil's Peak. From the Kloof Nek intersection you can descend to Cape Town directly or return to Camps Bay and follow the coastal road back to the city. This route takes you through the beautiful seaside communities of Clifton and Bantry Bay, and then along the seaside promenade in Sea Point.

53 **World of Birds.** Here you can walk through aviaries housing 450 species of indigenous and exotic birds, including eagles, vultures, penguins, and flamingos. No cages separate you from most of the birds, so you can get some pretty good photographs; however, the big raptors are kept behind fences. ✉ *Valley Rd., Hout Bay* ☎ *021/790–2730* ⊕ *www. worldofbirds.org.za* 🎫 *R55* ⊘ *Daily 9–5.*

BEACHES

With panoramic views of mountains tumbling to the ocean, the stunning sandy beaches of the Cape Peninsula are a major draw for Capetonians and visitors alike. Beautiful as the beaches may be, don't expect to spend hours splashing in the surf: the water around Cape Town is very, very cold (although you get used to it). Beaches on the Atlantic are washed by the Benguela Current flowing up from the Antarctic, and in midsummer the water hovers around 10°C–15°C (50°F–60°F). The water on the False Bay side is usually 5°C (9°F) warmer, so if it's warmer waters you seek, head to False Bay beaches such as Muizenberg, Fish Hoek, and Boulders. Cape beaches are renowned for their clean, snow-white, powdery sand. Beachcombers will find every kind of beach to suit them, from intimate coves to sheltered bays and wild, wide beaches stretching forever. If you are looking for more tropical water temperatures, head for the warm Indian Ocean waters of Kwa-Zulu-Natal or the Garden Route.

The major factor that affects any day at a Cape beach is wind. In summer howling southeasters, known collectively as the Cape Doctor, are all too common and can ruin a trip to the beach; during these gales you're better off at Clifton or Llandudno, on the Atlantic side; the sheltered but very small St. James Beach, on the False Bay side; and maybe even the southern corner of False Bay's Fish Hoek Beach or one of the pools along Jager's Walk. Boulders *(⇨above)* and Seaforth are also often sheltered from southeasters.

Every False Bay community has its own beach, but most are not reviewed here. In comparison with Atlantic beaches, most of them are rather small and often crowded, sandwiched between the sea and the commuter rail line, with Fish Hoek a major exception. South of Simon's Town the beaches tend to be wilder and less developed, except for the very popular Seaforth and Millers Point beaches.

TIMING & PRECAUTIONS

The closest beaches to town are Clifton and Camps Bay, which are just minutes away during non-rush-hour traffic. But in summer, when you can't move for traffic, getting anywhere—and especially to the beaches—can take a frustratingly long time. If you want an adventure and are eager to avoid the holiday traffic, jump on the train that runs by the False Bay beaches of Muizenberg, Fish Hoek, and Boulders. From the center of town it will take you about 40 minutes to get to Fish Hoek, and the views across the bay from Muizenberg onward are absolutely spectacular.

At many beaches there may be powerful waves, a strong undertow, and dangerous riptides. The lifeguard situation is haphazard, and varies according to funding and the availability of the lifeguards; the service combines voluntary and professional guards. Lifeguards work the main beaches, but only on weekends and during school breaks. Other beaches are unpatrolled. Although it's nice to stroll along a lonely beach, remember it's risky to wander off on your own in a deserted area. ⚠ **Toilet facilities at beaches are limited.**

Southeasters can also bring blue bottles—Portuguese men-of war. As these jelly fish–like creatures can sting, you should avoid swimming at these times. (If you see them washed up on the shore, that's a good sign to stay out of the water.)

The beaches below are marked on the Cape Peninsula map.

ATLANTIC COAST

Blouberg. Make the 25-km (16-mi) trip north from the city to the other side of Table Bay, and you'll be rewarded with an exceptional (and the most famous) view of Cape Town and Table Mountain. Blouberg is divided into two parts: Big Bay, which hosts surfing and windsurfing contests, and Little Bay, better suited to sunbathers and families. It's frequently windy here, which is fine if you want to fly a kite but a nuisance otherwise. (The Kite Shop in Victoria Wharf at the V&A Waterfront has many brightly colored high-tech numbers for sale.) Kite surfing has become extremely popular, and adrenaline junkies blow off work to come here and ride the waves. For safety, swim in front of the lifeguard club. The lawns of the Blue Peter Hotel are a favorite sunset cocktail spot, especially with tired kite- and windsurfers. ⊠*N1 north to R27 to Milnerton and Bloubergstrand, Blouberg.*

Camps Bay. The spectacular western edge of Table Mountain, known as the Twelve Apostles, provides the backdrop for this long, sandy beach that slopes gently to the very cold water from a grassy verge. Playing Frisbee or volleyball is very popular on this beach. The surf is powerful, but sunbathers can cool off in a tidal pool or under cool outdoor showers. The popular bars and restaurants of Camps Bay lie only yards away across Victoria Road. One drawback is the wind, which can blow hard here. It 's also a popular vacation resort for Cape

Town's beautiful people—models, movie stars, and the rest of the rich and famous. ⊠ *Victoria Rd., Camps Bay* Ⓜ *Hout Bay bus from OK Bazaars on Adderley St.*

★ **Clifton.** This is where the in crowd comes to see and be seen. Some of the Cape's most desirable houses cling to the slopes above the beach, and elegant yachts often anchor in the calm water beyond the breakers. Granite outcroppings divide the beach into four segments, unimaginatively known as First, Second, Third, and Fourth beaches. Fourth Beach is popular with families, whereas the others support a strong social and singles scene. Swimming is reasonably safe here, although the undertow is strong and the water, again, freezing. Lifeguards are on duty on weekends and in peak season. During holidays Clifton can be a madhouse, and your chances of finding parking at these times are nil. If you plan to visit the beaches in midsummer, consider renting a scooter or motorcycle instead of a car, taking a shuttle from your hotel, or going early in the morning, when the beautiful people are still sleeping off their champagne from the night before. ⊠ *Off Victoria Rd., Clifton* Ⓜ *Hout Bay bus from OK Bazaars on Adderley St.*

Hout Bay. Cradled in a lovely bay of the same name and guarded by a 1,000-foot peak known as the Sentinel, Hout Bay is the center of Cape Town's crayfishing industry, and the town operates several fish-processing plants. It also has a great beach with a knockout view of the mountains, gentle surf, and easy access to the restaurants and bars of Mariner's Wharf. Unfortunately, however, because this is a working harbor, the beach can be polluted, and the water often has an oily film on the surface. But people still swim here.

If you're getting hungry, head to Mariner's Wharf, which is Hout Bay's salty answer to the Waterfront in Cape Town. You can buy fresh fish at a seafood market and take it outside to be grilled. You should also try *snoek,* a barracuda-like fish that is traditionally eaten smoked. Cruise boats *(⇨ Tours in Cape Town Essentials, below)* depart from Hout Bay's harbor to view the Cape fur seal colony on Duiker Island. ⊠ *Off the M6, Hout Bay* Ⓜ *Hout Bay bus from OK Bazaars on Adderley St.*

Llandudno. Die-hard fans return to this beach again and again, and who can blame them? Its setting, among giant boulders at the base of a mountain, is glorious, and sunsets here attract their own aficionados. The surf can be very powerful on the northern side of the beach (where you'll find all the surfers, of course), but the southern side is fine for a quick dip—and in this water that's all you'll want. Lifeguards are on duty on weekends and in season. If you come by bus, brace yourself for a long walk down (and back up) the mountain from the bus stop on the M6. Parking is a nightmare, but most hotels run shuttles in summer. ⊠ *Llandudno exit off M6, Llandudno* Ⓜ *Hout Bay bus from OK Bazaars on Adderley St.*

Long Beach. This may be the most impressive beach on the peninsula, a vast expanse of white sand stretching 6½ km (4 mi) from the base of Chapman's Peak to Kommetjie. It's also one of the wildest and least populated, backed by a lagoon and private nature reserve. Because of the wind and the space, it attracts horseback riders and walkers rather than sunbathers, and the surfing is excellent. There are no lifeguards and there is no bus service, and as at some other beaches, there are real safety concerns. Despite patrollers on horseback and an all-terrain vehicle, crime is an issue here, and women in particular should be careful. You'd do well not to visit this beach unless it is well populated. ⊠ *Off M6, Noordhoek.*

> ### SPOTTING SHARKS
>
> Shark spotters are employed at several of Cape Town's beaches to warn bathers when sharks are out and about. Great white sharks are usually found close to the shore in the summer months (September–March), and spotters record around 170 sightings per year.

Sandy Bay. Backed by wild dunes, Cape Town's unofficial nudist beach is also one of its prettiest. Sunbathers can hide among rocky coves or frolic on a long stretch of sandy beach. Shy nudists will appreciate its isolation, 20 minutes on foot from the nearest parking area in Llandudno. That said, it's best to go to Sandy Bay with your eyes open (both literally and figuratively): amorous beachgoers have upon occasion been spotted in flagrante delicto behind boulders and bushes here, which can take unsuspecting sunbathers by surprise. Wind can also be a problem: if you're caught in the buff when the southeaster starts to blow, you're in for a painful sandblasting. Sandy Bay is also popular with gay men in summer and winter. Getting here by bus means a very long walk going down and up the mountain, but parking, too, is very difficult. ⊠ *Llandudno exit off M6, Llandudno* Ⓜ *Hout Bay bus from OK Bazaars on Adderley St.*

FALSE BAY

🕙 **Fish Hoek.** With the southern corner protected from the southeaster by Elsies Peak, this sandy beach attracts retirees and families with young kids, who appreciate the calm, clear water—it may be the safest bathing beach in the Cape, although sharks are sighted fairly regularly in the bay between September and March (though that doesn't stop people from swimming, surfing, and boogie boarding here); shark spotters are employed to keep an eye out. The middle and northern end of the beach are also popular with catamaran sailors and windsurfers, who often stage regattas offshore. Jager's Walk, from the south side of Fish Hoek Beach to Sunny Cove, is a pleasant, scenic, wheelchair-friendly pathway that meanders through the rocks, providing access to some sheltered natural rock pools that are just great for swimming. The snorkeling is good, too. This is also a great beach for boogie boarding. It's also one of the best places to see whales during calving season—approximately August to November—though there have been whale sightings as early as June and as late as January. Outside of peak traffic, it takes about 30 minutes to get from Cape Town to Fish Hoek, but over Christmas and New Year's the roads get very congested, so leave early to miss the crowds. ⊠ *Beach Rd., Fish Hoek.*

Muizenberg. Once the fashionable resort of South African high society, this long, sandy beach has, unfortunately, lost much of its glamour and now appeals to families and beginner surfers. A tacky pavilion houses a swimming pool, waterslides, toilets, changing rooms, and snack shops. The beach is lined with colorful bathing boxes of the type once popular at British resorts. Lifeguards are on duty, and the sea is shallow and reasonably safe. Many of the beautiful art-deco beachfront buildings that were fast becoming slums have been renovated into upscale apartments. New restaurants have opened, and property prices have soared. If you're keen on stretching your legs you can walk along the beach or take the picturesque concrete path known as the Catwalk, which connects Muizenberg to St. James. ⊠ *Off the M4, Muizenberg.*

WHERE TO EAT

By Brian
Berkman

Cape Town is the culinary capital of South Africa. Nowhere else in the country is the populace so discerning about food, and nowhere else is there such a wide selection of restaurants. Western culinary history here dates back more than 350 years—Cape Town was founded specifically to grow food—and that heritage is reflected in the city's cuisine. A number of restaurants operate in historic town houses and 18th-century wine estates, and many include heritage dishes on their menus.

Today dining in the city and its suburbs can offer a truly global culinary experience, since Cape chefs are now showing the same enthusiasm for global trends as their counterparts worldwide. French and Italian food has long been available here, but in the last decade, with the introduction of Thai and Pan-Asian flavors, locals have embraced the chili. Kurdish, Persian, Ethiopian, Lebanese, and regional Chinese cuisines are now easily available, and other Asian fare is commonplace. Sushi is ubiquitous. If there is a cuisine trend it is toward organic produce and healthful dishes made with foams rather than creams. Some ingredients, like foie gras and pork belly, are now so easily available that they're on most menus.

Wine lists at many restaurants reflect the enormous expansion and resurgence of the Cape wine industry since the 1990s, with some establishments compiling exciting selections of lesser-known gems. More and more restaurants employ a sommelier to offer guidance on wine, but diners, even in modest establishments, can expect staff to be well versed about both wine lists and menus. Wines are expensive in restaurants (often three times what you'd pay in a wineshop), and connoisseurs are often irritated at corkage charges (around R20). Only a handful of restaurants will refuse to open a bottle you bring, often the same ones that refuse to provide tap water despite its being perfectly potable.

During summer months restaurants in trendier areas are geared up for late-night dining, but will accept dinner orders from about 6. In winter locals tend to dine earlier, but there are venues that stay open late, particularly at the Waterfront and the strip along the main road between the city and Green Point. Other areas that are meccas for food lovers include Kloof Street (dubbed Restaurant Mile) in the City Bowl and the beachfront road in Camps Bay along the Atlantic seaboard. Many restaurants are crowded in high season, so it's best to book in advance whenever possible. With the exception of the fancier hotel restaurants—where a jacket is suggested—the dress code in Cape Town is casual (but no shorts).

For a description of South African culinary terms, see the Menu Guide in Understanding South Africa.

WHAT IT COSTS IN SOUTH AFRICAN RAND					
	¢	$	$$	$$$	$$$$
RESTAURANTS	under R50	R50–R75	R75–R100	R100–R125	over R125

Prices are per person for a main course at dinner, a main course equivalent, or a prix-fixe meal.

CAPE TOWN CENTRAL & CITY BOWL

The restaurants below are marked on the Where to Stay & Eat in Cape Town map.

$$$$ ✕**Haiku.** As this is widely regarded as the best Pan-Asian restaurant in town, it's worth putting up with the waiting lists, multiple seatings, and a complex menu that you'll probably need the server's help to wade through. The dim sum includes a spicy panfried lamb pot sticker with coriander and green chilies, and from the wok menu you can order salt-pepper calamari fried with five spices. Grills include mint lamb chops served with dry red chilies and garlic. On the sushi menu the salmon roses, thin sashimi curls filled with mayonnaise and topped with pink caviar, are outstanding. Multiple kitchens mean that cuisine arrives when it's ready. Although this provides the freshest dining experience, it may mean fellow diners watching while you eat, or vice versa. Haiku is owned by the same people who own Bukhara, the Indian restaurant above it. ⊠ *33 Burg St., Cape Town Central* ☎ *021/424–7000* ⌂ *Reservations essential* ⊟ *AE, DC, MC, V* ⊘ *No lunch Sun.*

$$$–$$$$ ✕**Cape Colony Restaurant.** Tall bay windows, a high domed ceiling, and a giant trompe-l'oeil mural—an inventive evocation of Table Mountain in days of yore—create a befitting setting for the city's most historic and unashamedly colonial hotel. This is a good place to come for a stylish night out, enhanced by a band. The menu includes such classic dishes as foie gras *ballentine* with apple-pear chutney and brioche, and lamb's kidney Bercy (with shallots and white wine). You'll also find Asian-inspired creations such as tomato-and-basil risotto in tomato water with fried dim sum, and Vietnamese black-lacquered roasted rack of lamb with fried bok choy. The Oasis, the hotel's Mediterranean poolside buffet restaurant, is outstanding. ⊠ *Mount Nelson Hotel, 76 Orange St., Gardens* ☎ *021/483–1000* ⌂ *Reservations essential* ⊟ *AE, DC, MC, V.*

$$–$$$$ ✕**Ginja.** Ginja's position in the culinary firmament is well deserved,
Fodor'sChoice but it does mean booking one month in advance and choosing one
★ of two sittings staggered from 7 PM. Order the Around the World in

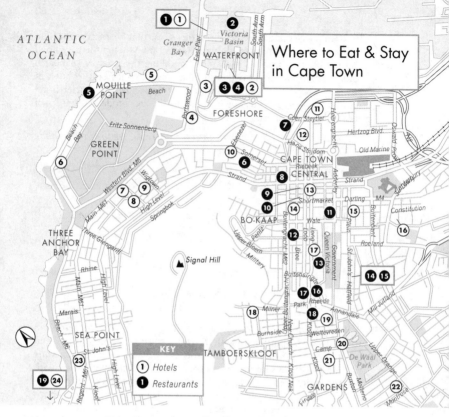

Where to Eat & Stay in Cape Town

KEY

① Hotels

● Restaurants

Restaurants

Africa Cafe **10**

Atlantic **1**

Aubergine **15**

Belthazar **2**

Birds Boutique Café **12**

Cape Colony Restaurant .. **14**

Ginja **8**

Haiku **11**

Manolo **18**

95 Keerom **13**

Ocean Basket **16**

one.waterfront **4**

Pigalle **6**

Panama Jack's **3**

Rozenhof **17**

Salt **19**

Savoy Cabbage **9**

The Showroom **7**

Wakame **5**

Hotels

Altona Lodge **8**

ArabellaSheraton
Grand Hotel Cape Town .. **11**

Ashanti Lodge **20**

A Sunflower Stop **7**

Best Western
Cape Suites Hotel **16**

Cape Grace **2**

Cape Heritage Hotel **14**

Cape Milner Hotel **18**

Cape Victoria
Guest House **9**

Daddy Long Legs
Boutique Hotel **17**

Ellerman House **24**

La Splendida
Luxury Suites **6**

Metropole **13**

Mount Nelson Hotel **19**

Peninsula
All Suites Hotel **23**

Protea Breakwater
Lodge **4**

Protea Hotel
Victoria Junction **10**

Radisson SAS Hotel **5**

Southern Sun Cullinan Cape
Town Waterfront **12**

Table Bay Hotel **1**

Townhouse Hotel **15**

Victoria & Alfred Hotel **3**

Villa Belmonte **22**

Welgelegen
Guest House **21**

a Spoon starter from the eclectic menu: six delicious mouthfuls, from eggplant with Parmesan to avocado sushi with ginger. Springbok Wellington with caramelized red cabbage and green beans is a delicious main course. End with Oreo mascarpone pudding served with an atomizer of Amaretto perfume. Service is slick, and the narrow entrance corridor, red walls, and black-and-white images of forks hint at the drama to unfold. Watch your step as you enter. ⊠ *121 Castle St., Cape Town Central, 8001* ☎ *021/426–2368* ⌂ *Reservations essential* ⊟ *AE, DC, MC, V* ✆ *Closed Sun. No lunch.*

$$–$$$$ ✕**one.waterfront.** With views over the yacht basin and working harbor, one.waterfront is a good spot for breakfast or lunch; come dinnertime, the watery reflection of lights only hints at the surrounding beauty. Seating is indoors, with a smattering of outdoor tables. Service is a hallmark at this hotel, and the attention that all guests, including diners, receive, is seductive. The menu reflects the hotel's position in the Cape and by the sea, with a focus on local ingredients. A three-mouthful starter, the smoked-duck-and-foie-gras pizza is packed with flavor and illustrates the kitchen's typical treatment: classic dishes updated. The coriander-crusted kingklip (a firm white fish similar to monkfish) served with prawn, potato, and a dill-and-caviar vinaigrette is also recommended. If all this sounds too fancy, the restaurant will accommodate requests for simpler dishes. The wine list includes local labels, and a sommelier can assist you with your choice. ⊠ *Cape Grace Hotel, West Quay Rd., Waterfront* ☎ *021/410–7100* ⊟ *AE, DC, MC, V.*

$$–$$$$ ✕**Pigalle.** One of the few stylish dinner-and-dancing venues near the city, Pigalle is an eclectic mix of sumptuous reds, art-nouveau-inspired light fixtures, and reproductions of Andy Warhol's Elvis images. Although it's open for lunch, the place comes alive at dinner, when a jazz band plays lounge-style tunes before upping the tempo and welcoming diners to the dance floor. The Portuguese cuisine includes starters of *trinchado* (panfried beef cubes with a tangy sauce) and grilled KwaZulu-Natal baby lobster served with a pineapple-chili salsa, but seafood (and langoustines in particular) is recommended simply grilled with either lemon-garlic or Portuguese-style *peri-peri* (a type of chili) bastings. The steaks are also delicious. The excellent staff seems to glide between tables as if still at the ice rink that used to be here. ⊠ *57a Somerset Rd., Green Point* ☎ *021/421–4848* ⌂ *Reservations essential* ⊟ *AE, DC, MC, V* ✆ *Closed Sun.*

$–$$$$ ✕**Panama Jack's.** In this raw-timber structure in the heart of the docks, the music is loud, the tables are crowded, and the decor is nonexistent, but nowhere in town will you find bigger crayfish. Your choice, made from large open tanks, is weighed before being grilled or steamed. Expect to pay about R460 per kilogram for this delicacy and a whopping R660 a kilogram for the scarce and endangered wild abalone, which is being poached nearly to extinction. Large prawns range in price from R199.50 for 10 to about R30 each for Mozambique langoustines. There is plenty of less expensive seafood as well, and daily specials such as baby squid and local line-caught fish are competitively priced. It can be difficult to find this place at night, so you may want to come for lunch if it's your first visit. ⊠*Royal Yacht Club basin, off Goliath Rd., Docks* ☎*021/447–3992* ▤*AE, DC, MC, V* ⊘*No lunch Sat.*

$–$$$$ ✕**Salt.** Floor-to-ceiling windows that overlook the sea afford marvelous views at this restaurant in the Ambassador Hotel, so be sure to ask for a window-side table. Although limited, Salt offers something for most palates, and the food is a surprisingly good value, considering the smart surroundings. The squid-ink tagliatelle is a bowl of freshness with tomato, parsley, lemon, and garlic swirling around the squid. The yellowtail (a flaky Cape fish) paired with bright yellow dal with tomato-and-cumin chutney is an inspired combination. The exciting panfried calf's liver comes with beetroot and horseradish fritters. Although desserts disappoint a little, the plate of cookies is a must-have, especially when the home-baked peanut-butter ones are available. ⊠*Ambassador Hotel, 34 Victoria Rd., Bantry Bay* ☎*021/439–7258* ⌂*Reservations essential* ▤*AE, DC, MC, V.*

$$$ ✕**Africa Cafe.** Tourist oriented it may be, but it would nevertheless be a pity to miss out on this vibrant restaurant in a historic 18th-century former home, with its African decor and city views. Fresh-fruit cocktails accompany a communal feast, with dishes originating from Ethiopia to Zambia, from Kenya to Angola. There are no starters or entrées, but rather a tasty series of patties, puffs, and pastries accompanied by addictive dips, along with dishes like West African shrimp-and-pepper salad, ostrich fillet in a cashew-nut sauce, and Ethiopian *doro wat* chicken, cooked in a mild *berbere* (Ethiopian spice mix) paprika sauce. Vegetarian dishes are plentiful, including the Soweto *chakalaka* (a fiery cooked-vegetable relish). The cost of this colorful prix-fixe abundance is R125 per person. Wines from Cape estates are available, or you can ask for *umqomboti* beer, brewed from sorghum or millet. ⊠*Heritage Square, 108 Shortmarket St., Cape Town Central* ☎*021/422–0221* ▤*AE, DC, MC, V* ⊘*Closed Sun. No lunch.*

$$$ ✕**Aubergine.** Aubergine's timber-and-glass interior matches chef-owner
Fodor'sChoice   Harald Bresselschmidt's classic-with-a-twist cuisine. A beaded Strelitzia
★   flower in the entrance hall is a clue to what will come: South African produce, prepared with strong classical methods, that surprises and requires a closer look. This is serious cuisine. You may notice yourself sitting more upright than usual—not because of stuffiness or any pretentious formality, but out of respect for the food. The fish-and-crayfish duo in a saffron gelée with mizuna (bitter-green) leaves served on a fragrant bell-pepper coulis is a fresh burst of clean flavors to start. Crocodile-tail fillets in a classic *piccata* (light batter) come with eggplant and geranium flowers. Most outstanding is the springbok medallion with bitter-chocolate flavors, celeriac, and baby carrots. Enjoy the accompanying mini potato soufflé as the comma before dessert. The highly recommended surprise du chef selection of mini-desserts might include melon soup with wine gelée and rhubarb sorbet, chocolate fondant with cherry ragout, crème brûlée, magnificent apricot linzer tartlet, and passion-fruit ice-parfait with deep-fried chocolate. The Cinq à Sept lunch menu is unexpectedly affordable. ⊠*39 Barnet St., Gardens,*

1

A Cape Town Celebration of Food

The **Gourmet Festival** (☎021/797–4500 ⊕www.gourmetsa.com) is an exclamation mark on the Cape culinary calendar. The festival usually begins in mid-May with the announcement of the Swiss Air wine awards, followed by the Table of Unity—a fundraising dinner on the slopes of Table Mountain. The last weekend in May, thousands visit the Good Food and Wine Show at the International Convention Centre for three days of foodie exhibitions and presentations by international celebrity (TV) chefs, cooking courses, wine tastings, coffee salons, and more. Food-related events throughout the city during this period in May include special-priced menus at restaurants to coax hibernating locals out as the chill of winter sets in. The festival culminates with a gala banquet prepared by a team of the visiting and local chefs.

8001 ☎*021/465–4909* ⚐*Reservations essential* ▤*AE, DC, MC, V* ◷*Closed Sun. No lunch Mon., Tues., and Sat.*

$$–$$$ ✕**Manolo.** If Spain's renowned chef Ferran Adria of El Bulli had a dis-
Fodor'sChoice   ciple in South Africa, it would be chef Richard Carstens, who is famous
★   here for his experimental flavor combinations and food alchemy. In February 2007 Carstens joined Manolo, giving the venue a cuisine to suit the Philippe Starck–inspired interior. A starter of foie gras *royale* is a rectangular block of smooth flavor served with tomato seeds, soy, and citrus redux (a pastille that dissolves) with ginger. The slow-roasted duck comes with Lego-like blocks of carrot and red-pepper gels and black-bean risotto with Cantonese sauce. For dessert try the pure-pink rose *sens:* rose-flavored *panna cotta* (custard), rose yogurt sorbet, marshmallow foam, and Turkish delight. You could also opt for the rich and delicious chocolate plate, a selection of chocolate mousse, white-chocolate fondant, truffles, ice cream, pistachio crumbs (an Adria hallmark), and citrus flavors. ⊠*30 Kloof St., Cape Town Central, 8001* ☎*021/422–4747* ⚐*Reservations essential* ▤*AE, DC, MC, V.*

$$–$$$ ✕**Savoy Cabbage.** Heritage Square, with its near-crumbling brick walls and original timber ceilings, is one of the oldest inner-city spaces, dating to the late 18th century. Today it houses a fine hotel and many good eateries, including the Savoy Cabbage, which attracts business deal-makers during the day and serious foodies by night. The place is famous for its themed events, where winemakers or opera-house stars make an evening of it, and mini-festivals such as chef Peter Pankhurst's paean to offal for an entire week in winter. Expect high-level service from the mostly career waiters. The menu changes daily, but the focus is on organic ingredients whenever possible, especially game. The fish of the day might be prepared with leeks and eggplant caviar. Brine-cured warthog is paired with sour fig sauce, and other game is often served with port sauce and spaetzle. The tomato tart with mozzarella encased in puff pastry is renowned. ⊠*101 Heritage Sq., Cape Town Central* ☎*021/424–2626* ▤*AE, DC, MC, V* ◷*Closed Sun. No lunch Sat.*

$$–$$$ ✕**The Showroom.** Bruce Robertson's training as a graphic artist before he became a chef is evident in the clean lines of the interior of the Showroom (so called for its view over a luxury-car showroom) and every plate he serves. The menu features basics done very well, but with a twist. He sets the benchmark for Caesar salad (prepared with Gruyère), and his simple lunchtime fish-and-chips—batter-fried kingklip with potato cubes on a stick—is delicious. For dinner lamb shoulder is served with sweetbread ravioli with lemon–crème fraîche noodles. ✉*10 Hospital St., Harbor Edge, Green Point* ☎*021/421–4682* ⌂*Reservations essential* ▭*AE, DC, MC, V* ⊘*Closed Sun. No lunch Sat.*

$$–$$$ ✕**Wakame.** The simple interior allows views over the Atlantic to take precedence here. The sushi, which Wakame does very well, is sufficient reason to visit. Other dishes, like the lightly seared tuna served with a tuna-confit emulsion and marinated snow peas, demonstrates the kitchen's culinary agility. Start with the crispy, fried, salted calamari with hoisin sauce, coriander, and lime. Then move on to the sesame-crusted tuna with *ponzu*-flavored greens (ponzu is a Japanese citrus-vinegar sauce) with deed-fried sweet potato, or Thai red-curry chicken with lime-fried rice. The dark-chocolate-and-cashew tart is rich, but not overly sweet. Smoking is permitted on the narrow balcony, which means that if the wind changes direction, nearby diners in the nonsmoking section may suffer the smell. Wafu, on the upper level, is excellent for drinks and serves a good dim sum menu. ✉*Surry Pl. and Beach Rd., Mouille Point* ☎*021/433–2377* ▭*AE, DC, MC, V* ⊘*Closed Mon.*

$–$$$ ✕**Atlantic.** The elegant flagship restaurant at the luxurious Table Bay Hotel holds a prime position at the city's waterfront. On balmy evenings diners seated on the terrace have stunning views of working docks against a mountain backdrop. A starter of salmon pastrami with pickled pear, ginger, cucumber, and a wasabi crème fraîche could precede sage-rubbed loin of springbok teamed with new potato, French beans, and white-bean puree. Vegetarians are limited to pasta dishes. Artistically plated desserts range from trendy lemon tart with berries to iced coconut and piña-colada soufflé with roasted pineapple, Jamaican-rum-pineapple jus, and coconut *tuile* (a thin cookie). The extensive wine list covers the best of the Cape, supplemented by a selection of New World labels. The Sunday jazz lunch is recommended. ✉*Table Bay Hotel, Quay 6, Waterfront* ☎*021/406–5688* ▭*AE, DC, MC, V* ⊘*Closed Sun. and Mon. No lunch.*

$–$$$ ✕**Rozenhof.** It's always a pleasure to revisit this 18th-century town house, home of stylish fare and an excellent wine list. Yellowwood ceilings and brass chandeliers provide historical Cape touches, and works by local artists adorn the walls. Inspiration from Asia and the Mediterranean is detectable, but the cuisine here is noted more for consistently good quality served in cozy and friendly surroundings. The signature cheese soufflé with mustard cream holds its own among trendier first courses like smoked marlin on sushi rice with cucumber and wasabi dressing. Crispy roast duck with a choice of fruity sauces is a time-honored favorite. Layers of local Gorgonzola and mascarpone paired with preserved figs and a glass of port make a savory-sweet alternative to more traditional desserts. ⊠*18 Kloof St., Gardens* ☎*021/424–1968* ▤*AE, DC, MC, V* ☉*Closed Sun. No lunch Sat.*

¢–$$$ ✕**Belthazar.** Claiming the largest selection of wines by the glass (about 100) in the land, Belthazar is also recommended for its consistently good steak and seafood. Steaks are cut and matured by an in-house butcher, and a team of sommeliers will recommend the best wine match for your meal. The springbok fillet served with a chocolate-chili sauce is a good choice. Be sure to order the deep-fried onion rose as an accompaniment. Outside seating under umbrellas (heated in winter) provides views over the harbor, though it's more comfortable inside. The service is excellent. ⊠*Victoria Basin, Waterfront* ☎*021/421–3753 or 021/421–3756* ≙*Reservations essential* ▤*AE, DC, MC, V.*

¢–$$ ✕**95 Keerom.** Chef-owner Giorgio Nava is so passionate about using only the finest ingredients that he catches his own fish and farms his own beef. Diners will be hard-pressed to find better Milanese cuisine. The paper-thin beef carpaccio "95" is drizzled with homemade mayonnaise and topped with fresh arugula and Parmesan shavings. When Nava manages to catch tuna, he serves it seared with cherry tomatoes, capers, and olives. The butternut-filled ravioli with brown sage butter is sublime. With its bentwood chairs, the upstairs interior is Eames-inspired; downstairs, the exposed stone reveals the building's history. ⊠*95 Keerom St., Cape Town Central* ☎*021/422–0765* ≙*Reservations essential* ▤*AE, DC, MC, V* ☉*Closed Sun. No lunch Sat.*

¢–$$ ✕**Ocean Basket.** On Restaurant Mile along the city fringe, this informal spot has few competitors in the field of bargain-price, ocean-fresh, well-cooked seafood. You can sit facing the street or find a table in the courtyard, complete with a fountain, at the back. Calamari—stewed, grilled, pickled, or in a salad—features prominently among the starters, which include a mezes selection. The catch of the day is listed on the many blackboards lining the mustard-yellow walls, but delicately flavored hake-and-chips is the budget draw card. Standard entrées range from excellent Cajun-style grilled calamari to a huge seafood platter for two. Prices for the seafood platters and crayfish run higher than for other dishes. Tartar, chili, and garlic sauces come on the side, and Greek salads are authentic. Desserts are average. ⊠*75 Kloof St., Gardens* ☎*021/422–0322* ≙*Reservations not accepted* ▤*AE, DC, MC, V.*

¢   ✕**Birds Boutique Café.** There's something so charming about this café that most diners are willing to overlook the discomfort of sitting on plastic milk crates or sharing a roughly hewn trestle table with other patrons. Bird-song records play, bird images abound, and the German owners roost over patrons like tall cranes. However inexplicable, it's so delightful that people tend to stay far longer than they intend. Teas are served sprouting fresh herbs and twigs, and for the most part salads and quiches incorporate organic produce. The chicken pie is legendary and big enough for two, and the butternut-and-feta quiche is delicious. Chocolate scones, like everything at Birds, are made daily and written up on the chalkboard menu. ⊠*127 Bree St., Cape Town Central* ☎*021/426–2534* ▤*No credit cards* ☉*Closed weekends. No dinner.*

ATLANTIC COAST

The restaurants below are marked on the Where to Stay & Eat in the Cape Peninsula map.

$$$–$$$$ ✗**Azure.** Blue leather armchairs and crisp white napery confirm the Twelve Apostle Hotel's nautical bent and Azure's smart interior. The menu—with its focus on seafood, game, and the indigenous fynbos plants—works well with views of the Atlantic Ocean as far as the eye can see and Table Mountain. Presented in a martini glass, the crayfish-and-prawn cocktail is retro-chic. The giant-tiger-prawn tempura, served with chili-tomato salsa and pickled cucumber, is an extravagant feast. Slow-roasted duck comes with *pomme* William (crumbed potato in the shape of a pear), mushrooms and roasted peppers, glazed baby apples, and a caramelized citrus reduction. Oversized napkins provide unexpected luxury for messy eaters. ■TIP➡**Ask for a window table.** ⊠*Twelve Apostles Hotel and Spa, Victoria Rd., Camps Bay* ☎*021/437–9029* ⚒*Reservations essential* ⊟*AE, DC, MC, V.*

$–$$$ ✗**Paranga.** Attracting models and folks hoping to spot celebrities along Camps Bay's beach strip, Paranga is a stylish vantage point and an acceptable place to eat. The terrace is shaded by a Bedouin-style tarpaulin. It's mostly popular with locals for a leisurely weekend breakfast, as the place can get very warm by lunchtime. A wide selection of salads will appeal to most palates. Start with the goat's-cheese cake served inside crispy deep-fried *kataifi* (Greek-style shredded phyllo dough) with a spicy chili jam; then move on to the fillet *tornadeo* (two circular-cut steak portions) with pepper sauce. Kingklip is served in three ways: prepared whole with lemon-butter sauce, crusted with fresh herbs and *haloumi* (a firm Greek cheese), or grilled with pineapple salsa. The lounge-style music selection is a focal point, and, as at Ibiza's famed seafront Café del Mar, it's available to purchase. Check menu prices carefully, as some are out of kilter. Reservations are essential for dinner. ⊠*Shop No. 1, The Promenade, Victoria Rd., Camps Bay* ☎*021/438–0404* ⊕ *www.paranga.co.za* ⊟*AE, DC, MC, V.*

¢–$$ ✗**Cafe Orca.** It may be laid-back and a trifle shabby, but this tiny eatery in a former fishing village enjoys views overlooking a stretch of pristine beach. There are salads, burgers, and toasted sandwiches on the menu, but the seafood combos and baskets—which combine fish with calamari, shrimp, mussels, or chicken—are the most popular items. At R175, the seafood platter is probably the best bargain of its kind. Service is friendly but can be slow. ⊠*88 Beach Rd., Melkbosstrand* ☎*021/553–4120* ⚒*Reservations essential* ⊟*AE, DC, MC, V* ⊗*No dinner Sun. and Tues.*

SOUTHERN SUBURBS

$$$–$$$$ ✗**Catharina's.** The old winery on this historic estate makes an elegant Cape Dutch home for the restaurant named after its original, feisty, and much-married 17th-century owner. At lunchtime you can sit on the oak-shaded terrace and enjoy sweeping mountain views. A global menu with Cape influences includes Cape West Coast mussels in a Thai curry broth and lamb with potatoes gratin, snow peas, olives, and

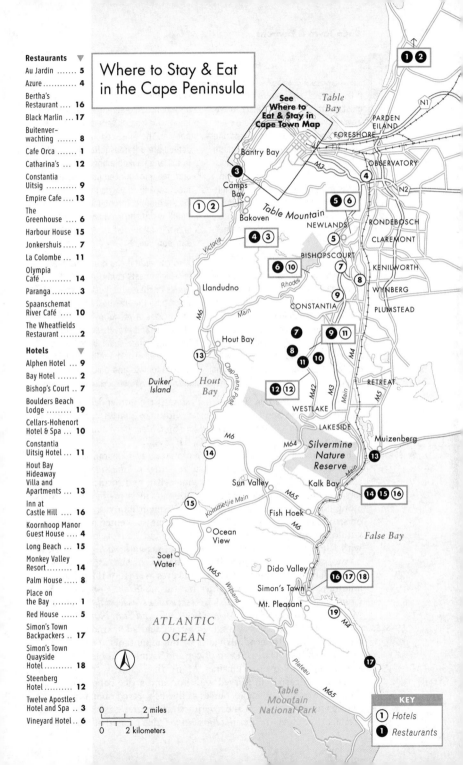

Where to Stay & Eat in the Cape Peninsula

See Where to Eat & Stay in Cape Town Map

Table Bay

PARDEN EILAND

N1

FORESHORE

OBSERVATORY

Bantry Bay

N2

Camps Bay

Table Mountain

Bakoven

NEWLANDS

RONDEBOSCH

CLAREMONT

BISHOPSCOURT

KENILWORTH

Rhodes

WYNBERG

Llandudno

Main

CONSTANTIA

PLUMSTEAD

Victoria

Hout Bay

RETREAT

Chapman's Peak

Duiker Island

Hout Bay

WESTLAKE

M42

M3

Main

M5

LAKESIDE

M6

M64

Silvermine Nature Reserve

Muizenberg

Sun Valley

Kalk Bay

Kommetjie Main

M65

Fish Hoek

M6

False Bay

Ocean View

Soet Water

Dido Valley

Simon's Town

Mt. Pleasant

M4

ATLANTIC OCEAN

Wildand

Plateau

M65

Table Mountain National Park

0   2 miles

0   2 kilometers

KEY

① Hotels

● Restaurants

Braai: The South African Cookout

If time, space, and weather permit, most South Africans will elect to *braai* (rhymes with rye), or barbecue, over the weekend. In black townships, literally hundreds will meet and socialize around an outdoor fire after purchasing meat from nearby butchers and drinks from a corner *shabeen* (neighborhood tavern). At recreation sites that allow fires, families and friends will gather to cook and eat together, but it is in the homes of South Africans that the braai comes to life.

The invite may be for lunch, but some folks will sit around drinking (beer or brandy and soda mostly) and chatting until 4 PM or so before even starting up the grill. Most favor the braai basics: *boerewors* (pronounced boo-ra-vorrs; beef and pork sausage with heady doses of coriander seed), lamb

chops, and chicken pieces. *Sosaties* (pronounced so-*sah*-teez), skewers of meat with fruit or vegetables, are also popular. The most common starches served are potatoes (often wrapped in foil and cooked among the coals) and pap (pronounced pup), maize meal cooked to varying consistencies—*krummel* (pronounced *krah*-muhl) is dry and crumbly, whereas *stywe* (pronounced *stay*-ver) is like a stiff porridge.

Also common is the bring-and-braai, in which guests come with meat and drinks to share. The host is expected to prepare the fire, best made with dried vines or *rooikrans* (wood or charcoal), and provide some sides (typically potato salad, baked beans, and coleslaw) and a relish (usually a cooked tomato-and-onion mix).

slow-roasted tomatoes. The tasting menu is recommended for serious foodies, and the Sunday lunch buffet with jazz quartet is the best the city has to offer. ⊠ *Steenberg Hotel and Spa, Steenberg and Tokai Rds., Tokai* ☎ *021/713–2222* ⊟ *AE, DC, MC, V.*

★ $$–$$$$ ✕ **Buitenverwachting.** On a historic wine estate in Constantia, this gracious restaurant occupies a modern building on one side of a grassy court ringed by the manor house, wine cellar, and former slave quarters. Window-side tables have views of the vineyards in serried rows along the lower mountain slopes. The cuisine is innovative, but based on strong French basics. A starter of lemongrass-scented bisque comes with a trio of prawns (tempura, panfried, and Thai-style). Springbok with Christine (the estate's flagship wine) jus and *madumbi* (African potato) croquette is recommended as a main dish. The raspberry soufflé with a parfait is as much a treat for the eyes as it is for the palate. The adjoining Café Petit serves lighter options. ⊠ *Klein Constantia Rd., Constantia* ☎ *021/794–3522* ⚱ *Reservations essential* ⊟ *AE, DC, MC, V* ☉ *Closed Sun. and Mon. May–Oct., and Sun. Nov.–Apr.*

$$–$$$$ ✕ **Constantia Uitsig.** Reserve a table on the enclosed veranda or outside on the patio for tremendous views of the mountains at this restored farmstead house. The menu is a pricey and harmonious blend of northern Italian and Provençal cuisines. Many diners start with homemade pasta or fish carpaccio (served with nori and a rice cube). They may then move on to such main courses as line fish served on mashed sweet potato with baby spinach and a verjuice (gentle grape astringent) vinaigrette, or the classic *trippa alla Fiorentina* (tripe braised in tomato, car-

rot, and celery sauce). The *marquise au chocolat* is calorific splendor: dark-chocolate mousse in a spider-web pool of crème anglaise. ⊠ *Constantia Uitsig Farm, Spaanschemat River Rd., Constantia* ☎ *021/794–4480* ☚ *Reservations essential* 🟰 *AE, DC, MC, V.*

$$–$$$$ ✕ **La Colombe.** Constantia Uitsig farm and winery is home to three good restaurants, but it is La Colombe, with chef Luke Dale Roberts's excellent Provence-inspired food, that attracts the most attention. The chorizo, tempura sweet potato, feta, and figs served on arugula, endive, and a soft-boiled egg is delicious to start. Most outstanding is panfried teriyaki-glazed salmon with chickpeas, roasted peppers, eggplant, pickled ginger, and a carrot-and-ginger-butter sauce. The dessert of warm figs on frangipane disks, served with cardamom ice cream and pink-peppercorn syrup, is a delight. The chalkboard menus are in French, but the staff delights in translating them. ⊠ *Constantia Uitsig Farm, Spaanschemat River Rd., Constantia* ☎ *021/794–2390* ☚ *Reservations essential* 🟰 *AE, DC, MC, V.*

$–$$$$ ✕ **Jonkershuis.** This 19th-century building adjoins the gracious manor house at Groot Constantia, the Cape's oldest wine estate. The Malay platter provides a hearty taste of the Cape's culinary heritage with *bobotie* (spiced minced beef studded with dried fruit and topped with a savory baked custard), lamb curry with *sambals* (condiments), chicken *breedie* (tomato-based stew), samosas, fish cakes, cinnamon-spiced butternut, rice, and *papadum* (crispy flatbread). Smoked snoek (fragrant Cape oily fish) pâté is a good way to start your meal. A wide selection of contemporary dishes, such as fig-and-*coppa* (Italian sausage) salad, is also available. The South African dessert *melktert*, or milk tart—similar to baked custard—is both traditional and delicious. ⊠ *Groot Constantia, Main Rd., Constantia* ☎ *021/794–6255* ☚ *Reservations essential* 🟰 *AE, DC, MC, V* ☾ *No dinner Sun.*

$$–$$$ ✕ **The Greenhouse.** Aptly named, this conservatory-like dining room built around a 350-year-old oak overlooks the beautiful gardens of the Cellars-Hohenort Hotel. The chef's French roots are evident in such dishes as home-smoked salmon with avocado chantilly (cream), which is perfect for a light starter, and the richer foie-gras terrine with duck breast, brioche, and berry compote. The slow-roasted duck with *pomme arlie* (refilled potato) is a signature dish, but the pork belly prepared with five spices and served with a coconut-and-lemongrass mousseline is outstanding. The kingklip with Parma ham risotto and Parmesan green beans is also good. Owner Liz McGrath's baked chocolate dessert is rich and heady, but the tiramisu soufflé (one of 12 dessert soufflés)—with espresso crème anglaise poured into its steaming center—takes the cake. Ask for senior sommelier Miguel Chan, who successfully secures rare wines, including every vintage of nearby Klein Constantia's famous Vin de Constance. ⊠ *Cellars-Hohenort Hotel, 15 Hohenort Ave., Constantia* ☎ *021/794–2137* ☚ *Reservations essential* 🟰 *AE, DC, MC, V.*

$–$$$ ✕ **Au Jardin.** Tucked away in a corner of the historic Vineyard Hotel, complete with fountain and views of Table Mountain, Au Jardin serves classic French cuisine imbued with subtle Cape and Mediterranean accents. The braised oxtail in phyllo with port and blue-cheese cream is good, as is the Mozambican crab cake accompanied by chilies, crab ice cream, and tomato-and-fennel coulis. Try the Karoo lamb with *imam biyaldi* (spicy Middle Eastern relish), garlic croquette, and rosemary jus as a main course. One dessert is reason alone to visit: a lemon trio in the form of lemon verbena and white-chocolate mousse served with lemon tart and lemon parfait. A seven-course tasting menu, including wine, costs R250. ⊠ *Vineyard Hotel, Colinton Rd., Newlands* ☎ *021/657–4545* ⊟ *AE, DC, MC, V* ☺ *Closed Mon. May–Sept. and Sun. No lunch.*

¢–$$ ✕ **Spaanschemat River Café.** For informal feasting on country fare in idyllic surroundings, this pretty spot with a lavender-fringed terrace is hard to beat. The place really shines at breakfast time with classics like eggs Florentine and Benedict, along with the usual fry-ups; on peak-season weekends cars line up waiting for the doors to the café to open. Norwegian-salmon fish cakes with tarragon-and-basil mayonnaise are good as a light lunch or a starter, whereas the butternut ravioli with a basil mousseline is richer. For a main dish, the Norwegian salmon on chive mashed potatoes with asparagus and a béarnaise sauce is a good option. Sticky pudding with star-anise caramel and vanilla ice cream is a nice way to round off the meal. ⊠ *Constantia Uitsig Farm, Spaanschemat River Rd., Constantia* ☎ *021/794–3010* ⊟ *AE, DC, MC, V* ☺ *No dinner.*

FALSE BAY

$$–$$$$ ✕ **Harbour House.** Don't be put off by the unremarkable entrance here; once you're upstairs and seated at a window table you'll be entranced by views across the bay, where fishing boats chug back and forth and whales spout for much of the year. Bring a keen appetite. Starter salads are substantial, and you can follow them with just-landed, olive-oil-brushed fish, or Mediterranean calamari with garlic, chili, black olives, and giant capers. There's also a tempting dessert list. ⊠ *Kalk Bay Harbour, Main Rd., Kalk Bay* ☎ *021/788–4133* ⊟ *AE, DC, MC, V.*

¢–$$$ ✕ **Bertha's Restaurant.** Alfresco dining at this waterfront venue offers a feast for both palate and eye. Boating activities from the naval dockyard on one side and yacht club on the other add action to a backdrop of sparkling water and mountain. The contemporary menu makes good use of local seafood, such as Atlantic black mussels and line-caught fish, which is grilled or fried. There are also reasonably priced burgers and yummy spiked ice-cream drinks and coffees. Lunch here is popular, so it's a good idea to reserve in advance. ⊠ *1 Wharf Rd., Simon's Town* ☎ *021/786–2138* ⊟ *AE, DC, MC, V.*

¢–$$$ ✕ **Olympia Café.** This tiny Kalk Bay landmark, furnished with mismatched tables and a counter along the window, has long been a well-kept secret among locals and regular visitors. The quality of the mostly Mediterranean fare is consistently high, and the servers are consistently sassy. A delectable dish of eggplant rolls—filled with butternut squash, ricotta, and sweet potato and sauced with piquant tomato—is always popular. Penne pasta topped with fresh tuna comes in two sizes, as do other specialties chalked up daily. The chef also serves more than

12,000 delicious omelets each year, accompanied by excellent croissants and crusty loaves from the café's bakery up the road. ⊠*134 Main Rd., Kalk Bay* ☎*021/788–6396* ⚐*Reservations not accepted* ☰*AE, DC, MC, V.*

$$ ✕**Black Marlin.** Black Marlin's position overlooking the Indian Ocean is unrivaled, and its popularity is well deserved (it's largely supported by tour-bus business). Ask for a table outside amid the bougainvillea. Seafood is the hero here, and it's fairly affordable. Calamari rings are paired with chili-mango jam, and the sesame-seed-covered kingklip *goujons* (strips) delivers a Middle Eastern flavor. The bayside platter, with fish, calamari rings, and mussels, is a good value, but be sure to leave room for angel's dark delight: a devilish dessert of baked dark-chocolate mousse with kirsch and black cherries. ⊠*Main Rd., Millers Pt., Simon's Town* ☎*021/786–1621* ⚐*Reservations essential* ☰*AE, DC, MC, V* ⊗*No dinner Sun.*

¢–$$ ✕**Empire Cafe.** A picture window overlooks the surfers' beach, and folks will visit barefooted with sand still between their toes. The food is unexpectedly good, even if the service isn't. The lamb rump steak is fabulous: it's served on sautéed spinach with chickpeas, *rooibos*-tea-soaked raisins (rooibos is a Cederberg mountain plant), garlic butter, and eggplant, with garlic aioli on the side. Also popular is the updated French toast with Thai-flavored prawns in caramelized lemon-scented honey with cumin. The café's confectionery skill is renowned, and people visit just to buy bread and pastries. As desserts go, they're pushing the envelope with a chocolate-chili cake and a mocha-pecan cake. The coffee is delicious. ⊠*11 York Rd., Muizenberg* ☎*021/788–1250* ⚐*Reservations essential* ☰*AE, DC, MC, V* ⊗*No dinner Sun.–Tues.*

NORTHERN SUBURBS

¢–$$ ✕**The Wheatfields Restaurant.** Celebrity chefs David Higgs and Wade van der Merve have brought such culinary renown to Meerendal Wine Estate in the Durbanville Hills that eating at any of their three restaurants is a treat. For fine dining though, Wheatfields, in the original manor house of the estate, is magnificent. Start with gnocchi with porcini or goat's cheese with peppers. The pork belly with smoked apple mash, lemongrass, and brown butter is fragrantly wonderful as a main dish. Wade's reputation as a confectioner is visible in each dessert; ask for the "busy plate of chocolate" to see why. Dining in the Barn & Lawn restaurant (open only for the Sunday family buffet) or the casual Deli is equally recommended. They also run a culinary academy, which means that many of the servers are chefs-in-training. ⊠*Visser-shok Rd., Meerendal Wine Estate, Durbanville* ☎*021/975–1655 or 072/856–6298* ⚐*Reservations essential* ☰*AE, DC, MC, V* ⊗*Closed Sun. and Mon.*

WHERE TO STAY

Finding lodging in Cape Town can be a nightmare during peak travel season (December–January), as many of the more reasonable accommodations are booked up. It's worth traveling between April and August, if you can, to take advantage of the "secret season" discounts. If you arrive in Cape Town without a reservation, head for the Tourism Office, which has a helpful accommodations desk.

Hotels in the city center are a good option if you're here on business or are here for only a short stay. During the day the historic city center is a vibrant place. At night, though, it's shut up tight (though this is changing slowly as some office buildings are converted into apartment complexes); night owls may prefer a hotel amid the nonstop action of the Waterfront. Hotels and bed-and-breakfasts in the Southern Suburbs, especially Constantia, offer unrivaled beauty and tranquillity and make an ideal base if you're exploring the peninsula. You'll need a car, though, and should plan on 15–30 minutes to get into town. Atlantic Coast hotels provide the closest thing in Cape Town to a beach-vacation atmosphere despite the cold ocean waters.

Keep in mind that international flights from the United States and Europe arrive in the morning and return flights depart in the evening. Because most hotels have an 11 AM checkout, you may have to wait for a room if you've just arrived; if you're leaving, you will be hauled kicking and screaming out of your room hours before your flight. Most hotels will try to accommodate you, but they often have no choice in peak season. Some of the larger hotels have residents-only lounges where you can spend the hours awaiting your flight. Note that many small luxury accommodations either do not permit children or have minimum-age restrictions. It's a good idea to inquire in advance if this will be an issue.

Another option is to stay in one of Cape Town's numerous guesthouses or B&Bs, which is what many South Africans do when they travel. Don't be put off by the names—choosing a B&B or guesthouse doesn't mean you'll have to eat breakfast with the family or help wash up afterwards! Instead, there are some very classy and professionally run establishments that offer everything a hotel does but on a smaller, more personal scale.

The most reliable source of good B&B establishments is **South African Accommodation** (☎021/794–0030 ⊕*www.bookabed.co.za*). The **Portfolio of Places** (☎021/689–4020 ⊕*www.portfoliocollection.com*) brochure includes guesthouses, B&Bs, villas, and more. If you don't like tiptoeing around someone's house or you want to save money, consider renting a fully furnished apartment, especially if you're staying two or more weeks. **CAPSOL Property & Tourism Solutions** (☎021/422–3521 ⊕*www.capsol.co.za*) has around 1,500 high-quality, furnished, fully stocked villas and apartments on its books. **Cape Stay** (☎021/674–3104 ⊕*www.capestay.co.za*) has a wide selection of accommodations to suit different needs.

De Waterkant Village & Life is Cape Town's first and only guest street, an entire little community near the harbor of houses to rent. There are more than 40 beautifully restored, self-catering (with cooking facilities) houses that are unusual, trendy, classy, and quite charming. The houses, which come with daily housekeeping services, have anywhere from one to four bedrooms. If you don't feel like cooking, you could also stay in the Village Lodge here. The high-season double-occupancy rate for one of the houses is around R2,000 per night. ⊠ *1 Loader St., Cape Town Central, 8000* ☎ *021/422–2721* ⊕ *www.dewaterkantvillage.com* ⊟ *AE, DC, MC, V.*

Cape Town is regarded as one of the top backpacker destinations in the world, with plenty of hostels to choose from. Contact **Backpacking South Africa** (*BTSA* ⊕ *www.btsa.co.za*) for information.

WHAT IT COSTS IN SOUTH AFRICAN RAND					
	¢	$	$$	$$$	$$$$
HOTELS	under R500	R500–R1,000	R1,000–R2,000	R2,000–R3,000	over R3,000

Prices are for a standard double room in high season, including 12.5% tax.

CAPE TOWN CENTRAL & CITY BOWL

The hotels below are marked on the Where to Stay & Eat in Cape Town map.

$$$$ 🏨 **ArabellaSheraton Grand Hotel Cape Town.** The super-sophisticated e-butler service in the foyer is enough to get excited about—and that's before you've even set foot in the rooms. Since the hotel is linked to the Cape Town International Convention Centre, rooms are geared toward working guests, but that doesn't mean they're spartan. The decor is modern minimalist with touches of African creativity, perhaps in pillowcases or a quirky wall color. Workstations are cleverly partitioned away from the sleeping area, so even if you have to burn the midnight oil, you can do it in comfort and style. Everything glides and whirls at the touch of a button, and service is seamless. Take special note of the artwork in the lobby and foyer area. This hotel group collects and supports local art. Don't miss the spa at the top of the hotel or a water-taxi ride from the hotel to the Waterfront. ⊠ *Convention Sq., Lower Long St., Cape Town Central* ⊕ *Box 50095, Waterfront 8002* ☎ *021/412–9999* ⊕ *www.sheraton.com/capetown* ⇗ *451 rooms, 32 suites* ⚭ *In-room: safe, refrigerator, dial-up (some), Wi-Fi. In-hotel: 2 restaurants, room service, bars, gym, spa, laundry service, concierge, executive floor, public Internet, public Wi-Fi, airport shuttle, parking (no fee), no-smoking rooms* ⊟ *AE, DC, MC, V* ⃝|BP.

$$$$ 🏨 **Mount Nelson Hotel.** This distinctive pink landmark is the grande
Fodor'sChoice dame of Cape Town. Since it opened its doors in 1899 to accommodate
★ passengers just off the Union-Castle steamships, it has been the focal point of Cape social life. It retains a traditional charm and gentility that other luxury hotels often lack: afternoon tea is served in the lounge to piano accompaniment, the Planet Champagne Bar is very glam, and

the staff almost outnumbers the guests. Rooms are decorated with fine antiques and fresh flowers and have an air of aristocracy about them. The hotel stands at the top of Government Avenue, but, surrounded as it is by 9 acres of manicured gardens, it might as well be in the country. Once a week the head gardener leads a guided tour through the magnificent gardens, and tea is served afterward. Very civilized! For peak season, December–March, it's advisable to book a year in advance. ⊠*76 Orange St., Gardens 8001* ☎*021/483–1000* ⊕*www.mountnelson.co.za* ⊅*145 rooms, 56 suites* ⚭*In-room: safe, refrigerator, DVD, VCR, Wi-Fi. In-hotel: 2 restaurants, room service, bar, tennis courts, pools, gym, spa, children's programs, laundry service, concierge, public Internet, public Wi-Fi, airport shuttle, parking (no fee), no-smoking rooms* ⊟*AE, DC, MC, V* ⦿❘*BP.*

$$–$$$ 🏨 **Metropole.** If it's style and a very central address you're after, then the Metropole is for you. The decor is a clever mix of old and new; art-deco furniture sits comfortably alongside stunning modern pieces. Rooms are simple and pared down. There's no extraneous clutter, but the attention to detail is superb. The Veranda restaurant is also excellent, and the M Bar & Lounge is a very trendy place to get a drink. ⊠*38 Long St., Cape Town Central 8001* ☎*021/424–7247* ⊕*www. metropolehotel.co.za* ⊅*23 rooms, 3 suites* ⚭*In-room: safe, refrigerator, ethernet, Wi-Fi. In-hotel: restaurant, room service, bar, laundry service, concierge, airport shuttle, parking (fee), no-smoking rooms* ⊟*AE, DC, MC, V* ⦿❘*BP.*

$$–$$$ 🏨 **Villa Belmonte.** In a quiet residential neighborhood on the slopes above the city, this small guesthouse offers privacy and luxury in an attractive Dutch Revival residence. The owners have sought to create the feeling of an Italian villa through the use of marbling, molded ceilings, and natural wood floors. Wide verandas afford superb views of the city, Table Mountain, and Devil's Peak. Rooms have colorful draperies, luxurious finishes, wicker furniture, and small-pane windows. It's a 20-minute walk to the city center. ⊠*33 Belmont Ave., Oranjezicht 8001* ☎*021/462–1576* ⊕*www.villabelmontehotel.co.za* ⊅*14 rooms* ⚭*In-room: safe, refrigerator, ethernet, dial-up. In-hotel: restaurant, room service, bar, pool, no elevator, laundry service, concierge, public Internet, airport shuttle, parking (no fee), no kids under 8, no-smoking rooms* ⊟*AE, DC, MC, V* ⦿❘*BP.*

$$–$$$ 🏨 **Welgelegen Guest House.** In Afrikaans, *welgelegen* means "well situated," and this classy guesthouse in two beautifully restored Victorian mansions is just that: it's nestled under Table Mountain and just minutes away from city attractions. Each room is individually and stylishly decorated. The look is a mixture of African chic and romantic whimsy, and the pretty courtyard is a good place to relax after a busy day. If you want more independence, you can opt for a two-bedroom, self-catering cottage down the road. ⊠*6 Stephen St., Gardens 8001* ☎*021/426–2373 or 021/426–2374* ⊕*www.welgelegen.co.za* ⊅*13 rooms, 1 cottage* ⚭*In-room: refrigerator, ethernet, Wi-Fi. In-hotel: room service, pool, no elevator, laundry service, concierge, public Internet, public Wi-Fi, airport shuttle, parking (no fee), no-smoking rooms* ⊟*AE, DC, MC, V* ⦿❘*BP.*

1

$$ ⊞ **Best Western Cape Suites Hotel.** This village-style hotel, with low buildings and adjoining individual units, is five minutes from the center of Cape Town, close to District Six, and a brisk 20-minute walk from the Waterfront. Although some guests find the complex security (high walls, electric fence, cameras) a bit off-putting, others like the peace of mind it gives them. Rooms are spacious and pleasantly furnished in a cheerful and contemporary style, and all come with a fully equipped kitchen. Some rooms have mountain views; others look into the city. Although it's on a corner site, the hotel is well insulated, so traffic noise is not a major problem; inner rooms tend to be quieter. If you have a car, you can park it virtually outside your room. A free shuttle takes you to popular sights within about 13 km (8 mi) of the hotel. Some stays include a full breakfast. ⊠ *Constitution and de Villiers Sts., Zonnebloem* ⬧ *Box 51085, Waterfront 8002* ☎ *021/461–0727* ⊕ *www. capesuites.co.za* 🗦 *123 suites* ⬧ *In-room: safe, kitchen, refrigerator. In-hotel: 2 restaurants, bars, pool, no elevator, laundry facilities, laundry service, concierge, public Wi-Fi, airport shuttle, parking (no fee), some pets allowed, no-smoking rooms* ▤ *AE, DC, MC, V.*

★ **$$** ⊞ **Cape Heritage Hotel.** Built as a private home in 1771, this friendly, attractive, well-run hotel is part of the Heritage Square development and as such has direct access to a host of restaurants and a couple of shops. Teak-beamed ceilings and foot-wide yellowwood floorboards echo the building's gracious past, and the spacious rooms are individually decorated. Some have four-poster beds, others exposed brickwork, but each has its own special charm. Rooms overlooking the pleasant courtyard—complete with tables sheltered by what is claimed to be the oldest grapevine in South Africa—may be a little noisy, but the revelry stops at midnight sharp, when the bar stops serving. Parking is across the street in a section of a public lot with good security. ⊠ *90 Bree St., Cape Town Central 8001* ☎ *021/424–4646* ⊕ *www.capeheritage. co.za* 🗦 *15 rooms* ⬧ *In-room: safe, refrigerator, DVD, ethernet, Wi-Fi. In-hotel: 6 restaurants, room service, bar, no elevator, laundry service, concierge, public Internet, public Wi-Fi, airport shuttle, parking (fee), no-smoking rooms* ▤ *AE, DC, MC, V* ⦿ *BP.*

$$ ⊞ **Cape Milner Hotel.** Tamboerskloof is an ideal location from which to explore the city and farther afield. The look at this attractive hotel is clean, classical, and contemporary, with rooms decorated in restful shades of gray, white, and black. And although the hotel might not be bursting with atmosphere, if you're not planning to spend much time in your room, it's ideal. Each room has a tea/coffeemaker, and there's a gym for those who need to work off some of their holiday excesses. The hotel shuttle service to the Waterfront and nearby beaches is also a real plus. The terrace has wonderful views of Table Mountain. ⊠ *2 Milner Rd., Tamboerskloof 8001* ☎ *021/426–1101* ⊕ *www.capemilner. com* 🗦 *56 rooms, 2 suites* ⬧ *In-room: safe, refrigerator, ethernet, Wi-Fi. In-hotel: restaurant, room service, bar, pool, gym, laundry service, concierge, public Internet, public Wi-Fi, airport shuttle, parking (no fee), no-smoking rooms* ▤ *AE, DC, MC, V* ⦿ *BP.*

$$ ⊞ **Townhouse Hotel.** Its proximity to government buildings and its easygoing atmosphere (not to mention extremely competitive rates) make the Townhouse a popular choice. Rooms are decorated in neutral shades and provide a restful retreat from the hubbub of the city. Request a room with a view of the mountain. ⊠ *60 Corporation St., Box 5053, Cape Town Central 8000* ☎ *021/465–7050* ⊕ *www.townhouse.co.za* ➾ *104 rooms* ⚷ *In-room: safe, refrigerator, ethernet, Wi-Fi. In-hotel: restaurant, room service, bars, pool, gym, laundry facilities, laundry service, concierge, public Internet, public Wi-Fi, airport shuttle, parking (fee), no-smoking rooms (some)* ⊟ *AE, DC, MC, V.*

★ $ 🏨 **Daddy Long Legs Boutique Hotel.** Being voted *House & Leisure*/Visa's best hotel in South Africa in 2006 and one of *Decorex's* top-10 boutique hotels in South Africa in 2007 puts DDL in a class of its own. Independent travelers with artistic streaks love this place. It was built to represent the creative community of Cape Town, and well-known local artists—including poet-author Finuala Dowling and architect Andre Vorster—were given a budget and invited to decorate a room to their tastes. The results are fantastic. In the Photo Booth room, a huge portrait behind the bed is made up of 3,240 black-and-white photos of Capetonians, while a funky room by the fusion band Freshlyground has a bright red throw, portraits of the band members, and music. But it's not all about show—the amenities are all in place as well. The linen is crisp and clean, the staff is friendly, and the only real drawback is finding parking on Long Street (it's fine after hours, but a crush during the day). ⊠ *134 Long St., Cape Town Central 8010* ☎ *021/422–3074* ⊕ *www.daddylonglegs.co.za* ➾ *13 rooms* ⚷ *In-room: no a/c, no phone, no TV (some), Wi-Fi. In-hotel: bar, no elevator, laundry service, public Wi-Fi, no-smoking rooms* ⊟ *AE, DC, MC, V.*

★ ¢ 🏨 **Ashanti Lodge.** A five-minute walk from the city center, Ashanti is a great place to stay if you're on a limited budget or just don't like the idea of spending a year's salary on one night's accommodation. The lodge has just about everything a backpacker or budget traveler might need—from laundry to a luggage-holding service to light meals. Rooms vary from cheerful dorms to smart doubles with private baths—great if you want more privacy. In addition to a communal kitchen and a TV lounge, there's a very organized travel center that can advise you on the rest of your stay. ⊠ *11 Hof St., Gardens 8001* ☎ *021/423–8721* ⊕ *www.ashanti.co.za* ➾ *20 rooms, 10 dormitories* ⚷ *In-room: no a/c, no phone (some), kitchen, no TV. In-hotel: bar, pool, no elevator, laundry service, public Internet, airport shuttle, parking (no fee), no kids under 18, no-smoking rooms* ⊟ *MC, V.*

WATERFRONT

$$$$ 🏨 **Cape Grace.** The exclusive and well-appointed Cape Grace, at the
Fodor's Choice   V&A Waterfront, is a hard act to follow. Built on a spit of land jut-
★   ting into a working harbor, it offers views of seals frolicking in the surrounding waters and seagulls soaring above. Large, elegant guest rooms have harbor or mountain views and are decorated with a combination of French period furnishings and wonderful modern design. The attention to detail throughout is outstanding, from the antique pieces to the fresh flowers in the rooms. There's a wonderful well-stocked

library for browsing, and the superb restaurant, one.waterfront, serves creative cuisine with a strong South African influence. Add to that a fantastic spa with treatments inspired by the spice route and African traditions. You also have free use of a nearby health club and the hotel's courtesy car for getting into the city and to the main beaches. Make time for at least one drink at Bascule, the hotel's sophisticated watering hole with an incredible selection of single-malt whiskies. ⊠ *West Quay Rd., Box 51387, Waterfront 8002* 🕾*021/410–7100* ⊕*www. capegrace.com* ⇌*122 rooms* ⚐*In-room: safe, refrigerator, ethernet. In-hotel: restaurant, room service, bar, pool, spa, no elevator, laundry service, executive floor, public Internet, public Wi-Fi, airport shuttle, parking (no fee), no-smoking rooms* ☰*AE, DC, MC, V* ❍|*BP.*

$$$$

FodorsChoice

★

Ellerman House. Without a doubt, this is one of the finest (and most exclusive) hotels in South Africa. Built in 1912 for shipping magnate Sir John Ellerman, the hotel sits high on a hill in Bantry Bay and has stupendous views of the sea. Broad, terraced lawns fronted by elegant balustrades step down the hillside to a sparkling pool. The drawing and living rooms, decorated in Regency style, are elegant yet not forbiddingly formal. Guest rooms have enormous picture windows, high ceilings, and spacious tile bathrooms. The hotel accommodates only a handful of guests, and a highly trained staff caters to their every whim. In the kitchen chefs prepare whatever guests request—whether it's on the menu or not. All drinks except wine and champagne are included in the rates. ⊠*180 Kloof Rd., Bantry Bay* ⚐*Box 515, Sea Point 8060* 🕾*021/430–3200* ⊕*www.ellerman.co.za* ⇌*11 rooms* ⚐*In-room: safe, refrigerator, DVD (some), Wi-Fi. In-hotel: restaurant, room service, bar, pool, gym, spa, laundry service, concierge, airport shuttle, parking (no fee), no kids under 14, no-smoking rooms* ☰*AE, DC, MC, V* ❍|*BP.*

$$$$

Table Bay Hotel. This glitzy hotel has a prime spot at the tip of the V&A Waterfront. The decor is sunny, with huge picture windows looking onto the mountain, marble mosaic and parquet floors, and lots of plants, including the hotel's trademark orchid arrangements. In the lounge you can browse through a selection of international newspapers as you sit by the fire, relaxing to live piano music. Rooms, although traditionally decorated with hints of dark wood, are bright and have marble-and-tile bathrooms with roomy showers. There's also a business center full of modern conveniences, including helpful administrators who can make your life easier. The hotel has direct access to the large Waterfront mall. ⊠*Quay 6, Waterfront 8002* 🕾*021/406–5000* ⊕*www.suninternational.com* ⇌*311 rooms, 18 suites* ⚐*In-room: safe, refrigerator, DVD (some), VCR (some), ethernet. In-hotel: 2 restaurants, room service, bar, pool, gym, spa, laundry service, concierge, public Internet, public Wi-Fi, airport shuttle, parking (fee and no fee), no-smoking rooms* ☰*AE, DC, MC, V.*

$$$$

Victoria & Alfred Hotel. This upscale hotel in a converted warehouse is smack in the middle of the Waterfront and surrounded by shops, bars, and restaurants. Rooms are huge and luxurious, with crisp linens and elegant throws. Views from the costlier mountain-facing rooms are spectacular, encompassing not only Table Mountain but the city and docks as well. The terrace is a great place to relax. ⊠*On the Waterfront Pierhead, Box 50050, Waterfront 8002* ☎*021/419–6677* ⊕*www.vahotel.co.za* ⟿*94 rooms* △*In-room: safe, refrigerator, dial-up, Wi-Fi. In-hotel: restaurant, room service, bar, gym, no elevator, laundry service, concierge, public Wi-Fi, airport shuttle, parking (no fee), no-smoking rooms* ▤*AE, DC, MC, V.*

$$$–$$$$ ▦ **Radisson SAS Hotel.** Location, location, location: when it comes to the perfect position, this hotel is one of Cape Town's front-runners, perched right on the edge of the Atlantic Ocean. You may only be a five-minute walk from the V&A Waterfront, but it's easy to imagine that you're on a yacht out at sea. The hotel overlooks a private marina, which explains why you'll find some wealthy yacht owners swanning about. The rooms are spacious and pleasantly decorated in neutral blues and cream; be sure to ask for a sea-facing room. Make time to enjoy the infinity pool and a drink at Tobago's Restaurant and Terrace, where Cape Town's cool set gathers for drinks after work. ⊠*Beach Rd., Granger Bay, Waterfront 8002* ☎*021/441–3000* ⊕*www.radissonsas. com* ⟿*182 rooms* △*In-room: safe, refrigerator, DVD (by request), Wi-Fi. In-hotel: restaurant, room service, bar, tennis court, pool, gym, spa, laundry service, public Wi-Fi, airport shuttle, parking (no fee), no-smoking rooms* ▤*AE, D, MC, V* ⦿|*BP.*

$$$ ▦ **Southern Sun Cullinan Cape Town Waterfront.** This sparkling white hotel is just opposite the entrance to the Waterfront. It has a spacious marble-tile lobby, huge picture windows draped in rose and gold that lead out to the pool, and an enormous double-curving gilt staircase that completes the picture. Rooms are quite restrained, with muted green carpets and floral notes, and bathrooms are well laid out, with separate showers in white tile and gray marble. But the views of Table Mountain and the harbor steal the show. There's an efficient shuttle service that runs 8 AM–11 PM, so you'll be able to get around easily. ⊠*1 Cullinan St., Waterfront 8002* ☎*021/418–6920* ⊕*www.southernsun.com* ⟿*410 rooms* △*In-room: safe, ethernet, Wi-Fi, In-hotel: restaurant, room service, bar, pool, gym, public Internet, public Wi-Fi, parking (fee), no-smoking rooms* ▤*AE, DC, MC, V.*

$$–$$$ ▦ **Peninsula All Suites Hotel.** In an 11-story building just across the road from the ocean, these accommodations are ideal for families or groups of friends. You can choose from a variety of rooms that sleep from four to eight people and have incredible views of the sea. The larger suites are the most attractive, full of light and air, thanks to picture windows, sliding doors, wide balconies, and white-tile floors. Small "studio suites" are more like conventional hotel rooms. Each unit has a fully equipped kitchen with a microwave oven. The hotel is a time-share property, so booking during the busy December holiday could be a problem. There are children's programs mid-December–mid-January. ⊠*313 Beach Rd., Sea Point* ⬧*Box 768, Sea Point 8060* ☎*021/430–7777* ⊕*www.peninsula.co.za* ⟿*100 suites* △*In-room: safe, kitchen, refrigerator, ethernet, Wi-Fi. In-hotel: restaurant, room service, bar, pools, gym, beachfront, children's programs (ages infant–12), laundry service, concierge, public Internet, public Wi-Fi, airport shuttle, parking (fee), no-smoking rooms* ▤*AE, DC, MC, V* ⦿|*FAP.*

$$-$$$ 🏨 **Protea Hotel Victoria Junction.** With a funky, art-deco-style decor, this hotel adjacent to the Waterfront and De Waterkant is popular with those looking for something different. Spacious high-ceilinged loft rooms have large double beds on an upper level; you have to be fairly nimble to climb in. Standard rooms have ordinary knee-level beds but are still quite chic. The Set, a trendy restaurant for business lunches, serves a great range of salads and innovative fare, and the bar always jumps at happy hour. ⊠*Somerset and Ebenezer Rds., De Waterkant* ⊡*Box 51234, Waterfront 8002* ☎*021/418–1234* ⊕*www.proteahotels.com/ victoriajunction* ⬦*172 rooms* ⚐*In-room: safe, kitchen (some), refrigerator (some), DVD (by request), VCR (by request), dial-up. In-hotel: restaurant, bar, pool, laundry service, public Wi-Fi, airport shuttle, parking (fee), no-smoking rooms* ⊟*AE, DC, MC, V.*

$$ 🏨 **Cape Victoria Guest House.** Only a five-minute drive and a brisk 20-minute walk from the Waterfront, this charming guesthouse is a luxurious refuge from the bustle of the city. Each room is individually decorated, and there are quirky touches throughout—from an enormous Victorian bath to an African-inspired room for those wishing they were on safari. The owner, Lily Kaplan, is a gem who knows Cape Town inside out, so she can give you all the hot tips when you arrive. The breakfasts are legendary; you will be fortified for the rest of the day, especially if you have a strong cup of coffee together with a slice of the freshly baked almond tart or Lily's special banana bread packed with fruit and nuts. The plunge pool on the terrace overlooking the city rooftops is a great place to unwind with a glass of wine at the end of a busy day. ⊠*13 Torbay Rd., Green Point 8005* ☎*021/439–7721* ⊕*www.capevictoria.co.za* ⬦*10 rooms* ⚐*In-room: no a/c (some), refrigerator, ethernet, dial-up. In-hotel: pool, no elevator, laundry service, concierge, airport shuttle, parking (no fee), no kids under 12, no-smoking rooms* ⊟*AE, DC, MC, V* ⦿*CP.*

$$-$$ 🏨 **La Splendida Luxury Suites.** Designed to look like an art-deco hotel in Miami's South Beach, this trendy all-suites lodging has a great location—the V&A Waterfront is a short walk away. Ask for a sea- or mountain-facing room, either of which will have great views. Natural fabrics decorate the well-proportioned rooms, and the overall feeling is light and airy. The hotel restaurant specializes in contemporary Italian food: great pizzas and pastas and fresh salads. You have a choice of executive or penthouse suites (slightly larger and a bit more expensive), but whichever you choose, you'll be very comfortable. ⊠*121 Beach Rd., Mouille Point 8005* ☎*021/439–5119* ⊕*www.lasplendida.co.za* ⬦*24 suites* ⚐*In-room: safe, refrigerator, Wi-Fi. In-hotel: restaurant, room service, bar, laundry service, public Wi-Fi, airport shuttle, parking (fee), no-smoking rooms* ⊟*AE, DC, MC, V.*

$$-$$ 🏨 **Protea Breakwater Lodge.** You won't find another hotel at the Waterfront offering rates so low. Built in a converted 19th-century prison on Portswood Ridge, the Breakwater certainly won't win any awards for charm or coziness. Its history is quite evident in the long, narrow corridors, which lead to tiny, sparsely furnished cells (sorry, rooms). Nevertheless, the rooms are clean and have TVs, phones, and tea/coffee-makers. Ask for a room with a view of Table Mountain. ⊠*Portswood*

Rd., Waterfront 🏠*Box 50683, Waterfront 8002* ☎*021/406–1911* ⊕*www.bwl.co.za* ❤*145 rooms, 65 with bath; 85 suites* ⬧*In-room: no a/c (some), safe (some), Wi-Fi. In-hotel: 2 restaurants, bar, laundry facilities, laundry service, public Internet, airport shuttle, parking (no fee), no-smoking rooms* ▭*AE, DC, MC, V.*

¢–$ 🏠**Altona Lodge.** If you don't want to spend an arm and a leg on accommodations, the Altona Lodge is a good alternative. This imposing 1890s mansion has been converted into a comfortable and homey B&B. Not all rooms have private bathrooms, so be sure to state your preference when you book. Ask for a room with a view of the sea. If this is full, inquire about the Wilton Manor, Altona's sister hotel. It's a bit pricier, but nothing like other hotels on the Atlantic seaboard. ✉*19 Croxteth Rd., Green Point 8001* ☎*021/434–2572* ⊕*www.wiltonmanor.co.za* ❤*19 rooms, 4 with bath* ⬧*In-room: no a/c, no phone. In-hotel: no elevator, laundry service, parking (no fee), no kids under 9* ▭*AE, MC, V* 🍴*BP.*

¢   🏠**A Sunflower Stop.** If your vocabulary is peppered with expressions such as *wicked, lethal,* and *cooool,* then this cheerful backpackers' lodge is a good stopover. It's close to the Waterfront, and the friendly staff can help you with everything you need to know about Cape Town and the surrounding area. It's also a great place to meet other travelers. You can use the kitchen, braai area, and TV lounge. Rooms are small, clean, and functional, but that's okay—you aren't going to be spending much time in them. ✉*179 Main Rd., Green Point 8001* ☎*021/434–6535* ⊕*www.sunflowerstop.co.za* ❤*15 rooms, 4 with bath; 3 dormitories* ⬧*In-room: no a/c, no phone, no TV. In-hotel: bar, pool, no elevator, laundry facilities, laundry service, airport shuttle, parking (no fee), no kids under 6* ▭*No credit cards.*

ATLANTIC COAST

The hotels below are marked on the Where to Stay & Eat in the Cape Peninsula map.

$$$$ 🏠**Bay Hotel.** This beach hotel in Camps Bay is the most relaxed and unpretentious of the luxury lodgings in and around Cape Town. It's across the road from a white-sand beach and is backed by the towering cliffs of the Twelve Apostles. From the raised pool deck you can look out over sea and sand and onto one of the coolest strips in South Africa, where all the beautiful people congregate. The decor is contemporary, clean, and bright, and the rooms incorporate a sophisticated range of neutral shades. Service is excellent, and although you're only 10 minutes from the hurly-burly of the city, it feels like a lifetime away. Ask for a premier room if you want a sea view. ✉*69 Victoria Rd., Box 32021, Camps Bay 8040* ☎*021/438–4444* ⊕*www.thebay.co.za* ❤*78 rooms* ⬧*In-room: safe, refrigerator, DVD, ethernet. In-hotel: 2 restaurants, room service, bars, pools, tennis court, gym, spa, beachfront, laundry service, concierge, public Internet, public Wi-Fi, airport shuttle, parking (no fee), no kids under 12, no-smoking rooms* ▭*AE, DC, MC, V* 🍴*FAP.*

★ $$$$ **Twelve Apostles Hotel and Spa.** Fancy taking a helicopter to the airport or lazing in a bubble bath while looking out floor-to-ceiling windows at sea and mountains? If this sounds like you, then opt for this luxurious hotel and spa. The only building between Camps Bay and Llandudno and bordering the Table Mountain National Park, it was built amid controversy just before the park's status was proclaimed. The hotel has spectacular views and an enormous indigenous garden that disappears up the mountain. Each room is unique, decorated in either cool blues and whites to reflect the colors of the ocean or warmer tones to conjure up the lifestyle of Africa's explorers. A shuttle runs to the Waterfront every hour during the day. Children's programs are available in December. ⊠ *Victoria Rd., Box 32117, Camps Bay 8040* ☎ *021/437–9000* ⊕ *www.12apostleshotel.com* ⤴ *46 rooms, 24 suites* ♿ *In room: safe, refrigerator, DVD, VCR (by request), ethernet. In-hotel: 2 restaurants, room service, bars, pools, gym, spa, laundry service, concierge, public Internet, public Wi-Fi, airport shuttle, no-smoking rooms* ☰ *AE, DC, MC, V* ❏| *BP.*

$$$–$$$$ **Place on the Bay.** These luxury self-catering apartments are on the beachfront in Camps Bay, within easy walking distance of a host of restaurants and bars. Apartments are tasteful, modern affairs that make extensive use of glass. Many units have good sea views from their balconies. If you really want to have it all, take the magnificent penthouse, which occupies the entire top floor and comes with its own plunge pool, for about R10,000 per day. All units have daily housekeeping service. ⊠ *Fairways and Victoria Rds., Camps Bay 8001* ☎ *021/437– 8200* ⊕ *www.theplaceonthebay.co.za* ⤴ *21 apartments* ♿ *In-room: no a/c (some), safe, kitchen, refrigerator, dial-up. In-hotel: restaurant, room service, pool, beachfront, laundry service, public Internet, public Wi-Fi, parking (no fee)* ☰ *AE, DC, MC, V.*

$$–$$$ **Hout Bay Hideaway Villa and Apartments.** You know you're in an exceptional place when you can lie in an outdoor bath surrounded by indigenous trees and an astonishing view of the mountains. Hout Bay Hideaway is a luxury retreat. All rooms are individually and beautifully decorated with original antiques and artwork. To complete the stylish picture, you can rent one of the beautifully restored Jaguars so that you can tool around Cape Town in style. ⊠ *37 Skaife St., Hout Bay 7806* ☎ *021/790–8040* ⊕ *www.houtbay-hideaway.com* ⤴ *5 suites* ♿ *In-room: no a/c, no phone, safe, kitchen, refrigerator, DVD, ethernet, Wi-Fi. In-hotel: room service, pool, no elevator, public Wi-Fi, airport shuttle, parking (no fee), no-smoking rooms* ☰ *MC, V* ❏| *CP.*

$$ **Long Beach.** It should come as no surprise that each of the rooms is
Fodor's Choice named after a game fish. Kommetjie is after all a pretty lobster-fishing
★ village, and your room is a stone's throw away from the water's edge. Management pays a lot of attention to details, such as offering cell phones with useful preprogrammed numbers that you can borrow for your Cape Town stay. The view is spectacular, rooms are serene yet luxurious, and spa treatments are on-site. When you're not basking on the sundeck (good for whale-watching during the season, approximately June–November), you can explore the Kommetjie beach. ⊠ *1 Kirsten Ave., Kommetjie 7975* ☎ *021/794–6561* ⊕ *www.thelastword.*

co.za 🏊6 rooms ♿*In-room: no phone, safe, refrigerator, DVD, ethernet, Wi-Fi. In-hotel: room service, bar, pool, beachfront, no elevator, laundry service, concierge, public Internet, public Wi-Fi, airport shuttle, parking (no fee), no-smoking rooms* ▭*AE, DC, MC, V* ◎⦚*BP.*

☾ ★ $$ ▦ **Monkey Valley Resort.** This secluded resort is one of the best places on the peninsula for families, and is very popular for small conferences. Built on stilts, the self-catering thatch log cottages lie in an indigenous milk-wood forest overlooking a nature reserve and the white sands of Noordhoek Beach. Cottages have two or three bedrooms, fully equipped kitchens, and large balconies. The wood interiors are attractive and rustic, brightened by floral fabrics, cottage-style furniture, and fireplaces. Rooms are similarly decorated, and some have pretty Victorian bathrooms. There's a large grocery store 5 km (3 mi) away. Owner Judy Sole runs an outstanding establishment and is a character in her own right. Children's programs for all ages can be arranged on request. ⊠*Mountain Rd., Box 114, Noordhoek 7985* ☎*021/789–1391* ⊕*www.monkeyvalleyresort.com* 🏊*32 rooms, 16 cottages* ♿*In-room: no a/c (some), kitchen (some), refrigerator, DVD, VCR (by request), ethernet, Wi-Fi. In-hotel: restaurant, room service, bar, pool, no elevator, laundry service, concierge, public Internet, public Wi-Fi, airport shuttle, parking (no fee), some pets allowed* ▭*AE, DC, MC, V* ◎⦚*BP.*

SOUTHERN SUBURBS

$$$$ ▦ **Bishop's Court.** Nestled in the exclusive suburb of Bishopscourt, where the bishop of the Anglican Church still has his residence, this boutique hotel with unrivaled views over Kirstenbosch and Table Mountain is a good combination of class and homey comfort. Thanks to a friendly and attentive staff, you may end up feeling as though you're staying with wealthy cousins. After browsing through the private library you can retreat to your gorgeous room. The decor is classical, and fine touches include fluffy robes, wonderful toiletries, and wonderful baths. Better still, there's a complimentary in-house chauffeur who is happy to shuttle you around. Groups can even rent the entire establishment. ⊠*18 Hillwood Ave., Bishopscourt 7708* ☎*021/797–6710* ⊕*www.thelastword.co.za* 🏊*5 rooms* ♿*In-room: no phone, safe, refrigerator, DVD, VCR, ethernet, dial-up, Wi-Fi. In-hotel: bar, tennis court, pool, no elevator, laundry service, concierge, public Internet, public Wi-Fi, airport shuttle, parking (no fee), no kids under 12, no-smoking rooms* ▭*AE, DC, MC, V* ◎⦚*BP.*

★ $$$–$$$$ ▦ **Cellars-Hohenort Hotel & Spa.** It's easy to forget the outside world at this idyllic getaway in Constantia. Set on acres of gardens on the slopes of the Constantiaberg, this luxury hotel commands spectacular views across Constantia Valley to False Bay. The 18th-century cellars of the Klaasenbosch wine estate and the Hohenort manor house form the heart of the hotel. Guest rooms are large and elegant, furnished in English-country style with brass beds, flowery valances, and reproduction antiques. Rooms in the manor house have the best views of the valley. The Presidential Suite sleeps six. ⊠*93 Brommersvlei Rd., Box*

1

270, Constantia 7848 ☎*021/794–2137* ⊕*www.cellars-hohenort.com* 📠*52 rooms, 1 suite* ♿*In-room: safe, refrigerator, DVD, dial-up. In-hotel: 2 restaurants, room service, bar, tennis court, pools, gym, spa, bicycles, no elevator, laundry service, concierge, public Wi-Fi, airport shuttle, parking (no fee), no kids under 12, no-smoking rooms* ▭*AE, DC, MC, V* ⏀*BP.*

★ $$$–$$$$ 🖼**Constantia Uitsig Hotel.** This 200-acre winery has an enviable setting, backed by the magnificent mountains of the Constantiaberg and overlooking the vineyards of Constantia Valley. You might be just 20 minutes from the center of town, but this is a little slice of rural paradise, with horses grazing just a few hundred yards away. Rooms, in whitewashed farm cottages set on manicured lawns and gardens, are luxurious and inviting. Brass bedsteads, timber ceilings, and sophisticated check and floral patterns evoke an upscale farmhouse feel. The two restaurants in the original farmhouse, La Colombe and Constantia Uitsig, draw diners from all over the Cape, and the manicured cricket pitch is the perfect place for a summer game. A stay includes a complimentary wine tasting. ✉*Spaanschemat River Rd., Box 32, Constantia 7848* ☎*021/794–6500* ⊕*www.constantiauitsig.co.za* 📠*16 rooms* ♿*In-room: safe, refrigerator, DVD (by request), VCR (by request). In-hotel: 3 restaurants, room service, bars, pool, spa, no elevator, laundry service, public Internet, airport shuttle, parking (no fee), no-smoking rooms* ▭*AE, DC, MC, V* ⏀*BP.*

$$$–$$$$ 🖼**Red House.** Once the hunting lodge of Lord Charles Somerset, this house, dating from 1729, is one of Cape Town's oldest surviving buildings. It's been lavishly restored, but the walls remain their signature red, the result of a former, eccentric owner who chose the bold color to "ensure protection against the elements." You won't have to worry much about the elements here, as the elegant rooms are extremely comfortable and decorated with heavy drapes, dark mahogany furniture, chandeliers, and bold gilt-frame mirrors. What's more, the guesthouse is nestled in the leafy suburb of Newlands, just five minutes from Kirstenbosch and 10 minutes from the city center. The terrace is a good place to relax after a busy day, and you can even get an on-site massage in the garden or near the pool. ✉*4 Hiddingh Ave., Newlands 7700* ☎*021/683–8000* ⊕*www.redhouse.co.za* 📠*5 rooms, 1 cottage* ♿*In-room: no a/c, ethernet, Wi-Fi. In-hotel: room service, pool, spa, no elevator, laundry service, public Wi-Fi, airport shuttle, parking (no fee), no kids under 12, no-smoking rooms* ▭*AE, DC, MC, V* ⏀*BP.*

$$–$$$ 🖼**Alphen Hotel.** Built in the mid-1700s in Cape Dutch style, this former manor house is now a national monument and one of the Cape's historic treasures. The owners are descendants of the distinguished Cloete family, which has farmed the land around Constantia since 1750. Cloete paintings and antiques, each with a story to tell, adorn the public rooms. Rooms range in size from compact to rather large. A small drawback is the slight traffic noise from the nearby highway in rush hour, but a health-and-wellness center on the grounds just might help you forget about it. Only luxury rooms have air-conditioning. ✉*Alphen Dr., Box 35, Constantia 7848* ☎*021/794–5011* ⊕*www.alphen. co.za* 📠*21 rooms* ♿*In room: no a/c (some), refrigerator, DVD, dial-*

up. *In-hotel: restaurant, room service, bar, pool, no elevator, laundry service, airport shuttle, parking (no fee), no-smoking rooms ▭AE, DC, MC, V ◯|BP.*

$$–$$$ 🏠 **Palm House.** Towering palms dominate the manicured lawns of this peaceful guesthouse straddling the border of Kenilworth and Wynberg, a 15-minute drive from the city. The house is an enormous, stolid affair, built in the early 1920s by a protégé of architect Sir Herbert Baker and filled with dark-wood paneling, wood staircases, and fireplaces. Bold floral fabrics and reproduction antiques decorate the large guest rooms. Upstairs rooms benefit from more air and light. Guests often meet for evening drinks in the drawing room. ✉ *10 Oxford St., Wynberg 7800* ☎ *021/761–5009* ⊕ *www.thepalmhouse.co.za* 🛏 *10 rooms* △ *In-room: no a/c (some), safe, refrigerator. In-hotel: bar, pool, no elevator, laundry service, public Wi-Fi, airport shuttle, parking (no fee), no-smoking rooms ▭DC, MC, V ◯|BP.*

★ $$–$$$ 🏨 **Steenberg Hotel.** Originally called Swaaneweide aan den Steenberg, this is one of the oldest estates in the area. It was granted to the four-time widow Catherina Ras in the late 17th century by her lover, Simon van der Stel, then governor of the Cape, making her the first woman to own land in South Africa. She was, by all accounts, wild, and legend has it that she was given to riding her horse naked around the grounds, which might explain van der Stel's generosity. The original buildings on this working wine estate have been painstakingly restored, the gardens manicured to perfection, and the vineyards replanted on the slopes of the Constantiaberg. The original vineyards have been converted into a championship 18-hole golf course. The spectacular buildings are all furnished with antiques, as are guest rooms, which are done in a Provençal style but with a modern touch. The hotel is exceptionally classy, as is its award-winning wine. Don't leave without buying some sauvignon blanc. ✉ *Steenberg and Tokai Rds., Tokai* 🖃 *Net Suite 150, Private Bag, X26, Tokai 7966* ☎ *021/713–2222* ⊕ *www. steenberghotel.com* 🛏 *30 rooms, 1 suite* △ *In-room: safe, refrigerator, DVD (on request), dial-up (some), Wi-Fi. In-hotel: restaurant, room service, bar, golf course, pools, gym, spa, no elevator, laundry service, concierge, public Wi-Fi, airport shuttle, parking (no fee), no-smoking rooms ▭AE, DC, MC, V ◯|BP.*

$$ 🏨 **Vineyard Hotel.** Set on 6 acres of rolling gardens overlooking the Liesbeek River in residential Newlands, this comfortable hotel was built around the 18th-century weekend home of Lady Anne Barnard. The views of the back of Table Mountain are spectacular, but for a better rate ask for a courtyard-facing room. Children's programs are available December–January. The hotel is 10 minutes by car from the city but within walking distance of the Newlands sports arenas and the shops of Cavendish Square. Au Jardin, the classic French restaurant, is very well regarded. ✉ *Colinton Rd., Box 151, Newlands 7725* ☎ *021/657–4500* ⊕ *www.vineyard.co.za* 🛏 *173 rooms* △ *In-room: safe, refrigerator, ethernet, Wi-Fi. In-hotel: 3 restaurants, room service, bar, pools, gym, spa, no elevator, children's programs (ages infant–11), laundry service, concierge, public Internet, public Wi-Fi, airport shuttle, parking (no fee), no-smoking rooms ▭AE, DC, MC, V.*

★ ¢–$ ⌂**Koornhoop Manor Guest House.** One of the best values in Cape Town is this lovely Victorian house set in a pretty garden. The unpretentious rooms vary in size, are simply decorated in pretty florals, and have private baths. The hotel is very central, and is within safe walking distance of a huge range of restaurants in the vibey young suburb of Observatory, five minutes' drive from the city and convenient to the railway station. A communal area with an honor bar is a convivial meeting place. You need to book quite far in advance to take advantage of this little gem. ⌧ *Wrench and London Rds., Observatory* ⓓ*24 London Rd., Observatory 7925* ☎*021/448–0595* ⊕*www.geocities. com/koornhoop* ⇦*8 rooms, 2 3-bedroom apartments* ⌂*In-room: no a/c, no phone, Wi-Fi. In-hotel: no elevator, laundry service, public Wi-Fi, airport shuttle, parking (no fee), no-smoking rooms* ⊟No *credit cards* ⓘⒷ*BP.*

FALSE BAY

$ ⌂**Boulders Beach Lodge.** Just a few steps from beautiful Boulders Beach—the best swimming beach in Cape Town—this comfortable guesthouse is a winner. The understated rooms are decorated with elegant black wrought-iron furniture and snow-white linen, creating a restful, minimalist feel. The adjacent restaurant and pub are a bit more boisterous. ⌧*4 Boulders Pl., Simon's Town 7975* ☎*021/786–1758* ⊕*www. bouldersbeach.co.za* ⇦*12 rooms* ⌂*In-room: no a/c, no TV, dial-up. In-hotel: restaurant, bar, no elevator, laundry service, public Wi-Fi, parking (no fee), no-smoking rooms* ⊟*AE, DC, MC, V* ⓘⒷ*BP.*

$ ⌂**Inn at Castle Hill.** The fishing village of Kalk Bay is a vacation destination in itself. From the inn you can stroll down to the beach, walk to the restaurants, or explore the antiques shops that this bohemian village is known for. The carefully restored Edwardian villa has a wonderful view over False Bay, and the spacious rooms are individually decorated. Be sure to ask for a room that opens onto the veranda. There's a communal TV lounge, and braai (South African barbecue) facilities are available on request. ⌧*37 Gatesville Rd., Kalk Bay 7975* ☎*021/788–2554* ⊕*www.castlehill.co.za* ⇦*5 rooms* ⌂*In-room: no a/c, no phone, no TV. In-hotel: bar, no elevator, laundry service, public Internet, parking (no fee), no kids under 12, no-smoking rooms* ⊟*AE, DC, MC, V* ⓘⒷ*BP.*

$ ⌂**Simon's Town Quayside Hotel.** On Jubilee Square, part of the Simon's Town Waterfront, this hotel is right in the action and has wonderful views over Simon's Bay, the harbor, and the yacht club. Almost all rooms have sea views, and all are light and airy, combining lime-washed wood with white walls and pale-blue finishes. Room service can be arranged from the adjacent Bertha's Restaurant. ⌧*Jubilee Sq., St. George's., Box 555, Simon's Town 7995* ☎*021/786–3838* ⊕*www. relaishotels.com* ⇦*26 rooms* ⌂*In-room: safe, refrigerator, dial-up, Wi-Fi. In-hotel: room service, no elevator, laundry service, public Wi-Fi, airport shuttle, parking (no fee), no-smoking rooms* ⊟*AE, DC, MC, V* ⓘⒷ*BP.*

¢   📺 **Simon's Town Backpackers.** Don't expect designer linen or glam furnishings at this backpackers' lodge. It's simple, cheap, cheerful, and spotlessly clean, and offers fantastic views from the upstairs balcony. Simon's Town is a great place to station yourself. It's only 45 minutes by car from Cape Town, it's on the railway line, and it's within walking distance of Boulders Beach and the penguin colony. You can also choose from plenty of nearby restaurants, serving everything from sushi to Nepalese fare. The historic building has been many things in its lifetime, including a brothel. A TV is available in the communal lounge. ✉*66 St. George's St., Simon's Town 7975* ☎*021/786–1964* ⊕*www. capepax.co.za* 🛏*6 rooms, 4 dormitories* ♿*In-room: no a/c, no phone, no TV. In-hotel: bar, bicycles, no elevator, laundry service, public Internet, airport shuttle, no-smoking rooms* ▭*No credit cards.*

NIGHTLIFE & THE ARTS

NIGHTLIFE

There's plenty to do in Cape Town after dark. The city's nightlife is concentrated in a number of areas, so you can explore a different one each night or move from one hub to another. After all, the city is small enough to get around in quite easily. That said, however, walking from one area to another isn't advisable, as there are some parts of the city that are completely deserted and unsafe. Women, in pairs or singly, and couples should not walk alone. One of the best—and safest—places to start is the Waterfront, where you can choose from movies, restaurants, bars, and pubs and walk between them quite happily, as there are plenty of security guards and other people walking around. The top end of Long Street is another good nightlife area. Here you'll find a couple of blocks of bars, restaurants, and backpacker lodges that are open late. And the area bounded by Loop, Long, Wale, and Orange streets is the best place to get a feeling for Cape Town's always-changing nightclub scene, but ask around for the latest on the current flavor of the month. De Waterkant is very busy at night; if you're in the area, you can also take in the Green Point strip, where restaurants and bars open out onto the streets. On weekends these bars are packed, and you'll get a good idea of how Capetonians let down their hair. Heritage Square, in the city center, is another vibey place to spend an evening. Here you'll find an ever-changing mix of bars and restaurants. Mouille Point's Platinum Mile is an excellent place for evening cocktails. The views over the Atlantic and onto Robben Island are breathtaking, and this is where the ultracool set hangs out after a hard day at the beach or gym. Be prepared to line up to get into places, especially on a Friday night.

BARS & PUBS

For a bird's-eye view of Cape Town and Table Mountain, head to **Hemisphere** (✉*31st fl., Absa Centre, 2 Riebeek St., Cape Town Central* ☎*021/421–0581* ⊕*www.hemisphere.org.za*) for sophisticated cocktails and oodles of style. The crowd is older, and the music is hugely accessible '70s, '80s, and '90s sounds. For a fab evening on Mouille Point's Platinum Mile, plan to have drinks at **Wafu** (✉ *1st fl., Beach Rd. and Surrey Pl., Mouille Point* ☎ *021/433–2377* ⊕ *www.wakame.co.za*) and then head to the downstairs restaurant, Wakame, for sushi and champagne. You'll have great views of the Atlantic and Robben Island.

Built right on the water's edge adjacent to the yacht marina, **Bascule Whisky Bar and Wine Cellar** (✉ *Cape Grace Hotel, West Quay Rd., Waterfront* ☎ *021/410–7238*) is a fancy watering hole for well-

> ### PINK AND PROUD TO PARTY
>
> A key event on Cape Town's social calendar is the **MCQP** (*Mother City Queer Party* ⊕ *www.mcqp.co.za*), which started in 1993. Party animals should definitely add this to their must-do list. It's part Mardi Gras, part Gay Pride March, and one enormous fancy-dress party. Each year the party is themed, and everyone goes all out to dress up in fantastic outfits. Everyone's welcome!

heeled, cigar-puffing locals. Its 450 whiskies are reputed to be the biggest selection in the southern hemisphere, so it's a great place to enjoy a good single malt or glass of bubbly while the light fades behind Table Mountain. **Quay Four** (✉ *Quay 4, Waterfront* ☎ *021/419–2008*) is a very relaxed option popular with visitors and locals, who clog picnic tables on the wooden deck overlooking the harbor before moving on to one of the many Waterfront restaurants. The **Sports Café** (✉ *Shop 256, 2nd fl., Victoria Wharf, Waterfront* ☎ *021/419–5558 or 021/419–5559*) is a huge place with big-screen TVs. The food isn't going to win any awards, but if you're homesick, this is the place to head. The bar gets into the spirit of major foreign sporting events, like the Super Bowl and the FA Cup Final (England's soccer championship), and is undoubtedly the best place to watch sports in the city.

In the city center, the **Long Street Café** (✉ *259 Long St., Cape Town Central* ☎ *021/424–2464*), an easygoing favorite with locals, serves light tasty dishes, coffee, and, of course, cocktails. Try the Long Street iced tea, but be warned: there's no tea in it. With its dark-wood paneling and hot-red upholstery, the **M Bar & Lounge** (✉ *38 Long St., Cape Town Central* ☎ *021/424–7247*) is home to the hip and happening. It's always busy with the after-work crowd looking for a bit of R&R. The **Planet Champagne Bar** (✉ *Mount Nelson Hotel, 76 Orange St., Gardens* ☎ *021/483–1000*) is a sophisticated spot that carries an excellent selection of local and international wines and champagnes by the glass. The decor is an interesting mix of retro and modern and the bar opens onto one of the Mount Nelson's magnificent garden terraces; on a hot summer night it's one of the coolest places to be seen.

You can watch the sun set at the hugely popular **Café Caprice** (✉ *37 Victoria Rd., Camps Bay* ☎ *021/438–8315*) while rubbing shoulders with beautiful bronzed bodies just off the beach. It's very LA. **Cafe Erte** (✉ *265a Main Rd., Sea Point* ☎ *021/434–6624*) is very gay-friendly. **Tank Restaurant & Sushi Bar** (✉ *Cape Quarter, 72 Waterkant St., Greenpoint* ☎ *021/419–0007*), in the trendy De Waterkant precinct, is a must for cool customers. It's been described as "schmodelly," which in Cape Town lingo roughly translates as a place where you can schmooze with models. The cocktails are made with the freshest ingredients. Try the signature Tank cocktail, a delicious mix of homemade lemongrass syrup, fresh litchi juice, and lots of alcohol.

Out of town in the quaint fishing village of Kalk Bay, **Polana** (✉*Kalk Bay Harbour, off Main Rd., Kalk Bay* ☎*021/788–7162*) has astonishing views across the bay. You can see all the way to Cape Hangklip, and when the weather is good they slide back the windows so you can enjoy the sea breeze while you sip a cold glass of South Africa's best.

DANCE CLUBS

Dance clubs open and close at a rapid rate in Cape Town. A club that's all the rage one month often closes while it's still hugely popular, only to be reinvented and reopened in a different guise. Your best bet is to ask around to find out what's hot or to check in one of the local entertainment guides such as *Cape etc.*

It's an easy move from supper in one of the many Long Street restaurants to clubbing at **Club Chrome** (✉*8 Pepper St., Cape Town Central* ☎*083/700–6079*), in the heart of Cape Town's nightlife strip. Dancers groove to R&B, hip-hop, and house music. **Club Roosevelt** (✉*160 Bree St., Cape Town Central* ☎No phone) draws the fickle Cape Town crowds with its Nina Simone–meets–The Prodigy mix of sounds. The balcony is great in good weather, as you can enjoy the vibe without the crush. The **Ivory Room** (✉*196 Loop St., Cape Town Central* ☎*021/422–3257*) always cooks until late. Think African colonial with a twist of R&B, funk, hip-hop, and lots in between. It's good for "everyone from 20 to old." **Rhodes House** (✉*60 Queen Victoria St., Cape Town Central* ☎*021/424–8844*) is one of the smarter places to boogie up a storm and, while you're at it, bump into a visiting celeb or two. Music varies from R&B to hip-hop, house, jazz, and funk. There are two dance floors and a cigar lounge to relax in.

Green Point has its share of clubs. **The Bronx** (✉*20 Somerset Rd., Green Point* ☎*021/419–9216*), one of the oldest kids on the block, is gay-friendly and plays disco (remember that?).

LIVE MUSIC CLUBS

The **Drum Café** (✉*32 Glynn St., Gardens* ☎*021/461–1305*) has live performances by percussionists from all over Africa. On Monday and Wednesday starting around 9, a drum circle lets you discover your inner rhythm. Among the clubs with live African music, a good bet is **Mama Africa** (✉*178 Long St., Cape Town Central* ☎*021/426–1017*). It has live music Monday through Saturday, and usually a marimba band on Monday, Wednesday, Friday, and Saturday night as well as authentic African food, music, and pulse.

Many of the mainstream jazz clubs in the city double as restaurants. Cover charges range from R15 to R30. Aside from the jazz clubs listed here, the hot venues change so quickly that it's best to get information when you're here. Cape Town Tourism has a list of good jazz venues

CLOSE UP

Jazz it Up

Music, especially jazz and local African music, was an extremely potent instrument for social change during the oppressive apartheid regime. Consequently, South Africans are passionate about music, and they celebrate their love of jazz with the **Cape Town International Jazz Festival** (⊕ www.capetownjazzfest.com), usually held in March. Started in 1999, this event (formerly known as the North Sea Jazz Festival) gets bigger and better each year. There's an even mix of local and international stars, and past festivals have included the likes of Randy Crawford, Abdullah Ibrahim, Gino Vannelli, Ladysmith Black Mambazo, and Nils Landgren and his Funk Unit.

The Independent Armchair Theatre (✉ 135 Lower Main Rd., Observatory ☎ 021/447–1514 ⊕ www.armchairtheatre.co.za) has a long history of promoting South African talent. It's close to town, but out of the immediate fray in the trendy suburb of Observatory—great if you

want to escape the frenzy of town on a Saturday night. You can hear rock, indie, electronica, jazz, and hip-hop here, but it's not just a music venue—it also stages theater and local comedy acts. At **Mercury Live** (✉ 43 De Villiers St., District Six, City Bowl ☎ 021/465–2106 ⊕ www.mercuryl.co.za) you'll find a regular lineup of South African bands such as Springbok Nude Girls (they're boys by the way) and the hugely popular Bed on Bricks, who pump out what's best described as South African rock and funk jazz. Regulars describe the place as "Fun with a capital F" and liken the relaxed atmosphere to partying in your own home. Book a show and a meal at the wheelchair-friendly **On Broadway** (✉ 88 Shortmarket St., Cape Town Central ☎ 021/424–1194 ⊕ www.onbroadway.co.za). The live acts—everything from jazz to '60s tunes—are usually extremely spirited, and audience participation is not uncommon.

and attempts to keep up with the frequent changes. The **Green Dolphin Jazz Restaurant** (✉ Victoria & Alfred Arcade, Pierhead, Waterfront ☎ 021/421–7471) attracts some of the best mainstream musicians in the country as well as a few from overseas. The cover charge is R20–R25. **Kenney's Cigar Lounge and Restaurant** (✉ 251 Long St., Cape Town Central ☎ 021/424–1212 ⊕ www.kennedys.co.za) is a relaxing place to have a drink and listen to live jazz acts. There's valet parking, which is fantastic if you're new to the city—Long Street at night is packed with partygoers, and parking is at a premium. **Mannenberg's Jazz Café** (✉ Clock Tower Precinct, Waterfront ☎ 021/421–5639), a longstanding Cape Town favorite, showcases talented musicians from South Africa and the rest of the continent. You can enjoy a sundowner or a meal while listening. **Winchester Mansions Hotel** (✉ 221 Beach Rd., Sea Point ☎ 021/434–2351) does a mellow Sunday brunch in the courtyard (11–2; about R165) with some of the city's best jazz musicians.

THE ARTS

The **Artscape** (⊠ *D. F. Malan St. and Hertzog Blvd., Foreshore* ☎ *021/410–9800* ⊕ *www.artscape.co.za*), a huge and unattractive theater complex, is the hub of performing arts and other cultural activities. Cape Town City Ballet, the Cape Town Philharmonic Orchestra, and the city's theater and opera companies perform in the center's three theaters. Since 1994 there's been a conscious effort to make the performing arts more representative and multicultural, and today there's a palpable African-arts excitement in the air. Classics are still well represented, as are more contemporary works.

CLASSICAL MUSIC

The **Cape Town Philharmonic Orchestra** (☎ *021/410–9809* ⊕ *www.cpo. org.za*) alternates performances between City Hall and Artscape. It's also relaxing to listen to the orchestra at one of its two open-air concerts at the Kirstenbosch gardens—usually the first and last concerts of the season. The orchestra has hosted several guest conductors from Europe and the United States and has an active program, which includes free concerts in the summer at the Waterfront's outdoor AGFA Amphitheatre. You can also make a day trip to hear the orchestra and other musical groups at the Spier Estate during the Spier Arts Summer Festival or at a music festival in Franschhoek in October *(⇨ Chapter 2).*

FILM

The Waterfront alone has two movie houses with a total of 19 screens. Check newspaper listings for what's playing. **Ster-Kinekor** (☎ *082/16789* ⊕ *www.sterkinekor.com*) has cinema complexes all over the city. **Nu Metro** (☎ *086/110–0220*) has several theaters throughout the city that screen mainstream movies.

At two locations, the **Cinema Nouveau** (⊠ *Cavendish Square shopping center, basement level, Cavendish Sq., Vineyard Rd., Claremont* ☎ *021/657–5620 or 082/16789* ⊠ *V&A Waterfront shopping center, ground floor, King's Warehouse, Waterfront* ☎ *082/16789*) concentrates on foreign and art films. The **Labia** (⊠ *68 Orange St., Gardens* ⊠ *50 Kloof St., Gardens* ☎ *021/424–5927* ⊕ *www.labia.co.za*) is an independent art house that screens good-quality mainstream and alternative films, including the works of some of the best European filmmakers. There are four screens at the Labia on Orange and two at the Labia on Kloof, just up the road. A small coffee bar serves snacks at both venues.

THEATER

The **Baxter Theatre Complex** (⊠ *Main Rd., Rondebosch* ☎ *021/685–7880* ⊕ *www.baxter.co.za*), part of the University of Cape Town, hosts a range of productions from serious drama to wacky comedies, as well as some rather experimental stuff. The complex includes a 666-seat theater, a concert hall, a smaller studio, and a restaurant and bar.

During the summer, when the weather's good, Cape Town has its own version of New York City's Central Park's Shakespeare in the Park at the excellent **Maynardville Open-Air Theatre** (⊠ *Wolfe and Church Sts.,*

1

Wynberg ☎*083/909–0909 Computicket* ⊕*www.artscape.co.za*). Theatergoers often bring a picnic supper to enjoy before the show.

The **Theatre on the Bay** (✉*1 Link St., Camps Bay* ☎*021/438–3301* ⊕*www.theatreonthebay.co.za*) features local and international drama and comedy, plus occasional cabaret and music. Its Act I Theatre Café is great for a preshow drink.

SPORTS & THE OUTDOORS

Cape Town is the adventure capital of the universe. Whatever you want to do—dive, paddle, fly, jump, run, slide, fin, walk, or clamber—this is the city to do it in. **Downhill Adventures** (☎*021/422–0388 or 021/422–1580* ⊕*www.downhilladventures.com*) books a range of activities via its Web site. **Siyabona Africa Travel** (☎*021/424–1037* ⊕*www.siyabona.com*) offers general travel advice and adventure booking.

For spectator sports, it's easy to get tickets for ordinary club matches and for interprovincial games. Getting tickets to an international test match is more of a challenge; however, there's always somebody selling tickets—at a price, of course.

BIKING
Downhill Adventures (☎*021/422–0388 or 021/422–1580* ⊕*www.downhilladventures.com*) offers great cycling trips around the peninsula. You can opt for a full day at the nature reserve at Cape Point, including a picnic lunch, or a leisurely cycle through the Constantia Winelands, stopping for wine tasting along the way. Those wanting something more hard-core might like mountain biking in the Tokai forest. Expect to pay R400–R500 per trip.

CLIMBING
Cape Town has hundreds of bolted sport routes around the city and peninsula, ranging from an easy 10 to a hectic 30. (To give you some idea of difficulty, a route rated a 10 in South Africa would be equivalent to a 5.5 climb in the United States. A 20 climb would register around 5.10c, while the hardest you'll find in South Africa is probably a 34, which American climbers would know as a 5.14b. The toughest climb up Table Mountain rates about 32, which is a 5.14a.) Both Table Mountain sandstone and Cape granite are excellent hard rocks. There are route guides to all the major climbs and a number of climbing schools in Cape Town. A few favorite climbs include Table Mountain (from various angles), Lion's Head, du Toit's Kloof, and Muizenberg Peak.

Cape Town School of Mountaineering (☎*086/110–6548*) is a good bet for day excursions and escorted walks. **High Adventure** (☎*021/689–1234* ⊕*www.highadventure.co.za*) specializes in climbing in the Cape Town area but also organizes trips farther afield.

FISHING

If you're keen to take to the open ocean for some deep-sea fishing, you'll have plenty of choices, as South Africa has excellent game fish, such as dorado, yellowfin tuna, and broadbill swordfish, which keep salty sea dogs going back for more. **Big Game Fishing Safaris** (☎021/674–2203 ⊕*www.simonstown.com/fishing/safaris*) operates a 39-foot luxury catamaran for a day of fishing. You can spend a day with **Reel Deep Charters** (☎083/414–6908 or 083/258–0707 ⊕*www.reeldeep.co.za*) out on the deep blue.

In the mountains, just an hour or so away from Cape Town, you'll encounter wild and wily fish in wild and wonderful rivers. The season runs September–May. **Inkwazi Fly-Fishing Safaris** (☎083/626–0467 or 021/788–7611 ⊕*www.inkwaziflyfishing.co.za*) offers escorted tours, all the equipment you'll need, and plenty of good advice.

GOLF

Most golf clubs in the Cape accept visitors, but prior booking is essential. Expect to pay R350–R400 for 18 holes and R120–R250 to rent golf clubs. Most clubs offer equipment rental. You can also rent golf carts for around R200, but you are encouraged to employ a caddie instead, as this offers valuable employment to local communities. Expect to pay around R100 and a tip of 10%–20% for good service. **Clovelly Country Club** (☎021/782–1118 ⊕*www.clovelly.co.za*), near Fish Hoek, is a tight course that requires masterful shot placement from tee to green. **Milnerton Golf Club** (☎021/552–1047 ⊕*www.milnertongolfclub.co.za*), sandwiched between the sea and a lagoon, is the Western Cape's only links course and can be difficult when the wind blows. **Mowbray Golf Club** (☎021/685–3018 ⊕*www.mowbraygolfclub.co.za*), with its great views of Devil's Peak, is a magnificent parkland course that has hosted several major tournaments; there are a number of interesting water holes. Unfortunately, noise from the highway can spoil the atmosphere. Founded in 1885, **Royal Cape Golf Club** (☎021/761–6551 ⊕*www.royalcapegolf.co.za*) is the oldest course in Africa and has hosted the South African Open many times. Its beautiful setting and immaculate fairways and greens make a round here a must for serious golf enthusiasts. The challenging and scenic **Steenberg Golf Estate** (☎021/715–0227 ⊕*www.steenberggolfclub.co.za*) is the most exclusive and expensive course on the peninsula. A round costs more than R600 per person unless you're staying at the hotel. Dress codes are strictly enforced here.

HIKING & CANYONING

Cape Town and the surrounding areas offer some of the finest hiking in the world, mostly through the spectacularly beautiful mountains. Kloofing, known as canyoning in the United States, is the practice of following a mountain stream through its gorge, canyon, or kloof by swimming, rock hopping, and jumping over waterfalls or cliffs into deep pools. There are some exceptional kloofing venues in the Cape. **Abseil Africa** (☎021/424–4760 ⊕*www.abseilafrica.co.za*) runs a kloofing and abseiling (rappelling) trip on the Steenbras River, better known as Kamikaze Kanyon. **Table Mountain Walks** (☎021/715–6136

⊕*www.tablemountainwalks.co.za*) offers various hikes, including options at Table Mountain and Silvermine Nature Reserve, with a well-informed guide.

There is a fantastic overnight hiking trail (part of the greater Hoerikwaggo Trail) in the Cape Point section of **Table Mountain National Park** (☎*021/780–9204* ⊕*www.cpnp.co.za*), but you need to book ahead—sometimes by as much as a year.

KAYAKING

You don't have to be a pro to discover Cape Town by kayak. **Coastal Kayak Trails** (☎*021/439–1134* ⊕*www.kayak.co.za*) has regular sunset and sunrise paddles off Sea Point. A two-hour paddle costs around R200. **Real Cape Adventures** (☎*021/790–5611* ⊕*www.seakayak.co.za*) offers regular scenic paddles off Hout Bay and from Simon's Town around to Boulders. Expect to pay R250–R450.

PARAGLIDING & SKYDIVING

Para-pax Tandem Paragliding (☎*021/461–7070* ⊕*www.parapax.com*) will take you flying off landmarks such as Lion's Head, Signal Hill, and Table Mountain, depending on the wind and weather conditions. You can do a tandem sky dive (no experience necessary) and have a video taken of you hurtling earthward with Table Mountain in the background with **Skydive Cape Town** (☎*082/800–6290* ⊕*www. skydivecapetown.za.net*). A tandem fall costs around R1,600, if you want a video of your madness.

RAPPELLING

Abseil Africa (☎*021/424–4760* ⊕*www.abseilafrica.co.za*) offers a 350-foot abseil (rappel) off the top of Table Mountain for about R350, not including cable car. Another excursion takes you over a waterfall in the Helderberg mountains, about an hour's drive away, for about R595, including transportation and lunch.

SAILING

Drum Africa (☎*021/782–2205* ⊕*www.drumafrica.co.za*) launches catamarans (and you) off Fish Hoek beach. Before you know it you'll be in a trapeze harness leaning over the side of the boat like an old pro. In whale season (June–November) you're bound to see plenty of whales in the bay, which is thrilling.

SCUBA DIVING

The diving around the Cape is excellent, with kelp forests, cold-water corals, very brightly colored reef life, and numerous wrecks. An unusual experience is a dive in the Two Oceans Aquarium. CMSA, NAUI, and PADI dive courses are offered by local operators, beginning at about R1,700. **Orca Industries** (☎*021/671–9673* ⊕*www.orca-industries. co.za*) offers dive courses and charters. **Pro Divers** (☎*021/433–0472* ⊕*www.prodiverssa.co.za*) runs dive tours to some of the many ships wrecked at the infamous Cape of Storms. The friendly **Scuba Shack** (☎*021/424–9368 Cape Town,* ☎*021/782–7358 Kommetjie* ⊕*www. scubashack.co.za*) has two outlets: one in town and one near Kommetjie. **Underwater World** (☎*021/461–8290*) is a city dive shop that offers only NAUI courses.

SURFING

Cape Town's surf is a bit erratic when compared with that of Durban or the revered J-Bay (Jeffreys Bay), but there are still some excellent spots. **Gary's Surf School** (☎*021/788–9839* ⊕*www.garysurf.com*) offers surfing lessons to youngsters and the young at heart in the relatively warm and gentle waters at Muizenberg. You can also rent boards and wet suits. Lessons last two hours and cost around R380 for adults, R300 for children, including suit and board; if you still feel strong after that, you can keep the equipment for the rest of the day. You do need to be aware, however, that you'll be sharing the ocean with plenty of sharks, but that never seems to stop anyone.

SHOPPING

When it comes to shopping, Cape Town has something for everyone—from sophisticated malls to trendy markets. Although African art and curios are obvious choices (and you will find some gems), South Africans have woken up to their own sense of style and creativity, and the results are fantastic and as diverse as the people who make up this rainbow nation. So in a morning you could bag some sophisticated tableware from Carrol Boyes, a funky wire-art object from a street vendor, and a beautifully designed handbag made by HIV-positive women working as part of a community development program.

Cape Town has great malls selling well-known brands, and the V&A Waterfront is an excellent place to start, followed by Cavendish Square in Claremont and Canal Walk at Century City, on the N1 heading out of town toward Paarl. But it's beyond the malls that you can get a richer shopping experience, one that will give you greater insight into the soul of the city and its people. Shopping malls usually have extended shopping hours beyond the normal 9–5 on weekdays and 9–1 on Saturdays. Most shops outside of malls (except for small grocery stores) are closed on Sunday.

MARKETS

Green Point. This flea market attracts a huge and diverse audience, which is not surprising, really, given that there's something for everyone here, from granny's old clothes to African artifacts, CDs, and T-shirts. It can get really hot and busy, so go early and then escape for a swim at one of the nearby beaches of Clifton or Camps Bay. ⊠ *Green Point Stadium parking lot, Somerset Rd., Greenpoint* ☎*021/439–4805* ⊙*Sun. and public holidays 9–5.*

Greenmarket Square. You can get good buys on clothing, T-shirts, handcrafted silver jewelry, and locally made leather shoes and sandals, and you can find African jewelry, art, and fabrics here, too. It's one of the best places in town to purchase gifts, but it's lively and fun whether or not you buy anything. More than half the stalls are owned by people not from South Africa. Here you'll find political and economic refugees from Ethiopia, Eritrea, Zimbabwe, and the Democratic Republic of Congo trying to eke out a living. Bargain, but do so with a conscience. ⊠*Longmarket, Burg, and Shortmarket Sts., Cape Town Central* ☎*No phone* ⊙*Mon.–Sat. 9–4:30.*

Obs Holistic Lifestyle Fair. For everything weird and wonderful, this market is an absolute winner. Cape Town is home to plenty of alternative-therapy practitioners, crystal gazers, and energy healers, and they congregate on the first Sunday of every month to sell their wares and trade spells. Food is abundant, healthful (of course), and vegetarian. Kids are not ignored; they run wild together with their parents. ⊠*Station and Lower Main Rds., Observatory* ☎*021/788–8088* ⊙*1st Sun. of month 10–4.*

Waterfront Craft Market. This indoor market contains an assortment of handcrafted jewelry, rugs, glass, pottery, and leather sandals. There's also a wellness center where you can have a shiatsu massage or some reflexology to pep you up if you're shopped out. ⊠*Dock Rd., Waterfront* ☎*021/408–7842* ⊙*Daily 9:30–6.*

Woodstock Neighbour Goods Market. A hot market destination, Woodstock is aimed at Cape Town's hip organic types on their Vespas looking for artisan breads, pesto, home-cured olives, and produce imported from France. It gets frantically busy, which indicates just how popular it is, but if you want to rub shoulders with trendy design types, this is the place to be. One of the stalls sells the very best falafel in Cape Town; it's worth standing in line for, as is the curry stall. When you're done browsing at the market, head to some of the great stores in the same complex. ⊠*373–375 Albert Rd. (Lower Main Rd.), Woodstock* ☎*No phone* ⊙*Sat. 9–3.*

SPECIALTY STORES

ARTS & CRAFTS A number of stores in Cape Town sell African art and crafts, much of which comes from Zululand or neighboring countries. Street vendors, particularly on St. George's Mall and Greenmarket Square, often sell the same curios for half the price.

Africa Nova. If you aren't crazy about traditional African artifacts, you might want to visit this store, which stocks contemporary African art that's quirky and interesting. Original African art is showcased for those looking for one-of-a-kind pieces. Come Christmastime, the store is transformed with beaded African Christmas decorations: gorgeous stars, divine angels, and brilliant nativity animals. Even if you aren't buying, it's worth visiting for the display. ⊠*72 Waterkant St., Cape Quarter* ☎*021/425–5123.*

African Image. Look here for traditional and contemporary African art and curios, colorful cloth from Nigeria and Ghana, plus West African masks, Malian blankets, and beaded designs from southern African tribes. A variety of Zulu baskets is also available. ⊠*52 Burg St., Cape Town Central* ☎*021/423–8385* ⊠*Shop 6228, Table Bay Hotel Mall, Waterfront* ☎*021/419–0382.*

Montebello Craft & Design Centre. This old building nestled under tall, shady trees houses a number of job-creation projects. This is a good place to shop if you have only a short time, as you'll find textiles, ceramics, jewelry, handbags, and sought-after Madiba dolls (*Madiba* is a term of endearment for Mandela; these soft dolls are fashioned after the great South African icon). For a break from shopping you can have a delicious light lunch or tea at the **Gardener's Cottage** (☎ *021/689–3158*) in the complex. ✉ *31 Newlands Ave., Newlands* ☎ *021/685–6445.*

Pan-African Market. The market, extending over two floors of a huge building, is a jumble of tiny stalls, traditional African hairdressers, tailors, potters, artists, musicians, and drummers. There is also a small, very African restaurant. If you're not going to visit countries to the north, come here for an idea of what you're missing. ✉ *76 Long St., Cape Town Central* ☎ *021/426–4478.*

Streetwires. You'll see street wire art everywhere in Cape Town, but this shop is a trove of the art form, which uses a combination of wire, beads, and other recycled materials to create bowls, lights, mobiles, and expressive sculptures. You might even want to buy a working wire radio. You won't find too many of those back home. ✉ *77 Shortmarket St., Cape Town Central* ☎ *021/426–2475.*

BOOKS &
MUSIC

African Music Store. The people who work here are passionate about African music and eager to pass on their love to anybody who lends them half an ear. You could easily spend a couple of hours listening to any- and everything in the store. You're bound to find something here that captures the heart of the country for you. ✉ *134 Long St., Cape Town Central* ☎ *021/426–0857.*

Clarke's Bookshop. At this local favorite you'll find a fantastic collection of both old and new books on southern Africa as well as general secondhand titles. ✉ *211 Long St., Cape Town Central* ☎ *021/423–5739.*

Exclusive Books. This is one of the best all-around bookshops in the country. The chain carries a wide selection of local and international periodicals and coffee-table books on Africa. A coffee bar allows you to browse at a comfortable table with an espresso or cappuccino. Be prepared, though, to pay at least twice as much for books here as you would in the United States or Britain. ✉ *Shop 6160, Victoria Wharf, Waterfront* ☎ *021/419–0905* ✉ *Lower Mall, Cavendish Sq., Vineyard Rd., Claremont* ☎ *021/674–3030* ✉ *Constantia Village Shopping Centre, Spaanschemat River Rd., Constantia* ☎ *021/794–7800* ✉ *Shop G55, Tygervalley Shopping Centre, Willie van Schoor Ave., Tygervalley* ☎ *021/914–9910* ✉ *Shop 428, Canal Walk, Century City Shopping Centre, Montague Gardens* ☎ *021/555–3720.*

Musica Mega Store. Looking for local music—or any music, for that matter? Musica Mega Store has an enormous selection of African music, and you'll find plenty of recordings from local artists as well as some from farther afield. The staff is knowledgeable and very helpful. ✉ *Dock Rd., Waterfront* ☎ *021/425–6300.*

Traveller's Bookshop. South Africa is astonishingly beautiful and diverse, and there are hundreds of books that capture both these qualities. This store, one of the best places to shop for travel books, stocks more than 25,000 titles, with everything from glossy coffee-table books to intimate portraits of a changing nation. It also stocks books about other countries. This store is linked to **Wordsworth Books,** an independent all-purpose bookstore next door. ⊠*Shop 2, King's Warehouse, Waterfront* ☎*021/425–6880.*

CLOTHING & FABRICS South African designers are flexing their creative muscles and coming up with innovative designs. Sure, there's traditional garb, such as a pretty *shweshwe* (traditional African print) skirt or a Madiba-style shirt, but also watch out for exciting interpretations on old themes.

Heartworks. Part of a job-creation initiative, this shop has people at its heart. And it happens to stock gorgeous things to wear. Buying something here means you can do good and look good at the same time. ⊠*98 Kloof St., Gardens* ☎*021/424–8419* ⊠*Gardens Centre, Gardens* ☎*021/465–1842.*

Mnandi Textiles. Here you'll find a range of African fabrics, including traditional West African prints and Dutch wax prints. The store sells ready-made African clothing for adults and children, and you can also have garments made to order. ⊠*90 Station Rd., Observatory* ☎*021/447–6814.*

N.C.M. Fashions–African Pride. This is the place to go for traditional clothing from all over Africa. One of the most striking outfits is the brightly colored *bubu,* a loose-fitting garment with a matching head wrap, or try a traditional Xhosa outfit, complete with braiding, beads, and a multilayer wraparound skirt. You can buy off the rack or order a custom outfit from a wide selection of fabrics. ⊠*152 Main Rd., Claremont* ☎*021/683–1022.*

HOUSEWARES **Carrol Boyes Functional Art.** Knives and forks need never be mundane again once you've seen Carrol Boyes's range of tableware and, more recently, leatherware. She works in pewter, aluminum, and stainless steel and weaves fluid female forms into functional items. ⊠*43 Rose St., Bo-Kaap* ☎*021/424–8263* ⊠*Shop 6180, Waterfront* ☎*021/418–0595.*

LIM. The name of the shop stands for "Less Is More," and these savvy designers have come up with a range of glassware, ceramics, and custom-made furniture that reflects this philosophy. The lines are clean and unfussy and the colors bold and unusual. ⊠*86a Kloof St., Gardens* ☎*021/423–1200.*

L'Orangerie. If knobbly imported linens, thick white ceramic bowls, and butcher blocks the size of a small car get you excited, then this is a good place to visit. The gardening shop is also enticing, and will make you want to rush home and start making things pretty. ⊠*7 Wolfe St., Wynberg* ☎*021/761–8355.*

WINE Most Capetonians wouldn't dream of having supper without a glass of wine, and most supermarket chains carry a good range of affordable local labels. A visit to Cape Town isn't complete until you've tasted and bought some of the wine the area is famous for. Your best bet is to buy directly from the vineyards, but if you don't manage to get out to the Winelands, head to one of the area stores that can fix you up with local or international wines.

Manuka Fine Wines. This store in the Southern Suburbs makes a point of stocking wines from the nearby Constantia Valley wine farms as well as those from the rest of the Cape. There are free wine tastings on Saturday morning and wine-tasting dinners once a month, at which winemakers introduce their product to appreciative imbibers. ⊠ *Steenberg Village Shopping Centre, Steenberg Rd. and Reddam Ave., Tokai* ☎ *021/701–2046.*

Vaughan Johnson's Wine & Cigar Shop. This wineshop has a terrific selection and staff members who know their stuff. They can even advise you about shipping if you decide to take a few cases home with you. And who could blame you? ⊠ *Dock Rd., Waterfront* ☎ *021/419–2121.*

CAPE TOWN ESSENTIALS

To research prices, get advice from other travelers, and book travel arrangements, visit www.fodors.com.

TRANSPORTATION

BY AIR

Cape Town International Airport lies about 20 km (12½ mi) southeast of the city center in the Cape Flats. The domestic and international terminals both have booths run by Cape Town Tourism, which are open from 7:30 until the last flight comes in.

International carriers flying into Cape Town include Air Namibia, British Airways, Globespan, KLM Royal Dutch Airlines, LTU, Lufthansa, Malaysia Airlines, Qatar Airways, Singapore Airlines, South African Airways, and Virgin Atlantic. Domestic flights are operated by British Airways/Comair/Kulula.com, Mango, Nationwide, 1time, and South African Airways/SA Airlink/SA Express.

There are no scheduled buses or trains to or from the airport, but there are plenty of private transportation operators. Shuttle services are based inside the domestic baggage hall and outside the international terminal, and can be phoned for airport drop-offs (as can other shuttle and taxi operators). Rates vary depending on the operator, the number in the group, the destination, and the time of arrival. As a single traveler, you can pay less if you're prepared to share the ride with others. One person going into the city center pays between R110 and R195, whereas the rate for a group of four is R140 to R210. A surcharge of up to 50% is usually levied from 10 PM until early morning, and some shuttles charge more for arrivals than for departures to cover waiting time. Metered taxis can also be found outside the terminals. ⚠ **Reports of overcharging are common, so check the fare first.** A ride into the center of town costs around R260 with Dalhouzie/Touch Down and about R240 with Marine Taxis. For the ultimate luxury ride you can hire a six-seat Lincoln stretch limo from Cape Limousine Services. Rates are R1,000 for the first two hours and R300 per hour thereafter (add extra for gas if you travel outside the Cape Town area).

Airlines **Air Namibia** (☎*021/936-2755* ⊕*www.airnamibia.com*). **British Airways/Comair/Kulula.com** (☎*021/936-9000 British Airways* ⊕*www. britishairways.com* ☎*011/921-0111 Comair* ⊕*www.comair.co.za* ☎*0861/585-852 Kulula* ⊕*www.kulula.com*). **Globespan** (☎*0044/1314-667-612 in the U.K.* ⊕*www.globespan.com*). **KLM Royal Dutch Airlines** (☎*086/024-7747* ⊕*www. klm.co.za*). **LTU** (☎*021/936-1190* ⊕*www.ltu.com*). **Lufthansa** (☎*011/975-0402* ⊕*www.lufthansa.com*). **Malaysia Airlines** (☎*021/934-8794* ⊕*www.malaysia airlines.com*). **Mango** (☎*021/936-1061 or 0861/162-646* ⊕*www.flymango.com*). **Nationwide** (☎*021/936-2050* ⊕*www.flynationwide.co.za*). **Qatar Airways** (☎ ⊕*www.qatarairways.com*). **1time** (☎*086/134-5345* ⊕*www.1time.aero*). **Singapore Airlines** (☎*021/674-0601* ⊕*www.singaporeair.com*). **South African Airways/SA Airlink/SA Express** (☎*021/936-1111* ⊕*www.flysaa.com*). **Virgin Atlantic** (☎*011/340-3400* ⊕*www.virgin-atlantic.com*).

Airport **Cape Town International Airport** (☎*021/937-1200, 086/727-7888 flight information* ⊕*www.airports.co.za*).

Airport Transfers **Cape Limousine Services** (☎*021/785-3100*). **Cape Town Sprinter** (☎*021/982-5815*). **City Hopper** (☎*021/934-4440*). **Dalhouzie/Touch Down Taxis** (☎*021/919-4659 or 021/919-2834*). **Dumalisile** (☎*021/934-1660*). **Legend Tours and Transfers** (☎*021/674-7055*). **Magic Bus** (☎*021/505-6300* ⊕ *www.magicbus.co.za* ✎*capemagic@magicbus.co.za*). **Marine Taxis** (☎*021/434-0434*). **Shawn Shuttle Service** (☎*082/954-4467*). **Way 2 Go** (☎*021/638-0505*).

BY BUS

Intercape Mainliner travels to Johannesburg, Durban, towns in the southwest Cape, and Windhoek, in Namibia. Greyhound offers daily overnight service to Johannesburg and Tshwane, but for Western Cape destinations Intercape Mainliner is a better option. Translux runs luxury vehicles between major cities, and its sister company City-to-City serves less well-serviced destinations like Umtata in addition to mainstream routes. BazBus offers a hop-on/hop-off service and other flexible tours aimed mostly at backpackers who don't want to travel vast distances in one day and can't easily get to train and bus stations. BazBus is more expensive than a regular bus but more convenient for covering distances in short stages. All the main bus companies operate from the bus terminal alongside the central train station on Adderley Street, and most have their offices there.

Daily overnight service to Johannesburg and Tshwane costs around R450–R500 one way. Cape Town to Springbok is about R250–R300, to Windhoek R450–R550, to George R150, and to Durban R450–R500. Round-trip tickets are roughly double. A BazBus Durban hopper ticket via the Wild Coast costs about R1,800 one way and R2,310 round-trip; travel cards are R850 for a seven-day pass and R1,600 for a 14-day pass.

Within Cape Town, Golden Arrow runs an extensive network of routes from the main Golden Acre terminal on the Grand Parade (Castle Street side). These subsidized buses are by far the cheapest form of transportation (much to the frustration of the minibus taxi operators). You'll get to most destinations for R5–R10, and you can save by buying 10-ride clip cards. ∎TIP➔ **The service has a timetable, but buses often run late and you'll need a certain level of knowledge regarding its operation.** Bus shelters and lamppost markers indicate stops. Route maps are not available in leaflet form, but they are displayed at all major depots. Alternatively, phone the Golden Arrow hotline, or ask people at a bus stop for info on which ones go your way.

For short trips locals generally use minibus taxis, which waste no time getting you to your destination and, for the modest fare of R5–R20, provide you with some local atmosphere. You can hop on and off the *combis* (vans) quite easily; small gatherings on the roadside usually indicate a stop. However, don't expect to leave the starting point until the taxi is full, which can slow you down outside of peak hours or away from busy routes. The main minibus stop in the city center is above the train station on Adderley Street, but you can flag combis down just about anywhere. Most taxis are sound, but watch out for those held together with tape and wire (literally). There are no route maps for minibus taxis; ask the drivers where they're going. If you don't have the exact change, you may have to wait until the guy taking the fares gets your change. Overcharging is not that common, but it's best to discreetly ask other passengers what the fare should be. Taxis are crowded, so watch out for pickpockets.

A few shuttle buses operate tourist-friendly routes around the city center. Shuttles to Kirstenbosch (R40 per person) and the Table Mountain cableway (R30) can be obtained from the V&A Waterfront's Cape Town Tourism office. A regular bus runs from the central train station to the Waterfront (R2.50), and there's also service from the Cape Town Tourism Information Office in the city center.

Bus Lines BazBus (☎ 021/439–2323 ⊕ www.bazbus.co.za). **Golden Arrow** (☎ 080/121–2111 ⊕ www.gabs.co.za). **Greyhound** (☎ 083/915–9000 ⊕ www.greyhound.co.za). **Intercape Mainliner** (☎ 0861/287–287 or 0861/287–329 ⊕ www.intercape.co.za). **Translux/City-to-City** (☎ 0861/589–282 ⊕ www.translux.co.za).

BY CAR & MOTORCYCLE

A car is by far the best way to get around Cape Town, particularly in the evening, when public transportation closes down. The Automobile Association has a presence, and if you're a member of any organization at home affiliated with AIT (Automobile International Travel), you qualify for basic benefits here, including breakdown service, towing, and transportation to the nearest provincial hospital. Fill in a form at the airport's Imperial Car Rental depot (Imperial has a rental-discount deal with the AA) or at any of the city's three AA auto shops.

Cape Town's roads are excellent, but they are unusual in a few respects and can be a bit confusing. Signage is inconsistent, switching between

1

Afrikaans and English, between different names for the same road (especially highways), and between different destinations on the same route. Sometimes the signs simply vanish. △ **Cape Town is also littered with signs indicating "Cape Town" instead of "City Center."** Good one-page maps are essential and are freely available from car-rental agencies and tourism information desks. Among the hazards are pedestrians, particularly those looking for a quick route across highways, and speeding vehicles, especially minibus taxis as they race to drop one load of passengers and pick up the next. Roadblocks for document and roadworthiness checks are also becoming more frequent, and there are concerted attempts to catch people who drink and drive.

Parking attendants organized by municipal authorities and private business networks provide a valuable service. Most wear brightly colored vests; pay them R2–R3 for a short daytime stop and R5–R10 in the evening. Parking in the city center can be a hassle. Longer-stay parking spaces are so scarce that most hotels charge extra for them, and even then you won't be guaranteed a space. For short stays you may get lucky and find metered parking; this requires a special parking card, which you can usually buy from nearby shops or from parking attendants. Be sure to watch while details are fed into the meter. There are numerous pay-and-display (i.e., put a ticket in your windshield) and pay-on-exit parking lots around the city. For central attractions like Greenmarket Square, Parliament, the Company's Gardens, museums, the South African National Gallery, and the Castle of Good Hope, park your car on the Grand Parade in Darling Street. The Sanlam Golden Acre Parking Garage, on Adderley Street, offers covered parking, as does the Parkade, on Strand Street.

The main arteries leading out of the city are the N1, which bypasses the city's Northern Suburbs en route to Paarl and, ultimately, Johannesburg; and the N2, which heads out past Khayelitsha and through Somerset West to the Overberg and the Garden Route before continuing on through the Eastern Cape to Durban. The N7 goes up to Namibia and leads off the N1. The M3 splits from the N2 at Hospital Bend, so called because of the high number of accidents and the presence of South Africa's leading teaching hospital, Groote Schuur. The M3 leads to Muizenberg via Claremont, Constantia, and Tokai, and is the main route to the False Bay suburbs on the city's south Peninsula. Expect delays in drive time from 7 to 9 and 4 to 6:30.

Most large car-rental agencies have offices in the city and major suburbs as well as at the airport, and all offer similar rates. You'll pay R200–R250 per day for a basic no-frills vehicle including standard insurance coverage (extended coverage costs more). If you want air-conditioning, power steering, or automatic transmission, you'll pay R250–R300. Rates come down by 10%–20% on longer rentals. Some companies include unlimited mileage, but more common is 200–300 km (125–185 mi) a day plus R1.50–R3 per km thereafter. Try to negotiate if it's low season or you're renting for a longer period. Some companies throw in free delivery and pickup. Expect to pay a bit more on one-way rentals. Airport rentals carry a 10% surcharge, so you may want to pick up a car elsewhere or have it delivered.

Another option is to rent a scooter or motorbike. African Buzz has scooters for around R190 a day (motorcycle license required). Motorcycles can be rented from Mitaka or Moto Berlin at R650–R800 a day for a 650-cc and R900–R1,000 for an 1100-cc machine. At Café Vespa you can rent a trendy Vespa and discuss the rental agreement over an excellent cappuccino.

Roadside Assistance Automobile Association (☎ 080/001–0101 or 080/011–1998 ⊕ www.aasa.co.za).

Car-Rental Companies Aroundaboutcars (☎ 021/422–4022 ⊕ www.around aboutcars.com). **Avis** (☎ 0861/113–748 ⊕ www.avis.co.za). **Beach Buggy Rentals** (☎ 021/423–1912 or 0860/000–060 ⊕ www.drivesouthafrica.co.za). **Budget** (☎ 0861/016–622 ⊕ www.budget.co.za). **CABS** (☎ 021/683–1932 ⊕ www.cabs.co.za). **Hertz** (☎ 0861/600–136 ⊕ www.hertz.co.za). **Imperial Car Rental** (☎ 086/113–1000 ⊕ www.imperialcarrental.co.za). **Value Car Hire** (☎ 0800/040–7557 ⊕ www.valuecarhire.co.za).

Motorcycle/Scooter-Rental Companies African Buzz (☎ 021/433–1244). **Café Vespa** (☎ 021/426–5042 ⊕ www.cafevespa.com). **Mitaka** (☎ 082/577–5797 ⊕ www.mitaka.co.za). **Moto Berlin** (☎ 021/421–3092 or 083/588–5225).

BY TAXI

Taxis are expensive compared with other forms of transportation but offer an easy, quick way to get around the city center. Don't expect to see the throngs of cabs you find in London or New York, as most people in Cape Town use public transportation or their own cars. You'll be lucky to hail one on the street. Taxis don't always use their roof lights to indicate availability, but if you flag down an occupied cab the driver may radio for another car for you. Your best bet is to summon a cab by phone or head to one of the major taxi stands, such as at Greenmarket Square or either end of Adderley Street, near the Slave Lodge, and outside the train station. For lower rates at night, try prebooking the Backpacker Bus, a shuttle service on Adderley Street. Sea Point Taxis charges R9 per kilometer and R48 an hour for waiting time. Expect to pay R40–R60 for a trip from the city center to the Waterfront. In the Southern Suburbs try phoning Unicab and in the Northern Suburbs Bellville Taxis, or ask at your lodging for local recommendations. In addition to these taxi companies, there are many taxis services listed in the Yellow Pages, but ask at your hotel or guesthouse which company they recommend. Often lodging establishments have an ongoing relationship with particular companies and/or drivers, and this way you will be assured of safe, reliable service.

Rikkis are little minivans with open sides that provide a cheap (but slow) alternative to taxis. Service is door-to-door, but they may stop at several other doors to pick up additional passengers en route. Rikkis operate limited hours in a limited area. Five rikkis work from the central business district, and three are based at the Simon's Town train station. Central rikkis run weekdays 7 AM–midnight, Saturday 8 AM–

midnight, and Sunday 8 AM–10 PM. They go everywhere (including the airport) and have a reasonable fare structure. For example, a one-way trip from the city center to Hout Bay for four people would cost R90. The Simon's Town rikkis (enclosed to protect you from the elements) can also take you anywhere, but the most popular trip is from Cape Town to Cape Point. A two-hour trip for two is about R538, including entry fees. Minibus taxis are another option *(⇨ Bus Travel, above).*

Taxi Companies **Backpacker Bus** (☎ *021/447–4991).* **Bellville Taxis** (☎ *021/949–6918).* **Marine Taxis** (☎ *021/434–0434).* **Rikkis (Central and Simon's Town)** (☎ *021/418–6713).* **Sea Point Taxis** (☎ *021/434–4444).* **Unicab** (☎ *021/447–4402 or 083/229–5125).*

BY TRAIN

Cape Town's train station is on Adderley Street, in the heart of the city, surrounded by lively rows of street vendors and a taxi stand. The station building and facilities are unattractive but functional (and a major renovation is planned), servicing local, interprovincial, and luxury lines.

Metrorail, Cape Town's commuter line, offers regular service to the Northern Suburbs, including Parow and Bellville; the Cape Flats townships Langa, Nyanga, Mitchell's Plain, and Khayelitsha; the Southern and False Bay suburbs of Observatory, Claremont, Wynberg, Muizenberg, St. James, Kalk Bay, Fish Hoek, and Simon's Town; and the Winelands towns of Paarl, Stellenbosch, and Franschoek *(⇨ Chapter 2).* The trip to Simon's Town takes 45–60 minutes and costs about R25 for a first-class round-trip ticket, R15 for third class. On weekends several trains carry a popular breakfast car. The train to Khayelitsha costs less than R20 round-trip first class, and a third-class ticket is around half that. The last train leaves about 7 PM on weekdays, and weekend service is reduced. Timetables change often. If you travel on Metrorail during off-peak periods, avoid isolated cars and compartments, and be alert to your surroundings when the train is stopped. Muggers work trains intensively, slipping on and off with ease. Train security is at best erratic. You're safer standing in a cramped third-class car than sitting comfortably in splendid isolation in an empty first-class one, but watch your pockets.

National carrier Shosholoza Meyl runs the *Trans-Karoo* daily between Cape Town and Johannesburg; the trip takes about 26 hours and costs R500 first class, R335 second class, and R200 economy. First- and second-class cars have sleeping compartments. A weekly train to Durban, the *Trans-Oranjia,* takes two days and costs R645 first class. You need to make first- and second-class reservations by phone (bookings open three months before date of travel) and then pay at the station in advance (not just before departure). For a third-class ticket you can pay just before you go. The reservations office at the train station is open 8–4 weekdays and 8–10 AM weekends. Transnet's *Union Limited* steam train and Shongololo Express's *Southern Cross* also run through the Karoo and the Garden Route to Johannesburg. The *Southern Cross* is

Riding in Style

CLOSE UP

A trip aboard the famous **Blue Train** (☎ 011/773–7631 ⊕ www.bluetrain. co.za) between Cape Town and Tshwane (Pretoria) has long been a highlight of a trip to South Africa. Compartments are individually air-conditioned and have remote-operated blinds and curtains, TV, CD player, and a personal mobile phone for contacting your butler/valet or making outgoing calls. The comfortably furnished lounge car offers refreshments and drinks throughout the day and is a good place to meet fellow travelers. There are two trains: the Classic and the African theme, which, while maintaining the same very high standard, is decorated with African touches such as faux animal-skin furniture and somewhat more exotic uniforms for the staff. In the well-appointed dining car, men are required to wear jacket and tie to dinner.

Another luxury option is **Rovos Rail** (☎ 012/323–6052 ⊕ www.rovos. co.za). Fifty-three beautifully restored cars make up three trains, which are drawn by a steam engine on certain sections. Some cars date to the Edwardian era. Each opulent train carries a maximum of 72 passengers, attended by up to 21 staff members, including two gourmet chefs. Regular weekly trips are run between Tshwane and Cape Town with a stop in Kimberly for a tour of the Big Hole and Diamond museum and Tshwane and Victoria Falls (both two nights). But, if you're looking for something even more epic, there's the journey in July from Cape Town to Dar es Salaam (and, of course, back again), as well as themed trips like the golf safari.

a night ride, so forget about seeing the splendors of the Garden Route en route.

Train Lines Metrorail (☎ 080/065–6463 ⊕ www.metrorail.co.za). **Shongololo Express** (☎ 011/781–4616 ⊕ www.shongololo.com). **Shosholoza Meyl** (☎ 086/000–8888 ⊕ www.spoornet.co.za/ShosholozaMeyl). **Transnet** (⊕ www. spoornet.co.za).

CONTACTS & RESOURCES

CONSULATE

United States **U.S. Consulate** (✉ 2 Reddam Ave., Westlake, Tokai 7966 ☎ 021/702–7300 ⊕ usembassy.state.gov/pretoria).

EMERGENCIES

There are several numbers you can call for general emergencies, including Vodacom mobile networks. Metrorail has its own security/emergency number. If you get lost on Table Mountain, call Wilderness Search and Rescue (WSAR), and for all sea emergencies, call the National Sea Rescue Institute (NSRI).

Emergency services at public hospitals are overworked, understaffed, and underfunded. They deal with a huge number of local people, most of whom cannot afford any alternative. Ambulances are provided by the state, but visitors are advised to use private hospitals, which are open 24/7 and have ambulances linked to their private hospital group (although these services can transport patients to any health facility). Most public hospitals have facilities for private patients at lower rates than the fully private hospitals. Make sure that you have medical insurance that's good in South Africa before you leave home.

A number of pharmacies are open from 8 AM to around 10 PM. Most pharmacies display telephone numbers on their door or storefront in case you have an emergency and need medicine during off-hours. (In a real emergency, head to the closest private clinic.)

Emergency Services Ambulance (☎10177). **Metrorail** (☎0800/210–081 or 0800/656–463). **National Sea Rescue Institute** (☎021/434–4011 head office, 082911 emergencies). **Police** (☎10111). **Police, Fire, and Ambulance services** (☎107 from landline). **Vodacom emergency services** (☎112 from mobile phone). **Weather** (☎082162). **Wilderness Search and Rescue** (☎021/948–9908).

Hospitals Christiaan Barnard Hospital (✉181 Longmarket St., Cape Town Central ☎021/480–6111). **Claremont Hospital** (✉Harfield and Main Rds., Claremont ☎021/670–4300). **Constantiaberg Medi-clinic** (✉Burnham Rd., Plumstead ☎021/799–2911). **Panorama Medi-clinic** (✉Rothchild Blvd., Panorama ☎021/938–2111).

Pharmacies Lite-Kem Pharmacy (✉Scotts Building, 24 Darling St., Cape Town Central ☎021/461–8040). **Rustenburg Pharmacy** (✉Rondebosch Shopping Centre, Main Rd., Rondebosch ☎021/686–3997). **Table Bay Pharmacy** (✉Shop 6108, V&A Waterfront, Waterfront ☎021/418–4556).

MONEY MATTERS

Most shops, restaurants, hotels, and B&Bs in Cape Town take credit cards, but you generally need cash to buy gas. Surveillance cameras cover most ATMs in the city center, but the money machines are still a magnet for fraudsters. Improvements in security in the central business district have led to increased ATM crime outside the center, so be alert wherever you withdraw cash. Keep your card in your hand, don't be distracted while using an ATM, and decline offers or requests for help. If your card gets swallowed, *stay at the ATM* and call the help line number displayed. If possible, withdraw money during the day and choose ATMs with security guards present or those inside stores.

■TIP➡ **Don't even think about changing money at your hotel.** The rates at most hotels are outrageous, and the city has plenty of banks and *bureaux de change* (exchange counters) offering better rates. Most suburbs have banks in the main streets and malls with currency-exchange facilities and American Express branches open during business hours (weekdays and Saturday mornings). Rennies Bank's Waterfront branch is open until 9 PM daily. At the airport, Foreign Exchange exchanges currency weekdays 7 AM–11 PM and weekends 8 AM–11 PM.

Exchange Services American Express (✉Ground fl., Thibault House, Thibault Sq., Cape Town Central ☎021/425–7991 ✉Shop 11A, Alfred Mall, Waterfront ☎021/419–3917 ⊕www.amex.co.za). **Rennies Bank** (✉2 St. George's Mall, Cape Town Central ☎021/418–1206 ✉Upper Level, Victoria Wharf, Waterfront ☎021/418–3744).

TOURS

Several companies offer guided tours of the city center, the south peninsula, the Winelands, and anyplace else in the Cape you might wish to visit. They differ in type of transportation used and tour focus.

BIKE TOURS   BazBus tours the south peninsula with a trailer full of bikes. You cycle the fun parts and sit in the bus for the rest. It costs about R385. Daytrippers specializes in bike tours but uses all sorts of modes of transportation, from bus to boat to foot, to explore the area.

Tour Operator **BazBus** (☎ *021/439–2323* ⊕ *www.bazbus.com*). **Daytrippers** (☎ *021/511–4766* ⊕ *www.daytrippers.co.za*).

BOAT TOURS   The Waterfront Boat Company offers trips on a range of boats, from yachts to large motor cruisers. A 1½-hour sunset cruise from the V&A Waterfront costs about R190, and includes a glass of bubbly. *Tigger 2* and Drumbeat charters both run a variety of trips in the Hout Bay area, ranging from sunset cruises to full-day crayfishing expeditions. A trip from Hout Bay to Seal Island with Drumbeat Charters costs R50 for adults, R20 for kids. ■ TIP→ The only boat trip to actually land on Robben Island is the museum's ferry.

Tour Operators **Drumbeat Charters** (☎ *021/791–4441 or 021/790–4859* ⊕ *www.drumbeatcharters.co.za*). **Tigger 2 Charters** (☎ *021/790–5256* ⊕ *www. tiggertoo.co.za*). **Waterfront Boat Company** (☎ *021/418–0134* ⊕ *www.water frontboats.co.za*).

BUS & CAR TOURS   Large- and small-group bus tours are operated by African Eagle Day Tours, Hylton Ross, Springbok Atlas, and Windward Tours, among many others. Expect to pay R300–R350 for a half-day trip and about R450–R600 for a full-day tour. There's a wide selection of tours to choose from. A day trip might include such Cape Town highlights as the Cape Point and Cape of Good Hope nature reserve, Chapman's Peak, and then onto Stellenbosch for some wine tasting; a half-day trip could involve a visit to a local township. Many of the companies will also tailor private trips to suit your needs.

Hylton Ross also sells tickets for the hop-on/hop-off CitySightSeeing Cape Town bus; a day ticket costs R100, and there are two routes to choose from. The Red Route runs through the city, and you can get on and off at major museums, the V&A Waterfront, Table Mountain Aerial Cableway, Two Oceans Aquarium, and other attractions. The Blue Route takes you farther afield—to Kirstenbosch National Botanic Gardens, Hout Bay, World of Birds, and Camps Bay, to name just a few destinations.

In addition to running the usual tours of the peninsula, city, and Winelands, iKapa Tours & Travel has a full-day Cape Safari tour, which is great if you won't have a chance to make it up north to one of the big-game reserves. The trip departs at around 6:30 AM and takes you over du Toit's Pass and on to the Aquila Private Game Reserve in the Southern Karoo Highlands. In addition to seeing animals on your three-hour game drive with an experienced ranger, you'll also get to visit world-renowned rock-art sites. Breakfast, lunch, a snack, and champagne are included in the tour.

Legend Tours offers a range of half- and full-day tours that include highlights of the peninsula, Table Mountain, and the city. With visits to the Bo-Kaap, District Six, and the Cape Flats, the comprehensive township tour demonstrates just how fragmented South African society is. The full-day version of this tour includes Robben Island as well.

Paradise Touring leads tours all around the Cape Town area. In addition to the usual Winelands and scenic peninsula tours, there are tours specifically designed to keep kids happy. The half-day family tour includes Two Oceans Aquarium, Table Mountain, and the South African Museum, plus time to play miniature golf and feed squirrels. The company also offers a township dinner-and-jazz experience and some exciting day courses with acclaimed local chefs. But if you want something really different, opt for the full-day trip around the peninsula in a World War II sidecar (your guide drives and you sit in the sidecar).

Friends of Dorothy leads small group tours of the Winelands, the peninsula, and more for gay travelers. Quite a few cultural tours are also offered. Thuthuka Tours leads music and gospel tours of the townships. You can develop your understanding of the destruction brought on by apartheid's forced removals while touring District Six with Our Pride-Bonani. A group of MK veterans (former cadres of the ANC's armed wing, Umkhonto we Sizwe), going by the name Western Cape Action Tours, provides insight into Cape Town's experience of apartheid and resistance. Tours include scenes of struggle and other historical sites as well as development projects, township markets, and housing programs. A half-day tour is R290 per person (minimum two people), a full-day tour including lunch costs R590 a head (minimum four people), and a customized day trip for a single individual is R950. Though these operators specialize in niche tours, most of them cover mainstream trips like Cape Point and the Winelands, too.

Tour Operators **African Eagle Day Tours** (☎021/464–4266 ⊕www.africa-adventure.org/a/africaneagle). **Friends of Dorothy** (☎021/465–1871 ⊕www.friendsofdorothytours.co.za). **Hylton Ross Tours** (☎021/511–1784 ⊕www.hyltonross.co.za). **iKapa Tours & Travel** (☎021/510–8666 ⊕www.ikapa.co.za). **Legend Tours** (☎021/674–7055 or 082/456–2014 ⊕www.legendtours.co.za). **Our Pride-Bonani** (☎021/531–4291 or 082/446–7974). **Paradise Touring** (☎021/713–1020 ⊕www.paradisetouring.co.za). **Springbok Atlas** (☎021/460–4700 ⊕www.springbokatlas.com). **Thuthuka Tours** (☎021/433–2429 or 083/979–5831). **Western Cape Action Tours** (☎021/448–5760 ⊕www.dacpm.org.za). **Windward Tours** (☎021/419–3475 ⊕www.windwardtours.co.za).

HELICOPTER & AIRPLANE TOURS Helicopters fly from the V&A Waterfront for a tour on a three- or four-seater chopper. Most operators charge between R1,300 and R1,800 for a 20-minute trip, and R4,900 to R5,400 for an hour in the air. Civair and NAC/Makana offer tours of the city and surrounding area ranging in length from 20 minutes to several hours. Custom tours can also be arranged, and the price varies according to how many people are flying. Downhill Adventures offers trips in a variety of light aircraft, including helicopters.

Tour Operators **Civair Helicopters** (☎ *021/419–5182* ⊕ *www.civair.co.za*). **Downhill Adventures** (☎ *021/422–0388 or 021/422–1580* ⊕ *www.downhilladventures. com*). **NAC/Makana Aviation** (☎ *021/425–3868* ⊕ *www.nacmakana.com*).

JAZZ SAFARI   Cape Town Jazz Safari offers jazz aficionados (and everyone else) a unique experience that takes you into the homes of some of Cape Town's greatest musicians. Visitors can relax in the lounge while the likes of the legendary Robbie Jansen, Mac McKenzie, and Hilton Schilder work their magic. This is a unique opportunity to experience the complexity of Cape Town jazz and get to know the musicians behind the music. The tour costs around R500 per person and a minimum of four people is needed to make the reservation.

Tour Operator **Cape Town Jazz Safari** (☎ *084/762–4944* ⊕ *www.jazzsafari.com*).

WALKING   Cape Town on Foot offers fun city walking tours lasting 1½–2½ hours.
TOURS   The tours cover major historical attractions, architecture, and highlights of modern-day Cape Town. A separate Bo-Kaap tour, which includes the Bo-Kaap Museum, is one of the best ways to explore this neighborhood. Expect to pay around R100 for 2½ hours.

Footsteps to Freedom has two really good walking tours—one of the city and its historical sites and the other of the V&A Waterfront. The guides are friendly and well informed, offer a rare insight into the city, and can help you with tours of the Bo-Kaap and townships. They also have great maps of the city, peninsula, and Winelands called *Serious Fun Guides,* which you can pick up at various outlets.

You can also do a walking tour of Langa township as part of Ilios Travel's *Walk to Freedom* portfolio. The guides explain the social structures and lifestyles of Cape Town's oldest African precinct, as well as the cultural history of the area.

Take some of the mystery out of Table Mountain with a guide who can share information on the incredible diversity of flora and fauna you'll come across. Join walking and climbing tours with Venture Forth International, or tag along on a group walk open to everyone (most are on weekends). Pick up a Cumhike timetable from any Cape Union Mart outdoor store (found in almost every mall). Pamphlets for a self-guided walking tour of city-center attractions can be picked up at Cape Town Tourism. Longer walking tours (four days and longer) outside Cape Town can be arranged through Active Africa, specialized birding walks through Bird-Watch Cape.

Tour Operators **Active Africa** (☎ *021/788–6083* ⊕ *www.active-africa.com*). **Bird-Watch Cape** (☎ *021/762–5059* ⊕ *www.birdwatch.co.za*). **Cape Town on Foot** (☎ *021/462–4252* ⊕ *www.wanderlust.co.za*). **Footsteps to Freedom** (☎ *021/426–4260 or 083/452–1112* ⊕ *www.footstepstofreedom.co.za*). **Ilios Travel** (☎ *021/697–4056* ⊕ *www.ilios.co.za*). **Venture Forth International** (☎ *0861/106–548* ⊕ *www.ctsm.co.za*).

Winelands & Beaches: The Western Cape

WORD OF MOUTH

"On our second day, we went to the Winelands. We decided to spend the day in Franschhoek, taking a circuitous route (via Sir Lowry's Pass) to get there. The scenery was amazing. One minute you feel like you're in Spain, the next like you're in the Western United States, and the next like you're in Provence. So varied and so spectacular. We very much enjoyed strolling through the delightful town of Franschhoek, and doing a wine tasting at Boschendal nearby."

—dlm

Updated by
Karena du
Plessis

THE WESTERN CAPE IS AN alluring province, a sweep of endless mountain ranges, empty beaches, and European history dating back more than three centuries and anchored by Cape Town in the southwest. The cultures of the indigenous Khoekhoen and San people—the first inhabitants of this enormous area—also contribute to the region's richness. In less than two hours you can reach most of the province's highlights from Cape Town, making the city an ideal base from which to explore.

The historic Winelands, in the city's backyard, produce fine wine amid the exquisite beauty of rocky mountains, serried vines, and elegant Cape Dutch estates. Here farms have been handed down from one generation to another for centuries, and old-name families like the Cloetes and Myburghs have become part of the fabric of the region. Even first-time visitors may notice subtle differences between these Cape Afrikaners and their more conservative cousins in the hinterland. For the most part they are descendants of the landed gentry and educated classes who stayed in the Cape after the British takeover in 1806 and the emancipation of the slaves in 1834.

The region they stayed behind in was one truly blessed by nature. Wildflowers are one extraordinary element of this natural bounty. The Western Cape is famous for its fynbos (pronounced *feign*-boss), the hardy, thin-leaf vegetation that gives much of the province its distinctive look. Fynbos composes a major part of the Cape floral kingdom, the smallest and richest of the world's six floral kingdoms. More than 8,500 plant species are found in the province, of which 5,000 grow nowhere else on earth. The region is dotted with nature reserves where you can hike through this profusion of flora, admiring the majesty of the king protea or the shimmering leaves of the silver tree. When the wind blows and mist trails across the mountainsides, the fynbos-covered landscape takes on the look of a Scottish heath.

Not surprisingly, people have taken full advantage of the Cape's natural bonanza. In the Overberg and along the West Coast, rolling wheat fields extend to the horizon, while farther inland jagged mountain ranges hide fertile valleys of apple orchards, orange groves, and vineyards. At sea hardy fisherfolk battle icy swells to harvest succulent crayfish (Cape lobsters), delicate *perlemoen* (abalone), and line fish, such as the delicious *kabeljou*. Each June–November hundreds of whales return to the Cape shores to calve, and the stretch of coastline that includes Hermanus, now referred to as the Whale Coast, becomes one of the best places for land-based whale-watching in the world.

For untold centuries this fertile region supported the Khoekhoen (Khoikhoi) and San (Bushmen), indigenous peoples who lived off the land as pastoralists and hunter-gatherers. With the arrival of European settlers, however, they were chased off, killed, or enslaved. In the remote recesses of the Cederberg mountains and along the West Coast you can still see the fading rock paintings left by the San, whose few remaining clans have long since retreated into the Kalahari Desert. The population of the Western Cape today is largely "coloured," a term used to describe South Africans of mixed race and descendants of imported slaves, the San, the Khoekhoen, and European settlers (⇨ *A Note on the Term "Coloured" box, below*).

ORIENTATION & PLANNING

2

ORIENTATION

The best way to explore the Western Cape is to rent a car and take to the roads. You need to be flexible to enjoy all this region has to offer, and public transportation is too limited. Navigating your way around is not difficult. There are three main routes out of the city: the N1, N2, and N7. The N1 and N2 take you to the Winelands of Stellenbosch, Franschhoek, and Paarl, and the N7 heads up the West Coast. To reach the Overberg, take the N2 out of town and head up over Sir Lowry's Pass. To the east is the historically significant and scenic Swellendam area, nestled under the towering Langeberg Mountains. Off the main road to the south are the coast and the southern tip of Africa, Cape Agulhas. This southern coastal part of the Overberg, containing the small towns and villages of Gordon's Bay, Betty's Bay, Kleinmond, Hermanus, Stanford, and Gansbaai, is usually referred to as the Overstrand. (*Strand* is Afrikaans for "beach.")

THE WINELANDS

This area lies only 45 minutes east of Cape Town, fanned out around three historic towns and their valleys. Founded in 1685, Stellenbosch is a gem. Its oak-lined streets bristle with historic architecture, good restaurants, and interesting galleries and shops, and it has a vibrant university community. Franschhoek, enclosed by towering mountains, is the original home of the Cape's French Huguenots, whose descendants have made a conscious effort to reassert their French heritage. Paarl lies beneath huge granite domes, its main street running 11 km (7 mi) along the Berg River past some of the country's most elegant historic monuments. Throughout the region you will find some of South Africa's best restaurants and hotels.

BREEDE RIVER VALLEY

Farms, vineyards, and orchards make up most of the Breede River valley. (So it should come as no surprise that one of the towns in the area is called Ceres, after the Roman goddess of agriculture.) Small-town hospitality, striking mountains, and wide-open spaces are hallmarks of this area. In summer the heat can be overwhelming, while in winter the mountain peaks are often covered with snow.

THE OVERBERG

The genteel atmosphere of the southwestern Cape fades quickly the farther from Cape Town you go. The Overberg, separated from the city by the Hottentots Holland Mountains, presides over the rocky headland of Cape Agulhas, where the Indian and Atlantic oceans meet (officially) at the southernmost tip of the continent. Unspoiled beaches, coastal mountains, and small towns are the lure of this remote area.

TOP REASONS TO VISIT

Land of Divine Wine Few places in the world can match the drama of the Winelands, where mountains rise above vine-covered valleys and 300-year-old homesteads. Against this stunning backdrop you can visit scores of wineries, tour their cellars, relax under old oaks with a picnic basket, and dine at the many excellent restaurants in the area. You'll be hard-pressed to decide which wines to take home with you.

Whale of a Time Come spring, when the winter rains are no longer lashing the Cape, the icy seas teem with Southern Right whales who come here to calve. Towns like Hermanus offer some of the best land-based whale-watching in the world, and you can also take a boat trip out to see these gentle giants. If it's adrenaline you're after, head to Gansbaai, where you can go diving amid great white sharks.

Flower Power In summer, when the temperatures soar and the land is dusty, parched, and brown, it's hard to imagine the transformation that takes place each spring when millions of flowers carpet the West Coast hills. It's a photographer's dream, with the blue ocean in the background and swaths of yellow, white, and orange daisies.

Fabulous Food South African food has come into its own. Boring *boerekos* (directly translated as "farmer's food"), characterized by meat and overcooked vegetables, has given way to an explosion of great cuisine. A new generation of chefs is making the most of the area's fabulous fresh produce, and restaurants in Franschhoek and Stellenbosch regularly get voted amongst the world's best.

The Great Outdoors The Western Cape's real charm lies outdoors. Erinvale and the Western Cape Hotel & Spa, near Kleinmond, have some of the most spectacular golf courses in the world. In the Cederberg you can hike for days and explore ancient rock formations while learning about the leopard-conservation programs. You can also ride horses through the vineyards of the Winelands, or go boating in the Klein River lagoon near Hermanus.

WEST COAST

North of Cape Town on the West Coast, civilization drops away altogether, save for a few lonely fishing villages and mining towns. Each spring, though, the entire region explodes in a spectacular wildflower display that slowly spreads inland to the desiccated Namaqualand and the Cederberg mountains. For nature lovers, the West Coast provides some unique opportunities, including birding at the West Coast National Park at the Langebaan Lagoon and hiking in the remote wilderness areas of the Cederberg.

PLANNING

Many people come to the Western Cape after getting a big-game fix in Mpumalanga. Although it's possible to explore Cape Town and the Winelands in three or four days—the area is compact enough to allow it—you need six or seven to do it justice. You can get a good sense of either the Overberg or the West Coast on a three- or four-day jaunt, but set aside a week if you plan to tackle more than one or two of the regions in this chapter.

TAKE IT ALL IN

3 Days: You could devote a couple of days to touring the wineries, spending perhaps one day visiting Stellenbosch-area wineries such as Simonsig and Villiera, and another day around Franschhoek or Paarl. Consider breaking up your wine touring with horseback riding at one of the vineyards and a night in Franschhoek. A third day could be devoted to a long, scenic route back to Cape Town after lunch at one of Franschhoek's many good restaurants. Another option is to spend the first day wine tasting, and then drive over Sir Lowry's Pass through Elgin and on to Greyton, where you can wander around the village and visit the Moravian Mission complex in Genadendal. The last morning of your stay could be spent in Greyton before you head back to Cape Town via the coastal road, Clarence Drive, that passes Kleinmond, Betty's Bay, Pringle Bay, and Gordon's Bay.

5 Days: With five days, you can work in time to see the Winelands as well as Clanwilliam, at the edge of the Cederberg. (The drive to the Clanwilliam area will take you through the Swartland and the beginning of the wildflower route, which is best in spring.) If nature beckons, head into the Cederberg, where you can easily spend two nights in some of the country's most spectacular scenery. You can hike, swim in crystal-clear rock pools, and admire ancient San rock art. You could also combine a trip to the Winelands or Cederberg with a visit to the coast's Langebaan and the West Coast National Park, where the birding is exceptional.

7 Days: A week would allow you to comfortably visit the Winelands, Cederberg, and the coast. You could spend a few days in the Cederberg and then head through Riebeek Kasteel and Wellington and on to the Winelands towns of Paarl, Stellenbosch, and Franschhoek, where you can linger for the next two or three days. You could easily spend your last days in the beautiful Franschhoek valley. Or you could take a scenic back route on the R45 and then the R321 into the Overberg. You could spend a couple of days exploring the coast, overnighting in Hermanus or Arniston. If it's winter, watch whales, and if you're not sick of wine by this point, sample some of the Overberg wines. Drive back to Cape Town via the spectacular coastal road of Clarence Drive.

EAT RIGHT, SLEEP WELL

The dining scene ranges from fine South African cuisine complete with silver service to local, laid-back, country-style cooking. Franschhoek restaurants attract some of the country's most innovative chefs, who aren't afraid to experiment with unusual ingredients or food-and-wine combinations, and offer up a very sophisticated dining experience in a gorgeous setting. West Coast fare is not as urban as what you find in the Winelands, and coastal towns usually concentrate on seafood, often served in open-air restaurants. Farther inland the cuisine tends to be less trendy and the portions more generous. Be sure to try some Cape Malay cuisine, characterized by mild, slightly sweet curries and

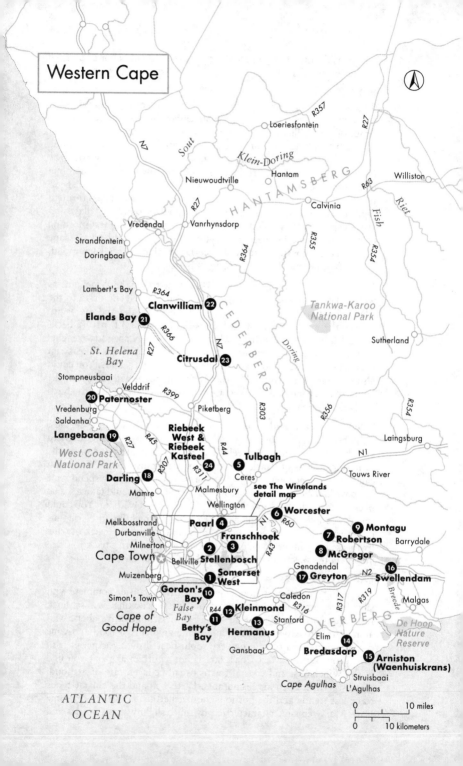

Western Cape

ATLANTIC
OCEAN

Loeriesfontein

Sout

Klein-Doring

Hantam

Nieuwoudtville

Williston

Calvinia

HANTAMSBERG

Vredendal

Vanrhynsdorp

Strandfontein

Doringbaai

Fish

Riet

Lambert's Bay

R364

Clanwilliam 22

Tankwa-Karoo National Park

Elands Bay 21

Sutherland

St. Helena Bay

Citrusdal 23

CEDERBERG

Stompneusbaai

Velddrif

Doring

20 Paternoster

Vredenburg

Saldanha

Piketberg

Laingsburg

Langebaan 19

West Coast National Park

N1

Touws River

Riebeek West & Riebeek Kasteel

Tulbagh 5

24

Ceres

Darling 18

Mamre

Malmesbury

see The Winelands detail map

Wellington

6 Worcester

Melkbosstrand

Durbanville

Milnerton

Paarl 4

9 Montagu

7 Robertson

Cape Town

Bellville

2

3

Franschhoek

Barrydale

8 McGregor

Stellenbosch

Genadendal

Muizenberg

1

Somerset West

17 Greyton

N2

16

Swellendam

Simon's Town

Gordon's Bay 10

Caledon

Malgas

False Bay

12 Kleinmond

R317

R319

Breede

OVERBERG

Cape of Good Hope

Betty's Bay 11

13

Stanford

De Hoop Nature Reserve

Hermanus

Elim

Gansbaai

14

Bredasdorp 15

Arniston (Waenhuiskrans)

Cape Agulhas

Struisbaai

L'Agulhas

0   10 miles

0   10 kilometers

aromatic spices. The only places you're likely to be disappointed in the food are in smaller agricultural towns in the Overberg or up the West Coast, where overcooked veggies and an uninspiring and indistinguishable roast are still the norm. But this is changing from month to month as weary city slickers are heading out of town to open lovely restaurants serving quality food.

Country restaurants tend to serve lunch from noon and dinner from 6, and do not cater to late diners except on weekends. Because these areas rely heavily on tourists and local day-trippers, most restaurants in the Winelands and seaside towns are open on weekends, especially for leisurely Sunday lunches, but may catch their breath on Sunday evenings or quieter Mondays. Dress codes vary as much as the dining experiences. Casual wear is acceptable during the day and at most restaurants in the evening. On the coast people pull shorts and T-shirts over their swimsuits before tucking into a plate of calamari and chips (fries), but some Winelands restaurants like their patrons to look as good as the cuisine they deliver. Even so, a nice pair of jeans or pants and a good shirt are usually enough; jackets and ties are rarely expected. If there's someplace you really want to eat, reserve ahead. In December and January, popular restaurants book up quickly, and reservations are advised at least a day or two in advance.

The Winelands are sufficiently compact that you can make one hotel your touring base. Stellenbosch and Paarl, situated close to dozens of wineries and restaurants as well as the major highways to Cape Town, offer the most flexibility. Here bed-and-breakfasts and self-catering (with cooking facilities) options are often less expensive than hotels, and provide a better taste of life in the country. Franschhoek is comparatively isolated, which many visitors consider a blessing. The West Coast, the Cederberg, and the Overberg are much more spread out, so you'll want to stay in one place for a day or two and then move on. During the peak season of December–January, book well in advance, and be prepared for mandatory two-night stays on weekends. Although the winter months of June–September are usually a lot quieter and bring negotiable rates, seaside towns get really busy (and booked up) when the whales arrive to calve. The same is true up the West Coast during flower season.

WHAT IT COSTS IN SOUTH AFRICAN RAND					
	¢	$	$$	$$$	$$$$
RESTAURANTS	under R50	R50–R75	R75–R100	R100–R125	over R125
HOTELS	under R500	R500–R1,000	R1,000–R2,000	R2,000–R3,000	over R3,000

Restaurant prices are per person for a main course at dinner, a main course equivalent, or a prix-fixe meal. Hotel prices are for a standard double room in high season, including 12.5% tax.

CLOSE UP

A Note on the Term "Coloured"

South Africa has come a long way since the first democratic elections in 1994. Parts of the country are, in fact, just about unrecognizable. What hasn't changed, however, is the enormous complexity surrounding language, race classification, and cultural identity. While for many Americans the term "colored" is offensive, the term (spelled "coloured") is widely used in South Africa to describe South Africans of mixed race, often descended from imported slaves, the San, the Khoekhoen, and European settlers. Over the years the term "coloureds" has lost any pejorative connotations. Most coloureds don't regard themselves as black Africans, and culturally they are extremely different. What is especially confusing to people just passing through South Africa is that many coloureds share so much in common with Afrikaners and are united in their love for and use of Afrikaans.

HEALTH & SAFETY

If you plan to go hiking in the mountains, come prepared with the right clothing and the correct attitude—each year tourists get lost in the mountains. Cape weather is notoriously changeable, so you need something warm and preferably waterproof. Take at least 2 liters of water per person and something to eat. If possible, hike with somebody who knows the area well, but if you're walking alone, be sure to take a cell phone and program in some emergency numbers (but be aware that cell phones won't work in all areas). Let somebody know of your route and when you expect to return, and don't stray from the paths if the mist closes in.

TIMING

Summer (late November–January) is high season in the Western Cape, and during that time you will seldom visit major places of interest without encountering busloads of fellow visitors. The weather is warm and dry, and although strong southeasterly winds can be a nuisance, they do keep the temperature bearable. If soaking up the sun is not of primary importance and you prefer to tour during quieter times, spring (September and October) and autumn–early winter (late March through May) are ideal. The weather is milder, and the lines are shorter. Spring also brings Southern Right whales close to the shores of the Western Cape to calve, and late August–October are the months to see the wildflowers explode across the West Coast. If the Winelands are high on your list of must-dos, remember that the busiest time in the vineyards and cellars is January–April, when they begin harvesting and wine making.

THE WINELANDS

Frank Prial, wine critic for the *New York Times,* wrote that he harbored "a nagging suspicion that great wines must be made in spectacular surroundings." If that's true, then the Cape Winelands are perfectly poised to produce fantastic wines, because the setting of dramatic mountains and lush valleys is absolutely stunning.

Although the Winelands region is largely thought of as the wine centers of Stellenbosch, Franschhoek, and Paarl, today these areas make up only 35% of all the land in the Cape under vine. This wine-growing region is now so vast you can trek to the fringes of the Karoo Desert, in the northeast, and still find a grape. There are around 18 wine routes in the Western Cape, ranging from the Olifants River, in the north, to the coastal mountains of the Overberg and beyond. There's also a well-established Winelands brandy route, and an annual port festival is held in Calitzdorp, in the Little Karoo.

The secret to touring the Winelands is not to hurry. Dally over lunch on a vine-shaded veranda at a 300-year-old estate, enjoy an afternoon nap under a spreading oak, or sip wine while savoring the impossible views. Of the scores of wineries and estates in the Winelands, the ones listed below are chosen for their great wine, their beauty, or their historic significance. It would be a mistake to try to cover them all in less than a week. You have nothing to gain from hightailing it around the Winelands other than a headache. If your interest is more aesthetic and cultural than wine driven, you would do well to focus on the historic estates of Stellenbosch and Franschhoek. Most Paarl wineries stand out more for the quality of their wine than for their beauty.

SOMERSET WEST (HELDERBERG)

❶ *40 km (25 mi) southeast of Cape Town on the N2.*

Though Helderberg is the official designation for this wine area on the edge of the Winelands, most people know it as Somerset West. Just before you reach the center of town you'll see the turnoff to Lourensford Road, which runs 3 km (2 mi) to Vergelegen and Morgenster.

★ **Vergelegen** was established in 1700 by Willem Adriaan van der Stel, who succeeded his father as governor of the Cape. His traditional Cape Dutch homestead, with thatch roof and gables, looks like something out of a fairy tale. An octagonal walled garden aflame with flowers surrounds it, and huge camphor trees, planted almost 300 years ago, stand as gnarled sentinels. The estate was purchased for Lady Florence Phillips by her husband, mining magnate Sir Lionel Phillips, in 1917, and she spent vast sums on the restoration of the homestead, library, and gardens. The homestead is now a museum and is furnished in period style. Other historic buildings include a magnificent library and the old stables, now the reception area and interpretive center. Behind the house, the Lady Phillips Restaurant serves lunch and tea, and the Rose Terrace café looks onto a formal rose garden.

Although Vergelegen still buys grapes from neighboring farms, the vineyards that were planted in 1989, during what is described as the renaissance of the farm, are beginning to give an inkling of some very good wines to come. The flagship Vergelegen is a Bordeaux-style blend, whereas the merlot has ripe, plummy flavors. The chardonnay

Behind Winelands Wine

The South African wine industry is booming. Buried by sanctions during apartheid, South African wines were largely unknown internationally. But today there's enormous interest in South African reds *and* whites, and good-quality wines at varied prices are readily available—even in supermarkets. Wine drinking has become part of daily life.

Currently red-wine production outstrips white; the quality continually improves for both. Cape reds regularly win international awards, and whites are gaining. Pinotage, South Africa's own grape variety, is a cross between pinot noir and cinsaut (formerly hermitage). Chenin blanc is used in everything from blends to bubbly (known in South Africa as Méthode Cap Classique).

Meanwhile, the industry is transforming itself slowly. Though illegal, the *dop* (drink) system, in which farmers pay some of laborers' wages in wine, is still practiced on some outlying farms, with disastrous results, as many workers suffer from alcoholism. But things are changing. Many international companies refuse to import wine from farms that don't secure their workers' rights, and some farms are working at black empowerment. Tukulu, Riebeek Cellars, Thandi Wines, and Ses'Fikile (which translated means "we have arrived") are just some of the pioneers, but only Mont Rochelle, in Franschhoek, is solely black owned.

If you're serious about wine, arm yourself with *John Platter's Wine Guide* or *Wine* magazine, featuring local wineries. For an in-depth read and fantastic photos, pick up *Wines and Vineyards of South Africa* by Wendy Torein or *New World of Wine from the Cape of Good Hope: The Definitive Guide to the South African Wine Industry* by Phyllis Hands, David Hughes, and Keith Phillips.

has touches of wood fermentation but is dominated by a fresh citrus nose. Reservations are essential for the tours. ⊠ *Lourensford Rd.* ☎ *021/847–1334* ⊕ *www.vergelegen.co.za* ☞ *Tastings R2–R10 per wine* ⊙ *Daily 9:30–4. Cellar tours Oct.–Apr., daily at 10:15, 11:30, and 3; May–Sept., daily at 10:15.*

Nestled against the base of Helderberg Mountain and shaded by giant oaks, the peaceful **Rust en Vrede** winery looks over steep slopes of vines and roses. This is a comparatively small estate that specializes entirely in red wine—and produces some of the very best in South Africa. Rust en Vrede Estate is the flagship wine, a blend of predominantly cabernet sauvignon, shiraz, and just over 10% merlot grapes. It has already won several awards both locally and abroad, but it would do well to mature in the bottle for another 10 years or more. Another interesting wine is the shiraz, which has an inviting, spicy bouquet with a mellowness imparted by the American oak in which it is matured, but none of the characteristic cloying sweetness; it will age from five to eight years. ⊠ *R44, between Somerset West and Stellenbosch* ☎ *021/881–3881* ⊕ *www.rustenvrede.com* ☞ *Tastings R20 (refundable on purchase)* ⊙ *May–Sept., weekdays 9–5, Sat. 9–3; Oct.–Apr., weekdays 9–5, Sat. 9–4.*

The Winelands

ATLANTIC OCEAN

Table Bay

CAPE TOWN

Camps Bay

Melkbosstrand

Bloubergstrand

Philadelphia

Durbanville

Kenridge

Bellville

Parow

Brackenfell

Kraaifontein

Villiera

Warwick

Simonsig

Mulderbosch

Jordan

Overgaauw

Neethlingshof

Spier

Meerlust

Rustenberg

Thelema

Morgenhof

Muratie

Kanonkop

Landskroon

Fairview

Glen Carlou

Backsberg

Rhebokskloof

Nelson's Creek

KWV

Avondale

Paarl 4

Plaisir de Merle

La Motte

L'Ormarins

Boschendal

Mont Rochelle

Cabrière

La Petite Ferme

Franschhoek 3

Tokara

Delaire

Stellenbosch 2

Rust en Vrede

Dombeya Farm

Somerset West 1

Vergelegen

Morgenster

Strand

False Bay

Mitchells Plain

Muizenberg

Noordhoek

Sun Valley

Villiersdorp

Theeuwaterskloof Dam

Wemmershoek Dam

Assegaaibos Dam

Paarl Mountain Nature Reserve

Hottentots Holland Nature Reserve

STELLENBOSCHBERG

FRANSCHHOEK MTNS.

Berg River

Helshoogte Pass

5 miles

5 kilometers

CLOSE UP

Cape Dutch Architecture

As you travel around the region, the most visible emblems of settler culture you'll encounter are the Cape Dutch–style houses. Here 18th- and 19th-century manor houses share certain characteristics: thick whitewashed walls, thatch roofs curving around elegant gables, and small-pane windows framed by wooden shutters. It's a classic look—a uniquely Cape look—ideally suited to a land that is hot in summer and cold in winter. The Cape Dutch style developed in the 18th century from traditional long houses: simple rectangular sheds capped by thatch. As farmers became more prosperous, they added the ornate gables and other features. Several estates, most notably Vergelegen (near Somerset West) and Boschendal (on the Franschhoek wine route), have opened their manor houses as museums.

Dombeya Farm, next door to Rust en Vrede, is one of the few places in the Western Cape to see spinning and hand weaving. The farm makes jerseys, blankets, and rugs from merino wool, all in the bright, floral patterns that are Dombeya's hallmark. The shop also sells knitting patterns and wool. A garden restaurant serves light lunches and snacks. ⊠ *Annandale Rd., between Somerset West and Stellenbosch* ☎ *021/881–3746* 🖅 *Free* 🕙 *Daily 9–4:30.*

WHERE TO STAY & EAT

$$–$$$$ ✕ **L'Auberge du Paysan.** This little cottage near Somerset West offers a formally presented mélange of southern and classic French cuisine that makes good use of South African game birds and venison. Tall upholstered chairs, small brass table lamps, and snowy linen create a Gallic setting for first courses like delicate *coquille de mer* (seafood in a lobster sauce topped with Parmesan cheese) or frogs' legs panfried in an herb-and-garlic butter. Guinea fowl is given traditional cassoulet treatment, and fish entrées could include fresh bouillabaisse or kabeljou topped with a *dijonnaise* (Dijon mustard seeds, sherry, and cream) sauce. Seasonal berries—filling meringue baskets, pureed into sorbets, and teamed with spiked chantilly cream—create irresistible desserts. ⊠ *Raithby Rd., off R44 between Somerset West and Stellenbosch* ☎ *021/842–2008* 🖃 *AE, DC, MC, V* 🕙 *Closed Sun. No lunch Mon.*

¢–$$ ✕ **Lady Phillips Restaurant.** In summer you need to reserve a table three weeks in advance at this idyllic country restaurant on the Vergelegen Estate. In pleasant weather ask for a table on the terrace, shaded by liquidambar trees. Consider starting with kudu carpaccio marinated in teriyaki sauce and served with a mustard-and-rosemary vinaigrette before moving on to homemade smoked-salmon pasta. The delicious lemon-thyme-marinated lamb rump is served with potatoes gratin and baby vegetables in season. Of the wide dessert selection, sticky-date-and-macadamia-nut pudding with cream and maple sauce is noteworthy, calorie-packed, and hugely delicious. If you can't get a reservation, head to the estate's Rose Terrace during summer for light meals.

CLOSE UP

From Soil to Oil

South Africans are beginning to produce extra-virgin olive oils that are as excellent as their wines. One place to learn about this fruit of the local fields is the historic estate Morgenster (*Morning Star*), which is part of Cape governor Simon van der Stel's original 17th-century farm. In the mid-'90s the estate was restored to its original splendor, and olive trees were planted; it's now producing some of the best oils in the country. Five different olive cultivars—frantoio, leccino, favoloza, coratina, and peranzana—are pressed individually before they're blended. For R10 you can taste the olives, the oil, and the delicious olive paste. Phone a day ahead if you're traveling in a group bigger than six. ⊠ *Vergelegen Ave., off Lourensford Rd., Somerset West* ☎ *021/852–1738* ⊕ *www.morgenster. co.za* ⊠ *Tastings R10* ⊗ *Daily 10–4.*

Kloovenburg Wine Estate. In addition to producing wine, this estate in the picturesque Riebeek Valley (⇨ *Riebeek West & Riebeek Kasteel, in West Coast, below*) also makes

olive oil and a delectable range of olive products that you can eat and rub on your body. Annalene du Toit, wife of the vineyard's owner, and one of her young sons took to the kitchen to come up with some of the olive concoctions, and they only sell what they like to eat. ⊠ *R46 just outside Riebeek Kasteel as you're coming down the pass into Riebeek Valley* ☎ *022/448–1635* ⊕ *www.kloovenburg.co.za* ⊠ *Tastings free (R20 per person for groups of more than 10)* ⊗ *Weekdays 9–4:30, Sat. 9–2.*

Fairview. This vineyard in the Suid-Agter-Paarl area has a range of olive oils they're proud of. You can taste single-cultivar oils and take home a bottle of your own particular blend. Or you can just buy the farm's oil, along with its excellent wines and goat's-milk cheeses. ⊠ *WR3, off R101 (Suid-Agter-Paarl Rd.), Suider-Paarl* ☎ *021/863–2450* ⊕ *www.fairview. co.za* ⊠ *Wine and olive-oil tasting R15* ⊗ *Weekdays 8:30–5, Sat. 8:30–4, Sun. 9:30–4.*

⊠ *Vergelegen Estate, Lourensford Rd.* ☎ *021/847–1346* ⊜ *Reservations essential* ▤ *AE, DC, MC, V* ⊗ *No dinner.*

¢–$$ ✕ **96 Winery Road.** This relaxed venue is always buzzing with folk from the wine industry, regulars, and up-country visitors. Inside, burgundy walls are cozy for winter, while outside terrace seating offers soothing mountain views. The menu changes regularly but tempts with such fresh and flavorful first courses as prawn tempura and salmon and line-fish sashimi. Steak lovers are treated well here; dry-aged cuts of prime beef are grilled and teamed with a variety of sauces. Vegetarians will find good choices, too, such as a salad of organic mixed leaves with grilled vegetables, feta, olives, Parmesan cheese, and toasted pine nuts. A good cheese board makes a savory—and many think, superior— option to rich desserts. The selection of wine is also impressive—in 2006 the restaurant won the Wine Spectator Grand Award for its comprehensive and innovative wine list. ⊠ *Zandberg Farm, Winery Rd., between Somerset West and Stellenbosch* ☎ *021/842–2020* ⊜ *Reservations essential* ▤ *AE, DC, MC, V* ⊗ *No dinner Sun.*

$$–$$$ ✕▥ **Willowbrook Lodge.** This lodge makes a good base for exploring the entire southwestern Cape, including the peninsula, the Winelands,

and the Overberg. The lodge lies hidden among beautiful gardens that extend down to the Lourens River; in the distance the peaks of the Helderberg are visible. It's a very peaceful place, with large, airy, comfortable rooms and sliding doors opening onto the gardens. D'Vine Restaurant ($–$$$) has equally high standards and regularly gets voted onto the country's top-100 list. The menu changes seasonally, but how's this for a delectable starter: wild mushrooms and chicken molded in a poppy-seed crepe and served with a duo of port and foie gras jus. It sounds complicated, but it's absolutely delicious. A simpler starter might be baked goat's cheese on walnut bread served with a honey-dressed salad of lemon, coriander, and green beans. For a main course, you'll be hard-pressed to choose between the likes of crispy aromatic duck or the springbok medallion served with berry compote, mushroom spaetzle, and sautéed green beans. ⊠ *Morgenster Ave., Box 1892, 7129* ☎ *021/851–3759* ⊕ *www.willowbrook.co.za* ⌘ *11 rooms, 1 suite* ♿ *In-room: safe, refrigerator, Wi-Fi (some). In-hotel: restaurant, bar, pool, no elevator, laundry service, public Wi-Fi, parking (no fee), no kids under 12, no-smoking rooms* ⊟ *AE, DC, MC, V* ⏺ *BP.*

SPORTS & THE OUTDOORS

The Gary Player–designed **Erinvale Golf Club** (⊠ *Lourensford Rd.* ☎ *021/847–1144*) is beautifully nestled beneath the Hottentots Holland Mountains. It costs around R495 to play 18 holes and about R330 for 9, R300 to rent clubs, and approximately R220 for a golf cart (there are no caddies). You can book only one week in advance during peak season (September–May); ask for availability when you phone. **Somerset West Golf Club** (⊠ *Rue de Jacqueline* ☎ *021/852–2925*) is an easy course with plenty of leeway for errant tee shots, except when the wind blows. Greens fees run about R275 for 18 holes, R150 for 9 holes; club rental is around R120. Golf carts are available for about R170, but you are encouraged to make use of the caddies for around R80, excluding tip.

EN ROUTE You can't drive down the R44 between Somerset West and Stellenbosch without noticing the remarkable scarecrows at **Mooiberge Farm Stall.** They're riding bicycles, driving tractors, and working in the strawberry fields, where you can spend a morning picking the luscious red fruit. The strawberry season varies from one year to the next but usually begins in October and runs to February. You pay for what you pick, and you can also buy jams, dried fruit, and other refreshments at the farm stall. Look for the interesting display of old farm implements at the side of the building. ⊠ *R44, between Somerset West and Stellenbosch* ☎ *021/881–3222* ⊠ *Free* ☉ *Daily 8–6.*

STELLENBOSCH

★ ❷ *15 km (9½ mi) north of Somerset West.*

You could easily while away a week in this small, sophisticated, beautiful, and absolutely delightful town. South Africa's second-oldest municipality, after Cape Town, Stellenbosch actually *feels* old, unlike so many other historic towns. Wandering the oak-shaded streets, which still have open irrigation furrows (known as the *lei water,* pronounced "lay vaater"), you'll see some of the finest examples of Cape Dutch, Georgian, Victorian, and Regency architecture in the country. The town was founded in 1679 by Simon van der Stel, first governor of the Cape, who recognized the agricultural potential of this fertile valley. Wheat was the major crop grown by the early set-

> **GOOD TO NOTE**
>
> A good place to start a tour of the town is at the corner of Dorp Street and the R44, where you first enter Stellenbosch. Look for street names written in yellow on curbs; they're easy to miss, so remember to look down and not up.

tlers, but vineyards now blanket the surrounding hills. Stellenbosch is considered the center of the Winelands, and many of the older and more established wineries are situated nearby. Wine routes fan out like spokes of a wheel, making excellent day trips if you're staying in town. The town is also home to the University of Stellenbosch, the country's first and most prestigious Afrikaner university.

Stroll up oak-lined **Dorp Street,** Stellenbosch's most historic avenue. Almost the entire street is a national monument, flanked by lovely restored homes from every period of the town's history.

Redolent of tobacco, dried fish, and spices, **Oom Samie Se Winkel** is a 19th-century-style general dealer and one of Stellenbosch's most popular landmarks. In addition to the usual Cape kitsch, Oom Samie sells some genuine South African produce, including *witblitz* and *mampoer,* both Afrikaner versions of moonshine. The shop has a wine-export business and restaurant, too. ⊠ *82–84 Dorp St.* ☎ *021/887–0797* ☾ *Weekdays 8:30–6, weekends 9–5.*

As you walk up Dorp Street, keep an eye out for the historic **La Gratitude home** (⊠ *95 Dorp St.*), built in the early 18th century in traditional Cape Dutch town-house style. The all-seeing eye of God molded on its gable was designed as a talisman to watch over the owner's property and keep him and his family safe from harm.

Voorgelegen (⊠ *176 Dorp St.*) and the houses on either side of it form one of the best-preserved Georgian ensembles in town.

Possibly the country's oldest boardinghouse, **d'Ouwe Werf** (⊠ *30 Church St.*) first took in paying guests in 1802. As you walk up Dorp Street, make a left onto Andringa Street and then a right onto Church (also called Kerk) Street to get here; d'Ouwe Werf will be on your left.

At the corner of Church and Ryneveld streets, the **Stellenbosch Village Museum** comprises four dwellings scattered within a two-block radius. Dating from different periods in Stellenbosch's history, the houses have been furnished to reflect changing lifestyles and tastes. The oldest is the very basic Schreuderhuis, built in 1709. The others date from 1789, 1803, and 1850. ⊠ *18 Ryneveld St.* ☎ *021/887–2902* ⊕ *www.museums.org.za/stellmus* ⊠ *R15* ☾ *Mon.–Sat. 9:30–5, Sun. 2–5.*

Some of Stellenbosch's most historic buildings face the town square, **Braak,** which is a national monument. To get here from the Stellenbosch Village Museum, continue down Ryneveld to Plein Street. Turn left and walk to the grassy square. At the southern end of the square is the **Rhenish Church** (⊠ *Bloem St.*), erected by the Missionary Society of Stellenbosch in 1823 as a training school for slaves and blacks. **St. Mary's Church** stands at the far end of the Braak. Built in 1852 as an Anglican church, it reflects the growing influence of the English in Stellenbosch. Across Bloem Street from St. Mary's is the **Burgher House,** built in 1797. Today it houses the offices of Historical Homes in South Africa.

Next to the Burgher House, on a traffic island in Market Street, stands the **V.O.C. Arsenal,** also known as the V.O.C. *Kruithuis* (powder house). It took 91 years for the political council to decide that Stellenbosch needed its own magazine, and just six months in 1777 to complete the structure. Today the arsenal contains a wide selection of guns, gunpowder holders, and cannons. If the arsenal is closed, call or pop into the **Toy and Miniature Museum** (☎ *021/886–7888*), on the Braak, and someone will open it up for you. ⊠ *Bloem St.* ☎ *021/886–4153* ⌨ *R5* ☉ *Sept.–May, weekdays 9–2.*

Walk down Market Street past the Tourist Information Bureau. On your left, facing a large lawn, is the **Rhenish Complex** (⊠ *Bloem St.*), one of the most impressive restoration projects ever undertaken in South Africa and a good example of what early Stellenbosch must have been like. The complex consists of an art center; the old Cape Dutch Rhenish parsonage (1815), which is now the Toy and Miniature Museum; the Leipoldt House, which melds elements of English and Cape architecture; and a two-story building that is typically English.

WINERIES

Delaire. This has to be one of the most spectacular settings of any winery in the country. Sit on the terrace of the tasting room or restaurant and look past a screen of oaks to the valley below and the majestic crags of the Groot Drakenstein and Simonsberg mountains. It's an ideal place to stop for lunch: you can order a picnic basket and relax on the lawn with a bottle of estate wine or visit the restaurant. The tasting room is unpretentious and casual. The Botmaskop Cabernet Sauvignon is highly rated, as is the 2006 sauvignon blanc. There are no cellar tours. At this writing the winery and restaurant were closed for renovation, but were scheduled to reopen in the first quarter of 2008. ⊠ *Helshoogte Rd., between Stellenbosch and Franschhoek* ☎ *021/885–1756, 021/885–1149 restaurant* ⊕ *www.delairewinery.co.za* ⌨ *Tastings R40 for 7 wines* ☉ *Weekdays 9–5, weekends 10–5.*

Jordan. At the end of the Stellenbosch Kloof Road, this meticulous winery, flanked by the Bottelary hills, overlooks rolling vineyards and jagged mountains. Husband-and-wife team Gary and Kathy Jordan studied at the University of California at Davis and worked at California's Iron Horse Winery. The family made their fortune producing practical shoes and now, although they produced their first vintage only in 1992, they have already established a formidable reputation.

Stellenbosch Wine Route

Along R310. West of Stellenbosch, the R310 (also known locally as Baden Powell Avenue) forks to the left, but go straight on the M12; **Neethlingshof** is on your left. Next turn right on the Stellenbosch Kloof Road, where **Overgaauw** is a merlot mainstay. Follow the winding road through pretty vineyards; at the end is **Jordan,** known for its whites. Double-back to the fork, and take the R310 to your right to the touristy but fun **Spier.** Next up this road is **Meerlust** with its submerged windmill.

If you drive east on the R310 from Stellenbosch, detour up the Idasvallei Road and follow a narrow lane through cattle pastures and oak groves to **Rustenberg,** which focuses on reds. Then it's up and over the scenic Helshoogte Pass to **Thelema Mountain Vineyards,** which has knockout reds and whites. Its neighbor, **Tokara,** is a great lunch spot, whereas **Delaire,** over the road, has breathtaking views (note that at this writing, Delaire was closed for renovation but scheduled to reopen in the first quarter of 2008).

Along R44. Some important wineries are on the R44 north of Stellenbosch. At **Morgenhof** you can sip chardonnay and pinotage and linger for lunch. About 3 km (2 mi) farther along on the R44, turn right on Knorhoek Road to reach low-frills **Muratie,** with some good reds. Back on the R44, travel a short way and then turn left on Kromme Rhee Road to visit **Simonsig,** home to wonderful bubbly. On the R44 once more, continue to **Kanonkop,** which has won numerous awards, and perhaps **Warwick,** with great red blends.

Along R304. This road shoots northwest from Stellenbosch past several wine farms. Stop at **Mulderbosch** for its excellent white wines. Cross over Kromme Rhee Road and on to **Villiera,** known for sparkling wine and lush sauvignon blanc.

The sauvignon blanc, with refreshing hints of asparagus, makes for good summer drinking, and the multi-award-winning dense but fruity chardonnay is extremely popular and has regulars stocking up on cases at a time. The two are combined in the versatile, flavorful, and well-priced Chameleon dry white. Other wines to try are the Cobblers Hill (get it?) Bordeaux blend and the Sophia CWG (Cape Winemakers Guild) Auction Reserve 2004 vintage, which is laden with stars. ⌂ *Stellenbosch Kloof Rd.* ☎ *021/881–3441* ⊕ *www.jordanwines.com* ▣ *Tastings R15* ☉ *Weekdays 10–4:30, Sat. 9:30–2:30, Sun 10–2:30; cellar tours by appointment.*

Kanonkop. In the days when ships of the Dutch East India Company used Cape Town as a refreshment station on the way to the East, a ship would fire a cannon as it entered the harbor to let farmers know provisions were needed, and a set of relay cannons, all set on hilltops, would carry the message far inland. One such cannon was on this farm, which was then called Kanonkop, Afrikaans for Cannon Hill. The beauty of Kanonkop today is not in its history or its buildings but in its wine. Winemaker Abrie Beeslaar has taken over from the legendary Beyers Truter (a very hard act to follow), but Kanonkop continues to reel in numerous awards and accolades. For example, the 1998 Paul Sauer, a blend of about 80% cabernet sauvignon with the balance made up of equal parts merlot and cabernet franc, was the grand champion at the South African Trophy Wine Show in 2002, and the 2003 vintage won a Veritas double gold. There are no guided cellar tours, but during harvest you can do a walkabout in the cellar to see all the action. ⊠ *R44, between Paarl and Stellenbosch* ☎ *021/884–4656* ⊕ *www.kanonkop.co.za* 🖃 *Tastings R10* ⊙ *Weekdays 8:30–5, Sat. 8:30–12:30.*

> **TAKE A LOOK**
>
> Architecture buffs will be happy to know that there are still examples of 19th-century Stellenbosch design around. To check them out, turn left off of Market Street onto **Herte Street.** The whitewashed cottages along this street were built by and for freed slaves after the Emancipation Act of 1834. Although they are no longer thatch, the houses on the left-hand side of the road are still evocative of this era.

Fodor'sChoice **Meerlust.** A visit to Meerlust, probably South Africa's most celebrated
★ estate, provides an introduction to Cape history. In the same family for generations, the wine farm was bought by Johannes Albertus Myburgh in 1757. When Nicolaas Myburgh, seventh-generation Myburgh and father of Hannes (the current owner), took over the reins in 1959, he began restoring the farm's Cape Dutch buildings. (The entire complex was declared a national monument in 1987.) But Nico Myburgh did more than just renovate. He took a fresh look at red wines and broke with tradition by deciding to make a red blend. In the '70s, conventional wisdom had it that cabernet sauvignon was king, but Nico went against the grain and opted for a Bordeaux-style blend, planting both merlot and cabernet franc. The first wine, made in 1980 and released in 1983, was named Rubicon (an allusion to Julius Caesar) to symbolize the crossing of a significant barrier. Although Rubicon rakes in the awards year after year, Meerlust's other wines—chardonnay, pinot noir, and merlot—are also notably good. The 2002 red blend, essentially a second-label Rubicon, is definitely worth buying, and it's also a little kinder on the wallet. ⊠ *Off R310* ☎ *021/843–3587* ⊕ *www.meerlust. co.za* 🖃 *Tastings R20* ⊙ *Weekdays 9–5, Sat. 10–2.*

Morgenhof Wine Estate. This beautiful Cape Dutch estate, with a history stretching back 300 years, lies in the lee of a steep hill covered with vines and pine trees. In 1993 Morgenhof was acquired by Anne Cointreau of Cognac, France, who spared no expense in making this a showpiece. The estate has a talented winemaker, Jacques Cilliers, and some distinguished wines. Try the chardonnay with fresh coconut nose and hints of lime, or the smoky, somewhat Burgundian pinotage. The estate's flagship wine is the wonderful Premiére Sélection, a Bordeaux blend. Morgenhof is an excellent place to stop for a simple lunch of homemade soup and freshly baked bread. Reservations are advisable in summer. ⊠ *R44, between Paarl and Stellenbosch* ☎ *021/889–5510* ⊕ *www.morgenhof.com* 🖃 *Tastings R10* ⊙ *May–Oct., weekdays 9–*

4:30, weekends 10–3; Nov.–Apr., weekdays 9–5:30, weekends 10–5; cellar tours by appointment.

Mulderbosch Vineyards. It's widely accepted that this small estate (only 67 acres are under vine) produces some of the best white wines around, thanks to Mike Dobrovic, an extremely talented cellar master. The robust, barrel-fermented chardonnay has a complex nose and a smooth, velvety finish; a sip might have you tasting buttered toast, citrus, vanilla, and wild herbs. The 2003 vintage sold out pretty quickly, so try to get a hold of the 2004 and 2005 while they are still available. The 2006 sauvignon blanc is also delicious; it's packed with gooseberry, nettle, and a touch of citrus. The Faithful Hound red blend was named after a dog who, when the current owners bought the farm in the late 1980s, refused to leave the house where he lived. A huge portion of the farm has been left to indigenous vegetation and wildlife. ⊠*R304, between Stellenbosch and Paarl* ☎*021/865-2488* ⊕*www. mulderbosch.co.za* ⌧*Fees vary* ⊗ *Mon.–Thurs. 8–5, Fri. 8–4; tastings by appointment.*

Muratie. Ancient oaks and a cellar that truly seems to be more concerned with the business of producing wine than with decor make this a refreshing change from the "prettier" wineries. It's a small estate, specializing in rich, earthy reds and full-bodied dessert wines. Muratie's port is an old favorite in the Cape, and the well-balanced amber is a fortified dessert wine of note, with pleasing citrus overtones to counter the sweetness. The cellar produces some fine red wines. Two worth looking out for are the pinot noir, from some of the oldest vines of this cultivar in the Cape; and Ansela van der Caab, a dry red blend of cabernet and merlot, named after the freed slave who married the first owner of the farm, Laurens Campher, and helped set up the vineyards in the early 1700s. Cellar tours are not offered. ⊠*Knorhoek Rd., off the R44, between Stellenbosch and Paarl* ☎*021/865-2330* ⊕*www. muratie.co.za* ⌧*Tastings R10* ⊗ *Weekdays 9–5, weekends 10–4.*

⟳ **Neethlingshof.** A long avenue of pines leads to this lovely estate, which traces its origins to 1692. The magnificent 1814 Cape Dutch manor house looks out across formal rose gardens to the Stellenbosch Valley and the Hottentots Holland Mountains. There's even a large play area, complete with jungle gyms, for kids. The wines produced on this estate and those from its sister farm, Stellenzicht, are highly regarded, so be prepared for a rush of tour buses during high season. The gewürztraminer is an off-dry, very elegant wine with rose-petal and spice aromas, and the Weisser Riesling Noble Late Harvest is one of the best of its kind, having scooped almost every local award since 1990. Two delicious wines worth stockpiling are the Stellenzicht Syrah and the farm's flagship wine, Lord Neethling Laurentius, a blend of cabernet sauvignon, cabernet franc, merlot, and shiraz. ⊠*M12* ☎*021/883-8988* ⊕*www.neethlingshof.co.za* ⌧*Tastings R30* ⊗ *Weekdays 9–5, weekends 10–4 (may stay open about 2 hrs later Dec. and Jan.); cellar tours by appointment.*

Overgaauw. Among the established estates on Stellenbosch Kloof Road, Overgaauw definitely deserves a visit. You can admire the pretty Victorian tasting room while exploring the range of big red wines. Overgaauw was the first South African estate to make a merlot, in 1982, and it's still up there with the leaders. The 2004 merlot is a wonderful, velvety wine that has rich chocolate, cherry, and raspberry flavors. It should age well. Try the Tria Corda, if you can get your hands on some; it sells out faster than it can be released. The 2004 vintage drew lots of accolades and is selling like hotcakes. The spicy, fruity sylvaner is named for a grape of the same name. To date, Overgaauw is the only Cape estate to grow this varietal, which comes from the Alsace region of France, so it's definitely worth exploring. ⊠ *Stellenbosch Kloof Rd.* ☎ *021/881–3815* ⊕ *www.overgaauw.co.za* ⊠ *Tastings R10* ☾ *Weekdays 9–12:30 and 2–5, Sat. 10–12:30.*

Rustenberg. This estate may date back to 1682, but it's been brought thoroughly up to date with a state-of-the art winery and underground vaulted maturation rooms. The estate is known for red wine, particularly its 100% cabernet Peter Barlow (named after the present owner's father), which is made from grapes from one lovely, well-tended vineyard. The Five Soldiers Chardonnay is also delicious and also made from a single vineyard, which gives it its unique character. It's named for the five tall pine trees that stand guard on top of the hill above the chardonnay grapes. The farm's second label, Brampton, also makes excellent wines. The 2004 cabernet sauvignon has won awards, but it's sold out, so scoop up some of the 2005 while it's still available and put it down for a couple of years. The 2005 shiraz is also wonderful. The farm uses screw caps for quality and environmental reasons. ⊠ *Off R310 (Rustenberg Rd.), Ida's Valley* ☎ *021/809–1200* ⊕ *www.rustenberg.co.za* ⊠ *Tastings free* ☾ *Weekdays 9–4:30, Sat. 10–1:30.*

☾ **Simonsig.** Sitting in a sea of vines is this estate with tremendous views back toward Stellenbosch and the mountains. Simonsig has more than a dozen white and red wines of impressive range, both in terms of taste and price. But quantity certainly doesn't mean that they have compromised on quality. This family-run farm produces exciting and consistent wines. Kaapse Vonkel was South Africa's first Méthode Cap Classique, and since 1971 this classic blend of chardonnay, pinot noir, and a touch of pinot meunier has been among the best. The 2000 Tiara is a great Bordeaux blend. The pinotage demonstrates how well this varietal fares with no wood aging, but the Red Hill Pinotage, from old bush vines, shows just how much good oaking can improve it. You can bring your own picnic to enjoy at tables by the small playground. ⊠ *Kromme Rhee Rd.* ☎ *021/888–4900* ⊕ *www.simonsig.co.za* ⊠ *Tastings R15 for 5 wines* ☾ *Weekdays 8:30–5, Sat. 8:30–4; cellar tours weekdays at 10 and 3, Sat. at 10.*

☾ **Spier.** Describing Spier Home Farms as simply a wine estate is doing it an enormous disservice. The vast complex comprises a manor house, wine cellars, wine and farm shop, rose garden, restaurants, equestrian facilities, a conference center, an open-air amphitheater featuring a variety of performances during summer, and a cheetah park, where you can watch the animals being fed daily 1–2. (A "private encounter" or photograph with a cheetah costs around R70 per person for an adult cat and R160 for a cub.) It's all designed in Cape-country style, with whitewashed walls and thatch roofs, set along the verdant north bank of the Eerste River. So, yes, it's seriously touristy, but still delightful. The Spier wines go from strength to strength. Try the cabernet sauvignon or the consistently good and well-priced chardonnay. ⊠*R310* ☎*021/809–1143* ⊕*www.spier.co.za* ✉*Informal tasting R10, educational tasting R18, reserve-wine tasting R20, cheese-and-wine tasting R25 for 3 wines and 3 cheeses* ⊙*Daily 9–5, tasting 10–4.*

Thelema Mountain Vineyards. On the slopes of the Simonsberg, just off the Helshoogte Pass, this is an excellent example of the exciting developments in the Cape Winelands since the early 1980s, when farmers began to eye land that hadn't traditionally been earmarked for wine farming. When Gyles and Barbara Webb started the farm in 1983, there was nothing here but very good soil and old fruit trees. It's a testament to their efforts that the winery has regularly won prizes for both its reds and whites ever since. To cap it all off, the view of the Groot Drakenstein mountains from the tasting room is unforgettable. Ever the pioneers, the Webbs have also bought Sutherland, an old fruit farm (not open to the public) in the Elgin area, an exciting new wine-growing region at the top of Sir Lowry's Pass. Be sure to taste Ed's Reserve, a dry white named after the late, legendary Edna McLean, Barbara's mother, who originally bought the Thelema farm and in later years was a stalwart in the tasting room. Also try the Thelema Sutherland Sauvignon Blanc, with its lovely mineral, grassy qualities. The 2004 mint cabernet sauvignon comes from a single block that produces a distinctively minty wine. For obvious reasons, it's been dubbed "The Full Minty." ⊠*Off R310, between Stellenbosch and Franschhoek* ☎*021/885–1924* ⊕*www.thelema.co.za* ✉*Tastings free* ⊙*Weekdays 9–5, Sat. 10–3.*

Tokara. Perched on the crest of the Helshoogte Pass between Stellenbosch and Franschhoek, Tokara is the brainchild of banker G. T. Ferreira. For a city slicker with lots of money, he's done everything right by employing an excellent winemaker in Miles Mossop and paying careful attention to the quality of his vines. The farm produces under two labels—Tokara and Zondernaam (which means "without name" in Old Dutch)—and the reds are big and powerful. The flagship red, a blend of cabernet sauvignon, merlot, petit verdot, and cabernet franc, is well worth taking home. They also have farms in the cooler Elgin and Hemel-en-Aarde regions, which means they can produce a stunning sauvignon blanc with plenty of complexity. Tokara also produces its own premium olive oil, which you can buy from the Olive Shed on the farm. Tokara's restaurant is a foodie's delight. ⊠*Off R310, between Stellenbosch and Franschhoek* ☎*021/808–5900* ⊕*www. tokara.com* ✉*Tastings free* ⊙*Weekdays 9–5, weekends and public holidays 10–3.*

Villiera. Since they started wine making in 1984, the Grier family has notched numerous successes. As John Platter, one of South Africa's foremost wine writers, says: "Other winemakers might jog or work out in the gym; Jeff Grier gets all the exercise he needs stepping up to the podium for wine industry awards." Try the Bush Vine Sauvignon Blanc, for which Grier was voted Winemaker of the Year in 1997, and you'll start to understand why it's become almost a cult wine. Then check out the range of Méthode Cap Classique sparkling wines—the Tradition Rosé Brut, for instance, is a delicate pink bubbly with soft, creamy overtones. This is one of the wineries that is, as far

> ### TASTING TIP
>
> One of the funny things about small, family-owned farms is that they won't charge you for a tasting if they don't feel like it. But it's at the owners' discretion, and it all depends on whether or not they wake up in a good or bad mood. If they like you, you could end up with a tasting, tour, and lunch at their home. So be at your best and most charming. But don't tell them we told you.

as possible, producing chemical-free wines. ✉*R101 and R304 (Old Paarl and Stellenbosch Rds.), Koelenhof* ☎*021/865–2002* ⊕*www.villiera.com* ✉*Tastings free* ☉ *Weekdays 8:30–5, Sat. 8:30–1; tours by appointment.*

Warwick. This Ratcliffe-family-run farm is all business. The tasting area is in a tiny cellar room cluttered with wine-making equipment, and the farm hubbub continues while you're tasting. Louis Nel, formerly from Neil Ellis estate, is the dynamic Warwick team's winemaker. The previous winemaker, Norma Ratcliffe, spent a couple of vintages in France perfecting traditional techniques, which have left their mark on Warwick's reds. The first female winemaker in South Africa, Norma pioneered the way for a new breed of young women who are now making their mark in the industry. Trilogy is a stylish and complex red made predominantly from cabernet sauvignon, with about 20% merlot and 20% cabernet franc. The 2004 Trilogy was voted one of the top five wines in the world by *Wine Spectator*—no mean feat! It retails at just over R100 a bottle, making it a bargain. Another great red, the Three Cape Ladies, was named after the indomitable Ratcliffe women. It's been described as a "feminine" blend of around 50% cabernet sauvignon, 20% merlot, and 30% pinotage. The cabernet franc is undoubtedly one of the best wines made from this varietal in the Winelands. There are no cellar tours. ✉*R44, between Stellenbosch and Klapmuts* ☎*021/884–4410* ⊕*www.warwickwine.com* ✉*Tastings R25* ☉ *Weekdays 10–5, weekends 10–4.*

WHERE TO STAY & EAT

★ $$–$$$$ ✗**Tokara.** At the top of the Helshoogte Pass with absolutely amazing views of the valley and mountains, Tokara is definitely a Winelands must-do. Chef Etienne Bonthuys is the acknowledged king of sauces—rich, slow reductions that you may be tempted to lick off your plate. His adventurous menu changes seasonally but could include such starters as chilled avocado soup with smoked salmon or warm oysters in a Cap Classique butter sauce (aah, therein lies his magic). For mains there are some unusual combinations that work brilliantly, such as grilled springbok served with a lobster sauce and mint oil, and the ostrich fillet accompanied by a mandarin-liqueur sauce and berries. The fantastic kids' menu doesn't list greasy fried chicken and fries, but rather miniburgers and calamari-and-prawn kebabs with pasta. ⊠ *Off R310, between Stellenbosch and Franschhoek* ☎ *021/808–5959* ⊟ *AE, DC, MC, V* ⊘ *Closed Sun. and Mon.*

★ $$–$$$ ✕ **Terroir.** The setting on a golf estate and wine farm is pretty, but it's the excellent food and service that really stand out here. Chef Michael Broughton does his best to honor the concept of *terroir* (from the French *terre* for "earth") and get as many ingredients from the surrounding area as possible. The menu changes regularly to make use of the fresh produce. Earthy and nutty cèpe mushrooms lightly fried in butter, garlic, and parsley make great starters. Main courses might include braised pork belly with ginger, juniper, and soy on smoked mash with braising juices and cabbage purée, or the duck-confit pancake with fig jam. Try the pear and Frangelica crème brûlée for dessert. Though the wine list is small, you can sample several different (and delicious) wines by the glass. Try the barrel-fermented chenin blanc, one of the estate's best-kept secrets. To avoid disappointment, be sure to book well in advance. ⊠ *Kleine Zalze Residential Golf Estate, R44, between Somerset West and Stellenbosch* ☎ *021/880–8167* ⌖ *Reservations essential* ⊟ *AE, DC, MC, V* ⊘ *Closed Mon. No dinner Sun.*

$–$$$ ✕ **Jonkershuis at Spier.** The culinary influences of traditional Cape cuisine are reflected in thoroughly modern food that you can savor under venerable oaks or inside the well-restored 18th-century homestead. To start, try the samosas of caramelized onion with feta and a coulis of sweet pepper, greens, and coriander. There's also a delicious local-venison carpaccio with arugula, Parmesan shavings, and raspberry dressing. Mains include masala chicken curry with all the trimmings, and beef *bobotie* (a light Malay curry of minced meat and dried fruit topped with a thin, baked, savory egg custard) with yellow rice and *sambals* (condiments). Look for the time-honored desserts of *malva* (a spongy, sweet pudding) with Amarula (a liqueur made from the fruit of the marula tree) sauce, or a delectable saffron poached-pear tart served with honey mascarpone. ⊠ *Spier Estate, Lynedoch Rd.* ☎ *021/809– 1172* ⊟ *AE, DC, MC, V.*

$–$$ ✕ **Olivello.** Be sure to book a table outside near the lily pond at this relaxed restaurant that serves Cape-meets-Mediterranean-style food in a fabulous country setting. Though the menu is fairly small, you'll still be hard-pressed to make a choice between such tasty options as lamb *tagine* (stew) served with preserved lemon, venison shanks slow-cooked in red wine and flavored with juniper, and beef fillet dressed with a cracked-peppercorn-and-brandy sauce. If all that sounds too rich for a hot summer's day, try the chicken salad with a lightly curried mayonnaise sauce, almonds, and apricots. On Sundays a Mediterranean buffet (R125) lets you choose from 20 tapas and four main courses. Little ones can have pasta with a homemade tomato sauce and grated cheese. ⊠ *Marianne Wine Farm, Valley Rd., off the R44* ☎ *021/875–5443* ⊟ *MC, V* ⊘ *Closed Mon. and Tues. No dinner.*

$$$–$$$$ ✕⊞**Lanzerac Manor.** The sense of history is almost tangible at this large working wine estate dating from 1692. The sheer beauty of the setting has not changed: a classic Cape Dutch manor house flanked by the rolling vineyards and mountains of the Jonkershoek Valley. The staff at this luxurious hotel and winery is friendly, and guest rooms are individually decorated with plush carpets, heavy drapes, and antiques. Some rooms have a floral theme; others are more masculine with animal-print cushions and bold stripes. You can eat casual alfresco meals at the Terrace Restaurant (weather permitting; $–$$$) or opt for fine dining at Ralph's ($$–$$$$), where chef Ralph van Pletzen pulls out all the stops. During summer a jazz band ups the tempo on the terrace. At Ralph's you can start with the "cappuccino" of porcini with white-truffle sauce and mushroom "biscotti." Main courses include Indian lamb curry and Karoo ostrich with fried banana, sweet potato, and other root vegetables. The legendary Lanzerac cheesecake is creamy, tangy, and utterly sublime. ⊠*Jonkershoek Rd., 1 km (½ mi) from Stellenbosch, Box 4, 7599* ☎*021/887–1132* ⊕*www.lanzerac.co.za* ⤳*43 rooms, 5 suites* ♿*In-room: safe, refrigerator, DVD (some), dial-up. In-hotel: 2 restaurants, room service, bars, pool, gym, spa, no elevator, laundry service, public Wi-Fi, airport shuttle, parking (no fee), no-smoking rooms* ☐*AE, DC, MC, V* �*♦OBP.*

$$–$$$ ⊞**Village at Spier.** The innovative design of these two-story buildings grouped around six courtyards, each with its own pool and leisure area, makes this complex feel like a Mediterranean village, albeit a very luxurious one. Rooms and suites are elegantly appointed, with Indonesian furniture, gas fireplaces, and stylish detail evident in the cotton throws and wide choice of pillows. The surrounding orchards and shade trees make the complex and walkways both verdant and private. ⊠*Spier Estate, Lynedoch Rd., 7600* ☎*021/809–1100* ⊕*www.spier. co.za* ⤳*155 rooms* ♿*In-room: safe, refrigerator. In-hotel: 4 restaurants, room service, bars, pool, no elevator, children's programs (ages 2–12), laundry service, public Wi-Fi, airport shuttle, parking (no fee), no-smoking rooms* ☐*AE, DC, MC, V* �*♦OBP.*

$$ ⊞**D'Ouwe Werf Country Inn.** A national monument, this attractive 1802 inn is thought to be the oldest in South Africa. From the street you enter the original living room, a beautiful space with a lofty beamed ceiling and elegant antiques. The hotel is divided into two parts: the old inn with luxury rooms on its Georgian second story and a new wing with more standard rooms. All luxury rooms are furnished with antiques, including four-poster beds, draped sash windows, and bronze bathroom fittings. The standard rooms have reproductions only. A lovely garden in a brick courtyard shaded by trellised vines is open for meals and drinks throughout the day. ⊠*30 Church St., 7600* ☎*021/887–4608* ⊕*www.ouwewerf.com* ⤳*32 rooms* ♿*In-room: safe, refrigerator, Wi-Fi. In-hotel: restaurant, room service, pool, bicycles, no elevator, laundry service, public Wi-Fi, parking (no fee), no-smoking rooms* ☐*AE, DC, MC, V* ⑩*♦OBP.*

¢   ⊞**Stumble Inn Backpackers Lodge.** Stellenbosch's original backpackers' lodging is within easy walking distance of most major town sights and is a great place to stay if you're traveling on a limited budget. You can choose from simple double rooms, dorm beds, and even limited camping facilities in the gardens. Other amenities include shared kitchen facilities and an on-site travel agent. The folks here will even arrange budget-minded packages that include wine tours and cheese tastings. ⊠*12 Market St., 7600* ☎*021/887–4049* ⊕*www.jump.to/stumble* ⤶*7 rooms, 6 dormitories* ⚫*In-room: no a/c, no phone, no TV. Inhotel: bar, pool, laundry service, public Internet, parking (no fee), some pets allowed* ⊟*AE, DC, MC, V.*

NIGHTLIFE & THE ARTS

NIGHTLIFE The **Dorp Street Theatre Café** (⊠*59 Dorp St.* ☎*021/886–6107*), usually open Tuesday–Saturday, always has a great lineup of local musicians. Take a stroll into the Church Street part of town, where shops stay open late and bars and cafés spill onto the streets. A good place to start, the **Wijnhuis** (⊠*Church and Andringa Sts.* ☎*021/887–5844*) quickly fills up with trendy locals wanting to unwind.

THE ARTS Each summer performances ranging from African jazz to opera to bal-
★ let are staged at the **Oude Libertas Amphitheatre** (⊠*Oude Libertas St.*), a delightful open-air venue across from and run and owned by Distell. For bookings contact **Computicket** (☎*083/909–0909*). The **Spier Arts Summer Festival** (⊠*Spier Estate, R310* ☎*021/809–1158*) runs from mid-November to mid-March and usually includes opera, classical music, and a host of other performances.

SPORTS & THE OUTDOORS

GOLF **Stellenbosch Golf Club** (⊠ *Strand Rd.* ☎*021/880–0103*) has long tree-lined fairways that will pose a problem if you don't hit the ball straight. Greens fees are R350 for 18 holes. A caddy costs R100, club rental R200, and a golf cart R200.

HORSEBACK **Spier Equestrian Centre** (⊠*Spier Estate, R310* ☎*021/881–3683 or*
RIDING *083/627–2282*) offers a gentle amble or a quick canter through the vineyards (R200 one hour, R250 two hours). If you don't fancy getting into a saddle, you can go on a horse-drawn wagon ride (R150 per person for an hour).

EN From Thelema the **R310** runs down into the fruit orchards and vines
ROUTE that mark the beginning of the Franschhoek Valley. The R310 dead ends at the R45. To the left is Paarl, to the right Franschhoek.

FRANSCHHOEK

★ ❸ *22 km (14 mi) northeast of Stellenbosch.*

Franschhoek (French Corner) takes its name from its first white settlers, French Huguenots who fled to the Cape to escape Catholic persecution in France in the late 1600s. By the early 18th century about 200 Huguenots had settled in the Cape; today their descendants—with names like de Villiers, Malan, and Joubert—number in the tens of thousands. With their experience in French vineyards, the early Huguenots were instrumental in nurturing a wine-making culture in South Africa.

Franschhoek is the most spectacular of the three wine centers, a long valley encircled by towering mountain ranges and fed by a single road that runs through town. As spectacular as the valley is today, it must have been even more so in the 17th century, when it teemed with game. In calving season herds of elephants would migrate to the valley via the precipitous Franschhoek Mountains. The last wild elephant in the valley died in the 1930s. Some leopards still survive high in the mountains, but you won't see them.

What you will see today is an increasingly upscale village with beautifully renovated cottages and gorgeous gardens. Although it can get very busy during the summer season, you will always be able to find a quiet spot with a view of the mountains, roses, and swathes of lavender, which do well here. Franschhoek has developed into something of a culinary mecca, with some of the country's best restaurants and cafés lining the pretty main street. In October the village hosts a music festival featuring many local and visiting artists. The town is more touristy than agrarian, although you will see the occasional wine farmer steaming into town with his dogs on the back of his *bakkie* (pickup truck), looking for tractor tires or other essentials. It's a great place for lunch or for a couple of days, as there are excellent small hotels and guesthouses to choose from.

The **Huguenot Monument** stands at the end of the main road through Franschhoek. It was built in 1948 to commemorate the contribution of the Huguenots to South Africa's development. The three arches symbolize the Holy Trinity, the sun and cross form the Huguenots' emblem, and the female figure in front represents Freedom of Conscience. ⊠ *Lambrecht and Huguenot Sts.* ☏ *No phone (contact Huguenot Memorial Museum at 021/876–2532)* ⊡ *R5* ⊙ *Daily 9–5.*

To trace the history of the Huguenot community here, visit the **Huguenot Memorial Museum.** Its main building is modeled after the Saasveld house, built in 1791 by renowned Cape architect Louis Thibault in Cape Town. Wall displays profile some of the early Huguenot families. Exhibits also focus on other aspects of the region's history, such as the development of Cape Dutch architecture and the relationship of the Huguenots with the Dutch East India Company. Displays in the annex cover the culture and life of the Khoekhoen, or Khoikhoi, once derogatorily known as Hottentots, as well as the role of slaves and local laborers in the development of the Franschhoek Valley. ⊠ *Lambrecht St.* ☏ *021/876–2532* ⊡ *R5* ⊙ *Mon.–Sat. 9–5, Sun. 2–5.*

WINERIES

It should come as no surprise that the Franschhoek Valley produces excellent wines. After all, the original French settlers brought with them an extensive and intimate understanding of viticulture. Some of the country's oldest estates nestle at the base of the spectacular Groot Drakenstein mountains, and the wine farmers here are constantly trying to top themselves.

Boschendal. With a history that dates back three centuries, this lovely estate is one of the Cape's major attractions. You can easily spend half

CLOSE UP

Franschhoek Wine Route

Along R310. The drive out of Stellenbosch up the Helshoogte Pass is spectacular. In winter you'll more than likely find snow on the mountain peaks; in summer, once you top the pass you enter a verdant valley of fruit trees and ordered vineyards. Be sure to stop in at **Hillcrest Berry Farm** (✉ *R310, Banhoek Valley* ☎ *021/885–1629*) for delicious tea and scones. Then head to **Boschendal,** one of the oldest and most established estates in the country.

Along R45. There are well more than 20 estates to choose from here, and there's something for everyone—from enormous farms covering hundreds of acres to smaller, boutique vineyards producing just a few hundred bottles each year. If you turn right on R45 from the R310, **L'Ormarins** is one of the first wine farms you'll come to (off the R45 through a tunnel of trees). It's a well-established estate that's undergoing some interesting changes. Just outside town, **La Motte** is a sister farm to L'Ormarins. Closer to town the estates come thick and fast. Amid this flurry—Môreson (up the aptly named Happy Valley Road), Rickety Bridge, Agusta, Chamonix, and Dieu Donne—is **Mont Rochelle,** the only fully black-owned vineyard in South Africa. Outside town and up the Franschhoek Pass toward Villiersdorp, the fabulous **Cabrière,** at Haute Cabrière, is built into the mountain. **La Petite Ferme** is worth phoning ahead for (you can't just pop in).

If you turn left on the R45 from the R310, you'll find more outstanding wine farms, including **Plaisir de Merle,** which makes a distinctive cabernet and sauvignon blanc.

2

---

a day here. Cradled between the Simonsberg and Groot Drakenstein mountains at the base of Helshoogte Pass, the farm—originally called Bossendaal—was originally granted to Jean le Long, one of the first French Huguenot settlers in the late 17th century.

Boschendal runs one of the most pleasant wine tastings in the region: you can sit inside at the Taphuis, a Cape Dutch *langhuis* (longhouse) and the oldest building on the estate, or outside at wrought-iron tables under a spreading oak. In 1981 Boschendal was the first to pioneer a Cape blanc de noir, a pink wine made in a white-wine style from black grapes. The Boschendal Blanc de Noir remains the best-selling wine of this style. Of the farm's extensive range of wines, a recent addition is the Cecil John Shiraz 2003, named after Cecil John Rhodes, the late-19th-century Cape prime minister who owned Rhodes Fruit Farms, of which Boschendal was once a part. This is a complex wine that's going to improve over time. From the Taphuis it's a two-minute drive through vines and fruit trees to the main estate complex. The excellent Boschendal Restaurant serves

DINING UNDER THE STARS

What could be more romantic than dining under the stars? During the summer months, Boschendal hosts a formal full-moon dinner under the oak trees to the accompaniment of a string quartet. Doesn't it sound lovely? Make sure you call for a reservation.

a buffet of Cape specialties, Le Café serves light meals at tables under the oaks leading to the manor house, and Le Pique Nique (October–May) provides picnic baskets that you can enjoy on the lawns. Reservations are essential for the restaurant and picnic services. The estate is wheelchair-friendly. ⊠ *R310, between Franschhoek and Stellenbosch, Groot Drakenstein* ☎ *021/870–4210 or 021/870–4211 for winery, 021/870–4274 for restaurants* ⊕ *www.boschendal.co.za* 🍷 *Tastings R15* ⊙ *Daily 10–6:30.*

Cabrière. Built in 1994 on the lower slopes of the Franschhoek Mountains, Cabrière is the brainchild of Achim von Arnim, one of the Cape's most colorful winemakers. To avoid scarring the mountain, the complex, which includes the fine Haute Cabrière restaurant, hunkers into the hillside. There are five Cap Classique sparkling wines under the Pierre Jordan label, and the fruity, mouth-filling Haute Cabrière pinot noir is consistently one of the best. Also delicious is the chardonnay-pinot noir blend, an ideal, extremely quaffable wine to enjoy at lunchtime. Take a Saturday-morning cellar tour with von Arnim, and watch him perform his trademark display of *sabrage*—the dramatic decapitation of a bottle of bubbly with a saber. ⊠ *R45* ☎ *021/876–2630* ⊕ *www.cabriere.co.za* 🍷 *Tastings and cellar tour R30* ⊙ *Weekdays 9–4:30, Sat. 11–3:30; tours Sat. at 11.*

La Motte Estate. This estate is owned by a branch of the same Rupert family that owns L'Ormarins, and is a partner in Rupert & Rothschild, a vineyard closer to Paarl. The elegant and rather formal tasting room, with its long marble-top table at which you sample the wines, looks into the cellars through a wall of smoked glass. The 2004 La Motte Shiraz, which needs about five years to reach its peak, is one of the biggest and boldest you'll taste of this variety, full of rich flavors. The 2004 Pierneef Collection Shiraz-Viognier is being snapped up for its whiffs of dark chocolate, smoked beef, black cherry, and blackberry. This wine is named in honor of the famous South African artist J.H. Pierneef, who was well known for his stunning landscapes from the first half of the 20th century. There are no cellar tours. ⊠ *R45 (Huguenot Rd.)* ☎ *021/876–3119* ⊕ *www.la-motte.com* 🍷 *Tastings R20* ⊙ *Weekdays 9–4:30, Sat. 10–3.*

La Petite Ferme. You'll have to phone ahead to arrange a tasting here, but it's worth it, because then you'll know what to have with your lunch if you decide to dine here. True to its name, this is a small, family-run estate producing just enough wine for the restaurant and to keep its faithful regular customers happy. Try the chardonnay. ⊠ *R45 (Franschhoek Pass Rd.)* ☎ *021/876–3016* ⊙ *Sales daily noon–4; tastings and tours by appointment at 11.*

L'Ormarins. Dating from 1811, the archetypal Cape Dutch manor house is festooned with flowers and framed by majestic peaks. At this writing, the farm was undergoing a major overhaul, so it will likely take a while for things to settle. But what is abundantly clear is the attention to detail at every turn. Two state-of-the-art cellars launched in 2007 are part of the farm's long-term plans to produce exceptional wines. Chat

2

with the winemakers and they'll tell you that the farm is introducing revolutionary farming practices, from transporting the grapes to the cellar in cool trucks to hand-sorting and -stemming. They're hoping to make full-bodied, bold wines that push the boundaries in every possible way. Keep an eye on this winery. In the meantime, the Terra del Capo range is going strong; the sangiovese is a brilliant, light drinking wine, and the pinot grigio is always a pleasure. ⊠*R45 (Franschhoek Rd.), Groot Drakenstein* ☎*021/874–9000* ⊕*www.lormarins.com* ✉*Tastings R20* ⊗*Weekdays 9–4:30, Sat. 10–3.*

Mont Rochelle. This is the only fully black-owned vineyard in the country. Owner Miko Rwayitare has injected new enthusiasm into the farm, which he bought in 2001, renovating the estate and replanting the vineyards. The barrel-fermented chardonnay has made everybody sit up and take notice; it sells out very quickly. The syrah is also noteworthy, and the sauvignon blanc reserve from 2006 is another winner. A swank hotel and the Mange Tout restaurant are also on-site. ⊠*Dassenberg Rd.* ☎*021/876–3000* ⊕*www.montrochelle.co.za* ✉*Tastings R15; cellar tour R10* ⊗*Daily 10–6; cellar tours weekdays at 11, 12:30, and 3.*

Plaisir de Merle. The name means "Pleasure of the Blackbird" and has its origins with the original French owners of the farm. This huge estate (2,500 acres) is the showpiece of Distell, a huge wine and spirit producer. With its innovative architecture and conservation area, it truly feels different from the ubiquitous "oak and gable" wineries that you see all over the Cape. But forget all the frills—it really is about the wine. Don't miss the cabernet franc. If you can get your hands on the exceptional 2003 vintage, you're in luck, but the 2004 is also good. The 2006 sauvignon blanc is brilliant—crisp, with plenty of hints of green asparagus. ⊠*R45, Simondium* ☎*021/874–1071 or 021/874–1072* ⊕*www.plaisirdemerle.co.za* ✉*Tastings R20; cellar tour with tastings R30* ⊗*Apr.–Oct., weekdays 9–5, Sat. 10–2; Nov.–Mar., weekdays 9–5, Sat. 10–4; cellar tours by appointment.*

WHERE TO STAY & EAT

$$$$ ✕**Boschendal Restaurant.** Reserve well in advance for the buffet lunch here at one of the Cape's most beautiful and historic wineries. A wide selection of soups, quiches, and pâtés prefaces a bewildering array of cold and hot main dishes, including pickled fish, roasts, and imaginative salads; traditional Cape dishes are well prepared. End with an excellent sampling of South African cheeses and preserves or a quintessentially Cape dessert such as malva pudding. Unobtrusive, professional, but friendly service complements the bounty, priced at R195 a head. ⊠*R310, between Franschhoek and Stellenbosch, Groot Drakenstein* ☎*021/870–4274* ⌂*Reservations essential* ▤*AE, DC, MC, V* ⊗*No dinner.*

$–$$$$ ✕**Reuben's.** Reuben Riffel is one of a small band of talented homegrown chefs who are breaking culinary rules with passion, and, more important, delectable results. Riffel is flexing his wings and "cooking food he would like to eat." And so, it seems, people would like to eat along with him. Choose from two menus—classic or contemporary—and

Fodor'sChoice
★

then have an even harder time choosing a meal. Do you opt for the crispy roast duck with noodles and an Asian-inspired sauce, or peppered rib-eye steak with a béarnaise sauce and lots of trimmings? The decor is minimalist but welcoming, with a roaring fire in winter, and the service impeccable. The waiters know their wine and are happy to make menu recommendations. Have a drink at the trendy bar, made from an airplane wing. ⊠ *19 Huguenot Rd., 7690* ☎ *021/876–3772* ⚕ *Reservations essential* ☰ *AE, DC, MC, V.*

★ ¢–$$$ ✕ **Haute Cabrière.** Try to reserve a window table for views across the vine-clad valley at this restaurant atop a working winery built into the mountainside. The mix-and-match menu is intended to complement the estate wines maturing in the cellar beneath you. You can opt for half or full portions of renowned chef Matthew Gordon's mouthwatering seasonal fare. Selections might include fresh mussels in white wine, cream, and garlic; a warm salad of marinated quail, foie gras, and fresh Japanese mushroom with ratafia vinaigrette; or Karoo lamb loin with lamb-shank ravioli, creamed spinach, and an Italian tomato sauce. Local Belgian-trained chocolatiers contribute to the luscious selection of desserts. ⊠ *Franschhoek Pass Rd. (R45)* ☎ *021/876–3688* ⚕ *Reservations essential* ☰ *AE, DC, MC, V.*

¢–$$ ✕ **Delicious!** If you're looking for a light lunch or quick snack, make for this fantastic deli on Franschhoek's main drag; find a spot on the sofas on the veranda and watch the world go by while you sip a cappuccino. The sticky buns are irresistible, as is the toasted *tremazzini* (pita-like bread) filled with smoked salmon, cream cheese, and avocado. This place has become so popular that it now stays open Wednesday evenings (reservations essential), when chef Neil Jewell comes to cook. His menu changes each week, but starters might include braised Italian plum tomatoes with eggplant ravioli and green-olive tapenade, or beech-smoked salmon with avocado cheesecake cream with a seaweed-and-lime dressing. Entrée options are porcini-dusted wildebeest loin with a smoked-beetroot custard, or pistachio-oil poached trout with roasted prawn, asparagus, and lemongrass stir-fry. In a word—delicious! ⊠ *Moreson Wine Farm, Main Rd.* ☎ *021/876–4004* ☰ *AE, DC, MC, V* ☉ *No dinner Thurs.–Tues.*

¢–$$ ✕ **Topsi & Company.** Chef Topsi Venter, doyenne of the Cape culinary scene, is as renowned as a raconteur as she is for her innovative country fare. The decor is simple and rustic, and local art lines the white walls. Blackboard menus change daily, and only fresh, local ingredients are used. Venter concentrates on traditional and indigenous Cape food, saying, "If somebody arrives with goat, we'll do goat. If they come with a zebra, then we'll do zebra." The food is not that intimidating, however. The beetroot with goat cheese and a rich pinotage syrup is a good start before you move on to the kudu fillet with pine-ring mushrooms. Mussel bobotie is an innovative take on the traditional South African dish, usually made with minced beef. The homemade ice cream is made from prickly pears, fresh figs, or tomatoes, depending on what's in season, and the old-fashioned apple-almond tart is sublime. In this valley of wonderful wines it's great to be able to BYOB. ⊠ *7*

Reservoir St. ☎021/876–2952 ⚐*Reservations essential* ⊟*AE, DC, MC, V* ⊘*Closed Tues.*

$$$$ ✕🔲 **Le Quartier Français.** Part of the Relais & Châteaux group, this
Fodor'sChoice classy guesthouse exuding privacy and peace is a Winelands favorite.
★ Rooms in two-story whitewashed cottages face a pool deck and central garden exploding with flowers. Decor is vibrant, with rustic furniture, sponge-painted walls, colorful drapes, and small fireplaces. Upstairs rooms have timber beams and mountain views, and suites have private pools. So which awards hasn't the restaurant won? None, by the looks of it, but chef Margo Janse and her team aren't resting on their laurels. You can eat at the Tasting Room, a formal restaurant, or the relaxed iCi ($–$$). Either way you won't likely be disappointed—unless you don't make reservations. Favorites from the iCi menu include the lamb burger with marinated tomatoes, pickled cucumber, and avocado, and the wild-mushroom-and-preserved-lemon risotto. The Tasting Room ($$$$; no dinner Sunday) offers four-course meals for R310 and six courses for R390. This is foodie territory—the menu is sprinkled with words like *ballotine* and *rillette,* but just ignore the complicated terminology and enjoy the creations on your plate. These could include inventive dishes like a roulade of sugar-cured tuna, salmon, and Alaskan snow crab; prawn tartare with horseradish cream; or crisp salmon trout with tomatoes, anchovy-and-basil terrine, and crushed potatoes. As you enter the boldly colored dining room, look for the exotic candelabras, made by iThemba, an organization providing employment for HIV-positive women. ⊠*16 Huguenot Rd., Box 237, 7690* ☎*021/876–2248 or 021/876–2151* ⊕*www.lequartier.co.za* 🛏*15 rooms, 2 suites* ⚒*In-hotel: 2 restaurants, bar, pool* ⊟*AE, DC, MC, V.*

$ 🔲 **Le Ballon Rouge.** If you fancy being in the heart of the village, Le Ballon Rouge makes a good base. Here you're just a five-minute walk from galleries, restaurants, and the general buzz. The guesthouse—in a restored 1904 Victorian homestead—is both welcoming and relaxing. The rooms are individually decorated in a pleasing mix of traditional and contemporary; a brass bedstead sits in one room, a modern four-poster in another. The Owner's Suite, which can be yours despite the name, has a private deck and Jacuzzi with a mountain view—just the thing for a starry evening with a glass of Franschhoek's best. ⊠*7 Reservoir St., Box 156, 7690* ☎*021/876–2651* ⊕*www.ballonrouge. co.za* 🛏*8 rooms, 2 suites* ⚒*In-room: no a/c (some), no phone (some), refrigerator (some). In-hotel: room service (by request), bar, pool, no elevator, laundry service, public Internet, airport shuttle, parking (no fee), no kids under 12, no-smoking rooms* ⊟*AE, DC, MC, V* ⊕*CP.*

$ 🔲 **Résidence Klein Oliphants Hoek.** Originally built as the home of a British missionary, this lovingly restored guesthouse also once served as a school. Now its rooms are decorated with rich fabrics and luxurious finishes. One has its own plunge pool, and others have generous fireplaces. On arrival, you're automatically booked in at Bouillabaisse, the sister seafood restaurant a five-minute stroll away, but you're welcome to eat anywhere in Franschhoek, the foodies' paradise. ⊠*14 Akademie St., Box 470, 7690* ☎*021/876–2566* ⊕*www.kleinoliphantshoek.com* 🛏*8 rooms* ⚒*In-room: no phone, safe, refrigerator (some), DVD. In-*

hotel: restaurant, room service, bar, pool, laundry service, public Internet, parking (no fee), no-smoking rooms ▭*AE, DC, MC, V* ⦿*I BP.*

PAARL

❹ *21 km (13 mi) northwest of Franschhoek.*

Paarl takes its name from the granite domes of Paarl Mountain, which looms above the town—*paarl* is Dutch for "pearl." The first farmers settled here in 1687, two years after the founding of Stellenbosch. The town has its fair share of historic homes and estates, but it lacks the charm of its distinguished neighbor simply because it's so spread out. Main Street, the town's oak-lined thoroughfare, extends some 11 km (7 mi) along the western bank of the Berg River. You can gain a good sense of the town's history on a drive along this lovely street.

Main Street North doglegs to the right at Lady Grey Street before continuing as Main Street South. On your left, the **Paarl Museum,** formerly the Oude Pastorie, occupies a gorgeous Cape Dutch home built as a parsonage in 1787. In fact, the building itself is of more interest than the collection, which includes odds and ends donated by local families, including silver, glass, and kitchen utensils. ✉*303 Main St.* ☎*021/872–2651* 🎟*R5* ⊙ *Weekdays 10–5, Sat. 9–1.*

It was from the Gideon Malherbe House, now the **Afrikaanse Taalmuseum** *(Afrikaans Language Museum),* that the Society of True Afrikaners launched its campaign in 1875 to gain widespread acceptance for Afrikaans, hitherto considered a sort of inferior kitchen Dutch. However, the museum may be of only limited interest to you because the displays are entirely in Afrikaans. To get here from the Paarl Museum, walk about 200 yards along Pastorie Street. ✉*11 Pastorie St.* ☎*021/872–3441* 🎟*R10* ⊙ *Weekdays 9–4, Sat. 9–1.*

Zeederberg Square is a grassy park bordered by some excellent examples of Cape Dutch, Georgian, and Victorian homes. It's on Main Street past the Paarl Tourism Bureau.

The old **Dutch Reformed Church,** a little farther down Main Street from Zeederberg Square on the left, is a thatch building dating from 1805. The cemetery contains the tombstones of the Malherbe family, which was instrumental in the campaign to gain official recognition for Afrikaans. The church is still active, and you can peek inside.

Like the Voortrekker Monument in Pretoria, the concrete **Afrikaanse Taalmonument** *(Afrikaans Language Monument),* set high on a hill overlooking Paarl, holds a special place in the hearts of Afrikaners, who struggled for years to gain acceptance for their language alongside English. The rising curve of the main pillar is supposed to represent the growth and potential of Afrikaans. When it was erected in 1973, the monument was as much a gesture of political victory as a paean to the Afrikaans language. Ironically, it may become the language's memorial. Under the new South Africa, Afrikaans has become just one of 11 official languages and is gradually losing its dominance, although

Paarl Wine Route

Wineries here are spread far apart, so you might want to select only a couple or take a whole day to taste at leisure. Start in Paarl, home to the impressive **KWV International,** with cellars covering 55 acres and a wide selection of wines.

Along R301/303. On its way to Franschhoek, the R301/303 runs past **Avondale Wine,** a relatively new farm with a state-of-the-art cellar, a gorgeous rose garden, and excellent wines.

Along WR1 between R44 and R45. On your way from Franschhoek to Paarl, take a quick detour down the WR1 (Simondium Road) to **Backsberg** and, a bit farther, **Glen Carlou.** Backsberg has more going on than Glen Carlou, but they both have wines that

are worth tasting and buying. Continue on, and turn right on the R44. At a four-way stop, turn right onto the R101 and cross over the N1. Follow the goat signs to Suid Agter Paarl Road and Fairview.

Along Suid and Noord Agter Paarl roads. Fairview is as famous for its goats and cheese as it is for its wines. Leave yourself plenty of time here. From Fairview, turn right onto the Suid Agter Paarl Road and make your way to **Landskroon,** known for full-bodied reds. Turn right on the R44 and, after about 10 km (6 mi), right onto the WR8 (Noord Agter Paarl Road), and then right again to **Rhebokskloof Private Cellar.** If you continue on the R44 toward Wellington, you'll pass **Nelson's Creek** (also known as Nelson's Wine Estate) on your left.

attempts are being made to ensure that the rich culture isn't lost. The view from the top of the hill is incredible, taking in Table Mountain, False Bay, Paarl Valley, and the various mountain ranges of the Winelands. You can buy a picnic basket at the monument's restaurant and find a pretty spot to enjoy the wonderful view; a basket costs around R60 for two people and is crammed with cold meats, salad, cheese, breads, fresh fruit, and something sweet. A short, paved walking trail leads around the hillside past impressive fynbos specimens, particularly proteas. After the N1 bridge, a sign on your right points the way to the monument. ⊠ *Afrikaanse Taalmonument Rd.* ☎ *021/863–4809* 🖃 *R10* 🕙 *Daily 8–5 (the monument sometimes stays open later in summer, but this varies).*

Halfway down the hill from the Afrikaans Language Monument is a turnoff onto a dirt road and a sign for the Paarl Mountain Nature Reserve. The dirt road is **Jan Phillips Mountain Drive,** which runs 11 km (7 mi) along the mountainside, offering tremendous views over the valley. Along the way it passes the **Mill Water Wildflower Garden** and the starting points for several trails, including hikes up to the great granite domes of Paarl Mountain. The dirt road rejoins Main Street at the far end of Paarl.

WINERIES

Avondale Wine. Although the farm was established as early as 1693, current owners Johnny and Ginny Grieve have done some serious reorganizing in the vineyards and built a state-of-the-art cellar, which is dug into a dry river bed. Avondale started producing wines only in 1999, making it one of the newer kids on the block. No matter. The winery has hit the ground running, and its wines are winning one award after another. The reds are especially good, and the intense Paarl summers result in full-bodied grapes that deliver knockout flavors. Be sure to try the 2002 Les Pleurs Syrah and the 2000 merlot in the same range. Both are delicious. The Grieves are also farming as biodynamically as possible, and Avondale is now registered as biodiversity-compliant by both South African and Dutch authorities. Many farms have absent owners, but the Grieve family takes a hands-on approach here. The casually dressed guy behind the wine-tasting counter might, in fact, be the owner. Once you've done your wine tasting and buying, be sure to visit Ginny's exquisite rose garden. ✉ *Lustigan Rd., off R301* ☎ *021/863–1976* ⊕ *www.avondalewine.co.za* 🍷 *Tastings R15* ⊙ *Mon.–Sat. 10–4; cellar tours by appointment.*

Backsberg. Framed by the mountains of the Simonsberg, this lovely estate is run by the Back family, well known for producing great wines of good value. Backsberg has a comprehensive range of red and white wines and a very fine brandy made from chenin blanc. Among the wines to look out for are the 2003 Babylons Toren Chardonnay, the 2003 Babylons Toren red blend, and the organic merlot. It also produces kosher wines and an organic unwooded chardonnay that has an interesting earthiness to it. The restaurant does a lamb spit every lunch, so you can taste some excellent wines before digging in to a typical South African meal. The estate also has self-guided cellar tours and the largest living maze in South Africa. Don't enter it after drinking too much wine; you might never come out! Concerned about climate change and the environment, the Back family has put measures in place to reduce the farm's carbon footprint. They've done a good job, and Backsberg is the first carbon-neutral wine estate in South Africa. Here's hoping others will soon follow suit. ✉ *WR1 (Simondium Rd.), between R44 and R45* ☎ *021/875–5141* ⊕ *www.backsberg.co.za* 🍷 *Tastings R10; cellar tours by appointment* ⊙ *Weekdays 8:30–5, Sat. 9:30–4:30, Sun. 10:30–4:30.*

☺ **Fairview.** This is one of the few wineries that are good for families. Children get a kick out of seeing peacocks roaming the grounds and goats clambering up a spiral staircase into a goat tower. In fact, Fairview produces a superb line of goat cheeses and olive oil, all of which you can taste. But don't let Fairview's sideshows color your judgment about the wines. Charles Back, a member of the family that runs Backsberg, is one of the most successful and innovative winemakers in the Cape, and the estate's wines are top-drawer and often surprising. Back does not stick to the tried-and-true Cape varietals. The zinfandel-cinsaut blend is quite unusual, as is the shiraz-mourvèdre-viognier blend. The winery also makes creative use of the farm's many Rhône varieties. Perhaps it's just because the pun was irresistible, but (as claimed by the label) goats are sent into the vineyard to personally select grapes for the Goats-do-Roam, which is indeed like a young Côtes du Rhône (infuriating French winemakers). Likewise, the very popular Goat-

Roti sounds awfully like Côte-Rôtie. If you care to linger, you can have a light meal and freshly baked bread at the Goatshed restaurant. ⊠ *WR3, off R101 (Suid-Agter-Paarl Rd.)* ☎ *021/863–2450* ⊕ *www. fairview.co.za* ✉ *Wine/cheese tastings: standard tasting R15, master tasting (with flagship wines) R30* ⊘ *Weekdays 8:30–5, Sat. 8:30–4, Sun. 9:30–4; cellar tours by appointment.*

Glen Carlou. What comes out of Glen Carlou is rather special. The chardonnay reserve is exceptional, the shiraz is noteworthy, and the Gravel Quarry Cabernet is making its mark. The cellar has undergone a major overhaul, and an art gallery that displays contemporary art has been added. There's also a Zen garden to relax in after you've stocked up on some seriously good wines. ⊠ *WR1 (Simondium Rd.), between R44 and R45, Klapmuts* ☎ *021/875–5528* ⊕ *www.glencarlou.co.za* ✉ *Tastings R15* ⊘ *Weekdays 8:45–4:45, weekends 10–3.*

KWV. Short for Ko-operatieve Wijnbouwers Vereniging (Cooperative Winegrowers' Association), KWV used to regulate and control the Cape wine industry for decades. This is no longer the case, and KWV is seeking to redefine itself as a top wine and spirit producer. Its brandies, sherries, and fortified dessert wines regularly garner gold medals, and it produces an enormous selection of excellent wines. KWV's cellars are some of the largest in the world, covering around 55 acres, and its cellar tours are the most popular and crowded in the Winelands. Among the highlights is the famous Cathedral Cellar, with a barrel-vaulted ceiling and giant vats carved with scenes from the history of Cape wine making. In an adjoining cellar you can see the five largest vats in the world under one roof. The tour begins with a short audiovisual presentation and ends with a tasting of some of KWV's products. ⊠ *André du Toit Bldg., Kohler St.* ☎ *021/807–3007* ⊕ *www.kwv.co.za* ✉ *Tastings R15; cellar tour with tastings R22* ⊘ *Mon.–Sat. 9–4:30; English tours at 10, 10:30, and 2:15.*

Landskroon. Landskroon means "crown of the land" in Afrikaans, and this venerable estate, run by the ninth generation of the de Villiers family, produces a lovely cabernet sauvignon—with hints of vanilla and oak—that's up there with the best. Look out for the premium-range 2002 Paul de Villiers Cabernet Sauvignon and the Landskroon 2005 Shiraz. For a little something to sip after a long, leisurely dinner, try the Murio Muscat Jerepico—a rich, velvety fortified wine with a fresh finish. They also produce an excellent port made from tinta barocca, tinta roriz, souzao, and touriga nacionale. ⊠ *Suid Agter Paarl Rd., off R44, Suider Paarl* ☎ *021/863–1039* ⊕ *www.landskroonwines.com* ✉ *Tastings free (groups of more than 10 will pay a fee)* ⊘ *Weekdays 8:30–5, Sat. 9–1.*

Nelson's Creek *(Nelson Wine Estate).* A huge geological fault runs through this wonderful estate and is partly responsible for the multiple soil types and microclimates here. But that's just the physical background. In 1997 owner Alan Nelson decided that land redistribution was a good idea, so he gave 24 acres of prime vineyard to the estate's farmworkers to inaugurate the New Beginnings program. From the proceeds of their first vintage, they bought another 20 acres. Matheus Thabo, who started off as a part-time gardener, is now producing three pretty respectable wines—two reds (a pinotage and a cabernet sauvignon) and a chardonnay. Nelson's Creek produces some fantastic reds, too. The 2002 Nelson Estate cabernet sauvignon–merlot blend is a big, ripe wine with hints of cassis and cigar box. The pinotage is also full-bodied, as is the chardonnay. The best buy is probably the inexpensive, very drinkable Albenet, a blend of merlot, ruby cabernet, and cabernet sauvignon. This is also a great place for a picnic or walk. ✉ *R44, Agter Paarl* ☎ *021/869-8453* ⊕ *www.nelsonscreek.co.za* ☜ *Tastings free; cellar tour with tastings R25* ⊙ *Weekdays 8–5, Sat. 9–2; cellar tours by appointment.*

Rhebokskloof Private Cellar. This winery sits at the head of a shallow valley, backed by hillsides covered with vines and fynbos. It's a lovely place for lunch on a sunny day, and you can also take horseback rides through the vineyards. The Victorian Restaurant serves à la carte meals and teas on an oak-shaded terrace overlooking the gardens and mountains; in inclement weather meals are served in the Cape Dutch Restaurant, which also has a Sunday buffet lunch. The Chardonnay Sur Lie 2005 is wonderful, with a lovely balance and fruity, toasty overtones, but the pick of the bunch has to be the 2000 Rhebokskloof Cabernet Sauvignon, which has scooped a whole array of awards. The estate has a number of different wine tastings; the gourmet tasting includes a cellar tour and pairs six dishes with six wines for around R150 per person. ✉ *WR8* ☎ *021/869-8386* ⊕ *www.rhebokskloof.co.za* ☜ *Tastings R15, cheese-and-wine tastings R30, formal tastings R45, gourmet tastings R150* ⊙ *Daily 9–5.*

WHERE TO STAY & EAT

$$$$ ✕ **Roggeland.** For an unforgettable Cape experience, make a beeline for this glorious Cape Dutch manor house on a farm outside Paarl. Meals are long, languid rituals, whether it's an alfresco lunch in the garden or a four-course dinner in the 18th-century dining room. The menu changes daily, but you might start with sweet-corn soup with cilantro cream followed by trout fillet on handmade pasta with a basil sabayon. A main course of lamb loin comes teamed with roasted butternut and shallots in muscadel, with an indigenous malva pudding with a *rooibos*-tea mousse as the finale. This feast is priced at R160 and includes a different wine with each course. ✉ *Roggeland Rd., North Paarl* ☎ *021/868-2501* ⚲ *Reservations essential* ▭ *AE, DC, MC, V.*

$$$–$$$$ ✕ **Bosman's.** Set amid the heady opulence of the Grande Roche hotel,
Fodor'sChoice this elegant restaurant and Relais & Châteaux member ranks as one
★ of the country's finest. The level of service is extraordinary, commensurate with that of the finest European restaurants. Once you overcome the hurdle of which menu to choose—seafood, tasting (8–12 dishes), Cape specialties, vegetarian, epicurean, or à la carte—you start with a complimentary *amuse-bouche* (literally, something to entertain your palate). A first course of baked goat's-cheese dumplings served with a Mediterranean vegetable salad and smoked-tomato coulis could precede a main course of springbok with mushroom-apple brioche and

port-wine jus. ⊠*Grande Roche, Plantasie St., 7622* ☎*021/863–5100* ▤*AE, DC, MC, V* ⊙*Closed mid-May–July.*

$–$$$ ✕**Marc's Mediterranean Cuisine & Garden.** Chef-owner Marc Friederich is a foodie with an instinctive feel for what will work. And work his restaurant does. It's consistently full, consistently interesting, and always a pleasure to eat in. One of the most popular starters is the trio of salmon, which comes smoked, as pastrami, and as gravlax, served with salad leaves and a lovely light lemon-and-olive-oil dressing. Opt for the springbok loin served with a berry-and-chocolate sauce on crushed potatoes for your main course, or the spicy paella, which gets snapped up when it's on the menu. The saffron rice is packed with flavor along with succulent chicken breast, black mussels, baby squid, and kingklip (a firm white fish similar to monkfish). Marc also serves as a sommelier, so the wine list is comprehensive and he can help you with food-and-wine pairings. ⊠*129 Main St.* ☎*021/863–3980* ▤*AE, DC, MC, V* ⊙*Closed July. No dinner Sun.*

$–$$ ✕**Pontac Manor.** Having established a popular small hotel in a striking Cape Victorian former farmstead, the owners added a restaurant that has become a Winelands favorite. The deep veranda is the place for lunch except on very hot days, when the elegant dining room makes a cooler option. Diners are only too happy to tuck into such dishes as rack of lamb served with a potato-and-tarragon galette and thyme-and-honey jus. Finish with country cheeses or try the chocolate-truffle gâteau with whiskey sponge and a gooseberry topping. ⊠*16 Zion St.* ☎*021/872–0445* ᯤ*Reservations essential* ▤*AE, DC, MC, V.*

$ ✕▥**Diemersfontein Wine & Country Estate.** Built in the 19th century, this historic farmstead is set in a lush garden with rolling lawns and abundant roses and azalea bushes. The farm has been transformed into a lifestyle estate—with private houses, a small school, and lovely cottages where you can stay. The rooms are comfortable and decorated in a relaxed country style with floral throws and fresh flowers. The farm produces a range of noteworthy wines, which you can taste; highlights include the flagship Carpe Diem Pinotage, the Carpe Diem Viognier 2006, and the Thokozani white blend of sauvignon blanc, chenin blanc, and viognier. Seasons restaurant ($–$$$$) serves, appropriately enough, seasonal meals and is a wonderful venue for a late brunch or leisurely lunch. If you want something low-key, order a picnic basket to take onto the grounds. If you're feeling energetic, try your hand at bass fishing or horseback riding on the estate. ⊠*Jan van Riebeek Dr. (R301), Wellington 7655* ☎*021/873–2671 lodging, 021/864–5060 restaurant* ⊕*www.diemersfontein.co.za* ⤶*17 rooms* ♿*In-room: no a/c (some), no phone (some), no TV. In-hotel: restaurant, bar, pool, laundry service, public Wi-Fi, airport shuttle, parking (no fee), no-smoking rooms* ▤*AE, DC, MC, V* ⍾*BP.*

★ **$$$–$$$$** ▥**Grande Roche.** A member of the prestigious Relais & Châteaux group, this establishment can stake a claim to being one of the best hotels in South Africa. In a gorgeous Cape Dutch manor house that dates from the mid-18th century, the hotel sits amid acres of vines beneath Paarl Mountain, overlooking the valley and the Drakenstein Mountains. Suites are either in the historic buildings—slave quarters, stables, and wine cellar—or in attractive terrace buildings constructed in traditional Cape Dutch style. Rooms are a tasteful mix of the modern and the old: reed ceilings and thatch comfortably coexist with heated towel racks and air-conditioning. Offering a level of service extremely rare in South Africa, the employees, many of whom trained in Europe, outnumber the guests by two to one. ⊠*Plantasie St., Box 6038, 7622* ☎*021/863–5100* ⊕*www.granderoche.co.za* ⬟*5 rooms, 29 suites* ⬧*In-room: safe, DVD (some). In-hotel: 2 restaurants, room service, tennis courts, pools, gym, no elevator, laundry service, concierge, public Internet, public Wi-Fi, parking (no fee), no-smoking rooms* ▤*AE, DC, MC, V* ⭘|*BP* ⊙*Closed mid-May–July.*

★ $$$ ▣ **Bartholomeus Klip Farmhouse.** For a break from a long bout of wine tasting, head to this Victorian guesthouse on a nature reserve and working farm. Its luxurious accommodations and excellent food come in the middle of 9,900 acres of rare *renosterveld* scrubland that is home to the endangered geometric tortoise. There's also plenty of eland, zebra, wildebeest, springbok, rhebok, bontebok, bat-eared fox, Cape buffalo, and birdlife in and around the mountains, streams, and plains, and the farm runs a growing Cape buffalo breeding program. Watch sheep shearing in action, hike, mountain bike, swim, or paddle. The farmhouse is decorated in old African colonial style, with plenty of floral fabrics, antique silver, and botanical art. Rooms have thick comforters and crisp linens. Ask for one that opens onto the veranda, especially in summer. Wild Olive House (R690 per person), a great self-catering option for families (though you can arrange to have your meals catered, too), is a five-minute walk from the farmhouse and has its own pool. High tea in the boathouse includes fabulous scones and cream and traditional *melktert* (cinnamon-sprinkled custard tart), a South African teatime institution. Rates include all meals, teas, and game drives. ⊠*Off the R44, near Bo-Hermon* ✑*Box 36, Hermon 7308* ☎*022/448–1820* ⊕*www.bartholomeus.co.za* ⬟*5 rooms, 1 suite, 1 house* ⬧*In-room: no TV, Wi-Fi. In-hotel: room service, bar, pool, water sports, bicycles, no elevator, laundry service, public Internet, public Wi-Fi, airport shuttle, parking (no fee), no kids under 16 in the main house, no-smoking rooms* ▤*AE, DC, MC, V* ⭘|*FAP.*

★ $$$ ▣ **Roggeland Country House.** Dating from 1693, this farm is one of the most delightful lodgings in the Winelands. The setting in the Dal Josaphat valley is breathtaking, with stunning views of the craggy Drakenstein Mountains. Guest rooms in restored farm buildings have reed ceilings, country dressers, and mosquito nets (not just for effect). The 1779 manor house, which contains the dining room and lounge, is a masterpiece of Cape Dutch architecture. If you have kids in tow, you'll need to contact Roggeland in advance to make arrangements. ⊠*Roggeland Rd., Box 7210, Northern Paarl 7623* ☎*021/868–2501* ⊕*www.roggeland.co.za* ⬟*10 rooms* ⬧*In-room: no a/c, no TV. In-hotel: restaurant, pool, no elevator, laundry service, parking (no fee), no-smoking rooms* ▤*AE, DC, MC, V* ⭘|*MAP.*

$ ▣ **Lemoenkloof Historical Hotel.** In the heart of Paarl, this national monument is decorated in sophisticated country style, with generous throws and flouncy curtains. The rest of the early-19th-century house is peppered with antiques and Oriental rugs. Modern accoutrements, such as television, air-conditioning, and tea- and coffeemaking facilities in each of the guest rooms, make your stay comfortable. The swimming pool and art gallery add an element of fun, and the private garden is a great place to relax after some hectic wine tasting. ⊠*396A Main St., 7646* ☎*021/872–7520 or 021/872–3782* ⊕*www.lemoenkloof.co.za* ⊅*26 rooms* ♿*In-room: safe, refrigerator, Wi-Fi. In-hotel: pools, no elevator, laundry service, public Internet, airport shuttle, no kids under 12, no-smoking rooms* ▤*AE, DC, MC, V* ⦿❙*BP.*

SPORTS & THE OUTDOORS

BALLOONING **Wineland Ballooning** (☎*021/863–3192 or 083/983–4687* ⊕*www.kap-info.com*) makes one-hour flights over the Winelands every morning from about November through April, weather permitting. The balloon holds a maximum of five passengers, and the trip costs about R1,950 per person. After the flight there's a champagne breakfast at the Grand Roche.

GOLF **Paarl Golf Club** (⊠*Wemmershoek Rd.* ☎*021/863–1140*) is surrounded by mountains, covered with trees, and dotted with water hazards. The greens fees are R330 for 18 holes for nonaffiliated members, golf-club rental is around R150, caddies cost around R150, and golf carts are approximately R190.

Pearl Valley Signature Golf Estate & Spa (⊠*R301* ☎*021/867–8000*) has a breathtaking setting in the valley, and the course, designed by Jack Nicklaus, has golfers in raptures. The greens fees are R595 for 18 holes, golf-club rental is around R280, and golf carts are approximately R210. There are no caddies. After your game you can relax at the great clubhouse, pool, or wellness center (which is also nice if some members of your party want to play while others want a bit of pampering).

HORSEBACK RIDING **Wine Valley Horse Trails** (⊠*Rhebokskloof wine farm, WR8, off the R44* ☎*083/226–8735 or 021/869–8687* ⊕*www.horsetrails-sa.co.za*) offers scenic rides around the Rhebokskloof vineyards or up into the surrounding Paarl Mountain Nature Reserve. If horses aren't your thing, you can have fun on an all-terrain vehicle. It costs about R200 for one hour on a horse or all-terrain vehicle.

EN ROUTE The **Bain's Kloof Pass Road,** built by engineer Andrew Geddes Bain and opened in 1853, links Wellington to Ceres and Worcester. The road (an extension of the R303 from Paarl through Wellington) winds north from Wellington, through the Hawekwa Mountains, revealing breathtaking views across the valley below. On a clear day you can see as far as the coast. The road has a good tar surface, but unlike many Western Cape passes, Bain's Kloof has not been widened much since it was built, so take your time and enjoy the views. There are places where you can park and walk down to lovely, refreshing mountain pools—great on a hot summer's day.

As you approach the initial slopes of Bain's Kloof, look out for the **Bovlei Winery,** on the right. Constructed in 1907 in traditional style, the building itself is not noteworthy, but it has a vast picture window offering a stupendous view of the undulating vineyards beyond. This winery celebrated its centennial in 2007, and its wines just keep getting better. Be sure to try the Centennial range shiraz-mourvèdre blend, which promises great things. With plenty of well-priced, good-quality wines to choose from, you likely won't go away empty-handed. ⊠ *Bain's Kloof Rd., Wellington* ☎ *021/873–1567* ⊕ *www.bovlei.co.za* ⌨ *Tastings free* ⊙ *Weekdays 8:30–5, Sat. 8:30–12:30.*

WINELANDS ESSENTIALS

To research prices, get advice from other travelers, and book travel arrangements, visit www.fodors.com.

TRANSPORTATION

BY BUS

There is no regular bus service to the Winelands suitable for tourists. If you are based in Stellenbosch, however, and don't want to drive to the wineries, you can make use of the Vine Hopper, a minibus that follows a fixed route to five wine farms. Tickets cost around R150, and you'll be given a timetable so that you can get on and off as you please.

Bus Line **Vine Hopper** (☎ *021/882-8112*).

BY CAR

Driving yourself is undoubtedly the best way to appreciate the Winelands. Each wine route is clearly marked with attractive road signs, and there are complimentary maps available at the tourism bureaus and at most wine farms. Roads in the area are good, and even the dirt roads leading up to a couple of the farms are nothing to worry about.

The best way to get to the Winelands is to take the N2 out of Cape Town and then the R310 to Stellenbosch. Outside of rush hour, this will take you around 45 minutes. Expect some delays during the harvest months (generally late January–late March), when tractors ferry grapes from farms to cellars on the narrower secondary roads. On your way back to Cape Town, stick to the R310 and the N2. Avoid taking the M12, as it gets very confusing, and you'll end up in suburbs that aren't on tourist maps.

If you spend a day out in the Winelands and return at dusk or after dark, be on the lookout for pedestrians, especially on weekends, when people are likely to have been drinking. There is, unfortunately, a high incidence of pedestrian-related accidents on these roads. Also be sure to designate a driver to avoid the risk of drinking and driving.

■ TIP➔ **South African drivers can be erratic, and the condition of their cars varies enormously.** There are lots of expensive SUVs on the roads, but also plenty of old bangers with no turn signals and dubious brakes, so watch for cars turning without warning. South African drivers tend to drive fairly fast and get very impatient when they're held up by slower vehicles. It's common practice to pull over onto the shoulder to let faster drivers pass you. If somebody flashes his or her lights behind you, that's what they're expecting you to do. If you do pull over, do

2

so briefly and with an eye out for pedestrians. Passing drivers usually acknowledge your courtesy by putting on their hazard lights for a few seconds or with a simple wave. If an oncoming driver flashes his or her lights, it's a warning to slow down, either for traffic police or for a dangerous situation, such as an accident or slippery road.

The major car-rental agencies have offices in the smaller towns, but it's best to deal with the Cape Town offices. Besides, you'll probably want to pick up a car at the airport. If you're already in the Winelands and would like a car for the day, try Wine Route Rent-a-Car, based in Paarl, which will drop off a car at your hotel. Since driving yourself around limits the amount of wine you can taste, unless you have a designated driver, it's best to join a tour, take a taxi, or—do it in style—rent a limo. Limos cost about R400 per hour, so they're particularly cost-effective if you have a group of four or five.

Rental Companies **Avis** (⊠ *123 Strand St., Cape Town* ☎ *021/424–1177, 021/934–0330 airport, 086/111–3748 reservations* ⊕ *www.avis.co.za*). **Budget** (⊠ *120 Strand St., Cape Town* ☎ *021/418–5232, 021/380–3140 airport* ⊕ *www. budget.co.za*). **Europcar** (⊠ *49 Loop St., Cape Town* ☎ *021/426–0939 or 021/426– 0940 rental, 082/305–0066 emergency* ⊕ *www.europcar.co.za*). **Hertz** (⊠ *40 Loop St., Cape Town* ☎ *021/410–6800* ⊕ *www.hertz.co.za*). **Wine Route Rent-a-Car** (☎ *021/872–8513 or 083/225–7089*).

Limousine Company **Cape Limosine Services** (☎ *021/785–3100*).

BY TAXI

Paarl Radio Taxis will transport up to three people at about R9 per kilometer (half mile). Waiting time is around R60 per hour. Larger groups can arrange transportation by minibus. Daksi Cab, based in Stellenbosch, works on a trip rate rather than a per-kilometer basis. A trip to a local restaurant costs around R70 regardless of the number of people. Daksi also provides shuttle service to the airport.

Taxi Companies **Daksi Cab** (☎ *082/854–1541*). **Paarl Radio Taxis** (☎ *021/872– 5671*).

BY TRAIN

Cape Metro trains run from Cape Town to Stellenbosch and Paarl, but owing to an increase in violent muggings the trains should be avoided.

CONTACTS & RESOURCES

EMERGENCIES

Emergency Services **Ambulance** (☎ *10177*). **Police** (☎ *10111*). **Police, Fire, and Ambulance** (☎ *107 from landline*). **Vodacom emergency services** (☎ *112 from mobile phone*).

Hospitals **Paarl Medi-Clinic** (⊠ *Berlyn St., Paarl North* ☎ *021/807–8000*). **Stellenbosch Medi-Clinic** (⊠ *Saffraan Ave. and Rokewood Rd., Die Boord, Stellenbosch* ☎ *021/883–8571*). **Strand Medi-Clini** (⊠ *Altena Rd., Strand* ☎ *021/854–7663*).

Late-Night Pharmacy **Die Boord Pharmacy** (⊠ *14 Saffraan Ave., Die Boord Shopping Centre, Stellenbosch* ☎ *021/887–9400*).

INTERNET

There are a couple of Internet cafés in the region's main towns, especially Stellenbosch. Some hotels and guesthouses also offer Internet connections, so ask at the front desk before heading into town. Where there are no Internet cafés, print shops are usually a good bet. Expect to pay around R5 for every 10 minutes of browsing.

Internet Access Fandango (✉ *Drostdy Sq., Bird St., Stellenbosch* ☎ *021/887–7501*). **Stellenbosch Adventure Centre** (✉ *36 Market St., Stellenbosch* ☎ *021/882–8112*).

MONEY MATTERS

Changing money in the Winelands is a breeze. Hotels, restaurants, and wineries are increasingly sophisticated and only too happy to swipe your credit card through their machines. There are also plenty of ATMs, banks, and *bureaux de change* (exchange counters), so you won't be stuck without cash. Be careful when withdrawing money from ATMs; don't let anyone distract you while your card is in the machine or while you're punching in your PIN.

TOURS

Most tours of the Winelands are operated by companies based in Cape Town, such as African Eagle Day Tours, Hylton Ross, iKapa, Springbok Atlas, Welcome Tourism Services, and Windward Tours. Most of these companies have half- or full-day tours, but they vary by company and might include a cheese tasting or cellar tour in addition to wine tasting. Expect to pay around R350 for a half day and R450 for a full day, including all tasting fees. Though you stop for lunch, it is not included. Most tour buses stop at Spier, as the cheetahs provide a magnetic pull.

The historic area of Stellenbosch is so pretty and compact that it's a pity just to drive through. Take a walking tour with Sandra Krige from Stellenbosch on Foot. Tours last around 1½ hours and take in all the well-known sights. Sandra is a mine of information about the town and even offers an evening ghost tour. Expect to pay around R70 per person for the evening tour.

Easy Rider Wine Tours has a great all-day tour that's very reasonably priced (around R300, including lunch in Franschhoek). You get picked up around Stellenbosch at about 10:30 for a visit to five estates in the three regions.

For those serious about wine, Vineyard Ventures offers the best of the Winelands tour companies. Sisters Gillian Stoltzman and Glen Christie are knowledgeable and passionate about wine and will tailor tours to your interests. The cost ranges from around R920 per person for four people to roughly R2,200 for one person and includes all tastings, museum entries, and a fabulous lunch (with wine, of course).

Lesley Cox from Amber Wine Tours is wildly enthusiastic about Cape wines, knows many of the Cape winemakers and wine-farm owners, and will personalize tours. Lesley prefers visiting boutique farms not on the tourist map, but she'll tailor tours to your tastes. So if you

2

want to only sample sauvignon blancs, for instance, she'll know just where to take you. If you're not crazy about wine, but want to tour the Winelands, Lesley can tell you about Cape Dutch architecture and the history of the area. Gourmet Wine Tours will also tailor a trip to the Winelands to suit your tastes.

The Wellington Wine Walk is a great way to combine wine tasting with exercise. This three-day walking tour, which caters to groups of 6–12 people (they'll group you with other people if you're on your own or in a small group), leads you from one upscale guesthouse to the next through vineyards and indigenous fynbos in the picturesque Wellington Valley. Your guides and hosts know all there is to know about the history and culture of the area, as well as the wines. They're also passionate about good food, and each day you'll have a picnic lunch and a gourmet dinner paired with the appropriate wines. The walking isn't tough, but you cover around 18 km (11 mi) each day. Your luggage is transferred for you from place to place, so all you have to carry is a light day pack. Expect to pay around R3,000 per person (all-inclusive, except for evening drinks). The best times to go are in autumn (April–May) and then again in spring (October–November) before the temperatures soar.

Tour Operators African Eagle Day Tours (☎ 021/464-4266 ⊕ www.africa-adventure.org/a/africaneagle). **Amber Wine Tours** (☎ 021/552-2137 or 083/448-7016 ⊕ www.ambertours.co.za). **Easy Rider Wine Tours** (☎ 021/886-4651 ⊕ www.jump.to/stumble). **Gourmet Wine Tours** (☎ 021/705-4317 or 083/299-3581 ⊕ www.gourmetwinetours.co.za). **Hylton Ross Tours** (☎ 021/511-1784 ⊕ www.hyltonross.co.za). **iKapa Tours & Travel** (☎ 021/510-8666 ⊕ www.ikapa.co.za). **Springbok Atlas** (☎ 021/460-4700 ⊕ www.springbokatlas.com). **Stellenbosch on Foot** (☎ 021/887-9150 or 083/218-1310). **Vineyard Ventures** (☎ 021/434-8888 or 082/920-2825 ⊕ www.vineyardventures.co.za). **Welcome Tourism Services** (☎ 021/532-6350 ⊕ www.welcome.co.za). **Wellington Wine Walk** (☎ 083/313-8383 ⊕ www.winescapetours.co.za). **Windward Tours** (☎ 021/419-3475 ⊕ www.windwardtours.co.za).

VISITOR INFORMATION

Yours truly, can get almost all the information you need about the Winelands and the rest of the Western Cape from the very organized Cape Town Tourism offices, which are open weekdays 8–6, Saturday 8:30–1, and Sunday 9–1. Cape Town Tourism's Helderberg branch is open weekdays 9–5 in winter (approximately March–October) and 9–6 in summer (about November–February), Saturday 9–1. Franschhoek Vallée Tourisme is open weekdays 9–6, weekends 9–5. Paarl Tourism Bureau is open Monday–Thursday 8–5, Friday 8–4:45, weekends 10–1. In summer Stellenbosch Tourism and Information Bureau is open weekdays 8–6, Saturday 9:30–5, Sunday 10–4; in winter it's open weekdays 8–5, Saturday 9:30–2, Sunday 10–2.

Tourist Offices Cape Town Tourism (✉ The Pinnacle, Burg and Castle Sts., Box 1403, Cape Town 8000 ☎ 021/487-6800 ⊕ www.tourismcapetown.co.za). **Cape Town Tourism–Helderberg Branch** (✉ 186 Main Rd., Somerset West 7129 ☎ 021/840-1400 ⊕ www.tourismcapetown.co.za). **Franschhoek Vallée Tourisme**

(⊠ *70 Main Rd., Franschhoek 7690* ☎ *021/876–3603* ⊕ *www.franschhoek.org.za*). **Paarl Tourism Bureau** (⊠ *216 Main St., Paarl 7646* ☎ *021/872–4842 or 021/ 872–6737* ⊕ *www.tourismpaarl.co.za*). **Stellenbosch Tourism and Information Bureau** (⊠ *36 Market St., Stellenbosch 7600* ☎ *021/883–3584* ⊕ *www.stellenboschtourism.co.za*).

BREEDE RIVER VALLEY

The upper and central part of the catchment of the Breede River extends over a large area. It's a beautiful part of the country, with a combination of fantastic mountain scenery, fabulous fynbos, pretty bucolic farmlands, and small towns. A short drive over any one of the scenic mountain passes is sure to bring you into a secluded valley resplendent with the greens of spring, the grape-laden vines of summer, the myriad colors of autumn, or the snowcapped peaks and crisp misty mornings of winter.

A natural climatic combination of comparatively mild but wet winters followed by long, warm summers makes this area perfectly suited for the cultivation of deciduous fruit, especially viticulture. In the summer the intense sunshine allows the wine and table grapes to develop rich ruby colors. Virtually deprived of rain in summer, the vines nurture their precious crop, irrigated from the meandering Breede River and the huge Brandvlei dam, near Worcester.

TULBAGH

❺ *60 km (37 mi) north of Paarl.*

Founded in 1743, the town of Tulbagh is nestled in a secluded valley bounded by the Witzenberg and Groot Winterhoek mountains. A devastating earthquake in September 1969 shook the city and destroyed many of the original facades of the historic town.

Much of the town is unlovely, having simply been rebuilt, often prefab style, on old foundations, but the real attraction of Tulbagh is **Church Street,** parallel to the main Van der Stel Street, where each of the 32 buildings was restored to its original form and subsequently declared a national monument.

The **Oude Kerk** *(Old Church)* museum stands at the entrance to Church Street, and is the logical departure point for a self-guided tour of the area, which is well marked. The church has been extensively restored and has an interesting collection of artifacts from the area, including carvings made by Boer prisoners of war. A ticket includes admission to another two buildings on Church Street, which operate as annexes of the main museum. These show a practical history of events before, during, and after the quake. The buildings have been painstakingly reconstructed. ⊠ *21 Church St.* ☎ *023/230–1041* 💰 *R7* ⊙ *Weekdays 8:30–5, Sat. 10–4 (opens Sat. at 9 Oct.–Apr.), Sun. 11–4.*

2

NEED A
BREAK?

Want to lie under a shady tree for a few hours and do some navel-gazing? If so, head to **Schoonderzicht Farm** (⊠ *Off Steinthal Rd.* ☎ *023/230–0673 or 072/504–9592* ⊕ *www.schoonderzicht.com*). Niki de Wolf puts together fantastic picnic baskets packed with quiches, marinated vegetables and gemsbok carpaccio, grilled chicken in chocolate-balsamic reduction, olives, smoked-salmon and cucumber rolls, a selection of cheese, wine, and chocolates. Phew! You may not be able to move after eating your way through this feast. Enjoy the food on the farm, which is high up in the Witzenberg Mountains, just five minutes out of Tulbagh, or at other venues in the area. Niki also makes fine Belgian chocolates and does chocolate and wine tastings.

Just 3 km (2 mi) out of town, set on high ground commensurate with its status, is the majestic **Oude Drostdy Museum.** Built by architect Louis Thibault in 1804, the structure was badly damaged by fire in 1934 and later by the 1969 quake, but it has been carefully restored and is a fine example of neoclassical architecture. The building now houses an impressive collection of antique furniture and artifacts. Look for the gramaphone collection and the Dutch grandfather clock that has a picture of Amsterdam harbor painted on its face. As the original magistrate's house, the Drostdy had a cellar that served as the local jail; it's now used for wine tastings and sales. ⊠ *Winterhoek Rd.* ☎ *023/230– 0203* ⌦ *Museum R7, tastings R8* ⊗ *Weekdays 10–5, Sat. 10–2.*

If you stand in front of the church on Van der Stel Street, you will see a wine barrel indicating the road to **Twee Jonge Gezellen,** which is about 8 km (5 mi) from town. One of the finest and oldest wineries in the area, it's a family-run estate best known for its fantastic Cap Classique—Krone Borealis Brut. But many Capetonians are more familiar with the old, tried, and trusted TJ39, an easily drinkable, well-priced blend of *weisser* (white) riesling, chardonnay, chenin blanc, and sauvignon blanc that has been making a regular appearance on local tables for years. The Krone Engeltjipipi (referring to—er—a certain body waste of little angels) is a blend made from grapes naturally infected with botrytis (a type of fungus) and considered a gift from the cherubs. The grapes are harvested by hand over a number of nights at the end of the season. ⊠ *Twee Jonge Gezellen Rd.* ☎ *023/230–0680* ⊕ *www. tjwines.co.za* ⌦ *Tastings free* ⊗ *Weekdays 9–4, Sat. 10–2; cellar tours weekdays at 11 and 3, Sat. at 11.*

WHERE TO STAY & EAT

★ ¢–$$ ✕ **Readers.** The historic residence of the former church reader makes a cozy setting for this restaurant with consistently high-quality food and service. Carol Collins's innovative fare offers sophisticated contrasts, although she keeps presentation simple and appetizing. Her small seasonal menu changes daily. Dinner could start with smoked chicken salad with papaw, nuts, and goat cheese, or a butternut-squash-and-zucchini soup. If the springbok fillet with gooseberry and Amarula sauce is listed, don't miss it. Any one of the dessert trio is sure to make a memorable finale. The carefully chosen and well-priced wine list reflects regional labels. ⊠ *12 Church St.* ☎ *023/230–0087* ⊟ *DC, MC, V* ✆ *Closed Tues.*

$ ✕**Paddagang.** Though built as a private residence in 1809, by 1821 Paddagang (Frog's Way) was already serving as one of South Africa's first tap houses (like a pub with wine on tap). Immaculately restored after the 1969 earthquake, it was turned into a restaurant and became a popular tourist destination. Although a little timeworn, the decor is authentic, as are the *riempie* (thong-upholstered) chairs. The vine-covered pergola makes a lovely place to eat in all but the hottest weather. Traditional Cape fare is your best bet here, from starters like *smoorsnoek* (local smoked fish braised with potato and onion) with grape jam on the side, to a main course of South Africa's national dish, bobotie. Though the establishment has much going for it, standards of both food and service aren't what they used to be. ⊠ *23 Church St.* ☎ *023/230–0242* ⊟ *AE, DC, MC, V* ✆ *No dinner Sun.–Tues.*

$–$$ ⌂**Rijk's Ridge Country House.** This spot is on the outskirts of the village, on a ridge overlooking a lake where you can enjoy sweeping views of the surrounding mountains. Each suite, decorated in a plush Cape-cottage style, has a private terrace leading to the poolside garden. ⊠ *Main Rd., Box 340, 6820* ☎ *023/230–1006* ⊕ *www.rijks.co.za* ⇆ *12 suites, 3 cottages* △ *In-room: no a/c, refrigerator (some). In-hotel: restaurant, room service, bar, pool, no elevator, laundry service, public Internet, public Wi-Fi, airport shuttle, parking (no fee)* ⊟ *AE, DC, MC, V* ⌶ *BP.*

$ ⌂**Tulbagh Country House.** Ginny Clarke, owner of this guesthouse with comfortable beds and hearty breakfasts, is warm, friendly, and open—just the sort of qualities you'd expect from somebody in a small country town. She's also a mine of information about the village. The house was built in 1809 and has been declared a national monument. There's even a resident ghost who appears periodically to make sure things are running as they should. If you don't feel like eating out, you can use the *braai* (barbecue) facilities, but there are a number of good restaurants within walking distance. Ginny will also pack you a picnic basket on request. ⊠ *24 Church St., 6820* ☎ *023/230–1171* ⊕ *www.tulbaghguesthouse.co.za* ⇆ *3 rooms, 1 suite* △ *In-room: no a/c, no phone, no TV (some). In-hotel: laundry service, parking (no fee)* ⊟ *MC, V* ⌶ *BP.*

WORCESTER

❻ *45 km (28 mi) southeast of Tulbagh; 50 km (31 mi) east of Paarl on the N1, on the other side of the du Toits Kloof Pass or tunnel.*

By far the largest town in the Breede River valley, Worcester is often termed the region's capital by locals, and with good cause. Much of the town's burgeoning commerce and industry is connected to agriculture—viticulture, in particular—and its brandy cellars produce the highest volume of the spirit in the country.

The **Karoo National Botanical Garden** includes several hundred species of indigenous flora, including succulents, aloes, and trees; it's been billed as one of the most important such collections in the world. The Braille Garden is geared toward the visually impaired. If you phone ahead, you can arrange to watch a slide show and take a guided walk through the gardens and the collection houses for around R60. The garden lies on the opposite side of the N1 highway from the town of Worcester, but is easy to find if you follow the signs eastward from the last set of traffic lights on High Street. Follow the road from the entrance to the garden to the main parking area, the starting point of three clearly marked walks. ☎*023/347–0785* ✉*R10* ☼*Daily 7–7.*

The **Kleinplasie Living Open-Air Museum** is a welcome change from dusty artifacts in glass cases. The fascinating museum is actually a collection of original buildings from the area that have been re-erected around a working farmyard. Following a narrated slide show, venture into the farmyard and watch the museum staff, intent on keeping traditional skills alive, as they bake bread, twist tobacco, make horseshoes in a smithy, and distill witblitz. The museum also has a shop where you can buy produce from the farmyard. ✉*Kleinplasie Agricultural Showgrounds, Traub St.* ☎*023/342–2225* ✉*R12* ☼*Mon.–Sat. 9–4:30.*

The **KWV Brandy Cellar** is the largest distillery of its kind in the world, with 120 pot stills under one roof. Informative guided tours, followed by a brandy tasting, will take you through the process of brandy making. The well-informed guide will give a layperson's rundown of the various methods used, the pros and cons of pot-still distillation as compared with the continuous-still method, as well as a description of the maturation process. In the cooperage you can watch traditional barrel making. ✉*Church and Smith Sts.* ☎*023/342–0255* ⊕*www.kwv-international.com* ✉*Tastings R25; tours R25 weekdays, R30 weekends* ☼*Weekdays 8–4; English tours weekdays at 2, weekends by appointment.*

WHERE TO STAY & EAT

¢–$$ ✕ **St. Geran.** Townsfolk and the local farming community form the bulk of the clientele, and most of them like red meat and plenty of it. Neither they nor the chef-owner see any need for change, so the menu, with its wide range of steak tempered by a good selection of seafood, has varied little since the start of the new century. The most popular dishes are peppered fillets panfried in cream and sherry or filled with ham and cheese, followed by kingklip topped with shrimp and cheese sauce. Starters and desserts are run-of-the-mill. ✉*48 Church St.* ☎*023/342–2800* ▤*AE, DC, MC, V* ☼*Closed Sun. No lunch Sat.*

$–$$ ▦ **Cumberland Hotel.** In a town that is, for its size, surprisingly short on accommodations, this central hotel is large, convenient, and well stocked with facilities. The reception area spreads out into a courtyard, and the dining area and spa and gym facilities have been placed around a central landscaped swimming pool. Rooms—all scrupulously clean and air-conditioned against the hot Boland summer—are reasonably priced. You can opt for a plan with no meals or one with breakfast included. ✉*2 Stockenstrom St., 6850* ☎*023/347–2641* ⊕*www.cumberland.co.za* ➳*54 rooms, 1 suite* ⚹*In-room: safe, refrigerator (on request). In-hotel: restaurant, room service, bars, tennis court, pool,* *gym, no elevator, laundry service, public Internet, airport shuttle, park-ing (no fee), no-smoking rooms* ☰*AE, DC, MC, V* ⦿*EP or BP.*

SPORTS & THE OUTDOORS

RAFTING & CANOEING   The Breede River has tiny rapids near Worcester, where it twists and turns between clumps of *palmiet* (river reeds) and the overgrown banks. Using two-person inflatables, **River Rafters** (☎*021/712–5094*) offers a one-day trip with wine tasting for R450 and a two-day, two-night trip for R950. **Wildthing Adventures** (☎*021/552–7753*) runs one- and two-day canoe trips. The one-day Wine Route trip (R425) is the most popular, and is more about food and drink than paddling. The highlight is the tasting of local wines during the extensive picnic lunch.

ROBERTSON

❼ *48 km (30 mi) southeast of Worcester.*

Robertson was founded primarily to service the surrounding farms, and it retains its agricultural and industrial character. The town largely lives up to its mantra of "small town, big heart"—the towns-folk are welcoming and friendly, which makes up for the lack of action. Some effort has been made to beautify the town with tree-lined roads, but there is little reason for visitors to come here, other than to stop off for lunch on the way to McGregor or Montagu. If you are in the area, however, you might consider visiting one of the well-known local wine farms.

Capetonians in the know have long considered **Rooiberg Winery,** between Worcester and Robertson, one of the best value-for-money wineries in the area. The red muscadel is reputedly one of the best in the world, and the shiraz, pinotage, chardonnay, and port are all good buys. A cabernet sauvignon–merlot blend, the Roodewyn (red wine) 2004 vintage is a good buy. Check out the latest installation by landscape-artist Strijdom van der Merwe outside the winery; it changes every year, but one past exhibit included 50 red socks blowing in the wind. The Bodega de Vinho deli serves light lunches, making this a good place to stop for something to eat. ✉*R60, about 10 km (6 mi) northwest of Robertson* ☎*023/626–1663* ⊕*www.rooiberg.co.za* ☜*Tastings free* ☉ *Weekdays 8–5:30, Sat. 9–3.*

Graham Beck, Robertson Cellar, on the road between Worcester and Robertson, is the sibling to a cellar of the same name in Franschhoek (Graham Beck has further extended his empire by acquiring Steenberg Estate in the Constantia Valley). This country cousin produces some very sophisticated wines, and winemaker Pieter Ferreira is known as Mr. Bubbles for his wonderful sparkling wines. The Rhona Muscadel 2002, a New Age muscat that's fruity but not cloying, and the excellent brut rosé are two favorites, but the reds are not to be ignored. Try the Ridge Syrah, which is garnering rave reviews, as is the Coffeestone Cabernet. ✉*R60, about 10 km (6 mi) northwest of Robertson* ☎*023/626–1214* ⊕*www.grahambeckwines.co.za* ☜*Tastings free*

2

⊗ *Weekdays 9–5, Sat. 10–3, first Sun. of the month 10–3; cellar tours by appointment.*

Van Loveren Winery, between Robertson and Bonnievale, produces 40 wines, so there's something to suit everybody's palate. In addition to sampling the unusual Fernão Pires and the big and bold 2005 cabernet sauvignon—both of which are very inexpensive—make sure you visit the unusual grounds of this family-owned and -run farm. An established garden of indigenous and exotic plants and trees surrounds a water fountain that supplies the entire farm. Instead of visiting the usual tasting room, you sit out under the trees and the various wines are brought to you. It's very relaxed and friendly, and you may feel like part of the family before you know it. ⊠ *Off R317, 15 km (9 mi) southeast of Robertson* ☎ *023/615–1505* ⊕ *www.vanloveren.co.za* ⊡ *Tastings free* ⊗ *Weekdays 8:30–5, Sat. 9:30–1.*

Abrie Bruwer, winemaker and viticulturist at **Springfield Estate,** has a fan club, for good reason. Although the cabernet has its loyal following, this innovative estate is best known for its unusual approach to white wines, especially chardonnay. The Méthode Ancienne Chardonnay is made in the original Burgundy style and is bottled only if it's perfect—which happens about two years in five. The creamy Wild Yeast Chardonnay, with its all-natural fermentation, is an unwooded version of the above and comes highly recommended. ⊠ *R317, just north of Robertson* ☎ *023/626–3661* ⊕ *www.springfieldestate.com* ⊡ *Tastings free* ⊗ *Weekdays 8–5, Sat. 9–4; cellar tours by appointment.*

WHERE TO EAT

★ $–$$$$ ✗ **Fraai Uitzicht.** In a deeply rural setting between Robertson and Ashton, this 200-year-old fruit and wine farm is home to a rustic restaurant where chef Sandra Burchardt whips up impressively sophisticated fare. Garden produce and herbs are transformed into a menu of culinary joy, and serious food lovers can opt for the six- or seven-course tasting menu with matching wines for each course. You might start with a bacon-wrapped salmon-trout fillet or the subtle smoked springbok carpaccio. Main courses might include roast rack of lamb with rosemary pesto or the tagine of free-range chicken cooked with fresh herbs and saffron and served with couscous and vegetables. Desserts are as admirable, their sauces as stellar as those of the savory variety. Try the "dream of Africa": a freshly baked mousse soufflé of Belgian chocolate served with vanilla yogurt cream and a mixed-berry coulis. The wine list does not disappoint, presenting a selection of the Robertson Valley's best augmented with French champagne. ⊠ *Off the R60, Klaas Voogds East* ☎ *023/626–6156* ⌔ *Reservations essential* ⊟ *AE, DC, MC, V* ⊗ *Closed June–mid-Aug. No lunch Mon. and Tues.*

EN ROUTE   On the R60 out of Robertson you can either take the clearly marked turnoff to McGregor, which snakes between vineyards and farms—a picture of bucolic charm—or continue on toward Montagu. Before reaching the latter, you'll pass through the unlovely agricultural town of Ashton. Keep left (don't turn off to Swellendam), and enter the short but spectacular **Cogman's Kloof Pass.** On either side of the pass, which runs in a river gorge, you can see the magnificent fold mountains, which are ultimately the source for Montagu's hot springs.

MCGREGOR

8 *20 km (12 mi) south of Robertson.*

Saved from development as a result of a planned mountain pass that never materialized, McGregor is the epitome of the sleepy country hollow, tucked away between the mountains, and is one of the best-preserved examples of a 19th-century Cape village. As you approach McGregor from Robertson, farmsteads give way to small cottages with distinctive red-painted doors and window frames. The McGregor Co-op Winery, on the left, heralds your entry into the town with its thatch cottages in vernacular architecture.

McGregor has become popular with artists who have settled here permanently and with busy executives from Cape Town intent on getting away from it all. Frankly, this is an ideal place to do absolutely nothing, but you can take a leisurely stroll through the fynbos, watch birds from one of several blinds on the Heron Walk, or follow one of the hiking or mountain-bike trails if you are feeling more energetic. There is a great hiking trail across the Riviersonderend Mountains to Greyton.

The **McGregor Co-op Winery** is a popular attraction, with surprisingly inexpensive wines, considering their quality. Try the unwooded chardonnay—the 2006 vintage won a Veritas Gold. The port is also exceptional and perfect for sipping near a log fire in winter, and the colombar gets rave reviews year after year. ⊠ *Main Rd.* ☎ *023/625-1741* ⊕ *www.mcgregorwinery.co.za* ✎ *Tastings free* ⊙ *Weekdays 8–5, Sat. 9–3; cellar tours by appointment.*

WHERE TO STAY

$ **Old Mill Lodge.** This simple thatch lodge, its adjacent 19th-century waterwheel still intact, dreams on among tall trees at the far end of the village. Accommodations are in thatch cottages with antique-style beds. Before dinner take a walk through the olive grove or a dip in the swimming pool. À la carte lunches and dinners are optional. ⌂ *Box 25, 6708* ☎ *023/625–1841* ⊕ *www.oldmilllodge.co.za* 🛏 *8 rooms* △ *In-room: no a/c, no phone, no TV. In-hotel: restaurant, bar, pool, no elevator, laundry service, parking (no fee), some pets allowed, no-smoking rooms* ▭ *AE, DC, MC, V* ⦿ *BP or FAP.*

SPORTS & THE OUTDOORS

HIKING   There are two wonderful two-day hikes through the **Vrolijkheid Nature Reserve** (⊠ *5 km [3 mi] outside McGregor* ☎ *023/625–1621*). For each you need to get a permit from the reserve and pay R18 per person for the two days. You'll also need to book accommodations.

MONTAGU

❾ *29 km (18 mi) northeast of Robertson.*

Montagu bills itself as "the Gateway to the Little Karoo," and its picturesque streets lined with Cape Victorian architecture lend this some credence. Today the town's main attraction is its natural hot springs, and many of the Victorian houses have been transformed into B&Bs and guesthouses. You know you're in a special place when farmers drop off their produce at the unmanned Honesty Shop and buyers leave money for what they owe.

There are a number of resorts where you can stay and "partake of the waters."

Popular **Avalon Springs,** the only resort open to day visitors, is not the most stylish, and the architecture leaves a lot to be desired. But if you look beyond this and the numerous signs carrying stern warnings and instructions, you'll get good insight into South African life and culture, as people float and splash around in the various pools. If you're not staying at the resort, you can rent bikes from the village and cycle to the springs, where you can spend a few hours before heading home again. ⊠ *Uitvlucht St., 3 km (2 mi) outside Montagu* ☎ *023/614–1150* ⊕ *www.avalonsprings.co.za* ✉ *R30 hot springs, R20 parking on weekends* ⊗ *Daily 8 AM–11 PM.*

The popular three-hour **Langeberg Tractor Ride** takes you to the summit of the Langeberg (Long Mountain) and back. The tractor winds up some tortuously twisted paths, revealing magnificent views of the area's peaks and valleys. After a short stop at the summit, a similarly harrowing descent follows, but you won't be disappointed by the views or the driver's chirpy banter. If you're here in spring or summer when the flowers are in bloom, you might even get to pick some gorgeous proteas on the way down. Following your trip, you can enjoy a delicious lunch of *potjiekos* (traditional stew cooked over a fire in a single cast-iron pot) for R60. Reservations are essential. ⊠ *Protea Farm, R318* ☎ *023/614–2471* ✉ *R60* ⊗ *Wed. and Sat. at 10 and 2.*

WHERE TO STAY & EAT

$–$$ ✕ **Jessica's Restaurant.** Housed within this Victorian structure is a restaurant with French colonial decor—with rich plummy colors, lots of candles, and dark wood—and pictures of the Staffordshire bull terrier for which the place is named. If you cannot make up your mind after perusing the menu, stick with the recommended daily specials, such as smoked kudu carpaccio with herb cream cheese and crispy onion bits. Follow that with tiger prawns and chicken breast in Thai spices and coconut cream, or butternut ravioli on roasted vegetables. Classic highlights are the crispy duck and satiny crème brûlée. In good weather, ask to sit in the garden. ⊠ *47 Bath St.* ☎ *023/614–1805* ✍ *Reservations essential* ▤ *AE, DC, MC, V* ⊗ *Closed Sun. May–Sept., and Dec. and Jan. No lunch.*

$–$$ ✕▥ **Montagu Country Hotel.** This salmon-color hotel was built in Victorian times but was extensively remodeled in the early 1930s. The present owner, Gert Lubbe, highlights its many art-deco features and collects furniture and artifacts from this era to complement the interior. A well-trained staff ensures efficient and personal service. The hotel has a wellness center and mineral pool. The Wild Apricot restaurant (¢–$) serves an excellent breakfast, satisfying no-frills lunch, and similarly straightforward dinner, with the addition of traditional country favorites like Karoo-lamb pie. ⊠27 Bath St., Box 338, 6720 ☎023/614–3125 ⊕www.montagucountryhotel.co.za ⬩34 rooms ⬩In-room: refrigerator (some). In-hotel: restaurant, room service, bar, pools, laundry service, parking (no fee), some pets allowed, no-smoking rooms ⊟AE, DC, MC, V ⦿IBP.

$ 🏠 **7 Church Street.** In the heart of the village sits this guesthouse in a lovingly restored Victorian home. Each room is individually and stylishly decorated with hand-embroidered cotton percale linens. The Honeymoon Suite, which is really more of a big room than a suite, has a big wrought-iron bed and a bathroom with a claw-foot tub. Ask for the Garden Suite if you want extra privacy. The pool is set in a magnificent garden and has stunning mountain views; it's the perfect place to relax with a book after a morning at the springs or exploring town. ⊠7 Church St., Box 43, 6720 ☎023/614–1186 ⊕www.7churchstreet. co.za ⬩3 rooms, 1 suite ⬩In-room: no a/c, no phone, refrigerator (some). In-hotel: pool, no elevator, laundry service, public Internet, no kids under 12, no-smoking rooms ⊟AE, MC, V ⦿IBP.

BREEDE RIVER VALLEY ESSENTIALS

To research prices, get advice from other travelers, and book travel arrangements, visit www.fodors.com.

TRANSPORTATION

BY BUS

Greyhound, Intercape Mainliner, and Translux provide daily service throughout most of the Western Cape, stopping at bigger towns such as Worcester and Robertson on their way upcountry. Although each company's timetable varies, most have approximately four trips a day from Cape Town. The journeys are not long. From Cape Town it takes about 1½ hours to Worcester and about 2 hours to Robertson. A one-way trip to Worcester costs around R150, and the drop-off spot is a service station on the side of the N1. It is a little way out of town, but shuttle buses will take you into town for a small fee.

Bus Lines Greyhound (⊠1 Adderley St., Cape Town ☎083/915–9000 ⊕www. greyhound.co.za). **Intercape Mainliner** (⊠1 Adderley St., Cape Town ☎0861/287–287, 083/909–0909 for alternate booking through Computicket ⊕www.intercape. co.za). **Translux Express Bus** (⊠1 Adderley St., Cape Town ☎0861/589–282 ⊕www.translux.co.za).

BY CAR

Driving is definitely the way to go when exploring the Breede River valley, as it will give you the flexibility you need to discover interesting back roads or to linger at a lovely lunch spot. The roads in the Western

Cape are generally good. Although you might have to navigate some dirt roads, they tend to be graded regularly and are in fine condition.

The major car-rental agencies have offices in some of the smaller towns, but it's best to deal with the Cape Town offices. An alternative is to pick up a car in Stellenbosch. *For car-rental agencies, see Winelands Essentials, above.*

The best way to get to this area is to take the N1 from Cape Town past Paarl. You can either go through the Huguenot toll tunnel (around R25 per vehicle) or over the spectacular Bain's Kloof mountain pass to Worcester. From there take the R60 to Robertson and Montagu.

CONTACTS & RESOURCES

EMERGENCIES

In the event of an emergency, you'll be able to track down medical professionals without too much trouble. Although Montagu and Robertson don't have any late-night pharmacies, small-town professionals are happy to open up after hours. Robertson and Montagu have small provincial hospitals, and Worcester has three, including the privately run Medi-Clinic.

Emergency Services Ambulance (☎10177). Police (☎10111). **Police, Fire, and Ambulance** (☎107 *from landline*). **Vodacom emergency services** (☎112 *from mobile phone*).

Hospitals **Montagu Hospital** (✉ *Church and Hospital Sts., Montagu* ☎023/614–8100). **Robertson Hospital** (✉ *Van Oudtshoorn St., Robertson* ☎023/626–3155). **Worcester Medi-Clinic** (✉67 *Fairburn St., Worcester* ☎023/348–1500).

INTERNET

Yours truly, won't find a slew of Internet cafés in these smaller rural towns, but you won't be completely stuck without access either. Some hotels and guesthouses will let you send and receive mail, but if your hotel does not offer access, ask the local tourism bureau for suggestions. Rates vary, but expect to pay around R24 for 30 minutes and R40 for an hour.

Internet Access **Printmor** (✉70 *Bath St., Montagu* ☎023/614–1838). **Rottó** (✉ *Van Rheenen St., Robertson* ☎023/626–5468).

MONEY MATTERS

Changing money isn't a problem in these outlying towns. They have banks and ATMs, and credit cards are widely accepted.

TOURS

Instead of big tour companies, there are a couple of individual guides operating in Breede River towns. Because the guides are usually from the area, they provide rare insights about the towns. Your best bet is to ask at local tourism offices for names and numbers. If you wish to hike in the Montagu Mountain Reserve, where trails are not well marked, go with someone familiar with the area, such as Patti van Dyk. She charges around R50 per person for a strenuous hike lasting 6–10 hours, including the park's entrance fee.

Tour Guide **Patti van Dyk** (☎023/614–1501 or 082/744–3655).

VISITOR INFORMATION

Cape Town Tourism offices are a good source of information on the whole Western Cape. Offices are open weekdays 8–6, Saturday 8:30–1, and Sunday 9–1. The Montagu Tourism Bureau is open weekdays 8–6 and weekends 9–noon. The Robertson Tourism Bureau is open weekdays 8–5, Saturday 9–4, and Sunday 10–2. Tulbagh Tourism is open weekdays 9–5, Saturday 9–4, and Sunday 10–4. The Worcester Tourism Bureau is open weekdays 7:45–4:30 and Saturday 7:45–12:30.

Tourist Offices **Cape Town Tourism** (⊠ *The Pinnacle, Burg and Castle Sts., Box 1403, Cape Town 8000* ☎ *021/487–6800* ⊕ *www.tourismcapetown.co.za*). **Montagu Tourism Bureau** (⊠ *24 Bath St., Montagu 6720* ☎ *023/614–2471* ⊕ *www.montagu-ashton.info*). **Robertson Tourism Bureau** (⊠ *Reitz and Voortrekker Sts.* ⌂ *Box 675, Robertson 6705* ☎ *023/626–4437* ⊕ *www.robertsonr62.com*). **Tulbagh Tourism** (⊠ *4 Church St., Tulbagh 6820* ☎ *023/230–1348* ⊕ *tulbaghtourism.org.za*). **Worcester Tourism Bureau** (⊠ *23 Baring St., Worcester 6850* ☎ *023/348–2795*).

THE OVERBERG

Overberg, Afrikaans for "over the mountains," is an apt name for this remote but beautiful region at the bottom of the continent, separated from the rest of the Cape by mountains. Before 19th-century engineers blasted a route over the Hottentots Holland mountain range, the Overberg developed in comparative isolation. To this day it possesses a wild emptiness far removed from the settled valleys of the Winelands.

It's a land of immense contrasts, and if you're planning a trip along the Garden Route, you would be well advised to add the Overberg to your itinerary. The coastal drive from Gordon's Bay to Hermanus unfolds a panorama of deserted beaches, pounding surf, and fractured granite mountains. Once you pass Hermanus and head out onto the wind-swept plains leading to Cape Agulhas, you have to search harder for the Overberg's riches. Towns are few and far between, the countryside an expanse of wheat fields, sheep pastures, and creaking windmills. The occasional reward of the drive is a coastline of sublime beauty. Dunes and unspoiled beaches extend for miles. Currently no roads run parallel to the ocean along this stretch, and you must repeatedly divert inland before heading to another part of the coast. But there are plans afoot for a major coastal highway, which has brought mixed reactions. It means economic growth for far-flung towns but threatens to destroy the peace and quiet that make these villages so attractive.

Unfortunately, the ocean's bounty has been the undoing of communities along this coastline. Perlemoen (abalone) poaching is an enormous problem. These sea mollusks are being illegally poached faster than they can reproduce and are then shipped to the East, where they are considered a powerful aphrodisiac. Violent Western Cape gangs are involved in perlemoen trafficking, and children as young as 11 are used as runners in exchange for drugs.

2

Naturally, the coast also has plenty of good on tap. Hermanus is one of the best places in South Africa for land-based whale-watching during the annual migration of Southern Right whales between June and November. Spring is also the best time to see the Overberg's wildflowers, although the region's profusion of coastal and montane fynbos is beautiful year-round. The raw, rugged beauty of Africa's southernmost coastline can be found at De Hoop Nature Reserve. The Whale Trail, a five-day hike mapped out through De Hoop, might just oust the Garden Route's Otter Trail as South Africa's most popular. In fact, walking is one of the Overberg's major attractions, and almost every town and nature reserve offers a host of trails.

The upper part of the Overberg, north of the N2 highway, is more like the Winelands, with 18th- and 19th-century towns sheltered in the lee of rocky mountains. Here the draws are apple orchards, inns, and hiking trails that wind through the mountains. The historic towns of Swellendam and Greyton are good places to spend a night before moving on to your next destination. Stanford, a tiny hamlet just outside of Hermanus, is also a lovely place to stay if you want to avoid the crowds that clog the streets of Hermanus on holidays.

To tour the whole area would take three to four days, but you could easily spend a week in the Overberg. For a shorter trip focus on the splendors of the coastal route from Gordon's Bay to Hermanus, and then head north toward Greyton and Swellendam.

GORDON'S BAY

⑩ *70 km (43½ mi) southeast of Cape Town.*

This attractive resort is built on a steep mountain slope overlooking the vast expanse of False Bay. You can often see whales and their calves in the bay in October and November. Gordon's Bay is a good point to start on the fantastic coastal route known as Clarence Drive.

EN ROUTE

From Gordon's Bay the road hugs the mountainside, slipping between the craggy peaks of the Hottentots Holland Mountains and the sea far below. The coastal drive, known as **Clarence Drive** (R44), between Gordon's Bay and Hermanus is one of the country's best, particularly if you take the time to follow some of the dirt roads leading down to the sea from the highway. There are numerous paths down to the seashore from the road between Gordon's Bay and Rooiels. It's worth walking down to watch the waves pounding the rocky coast, but take care. If there are no other people around and the waves are quite big, stay a few yards back from the water, as this section of coast is notorious for freak waves in certain swell and wind conditions. Note the many crosses on the side of the road—each one denotes somebody who has been swept off the rocks and drowned at sea.

The road passes the tiny settlement of **Rooiels** (pronounced *roy*-else), then cuts inland for a couple of miles. A turnoff leads to **Pringle Bay,** a collection of vacation homes sprinkled across the fynbos. The village has little to offer other than a beautiful wide beach (check out the sign warning of quicksand). If you continue through Pringle Bay, the tar road soon gives way to a gravel road, now closed by shifting sand dunes, that used to lead to Betty's Bay (you now have to backtrack and take the inland route to get to Betty's Bay).

BETTY'S BAY

⓫ *30 km (19 mi) southeast of Gordon's Bay.*

Betty's Bay, or Betty's, as the hamlet is fondly known, is worth visiting for its penguins and botanic garden. To get here from Pringle Bay, return to Clarence Drive (the R44) and continue 1½ km (1 mi) to the turnoff to Stony Point, on the edge of Betty's Bay. Follow Porter Drive for 3 km (2 mi) until you reach a sign marked MOOI HAWENS and a smaller sign depicting a penguin. Follow the penguin signs to a **colony of African penguins,** one of only two mainland colonies in southern Africa (the other is at Boulders Beach in Cape Town, where it is much easier to see these endangered seabirds). The colony lies about 600 yards from the parking area along a rocky coastal path. Along the way you pass the concrete remains of tank stands, reminders of the days when Betty's Bay was a big whaling station. The African penguin is endangered, so the colony has been fenced off for protection.

★ **Harold Porter National Botanical Garden** is a 440-acre nature reserve in the heart of the coastal fynbos, where the Cape floral kingdom is at its richest. The profusion of plants supports 78 species of birds and a wide range of small mammals, including large troops of chacma baboons. You couldn't ask for a more fantastic setting, cradled between the Atlantic and the towering peaks of the 3,000-foot Kogelberg Range. Walking trails wind through the reserve and into the mountains via Disa and Leopard's kloofs, which echo with the sound of waterfalls. Back at the main buildings, a pleasant restaurant serves light meals and teas. Book ahead for a volunteer guide to take you around the gardens, for which a donation is welcome. To get to the garden from the penguin colony, return to Porter Drive and turn right to rejoin the R44. Drive another another 2 km (1 mi) to get here. ⊠*R44* ☎*028/272–9311* 🖾*R10* ⊙ *Weekdays 8–4:30, weekends 8–5.*

WHERE TO STAY & EAT

$–$$ ✕**Hook, Line and Sinker.** Owners Jacqi and Stefan Kruger can be a bit gruff, though well-meaning. Only the most obedient diners will escape unscathed, but the trial, like all heroes' journeys, makes survival and the meal that much sweeter. Expect fish—which is fresher than you'll find just about anywhere else—prepared simply, usually with salsa verde or a bourbon-and-mustard sauce. The dishes, all cooked on a wood fire, come only with fries. Start with either the rich and fragrant crab bisque or mussels in a tomato-based soup. Try the prawn gumbo, if it's available. Steak is served Wednesday and Sunday nights. Beer-battered fish-and-chips (made with hake) is a lunch option. The restaurant is small, the waiting list long. ⊠*382 Crescent Rd., Pringle Bay* ☎*028/273–8688* ⚓*Reservations essential* ▭*AE, DC, MC, V* ⊙ *Closed most Mon.*

2

$–$$ 🛏 **Waterlilly Lodge.** Nestled in the little village of Betty's Bay and just a 10-minute stroll from the beach, Waterlilly Lodge is a great option if you don't want to take out a second mortgage on your house. The look is clean, modern, and devoid of the tacky knickknacks that often curse beachside guesthouses. Restful shades of cream, gray, and black decorate the stylish rooms. Your host, Bryan Charlton, has worked in the hospitality industry for years and knows how to make guests feel at home. Bryan is also a whiz in the kitchen, so you'll start your day with a hearty breakfast; he even puts together picnic baskets on request. There's even an honesty bar. Arrangements must be made in advance for children under 14. ⊠ *Porter and Angler Drs., Box 326, 7141* ☎ *028/272–9378* ⊕ *www.waterlillylodge.co.za* ➷ *6 rooms* ⌂ *In-room: no a/c, no phone, refrigerator. In-hotel: bar, no elevator, laundry service, public Internet, parking (no fee), no-smoking rooms* ▤ *AE, DC, MC, V* ⏀ *BP or CP.*

KLEINMOND

12 *25 km (15½ mi) southeast of Gordon's Bay.*

The sleepy coastal town of Kleinmond (Small Mouth) presides over a magnificent stretch of shoreline, backed by the mountains of the Palmietberg. It's a favorite among retirees, but more and more city-weary baby boomers are moving here as well. A harbor development near the old slipway is bustling with restaurants and shops.

NEED A BREAK?

Alive Alive-O-Shellfish Bar (⊠ *Kleinmond harbor* ☎ *028/271–3774*) is one of the places where you can try abalone quite legally. At the big abalone factory the mollusks are cultivated, harvested, and packaged for local restaurants and overseas markets.

Close to town, on the Cape Town side and clearly marked with signs from the main street, is the **Kogelberg Nature Reserve,** a 66,000-acre area of fynbos that extends from the mountains almost to the sea, and includes most of the course of the Palmiet River. Take one of the well-marked nature walks through the reserve and you are sure to see some of the area's magnificent flora and bird life. ☎ *028/271–5138* ▣ *R24* ⏱ *Apr.–Aug., daily 8–7; Sept.–Mar., daily 7:30–7.*

About 10 km (6 mi) of sandy beach fringes the impressive **Sandown Bay,** at the eastern edge of town. Much of the beach is nothing more than a sandbar, separating the Atlantic from the huge lagoon formed by the Bot River. Swift currents make swimming risky, although there is a sheltered corner near the rocks close to the Beach House hotel (which is closed due to fire damage). Keep an eye out for the famous Bot River horses that live on *vlei* (pronounced flay), or marsh. There are lots of theories about just how the horses got here. One has it that they were turned loose during the Boer War to save them from being killed, and ended up on the vlei for safety. DNA tests show that these horses are descendants of the Kaapse Waperd (Cape wagon horse), a sturdy breed used to help settle the wild regions of the Overberg.

WHERE TO STAY

★ $$$$ 🏨 **The Western Cape Hotel & Spa.** Gone are the days when heading out into the country meant staying in pokey hotels with dodgy beds. The Western Cape Hotel & Spa is luxurious lodging in the most amazing setting—on the edge of the Bot River lagoon. They have plenty to boast about. The 18-hole golf course has been voted the number-two course in South Africa by *Golf Digest,* and the AltiraSPA is highly regarded. Need any more prompting? The interior design is contemporary African, and bright bed throws and interesting signature pieces of furniture and art give each spacious room a unique feel. If you really want to splurge, the Presidential Suites, which include 24-hour butler service, will cater to your every need. The hotel is child-friendly, with extensive child-care programs during the holidays. ⊠ *Arabella Country Estate, R44, 7195* ☎ *028/284–0000* ⊕ *www.westerncapehotelandspa.co.za* 🛏 *117 rooms, 28 suites* ⚴ *In-room: safe, refrigerator, VCR (some), Wi-Fi. In-hotel: 2 restaurants, room service, bars, golf course, tennis court, pool, gym, spa, children's programs (ages 4–12), laundry service, concierge, public Wi-fi, airport shuttle, parking (no fee), no-smoking rooms* ⊟ *AE, DC, MC, V* ⦿ *BP.*

SPORTS & THE OUTDOORS

GOLF   The setting of the **Arabella Golf Club** (⊠ *R43* ☎ *028/284–9383* ⊕ *www. westerncapehotelandspa.co.za*) is so beautiful that you'd do well to take time to admire the views at the 8th hole, with the lagoon, the mountains, and the sea in the distance. The course is fairly challenging and quite expensive. Greens fees are R585 for 18 holes. A caddy costs R180, club rental R250, and a golf cart R210.

RAFTING   The Palmiet River is a low-volume, technical white-water river of about Grade 3. In high water in summer and winter, **Gravity Adventures** (⊠ *21 Selous Rd., Claremont* ☎ *021/683–3698 or 082/574–9901* ⊕ *www. gravity.co.za*) offers rafting trips in four- or two-seater inflatable rafts. In low water they do the same trip but on specially designed one-person inflatable crafts called "geckos." A full-day rafting trip (including a light breakfast and lunch) costs R380. Tubing costs R310 for a full day; you can order lunch for an extra R45 or bring your own. Remember to take along plenty of sun protection.

EN ROUTE   The R44 becomes the R41 and cuts inland around the Bot River lagoon. About 10 km (6 mi) past Kleinmond is the junction with the R43. Hermanus is to the right, but take a quick detour to the left through the sleepy town of Bot River to the big old white gates of **Beaumont Wines.** This is a fabulous family-run winery. It's just sufficiently scruffy to create an ambience of age and country charm without actually being untidy. But, charm aside, it's the wine you come here for, and it really is worth the detour. Beaumont produces a range of dependable, notable wines, like the new-wave pinotage and the first mourvèdre to be bottled in South Africa. ⊠ *R43, Bot River* ☎ *028/284–9194* 🍷 *Tastings free* ⊙ *Weekdays 9:30–12:30 and 1:30–4:30, Sat. 9:30–1:30.*

Head back toward Kleinmond, continuing on the R43 toward Hermanus and across the Bot River. The R43 swings eastward around the mountains, past the not particularly attractive fishing village of Hawston, one of the Overstrand communities hardest hit by abalone poaching, and the small artists' colony of **Onrus.** The Onrus lagoon is a great swimming spot for children. The water is always a couple of degrees warmer than the sea and is safe for the newly waterborne.

The Milkwood (⌗*Atlantic Dr., Onrus* ☎*028/316–1516*), overlooking the lagoon in Onrus, is a great place for a languid lunch. You can sit on the deck after a quick dip and eat some fresh fish (what kind of fish depends on the day's catch), grilled and served with a lemon or garlic-butter sauce, or one of several Thai-style stir-fries.

HERMANUS

🔞 *34 km (21 mi) southeast of Kleinmond on the R43.*

Pristine beaches extend as far as the eye can see, and the Kleinriviersberg provides a breathtaking backdrop to this popular resort, the Overberg's major coastal town. Restaurants and shops line the streets, and Grotto Beach was awarded Blue Flag status (an international symbol of high environmental standards as well as good sanitary and safety facilities) in 2003. Though the town has lost much of its original charm—thanks to the crowds and fast-food joints—it is still most definitely worth a visit.

Fodor'sChoice
★
Hermanus sits atop a long line of cliffs, which makes it one of the best places in South Africa for **land-based whale-watching.** (The town is packed during the Whale Festival in late September as well as over Christmas vacation.) The 11-km (7-mi) Cliff Walk allows watchers to follow the whales, which often come within 100 feet of the cliffs as they move along the coastline. Keep an ear and an eye out for the whale crier, Zolile Baleni, who makes his rounds during the season. Using horns made from dried kelp, he produces different codes indicating where to catch the best sighting of these mighty giants of the deep. A long note followed by a short one signals the new harbor, for instance.

Originally, Hermanus was a simple fishing village. Its Old Harbour, the oldest original harbor in South Africa that is still intact, has been declared a national monument. The **Old Harbour Museum** bears testimony to the town's maritime past. A small building at the old stone fishing basin displays a couple of the horrific harpoons used to lance whales and sharks as well as some interesting whale bones. There are also exhibits on fishing techniques, local marine life, and angling records. The white building next to the harbor parking lot on Market Square is **De Wet's Huis,** which houses the Old Harbour Museum Photographic Exhibition. Here are photos of old Hermanus, and many of the town's fishermen proudly displaying their catches of fish, sharks, and dolphins—yes, dolphins. The museum's third component is the **Whale House,** which currently houses a temporary exhibit of whale paintings. At this writing, the first phase of the permanent exhibition (of interactive exhibits and displays on whales) had been completed, but they were still busy with the second phase with no end date in sight.

A crafts market every weekend outside De Wet's Huis is fun for browsing. ✉ *Old Harbour, Marine Dr.* ☎ *028/312–1475* ✉ *R5* ⊙ *Weekdays 9–4:30, Sat. 9–4, Sun. 11–4.*

★ On the outskirts of town a pair of white gateposts set well back from the R43 signal the start of **Rotary Way.** This scenic drive climbs along the spine of the mountains above Hermanus, with incredible views of the town, Walker Bay, and the Hemel-en-Aarde (Heaven and Earth) Valley, as well as some of the area's beautiful fynbos. It's a highlight of a trip to Hermanus and shouldn't be missed. The entire mountainside is laced with wonderful walking trails, and many of the scenic lookouts have benches.

West of town off the R43, the R320 (Hemel-en-Aarde Valley Road) leads through the vineyards and orchards of the scenic Hemel-en-Aarde Valley and over Shaw's Pass to Caledon. The gravel road has some potholes and washboards, but nothing terrifying. A short way down the road in a thatch building overlooking a small dam, **Hamilton Russell Vineyards** produces some excellent wines. The pinot noir won loud acclaim from wine critic Frank Prial of the *New York Times,* and is one of the best produced in the country; it's served in two of the world's top restaurants, El Bulli in Spain and the Fat Duck in the England. The chardonnay comes closer to the French style of chardonnay than any other Cape wine, with lovely fruit and a touch of lemon rind and butterscotch. ✉ *Off Hemel-en-Aarde Valley Rd. (R320), Walker Bay* ☎ *028/312-3595* ✉ *Tastings free* ⊙ *Weekdays 9–5, Sat. 9–1.*

With only 44 acres under vine, **Bouchard Finlayson** nevertheless thrills critics and wine lovers year after year. Winemaker Peter Finlayson makes good use of the cool sea breeze and unique terroir of the estate to create some fantastic deep-south wines. Try the French-style Galpin Peak Pinot Noir. Finlayson, who has a great voice, maintains that pinot noir "is like opera. When it's great it is pure seduction, almost hedonistic. There is no middle road." You might wish to lay down a few bottles of the limited-release Tête de Cuvée Galpin Peak Pinot Noir, which gives off an exciting whiff of truffles; the 2005 vintage should be available. Bouchard is a short distance farther along the Hemel-en-Aarde Valley Road past Hamilton Russell Vineyards. ✉ *Off Hemel-en-Aarde Valley Rd. (R320)* ☎ *028/312-3515* ⊕ *www.bouchardfinlayson.co.za* ✉ *Tastings free* ⊙ *Weekdays 9:30–5, Sat. 9:30–12:30.*

WHERE TO STAY & EAT

If you want to avoid the crowds of Hermanus, consider lodging in the nearby tiny hamlet of Stanford.

$–$$$$ ✗**Burgundy.** In one of the village's original stone-and-clay fisherfolk cottages, the cozy Burgundy is one of Hermanus's oldest and best-loved restaurants. Not surprisingly, there's plenty of fish to be had on the extensive menu, from prawns and line fish to the specialty of the area—abalone, also known as perlemoen. The jury is out about just how tasty abalone is by itself, so it's usually served minced and highly flavored with other ingredients. Start with the delicate, delicious abalone with creamy mushrooms before you move on to succulent tiger

2

prawns or the fantastically fresh line fish served with lemon risotto, seasonal vegetables, and a lemon-dill sauce. The menu also includes a large choice of meat dishes, ranging from duck to venison, and a good vegetarian selection—something of a novelty in smaller towns. A creamy theme seems to run through the impressive dessert menu. The tiramisu is delicious, and you can even pretend it's good for you, as the menu describes it as "a nourishing dish to be eaten when feeling low." ⊠*Marine Dr.* ☎*028/312–2800* ▤*AE, DC, MC, V.*

$$–$$$ ✕**Mediterrea Seafood Restaurant.** You can't go wrong with excellent food and sweeping bay views, and Mediterrea regulars know to ask for a window seat. In whale season you can hear the giants blow just below you. The restaurant's owner is Greek and together with the chef strives to combine the best of Mediterranean cuisine with all that South African food has to offer. Favorite starters include baby calamari tubes flamed with vodka, capsicums, and fresh herbs and served on *tsatsiki* (Greek-style yogurt-cucumber-garlic dip), and prawns *lemoni*—tiger prawns simmered in a heavenly, creamy, garlic sauce and served with lightly toasted Mediterranean bread. For a main course, the lamb stuffed with garlic, rosemary, and apricots and slow-roasted in red wine and fresh herbs is out of this world, as are the medallions of ostrich fillet topped with a sweet-onion-and-chili marmalade. Or you could go straight for the ice-cream halvah (layers of phyllo and vanilla ice cream infused with pistachio halvah and drizzled with honey). ⊠*87 Marine Dr.* ☎*028/313–1685* ▤*AE, DC, MC, V* ☽*No lunch Mon.*

¢–$$$ ✕**Heaven.** If you're keen to escape the crush in Hermanus, Heaven is a good place to head for lunch. It's up the picturesque Hemel-en-Aarde Valley Road, where vines and fynbos cover the slopes and where you may wish you owned a country home. The view is wonderful, the service is attentive, and there's a good selection of local wines. The small, eclectic menu changes weekly but always emphasizes the best seasonal produce. Starters could include a salad of poached pears, greens, Brie, crispy bacon, fresh strawberries, pecan nuts, and pumpkin seeds. A main course might be substantial Mexican steak topped with a salsa of chopped avocado, red onion, tomato, and chilies, served with potato wedges and a side salad. ⊠*Hemel-en-Aarde Valley Rd. (R320)* ☎*072/905–3947* ▤*MC, V* ☽*Closed Mon. and May–Aug. No dinner.*

★ $–$$ ✕**Mariana's.** Mariana and Peter Esterhuizen started out selling organic vegetables at the Hermanus farmers' market before converting a house in the little village of Stanford, just 10 minutes away, into a restaurant. In just a few years they made their mark, and today Capetonians regularly make the trip for one of their memorable meals. What's the attraction? Excellent food, local wines, a relaxed setting, friendly hosts, and seasonal organic produce grown behind the restaurant. Mariana and Peter pick their ingredients moments before you arrive. You're welcome to wander around the garden, which is as much a tapestry as it is a veggie patch. The food is Mediterranean with a South African twist. The Gruyère soufflé is a sublimely light, cheesy concoction served in a pool of tomato cream. There's usually a warm trout or chicken salad, but if you're really hungry, go for the *skaap en dinge* (sheep and things), an enormous lamb shank served with mashed potatoes and seasonal vegetables. No children under 10 are permitted. ⊠ *12 du Toit St., Stanford* ☎*028/341–0272* ⚒ *Reservations essential* ☐*No credit cards* ⊘*Closed Mon.–Thurs. No dinner.*

$–$$ ✗**Mogg's Country Cookhouse.** Don't be put off by the bumpy dirt road heading up the Hemel-en-Aarde Valley. This restaurant on a fruit farm at the top of the valley is worth any amount of dust and corrugations. The converted laborer's cottage is as pretty as a picture in a tumble-down, overgrown kind of way, and the food is excellent in a relaxed and friendly setting. The seasonal menu is scribbled on a chalkboard. For starters you could expect beef carpaccio with a caper-and-olive dressing and pecorino cheese, or avocado-pear salad with hot walnut dressing and a sprinkle of blue cheese. Main courses might include chicken breast stuffed with tomatoes, olives, and feta and wrapped in phyllo, or homemade slow-roasted lamb shank accompanied by parsnip-potato mash with a mint-and-rosemary sauce. For dessert, homemade vanilla or Cointreau ice cream is served with a hot chocolate sauce. ⊠*Nuwe Pos farm, off the Hemel-en-Aarde Valley Rd. (R320)* ☎*028/312–4321* ☐*No credit cards* ⊘*Closed Mon. and Tues. No dinner Sun.–Fri.*

★ **$$$–$$$$** ✗▦**The Marine.** In an incomparable cliff-top setting, this venerable hotel has sumptuously decorated rooms. The sea-facing rooms, some with private balcony and all with under-floor heating, provide whale-watchers with grandstand views over Walker Bay. The revamped orangery invites you to linger over tea or drinks, and the two restaurants tempt with sophisticated menus. The Pavilion ($$$$), with wonderful views of Walker Bay, serves up-to-the-minute fare. Smoked snoek, calamari, prawn, and herb ravioli is a delicious first course, as is the potato gnocchi with wild mushrooms, cured ham, and celeriac velouté. Mains include roast rack of Karoo lamb with forest-mushroom mille-feuille, roasted beetroot, and lamb jus. Desserts are stunning, making many diners wish they'd left room for more. ⊠*Marine Dr., Box 9, 7200* ☎*028/313–1000* ⊕*www.marine-hermanus.co.za* ➬*43 rooms* ⚒*In-room: safe, refrigerator, DVD (some). In-hotel: 2 restaurants, room service, bar, pools, spa, no elevator, laundry service, concierge, public Internet, airport shuttle, parking (no fee), no kids under 12, no-smoking rooms* ☐*AE, DC, MC, V* ⓘ*BP.*

$$ ✗▦**Blue Gum Country Estate.** Husband-and-wife team Nic and Nicole Drupper run a top-notch establishment on the banks of the Klein River just 10 minutes from Stanford and 30 minutes from Hermanus. Blue Gum is a world away from the Hermanus crowds and a wonderful place to relax. The rooms are individually decorated in a style best described as English country house meets contemporary South African. The emphasis is on comfort, and the hotel seems like an extension of the Drupper's upscale home. The food (dinner only) is exceptional—Nicole is a trained chef, with a critical eye for detail—and you'll likely be only too happy to head back to Blue Gum at the end of a busy day exploring. The menu for the prix-fixe candlelighted dinners ($$$$) changes daily to make the most of seasonal ingredients, but you might start with chicken-tikka salad, followed by a tender beef fillet with spicy potatoes, roasted beetroot, and butternut squash. Weather permitting, you can have a predinner drink outside around the open fire. On the estate you can walk, trout fish, or wander around their small vineyard with the family dog—or give in to the luxury and just laze near the pool. ⊠ *Off R 326, Main Rd. to Caledon, Box 899, Stanford 7210* ☎ *028/341–0116* ⊕ *www.bluegum.co.za* ⟿ *12 rooms* ₺ *In-room: no a/c, safe, refrigerator. In-hotel: restaurant, room service (by request), bar, tennis court, pool, bicycles, no elevator, laundry service, public Internet, parking (no fee), no-smoking rooms* ⊟ *DC, MC, V* ⏇ *BP.*

$–$$ ▯ **Auberge Burgundy Guesthouse.** If you want to be in the center of the village, this stylish guesthouse is an excellent choice. You're a stone's throw from the famous whale-watching cliffs and the market, and three minutes from the Old Harbour Museum. When Hermanus took off as a tourist destination, this well-run and friendly operation was one of the first lodgings to take off with it. The rooms are comfortably decorated in French provincial style. Larger rooms with sleeper couches cost about a third more, but they're great for families or friends traveling together. Ask for a room with a balcony overlooking the bay or a suite that opens onto the pool. ⊠ *16 Harbour Rd., 7200* ☎ *028/313–1201* ⊕ *www.auberge.co.za* ⟿ *18 rooms* ₺ *In-room: no a/c, safe, kitchen (some), refrigerator. In-hotel: pool, no elevator, parking (no fee), no kids under 12, no-smoking rooms* ⊟ *AE, DC, MC, V* ⏇ *BP.*

$ ▯ **Whale Cottage, Hermanus.** Decorated in restful shades of blue and white, this is a great base from which to take long whale-watching walks. Ask for a room with a view, and put your feet up while you watch the Southern Right whales splashing in the bay below. Alternatively, take a stroll along the nearby whale-watching cliffs. An honor bar and tea and coffee are available throughout the day. ⊠ *38 Westcliff Dr., 7200* ☎ *028/313–0929* ⊕ *www.whalecottage.com* ⟿ *6 rooms* ₺ *In-room: no phone, safe, Wi-Fi. In-hotel: bar, pool, no elevator, public Wi-Fi, parking (no fee), no-smoking rooms* ⊟ *AE, DC, MC, V* ⏇ *BP.*

$ ▯ **Windsor.** If you come to Hermanus anytime from July to November, consider staying at this hotel in the heart of town. It's a family-run hostelry that offers comfort but little pretense. However, the hotel's position atop the cliffs makes it a great place to view the annual whale migration. Request one of the second-floor, sea-facing rooms, with huge sliding-glass doors and unbeatable views. ⊠ *Marine Dr., Box 3, 7200* ☎ *028/312–3727* ⟿ *70 rooms* ₺ *In-room: no a/c, refrigerator. In-hotel: room service, bar, no elevator, laundry service, public Internet, parking (no fee)* ⊟ *AE, DC, MC, V* ⏇ *BP.*

SPORTS & THE OUTDOORS

East of Hermanus the R43 hugs the strip of land between the mountains and the Klein River lagoon. The lagoon is popular with water-skiers, boaters, and anglers.

BOATING You can take a sunset cruise up the Klein River with **Walker Bay Adventures** (⊠ *Prawn Flats, off R43* ☎ *082/739–0159* ⊕ *www.walkerbay-adventures.co.za*). The cost is around R250 for the cruise and a braai afterward.

KAYAKING   For a really fun outing, join a gentle paddling excursion from the Old Harbour operated by **Walker Bay Adventures** (⊠ *Prawn Flats, off R43* ☎ *082/739–0159* ⊕ *www.walkerbayadventures.co.za*). You paddle in safe, stable double sea kayaks accompanied by a guide, and you pay around R250 for a two-hour morning trip. From July to December Walker Bay is a whale sanctuary, and this is the only company with a permit to operate here.

WHALE-
WATCHING &
SHARK DIVING   Although Hermanus is great for land-based whale-watching, you get a different perspective on a boat trip into Walker Bay. Boats leave on 2½-hour whale-watching trips (around R720) from both Hermanus and Gansbaai. **Dyer Island Cruises** (⊠ *Gansbaai* ☎ *082/801–8014* ⊕ *www.dyer-island-cruises.co.za*) is a good bet for whale-watching.

Shark diving is extremely popular (even Brad Pitt took the plunge), and Gansbaai has a number of operators working from the small harbor, including **White Shark Diving Company** (⊠ *Gansbaai* ☎ *082/559–6858*). A 4½-hour trip (with plenty of adrenaline) costs around R1,000, including breakfast and snacks on the boat. If you don't want to take the plunge (which you do in a cage, to keep you safe from the sharks), you can just stay in the boat and watch the sharks from the deck.

SHOPPING

Wine Village (⊠ *R43 and R320* ☎ *028/316–3988*) carries a good selection of South African wines, including wines from neighboring vineyards Hamilton Russell and Bouchard Finlayson as well as Southern Right.

BREDASDORP

14 *89 km (55 mi) east of Hermanus, 60 km (37 mi) east of Stanford.*

This sleepy agricultural town has a certain charm, as long as you don't catch it on a Sunday afternoon, when everything's closed and an air of ennui pervades the brassy, windswept streets. Each spring, however, the usual lethargic atmosphere is abandoned, and a radical sense of purpose takes its place when Bredasdorp hosts the Foot of Africa Marathon. Don't be lulled by the small-town country setting into thinking that this race is a breeze; word has it that the undulating landscape has the fittest athletes doubting their perseverance.

Housed in a converted church and rectory, the **Bredasdorp Museum** has an extensive collection of objects salvaged from the hundreds of ships that have gone down in the stormy waters off the Cape. In addition to the usual cannons and figureheads, the museum displays a surprising array of undamaged household articles rescued from the sea, including entire dining-room sets, sideboards, china, and phonographs. ⊠ *6 Independent St.* ☎ *028/424–1240* ⊕ *www.capeinfo.com/bredamuseum* 🎫 *R10* 🕒 *Weekdays 9–5, weekends 11–4.*

OFF THE
BEATEN
PATH   **Elim.** Little has changed in the last hundred years in this Moravian mission village founded in 1824: simple whitewashed cottages line the few streets, and the settlement's coloured residents all belong to the Moravian Church (⇨ *A Note on the Term "Coloured" box, above*).

2

At the Sunday 10 AM church service, which you're welcome to attend, just about the whole town turns out in their Sunday best, and voices soar in the white church at the top of the main street. The whole village has been declared a national monument, and it's the only town in the country that has a monument dedicated to the freeing of the slaves in 1838. It's also home to the country's oldest working clock and biggest wooden waterwheel. Elim is 36 km (22 mi) west of Bredasdorp and accessible only by dirt road. The easiest access is via the R317, off the R319 between Cape Agulhas and Bredasdorp.

Fodor'sChoice ★ **De Hoop Nature Reserve** is a huge conservation area covering 88,900 acres of isolated coastal terrain as well as a marine reserve extending 5 km (3 mi) out to sea. Massive white-sand dunes, mountains, and rare lowland fynbos are home to eland, bontebok, and Cape mountain zebra, as well as more than 250 bird species. Though the reserve is only three hours from Cape Town, it feels a lifetime away. Access is via the dirt road between Bredasdorp and Malgas. This is a fantastic place to watch whales from the shore—not quite as easy as in Hermanus but much less crowded. You can also hike the enormously popular **Whale Trail,** which runs through this reserve. A shuttle service takes your bags to each new stop, so all you have to carry is a small day pack and some water between overnight stops. You need to book up to a year in advance to enjoy the Whale Trail, or you might get lucky and snag a last-minute cancellation. In fact, this hike is now so popular that it's beginning to appear in online auctions. Self-catering cottages sleep up to four people and range from basic to fully equipped (weekdays R2,000, weekends R2,400). *Private Bag X16, 7280 028/425–5020 or 028/542–1253 www.capenature.org.za R24 Sat.–Thurs. 7–6, Fri. 7–7.*

Past De Hoop Nature Reserve on the dirt road from Bredasdorp is the small hamlet of **Malgas,** a major port in the 19th century before the mouth of the Breede River silted up. In addition to a tiny village, you will find the last hand-drawn car ferry in the country (R15 round-trip). It's fascinating to watch the technique, as the ferry operators "walk" the ferry across the river on a huge cable, leaning into their harnesses.

OFF THE
BEATEN
PATH

Cape Agulhas. From Bredasdorp it's just 41 km (25½ mi) through rolling farmland to the Cape Agulhas lighthouse. Although the cape is not nearly as spectacular as Cape Point, it's a wild and lonely place—rather fitting for the end of a wild and wonderful continent.

ARNISTON (WAENHUISKRANS)

★ ⑮ *25 km (15½ mi) southeast of Bredasdorp.*

Although its official name is Waenhuiskrans, and that's what you'll see on maps, this lovely, isolated vacation village is almost always called Arniston—after a British ship of that name that was wrecked on the nearby reef in 1815. Beautiful beaches, water that assumes Caribbean shades of blue, and mile after mile of towering white dunes attract anglers and vacationers alike. Only the frequent southeasters that blow off the sea and the chilly water are likely to put a damper on your enjoyment.

For 200 years a community of local fisherfolk has eked out a living here, setting sail each day in small fishing boats. Today their village, **Kassiesbaai** (translation: "suitcase bay," supposedly for all the suitcases that washed ashore from the frequent shipwrecks), is a national monument. It's fascinating wandering around the thatch cottages of this still-vibrant community, although declining fish stocks have left many families vulnerable. Abalone poaching is also a problem here. The adjacent village of Arniston has expanded enormously in the last two decades, thanks to the construction of vacation homes. Unfortunately, not all of the new architecture blends well with the whitewashed simplicity of the original cottages.

Waenhuiskrans is Afrikaans for "wagon-house cliff," and the village takes its other name from a vast **cave** 2 km (1 mi) south of town, which is theoretically large enough to house several wagons and their spans of oxen. Signs point the way over the dunes to the cave, which is accessible only at low tide. You need shoes to protect your feet from the sharp rocks, and you should wear something you don't mind getting wet. It's definitely worth the trouble, however, to see this stunning spot.

WHERE TO STAY & EAT

★ $$ ✕🏨 **Arniston Hotel.** You could easily spend a week here and still need to be dragged away. The setting, a crescent of white dunes, has a lot to do with the Arniston's appeal, but the hotel also strikes a fine balance between elegance and beach-vacation comfort. Request a sea-facing room, where you can enjoy the ever-changing colors of the horizon and have a grandstand view of the large concentration of cow-and-calf pairs found here during the whaling season, between June and November. The à la carte menu ($–$$$$) offers substantial variety, with few surprises, but the grilled catch of the day is as fresh as you can get. Oenophiles rejoice at the quality of the deservedly renowned wine list. Lunch, which is included in the rate along with a full breakfast, is served on the patio in fine weather. ✉ *Beach Rd., Arniston* 📮 *Box 126, Bredasdorp 7280* ☎ *028/445–9000* 🌐 *www.arnistonhotel.com* 🛏 *60 rooms* ⚴ *In-room: no a/c, safe, refrigerator, dial-up. In-hotel: restaurant, room service, bar, pool, spa, beachfront, laundry service, concierge, airport shuttle, parking (no fee), no-smoking rooms* ▭ *AE, DC, MC, V* 🍴 *BP.*

SWELLENDAM

★ ⑯ *72 km (45 mi) north of Arniston (Waenhuiskrans).*

Beautiful Swellendam lies in the shadow of the imposing Langeberg. Founded in 1745, it is the third-oldest town in South Africa, and many of its historic buildings have been elegantly restored. Even on a casual drive along the main street you'll see a number of lovely Cape

Dutch homes, with their traditional whitewashed walls, gables, and thatch roofs.

The centerpiece of the town's historical past is the **Drostdy Museum,** a collection of buildings dating from the town's earliest days. The Drostdy was built in 1747 by the Dutch East India Company to serve as the residence of the *landdrost,* the magistrate who presided over the district. The building is furnished in a style that was common in the mid-19th century. A path leads through the Drostdy herb gardens to Mayville, an 1855 middle-class home that blends elements of Cape Dutch and Cape Georgian architecture. Across Swellengrebel Street stand the old jail and the Ambagswerf, an outdoor exhibit of tools used by the town's blacksmiths, wainwrights, coopers, and tanners. ⊠*18 Swellengrebel St.* ☎*028/514–1138* ✉*info@drostdymuseum.co.za* 🖅*R15* ⏱*Oct.–Apr., daily 9–4:30; May–Sept., daily 10–4.*

Swellendam's **Dutch Reformed Church** is an imposing white edifice built in 1911 in an eclectic style. The gables are baroque, the windows Gothic, the cupola vaguely Eastern, and the steeple extravagant. Surprisingly, all the elements work together wonderfully. Inside is an interesting tiered amphitheater with banks of curving wood pews facing the pulpit and organ. ⊠*7 Voortrek St.* ☎*028/514–1225* 🖅*R5; services free* ⏱*Weekdays 8–4; services (in Afrikaans) Sun. at 9:30.*

If you'd like to stretch your legs, take a hike in the **Marloth Nature Reserve** in the Langeberg above town. Five easy walks, ranging from one to four hours, explore some of the mountain gorges. An office at the entrance to the reserve has trail maps and hiking information. There is a five-day trail, which costs R55 per person per day in addition to the park entrance fee. If you're doing a day walk, park outside the entrance boom. Although you can stay in the reserve until sunset, the gates close at the time advertised. ✛*1½ km (1 mi) from Voortrek St. on Andrew White St. to golf course, and follow signs* ☎*028/514–1410* ⊕*www.capenature.org.za* 🖅*R24* ⏱*Daily 7–4.*

Covering just 6,880 acres of coastal fynbos, **Bontebok National Park** is one of the smallest of South Africa's national parks. Don't expect to see big game here—the park contains no elephants, lions, or rhinos. What you will see are bontebok, graceful white-face antelope nearly exterminated by hunters in the early 20th century, as well as red hartebeest, Cape grysbok, steenbok, duiker, and the endangered Cape mountain zebra. Two short walking trails start at the campsite, next to the Breede River. ⊠*Off the N2, 5 km (3 mi) from Swellendam* ☎*028/514–2735* ⊕*www.sanparks.org* 🖅*R20* ⏱*May–Sept., daily 7–6; Oct.–Apr., daily 7–7.*

WHERE TO STAY & EAT

$$ ✕🏠 **Klippe Rivier Country House.** Amid rolling farmland 3 km (2 mi) outside Swellendam, this guesthouse occupies one of the Overberg's most gracious and historic country homes. It was built around 1825 in traditional Cape style, with thick white walls, a thatch roof, and a distinctive gable. Guests stay in enormous rooms in the converted stables. The three downstairs rooms are furnished with antiques in

Cape Dutch, colonial, and Victorian styles. Upstairs, raw-wood beams, cane ceilings, and bold prints set the tone for less expensive Provençal-style rooms with small balconies. Some public rooms have trouble supporting the sheer volume of antique collectibles, which gives them a museumlike quality. The delectable three-course dinners ($$$$) are table d'hôte and prepared with fresh herbs, vegetables, fruit, and cream from surrounding farms. ⊠ *On dirt road off R60 to Ashton, Box 483, 6740* ☎ *028/514–3341* ⊕ *www.klipperivier.com* ⇆ *6 rooms, 1 cottage* ☐ *In-room: no TV (some). In-hotel: restaurant, room service (by request), pool, no elevator, laundry service, public Wi-Fi, parking (no fee), no kids under 8, no-smoking rooms* ☐ *AE, DC, MC, V* ◎ *BP*.

$–$$ ☷ **Mardouw Country House.** The old Cape Georgian farmhouse on this working wine-and-olive farm has been beautifully converted into a luxury guesthouse with stunning views of the Langeberg mountains. Among the amenities are an infinity pool, wide verandas, under-floor heating, and an attentive staff. Clean, contemporary lines decorate the tasteful rooms. The estate produces its own pinotage and chenin blanc, which you can enjoy at Mardouw's sumptuous four-course dinners. The country house has its own herb-and-vegetable garden, so the emphasis is on fresh, seasonal food. The menu changes daily but might include a prawn starter and a main course of succulent beef medallions served with beetroot couscous and fresh ribbon vegetables. The chef's olive ice cream is a favorite on the dessert menu, and the cheese platter includes cheeses from a neighboring farm together with homemade preserves—figs in syrup, tomato jam, and marrow marmalade. Special arrangements must be made in advance for children. ⊠ *R60, between Ashton and Swellendam* ✉ *Box 625, Swellendam 6740* ☎ *023/616–2999* ⊕ *www.mardouw.com* ⇆ *3 rooms, 2 suites* ☐ *In-room: safe, refrigerator, DVD. In-hotel: room service, bar, golf course, pool, bicycles, no elevator, laundry service, public Wi-Fi, airport shuttle, parking (no fee), no-smoking rooms* ☐ *MC, V* ⊙ *Closed July* ◎ *BP*.

$ ☷ **Coachman Guesthouse.** Dating to the 18th century and declared a national monument in 1983, this guesthouse is in the historic heart of Swellendam, within easy walking distance of all the major sights and restaurants. A lovely garden surrounds the house; the rooms have entrances that open onto a courtyard, and two thatch garden cottages have their own verandas and great views over the Langeberg mountains. Rooms are charmingly furnished with brass beds and comfortable throws. The pool is an absolute necessity in summer, when temperatures soar. ⊠ *14 Drostdy St., 6740* ☎ *028/514–2294* ⊕ *www.coachman.co.za* ⇆ *4 rooms, 2 cottages* ☐ *In-room: no a/c, no phone, safe, kitchen, refrigerator, no TV, Wi-Fi. In-hotel: room service, bar, pool, no elevator, laundry service, public Wi-Fi, airport shuttle, parking (no fee), some pets allowed, no-smoking rooms* ☐ *AE, DC, MC, V* ◎ *BP*.

★ $ ☷ **The Hideaway.** The Victorian homestead and its three luxury cottages are set in a peaceful garden with literally hundreds of rosebushes. Although the setting and beautifully appointed cottages are excellent reasons to stay here, it's the level of hospitality that sets this place above the rest. The owners' dedication extends to providing lifts, planning routes, and presenting the best breakfast (complete with 38 homemade jams) for many miles around. ✉*10 Hermanus Steyn St., 6740* ☎*028/514–3316* ⊕*www.hideawaybb.co.za* ⤺*4 suites* ⬧*In-room: no phone, safe, refrigerator, no TV. In-hotel: pool, bicycles, no elevator, laundry service, public Internet, parking (no fee), some pets allowed, no kids under 10, no-smoking rooms* ▤*AE, MC, V* ◉*BP.*

2

SPORTS & THE OUTDOORS

HORSEBACK
RIDING

You can take just a little trot or a longer excursion through the Marloth Nature Reserve on horseback with **Two Feathers Horse Trails** (✉*Kolo-niesbos Hut* ☎*082/494–8279* ⊕*www.twofeathers.co.za*). Expect to pay between R150 for an hour and R850 for a full-day ride, including a packed lunch.

▌EN
ROUTE

From Swellendam return to the N2 and turn right toward Cape Town. The road sweeps through rich, rolling cropland that extends to the base of the Langeberg. A few kilometers after the town of Riverson-derend (pronounced riff-*ear*-sonder-ent), turn right onto the R406, a good gravel road that leads to the village of Greyton, in the lee of the Riviersonderend Mountains.

GREYTON

★ ⑰ *32 km (20 mi) west of Swellendam.*

The charming village of Greyton, filled with white thatch cottages and quiet lanes, is a popular weekend retreat for Capetonians as well as a permanent home for many retirees. The village offers almost nothing in the way of traditional sights, but it's a relaxing place to stop for a meal or a night, and a great base for walks into the surrounding mountains. There are plenty of small B&Bs and guesthouses to stay in, but no large hotels.

After Greyton the R406 becomes paved. Drive 5 km (3 mi) to the turnoff to **Genadendal** *(Valley of Grace)*, a Moravian mission station founded in 1737 to educate the Khoekhoen and convert them to Christianity. Seeing this impoverished hamlet today, it's difficult to comprehend the major role this mission played in the early history of South Africa. In the late 18th century it was the second-largest settlement after Cape Town, and its Khoekhoen craftspeople produced the finest silver cutlery and woodwork in the country. Some of the first written works in Afrikaans were printed here, and the coloured community greatly influenced the development of Afrikaans as it is heard today *(⇨A Note on the Term "Coloured" box, above)*. None of this went down well with the white population. By 1909 new legislation prohibited coloured ownership of land, and in 1926 the Department of Public Education closed the settlement's teachers' training college, arguing that coloureds were better employed on neighboring farms. In 1980 all the buildings on Church Square were declared national monuments (it's considered the country's most authentic church square), but despite a number of community-based projects, Genadendal has endured a long slide into obscurity and remains impoverished. In 1995, then-president Nelson Mandela renamed his official residence Genadendal. You can walk the streets and tour the historic buildings facing Church Square. Genadendal is still a mission station, and community tour guides show interested visitors around.

Of particular note in Genadendal is the **Genadendal Mission Museum,** spread through 15 rooms in three buildings. The museum collection, the only one in South Africa to be named a National Cultural Treasure, includes unique household implements, books, tools, and musical instruments, among them the country's oldest pipe organ. Wall displays examine mission life in the Cape in the 18th and 19th centuries, focusing on the early missionaries' work with the Khoekhoen. Unfortunately, many of the displays are in Afrikaans only. ⊠ *Off R406* ☎ *028/251–8582* ▭ *R10* ⊙ *Mon.–Thurs. 8:30–5, Fri. 8:30–3:30, Sat. 10–2.*

WHERE TO STAY

$ ▦ **Acorns on Oak.** A luxurious B&B, Acorns on Oak prides itself on repeat customers. Don't be put off by the seeming lack of amenities. There may be no TV in the rooms, but most guests don't miss it for one moment in this picturesque village. What you will find are mountain views, a pool, and a relaxing garden. Each peaceful, quiet suite was inspired by a different destination, such as Tuscany, Exmoor, and Provence. As soon as the weather gets chilly (in winter it's not unusual for there to be snow on the surrounding peaks), your hosts will light an enormous fire in the common-area fireplace. ⊠ *2 Oak St., 7233* ☎ *028/254–9567 or 082/367–2614* ⊕ *www.acorns-on-oak.co.za/* ⤶ *5 suites* ⌂ *In-room: refrigerator (some), no TV. In-hotel: pool, parking (no fee), no kids under 14, no-smoking rooms* ▭ *MC, V* ⦿ *BP.*

SPORTS & THE OUTDOORS

To get your heart rate up, your best bet is to contact **IntrApid Adventures** (☎ *021/461–4918 or 082/324–1188* ⊕ *www.raftsa.co.za*), which offers full-day adventures that include anything from a gentle rafting trip on the Sonderend River to a short mountain-bike ride to a scenic rappel. Trips cost R450–R900 for a full day (prices are based on a minimum of six people).

HIKING   In addition to day hikes and short walks, you can take the 32-km (20-mi) **Boesmanskloof Trail** through the Riviersonderend Mountains between Greyton and the exquisite hamlet of McGregor *(⇨ Breede River Valley, above).* In the good old days, youngsters used to walk from Greyton to McGregor for an energetic game of tennis before walking home again the same evening. Accommodations, in hiking huts on a private farm (R50 per person excluding bedding), can be booked through **Barry Oosthuizen** (☎ *023/625–1735*), who will also buy groceries and leave them at the hut, charging you only what he pays. Hikers often book the following night's accommodation at a local B&B, and have a good meal and a good night's sleep before heading home. In McGregor the trailhead is a ways from the town, but most guesthouses will pick you up and drop you off. Note that cell-phone coverage is sporadic on the trail.

To book the 25-km (15½-mi) **Genadendal Hiking Trail,** which costs R25 per person per day for a permit, contact the De Hoop Nature Reserve *(see Bredasdorp, above).* Accommodations (R30 per person) are in huts on the farm **De Hoek** (☎ *023/626–2176 or 082/400–6677)*, which has a gas stove, hot showers, flush toilets, a braai, and wood. If you like, you may spend a night at the **Moravian Mission Church** (☎ *028/251–8346)*, where the hike starts and ends.

EN ROUTE

To head back toward Cape Town, follow the R406 to the N2. After the town of Bot River the road leaves the wheat fields and climbs into the mountains. It's lovely country, full of rock and pine forest interspersed with orchards. **Sir Lowry's Pass** serves as the gateway to Cape Town and the Winelands, a magnificent breach in the mountains that opens to reveal the curving expanse of False Bay, the long ridge of the peninsula, and, in the distance, Table Mountain.

OVERBERG ESSENTIALS

To research prices, get advice from other travelers, and book travel arrangements, visit www.fodors.com.

TRANSPORTATION

BY BUS

Intercape Mainliner, Greyhound, and Translux have daily service throughout most of the Western Cape, especially to the bigger towns on the N2. Swellendam is a major hub and a good transit point, but to enjoy smaller towns such as Greyton or those along the coast, you'll need your own transportation.

Bus Lines **Greyhound** (⊠ *1 Adderley St., Cape Town* ☎ *083/915–9000* ⊕ *www. greyhound.co.za)*. **Intercape Mainliner** (⊠ *1 Adderley St., Cape Town* ☎ *0861/287– 287, 083/909–0909 for alternate booking through Computicket* ⊕ *www.intercape. co.za)*. **Translux Express Bus** (⊠ *1 Adderley St., Cape Town* ☎ *0861/589–282* ⊕ *www.translux.co.za)*.

BY CAR

Driving yourself is undoubtedly the best way to appreciate this lovely and diverse area. The roads in the area are generally good. They are signposted, and major routes are paved. For the most part, you'll come across gravel roads only around Elim and Napier and from Swellendam to Malgas, and they may be a bit rutted and bumpy. A two-wheel-drive vehicle is fine, but take it easy if it's been raining, as gravel roads can get slippery. You'll need a 4x4 only if you're planning to tackle some of the more remote back roads or want to do a 4x4 route.

The major car-rental agencies have offices in the bigger towns, such as Hermanus and Swellendam. However, it's best to deal with the Cape Town offices; you'll probably want to pick up a car at the airport anyway. *For car-rental agencies, see Winelands Essentials, above.*

The Overberg stretches over an enormous area, so you need to decide where you're heading before planning your route. If you want to enjoy the beauty of the coast, then take the N2 from Cape Town, but, instead of heading up Sir Lowry's Pass, turn off to Gordon's Bay and follow the R44, also known as Clarence Drive, along the scenic route. Just after Kleinmond the road becomes the R41 and turns inland to bypass the Bot River lagoon. It becomes the R43 as it makes its way toward Hermanus. If you want to explore inland, however, take the N2 over Sir Lowry's Pass and past Caledon and Swellendam. To get to the pretty hamlet of Greyton, take the R406 to your left just before Caledon.

Keep in mind that on Sunday afternoons and in early evenings traffic returning to the city via Sir Lowry's Pass can be very congested. Expect delays as you enter Somerset West, and be very careful if it is misty (which it often is on the pass), as this stretch of road sees numerous accidents each year. Leaving Cape Town on a Friday afternoon can also take time, so try to leave by lunchtime to avoid traffic jams.

CONTACTS & RESOURCES

EMERGENCIES

There are doctors and dentists in every town, as well as provincial hospitals in all but the smallest villages. Hermanus has a private hospital. Late-night pharmacies are a rarity in these small towns, but all pharmacies have emergency and after-hours numbers.

Emergency Services **Ambulance** (☎ *10177*). **Police** (☎ *10111*). **Police, Fire, and Ambulance** (☎ *107 from landline*). **Vodacom emergency services** (☎ *112 from mobile phone*).

Hospitals **Hermanus Medi-Clinic** (✉ *Hospital St., Hermanus* ☎ *028/313–0168*). **Otto du Plessis Hospital** (✉ *Dorpsig and van Riebeek Sts., Bredasdorp* ☎ *028/424–1167*). **Swellendam Hospital** (✉ *18 Drostdy St., Swellendam* ☎ *028/514–1142*).

INTERNET

You won't find an Internet café on every corner, though you will find some in the more touristy destinations, such as Hermanus. First inquire at your hotel or B&B, as many allow guests access for a small fee. Print shops also often have an Internet station. Expect to pay around R10 for 10 minutes, but this varies from shop to shop.

Internet Access **Comcell** (✉ *16 Donkin St., Caledon* ☎ *028/214–1732*). **Maxitec** (✉ *155 Main Rd., Hermanus* ☎ *086/123–4777*).

MONEY MATTERS

There are plenty of ATMs and banks throughout the region, so you won't have a problem withdrawing or exchanging money. As always, take care when getting large sums of money, and make sure you have your bank and credit cards with you at all times. You'll be able to use your credit card just about everywhere—except at some smaller farm stalls.

TOURS

There are a number of individuals and small companies offering customized tours. A day trip, which should cost R400–R500 including a packed lunch, could involve an excursion to De Hoop Nature Reserve, with plenty of time to admire the birds, fynbos, and whales; a ride on the ferry at Malgas; and time at Bontebok National Park. Or you

2

could start in Swellendam and then head over picturesque Tradouw Pass through the spectacular Cape Fold mountains to Barrydale, where you could do some wine tasting before heading on to Robertson. Other tours concentrate on the historic fishing village of Arniston (Waenhuis-krans), Bredasdorp, and Elim.

Having grown up in the Overber, Jacob Human from Ruggens en Rante knows the area well and can take you on customized day trips. Two of her favorite destinations are the De Hoop Nature Reserve and the quaint village of Elim, once a thriving Moravian mission station.

Wilson Salukazana, a former Hermanus whale crier, now conducts land-based whale-watching tours in the town. He's got all the experience in the world and can spot a Southern Right from miles away. When the whales aren't blowing in the bay, he conducts township tours. On a guided walk through the nearby township of Zwelihle, you can have a Xhosa meal, visit a traditional African healer, and meet local residents.

Tour Operators **Ruggens en Rante** (⊠ *Arniston* ☎ *028/445-9998 or 082/747-0141*). **Wilson Salukazana** (⊠ *Hermanus* ☎ *073/214-6949*).

VISITOR INFORMATION

Yours truly, can get plenty of information on the Overberg at the Cape Town Tourism offices; these are open weekdays 8–6, Saturday 8:30–1, Sunday 9–1. The Cape Agulhas Tourism Bureau has information for Bredasdorp, Elim, L'Agulhas, Struisbaai, and Arniston. It's open weekdays 8–5 and Saturday 9–12:30. The Greyton Tourism Bureau is open daily 9–5. The Hangklip-Kleinmond Tourism Bureau has information on Kleinmond, Betty's Bay, Pringle Bay, and Rooiels, and is open weekdays 8:30–5, Saturday 9–2, and Sunday 10–2. The Hermanus Tourism Bureau is open in summer weekdays 8–6, Saturday 9–5, and Sunday 10–3, and in winter Monday–Saturday 9–5. Overberg Tourism, open weekdays 8–4:30, is a good information clearinghouse and source of brochures. The Swellendam Tourism Bureau is open weekdays 9–5, weekends 9–1.

Tourist Offices **Cape Agulhas Tourism Bureau** (⊠ *Long St., Box 51, 7280 Bredasdorp* ☎ *028/424-2584*). **Cape Town Tourism** (⊠ *The Pinnacle, Burg and Castle Sts., Box 1403, Cape Town 8000* ☎ *021/487-6800* ⊕ *www.tourismcapetown.co.za*). **Greyton Tourism Bureau** (⊠ *29 Main Rd., Greyton 7233* ☎ *028/254-9414 or 028/254-9564* ⊕ *www.greyton.net*). **Hangklip–Kleinmond Tourism Bureau** (⊠ *14 Harbour Rd., Kleinmond 7195* ☎ *028/271-5657* ⊕ *www.ecoscape.org.za*). **Hermanus Tourism Bureau** (⊠ *Lord Robert and Mitchell Sts., Hermanus 7200* ☎ *028/312-2629* ⊕ *www.hermanus.co.za*). **Overberg Tourism** (⊠ *22 Plein St., Caledon 7230* ☎ *028/214-1466* ⊕ *www.tourismcapeoverberg.co.za*). **Swellendam Tourism Bureau** (⊠ *Oefeningshuis, Voortrek St., Swellendam 6740* ☎ *028/514-2770* ⊕ *www.swellendamtourism.co.za*).

WEST COAST

The West Coast is an acquired taste. It's dry and bleak, and other than the ubiquitous exotic gum trees, nothing grows higher than your knees. But it's a wild and wonderful place. An icy sea pounds long deserted beaches or rocky headlands, and the sky stretches for miles.

Historically, this area has been populated by hardy fisherfolk and tough, grizzled farmers. Over the years they have worked out a balance with the extreme elements—responding with a stoic minimalism that is obvious in the building styles, the cuisine, and the language.

Unfortunately, minimalism became fashionable, and urban refugees started settling on the West Coast. The first lot wasn't bad—they bought tattered old houses and renovated them just enough to make them livable. Then came those who insisted on building replicas of their suburban homes at the coast. And then—worst of all—came the developers. They bought up huge tracts of land and cut them into tiny little plots, popping horrid little houses onto them. Or perhaps they'd turn a whole bay into a pseudo-Greek village. As a result, the austere aesthetic that makes the West Coast so special is fast disappearing. But it's not gone—at least not yet.

Just inland from the West Coast is the Swartland (Black Ground, a reference to the fertile soil that supports a flourishing wheat and wine industry). Rolling wheat fields extend as far as the eye can see to mountains on either side. In summer the heat is relentless, and there's a sea of golden-brown grain, but in winter the landscape is a shimmery green, and when there's snow on the mountains, it's as pretty as can be. The Swartland includes Piketberg, Malmesbury, Darling (also considered part of the West Coast), and the twin towns of Riebeek West and Riebeek Kasteel.

To the north, the Cederberg is an absolutely beautiful and rugged range of mountains, most of which is a designated wilderness area. In South Africa that means you may hike there with a permit, but there are no laid-out trails and no accommodations or facilities of any kind. Fantastic rock formations, myriad flowering plants, delicate rock art, and crystal-clear streams with tinkling waterfalls and deep pools make this a veritable hiker's paradise.

A loop around the West Coast, Swartland, and the Cederberg, starting from Cape Town, will take a minimum of three days, but the distances are long, so plan to spend more time here if you can.

EN ROUTE   As you head out of Cape Town on the N1 or R27 on your way up the coast, it's easy to whiz past the tiny whitewashed settlement of Mamre on the R304. But it's worth turning off here to check out the old thatched buildings that made up the **Moravian Mission Station,** founded in 1808. The church here is usually always open, but phone ahead to make sure. All the buildings dating from this period have been restored and declared national monuments. Unfortunately, the rest of the town is unlovely and crippled with the usual ills of unemployment and poverty. ✉ *Church St.* ☎ *021/576–1296.*

DARLING

(18) *82 km (51 mi) north of Cape Town via the N7 and R315.*

Darling is best known for two draws: its sensational wildflowers and its sensational performer, Pieter-Dirk Uys, otherwise known as Evita Bezuidenhout. The wildflowers are usually at their best August–October, and there's an annual Wildflower and Orchid Show held in September. Evita is at her best all year-round *(see Nightlife, below)*. When driving into Darling, ignore the rather unattractive new houses on the Cape Town side of the village, and head straight through to the Victorian section of town, where pretty period houses line up amid lush gardens.

During the flower season the **Tienie Versfeld Wildflower Reserve** is just fantastic: a wonderful, unpretentious, uncommercialized little gem. ⊠ *R315, 12 km (7½ mi) west of Darling* 🎫 *Free* ⊘ *Daily 24 hrs.*

A more formal flower experience than Tienie Versfeld Wildflower Reserve, **Rondeberg Nature Reserve** is justly proud of the more than 900 species found here, including rare disas (a type of orchid), which you aren't likely to find elsewhere as easily. All visits are via guided tours of the grounds, so you must call ahead to reserve a tour. ⊠ *R27, 25 km (15½ mi) outside Darling* 🕿 *022/492-3099* ⊕ *www.rondeberg.co.za* 🎫 *R50* ⊘ *Flower season, usually Mar.–Oct.; call for tour times.*

Former dairy farmer Peter Pentz had enough of getting up at 4 AM to milk his cows, so together with his son Nick he turned instead to wine farming at **Groote Post Vineyard.** Groote Post fans couldn't be happier. The large, environmentally sensitive winery got off to a fantastic start when its maiden '99 sauvignon blanc was judged one of the best in the Cape, and Groote Post has been garnering awards ever since. Try the delicate 2006 sauvignon blanc, or the 2005 merlot with hints of chocolate and berries. There are no cellar tours. The restaurant, Hilda's Kitchen (named after the famous Hildagonda Duckitt, the Cape's answer to Mrs. Beeton), is an excellent choice for a lunch. A large portion of the farm has been left uncultivated and is covered with endangered *renosterveld* (literally, "rhino countryside" in Afrikaans) vegetation, which is only found in this area. These scrubby bushes might not look like much, but in the past they used to support large herds of game. Because the vegetation grows in fertile soil, a lot of renosterveld has been lost to agriculture. It's also very susceptible to fire and is the most endangered vegetation type in the Cape floral kingdom. At this writing, Groote Post was planning to introduce game drives through this unique vegetation. ⊠ *Off R307* 🕿 *022/492-2825* ⊕ *www.grootepost.com* 🎫 *Tastings free* ⊘ *Weekdays 8–5, weekends 9–3.*

Large **Darling Cellars** produces wines under a number of labels. In the Onyx range, look for the 2003 Kroon, the cellar's flagship wine and a stylish blend of pinotage, shiraz, grenache, and cinsaut. Other suggestions include the 2003 pinotage and the 2006 sauvignon blanc. The DC range has some pleasing reds, including the nice, spicy Black

Granite Shiraz and the 2005 Terra Hutton Cabernet Sauvignon. The newer Flamingo Bay range is proving that it can produce more than pleasant quaffs. In keeping with the West Coast, try the flamingo-pink Lagoon Rosé. ⊠*R315* ☎*022/492–2276* ⊕*www.darlingcellars.co.za* ▣*Tastings free* ⊙*Mon.–Thurs. 8–5, Fri. 8–4, Sat. 10–2; cellar tours by appointment.*

WHERE TO STAY & EAT

$ ✕▥ **Trinity Guest Lodge and Restaurant.** This old Victorian house has been elegantly transformed into a stylish and comfortable guest lodge. White linen and subtle furnishings create a restful atmosphere. Some bathrooms have Victorian claw-foot tubs. Regularly voted one of South Africa's top-100 dining establishments, the restaurant ($) will likely have you coming back for more, especially for dishes such as roast beef fillet with a verjuice-hollandaise sauce. The menu changes daily, and there are also interesting food-and-wine-pairing dinners that are worth inquiring about. For the lodge, arrangements must be made in advance for children. ⊠*19 Long St., 7345* ☎*022/492–3430* ⊕*www.trinitylodge.co.za* ➳*6 rooms* ⚘*In-room: no a/c, no phone, safe. In-hotel: restaurant, room service, pool, no elevator, laundry service, public Internet, parking (no fee), some pets allowed, no-smoking rooms* ▤*DC, MC, V* ⦿*BP.*

$ ▥ **Darling Lodge.** You'll soon be made to feel at home at this pretty Victorian B&B set in a lovely garden in the heart of the village. The three individually decorated rooms in the main house are all named after local artists whose prints hang on the walls, and all have en-suite Victorian bathrooms. There are also three pool-deck rooms. There's plenty going on in the area, and you'll probably be ready for a refuge at the end of the day, perhaps in one of the claw-foot tubs or with a drink from the honesty bar. ⊠*22 Pastorie St., 7345* ☎*022/492–3062* ⊕*www.darlinglodge.co.za* ➳*6 rooms* ⚘*In-room: no a/c, no phone, no TV, Wi-Fi. In-hotel: bar, pool, no elevator, laundry service, airport shuttle, parking (no fee), some pets allowed, no-smoking rooms* ▤*No credit cards* ⦿*BP.*

NIGHTLIFE & THE ARTS

Fodor'sChoice   One of Darling's main attractions is **Evita se Perron** (⊠*Darling station*
★   ☎*022/492–2831 or 022/492–2851* ⊕*www.evita.co.za*), the theater and restaurant started by satirist and drag-artist Pieter-Dirk Uys. The theater is on the platform of the Darling station (*perron* is the Afrikaans word for "railway platform"). Pieter-Dirk Uys has made his alter ego, Evita Bezuidenhout, a household name in South Africa. Performances cost R95 and take place Friday evening, Saturday afternoon and evening, and Sunday afternoon. Come early to enjoy a buffet meal in the restaurant. In the same complex, **Evita's A en C** is the gallery of an arts-and-crafts collective and skills-development center. Here you can see and buy works from West Coast artists. It's open daily 10–5.

Pieter-Dirk Uys: Everyone's Darling

It's fitting that Pieter-Dirk Uys (www.pdu.co.za) and his alter ego, Evita Bezuidenhout, live in a village called Darling. He's the darling of South African satire, and his speech is peppered with dramatic and warm-hearted "dahlings." *Tannie* (Auntie) Evita is as much a South African icon as braais and biltong.

But let's backtrack. Evita Bezuidenhout debuted in a newspaper column written by playwright Pieter-Dirk Uys in the 1970s. He dished the dirt as though he were an insider at the Nationalist Party. His mysterious source's voice grew so strong that she was soon nicknamed the "Evita of Pretoria." She hit the stage in the early 1980s, when apartheid was in full swing and the ruling Nationalist Party was short on humor.

Uys's first production, *Adapt or Dye*, was at a small venue in Johannesburg at 11 PM, a time when he hoped the censors would be in bed. The titles of his shows and some characters (all of which he plays himself) are intricately wound up with South African politics and life. *Adapt or Dye*, for instance, was based on a speech by former prime minister P. W. Botha, who said, "South Africans have to adapt to a changing world or die." For a country ripped apart by politics based on color, it was a play on words Uys couldn't resist.

Every performance shows an intricate understanding of the country and her people. Over the years, Uys's richest material has come from the government. Most politicians were happy to be lampooned; in an inhumane society, laughing at themselves made them seem more human. If there's any criticism leveled at Uys, it's that for all his biting remarks, he played court jester to the apartheid government and held back when he could have gone for the kill. He would argue that shows need a balance between punches and tickles. Too many punches don't put bums on seats; too many tickles can be vacuous.

Uys is not just about comedy and satire, however. He's deeply committed to transforming society. Before the first democratic elections in 1994, he embarked on self-funded voter-education tours. He's now channeling his considerable energy into tackling HIV/AIDS, which he believes the government is ignoring. He talks at schools, where he uses humor and intelligence and pulls no punches. During his talk he demonstrates how to put a condom on a banana. This he swiftly replaces with a rubber phallus, "because," he explains with a twinkle, "men and boys don't have bananas between their legs. A condom on a banana on the bedside table is not going to protect you!" Of course the kids shriek with laughter.

In 2002 Uys was nominated a national living treasure by the South African Human Sciences Research Council. Tannie Evita also has more than a few fans. She was awarded the Living Legacy 2000 Award in San Diego by the Women's International Center for "her contribution to the place of women in the last century." In 2005, Pieter-Dirk Uys wrote his autobiography, *Between the Devil and The Deep—A Memoir of Acting and Reacting*, in an attempt to capture a part of his extraordinary life. The book is good, but can only go so far in portraying a man and his alter ego, both of whom are larger than life. Here's to you, dahling.

—Karena du Plessis

LANGEBAAN

⑲ *50 km (31 mi) northwest of Darling.*

Probably the most popular destination on the coast, Langebaan is a great base from which to explore the region, and the sheltered lagoon makes for fantastic water sports, especially windsurfing, kite surfing, and sea kayaking. The town has a truly laid-back, beachy feel. To quote a local: "There is nowhere in Langebaan you can't go barefoot." Lots of Capetonians have weekend houses and head here on Friday afternoons with boats, bikes, and boards in tow. If you're not into water sports and serious tanning, however, Langebaan doesn't have that much to offer. The town grew up around a slipway, yacht club, and cluster of brick-faced beach houses, and the main drag is unexciting. Though the town comes alive in summer as youngsters crowd the beach and flex their muscles, during the off-season Langebaan quickly reverts to a quiet settlement where people retire to fish and mess about on boats.

Even if you don't stop in **West Coast National Park,** consider driving the scenic road that runs through it rather than the R27 to Langebaan. The park is a fabulous mix of lagoon wetlands, pounding surf, and coastal fynbos. On a sunny day the lagoon assumes a magical color, made all the more impressive by blinding-white beaches and the sheer emptiness of the place. Birders can have a field day identifying waterbirds, and the sandveld flowers are among the best along the West Coast. Postberg, the little mountain at the tip of the reserve where ships would drop off their mail on their trip around the Cape, is open only in flower season, which changes from year to year but usually falls between August and October, when the flowers are at their very best. It's easy to run out of superlatives when describing West Coast flowers, but imagine acres of land carpeted in multicolored blooms—as far as the eye can see. If you're lucky, you may catch glimpses of zebra, wildebeest, or bat-eared fox. Accommodation in the park is rarer than hen's teeth, and families book cottages at the little village of Churchhaven here for years at a time. If you really want to spend time in the area, contact **Langebaan Houseboats** (☎*021/689–9718 or 082/258–0929 ⊕www.houseboating. co.za*) to inquire about the houseboats moored in Kraalbaai. Some are superluxurious; others are simpler affairs. Either way, it's a great way to escape. ⊠*Off the R27, 11 km (7 mi) north of the R315* ☎*022/772– 2144 ⊕www.sanparks.org* 🔖*R30 in flower season, roughly ½ price other times* ⊙*Park: Apr.–Sept., daily 7 AM–6:30 PM; Oct.–Mar., daily 6:30 AM–7 PM. Postberg: flower season, usually Aug.–Sept., daily 9–5.*

WHERE TO STAY & EAT

★ ¢–$$$ ✕**Froggy's.** The food at this attractive and unpretentious establishment would be impressive even in a smart city restaurant, but in a town where most people consider steak, egg, and fries to be the height of culinary achievement, it really does stand out. The owner, Froggy, doesn't put on airs. The menu is eclectic—basically it's what Froggy likes to cook and eat. The caramelized-onion-and-Brie tart is a masterpiece, and the Mediterranean salad with grilled vegetables is a Langebaan institu-

2

tion. Other standouts are the Moroccan lamb shank—slow baked with cinnamon, coriander, cumin, ginger, and garlic—and the Thai curries. ✉ *29 Main Rd.* ☎ *022/772–1869* 🚫 *No credit cards* ⊗ *Closed Mon. No lunch Tues, no dinner Sun.*

$ ✕ **Geelbek.** Passionate about food and history, Elmarie Leonard created this restaurant to preserve the area's fast-disappearing old recipes. It's her way of paying homage to the different nationalities that helped shape the West Coast. The restaurant is in an old homestead dating to 1761, when it served as an outpost for people making the hard trip inland. Today the trip is a lot easier, but diners are still thrilled to tuck into Geelbek's venison carpaccio, fragrant Malay curry, and venison pie. If the stuffed harders (mullet) are on the menu, don't hesitate. These fish are filled with cheese, onions, and breadcrumbs, then wrapped in bacon and gilled. The combination is fantastic. If you're adventurous, try the snoek roe, which is deep-fried in beer batter. It's a local delicacy, commonly known as West Coast caviar. This is also a great place for tea. The lemon-meringue pie stands a mile high, and the chocolate cake is delicious. You can sit in the garden or on the veranda and watch the weaver birds go crazy in the nearby trees. ✉ *West Coast National Park* ☎ *022/772–2134* 🚫 *MC, V* ⊗ *No dinner.*

$–$$ ✕ ⊡ **The Farmhouse Hotel.** Centered on a restored farmstead built in the 1860s, this hotel has thick white walls, tile floors, and timber beams. Rustic pine furniture and bright floral fabrics decorate the rooms, some of which have fireplaces and views of the lagoon. The hotel's à la carte menu focuses on seafood and Cape cuisine, which is served in the attractive dining room ($–$$$$) notable for its Oregon-pine furniture, fireplace, and high ceiling. Breakfast is said to be the best in town—an enormous buffet of cheeses, cold meats, homemade breads and croissants, kippers, omelets, good coffee, and a view to die for. ✉ *5 Egret St., Box 160, 7357* ☎ *022/772–2062* ⊕ *www.thefarmhouselangebaan. co.za* 🛏 *18 rooms* ♿ *In-room: no a/c, refrigerator, Wi-Fi. In-hotel: restaurant, bar, pool, no elevator, laundry service, public Wi-Fi, parking (no fee), no-smoking rooms* 🚫 *AE, DC, MC, V* ⦿ *CP or BP.*

$ ⊡ **Friday Island.** If you like water sports or cycling or are generally active, then this guesthouse is a great choice. It's bright, airy, and right on the beach. Rooms are, not surprisingly, decorated in blue and white and have an outside shower for wet suits, boards, and such. Sea-facing rooms are ideal for families, with two beds downstairs and two in a loft. To top it off, the property is connected to the Cape Sports Centre complex. But Friday Island also has a lovely beachfront bar and restaurant and is a good place to stay even if you don't take to water in a big way. ✉ *Main Rd., Langebaan Lagoon, Box 280, 7357* ☎ *022/772–2506* ⊕ *www.fridayisland.co.za* 🛏 *12 rooms* ♿ *In-room: no a/c, no phone, safe, kitchen, refrigerator, no TV (some), Wi-Fi. In-hotel: restaurant, bar, no elevator, public Wi-Fi, parking (no fee), no-smoking rooms* 🚫 *DC, MC, V* ⦿ *BP.*

$ ⊡ **Langebaan Beach House.** On the beach with uninterrupted views of the lagoon and close to the nightlife of Langebaan (such as it is), this comfortable, friendly place even has dogs you can take for walks on the beach. Rooms are simply and tastefully furnished, with pine headboards and colorful comforters. Ask for a sea-facing suite; if there aren't any available, your room will look out onto the pool and garden instead. ✉*44 Beach Rd., 7357* ☎*022/772–2625* ⊕*www.langebaan-beachhouse.com* ⬃*2 rooms, 2 suites* ♦*In-room: no a/c, no phone, safe, refrigerator. In-hotel: pool, beachfront, no elevator, public Internet, parking (no fee), no kids under 12* ☰*AE, DC, MC, V* ❢*BP.*

SPORTS & THE OUTDOORS

The sheltered Langebaan Lagoon is a haven for water-sports enthusiasts, but you don't have to be energetic all the time. There are expansive stretches of beach that are good for walking, sunbathing, and kite flying. Be warned, however: the water might look calm and idyllic, but it's still cold, and the wind can blow unmercifully for days at a stretch. It's great for windsurfing, but not so great if you want to spend a peaceful day under your umbrella with a book.

Cape Sports Centre (✉*Main Rd.* ☎*021/772–1114* ⊕*www.capesport. co.za*) has everything you need if you want to kite surf, windsurf, kayak, or canoe or even learn how. You can rent gear or take lessons from qualified instructors, including packages consisting of a week of intensive lessons. Cape Sports Centre also rents mountain bikes.

EN ROUTE

About 20 minutes from Langebaan on the R45 on the way to Paternoster is the **West Coast Fossil Park,** one of the richest fossil sites in the world. It was discovered by chance while the area was being mined for phosphates in the 1950s. Since then, more than 200 kinds of fossilized animals have been collected, including the Africa bear, which used to roam this area. The park has been declared a national monument, and the curators have done much to make the park and information about the fossils as accessible as possible. There are interactive guided tours, cycle trails through the areas, and interesting archaeological workshops for all ages. ✉*R45* ☎*022/766–1606* ⊕*www.iziko.org.za/iziko/part-ners/wcfp.html* 🎫*R30* ⊗*Weekdays 8–4, weekends 9–noon; tours daily at 11:30.*

PATERNOSTER

20 *47 km (29 mi) northwest of Langebaan.*

Paternoster is a mostly unspoiled village of whitewashed thatch cottages perched on a deserted stretch of coastline. The population here consists mainly of fisherfolk, who for generations have eked out a living harvesting crayfish and other seafood. Despite the overt poverty, the village has a character and sense of identity often lacking in larger towns. It helps if you turn a blind eye to the rather opulent houses on the northern side of the village.

Along the coast just south of Paternoster, the **Columbine Nature Reserve** is a great spot for spring wildflowers, coastal fynbos, and succulents. Cormorants and sacred ibis are common here, and the population of the endangered African black oystercatcher is growing each year. You can walk anywhere you like in the 692-acre park (map provided); a round-trip through the reserve is 7 km (4 mi). It's very exposed, however, so

2

don't plan to walk in the middle of the day, or you'll end up with some serious sunburn. Die-hard anglers and their families camp here during the Christmas holidays and revel in the isolation and abundant fish. ☎022/752–2718 ✍R9 ⊙ Daily 7–7.

WHERE TO STAY & EAT

★ ¢–$ ✕**Voorstrand.** A little West Coast gem, this old corrugated-iron shack on the beach stood empty for years, then suddenly metamorphosed into a truly innovative seafood restaurant. It's literally set on the sand, so you can almost hear the ones that got away. Voorstrand serves all the expected seafood and fish, but the Malay-style fish curries and fresh local crayfish are favorites. You could also splash out and try the seafood platter, which has a little bit of everything. Although it's designed to serve two people, there's always some left over. ⊠ *Strandloper St.* ☎022/752–2038 ▤MC, V.

$ 🏨**Paternoster Lodge & Restaurant.** This lodge makes the most of the sweeping views of the Atlantic Ocean. The rooms are simply decorated, but who needs artwork when at every turn you catch glimpses of the azure sea and pretty bay? At any rate, the rooms are comfortable, with good linens and firm beds, and—a big plus—they all open onto verandas. The lodge has a restaurant that caters to just about every taste, as well as a bar so you can sip cocktails while watching one of the sunsets the West Coast is so famous for. ⊠ *64 St. Augustine Rd., 7381* ☎022/752–2023 ⊕ *www.paternosterlodge.co.za* ➔*7 rooms* ⌂ *In-room: no a/c, safe, refrigerator. In-hotel: restaurant, room service, bar, beachfront, laundry service, airport shuttle, parking (no fee), no-smoking rooms* ▤DC, MC, V ⫯⊙ IBP.

ELANDS BAY

㉑ *75 km (46½ mi) north of Paternoster.*

Mention eBay auctions here, and most people will stare at you blankly. But mention the E'bay left-hand break, and you'll get nods of approval and instant admission into the inner circle of experienced surfers, who make the pilgrimage to Elands Bay to experience some of the Western Cape's best surfing.

This lovely destination is at the mouth of the beautiful Verlorenvlei Lagoon. Verlorenvlei (Afrikaans for "lost wetland," a testimony to its remoteness) is a birder's delight; you're likely to see around 240 species, including white pelican, purple gallinule, African spoonbill, African fish eagle, and the goliath and purple herons. Nearby are some fantastic walks to interesting caves with well-preserved rock art that dates back to the Pleistocene era, 10,000 years ago.

WHERE TO EAT

$$$$ ✕**Muisbosskerm.** For the true flavor of West Coast life, come to this open-air seafood restaurant on the beach south of Lambert's Bay. It consists of nothing more than a circular *boma* (enclosure) of packed *muisbos* (a local shrub) and haphazardly arranged benches and tables. You'll watch food cook over blazing fires. Snoek is smoked in an old

drum covered with burlap, bread bakes in a clay oven, and everywhere fish sizzles on grills and in giant pots. Prepare to eat as much as you can of the prix-fixe meal, using your hands or mussel shells as spoons. Be sure to try some of the local specialties like *bokkems* (dried salty fish) and *waterblommetjiebredie* (water-flower stew). Crayfish costs extra (R30 for a half order, R60 for a whole one), but don't order it unless you have an enormous appetite. The only drawback is high-season crowding: when the restaurant operates at full capacity, your 150 fellow diners can overwhelm the experience. ⊠*Elands Bay Rd., 5 km (3 mi) south of Lambert's Bay* ☎*027/432–1017* ⌲*Reservations essential* ☐*AE, DC, MC, V.*

CLANWILLIAM

㉒ *46 km (28½ mi) northeast of Elands Bay.*

Although the town itself is uninspiring, it's no surprise that half the streets are named after trees or plants. Clanwilliam is at the edge of one of the natural jewels of the Western Cape—the Cederberg Wilderness Area, which takes its name from the cedar trees that used to cover the mountains. In spring the town is inundated with flower-watchers. Clanwilliam is also the center of the rooibos-tea industry.

Clanwilliam was home to Dr. Christiaan Louis Leipoldt, poet and Renaissance man. He is buried in a lovely spot in the mountains a little way out of town; you can visit his grave, which is on the way to the Pakhuis Pass (R364; there's a small signpost).

The **Ramskop Wildflower Garden** is at its best in August. (This is also when the Clanwilliam Flower Show takes place at the old Dutch Reformed church, and almost every available space in town is filled with flowers.) It's a wonderful opportunity to see many of the region's flowers all growing in one place. Even in other seasons the gardens are still quite attractive, but spring is orders of magnitude prettier. ⊠*Ou Kaapseweg* ☎*027/482–8000* ☞*R12* ⊗*Daily 7:30–5:30.*

East of Clanwilliam the R364 becomes a spectacularly scenic gravel road called **Pakhuis Pass.** Fantastic rock formations glow in the early morning or late afternoon. There's even a mountain range called the Tra-Tra Mountains, a completely fantastical name for a suitably fantastical landscape. A steep, narrow road to the right leads to the mission town of **Wuppertal,** with its characteristic white-thatch houses. You can drive this road in an ordinary rental car, but be very careful in wet weather. There are no guided tours, but there is a factory where you can see and buy sturdy handmade leather shoes and boots. Another way of seeing Pakhuis Pass is to take a Donkey Cart Adventure (⇨ *Tours in West Coast Essentials, below)* trip down to the tiny remote village of Heuningvlei, a former Moravian mission station. Currently only 20 families live here—eking out a living as subsistence farmers.

FodorsChoice ★   Clanwilliam is close to the northern edge of the **Cederberg,** a mountain range known for its San paintings, its bizarre rock formations, and, once upon a time, its cedars. Most of the ancient cedars have been cut

Rooibos Tea

Chances are you will either love or hate *rooibos* (red bush) tea, which South Africans drink in vast quantities. It has an unusual, earthy taste, and is naturally sweet. People drink it hot with lemon and honey or with milk or as a refreshing iced tea with slices of lemon and a sprig of mint. It's rich in minerals, such as copper, iron, potassium, calcium, fluoride, zinc, manganese, and magnesium; contains antioxidants; and is low in tannin. Best of all, it has no caffeine. Trendy chefs are incorporating it into their cooking, and you might see rooibos-infused sauces or marinades mentioned on menus. Rooibos leaves are coarser than regular tea and look like finely chopped sticks. When they're harvested they're green; then they're chopped, bruised, and left to ferment in mounds before being spread out to dry in the baking summer sun. The fermentation process turns the leaves red—hence the name.

down, but a few specimens still survive in the more remote regions. The Cederberg is a hiking paradise—a wild, largely unspoiled area where you can disappear from civilization for days at a time. About 172,900 acres of this mountain range constitute what has been declared the Cederberg Wilderness Area, and entry permits are required if you wish to hike here.

A scenic dirt road that heads south out of town, past the tourism bureau and museum, winds for about 30 km (18 mi) into the Cederberg to **Algeria,** a Cape Nature campsite set in an idyllic valley. Algeria is the starting point for several excellent hikes into the Cederberg. The short, one-hour hike to a waterfall is great, but it's worth going into the mountains for a day or two, for which you will need to book and obtain a permit through **Cape Nature** (☎*021/659-3500* ⊕*www.cap-enature.org.za*) or from one of the local farms, many of which have simple, self-catering cottages on their land.

The Cederberg might be the last place you'd expect to find a vineyard, but that's what makes **Cederberg Private Cellar** so unusual. It's been in the Nieuwoudt family for five generations. When old man Nieuwoudt, known to everyone as "Oom Pollie," planted the first vines in the 1970s, all his sheep-farming neighbors thought he had gone mad. Today, however, winemaker David Nieuwoudt and his viticulturist father, Ernst, are laughing all the way to the award ceremonies. At an altitude of around 3,300 feet, this is the highest vineyard in the Western Cape, and consequently is almost completely disease-free. They don't have to spray for the mildew and mealybugs that are the bane of wine farmers in the Winelands and Constantia. The 2006 sauvignon blanc has been voted among South Africa's top 10 by *Wine* magazine. The chenin blanc wins one award after another, and the bukettraube is a perfect accompaniment to South African curries. The exciting 2004 Teen die Hoog Shiraz is made from the upper portion of the best vineyard and coaxed to maturity in new oak. There's a limited number of bottles for sale, so don't hesitate if you stumble across

CLOSE UP

Leopard (and Sheep) Conservation

Sheep farming in the Cederberg is a precarious business. Not only are the winters harsh, but valuable sheep may be killed by the leopards that live in the mountains. Farmers have resorted to using gin traps to keep their flocks safe, but with devastating consequences for any animals caught in them. Two researchers, Quinton and Nicole Martins, in conjunction with the farmers in the area, were keen to find a solution to this problem. They established the **Cape Leopard Trust** (☎027/482–2785 or 073/241–4513

⊕www.capeleopard.org.za). The trust aims to track the movement of the predators to see exactly how many cats remain in the Cederberg and to pinpoint which farmers are most at risk. The trust is also working to introduce Anatolian Shepherds—dogs that are bred to bond with sheep and act as their protectors against leopards. Several farmers have already had great success with these dogs. Their flocks are safe, and the leopards aren't at risk of dying an agonizing death in a trap.

a couple. The farm has self-catering accommodations and is near the Wolfberg Cracks (cracks in the mountain that lure hikers) and Malgat (a huge rock pool), both well-known Cederberg attractions. The Cederberg Observatory also operates on this farm. It's an open-air wonder run by passionate stargazers, who give a slide presentation when the weather permits and then help you spot faraway galaxies on their superpowerful telescopes. ⊠*Dwarsrivier Farm, Algeria turnoff from the N7* ☎*027/482–2827* ⊕*www.cederbergwine.com* 🍴*Tastings R10* ☉*Mon.–Sat. 8–12:30 and 2–5.*

WHERE TO STAY

$$$$
FodorsChoice
★

🔲 **Bushmans Kloof Wilderness Reserve & Retreat.** It should come as no surprise that this fantastic wilderness reserve was ranked fifth in *Travel + Leisure*'s list of Top Hotels in the World in 2004. Bushmans Kloof is in an area of rich cultural significance and a South African National Heritage site. The stark beauty of the mountains, the incredible rock formations, and the waterfalls, pools, and potholes probably were as attractive to the San of long ago as they are to visitors today. More than 130 San rock-art locations can be seen on a tour with a trained guide, and you can also go hiking, mountain biking, fishing, and canoeing. The reserve used to be an overgrazed stock farm, and every attempt is being made to restore the land to a more pristine state. Only game endemic to the area has been reintroduced, including wildebeest, Cape mountain zebra, eland, genet, mongoose, blesbok, brown hyena, and the endangered bontebok. Freestanding thatch double cottages have all the modern conveniences, and the luxurious suites in the manor house are spacious and stylish. The food is exceptional, including the legendary springbok loin. The attention to detail is astonishing; you'll find flowers floating in the toilet bowl, and the library even has titles in Arabic and Chinese. Best of all, you can fly in from Cape Town. ⊠*Off Pakhuis Pass* 🕮*Reservations: Box 38104, Pinelands 7430* ☎*021/685–2598* ⊕*www.bushmanskloof.co.za* 🛏*13 rooms, 3 suites* ⚒*In-room: safe, refrigerator, no TV (some), dial-up. In-hotel: restau-*

rant, room service, bar, pools, gym, spa, bicycles, no elevator, laundry service, public Wi-Fi, airport shuttle, parking (no fee), no kids under 10, no-smoking rooms ⊟*AE, DC, MC, V* ⎟◎⎟*FAP.*

$$ 🔲 **Karu Kareb.** Frans and Beneta Bester are old hands (and some of the best hands) at the guesthouse business. Rooms are in a 100-year-old farmhouse surrounded by high mountains, a crystal-clear stream, and fantastic rock art. The Besters have mastered the art of excellent local cuisine, so guests are in for a real treat. Frans does incredible things with a braai or a potjie, and Beneta is surprisingly creative with dietary restrictions. She cooks for vegetarians, diabetics, and lactose-intolerant people without batting an eyelid—a rarity in this part of the world. Beneta is also something of a mini–tourism bureau, with tons of information at her fingertips. ✉*13 km (8 mi) from Clanwilliam on Boskloof Rd., Box 273, 8135* ☎*027/482–1675* ⊕*www.karukareb. co.za* ➥*5 rooms* △*In-room: no phone, safe, kitchen, refrigerator, no TV. In-hotel: restaurant, bar, pool, gym, bicycles, no elevator, laundry service, public Internet, parking (no fee), no kids under 12, no-smoking rooms* ⊟*No credit cards* ⎟◎⎟*MAP.*

$–$$ 🔲 **Clanwilliam Lodge.** In an area known more for its magnificent landscape than its fine lodging, Clanwilliam Lodge is something of an anomaly. Creams and taupe decorate the contemporary, sophisticated rooms, with nary a dried flower or knickknack in sight. The rooms at this lodge, which in its previous life was a drab girls' hostel, range from basic to luxurious. There's a simple hiker's room for those just wanting to crash for the night, as well as family suites and the Presidential Suite, with a four-poster bed and huge bathtub. When the temperatures rise in summer, the pool area, with its bedouin-style daybeds, is a great place to lounge with a cold drink in hand. There's also a treatment room, so after some hard days roughing it in the mountains you can freshen up with a facial and massage. The restaurant has a pizza oven and a nightly buffet that can satisfy even the hungriest hiker. ✉*Graafwaterweg, 8135* ☎*027/482–1777* ⊕*www.clanwilliamlodge. co.za* ➥*32 rooms* △*In-room: no phone (some), safe, refrigerator, DVD (some). In-hotel: restaurant, bar, pool, spa, no elevator, laundry service, public Wi-Fi, parking (no fee), no-smoking rooms* ⊟*AE, MC, V* ⎟◎⎟*BP or MAP.*

¢ 🔲 **Traveller's Rest.** If you're on a tight budget, this farm is the place to stay. There are no frills at these basic but comfortable cottages, but the surrounding mountain scenery is just as spectacular as it is at the expensive lodge next door. You can take a guided tour or explore on your own with a booklet (R60) that describes all the rock art on the farm. There's also a scenic drive for which you really need a 4x4, although it's not an off-road challenge. Owner Haffie Strauss is a mine of information and a force to be reckoned with. Her *boerewors* (spiced farm sausage) is legendary, and any bull who isn't performing on the farm ends up on the braai! During the flower season in spring, Haffie opens her restaurant, Khoisan Kitchen, where she serves typical boerekos, including curried offal, robust stews, *roosterbrood* (bread cooked on the coals), oxtail, and lamb cooked on the spit. Her rich malva pudding is perfect for cool Cederberg evenings, and her ice cream made with homegrown granadilla is sublime. ⊠*Off Pakhuis Pass, 8135* ☎*027/482–1824* ⊕*www.travellersrest.co.za* 🛏*14 cottages* ⚿*In-room: no a/c, no phone, kitchen, refrigerator, no TV. In-hotel: tennis court, pool, no elevator* ⊟*No credit cards.*

SHOPPING

Veldskoen, or *Vellies,* as they're fondly known, are something of a South African institution. All you have to do is think of the singer David Kramer and his signature red shoes to understand the place they hold in most South Africans' hearts. Vellies used to be the pre-serve of hardy farmers, who would wear these sturdy shoes with socks and shorts in winter, and without socks and shorts in summer. Thank-fully, the styles have changed somewhat, and now you can get the soft-est shoes made to order from the **Strassberger Veldshoe Factory** (⊠*Ou Kaapseweg* ☎*027/482–2141*). The shoemakers you see working here come from generations of craftspeople dating back to when the Mora-vian missionaries first started shoemaking in Wupperthal.

CITRUSDAL

㉓ *53 km (33 mi) south of Clanwilliam.*

As you might guess from the name, Citrusdal is a fruit-growing town. It sits by the Olifants River valley, surrounded by the peaks of the Ceder-berg, and is known as the gateway to the Cederberg. For the most part it's a sleepy farming town, but in spring the smell of fruit blossoms as you come over the Piekenaarskloof Pass (also known as the Piekenier-skloof Pass) is incredible.

After a grueling hike in the Cederberg, there's no better way to relax than at the **Baths,** where hot mineral water gushes from a natural spring. The waters' curative powers have been talked about for centu-ries, and although the formal baths were established in 1739, there's little doubt that indigenous San and Bushmen spent time here as well. In 1903 the hot springs were bought by James McGregor, and his great-grandchildren run them today. On-site are self-catering facilities and a restaurant. You can also go as a day visitor, but you must book ahead as they limit the number of people at the baths. ⊠*16 km (10 mi) out-side Citrusdal; follow signs* ☎*022/921–80267* ⊕*www.thebaths.co.za* 💵*Day of soaking R50* 🕘*Daily 8–5.*

EN ROUTE Once over the Piekenaarskloof Pass, you'll head toward the small town of Piketberg and enter the Swartland, the breadbasket of the Western Cape. On your left are the Groot Winterhoek Mountains and a road leading to the small town of Porterville. On your right is the village of Piketberg, where you can turn off for **Excelsior Farm** (⊠*Tar road off Versveld Pass* ☎*022/914–5853*), a small farm on top of the Piketberg Mountains. It offers day and overnight horseback rides (R150 for two hours, R450 for a full day with lunch) through the orchards and fynbos-clad mountains, and two simple, inexpensive, self-catering cottages.

RIEBEEK WEST & RIEBEEK KASTEEL

24 *104 km (65 mi) south of Citrusdal via the N7 and R311.*

Drive through the small agricultural town of Malmesbury and over the Bothman's Kloof Pass to these twin towns named after Jan van Riebeek, the 17th-century Dutch explorer of the Cape. The towns developed only a few miles apart because of a disagreement about where to build a church. In the end, two separate places of worship were built, and two distinct towns grew up around them.

Riebeek West is the birthplace of Jan Christiaan Smuts, one of the country's great politicians and leader of the United Party in the 1940s. D. F. Malan, prime minister of the Nationalist Party in 1948, was born on the farm Allesverloren, just outside Riebeek Kasteel. This wine estate produces some great red wines, an exceptional port, and world-class olives and olive oil. The *kasteel* or castle in question is the Kasteelberg (Castle Mountain), which stands sentinel behind the towns.

Disenchanted city dwellers have been buying up cottages here to use as weekend getaways, and others are moving out to the small towns and commuting into the city. It's not hard to understand why. Children play in the street and people keep sheep in their huge gardens—a far cry from Cape Town life. There are numerous restaurants, some galleries, and plenty of olive products to buy, including excellent olive oils and bottled olives. (Huge groves in the area do well in the Mediterranean climate; *for more on the production of olive oil in South Africa, including information on the area's Kloovenburg Wine Estate, see the From Soil to Oil box, above.*)

You'll hear the distinctive, rolling accent of the Swartland here. Known as the "Malmesbury *brei,*" it's characterized by long "grrrr" sounds that seem to run together at the back of the throat. In Afrikaans, *brei* means "to knit" or "temper," both of which make sense when listening to somebody from the Swartland.

Translated from Afrikaans, **Allesverloren** means "all is lost." The bleak name derives from a story from the early 1700s, when the widow Cloete owned this farm. Legend has it that she left the farm for a few weeks to attend a church gathering in town, and in her absence the resentful indigenous tribespeople set her homestead alight. When she came back to a smoldering ruin, she declared, "Allesverloren," and the name stuck. Today the farm's prospects are a lot brighter. It has been in the Malan family for generations. The infamous D. F. Malan, regarded as one of the architects of apartheid, gave up the farm for politics. Happily his descendents are doing a better job at winemaking than he did at shaping a country's destiny, and their reds are big, bold, and full of flavor. Delicious and packed with rich, pruney, nutty flavors, the port is perfect for cool winter evenings. A restaurant on the premises means you can dine in a beautiful setting. ⌧*R311 between Riebeek Kasteel and Riebeek West* ☎*022/461–2320* ⊕*www.allesverloren. co.za* ⌧*Tastings free (R10 for groups of 10 or more)* ⊙ *Weekdays 8:30–5, Sat. 8:30–2.*

You have to move fast if you want to snap up any wines from the **Kloovenburg Wine Estate.** This family-run farm has many awards under its belt and is probably best known for its excellent shiraz. In 2005 *Decanter* magazine awarded the 2002 vintage the only five-star "outstanding" honor among 95 other South African shiraz wines. The extravagant, full-bodied chardonnay is also wonderful, and you may want to snap up some of the 2006 vintage while it's still available. The 2003 Eight Feet cabernet sauvignon–merlot blend is a fun but very drinkable testimony to the generations of du Toits who have worked the land: it alludes to the eight grape-stomping feet of the owners' four sons. Don't miss out on Annalene du Toit's olive products. Her young son Daniel is chief taster, and the results are brilliant. ⊠ *R46 just outside Riebeek Kasteel as you're coming down the pass into Riebeek Valley* ☎ *022/448–1635* ⊕ *www.kloovenburg.co.za* 🍷 *Tastings free (R20 per person for groups of more than 10)* ☉ *Weekdays 9–4:30, Sat. 9–2.*

OFF THE BEATEN PATH

Swartland Winery. Because of its location in the less fashionable part of the Winelands, this large cellar a few miles outside Malmesbury has had to work hard for its place in the sun. Previously a well-kept secret among local cost- and quality-conscious wine experts, it's slowly garnering an international reputation. They are particularly proud of their Indalo range, and the cabernet sauvignon 2005 can hold its own in any company. The reserve range has a good selection of wines to choose from; the blend of chenin blanc, sauvignon blanc, and chardonnay has a firm following. If you're looking for something pleasant to knock back with lunch, try the low-alcohol (9%) Fernão Pires Light. ⊠ *R45, Malmesbury* ☎ *022/482–1134 or 022/482–1135* ⊕ *www.swwines.co.za* 🍷 *Tastings free* ☉ *Weekdays 8–5, Sat. 9–2; cellar tours by appointment.*

WHERE TO STAY

$ 🏨 **Riebeek Valley Hotel.** At the top of town, with a great view over vineyards and mountains, this small luxury hotel in a converted farmhouse is an oasis from the sweltering Swartland summer heat as well as a winter getaway. Each room has a different color palette: refreshing lavender, peaceful cream, warm rose, and bold red, to mention just a few. In addition to a regular pool, there's an indoor pool so you can swim even if the weather is iffy. A number of spa treatments such as massage and relexology are also available. The Sunday buffet draws crowds of day-trippers. ⊠ *4 Dennehof St., Riebeek West 7306* ☎ *022/461–2672* ⊕ *www.riebeekvalleyhotel.co.za* 🛏 *11 rooms, 5 suites* ♿ *In-hotel: restaurant, room service, bar, pool, no elevator, laundry service, public Internet, parking (no fee), no-smoking rooms* ▤ *AE, DC, MC, V* ❏ *BP.*

WEST COAST ESSENTIALS

To research prices, get advice from other travelers, and book travel arrangements, visit www.fodors.com.

TRANSPORTATION

BY BUS

Intercape Mainliner heads up the N7 daily. The bus stops at Malmesbury, Citrusdal, and Clanwilliam, but not coastal towns such as Langebaan and Elands Bay. Expect to pay around R85 for a one-way trip to Malmesbury, R140 to Citrusdal, and R150 to Clanwilliam. Malmesbury is only 70 km (43½ mi) from Cape Town, and the trip takes 1½ hours. The journey to Clanwilliam takes about four hours.

Bus Line **Intercape Mainliner** (✉ *1 Adderley St., Cape Town* ☎ *0861/287–287, 083/909–0909 for alternate booking through Computicket* ⊕ *www.intercape. co.za*).

BY CAR

Driving is undoubtedly the best way to appreciate this area. The roads up the West Coast are generally good, but some dirt roads on the West Coast and in the Cederberg are rutted and bumpy. If you plan to head into the Cederberg mountains rather than just sticking to the small towns, consider renting a 4x4, especially in winter, when roads become muddy and you run a small risk of being snowed in.

The major car-rental agencies have offices in the smaller towns, but it's best to deal with the Cape Town offices; you'll probably want to pick up a car at the airport anyway. *For car-rental agencies, see Winelands Essentials, above.*

To get up the West Coast and to the Cederberg, take the N1 out of Cape Town. Just before Century City shopping center, take Exit 10, which is marked GOODWOOD, MALMESBURY, CENTURY CITY DR. AND SABLE RD. and leads to the N7, the region's major access road. Though the highway is well marked, get yourself a good map from a bookstore or tourism office and explore some of the smaller roads, which offer surprising vistas or a glimpse into the rural heart of the Western Cape. The Versveld Pass, between Piketberg and the hamlet of Piket-Bo-Berg, at the top of the mountains, has views that stretch for miles. Driving to Clanwilliam takes close to three hours without stopping, but half the fun is checking out what local farm stands have to offer and stopping to admire the scenery. In spring this trip will take much longer, as you'll likely want to stop to photograph the flowers that carpet the countryside.

BY TRAIN

Although there is public train service to major West Coast towns, this isn't a recommended way to travel, as there have been regular on-board muggings. The train service is working hard to overcome these problems, but to date hasn't found a lasting solution.

CONTACTS & RESOURCES

EMERGENCIES

There are doctors and dentists in every town, as well as provincial hospitals in Citrusdal, Clanwilliam, Malmesbury, and Vredenburg (near Paternoster). The closest private hospital is at Milnerton, a Cape

Town suburb that has developed along the N7. Late-night pharmacies are a rarity in these small towns, but all pharmacies have emergency and after-hours phone numbers. If there isn't a pharmacy, head for the hospital.

Emergency Services Ambulance (☎10177). **Police** (☎10111). **Police, Fire, and Ambulance** (☎107 from landline). **Vodacom emergency services** (☎112 from mobile phone).

Hospitals **Citrusdal Hospital** (✉ Vrede St., Citrusdal ☎022/921–2153). **Clanwilliam Hospital** (✉35 Main Rd., Clanwilliam ☎027/482–1628). **Malmesbury Hospital** (✉ P.G. Nelson St., Malmesbury ☎022/482–1161). **Vredenburg Hospital** (✉ Voortrekker Rd., Vredenberg ☎022/713–1261).

INTERNET

There's public Internet access in several West Coast towns. For instance, you can have a cup of coffee while catching up on your e-mail at Saint du Barrys Country Lodge in Clanwilliam. You'll pay R15 for the first 15 minutes and R15 for every 30 minutes thereafter.

Internet Access **Bypass Café** (✉ Main Rd., Lambert's Bay ☎027/432–1120). **Evita se Perron** (✉ Darling station, Darling ☎021/492–2831 or 022/492–2851). **Friends** (✉ Marra's Sq., Bree St., Langebaan ☎082/447–4528). **Saint du Barrys Country Lodge** (✉13 Augsburg Rd., Clanwilliam ☎027/482–1537).

MONEY MATTERS

Credit cards are widely accepted at larger establishments, including shops and supermarkets. Smaller B&Bs and museums might operate on a cash-only basis, however, so ask ahead when you make your reservation. There are ATMs and banks in most towns on the West Coast.

TOURS

To Whom It May Concern: see the exceptional rock art in the Cederberg, it's recommended that you take a tour so that you can fully appreciate and understand this ancient art form, about which experts still have questions. The community-driven Clanwilliam Living Landscape Project has trained locals to act as guides. Expect to pay around R50 for a one-hour tour that includes a visit to two sites, and R80 for five sites, which takes about four hours. If you don't have your own vehicle, the guide can pick you up, but you'll be charged a little extra for gas.

Rooibos tea is a big part of this region's economy, and a rooibos tour with Elandsberg Eco-Tourism should fill you in on all you need to know about it. The shorter tour, around 1½ hours, costs R50, and the three- to four-hour tour costs around R80. Because the tour is out on a farm, they will arrange to pick you up in town.

For something completely out of the ordinary, try a Donkey Cart Adventure, which starts at the top of the Pakhuis Pass and ends a couple of hours later in the tiny hamlet of Heuningvlei in the heart of the Cederberg Wilderness Area. The donkey-cart route is windy and takes you through some spectacular scenery and flora. It's best to plan this trip for spring, when the fynbos is at its best, or in autumn. In summer, temperatures soar in the Cederberg.

During the orange-harvest season (April–September), you can gain insight into the fruit industry with an hour-long tour through the packing sheds at Goedehoop Citrus. These tours meet at the Citrusdal Tourism Bureau.

Tour Operators **Clanwilliam Living Landscape Project** (✉ *Clanwilliam* ☎ *027/482–1911*). **Donkey Cart Adventure** (✉ *Clanwilliam* ☎ *021/659-3500* ⊕ *www.capenature.org.za*). **Elandsberg Eco-Tourism** (✉ *Clanwilliam* ☎ *027/482-2022* ⊕ *www.africandawn.com*). **Goedehoop Citrus** (✉ *Clanwilliam* ☎ *022/921–3210*).

VISITOR INFORMATION

Yours truly, can get almost all the information you need about the Western Cape from the very organized Cape Town Tourism offices in Cape Town, which are open weekdays 8–6, Saturday 8:30–1, and Sunday 9–1. There are also tourist offices in most small towns along the West Coast, but the West Coast Regional Tourism Organisation has information on the entire area. Visit its Web site to get a good overview of the area. The Citrusdal Tourism Bureau is open weekdays 8:30–12:30 and 1–5, and Saturday 9–12:30. In the flower season (approximately August–October), the Clanwilliam Tourism Bureau is open daily 8:30–6. During the rest of the year it's open weekdays 8:30–5 and Saturday 8:30–12:30. The Darling Tourism Bureau, based at the Darling Museum, is open Monday–Thursday 9–1 and 2–4, Friday 9–1 and 2–3:30, and weekends 10–3. During the flower season, the Lambert's Bay Tourism Bureau is open weekdays 8–6 and Saturday 9–3. Off-season it's open weekdays 9–1 and 2–5 and Saturday 9–12:30. The Langebaan Tourism Bureau is open weekdays 9–5 and weekends 9–2. Piketberg Tourism is open weekdays 8:30–4:30. The Riebeek Valley Information Centre is open Monday–Saturday 9–4 and Sunday 9–1.

The Flowerline is a central hotline that provides details about where the flowers are best seen each day. You can call 24 hours a day July–September.

Flower Information **Flowerline** (☎ *083/910–1028*).

Tourist Offices **Cape Town Tourism** (✉ *The Pinnacle, Burg and Castle Sts., Box 1403, Cape Town 8000* ☎ *021/487-6800* ⊕ *www.tourismcapetown.co.za*). **Citrusdal Tourism Bureau** (✉ *39 Voortrekker St., Citrusdal 7340* ☎ *022/921–3210* ⊕ *www.citrusdal.info*). **Clanwilliam Tourism Bureau** (✉ *Main Rd.* ✍ *Box 5, Clanwilliam 8135* ☎ *027/482–2024* ⊕ *www.clanwilliam.info*). **Darling Tourism Bureau** (✉ *Pastorie and Hill Sts.* ✍ *Private Bag X1, Darling 7345* ☎ *022/492–3361* ⊕ *www.darlingtourism.co.za*). **Lambert's Bay Tourism Bureau** (✉ *5 Medical Centre, Main Rd., Lambert's Bay* ☎ *027/432–1000* ⊕ *www.lambertsbay.com*). **Langebaan Tourism Bureau** (✉ *Municipal Bldg., Langebaan 7357* ☎ *022/772–1515* ⊕ *www.langebaaninfo.co.za*). **Piketberg Tourism** (✉ *14 Church St., Piketberg 7320* ☎ *022/913–2063* ⊕ *www.piketberg.com*). **Riebeek Valley Information Centre** (✉ *7 Main St., Riebeek Kasteel 7307* ☎ *022/448–1584* ⊕ *www.capewestcoast.org/Towns/RiebMiddel.htm*). **West Coast Regional Tourism Organisation** (✍ *Box 242, Moorreesburg 7310* ☎ *022/433–8505* ⊕ *www.capewestcoast.org*).

The Garden Route & the Little Karoo

WORD OF MOUTH

"The Garden Route is one of the most beautiful places in all the world."

—pompous

"Storms River Mouth is well worth a visit, with a lovely forest walk to the suspension bridge over the river. It's a very scenic place."

—joode

"We stayed one night at the Hog Hollow Country Lodge. It's great.... Ask for the round room (it's in the old water cistern). While there, go to Monkeyland. It's a neat sanctuary for monkeys and other rescued primates."

—astein12

Updated by
Jennifer Stern

THIS REGION IS A STUDY IN CONTRASTS. The Outeniqua and Tsitsikamma mountains, forested ranges that shadow the coastline, trap moist ocean breezes, which then fall as rain on the verdant area known as the Garden Route. Meanwhile, these same mountains rob the interior of water, creating the arid semideserts of the Little and Great Karoo. Even within these areas, however, there is significant variety.

The Garden Route, the 208-km (130-mi) stretch of coastline from Mossel Bay to Storms River, encompasses some of South Africa's most spectacular and diverse scenery, ranging from long beaches and gentle lakes and rivers to tangled forests, impressive mountains, and steep, rugged cliffs that plunge into the wild and stormy sea. It's the kind of place where you'll have trouble deciding whether to lie on the beach, lounge in a pretty pastry shop, or go on an invigorating hike. For most people the Garden Route is about beaches, which are among the world's best. Though the ocean may not be as warm as it is in KwaZulu-Natal, the quality of accommodations tends to be far superior, and you can take your pick of water sports.

A trip into the Little Karoo, on the other hand, offers a glimpse of what much of South Africa's vast hinterland looks like. This narrow strip of land wedged between the Swartberg and Outeniqua ranges, stretching from Barrydale in the west to Willowmore in the east, is a sere world of rock and scrub. The area is most famous for its ostrich farms and the subterranean splendors of the Cango Caves, but there is much more for the discerning visitor to see. However, unlike those found on the classic safari destinations, these treasures are not handed to you on a plate. You have to really look. Scour the apparently dry ground to spot tiny and beautiful plants. Or spend time walking in the sun to discover some of the many bird species. A fairly energetic hike into the hills will reward you with fascinating geological formations, numerous fossils, and extensive rock art. You can also just stand still and enjoy the space and the silence. Even if all this leaves you cold, it is still worth the effort to explore spectacular passes that claw through the mountains into the desert interior.

ORIENTATION & PLANNING

ORIENTATION

Although it *is* possible to get from place to place by bus, the best way to explore this region is by car. There are two practical routes from Cape Town to Port Elizabeth. You can follow the N2 along the Garden Route, or you can take Route 62, which goes through the Little Karoo. These two roads are separated by the Outeniqua Mountains, which are traversed by a number of scenic passes. So it is possible—even desirable—to hop back and forth over the mountains, alternating between the lush Garden Route and the harsher Little Karoo. The inland border of the Little Karoo is formed by the Swartberg Mountains, which covers much of the interior of South Africa.

GARDEN ROUTE

This beautiful 208-km (130-mi) stretch of coast takes its name from a year-round riot of vegetation. Here you'll find some of the country's most inspiring scenery: forest-cloaked mountains, rivers and streams, and golden beaches. This area draws a diverse crowd, from backpackers and adventure travelers to family vacationers and golfers. Major resort towns here are Mossel Bay, George, Wilderness, Knysna, and Plettenberg Bay.

LITTLE KAROO

Presenting a striking contrast to the Garden Route is the semiarid region known as the Little Karoo (also known as the Klein Karoo). In addition to a stark kind of beauty that comes with its deep gorges and rugged plains, the Little Karoo has ostrich farms, the Sanbona Wildlife Reserve, the impressive Cango Caves, and even some vineyards.

PLANNING

There's no best time to visit the Garden Route, although the water and weather are warmest November through March. From mid-December to mid-January, however, the entire Garden Route is unbelievably crowded and hotel prices soar, so try to avoid visiting at this time. Between May and September the weather can be very cold and even rainy. But—and it's a big but—it makes all the more cozy the huge, blazing log fires and large bowls of steaming soup that local hostelries provide. And, of course, there are fewer tourists. Even in these colder months it's rarely cold for more than two or three days at a stretch, after which you'll get a few days of glorious sunshine. Wildflowers bloom along the Garden Route from July to October, the same time as the annual Southern Right whale migration along the coast.

The Little Karoo can be scorchingly hot in summer and bitterly cold at night in winter, but winter days are often warm and sunny. It really doesn't rain much in the Little Karoo.

TAKE IT ALL IN

3 days: Choose a home base in the Garden Route: either Mossel Bay, Knysna, or Plettenberg Bay (Plett). You'll encounter wonderful crafts shops and studios in all these towns, so keep your credit card handy. On your first day, take a half-day walk through Plett's Robberg Nature Reserve; along the Cape St. Blaize Trail, part of the larger Oyster-catcher Trail, in Mossel Bay; or at Knysna's Garden of Eden. Devote the afternoon to a boat or kayak trip; you may see dolphins, seals, and/or whales, particularly around Plett. Dedicate the second day to whatever activity suits your fancy—lounging on the beach, paddling, horseback riding, or abseiling (rappelling). If you're staying in Plett, you could drive out to Storms River on the third day to do the treetop canopy tour or, for the less adventurous, a tractor tour of the forest. If you're staying farther west, head over one of the scenic passes to Oudtshoorn, visit the Cango Caves, and take a different scenic drive back.

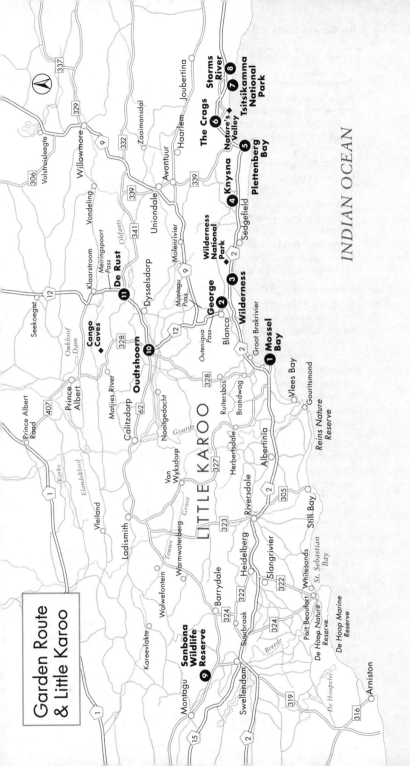

Garden Route & Little Karoo

INDIAN OCEAN

LITTLE KAROO

1 Mossel Bay
2 George
3 Wilderness
Wilderness National Park
4 Knysna
Nature's Valley
5 Plettenberg Bay
The Crags
6
7 Storms River
8 Tsitsikamma National Park
9 Sanbona Wildlife Reserve
10 Oudtshoorn
Cango Caves
11 De Rust

Prince Albert Road
Prince Albert
Seekoegat
Matjies River
Calitzdorp
Klaarstroom
Meiringspoort Pass
Dysselsdorp
Molenrivier
Montagu Pass
Outeniqua Pass
Blanco
Groot Brakrivier
Vlees Bay
Gouritsmond
Reins Nature Reserve

Willowmore
Volstruisleegte
Vondeling
Zaaimansdal
Avontuur
Uniondale
Haarlem
Joubertina
Sedgefield

Oukloof Dam
Noofgedacht
Ruitersbos
Brandwag

Vleiland
Ladismith
Van Wyksdorp
Herbertsdale
Albertinia
Riversdale
Still Bay

Wolwefontein
Warmwaterberg
Heidelberg
Slangrivier
Whitesands
St. Sebastian Bay

Kareevlakte
Barrydale
Suurbraak
Port Beaufort Nature Reserve
De Hoop Marine Reserve
De Hoop Nature Reserve

Montagu
Swellendam
De Hoopvlei
Arniston

Kerks
Elandskloof
Gourits
Groot
Touws
Breede

337
329
306
332
9
339
341
12
328
62
327
328
305
2
323
324
322
324
319
322
316
15
2
1
407
1
12
9
2
339

TOP REASONS TO VISIT

Cetacean Central Some of the best boat-based whale- and dolphin-watching in the world can be found at Plettenberg Bay. And although Plett is the best, there are also good trips to be had at Mossel Bay and Knysna (you probably won't see whales or dolphins at Knysna). You can often watch these friendly cetaceans frolicking from the shore, as well. If you really want to feel part of the ocean, your best bet is a kayaking trip in Plett, which might let you get up close and personal with these fascinating creatures.

Turning Wheels One unique way to enjoy the striking scenery of the Garden Route is to take a trip on the Outeniqua Choo-Tjoe, an authentic narrow-gauge steam train that runs between the Transport Museum in George and the Bartolomeu Dias Museum Complex in Mossel Bay. This is the last scheduled passenger steam train still operating in South Africa.

Animal Crackers The Crags area, just outside Plettenberg Bay, is a great place to spend the day with the animals. Visit with rescued primates at Monkeyland, amble through the world's largest free-flight aviary next door at Birds of Eden, and then finish the day off interacting with an elephant—and perhaps taking a ride—at the Elephant Sanctuary just down the road. Other spots for animal-watching include the ostrich farms and Cango Wildlife Ranch at Oudtshoorn and—for big game—the Sanbona Wildlife Reserve.

Soar through the Air If you just can't keep your feet on the ground, you've come to the right place. Hold your heart in both hands, close your eyes, and jump. Start off with a leap of faith via a bungee cord at the Gouritz Bridge at Mossel Bay, or try a bridge swing instead. If those prove too tame for you, move on to the highest bungee jump in the world (at 700 feet) at Bloukrans Bridge. If you must go higher, leap out of a plane with Skydive Plett. For something a little bit closer to the ground, nothing beats the canopy tour at Tsitsikamma, where you fly through the trees (via cables and a harness) with the greatest of ease.

Hike in Style Enjoy the best of nature in comfort on an escorted, guided, portered, and catered hike, locally called "slackpacking." Try the Dolphin Trail in Tsitsikamma National Park for remote and rugged coastal terrain and indulgent accommodation. The Oystercatcher Trail in Mossel Bay lets you explore a wide range of coastal scenery, ranging from cliff-top paths to long beaches, and the food emphasizes traditionally cooked local seafood. The Garden Route Trail combines long and short day hikes with some paddling through the wonderful wetlands of Wilderness National Park.

5 days: Start with the three-day itinerary above. Then spend the next two days at the Little Karoo's Sanbona Wildlife Reserve, where you can take in the big game and lovely flora. Alternatively, you could spend some extra time at any of the Garden Route destinations from the first itinerary; you may want to linger, for example, in Storms River, which will put you right near the spectacular Tsitsikamma National Park.

8 days: Spend the first day or two at Sanbona Wildlife Reserve. Then head east along the R62, stopping for lunch at the Joubert-Tradauw winery, or the Rose of the Karoo, in Calitzdorp, and ending up in Oudtshoorn. The next day, drive a long scenic loop, stopping at wineries and visiting the Cango Caves. Then head over either the Robertson, Montagu, or Outeniqua pass to Mossel Bay, Plettenberg Bay, Knysna, or Wilderness, where you'll have no trouble filling the rest of your time with shopping, beach lounging, kayaking, whale-watching, or any combination thereof. If you have an adventurous bent, spend the last two or three days at Storms River, where you can take the tree-top canopy tour, hit a mountain-bike trail, or go for a long walk in the Tsitsikamma National Park from Storms River Mouth. Want still more adventure? En route to Storms River, make the world's highest bungee jump at the Bloukrans River Bridge.

HEALTH & SAFETY

The whole area is malaria free, the climate is salubrious, and the water is safe to drink. Be careful of sunburn, and take care when swimming in the sea, as tides in some areas can be strong. Don't ever feed wild animals, even cute little dassies (hyraxes) or vervet monkeys.

MONEY MATTERS

There are ATMs all over, except in De Rust and Storms River; the closest ATMs to these towns, respectively, are in Oudtshoorn and at the fuel complex at the Storms River Bridge on the N2. Banks are open weekdays from 9 to 3 or 3:30 during the week and on Saturday mornings.

EAT RIGHT, SLEEP WELL

Most medium-size towns along the Garden Route offer a decent selection of restaurants, and the smaller towns of the Little Karoo usually have one or two good restaurants and a handful of lesser eateries. If you look around in the region, you'll find some fabulous places to eat; usually the emphasis will be on seafood in general and oysters in particular. (Knysna has an oyster festival in July.) The farms of the Little Karoo provide fresh ostrich meat and organic mutton or lamb, which stand up to South African red wines. Ostrich biltong (jerky) is widely considered the best variety of this national treat.

The region would not have such allure if it weren't for its exclusive seaside getaways and colonial manor houses, as well as its more rustic inland farms and national-park log cabins. Many of the better establishments are set on little islands of well-tended gardens within wild forests. Breakfast is included in many lodgings' rates, and if your guest-house serves dinner, eating the evening meal in situ often has a welcome intimacy after a day of exploring. On the flip side, some cottages are self-catering (with cooking facilities); pick up some local delicacies and make yourself a feast.

Note that the prices listed are for high season, generally October–April. In some cases these prices are significantly higher than during low season, and they may go up higher still for the busiest period—mid-December to mid-January. (If you're traveling during South Africa's winter, don't let high-season prices put you off before inquiring about seasonal specials.) The price categories in this chapter are applied differently to full-service safari lodges in Sanbona Wildlife Reserve than they are to other accommodations. This is because these safari lodges are all-inclusive experiences, with all meals and activities (like game-viewing) accounted for in the price. The chart below explains the differences in detail.

Keep in mind that although mailing addresses are provided for most of the lodgings below, you'll have a much easier time securing a reservation if you phone or, in some cases, book via the lodging's Web site.

WHAT IT COSTS IN SOUTH AFRICAN RAND				
	¢	$	$$	$$$	$$$$
RESTAURANTS	under R50	R50–R75	R75–R125	R125–R175	over R175
LODGING	under R250	R250–R500	R500–R1,000	R1,000–R2,500	over R2,500
FULL-SERVICE SAFARI LODGING	under R3,000	R3,000–R5,000	R5,000–R7,500	R7,500–R10,000	over R10,000

Dining prices are per person for a main course at dinner, a main course equivalent, or a prix-fixe meal. Lodging rates are for a standard double room in high season, including 12.5% tax.

GARDEN ROUTE

The Garden Route means different things to different people. The backpacking crowd loves it for the great beaches, exciting adventures, and parties, whereas more sophisticated visitors revel in the fantastic seafood, scenery, golf courses, and guesthouses and hotels—many with attached spas—where pampering is the name of the game. The Garden Route is also a fabulous family vacation destination, where little ones can frolic on the beach, visit Monkeyland and the Elephant Sanctuary, or go exploring in the forest. And almost no one passes up the opportunity to see whales and dolphins. With numerous guided, catered, and portered multiday hikes and loads of pretty day walks, the Garden Route is ideal for keen walkers and hikers.

EN ROUTE The small town of Albertinia, about 40 km (25 mi) west of Mossel Bay, is an interesting place to break your journey into the Garden Route from Cape Town or the Winelands. It's the center of the Aloe ferox industry. The gel of this indigenous aloe has even greater therapeutic benefits than the better known Aloe vera. Two factories in Albertinia make cosmetics and health-care products from this interesting plant. **Alcare House of Aloes** manufactures and sells a range of aloe products, and sometimes offers tours of the factory on request. There's also a coffee shop. ⊠N2 ☎028/735–1454 ⊕www.alcare.co.za ☉Weekdays 8–5, weekends 8–4.

MOSSEL BAY

❶ *384 km (238 mi) east of Cape Town via the N2.*

Mossel Bay's main attractions are an excellent museum complex; several beautiful historic stone buildings, some of which date back hundreds of years (the central part of Mossel Bay is exceptionally well preserved); some of the best oysters along the coast; golf; and good beaches with safe, secluded bathing. The area has most of the very few north-facing (read: sunniest) beaches in South Africa, but be warned: as it's very popular with local families, it is a writhing, seething mass of juvenile humanity every December. Dolphins—sometimes hundreds at a time—frequently move through the bay in search of food, and whales swim past during their annual migration (July–October). You could take a cruise out to Seal Island, home to a breeding colony of more than 2,000 Cape fur seals or, if you're feeling brave, a cage dive to view the numerous white sharks (blue pointers) that hang around the seal colony.

★ Named for the 15th-century Portuguese navigator, the **Bartolomeu Dias Museum Complex** concentrates on the early history of Mossel Bay, when it was a regular stopover for Portuguese mariners en route to India from Europe. Probably the most interesting exhibit is the full-size (340-foot-long) replica of Dias's ship (a caravel), which was sailed to Mossel Bay from Lisbon as part of the quincentenary celebrations in 1988. If you pay the extra fee to board it, you'll find it all pretty authentic, except for the modern galley and heads. Also here is the Post Office Tree. In the 15th century a few sailors decided that the tree—then a lone tree on a deserted beach on an unexplored coast—stood out sufficiently and left some letters here in an old boot, under a stone, in the hope they would be found and delivered. They were. Pop a postcard into the shoe-shape mailbox, and see if the service is still as good. Your mail will arrive with a special postmark. This museum is a terminus for the Outeniqua Choo-Tjoe train (⇨ *A Train Trip Back in Time box, below*). ✉ *Church and Market Sts.* ☎ *044/691–1067* ⊕ *www. diasmuseum.co.za* 💰 *R6, caravel additional R10* ⊗ *Weekdays 9–4:45, weekends 9–3:45.*

WHERE TO STAY & EAT

$–$$$ ✕ **Café Gannet.** Tour-bus crowds occasionally descend on this popular spot, but don't let that put you off. Justly renowned for its seafood—the oysters are extremely fresh and totally wild, not cultivated—it also has good general and vegetarian menus. Try a pizza from the wood-fired oven or something a bit more exotic, such as deep-fried Brie served with figs and drizzled with wild-forest-berry coulis, followed by skewered tuna cubes in a yogurt-and-dill sauce. The inevitable ostrich is here, served up skewered with sun-dried apricots, cheese sauce, and savory rice. In summer sit outside on the shaded terrace or inside with the eclectic collection of fish-themed African artifacts. ✉ *Church and Market Sts.* ☎ *044/691–1885* ▭ *AE, DC, MC, V.*

¢–$ ✕ **Delfino's Espresso Bar and Pizzeria.** Good coffee, yummy pizzas and pastas, tables on the lawn, and a fantastic view of the bay and the Cape

St. Blaize lighthouse make this a great place to spend a sunny afternoon. ⊠*2 Point Village* ☎*044/690–5247* ⊟*AE, DC, MC, V.*

$ ✕⊡ **Santos Express Train Lodge.** And now for something completely different. In an old train parked on the beach, this lodging uses real train compartments for accommodations. Though the place is not exactly luxurious, the location is hard to beat. Book way ahead to secure the Conductor's Suite, which has its own bathroom and a private deck. Popular with both backpackers and local families, this place buzzes. The restaurant (¢–$) is almost always busy and serves the usual fish, steak, and burgers. You'll also find a good range of traditional South African dishes, such as *bobotie* (a spicy ground-meat dish) and *waterblommetjiebredie* (water-flower stew)—don't knock it till you've tried it. ⊠*Santos Beach* ☎*044/691–1995* ⊕*www.santosexpress.co.za* ↩*29 rooms, 1 with bath; dormitory* ♿*In-room: no a/c, no phone, no TV. In-hotel: restaurant, bar, beachfront, laundry service, public Internet, parking (no fee), no-smoking rooms* ⊟*AE, DC, MC, V* ⦿*CP.*

$$–$$$ ⊡ **Protea Hotel Mossel Bay.** Just yards away from the museum complex, this comfortable hotel is close to most of what's happening in Mossel Bay. You can take in the great view of the harbor, beach, and sea while relaxing at the Blue Oyster Cocktail Bar. Strange nooks and crannies and yard-thick stone walls testify to the building's status as the third-oldest in Mossel Bay (built in the mid-19th century). Self-catering apartments have all the modern conveniences, and many overlook the water. Breakfast is served at the attached Café Gannet. ⊠*Market St.* ⌂*Box 349, 6500* ☎*044/691–3738* ⊕*www.oldposttree.co.za* ↩*23 rooms, 1 suite, 7 apartments* ♿*In-room: no a/c (some), safe, refrigerator, Wi-Fi. In-hotel: restaurant, room service, bar, pool, laundry service, airport shuttle, parking (no fee), no-smoking rooms* ⊟*AE, DC, MC, V.*

★ $$ ⊡ **Point Hotel.** Situated next to the Cape St. Blaize lighthouse, and overlooking a huge, linear tidal pool, the Point Hotel has incredible views over the ocean and the rugged coastline stretching west. In season (July–October), you may see whales from your private balcony. A neutral palette in the spacious, comfortable rooms means there's nothing to detract from the spectacular view. The start of the scenic and fragrant cliff-top Cape St. Blaize Trail is yards away from the front door, and the ocean is a stone's throw from your balcony. The tidal pool is public, but it's a short stroll from the hotel. One disadvantage of the location is that on foggy nights the lighthouse emits an aural rather than visual signal; this doesn't happen often, however, and when it does the noise is not that loud and can't be heard at all if you close the door to the balcony. (Most people, of course, leave the door open for the sound of the sea.) ⊠*Point Rd., Point Village* ⌂*Box 449, 6500* ☎*044/691–3512* ⊕*www.pointhotel.co.za* ↩*50 rooms* ♿*In-room: no a/c, safe. In-hotel: restaurant, room service, bar, laundry service, airport shuttle, parking (no fee), no-smoking rooms* ⊟*AE, DC, MC, V* ⦿*BP.*

SPORTS & THE OUTDOORS

BOATING   For a closer look at the Cape fur seals lounging around on Seal Island, or to check out whales and dolphins, take a trip with **Romonza Boat Trips** (☎*044/690–3101 or 082/701–9031* ⊕*www.mosselbay.co.za/*

romonza) on a 54-foot sailing yacht. Seal Island trips cost R70, and whale-watching trips R250.

From a convenient location near the harbor entrance, **Waverider Adventures** (☎076/335–1515 ⊕*www.waverider.co.za*) rents kayaks and Jet Skis and arranges parasailing and various boat trips. Prices range from R50 for a half-hour kayak rental to R300 for parasailing.

BUNGEE
JUMPING
& BRIDGE
SWINGING

The Gouritz Bridge is about 35 km (22 mi) from Mossel Bay. It's only 220 feet high, but it provides a range of wacky adrenaline opportunities. **Face Adrenalin** (☎044/697–7001 ⊕*www.faceadrenalin.com*) offers bungee jumps for R170 and tandem swings for R180. **Wildthing Adventures** (☎021/552–7753 ⊕*www.wildthing.co.za*) operates a bridge-swinging operation. You jump from one bridge with climbing ropes and swing from the adjacent bridge. The first jump costs R160 for a single (tandems and triples cost R110 per person), after which you get a "wild card," which entitles you to discounted jumps for the next two years.

HIKING

The spectacularly scenic cliff-top **Cape St. Blaize Trail** affords memorable views of the crashing waves below. The trail starts at the Cape St. Blaize Lighthouse, at the Point, and then meanders through fynbos (a local plant type) and past an interesting cave once inhabited by the San.

Fodor'sChoice
★

The guided, catered **Oystercatcher Trail** (☎044/699–1204 ⊕*www. oystercatchertrail.co.za*) offers the best of both worlds, providing a multiday hiking experience along the beach and over rocky shorelines while you carry only a day pack. The trail starts in Mossel Bay, with the first day spent on the lovely cliff-top Cape St. Blaize Trail, and continues to the mouth of the Gouritz River. At midday you'll be provided with a delicious picnic lunch. Nights are spent in a guesthouse or a thatched cottage, where delicious traditional food is prepared for you on open fires. Knowledgeable guides point out birds and plants, and discuss local history and customs. Walking on the beach can be hard if the tide is in, but most people of average fitness should manage. A typical trip is four days and starts at R3,850 per person (more for groups of fewer than six), but shorter hikes of one or two days can be arranged.

GEORGE

❷ *45 km (28 mi) northeast of Mossel Bay, 50 km (31 mi) southeast of Oudtshoorn.*

About 11 km (7 mi) from the sea, George is the largest town and the de facto capital of the Garden Route. Although the surrounding countryside is attractive and there is a thriving farming and crafts community on its outskirts, George itself is not particularly appealing unless you are a golfer or are interested in steam trains.

The **Outeniqua Transport Museum** is a huge hangarlike building with old steam trains on display. It's a real attraction for steam-train enthusiasts, as South Africa has a particularly good collection of preserved steam-driven rolling stock. This museum is a terminus for the Outeniqua

CLOSE UP

A Train Trip back in Time

 Fodor's Choice The **Outeniqua Choo-Tjoe**, an authentic narrow-gauge steam train, is the only scheduled passenger steam train still in operation in South Africa. This aged workhorse used to travel between George and Knysna until floods in 2006 temporarily closed the Kaaimans River Pass. Early in 2007 a new, more scenic, and infinitely more interesting route was started. The train now travels the two hours between the Outeniqua Transport Museum in George and the Bartolomeu Dias Museum Complex in Mossel Bay (you can also take the trip in the opposite direction). You may end up with a soot-blackened face if you succumb to the temptation of sticking your head out of the window to admire the beautiful Gwaing and Maalgate rivers as you cross them, or the crashing waves on the beaches stretching miles west of Mossel Bay, but it's so hard to resist.

It's also fun to wave at bystanders who gather to watch the immense billows of steam as the driver obliges keen photographers with an extra blast when the train passes particularly scenic sections. The train runs once a day Monday–Saturday; at this writing, there were plans to expand the service to two trips a day. Plans were also afoot to reinstate the original George–Knysna route in addition to the new one. In the off-season the train is also used to haul freight, but tourists are its main cargo. When weather and vegetation conditions are very dry, the steam engine poses a fire threat, so a diesel locomotive is used. Reservations are essential and should be made at least a day in advance. ⊠ *Station St., George* ☎ *044/801–8289* ⊕ *www.online-sources.co.za* ☞ *R85 one way, R100 round-trip* ⊙ *Mon.–Sat. 9:30–2.*

Choo-Tjoe train. ⊠ *2 Mission St.* ☎ *044/801–8289* ⊕ *www.online-sources.co.za* ☞ *R5* ⊙ *Weekdays 8–4:30, weekends 8–2.*

If you're into country life, pick up a map from George Tourism at 124 York Street and follow the **Outeniqua Hop,** a fun country route to hop farms (hops are used in beer making), strawberry farms, cheese farms, and numerous crafts outlets.

WHERE TO STAY & EAT

¢-$ ✕ **The Conservatory at Meade House.** Attached to the Meade Emporium, a book and flower shop, is this light and airy restaurant open only for breakfast and lunch. The Conservatory serves the usual sandwiches and salads, but it's locally renowned for some unusual combinations. The omelet with Chinese-style chicken, snap peas, and hoisin sauce is a new twist on an old breakfast favorite. Irish stew served with a pie crust and mash is the most popular lunch dish. You'll also find teas, coffees, and cakes, plus freshly squeezed juices. ⊠ *91 Meade St., Donerail Sq.* ☎ *044/873–3850* ⊟ *AE, DC, MC, V* ⊙ *Closed Sun. No dinner.*

★ ¢-$ ✕ **Leila's Arms.** Intended to be an example in sustainable living, this friendly and informal restaurant serves fabulous lunches—made mostly from organic ingredients—at a great price. The classic is a baked sweet potato smothered with cream cheese, olive oil, spinach, salsa, dates, and fresh herbs. There is always a slow-cooked lamb dish, either curry or *bredie* (stew). The crockery is from a local potter—and you won't find two matching plates. Leila's is on a farm just outside George; the turnoff is signposted on Montagu Street about 1 km (½ mi) on the airport side of Fancourt. Lunch is only served weekdays, though you can request Saturday lunch by appointment. ⊠ *Off Montagu St., Blanco* ☎ *044/870–7613* ⊕ *www.leilas.co.za* ⊟ *No credit cards* ⊗ *Closed Sun. No dinner.*

$$$$ ✕🖾 **Fancourt Hotel and Country Club Estate.** If you're one of those people who believe that we were created with opposable thumbs solely in order to hold a golf club, you'll *love* Fancourt. In the shadows of the Outeniqua Mountains, this luxury resort resembles a country club with numerous sports, leisure, and business facilities. Elegant rooms are either in an old 1860 manor house or in villas nestled in landscaped gardens. Whereas the rooms in the manor house have a classical air, the newer rooms are sleek and modern, with cream walls and pale stone finishes. Of the five restaurants, Sansibar ($–$$$$), with its Africa-theme menu, is the most popular. A bonus if you are flying in or out of George: Fancourt has its own private airport lounge at George Airport. ⊠ *Montagu St.* ☎ *Box 2266, Blanco 6530* ☎ *044/804–0000* ⊕ *www.fancourt.com* ⟿ *92 rooms, 57 suites* ♿ *In-room: safe, refrigerator, dial-up, Wi-Fi. In-hotel: 5 restaurants, room service, bars, golf courses, tennis courts, pools, gym, spa, bicycles, public Wi-Fi airport shuttle, no-smoking rooms* ⊟ *AE, DC, MC, V* ⦿ *BP.*

★ **$$–$$$** ✕🖾 **Hoogekraal.** About 16 km (10 mi) outside George, this historic farm sits on a grassy hill with panoramic views of the Outeniqua Mountains and the Indian Ocean. The public rooms are beautiful—filled with antiques and heirlooms—and just being in them makes a stay here worthwhile. Accommodations are in two sections, a building dating from 1760 and a newer one built in 1820. Although the buildings are full of character and have many lovely old pieces of furniture, the rooms suffer from problems often encountered in historic buildings: the bathrooms are somewhat cramped, and many rooms have unusual proportions. Suites have two bathrooms. Try to get the 1820 Suite, which is roomier than the others. The service is laid-back and friendly, so staying here is more like visiting distant relatives in the country than lodging at a hotel. Most guests choose to stay for the five-course dinner ($$$$) served on fine porcelain at a communal table in the magnificent dining room. (Nonguests may dine here if there's room, but must reserve at least a day in advance.) Almost all the vegetables come straight from the garden, the fish from the distantly glimpsed ocean, and the beef from the cows in the field. ⊠ *Glentana Rd., off N2 between George and Mossel Bay* ☎ *Box 34, 6530* ☎ *044/879–1277* ⊕ *www.hoogekraal.co.za* ⟿ *3 rooms, 3 suites* ♿ *In-room: no a/c, no phone, no TV. In-hotel: restaurant, bar, laundry service, airport shuttle, no kids under 13* ⊟ *DC, MC, V* ⦿ *BP.*

$$ 🖾 **Ambleside Country House.** One of the more reasonably priced options in town, this is a great base from which to play golf. The owner, a keen golfer himself, can book courses, arrange transportation, and generally make sure you play as much golf as you can handle. The lodge is unpretentious without compromising on comfort. The casual lounge, attractive pool area, and honor bar create a great home away from home for weary golfers. Although no dinner is served, many guests make use of the breakfast room and have food delivered. ⊠*Upper Maitland St., Blanco, 6530* ☎*044/870–8138* ⊕*www.ambleside.co.za* ⬎*12 rooms, 2 suites* ⬧*In-room: no a/c, no phone. In-hotel: bar, pool, no kids under 12, no-smoking rooms* ⊟*AE, DC, MC, V* ⦿⎮*BP.*

SPORTS & THE OUTDOORS

GOLF   Fancourt's Links, Montagu, and Outeniqua golf courses and the public George Golf Club are all regularly featured among South Africa's top 10 courses, and are never out of the top 20. Though you have to stay at **Fancourt Hotel and Country Club Estate** (⊠*Montagu St.* ☎*044/804–0000* ⊕*www.fancourt.com*) to play on two of its Gary Player–designed championship courses (Montagu and Outeniqua), Bramble Hill is open to the public. The Links, which is open to residents and members, is particularly challenging, and was the venue of the 2003 Presidents Cup. Greens fees for Bramble Hill fluctuate with the season; high-season rates are about R270 for 18 holes, R175–R200 for club rental, and R230 for cart rental. Outeniqua and Montagu cost R615 per person per day—but you can play both on one day for that price. The Links is expensive—R1,100. There is also an on-site golf academy.

Expect to pay about R400 in greens fees and R170 for a golf cart or R90 for a caddy at the top-rated public **George Golf Club** (⊠*Langenhoven St.* ☎*044/873–6116*). You can rent clubs (R150–R200 for 18 holes) and pull carts (R25) from the **George Golf Shop** (⊠*George Golf Club* ☎*044/874–7597*).

EN   ROUTE   From George the N2 descends steeply to the sea through a heavily forested gorge formed by the Kaaimans River. Look to your right to see a curved railway bridge spanning the river mouth. This is one of the most photographed scenes on the Garden Route (and was especially popular with shutterbugs when the Outeniqua Choo-Tjoe steam train used to puff over it). As you round the point, a breathtaking view of mile upon mile of pounding surf and snow-white beach unfolds before you. There is an overlook from which you can often see dolphins and whales frolicking in the surf, and if you look up, you may see a colorful paraglider floating overhead.

WILDERNESS

❸ *12 km (7 mi) southeast of George.*

Wilderness is a popular vacation resort for good reason. Backed by thickly forested hills and cliffs, the tiny town presides over a magical stretch of beach between the Kaaimans and Touw rivers, as well as a spectacular system of waterways, lakes, and lagoons strung out along the coast, separated from the sea by towering vegetated dunes.

Much of the area now falls under the control of **Wilderness National Park,** a 6,500-acre reserve that stretches east along the coast for 31 km (19 mi). This wetlands paradise draws birders from all over the country to its two blinds. Walking trails wend through the park, including the circular 10-km (6-mi) Pied Kingfisher Trail, which covers the best of what Wilderness has to offer: beach, lagoon, marsh, and river. ⊠*Off N2* ☎*044/877–1197* ⊕*www.sanparks.org* ⊡*R15* ☼*Daily 8–5.*

WHERE TO STAY & EAT

¢–$$ ✕**Pomodoro.** Conveniently located in the middle of town, friendly service, great food, and good value are the highlights of this Italian eatery. Pomodoro does breakfasts and throws in the odd burger to keep the masses happy, but the emphasis here is on crispy thin-crust pizzas—the butternut, feta, and rocket (arugula) is a favorite with locals—pastas, and other Italian dishes. Try the fish-fillet parcels with white wine, tomatoes, peppers, and fresh herbs. Even the ubiquitous ostrich is given a Mediterranean twist—grilled with a pancetta, vermouth, and cream sauce. ⊠*George St.* ☎*044/877–1403* ▤*DC, MC, V.*

$$$–$$$$ ▦**Xanadu.** Deep-pile carpets, double-volume spaces, spectacular floral arrangements, and voluminous drapes framing the sea-view windows add to the sense of opulence at this beachfront establishment. The classic, slightly over-the-top style—with dramatic shades of terra-cotta, and rich vibrant fabrics—tells you you're about to be pampered. Rooms are individually decorated, and all have balconies. The beach is just a short hop from the lawns or the saltwater pool. A small kitchenette means you can prepare a small snack or call for delivery. ⊠*43 Die Duin* ☐*Box 746, 6560* ☎*044/877–0022* ⊕*www.xanadu-wilderness.co.za* ➳*6 rooms* ⌂*In-room: no phone, DVD. In-hotel: pool, no elevator* ▤*AE, DC, MC, V* ⦿*BP.*

$ ▦**Wilderness Farm Backpackers.** Horses and cows in the field, a huge vegetable garden, and endless views over the ocean create a sense of space and abundance at this friendly, squeaky-clean hostel set high on a farm above Wilderness. Brothers Riaan and Theo, both qualified tour guides, offer excursions all over the Garden Route, as well as surfboard rentals and regular shuttles to and from Wilderness. You're welcome to use the well-equipped kitchen or barbecue, though you might want to opt to start the day off with a big farm breakfast for R25. ⊠*291 Whites Rd.* ☐*Box 366, 6530* ☎*082/838–5944 or 076/338–0512* ⊕*www.wildfarmbackpackers.co.za* ➳*1 room, 1 dormitory* ⌂*In-room: no a/c, no phone, safe, no TV. In-hotel: bar* ▤*AE, DC, MC, V.*

¢–$ ▦**Ebb and Flow Restcamp, Wilderness National Park.** Within Wilderness National Park is this rest camp divided into two sections, North and South. The South section is larger and consists of brick family cottages, which sleep up to six, as well as log cabins and forest huts, both of which sleep up to four. The log cabins are prettier than the cottages, but both are bright and pleasant, furnished in a plain but adequate manner with floral or geometric curtains and upholstery; both have bedrooms, kitchens, and bathrooms with balconies. Forest cabins are smaller but cute. Campsites, some of which directly overlook the river, are set on a wide lawn under trees. The much smaller North section has a few grassy campsites and 15 not particularly attractive *rondawels* (round huts). The communal bathroom areas are well maintained, clean, and adequate, and there are on-site laundry facilities. You can fish, hike, and boat here. ⊠*Off N2* ☎*044/877–1197* ⊕*www.sanparks.org* ➳*5 cot-*

*tages; 8 log cabins; 10 2-bed and 10 4-bed forest cabins; 12 rondawels,
10 with bath; 100 campsites* ☆ *No elevator* ▤ *AE, DC, MC, V.*

SPORTS & THE OUTDOORS

Wilderness National Park and environs provide opportunities for lovely
walks, fantastic paddling, and fishing.

CANOEING Based inside Wilderness National Park, **Eden Adventures** (☎ *044/877–*
★   *0179* ⊕ *www.eden.co.za*) offers a canoeing and mountain-biking
trip (R220), a kloofing (canyoning) excursion (R250), and abseiling
(rappelling) in Kaaimans Gorge (R250). These are all half-day trips
and include lunch, but they can be combined to form a full-day trip
(R440–R475). You can also rent a two-seater canoe for exploring the
wetlands (R120 per day). Eden Adventures also runs a two-and-a-half-
day guided canoeing and hiking trip in the park. It's fully catered, and
accommodation is in either a tented camp or chalets. Prices range from
R1,095 to R1,200, and custom tours can be arranged.

HIKING On the five-day, guided **Garden Route Trail** (☎ *044/883–1015 or*
082/213–5931 ⊕ *www.gardenroutetrail.co.za*) you start in the Ebb
and Flow Restcamp and then head east along the coast, taking in long
beach walks and coastal forest, before ending in Knysna. The emphasis
is on the natural environment, and knowledgeable guides provide commentary along the way. The trip is catered and portered, and you do
some canoeing in addition to hiking. The five-day trail costs R4,200; a
three-day trail is also available for R3,100.

PARAGLIDING Wilderness is one of the best paragliding spots in the country. You can
★   ridge-soar for miles along the dune front, watching whales and dolphins in the sea. If you've never done it before, don't worry: you can go
tandem (R350–R450) with an experienced instructor from **Cloudbase
Paragliding** (☎ *044/877–1414* ⊕ *www.cloudbase-paragliding.co.za*).

KNYSNA ★

❹ *40 km (25 mi) east of Wilderness.*

Knysna (pronounced *nize*-nuh) is one of the most popular destinations
on the Garden Route. The focus of the town is the beautiful Knysna
Lagoon, ringed by forested hills dotted with vacation homes. Several
walking and mountain-bike trails wind through Knysna's forests, many
offering tremendous views back over the ocean. With luck you may
spot the Knysna turaco, a brilliantly plumed and elusive forest bird also
known as the Knysna loerie, or the even more outrageously colored and
more elusive Narina trogon.

Towering buttresses of rock, known as the Heads, guard the entrance
to the lagoon, funneling the ocean through a narrow channel. The sea
approach is so hazardous that Knysna never became a major port,
which may explain why it developed instead into the modern resort
town it is today, with the attendant hype, commercialism, and crowds,
especially in summer. About the only aspect of the town that hasn't
been modernized is the single-lane main road (the N2 goes straight

through the middle of town), so traffic can be a nightmare. Walking is the best way to get around the town center, which is filled with shops, galleries, restaurants, and coffeehouses. Knysna's main claims to fame are edible and drinkable. The former are its famous—and abundant—cultivated oysters, and the latter is locally brewed Mitchell's beer, on tap at most bars and pubs.

Knysna Art Gallery is in the Old Gaol, a structure that dates to 1859. As well as constantly changing exhibitions of a high standard, there is a semipermanent exhibit of works by local artists, of which Knysna seems to produce an inordinate number. ⊠*Queen and Main Sts.* ☎*044/382–7124* ☒*Free* ☉ *Weekdays 9:30–4:30, Sat. 9:30–1.*

★ You can't come to Knysna without making a trip out to the **Heads,** at the mouth of the lagoon. The rock sentinels provide great views of both the sea and the lagoon. Only the developed, eastern side is accessible by car, via George Rex Drive off the N2. You have two options: to park at the base of the Head and follow the walking trails that snake around the rocky cliffs, just feet above the crashing surf, or to drive to the summit, with its panoramic views and easy parking.

Unlike its eastern counterpart, the western side of the Heads, part of the **Featherbed Nature Reserve** (☎*044/382–1693* ⊕*www.knysnafeatherbed. com*), is relatively unspoiled. In addition to a bizarre rock arch and great scenery, the reserve is home to various small mammals, more than 100 species of birds, and 1,000 plant species. There are two standard trips here, plus more in high season (generally October–April). The morning trip costs R300, leaves at 10, and lasts four hours. It consists of a ride on one of three ferries operated by the reserve, a tractor-trailer ride to the highest point, an escorted walk back, and buffet lunch. The afternoon trip leaves at 2:30, costs R190, takes three hours, and is identical except that it does not include lunch.

One of the most interesting buildings in the area stands across the lagoon from Knysna, in the exclusive community of Belvidere. The Anglican **Holy Trinity Church,** built in 1855 of local stone, is a lovely replica of a Norman church of the 11th century. Holy Trinity was erected by Thomas Duthie, a young ensign of the 72nd Highland Regiment who settled in Knysna in 1834. The interior is notable for its beautiful stinkwood and yellowwood timber and stained-glass windows. ⊠*N2 west out of Knysna to Belvidere turnoff just after bridge; then follow signs* ☎*No phone* ☒*Free* ☉*Daily 8:30–5, except during services.*

BEACHES

Although Knysna is very much a seaside destination, there are no beaches actually in the town—unlike Plett or Mossel Bay—but there are some fabulous ones nearby. **Leisure Isle,** in the middle of the lagoon, has a few tiny strands. The beach at **Brenton-on-Sea,** past Belvidere, is a beautiful, long white-sand beach on which you can walk for 6 km (4 mi) to Buffalo Bay. It's about a 10-minute drive; the turnoff from the N2 is about 12 km (7½ mi) west of Knysna. **Buffalo Bay Beach** is a wonderful little secret spot, with great walks in either direction—toward

Brenton-on-the-Sea or into the Goukamma Nature Reserve. The surfing is great, and you can go horseback riding here.

WHERE TO STAY & EAT

Of course there are restaurants that don't serve seafood, but very few of them are in Knysna. It's what the town's all about. There are more bed-and-breakfasts than you can possibly imagine, as well as some fantastic guesthouses, self-catering resorts, and hotels, so you will not be short of choices.

★ ¢–$$$$ ✕ **34° South.** Right on the water's edge in what appears to be a dolled-up warehouse, this place gives off a sense of abundance, with shelves, baskets, and display stands overflowing with all kinds of delicious goodies. Defying convention, 34° South manages to combine elements of a fishmonger, a bar, a bistro, a deli, a coffee shop, and a seafood restaurant. Choose from the huge array of fresh fish, including sushi, and enjoy your feast while sitting on the jetty looking at the boats. You could also opt for a delicious sandwich laden with avocados and peppadews (spicy pickled peppers). Or just fill a basket with delicious breads, pickles, cheeses, meats, and other delights. It's worth traveling halfway around the world just for the cilantro pesto. ⊠ *Knysna Quays* ☎ *044/382–7331* ▭ *AE, DC, MC, V.*

¢–$$ ✕ **Lush.** Depending on how you spent the '60s and '70s, you may think you're having an acid flashback as you walk into this stylish, retro-chic eatery with a red, black, and white pop-art vibe. But don't worry: the decor may hearken back to a different age, but the food is right here and now, and just a little bit different. The prawn tempura is fried in a pale-green batter made with cilantro and sesame seeds, and dipped in a sweet plum sauce; the kingklip (a firm white fish similar to monkfish) is baked in an olive puff-pastry crust. If you have a really sweet tooth, you may like the chocolate fondant with iced double cream. ⊠ *Sawtooth La., Thesen Harbour Town* ☎ *044/382–7196* ▭ *AE, DC, MC, V* ⊗ *No lunch.*

¢–$ ✕ **Ile de Pain.** Watch bakers hand-mix dough in the background before
Fodor's Choice consigning their huge assortment of European-style breads into wood-
★ fired ovens. All the meals on the seasonally changing menu are bread based, but they are definitely not your average sandwich. For breakfast try a rolled frittata with herbs, leeks, smoked salmon, horseradish sauce, cream cheese, and capers, or brioche French toast with caramelized pineapple, frozen yogurt, and passion-fruit syrup. Lunch favorites include a slice of ciabatta bread with sirloin steak, balsamic caramelized onions, and mustard butter, as well as a garden sandwich of mixed lettuce, avocado, pea-and-pistachio pesto, and tomato vinaigrette. All toppings are made on-site from fresh ingredients. And, of course, there are yummy pastries and good coffee. ⊠ *Boatshed, Thesen Island* ⊕ *Box 1366, Knysna 6570* ☎ *044/302–5707* ▭ *AE, MC, V* ⊗ *Closed Mon. No dinner.*

★ $$$$ ✕▭ **Phantom Forest Lodge.** Set on a private 300-acre nature reserve, this stunning lodge is built from sustainable natural materials. Accommodations are in luxury tree houses, and the living areas are joined by wooden walkways to protect the undergrowth. Rooms look straight out into the forest canopy. Though the original suites have natural tones and wood, thatch, and coir finishes, newer rooms are decorated in a vibrant North African style. Of the two restaurants, Chutzpah focuses on North African/Moroccan food, with tasty *tagines* (meat stews) and couscous in a variety of guises. Forest Boma produces contemporary classical cuisine with a local flavor, such as peppered springbok loin with asparagus, garlic mashed potatoes, and berry jus, or roasted butternut tortellini with apple, asparagus, and fennel salad. Desserts might include a fig, passion-fruit, and browned-butter pie with chili and vanilla ice cream. ⊠*Phantom Pass, Box 3051, 6570* ☎*044/386–0046* ⊕*www.phantomforest.com* ⌨*14 suites* ♿*In-room: no a/c, refrigerator. In-hotel: 2 restaurants, bar, pool, gym, spa, bicycles, no elevator, laundry service, public Wi-Fi, airport shuttle, parking (no fee), no kids under 12, no-smoking rooms* ☐*AE, DC, MC, V* ▮◎▮*MAP.*

★ $$$–$$$$ ▦**Belvidere Manor.** There are lovely views across the lagoon to Knysna, some 6½ km (4 mi) away, at this attractive establishment. Airy cottages face each other across a lawn that slopes down to a jetty. Choose from one- and two-bedroom units, all with dining areas, sitting rooms with fireplaces, and fully equipped kitchens. The manor house, a lovely restored 1834 farmstead, contains a restaurant and guest lounge. In summer breakfast is served on the veranda overlooking the lagoon. Sizable discounts are offered for long stays. ⊠*Lower Duthie Dr., Belvidere Estate* ⊕*Box 1195, 6570* ☎*044/387–1055* ⊕*www.belvidere. co.za* ⌨*30 cottages* ♿*In-room: no a/c. In-hotel: restaurant, room service, bar, pool, no elevator, parking (no fee), no kids under 10* ☐*AE, DC, MC, V* ▮◎▮*BP.*

★ $$$–$$$$ ▦**St. James of Knysna.** This elegant lodging is right on the edge of Knysna Lagoon. Outdoors you can enjoy a garden with tranquil koi ponds. Indoors the setting is light and bright, with some lovely antiques. Most of the individually decorated rooms have uninterrupted views of the water. Bathrooms range from Victorian fantasies to a brick-tone retreat with a glass wall that leads to a private leafy garden with an outside shower. ⊠*The Point, Main St.* ⊕*Box 1242, 6570* ☎*044/382–6750* ⊕*www.stjames.co.za* ⌨*2 rooms, 13 suites* ♿*In-room: safe, refrigerator. In-hotel: restaurant, room service, bar, pools, no elevator, laundry service, public Wi-Fi, airport shuttle, parking (no fee), no kids under 12, no-smoking rooms* ☐*AE, DC, MC, V* ▮◎▮*BP.*

$$ ▦**Brenton on Rocks.** It's unusual to find a self-catering establishment
Fodor'sChoice that is quite this sophisticated and understated, with clean lines, black
★ granite, and stainless-steel finishes. The suites and public rooms are spacious, and all share breathtaking ocean views. The two double rooms don't have a direct sea view, though you can see the water from the balconies, and they have only showers, whereas the suites have roomy showers and tubs. A steep, twisty path leads to a small beach that is easily seen from all the suites. All the accommodations have kitchenettes, but there are also two well-equipped communal kitchens (plus barbecues) where you can prepare a meal, which you can then serve in the big sea-view dining room or on the veranda. It's a bit like having your own beach house. The house next door, which isn't nearly as stylish but shares almost as good a view, is a great bargain for families.

✉ *276 Steenbras St., Brenton-on-Sea* ☎ *Box 3304, 6570* ✆ *044/381–0489 or 083/249–3644* ⊕ *www.brentononrocks.co.za* 🛏 *2 rooms, 5 suites, 1 4-bed house* ♿ *In-room: no a/c, safe, kitchen, dial-up. In-hotel: pool, beachfront, no elevator, laundry facilities, public Internet, parking (no fee), no-smoking rooms* ☰ *AE, DC, MC, V.*

$$ 🏠 **Cuningham's Island Guest House.** This casual beach house—okay, it's not actually on the beach, but it feels like it is—gets many return guests. Decorated with light lime-washed pine and wicker furnishings, it has an easy flow from the breakfast room to the sunny pool area. Owner Tim Cuningham will help make arrangements for golf, and can provide plenty of advice on other activities, too. Bathrooms don't have tubs, but the generously proportioned shower stalls make up for that. ✉ *Kingsway and Church St., Leisure Isle* ☎ *Box 3420, 6570* ✆ *044/384–1319* ⊕ *www.islandhouse.co.za* 🛏 *8 rooms* ♿ *In-room: no a/c, no phone. In-hotel: bar, pool, no elevator, laundry service, parking (no fee), no kids under 10, no-smoking rooms* ☰ *AE, DC, MC, V* ⊙*BP.*

$$ 🏠 **Lightleys Holiday Houseboats.** For a sense of freedom and adventure,

Fodor's Choice rent one of these fully equipped houseboats and cruise the lagoon. The

★ inside is compact, light, and bright, and outside there's an ever-changing vista of lagoon, forest, and mountain. This is self-catering at its very best. A four-berth boat costs R800 per day for two people and R1,265 for four; a six-berth boat costs about R1,635 per day. The longer you stay the cheaper it gets. If you don't fancy cooking, you can arrange to pick up meals or picnic baskets from the base or have them delivered to you at a mooring of your choice. Or you can just hop on a jetty and take your pick of Knysna's restaurants. ☎ *Box 863, 6570* ✆ *044/386–0007* ⊕ *www.houseboats.co.za* 🛏 *9 4-berth boats, 5 6-berth boats* ♿ *In-room: kitchen* ☰ *MC, V.*

SPORTS & THE OUTDOORS

BOATING   Boating on the lagoon is a scenic experience, and going through the Heads is quite dramatic. It makes you think about how dangerous it once was for big sailing ships to maneuver through narrow passages such as these without auxiliary engines.

Deep South Eco-Ventures (✉ *Knysna Quays* ✆ *044/382–2010 or 083/250–9441* ⊕ *www.deepsoutheco.com*) leads boat trips on the lagoon, starting at R270, that include commentary on the wildlife and sights. A boat trip can also be combined with a bike tour and lunch.

In addition to running the ferry to the nature reserve, the **Featherbed Company** (✉ *Ferry Terminus, Remembrance Ave.* ✆ *044/382–1693* ⊕ *www.knysnafeatherbed.com*) operates sightseeing boats on the lagoon (trips start at R75 per person), as well as a Mississippi-style paddle steamer that does lunch and dinner cruises.

★ **Springtide Charters** (✉ *Knysna Quays* ✆ *082/470–6022* ⊕ *www.springtide.co.za*) operates a luxury 50-foot sailing yacht for scenic cruises on the lagoon and through the Heads (weather permitting). You can have breakfast, lunch, or a romantic dinner on board—or even spend the night. The boat takes a maximum of 12 passengers, and dinner and overnight trips are limited to one party. Rates start at about R310 per person for a two-hour sail, or R470 for a three-hour trip with snacks.

GOLF Perched on the cliff top of the Eastern Head, the challenging 18-hole **Pezula Championship Golf Course** (⊠ *Lagoon View Dr.* ☎ *044/302–5300* ⊕ *www.pezula.com*) is one of South Africa's most scenic courses, designed by Ronald Fream and David Dale. It costs R700 per person, including a compulsory golf cart. Also available are a comfortable clubhouse with a great restaurant and lessons from resident pros.

HIKING The two-day **Harkerville Trail** (⊠ *N2, 15 km [9 mi] east of Knysna*) passes through the indigenous forests, pine plantations, and "islands" of fynbos, as well as fairly taxing sections on the coast. (This is not a beginner's trail.) Homesick Californians can hug a familiar tree in a small stand of huge redwoods (*Sequoia sempervirens*), planted as part of a forestry experiment years ago. Watch out for mountain bikers, who use sections of the trail, and usually shout a warning as they hurtle toward you. The trail costs R100 per person. For more information, contact **SANParks** (☎ *044/382–5606*).

If you'd like to sample the Harkerville Forest but don't want to commit to a strenuous, two-day, hike, try the easy stroll in the **Garden of Eden.** The short trail goes into the forest on a wheelchair-friendly wooden boardwalk. You'll see some big old trees, plus tables where you can picnic. The kiosk at the Garden of Eden is open daily 7:30–4, and entry is R6 per person. For more information, contact **SANParks** (☎ *044/382–5606*).

If you don't fancy heading off on your own, take a guided walk through the area with **Knysna Forest Tours** (☎ *044/382–6130* ⊕ *www.knysna foresttours.co.za*). Prices are about R350 for a half day, and R550 for a full day including lunch.

HORSEBACK If you've ever dreamed of riding a horse along a deserted beach, this is
RIDING your chance. From Buffalo Bay, **Garden Route Equestrian Adventure Tours**
Fodor'sChoice (⌂ *5, 12th Ave., Mossel Bay 6506* ☎ *082/835–9110* ⊕ *www.great.*
★ *co.za*) offers great sunrise and sunset horseback rides along Brenton Beach toward Brenton-on-Sea, and, during low tide, in the opposite direction along Goukamma Beach (where experienced riders who go fast enough can opt to return through the densely forested Goukamma Nature Reserve). Rides are 1½ hours long and cost R250. Longer rides are available by request.

MOUNTAIN The Garden Route is ideal for mountain biking. There are four circular
BIKING trails of varying length and difficulty at **Harkerville** (⊠ *N2, 15 km [9 mi]*
★ *east of Knysna*), all starting and ending at the Garden of Eden. If you're cycling without a guide, reservations are not necessary; just register when you start and pay the nominal fee (R25 per person). All the trails are great, but the last 6 km (4 mi) of the Petrus se Brand trail is widely considered to be the most fun (but not challenging) piece of single track in South Africa. Unlike the others, Petrus se Brand is not circular; it can be done either way between Diepwalle and Garden of Eden. It's tight and twisty, and you'll zip downhill (if you start at Diepwalle) over the

3

springy forest floor, dodging enormous trees. You can rent bikes (R125) from **Outeniqua Biking Trails** (✉ *Harkerville* ☎ *044/532–7644*), which is conveniently located right on the forest edge and close to the trails.

Deep South Eco-Ventures (☎ *044/382–2010 or 083/250–9441* ⊕ *www. deepsoutheco.com*) offers guided mountain-bike tours into the forests, starting at R260.

PLETTENBERG BAY

❺ *32 km (20 mi) east of Knysna.*

Plettenberg Bay is South Africa's premier beach resort, as the empty houses on Beachy Head Road (known as Millionaires' Mile) during the 11 months when it's not beach season will attest. But in December the hordes with all their teenage offspring arrive en masse. Even then you can find yourself a stretch of lonely beach if you're prepared to walk to the end of Keurboomstrand. Plett, as it is commonly known, is one of the best places in the world to watch whales and dolphins. Boat-based trips are run from Central Beach, as are sea-kayaking trips, which, although loads of fun, are not quite as efficient as the big motorboats.

It's fun to take a tour of the **Jacks Jungle Juice** *mampoer* (moonshine) distillery, located at the Buffalo Hills Game Reserve and Lodge. You can see how mampoer is made, and taste several mampoer-based liqueurs. ✉ *Stofpad, Wittedrif* ☎ *044/535–9739* 🎫 *Free* ⊙ *Weekdays 9–3.*

BEACHES

Plett presides over a stretch of coastline that has inspired rave reviews since the Portuguese first set eyes on it in 1497 and dubbed it *bahia formosa* (the beautiful bay). Three rivers flow into the sea here, the most spectacular of which—the Keurbooms—backs up to form a large lagoon. For swimming, surfing, sailing, hiking, and fishing you can't do much better than Plett, although the water is still colder than it is around Durban and in northern KwaZulu-Natal.

All the dolphin-watching boats and kayak trips leave from **Central Beach.** A constant stream of tenders going out to the fishing boats moored in the bay makes this area quite busy, but it's still a great spot. Just keep away from the boat-launching area, and swim in the southern section. Just on the other side of the Beacon Isle, the unmissable hotel at the end of the tòmbolo, is **Robberg Beach,** a great swimming beach that continues in a graceful curve all the way to Robberg Peninsula. You can get pretty good sightings of dolphins and whales just behind the back break.

Keurboomstrand is about 10 km (6 mi) from Plett—right on the eastern edge of the bay. If you're fit, you can walk all the way from here to Nature's Valley, but you need to watch both the tides and the steep, rocky sections. It's best to ask locals before tackling this. Even if you're not fit, you can still walk about a mile down the beach, relax for a while, and then walk back. **Lookout Beach** was Plett's flagship Blue Flag beach (indicating high environmental standards), but as the lagoon mouth shifts, the beach is disappearing. There's not much left of it, but it should still be around for a while, and it's great for swimming, body-surfing, and sunbathing. There's even a nice little restaurant-bar here.

WHERE TO STAY & EAT

As one of the most sophisticated destinations on the Garden Route, Plett has plenty of fabulous places to eat and overnight.

$–$$ ✕**Fushi.** Plett's slickest, sleekest eatery is all clean surfaces and clas-sical lines. In addition to sushi, there are unusual Pan-Asian dishes such as the deboned, pressed lamb shank with saffron rice, spicy chili sauce, and cucumber-yogurt dressing. The wasabi crème brûlée is a new twist on an old favorite. ⊠*Upper Deck, Marine Dr.* ☎*044/533–4440* ▭*AE, DC, MC, V* ⊘*No dinner Sun.*

¢–$$ ✕**Cornuti Al Mare.** The blue and white tiles on the facade of this popu-lar, casual Italian eatery—a favorite with locals that's usually pretty full—give the place a beach-house feel. Try the pastas or the thin wood-fired pizzas; the potato pizza is so much tastier than it sounds. In sum-mer, get there early to get a seat on the veranda. ⊠*Oddlands and Perestrello Sts.* ☎*044/533–1277* ⌂*Reservations not accepted* ▭*AE, DC, MC, V.*

¢ ✕**Plett Ski Boat Club.** Want to know a secret? Plett fisherfolk, ski-boat skippers, surfers, kayak operators, and other locals frequent this very, very casual eatery. It's right on the beach where the ski boats launch, so there's a great view—especially from the outside tables. It offers really good value for the money; well-cooked, fresh but not fancy seafood; the usual burgers and fries; and full breakfasts. Many locals can be reliably tracked down to the popular bar on weekday afternoons—especially if there is a rugby match on TV. ⊠*Central Beach* ☎*044/533–4147* ⌂*Reservations not accepted* ▭*AE, DC, MC, V* ⊘*No dinner.*

★ $$$$ ✕▥**Plettenberg.** High on a rocky point in Plettenberg Bay, this luxury hotel has unbelievable views of the bay, the Tsitsikamma Mountains, Keurbooms Lagoon, miles of magnificent beach, and, in season, whales frolicking just beyond the waves. Built around an 1860 manor house, the hotel is light and bright, decorated in shades of white and blue. Service is wonderfully attentive, with a front-desk staff that tries to anticipate your every need. Even if you don't stay here, treat yourself to lunch on the hotel terrace. Diners sit under large fabric umbrellas and look out over a pool that seems to extend right into the incredible views. The lunch menu is small: salads, sandwiches, a pasta dish, and the catch of the day. Dinner in the restaurant ($$; reservations essen-tial) is a fancier affair, focusing on local meat and seafood. Villas are self-catering. ⊠*Lookout Rocks* ✉*Box 719, 6600* ☎*044/533–2030* ⊕*www.plettenberg.com* ⌖*24 rooms, 12 suites, 2 villas* ⌂*In-room: kitchen (some), refrigerator. In-hotel: restaurant, bar, pools, spa, no ele-vator, laundry service, airport shuttle, parking (no fee), no kids under 12, no-smoking rooms* ▭*AE, DC, MC, V* ⎤⦿*BP.*

★ $$$–$$$$ ✕▥**Hunter's Country House.** Just 10 minutes from town, this tranquil property is set amid gardens that fall away into a forested valley. The heart of the lodge is an old farmstead, a lovely thatch building with low beams and large fireplaces. Guest rooms are in individual white thatch cottages, each with its own fireplace and veranda. Three suites have private plunge pools. Antiques grace the rooms, and claw-foot tubs are the centerpiece of many of the gigantic bathrooms. Service is outstanding. Most guests eat at the hotel's excellent table d'hôte restaurant ($$$$), which brings a French touch to local South African produce. Reservations are essential for nonguests. The lodge is very child-friendly, which makes it one of the few places where you don't have to sacrifice sophistication for family accommodations. ⊠ *Off N2, between Plettenberg Bay and Knysna* ⌂ *Box 454, 6600* ☎ *044/501–1111* ⊕ *www.hunter hotels.com* ⟿ *21 suites* ⌂ *In-room: safe. In-hotel: 2 restaurants, bar, tennis court, pool, children's programs, laundry service, public Internet, no-smoking rooms* ☰ *AE, MC, V* ⊙ *BP.*

★ $$$$ ⌂ **Plettenberg Park.** The setting of this stylish, minimalist lodge—in splendid isolation on a cliff top in a private nature reserve on the western (wild) side of Robberg Peninsula—is one of the best anywhere, and the view of the open ocean across fynbos-clad hills is spectacular. Rooms are decorated in an understated African colonial style in shades of white and cream; those that face the sea have dramatic views, and the others overlook a tranquil lily pond. A steep path leads to a private beach and natural tidal pool. ⊠ *Off Robberg Rd.* ⌂ *Box 167, 6600* ☎ *044/533–9067* ⊕ *www.plettenbergpark.co.za* ⟿ *9 rooms* ⌂ *In-room: no a/c, safe, refrigerator, VCR. In-hotel: restaurant, room service, bar, pool, gym, spa, beachfront, no elevator, laundry service, concierge, airport shuttle, no kids under 12, no-smoking rooms* ☰ *AE, DC, MC, V* ⊙ *BP.*

$$$$ ⌂ **Tsala Treetop Lodge.** Built on the same property as Hunter's, and also run by the Hunter family, this lodge combines the best of sleek design with spectacular natural surroundings. Fabulous glass, stone, metal, and wood chalets are built on stilts overlooking a steep forested gorge and, in some cases, extending into the forest canopy. Suites have plunge pools with fantastic views, verandas, and fireplaces, and the unusual decor includes specially manufactured oval baths, hand-beaten brass plumbing fittings, and loads of glass. Suites are connected by raised timber walkways. ⊠ *Off N2, between Plettenberg Bay and Knysna* ⌂ *Box 454, 6600* ☎ *044/532–7818* ⟿ *10 suites* ⌂ *In-room: no a/c, safe. In-hotel: restaurant, room service, bar, no elevator, laundry service, public Internet, airport shuttle, no kids under 10, no-smoking rooms* ☰ *AE, MC, V* ⊙ *BP.*

$$$ ⌂ **Buffalo Hills Game Reserve and Lodge.** Pockets of indigenous bush and tracts of fynbos alternate with old farmland on this fun property about 15 minutes outside Plett. It's not Mpumalanga—or even the Karoo or Eastern Cape—but it's a great place to see a variety of game, including buffalo and rhino. In this warm, friendly place, evening meals are taken around an enormous table, and outrageous stories are told. Try the game walk or even a multiday hike into the hills. Even little ones can do short game walks near the lodge at this child-friendly establishment. The rooms are in an old farmhouse, and there are also en-suite safari-style tents scattered around—some near the farmhouse and others across the river. The price includes game drives and walks, but not lunch, as most guests choose to spend the middle of the day in Plett,

where there are loads of restaurants. For R3,950, the fabulous three-day special includes lodging, breakfast and dinner, game drives, walks, a tour of the on-site Jacks Jungle Juice distillery, and four activities from a list of 26 of the most fun things to do in and around Plett. ⊠*Stofpad, Wittedrif* ✆*Box 1321, 6600* ☎*044/535–9739* ⊕*www.buffalohills.co.za* ✎*4 rooms, 11 tented rooms, 1 cottage* ⟨*In-room: no a/c, no phone, no TV. In-hotel: bar, pool, laundry service, airport shuttle, no-smoking rooms* ⊟*AE, DC, MC, V* ⍾*MAP.*

$$

Fodor'sChoice

★

Bitou River Lodge. Some places just seem to get everything right. This lovely, quiet, restful B&B has a wonderful location on the bank of the Bitou River, about 3 km (2 mi) upstream from the lagoon. Rooms overlook a pretty garden and a quiet bird-rich and lily-filled pond. The decor is understated and soothing, with neutral pastels dominating. Breakfasts are delicious affairs with freshly baked breads, muffins, and other goodies in addition to the usual fruit, cereal, and eggs. Bitou feels like it's in the middle of nowhere, but it's only a 10-minute drive from the center of town. Don't pass up the opportunity to explore the river in one of the available canoes. ⊠*About 3 km (2 mi) on the R340 to Wittedrif (off the N2)* ✆*Box 491, 6600* ☎*044/535–9577 or 082/978–6164* ⊕*www.bitou.co.za* ✎*5 rooms* ⟨*In-room: no a/c, no phone, refrigerator. In-hotel: pool, no kids under 12, no-smoking rooms* ⊟*MC, V* ⍾*BP.*

¢–$

Nothando Backpackers. This always-buzzing, warm, friendly hostel with some private rooms is light and bright, and is conveniently located near the middle of town. It's easy to find a sunny or shady spot in the garden to just relax with a book, and the lively bar is a great place to share adventures come evening. All in all, it's an excellent value. ⊠*5 Wilder St., 6600* ☎*044/533–0220* ⊕*www.nothando.com* ✎*8 rooms, 6 with bath; 1 dormitory* ⟨*In-room: no a/c, no phone, no TV (some). In-hotel: bar, laundry service, public Internet, parking (no fee), no-smoking rooms* ⊟*AE, DC, MC, V.*

SPORTS & THE OUTDOORS

HIKING

★

Robberg Nature Reserve (⊠*Robberg Rd. [on way to airport]* ☎*044/533–2125*), open daily 7:30–6, has three fabulous walks. The shortest takes about a half hour and offers great views of the ocean. A longer walk (1½ hours) passes above a seal colony and connects to the "island" via a tombolo. At 2½ hours or more, the longest walk goes right to the end of the peninsula. You need to watch the tides on this one. In addition to great sea views, dolphins, whales, birds, and seals, there are fantastic flowers and swimming beaches. You might also see abandoned gold mines. Admission is R25, and it's worth taking a picnic. A fascinating archaeological excavation at Nelson's Bay Cave has a display outlining the occupation of the cave over thousands of years.

KAYAKING

★

Kayaking on **Plettenberg Bay** is a great way to see the sights and possibly enjoy a visit from a whale or dolphin. Though you aren't likely to see as many animals as the people on the big boats will, it's a far more intimate and exciting experience if you do. You also get to paddle past the Cape fur seal colony on Robberg. Trips cost about R250 for three hours. **Dolphin Adventures** (⊠*Central Beach* ☎*083/590–3405* ⊕*www.*

dolphinadventures.co.za) offers regular trips in sleek but stable tandem kayaks. **Ocean Blue** (✉*Hopwood St., Central Beach* ☎*044/533–5083* ⊕*www.oceanadventures.co.za*) runs regular paddling trips on which you may see whales and dolphins.

SKYDIVING   If you want your views with a bit of adrenaline thrown in, consider a tandem skydive with **Skydive Plett** (✉*Plettenberg Bay Airport* ☎*082/905–7440* ⊕*www.skydiveplett.com*). Tandem jumps cost about R1,300, and it's worth the extra R300 to get the DVD so you can show your friends back home. You get nearly half a minute of free fall, during which you get to see Robberg and the whole of the Tsitsikamma coast. If you think you might get serious about this sport, you can take an Accelerated Free Fall (AFF) course.

WHALE-   **Plettenberg Bay** is one of the very best locations worldwide for boat-
WATCHING   based whale- and dolphin-watching. Most days visitors see at least two
☺   cetacean species and Cape fur seals, as well as a variety of seabirds,
Fodor'sChoice   including Cape gannets and African penguins. On some days people
★   have seen up to six cetacean species in the course of a few hours.

Two similar operators have you board an open vehicle outside a shop and from there step directly onto a boat at the beach. Boats are fast, safe, and dry. Both operators offer a standard trip (about R300), in which the boat must stay 975 feet from the animals, and a close-encounter trip (about R500) on a boat that is licensed to approach within 162 feet. These trips are limited in order to minimize disturbance to the whales. **Ocean Blue** (✉*Hopwood St., Central Beach* ☎*044/533–5083* ⊕*www. oceanadventures.co.za*) and **Ocean Safaris** (✉*Hopwood St., Central Beach* ☎*044/533–4963 or 082/784–5729* ⊕*www.oceansafaris.co.za*) run regular whale-and-dolphin-watching trips from the beach area.

SHOPPING

Plenty of shops in and around town sell casual beachwear and various crafts, but for a good concentration in a small place, you can't beat **Old Nick** (✉*N2, just east of town* ☎*044/533–1395*). Originally just a pottery and weaving studio, it has grown to include a host of other crafts—so many that you could spend a whole day here. Included are a weaving museum, a shop selling lovely woven goods, a crystal shop, and a few galleries. A handmade-soap factory beckons with the scent of essential oils and fruits, and the **Country Kitchen** competes for your olfactory attention with the heady aroma of freshly brewed espresso.

THE CRAGS

❻ *16 km (10 mi) northeast of Plettenberg Bay.*

Although technically part of Plett, the Crags is very different. It's rural and forested and is home to primate and elephant refuges, plus a free-flight aviary. Although there's no beach, the Crags region is close to the lovely beach at Nature's Valley. There are loads of fantastic accommodation options and exciting activities, most of which belong to a great little marketing initiative called **Cruise the Crags** (☎*044/534–8622* ⊕*www.cruisethecrags.co.za*).

☪ **Monkeyland** is a refuge for abused and abandoned primates, most of which were once pets or laboratory animals. They now roam in a huge enclosed area of natural forest and are free to play, socialize, and do whatever it is that keeps primates happy. There are lemurs, gibbons, spider monkeys, indigenous vervet monkeys, howler monkeys, and many more. Guided walks are run throughout the day, and the tamer "inmates" often play with guests. ⊠ *16 km (10 mi) east of Plettenberg Bay along the N2, just before Nature's Valley turnoff* ☎ *044/534–8906* ⊕ *www.monkeyland.co.za* ☜ *R100* ⊙ *Daily 8–5.*

☪ Built over a natural valley in the forest, **Birds of Eden** is the largest free-flight aviary in the world, spanning 5 dome-enclosed acres. A stream, waterfalls, ponds, paths, benches, and rest areas make it a great place to spend the day. About 200 species of birds, some of which are quite tame, fly freely in the huge space. ⊠ *16 km (10 mi) east of Plettenberg Bay along the N2, just before Nature's Valley turnoff* ☎ *044/534–8906* ⊕ *www.birdsofeden.co.za* ☜ *R100* ⊙ *Daily 8–5.*

Knysna Forest once harbored large herds of elephants, but hunting and habitat encroachment almost put an end to the wild population. At one time it was thought that there was only one old matriarch left, so a few young elephants were relocated from Kruger to keep her company and—with luck—breed. The new ellies couldn't cope with the forest, however, and after they wandered into farmland, the project was abandoned. Since then, more elephants, including a few young ones, have been found deep in the forest, but since they're not venturing near the more-traveled areas, it's extremely unlikely that you'll see one. Still it's nice to know they're there. If you want to see an elephant, your

☪ best bet is the **Elephant Sanctuary,** where you can go on a guided forest walk with these amazing animals, touch them, learn more about them, and take a short ride. ⊠ *16 km (10 mi) east of Plettenberg Bay along the N2, just before Nature's Valley turnoff* ☎ *044/534–8145* ⊕ *www. elephantsanctuary.co.za* ☜ *R250; additional R345 for elephant ride* ⊙ *Daily 8–noon; tours on the hr (on the ½ hr 1:30–3:30).*

WHERE TO STAY & EAT

★ $$$$ ✕▦ **Kurland.** On the road out of Plett toward Tsitsikamma, this magnificent 1,500-acre estate is centered on a lovely historic Cape Dutch homestead. Spacious guest suites are in separate buildings, and huge bathrooms, antique furniture, book-filled shelves, fireplaces, and private balconies give you the feeling you're staying in your own country home. A view of horse-filled paddocks makes it seem even more opulent. Ten rooms have staircases leading to charming children's attic rooms. The food in the restaurant ($$$–$$$$) is exactly what you might expect in such a refined atmosphere: well cooked, beautifully presented, and made from whatever's fresh. Guests have the use of a complimentary all-terrain vehicle for exploring, and polo packages for tournaments or clinics for groups and individuals are available. There are free pony rides for kids, plus children's programs during Easter and summer school holidays. ⊠ *N2* ✉ *Box 209, The Crags, 6602* ☎ *044/534–8082* ⊕ *www.kurland.co.za* 📛 *2 rooms, 10 suites* ♿ *In-*

room: no a/c, safe. In-hotel: restaurant, room service, bar, tennis court, pool, gym, spa, no elevator ☰ *AE, DC, MC, V* ⏵⏹*BP and MAP.*

★ $$$ ⌨**Hog Hollow Country Lodge.** Vistas stretch into the misty green distance at this lovely lodge set among gardens on the edge of a forested gorge. Rooms are decorated in a modern African motif, with cast-iron furniture, white linen, and African artwork. In summer the private verandas with hammocks are as popular as the fireplaces are in winter. The food is great, and meals are sociable affairs, taken around a huge table in the main house; breakfasts are taken on the patio. Local seafood and ostrich are well represented on the menu, but vegetarian food is handled with flair. An energetic one-hour walk through the forest will bring you to Monkeyland, Birds of Eden, and the Elephant Sanctuary. ✉*Askop Rd.* ⏢*Box 503, Plettenberg Bay, 6600* ☎*044/534–8879* ⊕*www.hog-hollow.com* ⤴*15 suites* ⌂*In-room: no a/c, no phone, refrigerator, no TV. In-hotel: bar, pool, no elevator, laundry service* ☰*AE, DC, MC, V* ⏵⏹*BP.*

EN
ROUTE

As you travel on the N2 east from Plett, you cross a flat coastal plain of fynbos, with the forested Tsitsikamma Mountains on your left. Just after The Crags, turn off onto the R102, an alternative to the toll road and a far more interesting and scenic route. The road passes through farmland before dropping suddenly to sea level via the Groot River Pass. It's a great descent, with the road worming back and forth through a tunnel of greenery, impenetrable bush pressing in on either side. At the bottom of the pass, turn right into **Nature's Valley,** where the Groot River forms a magnificent lagoon hemmed in by bush-cloaked hills before crossing a long, beautiful beach to enter the sea. An almost fairy-tale settlement nestles beneath the trees. This is the end point of the Otter Trail. At a small restaurant-cum-shop near the beach, weary hikers give their boots a solemn resting place if they're not fit for another hike. A walk to Salt River is another great way to spend the day, and there is a reasonable chance of spotting an otter.

From Nature's Valley the R102 climbs out of the Groot River valley and crosses the N2. Here you can choose to take the N2 or stay on the R102 through the incredibly scenic Bloukrans Pass and rejoin the N2 13 km (8 mi) farther on. From this point it's another 9 km (5½ mi) to the turnoff to Tsitsikamma National Park and the Storms River Mouth. The pretty and rather remote Storms River village is another 4 km (2½ mi) farther east on the N2.

TSITSIKAMMA NATIONAL PARK

➐ *31 km (19 mi) east of Nature's Valley, 42 km (26 mi) east of Plettenberg Bay.*

Tsitsikamma National Park, a narrow belt of coastline extending for 80 km (50 mi) from Oubosstrand to Nature's Valley, encompasses some of the most spectacular coastal scenery in the country, including deep gorges, evergreen forests, tidal pools, and beautiful empty beaches. The best way to see the park is on the five-day Otter Trail, South Africa's most popular hike, or the somewhat easier and more comfortable Dolphin Trail. A less-strenuous highlight is the Storms River Mouth, in the middle of the park. The river enters the sea through a narrow channel carved between sheer cliffs. Storms River was aptly named: when gale winds blow, as they often do, the sea flies into a pounding fury, hurling spray onto the rocks and whipping spume high up the cliffs. From the Tsitsikamma National Park's visitor center a trail descends through the forest (different tree species are all labeled) and over a narrow suspension bridge strung across the river mouth. It's a spectacular walk, a highlight of any trip to the Garden Route. On the other side of the bridge a steep trail climbs to the top of a bluff overlooking the river and the sea—the turning point of the Storms River MTB (mountain bike) Trail, which starts and finishes in Storms River village. Other trails, ranging from 1 to 3.2 km (½ to 2 mi), lead either to a cave once inhabited by hunter-gatherers or through the coastal forest. A pleasant, ordinary restaurant with great views of the river and the ocean serves breakfast, lunch, and dinner at the park. ⊠ *Off N2* ☏*042/281–1607* ⊕*www.sanparks.org* ⊠*R80* ⊗ *Daily 5:30* AM*–9:30* PM.

WHERE TO STAY

$-$$ 🏠 **Tsitsikamma National Park–Storms River Mouth.** The lodgings here are pretty basic, but they are clean and comfortable, and the setting, almost within soaking distance of the pounding surf, is spectacular. Log cabins sleep either two or four people, forest huts are the cheapest option and are very basic, "oceanettes" are attractive seaside apartments with fully outfitted kitchens, and the freestanding chalets are the closest to the sea. ⊠ *Off N2* ☏*012/428–9111* ⊕*www.sanparks.org* ⊠*21 cottages, 20 huts, 17 oceanettes, 16 chalets, 6 cabins* ⚘ *In-room: no a/c, no phone, no TV. In-hotel: restaurant, beachfront, diving, water sports, laundry facilities* ⊟*AE, DC, MC, V.*

SPORTS & THE OUTDOORS

BOATING For a really good look at the gorge, take a boat trip (R40) on the *Spirit of Tsitsikamma* (☏*042/281–1607* ⊕*www.sanparks.org*). The boat departs every 45 minutes between 9:30 and 2:45 from the jetty below the suspension bridge.

HIKING The **Dolphin Trail** (☏*042/280–3699 or 042/280–3588* ⊕*www.dolphin-*
Fodor'sChoice *trail.co.za*) is the perfect marriage between exercise and relaxation,
★ rugged scenery and comfort. Starting at Storms River Mouth, the trail continues east along the coast, with scenery similar to the Otter Trail's. Though the Dolphin is quite hard going, it covers just 20 km (12 mi) over two days, and the best part is that you carry only a day pack (your luggage is transported by vehicle to the next spot). Accommodations on the first night are in very comfortable cabins with private baths at Storms River Mouth. The next two nights are spent in lovely guesthouses with awesome views and great food. It costs R3,300 per person, which includes a guide, all meals, transportation, and three nights' accommodation.

★ The most popular of South Africa's hiking trails, the **Otter Trail** (☏*012/426–5111* ⊕*www.sanparks.org*) runs along the coast from the mouth of Storms River to Nature's Valley, passing rocky cliffs, beaches, fynbos, rivers, and towering indigenous forest. The trail is only 42 km (26 mi) long, but there are a lot of steep uphills and downhills. It's billed as a five-day hike to give you time to swim and hang out. Accommodations are in overnight huts equipped with sleeping bunks, *braais* (barbecues), and chemical toilets. You must carry in all food and carry out all trash. Only 12 people are allowed on the trail per day, making it vital to book at least a year in advance. However, because people sometimes book all 12 slots and then arrive with only four or five others, there are often cancellations. If you really want to hike this trail but can't get a reservation, you can try hanging around for a few days to see if a spot opens up. The trail costs R560 per person, plus an R80 conservation fee per person per night.

STORMS RIVER

★ ❽ *4 km (2½ mi) east of Tsitsikamma National Park.*

Although it's a small, isolated village, Storms River absolutely buzzes with activity. A hotel, a couple of guesthouses, and a smattering of backpackers' lodges all cater to the numerous adrenaline junkies and nature lovers who frequent this hot spot for adventure and ecotourism activities. Bear in mind that Storms River Mouth, the SANParks camp in the Tsitsikamma National Park, and Storms River village are not the same place.

NEED A BREAK?

Don't expect anything fancy, but do expect good value for the money at simple **Trees Fine Foods** (⊠ *Main Rd.* ☎ *042/281–1836*), which is part of a poverty-alleviation and employment program. Conveniently located in the heart of Storms River village, it serves burgers, sandwiches, and baked potatoes, plus full breakfasts.

WHERE TO STAY & EAT

$$ ✕⌂ **Protea Hotel Tsitsikamma Inn.** The guest rooms here are in pretty, colorful buildings that are neatly arranged around a village green, and the public rooms are in an old hunting lodge built in 1888. The inn is well known for its restaurant—De Oude Martha (¢–$$)—which was named after the hotel's first cook; though she has retired, her influence lingers. Food is mostly dependable standbys such as grilled line fish, chicken, and pastas, but there's a new twist on the inevitable ostrich steak: it's served with a creamy Amarula-and-gooseberry sauce. ⊠ *Main Rd.* ☝ *Box 53, 6308* ☎ *042/281–1711* ⊕ *www.village-inn.co.za* 🛏 *48 rooms, 8 apartments* ⟁ *In-room: no a/c (some). In-hotel: restaurant, bar, pool, no elevator, laundry service* ▤ *AE, DC, MC, V* ❙❉❙ *BP.*

★ $$ ⌂ **At the Woods Guest House.** Built with care and attention to detail, this lovely owner-managed guesthouse is a winner. The decor is understated, and most of the finishes are natural: stone tiles in the bathrooms, reed ceilings, and lots of woodwork, including some charming old wooden doors. All rooms have king-size beds, huge shower stalls, and roomy balconies with a mountain view. It's right in the village, so it's close to all the wonderful activities in Storms River. Hostess Bev Coetzee is a mine of information on the local area as well as the whole Garden Route. ✉*Formosa St.* ◎*Box 92, Tsitsikamma, 6308* ☎*042/281–1446* ⊕*www.atthewoods.co.za* ⬅*8 rooms* △*In-room: no a/c, safe, refrigerator. In-hotel: pool, no elevator* ⊟*MC, V* ⦿*BP.*

¢ ⊡**Tsitsikamma Backpackers.** This small, tidy hostel is a bit quieter than most, so it's a good place to stay if you're on a budget. The lovely garden has great mountain views. If you don't feel like making use of the communal kitchens, you can book meals (continental breakfast and dinner only) in advance. You can rent bicycles, shoot pool, and use the barbecue here. ✉*54 Formosa St., 6308* ☎*042/281–1868* ⊕*www. tsitsikammabackpackers.com* ⬅*3 rooms, 3 dormitories, 3 tents* △*In-room: no a/c, no phone, no TV. In-hotel: laundry facilities, public Internet* ⊟*No credit cards.*

SPORTS & THE OUTDOORS

BUNGEE JUMPING
Fodor's Choice
★

If you do only one bungee jump in your life, do it from the Bloukrans River Bridge with **Face Adrenalin** (✉*N2* ☎*042/281–1458* ⊕*www. faceadrenalin.com*). At 700 feet, it's the highest commercial bungee jump in the world. The span is the third-highest bridge in the world and the highest in the southern hemisphere. The jump costs R580, and the DVD to show your friends back home is an extra R120. A photo CD with about 30 images is another R50. If you want to see what it's all about but have no intention of flinging yourself off the bridge, you can do a walking tour for R70, but even that's not for the faint of heart, as it is pretty high, exposed, and scary. The flying fox—a cable on which you slide under the bridge and above the bridge arch to the jump-off spot—costs R150 for a single, and R200 for a tandem ride. The combo of fox and jump costs R680.

CANOPY TOUR
Fodor's Choice
★

Want a turaco's-eye view of the treetops? **Storms River Adventures** (✉*Main Rd.* ☎*042/281–1836* ⊕*www.stormsriver.com*) will take you deep into the forest, where you don a harness, climb up to a platform, clip in, and "fly" on long cables from platform to platform. You can even control your speed. The cost is R395, and the DVD with video and downloadable photos costs an extra R125.

FOREST TOUR
Storms River Adventures (✉*Main Rd.* ☎*042/281–1836* ⊕*www.stormsriver.com*) offers a gentle, open-vehicle tour of the forest and the old Storms River Pass. Knowledgeable guides expand on the flora and fauna, as well as the interesting history of the region. You end it all with lunch or tea at a beautiful picnic site next to the Storms River, where wagons would stop more than a century ago. The tea trip costs R90, and the lunch trip R175.

MOUNTAIN BIKING
The **Storms River Mountain Bike Trail** is a scenic, circular 22-km (14-mi) trail administered by the Department of Water Affairs and Forestry. It's free, and you don't need a reservation. Just go to the starting point, near the police station at Storms River, and fill out a form in a box at the gate to issue yourself a permit. **Tsitsikamma Backpackers** (✉*54 Formosa St.* ☎*042/281–1868* ⊕*www.tsitsikammabackpackers.com*) rents out mountain bikes for R20 per hour. Bikes can be rented for R100 per day at **Tube'n Axe Backpackers** (✉*Saffron and Darnell Sts.* ☎*042/281–1757* ⊕*www.tubenaxe.co.za*).

LITTLE KAROO

The landscape of the Little Karoo—austere, minimal, and dry—stands in stark contrast to the Garden Route. In summer it resembles a blast furnace, whereas winter nights are bitterly cold. In its own way, however, it is absolutely beautiful. The Little Karoo, also called the Klein Karoo (*klein* is Afrikaans for "small"; *karoo* derives from the San [Bushman] word for "thirst"), should not be confused with the Great Karoo, a vast semidesert scrub on the other side of the Swartberg Mountains. Everything here is a little surreal—giant birds soar overhead, huge caves stretch for miles underground, and bright green vineyards contrast with intricately eroded, deep red hills.

SANBONA WILDLIFE RESERVE

★ ❾ *27 km (17 mi) west of Barrydale.*

The Sanbona Wildlife Reserve was the first Big Five reserve in the Western Cape. Considering that the Karoo is technically semidesert, it's amazing how many absolutely beautiful plants there are here. Game drives concentrate on mammals and birds, but it's impossible to drive past the magnificent flowering shrubs without at least stopping for a better look. In addition to the usual big game you can see springbok, oryx, and other animals you won't see in Mpumalanga. Rugged gorges alternate with gently rolling plains to create an ever-changing vista. A big plus is that the reserve is entirely malaria-free.

WHERE TO STAY

$$ **Khanni Lodge.** Well-appointed rooms with light-wood finishes flow into luxurious bathrooms with double-sided tubs, indoor and outdoor showers, and double vanities. A central Zen-like water feature mitigates the heat of the Karoo, and you can watch animals at the water hole from the infinity pool, shaded veranda, or the private balcony of your room. Room layout—including interior connecting doors between rooms—is particularly family-friendly. Note that children under 7 are not allowed on game drives. *Box 149, Montagu 6720* *028/572–1077* *www.sanbona.com* *4 rooms* *In-room: safe, refrigerator. In-hotel: room service, pool, children's programs (all ages), laundry service, public Wi-Fi, no-smoking rooms* *AE, DC, MC, V* *FAP.*

$$ **Tilney Manor.** Accommodations here are spread out around an attractive lawn and garden and face the open Karoo. The spacious guest rooms are classically decorated with dark-wood finishes and neutral upholstery. The enormous bathrooms have indoor and outdoor showers as well as freestanding, double-sided tubs. The public rooms are in an old manor house built in 1894 for a former district magistrate. *Box 149, Montagu 6720* *028/572–1482* *www.sanbona.com* *6 rooms* *In-room: safe, refrigerator. In-hotel: room service, pool, spa, laundry service, public Wi-Fi, airport shuttle, no kids under 13, no-smoking rooms* *AE, DC, MC, V* *FAP.*

CLOSE UP

What the...?

No, your eyes are not playing tricks on you. That sign definitely says **Ronnie's Sex Shop**. And no, it's not a country brothel, nor does it purvey rubber garments and toys of an adult nature. It's actually a Route 62 icon that started out as a joke. Ronnie (a real person) returned to his farm one day to find his friends had decorated the disused laborer's cottage near the road, painting on it in big red letters RONNIE'S SEX SHOP. It stayed like that for years—a local landmark—until Ronnie thought he would cash in on the unintentional marketing, and opened a pub in it. It's a far cry from a sophisticated venue, but it's a great place to meet the less productive members of the local farming community, many of whom spend a large proportion of the day here. It's also a mandatory stop on most motorcycle rallies. It's open from 10 in the morning until the last person leaves at night, which is usually pretty late. You can't miss it—it's right on Route 62, just on the Ladysmith side of Barrydale. You may not want to go in, but you'll probably want to photograph it.

EN ROUTE

Set between Montagu and Barrydale on the R62, the Op-de-Tradouw region, named after a pass through the mountains, is best known for its excellent wines. **Joubert-Tradauw** is a great place to stop for a wine tasting or for lunch or tea. Owner Meyer Joubert makes wine in the age-old French tradition—unfiltered and unfined. His chardonnay is sublime, and he has publicly stated that it is his ambition to make the best syrah in the world. (Try it; he's definitely on the right track.) While he works his magic in the winery, his wife Beate waves her star-spangled wand over the small deli–cum–coffee shop, where you can sit under the pergola and spend ages over a superb cheese platter or Gruyère salad, or just have a quick coffee and cheesecake. It's tapas alfresco with a traditional Afrikaner touch. For a more adventurous dining experience, you can combine lunch or tea with a quad-bike (all-terrain-vehicle) tour. **Tradouw Quads** (⊠ *R62* ☎ *082/055–4096* ⊕ *www.tquads.co.za*) has great tours ranging from gentle rides through the orchards to Joubert-Tradauw for tea, lunch, or wine tasting, to a hectic mountain adventure. All tours can be combined with a picnic, which is supplied by the ever-talented Beate Joubert. ⊠ *R62, 12 km (7½) mi west of Barrydale* ☎ *028/572–1619* ⊕ *www.joubert-tradauw.co.za* 🖃 *Free* ☉ *Weekdays 9–5, Sat. 9–2.*

If you're heading down the R62 toward Oudtshoorn and you get a little peckish, stop at **Rose of the Karoo on Route 62** (⊠ *Voortrekker St., Calitzdorp* ☎ *044/213–3133* ⊕ *www.roseofthekaroo.co.za*). Options range from a light sandwich to a lamb- or ostrich-based Karoo specialty, and breakfast and tea are served here, too. And it's one of the few places in town where you can get really good coffee. Out back there's a lovely vine-covered patio with a couple of gift shops, and a small deli section sells home-baked goods and local preserves. An added bonus in summer: it's air-conditioned.

OUDTSHOORN

🔟 *201 km (125 mi) east of Sanbona Wildlife Reserve, 85 km (53 mi) north of Mossel Bay.*

Oudtshoorn has been famous for its ostriches since around 1870, when farmers began raising them to satisfy the European demand for feathers to adorn women's hats and dresses. In the years leading up to World War I, ostrich feathers were almost worth their weight in gold thanks to the continuing demands of fashion, and Oudtshoorn experienced an incredible boom. Many of the beautiful sandstone buildings in town date from that period, as do the "feather palaces," huge homes built by prosperous feather merchants and buyers. Although feathers are no longer a major fashion item, these huge birds are now bred for their tough and distinctive leather and almost completely fat- and cholesterol-free red meat. Almost as much of a moneymaker, though, is the tourist potential of these weird and wonderful birds. In addition to visiting an ostrich farm, you can buy ostrich products ranging from the sublime—feather boas—to the ridiculous—taxidermic baby ostriches emerging from cracked eggs. Several farms compete for the tourist buck, offering almost identical tours and a chance to eat an ostrich-based meal. Be warned—these can be real tourist traps: glitzy, superficial, and filled with horrendous crowds. As well as watching local "jockeys" racing on ostriches, you'll be offered the opportunity to ride one. This is pretty cruel; although the birds are incredibly strong, their legs are very thin, and many birds suffer broken legs when ridden. If this concerns you, visit instead the Cape Town ostrich farms, which do not allow this practice.

Note that most of the restaurants, guesthouses, and attractions listed below are on Baron van Reede Street. This street becomes the R328, which heads north from Oudtshoorn to the Cango Caves, the Swartberg Pass, and Prince Albert.

The **C.P. Nel Museum** focuses on the ostrich and Oudtshoorn's boom period at the beginning of the 20th century. The section on fashions of the feather-boom period are by far the most picturesque. The display that depicts the contribution of Lithuanian Jews to the economic development of Oudtshoorn and the feather industry contains a reconstruction of the town's first synagogue. ✉ *Baron van Reede St.* ☎ *044/272–7306* ⊕ *www.cpnelmuseum.co.za* 🏷 *R10 (includes admission to Le Roux's Town House)* 🕐 *Weekdays 8–5, Sat. 9–5.*

The most interesting remnants of the glory of the boom period are the magnificent palaces built by successful farmers. Most are private homes, but you can visit the sandstone **Le Roux's Town House**, built in 1909 and furnished in period style, to see just how good they had it in those heady days. ✉ *High and Loop Sts.* ☎ *044/272–3676* 🏷 *Free with ticket to C.P. Nel Museum* 🕐 *Weekdays 9–4.*

☾ The name **Cango Wildlife Ranch** is a bit misleading, as this is really just a glorified zoo, crocodile farm, and cheetah-breeding center, but it is great fun—especially for children. As well as the crocodiles and cheetahs, you may see pumas, jaguars, and lions in large pens. Other attractions include a snake park, pygmy hippos, a tropical house with birds and giant fruit bats: in short, loads of different animals that will keep the little ones amused for ages. You can even do a croc cage dive, which isn't as bizarre as it sounds: it's not really diving, as you are separated from the croc by glass and can stand up for a breath of air whenever you feel the need. For an extra fee (R130 to R300), you can cuddle one of the resident beasts (cheetahs, lions, pythons). The price, which includes a photograph, depends on the species you choose. ⊠ *Caves Rd.* ☎ *044/272–5593* ⊕ *www.cango.co.za* 🖃 *R80* ⊙ *Daily 8–5.*

☺ **Cango Ostrich Farm** is probably the least commercialized of the ostrich show farms. Guides take you through every step in the production of feathers, leather, and meat, and explain the bird's extraordinary social and physical characteristics. There are lots of interactive opportunities, including feeding and petting the ostriches and posing on one for a photograph. People who weigh less than 75 kilograms (165 pounds) are permitted to ride the ostriches as well, but many people consider this to be cruel. The farm is conveniently located en route to the Cango Caves from town. ⊠ *R328, 14 km (9 mi) north of Oudtshoorn* ☎ *044/272– 4623* ⊕ *www.cangoostrich.co.za* 🖃 *R45* ⊙ *Daily 8:30–4:45.*

★ Between Oudtshoorn and Prince Albert, the huge and stunningly beautiful **Cango Caves** are deservedly one of the most popular attractions in the area. Only a small fraction of the caves, which extend for several miles through the mountains, is open. The passage of countless people through these caves has turned the cave formations from milky white to red and brown because of a buildup of iron oxide and acid damage from human breath. You can choose between two tours: the hour-long standard tour and the aptly named adventure tour, which lasts 1½ hours. Think long and hard before opting for the latter if you're overweight, very tall, claustrophobic, or have knee or heart problems. It's exhilarating, but the temperature and humidity are high, there's not much oxygen, and you'll be shimmying up narrow chimneys on your belly, wriggling your way through tiny tunnels, and sliding on your bottom. Wear old clothes and shoes with a good tread. Standard tours leave on the hour, adventure tours on the half hour. ⊠ *Off R328, 32 km (20 mi) north of Oudtshoorn* ☎ *044/272–7410* ⊕ *www.cango-caves.co.za* 🖃 *Standard tour R48, adventure tour R62* ⊙ *Daily 9–4.*

NEED A BREAK?

At the turnoff to the Cango Caves, **Wilgewandel Coffee Shop and Country Farmstall** (⊠ *R328, 2 km [1 mi] from the caves* ☎ *044/272-0878*) serves well-cooked simple food such as hamburgers, toasted sandwiches, ostrich steaks, and sweet treats. Shady outdoor tables overlook a big lawn and duck-filled pond. Trampolines and camel, pony, and boat rides are offered for children.

WHERE TO STAY & EAT

★ ¢–$$ ✕ **Kalinka Café.** Set in a lovely old stone house with a small but tranquil garden, this is a pleasant option for dinner. Try the pancake filled with salmon-trout caviar and sour cream. Of course there has to be an

The Garden Route & the Little Karoo

CLOSE UP

Back & Forth

Part of the beauty of the Garden Route and Little Karoo is found in the spectacular passes that connect the two, and in those between the Little and Great Karoo. Be sure to see at least one.

Between Oudtshoorn and George, choose between the Outeniqua Pass (via the paved N12) and the more historic Montagu Pass (off the N9, after it diverges from the N12, on a narrow gravel road built in 1843 by Henry Fancourt White). The latter offers excellent views, picnic sites, and examples of Victorian road building, including a five-span arch bridge, railway viaduct, and expertly laid drystone embankments. An old tollhouse still sits at the bottom of the pass.

The Robertson Pass, between Oudtshoorn and Mossel Bay, is an easy tarred road with some fabulous views. One of the most interesting things about this route (especially if you're traveling from Mossel Bay) is that you can see the abrupt change of vegeta-

tion as you crest the ridge and drive over into the rain shadow.

For a great loop between the Great and Little Karoo, drive counterclockwise from Oudtshoorn through De Rust and the spectacularly scenic Meiringspoort. The road runs along the bottom of a deep gorge, crossing the pretty Meirings River 25 times as it cuts through red cliffs. Halfway through the pass is a rest area, where a path leads to a 200-foot waterfall. Head west on the R407 to Prince Albert; then head south through the Swartberg Pass on the R328 back to Oudtshoorn. (The views are more dramatic from this direction.) The road through this pass was built between 1881 and 1886 by the legendary engineer Sir Thomas Bain. At times the road barely clings to the mountainside, held only by Bain's stone retaining walls. From the top, at 5,230 feet, you can look out toward the hot plains of the Great Karoo and the distant mountains of the Nuweveldberg or down at the huge gorge and sheer walls of deep-red rock.

ostrich meal—the fillet baked with cheese and onions and served with roasted veggies and hash browns is a firm favorite. ⊠ *93 Baron van Reede St.* ☎ *MC, V* ⊘ *No lunch.*

★ ¢–$ ✕ **Jemima's Restaurant.** Named after the mythical guardian angel of love, good taste, and good cooking, this restaurant would not disappoint its muse. All the ingredients are sourced locally from farmers in the district, and the menu focuses on such local delicacies as olives, Karoo mutton, and, of course, ostrich. Meat lovers often opt for the Three Tenors—medallions of beef, ostrich, and venison fillet. Herbivores love the butternut, capsaicin, and feta cheesecake. There's an extensive list of local wines. ⊠ *94 Baron van Reede St.* ☎ *044/272–0808* ⧪ *Reservations essential* ▤ *AE, DC, MC, V* ⊘ *Closed Sun. No lunch Mon.*

$$ ☷ **Hlangana Lodge.** Conveniently situated on the edge of town on the road out to the caves, this great option strikes a nice balance between slick and stylish and warm and friendly. Superior rooms have baths and showers, whereas standard rooms have either showers or baths. Though only breakfast is served on the premises, you can arrange for a plan that includes a shuttle to dinner at Jemima's, just down the road.

In case you're wondering, it's pronounced *shlung*-gah-na. ⊠ *Baron van Reede and North Sts.* ☏ *51 North St., 6625* ☎ *044/272–2299* ⊕ *www. hlangana.co.za* ⤶ *18 rooms, 1 suite* ☖ *In-room: safe, refrigerator, Wi-Fi. In-hotel: bar, pool, airport shuttle, parking (no fee), no-smoking rooms* ▤ *AE, DC, MC, V* ⏐◯⏐*BP.*

★ **$$** ▦ **La Plume Guest House.** This stylish guesthouse is set on a working ostrich farm on the Calitzdorp side of Oudtshoorn. The rooms are all individually decorated with beautiful antiques, and some of the bathrooms have Victorian claw-foot tubs. Guests meet for predinner drinks in the elegant lounge or on the veranda overlooking the valley. If you're keen on seeing what ostrich farming is all about, you can do an informal and informative tour with the owner of the farm—so much better than all the hype you'd get at the show farms. The turnoff to the farm is 7 km (4 mi) west of Oudtshoorn and is well marked from the R62. ⊠ *Volmoed, 14 km (9 mi) west of Oudtshoorn* ☏ *Box 1202, 6620* ☎ *044/272–7516 or 082/820–4373* ⊕ *www.laplume.co.za* ⤶ *7 rooms, 3 suites, 1 2-bedroom cottage* ☖ *In-room: no phone, refrigerator, Ethernet. In-hotel: pool, bicycles, laundry service, public Internet, no-smoking rooms* ▤ *AE, DC, MC, V* ⏐◯⏐*BP.*

¢–**$$** ▦ **Kleinplaas.** The name means "small farm," and although it isn't really a farm, there are sheep, goats, ostriches, ducks, and other animals in small pens where children can gaze at them in wonder. Comfortable, well-appointed chalets with fully equipped cooking facilities are neatly arranged in a huge shady lawn area. There's also a pretty campsite with laundry facilities. Prices are per chalet for a maximum of four or six people (depending on the chalet). Extra people can be accommodated on sleeper-sofas. ⊠ *171 Baron van Reede St., 6620* ☎ *044/272–5811* ⊕ *www.kleinplaas.co.za* ⤶ *54 chalets* ☖ *In-room: no a/c (some), no phone. In-hotel: pool, laundry facilities, no-smoking rooms* ▤ *AE, DC, MC, V.*

$ ▦ **Backpackers Paradise.** A communal kitchen, pool table, swimming pool, bar, and TV lounge combine to create that typical hostel vibe where everyone becomes friends in half an hour. The dorms are on the small side; some have en-suite bathrooms, as do some of the doubles. Backpackers Paradise is conveniently located on Baron van Reede Street, just on the caves side of town. ⊠ *148 Baron van Reede St., 6625* ☎ *044/272–3436* ⊕ *www.backpackersparadise.net* ⤶ *10 rooms, 5 with bath; 3 dormitories* ☖ *In-room: no a/c, no TV. In-hotel: bar, pool, no elevator* ▤ *AE, DC, MC, V* ⏐◯⏐*BP.*

¢–**$** ▦ **Le Petit Karoo.** Perched high on a hill just off the R328, three en-suite tents with spa-baths on the veranda have fabulous views of the hills and pass. The tents are small and basic, but you feel like you're in your own little private paradise. There's also a campsite, and some families choose to bring a small tent for the kids while Mom and Dad enjoy the romance of the permanent tents. Dinner, which is by arrangement, usually has a French flair. There's a labyrinth for walking and musing, and you can also go horseback riding or hiking. This is not a good choice if you like to spend time in your room during the day, as the tents can get quite hot. Camping is R130 per site, which can hold up to four people. ⊠ *Off the R328, approx 14 km (9 mi) north of Oudtshoorn* ☏ *Suite*

24, Private Bag X600, 6620 ☎*044/272–7428* ⊕*www.lepetitkaroo. za.net* ⤴*3 tents, 14 campsites* ⚹*In-room: no a/c, no phone, no TV* ▭*AE, DC, MC, V* ⌇OI*BP.*

SPORTS & THE OUTDOORS

BALLOONING   **Oudtshoorn Ballooning** (☎*082/784–8539* ⊕*www.oudtshoornballoon- ing.co.za*) offers a scenic balloon flight over the town and neighboring farms at dawn. Flights are R1,760 per person and include tea and cof- fee on arrival, sparkling wine on landing, and breakfast.

HORSEBACK   Horse rides from **Le Petit Karoo** (☎*044/272–7428 or 073/457–3932* RIDING   ⊕*www.lepetitkaroo.za.net*) range from a gentle one-hour walk for beginners to an overnight trail or a game-viewing ride for experienced riders. Rates start at R120 for the one-hour ride and go up to R600 for the game-viewing ride.

SHOPPING

Oudtshoorn has loads of stores selling ostrich products, but it pays to shop around, as prices vary significantly. The smartest shops strung out along Baron van Reede Street have a great variety but are a tad pricey. **Lugro Ostrich** (☎*044/272–7012 or 082/788–7916* ⊕*www. lugro-ostrich.co.za*) is a small factory on a farm 10 km (6 mi) south of Oudtshoorn (8 km [5 mi] off the R62). Here you'll find great ostrich handbags and wallets as well as a few feather products. If you see some- thing you like but want it in a different color, the factory can make it up for you in 24 hours and will deliver anywhere. You can also take a short tour of the factory. The **Klein Karoo Co-op** (☎*044/203–5270* ⊕*www.kleinkaroofeathers.com*), which coordinates the marketing of ostrich products, has a boutique on its premises near the airport, on the western side of town. (This is really just an airfield, but it's called the airport.) Here you can purchase bags, feather boas, shoes, and other smaller items. It can be a little tricky to find, so it's best to phone for directions or ask for help at your hotel.

DE RUST

⓫ *40 km (25 mi) northeast of Oudtshoorn.*

De Rust is a sleepy little Karoo village. The main road is lined with crafts stores, coffee shops, restaurants, and wineshops.

★   **Domein Doornkraal** sells a superb range of fortified wines and a fan- tastic, inexpensive chardonnay-sémillon blend, but the red wines are what it's really all about—particularly the cabernet sauvignon–merlot blend, which you sometimes have to fight for. You may be lucky and find a few jars of homemade olives, but the small stock usually sells out pretty quickly. ✉*N12, about 15 km (9 mi) southwest of De Rust* ☎*044/251–6715* ▱*Free* ⊙ *Weekdays 9–5, Sat. 8–1 (Sat. 8–6 Dec. and Easter).*

Mons Ruber Estate is named after the Red Hills, which dominate the landscape and whose soil creates the perfect environment for grow- ing grapes with a high sugar content. So it's not surprising that this winery specializes in dessert wines as well as a fine brandy. There is a lovely restored 19th-century kitchen, and an easy hiking trail stretches 1½ hours into the fascinating Red Hills. ✉*N12, about 15 km (9 mi) southwest of De Rust* ☎*044/251–6550* 💲*Free* 🕑*Weekdays 9–5, Sat. 9–1.*

WHERE TO STAY

★ $$$ 🏠**Oulap Country House.** Oulap is an eclectic mix of textures and colors, winding staircases and little book-filled nooks, antiques and impressive contemporary South African art. Guest rooms are individually decorated with original artwork, and the owners grow their own olives and fruit, which they preserve. But what steals the show is the almost unbelievable star-studded Karoo sky; you haven't seen stars until you've spent a night in the Karoo. Four-course farmhouse suppers—Karoo lamb, hearty soups, and regional produce—are wonderful, and conversation around the huge dining table, which often carries on until late in the evening, is possibly even better. A large percentage of the money earned by this lodge has gone into building a village school, complete with school meals and 32 computers; even more community projects are planned. ✉*15 km (9 mi) from De Rust on R341* 📪*Box 77, 6650* ☎*044/241–2250* 🌐*www.classicafrica.com/portfolio/oulap.htm* 🛏*5 rooms* ♿*In-room: no a/c, no TV, dial-up. In-hotel: bar, pool, no elevator, laundry service, no-smoking rooms, some pets allowed* 🟰*AE, DC, MC, V* 🍴*MAP.*

GARDEN ROUTE & LITTLE KAROO ESSENTIALS

TRANSPORTATION

BY AIR
The only true airport serving the Garden Route and the Little Karoo is George Airport, 10 km (6 mi) southwest of town. George is well served by South African Airways (SAA), Kulula.com, 1time, and Nationwide. SA Airlink sometimes runs one flight a day between Johannesburg and the little airfield in Plett, 6 km (4 mi) west of town. African Ramble runs charters from Plett to Johannesburg and Cape Town, but more commonly to the Eastern Cape game reserves. These particularly scenic trips start by flying over Robberg and out over the bay (where you may see whales or dolphins) and then hugging the coast up to Nature's Valley before heading inland.

Airport George Airport (*GRJ* ☎*044/876–9310* 🌐*www.acsa.co.za*).

Airlines African Ramble Air Charter (✉*Plettenberg Bay Airport* ☎*044/533–9006* 🌐*www.aframble.co.za*). **Kulula.com** (☎*0861/585–852* 🌐*www.kulula.com*). **Nationwide Airlines** (☎*0861/737–737* 🌐*www.flynationwide.co.za*). **1time** (☎*0861/345–345* 🌐*www.1time.co.za*). **SA Airlink** (☎*0861/359–722* or *011/978–5313* 🌐*www.saairlink.co.za*). **South African Airways** (☎*0861/359–722* or *011/978–5313* 🌐*www.flysaa.com*).

BY BUS

Intercape Mainliner and Greyhound offer regular service between Cape Town and Port Elizabeth, stopping at all major Garden Route destinations on the N2. Neither of these services accesses out-of-the-way places like Barrydale, Oudtshoorn, Storms River, and De Rust, however. For them you need the Baz Bus, which does go to Storms River and also meets a shuttle in George that will get you to Oudtshoorn. The bus stops at all backpacker hostels along the Garden Route, so you don't have to arrange transportation from a bus station.

Bus Lines **Baz Bus** (☎ 021/439-2323 ⊕ www.bazbus.com). **Greyhound** (☎ 011/276-8500 or 083/915-9000 ⊕ www.greyhound.co.za). **Intercape Mainliner** (☎ 021/380-4400 ⊕ www.intercape.co.za).

BY CAR

Mossel Bay, at the western end of the Garden Route, lies 384 km (238 mi) east of Cape Town along the N2 highway. The road is in good condition and well signposted. It usually takes about four hours to drive from Cape Town to Mossel Bay—unless you stop to look at a view, have lunch, or browse in a roadside produce or crafts store. A few words of warning, however: there is a wide shoulder along most of the route, but pull onto it to let faster cars overtake you *only* when you can see a good few hundred yards ahead. ⚠ The area between George and Wilderness is notorious for speed traps, especially in the Kaaimans River Pass, just west of Wilderness. The fuel complex at the Storms River Bridge is your last eastbound chance to refuel before Port Elizabeth—more than 160 km (100 mi) away.

■ TIP→ An alternative to the N2 is the less traveled—some say more interesting—inland route, dubbed Route 62, even though some of it is on the R60. From Worcester, in the Breede River valley *(see Chapter 2)*, traveling on the R60 and R62 to Oudtshoorn provides a great view of the Little Karoo.

Avis, Budget, Europcar, and Hertz all have car-rental offices at George Airport. Avis and Budget also have additional offices in the area. Europcar rentals include a cell phone.

Rental Companies **Avis** (✉ George Airport ☎ 044/876-9314 ⊕ www.avis.co.za ✉ Knysna ☎ 044/382-2222 ✉ Oudtshoorn ☎ 044/272-4727 ✉ Plettenberg Bay ☎ 044/533-1315 ✉ Mossel Bay ☎ 044/695-3060). **Budget** (✉ George Airport ☎ 044/876-9204 ⊕ www.budget.co.za ✉ 9 Hill House, Main St., Plettenberg Bay ☎ 044/533-1858). **Europcar** (✉ George Airport ☎ 044/876-9070 ⊕ www.europcar.co.za). **Hertz** (✉ George Airport ☎ 044/801-4700 ⊕ www.hertz.co.za).

BY TRAIN

See A Train Trip Back in Time box, above, for information on the Outeniqua Choo-Tjoe train, which runs between George and Mossel Bay. The luxurious *Blue Train* (⇨ *Riding in Style box in Chapter 1)* travels between Port Elizabeth and Cape Town once a month, connecting with a shuttle at George for a day trip to Oudtshoorn.

Train Line **Blue Train** (☎ 021/449-2672 or 012/334-8459 ⊕ www.bluetrain.co.za).

CONTACTS & RESOURCES

EMERGENCIES

Most towns have late-night pharmacies, and if they don't, pharmacies usually have an emergency number on the door. Call the general-emergencies number for all emergencies. If you break down while driving, call your car-rental company or the company's designee. You can also call the Automobile Association (AA) for assistance. Call the National Sea Rescue Institute (NSRI) for local marine emergencies.

Emergency Services **Automobile Association** (☎ 083/84322). **General Emergencies** (☎ 10111 *from landline, 112 from mobile phone*). **National Sea Rescue Institute** (✉ *Knysna* ☎ 044/384–0211 or 082/990–5956 ✉ *Mossel Bay* ☎ 082/990–5954 ✉ *Plettenberg Bay* ☎ 044/533–2744 or 082/490–6226).

Hospitals **George Mediclinic** (✉ *York St. and Gloucester Rd., George* ☎ 044/803–2000). **Knysna Private Hospital** (✉ *Hunters Estate Dr., Knysna* ☎ 044/384–1083). **Medsac Private Health Centre** (✉ *Marine Dr., Plettenberg Bay* ☎ 044/533–0212).

MAIL & INTERNET

Each town's main post office usually stays open from about 9 to 4:30 on weekdays and on Saturday mornings. There are Internet cafés all over, and most lodgings offer Internet access to their guests. Most bigger towns also have Postnets (www.postnet.co.za), a franchise that offers business, mail, Internet, and courier services.

VISITOR INFORMATION

Most local tourism bureaus are very helpful. In peak season (generally October to April), you may find them open longer than their off-season hours, which are typically weekdays 8 or 8:30 to 5 or 5:30, Saturday 8 or 8:30 to 1 or 1:30. In very quiet periods the staff may close up shop early.

Tourist Offices **De Rust Tourism Bureau** (✉ *2 Schoeman St., De Rust* ☎ 044/241–2109 ⊕ *www.derust.org.za*). **George Tourism Information** (✉ *124 York St., George* ☎ 044/801–9295 ⊕ *www.georgetourism.co.za*). **Knysna Publicity Association** (✉ *40 Main St., Knysna* ☎ 044/382–5510 ⊕ *www.visitknysna. com*). **Mossel Bay Tourism** (✉ *Market Sq., Mossel Bay* ☎ 044/691–2202 ⊕ *www. visitmosselbay.co.za*). **Oudtshoorn Tourism Bureau** (✉ *21 Baron van Reede St., Oudtshoorn* ☎ 044/279–2532 ⊕ *www.oudtshoorn.com*). **Plettenberg Bay Tourism Association** (✉ *Shop 35, Melville's Corner, Marine Dr. and Main St., Plettenberg Bay* ☎ 044/533–4065 ⊕ *www.plettenbergbay.co.za*). **Wilderness Tourism** (✉ *Milkwood Village, Beach Rd., Wilderness* ☎ 044/877–0045 ⊕ *www.wildernessinfo.co.za*).

The Eastern Cape

WORD OF MOUTH

"Kwandwe is a great place to spend a few days on safari. The personnel is great, the setting is lovely, there are great animal sightings, and it's totally deserted (they can take like 30 guests on 30,000 acres). Pricey, but well worth it."

—astein12

"Port Elizabeth has great beaches and some great cliff-top walks; people always stay longer on their second visit."

—coline

Updated by
Jennifer Stern

THE EASTERN CAPE IS SOUTH AFRICA'S most diverse province and has some of its best vacation destinations, yet it is perhaps the most glossed over by overseas visitors. Starting where the Garden Route stops, it includes much of the Great Karoo—a large, semidesert region of ocher plains, purple mountains, dramatic skies, and unusual, hardy vegetation—and abuts KwaZulu-Natal in the northeast and Lesotho's mountain lands in the north. But a glance at a map will reveal the region's main attraction: its coastline, largely undeveloped and running for some 640 km (400 mi) from temperate to subtropical waters.

The climate is mild across the region and throughout the year, with temperatures at the coast ranging between winter lows of 5°C (41°F) and summer highs of 32°C (90°F). It has many of the country's finest and least crowded beaches, African montane forests and heathlands, an ever-increasing number of fantastic malaria-free game reserves, and some of the most interesting cultural attractions in South Africa.

There are a few areas of note. Formerly known as Settler Country, the area that stretches from the outskirts of Port Elizabeth to Port Alfred in the east, Grahamstown in the northeast, and the Zuurberg Mountains in the north is now referred to as Frontier Country. It was here that the early-19th-century immigrants (colloquially called the 1820 Settlers) tried to set up farms, some successfully, some not. Toward the end of the last century, many of the unprofitable farms were bought up and redeveloped as game reserves, thus adding superb game-viewing to the already existing cultural attractions. This area encompasses Addo Elephant National Park and the game reserves at Shamwari and Kwandwe, as well as Grahamstown itself. Towns are small and interesting, and the surrounding countryside alternates between hilly terrain, steep gorges, and gentle rolling hills.

Another noteworthy region on the Eastern Cape is the Wild Coast, which is aptly but perhaps a little unfairly named. Sure, it does get some monumental storms, when huge waves crash into the beach and cliffs, but it also has a gentler face. Lovely long beaches stretch as far as the eye can see, with only a few cows and a small herder to break the isolation. Strictly speaking, the Wild Coast originally stretched from the Kei River mouth to Port Edward (which were the borders of the then nominally independent Transkei), but today it has spread almost to the outskirts of East London.

Unfortunately, during the political uncertainty of the 1980s the Wild Coast lost a lot of its allure—more due to the perceived threat of violence than anything else. Hotels went out of business, the overnight huts on the fantastic Wild Coast Hiking Trail fell into disrepair, and the Transkei sank further into economic depression. For many years it was only die-hard locals with strong emotional ties, and hordes of backpackers who frequented these still-lovely and little-known places. Today, however, the area is going through a revival. Coastal hotels are being renovated one by one, and community projects are being put in place to ensure that the tourist dollar goes where it is intended. In addition to long, lovely beaches, the Wild Coast has crystal-clear turquoise

4

lagoons, some of which can be paddled for miles. The area is still virtually unspoiled, and the people who live here are mostly subsistence farmers and fisherfolk. It's not uncommon for a family who can't afford a loaf of bread to dine (reluctantly) on oysters and lobster. It's just another of the Eastern Cape's contrasts and seeming contradictions.

ORIENTATION & PLANNING

ORIENTATION

The Eastern Cape is a big space with many tiny gems. The towns, and even the cities, of the province are relatively small, often quaint, and the distances between them are fairly large. Since the only airports are in Port Elizabeth, East London, and Mthatha (previously Umtata), the best way to experience the region is on a driving tour, leaving yourself plenty of time to explore (but be prepared for some poorly maintained roads traveling east of Grahamstown on the N2 and in some regions of the Transkei).

PLANNING

Although winters are pretty mild, especially farther north along the Wild Coast, summer—from September to April—is the most popular time to visit, especially for sun worshippers. (The beaches are best avoided at Christmas and New Year's, as they become severely overcrowded with hordes of reveling locals.) But even winter has its attractions. The sardine run, usually in June or early July, is becoming a major draw, and July's National Festival of the Arts draws thousands of cultural pilgrims to the delightful university town of Grahamstown.

TAKE IT ALL IN

3 days: Fly in to Port Elizabeth in the morning, and head straight out to Grahamstown. Do a historical tour in the afternoon followed by dinner at your guesthouse or one of the many restaurants in town. The next morning, drive out to Shamwari, Kwandwe, or Addo; plan to spend two days in one of these reserves (staying at one of the private luxury lodges or, at Addo, at an inexpensive SANParks camp) and then drive back to Port Elizabeth to fly out. Alternatively, you could spend two days in Port Elizabeth—soaking up the sun, playing a round of golf, taking a cultural tour, and just relaxing—and a third day on a day trip to Addo for an animal fix.

5 days: With five days you could fly in and out of East London to join the Wild Coast Meander tour with Wild Coast Holiday Reservations (⇨ *Tours, below*)—your days filled with walking this wonderful coastline, and each night spent at a different beach hotel. For a glimpse of Africa not on the usual tourist route, fly to Mthatha from Johannesburg; spend two days and three nights at Bulungula, immersing yourself in the local culture, and then drive from Mthatha to either Addo, Shamwari, or Kwandwe for a good game fix. If you spend these

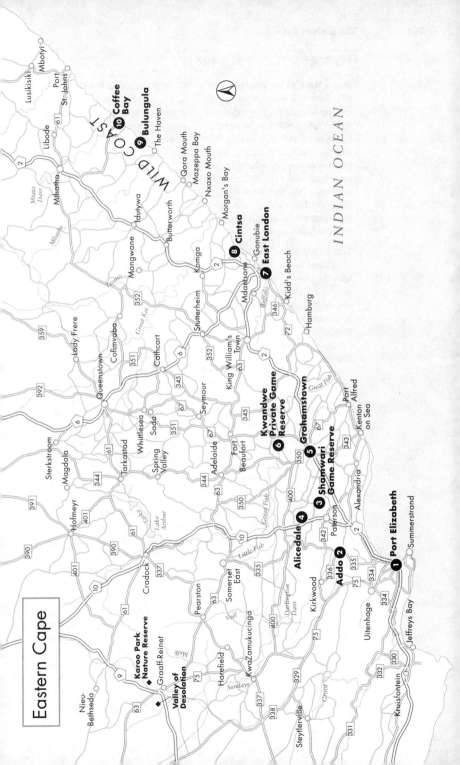

Eastern Cape

WILD COAST

INDIAN OCEAN

- Mbotyi
- Lusikisiki
- Port St. Johns
- Libode
- 61
- 2
- Mthatha
- Mtata Dam
- **10** Coffee Bay
- **9** Bulungula
- The Haven
- Qora Mouth
- Mazeppa Bay
- Nxaxo Mouth
- Morgan's Bay
- **8** Cintsa
- Gonubie
- **7** East London
- Kidd's Beach
- Butterworth
- Idutywa
- Mangwane
- Nqamakwe
- Komga
- Mdantsane
- Buffalo
- 346
- Hamburg
- 72
- Stutterheim
- King William's Town
- 63
- 352
- 2
- Great Kei
- Kuwa
- 359
- Lady Frere
- Cofimvaba
- 351
- Cathcart
- 6
- 345
- Seymour
- 67
- 345
- **6** Kwandwe Private Game Reserve
- **5** Grahamstown
- Great Fish
- 67
- Port Alfred
- Kenton on Sea
- 343
- 392
- Queenstown
- 6
- Whittlesea
- Sada
- 351
- Adelaide
- 67
- Fort Beaufort
- 344
- 63
- 350
- **3** Shamwari Game Reserve
- **4** Alicedale
- 342
- Paterson
- 10
- Alexandria
- 2
- Sterkstroom
- Magdala
- 61
- Tarkastad
- 344
- Spring Valley
- Lake Arthur
- Little Fish
- 400
- 335
- Kirkwood
- 336
- **2** Addo
- 335
- 75
- 334
- **1** Port Elizabeth
- Summerstrand
- 391
- Hofmeyr
- 401
- 61
- Cradock
- 337
- Pearston
- Somerset East
- Vlei
- 400
- Darlington Dam
- 75
- Uitenhage
- 334
- 390
- 401
- 10
- **Karoo Park Nature Reserve**
- 9
- Graaff-Reinet
- **Valley of Desolation**
- 63
- Harefield
- KwaZamukucinga
- Sundays
- 337
- Steytlerville
- 329
- Groot
- 75
- Jeffreys Bay
- 330
- Nieu-Bethesda
- 63
- Melk
- 338
- Kruisfontein
- 332
- 331

TOP REASONS TO VISIT

Take a Walk on the Wild Side The Wild Coast is a fabulous "slackpacking" destination. You can walk all day on long, lovely beaches, past turquoise lagoons, and through unspoiled villages. Wonderful day-hiking opportunities include the 37-km (23-mi) walk between Bulungula and Coffee Bay—which takes you along beaches, cliff tops, and rolling hills—plus guided hikes run by many of the lodges.

Take a Look at the Wildlife With its rich and varied topography and flora, the Eastern Cape supports a wide range of game, much of which was once hunted to near extinction by farmers and settlers. Initiatives to reclaim this area for its original inhabitants include Addo Elephant National Park, Shamwari Game Reserve, and Kwandwe Private Game Reserve. Most of the terrain here is hilly with thick bush, so you won't see vast herds of animals wandering across open plains, and some areas bear visible scars from farming. But the game is here: elephants, antelope, rhinos, buffalo, and much more. And best of all—it's malaria-free.

Take a Dive on the Wild Side If you've cage-dived with great whites, plumbed the depths of dark and narrow caves, and dived under ice, you probably think you've done it all. Wrong. Diving with a "baitball"—fish herded together by dolphins for dining purposes—in the sardine run off the Wild Coast is the ultimate adrenaline dive. Sharks, Bryde's and even humpback whales, and Cape gannets have all been known to join in the feast.

Take in the Culture and History From unsullied Xhosa villages—where women paint their faces with ocher clay, and boys undergo circumcision rites of passage—to colonial mansions, the range and depth of the Eastern Cape's cultural heritage is amazing. Since the early 19th century, the Eastern Cape has been a frontier and focus of black resistance. In almost every town you'll find fascinating museums and art galleries and a good tour operator who can expose you to the history and culture of this heterogeneous society. The cultural highlight of South Africa is the annual National Festival of the Arts, which runs for 10 action-packed days every July in Grahamstown.

See the Other Side The Transkei is the real Africa. Taking a tour will allow you to interact with locals while traversing the spectacular Wild Coast on foot, horse, bicycle, or ATV. If you're more interested in culture than adventure, a visit to Bulungula will let you meet locals and generally interact on a far more personal level.

last couple of nights at one of the private lodges, you can revel in the indulgence of absolute luxury after a few days of roughing it. Return to Port Elizabeth to fly out. A third option is to start in Grahamstown as for the three-day itinerary; two days in Grahamstown will give you the opportunity to fully appreciate the history and culture of this lovely town. Then spend two days at the game destination of your choice—Addo, Shamwari, or Kwandwe—and one more day in Port Elizabeth soaking up some culture, lounging on the beach, or playing golf.

7 days: Start off as you would for the three-day itinerary, but spend at least two days in Grahamstown and three days at your game destination. Then opt for a beach destination—Port Elizabeth, Coffee Bay, or Cintsa. Alternatively, fly into East London to join the Wild Coast Meander; then spend two days at Addo, Shamwari, or Kwandwe. Head to Port Elizabeth, and try to work in time to relax on the beach, play golf, or join a tour before flying out.

HEALTH & SAFETY

The Eastern Cape is malaria-free, and the climate is generally healthy. The tap water in the deep rural areas may be a bit dicey, but it's fine in the cities and towns. Avoid driving east of Grahamstown at night: the roads are unfenced, and animals wander onto—or even sleep on—the warm tarmac, which is a serious hazard. Be sure to bring protection against sunburn, and be careful swimming in the sea. The Wild Coast beaches don't have lifeguards.

EAT RIGHT, SLEEP WELL

Generally speaking, the restaurants of the Eastern Cape are good but not great. Of course there are always a few serendipitous exceptions to every rule, but for really good food, choose a great guesthouse—some of which are noted for their cuisine. Not surprisingly, most restaurants are reasonably casual, and there are none where you would be expected to wear a tie.

Most hotels along the coast get booked up over summer vacation (December–January), and the Wild Coast hotels are even busy over the winter school vacation, usually around June. Most establishments run winter specials, but there are exceptions. Grahamstown is packed the first week of July for the festival; every guesthouse is full, the campsite bulges, and even school and university dorms rent out rooms. Hotels on the Wild Coast often offer packages for the sardine run, usually in June or early July, but it's always a bit of a gamble. The sardines are just not as reliable as the artists of the Grahamstown festival.

Note that although mailing addresses are provided for most of the lodgings below, you'll have a much easier time securing a reservation if you phone or, in some cases, book via the lodging's Web site. Another thing to keep in mind is that many of the lodgings on the Eastern Cape are in a state of flux in terms of Internet service provided for guest use: some have limited service, others offer high-speed connections, and still others are planning to expand their service. In the facilities lists for the lodgings in this chapter, we've specified when a lodging has "Internet," but this could mean anything from a dial-up, broadband, or wireless connection in the guest rooms to a public Internet terminal. If the ability to connect to the Web is important to you, be sure to clarify the type of service available when you make your reservation.

The price categories in this chapter are applied differently to full-service safari lodges than they are to other accommodations. This is because safari lodges are typically all-inclusive experiences, with all meals, alcoholic beverages, and activities (like game-viewing) accounted for in the price. The chart below explains the differences in detail.

WHAT IT COSTS IN SOUTH AFRICAN RAND				
	¢	$	$$	$$$	$$$$
RESTAURANTS	under R40	R40–R75	R75–R125	R125–R175	over R175
LODGING	under R250	R250–R500	R500–R1,000	R1,000–R2,500	over R2,500
FULL-SERVICE SAFARI LODGING	under R3,000	R3,000–R5,000	R5,000–R7,500	R7,500–R10,000	over R10,000

Restaurant prices are per person for a main course at dinner, a main course equivalent, or a prix-fixe meal. Hotel and lodging prices are for a standard double room in high season, including 12.5% tax.

GET AROUND JUST FINE

MONEY MATTERS You will find ATMs even in really small towns—but not tiny villages like Coffee Bay or Alicedale—and full-service banks in Port Elizabeth, East London, and Grahamstown. Some of the smaller businesses do not accept credit cards, and some of the medium-sized ones do not accept American Express and/or Diners Club.

TOURS **African Heartland Journeys** (☎043/734–3415 or 082/269–6421 ⊕www.
★ africanheartland.co.za), based in Cintsa, arranges tours into the Transkei and Wild Coast for anywhere from R700 to R2,000 daily, depending on the nature of the trip and the number of guests. Tours generally focus on the people and culture, but all include an element of adventure and are tailor-made to suit the needs, interests, and fitness levels of participants. You can choose to travel by vehicle, ATV, horse, canoe, mountain bike, on foot, or a combination thereof. Overnight accommodation may be in a village or at hotels—again, usually a combination of the two.

If you dive and you think you've done it all, think again. The sardine run, which takes place in June or July, is the ultimate adrenaline dive. **Blue Wilderness** (☎083/303–1515 ⊕www.bluewilderness.co.za) runs mobile, dynamic charters along the coast, using air support to find out where the little guys (and the big guys—dolphins, sharks, and whales show up to partake of the feast) are, and then heading out to the appropriate spot. You really need to spend a good couple of days at sea if you want a chance of hitting the big time—a "baitball." Seven-night, six-day packages cost about R17,000, all-inclusive. This is for experienced divers only.

★ **Calabash Tours** (☎041/585–6162 ⊕www.calabashtours.co.za) offers the best cultural, township, and shebeen tours in Port Elizabeth. In recognition of its commitment to community development, this operator has been awarded a Fair Trade in Tourism, SA accreditation—one of only a few. You can choose between a tour of the local townships (R300), which usually includes a visit to the spectacular Red Location Museum. For the more adventurous, an evening shebeen tour (R330) includes visits to a couple of township taverns and, almost certainly, some good music. Calabash also has multiday tours to Addo Elephant National Park, as well as three- to five-day African heritage tours.

One of South Africa's most seminal historical incidents was the 1819 Battle of Grahamstown, when the Xhosa prophet Makana tried to rid his area of British colonizers. Makana was arrested and sent to Robben Island, where he died trying to escape. You can relive this battle from the point of view of young Xhosa historians with the Grahamstown-based **Egazini Tours** (☎ *046/637–1500*). The cost varies according to the number of people on the tour, but should be about R200 if you have a rental car and are prepared to drive the guide around. The tour usually includes a visit to the Egazini Outreach Project, where you can see and buy local artworks, screen-printed fabric, T-shirts, and bags.

From a short city or township tour to an all-day game-viewing excursion or an elephant ride, **Highwinds Adventure and Travel** (☎ *041/586–3721* ⊕ *www.highwinds.co.za*) offers a variety of tours in and around Port Elizabeth.

Based in East London, **Imonti Tours** (☎ *083/487–8975 or 043/741–3884* ⊕ *www.imontitours.co.za*) runs a three- to four-hour tour through the local township, including a visit to a *sangoma* (traditional healer) for about R220. On Sundays the same tour lasts an hour or two longer and includes a visit to a local shebeen where you can enjoy a *braai* (barbecue) lunch and drinks with the locals, and listen to some awesome jazz. A tour of a rural village takes the whole day and costs R350. Imonti's full-day Nelson Mandela Freedom Trail takes in Mandela's childhood home in Qunu and the Nelson Mandela Museum in Mthatha. The price ranges from R480 for groups of four or more to R1,040 for just one person, and does not include lunch.

FodorśChoice **Spirits of the Past** (☎ *046/622–7896 or 046/622–7897* ⊕ *www.spiritsof-*
★ *thepast.co.za*), run by Grahamstown oral historian Alan Weyers, has fascinating and informative full- and half-day tours of the surrounding countryside, including visits to local forts, a balanced but emotive relation of the Battle of Grahamstown, and a visit to the Valley of the Ancient Voices, which is rich in rock art (and is best appreciated with a knowledgeable guide like Weyers). Prices range from about R430 per person for a half-day trip to about R850 for a full day.

The Wild Coast has been a favorite hiking destination for years, but the overnight huts have practically disintegrated. Perhaps they will be repaired, but until then you can take advantage of some good options—perhaps better than the original—offered by the East London–based
★ **Wild Coast Holiday Reservations** (☎ *043/726–2310* ⊕ *www.wildcoasthol-idays.co.za*). The Wild Coast Meander and the Wild Coast Amble are five- or six-day guided hikes during which you walk between hotels and/or resorts on the southern section of the coast. Further north, the Hole-in-the-Wall and Wild Coast Pondo walks traverse more remote and less densely populated terrain. The Pondo Walk is a series of walks from a comfortable base camp over far more spectacular, but also much steeper, terrain than what you'll find on the other hikes. The trips are all catered, and you can arrange to have your luggage driven or portered. Costs start at R3,450 per person. Shorter walks can be organized by request. This really is the best of both worlds. You walk on deserted

beaches during the day and stay in comfy hotels with all the modern conveniences at night.

In Grahamstown, **Makana Tourism** (⊠*63 High St.* ☎*046/622–3241* ⊕*www.grahamstown.co.za*) is open weekdays 8–5 and Saturday 9–1.

Port Elizabeth's **Nelson Mandela Bay Tourism** (⊠*Donkin Reserve, Belmont Terr., Central* ☎*041/585–8884* ⊕*www.nelsonmandelabaytourism.co.za*) is open weekdays 8–4:30 and weekends 9:30–3:30.

Tourism Buffalo City (⊠*King's Tourism Centre, Aquarium Rd., Esplanade* ☎*043/722–6015* ⊕*www.visitbuffalocity.co.za*), in East London, is open weekdays 8–4:30, Saturday 9–2, and Sunday 9–1.

PORT ELIZABETH

❶ *770 km (477 mi) east of Cape Town.*

Port Elizabeth, or PE, is probably South Africa's best-kept secret. Along with its almost-perfect weather and wonderful beaches—from overdeveloped urban playgrounds to deserted snow-white sands—it has some fascinating cultural attractions, including beautifully preserved historic buildings. Most of these are in the older part of the city, called Central. A large part of the town's charm lies in its small size and quiet environment, but PE is not a total sleepy hollow. If you feel the need for a bit of nightlife, head to the Boardwalk complex, which has restaurants, theaters, and a casino in a pretty setting near the beach.

PE is also a good base for exploring some other fantastic destinations, both wild and cultural, including Addo Elephant National Park. The suburbs can be a little confusing, however. Humewood and Summerstrand are PE's two main coastal suburbs, with Humewood closer to the city center. The Humewood Golf Course, one of South Africa's best, is in Summerstrand, not Humewood, however (just to keep you on your toes).

South End was once the most vibrant part of Port Elizabeth, until it was flattened by the apartheid-era government to "tidy up" the city and put everything and everyone in their places. At the **South End Museum,** a map, photographs, and paintings give you an idea of what the old South End was like in its heyday. ⊠*Humewood Rd. and Walmer Blvd., Summerstrand* ☎*041/582–3325* 🖃*Donations welcome* ☉*Weekdays 9–4, Sat. 10–3.*

Red Location Museum won the inaugural World Leadership Award in the Architecture and Civil Engineering category for 2005. Innovative displays, including multimedia memory boxes exploring the experiences of individuals under apartheid, depict the history of forced resettlement in the area. The museum, on the outskirts of town, is well signposted and safe to visit, but you may be more comfortable viewing it as part of a guided tour. ⊠*Olaf Palme and Singaphi Sts., Red Location, New Brighton* ☎*041/408–8400* 🖃*R12* ☉*Weekdays 9–4, weekends 10–3.*

BEACHES

The beaches listed here are all lined with restaurants, shops, and coffee bars, and there are flea markets on weekends. Beyond Hobie Beach the seafront is still built up with houses and apartments, but the frenetic commercialism is missing.

Within the bay and starting closest to the city center and harbor (which is best avoided), the first
★ beach you come to is **King's Beach,** so named because King George VI slept in the Royal Train here dur-

> **DID YOU KNOW?**
>
> Port Elizabeth is the first South African city to supply off-road wheelchairs for use on the beach (either King's or Humewood). You can swap your regular street-legal chair for a "four-wheel-drive" model—and even get a lifeguard to help you in and out of the water. And, yes, it's free. Book the chairs through **PE Beaches** (☎ 041/586–1040).

ing a visit to the city before World War II. You may want to avoid the far end of King's Beach, as it can get pretty crowded. The section of beach near **McArthur Baths** (☎041/582–2282) is great for swimming and very popular. If you'd rather swim in flat water, head for the stylish bath complex (R30, open September–April), which has a range of pools—some heated, some not. **Humewood Beach** runs from King's Beach to Shark Rock Pier.

★ The pier marks the beginning of **Hobie Beach,** where sailing catamarans and Jet Skis launch. The section of beach closest to the pier is great for swimming.

★ **Pollock Beach,** adjacent to the suburb of Summerstrand, is one of the better swimming beaches, with a lovely, small natural tidal pool. It also offers great surfing. (Generally the surfing in PE is not too challenging, unlike at Jeffreys Bay, just over an hour's drive to the west, which has some pretty exciting waves.) The far end of Pollock Beach is best avoided, as it can get crowded with somewhat boisterous, picnicking, partying crowds. ■TIP→ For a truly fantastic beach experience, very little can beat **Sardinia Bay Beach,** outside the bay and about a 20-minute drive from the main beaches. Here miles and miles of deserted, snow-white sand are great for long walks.

WHERE TO STAY & EAT

The beachfront is lined with an enormous selection of reasonably priced hotels and restaurants, as well as a few higher-quality ones.

★ $–$$$$ ✕**Mauro's on the Beachfront.** Set on the beachfront, this popular eatery serves up fabulous views over the McArthur Baths complex and the beach in addition to great Italian food. If they're available, order the prawns baked in a white-wine-and-onion sauce with mozzarella, or else try the grilled sweet-and-sour ostrich steak. Linguine with creamy chicken sauce is one of the more-traditional choices. ✉1 *MacArthur Baths, Beach Rd., Humewood* ☎041/582–2700 ☜*Reservations essential* ☐*AE, DC, MC, V* ☯*Closed Sun. No lunch Sat.*

$–$$ ✕**34° South.** Sibling to the fabulous deli-cum-restaurant-cum-fishmonger of the same name in Knysna, this is the most popular restaurant at the well-frequented Boardwalk. The line fish is always fresh, and the best way to try it is as a *king-klip espatada*—skewered chunks of firm, white fish grilled with roasted peppers and onions and drizzled with lemon butter. For an equally fishy experience, fill a huge platter from the seafood meze. Even the snack-type options, like sandwiches, are big enough to qualify as a meal. ⊠*Boardwalk, Marine Dr., Summerstrand* ☎*041/583–1085* ⊟*AE, DC, MC, V.*

> **A WORD OF CAUTION**
>
> One thing to keep in mind is that although most of the Central area of PE is safe, a few parts of it can be dicey. The lower section along Govan Mbeki is lively and vibrant and the upper section is quiet and peaceful, but the bits in between have seen some crime. The area is slowly improving, but it's still best to get advice from your hotel or the tourism office before wandering around.

★ $$$ ✕⊠**La Provence Country House.** Rooms look out over lovely gardens, rolling lawns, and horse-filled paddocks on this large property. It's a quiet, restful place to stay, and the garden suites, which were once very roomy stables, are particularly soothing, with monastically understated decor. A quick drive will bring you to the lovely Sardinia Bay Beach, where you can go for a long, leisurely walk of up to 8 km (5 mi). It's worth staying for the delicious three-course dinners ($$$–$$$$), as this establishment is a member of Good Cooks and Their Country Houses. The menu changes constantly, and nonguests are accommodated if there is room. ⊠*Old Seaview Rd., 6011* ☎*041/368–1911* ⊕*www.laprovence.co.za* ⇗*10 rooms* ⌂*In-room: no a/c, safe, refrigerator. In-hotel: restaurant, tennis court, pool, no elevator, laundry service, Internet, airport shuttle, parking (no fee), no kids under 10, no-smoking rooms* ⊟*AE, DC, MC, V* ⊠*BP.*

★ $$$$ ⊠**Hacklewood Hill Country House.** For superbly comfortable and gracious lodgings, try this inn set in English-style gardens in the leafy suburb of Walmer. Beautiful antiques, such as four-poster beds, furnish the spacious rooms—some of which are downright enormous, with sofas and huge wardrobes. The Victorian baths are also huge, with separate showers and marble-top vanities. All rooms except one have balconies. ⊠*152 Prospect Rd.* ⊘*Box 319, 6000* ☎*041/581–1300* ⊕*www.hacklewood.co.za* ⇗*8 rooms* ⌂*In-room: safe, refrigerator. In-hotel: restaurant, room service, bar, tennis court, pool, no elevator, laundry service, Internet, airport shuttle, parking (no fee), no kids under 12, no-smoking rooms* ⊟*AE, DC, MC, V* ⊠*BP.*

★ $$–$$$ ⊠**King's Tide Boutique Hotel.** In a quiet part of Summerstrand, this hotel feels cocooned, but it's close to the Boardwalk and Humewood Golf Course and within easy walking distance of Pollock Beach. The rooms are richly furnished with heavy fabrics and dark wood (which is not as overpowering as it sounds). Most bathrooms have enormous tubs and triple-head showers in roomy stalls, though four rooms have showers only. ⊠*16 10th Ave., Summerstrand 6013* ☎*041/583–6023* ⊕*www.kingstide.co.za* ⇗*10 rooms* ⌂*In-room: no a/c. In-hotel: bar, Internet, parking (no fee), no kids under 13* ⊟*AE, DC, MC, V* ⊠*BP.*

$$ ⚟ **Summerstrand Hotel.** Two major attractions of this hotel are its good prices and its location—close to the beach on the quieter side of the bay and virtually on top of the excellent Humewood Golf Course—but it's the deeply entrenched culture of service that sets this large, comfortable, owner-managed hotel apart from the many other city hotels it otherwise resembles. Sea-facing rooms have lovely bay views, and golf-course-facing rooms have excellent views of the 4th and 5th holes plus a generous glimpse of sea. Rooms are spacious; singles have king-size beds, whereas doubles and suites have two double beds. Original artwork decorates the public rooms and suites. Guests here have golf privileges on the Humewood course. ✉ *Marine Dr., Summerstrand* 🖃 *Box 204, Port Elizabeth 6000* ☎ *041/583–3131* ⊕ *www.hotsummer.co.za* ⇆ *175 rooms, 5 suites* △ *In-hotel: restaurant, room service, bar, pool, concierge, Internet, laundry service, airport shuttle, parking (no fee), no-smoking rooms* ▭ *AE, DC, MC, V.*

¢ ⚟ **Jikeleza Lodge.** In a quiet part of the Central neighborhood, this hostel tends to attract mature backpackers who are more interested in culture and adventure activities than partying. Rooms are clean, comfortable, and basic, and the communal kitchen is well-appointed. Tables out in the garden make mealtimes a pleasure. ✉ *44 Cuyler St., Central Hill, 6011* ☎ *041/586–3721* ⊕ *www.jikelezalodge.co.za* ⇆ *6 rooms, 2 dormitories* △ *In-room: no a/c, no phone. In-hotel: bar, no elevator, airport shuttle, parking (no fee), no-smoking rooms* ▭ *AE, DC, MC, V.*

SPORTS & THE OUTDOORS

GOLF Consistently listed as one of the country's top 10 courses, the challeng-
★ ing championship **Humewood Golf Course** (✉ *Marine Dr., Summerstrand* ☎ *041/583–2137* ⊕ *www.humewoodgolf.co.za*) is set in undulating dunes on the edge of Algoa Bay, making it one of South Africa's few natural links courses. The late South African golfer Bobby Locke considered it the finest course in the country, and compared it favorably to the best of British links courses. At 7,100 yards and exposed to stiff sea breezes, it's not for the fainthearted. Greens fees are R425, cart fees R150, caddies R90, and club rental R185–R245.

ADDO

★ ❷ *72 km (45 mi) north of Port Elizabeth.*

Undoubtedly, the greatest attraction near the small town of Addo, which is smack in the middle of a citrus-growing and horse-breeding area, is the **Addo Elephant National Park.** Current population figures are estimated at 450 elephants, 400 buffalo, 48 black rhino, hundreds of kudu and other antelopes, and six lions. At present the park has about 300,000 acres, but it's expanding all the time and is intended to reach a total of about 890,000 acres. But Addo is a work in progress: not all of the land is contiguous, and parts of the land are not properly fenced in yet. The four most accessible parts of the park are the original, main section and the Colchester, Nyati, and Zuurberg sections. The original section of Addo still holds most of the game, and is served by Addo

Main and Gorah camps. The Colchester section, in the south, which has one South African National Parks (SANParks) camp, is contiguous with the main area but is not properly fenced yet, so there's not much game there. The scenic Nyati section is separated from the main section by a road and railway line (which will eventually be covered by huge land bridges); there are two luxury lodges in the Nyati section, and the game-viewing is excellent. Just north of Nyati is the mountainous Zuurberg section, which does not have great game but is particularly scenic, with fabulous hiking trails and horse trails. It is also the closest section of the park to Addo Elephant Back Safaris.

You can explore the park in your own vehicle, in which case you need to take the road signs that claim DUNG BEETLES HAVE RIGHT OF WAY seriously. Addo is home to the almost-endemic and extremely rare flightless dung beetle, which can often be seen rolling its unusual incubator across the roads. Watch out for them (they're only about 2 inches long, but they have the right-of-way—as well as sharp spines that can puncture tires), and watch them: they're fascinating. Instead of driving you could take a night or day game drive with a park ranger in an open vehicle from the main camp. A more adventurous option is to ride a horse among the elephants. Less-experienced riders may ride along the fence line. Warning: no citrus fruit may be brought into the park, as elephants find it irresistible and can smell it for miles. ☎042/233–0556 ⊕www.addoelephantpark.com ✉R80 ⊙Daily 7–7 (may vary with seasons).

★ ☾ **Addo Elephant Back Safaris** lets you get really up close and personal with a small group of trained African elephants. You get to do a short elephant ride and then go for a scenic walk through the bush with them. You can touch them, feed them, and watch them as they bathe themselves with sand, water, or both (i.e., mud). The whole experience lasts about 2½ hours. You can also arrange for a fly-in day trip from Port Elizabeth. ☎042/235–1400 or 083/283–2359 ⊕www.addoelephant-backsafaris.co.za ✉R650 ⊙Visits by appointment.

WHERE TO STAY

★ $$$–$$$$ ⌂ **Camp Figtree.** With extensive views of the deeply incised Zuurberg Mountains undulating into the blue-green distance, this beautiful lodge has the most fantastic location. The lodge is centered around an old wood-and-iron pioneer house, and it picks up the style in individual iron cottages and tented rooms, all overlooking the deep green valleys and distant mountains. You can do game drives from the lodge to main game area, although this is not included in the lodging price. It's relatively close to the horse trails at Zuurberg and Addo Elephant Back Safaris. ⊠On the R335, about 15 km (9 mi) from Addo Main Gate ☍Box 40283, Walmer 6065 ☎042/233–1291 ⊕www.campfigtree. com ⇱4 rooms, 2 tents ☍In-room: no a/c, no phone, no TV. In-hotel: room service, bar, pool, no elevator, laundry service, airport shuttle, no-smoking rooms ☐AE, DC, MC, V ☉MAP.

★ $$$ ⌂ **Gorah Elephant Camp.** A private concession within the main section of Addo, this lodge centers on an old farmhouse, which has been restored and filled with antiques. Roaring fires warm chilly winter nights, and the wide veranda provides cool shade in the heat of the day. The lodge overlooks a water hole where various animals come to drink, the stars of which are the elephants. Accommodations are in huge tents with private baths. Mosquito nets are more for effect than necessity, as this is a malaria-free area. Keep in mind that although this is a luxury lodge, there is no electricity, so you won't find hair dryers in the rooms. Meals are taken alfresco on the veranda or in the dining room. Cuisine and service are equal to the best in Africa. The lodge operates three game drives per day and/or escorted walks. ⊠ *Addo Elephant National Park* ⬧ *Box 454, Plettenberg Bay 6600* ☎ *044/532–7818* ⊕ *www.gorah. com* 🛏 *11 tents* ⚘ *In-room: no a/c, safe, no TV. In-hotel: bar, pool, no elevator, laundry service, Internet, airport shuttle, no kids under 10, no-smoking rooms* ▤ *AE, DC, MC, V* ⦿*FAP.*

$$$
Fodor's Choice
★
🏠 **Hitgeheim Country Lodge.** This lovely lodge is set on a steep cliff overlooking the Sundays River and the town of Addo. Classically decorated rooms, graced with lovely antiques, are in separate thatch buildings, all with verandas overlooking the river. The bathrooms are spacious and luxuriously appointed with large tubs and enormous shower stalls. Some rooms have indoor and outdoor showers. Birds frolic in the natural vegetation that has been allowed to grow up to the edge of the verandas, and tame buck often wander around the garden. Hitgeheim (pronounced *hitch-ee-hime*) is a working ostrich, citrus, and buffalo-breeding farm, and you can walk through the game areas to look at the buffalo, eland, sable, and other antelope. The food is fabulous, and most guests opt to stay for the six-course dinners (R220). ⊠ *18 km (11 mi) from Addo Main Gate on the R335, and then follow the R336 to Kirkwood* ⬧ *Box 95, Sunland 6115* ☎ *042/234–0778* ⊕ *www.hitge-heim-addo.co.za* 🛏 *8 rooms* ⚘ *In-room: no phone, no TV, refrigerator. In-hotel: bar, pool, laundry service, Internet, airport shuttle, no kids under 12, no-smoking rooms* ▤ *AE, DC, MC, V* ⦿*BP.*

$$–$$$
🏠 **Zuurberg Mountain Inn.** This characterful lodge has a sense of history: it dates from 1861, when the steep and twisty pass it's set on was on the main road from Port Elizabeth to the diamond fields of Kimberley. If you like, you can take a 4x4 tour following the old route. The public rooms have the feel of a traditional country hotel, in part because it seems like nothing much has changed here in a century or so. This slightly retro air is reinforced by the popular Sunday carvery lunches (R75). Rooms are in separate thatched *rondawels* (round buildings) scattered around the extensive grounds. Although the standard rooms are quite ordinary, the Upper Zuurberg Village rooms are a bit more stylish, with bathrooms tiled in slate and large shower stalls. The views across the valley and toward Addo stretch on forever, and there are hikes and guided horse rides into the beautiful forest. Although the Zuurberg Mountains are a part of Addo, the game is restricted to smaller species that are not often seen, but the birding is good. ⊠ *On the R335 Zuurberg Mountain Pass* ⬧ *Box 12, 6105* ☎ *042/233–0583* ⊕ *www.addo.co.za* 🛏 *36 rooms* ⚘ *In-room: no a/c, no TV. In-hotel: restaurant, bar, tennis court, pool, laundry service, no-smoking rooms* ▤ *AE, DC, MC, V* ⦿*BP.*

★ $$ ⛏**Nguni River Lodge.** Within the scenic Nyati section of Addo and close to the main game area is this stylish lodge notable for its unusual decor. Each room takes its name and theme from a particular color pattern of the indigenous Nguni cattle. Stone, thatch, rough metal sculptures, and, of course, the skins of Nguni cattle work together to produce a funky contemporary interpretation of African architectural styles and legends. Indoor and outdoor showers and private plunge pools increase the living space of the already quite large rooms. The food is cooked mostly on open fires and could best be described as fusion cuisine with an African twist. Game drives and guided walks are included. ⊠ *On the R342, about 7 km (4 mi) on the Paterson side of Addo Main Gate* ⌂ *Box 2513, North End 6056* ☎ *042/235–1022 reservations* ⊕ *www. ngunilodges.co.za* ⇗ *8 rooms* ⛄ *In-room: safe, no TV. In-hotel: bar, no elevator, laundry service, airport shuttle* ⊟ *AE, DC, MC, V* ⦿*FAP.*

★ $$ ⛏**River Bend Country Lodge.** A private concession within the Nyati section of Addo, River Bend perfectly balances the idea of a sophisticated, comfortable country house with all the facilities of a game lodge. The spacious public rooms, filled with antiques and comfy couches, are in a beautifully renovated farmhouse and outbuildings. The guest rooms are in individual cottages dotted around the lovely gardens; each is uniquely decorated with a different color scheme. In addition to the usual game drives, you can tour the adjacent citrus farm and a small game sanctuary, where you may see animals not found in Addo—giraffes, white rhinos, blue wildebeest, nyala, and impala. ⊠ *On the R335, about 70 km (43 mi) north of Port Elizabeth* ⌂ *Box 249, 6105* ☎ *042/233–8000* ⊕ *www.riverbendlodge.co.za* ⇗ *8 rooms* ⛄ *In-room: safe, refrigerator, DVD. In-hotel: room service, bar, pool, laundry service, Internet, airport shuttle, no-smoking rooms* ⊟ *AE, DC, MC, V* ⦿*FAP.*

$ ⛏**Matyholweni Camp.** Set in the quieter Colchester section in the south, this pleasant camp is close to the marine sections of the park and only a 16-km (10-mi) drive to the gate of the main game area. Pretty thatched chalets nestle in the thick bush, and a sense of peace and quiet pervades. The bathrooms have no tubs, only showers. Two rooms are accessible for people who use wheelchairs. ⊠ *N2* ☎ *012/428–9111* ⊕ *www. addoelephantpark.com* ⇗ *12 chalets* ⛄ *In-room: no a/c, kitchen, no TV. In-hotel: no elevator* ⊟ *AE, DC, MC, V.*

¢–$ ⛏**Addo Elephant National Park Main Camp.** Typical of SANParks rest camps, this location has comfortable chalets with cooking facilities and a shop that sells basic supplies as well as souvenirs. An à la carte restaurant is open for all meals, and a floodlighted water hole is nearby. Prices are calculated according to a complicated SANParks formula, which works out to anything from R140 to R480 per person sharing. Camping ranges from R40 to R60 per person. The most efficient way to book any SANParks accommodation is to phone. ☎ *012/428–9111* ⊕ *www.addoelephantpark.com* ⇗ *53 chalets, 5 tents, 20 campsites* ⛄ *In-room: no a/c (some), kitchen, no TV. In-camp: restaurant, pool* ⊟ *AE, DC, MC, V.*

SHAMWARI GAME RESERVE

❸ *72 km (45 mi) northeast of Port Elizabeth, 70 km (43 mi) west of Grahamstown.*

Shamwari is, in every sense of the word, a conservation triumph. Unprofitable farmland has been turned into a successful tourist attraction, wild animals have been reintroduced, and alien vegetation has been, and is still being, eradicated. The reserve is constantly being expanded and now stands at about 54,400 acres. Its mandate is to conserve not only the big impressive animals, but also small things: the plants, buildings, history, and culture of the area. Shamwari has been awarded the Global Nature Fund Award for Best Conservation Practice, and wildlife manager Dr. Johan Joubert was voted one of South Africa's top 10 conservationists by the Endangered Wildlife Trust. ☎*041/407–1000 or 042/203–1111* ⊕*www.shamwari.com.*

About 7,400 acres have been set aside as **Wilderness Area,** where only
FodorsChoice escorted walking safaris are allowed. You carry all your own stuff,
★ including food and sleeping bags, which are supplied, and head off into the wilds in the company of a ranger to sleep under the stars. A two-night, all-inclusive package costs R950 per person. Part of the reserve has been set aside as the **Born Free Centres** (there's one in the northern part and one in the southern part of the reserve). Here African animals rescued from around the world are allowed to roam in reasonably large enclosures for the rest of their lives, as they cannot safely be returned to the wild. Although these are interesting tourist attractions, the main purpose is educational, and about 500 local school children tour the centers every month.

WHERE TO STAY

$$$$ 🏨**Eagles Cragg.** Very different from the other Shamwari options, this
FodorsChoice sleek, modern lodge makes use of light wood, pale sandstone, and
★ stainless-steel finishes. It's light and airy and gives a sense of space. All rooms have indoor and outdoor showers and private decks with plunge pools. Glass walls fold away to bring the feel of the bush into the room. ✉*Box 113, Swartkops, Port Elizabeth 6210* ☎*041/407–1000* ⊕*www.shamwari.com* ➭*9 rooms* ☖*In-room: safe, refrigerator, no TV. In-hotel: bar, spa, no elevator, laundry service, concierge, airport shuttle, no kids under 16* ▭*AE, DC, MC, V* ⏀*FAP.*

★ $$$$ 🏨**Lobengula Lodge.** Though rooms are set around a central lawn and pool area, which makes the lodge compact, they face outward for privacy. Thatch roofs and muted earth tones are part of the African decor. All rooms open onto a private veranda and have indoor and outdoor showers. Two rooms and the suite have private plunge pools. Meals are served around a central fireplace, and you may choose wines from the extensive cellar. ✉*Box 113, Swartkops, Port Elizabeth 6210* ☎*041/407–1000* ⊕*www.shamwari.com* ➭*5 rooms, 1 suite* ☖*In-room: safe, refrigerator. In-hotel: bar, pool, gym, spa, laundry service, concierge, airport shuttle, no kids under 16* ▭*AE, DC, MC, V* ⏀*FAP.*

4

$$$$ ⊞ **Long Lee Manor.** Long Lee appeals to those looking for an *Out of Africa* romance, complete with four-poster beds, teak staircases, antique furniture, and manicured lawns. An authentic part of Eastern Cape history, this renovated salmon-pink Edwardian mansion was built in 1816, and served as the original owner's home. Ask for one of the designer-decorated suites in the main house. Other rooms are in separate buildings. Every other night, supper is an opulent African feast—corn on the cob, game stews, *mielie pap* (a gritslike corn porridge)—served in the courtyard. Of all the Shamwari lodges, this is the lodge most open to children. ⌂ *Box 113, Swartkops, Port Elizabeth 6210* 🕾 *041/407–1000* ⊕ *www.shamwari.com* 🛏 *17 rooms, 3 suites* ♿ *In-room: safe, refrigerator. In-hotel: room service, bar, spa, no elevator, laundry service, concierge, airport shuttle* ═ *AE, DC, MC, V* ⦿ *FAP.*

$$$ ⊞ **Bayethe Tented Lodge.** The huge air-conditioned safari tents have private decks with plunge pools that overlook the Buffalo River. One tent is wheelchair accessible. Suites, which are separated from the other rooms by the reception area and a walk of a hundred yards or so, are huge and impressive. Gleaming light-wood floors, fireplaces, and an enormous deck with the most beautiful loungers all contribute to a sense of restrained style and opulence. ⌂ *Box 113, Swartkops, Port Elizabeth 6210* 🕾 *041/407–1000* ⊕ *www.shamwari.com* 🛏 *9 rooms, 3 suites* ♿ *In-room: safe, refrigerator, no TV (some). In-hotel: bar, pool, laundry service, concierge, airport shuttle, no kids under 12* ═ *AE, DC, MC, V* ⦿ *FAP.*

★ $$$ ⊞ **Bushmans River Lodge.** This tastefully restored original settler's cottage can host up to eight guests in a homelike setting. A dedicated chef, hostess, and ranger make this a rather exclusive experience for small groups, who can book the whole house. ⌂ *Box 113, Swartkops, Port Elizabeth 6210* 🕾 *041/407–1000* ⊕ *www.shamwari.com* 🛏 *4 rooms* ♿ *In-room: safe. In-hotel: bar, pool, laundry service, concierge, airport shuttle* ═ *AE, DC, MC, V* ⦿ *FAP.*

★ $$$ ⊞ **Riverdene Lodge.** The public areas are in a period farmhouse, and accommodations are in three enormous renovated barns, which are long, yellow buildings with rooms opening onto private balconies. Weather permitting, meals are served on the large patio by the pool or around the fire in a spectacular wooden *boma* (thatched area) overlooking the Bushmans River. A collection of black-and-white photographs, all taken at Shamwari, adorns the walls of the lodge. ⌂ *Box 113, Swartkops, Port Elizabeth 6210* 🕾 *041/407–1000* 🖷 *041/407–1001* ⊕ *www.shamwari.com* 🛏 *9 rooms* ♿ *In-room: safe, refrigerator. In-hotel: bar, pool, laundry service, airport shuttle, no kids under 12* ═ *AE, DC, MC, V* ⦿ *FAP.*

ALICEDALE

❹ *5 km (3 mi) north of edge of Shawmari, 60 km (37 mi) west of Grahamstown.*

A tiny settlement west of Grahamstown, Alicedale was once an important railway town. The demise of the steam train, however, sent Alicedale into decline, turning it into a virtual ghost town populated by a depressed band of unemployed wraiths subsisting on meager railway pensions and funds sent home from family members working elsewhere. The development of a major golf course, hotel, and game reserve, however, has brought life back to Alicedale: property prices have risen, unemployment is down, and a sense of relative prosperity is slowly settling on the town.

WHERE TO STAY

$$$ 🏨 **Bushman Sands Hotel.** Built around a demanding Gary Player–designed, links-style golf course, and adjacent to the Bushman Sands Game Reserve, this hotel offers a number of leisure options—including golf, game drives, and sunset cruises on the nearly 500-acre New Year's Dam. Rooms are in separate structures that echo the style of the original Victorian school building, which forms the hotel's center. The decor is understated and classical, with black-and-white-tile bathroom floors and claw-foot tubs. The suites, which are renovated railway cottages, have fabulous bathrooms, with shower stalls just big enough for you and your favorite baseball team. The food served at the restaurant is nothing special, but the golf course setting makes this a pleasant enough place to eat. ✉ *Box 39, 6135* ☎ *041/407–1000* ⊕ *www.bushmansands.com* 🛏 *34 rooms, 5 suites* ♿ *In-room: safe, refrigerator. In-hotel: restaurant, bar, golf course, pools, gym, spa, laundry service, Internet, airport shuttle, no-smoking rooms* 🖃 *AE, DC, MC, V* ⫿⦿*BP.*

SPORTS & THE OUTDOORS

GOLF The challenging, links-style, 6,599-yard championship **Bushman Sands Golf Course** (☎ *042/231–8000* ⊕ *www.bushmansands.com*), designed by South African golfer Gary Player, undulates along the banks of the Bushman's and New Year's rivers. Greens fees are R310 (R165 for hotel guests), cart fees are R190, and club rental costs R170.

GRAHAMSTOWN

❺ *60 km (37 mi) east of Alicedale, 120 km (75 mi) northeast of Port Elizabeth.*

Although billed as a city, Grahamstown looks more like an English village than anything else—except, of course, for that alter ego of most South African towns, those desperately poor contiguous shanty townships. These are a big part of Grahamstown, and they contribute to the city's wealth of cultural history. Established as a garrison town to enforce the arbitrarily assigned border of the British Cape Colony, Grahamstown was the center of several battles during the last couple of centuries. It's worth spending a day or two to explore the sights and to perhaps take two different tours—just to reinforce the fact that history, no matter how accurately portrayed, is always subjective.

Home to Rhodes University and some of the country's top schools, Grahamstown is considered by many to be the seat of culture and learning in South Africa. This claim is given further credibility by its hosting of the country's premier cultural event—the 10-day **National Festival of the Arts** (☎046/622–4341 ⊕ *www.nafest.co.za*), which takes place in July and is purported to be second in size only to the Edinburgh Festival in Scotland. The festival includes local and international music, theater, ballet and modern dance, fine art, and more. The festival comprises the formal program, an official fringe festival, and even a fringe of the fringe that gets seriously alternative. Events are staged throughout town but mainly at the **1820 Settlers National Monument,** a concrete edifice on Gunfire Hill, next to the old garrison, Fort Selwyn

The **Cathedral of St. Michael and St. George** is Grahamstown's most prominent landmark, as much by virtue of its steeple—the highest in South Africa—as the strict geometry of the town. High Street runs in a straight line from the cathedral doors through the Drostdy Arch to the doors of the administration buildings of Rhodes University. The cathedral's eight bells, which you can hear ringing out on Sundays, were the first and still are the heaviest in Africa. Though started in 1824, the cathedral was only finally completed in 1952. ⊠ *High St.* ☎ *No phone* 🎫 *Free* ⊗ *Mon.–Sat. 9–3.*

The statue of the **Winged Angel of Peace** (⊠ *Bathurst St.*) commemorates the dead of the Second South African War (1899–1902), also called the Boer War. The site was chosen as one that was "in the midst of our daily work," so it would be seen often and would serve as an inspiration for peace. Irreverent students can't help pointing out that it looks as though the angel is supporting a drunk (not dying) soldier and pointing accusingly at one of the local pubs.

The **Observatory Museum** is an intriguing study of Victorian-era cutting-edge science. The building was constructed by a watchmaker and amateur astronomer, H. C. Gulpin, who built a cupola above his shop to house his instruments. The museum contains a two-story pendulum and the only genuine Victorian camera obscura in the southern hemisphere. You can stand in the tower and watch what's happening in the town below—pretty useful if you've lost your companions. ⊠ *Bathurst St.* ☎ *046/622–2312* ⊕ *www.ru.ac.za/affiliates/am* 🎫 *R8* ⊗ *Weekdays 9:30–1 and 2–5, Sat. 9–1.*

The **National English Literary Museum** houses a comprehensive collection of books, articles, and press clippings on South African writers in the English language, including some unpublished works. There is also a bookshop. ⊠ *87 Beaufort St.* ☎ *046/622–7042* 🎫 *Free* ⊗ *Weekdays 9–12:30 and 2–4:30.*

When Grahamstown was a garrison town, the **Drostdy Arch** (⊠ *High St.*) was the original entrance to the military parade ground. Now it is the gateway through which thousands of Rhodes students pass when leaving campus for town. There is a small **crafts market** "under the Arch" on weekdays 9–5 and Saturday 9–1.

The **International Library of African Music** is a teaching and research center for indigenous music. It has a collection of more than 200 traditional African musical instruments, including *djembes* (drums), *mbiras* (thumb pianos), and marimbas (xylophones). ⊠*Rhodes University, Prince Alfred St.* ☎*046/603–8557* ✉*Free* ✆*By appointment.*

WHERE TO STAY & EAT
Your best bet for help with lodging, especially at festival time, is the **Grahamstown Accommodation Bureau** (✍*Box 758, 6140* ☎*046/622–5777 or 082/758–4740* ⊕*www.grahamstownaccom.co.za*).

> ### THE ELASTIC CITY
>
> Most of the year Grahamstown is pretty small, but around festival time this elastic city expands to accommodate the tens of thousands of festival-goers. Come December, it shrinks to a mere ghost of itself as the students and scholars go home.

4

$ ✕**La Galleria.** Italian is South Africa's alternate gastronomic culture, and there's a good family *ristorante* in almost every town. Choose from a selection of starters presented on a trolley, then perhaps try the pan-fried fillet of beef in a red-wine-and-herb sauce or with blue cheese and brandy flambé. All pastas are homemade. ⊠*St Aidans Complex, Constitution St.* ☎*046/622–2345* ▭*AE, DC, MC, V* ✆*No lunch.*

$$ ✕▥**Cock House.** Over the years, this charming building has been the home of distinguished citizens, most notably academic and novelist André Brink, so it's fitting that the individually decorated rooms are named after previous owners. The small hotel suffers from (or is blessed by, depending on how you look at it) the rather haphazard improvements that have been made over time. It's worth staying here just for the food ($–$$), but you can also book a table for breakfast, lunch, or dinner if you're staying elsewhere. Try the delicious lamb shank, served in a thyme-and-rosemary sauce, or feta-cheese soufflé with *peppadews* (a cross between a sweet pepper and a chili). Dinner is usually a set menu, but à la carte is available. The next-door building has four self-catering apartments, which are good value for a longer stay, though less atmospheric than rooms in the main house. ⊠*10 Market St., at George St., 6140* ☎*046/636–1295* ⊕*www.cockhouse.co.za* ⇆*7 rooms, 2 suites, 4 apartments* ⌂*In-room: no a/c (some). In-hotel: restaurant, bar, no elevator, laundry service, Internet, parking (no fee), no-smoking rooms* ▭*AE, DC, MC, V* ⑩*BP.*

$$ ✕▥ **137 High St.** Conveniently located right on High Street, this warm, friendly coffee shop (¢–$) is popular with students. It serves the usual pastas, sandwiches, and salads—and arguably the best coffee in town. The bed-and-breakfast upstairs has fabulous yellowwood floors in the residents' lounge, but otherwise its main attraction is its good value. Rooms are small but clean and comfortable. One room has a tub; the others have showers only. ⊠*137 High St., 6140* ☎*046/622–3242* ⇆*7 rooms* ⌂*In-room: no a/c. In-hotel: restaurant, no elevator, laundry service, parking (no fee), no-smoking rooms* ▭*DC, MC, V* ✆*No dinner Sun.* ⑩*BP.*

★ $$$ ▥ **7 Worcester Street.** Built in 1888, this magnificent dressed-stone mansion has been meticulously restored and beautifully decorated with a subtle mix of local, Thai, and Indonesian artifacts. Rooms are elegantly proportioned and have high ceilings and large bathrooms. Dinner is by arrangement. As befits an establishment of this nature, the service is friendly and discreet, but no request seems too much trouble for the staff. You can arrange tours and activities through the inn. ⊠7 *Worcester St., 6140* ☎*046/622–2843* ⊕*www.worcesterstreet.co.za* ⊠*10 rooms* ᗧ*In-room: safe, refrigerator. In-hotel: bar, pool, no elevator, laundry service, Internet, parking (no fee), no-smoking rooms* ▤*AE, DC, MC, V* ⦿|*BP.*

KWANDWE PRIVATE GAME RESERVE

❻ *38 km (24 mi) northeast of Grahamstown.*

FodorśChoice
★

Kwandwe is set among about 50,000 acres of Karoo scrubland and succulent thicket, a mere 20 minutes from Grahamstown. Rolling hills, flowering plants, and endless vistas form a perfect backdrop for a good variety of game. Although the daytime game game-watching is excellent, Kwandwe is particularly renowned for its nocturnal animals. So it's worth opting for a night drive, during which you stand a pretty good chance of unusual sightings like aardwolf, aardvark, porcupine, genet, and other creatures of the night.

Carved out of old farmland, including the world's first commercial ostrich farm, which today serves as the lodge reception, this reserve has several beautifully renovated old buildings. The Great Fish River runs through the reserve, offering a change in scenery as the riverine vegetation gets thicker and higher. Air and road shuttles are available from Port Elizabeth.

WHERE TO STAY

All the lodges listed here have cable TV in a communal area, and the child-friendly ones have movies and games. In the single-use lodges, these are hidden away in a cupboard, so you can keep their existence a secret from your brood unless a rainy day makes them essential.

$$$$ 　▥**Melton Manor.** Although this single-use lodge is architecturally slick and contemporary, lovely antiques and rather whimsical old artifacts create an interesting sense of ongoing history—and a definite style statement. Built around a small central lawn with a swimming pool, the four spacious, light, and airy rooms look outward into the bush for privacy. You have your own chef and game ranger, and you call the shots. This is a great option for families, as you can take the little ones on game drives or leave them behind with babysitters. It's also a good deal for three couples traveling together (and a great deal for four). ⌂*CC Africa, Box X27, Benmore 2010* ☎*011/809–4300* ⊕*www. kwandwereserve.co.za* ⊠*4 rooms* ᗧ*In-room: no TV. In-hotel: bar, pool, no elevator, laundry service, Internet, airport shuttle* ▤*AE, DC, MC, V* ⦿|*FAP.*

$$$$ 　▥**Uplands Homestead.** To stay at Uplands you have to rent the whole house, but you get your own chef, game ranger, and vehicle. This renovated, century-old, Cape Dutch farmhouse was once a family home, and the feeling persists. A large lawn for little ones to play on and babysitting service make this a great choice for families with children. ⌂*CC Africa, Box X27, Benmore 2010* ☎*011/809–4300* ⊕*www.*

kwandwereserve.co.za ✎*3 rooms* ⚐*In-room: no TV. In-hotel: bar, pool, no elevator, laundry service, Internet, airport shuttle* ▤*AE, DC, MC, V* ⍾*FAP.*

$$–$$$$ 🏨**Ecca Lodge.** If you believe a game lodge has to have thatch, African artifacts, the heads of dead animals, and zebra-skin rugs, you'll hate Ecca. But if you like clean lines, unusual materials, and a sense of place, you'll love it. Built largely from gabions (those caged rocks used to shore up roads), bare concrete, and glass, and accented with bright orange, this is a masterpiece of design. It's different and vibrant. Huge, light rooms lead onto private decks with plunge pools and views of the surrounding bush. It's child-friendly, and a well-appointed activity center will keep

> ### THE WILD TIME
>
> The Eastern Cape was a hotbed of conflict during the early 19th century. Trekboers fleeing British bureaucracy tried to establish farms, British settlers were dumped in the Grahamstown area as a buffer between the established Cape Colony (the Western Cape) and the wilds of "Kaffraria" (a derogatory term applied to part of the Eastern Cape), and British soldiers tried to protect them from the starving Xhosa *impis* (regiments) made desperate by Britain's scorched-earth policy. A tour with either Spirits of the Past or Egazini Tours will give you an insight into this dramatic era.

the little ones amused between game activities. Game drives, guided hikes, and fishing are available. ⌕*CC Africa, Box X27, Benmore 2010* ☎*011/809–4300* ⊕*www.kwandwereserve.co.za* ✎*6 rooms* ⚐*In-room: safe, refrigerator, no TV. In-hotel: pool, no elevator, children's programs, laundry service, Internet, airport shuttle* ▤*AE, DC, MC, V* ⍾*FAP.*

★ $$–$$$$ 🏨**Great Fish River Lodge.** Built on a slope overlooking the river, this lodge consists of traditional-style, glass-fronted thatch rooms in individual buildings, with indoor and outdoor showers and every possible creature comfort. Each room has its own large, shaded deck next to a private plunge pool. A minibar and telephone for pool service ensure that you'll be well fed. Game drives, guided walks, and fishing are available. ⌕*CC Africa, Box X27, Benmore 2010* ☎*011/809–4300* ⊕*www.kwandwereserve.co.za* ✎*9 rooms* ⚐*In-room: safe, refrigerator, no TV. In-hotel: room service, bar, no elevator, laundry service, Internet, airport shuttle, no kids under 12* ▤*AE, DC, MC, V* ⍾*FAP.*

EAST LONDON

❼ *150 km (93 mi) east of Grahamstown.*

The gateway to the Wild Coast, East London was built around the mouth of the Buffalo River, which forms South Africa's only river port. Although fairly urban, East London is still close to the rural heartland, so it retains a pleasantly small-town air. There's a great museum here, and you can take a half-day city tour, an escorted visit to a local township, or a full-day tour of a rural village (⇨*Tours in Orientation & Planning, above*). Although the beaches on the outskirts of the city are wonderful, those within the central business district are crowded and not very pleasant.

There's definitely something fishy going on at the **East London Museum.** In addition to a whole section on the discovery of the coelacanth, the museum has a large display of preserved fish, including an enormous manta ray. For a different kind of fishy, check out what is claimed to be the world's only surviving dodo egg. *Jurassic Park,* here we come! Probably the most worthwhile exhibit, though, is the extensive beadwork collection; it's both culturally interesting and just plain beautiful. ⊠ *319 Oxford St.* ☎ *043/743–0686* ✍ *R7* ⊙ *Weekdays 9–4:30, Sat. 10–1, Sun.10–3.*

BEACHES

East London is just far enough north of PE that the water and the weather are a bit warmer, but the inner inner-city beaches are not that great and would appeal more to surfers than to general loungers.

Gonubie Beach is at the mouth of the Gonubie River, about half an hour northeast of the city. The riverbank is covered in dense forest, with giant *strelitzias* (wild banana trees) growing right to the water's edge. A lovely beach, tidal pools, and a 500-yard-long wooden walkway make this a fantastically user-friendly beach.

Nahoon Beach, at the mouth of the Nahoon River, about 20 minute's drive from the city, has some fantastic surf—but only for people who know what they're doing. Of course, it's also just a lovely beach for bathing, sunbathing, and watching surfers, and the lagoon is great for swimming and snorkeling.

WHERE TO STAY & EAT

$$–$$$ ✕⊡ **Blue Lagoon Hotel.** Overlooking the mouth of the beautiful Nahoon River and within easy reach of Nahoon Beach, this is a great place for a low-key family beach break. The standard rooms are quite ordinary and lack views, but the family suites have magnificent views of the lagoon, the sea, or both. Each suite has two bedrooms, one bathroom with tub and shower, a well-appointed kitchen, a living room, and a spacious balcony. The restaurants (¢–$$) are popular with locals—as much for the fabulous views as for the large menu of pastas, steaks, and fish dishes, plus a few interesting innovations thrown in. ⊠ *Blue Bend Pl.* ✉ *Box 2177, Beacon Bay, 5205* ☎ *043/748–4821* ⊕ *www.bluelagoonhotel.co.za* 🛏 *40 rooms, 36 suites* ⟁ *In-room: kitchen (some). In-hotel: 2 restaurants, bars, pool, spa, beachfront, no elevator, laundry service, Internet, parking (no fee), airport shuttle, no-smoking rooms* ⊟ *AE, DC, MC, V* ⦙⊙⦙*BP.*

$$ ⊡ **Meander Inn.** In the leafy suburb of Selborne, Meander Inn is close to the East London Museum, restaurants, and shops. It's a convenient place to stay on either side of a Wild Coast hike, but it's also great for business travelers, thanks to its business services. Of the older rooms in the main house, one is not en suite, but it does have its own bathroom across the hall. All rooms are predominantly white, with a different color accent in the soft furnishings. The newer rooms have wood accents and stylish bathrooms with black-granite finishes. All rooms have showers but no tubs. Dinner is available by request. ⊠8 *Clarendon Rd., Selborne* ⌂*Box 8017, Nahoon, East London 5210* ☎*043/726–2310* ⊕*www.wildcoastholidays.co.za* ⟲*10 rooms* ⚘*In-room: no a/c, no phone. In-hotel: bar, pool, no elevator, laundry service, Internet, parking (no fee), concierge, airport shuttle, no-smoking rooms* ⊟*AE, DC, MC, V* ⍾*BP.*

★ $$ ⌘ **Stratfords Guest House.** It's worth staying at this friendly, stylish guesthouse just to see the building. A masterpiece of design, it makes excellent use of space, and utilizes unusual materials like corrugated iron, bare concrete, wood, and glass in incredibly innovative ways to create a comfortable, stimulating environment. Built in 2000, it received a merit award from the SA Institute of Architects in 2001. Loft suites have microwaves, fridges, and combination tub-showers, whereas the other rooms have only showers. Centrally situated in the suburb of Vincent, Stratfords is close to the East London Museum, shops, and restaurants. It's particularly popular with business travelers. ⊠*31 Frere Rd., Vincent, 5247* ☎*043/726–9765* ⟲*12 rooms, 4 suites* ⚘*In-room: no a/c, refrigerator (some). In-hotel: bar, pool, no elevator, laundry service, Internet, parking (no fee), no-smoking rooms* ⊟*MC, V* ⍾*BP.*

¢ ⌘ **Sugarshack Backpackers.** The numerous wet suits and surfboards lying around make it clear that this fun, casual hostel is the place to go if you're after some waves. It's right on Eastern Beach in Quigney, a suburb of East London; the big open-air deck, which leads off the communal kitchen-lounge, is a great place to sit and watch the waves. Double rooms, which share bathrooms with dorm residents and campers, are in cute but tiny wooden cabins with their own sea-view verandas. Sugarshack serves a healthful Continental continental breakfast for R15–R25, and there are loads of restaurants and pubs within walking distance. Like most hostels, this place can get quite lively; drumming evenings are a regular occurrence. All kinds of adventure tours (such as paddling and sand-boarding) are on offer, along with surfing lessons. ⊠*Eastern Beach, Esplanade* ⌂*Box 18312, Quigney, 5201* ☎*043/722–8240* ⊕*www.sugarshack.co.za* ⟲*4 rooms without baths, 4 dormitories, camping* ⚘*In-room: no a/c, no phone, no TV. In-hotel: bar, beachfront, no elevator, laundry service, Internet, no-smoking rooms* ⊟*No credit cards.*

CINTSA

❽ *40 km (25 mi) northeast of East London.*

This lovely, quiet little seaside town a half-hour's drive from East London is a winner. A nice long beach, pretty rock pools, and a beautiful lagoon on which to paddle make this a coastal paradise. Not much happens here, which is its main attraction. The town—if it can be called a town—is divided by the river mouth into an eastern and a western side. It's a drive of about 10 km (6 mi) between them, although you can walk across the river at low tide (most of the time). The town has a couple of restaurants and small shops, plus a good choice of accommodations.

CLOSE UP

The Food Chain Up Close

Hailed by locals as "the greatest shoal on earth," the sardine run is, in terms of biomass, the world's largest animal migration. Cold water traveling up the coast moves closer to shore and brings with it untold millions of sardines (actually pilchards). These tiny fish are, of course, highly edible, so they have quite a following. Cape gannets, Cape fur seals, common and bottlenose dolphins, sharks, and Bryde's whales all follow this movable feast. The run coincides with the northern migration of the humpback whales, so the sea is teeming with life. Local fishing folk revel in the huge catches to be had simply by wading into the shallows with makeshift nets, and sightseers can watch for the bubbling water and attendant cloud of seabirds that signal shoals moving past.

There are boat trips aplenty to take you out for a closer look, but the real thrill is in diving the run. It's awesome just being amid all those fish, but you often are also among a thousand common dolphins. What everyone is really hoping for, though, is a "baitball"—when dolphins herd a big school of sardines into a circle, keep them there by swimming around them, and pick them off at will. Sharks almost always join in, and an acrobatic seal or two might take advantage of the free lunch. Bryde's, and even humpback, whales have been known to take a (rather large) passing bite out of the ball, and the sight of Cape gannets from underwater as they dive-bomb the fish is memorable. Of course, while you're watching this feeding frenzy, you're hovering on the edge of the food chain—ideally to stay there.

WHERE TO STAY

$ **Buccanneers Lodge and Backpackers.** Half hostel, half B&B, this very casual establishment is a shirts- and shoes-optional sort of place, and it does get quite lively. The dorms are what you'd find at any hostel, but there are also pretty chalets scattered across a wooded slope leading to the beach. Six have cooking facilities, and most have fantastic views over the lagoon and ocean. The platformed safari tents are small and basic, containing not much more than a bed and without private baths, but the privacy and views make them a good budget option. There's something happening at 4 every afternoon—a volleyball game, free sundowner cruise, or some other spur-of-the-moment activity. It's a great base from which to undertake a whole range of reasonably priced cultural tours and excursions. Breakfast is about R15–R45, lunch (usually served at the pool bar in summer) costs about R15–R50, and a hearty supper will set you back R45–R75. Children are permitted, and the self-catering cottages are family-friendly. But be warned: this is a PG-13 kind of place, as backpackers can be very casual, and the language might not be what you'd hear in church. ✉ *Cintsa West* 📭 *Box 13092, Vincent 5217* ☎ *043/734–3012* 🌐 *www.cintsa.com* *9 chalets, 5 safari tents without bath, 4 dormitories, camping* *In-room: no a/c, no phone, no TV. In-hotel: restaurant, bars, pool, beachfront, no elevator, laundry service, Internet, airport shuttle, no-smoking rooms* 💳 *MC, V.*

BULUNGULA

🟢 *295 km (183 mi) northeast of East London.*

Bulungula is a tiny community near the mouth of the Bulungula River, about a 25-km (16-mi) walk from Coffee Bay's Hole-in-the-Wall. There are no shops, no banks, and no post offices. There isn't even a decent road. The one lodge is run in partnership with the local community, making it a completely different destination for adventure travelers. This is the *real* Africa. Bulungula is a great place to just chill out on the beach, but there are also loads of great activities—all owned and run by members of the community in conjunction with the lodge. You can choose from a horseback ride, a canoe or fishing trip, an educational walk through the bush with an herbalist, a visit to a local restaurant, or a day spent with the women of the village, learning how they live. You might learn to carry water and firewood on your head, harvest wild foods and cook them for your lunch, make mud bricks, work in the fields, or weave baskets.

This is a really worthwhile destination, but it's not for everyone. But because Bulungula is such a small isolated community, crime is practically nonexistent and it is very safe.

WHERE TO STAY & EAT

Bulungula Lodge. Even though it is relatively isolated, Bulungula's one lodge is, in spirit, just an extension of the village. The fair-trade lodging is partly owned by the local community, which is not an uncommon thing on the Wild Coast. What makes it different, though, is that in contrast to what you'll find at smarter hotels, the local people are fully integrated in the running of the lodge. Accommodations are in traditional round thatched huts (rondawels) overlooking the lagoon and ocean. Furnishings are simple: a bed, a table, and a stick suspended from the roof on which to hang clothes. The ecofriendly, odor-free composting toilets and paraffin-fired hot showers are communal and situated in beautifully decorated colorful thatched buildings. Meals are served in a large lounge-cum-bar, where you can engage in a long discussion with one of the villagers or the other guests. You can use the cooking facilities, but it's far nicer to take advantage of the generous, simple, but well-cooked meals on offer. Lunches are usually a traditional dish (R15), and all meals include a good vegetarian option. Breakfast ranges from R12 to R22, and dinner costs R40. Bed linen is supplied, but you need to bring a towel and toiletries (including soap and shampoo). Babysitting is available. The lodge is inaccessible to all but 4x4s, but a shuttle is available from Mthatha and from closer destinations (where there is safe parking). Guided trips include abseiling (rappelling; R80), canoeing (R50), cultural tours (R20–R50), and horseback riding (R120). A 37-km (23-mi) guided walk to Coffee Bay via Hole-in-the-Wall costs R50 one way, and you can arrange to have your luggage transported; keep in mind that it's only for the relatively fit. You can also do the trip in reverse, from Coffee Bay to Bulungula. *Box 52913, Mthatha 5099* ☎*047/577–8900 or 083/391–5525* ⊕*www.bulungula.com* ⇌*7 rooms without bath, 2 dormitories,*

Fodor's Choice ★

camping ♿ *In-room: no a/c, no phone, no TV. In-hotel: restaurant, bar, beachfront, laundry service, airport shuttle* ▭*No credit cards.*

COFFEE BAY

★ ➓ *295 km (183 mi) northeast of East London.*

The village of Coffee Bay is a bit run-down, but the beaches and the scenery are great. (The surf is fantastic, but don't head out alone if you don't know what you're doing.) What makes Coffee Bay stand out from all the other lovely destinations, though, is its proximity—only 9 km (5½ mi)—to the spectacular **Hole-in-the-Wall,** a natural sea arch through a solid rock island. You can go here on a rather adventurous road from Coffee Bay, and it's included on almost any tour of the Wild Coast. The Xhosa name, Esikaleni, means "place of the water people," and it is believed to be a gateway to the world of our ancestors. If you try swimming through it in rough seas, it certainly will be, but some intrepid souls have made it on calm (very calm) days.

You can do a fabulous 37-km (23-mi) hike from Coffee Bay to Bulungula (or vice versa) via Hole-in-the-Wall, across the cliff tops, and along the beach. It's best to take a guide, who can cut about two or three hours from the journey by taking a shortcut through rolling hills dotted with thatched huts. Arrange for a guide through Bulungula Lodge (⇨*above*), where you should plan to overnight at the end of your hike; the lodge can transport your luggage while you walk. The cost for the guide and luggage transfer is R70 (R50 going from Bulungula to Coffee Bay).

WHERE TO STAY & EAT

★ $$–$$$ ✕▥ **Ocean View Hotel in Coffee Bay.** This old Wild Coast hotel is light and bright, with white walls and blue fabrics with marine motifs. Some rooms overlook the sea. A resident tour operator can arrange anything from day walks and gentle cruises to abseiling, quad biking, and canoeing. Activity prices range from R100 for a full day of hiking or abseiling (including lunch) to R300 for a two-hour quad-bike tour. Like all Wild Coast resorts, it's child-friendly. The food ($$) is good, well cooked, and unpretentious—just keep in mind that lobster and other seafood are considered unpretentious in this region, and you may well find wild coastal oysters offered as bar snacks. Nonguests may book for dinner if the hotel is not full (R90 for a three-course set menu). Like some other Wild Coast properties, this hotel is partly owned by the local community. ✉*Main Beach, Coffee Bay* ✍*Box 566, Umtate 5100* ☎*047/575–2005 or 047/575–2006* ⊕*www.oceanview.co.za* ⇖*30 rooms* ♿ *In-room: no a/c, no phone, safe, no TV. In-hotel: restaurant, bar, pool, beachfront, no elevator, children's programs (ages 3–12), laundry service, Internet* ▭*AE, DC, MC, V* ⏺*MAP.*

¢–$ ▥ **Coffee Shack on the Beach.** The main (but certainly not the only) attraction of this vibey backpackers' lodge is the free surfing lessons—possibly from former world pro-am surfing champion Dave Malherbe, who has moved here so he can surf the perfect wave whenever he wants—at least when he isn't running one of the better backpackers' lodges on the coast. You need to book pretty far ahead to secure the room with the private bathroom, or you may end up jostling for shower space or even sleeping in a dorm. As at all backpacker lodges, you don't need to be young to stay here, but an open mind and a sense of fun are prerequisites. Guided trips include abseiling (R85), canoeing (R80), cultural tours (R65), and hikes (R50). ⌂ *Box 54, Mthatha 5100* ☎*047/575–2048* ⊕*www.coffeeshack.co.za* ⇆*7 rooms, 1 with bath; 6 dormitories; 15 campsites* ⌂*In-room: no a/c, no TV. In-hotel: beachfront, laundry service, airport shuttle, Internet* ▭*AE, DC, MC, V.*

OFF THE BEATEN PATH

★

The **Nelson Mandela Museum** stands as evidence of the love and respect that this awesome statesman has inspired in people all over the world, from rural schoolchildren to royalty. The many gifts Mandela has received through his life say more about the givers than the receiver, and the Long Walk to Freedom display shows the political and personal journey of this beloved politician. In addition to the building in Mthatha, there are two other sites. **Qunu,** where Mandela spent his childhood and where he now has his permanent residence, is on the N2, 32 km (20 mi) south of Mthatha; you can see his home, a rather ordinary brick house, from the highway. A beautifully designed museum combines natural stone and unfinished wattle branches to create an interesting pattern of light and shade that complements the black-and-white photographs documenting Mandela's early life and his period of activism and incarceration. There's also a reconstruction of his prison cell on Robben Island. Huge glass windows overlook the fields where Madiba (an affectionate sobriquet for Mandela) herded cattle as a boy, and his present house can be seen in the distance. **Mvezo** was the birthplace of Mandela. Although the foundations of the house in which Mandela was born are visible and there is a small open-air museum, Mvezo is more a place of pilgrimage than a museum (since there isn't very much to see here). It's best to visit Mvezo as part of a tour—both because it's hard to find and because you'll get much more out of it with a knowledgeable guide—which you can arrange through the museum; you can also get directions from the museum in Mthatha if you want to go on your own. At this writing, the road to Mvezo was in a state of disrepair, making it suitable only for 4x4s. ⊠*Owen St. and Nelson Mandela Dr. (N2), Mthatha* ☎*047/532–5110* ⊕*www.mandela-museum.org.za* ▭*Free* ⊙*Weekdays 9–4, Sat. 9–noon.*

EASTERN CAPE ESSENTIALS

TRANSPORTATION

BY AIR

Port Elizabeth (PLZ) and East London (ELS) airports, which are both small and easy to navigate, are served daily by South African Airways and SA Airlink. SA Airlink also flies between the tiny airport at Mthatha (UTT)—for travel to the Wild Coast—and Johannesburg. Though East London and PE have all the expected facilities, Mthatha doesn't; it's a really small airport.

Airports **East London Airport** (☎043/706–0306 ⊕ www.acsa.co.za). **Mthatha Matanzima Airport** (☎047/536–0023). **Port Elizabeth Airport** (☎041/507–7319 ⊕ www.acsa.co.za).

Airlines **SA Airlink** (☎0861/359–722 ⊕ www.saairlink.co.za). **South African Airways** (☎0861/359–722 ⊕ www.flysaa.com).

BY BUS

Greyhound and Intercape Mainliner have pretty reliable and reasonably priced bus services, but the distances are long. Always arrange a shuttle ahead of time, as bus stations are not great places to hang around. If you are concerned about your budget, consider saving money by staying at a backpackers' lodge and spending a bit more on the Baz Bus (which travels door-to-door at these lodges); an added benefit is that you won't have to wander around town with your luggage, which is not a good idea.

Bus Lines **Baz Bus** (☎021/439–2323 ⊕ www.bazbus.com). **Greyhound** (☎011/276–8500 ⊕ www.greyhound.co.za). **Intercape Mainliner** (☎021/380–4400 ⊕ www.intercape.co.za).

BY CAR

It's easiest and best to tour this region by car. The major rental agencies have offices at all the airports and the downtown sections of bigger cities like East London and PE. They all provide one-way rentals. Roads are generally in good shape, but there's a distinct difference in road conditions east and west of Grahamstown. To the west (that is, on the PE side) roads are wide, often dual lane, and well maintained. East of Grahamstown the N2 is a single-lane road with no shoulders, few fences, and quite a few potholes. Northeast of East London there are long sections of road that are relatively broad and well maintained, but they are all unfenced—meaning livestock can wander onto the road—and some stretches have potholes.

Once off the N2 in the Transkei, the roads are very potholed indeed, and the livestock problem is much more serious, as cattle, dogs, horses, and sheep cross streets at will. On these secondary roads, aim for an average speed of 40 kph–50 kph (25 mph–30 mph). It's not uncommon to find spectacularly unroadworthy vehicles in this area, so be alert and don't drive here at night. You will need to travel on unpaved roads to get to some game lodges and to Bulungula and Alicedale.

Rental Companies **Avis** (☎043/736–1344 in East London, 046/622–2235 in Grahamstown, 041/363–3014 in PE, 047/536–0066 in Mthatha ⊕ www.avis.co.za). **Budget** (☎043/736–1084 in East London, 041/581–4242 in PE, 047/536–0917 in Mthatha ⊕ www.budget.co.za). **Europcar** (☎043/736–3092 in East London, 041/581–1547 in PE ⊕ www.europcar.com). **Hertz** (☎043/736–2116 in East London, 041/508–6600 in PE ⊕ www.hertz.co.za).

CONTACTS & RESOURCES

EMERGENCIES

In case of an emergency, call the general-emergencies number. For vehicle breakdown, call your car-rental company. If your car is not a rental, call the Automobile Association (AA). If you need an emergency pharmacist, ask at your hotel. For emergencies at sea, call the National Sea Rescue Institute (NSRI).

Emergency Services **Automobile Association** (☎ *083/84322*). **General Emergencies** (☎ *10111 from landline, 112 from mobile phone*). **National Sea Rescue Institute** (✉ *East London* ☎ *043/700–2100, 043/700–2142, or 082/990–5972* ✉ *Port Elizabeth* ☎ *041/507–3911, 041/507–2043, or 082/802–3014*).

Hospitals **Greenacres Hospital** (✉ *Rochelle and Cape Rds., Greenacres, Port Elizabeth* ☎ *041/390–7000*). **St. Dominic's Hospital** (✉ *45 St. Mark's Rd., Southernwood, East London* ☎ *043/743–4303*).

Pharmacies **Berea Pharmacy** (✉ *31 Pearce St., Berea, East London* ☎ *043/721–1300*). **Mount Road Pharmacy** (✉ *559 Govan Mbeki Ave., Port Elizabeth* ☎ *041/484–3838*). **RET Butler Pharmacy** (✉ *Bathurst St., Grahamstown* ☎ *082/568–8784*).

MAIL & INTERNET

There are post offices in all the towns except for the really small ones, such as Coffee Bay. In most of the bigger towns you will also find Postnets (⊕ *www.postnet.co.za*)—a franchise that provides business, mail, parcel, and courier services—in shopping malls and other convenient places. There are Internet cafés all over, and most accommodations have Internet facilities.

Durban & KwaZulu-Natal

WORD OF MOUTH

"We drove through Hluhluwe-Umfolozi and it was fabulous. We saw elephants, giraffe, zebra, wart-hogs, white rhino, nyala, wildebeest, baboons and lots of birds and lovely scenery up close to the car."

—stamiya

Updated by
Tara Turkington
and Kate
Turkington

KWAZULU-NATAL IS A PREMIER VACATION area for South Africans, though it's a comparatively small province. Here lie the highest and most beautiful mountains in southern Africa (the Drakensberg), some of the finest game reserves, and a landscape studded with memorials commemorating the great battles between Briton, Boer, and Zulu. The main draws, though, are the subtropical climate and the warm waters of the Indian Ocean. In fact, the entire 480-km (300-mi) coastline, from the Wild Coast in the south to the border with Mozambique in the north, is essentially one long beach, attracting hordes of swimmers, surfers, and anglers.

KwaZulu-Natal's two-part moniker is just one of the many changes introduced since the 1994 democratic elections. Previously the province was known simply as Natal (Portuguese for "Christmas"), a name bestowed by explorer Vasco da Gama, who sighted the coastline on Christmas Day, 1497. KwaZulu, "the place of the Zulu," was one of the nominally independent homelands created by the Nationalist government (1948–94). The Nationalist Party's strategy entailed declaring most of the country the province of whites, while carving out a tiny portion of the least arable and desirable land as "homelands" for black "tribes" (a term now politically incorrect). Black South Africans were then relegated to these homelands (which often had never been their homes previously), where they had to live except when they were working in the "white" areas, such as the cities. KwaZulu was carved out of the old Natal Province, but with the arrival of democratic South Africa the two were merged to form KwaZulu-Natal.

KwaZulu-Natal has long been politically volatile. In the run-up to the 1994 elections, there were certain "no-go" areas and many people were killed by rivals from opposing sides. Today, however, political violence is the exception rather than the rule.

During the years of white rule, parts of Natal were seen as a bastion of English-speaking South Africans and the province was known, rather derogatorily by outsiders, as the "Last British Outpost." There are still relatively few whites here who speak Afrikaans, and Zulu is the lingua franca of black KwaZulu-Natalians. Natal's first white settlers—a party of British officers seeking trade with the Zulu in ivory—established themselves in Port Natal (now Durban) in 1824. The colony of Natal was formally annexed by the British in 1843. Cities like Durban and Pietermaritzburg present strong reminders of the colonial past in their Victorian architecture and public monuments. The province's huge Indian population is another reminder of Britain's imperial legacy. In the 1860s the British brought thousands of Indians to South Africa to work as indentured laborers cutting sugarcane, which grows abundantly on the coastal hills. Today the Indian population of Durban alone numbers about 1 million of the city's total 3.2 million or so people, and it plays a major part in the economic, political, and cultural life of the province.

SWAZILAND

MOZAMBIQUE

KwaZulu–
Natal

Maputaland
Coastal
Reserve
76

N2

Phongola

Jozini

Itala
Game
Reserve
74

Phongola
Game
Reserve
75

Phongola

Louwsburg

Mkuze

ELEPHANT COAST

Amazulu
Private
Game
Reserve
73

Mkuze
Game
Reserve
72

Phinda
Private
Game
Reserve
71

R66

Nongoma

Msunduze

Black Umfolozi

70

Hluhluwe

ZULULAND

Thanda Private
Game Reserve

N2

69 Greater St. Lucia
Wetland Park

Ulundi

68

Cape Vidal

62

Hluhluwe-Umfolozi
Game Reserve

St. Lucia

White Umfolozi

Mtubatuba

2

61 Melmoth

Ngwelezana

R34

Empangeni

♦Shakaland

Richards Bay

60 Eshowe

Ezikhawini

Gingindlovu

N2

DOLPHIN COAST

Dukuza

INDIAN OCEAN

0   30 miles

0   30 kilometers

ORIENTATION & PLANNING

ORIENTATION

For tourism purposes, KwaZulu-Natal can generally be divided into eight areas: Durban (including the outlying Valley of a Thousand Hills), the Dolphin (also called North) Coast, the South Coast, Pietermaritzburg and the Midlands, the Drakensberg, Zululand, the Battlefields, and the Elephant Coast. But for our book, we've divided the chapter up into six sections: Durban (including the Valley of a Thousand Hills, the Dolphin Coast, and the South Coast); Pietermaritzburg and the KwaZulu-Natal Midlands; the Drakensberg; Zululand & the Battlefields; the Elephant Coast, which stretches in a narrow strip north along the coast from the Greater St. Lucia Wetland Park; and private game reserves.

DURBAN

Durban, South Africa's third-largest city, is Africa's busiest port (chiefly cargo). It's from here that many of South Africa's exports—from sugar to cars—set sail, and it's here that many of the country's imports arrive. Durban's chief appeal to tourists is its long strip of high-rise hotels and its popular promenade—known as the Golden Mile (though it's actually several miles long)—fronting its beaches. To find beaches unmarred by commercial development, you need to travel north to Zululand, where much of the coastline is protected. In addition, the entire area is becoming more and more tourist friendly.

VALLEY OF A THOUSAND HILLS
Travel 20 minutes northwest of bustling downtown Durban and you'll be in the rural Valley of a Thousand Hills, so called because of the hundreds of steep valleys that cut into the rolling countryside. This region is home not only to Zulus but also to many artists, who have shops and studios here. On weekends many Durbanites drive out into the country to enjoy the region's quaint restaurants, hotels, and rural activities.

DOLPHIN COAST
As you head north of Durban along the coast, you will pass through small coastal villages, sugarcane fields, and commercial forestry plantations. This coastal strip from Zimbali (south of Ballito) north to Zinkwazi Beach (about an hour's drive from Durban) is the Dolphin Coast, a popular local vacation spot that gets extremely busy during school and public holidays. The many beaches here are protected by shark nets and lifeguards, making them safe for swimming.

SOUTH COAST
Stretching south of Durban for 160 km (100 mi) or so to Port Edward is the similarly popular South Coast, also known as the Hibiscus Coast, which spans vacation towns like Scottburgh, Margate, and Ramsgate, and boasts terrific beaches that have garnered Blue Flag status (awarded for excellence in safety and security, environmental management, and water quality).

PIETERMARITZBURG AND THE KWAZULU-NATAL MIDLANDS

Nestled among the Midlands hills, Pietermaritzburg, often abbreviated to Maritzburg or PMB, is the current capital of KwaZulu-Natal. It's a pleasant town, with wide tree-lined streets and a temperate climate that escapes the worst of the coastal heat and humidity.

> **WARNING**
>
> It is essential that visitors to the northern parts of the province, including Zululand, take antimalarial drugs, particularly during the wet summer months.

Moving inland takes you to the KwaZulu-Natal Midlands, just off the N3 between Durban and Johannesburg. Here racehorse and dairy farms stud rolling green hills and lush pastures that are reminiscent of England. The Midlands Meander (a series of routes set up by the local tourism board) is a great way to experience the area's farms and crafts shops.

THE DRAKENSBERG

Just a couple of hours northwest of Durban—and also easily accessible from the N3—are the Drakensberg Mountains (aka the Berg), a spectacular wilderness national park offering tremendous hiking amid some of the country's most spectacular unspoiled scenery. Restaurants and hotels catering to all tastes are spread along the base of the range. Sharing the lowlands areas on the approach to the Drakensberg are white farmers, some of whose families settled in the area more than 100 years ago, and a number of sprawling villages and subsistence farms populated by Zulu people.

ZULULAND & THE BATTLEFIELDS

Zululand the region north of the Tugela River and south of Swaziland and Mozambique, is the traditional home of the Zulu people. Prominent towns (though these are all relatively small) in this region are the industrial towns of Empangeni and Richards Bay, Eshowe, Pongola, and Ulundi. The farther north you go, the less populated and more rural the area becomes, with traditional Zulu huts and herds of long-horned brown-and-white and black-and-white Nguni cattle tended by boys or young men scattering over the hills.

The Battlefields (Anglo-Zulu and Anglo-Boer) are inland, to the north of the Midlands and northeast of the Drakensberg. The towns dotted among the Zululand battlefields tend to be a little ugly and dusty during the dry winter months, but this is an area to visit more for its historic than its scenic value.

THE ELEPHANT COAST

In the province's northeast corner, this area is home to the Hluhluwe-Umfolozi, Ndumo, Tembe Elephant Park and Mkuze game reserves, the Greater St. Lucia Wetland Park, and Kosi Bay.

TOP REASONS TO VISIT

Beautiful Beaches Durban's beaches are some of the world's safest and most beautiful. The long, sandy beaches and inviting water temperatures extend all the way up the Dolphin (North) Coast and beyond, as well as south from Durban, down the Hibiscus Coast and into the Eastern Cape.

Dramatic Scenery The magnificent mountainscapes, sparkling air, forested streams, pristine waterfalls, soaring birds, and hiking opportunites are guaranteed to enthrall you, as will the rock paintings in the caves—one of the major reasons for the declaration of the Drakensberg as a World Heritage Site.

Reliving History Explore the battlefields of the Anglo-Zulu and Anglo-Boer wars making sure you visit the legendary sites of Isandlwana, Rorke's Drift, and Blood River.

Game-Viewing Although smaller than Kruger, the easily accessible Hluhluwe-Umfolozi Game Reserve, Mkuze, Ndumo, Tembe Elephant Park, Itala, and Pongola game reserves are all teeming with game (including the Big Five).

A Vibrant City Durban, Africa's busiest port, has a distinct feel, flavored by its diverse populations. In the city center, you'll find mosques, temples, and churches. Take a rickshaw ride along the beachfront after browsing for Zulu beadwork, or try a local "bunny chow" (curry inside a hollowed-out loaf of bread).

PRIVATE GAME RESERVES & LODGES

KwaZulu-Natal's best private lodges lie in northern Zululand and Maputaland, a remote region close to Mozambique. Unfortunately, most of the lodges we list do not offer the Big Five. But what they do offer is proximity to each other and to Hluhluwe-Umfolozi Game Reserve, which allows you to put together a bush experience that delivers the Big Five, superb bird-watching, and amazing beaches.

PLANNING

The best time to tour KwaZulu-Natal is early autumn through winter and into spring (April to October), with the coast particularly pleasant in winter—you'll see people swimming. April is a lovely time to visit the city (avoid Easter weekend if you can), though most of this time is pleasant enough, with warm air and sea temperatures.

Game-viewing is also better during winter (late June, July, and August), when the grass is shorter, many trees have lost their leaves, and animals tend to congregate around water holes. Northern parts of the province are dry and dusty in winter, but the frosty mornings, crisp late afternoons, and reduced risk of malaria make up for it. Cold weather doesn't deter thousands of folk-music lovers from congregating at the annual folk-music festival held at Splashy-Fen Farm (⊕ *www.splashyfen.co.za*), in the Drakensberg. Local and international folk musicians perform during this four-day celebration, which usually occurs close to Easter.

The height of summer (December and January) brings heat, humidity, higher prices, and crowds, who pour into "Durbs," as it's fondly known, by the millions. Locals know never to brave the beach on holidays or over the Christmas season except for an hour or two from 6 AM—one of the nicest times there. Some facilities in the Zululand game reserves close in summer because of the extreme and unpleasantly high temperatures.

TAKE IT ALL IN

2 Days: If you have just two days, spend it in Durban. Start with an early morning walk along the Golden Mile to watch the surfers. ⚠ **Always leave jewelry and valuables in your hotel safe.** Spend three or four hours on a guided walking tour of the Indian District or downtown Durban. Tours (reservations are a must) leave from the Tourist Junction (Old Station Building). Wilson's Wharf, which overlooks the Durban harbor, or Morningside's trendy Florida Road offer great options for lunch or dinner. If you dine on Florida Road, make sure you stop by the African Craft Market for beautiful Zulu beadwork, baskets, prints, and other crafts and curios. You can also spend the afternoon strolling around Mitchell Park, which is known for its colorful flowerbeds at the top of Florida Road (also be sure to visit the small zoo here). On your second day, visit the aquarium at uShaka Marine World, one of the largest and best in the world, perhaps lunching on seafood at Cargo Hold, adjacent to the shark tank. In the afternoon, visit the Natal Sharks Board for a show and fascinating shark dissection—yes, they actually do a dissection (Tuesday, Wednesday, Friday, and Sunday only). You could also visit the Umgeni River Bird Park whose live bird shows are a must-see (11 and 2 daily).

5 Days: Spend at least one day in Durban (see above) before or after you explore KwaZulu-Natal following one of two options: the Drakensberg and Zululand or Zululand and the more northern section, which takes in the coastal strip and some of the northern game parks and private lodges. If you opt for the mountains, plan a day or two of hiking and walking, overnighting in one of the reserves or small establishments in the Northern or Central Drakensberg; then head toward the battlefield sites of Isandlwana, Rorke's Drift, and the Talana Museum, at Dundee. If battlefields aren't your scene, try the Southern Drakensberg, where you can make your way up the spectacular Sani Pass. Afterward, travel north and take the R103 to pick up the Midlands Meander, which stretches north all the way to Mooi River, through the tranquil Natal Midlands.

If you decide to head up the north coast, spend a night at Shakaland or Simunye Zulu Lodge to get the total Zulu cultural experience. Then schedule at least two days in Hluhluwe-Umfolozi Game Reserve or Phinda Private Game Reserve to see the game that these reserves are known for. A trip to Greater St. Lucia Wetland Park to see hippos and crocodiles in the wild is another great experience.

7–10 Days: Spend a day or two exploring Durban and then head up to Zululand to start your grand loop. Visit Greater St. Lucia Wetland

Park on your way to the incredible wildlife of Hluhluwe-Umfolozi Game Reserve or Phinda Private Game Reserve. A three-day trail in the wilderness of Umfolozi could be the high point of your trip. For something more sedate, spend three days at Rocktail Bay Lodge in the Maputaland Coastal Reserve, close to the Mozambique border; it's especially interesting during turtle-breeding season, from November to early March. Another distant park near the edge of the province is the delightful, less-visited Itala Game Reserve. On your way back to Durban, drive through the battlefields.

EAT RIGHT, SLEEP WELL

Durban's dining public is fickle by nature, and restaurants tend to change hands fairly often. But don't be discouraged, because Durban offers some superb dining options, provided you eat to its strengths. Thanks to a huge Indian population, it has some of the best curry restaurants in the country, and the city's seaside location allows for the freshest seafood, especially prawns from the Mozambique coast.

Durbanites eat lunch and dinner relatively early, because they're early risers, particularly in summer, when it's light soon after 4. They're also generally casual dressers—you'll rarely need a jacket and tie, and jeans are rarely frowned upon.

Many of Durban's main hotels lie along the Golden Mile, Durban's beachfront. Southern Sun, the chain that operates Sun and Holiday Inn hotels in South Africa, has had a virtual monopoly on Durban accommodations, but this is changing as many outstanding boutique hotels and B&Bs open.

If you're staying in Drakensberg you'll find expensive hotels, lodges, and guesthouses, campgrounds, self-catering (with cooking facilities) cottages, and bed-and-breakfasts. The older Berg resorts tend to be family-oriented establishments that encourage guests to participate in outdoor activities and sports. Not to be left out, many area residents have opened B&Bs, which range from the warm and welcoming to the just plain mediocre. And speaking of quaint, many Midlands lodgings can be described with that adjective.

In northern Zululand and Maputaland, game reserves and lodges— both publicly and privately owned and managed—are smaller than what you'd find in Mpumalanga, but offer delightful game-viewing experiences. Many are all-inclusive (or nearly so), though some have self-catering options.

■ TIP➔ Prices, especially along the coast, tend to rise with the summer heat.

WHAT IT COSTS IN SOUTH AFRICAN RAND					
	¢	$	$$	$$$	$$$$
RESTAURANTS	under R50	R50–R75	R75–R100	R100–R125	over R125
LODGING	under R500	R500–R1,000	R1,000–R2,000	R2,000–R3,000	over R3,000
FULL-SERVICE SAFARI LODGING	under R2,000	R2,000–R5,000	R5,000–R8,000	R8,000–R12,000	over R12,000

Restaurant prices are per person for a main course at dinner, a main course equivalent, or a prix-fixe meal. Hotel and lodging prices are for a standard double room in high season, including 12.5% tax.

DURBAN

Durban has the pulse, the look, and the complex face of Africa. It may have something to do with the summer heat, a clinging sauna that soaks you with sweat in minutes. You don't need to take a township tour here to see the *new* South Africa. Hang out in Farewell Square in the city center (while hanging on to your valuables carefully) and you'll rub shoulders with just about every nationality. Wander into the Indian District or drive through the Warwick Triangle—an area away from the sea around Warwick Road—and the pulsating city rises up to meet you. Traditional healers tout animal organs, vegetable and spice vendors crowd the sidewalks, and minibus taxis hoot incessantly as they trawl for business. It is by turns colorful, stimulating, and hypnotic.

It's also a place steeped in history and culture. Gandhi lived and practiced law here, and Winston Churchill visited as a young man. It's home to the largest number of Indians outside India; the massive Indian townships of Phoenix and Chatsworth stand as testimony to the harsh treatment Indians received during apartheid, though now thousands of Indians are professionals and businesspeople in Durban.

By no means should you plan an entire vacation around Durban, because there is so much more to see beyond the city. Nevertheless, it's definitely worth a stopover. To get the most from a city visit, get ready to explore its five sections: the city center around Francis Farewell Square down to the bay front; the Indian District; the Beachfront; Umhlanga, to the north, which is popular for its beaches, hotels, and mall; and outlying attractions.

⚠As this book was going to press, the Durban municipality changed most of the city center's street names literally overnight, mostly to names of prominent and not-so-well-known members of the ruling African National Congress, causing a national outcry. The municipality has been forced to reconsider its actions, but at present, there has been no official decision regarding which names will be used. We have kept the old names in the book, but please be aware that new names may appear. The municipality has said, however, that even if the name changes did go through after a period of consultation, the old names would be displayed alongside the new ones for a period of one to two years.

SAFE AND
SOUND

Durban has not escaped the crime evident in every South African city. Particularly in the city center but also elsewhere, smash-and-grab thieves roam the streets, looking for bags or valuables in your car, even while you're driving, so lock any valuables in the trunk and keep your car doors locked and windows up at all times. While there's no need to be fearful, be observant wherever you go. Hire a guide to take you around the Farewell Square area and the Indian District, don't wander around the city center or outside your hotel alone at night, and keep expensive cameras and other possessions concealed. The Durban Beachfront, Umhlanga, and the outlying areas are safe to explore on your own, though you'll need a taxi or car to get between them. If you plan on taking a dip while you're at the beach, ask a neighboring beachgoer or lifeguard to keep an eye on your belongings, or put them in a locker—available between North and South beaches.

Numbers in the text correspond to numbers in the margin and on the Durban map.

CITY CENTER & THE BAYFRONT

TIMING

The center of the city can get horribly humid from December through February, so if you visit then, avoid walking too much during the midday heat. Browse the air-conditioned museums when it's hot, and save walking outside for later in the afternoon, making sure you get to the museums and galleries before they close, around 4:30.

WHAT TO SEE

★ ❽ **Bartle Arts Trust (BAT) Centre.** To some, this arts center resembles a giant flying bat when viewed from above, though this takes some stretch of the imagination. The vibrant center (though perhaps a little on the seedy side these days) is abuzz with Durban's trendy set: artists, musicians, and other hipsters. Most days—and some nights—you can watch sculptors, dancers, musicians, and painters at work, and at night the BAT comes alive with plays, music, and African film or video festivals. The center is home to several small galleries, which showcase the work of local artists. The center contains a restaurant, a coffee bar overlooking the bay, a nightspot with live music, and shops that sell an excellent selection of high-quality African crafts, fabrics, and ceramics. ⊠ *45 Maritime Pl., Small Craft Harbour, Victoria Embankment* ☎ *031/332–0468* ⊕ *www.batcentre.co.za* ✉ *Free* ⊘ *Daily 8:30–4:30.*

NEED A
BREAK?

Need a break? Walk over to the adjacent Wilson's Wharf, where you can have a cool cocktail or a meal on a deck out over the harbor at one of several restaurants ranging from high-end to pub to fast-food outlet.

❹ **City Hall.** Built in 1910 in Edwardian neo-baroque style, the hall looks as if it has been shipped straight from the United Kingdom column by column—hardly surprising, since it's an exact copy of Belfast City Hall. The main pediment carries sculptures representing Britannia, Unity, and Patriotism, and allegorical sculptures of the Arts, Music, and Literature adorn the exterior. City Hall still houses the mayor's parlor and other government offices, the Durban Art Gallery and Natural

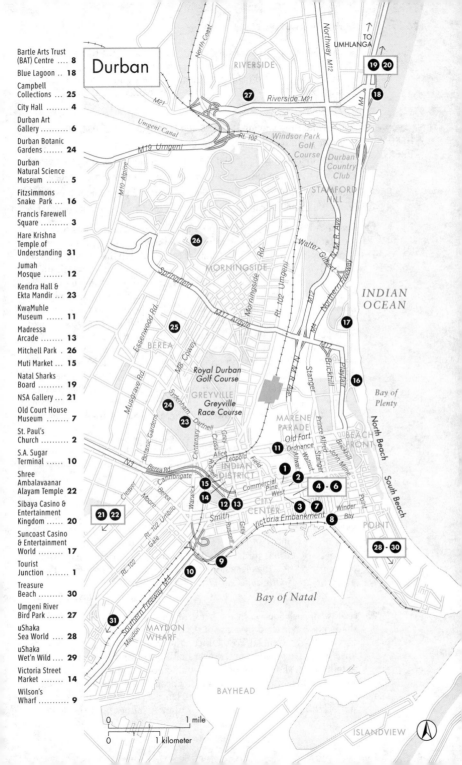

Durban

Science Museum, and the City Library. Ask the guard to let you in to see the huge theater's ornate molding and grand parterre boxes, or join an official tour run by Durban Africa. ⊠ *West and Church Sts., City Center* ☎ *031/304–4934* ⊕ *www.cityofdurban.co.za* ☞ *Free* ☉ *Daily 8:30–3:30.*

NEED A BREAK?.

The Royal Coffee Shoppe (⊠ *267 Smith St., City Center* ☎ *031/304–0331*), in the Royal Hotel, is a popular meeting place for Durban society and pre- and post-theater crowds. Crystal chandeliers, etched glass, formally dressed staff, and live piano music in the nearby lounge at lunchtime create a rich atmosphere of old-time colonial Durban. The café serves light breakfasts and lunch as well as coffees, teas, cakes, quiches, salads, and sandwiches.

6 **Durban Art Gallery.** The gallery presents a vibrant, contemporary mix of local, southern African, and international work, though the main focus is on work from KwaZulu-Natal. Recent exhibits have included the cultural diversity of South African handicrafts, forensic investigation, a project celebrating the paternal instinct, and a multimedia display highlighting Durban's annual events with work from Mozambique, Botswana, and Angola. Look out, too, for the traditional, patterned *hlabisa* baskets, regularly displayed at the gallery. Exhibits change every few months. The first Friday of every month is set aside for Red Eye, an initiative aimed at attracting younger audiences to the gallery. It showcases Durban's latest entertainment talent, with bands, African drummers, other musicians, and dancers performing among the exhibitions. ⊠ *City Hall, entrances in Smith and Church Sts., 2nd fl., City Center* ☎ *031/311–2264* ⊕ *www.durbanet.co.za/exhib/dag/dagmain. htm* ☞ *Free; small fee for Red Eye* ☉ *Mon.–Sat. 8:30–4 (1st Fri. of month to 10), Sun. 11–4.*

5 **Durban Natural Science Museum.** Despite its small size, this museum provides an excellent introduction to Africa's numerous wild mammals (the displays include a stuffed elephant, leopard, and smaller mammals like wild dogs and vervet monkeys), plants, birds, reptiles, and insects. It's a great place to bring the kids or to familiarize yourself with the local wildlife before heading up to the game parks in northern KwaZulu-Natal. At one popular gallery, the KwaNunu Insect Arcade, giant insect replicas adorn the wall; another, the bird gallery, showcases a variety of stuffed birds, including flamingos, ostriches, eagles, and penguins. ■ TIP→ **The museum offers Internet access at a minimal charge.** ⊠ *City Hall, Smith and Church Sts., 1st fl., City Center* ☎ *031/311– 2256* ☞ *Free* ☉ *Mon.–Sat. 8:30–4, Sun. and public holidays 11–4.*

3 **Francis Farewell Square.** In the heart of Durban, the square is a lovely shady plaza bordered by some of the city's most historic buildings, like City Hall, the Central Post Office, and the Royal Hotel. Walkways lined with stately palms and flower beds crisscross the square and lead to monuments honoring some of Natal's important historic figures. The square stands on the site of the first European encampment in Natal, established by Francis Farewell and Henry Fynn in 1824 as a trading station to purchase ivory from the Zulus. A statue representing Peace honors the Durban volunteers who died during the Second South African War (1899–1902), also known as the Boer War or Anglo-Boer War. The Cenotaph, a large stone obelisk, commemorates the South African dead from the two world wars. Apart from the historic attractions, it's an energetic, bustling part of the city center, with inexpensive street stalls selling flowers, clothes, and food for the Durban locals. You'll really feel the vibe of the city here. ⚠ **Pay attention to your valuables while walking in the square.** ✉ *Bounded by Smith, West, and Gardiner Sts. and the Church St. pedestrian mall, City Center.*

⓫ KwaMuhle Museum. Pronounced kwa-*moosh*-le (with a light *e*, as in *hen*), this small museum, housed in what used to be the notorious Department of Native Affairs, tells of Durban's apartheid history. During apartheid the department was responsible for administering the movement of black people in and out of the city, dealing with the dreaded passes that blacks had to carry at all times, and generally overseeing the oppressive laws that plagued the black population. Ironically, the name means "place of the good one," Kwa meaning "place of" and "Muhle" meaning "good one" (after J. S. Marwick, the benevolent manager of the municipal native affairs department from 1916 to 1920). Exhibits provide the often heartbreaking background on this period through old photographs and documents, replicas of passbooks, and lifelike models of people involved in the pass system, including *shebeen* (an informal bar) queens, who had to apply for permits to sell alcohol. ✉ *130 Ordnance Rd., City Center* ☎ *031/311–2223* ⊕ *www.durban.gov.za\museums\localhistory* 🎫 *Free* ⊗ *Mon.–Sat. 8:30–4, Sun. 11–4.*

❼ Old Court House Museum. This old courthouse was built in 1866, and during the Zulu War of 1879, when Durban was in danger of attack, the building's exterior was temporarily provided with holes so defenders could fire their rifles from inside it. Today it's a museum whose exhibits focus on Natal's colonial past, including a reconstruction of settler Henry Fynn's original 1824 wattle-and-daub hut, as well as simulated shopfronts of a turn-of-the-20th-century apothecary and department store. Upstairs is a display of miniature dolls, replicas of important people in Durban's history and development, including Zulu king Shaka. Local artists showcase mixed-media work at the museum. ✉ *77 Aliwal St., City Center* ☎ *031/311–2229* 🎫 *Free* ⊗ *Mon.–Sat. 8:30–4, Sun. 11–4.*

❷ St. Paul's Church. One of Durban's main Anglican churches, built in 1909 in Gothic Revival style, St. Paul's stands on the site of a previous church dating from 1847. From the outside it's not much to look at, but the interior is beautiful: notice the lovely wooden ceiling and the stained-glass chancel windows. ✉ *161 Pine St., City Center* ☎ *031/305–4666.*

❿ S. A. Sugar Terminal. Much of Durban's early economy was built on the sugar industry, and even today the hills and fields around the city and along the north and south coasts are covered with sugarcane. It's not surprising then that Durban's Sugar Terminal is the largest in southern Africa and one of the most advanced in the world. A short video presentation provides background on the sugar industry, and then you'll be taken on a walking tour of the terminal. Together, the tour and video presentation take 45 minutes. It's extraordinary to see the terminal's three enormous silos piled high to the domed ceiling with tons of raw sugar. The architectural design of the silos has been patented and used in other parts of the world. ✉ *25 Leuchars Rd., Maydon Wharf* ☎ *031/365–8100 or 031/365–8153* ✉ *R26* ☉ *Tours Mon.–Thurs. at 8:30, 10, 11:30 and 2* ☝ *Reservations essential.*

🕐 **Tourist Junction.** The city's principal tourist information outlet occupies Durban's old railway station, an attractive brick building constructed in 1894 in Flemish Revival style. The NGR above the main entrance stands for Natal Government Railways. Durban Africa, the city's tourist authority, is here, and the KwaZulu-Natal tourism authority also has a large office here, so it's a good place to pick up pamphlets and information for the city and province, and book tours or trips to any of the province's game reserves. ✉ *160 Pine St., at Soldier's Way, City Center* ☎ *031/304–4934* ☉ *Weekdays 8–5, weekends 9–2.*

🕘 **Wilson's Wharf.** Near the BAT Centre and on the edge of the harbor, this pleasant, privately developed section of waterfront is a lovely place to while away a few hours, soaking up the atmosphere, admiring the harbor view, and maybe having a meal or drink at one of the open-air restaurants on the expansive wooden deck. It's reminiscent of Cape Town's V&A Waterfront 20 years ago. In addition to restaurants and fast-food outlets, there are boat rentals and a market with 65 stalls, some selling classy local crafts, others selling cheaper trinkets from India and China. ✉ *Boatman's Rd., Maydon Wharf, Victoria Embankment* ☎ *031/307–7841* ⊕ *www.wilsonswharf.co.za* ☉ *Market daily 9–6, some restaurants daily 8:30–midnight.*

NEED A BREAK? The popular **Zack's** (✉ *Wilson's Wharf* ☎ *031/305–1677*) often hosts live music and an open mike on Monday evenings. It serves breakfast until late, as well as lunch and dinner.

INDIAN DISTRICT

TIMING   The best time of day to explore this area is in the morning. Set off before 9, when it's relatively cool. This also gives the street sellers time to set up their stalls. Their part of town can be quite grubby, and in the midday summer heat it can get unpleasantly humid.

WHAT TO SEE

🕛 **Jumah Mosque.** Built in 1927 in a style that combines Islamic and colonial features, this is the largest mosque in the southern hemisphere. Its colonnaded verandas, gold-domed minaret, and turrets give the surrounding streets much of their character. Tours (the only way to visit) are free and can be arranged through the Islamic Propagation Center, in a room at the entrance of the mosque, or through the Durban Africa offices at Tourist Junction. If you plan to go inside, dress modestly, as in most mosques around the world. Women should bring scarves to cover their heads out of courtesy, wear skirts below the knees, and cover

CLOSE UP

Bunny Chow

Contrary to what you might think, bunny chow is not about lettuce and carrots. This Durban specialty, prevalent in the Indian District, is a hollowed-out loaf of bread traditionally filled with bean curry, although mutton and sometimes beef and chicken are also used. The dish was popularized in the 1940s, during apartheid, when blacks were prohibited from entering Kapitan's Restaurant, in the city center, where traditional Indian beans in *roti* (pancakelike bread) were sold. The manager, known fondly as Bhanya, started offering takeout on the pavement, but the rotis often fell apart. So he started using a hollowed-out quarter loaf of bread as a

small pot for the beans, and the soft bread was used to soak up the gravy. "Bhanya's chow" became bunny chow, and meat was soon added as filling.

Good bunnies can be found at several Indian District eateries. **Patel Vegetarian Refreshment** (⊠ *Rama House, 202 Grey St.* ☎ *031/306–1774*), founded in 1912, has built a family legacy of good traditional food. **Victory Lounge** (⊠ *Grey and Victoria Sts.* ☎ *031/306–1906*) puts meat in its bunny chow and is usually very busy. In a quieter part of town, the vegetarian **Little Gujarat** (⊠ *43 Prince Edward St.* ☎ *031/305–3148*) has simple wooden decor.

5

their shoulders. Men should not wear shorts. A good idea is to keep a *kikoi* (a lightweight African sarong readily available in local markets) in your bag to use as a skirt or scarf. Men can use them, too, to cover bare legs. You'll have to take off your shoes as you enter, so wear socks if you don't want to go barefoot. No tours are offered during Islamic holidays, including Ramadan, which varies but lasts a whole month in the latter part of the year. ⊠ *Grey and Queen Sts.* ☎ *031/306–0026* 🖾 *Free* ☉ *Weekdays 9–4:30.*

⓫ **Madressa Arcade.** The thoroughfare has a Kiplingesque quality, recalling the bazaars of the East. Built in 1927, it's little more than a narrow, winding alley perfumed by spices and thronged with traders. You can buy everything from plastic trinkets to household utensils and recordings of Indian music. Bursts of color—from bright yellow material to dark red spices—create a refreshing and photogenic sight. You can buy striking costume jewelry that would cost three times more at major shopping centers, but be wary of pickpockets while browsing through the stores. ⊠ *Entrances on Queen and Cathedral Sts.* ☉ *Daily 9–5.*

⓯ **Muti Market.** For a uniquely African experience, hire a guide through Durban Africa at Tourist Junction to take you to southern Africa's largest and most extensive *muti* (traditional medicine, pronounced moo-tee) market. The market also serves as a distinctive traditional-medicine facility, where *sangomas* (traditional healers) offer consultations to locals in a bustling, urban atmosphere. If you're feeling bold, you might wish to consult a sangoma on matters of health, wealth, or personal problems. ⚠ **Don't go without a guide.** ⊠ *Warwick Junction* ☎ *No phone* ☉ *Weekdays 8–6, Sat. 8–1.*

★ ⑭ **Victoria Street Market.** Masses of enormous fish and prawns lie tightly packed on beds of ice while vendors competing for your attention shout their respective prices. In the meat section, goat and sheep heads are stacked into neat piles, and butchers slice and dice every cut of meat imaginable. The noise is deafening. The place pulsates with life, and even if you have no kitchen in which to cook, it's tough to resist joining the fray. In an adjacent building—where all the tour buses pull up— you'll discover a number of curio shops whose proprietors are willing to bargain over wood and stone carvings, beadwork, and basketry. You'll also find shops selling spices, recordings of African music, and Indian fabrics. The current structures stand on the site of an original, much-loved market, a ramshackle collection of wooden shacks that burned down during the years of Nationalist rule. ⚠**Watch your belongings closely.** ⊠*Queen and Russell Sts.* ☎*031/306–4021* ☉*Weekdays 8–5, weekends 10–2.*

BEACHFRONT

Either you will hate the Durban Beachfront for its commercial glitz, or you will love it for its endless activity. It extends for about 12 km (7½ mi) from South Beach, at the base of Durban Point, all the way past North Beach and the Suncoast Casino to Blue Lagoon, on the southern bank of the Umgeni River. The section of beachfront between South Beach and the Suncoast Casino is particularly safe, as police patrol often, though don't walk there late at night. It's lovely to take a stroll along here early or late in the day, when it's less busy. Walk out onto one of the many piers and watch surfers tackling Durban's famous waves. Of any place in Durban, the Beachfront most defines the city.

TIMING Depending on the weather, parts of the Beachfront can be quite busy, especially on weekends. There is always something to see, even in the early mornings, when people come to surf or jog before going to work. Head off early, but try to time your excursion so that you visit the snake park during feeding times or when there is a demonstration.

WHAT TO SEE

⑱ **Blue Lagoon.** About 3 km (2 mi) north of Suncoast, Durban's Umgeni River flows out to sea at the legendary Blue Lagoon, and on weekends local Indian families in particular gather for picnics and traditional South African *braais* (barbecues). The mood is often festive; cricket games and volleyball matches abound, and music plays on car stereos. There's also a minigolf course for those who want to engage in a quieter activity. ⊠*Snell Parade* ☎*No phone* ⊠*Free* ☉*24 hrs.*

☁ ⑯ **Fitzsimons Snake Park.** This small zoo houses a slithery collection of snakes, crocodiles, and other reptiles from around the world. Live snake demonstrations are held in a small amphitheater; on weekends these shows are followed by a feeding. There is also a snake breeding center and rehabilitation lab. ⊠*240a Lower Marine Parade, North Beach* ☎*073/156–9606* ⊠*R25* ☉*Weekdays 9–4:30, weekends 9–5; snake demonstrations daily at 10, 11:30, 1, 2:30, and 3:30; crocodile feedings Wed. and Sat. at 2.*

🕛 **⑰** **Suncoast Casino & Entertainment World.** Part of the rejuvenation of Durban's Golden Mile, this casino is done in the art-deco style for which Durban is famous. Colorful lights make it a nighttime landmark, but it's established itself as a daytime hot spot as well. There are deck chairs beneath umbrellas on a grassy sundeck, and a pretty beach. A paved walkway dotted with benches is a pleasant place to sit and watch cyclists, rollerbladers, and joggers. There's often a band playing directly in front of the complex on weekends, which you can listen to from the stairs. ✉ *20 Suncoast Blvd.* ☎ *031/328–3000* ⊕ *www.suncoastcasino. co.za* 🌐 *Pedestrians free, cars R5, sundeck R5* ⏱ *24 hrs.*

NEED A BREAK? Of the 20 or so restaurants, fast-food outlets, and coffee shops at Suncoast Casino, two are good for a respite. The **Mugg & Bean** (☎ *031/368–1848*), a popular chain, is open 24 hours a day near the west entrance. Besides excellent coffee, it turns out huge, good-value servings, from chocolate cake to well-roasted beef. Sit inside or on the terrace, with its beautiful view of the ships on their way to the harbor. You can choose from 39 flavors of smooth ice cream at **Mozart's** (☎ *031/332–9833*), including mint chocolate chip and blueberry.

UMHLANGA

Also known as Umhlanga Rocks, this used to be a small vacation town, but Durban's northward sprawl has incorporated it into a popular and upscale residential and business suburb, much like Sandton is to downtown Johannesburg. It's location, just 15 km (9 mi) from the city center along the M4 (Northern Freeway), makes it's close enough for those staying in the city center to come for a meal or a stroll along the promenade. To the north are the nicest sea views; to the south is Umhlanga's lighthouse. Umhlanga remains a popular vacation destination and boasts many of Durban's top hotels.

WHAT TO SEE

🕛 ★ **⑲** **Natal Sharks Board.** Most of the popular bathing beaches in KwaZulu-Natal are protected by shark nets maintained by this shark-research institute, the world's foremost. Each day, weather permitting, crews in ski boats check the nets, releasing healthy sharks back into the ocean and bringing dead ones back to the institute, where they are dissected and studied. One-hour tours are offered, including a shark dissection (sharks' stomachs have included such surprising objects as a boot, a tin can, and a car license plate!) and an enjoyable and fascinating audiovisual presentation on sharks and shark nets. An exhibit area and good curio shop are also here. You can also join the early morning trip to watch the staff service the shark nets off Durban's Golden Mile. Depending on the season, you will more than likely see dolphins and whales close at hand. Booking is essential for trips to the shark nets, and a minimum of six people is required; no one under six years of age is allowed. ■ TIP→ Book well in advance for this, it may turn out to be a highlight of your trip. ✉ *1a Herrwood Dr.* ☎ *031/566–0400* ⊕ *www.*

shark.co.za 🖂*Show R25, boat trips R200* ⊙*Trips to shark nets, daily 6:30–8:30* AM. *Shark show Tues., Wed., and Fri. 9 and 2, Sun. at 2.*

㉚ Sibaya Casino & Entertainment Kingdom. Opened in 2004, Sibaya is expansive—in size, decor, and number of activities—but is worth seeing for its grandiose architecture and decor, all styled along a Zulu theme. The buildings themselves, for example, echo a giant and opulent Zulu *kraal* (traditional village). Huge bronze statues of Zulu warriors and buffalos at the entrance provide a truly African welcome. Wherever you are at Sibaya, all 119 acres of it, a breathtaking view of the ocean is only a window or a balcony away. As you might expect, there are plenty of dining options. A 36-room, five-star hotel opened here in 2006. It's quite a way out of town, north of Umhlanga and about halfway between the city center and Ballito. 🖂*1 Sibaya Dr.* ☎*031/580–5000 or 0860/742–292* ⊕*www.sibaya.co.za* 🖂*Free.*

OUTLYING ATTRACTIONS

Directly west of the city center is Glenwood, an old leafy suburb with wide streets, big homes, the NSA gallery, and some pleasant new restaurants. Farther west, over the ridge, is Cato Manor (home to the Shree Ambalavaanar Alayam Temple) and then Westville (and, if you keep heading northwest, Pietermaritzburg, the Midlands, and ultimately Johannesburg). North of Glenwood is Berea, also an old and well-to-do suburb, built on a ridge overlooking the sea, and home to the Durban Botanic Gardens. To the east—toward the sea—are Greyville and the Kendra Hall & Ekta Mandir. Heading north toward Morningside you'll find the Campbell Collections and Mitchell Park, and farther north still, on the other side of the Umgeni River, are Durban North and the Umgeni River Bird Park. (Even farther north you reach Umhlanga and eventually the Dolphin Coast and Elephant Coast.) The neighborhood that's directly south of the main Durban beachfront and borders the north side of the harbor is called Point. Here is Durban's finest tourist attraction, uShaka Marine World, a large entertainment complex comprising four components—Sea World, Wet 'n Wild, uShaka Beach, and Village Walk—that's modeled on a mixture of Zulu, wider African, and maritime themes. On the south side of the harbor is a giant strip of dune covered by vegetation on which the suburb of Bluff is built, and where you find Treasure Beach. Surrounding Durban, many Indian and black "townships" are largely racially homogenous and mostly poor, a holdover from apartheid. Chatsworth, one such large Indian township, to the southwest, has the Hare Krishna Temple of Understanding.

WHAT TO SEE

★ ㉕ **Campbell Collections.** In the middle of bustling, suburban Berea, Muckleneuk is a tranquil Cape Dutch home in a leafy garden. It's much as it was when it was built in 1914 upon the retirement of Sir Marshall Campbell, a wealthy sugar baron and philanthropist who lived here with his wife, Ellen, and daughter, Killie. Today Muckleneuk houses a museum administered by the University of KwaZulu-Natal, including the **William Campbell Furniture Museum.** (William was the son of Sir Marshall.) The house is furnished similarly to when the Campbells lived here, and contains some excellent pieces of Cape Dutch furniture that belonged to them, an extensive collection of works by early European traveler artists, such as Angas, as well as paintings by prominent 20th-century black South African artists, including Gerard Bhengu, Daniel Rakgoathe, and Trevor Makhoba. The **Mashu Museum of Ethnology** displays the best collection of traditional Zulu glass beadwork in the country; African utensils, like tightly woven wicker beer pots; weapons dating from the Bambatha Uprising of 1906, during which blacks in Natal rebelled against a poll tax and were brutally put down; carvings; masks; pottery; and musical instruments. Paintings of African tribes-people by artist Barbara Tyrrell, who traveled around South Africa from the 1940s to 1960s capturing people in their traditional costumes and gathering valuable anthropological data, add vitality to the collection. The **Killie Campbell Africana Library,** which is open to the public, is a treasure trove of historical information on KwaZulu-Natal. It includes the papers of James Stuart, a magistrate and explorer during the early 20th century; the recorded oral tradition of hundreds of Zulu informants; a collection of pamphlets produced by the Colenso family in their struggle for the recognition of the rights of the Zulu people; and a good collection of 19th-century works on game hunting. ✉ *220 Marriott Rd., at Essenwood Rd., Berea* ☎ *031/207–3432 or 031/260–1722* ⊕ *http://campbell.ukzn.ac.za* ✍ *Muckleneuk tours R250, library free* ⊙ *Muckleneuk tours 11 and 2:30 daily; library weekdays 9–noon and 2–4:30, Sat. 9–noon* ♿ *Reservations essential for tours.*

24 Durban Botanic Gardens. Opposite the Greyville Racecourse, Africa's oldest surviving botanical garden is a delightful 150-year-old oasis of greenery interlaced with walking paths, fountains, and ponds. The gardens' orchid house and collection of rare cycads are renowned. The Garden of the Senses caters to the blind, and there's a lovely tea garden where you can take a load off your feet and settle back with a cup of hot tea and cakes. On weekends it's a popular place for wedding photographs, so you'll be sure to see retinues of colorfully clad bridesmaids. ✉ *70 St. Thomas Rd., Berea* ☎ *031/201–1303* ⊕ *www.durbanbotgardens.org.za* ✍ *Free* ⊙ *Mid-Apr.–mid-Sept., daily 7:30–5:15; mid-Sept.–mid-Apr., daily 7:30–5:45.*

31 Hare Krishna Temple of Understanding. This magnificent lotus-shaped temple opened in 1985 and is at the heart of activities run by the city's International Society for Krishna Consciousness. Gold-tinted windows adorn the outside of the temple, and the interior has floors made of imported Italian marble. Colorful laser drawings depicting the life of the Hindu god Krishna cover the ceiling, and statues of Krishna and his consort Radha are elaborately dressed in traditional Indian attire. You need to remove your shoes when entering the temple. ✉ *50 Bhaktivedanta Swami Circle, off Higginson Hwy., Unit 5, Chatsworth* ☎ *031/403–3328* ✍ *Free* ⊙ *Mon.–Sat. 10–1 and 4–8, Sun. 10–3:30; traditional singing and dancing Wed. 7–8 PM and Sun. 3–5 PM.*

NEED A BREAK? Govinda's (⊠*Hare Krishna Temple of Understanding* ☎031/403–4600) is an inexpensive yet excellent vegetarian restaurant. Hare Krishna devotees do not use onions, garlic, or mushrooms in their food. The traditional Indian *biryani*, a rice dish, is a favorite.

㉓ Kendra Hall & Ekta Mandir. One of the most easily accessible and opulent temples in the city center, the Kendra, adjacent to the Durban Botanic Gardens, opened in 2001 after two years of intricate work by sculptors in India. The structure is unmistakably Eastern, with golden domes that tower above a palm tree supported by ornately decorated columns and arches that give the temple an East-meets-West look. Inside are two halls: a small one on the ground level and a larger one upstairs, which is a popular venue for weddings and leads to the temple. Huge statues of Hindu gods, notably Ganesha, Krishna, and Ram, are garlanded and clothed in exquisite Indian fabric. You can join an early morning or evening prayer daily at 6:30 AM and 6:30 PM. ⊠*5 Sydenham Rd., Greyville* ☎*031/309–1824* ⊠*Free* ⊙*Daily 6–noon and 3–6.*

☾ ㉖ Mitchell Park. The magnificent rose garden, colorful floral displays, and leafy lawns here are real treats on a hot summer day. Attached to the park is a beautiful small zoo, named after Sir Charles Mitchell, an early governor of Natal. It was opened at the turn of the 19th century, and the Aldabra tortoises that were donated to the park in the early 1900s, now massive, are still in residence. There are also a number of small mammals, reptiles, tropical fish, and birds in large aviaries. The park has a popular playground, and the leafy terrace of the park's Blue Zoo Restaurant is a great place for breakfast or a light lunch. ⊠*10 Serndale Rd., Morningside* ☎*031/312–2318* ⊠*Gardens free; zoo R3* ⊙*Gardens daily 7:30 AM–8 PM; zoo daily 8–5.*

㉑ NSA Gallery. The National Society of the Arts' Gallery complex houses four exhibition areas, in addition to a crafts shop, the Durban Center for Photography, and a classy open-air restaurant. The center does not have a particular focus, but is committed to promoting emerging talent in the province. Exhibitions range in mediums, from photos and paintings to video installations. The center's clean architectural lines and leafy setting make this a popular venue with Durban's trendy set, and it's a lovely place to cool off after a hot morning touring the town. The gallery and crafts shop support and promote local art, so it's worth hunting for tasteful souvenirs. ⊠*166 Bulwer Rd. off the M8, Glenwood* ☎*031/277–1700* ⊕*www.kznsagallery.co.za* ⊠*Free* ⊙*Weekdays 9–5, weekends 10–4, public holidays 10–2.*

㉒ Shree Ambalavaanar Alayam Temple. One of Durban's most spectacular Hindu shrines is in Cato Manor. The temple's facade is adorned with brightly painted representations of the Hindu gods, notably Ganesha, Shiva, and Vishnu. The magnificent doors leading to the cellar were salvaged from a temple built in 1875 on the banks of the Umbilo River and subsequently destroyed by floods. During an important Hindu festival held annually in March, unshod fire walkers cross beds of burning, glowing coals. There are no set visiting hours; however if the temple is open you'll be welcome to go inside. If not, the exterior of the building is still worth seeing. ✉*890 Bellair Rd., Cato Manor* ✝*Take M13 (from Leopold St.) out of the city; at major fork in road after Westridge Park and high school, veer left onto Bellair Rd.* ☎*No phone* 🖃*Free* ☉*Hrs. vary.*

🐾 ③⓪ **Treasure Beach.** A visit to the Wildlife Society of South Africa's coastal reserve and environmental education center, on the Bluff, will give you an idea of what this section of the coast looked like before it was commercially developed. This is not a swimming beach but rather a good example of a rocky shore and narrow, sandy beach, accessed down a flight of almost 200 stairs and through a tropical dune forest. The center organizes night walks along the beach once or twice a month, after a new or full moon; they're very popular, especially with kids. The evening begins with a traditional braai at around 5:30 in the picnic area above the beach (bring your own meat, salad, and utensils). You're then led down to the shore, where society staff help you look for octopus, eels, mussels, oysters, crabs, and other sea creatures. Bring your own flashlight and shoes that don't come off easily but that you don't mind getting wet. ✉*835 Marine Dr., Bluff* ☎*031/467–8507 or 031/467–8508* ⊕*www.wessa.org.za* 🖃*R25 for an ecology tour and R25 for night walks (occur once a month)* ☉*9–1 for ecology tours.*

🐾 ★ ②⑦ **Umgeni River Bird Park.** This bird park, ranked among the world's best, is built under high cliffs next to the Umgeni River and has various walk-through aviaries. The variety of birds, both exotic and indigenous, is astonishing. You'll be able to take close-up photographs of macaws, giant Asian hornbills, toucans, pheasants, flamingos, and eight species of crane, including the blue crane, South Africa's national bird. Try to time your visit to take in the bird show, which is a delight for both children and adults, and afterward have your photo taken with Otis, a white-faced owl. Drinks and light lunches are served at the park's kiosk. ✉*490 Riverside Rd., off the M4, Durban North* ☎*031/579–4600* ⊕*www.umgeniriverbirdpark.co.za* 🖃*R25* ☉*Daily 9–4:30; bird shows daily at 11 and 2.*

🐾 ★ ②⑧ **uShaka Sea World.** The world's fifth-largest aquarium and the largest in the southern hemisphere, Sea World has a capacity of nearly 6 million gallons of water, more than four times the size of Cape Town's aquarium. The innovative design is as impressive as the size. You enter through the side of a giant ship and walk down several stories, past the massive skeleton of Misty, a Southern Right whale that died near Cape Town after colliding with a ship, until a sign welcomes you to the BOTTOM OF THE OCEAN. Here you enter a "labyrinth of shipwrecks"—a jumble of five different fake but highly realistic wrecks, from an early-20th-century passenger cruiser to a steamship. Within this labyrinth are massive tanks, housing more than 200 species of fish and other sea life and the biggest variety of sharks in the world, including ragged-tooth and Zambezi sharks (known elsewhere as bull sharks), responsible for more attacks on humans than any other species. Don't expect to see great whites, though; they don't survive in aquariums. While inside the aquarium, try to catch a fish feeding. The best is the open-ocean

5

feed in the afternoon, when divers hand-feed the fish. Look out for the interesting bottom feeders, like rays and sand sharks.

On dry land, 20-minute dolphin and seal shows, held in adjacent stadiums twice a day (three times during busy seasons), are both well worth attending. Watch for Gambit, the biggest dolphin in any dolphinarium in the world; the over-30-year-old dolphin jumps out of the water and perches on the side of the pool. Seals also strut their stuff in humorous, well-rehearsed shows. For the best views of dolphin and seal shows, sit in the middle of the stadium toward the back.

Add-ons include a 20-minute shark dive in an acrylic capsule, with instruction (R130; no children under 12); a snorkeling experience in the fish tanks (R70 for 45 mins or R160 whole-day pass); and ocean walking (R140; no children under 12), where you descend in a large bubblelike helmet in a fish tank, with the assistance of a guide. The add-ons don't take place on Monday and Tuesday. ⊠*1 Bell St., Point* ☎*031/328–8000* ⊕*www.ushakamarineworld.co.za* ✆*R92; R135 with Wet 'n Wild* ⊙ *Weekdays 9–5, weekends 9–6.*

♻ ★ ㉙ **uShaka Wet 'n Wild.** This extensive water fun park, run in tandem with Sea World, comprises slides, pools, and about 10 different water rides. There's something for everyone, from toddlers to adrenaline junkies. As you walk into uShaka Marine World, you'll see people lazily floating on giant red tubes in the Duzi Adventure River, a ride that circles the aquarium, descends down a long slide, and runs under waterfalls and past fish tanks in a nearly 1,500-foot loop that takes about 15 minutes. The giant, almost vertical Plunge is the most exciting slide, and the Zoom-Zoom, a five-lane racer, is also popular. A new slide, the Drop Zone, is one of the highest in Africa. You can easily spend the better part of a day here, and a combo ticket with Sea World lets you go back and forth between the two. Durban's moderate winter temperatures make it an attraction pretty much all year round, though it's especially popular in summer. Avoid it on public holidays. ⊠*1 Bell St., Point* ☎*031/328–8000* ⊕*www.ushakamarineworld.co.za* ✆*R70, R135 with Sea World* ⊙ *Weekdays 9–5, weekends 9–6.*

WHERE TO EAT

DURBAN

★ $$–$$$ ✕**Cargo Hold.** You might need to book several months in advance to secure a table next to the shark tank here, but if you do, it'll be one of your most memorable dining experiences ever. You can enjoy a trio of carpaccios—smoked ostrich, beef, and salmon—while 13-foot raggedtooth and Zambezi sharks drift right by your table. Aside from the array of fish dishes like sesame-seared tuna and kingklip à la Cargo (grilled kingklip topped with mussels poached in a passion-fruit-and-bourbon cream sauce), Cargo Hold also serves meat dishes like oxtail and rosemary-and-rock-salt leg of lamb. The restaurant is done up like a shipwreck; of three floors, two have tank frontage (the view of the shark tank from the bottom floor is best, so ask for this when booking). The restaurant is part of the Phantom Ship. Access to the ship costs

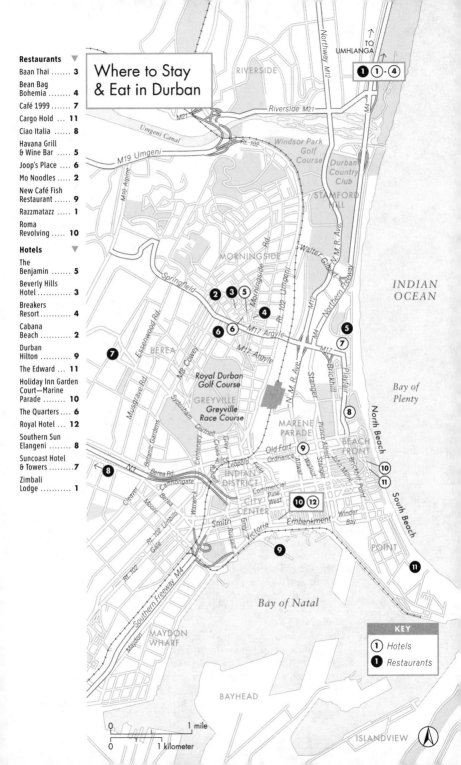

Where to Stay & Eat in Durban

Restaurants ▼

Baan Thai **3**

Bean Bag Bohemia **4**

Café 1999 .... **7**

Cargo Hold ... **11**

Ciao Italia **8**

Havana Grill & Wine Bar **5**

Joop's Place **6**

Mo Noodles **2**

New Café Fish Restaurant **9**

Razzmatazz **1**

Roma Revolving **10**

Hotels ▼

The Benjamin **5**

Beverly Hills Hotel **3**

Breakers Resort **4**

Cabana Beach **2**

Durban Hilton **9**

The Edward ... **11**

Holiday Inn Garden Court—Marine Parade **10**

The Quarters **6**

Royal Hotel ... **12**

Southern Sun Elangeni **8**

Suncoast Hotel & Towers **7**

Zimbali Lodge **1**

KEY

① *Hotels*

❶ *Restaurants*

0   1 mile

0   1 kilometer

R20, though this is refunded if you dine in Cargo Hold. ⊠*1 Bell St., Point* ☎*031/328–8065* ⊟*AE, DC, MC, V.*

★ $–$$$ ✕**Café 1999.** Trendy this restaurant may be, but the food is even more memorable than the shopping center setting. The husband-and-wife owners encourage you to celebrate taste with a menu of dishes that are meant for sharing, from the "titbits" (small servings) to the "bigbits." Let your fork and fingers wander between dishes like breaded olives stuffed with ricotta cheese and chicken kebabs with coriander-and-lemon pesto. The macadamia-nut-and-honey tart makes for a sweet finish. Café 1999 is a great place for lunch. ⊠*Shop 2, Silvervause Centre, 117 Vause Rd., Musgrave* ☎*031/202–3406* ⚄*Reservations essential* ⊟*AE, DC, MC, V* ⊗*Closed Sun. No lunch Sat.*

★ $–$$$ ✕**Havana Grill & Wine Bar.** The sea views and good food combine to make this one of Durban's finest restaurants, though most dishes are on the pricey side for Durban. It offers spectacular sea vistas (ask for a table with a view when making your reservation) and minimalist Afro-Cuban decor, with richly upholstered chairs, some leather couches, and antelope horns on the walls. Steak—aged on meat hooks in a giant fridge—and seafood are both specialties. Try Havana's tasting platter for starters (minimum of two people sharing): nachos, crumbed jalapeño poppers stuffed with cheese, grilled calamari, and spring rolls. For mains, consider the Lamb Tanganyika, which is rubbed with toasted cumin and coriander and served with a rich gravy, or line fish (likely sailfish, dorado, or Cape salmon) served in five different ways: grilled with lemon butter, topped with fresh pesto and fettucine, with a coriander dipping sauce and wasabi-infused mash, in a Thai green coconut curry, or in an Asian red curry. There's a good basic wine list as well as a walk-in cellar from which special bottles can be ordered. ⊠*Shop U2, Suncoast Casino & Entertainment World, Beachfront* ☎*031/337–1304* ⚄*Reservations essential* ⊟*AE, DC, MC, V.*

$–$$ ✕**Baan Thai.** On the second floor of a converted town house above the hustle and bustle of trendy Florida Road, this Thai restaurant, which has been around for 15 years, brings a refreshing flavor to Durban's dining scene. Thai chefs working in an open kitchen whip up authentic dishes that make heady use of lemongrass, coriander, and galangal (a type of ginger). Among the starters, the beef waterfall salad (thinly sliced grilled beef tossed with onions and coriander) is excellent, as are pad thai noodles. Other winners are the whiskey prawns, Thai crab, and the Baan Thai duck (deboned fillets basted in an almost-sweet sauce). *Brinjal* (eggplant) with chilies is a delicious vegetarian option. There is also a reasonably priced lunch menu. ⊠*138 Florida Rd., Morningside* ☎*031/303–4270* ⊟*AE, DC, MC, V* ⚇*BYOB* ⊗*Closed Sun. No lunch Sat.*

$–$$ ✕**Ciao Italia.** Don't expect anything traditional at this "modern trattoria" with its friendly, family atmosphere. The food is "zooped-up" Italian; for example, penne Oriental—a multi-culti mix of pasta, chicken breast, ginger, garlic, curry powder, coriander, and chutney. The most exciting dishes are often on the extensive specials list, which changes daily, according to which fresh ingredients are available. ⊠*Multichoice*

Centre, Shop 7A, Westville Rd., Westville ☎*031/267–1762* ⬧*Reservations essential* ▤*AE, DC, MC, V* ⊘*Closed Sun. No lunch Sat.*

$–$$ ✕**Roma Revolving.** In business since 1973, this slowly revolving restaurant, which takes about an hour to do one full rotation, offers what has to be the most spectacular views of the city, especially the harbor. It's run by the original Italian owners and staff, and its menu is extensive. While the restaurant is perched atop a high-rise building, its entrance is in an area which has become rather run-down over the years, and it's dangerous at night, so stick to lunch. ⬧*John Ross House, 32nd fl., Victoria Embankment* ☎*031/368–2275* ⬧*www.roma.co.za* ⬧*Reservations essential* ▤*AE, DC, MC, V* ⊘*Closed Sun.*

¢–$$$$ ✕**Bean Bag Bohemia.** One of the city's most intimate and most popular restaurants, Bohemia serves a mix of cosmopolitan and Mediterranean food. It's abuzz with Durban's young and trendy, especially late at night, when you can get a good meal after movies or the theater. Cocktails and lighter meals are served at the bar downstairs, where live musicians often play jazz or the piano. Up rickety wooden stairs at the main restaurant, a popular starter is the meze platter, with Mediterranean snacks such as hummus, baba ghanoush (an eggplant spread), olives, and pita. Bohemia is well known for its vegetarian meals, but dishes such as lamb shank and duck are also good. Finish your meal with the baked pecan praline cheesecake and then relax on the terrace. ⬧*18 Windermere Rd., Windermere* ☎*031/309–6019* ▤*AE, DC, MC, V.*

★ **¢–$$$** ✕**Joop's Place.** No trip to South Africa would be complete without a good traditional steak, and without a doubt, Joop's (pronounced "Yopes") is the best and most popular steak house in Durban. Most customers are regulars. It has an intimate, homely atmosphere, though the decor is nothing special. The food is the true focus, with Joop himself selecting and preparing the steaks in an open kitchen. The specialty here is panfried steak; the pepper steak and Hollandse (Dutch-style) *biefstuk* (a center-cut fillet panfried in black butter and flambéed in brandy) are tasty favorites. For the exceptionally hungry, try the 800-gram (about 21-ounce) T-bone. ⬧*Shop 14, Avonmore Centre, 9th Ave., Morningside* ☎*031/312–9135* ⬧*Reservations essential* ▤*AE, DC, MC, V* ⊘*Closed Sun. No lunch Sat.–Thurs.*

★ **¢–$** ✕**Mo Noodles.** Don't let the name or mostly outside location fool you: this is one of Durban's best restaurants, known for its huge portions, freshly prepared meals, and reasonable prices. The decor is chic and minimalist, but unpretentious and comfortable. Opt for a starter of prawn skewers in peanut dipping sauce or chicken teriyaki salad with a peanut dressing; then move on to chicken, prawn, and beef panfried noodles; a seared, marinated sesame fillet of beef; or any of the excellent Thai-style curries. Homemade ice cream comes in flavors like ginger, coconut, and honey and cashew. Because they don't take reservations, go early, especially on weekend nights. ⬧*Shop 5, Florida Centre, 275 Florida Rd., Morningside* ☎*031/312–4193* ⬧*Reservations not accepted* ▤*AE, DC, MC, V* ⊘*Closed Sun. No lunch Sat.*

¢–$ ✕**New Café Fish Restaurant.** This popular eatery juts out into the Durban Yacht Basin between the BAT Centre and Wilson's Wharf. Here the city's vertical lines—towering skyskrapers along the embankment and the slender masts of vessels anchored alongside the restaurant—tie sky and sea together in a memorable setting. The food is tasty, with fish a speciality, as the restaurant's name suggests. Try the mild Thai prawn curry or the pesto line fish, or order a seafood platter of special-order items like extra-large crayfish and prawns according to seasonal availabily (be prepared to pay quite a bit extra for seasonal specials). The bar upstairs (⇨ Nightlife & the Arts, below) is pleasant for sundowners and serves light meals and snacks. ✉ 31 Yacht Mole, Victoria Embankment ☎ 031/305–5062 or 031/305–5063 ☐ AE, DC, MC, V.

UMHLANGA

¢–$$ ✕ **Razzmatazz.** The ocean view is reason enough to enjoy an afternoon here—but so is the food in this value-for-money establishment. Weather permitting, book a sea view on the deck and dig into an order of fresh oysters or the line fish beurre blanc, grilled and served with a white-wine-and-butter sauce. The chef is well known for his game dishes, so the more adventurous might want to try the springbok carpaccio or the crocodile kebab for starters, and for mains either the kudu gently simmered in red wine, an ostrich fillet in gooseberry sauce, or warthog pie, depending on availability. There's usually a wide array of specials, too. ✉ Cabana Beach, 10 Lagoon Dr., Umhlanga ☎ 031/561–5847 ⚲ Reservations essential ☐ AE, DC, MC, V.

WHERE TO STAY

DURBAN

$$$ ⊡ **Southern Sun Elangeni.** One of the best hotels on the beachfront, this 21-story high-rise overlooks North Beach, and is a two-minute drive from the city center. It attracts a mix of business, conference, and leisure travelers. Though all rooms have views of the water, request a room on an upper floor for a full ocean view. Rooms are small and narrow and have a beachlike seaside feel at odds with the formality of the marbled lobby and public rooms. The hotel has one of the few Japanese restaurants in the city, as well as a first-class Indian restaurant. The hotel requires a minimum stay of two nights (price cited is for one night only). ✉ 63 Snell Parade, Box 4094, Beachfront, 4000 ☎ 031/362–1300 ⊕ www.southernsun.com ⇄ 449 rooms, 10 suites ⚹ In-room: ethernet, refrigerator, safe. In-hotel: 3 restaurants, room service, bars, pools, gym ☐ AE, DC, MC, V.

$$–$$$ ⊡ **Durban Hilton.** This massive luxury hotel adjacent to the International Convention Centre is relatively close (short taxi trip) to the city center and beachfront and is favored by businesspeople and conference-goers. The rooms are small but tastefully decorated in light wood with cream beddings and African touches, such as simple African patterns inlaid in the doors, and have views of either beach or city. Executive floors have a small club room, where guests can get breakfast and free Internet access. Large public areas come complete with marble pillars and a pianist tinkling away on a baby grand. The Rainbow Terrace restaurant has an excellent buffet and an unusual à la carte menu. The Hilton also boasts impeccable service, making it one of the top hotels in this chain

in Africa. Though expensive by Durban standards, rates can vary significantly based on how full the hotel is, which often relates to which conferences are being held at the convention center. ⊠ *12–14 Walnut Rd., Box 11288, Marine Parade, 4056* ☎*031/336–8100* ⊕*www.hilton. com* ➫*327 rooms, 16 suites* ⟡ *In-room: ethernet, Wi-Fi, refrigerator, safe. In-hotel: 2 restaurants, bar, pool, gym* ⊟*AE, DC, MC, V.*

\$\$–\$\$\$
Fodor'sChoice
★
🖫 **Royal Hotel.** Durban's best hotel, and a cherished institution, has often hosted British royals. Dating from 1842—the city's infancy—the original Royal was replaced by a high-rise in 1978, and all that remains of the old building is the grand Royal Grill. Nevertheless, the hotel maintains some classic touches, such as a butler for every floor and traditional shoe-shine service. Recently refurbished rooms are decorated with a mix of African and Indian influences in a classic, modern look. Bedrooms have dark-wood furniture with red cushions and white cotton bedding, and bathrooms have separate shower and tub. Request a room on an upper floor for a spectacular view of the harbor, which you can also get from the Top of the Royal, a great place for breakfast or brunch. ⊠ *267 Smith St., Box 1041, City Center, 4000* ☎*031/333–6000* ⊕*www.theroyal.co.za* ➫*196 rooms, 16 suites* ⟡ *In-room: ethernet, Wi-Fi, refrigerator, safe. In-hotel: 6 restaurants, room service, bars, pool, gym* ⊟*AE, DC, MC, V* ⦿*BP.*

\$\$
🖫 **The Edward.** Built in 1939 in classic colonial style, the Edward is one of Durban's oldest hotels. Although it's almost been restored to its former elegance, it seems to have lost a little of its soul. Nevertheless, service is excellent, and the stylish cut-glass chandeliers, molded ceilings, and subtle art-deco details bring to mind Durban's more refined past. Rooms are tastefully furnished; 10 have balconies overlooking the sea, and the others have bay windows with sea views. The hotel faces beautiful South Beach. ⊠ *149 Marine Parade, Box 105, Beachfront, 4000* ☎*031/337–3681* ⊕*www.proteahotels.com* ➫*101 rooms, 10 suites* ⟡ *In-room: ethernet, refrigerator, safe. In-hotel: restaurant, room service, bars, pool* ⊟*AE, DC, MC, V.*

★ \$\$
🖫 **The Quarters.** Four converted Victorian homes compose the city's most intimate boutique hotel, a contemporary European-style property with a colonial African feel. Rooms have mahogany furniture, cream damask-covered beds, and sunken tubs in luxurious bathrooms. Many of the rooms have small verandas facing onto Florida Road, with its swaying palm trees and sometimes busy traffic, but double-glazed windows keep it quiet. ⊠ *101 Florida Rd., Berea, 4001* ☎*031/303–5246* ⊕*www.quarters.co.za* ➫*25 rooms* ⟡ *In-room: ethernet, refrigerator, safe. In-hotel: restaurant* ⊟*AE, DC, MC, V* ⦿*BP.*

\$–\$\$\$\$
🖫 **Suncoast Hotel and Towers.** Durban's newest hotel, opened in December 2006, is situated adjacent to the Suncoast Casino and is a stone's throw from the beach. Like the casino, the hotel is designed in the art-deco style of the 1930s, in keeping with some of Durban's architectural heritage (the city is still home to a few beautiful art-deco apartment buildings). The hotel is furnished in pastel shades and is elegantly minimalist, though the rooms are rather small. The sea views from the higher floors are spectacular (sea-facing rooms are slightly more expensive, but worth it). The hotel mostly attracts businesspeople and

gamblers. The Suncoast Hotel is four star, while the 36 suites in the Towers are five star. ⊠*20 Battery Beach, Box 10690, Marine Parade, 4056* ☎*031/314–7878* ⊕*www.southernsun.com* ☞*165 rooms, 36 suites* ⚒*In-room: safe, Wi-Fi. In-hotel: restaurant, room service bar, pool, gym, spa* ☰*AE, DC, MC, V* ⍅*CP.*

$ 🏨**The Benjamin.** In one of Durban's transformed historic buildings, this small hotel offers excellent value for money. Its location is ideal—perched on trendy Florida Road, with its excellent restaurants and nightlife, and approximately five minutes from both the beaches and the city center. The residents' lounge is quiet and elegant but still warm and comfortable, as are the stylish rooms. The breakfast room has big glass doors opening out onto a small pool. ⊠*141 Florida Rd., Morningside, 4001* ☎*031/303–4233* ⊕*www.benjamin.co.za* ☞*45 rooms* ⚒*In-room: ethernet, refrigerator, safe. In-hotel: pool, no elevator* ☰*AE, DC, MC, V* ⍅*BP.*

$ 🏨**Holiday Inn Garden Court–Marine Parade.** You can't beat the location of this pleasant hotel midway between South and North beaches and only a five-minute drive from the city center. Rooms are attractive and modern, each with a small sitting area. All face the sea, but request an upper-floor room for the best views. Views from the pool deck on the 30th floor are superb. ⊠*167 Marine Parade, Box 10809, Beachfront, 4056* ☎*031/337–3341* ⊕*www.southernsun.com* ☞*340 rooms, 6 suites* ⚒*In-room: refrigerator, safe. In-hotel: restaurant, bar, pool* ☰*AE, DC, MC, V* ⍅*BP.*

UMHLANGA

★ $$$$ 🏨**Zimbali Lodge.** One of only two luxury lodges in the province with direct access to the beach, Zimbali's tranquil setting is in one of only a very few remaining coastal forests in the province. The decor is a stylish mix of African and Balinese, with lots of glass, dark wood, and rough woven fabrics. Rooms have an indulgently private and luxurious feel to them, with crisp white linen, wood carvings, large baths, and balconies that look out onto the forest, lake, and sea beyond. It's a wonderful place to laze around, enjoy afternoon tea, play a round of golf, or swim in the private Mauritian-style pool on the beach. The service is warm, friendly, and slick. ⊠*M4, 20 km (12 mi) north of Umhlanga, Box 404, Umhlali 4390* ☎*032/538–1007* ⊕*www.suninternational.com* ☞*76 rooms, 10 executive forest suites* ⚒*In-room: Wi-Fi, refrigerator, DVD, safe. In-hotel: room service, golf course, tennis courts, pools, gym, spa, beachfront, bicycles* ☰*AE, DC, MC, V.*

$$$ 🏨**Beverly Hills Hotel.** In a high-rise building right on the beach, this upscale hotel is popular with both vacationers and businesspeople, and has a longstanding reputation as one of the best in town. The service is excellent and the facilities superb. However, if you're the sort of beachgoer who likes to loll about in a bathing suit, you may find this hotel too formal. The public lounge, festooned with huge floral arrangements and yards of gathered drapes, serves a full silver-service tea in the afternoon, and a pianist plays in the evening. Guest rooms are fairly small, but all have terrific sea views, particularly those on the upper floors. For a more open, beachlike feel, take one of the cabanas, large duplex rooms that open onto a lovely pool deck. ⊠*Lighthouse*

Rd., Box 71, 4320 🕿*031/561–2211* ⊕*www.southernsun.com* ⤶*81 rooms, 7 suites.* ⚷*In-room: ethernet, refrigerator, safe. In-hotel: 2 restaurants, room service, bars, pool* ⊟*AE, DC, MC, V* ⦿|*CP.*

★ $$ 🔳**Cabana Beach.** Families who want a traditional beach vacation can't do better than this large resort, where children under 18 stay free. The bathing beach is directly in front of the hotel, and there are tons of activities to keep kids happy. Rooms are simple, but beach appropriate. Each cabana comes with a fully equipped kitchen, a dining-living area, and a veranda with great sea views. Request a tower or beachfront apartment for the most attractive and practical space configuration. Out of season, the rates can be reduced by up to about half. ⊠*10 Lagoon Dr., Box 10, 4320* 🕿*031/561–2371* ⤶*217 rooms* ⚷*In-room: kitchen, safe, refrigerator. In-hotel: 4 restaurants, bar, tennis courts, pools, gym* ⊟*AE, DC, MC, V* ⦿|*CP.*

$–$$ 🔳**Breakers Resort.** This property enjoys an enviable position at the northern tip of Umhlanga, surrounded by the wilds of the Hawaan Forest and overlooking the unspoiled wetlands of Umhlanga Lagoon. Of all the resorts in Umhlanga, this one suffers the least from crowds. The disadvantage though is that you probably need a car to get into town, and you can't swim directly in front of the resort because the surf's too dangerous. The building is unattractive, with long, depressing corridors, but the rooms themselves are fine, with fully equipped kitchens and great views of the beach and lagoon. There is a lovely grassed pool area with a beautiful view of the sea, from which you can order light meals. ⊠*88 Lagoon Dr., Box 75, 4320* 🕿*031/561–2271* ⊕*www.breakersresort.co.za* ⤶*80 rooms* ⚷*In-room: kitchen, safe, refrigerator. In-hotel: 2 restaurants, bar, tennis court, pool* ⊟*AE, DC, MC, V* ⦿|*CP.*

NIGHTLIFE & THE ARTS

What's on in Durban, a free monthly publication put out by the tourism office and distributed at popular sites, lists a diary of upcoming events. The "Entertainment" section of the Durban-based *Sunday Tribune* and the *Mail & Guardian,* a weekly national newspaper noted for its good nightlife reviews, are good information sources. *The Mercury* and *Daily News,* both published weekdays, also contain entertainment sections.

Tickets for shows, movies released by Nu Metro, concerts, and other events can be obtained through **Computicket** (🕿*083/915–8000 or 083/915–1234* ⊕*www.computicket.com*). Note, though, that Computicket does not accept foreign credit cards. Tickets for movies released by Ster Kinekor can be obtained from **Ticketline** (🕿*0861/300–444 or 082/16789* ⊕*www.sterkinekor.com*), which accepts foreign credit cards. Both ticket agencies have outlets in major shopping centers.

NIGHTLIFE
Durban's bars and nightclubs open and close almost as quickly as the tide changes. While a few popular and longer-lived spots are listed below, it's probably a good idea to ask at your hotel for suggestions.

That said, Florida Road in Morningside is a perennially popular location for trendy new bars, so it's worth taking a drive up it and seeing what attracts your fancy.

BARS   **Billy the BUMS** (⊠*504 Windermere Rd., Morningside* ☎*031/303–1988*) hums from the early evening until late. It also serves good food, like jalapeño poppers and other tasty tidbits. Durban's young and fashionable relax at the **Café Vacca Matta** (⊠*20 Suncoast Blvd., Beachfront* ☎*031/368–6535*), on the upper level of the Suncoast Casino. California-style **Joe Cool's** (⊠*137 Lower Marine Parade, Beachfront* ☎*031/332–9697*) is a popular nightclub and restaurant, right on the beach. A longstanding nightspot, Joe Cool's has recently been refurbished, and caters to a fairly upmarket crowd. You can sip a cocktail watching the sun go down over Durban's harbor at the **New Café Fish Bar** (⊠*31 Yacht Mole, Victoria Embankment* ☎*031/305–5062 or 031/305–5063*), in the Durban Yacht Basin. The refurbished **Zeta Bar** (⊠*258 Florida Rd., Berea* ☎*031/312–9436*) has a comfortable cocktail lounge and attracts an eclectic crowd.

CASINOS   The omnipresent sound of slot machines makes your ears ring at **Sibaya Casino** (⊠*1 Sibaya Dr., Umhlanga* ☎*031/580–5000 or 0860/742–292* ⊕*www.sibaya.co.za*). The casino area has more than 900 slot machines and 37 betting tables, among them roulette and poker. **Suncoast Casino** (⊠*20 Suncoast Blvd., Beachfront* ☎*031/328–3000* ⊕*www.suncoast casino.co.za*), a hub of dining, drinking, and gambling activity, has 1,250 slot machines and 50 gaming tables, including blackjack, roulette, and poker.

DANCE CLUBS   **Casablanca** (⊠*17 Florida Rd., Berea* ☎*031/303–7568* ⊕*http://club casablanca.co.za*), is trendy, upmarket, and plays music popular with the predominantly twentysomething crowd. **Tilt** (⊠*11 Walnut Rd., opposite Albert Luthuli International Convention CentreMarine Parade* ☎*031/306–9356* ⊕*www.clubtilt.co.za*) is popular with hip-hop and house music fans.

THE ARTS

The **Playhouse** (⊠*29 Acutt St. across from City Hall, City Center* ☎*031/369–9555* ⊕*www.playhousecompany.com*) stands at the heart of Durban's cultural life. The complex encompasses five performing-arts venues, and the Playhouse Company stages productions of music, ballet, drama, opera, and cabaret. The Playhouse is also home to the Natal Philharmonic Orchestra.

Located at the University of KwaZulu-Natal, the **Elizabeth Sneddon Theatre** (⊠*1 King George V Ave.,Glenwood* ☎*031/260–2296* ⊕*www.sneddontheatre.co.za*) hosts music and drama productions on a smaller scale than those at the Playhouse. Famous local, national, and international poets, writers, dramatists, and filmmakers gather at the Sneddon for annual festivals, such as the Durban International Film Festival in June and Poetry Africa in October.

Regular musical shows, such as those celebrating the music of the 1960s or the development of South African music, as well as cabaret performances are staged at the large, multitiered **Barnyard Theatre** (✉*Gateway Mall, 1st fl., Gateway Rd. and Sugar Close, Umhlanga Ridge* ☎*031/566–3045*). There's always something theatrical happening at the **BAT Centre** (✉*45 Maritime Pl., Small Craft Harbour, Victoria Embankment* ☎*031/332–0468* ⊕*www.batcentre.co.za*), from a drumming session to a live poetry festival. The intimate **Catalina Theatre** (✉*18 Boatman's Rd., Wilson's Wharf* ☎*031/305–6889* ⊕*www. catalinatheatre.co.za*) specializes in comedy, plays, and drama. Sibaya's **iZulu Theatre** (✉*1 Sibaya Dr., Umhlanga* ☎*031/580–5555* ⊕*www. sibaya.co.za*) can seat more than 600 people and stages the larger productions that come to town. A short distance from the restaurants at Florida Road, the small and intimate **KwaSuka Theatre** (✉*53 Stamford Hill Rd., Greyville* ☎*031/309–2236*) stages mostly local musicals and dramas. Suncoast's cinema complex, **Supernova** (✉*20 Suncoast Blvd., Beachfront* ☎*031/328–3333*) has the largest screen in the province, but is still cozy. It screens the latest releases from both Hollywood and Bollywood and is the only movie house in Durban to show midnight movies, on Saturday. It occasionally stages local dramas.

SPORTS & THE OUTDOORS

BEACHES

The sea near Durban, unlike that around the Cape, is comfortably warm year-round: in summer the water temperature can top 27°C (80°F), whereas in winter 19°C (65°F) is considered cold. The beaches are safe, the sand is a beautiful golden color, and you'll see people swimming all year round. All of KwaZulu-Natal's main beaches are protected by shark nets and staffed with lifeguards, and there are usually boards stating the wind direction, water temperature, and the existence of any dangerous swimming conditions. Directly in front of uShaka Marine World, **uShaka Beach** is an attractive public beach. The **Golden Mile,** stretching from South Beach all the way to Snake Park Beach, is packed with people, who enjoy the waterslides, singles' bars, and fast-food joints. A little farther north are the **Umhlanga beaches,** and on the opposite side of the bay are the less commercialized but also less accessible and safe beaches on **Durban's Bluff.** Another pretty beach and coastal walk, just north of the **Umhlanga Lagoon,** leads to miles of near-empty beaches backed by virgin bush. Please note: you should not walk alone on deserted beaches or carry any jewelry or other valuables, and should never walk at night.

BOATING & DOLPHIN-WATCHING

It's easy to charter all manner of boats, from a paddleski (a flat fiberglass board that you paddle) for a few rand to a deep-sea fishing vessel for a few thousand. Inexpensive harbor tours lasting a half hour, booze cruises, and dinner cruises can all be booked from the quayside at Wilson's Wharf. Shop around to find something that suits your budget, taste, and time frame.

FISHING

Deep-sea fishing is a popular activity, as there's almost always something biting. Summer (November–May) brings game fish like barracuda, marlin, sailfish, and dorado, whereas winter is better for the bottom fishes, like mussel crackers, salmon, and rock cod. Sharks are present year-round. Depending on the wind and conditions, charters are likely to head north, toward Tongaat, where the fishing is often better than south of the city.

Casea Charters (☎031/561–7381 or 083/690–2511 ⊕www.casea charters.co.za) offers trips on a ski boat from Granny's Pool, in front of Cabana Beach, that vary from three to five hours (R400–R550). Fish for dorado, yellowfin tuna, king and queen mackerel, garrick, rock cod, salmon, and other species. Bait and equipment are supplied, but bring your own food and drinks. You can keep the fish you catch. Booking is essential. **Lynski Charters** (☎031/539–3338 or 082/445–6600 ⊕www.lynski.com) offers deep-sea fishing for barracuda, sailfish, marlin, shark, and reef fish out of Durban's harbor. Trips, in a 35-foot game-fish boat, cost R4,000 for up to six people fishing for a day trip, although the boat can take nine people altogether. The price includes equipment, tackle, bait, and cold drinks. **Swissroll Charters** (☎031/467–2185 or 082/451–6567 ⊕www.swissroll.co.za) offers similar deep-sea fishing trips from the harbor. For R3,800, skipper-owner Ralph Nussbaumer takes a maximum of six people for a day on his 30-foot boat with a cabin. Sometimes he sets up a gas cooker and fries some fresh fish.

GOLF

Durban Country Club (☎031/313–1777 ⊕www.dcclub.co.za) has hosted more South African Opens than any other course, and is regularly rated the best in South Africa. Tees and greens sit atop large sand dunes, and trees add an additional hazard. Visitors can play all week, and fees for the 18-hole, par-72 course are R500. The first tee-off at 6:30 is popular with those who want to beat the heat. Rental clubs are available. Inside the Greyville Racecourse, the **Royal Durban Golf Club** (☎031/309–1373 ⊕www.royaldurban.co.za) offers no protection from the wind, which makes hitting the narrow fairways very difficult, but the surroundings are attractive and the venue is central. Fees for the 18-hole, par-72 course are R300, rental clubs are available, and reservations are essential. The course is open every day and the first tee-off is at 7 AM. **Zimbali Country Club** (☎032/538–1041 ⊕www.zimbali.org) is built in and around one of the few remaining coastal forests in the province. The world-class 18-hole course was designed by Tom Weiskopf and lies amid sand dunes above a secluded beach, natural springs, and a lake. There is a fully stocked pro shop. Greens fees for 18 holes are R235 midweek, R270 weekends. Compulsory cart rental is R180; rental clubs are available for R300 per set.

The **Roger Manning Golf Shop** (✉N.M.R. Ave., Windsor Park Golf Course, Stamford Hill ☎031/303–1728) rents clubs for R100 per set per day.

RUGBY

KwaZulu-Natal's Sharks play at the **ABSA Rugby Stadium** (✉ *Jacko Jackson Dr., Stamford Hill* ☎ *031/312–6368*). The Sharks are strong contenders in the annual Super Tournament 14 tournament, held between Australian, South African, and New Zealand teams between February and May, and in the South African round-robin ABSA Currie Cup competition, held from July to October, and KwaZulu-Natalians are known for supporting their team strongly. International rugby test matches are often played here, too.

SURFING

Surfing has a fanatical following in Durban, and several local and international tournaments are staged on the city's beaches, at nearby Umhlanga, or on the Bluff. Crowds of more than 10,000 are not unusual for night surfing competitions or the annual Mr. Price Pro championship (formerly the Gunston 500), a top World Qualifying Series event on the world surfing circuit. The Mr. Price Pro is held at Durban's most famous beaches, North Beach and New Pier. When the conditions are right, New Pier is one of the best beach breaks in the world.

Just the other side of Durban's protected bay, Cave Rock, on the Bluff, offers a seething right-hander that can handle big swell. It can be a tough paddle and is not for amateurs. Farther down the South Coast, surfers head for Scottburgh, Green Point, Park Rynie, or Southbroom. North of Durban, popular spots include Umhlanga, Ballito, Richard's Bay, and Sodwana Bay.

The more popular spots can get crowded, and locals are known to be territorial about certain sections. Be sure to obey the laws of surfing etiquette. Usually the best waves are found at dawn and dusk. If the southwester blows, the Durban beaches are your best bet. In the winter months look out for an early-morning land breeze to set up good waves along the whole coastline.

At the well-stocked **Pirana Surf Shop** (✉ *1 Bell St., Point* ☎ *031/337–6666, uShaka Marine World*) you can buy surf gear like sunglasses, wet suits, swimsuits, surfboards, and body boards. The shop also organizes surfing lessons and rents surfboards (R120 per hour) and body boards (R120 per hour). You can also arrange for surfing lessons (R150 per hour, including all equipment) with **Eli DeNysschen** (☎ *084/686–3923* ✉ *panacea1@telkomsa.net*) on North Beach or South Beach.

Wavehouse (✉ *Gateway mall, Gateway Rd. and Sugar Close, Umhlanga Ridge* ☎ *031/570–9200* ⊕ *www.wavehouse.co.za*), has outdoor wave pools in which waves are artificially created and are excellent for learning how to surf.

SHOPPING

Durban offers a great array of shopping experiences, from the Beachfront, where you can buy cheap beadwork and baskets, to enormous Western-style malls. In general, bargaining is not expected, though you might try it at the Beachfront or with hawkers anywhere. Look out for goods indigenous to the province: colorful Zulu beadwork and tightly handwoven baskets.

MALLS

One of the biggest malls in the Southern Hemisphere, **Gateway** (⊠ *1 Palm Blvd., Umhlanga Ridge* ☎*031/566–2332* ⊕*www.gatewayworld. co.za*) contains more than 300 stores ranging from clothing to music to jewelry, outdoor and indoor restaurants, the province's only IMAX theater, the live Barnyard Theatre, 23 movie screens, an adventure golf course (what Americans call miniature golf), a skate park, the Wavehouse, and a rock-climbing wall.

Village Walk (⊠ *1 Bell St., Point* ☎*031/328–8000* ⊕*www.ushaka marineworld.co.za*), part of uShaka Marine World, is a rather pricey shopping and restaurant mall containing about 100 stores, including photo, surf-gear, art, and good-quality curio shops. The main buildings are thatch, and eye-catching mosaics of lizards and snakes are inlaid into the walkways and echoed in the ceilings. Village Walk also has an American Express currency exchange, an Internet café, and a provincial Zulu Kingdom tourism office.

MARKETS

One of the nicest and most popular of Durban's many flea markets, the **Essenwood Flea Market** (⊠*Essenwood Rd., Berea* ☎*031/202–5632*) is held every Saturday until 2. Classy stalls sell handmade clothes and crafts, leatherwork, stained glass, and restored wooden furniture among many other items in a beautiful park setting. The **Stables** (⊠*Newmarket horse stables, Jacko Jackson Dr., next to the Absa Park Rugby Stadium* ☎*031/312–3752*) carries cheap imports from the East, but also an interesting selection of local crafts, such as beaded and leather goods. It's open Wednesday and Friday evenings 6–10 for a moonlight market and Sunday 10–5, except for June and July. The most exciting market in the city is the **Victoria Street Market** (⊠*Queen and Russell Sts., Indian District* ☎*031/306–4021*), where you can buy everything from recordings of African music to curios and curry spices. Bargaining is expected here, much as it is in India.

SPECIALTY STORES

ART & CRAFTS
★
The classy, nonprofit **African Art Centre** (⊠*94 Florida Rd., Morningside* ☎*031/312–3804 or 031/312–3805* ⊕*www.afriart.org.za* ⊙ *Weekdays 8:30–5, Sat. 9–3, Sun. and public holidays 10–3*) acts as a sales outlet for the work of rural and urban artisans, and is the best craft outlet in Durban. It carries an excellent selection of original African arts and crafts, including Zulu beadwork, ceramics, wood sculptures, and beautifully crafted wire baskets. The store will ship purchases overseas.

The small **Elizabeth Gordon Gallery** (⊠*120 Florida Rd., Morningside* ☎*031/303–8133*) carries a wide selection of work (including prints) by local and international artists and photographers. The crafts shop at the **NSA Gallery** (⊠*166 Bulwer Rd., Glenwood* ☎*031/202–3686*) also carries good-quality local crafts such as furniture, beadwork, and toys.

SIDE TRIPS FROM DURBAN

VALLEY OF A THOUSAND HILLS
45 km (27 mi) northwest of Durban.

In the early part of the 19th century, before cars were introduced, wagons traveled from the port of Durban up along the ridge of this region of plunging gorges, hills, and valleys into the hinterland, where the mining industry was burgeoning. Today the Old Main Road (M103) still runs between Durban and Pietermaritzburg, winding through a number of villages and offering stunning views of hills and valleys dotted with traditional Zulu homesteads. It is along this route that the Comrades Marathon—South Africa's most famous road race—is run.

For purposes of exploring, the area has been organized into routes by the local tourism office. A favorite with Durbanites, the routes wind through villages and past coffee shops, art galleries, restaurants, quaint pubs, small inns, farms, and nature reserves. There are a number of excellent B&Bs, small inns, and lodges in the area, often with fantastic views of the gorges.

The main route is called the T1. It follows the M13 out of Durban, up Field's Hill, through the village of Kloof, and past Everton, Gillits, and Winston Park; it then joins the Old Main Road (M103) at Hillcrest. A number of small shopping centers along the M103 sell a variety of goods, from crafts to old furniture, and there are some excellent coffee shops, restaurants, and small hotels as well as cultural attractions. At the end of the M103 is the small town of Monteseel. Drive along the dirt roads to the signposted overlook for one of the best uninterrupted views of the Thousand Hills. Other well-marked routes in the area are the Kranzkloof, Assagay Averston, and Isithumba routes and the Shongweni Shuffle, which all make for scenic drives.

Assagay Coffee. You can take a tour to see how this homegrown coffee, very popular with locals, is grown, roasted, and packaged. ⌧*Off Old Main Rd., Botha's Hill* ☎*031/765–2941* ⌧*Tours R10* ☉ *Weekdays 8–4, Sat. 10–4.*

PheZulu Safari Park. Popular with big tour buses, PheZulu is the equivalent of fast-food tourism, good for people who want a quick-fix African experience. A tour of the cultural village with its traditional beehive huts gives some insight into African traditions, and there are performances of traditional Zulu dancing, but the operation is not as vibrant or professional as the cultural villages up north in Zululand. An old-fashioned crocodile farm and snake park is fairly interesting, if a little tacky. The curio shop is enormous; you can probably get just about any type of African memento or booklet imaginable. ⌧*Old Main Rd., Drummond* ☎*031/777–1000* ⊕*www.phezulusafaripark.co.za* ⌧*R70* ☉*Daily 8–4:30; shows daily at 10, 11:30, 1, 2, and 3.*

SHOPPING   Most shopping centers do not post hours, as individual stores set their own opening and closing times. For the most part, hours are daily from 9 to 4:30.

The **Fainting Goat** (⊠ *Old Main Rd., Botha's Hill* ☎*No phone*), a fairly ordinary-looking shopping center, has a very good secondhand furniture shop, a coffee roaster, and a lively restaurant serving German specialties. Stop in at the fiber design shop for good-quality woven rugs and tapestries. The pseudo-Victorian **Heritage Market** (⊠ *Old Main Rd., Hillcrest* ☎*031/765–2500*) is charming and colorful, if a little contrived. It has more than 100 specialty stores dotted around a wonderful little central bandstand with rose gardens and twirling vines. There are a number of good coffee shops and restaurants, as well as secondhand bookstores and numerous crafts shops. Just before you start the steep ascent to Botha's Hill from Hillcrest and Assagay, you'll see the fairly scrappy-looking little **Sugar Loaf Centre** (⊠*Old Main Rd., Assagay* ☎*No phone*) on your left. Despite its appearance, it has some interesting shops selling handwoven rugs and fresh farm produce, all from the district, and some woodwork and furniture shops.

DOLPHIN COAST

Located about an hour north of Durban, the Dolphin Coast (aka North Coast) lies along the warm waters of the Indian Ocean, making it a popular vacation spot for South Africas. The area's many beaches are protected by shark nets and lifeguards, making them safe for swimming.

WHERE TO
STAY
☾ ★ $$

⌗ **Hotel iZulu.** This award-winning hotel, set in lush tropical gardens only 50 km (31 mi) north of Durban, was built using only local craftsmen and products. It's the perfect base for game-spotting in the nearby game reserves, which the hotel will arrange for you; visiting the great white sharks at uShaka Sea World; walking the historic battlefields where Brits battled Boers and Zulus; shopping till you drop on the Midlands Meander; or relaxing on the numerous nearby beaches. The comfortable suites with huge en-suite bathrooms are tastefully decorated in creams, greens, and browns, with sliding doors opening onto to the gardens. The food is outstanding, dreamed up and cooked by chef Floris Smith—one of the most sought-after young chefs in South Africa. Start with tandoori prawn vichyssoise, follow up with lamb shank bobotie (braised lamb shank spiced with Cape Malay spices, served in a savory pastry case topped with tarragon baked cream) and then go totally decadent with a chocolate study dessert (a chocolate brownie and hazelnut ice-cream sandwich served with a white-chocolate-and-passion-fruit mousse and a dark-chocolate-and-chili crème brûlée). Pamper yourself further with a restorative stress-relieving treatment at the in-house award-winning Impilo spa. ☖*Private Bag X004, Ballito 4420* ☎*27/32/946–3444* ⊕*www.hotelizulu.com* ⌻*18 suites* ♿*In-room: safe. In-hotel: bar, pool, Internet* ⊟*AE, DC, MC, V* ⏍*BP.*

SOUTH COAST

Vacation towns like Scottburgh, Margate, Ramsgate, Trafalgar, and Palm Beach dot KwaZulu-Natal's southern coast, which stretches for more than 200 km (125 mi) from Durban in the north to Port Edward in the south. The area has some of the country's best beaches, set against a tropical background of natural coastal jungle and palm trees. In fact, Blue Flag status has been conferred on the Marina (at

San Lameer), Ramsgate, Lucien, and Hibberdene beaches.

The South Coast is also famous for the annual sardine run, which usually occurs in June or July (though it has failed to occur in recent years). Colder currents in Antarctica at this time bring millions of sardines to local waters, and they often wash up right on the beach. Dolphins, seabirds, sharks, and whales follow in a feeding frenzy.

> **BLUE FLAG STATUS**
>
> Blue Flag status, which is awarded to more than 3,700 beaches and marinas in 37 countries by the Foundation for Environmental Education, changes every year. It's a good idea to check WESSA's (Wildlife and Environment Society of South Africa) Web site (☎ *033/330-3931* ⊕ *www.wessa. org.za*) to see who's on the list when you're planning a trip.

WHERE TO STAY & EAT
$–$$$$

San Lameer. This exclusive self-catering resort is a great getaway from noisy city life for a group of friends or a family. Spacious one- to five-bedroom Tuscan-style villas, many with breathtaking views of the sea or the bird-filled lagoons, are set among gardens and indigenous forest. At night it's lit by hundreds of twinkling lights. Stroll down paved walkways to the private beach, or meander through the woods, and you'll likely see small antelope and monkeys. Golf enthusiasts enjoy the championship course, which hosts major tournaments, and there's also a mashie (tiny) course. **Helen Fouche** (☎ *011/896–3544* ✉ info@sanlameer.com) handles bookings for privately owned villas at reduced rates or rent a villa through **Villa Rentals** (☎ *036/313–0450* ✉ villaren@venturenet.co.za). If DIY is not your style, opt for the recently refurbished on-site Mondazur Resort Estate Hotel. ✉ *Lower South Coast Main Rd., between Ramsgate and Palm Beach* 🖂 *Box 88, Southbroom 4277* ☎ *039/313–0011* ⊕ *www.sanlameer.com* 🛏 *40 rooms, 22 villas* ♿ *In-room: kitchen. In-hotel: restaurant, bar, golf course, tennis courts, pools, beachfront, bicycles, laundry service, airport shuttle, public Wi-Fi* ☰ *AE, DC, MC, V.*

$–$$
Fodor'sChoice
★

✕ **Lynton Hall.** This majestic, castlelike country house sits on 160 acres of gardens and coastal forests that extend down to the Indian Ocean. Built by sugar-baron brothers Charles and Sir Frank Reynolds in the late 1800s, it nestles next to the picturesque Umdoni Park golf course and has hosted royalty, prime ministers, and well-known literary figures. Each suite is different, boldly decorated with a mix of Victorian, Indian, and Southeast Asian furnishings. Large Victorian bathrooms have modern fittings, and even chandeliers. While the setting is romantic and tranquil, the multi-award-winning food is nothing short of poetic and adventurous. The cuisine (R215 prix-fixe dinner) is offered on a frequently changing menu—and might include mango soup with sorbet, tempura of line fish, red roast quail, or beef fillet with truffle-oil jus, followed by Gorgonzola ice cream with poached pears and red-wine jelly. 🖂 *Umdoni Park, Old South Coast Rd., Box 272, Pennington 4184* ☎ *039/975–3122* ⊕ *www.lyntonhall.co.za* 🛏 *11 suites* ♿ *In-room: refrigerator, safe. In-hotel: restaurant, room service, bar, tennis court, pool, beachfront, water sports, bicycles, laundry service,* *airport shuttle, parking (no fee), no kids under 12, no-smoking rooms, public Internet, no elevator* ⊟*AE, DC, MC, V* ◎*|BP.*

PIETERMARITZBURG AND THE MIDLANDS

80 km (50 mi) northwest of Durban.

'Maritzburg, as it is fondly known in South Africa, is a sleepy town with redbrick colonial architecture that offers tangible reminders of South Africa's British past; it's often referred to as the "Last British Outpost," even though it was first settled in 1838 by Voortrekkers. The city takes its name from two Voortrekker leaders, Gert Maritz and Piet Retief. Retief was murdered by the Zulu king Dingaan.

There is a relaxed, easygoing atmosphere here, which appeals to its residents, who are mainly involved in government or education—both the University of KwaZulu-Natal Pietermaritzburg and the provincial legislature are located here. The town lies at the foot of the KwaZulu-Natal Midlands, a lush farming area that has developed into a shopping and holiday destination with the development of the Midlands Meander—a series of arts-and-crafts routes.

⚠ Due to recent road name changes by the government, we've included both new names and the old road names, which are in parentheses, to help alleviate confusion as much as possible.

PIETERMARITZBURG

In a bowl of hills in the Natal Midlands, this city is the current capital of KwaZulu-Natal, and the legislature is in the busy city center. It's a pleasant town, with wide tree-lined streets and a temperate climate that escapes the worst of the coastal heat and humidity. Its redbrick colonial architecture offers tangible reminders of KwaZulu-Natal's and South Africa's British past; dozens of late-19th-century buildings line the streets in the center of town. It's worth visiting just to see this slice of Victorian England.

TIMING Even though many of the sidewalks are shaded, it's wise to get any serious exploring done either in the cooler earlier morning hours or in late afternoon, particularly in summer. When the heat begins to settle in, take a drive out to World's View for a panoramic view of the town.

Numbers in the text correspond to numbers in the margin and on the Pietermaritzburg map.

WHAT TO SEE

⓾ City Hall. Built in 1902, this grand building is the largest all-brick structure in the southern hemisphere. It's a classic Victorian edifice, notable for its stained-glass windows, soaring clock tower, and ornate gables and domes. You can take a self-guided tour; brochures are available at the reception desk. ✉*Church St. and Chief Albert Luthuli St. (formerly Commercial Rd).* ☎*033/395–1167* ✆*Free* ⊙ *Weekdays 8:30–4:30.*

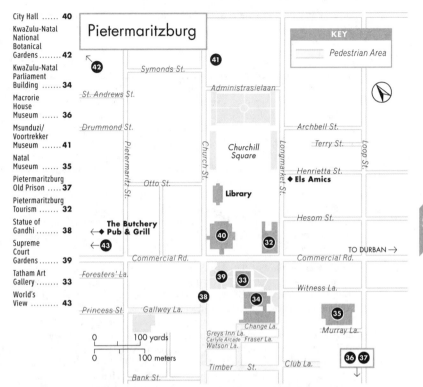

🖤 **42** **KwaZulu-Natal National Botanical Gardens.** Established in 1870, these gardens contain such colorful flowers as bougainvilleas and azaleas and provide a sanctuary for more than 100 species of birds. Rare and indigenous plants are preserved here, so it's no surprise that there is a muti garden (garden where traditional medicinal plants are grown) on-site. Small game, such as buck (in South Africa antelopes are called bucks regardless of sex), which have made the garden their home, can be spotted during guided tours. ✉ *Mayor's Walk, Prestbury* ☎ *033/344–3585* 💲 *R10* 🕙 *Daily 6–6.*

34 **KwaZulu-Natal Parliament Building.** This redbrick building, erected in 1889, formerly housed the twin chambers of the colonial parliament and is now used for the provincial legislature's sessions. Recent works of art promoting democracy and human rights by South African artists are displayed inside. A statue of Queen Victoria stands in front of the building. ✉ *Langalibalele (Longmarket St.) and Chief Albert Luthuli Sts. (Commercial Rd.)* ☎ *033/355–7600* ⊕ *www.kznlegislature.gov.za* 💲 *Free* 🕙 *Weekdays 8–4:30, free tours by appointment.*

🖤 **36** **Macrorie House Museum.** This lovely residence, described as the finest and best-built family house in the city, is typical of old Pietermaritzburg. Bishop Macrorie lived in the house from 1870 to 1892, and it's been furnished to reflect that period. A collection of dolls in period costume and the bishop's private chapel, dating back to 1869, are on display. ✉ *11 Jabu Ndlovu St. (Loop St.)* ☎ *033/394–2161* 🎫 *R5* 🕐 *Mon. 10–3, Tues.–Fri. 9–1.*

Ⓒ ❹ **Msunduzi/Voortrekker Museum.** This newly refurbished multicultural museum complex occupies the Church of the Vow, an immensely important monument in the eyes of many Afrikaners. After the murder of Voortrekker leader Piet Retief in 1838, the Voortrekkers sought revenge on the Zulus and their king, Dingaan. A Boer commando under the leadership of Andries Pretorius vowed to build a church if God granted them victory. The Battle of Blood River followed, in which 3,000 Zulus died and the Boers managed to emerge without a single casualty. Constructed in 1841 in typical Cape Dutch style, the church now houses a variety of Voortrekker artifacts, including an old wagon, flintlock rifles, and Piet Retief's prayer book. A reconstruction of Andries Pretorius's thatch home is also open to the public. A separate building houses various exhibitions—some still under construction—reflecting the culture and history of the peoples of KwaZulu-Natal. ✉ *351 Langalibalele St. (Longmarket St.)* ☎ *033/394–6834* 🎫 *R5* 🕐 *Weekdays 9–4, Sat. 9–1.*

Ⓒ ❸❺ **Natal Museum.** One of five national museums in South Africa and the largest museum in KwaZulu-Natal, this museum contains a little of everything. You'll find lifelike models of dinosaurs as well as stuffed African mammals, snakes, marine creatures, and local birds. The city's human history is revealed through a re-creation of an 1880s Pietermaritzburg street, complete with settler's cottage, shops, a pharmacy, and a blacksmith. San (Bushman) paintings are displayed in a replica of a Drakensberg cave. An exhibit on sub-Saharan cultures highlights religious, ceremonial, military, and household artifacts from across Africa. ✉ *237 Jabu Ndlovu St. (Loop St.)* ☎ *033/345–1404* ⊕ *www.nmsa.org. za* 🎫 *R5* 🕐 *Weekdays 9–4:30, Sat. 10–4, Sun. 11–3.*

❸❼ **Pietermaritzburg Old Prison.** The city's first jailhouse, built in 1862, is now used by Project Gateway, a church-based nonprofit organization that offers social development programs to the community. Key historical figures imprisoned here include Zulu king Dinizulu who in the late 19th century resisted the British, and Penuel Maduna, who was jailed for resisting apartheid and who later became minister of justice in the new South Africa. Don't miss the political graffiti on some of the prison walls. Guided tours by appointment. ✉ *2 Burger St.* ☎ *033/845–0400* ⊕ *www.projectgateway.co.za* 🎫 *R20 for the tour* 🕐 *Mon.–Thurs. 8–4:30, Fri. 8–4.*

❸❷ **Pietermaritzburg Tourism.** The office, in a classic redbrick building, distributes detailed pamphlets and maps of the town. Built in 1884 to house the Borough Police, the building included a bell tower used to signal a 9 PM curfew for blacks. ✉ *177 Chief Albert Luthuli St. (Commercial Rd.)* ☎ *033/345–1348* ⊕ *www.pmbtourism.co.za* 🕐 *Weekdays 8–5, Sat. 8–1.*

❸❽ **Statue of Gandhi.** On his arrival in the city in 1893, Mahatma Gandhi, then a young lawyer, was thrown out of a whites-only first-class train compartment. A statue of the Indian pacifist leader was erected in 1993 to mark the centenary of that day, of which he later said: "My active nonviolence began from that date." Gandhi lived in South Africa for 21 years before returning to India. ⊠*Maritzburg Mall.*

㊴ Supreme Court Gardens. This memorial park includes several monuments that commemorate those who died in wars that raged in this country and abroad: the Zulu War of 1879, the Anglo-Boer War (1899–1902), and World War I. The monuments all have a very English feel, emphasized by the legends on the commemorative stones extolling Queen, Country, and Empire. The gardens can get busy, as they are a popular thoroughfare and are not as well maintained as they used to be. ⊠*Chief Albert Luthuli St. (Commercial Rd.) at Church St.*

㉝ Tatham Art Gallery. Completed in 1871, the old Supreme Court building that houses this gallery is yet another of Pietermaritzburg's fine redbrick colonial structures. The museum is first-rate, with a solid collection of 19th- and 20th-century British and French paintings, including works by Picasso, Matisse, and Renoir. Of keenest interest, though, is the South African collection, which displays works by contemporary artists, including linocuts and traditional crafts such as beadwork, baskets, and tribal earplugs. The museum also presents temporary exhibits. The art gallery shop, though small, sells high-quality, locally produced contemporary crafts, such as woven baskets, beaded jewelry, African beaded Fabergé-style eggs, copper bracelets, and carved wooden angels. ⊠ *Opposite City Hall, Chief Albert Luthuli St. (Commercial Rd.)* ☎*033/342–1804* ⊒*Free* ☉*Tues.–Sun. 10–6.*

㊸ World's View. This spectacular overlook provides panoramic views of the city and surrounding countryside. The viewpoint lies on the route used by the Voortrekkers on their long migration from the Cape in the 19th century. A large diagram traces their route and labels the major landscape features. ⊠*Off Old Howick Rd. (R103).*

WHERE TO EAT

$–$$$ ✕**Else Amics.** This upmarket, à la carte restaurant, housed in one of the city's old Victorian houses, has been in operation since 1977. It serves seafood and game, including warthog and pheasant, as well as continental fare, and all dishes have a Spanish flair. Signature dishes include artichokes stuffed with crab, *sopa de ajo* (garlic soup), *chutetas de cerdo zingara* (grilled pork chops with a sauce of ham, mushrooms, tongue, onions, and red peppers), and gazpacho. ⊠*380 Langalibalele St. (Longmarket St.), City Center* ☎*033/345–6524* ⊟*AE, DC, MC, V* ⏚*BYOB* ☉*Closed Sun. and Mon. No lunch Sat.*

$–$$ ✕**The Butchery Pub & Grill.** The Butchery is a local favorite for those looking for traditional South African steaks, which range in size from 7 ounces to 35 ounces. The decor is distinctly African, with the chairs covered in zebra-skin material, elephant tusks on display, and Zulu spears over the doorways. Try the Bar-One cake for dessert. ⊠*101 Roberts Rd., Clarendon* ☎*033/342–5239* ⊕*www.thebutchery.co.za* ⊜*Reservations essential* ⊟*AE, DC, MC, V* ☉*Daily noon–late evening.*

SHOPPING

The large, upscale **Liberty Midlands Mall** (✉ *50 Sanctuary Rd., Chase Valley* ☎*033/342–0062*), a relatively new addition to Pietermaritzburg, is in the same vein as Durban's Gateway shopping center, but it offers many smaller clothing stores and shoe shops you won't find at either of these malls. There's also an extensive food court and banking facilities, and a pharmacy and Internet café.

KWAZULU-NATAL MIDLANDS

Set amid the rolling green foothills of the Drakensberg, the Midlands encompass waterfalls, lakes, dams (artificial lakes), forests, fields, Zulu villages, game reserves, and battle sites. The climate is pleasant most of the year, though summers tend to be hot. The area has long been an enclave for craftspeople—weavers, potters, woodcrafters, metalworkers, box makers, cheese makers, and beer brewers—who escaped the cities.

As a way to draw customers to the area, the crafters created four routes, called the Midlands Meander, in 1983, which include more than 160 shops, galleries, cultural activities, restaurants, and accomodations. The routes, which run through the towns of Curry's Post and Howick in the northeast and Nottingham Road, Balgowan, the Dargyle District, Lion's River, and Midmar in the southwest, provide a great opportunity to shop for authentic South African arts and crafts, while enjoying the tranquillity and beauty of the countryside. The area is filled with top accommodations and dining options.

TIMING   The most popular time to do the Meander is in the autumn (March to May), when it's not too hot or too cold. Many South Africans love the winters here; it often snows, particularly on the higher ground, and many establishments burn fires. No matter the time of year, though, there's always something to see and do, most of which involves shopping.

WHAT TO SEE

67 **Howick Falls.** Though this area is mainly about dining, shopping, and the arts, this waterfall is definitely worth a 10-minute stop. In the town of Howick, the Umgeni River plunges an impressive 300 feet into the gorge. There are numerous hikes of varying difficulty that provide different vantages of the falls. Contact or visit the Howick Tourism Office, which is just a few hundred yards from the falls, for information. ✉*Howick Tourism Office, 4 Fallview Dr.* ☎*033/330–5305.*

WHERE TO STAY & EAT

There are dozens of small hotels, guesthouses, and places to stop and eat along the Meander. The local tourism office, Midlands Meander Association, publishes a good, oversized magazine with maps of the routes and details of the various establishments, which is available free at most of the stops along the routes.

$$ **Brookdale Health Hydro.** Eat delicious, healthy (but small) meals; pamper yourself with the included massages and beauty treatments; and

relax for three nights (minimum stay) in this collection of comfortable, country-style cottages. Superb personal attention, professional treatments, lectures on topics ranging from stress management to dietary supplementation, late-night soaks in a whirlpool, early-morning walks over the mountains, and aquacise in the heated pool will get you into shape for the rest of your vacation—or cap it off with a feeling of rejuvenation. ☒ *R103, opposite Rawdons Hotel, Box 109, Nottingham Rd., 3280* ☎ *033/266–6208* ⊕ *www.brookdale.co.za* ⤴ *21 rooms, 2 suites* ♿ *In-hotel: pool, gym, spa* ☰ *AE, DC, MC, V* ⊠ *FAP.*

$–$$ ✕⊞ **Granny Mouse Country House.** One of the best-loved and oldest hotels on the Meander, Granny Mouse has cozy thatch rooms, all slightly different, with a river view, fireplace, and homey, though upmarket, atmosphere. Freestanding rooms offer privacy and peace, and the main hotel building—formerly an unusual farmhouse with doors and windows from an old church—offers conviviality and warmth in its several lounges. The on-site Mouse & Lion pub is locally famous for its lavish breakfasts and afternoon teas. Some of the best places on the Meander are within easy reach. ☒ *R103, 25 km (15½ mi) south of Nottingham Rd. exit off the N3* ⌖ *Box 22, Balgowan 3275* ☎ *033/234–4071* ⊕ *www.grannymouse.co.za* ⤴ *16 suites* ♿ *In-hotel: restaurant, bar, pools, bicycles, no elevator* ☰ *DC, MC, V* ⊠ *BP.*

★ $–$$ ✕⊞ **Hartford House.** Built in 1875, this inn is steeped in history and misty beauty. High up on the Meander, in the foothills of the Drakensberg, and adjacent to the Summerhill racing stud, it is a deliciously luxurious, if rather formal, escape for the lucky few. A few of the suites are in the original house, whereas others front an ethereal, lovely lake. Each suite is different, decorated in a gloriously eclectic collision of fabrics and furnishings from Africa, Europe, and the East. The food, which has garnered top honors, is just as rich and eclectically surprising. Dinner (R200 for five courses; reservations essential), which the chefs start preparing at dawn, is an unforgettable five-course event with wines to match. ☒ *Hlatikulu Rd., off road to Giant's Castle, Mooi River 3300* ☎ *033/263–2713* ⊕ *www.hartford.co.za* ⤴ *13 suites* ♿ *In-room: safe, ethernet, refrigerator. In-hotel: restaurant, bar, tennis court, spa, bicycles, laundry service, airport shuttle, no kids under 12, no-smoking rooms* ☰ *AE, DC, MC, V* ⊠ *BP.*

SHOPPING

Though on the whole the route is known for its quality, you can also find some establishments that are not up to standards of others. If you've only a limited time, head for the concentration of crafts shops on the R103 between Nottingham Road and Lion's River. If you have a couple of days, base yourself at one of the hotels and explore the Meander using the large-format, free guide available at most Meander stops. Many of the better establishments offer shipping services for those unusual items large and small.

A great place to buy handmade leather goods, especially shoes and beautiful bags and briefcases, is **Groundcover** (☒ *Curry's Post Rd., past Kingdom Weavers* ☎ *033/330–6092* ⊕ *www.groundcover.co.za*). The **Rosewood Embroidery Shoppe** (☒ *9 km [6 mi] northwest of the Curry's*

Post/Lion's River exit off the N3, then 5 km [3 mi] on the Dargyle Rd. ☎*033/234–4386* ⊕*www.rosewoodshoppe.co.za*) sells beautiful hand-stitched, pure cotton linens; upholstery; night wear; and gifts. At the **Woodturner** (✉*6 km [4 mi] from Rosewood, down the Dargyle Rd.* ☎*033/234–4548* ⊕*www.sculpturalwood.co.za*), father and son Andrew and John Early specialize in making elegant bowls, modern wood sculptures, and one-of-a-kind furniture pieces using salvaged, exotic woods like jacaranda and local woods like African mahogany and stinkwood. Their pieces are often snapped up by studios in New York and elsewhere. The studio is a delight; ask to see the Earlys at work in their workshop behind the sprawling farmhouse. Near the Woodturner is the **Dargyle Valley Pottery** (✉*1 km [½ mi] on the D666 off the Dargyle Rd.* ☎*033/234–4377*), where renowned potter Ian Glenny, whose work is in private collections and galleries worldwide, founded the Meander in 1983. Choose from porcelain, stoneware, or terra-cotta pots, bowls, and vases—or indulge in a fireplace. **Culamoya Chimes** (✉*3 km [2 mi] off the R103* ☎*033/234–4503 or 083/627–6195*), in the Dargyle District, has a 13-foot chime as well as other chimes that boom the sounds of Big Ben and St. Paul's Cathedral down to gentle tinkles of fairy magic. Near Culamoya and Granny Mouse, **Mole Hill** (✉*R103, 8 km [5 mi] south of Nottingham Road* ☎*033/234–4352* ⊕*www.millgate.co.za*) has a good reputation for high-quality men's and women's shirts with an African twist. Back toward Durban, the **Weaver's Hut** (✉*4 km [2½ mi] from the Howick/Midmar exit off the N3* ☎*033/330–4026* ⊕*www.weavershut.com*) in Howick has beautiful handmade rugs. Farther south, **Peel's Honey** (✉*N3, below the Midmar Dam* ☎*033/330–3762*) sells an assortment of honey, brittle, and other tasty treats.

DURBAN & PIETERMARITZBURG ESSENTIALS

TRANSPORTATION

BY AIR

Durban International Airport (DUR) is 16 km (10 mi) south of town along the Southern Freeway, or an easy 20-minute drive. South African Airways (SAA) flies to Durban via Johannesburg. Domestic airlines serving Durban include SAA, BA/Comair, Kulula, 1Time, SA Airlink, and Mango. Perhaps the easiest way to book a ticket to or from Durban is online. Check the various airlines' Web sites to compare prices. As with most other domestic flights, the further in advance you book, the more reasonable the fares will be. Kulula and 1Time are the more comfortable of the budget-priced airlines, as their seats are a little larger, but Mango is also well worth considering. If you're flying one of these three airlines, you'll be expected to buy your own snacks and drinks on board. SAA is usually the more expensive option, unless you're looking for a ticket at short notice (next day or two), when it may turn out to be cheapest.

The most inexpensive transfer into Durban and back is the Airport Shuttle Service, which costs R30 and departs a half hour after incoming flights arrive and leaves the city center every hour. Its drop-off points include the Hilton and Royal hotels, but it is likely to drop you any-where central if you request it first. Call ahead and the bus will pick you up at any hotel in the city; there's no need to reserve for the trip into Durban. If you want to go farther afield, call Mozzie Cabs or the Magic Bus.

Although Pietermaritzburg does have its own airport, it isn't used much by tourists because the town is so close to Durban—about 100 km (60 mi), or an easy hour's drive on a good road.

Airport Durban International Airport (☎ *031/408–1155*).

Airlines BA/Comair (☎ *031/450–7000* ⊕ *www.britishairways.com*). **Kulula** (☎ *0861/585–852* ⊕ *www.kulula.com*). **Mango** (☎ *0861/162–646* ⊕ *www. flymango.com*). **1Time** (☎ *086/134–5345* ⊕ *www.onetime.com*). **SA Airlink** (☎ *031/408–1029* ⊕ *www.saairlink.co.za*). **South African Airways** (☎ *0861/808– 808* ⊕ *www.flysaa.com*).

Airport Transfers Airport Shuttle Service (☎ *031/465–5573*). **Magic Bus** (☎ *031/263–2647*). **Mozzie Cabs** (☎ *0860/669–943*).

BY BUS

Greyhound and Translux Express offer long-distance bus service to cities all over South Africa. All intercity buses leave from New Dur-ban Station (off N.M.R. Avenue, between Old Fort Avenue and Argyle Road). Though you can often fly for much the same prices as traveling by bus, especially if you book well in advance or find a discount.

Durban Transport operates two types of bus service, but you need con-cern yourself only with the Mynah buses. These small buses operate from 6 AM to 11:45 PM along set routes every half hour through the city and along the Beachfront and cost a couple of rands per ride. Bus stops are marked by a sign with a mynah bird on it. The main bus depot is on Pine Street between Aliwal and Gardiner streets. You pay as you board; exact change is not required. Route information is also available at an information office at the corner of Aliwal and Pine streets.

Bus Lines Eldo Coaches (☎ *031/307–3363*). **Greyhound** (☎ *083/915–9000*). **Mynah Bus (Durban City Transport)** (☎ *031/309–5942*). **Raymond Nelson Land Transport** (☎ *031/307–3503*). **Translux Express** (☎ *031/361–7670*).

BY CAR

Durban is relatively easy to find your way around, because the sea is a constant reference point. Downtown Durban is dominated by two parallel one-way streets, West Street (going toward the sea) and Smith Street (going away from the sea, toward Berea and Pietermaritzburg); together they get you in and out of the city center easily. Parking down-town is a nightmare; head for an underground garage whenever you can. As with the rest of South Africa, wherever you go you'll be beset by self-appointed car guards, who ask if they can watch your car. The going rate for a tip—if you want to give one—is R2–R5, depending on how long you're away. The guards directly outside Joe Cool's, between North and South beaches, are said to be very trustworthy. ⚠**Don't leave your keys with anyone.**

The M4, which stretches north up to the Dolphin Coast—from Umhlanga to Ballito, about 40 km (25 mi), and beyond—is a particularly pretty coastal road, offering many views of the sea through lush natural vegetation and sugarcane fields. It's much nicer than the sterile N2 highway, which takes a parallel path slightly inland and offers no views.

The easiest way to reach Pietermaritzburg from Durban is along the N3, a direct 80-km (50-mi) run. Far more interesting and scenic, however, is the route that follows Old Main Road (R103) through the Valley of a Thousand Hills and rejoins the N3 east of Pietermaritzburg. Allow for an hour from Durban to PMB if you take the highway and add another half hour for the R103.

KwaZulu-Natal is particularly strict about speeding, and there are always either camera traps or police traps on the Durban–PMB road, so don't go more than 10 kph above the speed limit. On the whole, you'll find KZN drivers a lot slower, friendlier, and more accommodating than drivers from Gauteng.

Avis, Budget, EuropCar, Imperial, and Tempest have rental offices at the airport. The cheapest car costs about R350 per day, including insurance, plus R1.50 per kilometer (per half mile), or about R800 for the weekend. Avis offers unlimited mileage to international visitors, as long as you can produce your return ticket as proof.

Rental Companies **Avis** (⊠ *Ulundi Pl., City Center, Durban* ☎ *031/304–1741* ⊠ *1 Pharazyn Rd., Oribi, Pietermaritzburg* ☎ *033/386–6101* ⊕ *www.avis.co.za*). **Budget** (⊠ *Durban International Airport* ☎ *031/408–1809*). **EuropCar Hire** (⊠ *Durban International Airport* ☎ *031/469–0667*). **Imperial Car Rental** (⊠ *52 Stanger St., Morningside, Durban* ☎ *031/337–3731*). **Tempest Car Hire** (⊠ *47 Victoria Embankment, Victoria Embankment, Durban* ☎ *031/469–0660*).

BY RICKSHAW

Colorfully decorated rickshaws are unique to Durban—you won't find them in any other South African city. Though their origins lie in India, these two-seat carriages with large wheels are all over the city and are pulled exclusively by Zulu men dressed in feathered headgear and traditional garb. The rickshaw runners ply their trade all day, every day, mostly along the Golden Mile section of the beachfront. The going rate is R30 for a ride (2 people) for about 15 minutes, and R10 for a photo (don't assume you can take a picture without paying for the privilege). While it's worth doing because it will be memorable and won't have the opportunity anywhere else—negotiate the rate before climbing on.

BY TAXI

Taxis are metered and start at R5, with an additional R7 per kilometer (per half mile). Expect to pay about R60 from City Hall to North Beach and R200 to the airport. The most convenient taxi stands are around City Hall and in front of the beach hotels. Some taxis display a "for-hire" light, whereas others you simply hail when you can see they're empty. Major taxi companies include Bunny Cabs, Checker Radio Taxis, Deluxe Radio Taxis, and Morris Radio Taxis. Eagle Radio

Taxis is a little more expensive than other companies. If you're headed to the Indian Market on a weekend, consider having your taxi wait for you, as it can be difficult to flag a taxi in this neighborhood.

Taxi Companies **Bunny Cabs** (☎ *031/332-2914*). **Checker Radio Taxis** (☎ *031/465-1660*). **Deluxe Radio Taxis** (☎ *031/337-1661*). **Eagle Radio Taxis** (☎ *031/337-8333*). **Morris Radio Taxis** (☎ *031/337-2711*).

BY TRAIN

The Durban railway station is a huge, ghastly place that is difficult to find your way around. It's dirty and crowded, and petty theft is a problem. Spoornet's *Trans-Natal* train runs daily between Durban and Johannesburg, stopping at Pietermaritzburg, Estcourt, and Ladysmith. The trip to Jo'burg takes 13 hours and costs about R300 one way.

Train Station **Durban Railway Station** (✉ *N.M.R. Ave., City Center, Durban* ☎ *031/361-7609*).

Train Line **Spoornet** (☎ *031/361-7609* ⊕ *www.spoornet.co.za*).

CONTACTS & RESOURCES

EMBASSY

United States **U.S. Embassy** (✉ *Durban Bay House, 333 Smith St., City Center, Durban* ☎ *031/305-7600*).

EMERGENCIES

The best hospitals in central Durban are Entabeni and St. Augustine's, both private hospitals in the Glenwood area with 24-hour emergency rooms. Umhlanga Hospital is the best north of the city. Addington Hospital, a massive public hospital on the Beachfront, operates a 24-hour emergency room; though it's cheaper, it's not recommended. Daynite Pharmacy is open daily until 10:30.

In Pietermaritzburg, the best hospital is St. Anne's Hospital.

Emergency Services **Ambulance** (☎ *10177*). **Fire** (☎ *031/361-0000*). **General Emergencies** (☎ *10111*). **Police** (☎ *10111*).

Hospitals **Addington Hospital** (✉ *Erskine Terr., South Beach, Beachfront, Durban* ☎ *031/327-2000*). **Entabeni Hospital** (✉ *148 S. Ridge Rd., Glenwood, Durban* ☎ *031/204-1300*). **St. Anne's Hospital** (✉ *331 Burger St., City Center, Pietermaritzburg* ☎ *033/897-5000*). **St. Augustine's** (✉ *4 Cato Rd., Glenwood, Durban* ☎ *031/268-5000, 031/268-5559 trauma*). **Umhlanga Hospital** (✉ *323 Umhlanga Rocks Dr., Umhlanga* ☎ *031/560-5500, 080/033-6967 trauma*).

Late-Night Pharmacy **Daynite Pharmacy** (✉ *West St., City Center* ✉ *Point Rd., Point, Durban* ☎ *031/368-3666*).

INTERNET

Most hotels provide access to the Internet through business centers or Internet cafés, as well as through connections in the rooms if you have your own computer. Outside of hotels, Internet cafés seem to come and go quickly, so ask around. An Internet café at uShaka Marine World is open 8 AM–10 PM.

MONEY MATTERS

There are plenty of ATMs in and around Durban—at shopping centers, large attractions like Suncoast and uShaka, and even some of the smaller supermarkets. Most bank branches exchange money, and the airport and uShaka have money exchanges, as do Rennies and the AmEx foreign-exchange bureau. Shops in the bigger malls like Gateway, Pavilion, Musgrave, and La Lucia often take traveler's checks. Though you will need cash at the markets, don't carry too much. Use credit cards where you can.

Exchange Services **AmEx foreign-exchange bureau** (⊠ *350 Smith St., City Center, Durban* ☎ *031/301–5541*). **Rennies** (⊠ *Durban Bay House, 333 Smith St., City Center, Durban* ☎ *031/307–2625*).

TOURS

Durban Africa has a series of city walking tours for R40 per person. Tours depart from the Tourist Junction weekdays at 9:45 and return at 12:30, but you need to book in advance, as the tour guide only arrives if reservations have been made. The Oriental Walkabout explores the Indian District, including Victoria Market and several mosques. The Historical Walkabout covers the major historic monuments in the city, and the Feel of Durban Walkabout explores some of the city's military past, including the Old Fort, Warrior's Gate, and the original armory. Durban Africa offers other tour options as well; a comprehensive list of tour options is on its Web site.

Trips 'n Transport has standard sightseeing tours of Durban, including the National Botanic Gardens, as well as tours to the Thousand Hills area and further afield. They can tailor-make trips to any interest.

Zulwini Safaris provides standard tours (including the Drakensberg, the battlefields, game parks, and adventure travel) and designs custom tours to anywhere in the province; it also does tours for small groups. Its specialties are unusual, adventure, and off-the-beaten-path trips.

Sarie Marais Pleasure Cruises and Isle of Capri offer sightseeing cruises around Durban Bay or out to sea. Tours, which last about 90 minutes and cost about R60 per person, depart from the jetties next to the Natal Maritime Museum, on the Victoria Embankment at Aliwal Stand, the Point.

Tours of the Jumah Mosque can be arranged through the Islamic Propagation Center, inside the mosque, or through Durban Africa.

Urmilla Singh, who runs Tours of Remberance, specializes in taking tourists to off-the-beaten cultural and heritage sites, such as the Bhambayi informal settlement outside Durban and a memorial to John Dube, founding president of the ANC.

Tour Operators **Durban Africa** (☎ *031/304–4934* ⊕ *www.durban.kzn.org.za*). **Islamic Propagation Center** (☎ *031/306–0026*). **Isle of Capri** (☎ *031/337–7751*). **Sarie Marais Pleasure Cruises** (☎ *031/305–2844*). **Tours of Remembrance** (☎ *031/337–7879 or 083/560–9999* ✍ *uritours@absamail.co.za*). **Trips 'n Transport** (☎ *031/337–0230* ⊕ *http://users.iafrica.com/t/tr/trips*). **Zulwini Safaris** (☎ *033/347–1579* ⊕ *www.zulwini.com*).

TRAVEL AGENCIES

Rennies is the South African representative of Thomas Cook. It is open weekdays 8:30–4:30 and Saturday 8:30–noon. American Express is open weekdays 8–5 and Saturday 8:30–11, and has a full range of client services.

Travel Agents **American Express** (✉ *2 Durban Club Pl., off Smith St., City Center, Durban* ☎ *031/301–5541*). **Rennies** (✉ *Durban Bay House, 333 Smith St., City Center, Durban* ☎ *031/304–1511*).

VISITOR INFORMATION

The Tourist Junction, in the restored Old Station Building, houses a number of tourist-oriented companies and services, where you can find information on almost everything that's happening in Durban and KwaZulu-Natal. Among the companies represented are Durban Africa, the city's tourism authority; an accommodations service; an intercity train reservations office; a KwaZulu-Natal Nature Conservation Service booking desk; regional KwaZulu-Natal tourist offices; and various bus and transport companies. It is open weekdays 8–5 and weekends 9–2. Sugar Coast Tourism (covering the Umhlanga and nearby Umdloti areas), is open weekdays 8–4:30 and Saturday 9–noon. The Thousand Hills Tourism Association covers this area.

If you're looking to explore the Midlands on the Midlands Meander, contact the Midlands Meander Association for their magazine that includes maps of the routes and details of the various establishments.

An excellent Web site for all areas in KwaZulu-Natal is the official provincial tourism site, Zulu Kingdom.

Tourist Offices **Midlands Meander Association** (☎ *033/330–8195* ⊕ *www.midlandsmeander.co.za*). **Sugar Coast Tourism** (✉ *Chartwell Dr., off Lighthouse Rd., Umhlanga 4320* ☎ *031/561–4257*). **Thousand Hills Tourism Association** (✉ *Old Main Rd., Botha's Hill 3660* ☎ *031/777–1874* ⊕ *www.1000hills.kzn.org.za*). **Tourist Junction** (✉ *160 Pine St., City Center, Durban 4001* ☎ *031/304–4934*).

Web Sites **Dolphin Coast** (⊕ *http://dolphincoast.kzn.org.za*). **Zulu Kingdom** (⊕ *www.kzn.org.za*).

THE DRAKENSBERG

Afrikaners call them the Drakensberg: the Dragon Mountains. To Zulus they are uKhahlamba (pronounced Ooka–hlamba)—"Barrier of Spears." Both are apt descriptions for this wall of rock that rises from the Natal grasslands, forming a natural fortress protecting the mountain kingdom of Lesotho. The Drakensberg is the highest range in southern Africa and has some of the most spectacular scenery in the country. It's a hiker's dream, and you could easily spend several days here just soaking up the awesome views. uKhahlamba/Drakensberg Park, a World Heritage Site, is the first site in South Africa to be recognized for its combination of natural and cultural attractions.

Bushman Paintings

Besides the hiking opportunities and the sheer beauty of the mountains, the other great attraction of the Berg is the San (Bushman) paintings. The San are a hunter-gatherer people who once roamed the entire country from 8,000 years ago to the 1800s. More than 40,000 of their paintings are sprinkled in scores of caves and on rock overhangs throughout the Berg in more than 550 known San rock-art sites—probably the finest collection of rock paintings in the country. They tell the stories of bygone hunts, dances, and battles as well as relating and representing spiritual beliefs and practices. Images of spiritual leaders in a trance state, their visions, and their transformations into animals have now been studied and written about, although some of the mean- ings are still not fully understood. With the arrival of the Nguni peoples from the north and white settlers from the southwest in the 18th century, the San were driven out of their tradi- tional hunting lands and retreated into the remote fastnesses of the Drak- ensberg and the Kalahari Desert. San cattle raiding in Natal in the late 19th century occasioned harsh punitive expeditions by white settlers and local Bantu tribes, and by 1880 the last San had disappeared from the Berg. Today only a few clans remain in the very heart of the Kalahari Desert. For more information on viewing rock-art sites, contact **Ezemvelo KZN Wildlife** (☎ *033/845–1999* ⊕ *www.kznwildlife. com*), the province's official conserva- tion organization.

The blue-tinted mountains seem to infuse the landscape, cooling the "champagne air"—as the locals refer to the heady, sparkling breezes that blow around the precipices and pinnacles. The mountains, with names like Giant's Castle, Cathedral Peak, and the Sentinel, seem to have a special atmosphere, as well as a unique topography. It's no surprise that South African–born J.R.R. Tolkien—legendary author of *The Lord of the Rings*—was inspired by the fantastic shapes of the Drakensberg massif when he created the phantasmagorical settings of his Middle Earth.

The Drakensberg is not a typical mountain range—it's actually an escarpment separating a high interior plateau from the coastal low- lands of Natal. It's a continuation of the same escarpment that divides the Transvaal Highveld from the hot malarial zones of the lowveld in Mpumalanga. However the Natal Drakensberg, or Berg, as it is com- monly known, is far wilder and more spectacular than its Transvaal counterpart. Many of the peaks—some of which top 10,000 feet—are the source of crystalline streams and mighty rivers that have carved out myriad valleys and dramatic gorges. The Berg is a natural watershed, with two of South Africa's major rivers, the Tugela and the Orange, rising from these mountains. In this untamed wilderness you can hike for days and not meet a soul, and the mountains retain a wild majesty missing in the commercially forested peaks of Mpumalanga.

TIMING &
PLANNING

If possible, plan your visit to the Berg during the spring (September– October) and late autumn (late April–June), because although summer sees the Berg at its greenest, it's also the hottest and wettest time of the year. Vicious afternoon thunderstorms and hailstorms, which can put a severe damper on long hikes, are an almost daily occurrence. In winter the mountains lose their lush overcoat and turn brown. Winter days in the valleys, sites of most resorts, are usually sunny and pleasant, although there can be cold snaps, usually accompanied by overcast, windy conditions, depending on the severity of the winter. Nights are chilly, however, and you should pack plenty of warm clothing if you plan to hike the mountains or camp overnight. Snow is common at higher elevations. Hikers heading above the 10,000-foot level are obliged to sign the mountain register at the nearest Natal Parks Board/KwaZulu-Natal Nature Conservation Service office in case of emergency. Don't forget to sign out again on your return. It's also a good idea to check the weather forecast beforehand, particularly in winter (June–September), as extreme cold conditions may be experienced, many roads are closed, and hiking is prohibited.

⚠ **The Natal Drakensberg is not conducive to traditional touring because of the nature of the attractions and the limited road system.** It's best to check into a hotel or resort for two or three days and use it as a base for hiking and exploring the immediate area. If you decide to stay at one of the self-catering camps, it's best to do your shopping in one of the bigger towns, such as Winterton or Harrismith for Tendele, and Bergville or Estcourt for Giant's Castle, Kamberg, and Injasuti. The whole Drakensberg area has now become well established as a tourist attraction, particularly since its declaration as a World Heritage Site. Coffee shops, curio stores, visitor centers, and galleries abound, so you can spend a full day driving around the area, taking in the local art and handicrafts, or going for any one of the local activities.

Numbers in the margin correspond to points of interest on the Drakensberg map.

NORTHERN DRAKENSBERG

43 Access to **Royal Natal National Park** is via the R74, north of Bergville. The park contains some of the most stunning mountain scenery in the Drakensberg. The highlight is the Amphitheatre, a sheer rock wall measuring an unbelievable 5 km (3 mi) across and more than 1,500 feet high. Another showstopper is the Tugela River, which flows off Mont-aux-Sources (10,836 feet) and plunges nearly 3,000 feet over the plateau in a series of five spectacular falls that make up the Tugela Falls, the longest in South Africa. The park's most popular and scenic walk winds up the Tugela Gorge, a six-hour hike that crosses the river several times and passes through a tunnel before emerging into the Amphitheatre. Hikers often turn back at the first fording of the river, because the hike looks difficult. Persevere, for the scenery gets better and better, and the walk's not as tough as it appears. ■TIP➡ **Buy a comprehensive hiking guide with information about all the hikes at the visitor center, the main entrance gate, or at Thendele Camp office.** ⊠ *N. Berg Rd., 19 km (8* *mi) off R74* ☎*036/438–6303* ⊕*www.drakensberg.org.za* ☜*R25 plus R35 per vehicle* ⊙ *Apr.–Sept., daily 6–6; Oct.–Mar., daily 5* AM*–7* PM.

Just past the turnoff to Royal Natal National Park, the northbound
④④ R74 begins a twisty ascent up the **Oliviershoek Pass** (6,912 feet), offering tremendous views over the plains and hills. If these views don't satiate you, continue on the R74 past the Sterkfontein Dam until the road ends at a T. Turn left onto the R712 and head into Qwa Qwa, also known as Phuthaditjhaba. Follow signs to the Witsieshoek Mountain Resort.

Just before the resort, the road splits and continues for about 13 km (8
④⑤ mi) to the **Sentinel** (8,580 feet), where a path takes you to the edge of the Drakensberg escarpment. The views from here are breathtaking—the entire Royal Natal National Park lies below you and you can see all the way to Estcourt. You will need to purchase a permit from the guard at the parking lot before venturing onto the path. The number of people going to the overlook is restricted; it's based on the number of cars, so it's best to arrive before noon to avoid disappointment, especially during popular vacation periods. The parking lot is also the starting point for a strenuous hike to the top of Mont-aux-Sources. From the parking lot it's an easy drive back down the R712 to Harrismith and the N3 to Johannesburg and Durban.

WHERE TO STAY

¢ ⛺**Tendele Hutted Camp.** Smack in the middle of Royal Natal National Park, this popular camp makes a great base for long hikes into the mountains. Accommodations are in a variety of bungalows, cottages, and chalets, each with excellent views of the sheer rock face of the Amphitheatre. You must bring all your own food, although you can purchase staples and frozen meat at the main visitor center. In the bungalows and cottages all food is prepared by camp staff, but you can do your own cooking in the chalets. There is one lodge, which accommodates six people. ⟋*KwaZulu-Natal Nature Conservation Service, Box 13069, Cascades 3202* ☎*033/845–1000* ⟋*26 chalets, 2 cottages, 1 lodge* ⟐*In-room: kitchen (some)* ▭ *AE, DC, MC, V.*

CENTRAL DRAKENSBERG

④⑥ The small but fascinating **Winterton Museum** provides a nice overview of the Berg. Most exhibits were donated, made, or built by people from the Winterton and other nearby communities. If you are planning to hike to see any San (Bushman) paintings later in the day, first take a look at the museum's San Art Gallery. If you are planning a tour of the battlefields, pop into the reading room, where an outstanding private collection of books on the South African War is available for perusal. These volumes are used as reference sources by many of the professional battlefield tour guides. ⊠*Church St., Winterton Village* ☎*036/488–1620* ☜*Free* ⊙*Mon.–Thurs. 9–3, Sat. 9–noon.*

④⑦ Just outside Winterton is the **Central Drakensberg Information Centre,** which is located in the Thokozisa Centre, home to a variety of shops, the Thokozisa Restaurant, and the Thokozisa Deli and Wine Cellar.

Sterkfontein Dam

Babangiboni ▲
Hlolela ▲

R72

44 **Oliviershoek Pass**

Geluksburg

Sand River Valley

R103

43 **Royal Natal National Park**

R74

45 **Sentinel**

Mont-Aux-Sources

Woodstock Dam

M'Weni

Bergville

Ladysmith 11

Spioenkop Public Resort Nature Reserve

Roosboom

R600

R103

3

46 **Winterton Museum**

Winterton

R74

Colenso

Zunckels

47 **Central Drakensberg Information Centre**

Cathedral Peak ▲

Cleft Peak ▲

48 **Cathedral Peak Hotel**

Mambonja

R600

R74

R74

Bushmans

49 **KwaZulu Weavers and Candles**

Drakensberg Boys' Choir School

51 **Ardmore Guest House, Ceramic Art Studio, and Tea Garden**

R103

50

52

Four Rivers Rafting & Adventures

Cathkin Peak ▲

Little Tugela

53 **Monk's Cowl**

Champagne Castle ▲

Estcourt

LESOTHO

Mafadi ▲

54 **Injasuti**

KWAZULU-NATAL

Wagendrift Nature Reserve

R103

Popple Peak ▲

Mokhotlong

Rockmount

South Downs

55 **Giant's Castle Game Reserve**

Little Mooi

Mooi River

Rosetta

Giant's Castle ▲

3

Masenkeng

Redcliffe

Nottingham Road

R103

Redi ▲

Ukhahlamba/ Drakensberg Park

56 **Kamberg Nature Reserve**

Nottingham

Lidgetton

Lower Loteni

Umgeni

Umkomanazana

Dargle

Umkomaas

Mpendle

Sani Pass **57**

Himeville Nature Reserve

R617

Himeville Museum **58**

Himeville

R626

59 **Underberg**

Deepdale

R617

Bulwer

R617

R612

The Drakensberg

0 — 10 miles
0 — 10 kilometers

CLOSE UP

Fabulous Fishing

The Drakensberg and its low-lying areas are not only famous for spectacular scenery, but are also popular with fly fishermen. The crystal-clear Drakensberg streams are good for rainbow and brown trout, and many farmers stock their ponds specifically for fly-fishing. With its long stretch of coastline, saltwater fly-fishing is growing as a sport, and an early morning or an evening on the long, empty beaches of the north coast can provide some wonderfully rewarding fishing. Bear in mind, however, that most resorts require anglers to bring their own tackle. In winter, when huge shoals of sardines usually pass along the KwaZulu-Natal coast, rock and surf anglers follow flocks of seabirds in the hopes of catching some of the accompanying game fish. Obtain permits from the KwaZulu-Natal Nature Conservation Service or at post offices in larger cities and towns.

The information center can help with queries about local tourism attractions, excursions, travel advice, and lodging. The Thokozisa Centre has quirky and original architecture and includes colorful mosaics, handcrafted wooden statues, and painted walkways. The shops offer a variety of African curios, jewelry, clothes, arts and crafts, organic herbal and health products, ironware and candles, and hiking and camping gear. ⊠ *R600, Central Berg* ☎ *036/488–1207* ⊕ *www.cdic. co.za* ⊠ *Free* ☉ *Weekdays 9–5.*

48 The **Cathedral Peak Hotel,** accessible from Winterton or via dirt roads off the R600, is a tremendous base for hikes—and drives—into the mountains. Although KZN Wildlife levies a fee to enter the area, the hotel acts as the de facto center for hikers heading into the surrounding mountains. Leaflets, available at reception, give information on area trails—from easy strolls to demanding hikes. A scale model in the hotel lobby gives you the lay of the land before you set off. Cathedral Peak (9,900 feet) is the easiest of the major peaks to scale. Anyone who is fit and accustomed to long hikes can make the 19-km (12-mi) round-trip from the hotel to the summit and back; only the last portion near the summit is difficult. Budget 9 to 10 hours to get up and down, allowing plenty of time to drink in the view from the top, surely one of the highlights of the region. Another recommended route is the hike to Rainbow Gorge, about a six-hour trip, encompassing indigenous forest, pools, streams, and panoramic views. If you're traveling by car, drive up Mike's Pass (the road is a little rough, so take it slowly) to experience a magnificent vista of the entire Champagne Range and valley. ⊠ *Cathedral Peak Rd., Winterton* ☎ *036/488–1000* ⊕ *www. cathedralpeak.co.za* ⊠ *R20* ☉ *Daily 7–sunset.*

Seventeen km (8 mi) down the R600 from Winterton is the turnoff **51** to the **Ardmore Guest House, Ceramic Art Studio, and Tea Garden.** Started on a farm by artist Fée Berning in 1985, the studio is now home to several dozen Zulu and Sotho artists, each pursuing his or her own artistic visions in clay. Their colorful, totally nontraditional ceramics, which incorporate zebras and giraffes as handles on teapots, bowls, and platters, have won national and international awards and are displayed in galleries around the world. It's a small, modest studio where you can watch artists at work or just browse through the limited collection, which is housed in a converted farm shed. The ceramics are not cheap (they are regarded as collectors' pieces), and can be shipped overseas for you. Have tea and scones in the tea garden or stay a night in one of the pretty basic but inexpensive bungalows (R296 per night). ✉ *D275, off R600, Central Berg* ☎ *036/468–1314* ⊕ *http://ardmore. co.za* ✉ *Free* ⊙ *Weekdays 9–4:30.*

★ ⑤⓪ A couple of miles farther down the R600 is the turnoff to the **Drakensberg Boys' Choir School.** Mentioned in the same breath as the Vienna and Harlem boys' choirs, this is one of the most famous choral groups in the world. It's worth coming for one of the weekly performances in the auditorium, which run the musical gamut from Mozart to Freddy Mercury. Reservations are essential. There are no performances during school vacations. ✉ *Off R600, Central Berg* ☎ *036/468–1012* ✉ *R70* ⊙ *Performances Wed. at 3:30.*

④⑨ Also on R600, between the Ardmore Guest House and Winterton, is the popular tourist stop **KwaZulu Weavers and Candles.** This factory outlet has great value for the money and ships your orders to your door. There are a wide range of handmade wool and cotton rugs and carpets woven on the premises by local crafters. The outlet also includes a candle shop with a range of handmade aromatherapy candles in a wide selection of styles, colors, and designs. Adjacent to the outlet is the busy Waffle Hut, where you can satisfy your breakfast cravings with decadent chocolate-drizzled or fruit-filled pancakes. ✉ *On R600, Central Berg* ☎ *036/488–1657* ⊕ *www.kwazuluweavers.com* ✉ *Free* ⊙ *Daily 9–5.*

⑤② If you are staying in the region and want to do something more strenuous for the day, check out **Four Rivers Rafting & Adventures,** which is situated on the R600 approximately 2 km (1 mi) from Thokozisa heading toward Monk's Cowl. You can choose from a wide variety of adventure tours including white-water rafting, quad-bike trails (for adults or children), abseiling (rapelling), archery, mountain boarding, and mountain and rock climbing. ✉ *On R600, Central Berg* ☎ *083/785–1693* ⊕ *fourriversadventures.co.za.*

⑤③ The R600 runs directly into the mountains, ending at **Monk's Cowl,** a Natal Parks Board/KwaZulu-Natal Nature Conservation Service station. This is the gateway to several day and overnight hikes into the high Drakensberg from extreme to easy. Choose from a pleasant 30-minute amble along a stream to Fern Forest, to a moderate-severe six-hour walk to Sterkspruit Falls, the largest waterfall in the area, or an extreme 19-hour hike to Champagne Castle via Gray's Pass, where the views will take your breath away. Hikers who wish to camp out in the mountains must sign the mountain register and pay R30 per person per night. ✉ *Private Bag X2, Winterton 3340* ☎ *036/468–1103* ⊕ *www. kznwildlife.com* ✉ *R25* ⊙ *Daily 6 AM–7 PM.*

❺❹ Injasuti, 32 km (20 mi) down a dirt road off the Central Berg/Loskop Road, is a collection of huts set in the northern section of the Giant's Castle Game Reserve. A number of spectacular hikes start from here, including a guided 5-km (3-mi) walk (R35) up the Injasuti Valley to **Battle Cave,** which holds one of the most fascinating collections of San paintings in the country. Some 750 paintings cover the rock walls of the cave, but it's the subject matter that is most enthralling: one clearly depicts two Bushman clans at war—with some figures falling, others running away. Tours of Battle Cave leave daily at 8:30 from the camp office, which is 5 km (3 mi) from the gate and well marked, and return around 1. There's drinkable water all the way, but wear good shoes—hiking boots if possible—and take a hat and rain gear, as there are frequent thunderstorms. Reservations are essential. ✉*PO Box 13069, Pietermartizburg 3202* ☎*033/845–1000* ⊕*www.kznwildlife. com* 🎫*R20* ⏰*Apr.–Sept., daily 6–6; Oct.–Mar., daily 5 AM–7 PM.*

❺❺ South of Monk's Cowl is **Giant's Castle Game Reserve,** an 85,500-acre reserve encompassing rolling grasslands as well as some of the highest peaks in the Drakensberg. A host of trails, ranging in length from two hours to overnight, start at the main visitor center. The most popular tourist attraction is the **Main Caves,** which have the finest collection of San paintings in the Drakensberg. More than 500 paintings, some barely discernible, adorn the faces of two huge rock overhangs just an easy 45-minute walk from the camp office. Many paintings depict eland hunts, as the huge antelope held a special religious significance for the San. Guided tours start from the caves themselves. Take binoculars if you can; some of the paintings are hard to see with the naked eye.

♻ **Lammergeyer Hide,** set high on a cliff, is where bird-watchers can observe the endangered lammergeyer, or bearded vulture, and other birds of prey. On weekend mornings between May and September, rangers put out meat and bones for these birds below the hide (blind). In addition to giving birders a close-up view of the vultures, the feeding program is intended to draw the birds away from nearby farmland, where they might eat poisoned carcasses. Afrikaner farmers erroneously believe that the birds kill their young livestock, hence the name *lammergeyer,* or "lamb killer." The hide accommodates a maximum of six people. If you don't have a 4x4, take one of the extremely popular hide tours, which are sometimes fully booked six months in advance. Make sure you reserve a spot before leaving home, or call to see if there is availability the minute you arrive in the country. A ranger drives you up to the blind, and you're on your own for the walk back. ✉*Mooi River or Central Berg/Giant's Castle exit off N3, near Estcourt.* ✉*Hide bookings, Giant's Castle Game Reserve, Private Bag X7055, Estcourt 3310* ☎*036/353–3718* 🎫*R20; cave tours R35; hide tours R150 (if there are fewer than 6 people, the fee is R480 per person)* ⏰*Apr.–Sept., daily 6–6; Oct.–Mar., daily 5 AM–7 PM; cave tours daily, 9–3 hourly; hide tours May–Sept. at 7:30 AM.*

❺❻ Kamberg Nature Reserve, in the foothills of the uKhahlamba/Drakensberg Park, is best known for its superb collection of San rock-art paintings. Visit the **Kamberg Rock Art Centre** (wheelchair friendly) to watch a

FodorsChoice
★

video (R25) about the hunter-gatherer world of the San before taking a 2½- to 3-hour guided walk (R25) to **Game Pass Shelter,** along the same routes taken by the San to their rock shelters. One of the first rock-art sites recorded by Europeans and subsequently written up in a 1915 issue of *Scientific American,* Game Pass Shelter and its paintings are sometimes called the Rosetta Stone of San rock art, because it was here that archaeologists first came to understand the spiritual significance of rock paintings. ⌧*Mooi River or Central Berg/Giant's Castle exit off N3, near Estcourt.* ☎*KZN Wildlife, Box 13053, Cascades, Pietermaritzburg 3202* ☎*033/267–7251 or 031/845–1000* ✍kamberg@ kznwildlife.com ☎*R20* ☉*Daily 8–4.*

WHERE TO STAY & EAT

$$
FodorsChoice
★

⌧ **Cleopatra Mountain Farmhouse.** It would be difficult to find better lodging or dining anywhere in southern Africa than at this enchanting hideaway tucked away at the foot of the Drakensberg Range. The lodge overlooks a trout-filled lake and is encircled by mountains and old trees. Richard and Mouse Poynton, legendary South African chefs and hosts, have renovated the 1936 family fishing farm and created a perfect combination of comfort, tranquillity, style, and exceptional food. Homemade biscuits, hand-painted and stenciled walls, lovingly embroidered cushions and samplers, fluffy mohair blankets, and heated towel racks are just a few of the details you'll find here. You'll eat truly sumptuous meals with ceremony but no pretension in an intimate dining room warmed on cold days by a blazing log fire. ☎*Box 17, Balgowan 3275* ☎*033/267–7243* ⊕*www.cleomountain.com* ☞*6 rooms, 3 suites* ⊟*AE, DC, MC, V* ⎮⊚⎮*MAP.*

☼ ★ $ ⌧ **Cathedral Peak Hotel.** You'll get breathtaking views from almost every spot in this friendly and delightful hotel. It's an ideal family resort with an impressive range of activities with something for everyone. Go horseback riding or mountain biking, follow bird-watching trails, play bowls (lawn bowling) or a round of golf, or just soak up the heady mountain air. Accommodations include basic single standard rooms to slightly bigger family units, deluxe suites, honeymoon suites, and a presidential suite. The deluxe suite with adjacent rooms and connecting door is ideal for families. The tasty, hearty food is buffet style, and it's worthwhile taking afternoon tea outside so you can soak up the glorious views. You'll get excellent value here—prices include breakfast and dinner buffets as well as most activities. And whether you're mildly active or a seasoned mountain hiker or climber, trained and experienced guides take you on daily walks and trails through the Berg. There's a children's dining room and a babysitting service. Children under 3 stay free. ⌧*Cathedral Peak Rd., 43 km (27 mi) from Winterton 3340* ☎*036/488–1888 or 036/488–1889* ⊕*www.cathedralpeak.co.za* ☞*96 rooms* ☾*In-hotel: restaurant, room service, bars, golf course, tennis courts, pool, gym, spa* ⊟*AE, DC, MC, V* ⎮⊚⎮*MAP.*

$ ⌧ **Champagne Castle.** Along with Cathedral Peak, this old family-style hotel enjoys one of the best settings of any of the Berg resorts. It lies right in the mountains, with magnificent views down Champagne Valley to the towering massifs of Champagne Castle and Cathkin Peak. A host of hiking trails begins practically on the hotel's doorstep and the trailheads at Monk's Cowl lie just minutes away. There's nothing remotely fancy about the hotel itself, but it's a peaceful haven where genteel traditions linger—gentlemen are still required to wear ties to dinner. It also has a family-oriented bent, so expect to encounter South African families en masse during school vacations. Rooms, in thatch rondavels and bungalows scattered through the gardens, are pleasantly furnished and comfortable. Meals are served buffet style, with an emphasis on traditional South African roasts and vegetables. ⊠R600, Central Berg ⌂Private Bag X8, Winterton 3340 ☎036/468–1063 ⊕www.champagnecastle.co.za ⌨56 rooms ♿In-hotel: restaurant, bars, tennis court, pool ☰AE, DC, MC, V †◎†FAP.

♻ $ ⊞**The Nest.** This old-style hotel, built by Italian POWs in 1943, has been family owned since 1988, and is surrounded by rolling lawns with distant views of the mountains. Repeat guests comprise families or bowling enthusiasts, as the hotel hosts regular bowling tournaments and events. The atmosphere is relaxed and laid-back, the food wholesome and hearty. If you're looking for beautiful vistas and good walks, try one of the daily outings to the Monk's Cowl trails or mountain biking or horseback riding. Accommodations range from garden rondavels (traditional round huts)—be sure to get one with a mountain view—to the more comfortable and well-appointed executive suites (although these are situated in the new conference center away from the main hotel and other rooms). Babysitting services are also available. ⊠R600, Central Berg ⌂Private Bag X14, Winterton 3340 ☎036/468–1068 ⊕www.thenest.co.za ⌨54 rooms ♿In-room: no TV (some). In-hotel: restaurant, bar, tennis court, pool, bicycles ☰AE, DC, MC, V †◎†FAP.

¢   ⊞**Didima Camp.** This delightful self-catering camp is built to represent and celebrate San culture and art. And while the shapes of the brightly colored thatch-and-stone chalets may mimic the tribes' temporary dwellings, inside they're ultraluxurious with stone fireplaces and satellite TV. Visit the San Rock Art Interpretive Center to bring you up to speed on this fascinating culture—if you can't make it to any of the actual rock-art sites, the displays and video presentations here are the next-best thing. There is a grocery and curio shop on the premises. ⊠Cathedral Peak Rd., 43 km (27 mi) from Winterton, 3340 ⌂KZN Wildlife, Box 13053, Cascades, Pietermaritzburg 3202 ☎031/267–7251 or 031/845–1000 ⊕www.kznwildlife.com ⌨62 rooms ♿In-room: kitchen, TV. In-hotel: restaurant, bar ☰AE, DC, MC, V.

¢   ⊞**Giant's Castle.** This luxurious camp not only offers comfortable and well-equipped self-catering accommodations but is also ideally situated in Giant's Castle Game Reserve. Hidden away in a beautiful valley close to the sheer face of the High Drakensberg, it is an ideal base for viewing the San paintings in the main caves and bearded vultures from the Lammergeyer Hide. Accommodations are either in chalets, which share communal kitchens, or in self-contained cottages with either four or six beds. If you rent the lodge, which accommodates seven people, you must provide your own food, which is then cooked by camp staff. A store in the main office sells staples like milk, bread, charcoal, and packs of meat, and some good curios and souvenirs. ⊠Mooi River exit *off the N3* 🖰 *KZN Wildlife, Box 13053, Cascades, Pietermaritzburg 3202* 🕾 *031/845–1000* 📞 *37 chalets, 6 cottages, 1 lodge* ⚒️ *In-room: kitchen (some). In-hotel: restaurant* ☰ *MC, V.*

¢ 🖳**Injasuti.** At the head of Injasuti Valley in the northern section of the Giant's Castle Game Reserve, this self-catering camp has great views of Cathkin Peak, Monk's Cowl, and Champagne Castle. Cabins sleep up to six people, and all have kitchens and dining-living rooms. Electricity is available only from 5:30 to 10 each night. ✉️*1 McKenzie Dr., Cascades, Pietermaritzburg* 🖰 *KZN Wildlife, Box 13069, Cascades, Pietermaritzburg 3200* 🕾 *033/845–1000* ⊕ *www.kznwildlife.com* 📞 *18 cabins* ⚒️ *In-room: kitchen* ☰ *AE, MC, V.*

¢ 🖳**Kamberg Camp.** Deep in the mountains of the Kamberg Nature Reserve, these rustic self-catering accommodations are a good base from which to see the famous San rock paintings. Options range from two- and six-bed chalets to an eight-bed cottage, all with bathrooms and kitchenettes. A small café serves tea, coffee, muffins, and toasted sandwiches. ✉️*Mooi River or Central Berg/Giant's Castle exit off N3, near Estcourt.* 🖰 *KZN Wildlife, Box 13053, Cascades, Pietermaritzburg 3202* 🕾 *033/267–7251 or 031/845–1000* ✉️ *kamberg@kznwildlife.com* 📞 *6 chalets, 1 cottage* ⚒️ *In-room: kitchen. In-hotel: bar* ☰ *AE, DC, MC, V.*

SOUTHERN DRAKENSBERG

This attractive region is a about a two-hour drive south of Pietermaritzburg along pretty country roads. Its slightly remote location keeps it far from the madding tourist crowds. Much of the area is accessed by a network of rough dirt roads. Although most are suitable for regular cars, drive carefully and slowly. ■TIP→ **If you should get a flat, stop and fix it immediately; you could severely damage your tire rims on pebbles if you don't.**

59 The tiny town of **Underberg,** set in a fertile green valley with views of the Drakensberg, is accessed via the R617, a long but very pretty road from the town of Howick. The **Tourist Information Centre** (🕾 *033/701–1628*) can provide details on the Southern Drakensberg Sani Saunter, a tourist route which covers most area restaurants, accommodations, and attractions; not all are recommended, however.

What is worth visiting is Catherine and Lawrence Brennon's **Underberg Studio.** The art gallery showcases the Brennons' work, as well as the work of several local photographers and ceramists, and numerous creative workshops are offered in the studio. ✉️*21 Ridge Rd., Underberg* 🕾 *033/701–2440* ⊕ *www.africanlight.co.za* 🗒️ *Free* 🕙 *Mon.–Sat. 10–4:30, Sun. 11–4. Closed Tues. in the off-season.*

Another 5 km (3 mi) along the road to Sani Pass brings you to Himeville, where you might want to stop for a pint at the Himeville Arms

58 Hotel or drop by the **Himeville Museum,** across the street. Built as a fort on Natal Crown Colony lands in 1899 to protect the region's pioneer farmers, the building was later converted to a prison and used as such until the early 1970s. It became a museum in 1976, and the premises were subsequently declared a national monument. One of the best rural museums in the region, it houses an open-air display on the early European settlers in Himeville, Underberg, and Bulwer, as well as traditional weapons and ornaments of the San and other African tribes who once lived here. There are also displays on the area's fauna and flora, geography, and topography. ⊠ *Main St., Himeville* ☎ *033/702–1184* ⬚ *Free* ⊙ *Tues.–Sun. 9–1.*

⑤ **Sani Pass** attracts local 4x4 enthusiasts who test man and machine all the way into Lesotho. The pass, one of the traditional routes over the Drakensberg into the Lesotho highlands, ascends an incredible 5,730 feet through the upper valley of the Mkomazana River. From the top, the view of row upon row of tall peaks is truly stupendous. Just inside the Lesotho border is a mountaineer's chalet known as Sani Top, the highest pub in Africa. The pass is accessible only by 4x4 vehicle, and most accommodations in the nearby country towns of Himeville and Underberg can arrange tours to the top. ■TIP➜ **Remember to take your passport with you, as you will enter Lesotho on these excursions.** The cost is approximately R200 per person for a full day, which usually includes lunch and teas. The beautiful Giant's Cup Hiking Trail (⇨ *Sports & the Outdoors, below)* begins halfway up the pass.

WHERE TO STAY

$ 🏨 **Sani Pass Hotel.** Just 11 km (7 mi) from Himeville at the base of the spectacular Sani Pass, this attractive country hotel is close to the Roof of Africa and so is a favorite with international guests. The tranquil valley setting offers spectacular mountain views. Accommodations are either in attractive garden cottages or larger, more luxurious rooms in the main building. The latter rooms all have mountain views. The food is delicious country fare, and candlelit dinners are a hotel specialty. Activities include a challenging 9-hole golf course, scenic walks and drives, quad biking, a choice of horseback rides (including plateau and sunset rides), and, of course, regular trips up that fabulous pass. ⊠ *Sani Pass Rd., 11 km (7 mi) north of Himeville* ⬚ *Box 44, Himeville 3256* ☎ *033/702–1320* ⊕ *www.sanipasshotel.co.za* ➶ *43 rooms, 44 cottages* ⬚ *In-room: no a/c. In-hotel: restaurant, bars, golf course, tennis court, pool* ⊟ *AE, DC, MC, V* ⦿ *MAP.*

¢ 🏨 **Taylor's B&B.** A delightful respite is just off the R617, 2 km (1 mi) from Underberg on the Swartberg road (look for the sign to the Banks, on the left). All rooms are attractively and individually decorated; upstairs units have lovely views across the surrounding countryside. Each room has snack-making facilities, including a toaster and a *skottel-braai* (gas wok). A huge farm breakfast is included, and dinners can be arranged beforehand on request. Hosts Edith and John Taylor are extremely friendly and helpful and can arrange trips to Sani Pass as well as tennis, fishing, canoeing, and horseback-riding excursions. ⬚ *Box 33, Underberg 3257* ☎ *033/701–2011* ⊕ *www.taylorsguesthouse.com* ➶ *3 suites* ⬚ *In-room: refrigerator. In-hotel: no-smoking rooms (all).* ⊟ *No credit cards* ⦿ *BP.*

SPORTS & THE OUTDOORS

HIKING If you're into backpacking and want to see this beautiful region on foot, don't miss the **Giant's Cup Hiking Trail** (☎033/845–1000 ⊕*www. kznwildlife.com*). There are two-, three-, four- or five-day trail hikes from Sani Pass to Bushman's Nek in the Southern Drakensberg. Giant's Cup winds through the Little Berg, as this part of the southern Drakensberg is known, with incredible views of the escarpment at every turn. It passes by a petrified forest, San paintings, rock shelters, streams, and deep blue pools. If you like swimming, definitely come in summer. Accommodations are in old foresters' houses. The supply of firewood is plentiful, and roaring log fires will warm you. There aren't any comforts, though—water is usually heated by a wood-burning stove, bunks have mattresses but no bedding, and only one hut has electricity, so don't forget your flashlight. You'll need to carry your own food, sleeping bag, hiking stove and fuel, eating utensils, and clothing. If you're equipped for backpacking and are reasonably fit, this is a real treat, beginning halfway up Sani Pass and ending near the Lesotho border post at Bushman's Nek. The trail costs approximately R60 per person per night. For the not-so-fit or less energetic, who still want to hike the five-day trail, try "slack packing" (☎033/845–1000). Porters carry your packs and you stay in comfortable guesthouses each night.

DRAKENSBERG ESSENTIALS

TRANSPORTATION

BY BUS

On request, most resorts will pick up guests at the Greyhound or Translux terminal in Estcourt or Ladysmith or at the Montrose Service Area, one of the busiest gas stops on the N3, halfway between Johannesburg and Durban. Buses from both lines stop at these towns at least once a day on their runs between Durban and Johannesburg. Ladysmith to Jo'burg costs about R175 and takes roughly six hours, and Ladysmith to Durban is about R140 and takes roughly three hours.

Bus Stations **Estcourt terminal** (✉*Municipal Library, Victoria St., Estcourt* ☎*No phone*). **Ladysmith terminal** (✉*Murchison St., Ladysmith* ☎*No phone*). **Montrose Service Area** (✉ *City Shell Complex, Swinburne* ☎*058/672–1044*).

Bus Lines **Greyhound** (☎*083/915–9000, 011/249–8700, or 031/334–9720* ⊕ *www.greyhound.co.za*). **Translux** (☎*031/361–8132*).

BY CAR

The main resort area of the Drakensberg lies 380 km (250 mi) from Johannesburg and 240 km (150 mi) from Durban—an almost direct shot along the N3. A car is not strictly necessary for a trip to the Berg, although it is certainly a convenience, and though a 4x4 would be an advantage, it, too, is not a necessity. Gas stations can be found in Bergville, Winterton, and at the foot of Champagne Castle. Driving in this area is time-consuming. Trucks often slow up traffic, and you should be vigilant of animals on and attempting to cross the road.

CONTACTS & RESOURCES

EMERGENCIES

A dispensary and health-care clinic can be found at the Winterton Pharmacy. For mountain rescue, contact the Search & Rescue Section of the Mountain Club of South Africa.

Emergency Services Police (☎ *036/448–1095 Bergville, 036/352–2280 Estcourt, 036/488–1502 Winterton*). **Search & Rescue Section of the Mountain Club of South Africa** (☎ *082/990–5877*).

Hospital **Estcourt Hospital** (✉ *Old Main Rd., Estcourt* ☎ *036/342–7000*).

Pharmacies **Estcourt Pharmacy** (✉ *126 Victoria St., Estcourt* ☎ *036/352–3506*). **Winterton Pharmacy** (✉ *Springfield Rd., Winterton* ☎ *036/488–1177, 036/468–1303 after hours*).

MONEY MATTERS

Most larger towns have ATMs and banks, but don't count on finding one everywhere. Make sure you travel with enough cash. Both Winterton and Estcourt have an FNB (First National Bank), ABSA, and Standard Bank. Bergville has ABSA and FNB ATMs. Hours for all banks are weekdays 9–3:30 and Saturday 8:30–11.

VISITOR INFORMATION

Drakensberg Tourism is open weekdays 9–4. Underberg Tourist Information is open Monday–Saturday 8:30–4:30. Also vist the Zulu Kingdom's Web site (⊕ *www.kzn.org.za*) for helpful information.

Tourist Offices **Drakensberg Tourism** (✉ *Tugela Square, Kingsway St., Bergville* ☎ *036/448–1296* ⊕ *www.drakensberg.org.za*). **Underberg Tourist Information** (✉ *Clocktower Center, Main St.* ✎ *Box 230, Underberg 3257* ☎ *033/701–1471*).

ZULULAND & THE BATTLEFIELDS

Zululand stretches north from the Tugela River all the way to the border of Mozambique. It's a region of rolling grasslands, gorgeous beaches, and classic African bush. It has also seen more than its share of bloodshed and death. Modern South Africa was forged in the fiery crucible of Zululand and northern Natal. Here Boers battled Zulus, Zulus battled Britons, and Britons battled Boers. The most interesting historic sites, however, involve the battles against the Zulus. Names like Isandlwana, Rorke's Drift, and Blood River have taken their place in the roll of legendary military encounters.

No African tribe has captured the Western imagination quite like the Zulus. A host of books and movies have explored their warrior culture and extolled their martial valor. Until the early 19th century the Zulus were a small, unheralded group, part of the Nguni peoples who migrated to southern Africa from the north. King Shaka (1787–1828) changed all that. In less than a decade Shaka created a military machine unrivaled in black Africa. By the time of his assassination in 1828, Shaka had destroyed 300 tribes and extended Zulu power for 800 km (500 mi) through the north, south, and west.

Boers, Brits & Battlefields

The Boer War (1899–1902), now referred to as the South African War, was the longest, bloodiest, and costliest war fought by Britain for nearly 100 years. The Brits and the Boers, Afrikaner descendants of 17th-century Dutch settlers fighting for independence from Britain, engaged in numerous battles in which the little guys (the Boers) often made mincemeat of the great British colonial army sent out to defeat them. Britain marched into South Africa in the spring of 1899, confident that it would all be over by Christmas. However, the comparatively small bands of volunteers from the republics of the Transvaal and the Orange Free State were to give Queen Victoria's proud British army, as Kipling wrote, "no end of a lesson." Today history has also revealed the part played by hundreds of thousands of black South Africans in the war as messengers, scouts, interpreters, and laborers—hence the renaming of the war.

The most famous—or infamous—of the battles was fought on top of Spion Kop, in KwaZulu-Natal, where the mass grave of hundreds of British soldiers stretches from one side of the hill to the other. Of interest is that three men who were to change the course of world history were there on that fateful day: Winston Churchill, Mahatma Gandhi (who was a stretcher bearer), and Louis Botha, the first prime minister of the Union of South Africa.

–Kate Turkington

Fifty years after Shaka's death, the British still considered the Zulus a major threat to their planned federation of white states in South Africa. The British solution, in 1879, was to instigate a war to destroy the Zulu kingdom. They employed a similar tactic 20 years later to bring the Boer republics to heel and the rich goldfields of the Witwatersrand into their own hands.

Recently, interest in the battlefields has been growing, particularly in light of the Boer and Zulu War centenary celebrations, which started in 2000. If you're not a history buff, the best way to tour the battlefields is with an expert guide, who can bring the history to life because many of the battle sites are little more than open grassland, graced with the occasional memorial stone.

TIMING There is no bad time to visit Zululand and the battlefields. But when you do visit, make sure you wear comfortable shoes and plenty of sunblock and don't forget the binoculars.

Towns and sights on this tour appear on the KwaZulu-Natal map.

ESHOWE

 45 km (28 mi) northwest of Dukuza on the N2 and R66.

High up in the hills, this oldest town in Zululand has great views of the Dhlinza Forest and fields of sugarcane. The town is the birthplace of King Cetshwayo, the son of King Shaka's half brother Mpande.

Eshowe is the site of **Fort Nongqoi,** which houses the Zululand Histori-cal Museum, a good place to see displays of Zulu cultural items. The fort was built in 1883 and served as the headquarters of the Nongqoi Police, a black police contingent under British command. A particularly interesting exhibit deals with John Dunn (1834–95), the son of settler parents, who was fluent in Zulu, Afrikaans, and English. He became Chief Cetshwayo's political adviser in 1856, and was given the status of a Zulu chief. Dunn observed Zulu customs and laws, going so far as to marry 49 Zulu wives, by whom he had 117 children. Periodi-cally, the descendants of John Dunn stage reunions. ⊠*Nongqoi Rd.* ☎*035/474–1141* ✉*Tours, including 3 museums R25* ☉*Daily 9–4.*

Shakaland, a living museum of Zulu culture, is one of the most popular tourist stops in the region. Originally the movie set for *Shaka Zulu (1987),* Shakaland consists of a traditional Zulu kraal, with thatch beehive huts arranged in a circle around a central cattle enclosure. The emphasis here is on Zulu culture as it existed under King Shaka in the 19th century. You can watch Zulus dressed in animal skins or beaded aprons engaged in everyday tasks: making beer, forging spears, and crafting beadwork. Opt for a three-hour day tour or spend the night. A Zulu cultural adviser leads you through the kraal, explaining the significance of the layout and the roles played by men and women in traditional Zulu society. A highlight of the visit is a half-hour dance performance, featuring a variety of Zulu and other traditional dances. The whole setup is touristy, and some critics have labeled it a Zulu Disneyland, but it's fun and you learn a great deal about Zulu culture nevertheless. A buffet lunch is included in the tour. ⊠*Off R66, 13 km (8 mi) north of Eshowe* ☎*035/460–0912* ⊕*www.shakaland.com* ✉*R195* ☉*Tours daily at 11 and 12:30.*

WHERE TO STAY & EAT

$$ ✕🏠 **Protea Shakaland.** Staying overnight at Shakaland is far more rewarding than the three-hour daytime tour. Overnight guests see a more extensive program of cultural events and get to experience a night in a quasi-traditional Zulu dwelling. The rooms here are attractive and luxurious Africa-inspired accommodations. Enormous thatch beehive huts supported by rope-wrapped struts are decorated with African bed-spreads, reed matting, and interesting African art, creating an appeal-ing ethnic elegance. All have modern bathrooms and superb views. All meals are included in the price, though day-trippers can purchase lunch or dinner ($$; reservations essential), which feature a selection of Western-style dishes and some Zulu specialties. ⊠*Off R66, 13 km (8 mi) north of Eshowe* 🖃*Box 103, Eshowe 3815* ☎*035/460–0912* ⊕*www.proteahotels.com* ➥*48 rooms, 45 with bath* ♿*In-hotel: res-taurant, bar, pool* ☐*AE, DC, MC, V* ⍟*FAP.*

MELMOTH

61 *30 km (19 mi) north of Eshowe.*

As you drive along the R66, follow signs for the **Nkwalini Pass.** The road snakes up and over the mountains, revealing knockout views of valleys and hills dotted with Zulu kraals.

WHERE TO STAY

★ $ ▣ **Simunye Zulu Lodge.** If Shakaland is too commercial for your tastes, consider this small settlement tucked away in a remote valley of Zululand. Like Shakaland, Simunye attempts to introduce you to traditional Zulu culture, but the emphasis here extends to contemporary Zulu lifestyles, too. Leave your luggage, labels, and bling in Depart Point and just take an overnight bag. You'll reach the camp on an ox wagon, on horseback, or by 4x4, and the one-hour ride into the valley along upgraded roads and over the new bridge is one of the highlights of a visit. During a stay you'll watch Zulu dancing and visit a working kraal, complete with traditional beehive huts, where you'll learn about the culture and meet the residents. You can opt to sleep overnight in one of the guest beehive huts or stay in the more luxurious main camp, built into the side of a hill overlooking the Mfule River. The rooms, built of stone and thatch, are a classy mix of Zulu and pioneer cultures. You'll sleep in a wooden bed handmade by local villagers in a room decorated with Zulu cooking pots, cow-skin rugs, and handmade wooden African chairs. All the rooms have electricity and hot water. Most people stay only one night, but try to book for two nights over a weekend and arrange to attend a wedding or coming-of-age ceremony in a neighboring village (if one is happening while you're there). These ceremonies are purely local affairs, and you won't experience a more authentic celebration of rural Zulu culture elsewhere. ⊠*D256, off the R34, 6 km (4 mi) south of Melmoth* ✆*Box 248, Melmoth 3835* ☎*035/450–3111 or 035/450–7103* ☞*6 rock rooms, 5 lodge rooms, 5 rondavels, 3 beehive huts, 3 Africa rooms* ⌂*In-hotel: bar* ▤*AE, DC, MC, V* ⍼*FAP.*

ULUNDI

62 *35 km (22 mi) north of Melmoth.*

Ulundi is the joint capital—with Pietermaritzburg—of KwaZulu-Natal. Except for a huge legislative complex, however, it's a small, unremarkable town with a shopping complex and not much more.

Two kilometers (1 mi) south of town, you'll see the turnoff to the **Battle of Ulundi Memorial.** A stone temple with a silver dome marks the site of the battle, which marked the culmination of the Zulu War of 1879. Lord Chelmsford, smarting from his defeat at Isandlwana, personally led the march on Ulundi and defeated King Cetshwayo's 15,000 force and finally shattered the Zulu empire. ⊠*Cetshwayo Hwy.* ☎*No phone.*

Continue down the dirt road to the **KwaZulu Cultural Museum,** the original site of King Cetshwayo's royal kraal. Ondini was modeled after the kraal of Shaka's younger brother, Dingane, at Mgungundlovu *(see below).* At the time of its destruction in 1879, the kraal consisted of 1,500 huts and was home to some 5,000 people. Today only the royal enclosure has been restored, but a stroll among the deserted beehive huts gives you a feel for the kraal's size and scope. A site museum at the entrance traces the history of the Zulu kings and displays the silver mug and Bible presented to King Cetshwayo by Queen Victoria in 1882. The Cultural Museum, in a separate building, houses a superb collection of beadwork from various tribes, plus detailed exhibits on Zulu life. ⊠ *King Cetshwayo Hwy.* ☎*035/870–2050* ⌦*R15* ☉*Weekdays 8–4, weekends 9–4.*

EN ROUTE — From Ulundi retrace your route back down the R66 and turn right onto the R34 toward Vryheid. The turnoff to **Mgungundlovu** and the **Grave of Piet Retief** lies just a couple of miles farther on. Mgungundlovu was the site of Dingane's royal kraal and home to his 500 wives. Dingane, Shaka's younger brother, killed Shaka in 1828 to seize power for himself, and a few years later massacred Piet Retief and his party of almost 100 Voortrekkers who were petitioning Dingane for land. A monument now stands on the hill where Piet Retief and his men are buried. The beehive huts of the royal enclosure have been reconstructed on their original foundations, and a guide leads short tours of the kraal. There's also a small site museum. ⊠*R34* ☎*035/450–2254* ⌦*R15* ☉*Daily 8–5.*

BABANANGO

 38½ km (24 mi) northwest of Mgungundlovu and the grave of Piet Retief.

A dirt road connecting the R34 to Babanango passes through some of the most beautiful countryside in Zululand, with seemingly endless views over rolling grasslands. The road ends at the tarred R68. Turn right and drive less than 2 km (1 mi) into the pleasant hamlet of Babanango.

From Babanango follow the R68 for 48 km (30 mi) to the turnoff to **Isandlwana.** The Battle of Isandlwana, on January 22, 1879, was a major defeat for the British army. Coming as it did at the very beginning of the Zulu War, the defeat sent shudders of apprehension through the corridors of Whitehall and ultimately cost Lord Chelmsford his command. Chelmsford was in charge of one of three invasion columns that were supposed to sweep into Zululand and converge on Cetshwayo's capital at Ulundi. On January 20 Chelmsford crossed the Buffalo River into Zululand, leaving behind a small force at Rorke's Drift to guard the column's supplies.

Unknown to Chelmsford, the heart of the Zulu army—20,000 men—had taken up a position just 5 km (3 mi) away. Using Shaka's classic chest-and-horns formation, the Zulus swept toward the British positions. The battle hung in the balance until the Zulus' left horn out-flanked the British. The fighting continued for two hours before the British fled the field, with the Zulus in triumphant pursuit. About 1,000 Zulus perished in the attack, as did 1,329 British troops. Today the battlefield is scattered with whitewashed stone cairns and memorials marking the resting places of fallen soldiers. The visitor center houses a small but excellent museum of mementos and artifacts, following the course of the battle in marvelous detail—a good place to start if you're here without a guide. Allow at least two or three hours for a visit. ⊠ *Off R68* ☎ *034/271–8165* ⊟ *R15* ⊘ *weekdays 8–4, weekends 9–4.*

WHERE TO STAY & EAT

$ ✕▥**Babanango Hotel.** In the small Babanango Hotel you can relax in one of the country's most famous watering holes. It's a tiny place decorated in country style, with lots of wood and earthy colors. The pub serves a variety of inexpensive meals ($) including grilled rump steak and french fries. ⊠ *16 Justice St., 3580* ☎ *035/835–0029* ⇆ *5 rooms* △ *In-hotel: restaurant, bar* ⊟ *AE, DC, MC, V* ⊙*MAP.*

$$ ▥**Babanango Valley Lodge.** This tiny guest lodge lies at the end of a rutted dirt road on an 8,000-acre cattle farm. Obviously, it's not the sort of place where you constantly pop in and out, but that's okay—you probably won't want to leave anyway. The lodge sits at the head of a steep valley, far from any other buildings and with tremendous views of acacia-studded grasslands and hills. John and Meryn Turner, the charming hosts, and their very hospitable team, go out of their way to make you feel at home. John is a registered guide, and many people stay at the lodge as part of his battlefield tour. Rooms are decorated in contemporary style with fluffy white duvets and raw-silk lamp shades—simple, comfortable, and elegant. The four-course table d'hôte dinner focuses on traditional South African fare, including fresh farm produce. Battlefield tours, including a picnic lunch, cost R730. ⊠ *15 km (9 mi) off R68, near Babanango* ⌂ *Box 160, Dundee 3000* ☎ *035/835–0062* ⇆ *9 rooms* △ *In-hotel: pool* ⊟ *MC, V* ⊙*MAP.*

$$ ▥**Isandlwana Lodge.** It's said that during the Battle of Isandlwana, the chief of the Zulu army stood on Nyoni Rock where this lodge is now built. With sweeping views of the entire Isandlwana battlefield, the building, shaped like a Zulu shield, commemorates Isandlwana. The comfortable rooms are named for Zulus significant in the war, and bathrooms contain shield-shape sink pedestals. Decor is modern yet Afrocentric, with African prints and wooden furniture. Picture windows in public areas make the most of the incredible battlefield views. Trips to the local battlefields conducted by brilliant historian, lecturer, and fellow of the The Royal Geographical Society Rob Gerrard, will be a highlight of your stay. ⌂ *Box 30, 3005* ☎ *034/271–8301* ⊕*www.isandlwana.co.za* ⇆ *13 rooms* △ *In-hotel: bar, pool* ⊟ *AE, DC, MC, V* ⊙*MAP.*

RORKE'S DRIFT

★ ⑥₄ *35 km (22 mi) west of Isandlwana.*

Rorke's Drift is by far the best of the Zulu War battlefields to see without a guide. An excellent museum and orientation center retells the story of the battle, with electronic diagrams, battle sounds, and dioramas. From the British perspective this was the most glorious battle of the Zulu War, the more so because it took place just hours after the disaster at Isandlwana. The British force at Rorke's Drift consisted of just 141 men, of whom 35 were ailing. They occupied a Swedish mission church and house, which had been converted into a storehouse and hospital. The Zulu forces numbered some 3,000–4,000 men, composed of the reserve regiments from Isandlwana. When a survivor from Isandlwana sounded the warning at 3:15 PM, the tiny British force hastily erected a stockade of flour bags and biscuit boxes around the mission. The Zulus attacked 75 minutes later, and the fighting raged for 12 hours before the Zulus faltered and retreated. To this day, historians cannot figure out why the Zulus failed to press their huge advantage. When the smoke cleared, 500 Zulus and 17 Britons lay dead. ⊠ *Rorke's Drift Rd., off the R68* ☎ *034/642–1687* ✉ *R15* ⊙ *Weekdays 8–4, weekends 9–4.*

WHERE TO STAY

$$$ 🏠 **Fugitives' Drift Lodge.** Set on a 4,000-acre game farm, this attractive lodge lies just a couple of miles from the site of the famous engagement at Rorke's Drift and overlooks the drift where survivors of the British defeat at Isandlwana fled across the Buffalo River. The family of the late, legendary David Rattray, who owned and ran this lodge before his untimely death in January 2007, continues his lifelong commitment to Zululand, and the David Rattray Foundation has been established to carry on his community projects with the local people. Rooms, in individual cottages that open onto gardens, have fireplaces and wood furniture. You can rent a room in a cottage or the whole cottage, depending on your group size. The focal point of the lodge is the lounge and dining room, decorated with old rifles, British regimental flags, Zulu spears, and antique military prints. Battlefield tours cost R750 per person. ⊠ *Rorke's Drift Rd.* ⌂ *Rorke's Drift 3016* ☎ *034/271–8051* ⊕ *www.fugitives-drift-lodge.com* 🛏 *8 chalets, 2 cottages* ⌂ *In-hotel: bar, pool* ☰ *AE, DC, MC, V* ⦿ *FAP.*

$$ 🏠 **iSibindi Lodge.** This lodge within the iSibindi Eco Reserve combines game-viewing and Zulu cultural experiences with battlefield tours (R465) led by excellent local guides and historians. You'll see antelopes, giraffes, zebras, and wildebeests on your early-morning and evening game drives, and during cultural evenings you'll see traditional Zulu dancers and enjoy traditional delicacies. Another highlight will be a visit to a traditional village across the river where the *sangoma* (traditional healer) will "throw the bones" for you and read your fortune. In summer, river rafting is possible on the Buffalo River. Rooms, in elevated Zulu-style beehive huts with private decks, face glorious vistas of hill and valley. An attractive lounge and bar area shows off African prints and Zulu artifacts, and an outdoor bar and sunken pool

look out at the view. ⊠9 km (4 mi) from Rorke's Drift ⌂Box 275, Umhlali 4390 ☎034/642–1620 ⊕www.zulunet.co.za ☞6 huts ⚐In-hotel: bar, pool ☰AE, DC, MC, V ⵔⵔMAP.

SHOPPING

Rorke's Drift is still a mission station, run by the Evangelical Lutheran Church. The **Rorke's Drift ELC Art and Craft Centre** (⊠Rorke's Drift Rd., off R68 ☎034/642–1627), at the mission, sells wonderful pottery, handwoven rugs, and linocuts, all created by mission artists.

DUNDEE

65 35 km (22 mi) north of Rorke's Drift.

Once a busy coal-mining town, Dundee still has straight roads wide enough for the ox wagons of pioneer days to turn in, but today it's just a small commercial center in an area of subdued farming activity.

The first-rate **Talana Museum,** on the outskirts of Dundee, encompasses 10 buildings. Fascinating exhibits trace the history of the area, from the early San hunter-gatherers to the rise of the Zulu nation, the extermination of the cannibal tribes of the Biggarsberg and, finally, the vicious battles of the South African War. The museum stands on the site of the Battle of Talana (October 20, 1899), the opening skirmish in the South African War, and two of the museum buildings were used by the British as medical stations during the battle. The military museum here is an excellent starting point for the Battlefields Route, along which you follow in the footsteps of the Zulus, Brits, and Boers as they battled it out for territory and glory. ⊠R33, 2 km (1 mi) east of Dundee ☎034/212–2654 ☞R15 ⊙ Weekdays 8–4, Sat. 10–4, Sun. noon–4.

NEED A BREAK?

The Miner's Rest Tea Shop, in a delightfully restored miner's cottage at the Talana Museum, serves refreshments as well as more substantial dishes like peri-peri chicken livers and spinach, feta, and chicken pie in phyllo pastry. The food is good and the atmosphere most welcoming. Alternatively, you can take advantage of the braai and picnic facilities on the museum grounds.

Off the R33 northeast of Dundee is the **site of the Battle of Blood River,** one of the most important events in the history of South Africa. This battle, fought between the Boers and the Zulus in 1838, predates the Anglo-Zulu War by more than 40 years. After the murder of Piet Retief and his men at Mgungundlovu in February 1838, Dingane dispatched Zulu impis to kill all the white settlers in Natal. The Voortrekkers bore the brunt of the Zulu assault. For the next 10 months their future hung in the balance: entire settlements were wiped out, and a Boer commando was smashed at the Battle of Italeni. By November a new commando of 464 men and 64 wagons under Andries Pretorius had moved out to challenge the Zulus. On Sunday, November 9, the Boers took a vow that should God grant them victory, they would forever remember that day as a Sabbath and build a church in commemoration. They repeated the vow every night for the next five weeks. On December 16 an enormous Zulu force attacked the Boers, who had circled their wagons in a strategic position backed by the Blood River and a deep *donga,* or gully. Armed with only spears, the Zulus were no match for the Boer riflemen. At the end of the battle 3,000 Zulus lay dead, but not a single Boer had fallen. The immediate effect of the victory was to open Natal to white settlement, but the long-term effects were far more dramatic. The intensely religious Voortrekkers saw their great victory as a confirmation of their role as God's chosen people. This deeply held conviction lay at the spiritual heart of the apartheid system that surfaced more than a century later, in 1948. Indeed, when you see the monument here, there's no mistaking the gravity and importance that the Nationalist government ascribed to its erection. The laager, a defensive circle of 64 wagons, has been reconstructed in exacting detail, made from a mix of cast steel and bronze. It's a truly haunting monument, made even more so by its position on empty grasslands that seems to stretch for eternity. ⊠ *Off R33, between Dundee and Vryheid* ☎ *072/088–3544* ☞*R20* ⊙ *Daily 8–4.*

WHERE TO STAY

🏠 **Lennox Cottage.** This active farm is owned and run by ex-South African National Team Springbok rugby center Dirk Froneman and his wife, Salomé. After a day touring the battlefields (they will recommend superb guides), if you've still got some energy left you can ride, swim in the large pool, play tennis or snooker, or go on an evening game drive around the farms before sinking into a comfortable bed in your country-style room. Salomé's home cooking is superb, and each evening she serves such traditional Afrikaans dishes as butternut soup, *bobotie* (a spicy ground-meat dish), and local venison on an antique dining table as guests discuss the day's doings over a *dop* (drink) or two (dinner R180). ⊠ *R68, Box 197, 3000* ☎ *082/574–3032* 🖃 *lennox@dundeekzn.co.za* 🛏 *10 rooms* ♿ *In-hotel: bar, tennis court, pool* 🗖 *AE, DC, MC, V* 🍴*MAP.*

LADYSMITH

66 *60 km (37 mi) southwest of Dundee.*

Ladysmith, dating back to the middle of the 19th century, became famous around the world during the South African War, when it outlasted a Boer siege for 118 days. Nearly 20,000 people were caught in the town when the Boers attacked on November 2, 1899. Much of the early part of the war revolved around British attempts to end the siege. The incompetence of British general Sir Redvers Buller became apparent during repeated attempts to smash the Boer lines, resulting in heavy British losses at Spionkop, Vaalkrans, and Colenso. Finally, the sheer weight of numbers made possible the British defeat of the Boers in the epic 10-day Battle of Tugela Heights and ended the siege of Ladysmith on February 28, 1900.

Today Ladysmith is a small provincial town with a haphazard mix of old colonial and newer buildings and the same inhospitable climate (scorchingly hot in summer, freezing in winter). Look out for the elegant, historic Town Hall built in 1893, and visit the gleaming white Soofie Mosque on the banks of the Klip River; it's a national monument and is regarded as one of the most beautiful mosques in the southern hemisphere. On Murchison Street (the main street) is Surat House, a shop built in the 1890s, where Ghandi used to shop on his way through Ladysmith.

The **Ladysmith Siege Museum** brings the period of the siege skillfully to life, with the use of electronic mapping, artifacts from the period, and black-and-white photos. The museum can arrange guided tours, but it also sells two pamphlets that outline self-guided tours: the "Siege Town Walkabout" and the "Siege Town Drive-About." ⊠ *151 Murchison St., next to Town Hall* ☎*036/637–2992* ⊠*R2* ☉ *Weekdays 9–4, Sat. 9–1.*

In the courtyard of the Siege Museum stands a replica of a Long Tom, the 6-inch Creusot gun used by the Boers during the siege to terrify the inhabitants of Ladysmith. In front of the Town Hall are two howitzers used by the British and christened Castor and Pollux.

WHERE TO STAY & EAT

$ ✕🏨 **Royal Hotel.** This recently refurbished typical South African country hotel shares much of Ladysmith's historic past. The hotel was built in 1880, just 19 years before the town was attacked by the Boers during the war. Expect small rooms, although TVs and air-conditioning are standard features. The hotel serves a buffet for lunch and dinner at R80 a head and offers an à la carte menu on weekends. ⊠*140 Murchison St., 3370* ☎*036/637–2176* ⊕*www.royalhotel.co.za* ⌦*71 rooms* ⌕*In-hotel: restaurant, bar* ⊟*AE, DC, MC, V* ⧖|*BP.*

ZULULAND & THE BATTLEFIELDS ESSENTIALS

TRANSPORTATION

BY CAR

Unless you're on a tour, it's almost impossible to see this part of the country without your own car. Your best bet is to rent a car in Durban and perhaps combine a trip to the battlefields with a self-drive tour of KwaZulu-Natal's game reserves. Roads are in good condition, although some of the access roads to the battlefields require more careful and slower driving, as dirt roads can be bumpy and muddy when wet.

CONTACTS & RESOURCES

EMERGENCIES

Of Ladysmith's two hospitals, the state-run Ladysmith Provincial Hospital and the Netcare's private Laverna Hospital (which has full emergency services and a pharmacy that's open 8–5), Laverna is probably a better bet. Elsewhere, call the general police number to be put in touch with the nearest hospital.

Emergency Services Police (☎*036/638–3300 Ladysmith, 10111*).

Hospitals Ladysmith Provincial Hospital (⊠ *36 Malcolm Rd., Ladysmith* ☎*036/637–2111*). **Laverna Hospital** (⊠*1 Convent Rd., Ladysmith* ☎*036/631–0065*).

Pharmacy **Ladysmith Pharmacy** (⊠ *262 Murchison St., Ladysmith* ☎ *036/631–0648, 036/637–7891, or 082/542–7677.*).

MONEY MATTERS

There are plenty of banks and ATMs in all towns and at the larger filling stations. Ladysmith has branches of all the main banks, with ABSA, FNB, Standard Bank, and Nedbank ATMs on Murchison Street.

TOURS

The visitor information offices at Dundee's Talana Museum and in Ladysmith have lists of registered battlefield guides including John Turner of the Babanango Valley Lodge, Rob Gerrard of Isandlwana Lodge, and Neville Worthington, who are experts on the Zulu battlefields. For ethnic and cultural tours, you'll want to look up Bethuel and Dudu Manyathi and for Berg, bush, and battlefield tours, use the Dunbars of Parker Tours. If you're interested in self-guided tours, stop by the Talana Museum to rent or buy cassette tapes and CDs that describe the events at Rorke's Drift and Isandlwana, including some narrated the late David Rattray. Information about battlefield guides and guides specializing in authentic Zulu culture can be obtained at any information center or tourism office.

Tour Operators **Rob Gerrard** (☎ *034/271–9710 or 083/531–0061*). **Bethuel and Dudu Manyathi** (☎ *034/271–9710, 083/531–0061 cell*). **Parker Tours–Ken and Jane Dunbar** (☎ *082/679–0133 or 035/590–1576*). **Rattray Tours** (☎ *034/271–8051 or 034/642–1843*). **John Turner** (☎ *035/835–0062*). **Neville Worthington** (☎ *034/212–1347*).

VISITOR INFORMATION

Battlefields Route is a good source for information on the battlefields. Dundee's Regional Information Tourism Office is open weekdays 7:30–4. The Talana Museum visitor information office is open weekdays 8–4:30 and weekends 10–4:30. The Ladysmith Information Bureau is open weekdays 9–4, Saturday 9–1, and Sunday by request. For information on Ulundi, check with the Ulundi Tourism Office, weekdays 9–4, or the KZN Wildlife office. For a good overview covering this area, go to Tourism KwaZulu-Natal's Web site.

Tourist Offices **Battlefields Route** (⌂ *Box 3330, Ladysmith 3370* ☎ *082/802–1643* ⊕ *battlefields.kzn.org.za*). **KZN Wildlife** (⊠ *Prince Mkabayi St., Ulundi* ☎ *035/473–0700*). **Ladysmith Information Bureau** (⊠ *Siege Museum, Town Hall, Murchison St., Ladysmith* ☎ *036/637–2992*). **Regional Information Tourism Office** (⊠ *Main St. and Osborn Rd., Dundee* ☎ *035/473–3474* ✎ *tourism@dundee.kzn.co.za*). **Talana Museum** (⊠ *R33, 2 km [1 mi] east of Dundee* ☎ *034/212–2654*). **Ulundi Tourism Office** (⊠ *Kulani Park, 93 Princess Mkabayi St., Ulundi* ☎ *035/874–5607*).

Web Site **Tourism KwaZulu-Natal** (⊕ *www.zulu.org.za*).

THE ELEPHANT COAST

CALLING ALL WHALES

For up-to-the-minute information about whale sightings off the coast, keep the toll-free **Whale Hotline** (☎ *083/910–1028*) handy. The hotline also gives information about whale-watching excursions.

The Elephant Coast is bordered in the northwest by the Ubombo Mountains, in the east by the Indian Ocean, and in the south by the Umfolozi River, which is just below the St. Lucia Estuary. The estuary is part of the Greater St. Lucia Wetland Park, a recently declared World Heritage Site. Although the area is only 200 km long (320 mi long) and 70 km wide (110 mi wide), its ecodiversity offers some of South Africa's most varied and gorgeous scenery: pristine coastal bird-rich forests, floodplains and inland lakes, unspoiled miles-long beaches, deep rivers, and unique sand forests. It's an outdoor lover's paradise, where you can swim (with sharks!), snorkel, surf, watch turtles, go hiking, mountain biking, deep-sea fishing or diving, check out the Big Five, or see dolphins and whales.

TIMING This area is hot and humid in summer, but if you can stand the heat it's a great time to visit, because the scenery is at its greenest and most spectacular. Want to see turtles or whales? November through March is turtle-tracking time and July through December is whale-watching time. Witnessing these magnificent creatures leaping or breaching above the waves is an unforgettable and somehow spiritual sight. From July to September you can spot humpback whales, and occasionally see Southern Right whales moving north to their breeding grounds off Mozambique; in September and November you can spot them on their way back to their Antarctic feeding grounds.

HLUHLUWE-UMFOLOZI GAME RESERVE

  264 km (165 mi) northeast of Durban.

Reputedly King Shaka's favorite hunting ground, Zululand's Hluhluwe-Umfolozi (pronounced Shloo-*shloo*-ee Im-fuh-*low*-zee) incorporates two of Africa's oldest reserves: Hluhluwe and Umfolozi, both founded in 1895. In an area of just 906 square km (325 square mi), Hluhluwe-Umfolozi delivers the Big Five plus all the plains game as well as species like nyala and red duiker that are rare in other parts of the country. Equally important, it boasts one of the most biologically diverse habitats on the planet, a unique mix of forest, woodland, savanna, and grassland. You will find about 1,250 species of plants and trees here—more than in some entire countries.

The park is administered by Ezemvelo KZN Wildlife, the province's official conservation organization, which looks after all the large game reserves and parks as well as many nature reserves. Thanks to its conservation efforts and those of its predecessor, the highly regarded Natal Parks Board, the park can take credit for saving the white rhino from extinction. So successful was the park at increasing white rhino numbers that in 1960 it established its now famous Rhino Capture Unit to relocate rhinos to other reserves in Africa. The park is currently trying to do for the black rhino what it did for its white cousins. Poaching had decimated Africa's black rhino population, but remarkable conservation efforts have increased the population, and about 20% of Africa's remaining black rhinos now live in this reserve.

Until 1989 the reserve consisted of two separate parks, Hluhluwe in the north and Umfolozi in the south, separated by a fenced corridor. Although a road (R618) still runs through this corridor, the fences have been removed, and the parks now operate as a single entity. Hluhluwe and the corridor are the most scenic areas of the park, notable for their bush-covered hills and knockout views, whereas Umfolozi is better known for its broad plains.

WHERE TO STAY

IN HLUHLUWE-UMFOLOZI
Hluhluwe-Umfolozi offers a range of accommodations in government-run rest camps, with an emphasis on self-catering (only Hilltop has a restaurant). Unfortunately, most foreign visitors can't avail themselves of the park's secluded bush lodges and camps, as each of them must be reserved in a block, and the smallest accommodates at least eight people. At Hilltop you can expect to pay R510 per person for a self-catering en suite chalet with cooking facilities. Conservation levies are R80 per person.

$ 🏠 **Hilltop Camp.** It may be a government-run camp, but this delightful award-winning lodge in the Hluhluwe half of the park matches some of South Africa's best private lodges. Perched on the crest of a hill, it has panoramic views over the park, the Hlaza and Nkwakwa hills, and Zululand. Thatch and ocher-colored walls give it an African feel. Scattered across the crown of the hill, self-contained chalets have high thatch ceilings, rattan furniture, and small verandas. If you plan to eat all your meals in the restaurant or sample the evening braai, forgo the more expensive chalets with fully equipped kitchens. If you're on a tight budget, opt for a basic rondawel with two beds, a basin, and a refrigerator; toilet facilities are communal. There's an à la carte restaurant, an attractive pub, and a convenience store. Take a stroll along a forest trail rich with birdsong, or take a bottle of wine to Hlaza Hide and join the animals as they come for their sundowners. There is a gas station on the premises. ☝*KZN Wildlife, Box 13069, Cascades, Pietermaritzburg 3202* 🕾*033/845–1000* @*www.kznwildlife.com* 🛏*20 rondavels, 49 chalets* ⚒*In-room: kitchen (some). In-hotel: restaurant, bar* ☰*AE, DC, MC, V.*

¢ 🏠 **Mpila Camp.** In the central Imfolozi section of the park, Mpila is humbler than the classy Hilltop Camp, more reminiscent of some of Kruger's older camps. Choose between one-room huts sharing communal facilities, two- and three-bedroom cottages, an en-suite safari tent, or three secluded lodges. Gas is available, but you can only buy curios and sodas at the camp shop, so stock up with groceries before you arrive. Book your bush walks and game drives on arrival, as they work on a first-come, first-served basis. ☝*KZN Wildlife, Box 13069, Cascades, Pietermaritzburg 3202* 🕾*033/845–1000* @*www.kznwild-*

CLOSE UP

How to See the Hluhluwe-Umfolozi Reserve

Hluhluwe-Umfolozi may be less than 6% of Kruger's size, but it has many advantages over Kruger. Game-viewing is good year-round and it's very close to Mkuze Game Reserve and the spectacular coastal reserves of Greater St. Lucia Wetland Park. The park is also close enough to Durban to make it a worthwhile one- or two-day excursion. For bush walks and game drives, make reservations through Hilltop Camp reception (☎035/562–0848).

BUSH WALKS

Armed rangers lead groups of eight on two- to three-hour bush walks departing from Hilltop or Mpila Camp. You won't see a lot of game (birds galore), but you'll learn a great deal about the area's ecology and tips on how to recognize the signs of the bush, including animal spoor. Walks leave daily at 5:30 AM and 3:30 PM (6 and 3 in winter) and cost R200.

GAME DRIVES

These ranger-led drives (R200 per person) hold several advantages over self drives: you sit high up in an open-air vehicle; a ranger explains the finer points of animal behavior and ecology; and your guide has a good idea where to find animals like leopards, cheetahs, and lions. Game drives leave Monday–Saturday at 5:30 AM in summer, 6:30 AM in winter. The park also offers three-hour night drives—rangers search for nocturnal animals with powerful spotlights. These three-hour drives depart at 7.

WILDERNESS TRAILS

The park's wilderness trails are every bit as popular as Kruger's, but they tend to be tougher and more rustic. Led by an armed ranger, you should be fit enough to walk up to 16 km (10 mi) a day for a period of three days and four nights. All equipment, food, and baggage are carried by donkeys. The first and last nights are spent at Mndindini, a permanent tented camp. The other two are spent under canvas in the bush. While in the bush, hikers bathe in the Umfolozi River or have a hot bucket shower; toilet facilities consist of a spade and toilet-paper roll. Trails, open March–November, are limited to eight people and should be reserved a year in advance (R2,700 per person per trail).

If that sounds too easy, you can always opt for the four-night, ranger-guided **Primitive Trails** (R1,800 per person per trail). You'll carry your own pack and sleep outside, although there are lightweight tents if the weather is bad, and each participant is expected to sit a 90-minute watch.

A less rugged wilderness experience—you're guaranteed a bed and some creature comforts—is **Bushveld Trails** (R1,800 per person per trail), based out of the tented Mndindini Camp. The idea behind these trails is to instill in the participants an appreciation for the beauty of the untamed bush. You can join the Mpila night drive if you wish. Participation is limited to eight people.

Bookings may be made through **KZN Wildlife** (☎033/845–1000 ⊕www.kznwildlife.com).

5

life.com ☞12 rest huts, 2 cottages, 6 chalets, 9 safari tents, 3 bush lodges ⚓In-room: kitchen (some) ▤AE, DC, MC, V.

NEAR
HLUHLUWE-
UMFOLOZI

☺ $$

🏠**Hluhluwe River Lodge.** Overlooking False Bay Lake and the Hluhluwe River floodplain, this luxurious, value-for-money, spacious, family-owned lodge set in indigenous gardens is the ideal base for visiting the game reserves and the Greater St. Lucia Wetland Park. After a day spent game-viewing, canoeing, bird-watching, boating, fishing, or walking in the pristine sand forest, you can relax in a terra-cotta-colored A-frame chalet with cool stone floors, wood and wicker furniture, and cream-and-brown decor and furnishings. Alternatively, sit out on your wooden deck overlooking the bush, the floodplain, and the lake. This lodge is the only one with direct access to the lake, and as you chug along through bird-filled papyrus channels decorated with water lilies en route to the broad expanses of the main body of water, you might easily feel as though you were in Botswana's Okavango Delta. Water activities are dependent on the seasonal rains, so check with the lodge in advance. The food is excellent—wholesome country cooking with lots of fresh vegetables and good roasts. ✉Follow signs from Hluhluwe village ⌂Box 105, Hluhluwe 3960 ☎035/562-0246 ⊕www.hluhluwe.co.za ☞12 chalets ⚓In-hotel: restaurant, bar, pool ▤AE, DC, MC, V ⭐MAP.

$$

🏠**Zululand Tree Lodge.** Sixteen kilometers (10 mi) from the park, this lodge lies in a forest of fever trees on the 3,700-acre Ubizane Game Reserve, a small park stocked with white rhinos and plains game. It makes a great base from which to explore Hluhluwe, Mkuze, and St. Lucia. Built of thatch and wood, the open-sided lodge sits on stilts overlooking the Mzinene River. Rooms are in separate cottages, also on stilts, along the riverbank. The rooms themselves are small, but tastefully decorated with mosquito nets covering old-fashioned iron bedsteads made up with fluffy white duvets, African-print cushions, wicker, and reed matting. If you want the experience of sleeping alfresco, fold back the huge wooden shutters dividing the bedroom from the open deck. A qualified ranger will take you for a bush walk or a game drive (included) through the small reserve, or a little farther afield for a game drive in the nearby Hluhluwe-Umfolozi reserve. Try to visit the nearby Illala Weavers, where you can buy superb Zulu handwoven baskets. ✉Hluhluwe Rd. ⌂Box 116, Hluhluwe 3960 ☎035/562-1020 ☞24 rooms ⚓In-hotel: restaurant, bar, pool ▤AE, DC, MC, V ⭐MAP.

MKUZE GAME RESERVE

🔟 48 km (30 mi) north of Hluhluwe-Umfolozi.

This 88,900-acre reserve lies in the shadow of the Ubombo Mountains, between the Mkuze and Msunduze rivers, which makes up the northwestern spur of the Greater St. Lucia Wetland Park. If you're a birder you will think you've died and gone to Heaven—more than 400 bird species have been spotted here, including myriad waterfowl drawn to the park's shallow pans in summer. Several blinds, particularly those overlooking Nsumo Pan, offer superb views. ■TIP➔ **Don't miss out on the awesome 3-km (2-mi) walk through a spectacular, rare forest of tow-**

ering, ancient fig trees, some as big as 82 feet tall and 39 feet around the base. Although only a fraction of Kruger's size, this is the place to find rhinos; there's a healthy population of both black and white rhinos. You won't find lions, buffalo, or elephants, but the low-lying thornveld supports lots of other game, including zebras, giraffes, kudus, and nyalas. ⊠*Off the N2* ☎*035/573–9004* ⊠*R35 per vehicle, plus R35 per person* ⊙*Daily 6–6.*

WHERE TO STAY

¢ ⛺**Ghost Mountain Inn.** Swathes of scarlet bougainvillea run riot in the lush gardens of this family-owned country inn near Mkuze. It was here that Rider Haggard wrote some of his adventure stories, inspired perhaps by the mysterious lights and elusive flickering flames that give the mountain its spooky name. Rooms, each with a small veranda, are tastefully furnished in understated creams and browns with interesting historical prints. Large, invitingly restful public areas have terracotta tiles and comfortable cane furniture, and the cozy African lounge makes you feel like you've slipped back to the past. Don't miss the enthusiastic Zulu dancing before a succulent barbecue under the stars. At first light, wander down to the lake and watch the waterbirds wake up, or, later in the day, sit in the blind and watch them come home to roost. There is an excellent curio shop. The friendly staff can arrange tours to the neighboring game reserves and cultural sights, or will fix you up to go bird-watching or fishing. ⊠*Fish Eagle Rd.* ⌂*Box 18, Mkuze 3965* ☎*035/573–1025* ⊕*www.ghostmountaininn.co.za* ⇔*33 rooms* ��*In-hotel: restaurant, bar, pool* ⊟*AE, DC, MC, V* ⎢⎢*BP.*

GREATER ST. LUCIA WETLAND PARK

69 *133 km (83 mi) from Mkuze Game Reserve.*

This huge park, a World Heritage Site, is one of the most important coastal and wetland areas in the world, with five interlinked ecosystems: a marine system, a coastal dune system, lake systems, swamps, and inland savanna woodlands. It is this often pristine diversity that makes it both important and amazingly beautiful. The focal point is Lake St. Lucia, a broad 95,545-acre lake dotted with islands and populated by crocodiles and hippos. Bird-watchers rave about the avian life, too—at times the lake is pink with flamingos. KZN Wildlife offers guided trips up the estuary aboard the *Santa Lucia,* an 80-seat motor launch that makes the 90-minute voyage several times daily (reservations are essential). KZN Wildlife maintains an office and self-catering camp in the small but rapidly expanding fishing resort of St. Lucia, near the mouth of the estuary. The village is also the access point to the thin strip of land that runs up the coast between Lake St. Lucia and the Indian Ocean, with terrific beaches as well as the highest vegetated dunes in the world. There's a small KZN Wildlife base at Cape Vidal, 20 km (12 mi) north of St. Lucia, where you can visit privately owned whale-watching towers to spy on Southern Right whales and humpbacks, which drift south on the warm Aghulas current around October each year. Check out the Crocodile Center at St. Lucia village, where a registered guide will induct you into the habitat and habits of one of the world's oldest living creatures. ⊠*24 km (15 mi) east of Mtubatuba exit off the N2* ✆*Officer-in–Charge, Cape Vidal, Private Bag X04, St. Lucia Estuary 3936* ☎*035/590–1340* 🚤*Boat tours R90* ☉*Tours daily, check in advance.*

ITALA GAME RESERVE

🅭 *221 km (138 mi) northwest of Hluhluwe-Umfolozi.*

In northern KwaZulu-Natal, close to the Swaziland border, Itala, at 296 square km (107 square mi), is small even compared with the relatively compact Hluhluwe-Umfolozi. Its size and its dearth of lions are probably why this delightful park is usually bypassed, even by South Africans—although they clearly don't know what they're missing. The other four of the Big Five are here—it's excellent for black and white rhinos—and the park is stocked with cheetahs, hyenas, giraffes, and an array of antelopes among its 80 mammal species. It's also an excellent spot for birders. The stunning landscapes and the relaxed game-viewing make this area a breath of fresh air after the Big Five melee of Mpumalanga.

Founded in 1972, the reserve, run by KZN Wildlife, is a rugged region that drops 3,290 feet in just 15 km (9 mi) through sandstone cliffs, multicolored rocks, granite hills, ironstone outcrops, and quartz formations. Watered by nine small rivers rising in its vicinity and covered with rich soils, Itala supports a varied cross section of vegetation, encompassing riverine thicket, wetland, open savanna, and acacia woodland. Arriving at its Ntshondwe Camp is nothing short of dramatic. The meandering road climbs from open plains to the top of a plateau dotted with granite formations, which at the last minute magically yield the rest camp at the foot of pink and russet cliffs.

SELF-GUIDED TRAILS An unusual feature of Itala is its self-guided walking trails in the mountainside above Ntshondwe Camp. It gives you a chance to stretch your limbs if you've just spent hours cooped up in a car. It also has the advantage of giving you the chance to get really close to the euphorbias, acacias, and other fascinating indigenous vegetation that festoon the hills. Ask at the camp reception for further information.

WHERE TO STAY

Although Itala has several exclusive bush camps, these are booked up months in advance by South Africans, making the chalets at its main camp the only practical accommodations for foreign visitors. Two people sharing a two-bed unit at Ntshondwe will pay about R350 per person per night.

★ ¢ 🏨**Ntshondwe Camp.** In architecture, landscaping, and style, this beautiful government-run rest camp, 69 km (43 mi) from Vryheid, comes closer than any other in the country to matching the expensive private lodges. Built around granite boulders and vegetation lush with acacias, wild figs, and giant cactuslike euphorbias, airy chalets with steep thatch roofs blend perfectly with the surroundings. Its two-, four-, and six-bed units can accommodate a total of 200 guests. Each self-catering chalet has a spacious lounge simply furnished with cane chairs, a fully equipped kitchen, and a large veranda surrounded by indigenous bush. Keep an eye open for eagles soaring above the pink and russet sandstone cliffs. A magnificent game-viewing deck juts out over a steep slope to provide views of a water hole and extensive panoramas of the surrounding valleys. Take a guided game drive (R150) or guided walk (R140), hike a self-guided trail, or follow one of the well-laid-out drives with markers at points of interest. Picnic at one of the many scenic picnic spots, all of which have barbecue facilities and toilets. There's a gas station, a store (with great curios), and a good restaurant on the premises. ✍*KZN Wildlife, Box 13069, Cascades, Pietermaritzburg 3202* ☎*033/845–1000 or 034/983–2540* 🏠*39 chalets* ♿*In-room: kitchen. In-hotel: restaurant, bar, pool* ▤*AE, DC, MC, V.*

ELEPHANT COAST ESSENTIALS

5

TRANSPORTATION

BY AIR

The closest airport to this area is at Richards Bay, about 100 km (60 mi) south of Hluhluwe-Umfolozi and about 224 km (140 mi) south of Itala. The airport is served by SA Express Airways, which has daily flights from Johannesburg.

Airline SA Express Airways (☎*035/786–0301*).

BY CAR

If you're traveling to Hluhluwe-Umfolozi from Durban, drive north on the N2 to Mtubatuba; then cut west on the R618 to Mambeni Gate. Otherwise, continue up the N2 to the Hluhluwe exit and follow the signs to the park and Memorial Gate. The whole trip takes about three hours, but watch out for potholes.

If you're headed to Itala from Durban, drive north on the N2 to Empangeni, and then head west on the R34 to Vryheid. From here cut east on the R69 to Louwsburg. The reserve is immediately northwest of the village, from which there are clear signs. The journey from Durban takes around five hours, and from Hluhluwe-Umfolozi about 2½ hours. Roads are good, and there are plenty of gas stations along the way.

Avis and Imperial have car-rental offices at the Richards Bay airport.

Rental Companies Avis (☎*035/789–6555*). Imperial (☎*035/786–0309*).

CONTACTS & RESOURCES

TOURS

Umhluhluwe Safaris is by far the largest tour operator in Zululand and offers a full range of half- and full-day game drives in Hluhluwe-Umfolozi, as well as night drives and bush walks. The company also leads game drives into the Mkuze Game Reserve and guided tours to the bird-rich wetlands and beaches of St. Lucia. If you're interested in the trail hikes through Hluhluwe-Umfolozi, contact KZN Wildlife.

Tour Operator **KZN Wildlife** (☎ *033/845–1000* ⊕ *www.kznwildlife.com*). **Um-hluhluwe Safaris** (☎ *035/562–0414*).

VISITOR INFORMATION

The Elephant Coast's Web site has information about dining and lodging, as well as attractions, towns you'll pass through, sports facilities, and much more. If you're visiting the Hluhluwe-Umfolozi Game Reserve, all activites can be booked through the Web site of the province's official conservation organization, Ezemvelo KZN Wildlife.

Web Sites Elephant Coast (⊕ *www.elephantcoast.kzn.org.za*). **Ezemvelo KZN Wildlife** (⊕ *www.kznwildlife.com*).

PRIVATE GAME RESERVES & LODGES

KwaZulu-Natal's best private lodges lie in northern Zululand and Maputaland, a remote region close to Mozambique. With one exception, the lodges reviewed here do not offer the Big Five. However, they are sufficiently close to one another and Hluhluwe-Umfolozi Game Reserve to allow you to put together a bush experience that delivers the Big Five and a great deal more, including superb bird-watching opportunities and an unrivaled beach paradise. Malaria does pose a problem, however, and antimalarial drugs are essential. Summers are hot, hot, hot. If you can't take heat and humidity, then autumn, winter, and early summer are probably the best time to visit.

PHINDA PRIVATE GAME RESERVE

71 Established in 1991, this flagship CC Africa reserve is a heartening example of tourism serving the environment with panache. Phinda (*pin*-duh) is Zulu for "return," referring to the restoration of 54,360 acres of overgrazed ranchland in northern Zululand to bushveld. It's a triumph. You'll find it impossible to believe the area wasn't always the thick bush you see all around you. The Big Five have established themselves firmly, and Phinda can claim a stunning variety of five different ecosystems: sand forest (which grows on the fossil dunes of an earlier coastline), savanna, bushveld, open woodland, and verdant wetlands.

Phinda can deliver the Big Five, although not as consistently or in such numbers as its sister lodge, Londolozi, in Mpumalanga. Buffalo, leopards, lions, cheetahs, spotted hyenas, elephants, white rhinos, hippos, giraffes, impalas, and the rare, elusive, tiny Suni antelope are all here, and rangers provide exciting interpretive game drives for guests. Birdlife is prolific and extraordinary, with some special Zululand finds: the pink-throated twin spot, the crested guinea fowl, the African broadbill, and the crowned eagle. Where Phinda also excels is in the superb quality of its rangers, who can provide fascinating commentary on everything from local birds to frogs. You'll be amazed at just how enthralling the love life of a dung beetle can be! There are also Phinda adventures (optional extras) down the Mzinene River for a close-up look at crocodiles, hippos, and birds; big-game fishing or scuba diving off the deserted, wildly beautiful Maputaland coast; and sightseeing flights over Phinda and the highest vegetated dunes in the world.

WHERE TO STAY

For all reservations, contact **CC Africa** ☎*011/809–4300* ⊕*www.phinda. com* ⊟*AE, DC, MC, V* ⊚*FAP.*

☾ $$$$ ☷**Phinda Zuka Lodge.** An exclusive sole-use villa for a family or small group of friends, Zuka (Zuka means "sixpence" in Zulu) is a couple of miles from the bigger lodges. The area that this lodge is on was recently added to Phinda to accommodate black rhinos. Thatch cottages overlook a busy water hole, and you'll be looked after by the camp's personal ranger-host, butler, and chef. Children are welcome. ⤳*4 cottages* ⌂*In-hotel: bar, pool.*

★ $ ☷**Forest Lodge.** Hidden in a rare sand forest, this fabulous lodge overlooks a small water hole where nyalas, warthogs, and baboons frequently come to drink. The lodge is a real departure from the traditional thatch structures so common in South Africa. It's very modern, with a vaguely Japanese Zen feel thanks to glass-paneled walls, light woods, and a deliberately spare, clean look. The effect is stylish and very elegant, softened by modern African art and sculpture. Suites use the same architectural concepts as the lodge, where walls have become windows, and rely on the dense forest (or curtains) for their privacy. As a result, you feel very close to your surroundings, and it's possible to lie in bed or take a shower while watching delicate nyalas grazing just feet away. ⤳*16 suites* ⌂*In-hotel: pool.*

☾ $ ☷**Mountain Lodge.** This attractive thatch lodge sits on a rocky hill overlooking miles of bushveld plains and the Ubombo Mountains. Wide verandas lead into the lounge and bar, graced with high ceilings, dark beams, and cool tile floors. In winter guests can snuggle into cushioned wicker chairs next to a blazing log fire. Brick pathways wind down the hillside from the lodge to elegant split-level suites with mosquito nets, thatch roofs, and large decks overlooking the reserve. African baskets, beadwork, and grass matting beautifully complement the bush atmosphere. Children are welcome, although those under 5 are not allowed on game drives and 6- to 11-year-olds are permitted only at the manager's discretion. ⤳*20 suites, 7 chalets* ⌂*In-hotel: bar, pool.*

$ ☷**Rock Lodge.** If you get tired of the eagle's-eye view of the deep valley below from your private veranda, you can write in your journal in your luxurious sitting room or take a late-night dip in your own plunge pool. All of Phinda's activities are included, including twice-daily game drives, nature walks, riverboat cruises, and canoe trips along the Mzinene River. Scuba diving, deep-sea fishing, and spectacular small-plane flights are extras. Don't miss out on one of Phinda's legendary bush dinners, when hundreds of lanterns light up the surrounding forest and bush and the food is unforgettable. ⤳*6 suites* ⌂*In-hotel: bar, pool.*

$ ☷**Vlei Lodge.** Accommodations at this small and intimate lodge are nestled in the shade of the sand forest and are so private it's hard to believe there are other guests. Suites—made of thatch, teak, and glass—have a distinct Asian feel and overlook a wet marshland on the edge of inviting woodland. The bedrooms and bathrooms are huge, and guests have private plunge pools (a recent visitor found a lion drinking from his) and outdoor decks. The lounge/living area of the lodge has two fireplaces on opposite glass walls, a dining area, and a large terrace under a canopy of trees, where breakfast is served. The bush braai, with its splendid food and fairy-tale setting, is a memorable occasion after an evening game drive. ↩6 suites ⚭In-hotel: bar, pool.

¢ 📷 **Phinda Walking Safari.** This unusual experience is a really delightful way to get close to the bush. Your home for three nights is a spacious safari tent (with bathroom) in the middle of a rare sand forest. Here crowned eagles may survey you as you take a postprandial nap in a hammock under giant fig trees, or a fishing owl may call as you swap safari stories under the stars. An armed security guard–ranger makes sure you get home safely, and the camp chef keeps the calories coming. Each morning (depending on the consensus of the group) you amble through the forest or over the plains for four or five hours; then it's back to camp for a pre-sunset walk and game drive. The walking safari is not offered in summer because of the heat. ↩4 luxury tents ⚭In-hotel: bar, no kids under 16 ⊗Closed Dec.–Feb.

THANDA PRIVATE GAME RESERVE

70 Located in a wildly beautiful part of northern Zululand, award-winning Thanda is one of KwaZulu-Natal's newer game reserves, and, like its neighbor Phinda did more than a decade ago, it is restoring former farmlands and hunting grounds to their once-pristine state. The reserve occupies 37,000 acres of these former farmlands and hunting grounds, thanks to a joint venture with local communities and the king of the Zulus, His Majesty Goodwill Zweletini, who gave some of his royal hunting grounds to the project. Game that used to roam here centuries ago have been reestablished, including the Big Five. Thanda (tan-duh) is Zulu for "love," and its philosophy echoes just that: "for the love of nature, wildlife, and dear ones." Rangers often have to work hard to find game, but the rewards of seriously tracking lions or rhinos with your enthusiastic and very experienced ranger and tracker are great. Because its owner is passionately committed not only to the land but also to the local people, there are many opportunities to interact with them. Don't miss out on Vula Zulu, one of the most magical and powerful Zulu experiences offered in South Africa; you can have the bones thrown and read at the sangoma's hut or visit the chief's kraal. After exploring the village, you'll be treated to the Vula Zulu show, a memorable blend of narration, high-energy dance, song, and mime that recounts Zulu history. The lodge can also arrange golf, scuba diving, snorkeling, whale-watching, and fishing expeditions.

WHERE TO STAY

For all reservations, contact **Thanda.** Both the tented camp and the main lodge offer kids' programs and a customized Junior Ranger's course. ☎011/704–3115 ⊕www.thanda.com ☰AE, DC, MC, V ⼌FAP.

☾ ★ $ 📷 **Thanda Main Lodge.** There's a palpable feeling of earth energy in this magical and exquisite lodge that blends elements of royal Zulu with an eclectic pan-African feel. Beautiful domed, beehive-shape dwellings perch on the side of rolling hills and overlook mountains and bushveld. On the inside it's contemporary Scandinavian meets pan-African chic. Both are works of art, from the "eyelashes" of slatted poles that peep out from under the thatch roofs to the embedded mosaics in royal Zulu red and blue that decorate the polished, honey-colored stone floors. Check out the creative light fixtures—no two are alike—from chandeliers made of handcrafted Zulu beads or twisted wire to lamps made of straw or filmy cotton mesh. A huge stone fireplace divides the bedroom area—which has drawn threadwork bed linens and a curtain of river pebbles and wire behind the bed—from the comfortable and roomy lounge. Each chalet has a different color scheme and is decorated with beaded, hand-embroidered cushions and throws. Dip in your personal plunge pool after an exciting game drive; then sunbathe on your private deck or commune with the surrounding bushveld in your cool, cushioned *sala* (outdoor covered deck). Later, after a meal that many a fine restaurant would be proud to serve, come back to your chalet to find a bedtime story on your pillow, marshmallows waiting to be toasted over flickering candles, and a glass of Amarula cream. Or dine alone with your loved one in your private *boma* (outdoor eating area) by the light of the stars and the leaping flames of a fragrant wood fire. The spacious, uncluttered public areas—dining decks, bomas, library, and lounge—are decorated in restful earth tones accented by royal Zulu colors, beads from Malawi, Ghanaian ceremonial masks, and Indonesian chairs. ➡9 *chalets* ⚐*In-hotel: bar, pool, spa, children's programs (ages 5–15).*

⏱ $ ▦**Thanda Tented Camp.** Perfect for a family or friends' reunion, this unelectrified intimate camp deep in the bush brings you into even closer contact with your surroundings. Wake up in your spacious safari tent with en-suite bathroom and private veranda to find a warthog or nyala or three grazing outside. The camp has its own vehicle, ranger, and tracker, and a huge sala with pool and sundeck. ➡4 *tents* ⚐*In-hotel: bar, pool, spa, children's programs (ages 5–15).*

PHONGOLA GAME RESERVE

🅱 One of the largest inland bodies of water in Zululand, the Jozini Dam covers an area of some 39,520 acres along the Phongola (also called Pongola) River, close to the southern Swaziland border. Some 200 km (120 mi) of its pristine shoreline is bounded by the Phongola Game Reserve, today only a part of the original area declared a reserve in 1894 by President Paul Kruger. The dam (artificial lake), built in the 1960s to provide irrigation to sugarcane farmers and hydroelectric power to the region, was never used for those purposes, and for many years was something of a white elephant. Today it has found its niche, becoming a magnet for tourists to northern KwaZulu-Natal. Surrounded by pristine bushveld and scrub, the lake provides sanctuary to a large number of crocodiles and hippos. Tiger fish that had nowhere to swim to after the river was dammed stayed put, and now fish of up to 24 pounds have been caught in the lake's waters. The region hosts an annual tiger-fishing competition in late September, drawing fishing enthusiasts from around the country. The lake has also ensured that the area is a birding hot spot, with more than 350 species of bushveld and waterbirds recorded. The purple-blue Lebombo Mountains looming behind the lake add majesty to the landscape.

Game here includes four of the Big Five (except lions), all of which have been reintroduced. The most interesting are the elephants, to the south of the reserve. It is the first time in more than 100 years that the great beasts have populated the region, and their effect on bushveld ecology is being monitored by a dedicated team. In addition, you may see warthogs, wildebeests, giraffes, zebras, and a variety of antelopes, including nyalas.

But it's not just game at this bushveld destination, which has six luxury lodges, four of them self-catering. Although activities include traditional game drives in open safari vehicles, big-game tracking and guided bush walks, there's also very exciting fishing, canoeing, and daylong boat trips on the Phongola River and Jozini Dam.

WHERE TO STAY

NORTHERN SECTION   To access the northern part of the reserve, travel north on the N2, past Umfolozi and Hluhluwe, toward the town of Phongola. Approximately 30 km (19 mi) south of Phongola, look for the sign to Golela and take this road to the right. After about 4 km (2 mi) you will see a sign to Phongola Game Reserve. The gate is on the right-hand side. *Note: Do not take the first right-hand turn, also signposted* PHONGOLA GAME RESERVE, *off the N2. This accesses the southern part of the reserve only.*

$ 🔲 **Mvubu Lodge.** This beautiful and affordable lodge high on the banks of the Phongola River has endless, unspoiled views of silver river, blue sky, and rolling green hills. Attractive thatch-and-wood chalets face the magnificent panorama, but bathrooms are rather small, containing only a sink, toilet, and shower. A stone-walled communal lounge-bar area, attractively furnished with huge basket chairs, has sliding doors that open onto a wooden deck. Breakfasts are usually served on a thatch deck, and a traditional boma is the place for dinner, where, if you're adventurous, you can try such meats as kudu rumps or impala schnitzel. There's also a swimming pool—a must during summer, when temperatures soar beyond 38°C (100°F). ⊠ *Golela Rd., off the N2, Box 767, 3170* 🕾 *034/435–1123 or 034/435–1104* ⊕ *www.pongolagamereserve.co.za* 🛏 *11 chalets* ⌂ *In-hotel: bar, pool* ⊟ *MC, V* ⦿ *MAP.*

SOUTHERN SECTION   To access the southern part of the reserve, travel north on the N2, past Umfolozi and Hluhluwe, toward the town of Phongola. Fifty kilometers (31 mi) from Phongola, look for the brown sign to Phongola Game Reserve and turn right.

★ **$** 🔲 **White Elephant Lodge.** Built in the 1920s, White Elephant is a lovely lodge that captures the elegance of colonial Africa, with white furniture, African prints, sepia photographs of local historical scenes, and antiques. The lounge and dining room are in a historic farmhouse, with wide verandas providing sweeping views of the bushveld and Lebombo Mountains. Behind the house, sheltered from the prevailing winds, a traditional Zulu boma is the site of dinners and Zulu dancing. Accommodations are in luxurious East African safari tents—airy, cool, and perfect for hot subtropical nights. Each tent has a private bathroom with a claw-foot tub, an outdoor shower surrounded by canvas screens, and a private veranda. Paths link the tents and the main house. You can choose between taking part in the lodge's elephant monitoring program or going rhino tracking (no kids under 12), viewing game from an open vehicle, or fishing for a whopping tiger fish or two. Rates include two activities per day. Once you are in the Phongola Game Reserve, follow the Pongolwane signs (painted on rocks) and white arrows (*do not turn off to Mpelane*) and the logos of white elephants. ⊠ *Off the N2, south of Phongola* ▢ *Box 792, Phongola 3170* ☎ *034/413–2489* ⊕ *www. whiteelephantlodge.co.za* ⊶ *8 tents* ☐ *In-hotel: bar, pool* ▭ *AE, DC, MC, V* ⓘ *FAP.*

¢ 🖼 **White Elephant Bush Camp.** If you're watching pennies and want a back-to-nature experience, then this lovely little camp will hit the spot. Thatch chalets have private verandas with great views, ceiling fans, and the ubiquitous mozzie nets. Chill out at the swimming pool, sit quietly in the blind, or watch the passing show at the water hole. Go for a bush walk or game drive, catch a tiger fish or two, or go "elephant-ing" (no kids under 12). Rates include one activity per day. ⊠ *Off the N2, south of Phongola, Box 792, Phongola 3170* ☎ *034/413–2489* ⊕ *www.whiteelephantlodge.co.za* ⊶ *7 chalets* ☐ *In-hotel: pool* ▭ *AE, DC, MC, V* ⓘ *FAP.*

AMAZULU PRIVATE GAME RESERVE & AMAKHOSI LODGE

73 Forty kilometers (21 mi) south of Phongola lies AmaKhosi Lodge, in the Amazulu Private Game Reserve, which covers some 25,000 acres of pristine wilderness on the perennial Mkhuze River. Different habitats range from rocky hillsides to thick bushveld, tamboti forests to broad wetlands. AmaKhosi has all of the Big Five, in addition to wildebeests, zebras, giraffes, and a variety of antelopes, including the shy nyala. Most animals have been reintroduced, with the exception of leopards, which remain secretive and very difficult to spot. In addition, a wide variety of bird species will delight birders.

★ $ 🖼 **AmaKhosi Lodge.** In the heart of northern KwaZulu-Natal, amid countryside that Alan Paton would have described as beautiful beyond any singing of it, this spectacular lodge overlooks the Mkhuze River, which carves its way through mountains, rolling hills, open plains, thick thornveld, and riverine bush. Birdlife is abundant, the Big Five are all here, and rangers work hard to find game, instead of relying on animals habituated to vehicles, as at some of the older camps. Superb air-conditioned suites (big enough to swing a pride of lions) have huge decks from which you can survey the river below. The staff excels, from management right down to the friendly gardeners, and the food would put many a posh restaurant to shame. Dine under the stars on a sprawling deck overlooking the river, in a gracious dining room if the weather is inclement, or in the staff-built branch-enclosed boma, entertained by local schoolchildren who practice their singing and dancing hard to help pay their school fees. For something very different, try a frog or insect safari: after a bush braai, you'll be supplied with gum boots and miners' lamps, and led on a hunt for more than 30 species of these fascinating and little-known creatures with the resident frog or insect expert. ⊠ *Off the N2, south of Phongola* ⊡ *Box 354, Phongola 3170* ☎ *034/414–1157* ⊕ *www.amakhosi.com* ➥ *6 suites* ⚒ *In-room: safe. In-hotel: bar, pool* ⊟ *AE, DC, MC, V* ⊚ *FAP.*

MAPUTALAND COASTAL RESERVE

76 If Robinson Crusoe had washed ashore on the pristine coastline of Maputaland, he wouldn't have found anybody to call Friday—and he certainly wouldn't have cared what day of the week it was. It's that empty and that magnificent. No other buildings lie within 16 km (10 mi) of Rocktail Bay Lodge, tucked away in Maputaland Coastal Reserve, a narrow strip of wilderness that stretches from St. Lucia all the way to Mozambique. If you love exploring along untouched beaches, fishing, scuba diving, snorkeling, and walking, coming here will be one of the highlights of a visit to South Africa. Rocktail Bay is not a game lodge—the only animals you're likely to see are loggerhead and leatherback turtles. It is included in this section because it lies far from any other major tourist destination and operates much like a game lodge. In fact, unless you have a four-wheel-drive vehicle, the lodge must pick you up for the final 11-km (7-mi) journey along deep sand tracks carved through coastal dune forest.

Rocktail Bay *does not offer traditional game-viewing,* although you can combine a visit here with a trip to Phinda, about 95 km (60 mi) to the south. Besides glorious beaches, its major attraction is the annual arrival of giant loggerhead and leatherback turtles to lay their eggs. The beaches here are one of the few known egg-laying areas of these endangered animals, and the season extends from the November through early March. During these months rangers lead after-dinner drives and walks down the beach to look for turtles, and you can expect to cover as much as 16 km (10 mi) in a night. From a weather standpoint, the best times to visit the lodge are probably spring (September–October) and autumn (March–May). In summer the temperature regularly soars past 38°C (100°F), and swimming during winter is a brisk proposition. August is the windiest month, and it's in summer that the turtles come ashore to dig their nests and lay their eggs—an awesome spectacle.

WHERE TO STAY

¢   **Rocktail Bay Lodge.** The lodge lies in a swale formed by enormous dunes fronting the ocean. Walkways tunnel through the dune forest to a golden beach that sweeps in a gentle arc to Black Rock, several miles to the north. There are no lifeguards or shark nets, but the swimming and snorkeling are fabulous. The lodge consists of simple A-frame chalets raised on wooden platforms above the forest floor. Wood and

Fodor's Choice
★

thatch create a rustic ambience, complemented by solar lighting and basic furnishings. A large veranda and adjoining thatch bar provide the backdrop for alfresco meals under a giant Natal mahogany tree. Activities include great surf fishing (tackle provided), snorkeling, and walking through the forest or along the beach. Rangers lead excursions to see hippo pools, the rich birdlife of Lake Sibaya, and Kosi Bay, where the local Tembe people catch fish using the age-old method of basket netting, and Tsonga descendants also use ancient woven fish traps. For many people, though, a trip to Rocktail Bay is a chance to kick back and just soak in the atmosphere of an unspoiled coastal wilderness. ✉ *Box 78573, Sandton 2146* ☎ *011/883–0747* ⊕ *www.rocktailbay. com* ⤴ *10 chalets* ♿ *In-hotel: bar, pool* ▤ *AE, DC, MC, V* ⏐◎⏐ *FAP.*

SPORTS & THE OUTDOORS

DIVING At Manzengwenya, 11 km (7 mi) south of the camp, you'll find some of the best (some say the best) scuba-diving sites in the country. This is the only diving concession in the marine reserve, so you'll be diving from the only boat in the area and should have the pristine reefs all to yourself (R350 for the first dive, R300 for the second). The **Rocktail Bay Dive Centre** (☎ *035/574–8557*) is fully outfitted, and you can dive reefs that have never been dived on before. In December and January pregnant ragged-tooth sharks migrate to the area and rest placidly in reef caves.

Johannesburg & Environs

WORD OF MOUTH

"With kids, a visit to the Lion Park, just on the outskirts north-west of Johannesburg, is a great way
to spend a few hours. Drive around the park, drive
through the lion enclosures, and also get the kids
to hold a lion cub."

—RKR

"I would definitely suggest doing a tour of Soweto.
To visit South Africa without doing a Soweto Tour
is to ignore the history of South Africa. However,
that is not to say that it will not, ultimately, be a
fun and uplifting tour. Also, I suggest staying in the
Sandton area as there are nice restaurants and
great shopping and Sandton Square is totally safe
to walk around day and night.'"

—Roccco

Updated by
Tara Turkington

JOHANNESBURG, EGOLI, JOZI: THE PLACE where the gold is. Johannesburg is the center of a vast urban industrial complex that covers most of the province of Gauteng (pronounced *Ggggow*-teng, with a gutteral g), which is Sotho for "place where the gold is." But more than 100 years ago it was just a triangular, rocky piece of unwanted Highveld land. It remained so until gold was officially discovered in 1886 by an Australian, George Harrison. The discovery allowed Johannesburg to become a modern metropolis that still powers the country's economy; it produces nearly 20% of the country's wealth. Its population, about 3.2 million, is mostly young, and despite being a commercial center, Johannesburg is a green city, with more than 10 million trees, and parks and nature reserves that hug the outskirts of the city.

In the late 1980s Johannesburg's big business fled north from crime and urban decay to the suburb of Sandton, about 10 mi from the city center. But lately local government and business have been reinvesting in the inner city, particularly with an eye to the 2010 World Cup, when it will welcome millions of visitors. The beautiful Nelson Mandela Bridge, which spans the railway tracks close to the Newtown Cultural Precinct, has been decorated with wonderful street sculpture. Even the streets in downtown Johannesburg have been renamed: Bezuidenhout Street is now called Miriam Makeba Street, which is next to Dolly Rathebe Street, named for two of South Africa's jazz legends.

ORIENTATION & PLANNING

ORIENTATION

South Africa's biggest city is in the middle of Gauteng, South Africa's smallest but wealthiest province. The M1, a large highway, runs centrally through the city and its suburbs. The city is circled by two adjoining highways, the N3 to the east and the N1 to the west; the M1 bisects this circle.

Tshwane's city center, Pretoria, is about 30 mi (50 km) directly north of Johannesburg's city center, and the two are connected by the N1, which runs the full length of South Africa, from Musina on the Zimbabwe border in the north to Cape Town in the south.

JOHANNESBURG

Jo'burg was born as a mining camp, and its downtown area—the oldest part—is a jumbled grid of one-way streets heading in opposite directions reflecting its hasty start to life. Although the city center is experiencing a revival, it's not somewhere that everyone will choose to visit. The attractions in or close to the city center include the Nelson Mandela Bridge, MuseuMAfricA, and the SAB World of Beer in the Newtown area, the Johannesburg Art Gallery, the Standard Bank Gallery, and Diagonal Street in the downtown area, and Constitution Hill, the Civic Theatre, and the Johannesburg Planetarium in Braamfontein.

About 12 mi (20 km) to the south of downtown Johannesburg lies the vast township of Soweto, where you can take a township tour and visit the Hector Pieterson Museum. Between Soweto and the city are Gold Reef City and the Apartheid Museum.

Most of the city's good hotels and major malls are in the northern suburbs: Melville (closest to the city center), Greenside, Parkhurst, Sandton, and Rosebank, among many others. The burgeoning "new north," comprising Fourways, Kyalami, Midrand, and others is farther north. This area has been expanding rapidly since the 1990s, causing an almost continuous traffic snarl-up. There are no must-see sights (though Montecasino is a popular attraction), but the shopping is good.

PRETORIA AND TSHWANE
About an hour north of Johannesburg (traffic-depending—on a bad day it can take more than two hours), Pretoria, the country's capital, is within the larger metropolitan area of Tshwane (pronounced *Chwa*-aah-nie). Though it was once a bastion of hard-line Afrikanerdom, the city now has a refreshing cosmopolitan breeze blowing through its streets. In addition to its several historic buildings, it's renowned for its jacaranda trees, whose purple blossoms blanket the city in September and October.

CRADLE OF HUMANKIND
The Cradle of Humankind, a World Heritage Site, has a rich fossil record that reflects the history of humanity over the past 3 million years. More fossils of hominids (human ancestors) have been found here than anywhere else on earth. There is a visitor center at the Sterkfontein Caves and at Maropeng.

THE MAGALIESBERG
To the north of Johannesburg lies the Magaliesberg (pronounced "Mu-*Ggggu*-lees-berg," with a gutteral g). The name means "the mountains of Magalie" or Mogale, who was a famous Setswana chief in the area, and refers to both a small "dorp" (country town) and a wider region. Here you can get a restful break amid lovely mountain scenery, farmlands, and quiet country roads. Though now more pleasantly rolling than spectacular, the Magaliesberg is one of the world's oldest mountain ranges.

SUN CITY & PILANSBERG
Sun City, a multifaceted entertainment and casino complex comprising hotels, championship golf courses, and a water park, is about a 90-minute drive from Johannesburg. Each year in early December the resort hosts the Nedbank Golf Challenge, which regularly draws big names in golf, such as Tiger Woods, Colin Montgomerie, Vijay Singh, and local favorites Ernie Els and Retief Goosen. Adjacent to Sun City is the Pilansberg National Park, a small reserve that's home to the Big Five and has excellent accommodations ranging from upmarket timeshares to camp sites.

TOP REASONS TO VISIT

Cradle of Humankind. Visit the **Sterkfontein Caves** and **Maropeng** visitor centers at this World Heritage Site, about an hour from Johannesburg, to view the ancient history of humanity, fossils, and paleontology.

History In Your Lifetime. Do a tour of the **Constitutional Court,** South Africa's highest court, built on the site of an infamous Johannesburg prison. Famous inmates have included Mahatma Gandhi and Nelson Mandela. The award-winning architecture includes elements of the past such as bricks from the old jail

and art marking South Africa's transition to democracy. Also check out the Apartheid Museum for a harrowing look at South Africa's apartheid history and road to democracy.

Mall Fancy. Enjoy a few hours in Sandton City, a glitzy mall where you can buy everything from gold jewelry to camping gear. Eat outside at one of the upmarket restaurants in the adjacent **Nelson Mandela Square**, ironically presided over by a giant statue of the champion of the poor and oppressed.

PLANNING

6

To residents, Johannesburg is a ghost town over the December holidays, when most leave for the seaside or the bush for the summer holidays. It's hot, but dry, and there's often an afternoon thunderstorm. There's little or no rain in winter (from March to September), and it gets bitterly cold, often dropping below freezing at night, though its often pleasant during the day. Johannesburg seems stark, with the cold gripping the concrete, but at least the aloes flower, some a deep red. Then the city starts to thaw. Jacaranda trees bloom, carpeting the streets with purple blossoms, and a local arts festival, Arts Alive, harkens the change of seasons. Jo'burgers boast that they enjoy the best climate in the world: not too hot in summer, not too cold in winter, and not prone to sudden temperature changes. Summer may have the edge, though: it's when the gardens and open spaces are at their most beautiful.

TAKE IT ALL IN

1 or 2 days: If you have only one day in Jo'burg, take a tour of Soweto, visit the Apartheid Museum, go shopping, and then head out to Muldersdrift for a wild and wacky African dinner at the Carnivore restaurant. If you have a second day, focus on what interests you most: perhaps a trip to the Cradle of Humankind, where you can explore the sites of some of most significant paleontological discoveries, or a jaunt to Sun City. You could start off with a balloon ride and then amble through the

GOOD TO KNOW

It's virtually impossible to see anything of the Johannesburg area without a car. Your best bet is to rent one, decide what you want to see, and get a good road map or rent a GPS navigator. Service-station attendants can also point you in the right direction. If you're staying only a day or two, stick to escorted trips.

Magaliesberg area, wandering from coffee shop to art studio. Other options include a tour of the Cullinan Diamond Mine, near Pretoria, or a visit to Gold Reef City. Each of these options could take up a half or full day.

3 or 4 Days: Spend Days 1 and 2 as described above, overnighting, perhaps, at the Misty Hills Country Hotel after your visit to the Cradle of Humankind. En route back to Johannesburg on Day 3, visit the Cullinan mine and do a short walking tour of central Pretoria. On Day 4 shop in the morning, visiting the Bruma flea market or the African market outside Rosebank Mall. If you'd rather mix your energy with some peace and quiet, you can stay in a chalet at Mountain Sanctuary Park, in the Magaliesberg, for a night or two.

SAFETY

Johannesburg is notorious for being South Africa's most dangerous city. It's quite common to hear about serious crimes such as armed robbery and murder. Even South Africans fear it, regarding it as some Americans regard New York City: big and bad. That said, it's safe for visitors if they take reasonable precautions. These include not leaving bags or valuables visible in a car and keeping the doors locked, even while driving (to minimize the risk of smash-and-grab robberies or being hijacked), not carrying large wads of cash, and not walking in the city center or any of the townships with flashy jewelry or expensive equipment.

MONEY MATTERS

You can exchange currency at Johannesburg International Airport or at the larger branches of South Africa's banks, such as ABSA, Standard Bank, and Nedbank's operations in Rosebank and Sandton. Look for the BUREAU DE CHANGE signs at these banks. ATMs are all over the city, especially at shopping centers. Be careful when using them, though. Don't let anybody distract your attention, and avoid ATMs in quiet spots at night. Traveler's checks are welcome, but more and more businesses are switching over to credit cards.

VISITOR INFO

The helpful **Gauteng Tourism Authority** (☎011/ 832–2780 ⊕*www. gauteng.net*) has information on the whole province, but more detailed information is often at local tourism associations. The **Johannesburg Tourism Company** (☎011/214–0700 ⊕*www.joburg.org.za*) has an excellent Web site. The **Soweto Accommodation Association** (☎011/936–8123 ⊕*www.sowetobedandbreakfast.co.za*) lists more than 20 lodgings. Covering Pretoria, Centurion, Atteridgeville, Mamelodi, and surrounds, the **Tshwane Tourism Information Centre** (☎012/358–1430, 082/239–2630 24 hrs ⊕*www.tshwane.gov.za*) has friendly staff, plenty of pamphlets and printed guides, and a 24-hour info line. The **Cullinan Info Shop** (☎012/734–2170 ⊕*www.cullinanmeander.co.za*) provides information about tours and attractions in and around Cullinan. **Magalies Reservations** (☎014/577–1733 ⊕*www.magaliesinfo. co.za*) covers accommodations and attractions in the Magaliesberg area. The **Maropeng Vistor Centre** (☎014/577–9000 ⊕*www.maropeng.*

co.za) provides information about the visitor centers in the Cradle of Humankind. For further inquiries about the Cradle of Humankind and Magaliesberg areas—including suggestions for restaurants, small lodges, and routes to take—contact the **Crocodile Ramble Information Centre** (☎*014/577–9323, 082/923–6120, or 083/284–3523* ⊕*www. theramble.co.za*).

EAT RIGHT, SLEEP WELL

Jo'burgers love eating out, and there are thousands of restaurants throughout the city to satisfy them. Some notable destinations for food include Melrose Arch, Parkhurst, Sandton, the South (for its Portuguese cuisine), Melville, and Chinatown in the CBD (Central Business District). There's also a new Chinatown—a strip of restaurants and Asian grocery stores in Cyrildene, just above Bruma Lake. Check out the restaurants recommended on the official Johannesburg Web site ⊕*www. johannesburg.gov.za*. "Smart casual" dress is a good bet, as is making reservations. Most places are open for lunch and dinner, though many establishments are closed on Sunday nights and Monday.

Most, if not all, of the good hotels are in the northern suburbs. Many of the hotels are linked to nearby malls and are well policed. Boutique hotels have sprung up everywhere, as have bed-and-breakfasts from Melville to Soweto. Hotels are quieter in December and January, and their rates are often cheaper. Generally the busy months in Jo'burg are from June to August. If there's a major conference, some of the smaller hotels can be booked months in advance.

6

WHAT IT COSTS IN SOUTH AFRICAN RAND					
	¢	$	$$	$$$	$$$$
RESTAURANTS	under R50	R50–R75	R75–R100	R100–R125	over R125
LODGING	under R500	R500–R1,000	R1,000–R2,000	R2,000–R3,000	over R3,000

Restaurant prices are per person for a main course at dinner, a main course equivalent, or a prix-fixe meal. Hotel and lodging prices are for a standard double room in high season, including 12.5% tax.

EXPLORING JOHANNESBURG

Johannesburg epitomizes South Africa's paradoxical make-up—it's rich, poor, innovative, and historic all rolled into one. And it seems at times as though no one actually comes *from* Johannesburg. The city is full of immigrants: Italians, Portuguese, Chinese, Hindus, Swazis, English, Zimbabweans, Nigerians, Xhosa. And the streets are full of merchants. Traders hawk *skop* (boiled sheep's head, split open and eaten off newspaper) in front of polished glass buildings, as taxis jockey for position in rush hour. *Sangomas* (traditional healers) lay out herbs and roots next to roadside barbers' tents, and you never seem to be far from a woman selling *vetkoek* (dollops of deep-fried dough), beneath billboards advertising investment banks or cell phones.

The Greater Johannesburg metropolitan area is massive—more than 1,300 square km (800 square mi)—incorporating the large municipalities of Randburg and Sandton to the north. Most of the sights are just north of the city center, which degenerated badly in the 1990s but is now being revamped.

To the south, in Ormonde, are the Apartheid Museum and Gold Reef City, and the sprawling township of Soweto is farther to the southwest. Johannesburg's northern suburbs are its most affluent. On the way to the shopping meccas of Rosebank and Sandton you can find the Johannesburg Zoo and the South African Museum of Military History, in the leafy suburb of Saxonwold.

> ### A JO'BURG BEACON
>
> If there's a symbol of Johannesburg, it's **Ponte City** (⌧1 Lily St., Hillbrow) a massive, hollow, 54-story cylinder of apartments perched on the edge of the central business district. Built in 1975, and standing at a height of 567 feet with a flashing cell-phone ad at the top, it's the tallest residential building in the southern hemisphere.

Numbers in the margin correspond to numbers on the Johannesburg map.

DOWNTOWN JOHANNESBURG

You'll find plenty to do in the city center including a visit to the impressive Standard Bank Gallery and Johannesburg Art Gallery. Diagonal Street runs—you guessed it—diagonally through the city center. The 768 foot Brixton Tower in Auckland Park and the tall, round Ponte City apartment block near Hillbrow are focal points and can be seen from almost all parts of the city.

WHAT TO SEE

❺ **Diagonal Street.** This street in the city center is lined with African herbalists' shops, where you can acquire a mind-boggling array of homeopathic and traditional cures for whatever ails you. If you're lucky, a sangoma might throw the bones and tell you what the future holds. This is also the site of the old Johannesburg Stock Exchange building (the modern version is in Sandton).

❸ **Johannesburg Art Gallery.** This three-story museum hosts excellent local and international exhibitions in 15 halls, and has collections of 17th-century Dutch art, 18th-century French art, and paintings by great South African artists such as Jacob Hendrik Pierneef, Ezrom Legae, Walter Battiss, Irma Stern, Gerard Sekoto, and Anton van Wouw. It exhibits 10% of its treasures at a time. You can also admire a large selection of traditional African objects, such as headrests, tree carvings, and beadwork. ⌧*King George and Klein Sts., Joubert Park* ☎*011/725–3130* ✉*Free* ◷*Tues.–Sun. 10–5.*

❹ **Standard Bank Gallery.** At the home of the Standard Bank African art collection you can admire contemporary South African artwork. The gallery hosts high-quality, ever-changing local and international exhibitions, including the annual traveling World Press Photo show. ⌧*Fred-*

erick and Simmonds Sts., City Center ☎*011/631–1889* ⊕*www.sbgallery.co.za* ✉*Free* ⊙ *Weekdays 8–4:30, Sat. 9–1.*

NEWTOWN

Located in the western section of the city, Newtown, which is connected to Braamfontein via the Nelson Mandela Bridge, was once one of the city's most run-down neighborhoods. Today it is known as the city's Cultural Precinct, as it's home of MuseuMAfricA, Newtown Music Centre, Market Theatre, and the National Design and Craft Centre.

WHAT TO SEE

★ **6** **MuseuMAfricA.** Founded in 1935, this was the first major museum to acknowledge black contributions to the city's development. The museum houses geological specimens, paintings, and photographs relating to South Africa's complex history. You can step into a re-creation of a 1950s *shebeen* (township bar) or view the ever-changing exhibits of pottery, photography, and other arts and crafts. Seven permanent displays include a look at the history of gold mining in Johannesburg and a journey through the history of South African music, such as township jazz, kwela, and *mbaqanga,* a form of driving township pop-jazz. Another display illustrates the life of Mahatma Gandhi, who once lived in Jo'burg. Upstairs, the Bensusan Museum examines the art, development, and technology of photography with fun, hands-on exhibits. ✉*121 Bree St., Newtown* ☎*011/833–5624* ✉*Free* ⊙ *Tues.–Sun. 9–5.*

8 **Nelson Mandela Bridge.** This modern, 931-foot-long bridge with sprawling cables spans the bleak Braamfontein railway yard, connecting Constitution Hill and Braamfontein to the revamped Newtown Cultural Precinct. A symbol of the renewal process going on in the city, the bridge is especially beautiful at night, when it is lighted in white and blue. ✉*Take Queen Elizabeth St. from Braamfontein, or follow signs from central Newtown or from M1 south, Braamfontein and Newtown.*

7 **World of Beer.** This unusual museum is dedicated to a great South African favorite—beer! SABMiller is the country's—and Africa's—largest beer company. You can find out all about the history of beer brewing in South Africa and the process of beer making, including African brewing traditions. After a 90-minute tour you can enjoy two complimentary beers in the tap room. The World of Beer went through a major revamp in 2007. ✉*15 President St., Newtown* ☎*011/836–4900* ⊕*www.worldofbeer.co.za* ✉*R10* ⊙ *Tues.–Sat. 10–6.*

BRAAMFONTEIN

Braamfontein is home to Constitution Hill and the University of the Witwatersrand, one of South Africa's oldest and most respected universities.

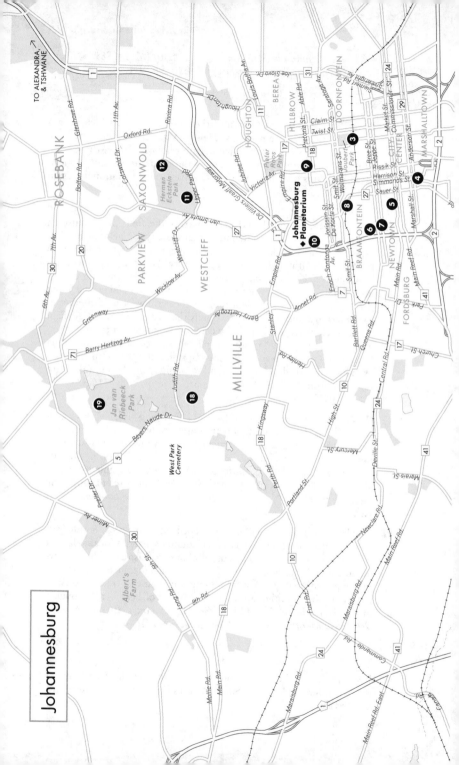

Johannesburg

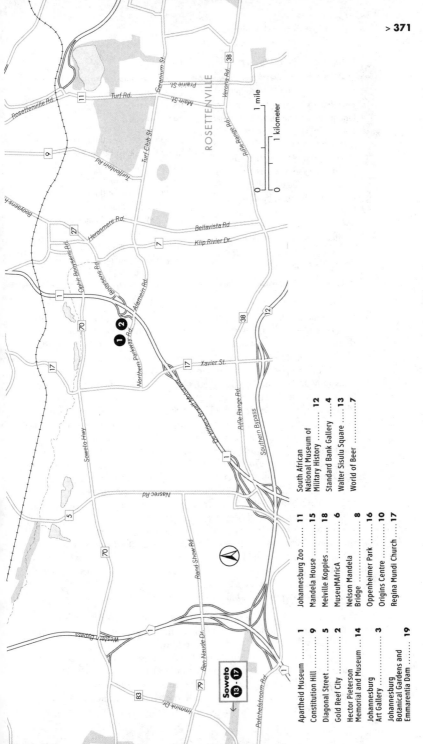

6

ROSETTENVILLE

1 mile

1 kilometer

South African
National Museum of
Military History **12**
Standard Bank Gallery **4**
Walter Sisulu Square **13**
World of Beer **7**

Johannesburg Zoo **11**
Mandela House **15**
Melville Koppies **18**
MuseuMAfricA **6**
Nelson Mandela
Bridge **8**
Oppenheimer Park **16**
Origins Centre **10**
Regina Mundi Church **17**

Apartheid Museum **1**
Constitution Hill **9**
Diagonal Street **5**
Gold Reef City **2**
Hector Pieterson
Memorial and Museum ... **14**
Johannesburg
Art Gallery **3**
Johannesburg
Botanical Gardens and
Emmarentia Dam **19**

Soweto **13 - 17**

CLOSE UP

Posing on a Gold Mine (Dump)

In 1952 the young Dolly Rathebe, who was to become a jazz singing legend, and a young, white German photographer, Jürgen Schadeberg, scrambled to the top of a mine dump for a *Drum* magazine photo shoot. The photograph looks like it was taken on some strange beach: Rathebe smiles, posing in a bikini. They were spotted by the police and arrested under the Immorality Act, which forbade extra-marital intercourse between blacks and whites. This dump was in the Crown Mines, and is now the site of the Crown Mines Golf Course. Today there's a street in Newtown named after Rathebe.

Today you can see gold-mine dumps along the edge of town marching east and west along the seam of gold. Some are close to 300 feet high. Many people are fond of them—it's one of the city's defining characteristics—but those who live nearby are blinded by the dust, and little grows on them. Since they're also rich in minerals, they're slowly being chipped away and remined.

WHAT TO SEE

9 **Constitution Hill.** Overlooking Jo'burg's inner city and suburbs, Constitution Hill houses the Constitutional Court set up in 1994 with the birth of democracy, as well as the austere Old Fort Prison Complex (also called Number Four), where thousands of political prisoners were incarcerated, including South African Nobel Peace laureates Albert Luthuli and Nelson Mandela, and iconic Indian leader Mahatma Gandhi. The court decides on the most important cases relating to human rights, much like the Supreme Court in the United States. Tours and exhibits in the visitor center portray the country's journey to democracy. You can walk along the prison ramparts (built in the 1890s), read messages on the We the People Wall (and add your own), or view the court itself, in which large, slanting columns represent the trees under which African villagers traditionally met to discuss matters of importance. A restaurant, a coffee shop, and a museum shop are found on Constitution Square, a central piazza, as well as a children's room with special programs. The daily tour now includes a visit to the women's jail, where photographs and exhibits of how women were treated in the prison system and how they contributed to the struggle against apartheid are displayed. Future plans for Constitution Hill include restaurants, apartments, and hotels. ✉ *Joubert and Kotze Sts., entrance on Sam Hancock St., Braamfontein* ☎ *011/274–5300* ⊕ *www.constitutionhill.org.za* 💰 *R22 for tourists and R15 for citizens* ⏱ *Daily 9–5; last entry at 4.*

Fodor's Choice ★

10 **Origins Centre.** The Origins Centre based at the University of the Witwatersrand is a modern museum dedicated to exploring human development over the past 100,000 years, and in particular the tradition of rock art—of which Southern Africa has some of the richest and oldest in the world. It's complementary to Maropeng, which details the past 4 million years or so of human evolution, and the history of earth since its formation. The two experiences enhance one another rather than compete. Origins is spacious and elegantly designed, with

Fodor's Choice ★

multimedia displays, photographs, and text catering to a range of tastes, from kids to visiting professors. The shop sells high-quality crafts and hard-to-source books on rock art in southern Africa, and Café Fino serves good, light meals. ⊠ *Yale Rd., University of the Witwatersrand, Braamfontein* ☎ *011/717–4700* ⊕ *www.origins. org.za* ✉ *R45, including audio tour* ☉ *Mon.–Thurs. 9–6, Fri. 9–8, weekends 9–5.*

> **DID YOU KNOW?**
>
> South Africa can proudly claim four Nobel Peace Prize winners among its citizens. The first was African National Congress (ANC) founder Albert Luthuli, in 1960. Anglican archbishop Desmond Tutu won his in 1984, and Nelson Rolihlahla Mandela and ex-president F. W. de Klerk won theirs in 1993.

SOWETO & THE SOUTH

Between downtown Johannesburg and Soweto lie several suburbs less affluent than their northern counterparts, including Ormonde, where Gold Reef City and the Apartheid Museum are. Both are well signposted from the N1 highway going both south and north.

Farther south, you can find Soweto, an acronym for *South Western Townships,* which was founded in 1904, when city councilors used an outbreak of bubonic plague as an excuse to move black people outside the town. Today it's home to about a million residents. What it lacks in infrastructure, it more than makes up for in soul, energy, and history. The largely working-class population knows how to live for today, and Soweto pulsates with people, music, and humor.

Other Soweto neighborhoods worth touring include old-town neighborhood Diepkloof, just beyond Orlando West, and its neighbor, the new Diepkloof Extension, which dates from the mid-1970s, when bank loans first became available to black property owners. The difference between the two is startling: the dreary prefabricated "matchbox" houses of Diepkloof next to what looks like a middle-class suburb anywhere. In nearby Dube, many of the evicted residents of Sophiatown—a freehold township west of the city and a melting pot of music, bohemianism, crime, and multiracialism that insulted Afrikaner Calvinism and nationalism—were resettled in 1959. At the time they brought an exciting vibe to the dreary, homogenous dormitory town.

■ TIP➡ **Soweto is a chaotic, virtually indistinguishable sprawl that, even if you found your way in, you'd struggle to find your way out of—let alone around in.** It's best to take a guided tour *(⇨Johannesburg & Environs Essentials, below).* Bus tours are offered by various companies, but we suggest hiring a private guide or joining a smaller group tour because you'll get one-on-one attention and be able to ask any and all questions. You can also ask for a special-interest tour, such as art, traditional medicine, restaurants, nightlife, or memorials.

WHAT TO SEE

① Apartheid Museum. The Apartheid Museum leaves no stone unturned, black or white, as it takes you on a journey through South African apartheid history—from the entrance, where you pass through a turnstile according to your assigned skin color, to the myriad historical, brutally honest, and sometimes shocking photographs, video displays, films, documents, and other exhibits. It's an emotional, multilayered journey. As you walk chronologically through the apartheid years and eventually reach the country's first steps to freedom, with democratic elections in 1994, you experience a taste of the pain and suffering with which so many South Africans had to live. A room with 121 ropes with hangman's knots hanging from the ceiling—one rope for each political prisoner executed in the apartheid era—is especially chilling. ⊠ *Northern Pkwy. and Gold Reef Rd., Ormonde* ☎ *011/309–4700* ⊕ *www.apartheidmuseum.org* ⊡ *R25* ⊙ *Tues.–Sun. 10–5.*

FodorsChoice ★

② Gold Reef City. This theme park lets you step back in time to 1880s Johannesburg, and see why it became known as the City of Gold. One of the city's most popular attractions (avoid it on public holidays or weekends), it has good rides, and is based on the real history of Jo'burg. In addition to riding the Anaconda, a scary roller coaster on which you hang under the track, feet in the air, you can descend into an old gold mine (additional fee), see molten gold being poured, or watch a gumboot dance, a riveting dance developed by black miners. The reconstructed streets are lined with operating Victorian-style shops and restaurants. And for those with money to burn, the large, glitzy Gold Reef Village Casino beckons across the road. ⊠ *Gold Reef Rd., 6 km (4 mi) south of city center, Ormonde* ☎ *011/248–6800* ⊕ *www.goldreefcity.co.za* ⊡ *R100* ⊙ *Tues.–Sun. 9:30–4; mine tours 10–4 every 30 min.*

⑭ Hector Pieterson Memorial and Museum. Opposite Holy Cross Church, a stone's throw (literally, in those days) from the Tutu and Mandela homes, the Hector Pieterson Memorial and Museum is a crucial landmark. Pieterson, a 14-year-old student, was the first victim of police fire on June 16, 1976, when schoolchildren rose up to protest their second-rate *Bantu* (black) education system. The memorial is a paved area with benches for reflection, an inscribed stone and simple water feature, but in the museum are grainy photographs and films that bring that fateful day to life. Small granite blocks in the museum courtyard are a tribute to the 350 children among the more than 500 people who died during this violent time. ⊠*Khumalo and Phela Sts., Orlando West* ☎*011/536–0611* ⊠*R15* ⊙*Mon.–Sat. 10–5, Sun. 10–4.*

⑮ Mandela House. The former president lived in this small house until his arrest in 1961, with his now disgraced ex-wife Winnie Madikizela-Mandela, who owns a high-security mansion higher up the street. The house is now a museum containing Mandela memorabilia from the 1960s. ⊠*Vilakazi St., Orlando West* ☎*011/936–7754* ⊠*R20* ⊙*Weekdays 9:30–5:15, Sat. 9:30–4:30, Sun. 9:30–4:15, holidays 9:30–3.*

⑯ Oppenheimer Park. Named after mining magnate Ernest Oppenheimer, who established the De Beers diamond mining company as a powerful global brand, this park is one of the few green spaces in Soweto, and is rich in flora and birdlife. The park's big trees give an impression of a forest. It's dominated by a large tower built as a tribute to Oppenheimer, who helped resettle people displaced by the apartheid government in the 1950s. Here you can also see **Khayalendaba,** a cultural village built in the 1970s by South Africa's best-known traditional healer, artist, and oral historian, Credo Mutwa. Some of his statues here portray African gods, warriors, and mythical figures, even sculptures of prehistoric African animals. It's best to visit the park with a guide in daytime for safety reasons. ⊠*Majoeng St., Central Western Jabavu* ☎*No phone* ⊠*Free* ⊙*Daily 24 hrs.*

⑰ Regina Mundi Church. Central to the liberation struggle, this Catholic church was a refuge of peace, sanity, and steadfast moral focus for the people of Soweto through the harshest years of repression. Archbishop Desmond Tutu often delivered sermons in this massive church during the apartheid years. It has a black Madonna and Child inside and an art gallery upstairs. ⊠*1149 Khumalo St., Rockville* ☎*011/986–2546* ⊠*Donations requested* ⊙*Weekdays 9–5.*

⑱ Walter Sisulu Square (formerly Freedom Square). In 1955 the Freedom Charter was adopted here by the Congress Alliance, a gathering of political and cultural groups trying to map a way forward in the repressive 1950s. The charter, the guiding document of the African National Congress, envisaged an alternative nonracial dispensation in which "all shall be equal before the law." It has the same significance in South Africa as the Declaration of Independence has in the United States. ⊠*Close to Union St. and Boundary Rd., Kliptown.*

NORTHERN SUBURBS

Johannesburg has dozens of northern suburbs, ranging in size from the huge and diverse Sandton, which includes the entire township of Alexandra, among other suburbs, to the smaller, leafy Saxonwold near the zoo. The northern suburbs highlighted here—from southernmost to northernmost—are by no means the only ones—they simply have the most attractions.

6

MELVILLE

The trendy suburb of Melville essentially grew around the South African Broadcasting Corporation (SABC) in nearby Auckland Park. It
was once an average middle-class enclave but has become one of the
hippest places around Johannesburg. Here you can eat at a variety of
restaurants, from African to Portuguese or Thai, and enjoy an evening
out at one of the many vibey bars. Seventh Street has pleasant shops
and sidewalk cafés.

⟲ ⑲ The large and beautiful **Johannesburg Botanical Gardens and Emmarentia
Dam** are five minutes down the road from Melville. This gigantic parkland dotted with trees, statues, fountains, and ponds, is a wonderful
haven. You can relax on benches beneath weeping willows surrounding the dam (lake), where canoeists and windsurfers brave the water,
or wander across to the 24-acre rose and herb gardens. The gardens'
flowers include an alpine collection and a cycad collection. On weekends bridal parties use the gardens as a backdrop for photographs.
✉ *Thomas Bowler St., Roosevelt Park* ☎ 011/407-6111 ⌨ *Free*
🕒 *Daily sunrise–sunset.*

⟲ ⑱ A small nature reserve on the southern side of the Johannesburg Botanical Gardens, **Melville Koppies** has guided ecology walks; many of the
guides are members of the local botanical society and can introduce
you to the rich diversity of highveld flora found here. Bird-watching is
also excellent: expect to see more than 200 varieties of grassland and
highveld birds, as well as suburban garden species and small mammals.
An archaeological site contains a furnace dating from the Iron Age.
The reserve is managed by volunteers, and you can reserve a special
three-hour tour with them by booking ahead. ✉ *Judith Rd., Emmren-
tia* ☎ *011/788-7571, 011/482-4797 special tours* ⊕ *www.veld.org.za*
⌨ *Free, but a R10 donation is advised; tour R100 per hour for guide.*
🕒 *Every Sun., times vary.*

PARKTOWN, PARKVIEW & SAXONWOLD

Perched on the Braamfontein Ridge, Parktown was once the address
du jour for the city's early mining magnates. Most of the magnificent
houses have since met their demise, but those that are left are worth a
look. The small, but picturesque suburbs of Parkview and Saxonwold
are nearby.

⟲ ⑪ **Johannesburg Zoo.** Smaller than its Pretoria counterpart but no less
impressive, the city's zoo makes for a pleasant day trip, with plenty of
lawns and shade—good for a picnic. The large variety of species (more
than 250) includes rare white lions and highly endangered red pandas.
The polar bear enclosure has a viewing tunnel where you can see the
bears cavorting underwater (the zoo has the only two polar bears in
Africa). Perhaps the best way to see the zoo is to rent a golf buggy for
about R100 per hour, as it's so large that walking around it can be
very tiring. (Get there early on a weekend to reserve a buggy.) Afterward, stroll past Zoo Lake in the large peaceful park across the road.
✉ *Opposite Zoo Lake, Jan Smuts Ave., Parkview* ☎ 011/646-2000
⊕ *www.jhbzoo.org.za* ⌨ *Free* 🕒 *Daily 8:30–5:30.*

CLOSE UP

Victorian Parktown

Parktown was once a gated community for the area's mining magnates, but most of its Victorian mansions fell victim to the wrecking ball long ago. Luckily, a few managed to survive. Perhaps the cream of the crop is **Northwards** (⌂ *Rock Ridge Rd., near Oxford Rd.*), designed by Sir Herbert Baker. For many years it was the home of socialite Jose Dale Lace, whose ghost is said to still grace Northwards's minstrel gallery. Another gem is **Outeniqua** (⌂ *St. David's Pl.*), a mansion built in 1906 for the managing director of Ohlssons Breweries. Today it's part of the Wits Business

School. Across the road you'll find **Eikenlaan** (⌂ *St. David's Pl.*), which was built in 1903 for James Goch, a professional photographer and the first to use flash photography in South Africa. In 1985 the home was turned into a rather garish franchise of the Mike's Kitchen steak-house chain.

Interested in checking out these architectural treasures? Most are closed to the public, but the Parktown and Westcliff Heritage Trust (☎ *011/482–3349* ⊕ *www.parktownheritage.co.za*) organizes tours of the houses and gardens, which allow you a glimpse of turn-of-the-century grandeur.

6

⑫ **South African National Museum of Military History.** Set in a park, this museum has two exhibition halls and a rambling outdoor display that focus on South Africa's role in the major wars of the 20th century, with an emphasis on World War II. On display are Spitfire and Messerschmidt fighters (including what is claimed to be the only remaining ME110 jet night fighter), various tanks of English and American manufacture, and a wide array of artillery. Among the most interesting objects are the modern armaments South Africa used in its war against the Cuban-backed Angolan army during the 1980s, including French-built Mirage fighters and Russian tanks stolen by the South Africans from a ship en route to Angola. More recent exhibits include the national military art collection, memorabilia from the Anti-Conscription Campaign, and an exhibit on the history of Umkhonto weSizwe (Spear of the Nation, or MK, the African National Congress's military arm) from its inception until its incorporation into the South African National Defence Force. The tall, freestanding South African (Anglo-Boer) War memorial, which looks like a statue-adorned mini Arc de Triomphe, is the most striking landmark of the northern suburbs. ⌂ *22 Erlswold Way, Saxonwold* ☎ *011/646–5513* ⊕ *www.militarymuseum. co.za* ⌂ *R20* ⊙ *Daily 9–4:30, weekends 9:30–4:30.*

ROSEBANK

Originally a farm known as Rosemill Orchards, today Rosebank is a chic commercial center where worlds collide: the African crafts on display at the no-frills African Craft Market vie with designer clothes adorning expensive shop windows; saxophone players perform for small change while Jo'burg's elite sip capuccinos at street cafés. Home to shopping malls, restaurants, hotels, and art galleries, Rosebank is frequented by well-to-do locals and tourists. At the Rosebank Rooftop Market, in a large parking lot in Rosebank Mall and open every

Sunday, everything and anything can be purchased from crafts to jewelry, to clothes or plants. The African Craft Market, open daily, is adjacent to the shopping center, the Mall of Rosebank, which is popular for its curios and African art. Clubs, bars, galleries, and an art-house cinema add flavor to this trendy area.

GREENSIDE & PARKHURST

These two suburbs, close to Rosebank, are popular for eating out—often at tables cramming the pavements. Gleneagles Road in

> **DRIVERS TAKE NOTE**
>
> The building of the Gautrain, a high-speed train that will join Johannesburg and Pretoria, has greatly affected traffic flow in this area—numerous roads have been closed, causing heavy traffic congestion during rush hour. However the roads and alternative routes are clearly signposted. Fingers are crossed that this section of the Gautrain will be finished, as scheduled, by the end of 2009.

Greenside and 4th Avenue in Parkhurst are lined with small eateries, including Italian, Indian, Portuguese, and Japanese restaurants, along with those offering a more conventional range of meats, fish, and pasta. Over the weekend, cars fill the streets and people pack the sidewalks. The adjacent suburb of Emmarentia is also benefiting from Greenside's popularity, with small restaurants popping up. The Emmarentia Dam and gardens, a popular dog-walking and picnic spot, is also a draw card.

Parkhurst, a neighborhood full of freshly renovated homes and young couples, has some of the trendiest restaurants in Johannesburg. There are more than a dozen places to eat on 4th Avenue alone. Antiques shops and boutique stores selling furniture and children's clothes also dot the street.

SANDTON

Sandton is the new financial center of South Africa, with skyscrapers housing banks, businesses, and law firms. It was originally a residential area, but with the shift from the city center to Sandton, it's now home to the Johannesburg stock exchange and the enormous Sandton Convention Centre, which hosts large conferences and concerts.

Near the large and expensive Sandton City shopping center and the open-air Nelson Mandela Square (also known as Sandton Square), you'll find trendy restaurants selling good but pricey food. There's also a small theater, which favors short local productions such as one-person comedy shows, and can be a fun, light diversion. The convention center is next to the square.

But Sandton is not all glitz and glamour—a few miles from Sandton City and part of the large suburb is the township of Alexandra, home to an estimated 350,000 people, mostly living in overcrowded, squalid conditions in shacks and rented run-down houses.

WHERE TO EAT

There's no way to do justice to the sheer scope and variety of Johannesburg's restaurants in a few pages. What follows is a (necessarily subjective) list of some of the best. Try asking locals what they recommend; eating out is the most popular form of entertainment in Johannesburg, and everyone has a list of favorite spots.

DOWNTOWN

$–$$ ✕**Gramadoelas at the Market Theatre.** Crossing the threshold here is like stepping into a strange old museum: African artifacts and mirrors litter the huge room. Established in 1967, Gramadoelas has hosted an impressive list of guests including Nelson Mandela, Elton John, the Queen of England, Bill and Hillary Clinton, and many others. The restaurant specializes in South African fare, but does have a few dishes from farther north in the continent. Try *umngqusho* (beans and whole corn) or, if you're feeling adventurous, *mogodu* (unbleached ox tripe) or *masonja* (mopane worms). Traditional Cape Malay dishes include *bredie* (lamb casserole in a tomato sauce) and *bobotie* (a casserole of minced lamb). Meat lovers will like the selection of game meats such as the kudu (antelope) panfried with dried fruit and spices. The popular buffet is available most evenings for R150. ☒*Market Theatre, Margeret Mcingana St., Newtown* ☎*011/838–6960* ⊕*www.gramadoelas. co.za* ⊟*AE, DC, MC, V* ☽*Closed Sun. No lunch Mon.*

¢–$$ ✕**Shivava Café.** Although not in the same league as the more famous Nambitha's and Wandie's traditional township restaurants in Soweto, the Shivava Café in Newtown is popular and easier to find. Jazz music vies for attention with the rather boisterous crowd, and the place has the feel of a *shebeen* (township bar). The food is speedily prepared, and is a good example of black South African cuisine. A specialty is pap (a traditional South African maize-meal porridge that is white and stiff) and mogudo (tripe), which is something of an acquired taste. The café serves other dishes popular in the townships, such as chicken livers and giblets, masonja (mopane worms) and morogo (wild spinach). Simpler meals like steak are also served—with a certain African panache. ☒*1 President St., at Miriam Makeba and Jeppe Sts., Newtown* ☎*011/834–8037 or 072/449–2199* ⊟*AE, DC, MC, V* ☽*Closed Mon.*

THE SOUTH & SOWETO

¢–$$ ✕**Nambitha.** You can't actually see Nelson Mandela's old house from this popular restaurant, which means that you're less likely to run into a tour bus. Nambitha has evolved from a township restaurant catering only to African tastes into a more versatile establishment. It plays an eclectic selection of music—soul, jazz, R&B, and more traditional African—and is constantly buzzing with people. A standard meal of mutton stew, served in a rich tomato gravy with little piles of spinach, pumpkin, and potato salad, costs R44, but food is less Nambitha's strength than its busy vibe. Many locals pop in just to chat and mingle. ☒*6877 Vilakazi St., Orlando West* ☎*011/936–9128* ⊕*www.nambitha.biz* ⊟*DC, MC, V.*

★ $ ✕**Wandie's Place.** Wandie's isn't the only good township restaurant, but it's the best-known and one of the most popular spots in Jo'burg. The

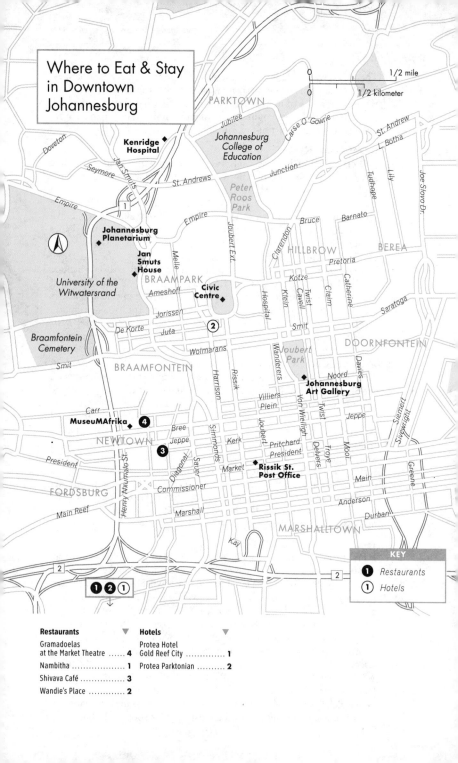

Where to Eat & Stay in Downtown Johannesburg

Restaurants

Gramadoelas
at the Market Theatre **4**

Nambitha **1**

Shivava Café **3**

Wandie's Place **2**

Hotels

Protea Hotel
Gold Reef City **1**

Protea Parktonian **2**

KEY

1 *Restaurants*

① *Hotels*

decor is eclectic township (a bit makeshift), and the walls are adorned with signatures and business cards of tourists that have crossed its path. The waiters are smartly dressed in bow ties, and the food is truly African. Meat stews, *imifino* (a leafy African dish), sweet potatoes, beans, corn porridge, traditionally cooked pumpkin, chicken, and tripe are laid out in a buffet in a motley selection of pots and containers. The food is hot, the drinks are cold, and the conversation flows. You may end up here with a tour bus, but it's big enough to cope and Wandie's now has an on-the-property guesthouse in case the alcohol flows too much. It's not that difficult to find, and parking is safe, but it's probably better to organize a visit on a guided trip. ⊠ *618 Makhalamele St., Dube* ☎ *011/982–2796* ⊕ *www.wandies.co.za* ⊟ *AE, DC, MC, V.*

NORTHERN SUBURBS

SANDTON
$$$–$$$$
Fodor'sChoice
★

✕ **Linger Longer.** Set in the spacious grounds of a grand old home in Wierda Valley, in the business center of Sandton, Linger Longer has an air of gracious elegance. The wooden floors, colored walls, and striped curtains give this restaurant a Wedgewood-like quality. Diners can reserve a table in the newly built conservatory. Though upmarket, this restaurant has a warm atmosphere, and the hospitable staff and personal service of Chef Walter Ulz attract local and international diners. The menu is varied and includes an array of seasonal specials. Start with the prawn firecracker, followed by the Asian split duck or the lamb rack cooked with crushed chermoula, a North African spice mix. The delicious porcini ravioli is the best choice on the vegetarian main menu, and a good finale is the trio of sorbets. There's also a good wine list. ⊠ *58 Wierda Rd., Wierda Valley, Sandton* ☎ *011/884–0465* ⌂ *Reservations essential* ⊟ *AE, DC, MC, V* ☾ *Closed Sun. and public holidays. No lunch Sat.*

$$–$$$$ **Le Carnard.** In an old house off the busy arterial Rivonia Road, Le Canard provides a tranquil break from the hub of metropolitan Sandton. It has classically romantic touches—crystal glasses, small rose bowls, chandeliers—and the service is excellent. Le Carnard means "the duck" in French and duck is the specialty. The food is rich in flavor with some unique twists, including the tomato bomb, a cold chili tomato soup with a shot of Russian vodka, or the chocolate sauce for duck. Between courses expect little treats from the chef such as vegetable soup and duck-liver pâté. Le Carnard has an extensive wine list of South African and international wines, champagnes, and liquors. ⊠ *163 Rivonia Rd., Morningside, Sandton* ☎ *011/884–4597* ⌂ *Reservations essential* ⊟ *AE, DC, MC, V* ☾ *Closed Sun. and public holidays. No lunch Sat.*

$–$$$$ ✕ **Moyo.** Now with four locations (in Johannesburg at Melrose Arch in Melrose North, the Market Theatre in Newtown, and at Zoo Lake in Parktown, and outside Cape Town at the Spier wine estate), Moyo is strongly African in theme, from the food and decor to the music and live entertainment. The focus of the rich and varied menu is pan-African, incorporating tandoori cookery from northern Africa, Cape Malay influences such as lentil bobotie, Moroccan-influenced tasty *tagines* (stews with lamb, chicken, fish, or seven vegetables), and ostrich burgers and other dishes representing South Africa. Diners are often entertained by storytellers, face painters, and musicians. Moyo at Zoo Lake in Parktown is the nicest in Jo'burg during the day, as you can dine with a view of the lake and take a stroll or a ride in a rowboat afterwards. At night or in wintertime, try the Melrose Arch or Newtown branches. ⊠*Melrose Arch, Shop 5, High St., Melrose North* ☎*011/684–1477* ⊕*www.moyo.co.za* ⌂*Reservations essential* ⊟*AE, DC, MC, V.*

$–$$$ ✕**The Butcher Shop and Grill.** This is a good place for hungry carnivores. It specializes in prime South African meat aged to perfection by Alan Pick, the butcher–owner. An operating butchery features prominently in the restaurant, and special cuts can be ordered for the meal or to take home. Kudu, springbok, ostrich, and other game are often on the specials list, and only the tenderest cuts are served. For lighter appetites, try the chicken or line fish. Jelly and custard pudding is a favorite with regulars. Plus, there's an excellent wine cellar. ⊠*Nelson Mandela Sq., Sandton* ☎*011/784–8676* ⊕*www.thebutchershop.co.za* ⊟*AE, DC, MC, V.*

ILLOVO ✕**Parea.** Previously known as Plaka, this Greek taverna, grill, and meze
$–$$ café is the best of its kind in the city. Greek music floats above the buzz of conversation, a souvlaki spit turns slowly near the door, and a refrigerated case displays an array of meze (small appetizers). Most people sit on the roofed terrace or at the few street-side tables; the spacious inside dining area is slightly more formal. Start with a meze platter of souvlaki, feta, olives, cucumber, and tomato, followed by the line fish, grilled on an open flame with olive oil and lemon, or kleftiko (lamb slow cooked in a clay oven) and a carafe of wine. On weekend evenings, belly dancers perform between the tables, and Greek dancers do the Zorba to a backdrop of "controlled" plate breaking—all while patrons find it hard to resist a glass of ouzo. Even the manager is known to let his hair down and perfom for the patrons once in a while. Set menus range from R110 to R180. ⊠*3 Corlett Dr., at Oxford Rd., Illovo* ☎*011/788–8777* ⊟*AE, DC, MC, V.*

¢–$ ✕**Trabella Pizzeria.** This intimate restaurant of 10 tables or so is on a busy street corner around the corner from Parea—an accessible but not attractive position. Trabella's strength is its designer pizza, some of the best you'll ever taste, whether it's with the brie and cranberry topping, Parma ham, rocket and Parmesan, or smoked salmon, sour cream, and caviar, sprinkled with spring onion. The pasta and gnocchi are good options as well. ⊠*Number 3, Galen House, Oxford Rd., at Corlett Dr., Illovo* ☎*011/442–0413 or 011/442–0414* ⊟*AE, DC, MC, V* ⊙*Closed Mon. No lunch Sun.*

PARKTOWN ✕**La Cucina di Ciro.** This is one of the best Italian restaurants in Johan-
NORTH nesburg. The owner and chef, Ciro, says the cuisine is "very much
$–$$ my own," which means you can find truly inventive dishes on his
Fodor's Choice seasonally changing menu. The pasta is made on the premises. His
★ most popular dishes are the duck and the variety of homemade pasta dishes, especially the seafood pasta. Be warned: Ciro will chat with complete strangers as if they've been friends for years. La Cucina di Ciro serves breakfast, lunch, and dinner. ⊠*17 4th Ave., Parktown North* ☎*011/442–5346* ⌂*Reservations essential* ⊟*AE, DC, MC, V* ⊙*Closed Sun. No dinner Sat.*

¢–$$$$ ✕**Ruby Grapefruit** This Japanese and Chinese restaurant is in the heart of Parkhurst's restaurant hub and sports a red-and-white color scheme, Asian-inspired lanterns, and a large painting of a Japanese woman. It's most popular for its variety of sushi, including creations such as bacon and avocado or pecan and avocado pieces. Begin a meal with the miso soup or some crispy spring rolls with sweet chili sauce and end it with an herbal tea. Be warned: The service is not as good as the food. ✉*24C 4th Ave., Parkhurst* ☎*011/880–3673* ✍*Reservations essential* ▤*DC, MC, V.*

$–$$ ✕**Café Flo, Oveflo.** This pair of easygoing, unpretentious restaurants are always busy, perhaps because the food is so fresh and good. Once Café Flo is full, you "oveflo" next door. You can order from both menus in either one. Café Flo serves unusual pizzas, like roast lamb, eggplant or *peri-peri* (a hot chili sauce) prawn, and a prawn, artichoke, and spring-onion pizza with a milder sweet chili sauce. Favorites at Oveflo are prawn-stuffed calamari and the lamb shank. Oveflo also serves breakfast. ✉*116 Greenway, Greenside* ☎*011/646–6817* ▤*AE, DC, MC, V* ☾*Closed Sun.*

HOUGHTON **La Rustica.** Set in an old house, this restaurant has outside covered areas
¢–$$ that extend around a lovely garden with fountains. The weekend buffet (R140) is sumptuous, with meze-style starters like eggplant baked in napoletana sauce, Parma hams, salads, and calamari, followed by spit-braised meats including lamb and beef, and dessert items such as brandy snaps, ice cream, crème brûlée, and cheesecake. During the week, dine from the à la carte menu. Try the tagliolini panna e salmone, thin ribbon noodles served with a smoked salmon and cream sauce or the Fegato alla Veneziana, calves' liver sauteed with caramelized onion, white wine, and sage, served with polenta. There's also a good wine list. ✉*103 Houghton Dr., at Lloyd Ellis Ave., Houghton* ☎*011/728–2092* ⊕*www.larustica.co.za* ✍*Reservations essential* ▤*AE, DC, MC, V.*

NORWOOD ✕**Singing Fig.** The decor at this popular neighborhood restaurant can
$$–$$$ only be described as Karoo meets Tuscany, with apricot walls, white tablecloths, and beautiful old globe chairs. The menu, scribbled on a blackboard, changes daily. For starters try the mussels steamed in white wine and flavored with orange and fennel. The duck à l'orange and oxtail are two classics that keep the regulars coming back. But for something a little different, try the Norwegian salmon skewered with pickled ginger, crusted with lime and wasabi, and grilled. For dessert, indulge in the signature homemade fig-and-vanilla ice cream, made with dried figs cooked in port. ✉*44 the Ave., Norwood* ☎*011/728– 2434* ⊕*www.singingfig.co.za* ✍*Reservations essential* ▤*AE, DC, MC, V* ☾*Closed Mon. No dinner Sun.*

WHERE TO STAY

DOWNTOWN

$ ▦**Protea Parktonian.** Close to the Civic Theatre and a three-minute drive from the central business district, this property offers the best value in the city and a view of the cityscape. Suites are all air-conditioned, and each has a separate lounge and balcony. You can enter the hotel directly from a secure parking garage. A word of warning: the neighborhood isn't safe to walk in at night. ✉ *120 De Korte St., Braamfontein* ⌂ *Box 32278, Braamfontein 2017* ☎ *011/403–5740* ⊕ *www.proteahotels. com* ⇔ *294 suites* ⚭ *In-room: refrigerator. In-hotel: 2 restaurants, room service, bar, pool, gym* ☰ *AE, DC, MC, V* ❤| *BP.*

SOWETO & THE SOUTH

$$ 🔲 **Protea Hotel Gold Reef City.** Small buildings with Victorian-style wrought-iron trim make up this hotel spread over a large part of the Gold Reef City theme park. All rooms are furnished in Victorian period style, with claw-foot tubs and reproduction furniture. There's an in-house restaurant called Braney's. Since the entire hotel is within the theme park, it's safe to walk around at night—even across the highway on the pedestrian bridge to the nearby casino. Access to the theme park is free for hotel visitors. But by staying in the south, you're farther from most good restaurants than you would be staying in the north. You're relatively close to Soweto and downtown Johannesburg, however. ✉ *Shaft 14, Northern Pkwy., Ormonde* ⌂ *Box 25, Gold Reef City 2159* ☎ *011/248–5700* ⊕ *www.proteahotels.com* ⇔ *74 rooms* ⚭ *In-hotel: restaurant, bar, pool, no elevator* ☰ *AE, DC, MC, V* ❤| *BP.*

NORTHERN SUBURBS

SANDHURST   🔲 **Saxon.** In the exclusive suburb of Sandhurst, adjacent to the com-
$$$$ mercial and shopping center of Sandton, Saxon was voted the World's
Fodor's Choice Leading Boutique Hotel by the prestigious World Travel Awards from
★ 2001 to 2006 consecutively. Heads of state have stayed here, including Nelson Mandela, who came here after his release from prison and to work on his autobiography, *Long Walk to Freedom*. The butlers pride themselves on keeping files on their guests, right down to what they order from the bar. An azure pool adjoins the sleek modern building. Inside, the feeling is calm and classical, and there's an extensive African art collection on display throughout the hotel. Rooms are huge, and have big bay windows overlooking the gardens or pool. Large-screen TVs, DVD players, surround sound, and a workstation with a fast Internet connection are standard. The delightful restaurant has a wonderful setting. ✉ *36 Saxon Rd., Sandhurst* ☎ *011/292–6000* ⊕ *www. thesaxon.com* ⇔ *27 suites* ⚭ *In-room: minibar, data ports, internet. In-hotel: restaurant, bar, 2 pools (1 heated), gym, spa, concierge.* ☰ *AE, DC, MC, V* ❤| *BP.*

SANDTON   🔲 **InterContinental Sandton Sun & Towers.** These two high-rise hotels are
$$–$$$$ right next to Johannesburg's premier mall, Sandton City, and the adjoining Nelson Mandela Square. Guest rooms are small but superbly laid out, with understated lighting and elegant decorative touches. There's little to recommend one hotel over the other, although the towers are smaller and farther removed from the bustle of Sandton City. The towers also have two full floors of executive suites, which have their own bar, breakfast room, and full-time staff. ✉ *Sandton City, 5th St. and Alice La., Sandton 2146* ☎ *011/780–5000* ⊕ *www.southernsun.com* ⇔ *Sun: 311 rooms, 22 suites; Towers: 214 rooms, 17 suites* ⚭ *In-*

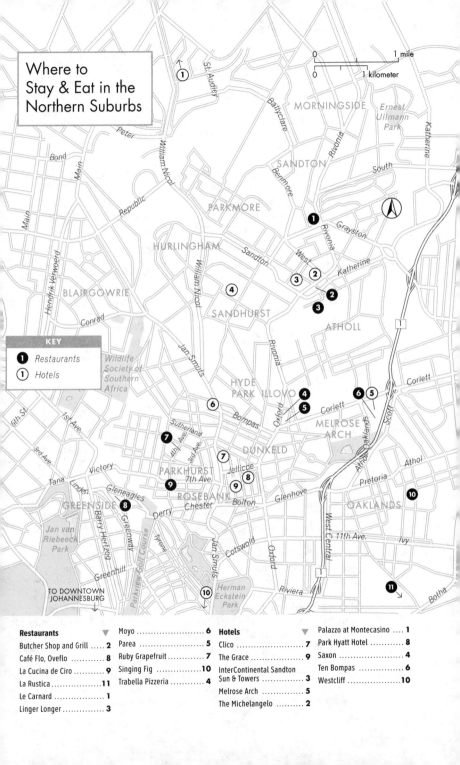

Where to Stay & Eat in the Northern Suburbs

0 ___ 1 mile
0 ___ 1 kilometer

KEY

❶ Restaurants

① Hotels

MORNINGSIDE

Ernest Ullmann Park

SANDTON

PARKMORE

HURLINGHAM

BLAIRGOWRIE

SANDHURST

ATHOLL

Wildlife Society of Southern Africa

HYDE PARK ILLOVO

MELROSE ARCH

DUNKELD

PARKHURST

ROSEBANK

GREENSIDE

Jan van Riebeeck Park

OAKLANDS

Herman Eckstein Park

TO DOWNTOWN JOHANNESBURG

Restaurants ▼		Moyo 6	Hotels ▼	Palazzo at Montecasino 1
Butcher Shop and Grill 2		Parea 5	Clico 7	Park Hyatt Hotel 8
Café Flo, Oveflo 8		Ruby Grapefruit 7	The Grace 9	Saxon 4
La Cucina de Ciro 9		Singing Fig 10	InterContinental Sandton	Ten Bompas 6
La Rustica 11		Trabella Pizzeria 4	Sun & Towers 3	Westcliff 10
Le Carnard 1			Melrose Arch 5	
Linger Longer 3			The Michelangelo 2	

room: refrigerator, Ethernet. In-hotel: 5 restaurants, room service, gym, laundry service, executive floor. ⊟*AE, DC, MC, V.*

$$$ ⚏**The Michelangelo.** As though taken from a street in Florence, this hotel forms the northern facade of much-touted piazza-inspired Nelson Mandela Square, also called Sandton Square. Although the hotel is unusually tasteful, even grand, the square lacks the authenticity of an Italian piazza. Still, this hotel has all the class, comforts, and facilities you'd expect from a top establishment. The atrium-style pool area is notable. The restaurant, Piccolo Mondo, focuses on Mediterranean cuisine, which means plenty of seafood from Mozambique, such as rock cod, prawns, lobsters, langoustines, and mussels. ⊠ *West St., Nelson Mandela Sq., Sandton* ✉*Box 784682, Sandton 2146* ☎*011/282-7000* ⊕*www.michelangelo.co.za* ⇖*242 rooms* ⚍*In-hotel: restaurant, room service, bars, pool, gym* ⊟*AE, DC, MC, V.*

ROSEBANK   ⚏**Park Hyatt Hotel.** This Hyatt is trendy and opulent, with lots of black, $$$–$$$$ gold, and glass. Enormous picture windows reveal stunning views of the northern suburbs. Local art lines the walls in discreetly lit passageways, and there's an ultramodern restaurant, a wine bar, and a solar-heated pool on the roof. Sunday brunch is a favorite with guests and local families, and the lobby serves coffee and light meals. The hotel is adjacent to Rosebank's major shopping malls. ⊠*191 Oxford Rd., Rosebank* ✉*Box 1536, Saxonwold 2132* ☎*011/280-1234* ⊕*www.johannesburg.park.hyatt.com* ⇖*244 rooms* ⚍*In-room: Ethernet. In-hotel: 2 restaurants, room service, bar, pool, gym, laundry service, airport shuttle* ⊟*AE, DC, MC, V.*

$$$ ⚏**The Grace.** Most of the visitors to the Grace are businesspeople
Fodor'sChoice   drawn to the old-world elegance behind the towering brick facade and
  ★   concrete columns. It's also in the center of Rosebank and linked to the nearby mall and African crafts market. Travelers rave about the breakfast, and the restaurant, called simply the Dining Room, has established itself as one of Johannesburg's culinary centers. One of the hotel's finest features is the rooftop garden and pool area, which has amazing views of the northern suburbs' greenery. Thoughtful extras include transportation within a 10-km (6-mi) radius and tea and cake served in the lounge. ⊠*Bath and Tyrwhitt Aves., Rosebank 2196* ☎*011/280-7200* ⊕*www.thegrace.co.za* ⇖*60 rooms, 15 suites* ⚍*In-hotel: restaurant, bar, pool, gym, airport shuttle, spa* ⊟*AE, DC, MC, V* ⦿*BP.*

$$ ⚏**Clico.** This small, upmarket guesthouse in central Rosebank is a 60-year-old Cape Dutch house with a gracious garden, and offers perhaps the best value in an area known for expensive accommodation. It has an engaging mix of old and new—Oregon pine floorboards, antique inlaid-wood side tables from Morocco, custom-made couches, and modern, whimsical sculptures like one of a woman floating above water by Anton Smit. The bedroom suites are luxurious and have heated floors; one has wheelchair access. The superb food has a strong French influence, though often with a local twist, and the chef adapts his menu daily to whatever fresh ingredients he can purchase. ⊠*27 Sturdee Ave., at Jellicoe, Rosebank 2196* ☎*011/252-3300* ⊕*www.clicoguesthouse.com* ⇖*9 suites, including 1 room self-catering* ⚍*In-*

hotel: pool, airport shuttle, no elevator. In-room: refrigerator, safe, Wi-Fi. ⊟*DC, MC, V* ⦿❘*BP.*

DUNKELD
WEST
$$$
★

🏨 **Ten Bompas.** This is a hotel-cum-restaurant and art gallery. It's small and luxurious, and the decor is minimalist, with carefully chosen African art. Suites, each done by a different interior designer, have separate lounges and bedrooms, fireplaces, complimentary minibars, and satellite TV. You can also ogle brochures for the hotel's partner game lodges in the far north of Kruger National Park. Sides, the restaurant, turns in consistently good reviews. Its menu changes with the seasons. The food is exciting and fresh: roasted artichoke, mozzarella, and olive salad and roast-duck-and-orange risotto, for example. It also has a well-stocked wine cellar. ⊠*10 Bompas Rd., Dunkeld West* ⟗*Box 786064, Sandton 2146* 📞*011/325–2442* ⊕*www.tenbompas.com* ⤴*10 suites* ⧉*In-hotel: restaurant, bar, pool* ⊟*AE, DC, MC, V* ⦿❘*BP.*

MELROSE
NORTH
$$$

🏨 **Melrose Arch.** This is an ultramodern hotel within the shopping, dining, and residential enclave Melrose Arch. The minimalist decor is an eclectic mix of modern and African influences, with high-tech colored lighting throughout and sculptures, baskets, and furnishings all highlighting the African locale. Even the elevators reflect this mix, with one representing the African day and the other, almost completely dark, suggesting the night. Mainly catering to businesspeople, the hotel has free high-speed Internet access in each room and a Wi-Fi hot spot in the warm mahogany-clad library bar. The rooms are well equipped and each has a view of the pool and garden. The pool area highlights the eccentric and modern taste that is echoed throughout the hotel, with trees planted in larger-than-life steel buckets and table and chairs set out in a few inches of water. Sip a cocktail here while soaking your feet in the heated pool, which has piped underwater music. Meals are offered at the stylish fusion restaurant, March. ⊠*1 Melrose Sq., Melrose Arch* 📞*011/214–6666* ⊕*www.africanpridehotels.com/melrosearch* ⤴*117 rooms, 1 suite* ⧉*In room: minibar, DVDs, Ethernet. In-hotel: restaurant, 2 bars, pool, public Internet* ⊟*AE, DC, MC, V.*

WESTCLIFF
$$$$
★

🏨 **The Westcliff.** This landmark hotel and Johannesburg icon was built on a steep hill and has amazing views of the northern suburbs and the Johannesburg Zoo. You're taken to your destination by a shuttle service, winding your way up twisting lanes. Bedrooms are in multistory villas, each with its own balcony. Enormous bathrooms have marble vanities and huge soaking tubs. The cuisine, service, and facilities are all top-notch. The Westcliff is known throughout the city for its lavish high teas, served every afternoon. ⊠*67 Jan Smuts Ave., Westcliff 2193* 📞*011/646–2400* ⊕*www.westcliffhotel.orient-express.com* ⤴*104 rooms, 14 suites* ⧉*In-room: dial-up. In-hotel: 2 restaurants, room service, bar, tennis court, pool, gym, no elevator* ⊟*AE, DC, MC, V.*

FOURWAYS
★ $$$

🏨 **Palazzo at Montecasino.** Built in the style of a Tuscan villa, the hotel is set among formal herb gardens. Public rooms are on a grand scale, and the whole hotel is decorated in gilt, marble, and terra-cotta, with small touches of trompe l'oeil. The rooms are spacious, with rich tapestry-style draperies, canopied beds, and gilt-framed mirrors and prints.

6

Large picture windows and light terra-cotta tiles lighten the effect. The hotel is done with so much more style, attention to detail, and class than the adjacent casino and mall that it's almost impossible to believe they're connected. This is a good choice for a business stay, though be aware that its relatively northern location is closer to the business area of Bryanston and Sandton than downtown Johannesburg. Service is impeccable. ✉ *Montecasino Blvd., Fourways* 📫 *Private Bag X125, Bryanston 2021* ☎ *011/510–3000* 🌐 *www.ichotelsgroup.com* ⇨ *246 rooms, 12 suites* ♨ *In-room: Ethernet. In-hotel: restaurant, bar, pool, gym* 💳 *AE, DC, MC, V.*

NIGHTLIFE & THE ARTS

The best place to find out what's going on is in the "Tonight" section of the *Star,* Johannesburg's major daily. For a comprehensive guide, get the "Friday" supplement of the weekly *Mail & Guardian* (🌐 *www.mg.co.za*). A useful Web site for event details is **JHBLive** (🌐 *www.jhblive.com*). Almost all major performances and many smaller ones can be booked through **Computicket** (☎ *083/915–8000 or 011/340–8000* 🌐 *www.computicket.com* ⏲ *Mon.–Sat. 8–8* ⏲ *Closed Sun. and some public holidays*).

NIGHTLIFE

Johannesburg comes alive after dark, and whether you're a rebellious punk rocker or a suave executive, there's always something to do. Rivonia and the business district of Sandton have become trendy spots for young and hip executives and their style-conscious friends, and the old neighborhood of Melville still has streets filled with lively little bars and restaurants and a sprinkling of clubs. The Newtown Cultural Precinct, an old area that started as a produce market, has undergone a successful rejuvenation. Now clean and brightly lighted, it's home to the Market Theatre complex, which includes dance club Carfax, and other entertainment venues. The suburb of Norwood also has a central street with a good selection of small restaurants and bars. To dine and dance in one go, you should venture to one of these suburbs or visit one of the casino complexes, such as the popular Montecasino in Fourways or Emperor's Palace next to the O.R. Tambo Airport.

BARS & PUBS

★ Dress stylishly for **Café Vacca Matta** (✉ *Montecasino, William Nicol Dr., Fourways* ☎ *011/511–0511*), a trendy bar and restaurant where a sometimes snobbish crowd dances to Top-40 hits.

★ **Capitol Music Café** (✉ *Tyrwhitt and Keyes Aves., Rosebank* ☎ *011/880–0033*) is a happening vinyl shop and bar, where DJs play what they have just bought and an eclectic crowd gathers. **Cool Runnings** (✉ *4th Ave., Melville* ☎ *011/482–4786*) is a lively, Jamaican-theme chain of bars, where rock bands and stand-up comedians often perform. The huge Jo'burg branch has excellent stand-up comedy on Sunday night.

Designer venue **88** (✉ *114 Ivy Rd., Norwood* ☎ *011/728–8417*) has a retro feel to the beat of drum 'n' bass, funk, soul, house, and jazz Tuesday–Saturday. **Katzy's** (✉ *The Firs, Cradock Ave., Rosebank*

CLOSE UP

Kwaito

Kwaito is a uniquely South African music genre, rooted in house, raga (a subgenre of reggae), hip-hop, and local rhythms. It emerged from the country's townships post-apartheid and gets its name, some say, from township slang for "cool talk." Its hard-pumping bass beats, lightly slowed down from a house rhythm, are topped with rambled-off lyrics in style reminiscent of American rap. It's as much a lifestyle as it is a music genre, with its own ways of dancing and dressing.

The best-selling kwaito musicians (and kwaito DJs) have superstar status in South Africa, but they have a less unsavory reputation than their American hip-hop equivalents. Though some kwaito acts stand accused of sexism and vulgar lyrics, the kwaito attitude is generally respectable. Lyrics are often about banning guns or respecting women, or they comment on murder, rape, AIDS, and unemployment. One kwaito star, Zola—named after an impoverished Soweto community—has his own long-running TV series, in which he works to improve people's lives. His music is featured in the 2006 Academy award-winning movie *Tsotsi*. Other chart-topping kwaito stars include Mandoza, whose catchy, powerful songs have earned him several awards and crossover appeal; Arthur Mafikizolo; Mdu; the Brothers of Peace; and Mzekezeke, an enigmatic masked singer.

–Riaan Wolmarans

6

☎011/447–5162) is a cigar lounge where the connected get together over a stogie or an expensive single-malt whiskey. Often a jazz band plays. **Oh!** (✉*4th Ave. and Main Rd., Melville* ☎*011/482–4789*) is the city's busiest gay bar. On summer weekend nights an entertaining crowd gathers on the balcony. At the Westcliff, one of Jo'burg's most stylish hotels, the **Polo Lounge** (✉*67 Jan Smuts Ave., Westcliff* ☎*011/646–4062*) is a sexy spot with an excellent view for pricey sundowners (cocktails). The **Radium Beer Hall** (✉*Louis Botha Ave. and 9th St., Orange Grove* ☎*011/728–3866*) opened in 1929, and is one of the oldest pubs in the city. It's got spicy Portuguese food and blues and jazz on Wednesday, Friday, and Saturday.

★ Melville's **7th Street** is the place to go for a night of bar-hopping. It varies from stylish spots, such as the Mozambique-style **Xai Xai Lounge** (✉*Shop 7, Melville Gardens, 7th St., Melville* ☎*011/482–6990*) to glitzy, vibey bars, such as **Unplugged on 7th** (✉*Shop 4, 7th St., Melville* ☎*011/482–5133*), psychedelic trance hangout **Trance-Sky Beat Bar** (✉*7 7th St., Melville* ☎*083/604–0832*), **Buzz 9** (✉*At 3rd Ave. and 7th St., Melville* ☎*011/726–2019*), and the kitsch-but-cool **Tokyo Star** (✉*At 4th Ave. and 7th St., Melville* ☎*072/478–2529 or 084/208–0236*), which is frequented by an young, energetic crowd.

CLUBS Jo'burg's clubs are usually not too expensive. On a normal club night, or for B-list local bands, it's between R20 and R50 to get in. When dance parties or bigger events take place (or big-name DJs and musicians appear), you pay R60 to R150. Below are just some of the city's established clubs.

Yeoville and Hillbrow were hot spots for nightlife in the 1980s and 1990s; this is true no more. Crime is rife in these areas, and they are best avoided. Though the Newtown Cultural Precinct has been much enhanced and is a lively area worth visiting, it's still not an entirely safe area at night, so take care, especially if you're unaccompanied.

★ **Back 2 Basix** (⊠*Perth and Lancaster Rds., Westdene* ☎*011/726–6857*) is a laid-back restaurant and music venue with top local folk, pop, and rock musicians performing weekends and most weeknights. **Back o' the Moon** (⊠*Gold Reef City Casino, Ormonde* ☎*011/496–1423* ⊕*www. backofthemoon.co.za*) is a modern interpretation of an iconic 1950s bar in Sophiatown, a suburb destroyed during apartheid by forced removals. Live entertainment every evening counters the clanging slot machines outside. It's closed Monday, and reservations are essential. The **Blues Room** (⊠*Village Walk, Sandton* ☎*011/784–5527*) is one of the city's most dependable blues, rock, and jazz venues. It serves good food and is open Tuesday–Saturday.

Fodor'sChoice   Big parties happen at **Carfax** (⊠*39 Pim St., Newtown* ☎*011/834–*
★   *9187*), a converted factory building. Performance art, dance events with guest DJs, and rock shows draw a selection of the town's more interesting people. **The Palms** (⊠*Rivonia and Linden Rd., Sandton* ☎*011/783–7148*) is an ultratrendy dining venue in the evening, and then tables are shifted and the dancing begins. **Sudada** (⊠*12 Fredman Dr., Nedbank House, Sandton* ☎*011/884–1980*) is a stylish cocktail bar frequented by young up-and-coming businesspeople. On the weekend Sudada hosts popular South African DJs. **Taboo** (⊠*24 Central, Fredman Dr., Sandton* ☎*011/783–5805*) is a club catering to the hip and happening South African. This multistory club hosts a variety of parties from grand prix, Greek socials, and gay nights.

Close to the Jo'burg airport, **Monsoon Lagoon** (⊠*Caesars Gauteng, 64 Jones Rd., Kempton Park* ☎*011/928–1280*) is a glittery casino with weekend party nights ranging from bhangra (Punjabi folk music) bashes to R&B, kwaito, and dance events. Since the late 1980s, **Roxy's** (⊠*20 Main Rd., Melville* ☎*011/726–6019*) has brought the country's best new and old rock bands to a rowdy student crowd.

THE ARTS

CLASSICAL   The **Linder Auditorium** (⊠*27 St. Andrews Rd., Wits Education Campus,*
MUSIC   *Parktown* ☎*011/643–6413*) hosts classical performances almost every week. It's the home of the Johannesburg Philharmonic Orchestra's seasonal series. A bit far out of town, the **Pro Musica Theatre** (⊠*Christiaan de Wet Rd., Florida Park, Roodepoort* ☎*011/672–2217*) has a year-round program of classical music and dance and its own orchestra, the Sasol Pro Musica Orchestra.

FILM   The best art-house and foreign-language films are shown at the large
Fodor'sChoice   **Cinema Nouveau** (⊠*Rosebank Mall, Bath Ave., Rosebank* ☎*082/16789*
★   *Ster Kinekor Ticketline, 083/915–8000 Computicket* ⊕*www.sterki-nekor.com*). Movies change every Friday, and several film festivals, such as the Gay and Lesbian Film Festival (usually in March), run yearly.

THEATER The **Civic Theatre** (✉ *123 Loveday St., Braamfontein* ☏*011/877–6800* ⊕*www.showbusiness.co.za*) is Jo'burg's main cultural venue and the home of the South African Ballet Theatre. It contains the enormous Nelson Mandela Theatre and the smaller People's and Tesson theaters. Many productions have a South African focus, such as works by local talents Pieter-Dirk Uys and Paul Slabolepszy.

Occupying an old produce market that dates from the early 1900s, the **Market Theatre** (✉ *Bree and Margret Mcingana Sts., Newtown* ☏*011/832–1641* ⊕*www.markettheatre.co.za*) has a delightful vintage look. In the 1980s the Market played a key role in bravely staging Protest Theater against the apartheid regime—often to local and eventually critical acclaim. Plays like *The Island* about Robben Island and *Sarafina!* denouncing the inferior Bantu education made their debuts here. Today theater productions encompass everything from plays with an African focus by Athol Fugard and Gibson Kente to comedies imported from London's West End. The theater occasionally features traditional African music and jazz performances. Experimental plays test audience approval at the Market Theatre Laboratory, just across Bree Street. The complex also has a great bar and restaurant, and an art gallery. The **Liberty Theater on the Square** (✉ *Nelson Mandela Sq., Maude and West Sts., Sandton* ☏*011/883–8606*) is a smaller theater, easily accessible from the restaurants on Nelson Mandela Square. Its productions are usually short and entertaining, but not as challenging for actors or audiences as those put on at the larger Market and Civic theaters.

Pieter Toerien's Montecasino Theatre (✉ *Montecasino, William Nicol Dr., Fourways* ☏*011/511–1988*), a large casino venue, often hosts famous playwright and satirist Pieter-Dirk Uys's satirical shows, comedies, and appearances by international theater stars. The newly built **Teatro Montecasino Theatre** (☏*011/510–7472*) has recently opened in the same casino complex and is much bigger than the Pieter Toerien Theatre. The first production staged there was the internationally acclaimed musical *The Lion King*.

The city has many smaller venues that cater to experimental and amateur productions. The **Wits Theater Complex** (✉ *University of the Witwatersrand, Jorissen St., Braamfontein* ☏*011/717–1372*) is a center of student drama. All the town's casino complexes have a cabaret venue or two hidden among the slot machines.

SHOPPING

Whether you're after designer clothes, the latest books or DVDs, high-quality African art, or glamorous gifts, Johannesburg offers outstanding shopping opportunities. Dozens of malls, galleries, and curio shops are scattered throughout the city, often selling the same goods at widely different prices. It's best to shop around.

6

MALLS

Johannesburg has more malls than seems healthy, especially in the northern suburbs. Most are quite exclusive, with shops selling the latest from Italy, France, and the States, but you might get it cheaper at home. Most malls also have department stores, such as Edgars and Woolworths (which stocks good-quality food and clothes). Mall hours are usually Monday–Saturday 9–5, 9–2 on Sunday.

You can eat a spicy samoosa and haggle over the massive selection of textiles, clothes, and the like at the maze of little shops in the **Oriental Plaza** (⌗*Bree St., Fordsburg* ☎*011/838–6752*), which is more like a Mumbai market than the glitzy malls of northern suburbs, and where you're sure to find a bargain.

The **Rosebank Mall** (⌗*Bath Ave., Rosebank* ☎*011/788–5530*) has a good selection of shops as well as Cinema Nouveau, Jo'burg's best art-house complex. Across the street, the **Zone** (⌗*Oxford Rd., Rosebank* ☎*011/788–1130*) is a trendy mall aimed at under-twenty-fives. It contains clothing stores, a cinema, Exclusive Books, and the massive CD Wherehouse, which is a good place to pick up South African and African music. **Hyde Park Corner** (⌗*6th and Jan Smuts Aves., Hyde Park* ☎*011/325–4340*) is an upscale shopping center where fashionistas sip cappuccinos and browse in Exclusive Books—the country's best bookstore chain.

Melrose Arch (⌗*32 Melrose Blvd., Melrose North* ☎*011/684–0000*) is a shopping, residential, and business district where you can walk among sidewalk cafés and specialty shops. When night falls, savor North African flavors at Moyo.

The best—but expensive—mall in Johannesburg is **Sandton City** (⌗*Sandton Dr. and Rivonia Rd., Sandton* ☎*011/217–6000*). The center has 1,550,000 feet of shopping space with some 300 stores, from high-end boutiques to franchise fast-food outlets, and a tax-refund center for tourists. Adjoining Sandton City is **Nelson Mandela Square** (⌗*5th St., Sandton* ☎*011/217–6000*), a popular meeting place for Jo'burg's wealthier residents and visitors. It has sidewalk cafés, fine restaurants, a theater, and 93 exclusive shops.

Montecasino (⌗*William Nicol Dr., Fourways* ☎*011/510–7777*) is a reproduction of a Tuscan village, with a painted ceiling resembling the sky. Some hate it, some love it, but it's a favorite tourist destination nonetheless. It has restaurants, movie theaters, a casino, and a lovely bird park with birds from around the world, like huge gold and blue macaw parrots and startlingly bright scarlet ibises from South America.

MARKETS

At the city's several markets, bargaining—although not as expected as in other countries—can still get you a great price. Watch out for inferior goods, pirated DVDs and CDs, and fake designer clothes.

The **African Craft Market,** between the Rosebank Mall and the Zone, has a huge variety of African crafts from Cape to Cairo, all displayed to the background beat of traditional African music. ⊠*At Cradock and Baker St., Rosebank* ☎*011/880–2906* ⊙*Daily 9–5.*

Bigger is better at **Bruma Market World,** one of the biggest flea markets in South Africa. You can find anything you can imagine here—and probably a whole lot you can't. Search for it between the West African wood crafts, "designer" clothing (but check the quality before you buy), wire sculptures, cheap plastic gadgets, home crafts, homemade toys, and the like. African dancers perform twice daily. ⊠*Ernest Oppenheimer and Marcia Sts., Bruma* ☎*011/622–9647* ⊙*Tues.–Fri. and Sun. 9:30–5, Sat. 8:30–5.*

Into healthful living? Then visit the **Michael Mount Organic Market,** where homemade and organically grown food, flowers, handmade clothes and shoes, and other products clamor for your clean-living attention. Remember to taste the cheeses. The quality is probably the best you'll find at any market in the country, but the selection is relatively small. ⊠*Bryanston and Culross Aves., Bryanston* ☎*011/706–3671* ⊙*Thurs. 9–1, Sat. 9–2.*

Newtown Market Africa, across the street from the Market Theatre, is a good option for African art and artifacts. Craftspeople from as far away as Cameroon and Zaire sell their masks, wooden artworks, fabrics, and blankets, often at cheaper prices than elsewhere in town. ⊠*Bree and Wolhuter Sts., Newtown* ☎*083/732–0302* ⊙*Sat. 9–5.*

Rosebank's **Rooftop Market** has become a Sunday tradition in the city. More than 600 stalls sell African and Western crafts, antiques, books, food, art, trinkets, CDs, jewelry and clothes. Frequently African musicians, dancers, and other entertainers delight the crowds. ⊠*Rosebank Mall, 50 Bath Ave., Rosebank* ☎*011/442–4488* ⊙*Sun. 9–5.*

SPECIALTY STORES

AFRICAN ARTS & CRAFTS

Art Africa brings together a dazzling selection of ethnic arts, crafts, and artifacts from across the continent, and also sells funky items produced in self-help projects, such as tin lizards and wooden animals. ⊠*62 Tyrone Ave., Parkview* ☎*011/486–2052.*

The **Everard Read Gallery,** established in 1912, is one of the largest privately owned galleries in the world. It acts as an agent for several important South Africans. The gallery specializes in wildlife paintings and sculpture. ⊠*6 Jellicoe Ave., Rosebank* ☎*011/788–4805.*

The highly successful, three-decade-old **Goodman Gallery** presents exciting monthly exhibitions by the stars of contemporary South African art, including Norman Catherine, William Kentridge, and Deborah Bell. ⊠*163 Jan Smuts Ave., Parkwood* ☎*011/788–1113.*

The **Kim Sacks Gallery,** in a lovely old home, has a superb collection of authentic African art. Displayed throughout its sunny rooms are Zairian raffia cloth, Mali mud cloth, Zulu telephone-wire baskets, wood sculptures, and original masks and carvings from across the continent. It's also a good place to find ceramic art. Prices are steep. ⊠*153 Jan Smuts Ave., Parkwood* ☎*011/447–5804.*

Totem Gallery specializes in artifacts from west and central Africa, including Kuba cloth from Zaire, Dogon doors from Mali, glass beads, masks from Burkina Faso, and hand-painted barbershop signs. Prices are high. ⊠*U17a level 6, Sandton City, Sandton* ☎*011/884–6300* ⊠*The Firs, Rosebank* ☎*011/447–1409.*

BOOKS   If you're looking for a cheap vacation read or out-of-print books, go to one of the **Bookdealers** chain of secondhand bookstores for an excellent selection. ⊠*Mutual Gardens, Rosebank* ☎*011/442–4089* ⊠*12 7th St., Melville* ☎*011/726–4054* ⊠*Rivonia Sq., Rivonia* ☎*011/234–0486.*

Exclusive Books is the best chain of bookstores in the country, with an impressive selection of African literature, history, travel, and culture. You can select a book, order a designer coffee, and read in comfort all day. In Johannesburg, the Hyde Park store is the best. ⊠*Sandton City, Sandton* ☎*011/883–1010* ⊠*Hyde Park Corner, Hyde Park* ☎*011/325–4298* ⊠*The Zone, Rosebank* ☎*011/327–5736* ⊠*Rosebank Mall, Rosebank* ☎*011/784–5419.*

GOLD &   Krugerrands, which carry images of President Paul Kruger and a
DIAMONDS   springbok on either side, are among the most famous gold coins minted today. They lost some of their luster during the apartheid years, when they were banned internationally. Krugerrands are sold individually or in sets containing coins of 1 ounce, ½ ounce, ¼ ounce, and [1//10] ounce of pure gold. You can buy Krugerrands through most city banks, and several branches of First National Bank sell them over the counter. The most convenient branches are in Sandton City and Rosebank.

South Africa is also diamond country. The world's biggest diamond, the 3,106-carat Cullinan, was found in the town of the same name (near present-day Tshwane) in 1905, and is now among the British crown jewels. For a comprehensive list of diamond retailers, contact the **Shining Light of South Africa** (☎*011/880–0230* ⊕*www.sadiamond.com*).

Charles Greig (⊠*Hyde Park Corner, Jan Smuts Ave., Hyde Park* ☎*011/325–4477* ⊕*www.charlesgreig.co.za*) sells a dazzling array of diamonds.

Schwartz Jewellers (⊠*Sandton City, Sandton* ☎*011/783–1717*) is a diamond wholesaler and manufacturing jeweler. It offers a large range of classical and ethnic African pieces and a custom design service.

For something shiny but less expensive, try **De Klerk's Coppersmith** (⊠*24 Currey St., Doornfontein* ☎*011/402–7644*). The only remaining authentic coppersmith in South Africa, it turns out anything copper.

PRETORIA/TSHWANE

While Johannesburg's greater metropolitan area is called Johannesburg like the city, Pretoria, which used to refer to the entire urban area, now refers only to the city center area of the Tshwane metropolitan area. The city, while being the country's administrative capital and home of many senior politicians (including the president) and diplomats, is overshadowed by Johannesburg, 48 km (30 mi) to the south. It's a pleasant city, with many historic buildings and a city center that is easily explored on foot. One thing that doesn't change is the many clusters of jacaranda trees, which blanket the city with their purple blossoms in spring (September and October).

Founded in 1855, the city was originally named after Afrikaner leader Andries Pretorius, the hero of the Battle of Blood River (1838) and one of the Voortrekkers (pronounced *Foo-er*-treka) who moved from the Cape to escape British rule. For many years the city remained a bastion of Afrikaner culture. In 1860 Pretoria was named the capital of the independent Transvaal Voortrekker Republic, and in the late 1870s the Transvaal war of independence was successfully waged against the British, who wished to annex the area (the proclamation of annexation was read on Church Square). The British withdrew—temporarily. After the South African War of 1899–1902 (also called the second Anglo-Boer War), however, the city became the capital of the then British colony, and in 1910 it was named the administrative capital of the Union of South Africa. Jumping ahead to 1948, when the National Party came to power, Pretoria also became the seat of the apartheid government, and the city developed a reputation for hard-line insularity. In 1964 the Rivonia treason trial (named for the Johannesburg suburb where 19 ANC leaders had been arrested in 1963) was held here, and Nelson Mandela and seven of his colleagues were sentenced to life in prison.

The Tshwane metropolitan council is responsible for all the areas within the municipality, including the city center of Pretoria, but also nearby Centurion; the sprawling townships of Atteridgeville, Mamelodi, and Soshanguve; and other neighboring areas. "Tshwane" is a reference to the indigenous people who lived in the area before the first white Afrikaners arrived. The name Pretoria is still used for the city center, however, which is now basically a neighborhood of Tshwane.

Numbers in the text correspond to numbers in the margin and on the Pretoria map.

TIMING & PRECAUTIONS

It takes at least an hour to travel from Johannesburg to Pretoria in the Tshwane Metropole on the N1 (two hours if the traffic is bad, which happens quite regularly). If you want to see everything, schedule an entire day here. A side trip to the Cullinan diamond mine will take at least half a day. Pretoria is not as notorious as Johannesburg for crime, but drive with your car doors locked and don't have bags or valuables visible or you could become a target of a "hit-and-grab."

WHAT TO SEE

26 **African Window.** Part of the National Cultural History Museum, this cultural center offers song and dance programs, a traditional crafts shop, exhibitions (including Bushman, or San, art), and an archaeology program. Don't miss the stunning, full-color Ndebele mural along the

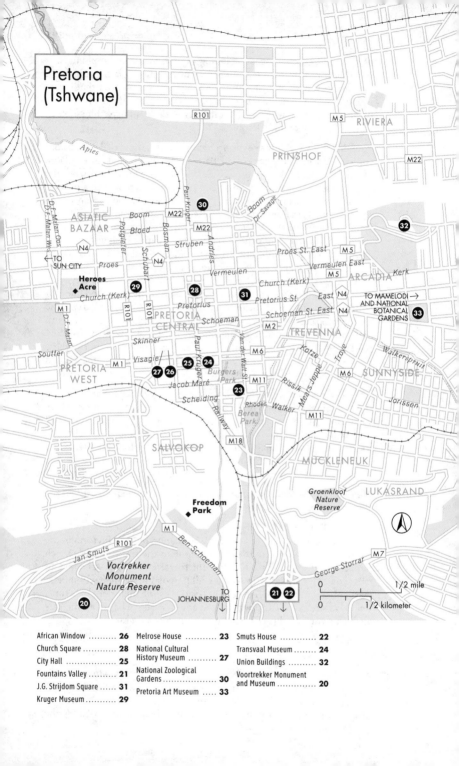

Pretoria (Tshwane)

RIVIERA

PRINSHOF

M5

M22

R101

Apies

M22

ASIATIC BAZAAR

D.F. Malan Oos
D.F. Malan Wes

N4

←TO SUN CITY

Boom

Bloed

Polgieter

Schubart

Proes

N4

Bosman

Paul Kruger

M22

M22

Andries

Struben

Vermeulen

Heroes Acre

Church (Kerk)

Church (Kerk)

Proes St. East

Vermeulen East

M5

M5

Kerk

ARCADIA

M1

D.F. Malan

R101

R101

29

30

28

31

Pretorius

Pretorius St.

Schoeman

Schoeman St. East

East

N4

N4

TO MAMELODI →
AND NATIONAL
BOTANICAL
GARDENS

33

32

PRETORIA CENTRAL

M2

TREVENNA

Souttter

Skinner

Visagie

Paul Kruger

Van der Watt St.

M6

Kotze

Troye

Walkerspruit

PRETORIA WEST

M1

27 **26**

25 **24**

Burgers Park

23

M11

Rissik

Mears
Jeppe

M6

SUNNYSIDE

Jacob Maré

Scheiding

Railway

Rhodes
Berea
Park

Walker

M11

Jarissen

SALVOKOP

M18

MUCKLENEUK

LUKASRAND

Groenkloof
Nature
Reserve

Freedom Park

M1

Ben Schoeman

Jan Smuts

R101

Vortrekker
Monument
Nature Reserve

TO JOHANNESBURG ↓

George Storrar

M7

21 **22**

↓

20

0   1/2 mile
0   1/2 kilometer

entrance wall. ⊠*149 Visagie St.,* ☎*012/324–6082* ⊕*www.nfi.org.za* ⊠*R20* ⏱*Daily 8–4.*

🔵**28** **Church Square.** Anton van Wouw's statue of President Paul Kruger, surrounded by sentries, dominates this pleasant square, which is flanked by some of the city's most historic buildings: the Old Raadsaal (Council Chamber), designed by Dutch architect Sytze Wierda; the Palace of Justice (used as a military hospital during the South African War), built in early Italian Renaissance style; and the modern Provincial Administration Building. On Wednesday mornings you can watch a military parade and flag-raising. ⊠*Bordered by Paul Kruger and Church Sts..*

NEED A BREAK? In a building dating from 1904, **Café Riche** (⊠*Church Sq.* ☎*012/328–3173*) is one of the better coffee shops in the center of town. They also serve *tramezzini* (toasted sandwiches) and salads.

🔵**25** **City Hall.** This imposing structure has a semi-Italian style that borrows freely from classical architecture. A tympanum on the front, by Coert Steynberg, one of South Africa's most famous sculptors, symbolizes the growth and development of the city. Statues of Andries Pretorius, the city's founder, and his son Marthinus, stand in the square fronting the building, and relief panels depict the founding in 1855. ⊠*Visagie and Paul Kruger Sts.* ☎*012/358–8949* ⊕*www.museumpark.co.za/cityhall. htm* ⊠*Free* ⏱*Weekdays 8–4.*

👣🔵**21** **Fountains Valley.** The Apies River, which flows through Tshwane, originates in this 24-acre park with a game and bird sanctuary. The springs drew early humans to the area and was one of the reasons this river valley was originally chosen as the site for Pretoria. You can hike, swim, or picnic here while the kids enjoy the play area and miniature locomotive. There's also a restaurant. ⊠*Christina de Wit Dr. and Eeufees Rd.* ☎*012/440–2121* ⊠*R15* ⏱*Daily 7–7.*

🔵**30** **J. G. Strijdom Square.** This square was once dominated by a huge bust of former pro-apartheid prime minister J. G. Strijdom. However, on May 31, 2001—exactly 40 years to the day after the government declared South Africa a republic—the supporting structure of the whole edifice crumbled, and Strijdom fell unceremoniously into the parking garage under the square. All that remains is a statue by Danie de Jager of charging horses atop a high column. ⊠*Church and van der Walt Sts.*

🔵**29** **Kruger Museum.** This was once the residence of Paul Kruger, president of the South African republic between 1883 and 1902 and one of the most revered figures in South African history. The home, still fully furnished, is humble and somber, befitting this deeply religious leader who loved to sit on the front *stoep* (veranda) and watch the world go by. Exhibits in the adjoining museum trace Kruger's career, culminating in his exile by the British and eventual death in Switzerland in 1904. Of particular interest are the letters of support that Kruger received from all over the world, including the United States, when Britain instigated the South African War (1899–1902), also known as the Anglo-Boer War. Across the road is the Dutch Reformed Church, where Kruger's wife is buried. ⊠*60 Church St. W, at Potgieter St.* ☎*012/326–9172*

6

⊕*www.nfi.org.za* ✇*R18; guided tours R25* ⊙*Weekdays 8:30–5:30, weekends 8:30–5.*

㉓ **Melrose House.** Built in 1886, this opulent structure is one of South Africa's most beautiful and best-preserved Victorian homes, furnished in period style. It has marble columns, mosaic floors, lovely stained-glass windows, ornate ceilings, porcelain ornaments, and richly colored carpets. On May 31, 1902, the Treaty of Vereeniging was signed in the dining room, ending the South African War. You can view a permanent exhibit on the war or arrange for a guided tour (R50 for a group of 20 or fewer; by appointment). ⊠*275 Jacob Maré St.* ☎*012/322–2805* ⊕*www.melrosehouse.co.za* ✇*R8* ⊙*Tues.–Sun. 10–5.*

★ **㉗** **National Cultural History Museum.** This museum offers an insightful look at the country's indigenous cultures. You can marvel at San rock art, African headdresses, clay sculptures, and several permanent collections of archaeological material dealing with Pretoria, South Africa, and the many people who call this country home. The museum also has a restaurant. ⊠*149 Visagie St., between Bosman and Schubart Sts.* ☎*012/324–6082* ⊕*www.nfi.co.za* ✇*R20* ⊙*Daily 8–4.*

☾ **㉚** **National Zoological Gardens.** The city's zoo, covering nearly 200 acres,
FodorśChoice is considered one of the world's best, with about 9,000 animals from
★ almost every continent (including rare Komodo dragons, the world's largest lizards). The animal enclosures here are much larger than those of most zoos. However, like any modern zoo worth its name, this is just the public facade for a much larger organization that specializes in the research and breeding of endangered species. It includes an aquarium (with Africa's largest collection of freshwater fish) and reptile park, where the king crocodiles and the impressive collection of snakes won't fail to intimidate you. A cable car transports you high above the zoo to a hilltop lookout, and it's a fun, worthwhile ride. It's also a good idea to rent a golf cart, so you can move more quickly between enclosures for the staggered feeding times each morning and afternoon. ⊠*Boom St.* ☎*012/328–3265* ⊕*www.zoo.ac.za* ✇*R34* ⊙*Daily 8–6.*

㉝ **Pretoria Art Museum.** Despite its dull exterior, this gallery houses an impressive collection of South African art in constantly changing exhibitions. The collection includes works by South African masters, painter Jacob Hendrik Pierneef and the more contemporary Anton van Wouw, and such international heavyweights as Salvador Dalí and Pablo Picasso, collections of 17th-century Dutch art, and international graphic art. Guided tours are available for an extra R5. The museum also has a sculpture garden. ⊠*Schoeman and Wessels Sts., Arcadia* ☎*012/344–1807* ⊕*www.pretoriaartmuseum.co.za* ✇*R5* ⊙*Tues. and Thurs.–Sun. 10–5, Wed. 10–8.*

▌OFF THE
BEATEN
PATH
Sammy Marks Museum About 23 km (14 mi) outside Pretoria, this furnished Victorian mansion and its outbuildings, surrounded by gardens, were built in 1884 for mining and industrial magnate Sammy Marks. You can relax at the restaurant after visiting the 48 rooms (in a mixture of grand styles) or have a picnic on the grounds. Guided tours take place every 90 minutes on weekdays; there are ghost tours at night.

✉ *Off Centurion exit of N4; follow signs* ☎*012/802–1150* ⊕*www. nfi.org.za* ✆*R20* ⊙ *Tues.–Fri. 10–5, weekends 10–4.*

㉒ Smuts House. This small wood-and-iron country house was the residence of three-time South African prime minister Jan Christian Smuts, who played active roles in the South African War and World Wars I and II and was instrumental in setting up the League of Nations (forerunner of the United Nations). Despite his military background, he was committed to working for peace and remains one of South Africa's most interesting historical characters. His home illustrates the simple manner in which he lived until his death in 1950. There's a tea garden on the large grounds; an adjacent campsite; and easy trails up a nearby hill. Ask about guided bird-watching and other tours. On the second and last Saturday of each month a crafts market takes to the grounds. ✉*Off Nelmapius Rd., Irene* ☎*012/667–1176* ✆*R10* ⊙ *Weekdays 9:30–4:30, weekends 9:30–5.*

㉔ Transvaal Museum. This massive natural-history museum has an extensive collection of land and marine animals from around the world, with an emphasis on African wildlife. The beautiful building also contains the Austin Roberts Bird Collection, the most comprehensive display of taxidermied African birds in southern Africa. Of particular interest are the Genesis exhibits, tracing the evolution of life on Earth, and the geology section, with displays of weird and wonderful rocks and minerals. Mrs Ples, the famous Australopithecus skull found at the Sterkfontein Caves in the Cradle of Humankind, resides here. Tours cost an extra R3. ✉*Paul Kruger St., across from City Hall* ☎*012/322–7632* ⊕*www.nfi.org.za* ✆*R20* ⊙ *Daily 8–4.*

6

OFF THE BEATEN PATH

Tswaing Crater Museum. This huge meteorite crater was formed about 220,000 years ago. Today it's home to 340 bird species and even more plant species. Browse through the crater's ecomuseum (guided or unguided) to learn more about the area or explore an Ndebele cultural village. A three-hour guided tour (R80 a guide) includes a walk to the crater. ✉*Old Soutpan Rd. (M35), about 40 km (25 mi) outside Tshwane* ☎*012/790–2302* ⊕*www.nfi.org.za* ✆*R15* ⊙ *Daily 7:30–4.*

㉜ Union Buildings. Built in 1901, this impressive cream-sandstone complex—home to the administrative branch of government—was designed by Sir Herbert Baker, one of South Africa's most revered architects. It is his masterpiece, and closely resembles the Parliament Buildings in New Delhi, where he went on to work. The complex incorporates a hodgepodge of styles—an Italian-tile roof, wooden shutters inspired by Cape Dutch architecture, and Renaissance columns—that somehow works beautifully. Expansive formal gardens step down the hillside in terraces, dotted with war memorials and statues of former prime ministers. There's no public access to the building, but the gardens are perfect for a picnic lunch. ✉*Off Church St., Meintjeskop* ⊙ *Gardens open 24 hrs.*

㉐ Voortrekker Monument and Museum. This monument lies at the heart of Afrikaner nationalism. Completed in 1949, it honors the Voortrekkers who rejected British rule and trekked into the hinterland to found their own nation. The Hall of Heroes traces in its marble frieze their momentous Great Trek, culminating in the Battle of Blood River (December 16, 1838), when a small force of Boers defeated a large Zulu army without losing a single life. The Voortrekkers considered this victory a special gift from God. An adjoining museum displays scenes and artifacts of daily Voortrekker life, as well as the Voortrekker Tapestries, 15 pictorial weavings that trace the historical high points of the Great Trek. The monument is in a nature reserve, which has a picnic area and hiking and biking trails. You can dine in the restaurant and tea garden if you don't like to rough it. Also on-site is **Fort Schanskop,** the best-preserved of four area forts commissioned by President Paul Kruger in about 1897. The fort houses a South African (Anglo-Boer) War museum and gift shop. ⊠ *Off R28* ☎ *012/326–6770* ⊕ *www.voortrekkermon.org.za* 🎫 *R25* ⊙ *May–Aug., daily 8–4:30; Sept.–Apr., daily 8–6.*

> **FREEDOM PARK**
>
> Though it's already possible to do a two-hour tour of Freedom Park (☎ 012/361–0021 ⊕ www. freedompark.org.za), when finished in 2009 the site will be a "one-stop-heritage-shop" for South Africa, dedicated to the struggle for freedom and humanity, as well as other aspects of South African heritage, including human evolution. It will comprise a memorial, interactive museum, archives, and a garden of remembrance. Tours start every day at 8 AM. Bookings are essential, and admission is free until construction is complete.

WHERE TO STAY & EAT

$–$$$$ ✕ **Cynthia's Restaurant and Art Gallery.** This bistro-style restaurant has good local game and seafood. Locals flock here for the line fish cooked on an open grill. All the art on the walls is for sale. ⊠ *Maroelana Centre, Maroelana St., Maroelana.* ☎ *012/460–3220* ⊕ *www.cynthias. co.za* 🖃 *AE, DC, MC, V* ⊙ *No lunch Sat., no dinner Sun.*

★ $–$$$$ ✕ **La Madeleine.** Noted for its classic and creative French cuisine, this restaurant is frequently ranked among the country's top 10. Belgian-French chef Daniel Leusch opened the restaurant in his former home. The menu is set, with a few choices for each course, and changes daily, depending on what's at the market. For starters he might serve calamari tubes stuffed with ratatouille or oysters and mussels in a curry cream sauce. For a main dish, there's a choice: perhaps between a rack of lamb with fresh vegetables and olives, line fish in champagne sauce, ostrich fillet with cranberry sauce, or veal in muscat sauce. Don't miss the fine selection of cheeses served after dinner. ⊠ *122 Priory Rd., Lynwood Ridge* ☎ *012/361–3667* 🖎 *Reservations essential* 🖃 *AE, DC, MC, V* ⊙ *Closed Sun. and Mon. No lunch, except Fri.*

$–$$$$ ✕ **O'Galito's.** You'll find it hard to believe you're nearly 500 km (300 mi) inland at this seafood restaurant. But if you have an enormous imagination, the big spaces and white tables bring to mind the beach. The popular shellfish platter contains langoustines, king prawns, small crayfish (lobster), mussels, grilled calamari, french fries, and rice. There's a limited vegetarian menu, too. O'Galito's now has branches in Centurion, a suburb south of Pretoria, and in the Village Walk Shopping Centre in Sandton, Johannesburg. ✉*367 Hilda St., Hatfield* ☎*012/342–6610* ⊕*www.ogalito.com* ▭*AE, DC, MC, V.*

¢–$ ✕**Carlton Café Delicious.** If you weren't looking for it, this little café might just disappear into the facade of suburban mall shops. If you're hungry at lunchtime, however, make a point of seeking it out. The home-style food is prepared by owner and chef Rachel Botes and her all-woman team, offering leg-of-lamb pies, massive deli "designer sandwiches" like toasted biltong and Gorgonzola, and cashew-and-chicken salad. The array of desserts includes good cheesecake. ✉*Shop 55A, Menlo Park Centre, 71 13th St., Menlo Park* ☎*012/460–7996* ⊕*www.carltoncafe.co.za* ▭*AE, MC, V* ☉*Mon. noon–4, Tues.–Fri. 8–5, Sat. 8–1* ☉*Closed Sun.*

★ $$$ ▦**Illyria House.** Although there are grander hotels in town, sheikhs and presidents have requested this small suburban guesthouse on Muckleneuk Hill, overlooking the city bowl. The house takes its name from the setting of Shakespeare's romantic comedy *Twelfth Night,* and the house and gardens feel as though they're part of an elaborate stage. Presiding over the array of French antiques and over-the-top Venetian light fixtures is vivacious owner Marietjie van der Walt. There's a dining room but no set menu; the butler and chef will discuss options with you each day and then shop just for you. Nothing is too much, which explains something of the lodge's appeal. If it's available, ask for the Katarina Suite, with its view of the Union Buildings. Horseback riding, golf, tennis, and hiking can also be arranged. ✉*327 Bourke St., Muckleneuk 0002* ☎*012/344–5193 or 012/344–4641* ⊕*www.illyria. co.za* ⇖*6 suites* ⌂*In-hotel: spa, Wi-Fi, no elevator.* ▭*AE, DC, MC, V* ⦿*MAP.*

$$ ▦**Sheraton Pretoria.** The first five floors consist of standard or classic rooms, all decorated in shades of cream with Italian marble tiles. The top two floors are towers: 36 executive rooms and 7 suites, each with a personal computer. Ask for a room overlooking the Union Buildings' gardens. ✉*643 Church St., at Wessels St., 0002* ☎*012/429–9999* ⊕*www.sheraton.com/pretoria* ⇖*175 rooms, 7 suites* ⌂*In-hotel: 3 restaurants, bars, pool, gym* ▭*AE, DC, MC, V.*

¢ ▦**Pretoria Backpackers.** This backpackers' hostel is run more like a family guesthouse. All the beds have electric blankets in winter, and the rooms have fans for the hot summer. There's a dormitory, but also 14 rooms and wooden cabins in the lush, tropical garden. The owner, Francois Van Rooyen, can take you on a daylong sightseeing tour to Johannesburg, Soweto, and the Apartheid Museum, and will also pick you up from the Johannesburg airport. ✉*425 Farenden St., Clydesdale 0002* ☎*012/343–9754* ⊕*www.pretoriabackpackers.net* ⇖*14 rooms, 13-bed dormitory* ⌂*In-room: kitchen. In-hotel: bar, pool, no elevator* ▭*AE, DC, MC, V* ⦿*CP.*

¢ ▦**Ted's Place.** In a sleepy cul-de-sac on the spectacular Bronberg mountain, Ted's Place looks like a large, smart suburban home. From a large veranda you can watch the abundant bird life that has taken sanctuary on the mountain. Annemarie, Ted's wife, serves a full bacon-

and-egg breakfast, sometimes with pancakes, too. Ted is a registered tour guide and can show you the sights, such as the hulking Voortrekker Monument or the Cullinan Diamond Mine. ✉*961 Wagon Wheel Ave., Wapadrand 0050* ☎*012/807–2803 or 083/452–5546* ⊕*www.teds-place.za.net* ⟳*4 rooms* ♿*In-hotel: bar, no elevator* ☰*AE, DC, MC, V* ⏏*BP.*

NIGHTLIFE & THE ARTS

NIGHTLIFE

For such a large city, Pretoria is on the quiet side, and has far fewer nightspots than Johannesburg. Hatfield—the area defined by Burnett, Hilda, and Festival streets and just off Duncan Street—is the liveliest area at night. It's a hodgepodge of bars, coffeehouses, and restaurants and is reasonably safe to walk in at night. You can find an interesting mix of slightly rowdy students, young professionals, diplomats, politicians, and a few creative types.

Cool Runnings (✉*1071 Burnett St., Hatfield* ☎*012/362–0100*) has rock bands, DJs, and good meals, and stand-up comedians often perform.. **Tings an' Times** (✉*1065 Arcadia St., Hatfield* ☎*012/362–5537*) is Hatfield's most atmospheric student eatery, with a reggae theme, tasty and cheap food, and bands or DJs playing. The two-story **Cuban Café** (✉*129 Duxbury Rd., Hatfield* ☎*012/362–1800*) is a cocktail haven that also serves excellent food.

★ Pop in at the chilled-out **Izzy's Café** (✉*Brooklyn Mall, Veale St., Brooklyn* ☎*012/346–4296*) to chat with friends over a slow drink. **Legends** (✉*President Arcade, Schoeman and Pretorius Sts.* ☎*084/400–1271*) is Tshwane's biggest gay club, but it attracts a very mixed crowd of straight and gay. On Friday, resident DJs play funky house, and on Saturday the music is commercial. **Lucit Restaurant** (✉*42 Belrene St., Rietondale* ☎*012/329–4180 or 083/306–2830*) is one of the city's best spots for weekend performances of classical music, jazz, and cabaret—all in a garden surrounded by a legion of candles. The restaurant is open Tuesday to Sunday and booking is essential. **Zeplin's** (✉*384 Pretorius St.* ☎*082/787–9532*) is the city's largest and darkest venue for rock lovers, with separate areas for goth, industrial, and metal beats. Rock bands often perform on weekends.

THE ARTS

The **South African State Theatre** (✉*Church St.* ☎*012/392–4114* ⊕*www.statetheatre.co.za*) is the largest theater in Africa. It hosts local and international touring productions of ballet, musical theater, and dramas in its two large venues, one smaller theater, and one intimate cabaret theater.

SHOPPING

GALLERY

At the **Association of Arts Pretoria** (⊠*173 Mackie St., Nieuw Muckle-neuk* ☎*012/346–3100* ⊕*www.art.co.za/artspta*) you can admire or buy contemporary paintings, prints, and sculpture.

MARKETS

The **Hatfield Market** (⊠*Burnett St., Hatfield* ☎*011/442–4488*) spreads out over a central parking lot in Hatfield every Sunday. Hundreds of stalls sell crafts, toys, goldfish, food, secondhand books, and other titbits. The **Irene Village Market** (⊠*Nelmapius Rd., Irene* ☎*012/667–1659*) appears on the second and last Saturday of the month from 9 to 2, with about 300 stalls of art, fresh produce, flowers, hand-painted African fabrics, and toys. When you're tired, head for the tea garden. **Magnolia Dell** (⊠*Queen Wilhelmina Dr., Nieuw Muckleneuk* ☎*072/836–2446*) comes alive on the first Saturday of each month from 9 to 3, when it's home to a large arts-and-crafts market. On the last Saturday of the month, shop for bargains when up-and-coming artists show their works at Art in the Park.

6

CRADLE OF HUMANKIND

The original Cradle of Humankind World Heritage Site (excluding Taung and the Makapans Valley, which lie farther away, though they were included in the World Heritage Site declaration in 2005) stretches over an area of about 470 squre km (181 square mi) with about 300 caves. Inside these caves, palaeoanthropologists have discovered thousands of fossils of hominids and other animals, dating back about 4 million years. The most famous of these fossils are "Mrs Ples," a skull more than 2 million years old, and "Little Foot," a skeleton more than 3 million years old. While the Cradle does not have the world's oldest hominid fossils, it has the most complete fossil record of human evolution of anywhere on earth, and has produced more hominid fossils than anywhere else.

Archaeological finds at the Cradle of Humankind include 1.7-million-year-old stone tools, the oldest recorded in southern Africa. At Swart-krans, near Sterkfontein, a collection of burned bones tells us that our ancestors could manage fire more than 1-million years ago.

Not all the fossil sites in the Cradle are open to the public, but a tour of the Sterkfontein Caves and the visitor center provides an excellent overview of the archaeological work in progress, and a trip to Maropeng, a much larger visitor center 10 km (6 mi) from the Sterkfontein Caves, provides even more background. Special tours to fossil sites with expert guides can be booked at either of the visitor centers.

WHAT TO SEE

The **Sterkfontein Caves** are the best known of the Cradle's fossil sites. It
was here, in 1936, that Dr. Robert Broom discovered the now famous
Mrs. Ples, as she is popularly known—a skull of an adult *Australo-pithecus africanus* that is more than 2-million years old. The find
reinforced the discovery of a skull of an *Australopithecus* child, the
"Taung Skull," by Prof. Raymond Dart in 1924, which was the first
hominid ever found. At the time, Dart was ostracized for claiming the
skull belonged to an early human ancestor. Scientists in Europe and the
United States simply didn't believe that humanity could have originated
in Africa. Today, few disagree with this theory. Another important find
was the discovery in the 1990s of "Little Foot," a near-complete skeleton of an Australopithecus, embedded in rock deep inside the caves.
Guided tours of the excavations and caves, which are spacious and not
claustrophobic, last an hour and leave on the half hour. Wear comfortable shoes. Before or after the tour, spend some time in the small
but excellent **Sterkfontein Visitor Centre**, which has exhibits depicting
the origins of the earth, life, and humanity. There's a small restaurant
that serves pleasant meals on-site (open Wednesday–Sunday). ⊠*Sterkfontein Caves Rd., off R563, Kromdraai* ☎*011/668–3200* ⊕*www.
maropeng.co.za* ⊠*R68* ☉*Daily 9–5; last tour departs at 4.*

The impressive **Maropeng Visitor Centre** comprises displays, interactive
exhibits, and even an underground boat ride through the elements of
water, air, wind, and fire that the kids will enjoy. Maropeng means
"returning to the place of origin" in Setswana, the area's main indigenous language. It's a one-stop tourist destination with restaurants, a
boutique hotel, arts-and-crafts market, and interpretive center, and
you can attend cultural events in its amphitheater. The exhibits are vast,
and are mostly housed in a giant underground chamber. A large area is
dedicated to human evolution, and the lifelike models of human ancestors draw much attention. Visit the Web site for a downloadable map
of the area. ⊠*R24, off R563, Kromdraai* ☎*014/577–9000* ⊕*www.
maropeng.co.za* ⊠*R80* ☉*Daily 9–5; last boat ride at 4.*

For more recent history, tour the **Old Kromdraai Gold Mine,** one of the
country's oldest gold mines, where gold was found in 1881. Frankly,
it's a little spooky. You don a miner's helmet and wander into the mine's
murky depths as part of one-hour guided tours, which leave on the
hour. It's not a difficult walk, and if you're lucky, you'll see bats roost-
ing. ⊠*Ibis Ridge Farm, Kromdraai Rd., Kromdraai* ☎*011/957–0205
or 011/957–0211* ⊠*R45* ☉*Weekends 9–5, last tour at 4, weekdays
by appointment.*

Rhinos, lions, wild dogs, cheetahs, hippos, and crocodiles are among
the animals you can see at the **Rhino and Lion Park.** You can spot about
600 head of game; visit the lion, wild dog, and cheetah enclosures (be
careful of lions approaching vehicles) or vulture blind; or be thrilled
by live snake shows on weekends and holidays. You can also visit the
endangered species breeding center (and the magnificent white lions)
or cuddle a baby animal at the nursery for young orphaned animals.

In addition to the self-driving tour, you can book an escorted game drive or horseback ride. The visitors' area has a pool, the Croc Pub and Diner, and a curio shop, as well as a small rest camp with three self-catering chalets. ⊠*Kromdraai Rd., Kromdraai* ☎*011/957–0109* ⊕*www.rhinolion.co.za* ⊠*R70* ⊙ *Weekdays 8–5, weekends 8–6.*

The **Wonder Cave** is a huge single-chamber cave with a number of intact stalagmites and stalactites and formations up to 50 feet high. An elevator takes regular guided tours all the way down, but if you're feeling adventurous you can rappel down (by prior arrangement only). You can also book evening tours. ⊠*Kromdraai Rd., Kromdraai* ☎*011/957– 0106 or 011/957–0109* ⊠*R45* ⊙ *Weekdays 8–5, weekends 8–6.*

WHERE TO STAY & EAT

★ **$$$$** ✗**The Carnivore.** Don't come expecting a quiet romantic dinner, as the huge space lends itself to a loud and sometimes frenetic scene. Game meat such as warthog, impala, and crocodile vies for space around an enormous open fire with tamer fare such as pork and mutton. Great hunks of meat are brought around to your table on Masai spears and carved directly onto your plate until you (literally) surrender by lowering the flag on your table. Vegetarians won't feel left out, with an excellent vegetarian à la carte menu featuring uniquely African dishes such as *aviyal* (a spicy mixed vegetable dish cooked in coconut milk). ⊠*Misty Hills Country Hotel, 69 Drift Blvd., Muldersdrift* ☎*011/950– 6000* ⊟*AE, DC, MC, V.*

$–$$ ✗◫ **The Cradle.** The forest camp in the Cradle conservation area has eight self-catering thatch A-frame cottages on the banks of a stream. Each cottage is fully equipped with a fridge, stove, dishes, and other necessities. Game drives and guided walks can be arranged. The Cradle restaurant has tables overlooking a 7,413 acre game reserve. The overall impression is one of space and silence. The frequently changing menu is impressive, too. Dishes include sage pork chops, lamb shank, veal saltimbocca (a sauce with white wine, vinegar, sage, and butter), and venison and pancetta stew. The extensive wine list has many local specialties. ⊠*Cradle of Humankind, Kromdraai Rd., Mogale City* ☎*011/659–1622* ⊕*www.thecradle.co.za* ⤶*8 cottages* ⌂*In-room: kitchen. In-hotel: restaurant* ⊟*AE, DC, MC, V.*

$$$ ◫ **Forum Homini.** As its overriding theme, this boutique hotel in a game estate in the Cradle of Humankind aptly alludes to the mysterious and fascinating story of the development of humanity. Artworks of bygone years adorn the walls and the modern architecture takes into account the landscape. The windows have sweeping views and natural veld (pronounced "felt")—long, African grasses—grows on the rooftops. Ideally located within the World Hertage Site, the hotel offers patrons visits to the Sterkfontein Caves and the Wonder Caves, famous for their stalactites and stalagmites. The superb in-house restaurant, Roots, specializes in French cooking. There's also a gallery and wine cellar on the property. ⊠*Letamo Game Estate, Bartlet Rd., Kromdraai, Mogale City* ☎*011/668–7000* ⊕*www.forumhomini.com* ⤶*14 rooms* ⌂*In-*

room: *Internet, safe, minibar. In-hotel: pool, restaurant, spa, room service* ⊟*AE, DC, MC, V* ⏀*BP.*

$$ ☒**Toadbury Hall.** This small country hotel is on lovely grounds. The rooms are predominantly white, enlivened with botanical prints; two rooms are given a New Orleans treatment. All rooms have under-floor heating, and bathrooms have separate showers and two sinks. ⊠*M5, Elandsdrift* ✆*Box 746, Muldersdrift 1747* ☎*011/659–0335* ⊕*www. toadburyhall.co.za* ⇆*5 rooms, 5 suites* ♿*In-hotel: restaurant, bar, tennis courts, pool, no kids under 12* ⊟*AE, DC, MC, V* ⏀*BP.*

SHOPPING

The **Crocodile Ramble** (☎*014/577–9323* ⊕*www.theramble.co.za*) is an arts, crafts, and restaurant route set up by local artists, potters, sculptors, and other craftspeople. It meanders through the Cradle of Humankind area on up to the Hartbeespoort Dam in the Magaliesberg. Whether you're shopping for jewelry, antiques, or art, or looking for a restaurant or pub, it's all on the Ramble. The Web site has a handy interactive road map.

THE MAGALIESBERG

The Magaliesberg mountains (or rolling hills) stretch 120 km (74 mi) between Pretoria and the town of Rustenburg, about a 90-minute drive northwest of Johannesburg. The South African War once raged here, and the remains of British blockhouses can still be seen. The region is most remarkable, however, for its natural beauty—grassy slopes cleft by ocher cliffs, streams running through the ferns, waterfalls plunging into pools, and dramatic rock formations. It's an outdoor lover's paradise: go hiking, mountain biking, or horseback riding; swim in crystal streams; picnic in one of the natural hideaways; or take a balloon flight at dawn followed by a champagne breakfast. It's also home to the large Hartbeespoort Dam, a water-sports hot spot.

TIMING & PRECAUTIONS

The main areas and attractions become extremely crowded on weekends. On Friday evenings and Sunday afternoons there's always a wait—sometimes an hour or more—to cross the one-way bridge over the Hartebeestport Dam.

WHAT TO SEE

★ The **De Wildt Cheetah Centre** is respected for its conservation and breeding programs. They offers three-hour guided tours in vehicles (included in the price of admission) and a guided walking trail. A beautiful stone lodge has nine guest rooms. No children under six are permitted. Book visits to the center in advance. ⊠*R513, near Hartbeespoort Dam* ☎*012/504–1921* ⊕*www.dewildt.org.za* ✑*R180, R280 including lunch* ☉*Tours Tues., Thurs., and weekends at 8:30 and 1:30.*

The **Elephant Sanctuary** is home to 10 of the big mammals. Advanced booking is essential. A small lodge sleeps up to 12. ⊠*Rustenburg Rd. (R112), about 2 km (1 mi) from Hartbeespoort Dam* ☎*012/258-0423* ⊕*www.elephantsanctuary.co.za* ⊠*R350 including a ride, or R325 for 1-hr interactive and educational session, R425 for 2-hr session* ⊙*Sessions daily at 8, 10, and 2.*

The **Snake and Animal Park** is not big (you can walk through in less than two hours) but has rare white lions, gray wolves, many primate species, and birds of prey. Its selection of reptiles is overwhelming. Snake cages line the walkways, containing anything from harmless little garden snakes to poisonous cobras and giant pythons. Keep an eye out for snake shows, especially on weekends. The park has a ferry restaurant on the dam and a tea garden. ⊠*1 Scott St., Hartbeespoort* ☎*012/253-1162* ⊕*www.hartbeespoortdam.com* ⊠*R50* ⊙*Daily 8-5.*

For a panoramic view from the top of the mountain range, take a ride on the **Hartbeespoort Cableway.** You can see the Hartbeespoort Dam on one side and the North West Province on the other. You can pack a picnic to enjoy on the mountain, where there's a small shop selling beer and snacks, and a few picnic tables, or eat afterward at the base station restaurant. ⊠*1 km (½ mi) from Brits turnoff on R511, Hartbeespoort* ☎*012/253-1706* ⊕*www.hartbeespoortdam.com/cableway* ⊠*R30* ⊙*Weekdays10-3:30, weekends 10-5.*

WHERE TO STAY & EAT

$$$ ✕🏠 **De Hoek Country House.** In France this exclusive establishment would be called an *auberge*, and the two-story stone-and-heavy-timber building along the river would not be out of place in Provence. De Hoek is in semi-indigenous gardens in the exquisite Magalies River valley. The quiet rooms have golden walls and dark mahogany furniture. Some of the superior suites have fireplaces, and all rooms have underfloor heating. Programs offered include archery, croquet, lawn bowling, and mountian walks. However, the food is what brings most people. Classic French techniques applied to contemporary ingredients result in an eclectic menu, with dinner (reservations essential) a five-course affair that changes daily according to ingredients available. Starters can include homemade tagliolini with shredded crab meat in a chili, cream, and tomato sauce, followed by roast rack of lamb rubbed with Moroccan-style spice served with curried vegetables, couscous and tamarind

sauce, and chocolate and coconut ice cream with a wafer teardrop, raspberry sauce, and chocolate garnish for dessert. ✉ *Off R24, north of Magaliesberg* 🖂 *Box 117, Magaliesberg 2805* 🕾 *014/577–1198* ⊕ *www.dehoek.com* 🛏 *4 rooms, 16 suites* ⚿ *In-hotel: pool, no elevator* ▤ *AE, DC, MC, V* ⍩*BP.*

$$–$$$ ✕⊞ **Budmarsh Country Lodge.** Surrounded by a lush garden in the heart of the Magaliesberg, this lodge has rooms with beautiful antique furniture. It's a good place for a river ramble or a mountain hike. Even if you don't stay overnight, drive through for dinner or a light lunch. It's a beautiful drive, and the always-changing menu is prepared by a master chef, Zhan Steyn. Dinner (reservations essential) is a six-course set menu of French-influenced cuisine that changes daily. ✉ *T1, off R24 Magaliesberg* 🖂 *Box 1453, Highlands North 2037* 🕾 *011/728–1800* ⊕ *www.budmarsh.co.za* 🛏 *18 rooms* ⚿ *In-hotel: restaurant, pool, no elevator* ▤ *AE, DC, MC, V* ⍩*BP.*

$$–$$$ ⊞ **Mount Grace Country House Hotel.** This village-style bed-and-breakfast near the town of Magaliesberg has accommodations in a variety of delightful country-style buildings. All have glorious views of the mountains, valley, and the landscaped gardens. The Mountain Village is the most luxurious lodging, with sunken baths and heated towel bars. For more privacy, stay at Grace Village, which is farther down the mountain. The most reasonable lodging is the Thatchstone Village. The food is wholesome country fare with a Mediterranean influence, and the Mount Grace is famous for its Sunday lunches. ✉ *R24 to Hekpoort, near Magaliesberg* 🖂 *Private Bag 5004, Magaliesberg 1791* 🕾 *014/577–1350* ⊕ *www.grace.co.za* 🛏 *81 rooms* ⚿ *In-room: refrigerator (some). In-hotel: 2 restaurants, bar, tennis court, pools, spa, bicycles* ▤ *AE, DC, MC, V* ⍩*BP.*

$ ✕⊞ **Goblin's Cove.** You can find this delightful little restaurant and hotel, the creation of sculptor Charles Gotthard, amid trees next to a river. It's made up like a fantasy fairy world, with three stories of little rooms, winding passageways, and stairs leading to colorful private alcoves and balconies. The restaurant has tasty, creative cuisine, such as South African sushi (made with springbok carpaccio), Thai chicken salad, and lime-marinated chicken breasts. A set menu (about R170) is offered on Sunday and holidays. The restaurant is open from Wednesday to Sunday, and bookings are essential. A small shop sells dream catchers, small fairy statues, and the like, and the Gobble D'Gook coffee shop serves homemade cakes on weekends and holidays. There are three B&B units in a restored vintage train car and two forest cabins. (Less than 10 km [6 mi] away and also operated by Gotthard are the smaller Out of Africa Guest Lodge, which has five two-story thatch cottages, and La Provence, which has seven suites, each with a lovely antique Victorian bath, in an old stone sculptor's studio.) ✉ *Off R24, Bekker School Rd., Box 98, Magaliesberg 1991* 🕾 *014/576–2143,014/577–1126 Out of Africa and La Provence* ⊕ *www.goblins.co.za* 🛏 *3 rooms, 2 cabins* ⚿ *In-hotel: restaurant, no elevator* ☉ *Open Wed. and Thurs. breakfast and lunch, Fri. and Sat. breakfast, lunch, and dinner, Sun. lunch only* ▤ *AE, DC, MC, V* ⍩*BP.*

$ ✕🏠**Lesedi Cultural Village.** This is not just a place to stay and eat; it's a place to learn about the cultures and history of South Africa's Basotho, Ndebele, Pedi, Xhosa, and Zulu nations. Daily shows of dancing and singing, tours of traditional homesteads, and a crafts market complement the dining, lodging, and conference facilities. The large Nyama Choma restaurant ($$–$$$$) serves food from all over the continent so you can taste North African fare, East African cuisine, or opt for a South African barbecue. Dishes include roast meats, porridge and vegetables, often cooked in traditional African three-legged iron pots. Most of the Africa-theme guest rooms have two beds. Packages can include breakfast, dinner, and the tours. ✉*R112, 12 km (7½ mi) north of Lanseria* ☎*012/205–1394 or 012/205–1395* ⊕*www.lesedi. com* 📶*38 rooms* 🛗*In-hotel: restaurant, bar* ⦿*BP.*

¢–$ 🏠**Valley Lodge.** Although it's too big to be called a hideaway, this B&B has a bird sanctuary, 250-acre nature reserve, and a stream running through it. The lodge is popular with corporate groups, but it's big enough to find quiet (the Nature Rooms offer the most privacy). It's also one of few hotels in the area that accept small children. Rooms have small sitting areas and some have four-poster beds and fireplaces; all have covered patios. ✉*Jennings St.* ✉*Box 13, Magaliesberg 1791* ☎*014/577–1301 or 014/577–1305* ⊕*www.valleylodge.co.za* 📶*68 rooms* 🛗*In-room: dial-up. In-hotel: restaurant, bar, tennis courts, pool, gym* ▱*AE, DC, MC, V* ⦿*BP.*

★ ¢ 🏠**Green Hills.** This romantic B&B is just right for a break from the city. Rooms are in three separate cottages in a lovely garden and have ceramic fireplaces. The bathrooms are spacious, with large showers and separate baths. Nothing is too much trouble for hosts Etaine and Sarah Hewitt, who make a delicious English breakfast every morning, as well as dinner, picnic hamper, or a braai by arrangement. ✉*T1, 11 km (7 mi) from Magaliesberg, after Bekker School Rd.* ✉*Box 286, Magaliesberg 1791* ☎*014/577–2063* ⊕*www.greenhills.co.za* 📶*3 cottages* 🛗*In-room: no TV* ▱*No credit cards* ⦿*BP.*

¢ 🏠**Jameson Country Cottages.** These pretty, well-appointed self-catering cottages can sleep four or six people and have stoves, fridges, TVs, and a good selection of culinary appliances. Set in an attractive garden around a pool and adjacent to a cane-furniture factory and shop, they offer excellent value for the money. A tea garden serves breakfast and lunch. ✉*R509 (Koster Rd.), 10 km (6 mi) from Magaliesberg* ✉*Box 96, Magaliesberg 1791* ☎*014/577–1361 or 083/301–5791* ⊕*www. westcane.co.za* 📶*6 cottages* 🛗*In-room: kitchen. In-hotel: pool* ▱*AE, DC, MC, V.*

☞ ★ ¢ 🏠**Mountain Sanctuary Park.** Don't let the rather terse list of rules at the entrance put you off; the owners are fiercely protective of their little piece of paradise—and justly so. This is a simple campsite, with spotless bath facilities, on-site trailers, and some basic but comfortable self-catering cottages with electricity, hot water, and cooking facilities. The emphasis is on the surrounding 2,200 acres of mountains, pools, waterfalls, and streams, where you can hike a different route every day—each more beautiful than the last. Pets and radios are forbidden, but children's laughter is welcome. ✉*40 km (25 mi) from Magaliesberg on*

6

dirt road, 15 km (9 mi) from N4 ☎014/534–0114 or 082/371–6146 ⊕www.mountain-sanctuary.co.za 🛏3 chalets, 3 trailers, 30 campsites ♨In-hotel: pool ▤No credit cards.

SHOPPING

Stretching from the Cradle of Humankind to the Magaliesberg area, the **Crocodile Ramble** (☎011/957–3745 ⊕www.theramble.co.za) includes restaurants, shops, and attractions. Most visitors amble around exploring the many crafts shops and studios and coffee shops.

The **Chameleon Village Lifestyle Junxion** (✉Hartebeespoort Dam ☎012/253–1451 ⊕www.chameleonvillage.co.za) has shops, fast-food outlets, and restaurants lined up alongside art studios. You can visit an ostrich show farm, a Bushman village, pet a pony (and put the kids on one), browse through the Crafters Junxion market, or enjoy live music on weekends. **Crystal Feeling** (✉Akasha Centre, 15 Rustenburg Rd., Magaliesberg ☎014/577–2182) has many fascinating decorative and healing crystals, dream catchers, books, and jewelry. The **Welwitschia Country Market** (✉R104 [Rustenburg Rd.], 2 km [1 mi] from Hartbeespoort Dam, at Doryn 4-way stop ☎083/302–8085 ⊕www.countrymarket.co.za) sells arts and crafts among other goodies at 38 little shops and three restaurants. At **Western Cane Trading** (✉R509, 10 km [6 mi] from Magaliesberg ☎014/577–1361 ⊕www.westcane.co.za) you can browse through a huge warehouse of cane, wood, and iron furniture. There's a good tea garden and even a driving range.

SUN CITY & PILANESBERG

SUN CITY

177 km (110 mi) northwest of Jo'burg.

Sun City is a huge entertainment and resort complex in the middle of dry bushveld in the North West Province. It's very popular with golfers and families, and South Africans and foreign tourists alike. It's the dream child of Sol Kerzner, the South African entrepreneur who first saw the possibilities of a casino in the rocky wilds of the Pilanesberg mountains, formed by an ancient volcano. The area was in the then Bantustan of Bophuthatswana—one of several areas during apartheid set aside for black ethnic groups, with a semblance of self-government. As such, it was exempt from South Africa's then strict anti-gambling laws. Today Sun City comprises four luxurious hotels, two casinos, major amphitheaters that host international stars, and a host of outdoor attractions. The complex is split into two parts: the original Sun City and Lost City, which is anchored by the magnificent Palace Hotel.

Though it's quite possible to enjoy a week at the resort without setting foot in a casino, Sun City has its slot machines, card tables, and roulette wheels. It stages rock concerts, major boxing bouts, the annual Sun City Golf Challenge, and the occasional Miss World pageant. At

Lost City, painted wild animals march across the ceilings, imitation star-spangled skies glitter even by day, lush jungles decorate the halls, and stone lions and elephants keep watch over it all.

Sun City's appeal is vastly enhanced by the nearby Pilanesberg National Park and a full round of outdoor sports and activities, including two Gary Player–designed world-class golf courses, elephant-back riding, archery, and surfing in the Valley of the Waves, a water park with a giant pool that creates perfect waves for bodysurfing.

Elsewhere the resort offers visits to the Motsaeng Cultural Village, a crocodile sanctuary, horseback riding, jogging trails, large botanical gardens, helicopter trips, balloon safaris, and the Zip 2000—the world's longest, highest, and fasted zip line. It's 2 km (1 mi) long and reaches speeds of 120 km/h (75 mi/h).

WHERE TO STAY & EAT

Accommodations in Sun City are generally expensive, and more so at the Palace—though the prices are probably worth it if you can afford them. You may opt to stay instead in the nearby rest camps and private lodges of Pilanesberg National Park, which are much more basic but pleasant. Kwa Maritane, an upmarket timeshare resort in the park, is worth staying at if you can get in.

There's a wide variety of dining options at Sun City and the Palace, from upmarket and glitzy to poolside cafés selling light meals like toasted sandwiches. Generally, though, they're all rather pricey.

★ $$$$ 📅**Palace of the Lost City.** You might think any hotel based on the concept of a lost African palace would suffer from theme-park syndrome, but happily that's not the case here. Sculpted cranes and leaping kudu appear to take flight from the hotel towers, elephants guard stairways and bridges, and graceful reminders of ersatz Africa strike you at every turn. No expense has been spared, and the attention to detail is mind-boggling. All rooms have hand-carved doors and furnishings, the jungle paintings on the ceiling of the lobby's rotunda took 5,000 hours to complete, and the hand-laid mosaic floor is made up of 300,000 separate tiles. Guest rooms, done in rich earth tones, blend African motifs with delicate Eastern touches. ✉ *Box 308, Sun City 0316* ☎ *014/557–3131, 011/780–7800 reservations* ⊕ *www.suninternational.com* 🛏 *338 rooms* 🔧 *In-hotel: 2 restaurants, room service, bars, pool* 🟰 *AE, DC, MC, V* ⧉ *BP.*

$$$-$$$$ 📅**Sun City Hotel and Casino.** This is the original Sun City property, and it still houses the gaming casino, banks of slot machines, and other gaming activities. If gambling and nonstop action are your scene, this will appeal to you, but otherwise it probably won't. The main room is decked out like a Tarzan jungle, with palms, artificial waterfalls, and rope walkways. The sound of rushing water drowns out the jangle of the slots somewhat, but it's still a somewhat lurid spectacle. Thankfully, the rooms are more sedate. ✉ *Box 2, Sun City 0316* ☎ *014/552–1001, 011/780–7800 reservations* 🛏 *340 rooms* ⊕ *www.suninternational.com* 🔧 *In-hotel: 4 restaurants, room service, bars, pool* 🟰 *AE, DC, MC, V* ⧉ *BP.*

$$ ⊡ **The Cabanas.** Paths thread through pleasant gardens to rooms in small apartment blocks overlooking a manmade lake. Though small, the rooms are clean and cheerful, with tile floors, bright bedspreads, and sliding glass doors that open onto the lawns. All have TV, tea/coffeemakers, and air-conditioning. The hotel is popular with families. ⊡*Box 3, Sun City 0316* ☎*014/557–1000, 011/780–7800 central reservations* ⇌*380 rooms* ⌂*In-hotel: 2 restaurants, bars, pool* ▭*AE, DC, MC, V* ⎮⊙⎮*BP.*

⟳ $$ ⊡ **Santorini.** At this Cascades Hotel restaurant you can dine beside a sparkling pool and surrounded by lush tropical gardens and cascading waterfalls. The pool deck is relaxed and casual, while inside is more formal, although the menu is the same. The restaurant has a reasonably priced menu and wine list and consistently good food. Start with homemade bread and traditional Greek dips, followed by calamari grilled with olive oil, lemon juice, garlic, oregano, and a hint of chili, or slovaki—sirloin skewers marinated in garlic, mint, coriander, and lemon juice served with tzatziki. The Amarula crème brûlée, made with a South African liqueur, is a sweet way to finish. There's also a good children's menu. ☎*014/557–3131 or 011/780–7800* ⊙*Daily 10–5* ▭*AE, DC, MC, V.*

PILANESBERG

150 km (93 mi) northwest of Jo'burg.

The 150,000-acre **Pilanesberg National Park** is centered on the caldera of an extinct volcano dating back 1,200 million years, and which may well have once been Africa's highest peak. Concentric rings of mountains surround a lake filled with crocodiles and hippos. Open grassland, rocky crags, and densely forested gorges provide ideal habitats for a wide range of plains and woodland game, including rare brown hyenas, sables, and gemsbok. Since the introduction of lions in 1993, Pilanesberg (pronounced "Pee-luns-berg") can boast the Big Five. It's one of the best places in the country to see rhinos, and is a bird-watcher's paradise, with a vast range of grassland species, waterbirds, and birds of prey. A huge plus is that this reserve is in a malaria-free area, unlike many of the reserves in Mpumalanga, including the Kruger National Park. You can drive around the park in your own vehicle or join guided safaris with Pilanesberg Safaris (⇨*Johannesburg & Environs Essentials, below*).

WHERE TO STAY

★ $$$$ ⊡ **Tshukudu Game Lodge.** The most stylish option in the area, Tshukudu is built into the side of a steep, rocky hill and overlooks open grassland and a large water hole where elephants bathe. If you watch long enough, you can probably see most of the Big Five from your veranda. Winding stone stairways lead up the hill to thatch cottages with private balconies, wicker furniture, African materials, and black-slate floors. Fireplaces and mosquito nets are standard, and sunken bathtubs have spectacular views of the water hole. It's a long, 132-step climb to the main lodge on the summit, making this an impractical choice for those with mobility problems. At night you can use a spotlight to illuminate game at the water hole below. ⊠ *Pilanesberg National Park, Box 6805, Rustenburg 0300* ☎ *014/552–6255, 011/806–6888 reservations* ⊕ *www.legacyhotels.co.za* ⬎ *6 chalets* ♿ *In-hotel: pool, restaurant, no elevator* ☰ *AE, DC, MC, V.*

☾ ★ $$$ 🏨 **Kwa Maritane.** This hotel, primarily a timeshare resort, is in a bowl of rocky hills on the edge of the national park—definitely its greatest asset. It's best to secure a unit far from the reception, dining, and pool area. The resort has a terrific blind, overlooking a water hole and connected to the lodge via a tunnel, and TVs in the rooms have a channel dedicated to watching what's there round the clock. Guest rooms have high thatch ceilings, air conditioning, and large glass doors that open onto a veranda. You can pay to go on day or night game drives in open-air vehicles or to go on guided walks with an armed ranger—both worthwhile. The breakfasts at the restaurant are legendary. ⊠ *Pilanesberg National Park* 🖃 *Box 39, Sun City 0316* ☎ *014/552–5100, 011/806–6888 reservations* ⊕ *www.legacyhotels.co.za* ⬎ *90 rooms* ♿ *In rooms: kitchen, refrigerator. In-hotel: restaurant, bar, pools, no elevator* ☰ *AE, DC, MC, V* ⦿ *BP.*

$$–$$$ 🏨 **Bakubung.** Abutting the national park, this lodge sits at the head of a long valley with terrific views of a hippo pool that forms the lodge's central attraction—it's not unusual to have hippos grazing 100 feet from the terrace restaurant. Despite this, the lodge never really succeeds in creating a bush feel, perhaps because it's such a big convention and family destination. Its brick buildings feel vaguely institutional. Nevertheless, the guest rooms, particularly the executive studios, are very pleasant, thanks to light pine furniture, colorful African bedspreads, and super views of the valley. The lodge conducts game drives in open-air vehicles, as well as ranger-guided walks. A shuttle bus (R40 round-trip) runs to Sun City, 10 km (6 mi) away. ⊠ *Bakubung Gate, Pilanesberg National Park* 🖃 *Box 294, Sun City 0316* ☎ *014/552–6000, 011/806–6800 reservations* ⊕ *www.legacyhotels.co.za* ⬎ *76 rooms, 56 timeshare chalets* ♿ *In-hotel: restaurant, bar, tennis court, pool, no elevator* ☰ *AE, DC, MC, V* ⦿ *BP.*

$–$$ 🏨 **Manyane.** This resort is in a thinly wooded savanna east of the Pilanesberg's volcanic ridges. Offering affordable accommodations in the Sun City area, Manyane is simple, but well located, efficiently run and clean. Thatch roofing helps soften the harsh lines of bare tile floors and brick. You can choose either a two- or four-bed chalet, all with fully equipped small kitchens and bathrooms, and the camping facilities are also very popular. Self-guided nature trails lead from the chalets, providing interesting background on the geology and flora of the park. You can also take advantage of the outdoor chess and trampoline. ⊠ *Pilanesberg National Park, Rustenburg 0300* ☎ *014/555–1000* ⊕ *www.goldenleopard.co.za* ⬎ *30 4-sleeper chalets and 15 2-sleeper chalets* ♿ *In-room: kitchen. In-hotel: restaurant, bar, pools* ☰ *AE, DC, MC, V* ⦿ *BP.*

6

JOHANNESBURG & ENVIRONS ESSENTIALS

To research prices, get advice from other travelers, and book travel arrangements, visit www.fodors.com.

TRANSPORTATION

BY AIR

O.R. Tambo International Airport (formerly Johannesburg International Airport) is Africa's busiest airport. More than 17 million travelers pass through every year. It's about 19 km (12 mi) from Johannesburg and is linked to the city by a fast highway, which is always busy, but especially so before 9 AM and 4–7 PM, when commuters use it most. Most international flights depart from this airport, which has been refurbished in the last several years and now looks a bit like an upscale mall. There's a tourist information desk in the international arrivals terminal, and the domestic terminal offers a slew of restaurants and coffee shops. There's also a duty-free mall and V.A.T. refund office. You can also leave your bags at Lock-Up Luggage, which is one level below international departures. It costs about $5 per bag per day. Information and airport maps can be obtained from the ACSA Web site. Flight and general information is available from the airport itself. There are a number of hotels near the airport, as well as one within the airport precinct.

Expect long lines at check-in counters in the early evening, when many long-distance flights depart, but the lines move quickly; it shouldn't take more than a half hour to get through. Baggage claim usually takes about 15 minutes. The airport has its own police station, but security has been a problem in recent years, with many people's baggage being stolen either in transit or even within the airport itself. Be vigilant and keep your belongings close and within your sight at all times.

Major airlines serving Johannesburg include Air Namibia, British Airways, KLM Royal Dutch Airlines, Qantas, Singapore Airlines, South African Airways, and Virgin Atlantic, among others. In addition to South African Airways, the major domestic carriers serving Johannesburg are British Airways, operated by Comair, and SA Airlink. In the past few years several good-quality, low-cost domestic airlines have sprung up, and all are worth flying—they tend to have less legroom and smaller seats, and you will need to pay for snacks on board, but they're usually considerably cheaper than SAA and its affiliates.

GROUND TRANSFERS
Magic Bus operates a minibus service that connects to all the major hotels in Sandton. It runs all day on the half hour, costs R110, and takes 30 minutes to an hour. Airport Link will ferry you anywhere in Johannesburg in a Toyota Camry or Mercedes minibus for R255 per person. Wilro Tours charges R465 to Sandton for three people. In addition, scores of licensed taxis line up outside the airport terminal. By law they must have a working meter. Expect to pay about R250–R350 for a trip to Sandton. If you're transferring directly between a train or an intercity bus and the airport, head to the Rotunda; the main

hub for airport shuttles, it's outside the Johannesburg train station at Leyds and Loveday streets. It's not a particularly safe area, so avoid it if you can.

Airlines **American Airlines** (☎ *021/440–6440*). **British Airways** (☎ *011/441–8600*). **KLM Royal Dutch Airlines** (☎ *011/881–9696*). **Qantas** (☎ *011/441–8550*). **SA Airlink** (flies to some of the smaller, out-of-the-way domestic locations; ☎ *011/978–1111*). **Singapore Airlines** (☎ *011/880–8566*). **South African Airways** (☎ *011/978–1111*). **Virgin Atlantic** (☎ *011/340–3400*).

Airport **ACSA** (⊕ *www.acsa.co.za*). **O.R. Tambo International Airport** (☎ *086/727–7888 help line*).

Airport Transfers **Airport Link** (☎ *011/792-2017 or 083/625-5090* ⊕ *www.airportlink.co.za*). **Magic Bus** (☎ *011/548–0822* ⊕ *www.magicbus.co.za*). **Wilro Tours** (☎ *011/789–9688* ⊕ *www.wilrotours.co.za*).

Low-Cost Domestic Airlines **Kulula.com** (☎ *0861/585–852* ⊕ *www.kulula.com*). **Mango** (☎ *0861/162–646* ⊕ *www.flymango.com*). **1Time** (☎ *0861/345–345* ⊕ *www.1time.co.za*).

BY BUS

Intercity buses depart from Braamfontein's Rotunda, the city's principal transportation hub, opposite the main train station at Leyds and Loveday streets. It's a reasonably well-run operation, but gets quite busy and is not in a very safe area—avoid it at night. Be attentive at all times—tourists are sometimes mugged here. Greyhound and Translux operate extensive routes around the country. Intercape Mainliner runs to Cape Town. The Baz Bus does not depart from the Rotunda but operates a hop-on, hop-off door-to-door service, stopping at backpackers' hostels between Johannesburg and Durban or Jo'burg and Cape Town on two routes—via the Drakensberg or via Swaziland.

Bus Lines **Baz Bus** (☎ *021/439–2323* ⊕ *www.bazbus.com*). **Greyhound** (☎ *083/915-9000, 083/915-8000 Computicket* ⊕ *www.greyhound.co.za*). **Intercape Mainliner** (☎ *0861/287-287, 083/915-8000 Computicket* ⊕ *www.intercape.co.za*). **Translux** (☎ *0861/589-282, 083/915-8000 Computicket* ⊕ *www.translux.co.za*).

BY CAR

Traveling by car is the easiest way to get around Johannesburg, as the city's public transportation is not that reliable or extensive. The general speed limit for city streets is 60 kph (37 mph), for main streets it's often 80 kph (50 mph), and for highways it's 100 kph or 120 kph (62 mph or 75 mph). Be warned, though: Jo'burgers are known as the most aggressive drivers in the country, and minibus taxis are famous for not obeying the rules of the road. Most city roads are in good condition, with plenty of signage, and main roads in the countryside are also very passable. Street names are sometimes visible only on the curb, however. Try to avoid driving in rush hours, 7–8:30 AM and 4–6:30 PM, as the main roads become terribly congested. Gas stations are plentiful in most areas. (Don't pump your own gas though, every station employs operators to do that for you.)

Almost everywhere there are security guards who look after parked cars, as street parking is always risky because of car burglaries. It's customary to give these guards a small tip when you return to your car. Most big shopping centers have parking garages, where you pay about R5 per hour.

Most visitors need concern themselves only with the city center and the northern suburbs. The city center is laid out in a grid, making it fairly easy to get around if you can keep track of the many one-way streets. ⚠️**It's not advisable to tour the area on foot, except in groups or with a local guide.** If you plan to drive yourself around, get a *good* map or buy or rent a GPS (for hire at the airport and most car-rental agencies). Map-Studio prints excellent complete street guides, available at bookstores, and tourism operators often have maps of the area.

Major rental agencies have offices in the northern suburbs and at the airport. Most are open 24/7.

Rental Companies **Avis** (✉ *167A Rivonia Rd., Sandton* ☎ *011/884–2221* ✉ *O. R. Tambo International Airport* ☎ *011/394–5433* ⊕ *www.avis.co.za*). **Budget** (✉ *Holiday Inn Crowne Plaza, Rivonia Rd. and Grayston Dr., Sandton* ☎ *011/883–5730* ✉ *O. R. Tambo International Airport* ☎ *011/394–2905* ⊕ *www.budget.co.za*). **Europcar** (✉ *Sandton Holiday Inn Garden Court, Maude and West Sts., Sandton* ☎ *011/883–8508* ✉ *O. R. Tambo International Airport* ☎ *011/394–8832* ⊕ *www.europcar.co.za*). **Hertz** (✉ *Sandton Hilton, Rivonia Rd. at Chaplin St., Sandton* ☎ *011/322–1598* ✉ *O. R. Tambo International Airport* ☎ *011/390–9700* ⊕ *www.hertz.co.za*). **Imperial** (✉ *Sandton Sun hotel, 5th St. and Alice La., Sandton* ☎ *011/883–4352* ✉ *O. R. Tambo International Airport* ☎ *011/390–3909* ⊕ *www.imperialcarrental.co.za*). **Tempest Car Hire** (✉ *Village Walk, Maude St., Sandton* ☎ *011/784–3343* ✉ *O. R. Tambo Airport International* ☎ *011/394–8626* ⊕ *www.tempestcarhire.co.za*).

BY TAXI

The city has a great number of minibus taxis, which form the backbone of Jo'burg's transportation. They're very cheap and run on main routes; often, however, they're not roadworthy, and drivers can be very irresponsible, so you ought to avoid using them. Also, there's no real way to know where these taxis go without stopping one and asking. Car taxis, which are much more expensive, have taxi stands at the airport, the train station, and the Rotunda, but otherwise you must phone for a cab. They don't tend to drive around waiting for a fare. Taxis should be licensed and have a working meter. Ask the taxi company how long it will take the taxi to get to you. The meter starts at R2 and clicks over at a rate of R8 per kilometer. Expect to pay about R150–R240 to the airport from town or Sandton and about R120 to the city center from Sandton.

Taxi Companies **Maxi Taxi** (☎ *011/648–1212*). **Rose Taxis** (☎ *011/403–9625 or 011/403–0000* ⊕ *www.rosetaxis.com*).

BY TRAIN

Johannesburg's train station is opposite the Rotunda in Braamfontein, at Leyds and Loveday streets. The famous, luxurious *Blue Train,* which makes regular runs to Cape Town, departs from here, as do Shosholoza Meyl trains to cities around the country, including the *Trans-Karoo* to Cape Town, the *Komati* to Nelspruit in Mpumalanga, and the *Trans-Natal* to Durban. Many of these trains have overnight service, but they're not terribly comfortable because they can get crowded. There's no air-conditioning, but you can open the window.

Train Lines **Blue Train** (☎ *012/334–8459* ⊕ *www.bluetrain.co.za*). **Shosholoza Meyl** (☎ *086/000–8888* ⊕ *www.spoornet.co.za*).

CONTACTS & RESOURCES

EMBASSY
U.S. Embassy (✉ *877 Pretorius St., Arcadia, Tshwane* ☎ *012/431–4000*).

EMERGENCIES
In the event of a medical emergency, seek help at one of the city's private hospitals. Among the most reputable are Milpark Hospital and Sandton Medi-Clinic. You'll find pharmacies all over the city, but when in doubt, there are pharmacies in every Clicks and Dischem store located in shopping complexes citywide.

Emergency Services **Ambulance** (☎ *999 or 011/375–5911*). **General Emergencies** (☎ *10111 from landline, 112 from mobile line*). **Police** (☎ *10111*).

Hospitals **Milpark Hospital** (✉ *9 Guild Rd., off Empire Rd., Parktown* ☎ *011/480–5600*). **Sandton Medi-Clinic** (✉ *Main St. and Peter Pl., off William Nicol Dr., Lyme Park* ☎ *011/709–2000*).

Pharmacies **Brug Pharmacy** (✉ *Jacob and Frads Sts., Rietfontein, Tshwane* ☎ *012/329–2664*). **Bruma Pharmacy** (✉ *Bruma Boardwalk, Bruma* ☎ *011/622–1472*).

MAIL & INTERNET
Internet Cafés **Milky Way** (✉ *Rosebank pedestrian boulevard, Rosebank* ☎ *011/447–1295*). **SOHO on 4th** (✉ *At 4th Ave. and 10th St., Parkhurst* ☎ *011/880–1523*). **Odyssey Internet Cafe** (✉ *CL5 Village Walk Shopping Centre, Sandton* ☎ *011/884–0377*).

Post Offices **Johannesburg** (✉ *Jeppe and Small Sts., City Center, 2000* ☎ *011/336–1361*). **Sandton** (✉ *5th Ave., Sandton, inside Sandton City, 2146* ☎ *011/783–7364*). **Pretoria** (✉ *Church Sq., Pretoria, 0001* ☎ *012/339–8000*).

TOURS
GENERAL-INTEREST TOURS Springbok Atlas and Gold Reef City Tours offer two- to three-hour tours (including self-drive tours) of Johannesburg that include visits to the city center, Soweto, the Apartheid Museum, Gold Reef City, and some of the city's more interesting parks and suburbs. Other tours explore Tshwane; Cullinan, including a working mineshaft; Sun City; and Pilanesberg National Park. Tour fees start around R350 per person for half-day tours and R150 per person for five-hour game drives. Wilro Tours conducts various tours to Soweto, Johannesburg, and the Pilanesberg. The Johannesburg Tourism Company has customized

tours (golf anyone?) that include visits to the Apartheid Museum, the Tswaing Meteorite Crater, and Soweto. The company also has information on the city's accommodations, sights, nightlife, and restaurants. Observer Tours and Charters will do tailor-made, chauffeur-driven tours for one or two people or small groups, costing up to R1,200 for an eight-hour tour of the city. It also has shorter tours to Soweto and Tshwane. JMT Tours and Safaris can arrange trips to Soweto, Sun City, the Lesedi Cultural Village in Magaliesberg, or Kruger National Park and other destinations. Parktown–Westcliff Heritage Trust offers tours of the area's gardens and homes (the exteriors, anyway), as well as theme tours throughout Johannesburg such as mining and the South African (Anglo-Boer) War.

The Adventure Bus is an excellent way to see Johannesburg's main sights in about three hours, with plenty of stops. Tours leave several times a day from Sandton (except Monday). Your ticket is valid for 24 hours, so you can jump on and off as many times as you like. For something completely different, try the Mystery Ghost Bus Tour (5½ hr tour R195; 2½ hr tour R80), which stops at haunted houses (and lively pubs). You can book these tours through Computicket.

Africa Explore offers full-day and half-day tours of the Cradle of Humankind area; the full package (from R780 per person sharing per day) includes the Kromdraai Gold Mine, Sterkfontein Caves, and Rhino and Lion Park. Palaeo-Tours runs full- and half-day trips to local paleontological sites.

If you choose not to drive around Pilanesberg National Park on your own, you can join a 2½-hour escorted safari with Pilanesberg Mankwe Safaris for R230. Or you can embark on an elephant safari offered by Game Trackers Outdoor Adventures, offered three times daily for R1,090. The outfit also has balloon safaris. Kids under 5 are not allowed, and the maximum number of riders is 10. A one-hour flight (R2,750 per person) includes a game drive, sparkling wine, and a full English breakfast at the Bakubung game lodge. Bookings are essential.

Tour Operators **Adventure Bus** (☎ 011/975–9338). **Africa Explore** (☎ 011/917– 1999 ⊕ www.africa-explore.co.za). **Game Trackers Outdoor Adventures** (☎ 014/552–5020 ⊕ www.gametrac.co.za). **Gold Reef City Tours** (☎ 011/917– 1999). **JMT Tours and Safaris** (☎ 011/980–6038 ⊕ www.jmttours.co.za). **Johannesburg Tourism Company** (☎ 011/214–0700 ⊕ www.joburgtourism.com). **Mystery Ghost Bus Tour** (☎ 083/915–8000 Computicket ⊕ www.mysteryghost-bus.co.za). **Observer Tours and Charters** (☎ 011/609–4752). **Palaeo-Tours** (☎ 011/726–8788 ⊕ www.palaeotours.com). **Parktown–Westcliff Heritage Trust** (☎ 011/482–3349 ⊕ www.parktownheritage.co.za). **Pilanesberg Mankwe Safaris** (☎ 014/555–7056 ⊕ www.mankwesafaris.co.za). **Springbok Atlas** (☎ 011/396–1053 ⊕ www.springbokatlas.com). **Wilro Tours** (☎ 011/789–9688 ⊕ www.wilrotours.co.za).

DIAMOND &
GOLD TOURS Mynhardts Diamonds, which sells diamonds and jewelry, gives audiovisual presentations by appointment. Schwartz Jewellers conducts one-hour tours of its workshops in Sandton by appointment. You can see

Mining Diamonds

Anyone can go to a jewelry store and bring home South African diamonds, but how many people can say they got their sparkler from an actual mine? At **Cullinan Diamond Mine** (✉ *Mine: Oak Ave., west of Olienhout Ave.; Cullinan Tours: 95 Oak Ave., Cullinan* ☎ *012/734–0260*), not only can you buy diamonds, but you can get custom-made pieces from the resident jeweler, though don't expect your piece to include the world's largest diamond—the 3,106-carat Cullinan diamond unearthed here in 1905 is now in the Crown Jewels in London.

If you're interested in checking out the mine, tours are offered every day, ranging from the standard mine tour (R50, weekdays at 10 and 2:30, week-ends at 10 and noon) to the four-hour underground tour (R400, daily at 8 AM); we suggest the underground tour—you get to experience what it's like being underground and see the miners' working conditions. It's essential to reserve tours in advance. No children under 10 are permitted on the standard tour and no children under 16 are permitted on the underground tour.

If looking at all those carats makes you hungry, Cullinan's delightful old Victorian mine director's house has been turned into a guesthouse and tea garden. **Oak House** (✉ *103 Oak Ave.* ☎ *012/305–2364*) serves breakfast, lunches, and afternoon teas from 8 daily.

6

stone grading, diamond setting, and gold pouring, and, of course, you can buy the finished product. Tours are free and include refreshments, and you need to take your passport along for security reasons.

Tour Operators Mynhardts Diamonds (☎ *011/484–1717* ⊕ *www.mynhardts. com*). **Schwartz Jewellers** (☎ *011/783–1717* ⊕ *www.schwartzjewellers.com*).

TOWNSHIP TOURS Tours of Soweto are offered by many of the above operators as well as Jimmy's Face to Face Tours. Information on Soweto tours can also be obtained from the Soweto Tourism Association and Soweto.co.za.

Tour Information Jimmy's Face to Face Tours (☎ *011/331–6109* ⊕ *www. face2face.co.za*). **Soweto.co.za** (☎ *011/326–1600* ⊕ *www.soweto.co.za*). **Soweto Tourism Association** (☎ *011/938–3337*).

WALKING TOURS Walk Tours offers tours of the city center, Kensington, Parktown, and Melville Koppies, as well as "dinner hops," a dinner tour with stops all over town. Group tours can be arranged for eight or more, and electronic self-guiding systems are available.

Tour Operator Walk Tours (☎ *011/444–1639* ⊕ *www.walktours.co.za*).

Mpumalanga & Kruger National Park

WORD OF MOUTH

"After falling asleep to the sounds of hippos and frogs, I woke up to the sounds of the birds . . . and then to a loud banging and clanging. It was the baboons making their morning rounds, emptying the contents of every metal trash can in Kruger."

—Lisa

Updated by
Kate Turkington

IN MANY WAYS MPUMALANGA ("where the sun rises") is South Africa's wildest and most exciting province. Its local history is action-packed: local wars, international battles, and a gold rush every bit as raucous and wild as those in California and the Klondike. Legend has it that you can still find a few old-time prospectors panning for gold in the rivers and streams of the Pilgrim's Rest area.

Kruger National Park and the private game reserves abutting its western borders provide the country's best and most fulfilling game experience; in fact, it's highly probable that you will see all of the Big Five during an average two- to three-night stay at one of the private reserves.

ORIENTATION & PLANNING

ORIENTATION

Mpumalanga spreads east from Gauteng to the border of Mozambique. The 1,120-km (700-mi) Drakensberg Range, which originates in KwaZulu-Natal, divides the high, interior plateau from a low-lying subtropical belt that stretches to Mozambique and the Indian Ocean. The lowveld (the subtropical region of northeastern South Africa), where Kruger National Park alone covers a 320-km (200-mi) swath of wilderness, is classic Africa, with as much heat, dust, untamed bush, and big game as you can take in.

The Drakensberg Escarpment rises to the west of Kruger and provides a marked contrast to the lowveld; it's a mountainous area of trout streams and waterfalls, endless views, and giant plantations of pine and eucalyptus. Lower down, the forests give way to banana, mango, and papaya groves. People come to the escarpment to hike, unwind, soak up its beauty, and get away from the summer heat of the lowveld. Touring the area by car is easy and rewarding, and you can reach many of the best lookouts without stepping far from your car.

MPUMALANGA (MM-PUMA-LANGA)
Mpumalanga offers a wealth of activities, from poking around cultural villages and hiking on mountain trails to driving through game reserves. The best way to get around Mpumalanga is by car, either from Johannesburg or from the airports at Nelspruit, Hoedspruit, or Phalaborwa (if you're going into the central section of Kruger). Plan your road trip with booked-in-advance accommodations (there are superb options all over the province), and visit at least one of the farm stalls that dot country roads for fresh fruit and veggies (in season), nuts, and creamy farm milk.

KRUGER NATIONAL PARK
Larger than Israel and approximately the same size as Wales, Kruger National Park encompasses diverse terrain ranging from rivers filled with crocodiles and hippos to rocky outcrops where leopards lurk and thick thorn scrub shelters lions and buffalo. Roaming this slice of quintessential Africa are animals in numbers large enough to make a

TOP REASONS TO VISIT MPUMALANGA

Classic Africa Apart from the tarred roads and rest camps, Kruger Park is the legendary Africa of Dr. Livingstone, the Rain Queen, and Karen Blixen, where countless animals, birds, insects, and reptiles freely roam the plains, rivers, and forests.

Discovery Channel Comes Alive From grasses and flowers to trees and shrubs, from comical dung beetles to gaudy butterflies, from tiny colorful lizards to huge dozing crocodiles, from dainty bushbuck to giant giraffes, from leaping bush babies to languorous lions, you'll marvel at them all.

A Total Escape When you're steeped in the bush, watching that approaching elephant or a pod of harrumphing hippos, you'll forget all the pressures of today's living.

Safari Opulence Stay for a couple of nights at one of Sabi Sands' private game reserves. You're guaranteed luxury accommodation, impeccable service, and probably Big Five sightings. Kids are usually welcome, but check before you book.

Blyde River Canyon The gigantic rocks, deep gorges, and high mountains of the Three Rondawels create one of South Africa's great scenic highlights.

conservationist squeal with delight: in all, there are nearly 150 mammal species and more than 500 species of birds.

PLANNING

Where you stay on the escarpment may well dictate the kind of weather you get. High up, around Pilgrim's Rest and Sabie, the weather can be chilly, even in summer. Pack a sweater whatever the season. At these elevations fog and mist can be a hazard, especially while driving. On the other hand, the lowveld, especially in summer, is downright sultry.

Kruger National Park is hellishly hot in midsummer (November–March), with afternoon rain a good possibility, though mostly in the form of heavy short showers that don't interfere with game-viewing for long. If you plan your drives in the early morning (when the gates first open) or in the late afternoon, you will manage even if you are extremely heat sensitive. ■TIP➔**Don't drive with the windows up and the air conditioner on—you'll cocoon yourself from the reason you're there.** In summer the bush is green, the animals are sleek and glossy, and the birdlife is prolific, but high grasses and dense foliage make spotting animals more difficult. Also, because there's plenty of surface water about, animals don't need to drink at water holes and rivers, where it's easy to see them. There are also more mosquitoes around then, but you'll need to take malaria prophylactics whatever time of year you visit.

In winter (May through September), the bush is at its dullest, driest, and most colorless, but the game is much easier to spot, as many trees are bare, grasses are low, and animals congregate around the few available permanent water sources. Besides, watching a lion or leopard pad across an arid but starkly beautiful landscape could be the highlight of your trip. It gets very cold in winter (temperatures can drop to almost freezing at night and in the very early morning), so wear layers of warm clothes you can shed as the day gets hotter. Lodges sometimes drop their rates during winter (except July), because many foreign tourists prefer to visit in the South African summer months, which coincide with the northern hemisphere winter.

Spring (September and October) and autumn (March to early May) are a happy compromise. The weather is very pleasant—warm and sunny but not too hot—and there are fewer people around. In October migratory birds will have arrived, and in November many animals give birth. In April some migrating birds are still around, and the annual rutting season will have begun, when males compete for females and are often more visible and active.

TAKING IT ALL IN

If you have more than a handful of days in the area, split them between the mountain scenery of the escarpment and wildlife viewing in the lowveld. You could complete a tour of the Drakensberg Escarpment area in two days, but you're better off budgeting three or more if you plan to linger anywhere. To take in parts of Kruger National Park or one of the private game lodges, which are simply a must, add another three days or more.

3 Days: One of the prime reasons for visiting Mpumalanga is for big game, so fly into the airport nearest your destination and either rent a vehicle and take off into Kruger or get picked up by the private game lodge of your choice. Driving anywhere else in such a short time is not really an option.

5 Days: Your biggest decision will be how much time to spend wildlife-watching and how much to spend exploring the escarpment and its historic towns. A good suggestion is two days for the mountains and three in Kruger. Driving from Johannesburg, plan an overnight in Sabie after driving the awesome Long Tom Pass. The next day, head to the former mining town of Pilgrim's Rest and soak up some of the colorful local history, but make sure you get to Kruger or your private lodge in time for the afternoon game drive. Spend the night at Pilgrim's Rest or in the vicinity, and start out early the next morning for Blyde River Canyon, with its hiking trails and magnificent escarpment scenery. Then it's off to Kruger, Sabi Sands, Manyeleti, or Timbavati game reserves.

7 to 10 Days: Spend four or more days in the bush—half at Kruger and half at a private lodge, perhaps. A minimum of two nights at either one is non-negotiable. Then split the rest of your time between the escarpment and the lowveld outside Kruger, as in the previous itinerary.

HEALTH & SAFETY

The lowveld area, which stretches from Malelane (east of Nelspruit) to Komatipoort, on the Mozambique border, and up throughout Kruger National Park, is a malarial zone, and you should take antimalarial drugs. Note: malaria prophylactics may be unsuitable for children under six. Consult your doctor regarding the best options when plan-

Mpumalanga & Kruger National Park

ning your trip. ■TIP→ Prevention is the best medicine: at dawn and dusk, smother yourself with insect repellent, and wear long sleeves, long pants, socks, and covered shoes. The private camps all have mosquito (*mozzie*) nets, but not Kruger, so spray yourself again before you go to sleep.

ON THE CHEAP

If you're watching your pennies, look into staying at regular hotels, B&Bs, or self-catering (with cooking facilities) places instead of the luxury lodges.

EAT RIGHT, SLEEP WELL

Because Mpumalanga is a sought-after tourist destination, its culinary scene keeps getting better and better, both in *larney* (South African slang for "posh") restaurants and attractive cafés. Cuisines range from Mediterranean to Pan-African, and many places serve local delicacies such as fresh trout, venison, Cape Malay favorites such as *bobotie* (a spicy meat-and-egg dish), and curries.

Food is cheap and cheerful in Kruger's cafeterias and restaurants, and usually excellent in the private game lodges. Dinner is eaten 7:30-ish, and it's unlikely you'll get a meal in a restaurant after 9. The more larney the restaurant, the more formal the dress, with "smart casual" the norm. In Kruger you might put on clean clothes for an evening meal in a restaurant, but that's how formal it gets. After an exciting night game drive in a private reserve, you'll want to change or at least freshen up, but keep the clothes very casual. Wear long sleeves and long pants because of mosquitoes. Many higher-end restaurants close on Monday, and it's always advisable to make reservations at these in advance.

You may be in darkest Africa, but you'll be amazed by the very high standards you'll encounter for both service and accommodations. The latter range from fairly basic in the Kruger Park huts to the ultimate in luxury at most of the private camps. You may forget that you are in the bush until an elephant strolls past. The advantage of a private lodge (apart from superb game-viewing) is that often everything is included—lodging, meals, beverages including excellent house wines, game drives, and other activities. The price categories used for lodging in this chapter treat all-inclusive lodges differently than other lodgings; see the price chart below for details. It's essential to note that there are no elevators in any lodging facility in Mpumalanga or in Kruger.

Prices at most guest establishments on the escarpment include a three- to five-course dinner plus a full English breakfast. Most places have at least one vegetarian course on the menu. Many lodges and hotels offer special midweek or winter low-season rates. If you're opting for a private game lodge, find out whether they accept children (many specify only kids over 12), and stay a minimum of two nights, three if you can.

In Kruger National Park you have the choice between budget self-catering huts from R250 per couple per night and much more expensive (but worth it) self-catering cottages in the more remote and exclusive bushveld (*bushveld* is the generic term for the wild indigenous vegetation of the lowveld) camps which range from R600 to

R1100. Visit the South African National Parks Web site (⊕*www. sanparks.org*) to get information and book accommodations. ▇TIP➔ Bookings open every September 1 for the following 12 months. Make sure you book well in advance and, if possible, avoid July, August, and December, which are South African school vacations.

WHAT IT COSTS IN SOUTH AFRICAN RAND					
	¢	$	$$	$$$	$$$$
RESTAURANTS	under R50	R50–R75	R75–R100	R100–R125	over R125
LODGING	under R500	R500–R1,000	R1,000–R2,000	R2,000–R3,000	over R3,000
FULL-SERVICE SAFARI LODGING	under R2,000	R2,000–R5,000	R5,000–R8,000	R8,000–R12,000	over R12,000

Restaurant prices are per person for a main course at dinner, a main course equivalent, or a prix-fixe meal. Hotel and lodging prices are for a standard double room in high season, including 12.5% tax.

MPUMALANGA

In addition to Cape Town and the Winelands, Mpumalanga should be high on any South African list. Nowhere else in the country can you spend one day seeing spectacular wildlife, the next climbing or gazing over the escarpment, and a third poking around some of the country's most historic towns—all within close proximity of each other. The local history is fascinating. In the late 1800s skirmishes and pitched battles pitted the local Pedi against the Boers (the original Dutch farmers who moved here from the Cape to escape British oppression), as well as the Brits against the Boers (in the First South African War). At the turn of the 20th century, the Brits and Boers fought again (the Second South African War), when England's Queen Victoria brought some of her finest troops from all corners of the British Empire to South Africa, hoping for a final victory over the Boers. Gold and diamonds had been discovered in South Africa, and there was more at stake than political games. The Pilgrim's Rest gold strike of 1873 was minor compared with those in and around Johannesburg, but it nevertheless provided inducement for gold-hungry settlers.

These early gold-mining days have been immortalized by Sir Percy Fitzpatrick in *Jock of the Bushveld,* a classic of South African literature. Jock was a Staffordshire terrier whose master, Percy (he was later knighted by the British crown), worked as a transport rider during the gold rush. Sir Percy entertained his children with tales of his and Jock's adventures braving leopards, savage baboons, and all manner of dangers. Rudyard Kipling, who wandered this wilderness as a reporter covering the First South African War in the early 1880s, encouraged Fitzpatrick to write down the stories. Jock is still a household name in South Africa today. You'll see lots of Jock of the Bushveld signs all over Mpumalanga, seemingly wherever he cocked a leg.

Numbers in the text correspond to numbers in the margin and on the Mpumalanga map.

SABIE

❹ *355 km (220 mi) east of Johannesburg on the N12.*

As you descend Long Tom Pass, the town of Sabie (sah-bee) comes into view far below, in a bowl formed by the surrounding mountains. It's by far the pleasantest and most enjoyable town in the region, with restaurants, shops, and bars. The name Sabie is derived from the Shangaan word *uluSaba,* which described the "fearful river," home to many crocodiles. Today it makes a great base for exploring.

In the 1900s gold provided the community's livelihood, but today it's been replaced by timber, and Sabie sits in the heart of the world's largest man-made forest—more than a million acres of exotic pine and eucalyptus. The first forests were planted in 1876 to provide the area's mines with posts and supports. Today much of the timber is still used to prop up shafts in the Gauteng gold mines.

Sabie itself is a busy little town with a farming feel. It boasts some of the biggest traffic humps in South Africa, ensuring that farmers' and visitors' tractors and cars drive slowly through the broad, shady, tree-lined streets. It's easy to walk from one end of the central part of town to the other, taking in sights like **Market Square,** the commercial hub of Sabie in its early days. Here St. Peter's Anglican Church, designed by the famous architect Sir Herbert Baker and built by Italians in 1913, stands in its own pleasant gardens. Also in the square is a Jock of the Bushveld sign, said to commemorate Jock and Percy's arrival in 1885.

Make time to visit the **Sabie Forestry Museum,** which not only details the history of this attractive and friendly small town but also provides a wealth of information on wood and the timber industry. ⊠*Between 10th Ave. and 4th St.* ☎*013/764–1058* ⬧*klfmuseum@mweb.co.za* 🖾*R5* ⊙ *Weekdays 8–1 and 2–4:30, Sat. 8–noon.*

❸ **Lone Creek Falls** is the prettiest, most peaceful, and last of three local waterfalls on a dead-end road (the others are Bridal Veil Falls and Horseshoe Falls). An easy paved walkway leads to the falls, which plunge 225 feet from the center of a high, broad rock face framed by vines and creepers. The path crosses the river on a wooden bridge and loops through the forest back to the parking lot. If you're feeling energetic, follow the steep steps leading up to the top of the falls. Lone Creek is accessible to the elderly and those with disabilities because of its easy approach. ⊠*6½ km (4 mi) down Old Lydenburg Rd., off Main Rd.* ☎*No phone* 🖾*R5* ⊙*Daily 8–5.*

❻ Set in an ampitheater of towering cliffs, **Mac Mac Falls** is arguably the most famous waterfall in Mpumalanga. The water plunges 215 feet into a pool, and rainbows dance in the billowing spray. It's worth the small entry fee to go through the gate to get a closer look. The falls owe their name to President Thomas Burger, who, while visiting

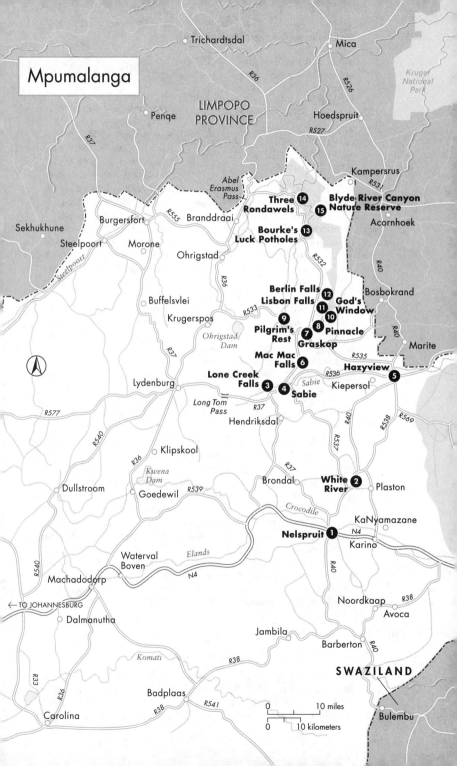

Mpumalanga

Trichardtsdal

Mica

Kruger National Park

R36

R526

LIMPOPO PROVINCE

Penge

Hoedspruit

R527

R37

Kampersrus

R531

Abel Erasmus Pass

Sekhukhune

Burgersfort

Branddraai

Three Rondawels **14**

Blyde River Canyon Nature Reserve

15

R555

Acornhoek

Steelpoort

Morone

Ohrigstad

Bourke's Luck Potholes **13**

Steelpoort

R36

R532

Bosbokrand

Buffelsvlei

Berlin Falls **12**

R533

Lisbon Falls

11 God's Window

10

R40

Krugerspos

Ohrigstad Dam

Pilgrim's Rest **9**

7

8 Pinnacle

Graskop

R37

Mac Mac Falls **6**

R535

Marite

Lone Creek Falls **3**

4 Sabie

Sabie

R536

Hazyview **5**

Lydenburg

Long Tom Pass

R37

Hendriksdal

Kiepersol

R40

R538

R569

R577

Klipskool

R540

Kwena Dam

R36

R539

Goedewil

Brondal

R37

White River 2

Plaston

Dullstroom

Waterval Boven

Elands

KaNyamazane

N4

Nelspruit 1

Karino

Crocodile

Machadodorp

N4

R540

R40

Dalmanutha

← TO JOHANNESBURG

Noordkaap

R38

Avoca

R33

R26

Jambila

Barberton

R40

Badplaas

Komati

R38

SWAZILAND

0   10 miles

R38

R541

Carolina

0   10 kilometers

Bulembu

some nearby gold diggings in 1873, noticed that many miners' names began with "Mac," revealing their Scottish background. He promptly dubbed the area Mac Mac. At the gate a number of peddlers sell very cheap curios. ⊠*R532, 15 km (9 mi) northeast of Sabie* ☎*No phone* 🎫*R5* ⊙*Daily 8–5.*

On November 6, 1872, a prospector located deposits of gold in a creek on the Hendriksdal farm, now a small hamlet about 16 km (10 mi) from Sabie. Sabie itself owes its origins to an altogether luckier strike. In 1895 Henry Glynn, a local farmer, hosted a picnic at the Klein Sabie Falls. After a few drinks, his guests started taking potshots at empty bottles on a rock ledge. The flying bullets chipped off shards of rock revealing traces of gold. Fifty-five years later, when mining operations closed down, more than 1 million ounces of gold had been taken from the Klein Sabie Falls.

WHERE TO STAY & EAT

¢–$ ✕**Wild Fig Tree Restaurant and Pub.** This excellent and casual eatery, in the shade of a huge wild fig tree, is open daily from 8 AM to 9 PM for breakfast, light lunches, and dinner. The emphasis is on local specialties such as crocodile, roast saddle of warthog, and variety of local trout dishes, including the unusual avocado bake with trout and crumbled cheese. Eat on the patio in summer or enjoy the warmth of a cozy log fire for chilly winter evenings. Tourist information and Internet services are available as well as a licensed bar and lounge area. After your meal, pop into the adjoining Wild Fig Tree shops, where arts, crafts, jewelry, and handmade clothing are for sale. ⊠*Corner of Main and Louis Trichardt Sts.* ☎*013/764–2239* ⊟*AE, DC, MC, V.*

$ 🏠**Sabie Town House.** Built of local Sabie stone, this beautifully appointed bed-and-breakfast has sweeping views of the Sabie Gorge. The attractive atrium entrance sets the scene for the rest of the establishment, which has spacious guest rooms, including one for families. Four rooms have separate entrances, and all have a minibar-refrigerator and tea/coffeemaker. Guests have free use of the garden, guest lounge, swimming pool, and patio. Barbecue facilities are available, and by special arrangement hosts Frikkie and Louma Van Rooyen will arrange a complete evening *braai* (barbecue) for guests in the *boma* (outdoor eating area) overlooking the gorge. Breakfast is served in the breakfast room or on the patio. ⊠*Power St., 2060* ☎*013/764–2292* ⊕*www. sabietownhouse.co.za* 🛏*5 rooms, 1 suite* ♿*In-room: refrigerator. In-hotel: bar, pool, Internet* ⊟*AE, DC, MC, V* ⊗*BP.*

PILGRIM'S REST

➒ *16 km (10 mi) north of Sabie on R533.*

The charming village of Pilgrim's Rest—also a national monument—dates back to the 1870s gold-rush days when it was the first proper gold-mining town in South Africa. Alec "Wheelbarrow" Patterson abandoned the overcrowded Mac Mac diggings, and, carting all his belongings in a wheelbarrow, left to search elsewhere for gold. He found it in Pilgrim's Creek, setting off a new gold rush in 1873. Rumors about the richness of the strike carried quickly around the world, bringing miners from California, Australia, and Europe. Within a year 1,500 diggers, living in tents and huts, had moved to the area. Most of the alluvial gold was found by individuals who recovered more than R2 million worth of gold dust and nuggets using pans, sluice boxes, and cradles. It wasn't until about 1876 that most of the tents were replaced by buildings. Most of the beautifully restored houses seen in the village today are from the more staid period of the early 1900s.

Your first stop should be the **Pilgrim's Rest Information Centre,** in the middle of town, opposite the Victorian-era Royal Hotel, which is the town's focal point and well worth a visit for its history. The center offers various tours, such as panning for gold and the Prospector's Hiking Trail, as well as maps and tickets for all the museums in the village. ⊠ *Main St.* ☎ *013/768–1080 or 013/768–1471* ⊙ *Daily 9–12:45 and 1:45–4.*

Main Street is where most of the attractions are, including **St. Mary's Anglican Church** (⊠ *Main St.* ☎ *No phone*). Built in 1884, the iron-roofed stone building replaced the original makeshift wattle-and-daub structure. It was an uphill battle for the early ministers to lure miners from the town's 18 canteens. After a backbreaking week spent on the sluices, Holy Communion just didn't pack the punch of a belt of Cape brandy or Squareface gin.

The tiny **Pilgrim's and Sabie News Printing Museum** is full of displays of antique printing presses and old photos. The building, constructed in the late 19th century as a residence, later served as the offices of the weekly *Pilgrim's and Sabie News.* The first newspaper in Pilgrim's Rest was the *Gold News,* published in 1874 and notable for its libelous gossip. The editor, an Irishman by the name of Phelan, felt obliged to keep a pair of loaded pistols on his desk. ⊠ *Main St., Uptown* ☎ *No phone* ⊠ *R5* ⊙ *Daily 9–4.*

The **House Museum,** across and up the street from the Royal Hotel, re-creates the way of life of a middle-class family in the early part of the 20th century. The house was built in 1913 of corrugated iron and wood and is typical of buildings erected at the time. ⊠ *Main St., Uptown* ☎ *No phone* ⊠ *R5* ⊙ *Daily 9–12:45 and 1:45–4.*

The **Pilgrim's Rest Cemetery** sits high on the hill above Main Street. The fascinating inscriptions on the tombstones evoke the dangers and hardship of life in Mpumalanga a century ago. Tellingly, most of the dead were in their twenties and thirties and hailed from Wales, Scotland, and England. The cemetery owes its improbable setting to the Robber's Grave, the only grave that lies in a north–south direction. It contains the body of a thief who was banished from Pilgrim's Rest for stealing gold from a tent, after which he was tarred and feathered and chased out of town; the man foolishly returned and was shot dead. He was buried where he fell, and the area around his grave became the town's unofficial cemetery. To get here, follow the steep path that starts next to the picnic area, near the post office.

In 1930, 16 general stores lined the streets of Pilgrim's Rest. By 1950 mine production had taken a nosedive, and most of the businesses had shut down. The **Dredzen Shop and House Museum** re-creates the look of a general store during those lean years, with shelves displaying items that would have been on sale, from jams and preserves to candles and matches. The attached residence focuses on life in Pilgrim's Rest in the years immediately following World War II. After you come down the hill from the cemetery, turn left on Main Street to get to the museum. ⊠ *Main St., Uptown* ☎ *No phone* 🖃 *R5* ⊙ *Daily 9–1 and 1:30–4.*

Guided tours, including refreshments, are offered at **Alanglade,** the beautiful home of the Transvaal Gold Mining Estates' mine manager, set in a forested grove 2 km (1 mi) north of town. The huge house was built in 1916 for Richard Barry and his family, and is furnished with pieces dating from 1900 to 1930. Look carefully at the largest pieces— you will see that they are segmented, so they could be taken apart and carried on ox wagons. Tour tickets are available at the information center and should be reserved 30 minutes in advance. ⊠ *Vaalhoek Rd., off R533* ☎ *No phone* 🖃 *Tours R20* ⊙ *Tours Mon.–Sat. at 11 and 2.*

At the **Diggings Museum,** in the creek where the alluvial gold was originally panned, you'll find displays of a water-driven stamp battery and some of the tents and wattle-and-daub huts typical of the early gold-rush years. The tour lasts about an hour and is more of an enjoyable experience than an informative one. The retired prospector who conducts the tours enlivens the proceedings with yarns about the old days. You'll also see a display of gold panning and get to poke around in some of the old diggings. Tickets are available at the information center. ⊠ *R533, 2 km (1 mi) south of Pilgrim's Rest* ☎ *No phone* 🖃 *R5* ⊙ *Tours daily at 10, 11, noon, 2, and 3.*

WHERE TO STAY & EAT

$ ✕ **Vine Restaurant and Pub.** In a former trading store dating from 1910, the Vine uses antique sideboards, sepia photos, and country-style wooden furniture to recapture that heady gold rush–era feeling. The food is straightforward and hearty. Try traditional South African *bobotie* (curried ground mutton topped with egg), *potjiekos* (lamb stew), digger's stew (beef and veggies) served in a digger's gold-prospecting pan, or *samp* (corn porridge). The pub is a good place to sit outside and watch the world go by. ⊠ *Main St., Downtown* ☎ *013/768–1080* ⊟ *DC, MC, V* ⊙ *8–6.*

¢ ✕ **Scott's Café.** Dozens of varieties of crepes—both savory (stir-fried chicken) and sweet (fried nuts and cinnamon with chocolate sauce)— are the draw at this restaurant. Also on the menu are sandwiches and salads. Meals can be eaten outside on the pleasant wide veranda. There's also an interesting little arts-and-crafts gallery, which, like the café, is open from 8 to 7. ⊠ *Main St.* ☎ *013/768–1061* ⊟ *DC, MC, V.*

¢ ✕🏠 **Royal Hotel.** Established in 1873, this hotel dates from the very beginning of the gold rush in Pilgrim's Rest—you'll see its corrugated-iron facade in sepia photos displayed around town. The hotel is spread out over 10 quaint wood-and-tin buildings, and rooms are decorated with reproduction four-poster beds, wood ceiling fans, sumptuous deep baths, and marble-and-oak washstands. The Church Bar was formerly a chapel in a Cape Town girls' school, which was dismantled, shipped to Mozambique, and transported to Pilgrim's Rest by ox wagon. The wood-paneled walls, old wooden bar counter, antique cash register, and a fascinating display of photographs depicting early life in the village all add to the convivial gold-rush atmosphere of the bar. Choose a book from the small library or watch TV in the elegant old-world-styled lounge. If you're feeling energetic, take advantage of the horseback riding, gold panning, hiking, golfing, or trout fishing offered by the hotel. A restaurant offering à la carte and buffet meals is adjacent to the hotel. Don't miss out on the delicious cream scones served all day with tea or coffee. ☒ *Main St., Uptown* ☏ *Box 59, 1290* ☎ *013/768–1100* ✎ *royalres@rhpilgrims.co.za* ☞ *50 rooms* ☝ *In-room: no a/c, no TV. In-hotel: restaurant, bar* ☰ *AE, DC, MC, V* ☝ *BP.*

¢–$ 🏨 **District 6 Miners' Cottages.** On top of a hill a few minutes' walk from the center of town, these self-catering cottages are a very good value. The delightful cottages are all miners' homes dating from 1920. From their verandas are spectacular views of the town and surrounding mountains. Interiors are furnished with period reproductions, complete with wooden floors, brass bedsteads, and claw-foot tubs. Each cottage consists of a small living room, two double bedrooms, a fully equipped kitchen, and a bathroom. There's also a 3-bedroom cottage and a 6-person house. Phone reservations can be made only weekdays 9–4, and if you arrive after hours, you'll pick up keys from the Royal Hotel. ☒ *District 6* ☏ *Private Bag X516, 1290* ☎ *013/768–1211* ☞ *6 cottages* ☝ *In-room: kitchen, no TV (some)* ☰ *No credit cards.*

SPORTS & THE OUTDOORS

HIKING Ranging from two nights to five days, several area hiking trails are part of the **Prospector's Hiking Trail.** You follow in the footsteps of the old miners as you walk through indigenous forest and over rolling hills. Overnight accommodations are very basic 16-bunk huts, good if you're hardy and love unspoiled countryside. The birdlife is superb, and you may even see a small antelope or two. Book trails well in advance through **Komatiland Forest Ecotourism** (☎ *012/481–3615* ⊕ *www.komatiecotourism.co.za*).

GRASKOP

❼ *25 km (16 mi) northeast of Sabie, 15 km (9 mi) southeast of Pilgrim's Rest.*

Graskop (translation: "grass head") was so named because of the vast tracts of grassveld and singular lack of trees in the area. Like so many of the little towns in this area, it started as a gold-mining camp in the 1880s, on a farm called Graskop that was owned by Abel Erasmus, who later became the local magistrate. After the gold mines closed down, the town served as a major rail link for the timber industry.

Today the main features of this rather featureless little town are its curio shops and eateries. Perched on the edge of the Drakensberg/Mpumalanga Escarpment, Graskop considers itself the window on the lowveld, and several nearby lookouts do have stunning views over the edge of the escarpment. It's an ideal base for visiting scenic hot spots, including Mac Mac Falls and the beauties in and around the Blyde River Canyon Nature Reserve.

Traveling east toward Hazyview, you enter the lovely Koewyns Pass, named for a local Pedi chief. Unfortunately, there are few scenic overlooks, but you'll still get sweeping views of the Graskop gorge. Look for the turnoff to Graskopkloof on your left as you leave town, and stop to get a closer view into this deep, surprisingly spectacular gorge, where in the rainy season two waterfalls plunge to the river below.

WHERE TO STAY

¢   ⊞ **West Lodge.** This attractive Victorian-style B&B is set in a delightful garden bursting with roses. Luxurious bedrooms are decorated in pastels and have crisp white linens, both bath and shower, satellite TV, and tea/coffeemakers. The two rooms on the first floor of the main building are completely private but share a balcony and lounge; they look out over an area known as Fairyland, a communal farm area where Sir Percy Fitzpatrick set up camp on his way to Lydenburg. Two garden suites are in a detached building and have private entrances. Guests can use a visitors' lounge as well as a refrigerator in the main house. A small chapel in the garden is the spot for tying the knot, renewing wedding vows, or just meditating quietly. A wide choice of eateries and the town center are only minutes away. ⊠ *12/14 Huguenot St.* ✆ *Box 2, 1270* ☎ *013/767–1390 or 082/429–2661* ⊕ *www.west-lodge.co.za* ➷ *4 rooms* ⚐ *In-hotel: bar, no kids under 16, no-smoking rooms* ⊟ *AE, MC, V* ⫶◯⫶ *BP.*

BLYDE RIVER CANYON NATURE RESERVE

★ ⑮   15 km (9 mi) northeast of Graskop.

Just north from the town of Graskop, the dense plantations of gum and pine fall behind, and the road runs through magnificent grass-covered peaks. This lush land is fed by two rivers, the Treur and the Blyde; how they came to be named is part of Mpumalanga lore. The story goes that Voortrekker leader Hendrik Potgieter led an expedition to Lourenço Marques in 1840, leaving the womenfolk behind near Graskop. The men took so long to return that the women gave them up for dead, named the river beside which they camped the Treur (sorrow), and set off for home. As they were about to wade across another river, they were met by the returning men and were so overjoyed that they named the river the Blyde (joy). This is the setting for the Blyde River Canyon, nearly 30 km (19 mi) long, and the nature reserve of the same name, which stretches for 60 km (37 mi) from its entrance just north of the town of Graskop up to the Abel Erasmus Pass. The reserve has gigantic rocks, deep gorges, and high mountains. ⊠ *Along the R532*

☎013/761–6019 ✉R25 *(payable at Bourke's Luck Potholes)* ◷*Reserve daily 7–5, visitor center daily 7:30–4.*

⑧ **Pinnacle** is a 100-foot-high quartzite "needle" that rises dramatically out of the surrounding fern-clad ravine, as it has for countless millennia. Way down below, beneath and to the right of the viewing platform, you can see the plateau beneath the escarpment. The watercourse drops down some 1,475 feet in a series of alternating falls and cascades. From Graskop take the R532 north and turn right after 2½ km (1½ mi) onto the R534, marked GOD'S WINDOW. To reach the Pinnacle, continue 1½ km (1 mi) and look out for the brown sign reading PINNACLE.

⑩ **God's Window** is the most famous of the lowveld lookouts. It got its name because as you peer through the rock "window" at the sublime view below, or gaze out into seeming infinity from the edge of the escarpment (which drops away almost vertically), you feel you're on top of the world. Geared to tourists, it has toilet facilities, paved parking areas, curio vendors, and paved, marked walking trails leading to various lookouts. The God's Window lookout has a view back along the escarpment framed between towering cliffs. For a broader panorama, make a 10-minute climb along the paved track through the rain forest to a small area with sweeping views of the entire lowveld. The altitude here is 5,700 feet, just a little lower than Johannesburg. If you're traveling from the Pinnacle, turn right on the R534, pass two overlooks, and travel another 4½ km (nearly 3 mi).

⑪ Set in a bowl between hills, **Lisbon Falls** cascades 120 feet onto rocks below, throwing up spray over a deep pool. You can hike down to the pool on a path from the parking area. From God's Window turn right on the R534 and continue 6 km (4 mi). At the T with R532, turn right onto the road marked LISBON FALLS.

⑫ A small stream, Waterfall Spruit, runs through a broad expanse of grassland to **Berlin Falls**. A short walk takes you to the cascade, which is a thin stream that drops 150 feet into a deep-green pool surrounded by tall pines. Berlin Falls is a little over 2 km (1 mi) north of Lisbon Falls off the R532.

⑬ Another 27 km (17 mi) north of Berlin Falls on the R532 are **Bourke's Luck Potholes** and the nature reserve visitor center. Named after a gold prospector, the cylindrical and rather alien-looking deep potholes filled with green water are carved into the rock by whirlpools where the Treur and Blyde rivers converge. The visitor center has interesting information on the flora, fauna, and geology of the canyon. Several long canyon hiking trails start from headquarters, as do shorter walks and trails. A three-hour walk, for example, could take you down into the bottom of the canyon, where you follow a trail marked by rocks painted with animal or bird symbols as the gorge towers above you.

⑭ Continuing north from Bourke's Luck Potholes, you get occasional glimpses of the magnificent canyon and the distant cliffs of the escarpment. Nowhere, however, is the view better than from the **Three Rondawels** *(Drie Rondawels)*, 14 km (9 mi) from the potholes. This is one of the most spectacular vistas in South Africa—you'll find it in almost every travel brochure. Here the Blyde River, hemmed in by towering buttresses of red rock, snakes through the bottom of the canyon. The Three Rondawels are rock formations that bear a vague similarity to the round, thatch African dwellings of the same name. Before Europeans moved into the area, the indigenous local people named the formations the Chief and His Three Wives. The flat-top peak to the right is Mapjaneng (the Chief), named in honor of a Mapulana chief, Maripe Mashile, who routed invading Swazi at the battle of Moholoholo ("the very great one"). The three "wives," in descending order from right to left, are Maseroto, Mogoladikwe, and Magabolle.

WHERE TO STAY

$ 🏠 **Belvedere Guest House.** You would be hard-pressed to find a more perfect place to experience the awesome beauty of the Blyde River Canyon than this self-catering establishment, which was built in 1915 for the manager of the old Belvedere Power station that provided electricity for the Pilgrim's Rest mining operations. Double up in nine twin-bedded rooms, or go it alone in the single room. When it's cold, get cozy by a roaring fire in the comfortable lounge; on warmer nights you can sit out on the wrap-around veranda. Plenty of refrigerators, freezers, and stoves make self-catering a pleasure. Several walks, some more gentle than others, take you straight from the house into the surrounding indigenous forests with abundant birdlife and splendid views. Access is via the Belvedere Nature Reserve and down a steep but easily negotiated concrete strip road. The house is fully equipped with linen, towels, cutlery, and crockery, and has a cleaning staff. ⊠ *Off the R532, 5 km (3 mi) north of Bourke's Luck Potholes* ℗ *Mpumalanga Parks Board, Central Reservations, Box 1990, Nelspruit 1200* ☎ *013/759–5432* 🛏 *1 house* ⚅ *In-hotel: kitchen, lounge* ☰ *MC, V.*

SPORTS & THE OUTDOORS

HIKING   The **Blyde River Canyon Trail** is a 29-km (18-mi) three-day hike that runs from God's Window right along the edge of the escarpment to the Sybrand van Niekerk Resort. The mountain scenery is spectacular, making it one of the most popular trails in the country. Several shorter trails explore the canyon from trailheads at Bourke's Luck Potholes. The number of hikers on the multiday trails is controlled, so it's essential to reserve far in advance (contact the nature reserve).

EN
ROUTE   The descent out of the nature reserve, down the escarpment, and through **Abel Erasmus Pass** is breathtaking. (From the Three Rondawels, take the R532 to a T, and turn right onto the R36.) Be careful as you drive this pass. Locals graze their cattle and goats on the verges, and you may be surprised by animals on the tarmac as you round a bend. The J. G. Strijdom Tunnel serves as the gateway to the lowveld. At the mouth of the tunnel are stands where you can buy clay pots, African masks, wooden giraffes, and subtropical fruit. As you emerge from the dark mouth of the tunnel, the lowveld spreads out below, and the views of both it and the mountains are stunning. On the left, the Olifants River snakes through the bushveld, lined to some extent by African subsistence farms.

HAZYVIEW

⑤ *45 km (28 mi) east of Sabie.*

Named for the heat haze that rises from the fruit plantations and bush in the surrounding area, Hazyview is a boomtown. Situated in the center of the prime tourist attractions, it's also the gateway to Kruger through the nearby Phabeni, Numbi, and Kruger gates. There are plenty of good places to stay and eat, and Hazyview is also the adventure mecca of the region. Here you can try your hand at horseback riding, helicopter trips, river rafting, hiking, ballooning, quad biking, golf, and game-viewing safaris.

The **Shangana Cultural Village** is a genuine Shangaan village that's presided over by Chief Israel Ngobeni, who has lived here for nearly 40 years. An hour-long tour of the *kraal* (traditional rural village) includes a meeting with the chief and a visit to the sangoma (traditional healer). Guests can enjoy a traditional lunch or a light meal in the tea garden after visiting the Marula Market, where good-quality handcrafted items can be purchased. During the evening the chief hosts a memorable firelight song-and-dance performance portraying the history of the Shangaan people. A traditional dinner is included. Booking for the performance (6 PM in summer, 5:15 PM in winter) is essential. ✉*R535, 5 km (3 mi) northwest of Hazyview* ☎*013/737–7000* ⊕*www.shangana.co.za* ☞*Day tour R70, day tour and meal R140, evening festival R240* ☉*Daily 9–5, to 8 for evening shows.*

At **Sabie Valley Coffee** you can take a coffee tour, led by owner Tim Buckland, through the whole coffee-making process—from orchards to roasting to packaging. Challenge your taste buds with a tasting of homegrown, 100% pure Arabica specialty coffees, before sampling some of the coffee-related goodies for sale: coffee liqueur, cake, and candies. Reservations are essential. ✉*R536, 18 km (11 mi) west of Hazyview* ☎*013/737–8169* ☞*Tours with tastings R25, children R15* ☉*Wed. at 3, Sat. at 10.*

WHERE TO STAY & EAT

★ $$–$$$$ ✕🏨 **Cybele Forest Lodge and Spa.** Indulge all your senses at this truly tranquil hideaway nestled in the subtropical splendor of the surrounding forests and overlooking the rolling hills of the lowveld. A wide range of indigenous flowering trees surround the lodge's gardens and create secluded spaces for the 12 luxury suites and cottages, many of which have their own heated swimming pool and outdoor shower. ▮TIP➜ **Keep an eye on the mischievous monkeys swinging from the trees that overlook the deep verandas.** The cuisine at this romantic retreat is regarded as some of the best in South Africa, and features organic free-range produce served in five-course dinners, generous breakfasts, and à la carte lunches. A typical five-course dinner (R195, reservations essential) could include Swiss cheese crepes, followed by panfried Atlantic salmon in hollandaise sauce, and fig pâté and passion-fruit brûlée tart for dessert. Activities include forest walks, horseback riding, a well-equipped gym, and a wide range of spa treatments. ✉*Off R40, between Hazyview and White River, near the Phabeni Gate into the*

Kruger National Park ⌂ *Box 346, White River 1240* ☎ *013/764–9500* ⊕ *www.cybele.co.za* ⇝ *6 cottages, 6 suites* ♿ *In-room: safe, minibar. In-hotel: bar, pools, gym, spa, no kids under 10, Internet* ☰ *AE, DC, MC, V* ⊙ *MAP.*

★ $ ✕▥ **Böhm's Zeederberg Country House.** Expect a warm, sincere welcome at this owner-run guesthouse situated on spacious grounds with verdant lawns shaded by indigenous trees. Mrs. Böhm and her German-speaking family have been dispensing good old-fashioned hospitality here for more than 30 years. Chalets are perfect for groups and come fully equipped, with bathrooms, tea/coffeemaker, a heater, air-conditioning, and hair dryers. Take time to sit on your private veranda and gaze at the spectacular view of the Sabie River Valley and the prolific birdlife, order a picnic lunch, or walk the steep 4-km (2½-km) walking trail down to the river. A four-course dinner (R120) includes Sabie trout, succulent Karoo lamb, ostrich and venison, and local mushrooms served with fresh herbs and vegetables from the lodge's own garden. ⊠ *R536, 18 km (11 mi) west of Hazyview* ⌂ *Box 94, Sabie 1260* ☎ *013/737–8101* ⊕ *www.bohms.co.za* ⇝ *10 rooms* ♿ *In-room: minibar. In-hotel: restaurant, bar, pool* ☰ *AE, DC, MC, V* ⊙ *BP.*

¢ ✕▥ **Rissington Inn.** This relaxed and reasonably priced lodge offers fine food, superb hospitality, and all the facilities you'd expect at a top lodge. Whitewashed walls, thatch roofs, delightful gardens, and panoramic views over the rolling Sabie River valley make for a country-house atmosphere. Gaily colored checked or striped bedspreads, pine furniture, and rush mats add to the rustic ambience, and—a special bonus—all rooms have verandas. Not surprisingly, the inn gets lots of repeat visitors. Meals are served in the restaurant or on the patio overlooking the pool. For breakfast choose continental fare or the Full Monty, a full English feast. If you're looking for a snack, the à la carte menu offers light lunches and a variety of teas. For dinner, dishes range from pasta to fish, including local fare such as venison stew or tarragon trout, and tasty vegetarian specialties. The excellent wine list features a wide choice of South African wines. The lodge will arrange hot-air ballooning, adventure sports, or Kruger Park tours for you, supplemented with a tasty picnic basket. ⊠ *Off the R40, 1 km [¾ mi] from Hazyview and down a dirt road* ⌂ *Box 650, 1242* ☎ *013/737–7700* ⊕ *www.rissington.co.za* ⇝ *14 rooms* ♿ *In-hotel: restaurant, bar, pool* ☰ *AE, DC, MC, V* ⊙ *BP.*

SHOPPING

Stop in at the **Windmill Wine Shop** (⊠ *R536, 18 km [11 mi] west of Hazyview* ☎ *013/737–8175*), on the same property as Böhm's Zeederberg, to pick up excellent Cape wines, ports, and brandies, local beer made by Hops Hollow Brewery, and local cheeses, olives, olive oil, and coffee grown and processed at nearby Sabie Valley Coffee. You can also get a light meal of local cheese, cold meats, pâté, and olives.

Rock Art

An important key to understanding humankind's past, rock art is a fascinating aspect of the South African and world heritage. Engravings (made by scratching into the rock surface), paintings, and finger paintings proliferate throughout the province and carry an air of mystery, since relatively little is known about them. Although some archaeologists have attributed the origins of rock art to ancient Egyptians, Phoenicians, and even extraterrestrial races, the rock art found here was created by ancestors of the San. Materials came from the immediate environment. Ocher (red iron-oxide clay) was used to obtain red, charcoal for black, and white clay for white. Blood, egg, and plant juices were used for binding, creating a paint with obvious staying power.

Most rock art illustrates the activities and experiences of the African medicine people, or shamans. Religious rituals, such as those for making rain and healing the sick, involved trances and inspired visions, from which rock-art images were created. The images included large animals, such as the highly regarded eland and rhino, which were believed to possess supernatural power. Half-animal, half-human representations and geometric patterns and grids are also featured. The shamans believed that when an image was drawn, power was transferred to the people and the land.

WHITE RIVER

2 *35 km (22 mi) southeast of Sabie.*

This pleasant little town is set amid nut and tropical-fruit plantations and is one of the gateways to the escarpment's major sights. Settled by retired British army officers in the early 20th century, it still has a colonial feel, although there's plenty of new development.

If you're into automobiles and their history, travel to the Casterbridge Farm shopping and entertainment center for the **White River Motor Museum.** It has an impressive collection of more than 60 vehicles, dating from as early as 1911, including a 1936 Jaguar SS100, one of only 314 ever built. ⊠*R40 and Numbi Rd.* ☎*013/750–2196* ⊕*www.casterbridge.co.za* ⊠*Free* ⊗ *Weekdays 9–4:30, weekends 9:30–4:30.*

WHERE TO STAY & EAT

$–$$ ✕🏨 **Jatinga Country Lodge and Restaurant.** Only 38 km (24 mi) from Kruger, this boutique hotel, originally a hunting lodge built in the 1920s, is situated on the banks of the White River. Rooms, most of which have magnificent private gardens and outside showers, are individually furnished in colonial, Victorian, Provençal, or English-country styles. High tea is a specialty, which includes cucumber sandwiches and cream scones. Sundowners are enjoyed every evening, and you can dine on a medallion of venison and homemade ice cream under the stars ($$). Fly-in guests receive complimentary transfers to Kruger Mpumalanga International Airport, only 4½ km (3 mi) from the lodge, and hot-air balloon flights, helicopter trips, Kruger Park excursions, and scenic trips along the Panorama Route can be arranged. You can also order a well-packed picnic basket to take with you. There's croquet and lawn bowling and an attractive, country-style wedding chapel on the grounds. ⊠*Jatinga Rd.* ☎*Box 3577, 1240* ☎*013/751–5059 or 013/751–5108* ⊕*www.jatinga.co.za* ⊲*20 rooms* ⌂*In-room: safe, minibar. In-hotel: restaurant, bar, pool, airport shuttle* ☰*AE, DC, MC, V* ⦿*MAP.*

$ ╳⊡ **Oliver's Restaurant and Lodge.** This large, white-walled, red-roofed country house situated among pine trees and lush forest overlooks lovely gardens and the 1st hole of the White River Golf Course. It's an excellent touring base for both Kruger and the escarpment. The comfortable, spacious en-suite rooms are decorated with floral artworks and coordinating flower-print linen. There's an in-house Wellness and Beauty Clinic that offers a variety of treatments including facials and massage. The à la carte dining room ($$) more than lives up to its reputation for delectable continental and Mediterranean cuisine, including house specials such as *eisbein* (the German name for a culinary dish involving the lower part of hams hocks) and roast rack of lamb followed by Oliver's special crème brûlée. You can also enjoy raclette and fondue evenings in the wine cellar. Work all that yummy food off with a game of tennis or squash, or a round of golf at the White River Golf Course. ⊠*R40, between Hazyview and White River* ☎*Box 2809, White River 1240* ☎*013/750–0479* ⊕*www.olivers.co.za* ⊲*9 rooms* ⌂*In-room: safe, minibar. In-hotel: restaurant, bar, pool, gym, spa* ☰*AE, DC, MC, V* ⦿*BP.*

SHOPPING

You can browse in White River's noted art and crafts galleries or venture to **Casterbridge Farm** (⊠*R40 and Numbi Rd.* ☎*013/750–2196* ⊕*www. casterbridge.co.za*), a shopping and entertainment center that was once a rambling mango estate. It now houses stores selling designer clothing, jewelry, local pottery, and art, as well as a range of excellent restaurants offering everything from Portuguese cooking to wood-oven pizza.

NELSPRUIT

❶ *19 km (12 mi) southwest of White River on the R40.*

Nelspruit (nel-sprate), the capital of Mpumalanga and home of the provincial government, is a modern, vibrant city of just over 250,000 people. It's a notable stop on the main route between Gauteng and Maputo, Mozambique, as well as a gateway town to the lowveld and Kruger. The compact town sits in the middle of a prosperous agricultural community, which farms citrus (a third of South Africa's citrus exports come from here), subtropical fruit, tobacco, and vegetables. It has an international airport and excellent hospitals. If you have time, it's worth having a look at the **Lowveld National Botanical Gardens,** where more than 500 plant species indigenous to the valley are on display, including a spectacular

IT HAPPENED HERE

Tiny fossils, which are thought to be about 3.3 billion years old, were found in the mountains around Barberton, which is 43 km (27 mi) south of Nelspruit.

collection of cycads and ferns. ✉ *White River Rd., 3 km (2 mi) outside Nelspruit* ☎ *013/752–5531* 📠 *R12.50* ⊙ *May–Sept., daily 8–5:15; Oct.–Apr., daily 8–6.*

KRUGER NATIONAL PARK

Visiting Kruger is likely to be one of the great experiences of your life. You'll be delighted and amazed not only with the diversity of life forms, but also its San (Bushman) rock paintings and major archaeological sites. (There is ample evidence that prehistoric humans—*Homo erectus*—roamed the area between 500,000 and 100,000 years ago.) Founded in 1898 by Paul Kruger, president of what was then the Transvaal Republic, the park is a place to safari at your own pace, choosing between upscale private camps or simple campsites.

Kruger lies in the hot lowveld, a subtropical section of Mpumalanga and Limpopo provinces that abuts Mozambique. The park cuts a swath 80 km (50 mi) wide and 320 km (200 mi) long from Zimbabwe and the Limpopo River in the north to the Crocodile River in the south. It is divided into 16 macro ecozones, each supporting a great variety of plants, birds, and animals, including 145 mammal species and almost 500 species of birds, some of which are not found elsewhere in South Africa. In 2002 a treaty was signed between South Africa, Zimbabwe, and Mozambique to form a giant conservation area, the Great Limpopo Transfrontier Park. It's a complex ongoing process, but once the fences between Kruger, the Gonarezhou National Park in Mozambique, and the Limpopo National Park in Zimbabwe are finally removed, the Peace Park will be the largest conservation area in the world.

EXPLORING KRUGER NATIONAL PARK

The southern and central sections of the park are where you will probably see the most game. Riverine forests, thorny thickets, and large, grassy plains studded with knobthorn and marula trees are typical of this region and make ideal habitats for a variety of animals, including black and white rhinos (once on the verge of extinction), leopards, giraffes, hyenas, numerous kinds of antelope, lions, and the rare "painted wolf"—a wild dog.

As you drive north to Olifants and Letaba, you enter major elephant country, although you're likely to spot lots of other game, too, including lions and cheetahs. North of Letaba, however, the landscape becomes a monotonous blur of mopane trees, the result of nutrient-poor land that supports smaller numbers of animals, although the lugubrious-looking *tsessebe* (sess-a-bee) antelope and the magnificent and uncommon roan antelope, with its twisty horns, thrive here. Elephants love mopane, and you'll certainly see plenty of them. The Shingwedzi River Drive is one of the park's most rewarding drives, with elephants, leopards, giraffes, and other game regularly seen. Park your vehicle underneath the lovely hide on this drive, and take in life on the river, including waterbirds, hippos, and basking crocs. To experience the full richness of the northern Kruger, visit the Pafuri Picnic Site (hot water and braais

Kruger National Park

KEY
- ⚠ Bushveld Camp
- 🛖 Rest Camps
- ⊠ Entrance Gate

MOZAMBIQUE

LIMPOPO PROVINCE

MPUMALANGA

⊠ Pafuri

🛖 Punda Maria

⚠ Sirheni

Shingwedzi

⚠ Bateleur

Thohoyandou

Giyani

Mopani

Shimuwini ⚠

Letaba 🛖

Phalaborwa ⊠ Phalaborwa

Olifants 🛖

Balule 🛖

Hoedspruit

Timbavati Game Reserve ◆
Maroela 🛖

Thornybush Game Reserve ◆

⊠ Tamboti
⊠ Orpen

Satara 🛖

⚠ Talamati

Manyeleti Game Reserve ◆

Pilgrim's Rest

Sabi Sands Game Reserve ◆

Graskop

Hazyview

Sabie

⊠ Paul Kruger
⚠ Rhino Camps

🛖 Skukuza

⊠ Phabeni Gate

⊠ Numbi
🛖 Pretoriuskop

Lower Sabie 🛖

Biyamiti ⚠
⊠ Crocodile Bridge

Berg-en-Dal 🛖
Malelane ⊠

Nelspruit

Massingir Dam

0 —— 20 miles
0 —— 20 kilometers

available), where ancient massive leadwood and jackalberry trees lean over the often dry Luvuvhu River, the haunt of the scarlet-and-green Narina trogon (a bird) and the much-sought-after Pel's fishing owl. But don't leave your picnic unattended while you look for more special birds, such as the wattle-eyed flycatcher, because the vervet monkeys will have it in a flash.

Since the bush is unpredictable, you may get some of your best sightings where and when you least expect them: a pack of wild dogs lying in the road just outside the Skukuza camp gate or a cheetah and two cubs sitting in the middle of the tar road 100 yards inside the Orpen Gate. ■TIP➡ **If you have a week in Kruger, it's worth driving north, as there are always fewer people here. However, if you are short on time, then stick to the south or central sections of the park.** But wherever you go, **don't get out of your vehicle** except at certain well-marked picnic sites or view sites, unless you want to make an international headline.

There are nine entrance gates to Kruger, namely (counterclockwise from the north) Pafuri, Punda Maria, Phalaborwa, Orpen, Paul Kruger, Phabeni, Numbi, Malelane, and Crocodile Bridge. National access roads to all the entrance gates are paved. You can arrange for a late-entry escort (R150) until 9 PM for the following gates (and their nearby camps): Paul Kruger (Skukuza), Numbi (Pretoriuskop), Malelane (Berg-en-Dal and Malelane), Crocodile Bridge (Crocodile Bridge), Punda Maria (Punda Maria), and Orpen (Orpen). Always check at your gate for pamphlets, maps, and books (also available in the camp shops).

There is a daily conservation fee, but Wild Cards, available at the gates or online, are more economical for stays of more than a few days. Reservations for all accommodations, bush drives, wilderness trails, and other park activities must be made through South African National Parks (SANParks). *Box 787, Pretoria 0001* *012/343–1991* *www.SANParks.org* *R120* *Gates Apr.–Sept., daily 6–5:30; Oct.–Mar., daily 5:30 AM–6:30 PM, but sometimes vary.*

BUSH DRIVES

First-time visitors sometimes feel a little lost driving themselves through the park. They don't know what to look for, and they can't always identify the animals they see. Besides, not everyone knows what to do when a herd of elephants blocks the road. An affordable solution is to hire a game ranger to show you the park and its animal and bird inhabitants. All the major rest camps offer ranger-led bush drives in open-air vehicles (minimum of two people). Not only can rangers explain the finer points of what you're seeing, but they can also take you into areas off-limits to the public. There are also bush walks on offer at the different camps, something else you can't do on your own. Sunrise and sunset drives cost R155 (R80 per child); guided bush walks R230 (no children). Book drives at least two weeks in advance or when you make your park reservations.

DAY & NIGHT DRIVES

Even if you tour the park by yourself during the day, don't miss out on a ranger-led night drive, when the park is closed to regular visitors. You'll sit in a large open-air vehicle, scanning the bush with the ranger, who uses a powerful spotlight to pick out animals, including nocturnal creatures that you would never see otherwise. You might see bush babies (enchanting furry, bigeared, big-eyed little primates that

> ### A GOOD DRIVE
>
> One of the most consistently rewarding drives in the park is along the H4, running along the Sabie River from Skukuza to Lower Sabie. It can be crowded, however, particularly on weekends and public holidays and especially during the July and December school vacations.

leap from bush to bush), servals (mini leopard-looking felines), civets (black and white possum look-alikes), genets (spotted catlike creatures with bushy tails), or an aardvark ambling along in the moonlight. Scrutinize branches of big trees for the giant eagle owl, with its pink eyelids, or a leopard chewing on its kill. Night is also the time when hyenas and lions hunt. These opportunities alone make a night drive an unforgettable experience. The three- to four-hour trip leaves the rest camps half an hour before the gates close. ■TIP→ **Book as far in advance as possible.** Night drives cost R105 per person (depending on the size of the vehicle—smaller vehicles cost more), half price for kids. Don't forget your binoculars, a snack or drink, and a warm jacket whatever the season.

Day drives follow the same format as night drives. Choose between sunrise, mid-morning, and sunset drives. The cost is approximately the same as for night drives. Check the SANParks' Web site (⊕*www.sanparks.org*) for more details.

WILDERNESS TRAILS

Spend a few days hiking through the wilds of Africa and you may never again be satisfied with driving around a game reserve. On foot you gain an affinity for the animals and the bush that's impossible in the confines of a vehicle. Kruger has seven wilderness trails, each accommodating eight people. You need to be walking-fit and reasonably adventurous. Led by an armed ranger and local tracker, you'll go out in the morning for a few hours, come back at lunchtime for a meal and a siesta, and go out again in the early evening before returning to the same trail camp to relive the day's adventures around a cheerful campfire. These are not military-style marches but slow meanders, the point being to learn about your surroundings: the medicinal uses of trees and plants, the role of dung beetles and wasps in the ecology, and how to recognize animals by their spoor. In general, you don't get as close to animals on foot as you can in a vehicle. You will see animals, though, and many hikers can recount face-to-face encounters with everything from rhinos to elephants and lions.

Hikes last three nights and two days (starting on Sunday and Wednesday), and you should be prepared to walk as far as 19 km (12 mi) a day, although this will depend on the consensus of the group. Don't be

Spotting Kruger's Big Game

Watching game in the bush is very different from watching it on the Discovery Channel with its nonstop action. The former demands energy, concentration, patience, and luck, and with these you'll probably see wonderful game at Kruger, including the Big Five. The easy option is to visit a private game reserve, where knowledgeable rangers take you out in open vehicles or on foot and find game for you. You might spend two or three nights at a private reserve and then rent a vehicle and strike out on your own into Kruger's unknown territory. There's nothing quite like the thrill of finding your "own" elephant or identifying that psychedelic turquoise-and-lilac bird for yourself. Bring a couple of good field guides, available at bookstores and Kruger camp shops.

Drive slowly, stop at water holes, and keep your eyes and ears open. Talk to other visitors, and read the "game sightings" notice board and visitor's book at each camp. If other vehicles are stopped on the road, be courteous. Don't drive in front of or beside them and block their view, but edge along and find out what's being looked at. Don't forget to absorb the total bush experience—big and little creatures, trees, plants, sounds, colors, shapes, and smells. Look for the Little Five: the elephant shrew, lion ant, leopard tortoise, buffalo weaverbird, and rhinoceros beetle. You'll often find these in camp along with hundreds of birds that are habituated to visitors, good for up-close pictures.

afraid to make your wishes heard; have a group chat with your ranger on the first night and decide on the walking agenda. No one under 12 or over 60 is allowed, although if you book the whole trail and produce a doctor's certificate, over-60s are allowed. Hikers sleep in rustic A-frame two-bed huts and share a reed-wall bathroom with flush toilets and bucket showers. Meals are simple bush fare, including stews and barbecues; you provide your own booze and soft drinks (which you can purchase from the camp where you meet before the trail). In summer the trails are often cheaper (it's uncomfortably hot to walk at this time), and in winter nights can be freezing, so take very warm clothes and an extra blanket. These trails are incredibly popular; try to reserve 13 months in advance. The cost is approximately R2,350 per person per trail.

Bushman Trail. In the southwestern corner of the park, this trail takes its name from the San rock paintings and sites found in the area. The trail camp lies in a secluded valley dominated by granite hills and cliffs. Watch out for white rhinos, elephants, and buffalo. Check in at Berg-en-Dal.

Metsi Metsi Trail. The permanent water of the nearby N'waswitsontso River makes this one of the best trails for winter game-viewing. Midway between Skukuza amd Satara, the trail camp hunkers in the lee of a mountain in an area of gorges, cliffs, and rolling savanna. Check in at Skukuza.

Mpumalanga & Kruger National Park

Napi Trail. Sightings of white rhinos are common on this trail, which runs through mixed bushveld between Pretoriuskop and Skukuza. Other frequent sightings include black rhinos, cheetahs, leopards, and elephants. If you're lucky, you may also see the nomadic wild dogs. The trail camp is tucked into dense riverine forest at the confluence of the Napi and Biyamiti rivers. Check in at Pretoriuskop.

★ **Nyalaland Trail.** If it's untouched wilderness and remoteness you're after, then this camp in the far north of the park is for you. The camp is situated among ancient baobab trees near the Luvuvhu River, and you'll walk at the foot of huge rocky gorges as well as in dense forest. Some highly sought-after birds, such as Bohm's spinetail, crested eagle, and Pel's fishing owl, can be found in this birding mecca of huge baobabs and sinister-looking slime-green fever trees. You're almost certain to see hippos, crocodiles, elephants, buffalo, and the strikingly colored nyala antelope, with its dark fur, white spotted nose, and yellow "soccer stockings." Check in at Punda Maria.

Olifants Trail. With one of the most spectacular sites of all trail camps, this camp sits on a high bluff overlooking the Olifants River and affords regular sightings of elephants, lions, buffalo, and hippos. You'll walk through landscape varying from riverine forest to the rocky foothills of the Lebombo Mountains. Check in at Letaba.

Sweni Trail. East of Satara, this trail camp overlooks the Sweni Spruit and savanna dotted with marula and knobthorn trees. The area attracts large herds of zebras, wildebeests, and buffalo with their attendant predators: lions, spotted hyenas, and, if you're very lucky, wild dogs. Check in at Satara.

Wolhuter Trail. If you want to come face-to-face with a white rhino, choose this trail midway between Berg-en-Dal and Pretoriuskop. The undulating bushveld, interspersed with rocky *kopjes* (small hills), is ideal habitat for these tremendous, somehow anachronistic beasts, but you're also likely to see elephants, buffalo, and lions. Check in at Berg-en-Dal.

WHERE TO STAY IN KRUGER NATIONAL PARK

REST CAMPS

Rest camps include a variety of accommodations with prices to match—from R110 for a campsite for two people through basic two-person huts at R235 up to R1,870 for a luxury guesthouse for up to eight people. Options include rondawels (round beehive huts), cottages, bungalows, guest cottages (usually larger than the regular cottages), guesthouses, and safari tents. As a rule of thumb, here's what's meant by these terms (keeping in mind that each camp is different): rondawels or huts consist of one or two small rooms that can accommodate one or two people with electricity; you'll share a communal bathroom facility (always clean and with hot and cold running water) and communal kitchen with hot plates, sinks, and refrigerator. Cottages have at least one bedroom, a living room, bathroom, and a partially equipped kitchen or

Splendor in the Grass & Bush

If you can afford it, a splurge on a Kruger SKI (Spend the Kids' Inheritance) vacation could be the experience of a lifetime. Staying for a couple of nights at a private game lodge combines superb accommodations, service, and food with equally excellent game-viewing opportunities. Exclusivity on game drives (most lodges put only six people per vehicle with a dedicated ranger and tracker) almost guarantees sightings of the Big Five. Words like *elegance, luxury,* and *privacy* are overused when describing the accommodations, but the lodges are not all the same. One place might feature chalets done in modern chic, another lodges with an African-colonial feel, and a third open-air safari tents whose proximity to the bush makes up for what they lack in plushness. And you'll be treated like royalty, with whom you may well rub shoulders.

kitchenette, and a family cottage will have one, two, or three bedrooms with kitchenette. Bungalows have one room and a bathroom; some have their own kitchenettes, whereas others share communal kitchen facilities. Units with cooking facilities have basic kitchen equipment, dishes, and cutlery. Guest cottages and guesthouses are secluded units within a rest camp and have three or four bedrooms, most of which have private bathrooms. Each has a fully equipped kitchen, a communal lounge–living room, or an open veranda. Permanent, comfortable, large walk-in East African–style safari tents with insectproof flaps and windows sleep one or two people. Very popular, they give an *Out of Africa* feel and are equipped with beds, a cupboard, table and chairs, refrigerator, and electric fan. Communal kitchen and bathroom facilities are provided. In all accommodations, beds are comfortable, linens are always impeccable, soap and towels are provided, and units are serviced on a daily basis. A site to pitch your own tent (the best option if you're looking to do things on the cheap) costs approximately R110 for up to two people throughout the park. All campsites have excellent cooking and bathroom facilities.

All the major rest camps have electricity; a first-aid center; a shop selling food, drink (including alcohol—local wine is particularly good), curios, wildlife books, videos, and DVDs; barbecue and communal kitchen facilities; a self-service laundry or laundry tubs; public telephones (cellphone reception is usually possible at most of the major rest camps and environs); a gas station; and a restaurant and/or self-service cafeteria. However, most people bring their own food and drink (or buy it), and the evening braai (most rooms have individual open-air barbecue facilities) is a friendly park ritual; visitors build their fires as night falls and lions and hyenas start their nocturnal choruses. Holiday programs and evening shows on wildlife and conservation are arranged at many of the rest camps. Nature trails have been laid out in Punda Maria, (also accessible to blind/visually impaired visitors), and Pretoriuskop.

■ TIP→ There are no age limits for kids except on the walking trails.

All rest camps have their own individual character and charm. However, Skukuza, the hub of the park, is more like a small town than a rest camp. Avoid it if you dislike crowds, particularly in summer. There are swimming pools for residents only at Berg-en-Dal, Lower Sabie, Pretoriuskop, Mopani, Shingwedzi, and Skukuza. Skukuza also has a post office and a bank. There is an additional pool for day visitors at the Skukuza Day Visitor Area (to be avoided if possible, as it's nearly always packed). All rest camps are protected and enclosed by electrified fences, which are highly functional but don't prevent good game-viewing through the wire. ■TIP→ **It's always worth a dawn patrol or sunset stroll around your camp fence; you never know what you may spot.**

The golden rule when booking your accommodation is to get as much information as possible about the different types before you make your decision. It's often necessary to reserve a year in advance if you want to come during peak seasons (December–January and July). Reservations should be made with the **South African National Parks.** ☎*012/343–1991* ⊕*www.SANParks.org* ▤*AE, DC, MC, V.*

★ $ 🏠**Berg-en-Dal.** At the southern tip of the park, in a basin surrounded by rocky hills, Berg-en-Dal is known for its white rhinos, leopards, and wild dogs, but it lacks the tremendous game intensity of some of the camps to its north. A dam—in southern Africa, all man-made lakes, ponds or pools are called dams—by one side of the perimeter fence offers good game-viewing, including a close look at cruising crocodiles and munching elephants. One of the more attractive camps, it has thoughtful landscaping, which has left much of the indigenous vegetation intact, making for more privacy. ⟋*63 chalets, 23 family cottages, 2 guesthouses, 70 campsites* ⟋*In-room: kitchen. In-hotel: restaurant, pool, laundry facilities.*

   $ 🏠**Crocodile Bridge.** In the southeastern corner of the park, this superb small rest camp (it's won several awards for good service) doubles as an entrance gate, which makes it a convenient stopover if you arrive near the park's closing time and thus too late to make it to another camp. Although the Crocodile River provides a scenic backdrop, any sense of being in the wild is quickly shattered by views of power lines and farms on the south side. The road leading from the camp to Lower Sabie is famous for sightings of general game as well as buffalo, rhinos, cheetahs, and lions, but it's often crowded on weekends and holidays and during school vacations. A hippo pool lies just 5 km (3 mi) away. ⟋*20 bungalows (2 wheelchair accessible), 8 safari tents, 12 campsites* ⟋*In-room: kitchen. In-hotel: laundry facilities.*

   $ 🏠**Letaba.** Overlooking the frequently dry Letaba River, this lovely camp sits in the middle of elephant country in the central section of the park. There's excellent game-viewing on the roads to and all around the Engelhardt and Mingerhout dams. The camp itself has a real bush feel: all the huts are thatch (ask for one overlooking the river), and the grounds are overgrown with apple-leaf trees, acacias, mopane, and lala palms. The restaurant and snack bar, with attractive outdoor seating, look out over the riverbed. Even if you're not staying at Letaba, stop at the superb elephant exhibit at the Environmental Education

Centre and marvel at just how big elephants' tusks can get. Campsites, on the camp's perimeter, offer lots of shade for your tent or trailer. ⌂ *8 bungalows, 5 huts, 10 guest cottages, 2 guesthouses, 20 safari tents, 35 campsites* ⌂ *In-room: kitchen. In-hotel: restaurant, laundry facilities.*

★ $ ✕ ▦ **Lower Sabie.** This is one of the most popular camps in Kruger for good reason: it has tremendous views over a broad sweep of the Sabie River and sits in one of the

> **GOING ON A SAFARI?**
>
> Here are some items our readers suggest you not forget to pack:
>
> Wet wipes
>
> Converter
>
> Sports bra
>
> Tissues
>
> Eye drops

best game-viewing areas of the park (along with Skukuza and Satara). White rhinos, lions, cheetahs, elephants, and buffalo frequently come down to the river to drink, especially in the dry winter months when there is little surface water elsewhere. Long wooden walkways that curve around the restaurant and shop are particularly attractive; you can sit here looking out over the river. Half the safari tents have a river view. The vegetation around the camp is mainly grassland savanna interspersed with marula and knobthorn trees, and there are also lots of animal drinking holes within a few minutes' drive. Don't miss the H10 road from Lower Sabie to Tshokwane, where you'll almost certainly see elephants. ⌂ *30 huts, 62 bungalows, 24 safari tents, 1 guest cottage, 1 guesthouse, 33 campsites* ⌂ *In-room: kitchen. In-hotel: restaurant, pool, laundry facilities.*

$ ▦ **Mopani.** Built in the lee of a rocky kopje overlooking a lake, this camp in the northern section is one of Kruger's biggest. The lake and the camp are an oasis for both animals and people amid not very attractive surrounding mopane woodlands. If it's hippos you're after, sit on your veranda overlooking the lake and feast your eyes on a cavalcade of these giants mating, frolicking, or just mooching about. Constructed of rough stone, wood, and thatch, the camp blends well into the thick vegetation. Shaded wooden walkways connect the public areas, all of which overlook the lake, and the view from the open-air bar is awesome. The à la carte restaurant (reserve before 6 PM) serves better food than most of the other camps, and the cottages are better equipped and larger than their counterparts elsewhere in Kruger. Ask for accommodations overlooking the lake when you book. Mopani lacks the intimate charm of some of the smaller camps, and the surrounding mopani woodland doesn't attract much game, but it's a really comfortable camp to chill out in for a night or two if you're driving the length of the park. ⌂ *45 bungalows, 12 cottages, 45 guest cottages, 1 guesthouse* ⌂ *In-room: kitchen. In-hotel: restaurant, bar, pool, laundry facilities.*

$ ▦ **Olifants.** In the central section of the park, Olifants has the best setting of all the Kruger camps, high atop cliffs on a rocky ridge with panoramic views of the distant hills and the Olifants River below. A lovely thatch-sheltered terrace allows you to sit for hours with binoculars and pick out the animals below. Lions often make kills in the river valley, and elephants, buffalo, giraffes, kudu, and other game come to drink and bathe. Try to book one of the thatch rondawels overlooking the river for at least two nights (you'll need to book a year in advance) so you can hang out on your veranda and watch Africa's passing show below. Olifants offers more than a good view, however. It's a charming old camp, graced with wonderful indigenous trees like sycamore figs, mopane, and sausage trees—so called because of the huge, brown, sausage-shape fruits that weigh down the branches. A big drawback, particularly in the hot summer months, however, is that it has no pool. ➥*97 rondawels, 2 guesthouses ☼In-room: kitchen. In-hotel: restaurant, laundry facilities.*

$ 🏠**Orpen.** Don't dismiss this tiny Cinderella rest camp in the center of the park because of its proximity to the Orpen Gate. It may not be a particularly attractive camp—the rooms, arranged in a rough semicircle around a large lawn, look out toward the perimeter fence, about 150 feet away—but there's a permanent water hole, where animals come to drink, and plenty of game in the vicinity, including cheetahs, lions, and rhinos. The two-bedroom huts are a bit sparse, with no bathrooms or cooking facilities (although there are good communal ones), but there are three comfortable family cottages with bathrooms and kitchenettes. And it's a blissfully quiet camp, as there are so few accommodations. ➥*12 huts, 3 guest cottages ☼In-room: kitchen (some).*

$ 🏠**Pretoriuskop.** This large, bare, but nostalgically old-fashioned camp, conveniently close to the Numbi Gate in the southwestern corner of the park, makes a good overnight stop for new arrivals. The rocky kopjes and steep ridges that characterize the surrounding landscape provide ideal habitat for mountain reedbuck and klipspringers—antelope not always easily seen elsewhere in the park. The area's sourveld (so named because its vegetation is less sweet and attractive to herbivores than other kinds of vegetation) also attracts browsers like giraffes and kudu, as well as white rhinos, lions, and wild dogs. There's not a lot of privacy in camp—accommodations tend to overlook each other—but there is some shade and a great swimming pool. ➥*82 rondawels, 52 bungalows, 6 cottages, 45 campsites ☼In-room: kitchen. In-hotel: restaurant, pool, laundry facilities.*

$ 🏠**Punda Maria.** Not many foreign visitors make it to this lovely little camp in the far end of the park near Zimbabwe, but if you have time, try to get there. In some ways it offers the best bush experience of any of the major rest camps and it's considered to be Kruger's best birding camp. Tiny whitewashed thatch cottages arranged in terraces on a hill make up the camp, which lies in a sandveld (a botanically rich area notable for its plant and birdlife). ■TIP→ **If you're into birds, make sure you find the tiny, stone birdbath by the barbecue site, because dozens of really special birds visit daily.** The camp also offers a guided walking tour of the Thulamela Ruins (AD 1250–1700), one of South Africa's most interesting archaeological sites. Reservations are advised for the restaurant, but don't expect too much from the food. ⚠ **Only some of the campsites have power.** ➥*18 bungalows, 2 family* *bungalows, 7 safari tents, 50 campsites* ♿ *In-room: kitchen (some). In-hotel: restaurant.*

$ 🏠 **Satara.** Second in size only to Skukuza, this camp sits in the middle of the hot plains between Olifants and Lower Sabie, in the central section of Kruger. The knobthorn veld surrounding the camp provides the best grazing in the park and attracts large concentrations of game, which in turn brings the predators—lions, cheetahs, hyenas, and wild dogs—making this area great for game-viewing, especially on the N'wanetsi River Road (S100). You may see giraffes, zebras, waterbucks, and other antelopes around the perimeter fence. Despite its size, Satara has far more appeal than Skukuza: the huts aren't all piled on top of one another and there's tremendous birdlife. The restaurant and cafeteria are very pleasant, with shady seating overlooking the lawns and the bush beyond. Accommodations are in large cottages and two- or three-bed thatch rondawels, some with kitchenettes (no cooking utensils). The rondawels, arranged in large circles, face inward onto a central, open, grassy area. Campsites are secluded, with an excellent view of the bush, although they don't have much shade. ➥ *153 rondawels, 10 guest cottages, 3 guesthouses, 74 campsites* ♿ *In-room: kitchen (some). In-hotel: restaurant, laundry facilities.*

$ 🏠 **Skukuza.** It's worth popping in to have a look at this huge camp. More like a small town than a rest camp, it has a gas station, police station, airport, post office, car-rental agency, grocery store, and library. It's nearly always crowded, not only with regular visitors but with busloads of noisy day-trippers, and consequently has lost any bush feel at all. Skukuza is popular for good reason, though. It's easily accessible by both air and road, and it lies in a region of thorn thicket teeming with game, including lions, cheetahs, and hyenas. The camp itself sits on a bank of the crocodile-infested Sabie River, with good views of thick reeds, dozing hippos, and grazing waterbuck. Visit the worthwhile museum and education center to learn something about the history and ecology of the park. However, if you're allergic to noise and crowds, limit yourself to a stroll along the banks of the Sabie River before heading for one of the smaller camps. ➥ *199 bungalows, 16 cottages, 15 guest cottages, 7 guesthouses, 20 safari tents, 80 campsites* ♿ *In-hotel: restaurant, pool.*

¢   🏠 **Balule.** On the banks of the Olifants River, Satara's rustic satellite camp differs radically from the others because it really is simple, appealing to those who don't mind roughing it a bit and want to experience the true feel of the bush. There are no shops or restaurants, and there's no electricity either—only lanterns—so bring your own food. Accommodations are in basic three-bed huts with no windows (vents only) and shared bathroom facilities with running water. You must check in at Olifants, 11 km (7 mi away). ➥ *15 campsites, 6 huts.*

¢   🏠 **Malelane.** This very small, intimate little camp, ideal for backpackers and do-it-yourselfers, offers privacy and a "close-to-the bush" feeling. If you need supplies, a swim, or a bit more sophistication, Bergen-Dal is only a few kilometers away. A bonus is that you're within easy driving distance of good game areas around and towards Lower Sabie, and guided bush drives are on offer. Check in at Malelane Gate, from where the camp is managed. There's a communal kitchen and bathrooms near the camp's perimeter, within easy reach of camping sites and rondawels. ➩*3 bungalows, 5 rondawels, 15 campsites* ⚗*In-room: kitchen.*

¢ 🏕 **Maroela.** Orpen's small, cosy satellite campsite (the only camp in Kruger that caters exclusively to campers and caravans) is just 3 km (2 mi) away from the Orpen Gate. It can be hot, dry, and dusty at any time of the year, but you'll

feel close to the bush among thorn trees and maroela trees, and there's a small hide (blind) overlooking a waterhole. There are spic-and-span bathrooms, and good cooking, washing, and braii facilities. ➩*24 campsites (20 with power hook ups).*

¢ 🏕 **Tamboti.** Kruger's first tented camp, a satellite of Orpen and very close to the Orpen Gate, is superbly sited on the banks of the frequently dry Tamboti River, among sycamore fig and jackalberry trees. Communal facilities make it a bit like an upscale campsite, but nevertheless it's one of Kruger's most popular camps, so book well ahead. From your tent you may well see elephants digging in the riverbed for water just beyond the barely visible electrified fence. Each of the walk-in, permanent tents has its own deck overlooking the river, but when you book, ask for one in the deep shade of large riverine trees—worth it in the midsummer heat. All kitchen, washing, and toilet facilities are in two shared central blocks. Just bring your own food and cooking and eating utensils. There are braai facilites on-site. ➩*30 safari tents.*

¢ 🏠 **Shingwedzi.** Although this camp lies in the northern section of the park, amid monotonous long stretches of mopane woodland, it benefits enormously from the riverine growth associated with the Shingwedzi River and Kanniedood (Never Die) Dam. As a result, you'll probably find more game around this camp than anywhere else in the region—lots when you drive the Shingwedzi River Road early in the morning or just before the camp closes at night (but don't be late or you'll catch a hefty fine). The roofs of thatch and rough tree trunks give the camp a rugged, pioneer feel. Both the à la carte restaurant and the outdoor cafeteria have views over the Shingwedzi River. Accommodations are of two types: A and B. Try for one of the A units, whose steeply pitched thatch roofs accommodate an additional two-bed loft; some also have fully equipped kitchenettes. The huts face one another across a fairly barren expanse of dry earth except in early spring, when the gorgeous bright pink impala lilies are in bloom. ➩*24 huts, 54 bungalows, 1 cottage, 1 guesthouse, 50 campsites* ⚗*In-room: kitchen (some). In-hotel: restaurant, pool, laundry facilities.*

BUSHVELD CAMPS

Smaller, more intimate, more luxurious, and consequently more expensive than regular rest camps, Kruger's bushveld camps are in remote areas of the park that are often off-limits to regular visitors. Access is limited to guests only. As a result you get far more bush and fewer fellow travelers. Night drives and day excursions are available in most of the camps. There are no restaurants, gas pumps, or grocery stores, so bring your provisions with you, though you can buy wood for your barbecue. All accommodations have fully equipped kitchens, bathrooms, ceiling fans, and large verandas, but only Bateleur has air-conditioning and TV, the latter installed especially for a visit by South Africa's president. Cottages, in stands of trees or clumps of indigenous bush for maximum privacy, have tile floors and cane patio furniture. Many face directly onto a river or water hole. There are only a handful of one-bedroom cottages (at Biyamiti, Shimuweni, Sirheni, and Talamati), but it's worth booking a four-bed one and paying the extra, even for only two people. The average cottage price for a couple is R850, with extra people (up to five or six) paying R180 each. Reservations should be made with **South African National Parks.** ⌂ *Box 787, Pretoria 0001* ☏ *012/343–1991* ⊕ *www.SANParks.org* ▭ *AE, DC, MC, V.*

$ ⌂ **Bateleur.** Hidden in the northern reaches of the park, this tiny camp, the oldest of the bushveld camps, is one of Kruger's most remote destinations. Shaded by tall trees, it overlooks the dry watercourse of the Mashokwe Spruit. A raised platform provides an excellent game-viewing vantage point (don't forget to apply mosquito repellant if you sit here at dawn or dusk), and it's only a short drive to two nearby dams, which draw a huge variety of animals, from lions and elephants to zebras and hippos. The main bedroom in each fully-equipped cottage has air-conditioning (all other rooms have ceiling fans), a microwave, and a TV. ⇲ *7 cottages.*

$ ⌂ **Biyamiti.** Close to the park gate at Crocodile Bridge, this larger-than-average, but very beautiful and sought-after bush camp overlooks the normally dry sands of the Biyamiti River. It's very popular because it's close to the southern gates, and the game is usually prolific. A private sand road over a dry riverbed takes you to the well-sited camp, where big shade trees attract birds and make you feel truly cocooned in the wilderness. The vegetation is mixed woodland, which attracts healthy populations of kudu, impalas, elephants, lions, and black and white rhinos. After the stars come out you're likely to hear lions roar, nightjars call, and jackals yipping outside the fence. ⇲ *15 cottages.*

$ ⌂ **Shimuwini.** Birders descend in droves on this isolated and peaceful camp set on a lovely dam on the Letaba River. Away from the river, the riverine forest quickly gives way to mopane woodland, which is not particularly good for abundant game. Even so, the beautiful roan antelope and handsome, rare black and white sable antelope, which has back-sweeping scimitarlike horns, move through the area. Resident leopards patrol the territory, and elephants are usually browsing in the mopane. Be sure to visit one of the huge ancient baobab trees on the nearest loop road to the camp; Shimuweni is the Shangaan word for "Place of the Baobab," and there are lots of these striking, bizarre trees in the surrounding area. One disadvantage is that the camp is only accessed by a single road, which gets a bit tedious when you have to drive it every time you leave or come back to the camp. Cottages have one, two, or three bedrooms. ◄*15 cottages.*

★ $ Sirheni. The most remote of all the bushveld camps and one of the loveliest, Sirheni, another major bird-watching camp, sits on the edge of the Sirheni Dam, in the far north of the park. Because there is permanent water, game—including lions and white rhinos—can often be seen at the dam, particularly in the dry winter months. Keep your eyes open for the resident leopard which often comes down to drink in the evening. A rewarding drive for birders and game spotters alike runs along the Mphongolo River. Watch the sun set over the magnificent bush from one of two secluded viewing platforms at either end of the camp, but be sure to load on the mosquito repellent. ◄*15 cottages.*

  $ Talamati. On the banks of the normally dry N'waswitsontso River in Kruger's central section, this peaceful camp in the middle of a wide, open valley offers excellent game-viewing. Grassy plains and mixed woodlands provide an ideal habitat for herds of impalas, zebras, and wildebeests, as well as lions, cheetahs, and elephants. You can take a break from your vehicle and watch birds and game from a couple of raised viewing platforms inside the perimeter fence. The accommodations are well equipped and comfortable, with cane furniture and airy verandas. ◄*15 cottages.*

CONCESSIONS WITHIN KRUGER

Among the privately operated areas within the boundaries of the park is the 37,000-acre N'wanetsi concession in the extreme northeast of the park. Here two lodges, Singita Lebombo and Sweni, are located at the confluence of the N'wanetsi and Sweni rivers (not to be confused with their sister Singita camps in Sabie Sands private reserve). The area was once the base for the park's foot and horse patrols, and until the building of the lodges it had never been traversed by vehicles. Today it's home to the Big Five as well as zebras, giraffes, wildebeests, hippos, hundreds of bird species, and varied flora. Twice-daily game drives (dawn and late afternoon) in an open vehicle are led by a highly experienced and knowledgeable ranger. You can also take a bush nature walk, camp out under the stars, or try your hand at archery.

The Rhino Plains Concession, made up of the Rhino Walking Safari, Rhino Post Safari Lodge, and Plains camps, are situated in about 30,000 acres of pristine bushveld in the Mutlumuvi area of Kruger, which is 10 km (6 mi) northeast of Skukuza, the heart of Kruger Park. This location makes the concession easily accessible by road or air and allows for a shared 15-km (9-mi) boundary with Mala Mala, in the Sabi Sands Game Reserve, allowing for plenty of game movement between the two. The environmental impact of the lodge and tented camp is minimal; no concrete was used in buildings, battery power is used for lighting, and a special reedbed system processes bathroom waste. The area is home to the Big Five as well as many other mammals, birds, trees, and other plants. Activities include twice-daily game drives with professional guides in specially adapted open Land Rovers (the camps have access to some of Kruger's public roads at night), a sleep-out on an elevated wooden platform overlooking a water hole, a guided bush walk, a half- or full-day drive on public roads (with picnic lunch), or a game of golf, which can be arranged at the 9-hole Skukuza course. Trail packages, which include lodging, encourage a sense of companionship among the group (maximum eight), which decides together on speed and length of walks; feats of endurance are not the name of the game.

★ $$ 🏠 **Singita Lebombo Lodge.** Taking its name from the Lebombo Mountain Range and ecodriven in concept, Singita Lebombo, winner of numerous international accolades, has been built "to touch the ground lightly." It hangs seemingly suspended on the edge of a cliff, like a huge glass box in space. Wooden walkways connect the aptly named "lofts" (suites), all which have an uncluttered style and spectacular views of the river and bushveld below. Outdoor and indoor areas fuse seamlessly. Organic materials—wood, cane, cotton, and linen—are daringly juxtaposed with steel and glass. This is Bauhaus in the bush, with a uniquely African feel. Soak in perfumed luxury in a big sunken tub in your massive bathroom while you gaze at the river. Public areas, built around stately candelabra euphorbias (succulents) endemic to the area, are light, bright, and airy, furnished with cane furniture, crisp white cushions, comfy armchairs, and recliners. Service is superb, as is the food, and nothing is left to chance. At the classy Trading Post you can buy African art and artifacts, snakeskin purses, or a diamond or two. You can also treat yourself to a beauty treatment at the spa. ⌂ *Box 650881, Benmore 2010* ☎*011/234–0990* ⊕*www.singita.co.za* 🛏*15 suites* ⌂*In-room: safe, minibar. In-hotel: bar, pool, gym, spa, Internet* ▤*AE, DC, MC, V* ⧖*FAP.*

$$ 🏠 **Sweni Lodge.** Built on wooden stilts, Sweni, the smallest of all the Singita lodges, is cradled on a low riverbank amid thick virgin bush and ancient trees. More intimate than its sister camp, Lemombo, it has six huge river-facing suites glassed on three sides, wooden on the other. At night khaki floor-to-ceiling drapes lined with silk divide the living area from the bedroom, which has a king-size bed with weighted, coffee-colored mosquito netting and a cascade of ceramic beads. Hanging lamp shades of brown netting fashioned like traditional African fish traps, cream mohair throws, and brown leather furniture enhance the natural feel and contrast daringly with the gleam of stainless steel in the living room and bathroom. Chill out on your large reed-shaded deck while watching an elephant herd drink, or spend the night under the stars on a comfy, mosquito-net-draped mattress. A fully stocked bar and your own library of bird and mammal books, wildlife magazines, and board games are available if you decide to do your own thing for an hour or three. ⌂ *Box 650881, Benmore 2010* ☎*011/234–0990* ⊕*www.singita.co.za* 🛏*6 suites* ⌂*In-room: safe, minibar. In-hotel: bar, pool, gym, spa, Internet* ▤*AE, DC, MC, V* ⧖*FAP.*

$ 🏠 **Rhino Post Plains Camp.** Overlooking a water hole amid an acacia knobthorn thicket deep in the heart of the Timbitene Plain, Plains Camp has comfortably furnished tents with wooden decks and great views of the plains. A deck with bar and plunge pool are great for post-walk get-togethers, and there's a small tented dining area. Simple, unpretentious, and very friendly, the camp has great food. ⌂ *Box 1881, Juskei Park 2153* ☎ *011/467–1886* ⊕ *www.zulunet.co.za* ⟿ *4 tents* ⌂ *In-hotel: bar* ☰ *AE, DC, MC, V* ⎮○⎮ *FAP.*

> **WHAT'S A CONCESSION?**
>
> Concessions are certain areas within national parks that are leased to private companies. These companies then build, run, and maintain lodges within their concession.

$ 🏨 **Rhino Post Safari Lodge.** The lodge comprises eight spacious suites on stilts overlooking the Mutlumuvi riverbed. Open-plan suites built of canvas, thatch, wood, and stone each have a bedroom, private wooden deck, bathroom with a deep freestanding bath, his-and-hers sinks, a separate toilet, and an outdoor shower protected by thick reed poles. ⌂ *Box 1881, Juskei Park 2153* ☎ *011/467–1886* ⊕ *www.zulunet. co.za* ⟿ *8 suites* ⌂ *In-hotel: bar, pool* ☰ *AE, DC, MC, V* ⎮○⎮ *FAP.*

☾ ¢ 🏨 **Pafuri Camp.** This gorgeous, sprawling camp—Wilderness Safari's first game lodge in South Africa—stretches for almost a mile along the banks of the Luvuvhu River. The 59-acre area is home to an amazing variety of landscapes. It's also in one of the wildest and most inaccessible parts of Kruger and is the ancestral home of the Makuleke people, who, in partnership with Wilderness Safaris, act as landlords for this camp and the area. Pafuri is one of the few places on earth where a fever tree forest and a baobab forest intermingle. At Crooks Corner, where the villains of yesteryear hid and made mischief, there is a wide swath of sand stretching as far as the eye can see, linking the three countries of Mozambique, South Africa, and Zimbabwe. There's great game—you could wake up in the morning and find a herd of 60 nyala around your tent accompanied by more than 20 bushbuck—and the area is covered in stone-age tools, rock engravings, and rock paintings that are more than 1.5 million years old; dinosaur fossils have been found too. You can also visit one of the biggest baobabs in the world; it takes at least 10 people holding hands to encircle it. Pafuri has the best birding in Kruger—if you've never seen or heard the rare and elusive Pel's fishing owl, then this is the place to find it. It's a long but easy drive from Johannesburg, and you can bring the kids, because there's a superb children's program and special family accommodations which give both you and the kids privacy. ⌂ *Wilderness Safaris, Box 5219, Rivonia 2120* ☎ *027/11/807–1800* ⊕ *www.wilderness-safaris.co.za* ⟿ *20 tented river-facing rooms* ⌂ *In-room: safe. In-hotel: restaurant, bar, pool, airport shuttle* ☰ *AE, DC, MC, V* ⎮○⎮ *FAP.*

WHERE TO STAY NEAR KRUGER NATIONAL PARK

The hotels and lodges reviewed below lie in private game reserves adjoining Kruger National Park, and game roams freely between the reserves and the park.

Lodges are substantially more expensive than the rest camps and bushveld camps in Kruger, but there's a reason. Service is more personalized, accommodations are plusher, the food is usually excellent, game-viewing opportunities are superb, and generally everything's included. Don't worry if you're averse to venison or are a vegetarian; there are tempting, creative dishes for all tastes. Most accommodations have air-conditioning, minibars, room safes, a ceiling fan, tea/coffeemakers, and bathrooms offering the most gorgeous "smellies"—shampoo, body lotion, shower gels—plus insect repellent. If landline reception is available, there are room telephones. Cell-phone reception is patchy (depending on the area), but never take your cell phone on a game drive for obvious reasons. All camps have radio telephones if you need to make contact with the outside world. Chartered flights to and from the camps on shared private airstrips are available, or lodges will collect you from Hoedspruit Airport or KMIA. Most lodges recommend a two- to three-night stay (try for three nights) so that you can experience as much as possible, from starlit dinners to ranger-led bush walks.

The daily program at each lodge rarely deviates from a pattern, starting with a light breakfast before an early-morning game drive (usually starting at dawn, later in winter). At 10, when you get back to the lodge, you get a full English breakfast or brunch. You can then choose to go on a bush walk with an armed ranger, where you learn about some of the minutiae of the bush (including the Little Five), although you could also happen on giraffes, antelopes, or any one of the Big Five. But don't worry; you will be well briefed in advance on what you should do if you come face-to-face with a lion, for example. The rest of the day, until the late-afternoon game drive, is spent at leisure, so read up on the bush in the camp library, snooze, or have a swim. A sumptuous afternoon tea is served at 3:30 or 4 before you head off back into the bush for your night drive. During the drive, your ranger will find a peaceful spot for sundowners (cocktails), and you can sip your drink and nibble snacks as you watch one of Africa's spectacular sunsets. As darkness falls, your ranger will switch on the spotlight so you can spy nocturnal animals: lions, leopards, jackals, porcupines, servals, civets, and bush babies. You'll get back to the lodge around 7:30, in time to freshen up before a three- or five-course dinner in an open-air boma around a blazing fire. Often the camp staff entertains after dinner with local songs and dances—an unforgettable experience. Children under 12 are not allowed at some of the camps (unless the whole camp is booked), and if they are, those six years or under are not allowed to take part in game activities.

¢ **Protea Hotel Kruger Gate.** Set in its own small reserve only 110 yards from the Paul Kruger Gate, this comfortable hotel gives you a luxury alternative to the sometimes bare-bones accommodations of Kruger's rest camps. The hotel has two major advantages: fast access to the south-central portion of the park, where game-viewing is best, plus the impression that you are in the wilds of Africa. Dinner, heralded by beating drums, is served in a boma, a traditional open-air reed enclosure around a blazing campfire. Rangers lead guided walks through the surrounding bush, you can even sleep overnight in a tree house, or you can book a guided game drive (all these activities are at extra cost).

Rooms, connected by a raised wooden walkway that passes through thick indigenous forest, are not very imaginative. They have Spanish-tile floors and standard hotel furniture, as well as air-conditioning, TV, minibar, and tea/coffeemakers. There are also self-catering chalets that sleep six. Relax on the pool deck overlooking the Sabie River, have a cocktail in the cool bar, or puff on a cheroot in the sophisticated cigar bar while the kids take part in a fun-filled Prokidz program (during school vacations only). ⊠ *Kruger Gate, Skukuza 1350* ☎ *013/735–5671* ⊕ *www.proteahotels.co.za* ⊅ *96 rooms, 7 chalets* ⌂ *In-hotel: restaurant, bar, pool* ⊟ *AE, DC, MC, V* ⍓ *FAP.*

SABI SANDS GAME RESERVE

This is the most famous and exclusive of the private reserves, which boasts perhaps the highest game density of any private reserve in southern Africa. Collectively owned and managed, the 153,000-acre reserve is home to dozens of private lodges, including the world-famous Mala Mala and Londolozi.

Although not all lodges own vast tracts of land, most have traversing rights over most of the reserve. With an average of 20 vehicles (from different camps) watching for game and communicating by radio, you're bound to see an enormous amount of game and almost certainly the Big Five, but since only three vehicles are allowed at a sighting at a time, you can be assured of a grandstand seat. Expect to see large herds of elephants, particularly in the fall (March–May), when they migrate from Kruger in search of water and better grazing. The Sabi Sands is also the best area for leopard sightings. (In fact, the Londolozi leopards are world famous.) It's a memorable experience to see this quite beautiful, powerful, and often elusive feline—the most successful of all feline predators—padding purposefully through the bush at night, illuminated in your ranger's spotlight. There are many lion prides, and occasionally, the increasingly rare wild dogs will migrate from Kruger to den in the Sabi Sands. You'll also see white rhinos, zebras, giraffes, wildebeests, and most of the antelope species, plus birds galore. Before you go on your first game drive, if there's a special animal or bird you would really love to see, tell your ranger, who will try to find it for you.

DJUMA   Shangaan for "roar of the lion," Djuma is in the northeast corner of the Sabi Sands Game Reserve. It was the first game reserve in Africa to place permanent cameras at water holes and on a mobile vehicle so that Web surfers (www.africam.com) can watch the goings-on in the African bush without leaving home. Your hosts are husband-and-wife team Jurie and Pippa Moolman, who are passionate about their work (Jurie has a B.S. in ecology). Although there's a good chance of seeing the Big Five during the bush walk after breakfast and the twice-daily game drives, Djuma also caters to those with special bushveld interests, such as bird-watching or tree identification. Djuma's rangers and trackers are also adept at finding seldom-seen animals, such as wild dogs, spotted hyenas, and genets. You'll find none of the formality that sometimes prevails at the larger lodges. For example, members of the staff eat all meals with you and join you around the nighttime fire. In fact,

Djuma prides itself on its personal service and feeling of intimacy. Your dinner menu is chalked up on a blackboard (try ostrich pâté with cranberry sauce for a starter), as is the evening cocktail menu (how about a Screaming Hyena or African Sunrise?). ⌂ *Box 338, Hluvukani 1363* ☎ *013/735–5118* ⊕ *www.djuma.com* ✉ *AE, DC, MC, V* ⏺ *FAP.*

$ 🔲 **Bush Lodge.** Sitting in a lush grove of tamboti trees and overlooking a water hole, this camp contains thatch chalets with rugged wooden furniture and faux-animal-skin fabrics. Don't miss out on a trip to the local villages (not tourist traps) of Dixie and Utah, where you'll be introduced to the families of the people looking after you at camp. 🛏 *8 chalets* ♿ *In-hotel: bar, pool.*

$ 🔲 **Vuyatela.** Djuma's vibey, most upscale camp mixes contemporary African township culture with modern Shangaan culture. It's quite different from most of the other private camps with its bright colors, trendy designs, hand-painted napkins, and candy-wrapper place mats that mix with traditional leather chairs, thatch, and hand-painted mud walls. Look out for some great contemporary African township art, both classic and "naïf" artifacts, and especially for the chandelier made with old Coca-Cola bottles above the dining table. The camp is unfenced, and it's quite usual to see kudu nibbling the lawns or giraffes towering above the rooftops. Accommodations are in beautifully decorated chalets with private plunge pools. For something different in between drives, get your hair braided African style at the Comfort Zone, the in-camp spa. 🛏 *8 suites* ♿ *In-hotel: bar, spa.*

¢ 🔲 **Galago.** A delightful and affordable alternative to the upscale lodges, Galago, which means "lesser bush baby" in Shangaan, is a converted U-shape farmhouse whose five rooms form an arc around a central fireplace. There's a big, shady veranda where you can sit and gaze out over the open plain before cooling off in the plunge pool. You can bring your own food and do your own cooking for less than half the all-inclusive price, or you can bring your own supplies and hire the camp's chef (R300 per day) to cook it for you. Game drives and walks are led by your own ranger. This is a perfect camp for a family safari or friends' reunion. 🛏 *5 rooms* ♿ *In-hotel: pool.*

LEOPARD HILLS $$ **Leopard Hills Lodge.** Owned by the Kruger family, distant relatives of Paul Kruger, president of the then Transvaal Republic and founder of Kruger National Park, this hilltop lodge was built 100 years after Kruger's foundation in 1898. Set on a rocky outcrop with panoramic views of the surrounding bushveld, the lodge's main draw is its game-viewing; during a two-night stay guests can almost be guaranteed to see the Big Five. Guests can also take a guided bush walk, fly over the Blyde River Canyon in a helicopter, or visit the local village. The lodge's decor has an authentic bush theme, which gels well with the surroundings. Each double room has its own private heated pool (in addition to the main pool) and deck overlooking the bushveld. Bathrooms have his-and-hers showers both indoors and out. Attention to detail is manifested in the leopard tracks and similar African motifs that appear in walkways, bedrooms, and bathrooms; check out the ceramic chameleon around the dressing table. As with many lodges in the area, Leopard Hills gives back to the community, and its junior school on the premises provides excellent schooling for the children of lodge staff throughout the Sabi Sands area. A library and traditional Shangaan boma are on the grounds. No kids under 10 are allowed. ◻ *Box 612, Hazyview 1242* ☎ *013/737–6626 or 013/737–6627* ⊕ *www.leopardhills.com* ⬚ *8 rooms* ⚲ *In-room: safe, minibar. In-hotel: bar, pool, gym, spa, Internet* ▤ *AE, DC, MC, V* |◯| *FAP.*

LION SANDS   Guests of the Lion Sands Private Game Reserve can take direct scheduled flights to the Mala Mala airfield through SA Airlink (⇨ *Mpumalanga & Kruger National Park Essentials, below*). ◻ *Box 30, White River 1240* ☎ *013/735–5330* ⊕ *www.lionsands.com* ▤ *AE, DC, MC, V* |◯| *FAP.*

★ $$ ▣ **Ivory Lodge.** If you're looking for ultimate luxury, solitude, and total relaxation, this is the place for you. Six simple and uncluttered, Afro-European-styled suites offer absolute exclusivity, operating as private villas with private entrances and superb views overlooking the Sabi River, Kruger, and beyond. Chill out with intimate dinners and on-the-spot spa treatments, attend a wine-tasting at the on-site wine cellar that features some of South Africa's finest wines, or opt for game drives in a private game vehicle with your own personal ranger. You also have a personal butler and plunge pool. ⬚ *6 suites* ⚲ *In-room: safe, minibar. In-hotel: spa, restaurant.*

$ ▣ **River Lodge.** This friendly lodge is set on one of the longest and best stretches of river frontage in Sabi Sands. You can watch the passing animal and bird show from your deck or from the huge tree-shaded wooden viewing area that juts out over the riverbank facing Kruger National Park. Although the guest rooms are small, they are comfortable and attractively Africa themed, with honey-colored stone floors with pebble inlays, cream wooden furniture, embroidered white bed linens, and lamps and tables of dark indigenous wood. The food is imaginative and tasty (try kudu stuffed with peanut butter with a mushroom and Amarula sauce), the young staff cheerful and enthusiastic, and the rangers highly qualified. After an exhilarating game drive, take a leisurely bush walk, go fishing, sleep out under the stars, or relax with a beauty treatment at Lalamuka Spa (*Lalamuka* means "unwind" in Shangaan). Public spaces are large and comfortable and lack the African designer clutter that mars some other lodges. There's a resident senior ecologist and a classy and interesting curio shop. ⬚ *20 rooms* ⚲ *In-room: safe, minibar. In-hotel: bar, pool, spa.*

LONDOLOZI   Since its inception in 1974 (it was a family farm and retreat before that), Londolozi has become synonymous with South Africa's finest game lodges and game experiences. (*Londolozi* is the Zulu word for "protector of all living things.") Brother-and-sister Bronwyn and Boyd Varty, the third generation of the Varty family, are now in charge with a mission to reconnect the human spirit with the wilderness and to carry on their family's quest to honor the animal kingdom. The Big Five are all here, as are the world famous leopards of Londolozi. (You are guaranteed to see at least one.) There are five camps, each representing a different element in nature: Pioneer Camp (water), Tree Camp (wood),

Granite Suites (rock), Varty Camp (fire), and Founders Camp (earth). Each is totally private, hidden in dense riverine forest on the banks of the Sand River. The Varty family live on the property, and their friendliness and personal attention, along with the many staff who have been here for decades, will make you feel part of the family immediately. The central reception and curio shop are at Varty Camp. ☒*Londolozi, Box 41864, Hyde Park 2024* ☎*011/280–6655* ⊕*www.londolozi.com* ☰*AE, DC, MC, V* ⦿*FAP.*

$$$ ⛁**Granite Suites.** Book all three private suites or just hide yourself away from the rest of the world like the celebrities and royals who favor this gorgeous getaway. Here, it's all about location, location, location. Huge, flat granite rocks in the riverbed, where elephants chill out and bathe, stretch almost to the horizon in front of your floor-to-ceiling picture windows, and the elephant prints and furnishings done in velvets and silvers, grays and browns, echo the shifting colors and textures of the mighty pachyderms. Bathe in your own rock pool, then at night, when your suite is lit by scores of flickering candles, feel truly in wonderland. ⇔*3 suites* ⛁*In-room: minibar, safe. In-hotel: bar, pool, public Wi-Fi.*

☺ $$ ⛁**Founders Camp.** This camp takes you back to the early days of Londolozi, before ecotourism was invented—when it was more important to shoot a lion than to take the perfect shot of it. The stone-and-thatch chalets are situated among thick riverine bush and are linked to the other chalets by meandering pathways. Each has its own wooden viewing deck and is decorated in classic black-and-cream ticking fabric, with compass safari lamps, military chests, and faded family documents. Relax on the thatch split-level dining and viewing decks that jut out over a quiet backwater of the Sand River, and watch the mammals and birds go by. After your game drive or walk, cool off in the tree-shaded swimming pool, which also overlooks the river. ⇔*5 chalets* ⛁*In-room: minibar, safe. In-hotel: bar, pool, public Wi-Fi.*

$$ ⛁**Pioneer Camp.** Pioneer Camp and its suites are a loving tribute to the early days and legendary characters of Sparta, the original name of the Londolozi property. Channel into a past world through faded sepia photographs, old hunting prints, horse-drawn carts, gleaming silverware, and scuffed safari treasures, taking you back in time to the day when it took five days by ox wagon to get to Londolozi. In winter sink deeply into your comfortable armchair in front of your own blazing fireplace; in summer sit outside in your outdoor dining room and listen to Africa's night noises. Keep your ears and eyes open for the resident female leopard as she hunts at night. The public rooms comprise a small, intimate boma, inside and outside dining areas, viewing decks, and a gorgeous S-shaped pool nestling in the surrounding bush, where after your dip you can laze on padded lie-out chairs and be lulled to sleep by the birdsong. ⇔*6 cottages* ⛁*In-room: minibar, safe. In-hotel: bar, pool, public Wi-Fi, no kids under 12.*

★ $$ ⛁**Tree Camp.** The first Relais & Chateaux game lodge in the world, this gorgeous camp, now completely rebuilt and redesigned (think leopards, lanterns, leadwoods, and leopard orchids), is shaded by thick riverine bush and tucked into the riverbank overlooking indigenous

7

forest. Dave Varty has built well over 20 lodges around Africa, and he feels that this is his triumph. The lodge is themed in chocolate and white, with exquisite leopard photos on the walls, airy and stylish interiors, and elegant yet simple furnishings. Huge bedrooms, en-suite bathrooms, and plunge pools continue the elegance, simplicity, and sophistication, and all suites have their own plunge pools. From your spacious deck you look out onto a world of cool green forest dominated by ancient African ebony and marula trees. Treat yourself to a bottle of bubbly from the Champagne Library and then dine with others while swapping bush stories, or alone on your private *sala* (outdoor covered deck). ⌑6 suites ⌂ In-room: minibar, safe. In-hotel: bar, pool, public Wi-Fi.

⌂ $ ⊞**Varty Camp.** This camp's fire has been burning for more than 80 years, making this location the very soul and center of Londolozi. It's also the largest of Londolozi's camps, centered on a thatched A-frame lodge that houses a dining room, sitting areas, and lounge. Meals are served on a broad wooden deck that juts over the riverbed and under an ancient jackalberry tree. The thatch rondavels, which were the Varty family's original hunting camp, now do duty as a library, a wine cellar, and an interpretive center, where you can listen to history and ecotourism talks—don't miss the Londolozi Leopard presentation. If you're looking for romance, have a private dinner on your veranda and go for a moonlight dip in your own plunge pool. In suites, the pool leads right to the riverbed. All rooms are decorated in African ethnic chic—in creams and browns and with the ubiquitous historic family photographs and documents—and have great bushveld views. Families are welcome and the fascinating kids' programs will turn any couch potato into an instant wannabe ranger. ⌑2 suites, 8 chalets ⌂ In-room: minibar, safe. In-hotel: bar, pool, public Wi-Fi.

MALA MALA This legendary game lodge, which along with Londolozi put South
Fodor'sChoice African safaris on the international map, has been tops in its field for
★ more than 40 years. Visitors will be delighted with incomparable personal service, superb food, and discreetly elegant, comfortable accommodations, where you'll rub shoulders with statesmen and -women, aristocrats, celebrities, and returning visitors alike. Mike Rattray, a legend in his own time in South Africa's game-lodge industry, describes Mala Mala as "a camp in the bush," but it's certainly more than that, although it still retains that genuine bushveld feel of bygone days. Both the outstanding hospitality and the game-viewing experience keep guests coming back. Mala Mala constitutes the largest privately owned Big Five game area in South Africa, and includes an unfenced 30-km (19-mi) boundary with Kruger National Park, across which game crosses continuously. The variety of habitats ranges from riverine bush, favorite hiding place of the leopard, to open grasslands, where cheetahs hunt. Mala Mala's animal-viewing statistics are impressive: the Big Five are spotted almost every day. At one moment your well-educated, friendly, articulate ranger will fascinate you with the description of the sex life of a dung beetle, as you watch the sturdy male battling his way along the road pushing his perfectly round ball of dung with wife-to-be perched perilously on top; at another, your adrenaline will flow as you

follow a leopard stalking impala in the gathering gloom. Along with the local Shangaan trackers, whose eyesight rivals that of the animals they are tracking, the top-class rangers ensure that your game experience is unforgettable. ⌂ *Box 55514, Northlands 2116* ☏*011/268–2388* ⊕*www.malamala.com* ▱*AE, DC, MC, V* ◯❙*FAP.*

$$ ⊞**Rattray's on Mala Mala.** The latest addition to Mala Mala is breathtakingly beautiful. Original bushveld style has been merged with modern touches that run the risk of being out of place, but work wonderfully well. Tuscan-style villas with spacious en-suite his-and-hers bathrooms, dressing rooms, and private heated plunge pools blend astonishingly well with the surrounding landscape. Each villa's entrance hall, with original art by distinguished African wildlife artists such as Keith Joubert, leads into a huge bedroom with a wooden four-poster bed. Beyond that is a lounge with deep sofas, comfy armchairs, padded ottomans, writing desks (for those crucial nightly journal entries), antique Persian rugs and carpets, and a dining nook for those intimate dinners à deux. Floor-to-ceiling picture windows with insect-proofed sliding doors face the Sand River, and the massive deck will tempt you onto the cushioned chairs to view the passing wildlife. You also have your own attractive indigenous garden, alive with colorful butterflies. The main lodge (also a Tuscan-style villa) includes viewing and dining decks, a horizon pool, and lounge areas that offer tantalizing views of the Sand River. You'll find it difficult to tear yourself away from the paneled library, with its plush sofas, inviting leather chairs, antique carpets, old prints and photographs, and well-traveled leather suitcases. Complete works of Rudyard Kipling, Dickens, and Thackeray rub shoulders with 100-year-old bound copies of England's classic humor magazine *Punch* and contemporary classics. The wine cellar has an impressive array of fine wines, and the bar, made of polished cherrywood, has a huge fireplace, old photographs, leather seats, and an antique card table. Ernest Hemingway would have loved it. ⇝*8 villas* ⌂ *In-room: safe, minibar, Internet, DVD. In-hotel: bar, pool, gym, no kids under 16.*

$$ ⊞**Sable Camp.** This fully air-conditioned, exclusive camp at the southern end of Main Camp overlooks the Sand River and surrounding bushveld. With its own pool, library, and boma, it's smaller and more intimate than Main Camp, although it shares the same magnificent all-around bush and hospitality experience. There's a shop and a library as well. ⇝*7 suites* ⌂ *In-room: safe, minibar, Internet. In-hotel: bar, pool, gym, no kids under 12.*

♺ $ ⊞**Main Camp.** Ginger-brown stone-and-thatch air-conditioned rondawels with separate his-and-hers bathrooms are decorated in creams and browns and furnished with cane armchairs, colorful handwoven tapestries and rugs, terra-cotta floors, and original artwork. Public areas have a genuine safari feel, with plush couches, animal skins, and African artifacts. A huge deck is shaded by ancient jackalberry trees and overlooks the Sand River. Browse in the air-conditioned Monkey Room for books and wildlife videos, sample the magnificent wine cellar, sun yourself by the pool, or stay fit in the well-appointed gym. The food (among the best in the bush) is tasty, wholesome, and varied, with a full buffet at both lunch and dinner. Children are welcome, and there are special children's programs, but children under 12 are not allowed on game drives unless with their own family group. Children under five are not allowed on game drives. ⤳*18 rooms (1 with wheelchair accessability).* ♿*In-room: safe, Internet, refrigerator. In-hotel: bar, pool, gym.*

SABI SABI   Founded in 1978 at the southern end of Sabi Sands, Sabi Sabi was one of the first lodges, along with Londolozi, to offer photo safaris and to link ecotourism, conservation, and community. Superb accommodations and the sheer density of game supported by its highly varied habitats draw guests back to Sabi Sabi in large numbers. There's a strong emphasis on ecology: guests are encouraged to look beyond the Big Five and to become aware of the birds and smaller mammals of the bush. 🖂*Box 52665, Saxonwold 2132* ☎*011/483–3939* 🌐*www.sabisabi.com* ▤*AE, DC, MC, V* ❙⊙❙*FAP.*

$$ 🏨**Earth Lodge.** This multi-award-winning ecofriendly lodge was the first to break away from the traditional safari style and go for a contemporary theme that's a cross between a Hopi cave dwelling and a medieval keep. On arrival, all you'll see is bush and grass-covered hummocks until you descend a hidden stone pathway that opens onto a spectacular landscape of boulders and streams. The mud-domed suites are hidden from view until you are practically at the front door. Each one has a huge living space with a sitting area, mega bathroom, private veranda, and plunge pool. A personal butler takes care of your every need, and there's a meditation garden for the lodge. Dine in a subterranean cellar or in the boma fashioned from roots and branches and lighted at night by dozens of lanterns. ⤳*13 suites* ♿*In-room: safe, minibar. In-hotel: bar, pool, spa.*

$ 🏨**Bush Lodge.** This large lodge overlooks a busy water hole (lions are frequent visitors) and the dry course of the Msuthlu River. The thatch, open-sided dining area, observation deck, and pool all have magnificent views of game at the water hole. Thatch suites are connected by walkways that weave between manicured lawns and beneath enormous shade trees where owls and fruit bats call at night. All have a deck overlooking the dry river course (where you may well see an elephant padding along) and outdoor and indoor showers. Chalets are older and smaller—although more intimate in a way—but still roomy; they are creatively decorated with ethnic designs and have a personal wooden deck. ⤳*21 chalets, 5 suites* ♿*In-room: safe, minibar. In-hotel: bar, pool, spa.*

☾ **$**   🏨**Little Bush Camp.** This delightful family camp easily meets Sabi Sabi's high standards. At night glowing oil lanterns lead you along a wooden walkway to your comfortable thatch-roofed suite, decorated in an African style in brown, cream, and white earth tones. A delicious brunch and some serious chill time follow your action-packed morning game drive: lounge on the wooden deck overlooking the bush, have a snooze in your air-conditioned bedroom, or laze by the pool area. At night sip a glass of complimentary sherry as you watch the stars—you'll swear you've never seen such bright ones. ⤳*6 suites* ♿*In-room: safe, minibar. In-hotel: bar, pool, spa.*

★ $ ⊞ **Selati Lodge.** For that genuine *Out of Africa* feel, Selati, formerly the private hunting lodge of a famous South African opera singer, is an intimate, stylish, colonial-style camp. The early-1900s atmosphere is created by the use of genuine train memorabilia—old leather suitcases, antique wooden chairs, nameplates, and signals—that recall the old Selati branch train line, which once crossed the reserve, transporting gold from the interior to the coast of Mozambique in the 1870s. At night the grounds of this small, secluded lodge flicker with the lights of the original shunters' oil lamps. You'll dine in a boma, and eat brunch in the friendly farmhouse kitchen. Members of the glitterati and European royalty have stayed at the spacious Ivory Presidential Suite, with its Persian rugs and antique furniture. ⌂*8 chalets, 1 suite* ♿*In-room: safe, minibar. In-hotel: bar, pool, no kids under 10.*

SINGITA   Although Singita (Shangaan for "the miracle") offers much the same bush experience as the other lodges, its huge public areas, extravagant megasize accommodations, and superb dining options help set it apart. Enjoy a riverside breakfast, picnic lunch, or starlit supper in the bush; browse in the reading rooms and wine cellar, which has a superb stock of vintage wines; relax in your huge, private suite; or shop at the Trading Store for African artifacts, bush clothes, handmade jewelry, and ostrich-skin purses. ⌂*Box 650881, Benmore 2010* ☎*011/234–0990* ⊕*www.singita.co.za* ▤*AE, DC, MC, V* ❖*FAP.*

★ $$ ⊞ **Boulders Lodge.** The style is traditional African at this ultraluxurious camp, whose exterior echoes the great Zimbabwe ruins. Large ponds guard the entrance to the public areas, where decor combines modern with bushveld. An entrance hall with fully stocked bar and pantry welcomes you into your enormous suite, where a glass-sided lounge is dominated by a freestanding fireplace. Dark brown, cream, and pale blue fabrics complement leather and wicker armchairs, a zebra-skin ottoman, and antique pieces from owner Luke Bailes's original family home. Occasional touches of steel—candleholders, mirrors, and lamps—provide a nice contrast. A herd of impalas could easily fit into the bathroom, which has dark stone floors, a claw-foot tub, his-and-hers sinks, and massive indoor and outdoor showers. All the doors in the suite lead directly onto a wooden deck with mattresses, chairs, and a bubbling infinity pool with views of the surrounding bushveld. ⌂*9 suites* ♿*In-room: safe, minibar. In-hotel: bar, pool, spa.*

$$ ⊞ **Ebony Lodge.** Gardens, well-worn polished terra-cotta tile and mud floors, overstuffed armchairs and sofas, and antiques make you feel like a houseguest in somebody's old family lodge. The cozy library with its leather-bound books, period prints, leather armchairs, and silver trophies is a little gem. The bright yellow-and-orange walls in the suites contrast surprisingly well with the soft colors of the bush outside. Each suite has a double-sided fireplace, separate living room, enormous veranda, and bathroom with indoor and outdoor showers, plus a personal deck and plunge pool. ⌂*9 suites* ♿*In-room: safe, minibar. In-hotel: bar, pool, spa.*

MANYELETI GAME RESERVE

North of the Sabi Sands, Manyeleti ("the place of the stars" in Shangaan) is a public park covering 59,280 acres bordering Kruger, Sabi Sands, and Timbavati, but it's something of a Cinderella reserve compared with its more famous neighbors. Away from the major tourist areas, it's amazingly underused; you'll probably see very few vehicles while you're here. The park's grassy plains and mixed woodland attract good-size herds of general game and their attendant predators. You have a strong chance of seeing the Big Five, but the Manyeleti lodges focus more on providing an overall bush experience than simply rushing after big game. You'll learn about trees, birds, and bushveld ecosystems as you go on guided bush walks.

HONEYGUIDE TENTED SAFARI CAMPS ★ Honeyguide Tented Safari Camps offer some of the best value in Mpumalanga, achieving the delicate balance of providing professional service with a casual atmosphere, a welcome relief if the over-attentiveness of some of the more upscale lodges isn't to your taste. Because the camps are small, an added bonus is that there are only six people per game vehicle. ⌂ *Box 781959, Sandton 2146* ☎ *011/341–0282* ⊕ *www.honeyguidecamp.com* ☰ *AE, DC, MC, V* ⎢⎢*FAP.*

☺ $ 🏕 **Khoka Moya.** This delightful, value-priced camp is situated on both sides of a riverbed. Simply designed and built of corrugated iron, the large lounge and dining areas overlook green lawns leading to the pool and outside bar. There's a private space in front of each tent, where you can chill out and take in the sights and sounds of the surrounding bush. Each open-air bathroom has a concrete tub, double shower, and separate toilet. Nice touches in your tent include a leather couch, cotton sheets, and damask linen bedspreads. As part of the Children's Safari program, kids can make clay footprints, learn about the little bugs and critters they see on their guided walks, play soccer, swim, relax in the playroom, and then dig into a special kids' menu. ⇲ *12 tents* ⌂ *In-hotel: bar, pool, children's programs (ages 4–14).*

$ 🏕 **Mantonbeni.** This tented camp, minimalist but with surprising luxury touches, gives you the total bush experience without some of the bells and whistles of more upscale camps and at half the price. Designed to reflect Hemingway's Africa, it sits in a tamboti grove overlooking a dry riverbed. You'll feel very close to the bush (but quite safe and secure) in your large, comfortable tent with its leather couch and open-air bathroom with concrete bath, double shower, and separate toilet. Spot game as you lounge on the swimming pool deck, or browse in the temperature-controlled wine cellar. Tea or coffee is served in your tent at dawn, and meals are served in a big safari tent around a long wooden table, where you can swap animal war stories with your fellow guests in an intimate, relaxed atmosphere. Children under 12 are not allowed. ⇲ *12 tents* ⌂ *In-hotel: bar, pool.*

TINTSWALO ☺ $$$ 🏕 **Tintswalo Safari Lodge.** This gorgeous new lodge, which aims to recapture the mid-19th century, is sited under huge jackalberry and fig trees overlooking a seasonal river, where game come down to drink and bathe. Each suite is themed for one of the great African explorers, including Burton, Speke, Livingstone, and Stanley, who would undoubtedly be amazed by such modern conveniences as air-conditioning, hair dryers, en-suite bathrooms, and personal plunge pools. The suites are warmed by Persian rugs and honey-colored velvet chairs and ottomans. Dining is under the stars or in an elegant thatch dining room with open fireplace and sparkling chandelier. Although it's great to have a personal butler, sometimes it's rather disconcerting to be offered something every time you move a muscle. Stargaze by telescope, enjoy a complimentary spa treatment, visit a local Shangaan village, or, if you're both adventurous and romantic, opt for a moonlight sleep-out in the bush. There's a good children's program, but children are allowed only in the Presidential Suite. ⌂*Box 70378, Bryanston 2021* ☎*011/706–7207* ⊕*www. tintswalo.com* ⇥*7 suites* ⌂*In-room: safe, minibar. In-hotel: bar, pool, spa* ⊟*AE, DC, MC, V* ⧖*FAP.*

TIMBAVATI GAME RESERVE

The 185,000-acre Timbavati, the northernmost of the private reserves, has been collectively owned and managed since 1962 by the Timbavati Association, a nonprofit organization that strives to conserve the biodiversity of the area. Timbavati is home to more than 40 mammal species, including the Big Five, and over 360 species of birds. It's famed for its rare white lions; if you miss them here, you can see more at the National Zoological Gardens in Tshwane. Timbavati also has a large population of "regular" lions, and there's a good chance of finding leopards, elephants, buffalo, and spotted hyenas. Rhinos are scarcer, however. Rumor has it that they keep crossing back into Kruger. You might get lucky and see wild dogs, as they migrate regularly to this region from Kruger.

NGALA **Ngala** means "the place of the lion" and certainly lives up to its name. There's wall-to-wall game, and you'll almost certainly see the King of Beasts as well as leopards, rhinos, elephants, and buffalo, among others. Ngala lies in Timbavati's mopane shrubveld, and its main advantage over Sabi Sands is its proximity to four major ecozones—mopane shrubveld, marula combretum, acacia shrub, and riverine forest—which provide habitats for a wide range of animals. As this camp is unfenced, always be sure to walk with a guide after dark. Ngala welcomes kids and puts on a range of activities for them. Ngala rangers, trackers, and general staff are specially trained to look after children and their needs, and, what's more, they seem to delight in their company. After the morning game drive, the kids are whisked away to go on a bug hunt, visit a local village, or bake cookies. ✉*CC Africa, Private Bag X27, Benmore 2010* ☎*011/809–4447* ⊕*www.ngala.co.za* ⊟*AE, DC, MC, V* ⧖*MAP.*

♻ $ ▦ **Main Camp.** This camp has Mediterranean style and a sophistication that is refreshing after the hunting-lodge decor of some other lodges. Track lighting and dark-slate flooring and tables provide an elegant counterpoint to high thatch ceilings and African art. A massive, double-sided fireplace dominates the lodge, opening onto a lounge filled with comfy sofas and chairs on one side and a dining room on the other. Dinner at Ngala is quite formal (kids on their best behavior, please!); it's served in a reed-enclosed boma or a tree-filled courtyard lighted by lanterns with crystal and silver. Air-conditioned guest cottages, in mopane shrubveld with no views, comprise two rooms, each with its own thatch veranda. Rooms make extensive use of hemp matting, thatch, and dark beams to create an appealing, warm feel. 🖃20 *rooms, 1 suite* ⌂*In-hotel: bar, pool.*

★ $　🖃**Ngala Tented Safari Camp.** It seems that the marula seeds softly falling on the tents are applauding this gorgeous little camp shaded by a canopy of giant trees. You'll feel like a sultan as you lie beneath your billowing, honey-colored canvas roof, which acts as a ceiling for your basket-weave handmade bed and headboard. Polished wooden floors, gauze-screened floor-to-ceiling windows, and a dressing area with his-and-hers stone washbasins and gleaming old-fashioned bath create a feeling of such roominess and elegance that it's hard to believe you're in a tent. The camp's dining area and lounge have an almost nautical feel. Huge wooden decks are tethered by ropes and poles on the very edge of the Timbavati River. It seems as if at any moment you could be gently blown into the sky over the surrounding bushveld. 🖃6 *tents* ⌂*In-hotel: pool, no kids under 12.*

TANDA TULA　🖃**Tanda Tula Safari Camp.** With a well-deserved reputation as one of
★ $　the best bush camps in Mpumalanga, Tanda Tula is very professional, yet makes you feel at home. When lions roar nearby, the noise sounds like it's coming from under the bed. The reason is simple: you sleep in a large safari tent with huge window flaps that roll up, leaving you gazing at the bush only through mosquito netting. Tanda Tula is decorated with colorful Africa-themed furnishings. Each thatch tent has electricity, a freestanding fan, a private bathroom with a Victorian-style tub and outdoor shower, and a private wooden deck overlooking the Nhlaralumi River. You'll eat breakfast and lunch in a large, open, thatch lounge, but for dinner enjoy one of Tanda Tula's famous bush braais in the dry riverbed, with the moon reflecting off the dry sand. Although the lodge can sleep 24, it usually keeps numbers down to 16, which makes for added intimacy. First-class rangers give you a very thorough understanding of the environment, local history, and animals without concentrating solely on the Big Five. The Elephant Research Program's camp is housed here and accepts visitors. If you want real privacy, book the luxurious two-person lodge next to the tented camp; it comes with its own butler, vehicle, plunge pool, and in-house catering. 🖃*Box 32, Constantia, Cape Town 7848* 🕾*021/794–6500* ⊕*www.tandatula.co.za* 🖃*12 tents, 1 lodge* ⌂*In-hotel: bar, pool, no kids under 12* ▤*AE, DC, MC, V* ❙◎❙*FAP.*

THORNYBUSH GAME RESERVE

This small game reserve, 35 acres of pristine Limpopo bushveld, is known for its fine lodges and good game sightings. It abuts the western boundary of Timbavati and Kruger.

🕓 $　🖃**Jackalberry Lodge.** This lodge offers understated luxury, excellent food, superb guiding, and the Big Five at half the price of some of the better-known lodges. The air-conditioned thatch-and-stone chalets face the purple Drakensberg Mountains and lie in pristine bushveld that nudges the public areas and pool. It's commonplace to watch a warthog munching while you do, or a giraffe wander past as you sun yourself. Chalets have stone floors, braided straw rugs with leather bindings, deep armchairs, and beaded cushions in soft earth tones, all echoing a simple but elegant African theme. Spacious bathrooms have his-and-hers sinks, a tub with a bushveld view, and indoor and outdoor showers. The rangers are terrific, the staff friendly and efficient, and a particular bonus is that kids of all ages are welcome. Trained babysitters keep them occupied while you are off on game drives. For a little extra you can book the two-bedroom family chalet or one of the two large rooms where the bush comes right up to your doorstep. Don't be surprised if a herd of curious zebras eyeballs you as you sit on your large, private stoop. *Box 798, Northlands 2116 ☎015/793–2980 ⊕www.jackalberrylodge.co.za ⇩7 rooms, 1 suite ☐In-hotel: bar, pool ☐AE, DC, MC, V ⎮◎⎮FAP.*

MPUMALANGA & KRUGER NATIONAL PARK ESSENTIALS

TRANSPORTATION

BY AIR

Three airlines—SA Airlink, SA Express, and Nationwide—link Johannesburg to KMIA (Kruger Mpumalanga International Airport), at Nelspruit, which is equipped to handle the largest and most modern aircraft. KMIA has a restaurant, curio shops, banking facilities, car-rental agencies, VIP lounges, information desks, and shaded parking. SA Airlink has daily flights, SA Express flies on Saturday and Sunday, and Nationwide has flights on Wednesday, Friday, and Sunday. SA Airlink also flies directly to Mala Mala airstrip, which serves the Sabi Sands lodges.

Hoedspruit is an attractive little Africa-themed airport with a restaurant and curio shop. Connected to Johannesburg by SA Express daily, it is close to Kruger's Orpen Gate and serves the Timbavati Game Reserve. SA Airlink has daily flights between Johannesburg and Phalaborwa, a mining town on the edge of central Kruger.

Nelair Charters and Travel, one of the largest privately owned aviation companies in South Africa, is operational 24 hours a day. It operates out of KMIA and does lodge hops within the Sabi Sands, Manyeleti, and Timbavati reserves as well as flights to and from Johannesburg.

Airlines **Nationwide** (☎011/395–7699 ⊕ www.flynationwide.co.za). **Nelair Charters and Travel** (☎013/751–1870 ⊕ www.nelair.co.za). **SA Airlink** (☎015/781–5823 or 015/781–5833 ⊕ www.saairlink.co.za) . **SA Express** (☎011/978–5577 ⊕ www.flysax.com).

Airports **Hoedspruit** (HDS) (⊕ http://hoedspruit-hds-airport.webport.com). **Kruger Mpumalanga International Airport (KMIA)** (☎27/13/753–7502 ⊕www.kmiairport.co.za).

BY BUS

Greyhound runs daily between Johannesburg and Nelspruit, stopping in the city of Louis Trichardt opposite the Promenade Hotel. The direct trip takes five to six hours, but there are also buses that stop along the way. A round-trip ticket is R330, one way R165. Nelspruit is 50 km (31 mi) from Kruger's Numbi Gate and 64 km (40 mi) from Kruger's Malelane Gate.

Public bus service is limited or nonexistent in Mpumalanga. If you don't have your own car, you're dependent on one of the tour companies to get around the escarpment and into the game reserves. Many of these companies also operate shuttle services that transfer guests between the various lodges and to the airport. It's usually possible to hire these chauffeured minibuses at an hourly or daily rate.

Only tour-company buses actually go through Kruger, but they're not recommended. Being in a big tour bus in the park is like being in an air-conditioned bubble, totally divorced from the bush. Also, the big tour buses aren't allowed on many of Kruger's dirt roads and have to stick to the main paved roads.

Bus Line Greyhound (☎ 013/753–2100, 011/276–8500 24-hour call line ⊕ www. greyhound.co.za).

BY CAR

The road system in Mpumalanga is excellent, making it a great place to travel by car. Three principal routes—the N4, N11, and R40—link every destination in the province. From Johannesburg drive north on the N1, and then head east on the N4 to Nelspruit, which is close to many of Kruger's well-marked gates. It's best to arm yourself in advance with up-to-date maps, available at most large gas stations or bookstores, and plan your route accordingly.

The N4 is an expensive toll road (approx R150 for the one-way trip between Johannesburg and Kruger). You can use plastic or cash at the toll booths, where tolls vary between R16 and R40. Though it's a very good, well-maintained road, always look out for the ubiquitous, often reckless taxi drivers in their overcrowded *combis* (vans). Traffic jams are common on weekends and at the beginning and end of school vacations. Secondary roads are also well maintained, but watch out for goats and donkeys that stray from the villages.

The best places to pick up rental cars are at the KMIA, Hoedspruit, and Phalaborwa airports. Avis, Budget, and Imperial all have desks at KMIA and Phalaborwa, whereas Hoedspruit offers Avis and Budget.

Maps of Kruger are available at all the park gates and in the camp stores, and gas stations are available at the park gates and at the major camps. Once in the park, observe the speed-limit signs carefully (there are speed traps): 50 kph (31 mph) on paved roads, 40 kph (25 mph) on dirt roads. Leave your vehicle only at designated picnic and view sites, and if you do find animals on the road, allow them to pass before moving on. Sometimes you have to be very patient, especially if a breeding herd of elephants is blocking your way. ■ TIP→ Animals always have the right-of-way. Always be cautious. Kruger is not a zoo; you are entering the territory of wild animals, even though many may be habituated to the sights and sounds of vehicles.

If you are planning to go into Kruger or one of the private reserves, it's worth renting an eight-seater combi (van) or SUV. Though more expensive than a car, they provide more leg room and you'll probably spot more game and see it better from your lofty perch. It's best to reserve well in advance, particularly if you want a bigger vehicle. Opt for the "supercover" insurance; it's not that much more expensive, but if you do get bumped by an elephant, you'll be covered.

Rental Companies **Avis** (⊠ KMIA, Nelspruit ☎ 013/750–1015 ⊠ Hoedspruit Airport ☎ 015/793–2014 ⊠ Phalaborwa ☎ 015/781–3169 ⊕ www.avis.co.za). **Budget** (⊠ KMIA, Nelspruit ☎ 013/751–1774 ⊠ Hoedspruit Airport ☎ 015/79–2806 or 24-hour call line 011/398–0123 ⊠ Phalaborwa ☎ 015/781–5822 ⊕ www.budget.co.za). **Imperial** (⊠ KMIA, Nelspruit ☎ 013/750–2871/2 ⊠ Phalaborwa ☎ 015/781–0376 ⊕ www.fairestcapecarhire.co.za).

BY TRAIN
Shosholoza Meyl/Spoornet's *Komati* train travels between Johannesburg and Nelspruit via Tshwane daily, and although it's comfortable and has a dining car, it's very slow (10 hours). It departs from Johannesburg at 5:45 PM and arrives in Nelspruit at 3:32 AM, so make sure there's somebody to meet you at that early hour. A one-way, first-class ticket costs R175, round-trip R350.

The luxurious *Blue Train* also makes occasional runs from Tshwane to Nelspruit; Rovos Rail, the Edwardian-era competitor of the *Blue Train,* travels from Tshwane to Komatipoort, just outside Kruger National Park. Most passengers combine a journey on Rovos Rail with a package trip to a game reserve or one of the exclusive lodges on the escarpment.

Train Lines **Blue Train** (☎ 012/334–8459 ⊕ www.bluetrain.co.za). **Rovos Rail** (☎ 012/315–8242 ⊕ www.rovos.co.za). **Shosholoza Meyl/Spoornet** (☎ 011/774–4555 or 013/752–9207 ⊕ www.spoornet.co.za).

CONTACTS & RESOURCES
EMERGENCIES
In case of an emergency, contact the police. In the event of a serious medical emergency, contact Med Rescue International (MRI). Nelmed Forum provides a 24-hour GP service and an emergency service. Nelspruit Medi-Clinic is an excellent, well-equipped hospital with a 24-hour pharmacy.

Emergency Services **Police** (☎ 10111).

Hospitals and Medical Services **MRI** (☎ 011/359–5000). **Nelmed Forum** (⊠ Nel and Rothery Sts., Nelspruit ☎ 013/755–5000 or 013/755–1541). **Nelspruit Medi-Clinic** (⊠ Louise St., behind West End Shopping Centre, Nelspruit ☎ 013/759–0645).

INTERNET
Most hotels, guesthouses, and some game lodges have Internet ethernet facilities: only a few have Wi-Fi. Check with the tourist office in each town for Internet cafés.

MONEY MATTERS

There are plenty of banks and ATMs in lowveld towns and at KMIA, and there is a bank at Skukuza. Kruger accepts credit cards, which are also useful for big purchases, but always have some small change for staff tips (tip your cleaning person R20 per hut per day) and for drinks and snacks at the camp shops.

TOURS

All tour operators offer an assortment of trips and tours that cover the Panorama Route, which links the major escarpment sights, as well as game-viewing trips into Kruger National Park and the private reserves. Fausto Carbone of Matsimba Safaris is a superb personal tour guide. Springbok Atlas, Trips SA, Welcome Tours, and Cybele Tours and Transfers are just some of the many operators that lead trips in the area. It's pricey, but worth it, to take Cybele's Magic Mountain helicopter trip (R6,275). The helicopter journeys from one sight (including waterfalls) to another, stopping off at the Pinnacle, near Graskop, for a picnic champagne breakfast.

Expressions of Africa, the leisure division of SA Express Airways, has more than 25 years of tour-operating experience in South Africa as well as good access to the most exclusive game lodges. Packages range from standard to luxurious, and Expressions also customizes packages.

Tour Operators **Cybele Tours and Transfers** (☎ *013/764–9500 or 013/219–5600* ⊕ *www.cybele.co.za*). **Expressions of Africa** (☎ *011/978–5577 or 011/978–6384* ⊕ *www.saexpress.co.za*). **Matsimba Safaris** (☎ *072/159–4180 or 083/226–6239).* **Springbok Atlas** (☎ *011/396–1053* ⊕ *www.springbokatlas.com*). **Trips SA** (☎ *013/764–1177* ⊕ *www.sabie.co.za*). **Welcome Tours** (☎ *011/676–3300* ⊕ *www.welcome.co.za*).

VISITOR INFORMATION

Mpumalanga Tourism Authority has a host of information. There are also tourist information offices for Hoedspruit, Nelspruit, and White River. The Golden Monkey offers a free booking service for places to stay and things to do in the lowveld and escarpment. Their office is open seven days a week. Sabie and Lowveld Info have Web sites for additional information.

In Kruger there are information centers at the Letaba, Skukuza, and Berg-en-Dal rest camps.

Tourist Offices **Golden Monkey** (✉ *Hazyview* ☎ *013/737–8191* ⊕ *www. big5country.com*). **Hoedspruit tourist information** (✉ *Unit 1, Maroela Park, Kudu St., Hoedspruit* ☎ *015/793–2996* ⊕ *www.hoedspruit.co.za*). **Mpumalanga Tourism Authority** (✉ *Box 679, Nelspruit 1200* ☎ *013/752–7001* ⊕ *www.mpumalanga. com*). **Nelspruit tourist information** (✉ *The Crossing shopping center, N4, Nelspruit* ☎ *013/755–1988*). **White River tourist information** (✉ *Casterbridge Farm, White River* ☎ *013/750–1073*).

Web Sites **Lowveld Info** (⊕ *www.lowveld.info*). **Lowveld Tourism** (⊕ *www.lowveld-info.com*). **SA-Venues** (⊕ *www.SA-Venues.com*). **Sabie** (⊕ *www.sabie.co.za*).

Victoria Falls

WORD OF MOUTH

"I was at Victoria Falls and thought they were spectacular. I saw them from the Zim side and also took a helicopter ride which I highly recommend."

—CarlaM

"Check out Ilala Lodge. It has good food, a swimming pool, clean rooms, and air conditioning. Plus, it's close to the falls and the markets and animals roam the grounds."

—matnikstym

Updated by
Sanja Cloete-
Jones

ROMANCE, INTRIGUE, MYTH, DECADENCE, AWE, and terror: the larg-est curtain of falling water known to humankind reveals itself like an irresistible read. Roughly 1,200 km (750 mi) from its origin as an insignificant spring, the Zambezi River has grown more than a mile wide. Suddenly there's a bend to the south, the current speeds up, and a few miles downstream the entire river is forced into a fissure created in the Jurassic age by the cooling and cracking of molten rock. Nearly 2½ million gallons of water disappear over a vertical drop 300 feet high in a matter of seconds. The resulting spray is astounding, the force splashing drops of water up into the air to form a smokelike cloud that is visible 65 km (40 mi) away on a clear day. Dr. David Livingstone, a Scottish medical doctor and missionary, visited the area in 1855 and is widely credited with being the first European to document the exis-tence of this natural wonder. He named it Victoria Falls in honor of his queen, although the Makololo name, Mosi-oa-Tunya (literally, "the Smoke that Thunders"), remains popular.

Livingstone fell madly in love with the falls, describing them in poi-gnant prose. Other explorers had slightly different opinions. E. Holub could not contain his excitement, and spoke effusively of "a thrilling throb of nature," A. A. de Serpa Pinto called them "sublimely horrible" in 1881, and L. Decle (1898) expected "to see some repulsive monster rising in anger." The modern traveler can explore all of these points of view. There is so much to do around the falls that your only limitations will be your budget and sense of adventure (or lack there of).

ORIENTATION & PLANNING

ORIENTATION

The fissure containing the falls stretches over a mile, roughly from southwest to northeast. Livingstone lies to the north and the town of Victoria Falls immediately to the south.

Located at the falls, the border between the countries is within walking distance of the compact town of Victoria Falls. Livingstone, however, was settled 10 km (6 mi) from the falls in an attempt to avoid malaria, believed to be caused by the swampy Zambezi. ⚠ **The stretch between the falls border and town center should not be attempted on foot, because of the dangers of wandering elephants, the African sun, and the occasional opportunistic thief.**

LIVINGSTONE, ZAMBIA

Zambian lodge owners are quite used to coping with limited supply, and their knack for innovation is tangible, from the fabulously unusual decor finishes to astoundingly inspired food. Individual attention is the norm, and you can expect to have a lot of control over your schedule. Service can be a bit slow and infuriating at times. As for the falls them-selves, the view is spectacular year-round, though it does vary based on time of year. If you travel halfway across the world for a lot of water, come during the wet season (January through June) when the falls are

TOP REASONS TO VISIT

The Phenomenon Not only can you experience Victoria Falls and the Batoka Gorge from up, down, and even inside—the sheer size still allows for the experience to have an exclusive feel.

Fundamental Adrenaline Looking for an adventure to get your heart pounding? From bungee jumping to elephant-back riding and skydiving, Victoria Falls has it all.

Ultimate Relaxation Massages are offered on the banks of the Zambezi River, sumptuous food is served wherever you turn, and there is nothing like having a gin and tonic while the spray of the falls fades in the evening light to end the perfect day.

Africa Central With direct flights from London to Livingstone, you'll be within spitting distance of the Okavango Delta and the Big Five in record time.

full. During the dry season you see fantastic rock formations, as the basalt gorge is exposed. It's also possible to walk across a large part of the falls on this side during the drier months—an awe-inspiring activity. The climb down into the gorge for your rafting trip happens at the Boiling Pot (the first bend of the river after the falls), which gives you an interesting view of the bridge. The Ecolift, a cable car that opened in August of 2006, means no more walking out of the gorge at the end of a hard day's rafting.

VICTORIA FALLS, ZIMBABWE

8

The Zimbabwe side is currently a buyer's market, with hotel prices negotiable up to 20% less than the advertised price. Service is still superb, and up until the recent shifts in the political climate this was the preferred destination, so the people here are definitely comfortable with anticipating visitors' needs. The majority of operators are all one-stop shops, which makes booking activities straightforward. The view of the falls can be a little overwhelming in the flood season, an experience similar to being caught in a blizzard, and the climb out of the gorge following rafting is also pretty daunting, with no plans for any automated aids at the moment. Finally, although the town is perfectly safe, the atmosphere can be understandably negative, as inhabitants struggle to cope with the tyrannical rule of President Mugabe, which affects their access to basics such as bread and milk.

PLANNING

The settlements of Livingstone, Zambia, and Victoria Falls, Zimbabwe, both owe their existence to the falls. In different countries and intriguingly diverse in character, they nevertheless function like two sides of one town. Crossing the border is a formality that generally happens with minimum fuss. Although the Zimbabwean town of Victoria Falls remains perfectly safe and far away from the documented strife, Livingstone, on the Zambian side, is currently the favored destination. Not

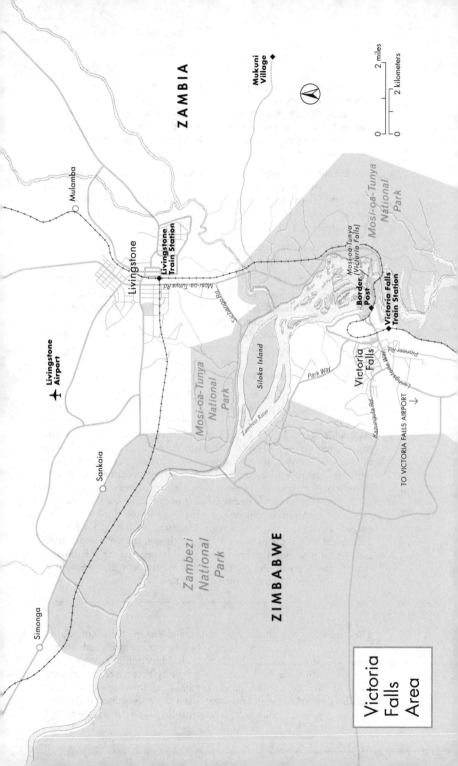

Victoria Falls Area

ZAMBIA

Mukuni Village

2 miles
2 kilometers

Mulamba

Livingstone

Livingstone Train Station

Livingstone Airport

Sankaia

Simonga

Mosi-oa-Tunya Rd.

Sichango Rd.

Mosi-oa-Tunya National Park

Siloka Island

Zambezi River

Mosi-oa-Tunya National Park

Mosi-oa-Tunya (Victoria Falls)

Border Post

Victoria Falls Train Station

Victoria Falls

Park Way

Livingstone Way

Pioneer Rd.

Kazungula Rd.

TO VICTORIA FALLS AIRPORT

Zambezi National Park

ZIMBABWE

only are visitors spoiled with choices in Zambia, which has a plethora of top-class safari lodges along the Zambezi, but strong competition places the emphasis on individualized service, which enables you to tailor your visit. In Zimbabwe the general mood is not always upbeat, but the absence of throngs of travelers is lovely, and it currently provides excellent value for money. The region deserves its reputation as an adventure center and offers adrenaline-inducing activities by the bucketful. The backdrop for any of these is stunning, and the safety record superb.

HEALTH & SAFETY

Wild animals abound throughout this area, and must invariably be given a lot of room and respect. Zimbabwe and Zambia are relatively poor. Both countries have tourism police, but opportunistic thieving still happens occasionally. Although crime is generally nonviolent, losing your money, belongings, or passport will result in spending the remainder of your trip with various officials in stuffy, badly decorated offices instead of sitting back on the deck of your sunset cruise, drink in hand.

As for the water, it's always advisable to drink bottled water, although the tap water in Zambia is generally safe. If you develop an upset stomach, be sure to contact a physician, especially if you are running a fever, in order to rule out malaria or a communicable disease.

Finally, confirm that your insurance covers you for a medical evacuation should you be involved in a serious accident, as the closest intensive-care facilities of international standard are in South Africa.

COMING & GOING

You'll need a valid passport and visa to enter **Zambia,** but it's very simple to purchase a visa when you enter the country, so don't stress yourself out by going through the trouble of getting one ahead of time. A multiple-entry visa costs US$100 (ZK404) and is valid for three years; a single-entry or transit visa is not necessary provided you do not leave the airport terminal. Day-trip visas cost US$10(ZK40); this is often included in the cost of prebooked activities, so check with your booking agent. If you leave Zambia at any time, but intend to return the same day or some days later, you will need to purchase a reentry visa (ZK5,000), or buy a new one at full price at the border. Make sure you take care of this before you leave for your trip or as you leave Zambia. If you're doing an organized tour, the operator should take care of it, but double-check anyway. If you're staying in Zambia, make sure you are included on the lodge or hotel's visa manifest. This manifest needs to be stamped at least 24 hours before your arrival, so make sure you forward your name as it appears in your passport, as well as your nationality, passport number, and expiration date well in advance. The manifests are kept at the point of entry so when you arrive simply give the immigration official the name of your lodging.

You can buy point-of-entry visas for **Zimbabwe** for US$30 for a single entry. If you leave Zimbabwe for more than 24 hours, you will need to buy another to reenter (unless you bought a double-entry visa for

US$45), so think before you travel. To cross the border into Zambia for a day, you'll need to purchase a Zambian day visa for US$10, unless you have booked an activity that includes this cost. Visas can be purchased from an embassy before departure, but it will almost certainly be more trouble and generally cost more than buying them at the border.

> **DID YOU KNOW?**
>
> The first uttering of the popular phrase "Dr. Livingstone, I presume?" may never have happened. Although Livingstone did meet John Rowlands (the assumed utterer of the phrase) in Tanzania in 1871, the famous quote is widely considered a figment of Rowlands's imagination.

Zambian Missions Abroad **United States** (⌧ *2419 Massachusetts Ave., NW, Washington, DC 20008* ☎ *202/265–9717* ⊕ *www.zambiaembassy.org*).

Zimbabwean Missions Abroad **United States** (⌧ *1608 New Hampshire Ave., NW, Washington, DC 20009* ☎ *202/332–7100*).

IN THE KNOW

ZAMBIA   Although the Zambia National Tourist Board (open weekdays 8–1 and 2–5, Saturday 8–noon) is very helpful and friendly, you might be better off visiting the Zigzag coffeehouse for serious unbiased advice. It's open daily 8–8.

Tourist Offices **Zambia National Tourist Board** (⌧ *Tourist Centre, Mosi-oa-Tunya Rd.* ☎ *213/32–1404* ⊕ *www.zambiatourism.com*). **Zigzag** (⌧ *The Warehouse, Mosi-oa-Tunya Rd.* ☎ *213/32–2814* ⊕ *www.zigzagzambia.com*).

ZIMBABWE   The Victoria Falls Publicity Association is fairly well stocked with brochures. It's open weekdays 8:30 to 4:30 and Saturday 8:30 to 1. It's also a good idea to seek advice from the many safari companies in town.

Tourist Office **Victoria Falls Publicity Association** (⌧ *412 Park Way* ☎ *013/4–4202*).

MONEY MATTERS

ZAMBIA   Kwacha and U.S. dollars are welcomed everywhere from street vendors to big hotels. It's a good idea to travel with plenty of small U.S. denominations for tips and small purchases. Make sure you have only "big head" dollars, as the older, "small head" ones are no longer accepted. International banks, located along Mosi-oa-Tunya Road, have ATMs and exchange services. Banking hours are generally weekdays 8–2 (although some do open the last Saturday of the month). Bank ATMs accept only Visa.

⚠ **You may be invited to do a little informal foreign exchange by persuasive street financiers, who will offer you excellent rates.** Resist the temptation—it's not worth the risk of being ripped off or caught and arrested. There are many reputable exchange bureaus throughout town, though they are sometimes flooded with dollars and low on kwacha, generally toward the end of the month. MasterCard and Visa are preferred by business owners and banks to American Express or Diners Club. Business owners in Zambia always prefer cash (or traveler's checks) to credit cards, and some smaller hotels levy fees up to 10% to use their credit-card facilities.

ZIMBABWE If you limit your Zimbabwe visit to Vic Falls, it's not absolutely necessary to change money into Zimbabwean dollars, because everyone from taxi drivers to curio vendors accepts foreign currency (the same applies on the Zambian side of the falls). However, you will be given change in Zimbabwean dollars—probably at a pretty bad exchange rate.

Tour operators accept U.S. dollars, and it's advisable to stick to this currency for all activity payments to both the Zimbabwean- and the Zambian-based operators. Credit-card facilities are not readily available, but traveler's checks are accepted.

Change your money only at banks, located around Livingstone Way and Park Way, and generally open only during the morning. It is illegal to change money on the black market, and street vendors are world-class con artists who will rip you off in ways you never would have believed possible. All official *bureaux de change* have been closed down by the government.

EAT RIGHT, SLEEP WELL

Welcome to carnivore country! Superior free-range beef and chicken are available everywhere, and the portions can be daunting. In Zimbabwe, game meat can be found on almost any menu, but it is something of a delicacy in Zambia. The local bream, filleted or whole, is quite good, and the staple starch, a thick porridge similar to polenta and called *sadza* in Zimbabwe and *nsima* in Zambia, is worth a try. Expect to be given a finger bowl, as the initiated roll the corn into a ball and eat it with their fingers. More adventurous travelers can try *macimbi* or *vinkuvala* (sun-dried mopane worms) and, in the flood season, *inswa* (flash-fried flying ants).

Meals are taken at regular hours, with breakfast from 7 on, lunch around midday, and dinner served at 8 in most lodges. During the week, restaurants close around 10. Dress tends to be extremely casual, although you will never be out of place in something more formal.

Livingstone has seen a dining boom in recent years, with culinary options ranging from wasteland to worth making that reservation for. Service is slow, as the town comes to grips with the increase in tourist volume, and it's a good idea to ask your waiter to repeat your order to avoid communication errors. Although the culinary focus tends to be in town, the lodges all take their cuisine seriously and spoil guests with freshly prepared and beautifully presented meals. Though breakfast and dinner buffets at the Zambezi Sun are awe-inspiring, hotel prices are generally very high. Restaurants use locally grown ingredients and serve both local and international fare.

Sun International has excellent package deals to Zambia from South Africa, although the cost of eating and drinking at the hotels is exorbitant and could easily double the price of a three-night stay. Lodge reservations can be made at any time, but flight availability can be a problem, especially traveling from South Africa on a Friday and to South Africa on a Sunday (due to the Sun hotels' special packages). Lodges tend to have inclusive packages, whereas the hotels generally include only breakfast. All hotels and lodges quote in U.S. dollars, and accept payment in other currencies only at unfriendly exchange rates. Though hotels in Zimbabwe have set rates, they are currently desperate for business, and you can bargain them down 20% in many instances. A 10% service charge is either included or added to the bill (as is the value-added tax) in both countries, which frees you to include an extra tip only for exceptional service.

> **WHEN IN ROME...**
>
> Fearing a few weeks without your Coors Light or Budweiser? No worries. There are a couple of great local brews for you to try on both sides of the falls: Mosi in Zambia and Zambezi in Zimbabwe. Both are crisp, light, and thirst-quenching beers. What about after your meal? Order an Amarula on ice. Not unlike Baileys Irish Cream, this liquor is made from the fruit of the marula tree, a well-documented delicacy for elephants.

Although air-conditioning can be expected in the hotels, lodges tend to have fans. ■ TIP→ **During very hot months it is advisable to travel with a sarong (locally available as a *chitenge*), which you can wet and wrap around you for a cooler siesta.**

WHAT IT COSTS IN U.S. DOLLARS					
	¢	$	$$	$$$	$$$$
RESTAURANTS	under $5	$5–$10	$10–$15	$15–$25	over $25
HOTELS	under $50	$50–$100	$100–$200	$200–$350	over $350

Restaurant prices are per person for a main course at dinner, a main course equivalent, or a prix-fixe meal. Lodging prices are for a standard double room in high season, including 12.5% tax.

TIMING

If you are at all sensitive to heat and humidity, visit from May through August, when it is dry and cool. Although the bush can resemble a wasteland, with short brown stubble and bare trees, it does improve game-viewing, and most other adventure activities are more comfortable in the cooler weather. This is also the time when the mosquitoes are less active, although it remains a malaria area year-round, and precautions should always be taken. ■ TIP→ **Consult your medical practitioner a minimum of four weeks prior to your trip.**

The rainy season starts sometime around late October and generally stretches well into April. Following the first rains, the mopane forests are clad in a shiny, psychedelic light green as they come into new leaf, which becomes an intense emerald green by the end of the rains. With the first rains also comes the "time of the bugs," with tsetse flies, mosquitoes, and the harmless but aptly named stink bug seemingly running the show for a couple of months. Of course, the abundance of insect life also leads to great bird-watching. Although the rain showers tend to be of the short and spectacular kind, they can interfere with some activities, especially if your visit is a short one. As a rule of thumb, try to arrange your activities for the early hours, as the rain generally falls in the late afternoon.

The water plunging over the falls relies on the rainfall in Angola, and therefore the Zambian side dries up almost completely at the beginning of the year (in the middle of the rainy season). Peak flow is achieved in late April and May, when rafting and visiting Livingstone Island might not be possible. If you would like to see a lunar rainbow, plan your trip to coincide with the full moon; Victoria Falls park areas are only accessible on the night leading up to a full moon. Finally, make sure your visit does not coincide with school vacations in South Africa.

LIVINGSTONE, ZAMBIA

This marvelous old town has a wealth of natural beauty and a surplus of activities. It was the old colonial capital, but after a few decades of neglect it has recast itself as Zambia's tourism and adventure capital. There is a slight air of the past here: historic buildings outnumber new ones, and many inhabitants live a life not unlike that of 100 years ago. Livingstone handles the surge of tourists with equal parts grace, confidence, African mischief, and nuisance.

Many visitors to this side of the falls opt to stay in one of the secluded safari-style lodges on the Zambezi River. The Zambian experience offers a tranquil respite from the compact Victoria Falls town across the border in Zimbabwe, that can easily be busy and noisy.

WHAT TO SEE

Numbers in the margin correspond to numbers on the Livingstone map.

❺ **Batoka Gorge.** Located just below the falls, the gorge is split between Zambia and Zimbabwe and is more than 120 km long (75 mi long) and 1,950 feet deep. It lies mostly within the Hwange Communal Land and is covered with mopane and riparian forests that are interspersed with grassland. On the Zambian side, the gorge is surrounded by Mosi-oa-Tunya National Park, with a tropical rain forest that thrives on the eternal rainfall from the falls. Victoria Falls National Park in Zimbabwe surrounds the other side of the gorge.

Operators from both countries offer excursions to what is reputed to be the world's best one-day white-water rafting, with class 5 rapids that have been lovingly nicknamed "The Ugly Sisters" and "Oblivion." If you're *lucky* enough to experience what locals call a "long swim" (falling out of the raft at the start of a rapid and bodysurfing through), your definition of the word *scary* will surely be redefined. The walk in and out of the gorge is quite strenuous on the Zimbabwe side, but as long as you're reasonably fit and looking for adventure, you need no experience. On the Zambian side, operators use the Ecolift to transport

8

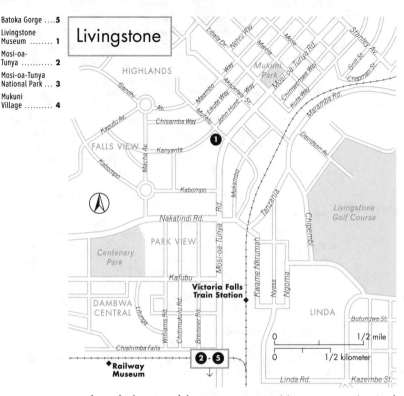

you from the bottom of the gorge to your waiting transportation (and beverage) at the top.

🐾 ❶ **Livingstone Museum.** The country's oldest and largest museum contains history, ethnography, natural history, and archaeology sections and includes materials ranging from newspaper clippings to photographs of Queen Elizabeth II dancing with Kenneth Kaunda (Zambia's first president) to historical information dating back to 1500. Among the priceless David Livingstone memorabilia is a model of the mangled arm bone (he was attacked by a lion) used to identify his body, and various journals and maps from the period when he explored the area and claimed the falls for his queen. ✉ *Mosi-oa-Tunya Rd., between civic center and post office* ☎ *213/32–0495* 🖃 *US$5* ⊙ *Daily 9–4:30.*

❷ **Mosi-oa-Tunya.** Literally translated as "The Smoke that Thunders," the
Fodor'sChoice falls more than live up to their reputation as one of the world's great-
★ est natural wonders. No words can do these incredible falls justice, and it's a difficult place to appreciate in just a short visit, as it has many moods and aspects. Though the Zimbabwean side may offer more panoramic views, the Zambian side—especially the **Knife Edge** (a sharp headland with fantastic views)—allows you to stand virtually suspended over the Boiling Pot (the first bend of the river after the falls), with the deafening water crashing everywhere around you. From

around May to August the falls are a multisensory experience, though you'll get absolutely drenched if you venture onto the Knife Edge, and there may be too much spray to see the bottom of the gorge. If you get the sun behind you, you'll see that magic rainbow. A network of paths leads to the main viewing points; some are not well protected, so watch your step and wear good, safe shoes, especially at high water, when you are likely to get dripping wet. You'll have dramatic views of the full 1½ km (1 mi) of the ironstone face of the falls, the Boiling Pot directly below, the railway bridge, and Batoka Gorge. At times of low water it's possible to take a guided walk to Livingstone Island and swim in the **Devils Pool,** a natural pond right on the lip of

> ## A THREE-HOUR TOUR
>
> Many park guides are knowledgeable, but the ultimate Mosi-oa-Tunya National Park experience is the three-hour guided walking safari offered by **Livingstone Safaris** (☎ *213/32–2267*). Not only can you see the endangered white rhino and other plains game, but your professional guide and park scout will impart detailed information on birding, flora, and the modern use of plants by local people. Walks are conducted early in the morning and late in the afternoon and cost US$65, including transfers within Livingstone. Hopefully, your trip won't turn out like Gilligan's.

the abyss. ✉ *Entrance off Mosi-oa-Tunya Rd., just before border post* ☎ *No phone* 🎟 *US$10* ⊗ *Daily 6–6, later at full moon.*

☻ ❸ **Mosi-oa-Tunya National Park.** This park is a quick and easy option for viewing plains game. In fact, you're almost guaranteed to spy white rhinos. You can also visit the Old Drift graveyard, as the park includes the location of the original settlement here. The park's guides are knowledgeable, but you can visit without one, though the roads get seriously muddy in the rainy season, and a guide who knows where to drive becomes a near necessity. ✉ *Sichanga Rd., off Mosi-oa-Tunya Rd., 3½ km (2 mi) from Livingstone* 🎟 *US$10* ⊗ *Daily from 6–6.*

☻ ❹ **Mukuni Village.** Fascinated by the history, customs, and traditions of the area? Local guides can escort you on an intimate visit inside a local house and explain the customs of the village. This is not a stage set but a very real village, so your tour will be different depending on the time of day you go. For example, at mealtimes you can see how local delicacies are prepared. It's customary to sign in the visitor book and to pay a small fee to your guide. Bushtracks (⇨ *Livingstone and Zambia Essentials, below*) conducts organized visits. ⊗ *Daily 6–6.*

WHERE TO STAY & EAT

$$$$ ✕ **Livingstone Island Picnic.** Available throughout the year except for a couple of weeks when the water level is too high, this is a spectacular, romantic dining option. Livingstone Island is perched right on the edge of the abyss, where you'll sit around a linen-decked table and dine on a delicious buffet lunch (with salads); drinks are delivered by waiters. You get here by boat (two engines, just in case). Brunch and afternoon

Fodor'sChoice
★

8

tea are US$47and US$63, respectively, and lunch is US$99, including transfers. The trips are run by Tongabezi Lodge, and there is a maximum of 12 guests. ⊠*Livingstone Island* ⌖*Box 31* ☎*213/32–7450* 🖃*MC, V* ☽*Closed a couple of months around Feb.–June, depending on water level. No dinner.*

$–$$ ✕**Kamuza.** The Moghuls themselves might declare a meal here a feast. Spicy but not hot, the curries are lovingly prepared from ingredients imported from India. The chicken tikka masala is a house specialty, and the handmade saffron *kulfi* (an Indian ice cream made with milk, white bread, and a whipped topping) is a great way to end a hot day in Africa. ⊠*Ngolide Lodge, Mosi-oa-Tunya Rd.* ☎*213/32–1091* 🖃*MC, V* ☽*No dinner Mon.*

¢–$ ✕**Funky Munky.** Cheap and cheerful, this small pizzeria's reputation keeps spreading. On offer find thin-crust pizzas baked in a traditional wood-fired oven and named after primates. Try the popular bacon and mushroom Baboon, the Chimpancheese four-cheese extravaganza, or build your own. If you seek lighter fare, have a fresh baguette stuffed with various traditional lunch fillings. And on those unbearably hot summer days pop in for shave ice that might make you forget you are about as far from Hawaii as possible! ⊠*Mosi-oa-Tunya Rd.* ☎*213/32–0120* 🖃*No credit cards.*

♺ $$$$ ✕🏨 **Zambezi Sun.** Part of the same complex as the Royal Livingstone, this hotel is less expensive, less pretentious, and a whole lot more welcoming than its pricier cousin. The design borrows freely from a variety of (mostly African) cultures and is vibrantly colorful, sparkly, and fun. Buildings are earth-red and round-cornered, blending in with the surroundings. Rooms are decorated with bright primary-color murals, and the spacious bathrooms have colorful tiles and handmade sinks. The hotel is child-friendly, with family rooms and a play center. The buffet breakfasts and dinners are gastronomic feasts, but all food and drink are exorbitantly priced. Although the Zambezi Sun doesn't share the Livingstone's fantastic view, it's even closer to the falls—within walking distance. ⊠*Mosi-oa-Tunya Rd.* ☎*213/32–1122, 27/11/780–7444 reservations (South Africa)* ⊕*www.suninternational.co.za* ⇗*208 rooms, 4 suites* ⚿*In-hotel: 2 restaurants, bar, pool, a/c, children's programs (all ages), no elevator* 🖃*AE, DC, MC, V* ⍟*CP.*

♺ $ ✕🏨 **Zigzag Coffee House.** First came the coffee shop, which still serves the best coffee in town, including a choice of flavored espresso and cappuccino. Then its owners added the Warehouse complex, with a swimming pool, crafts market, children's play area and B&B. Meals are simple and good—soups, ciabatta bread, nachos, muffins, and all-day breakfasts, which you can eat while catching up on all the scandalous gossip Livingstone town can provide. ⊠*Mosi-oa-Tunya Rd.* ☎*213/32–2814* ⊕*www.zigzagzambia.com* ⇗*12 rooms* ⚿*In-hotel: pool, no elevator* 🖃*No credit cards* ⍟*BP.*

★ $$$$ 🏨 **River Club.** With split-level rooms that cling to the edge of the great Zambezi, the River Club puts a modern spin on a Victorian house party. The view from the infinity pool seems unbeatable, until you watch the sun set from your claw-foot tub. Clever cooling mists of water draw flocks of birds to the massage tent, and the library begs for a glass of port and a serious book. History clings to the structure, built to the plans of the original house, but decorations have been lovingly collected from past and present. You could spend an entire day reading interesting anecdotes, old maps, *Punch* cartoons, and updates about the River Club's support of the local village. A candlelight dinner is followed by croquet on the floodlit lawn before you retire to your partially starlit room. You approach the lodge from the river—purely for the spectacular effect—but it necessitates negotiating some steep stairs. If you think you'll struggle, ask to be transferred by vehicle. ✍*Box 60469* ☎*213/32–3672* ➥*10 rooms* ♿*In-hotel: pool, no elevator* ▤*MC, V* ☒*FAP.*

$$$$ 🏨 **Royal Livingstone.** This high-volume, high-end hotel has an incredibly gorgeous sundowner deck, arguably on the best spot on the river, just upstream from the falls. The attractive colonial safari-style buildings are set amid sweeping green lawns and big trees and have fantastic views, but passing guest traffic makes for a lack of real privacy. The decor of both the guest rooms and public rooms is deliberately ostentatious. This resort is tremendously popular and can be extremely busy, especially during peak times, but the staff is always friendly and helpful. Unfortunately, the volume of people can lead to problems, omissions, and errors, with service standards struggling to match the high costs. ⚠ **Vervet monkeys are an entertaining nuisance, so hang on to your expensive cocktail.** ✉*Mosi-oa-Tunya Rd.* ☎*213/32–1122* ⊕*www.sun-international.co.za* ➥*173 rooms* ♿*In-hotel: restaurant, room service, bar, pool, no elevator, a/c* ▤*AE, DC, MC, V* ☒*CP.*

$$$$
FodorśChoice
★
🏨 **Tongabezi and Sindabezi Island.** If you're looking for a truly African experience, Tongabezi and Sindabezi, its satellite island 4 km (2½ mi) downriver, won't disappoint. Never formal but flagrantly romantic, they are the frame around the picture, so to say, and do not upstage the reason you have come: the flora and fauna. At Tongabezi, standard rooms are spacious cream-and-ocher *rondawels* (round thatch huts) featuring private verandas that can be enclosed in a billowing mosquito net. Three suites are built into a low cliff, and incorporate the original riverine forest canopy. King beds set in tree trunks and covered by curtains of linen netting, oversize sofas in the sitting area, and giant bathtubs on the private decks are all unashamedly romantic. Every room has a local guide who acts as a personal valet and delights in catering to your every decadent whim. Room service is ordered via antique telephones, and the lodge has an in-house holistic therapist. Small **Sindabezi Island,** which has a 10-guest maximum, is separated by a stretch of river from Zambezi National Park. Each of the island's huts has an open front with a private view, and your every need is anticipated, but there's no electricity, and hot bucket showers are by demand only. If your party takes Sindabezi for yourselves, the guide, boat, and land vehicle are at your disposal. Dinner is served by lantern and candlelight on a sandbank under the stars. ✍*Box 31* ☎*213/32–7450 or 213/32–7468* ⊕*www.tongabezi.com* ➥*5 suites, 5 cottages* ♿*In-hotel: pool* ▤*MC, V* ☒*FAP.*

$$ 🏨 **Zambezi Waterfront.** There's a hive of happy activity here ranging from opportunistic monkeys relieving unsuspecting tourists of their lunch to serious late-night boozing to adventure enthusiasts (hangover optional) being whisked off to do their thing at all hours of the day. Curiously, the spacious rooms where families can stay can be reached only via a steep exterior wooden staircase, but this is also a popular spot for camping. Restaurant service is notoriously slow and mediocre. ⊠*Sichanga Rd., just off Mosi-oa-Tunya Rd.* ☎*213/32–0606* ⊕*www.safpar.com* ⌨*21 chalets, 24 adventure village tents, campsites accommodating 86 campers* ⚲*In-hotel: restaurant, bars, pools, no elevator, no a/c* ▭*MC, V* ⦿*BP.*

¢ 🔲**Bovu Island.** The vibe of California and Marrakesh in the '60s and '70s is alive and well at this collection of thatched huts and campsites along the banks of the Zambezi, 52 km (32 mi) upstream of the falls. This is the place to chill out. Take a good book or an excellent companion. Accommodations are basic but somehow quite perfect, each with gorgeous river views, and there are hot showers and flush toilets. The food is good and the coffee better than most of what the upscale lodges serve. You can swim in a shallow section of small rapids naturally protected from crocodiles or hippos (or this is the theory). Warning: "island time" operates here and anything goes, so the staid or conservative are likely to find it unsuitable. Return transfers cost US$50 and include a guided sunset cruise in a *mokoro* (an African canoelike boat) and village walks. Meals are provided but cost extra. Don't forget to check out the hat collection behind the bar in the main camp and add your own to the mix. ⌂*Box 61122* ☎*213/32–3708* ⊕*www.jungle-junction.info* ⌨*8 huts* ⚲*In-hotel: bar, no elevator.*

¢ 🔲**Fawlty Towers.** Centrally located to town, this old textile factory was named after the popular British comedy from the 1970s and has become the most popular backpacker's lodge in the area. There's a big lawn with a pool and a popular restaurant and bar. Very comfortable rooms with private bath are available, as are dorm rooms, but they have communal baths. ⊠*Mosi-oa-Tunya Rd.* ☎*213/32–3432* ⊕*www.adventure-africa.com* ⌨*23 rooms, 6 dormitories* ⚲*In-hotel: restaurant, bar, pool, no elevator* ▭*MC, V* ⦿*EP.*

SPORTS & THE OUTDOORS

Livingstone can compete with the best as far as indulging the wildest fantasies of adrenaline junkies and outdoor enthusiasts goes. You can reserve activities directly with any of the operators listed below, let your hotel or lodge handle it, or book through a central booking group.

Safari Par Excellence (☎*213/32–1629* ⊕*www.safpar.net*) offers elephant-back safaris, game drives, river cruises, canoeing, kayaking, and rafting. They also have trip combinations (a good option if your time is limited or you just want to go wild) such as the Raft-Heli which offers a spectacular view of the gorge at the conclusion of a hard day's rafting—you can substitute tandem kayaking or river boarding for rafting—or the Heli-Jet which involves no strenuous walking as you helicopter in, go wild in a jetboat, and then helicopter out. Prices for combinations are available on request.

Livingstone's Adventure (☎*213/32–0058* ⊕*www.livingstonesadventure. com*) offers a central booking service as well as operating Batoka Sky, *African Queen,* and Livingstone Quad Company.

ATVING Riding a quad through the mopane forest, seeing local villages, and playing in Batoka Gorge is possible courtesy of Livingstone Quad Company. A one-hour ecotrail adventure costs US$65. The minimum age is 16, but even absolute beginners are welcome.

BOATING Truly the monarch of the river, the *African Queen* is an elegant colonial-style riverboat. Sunset cruises offer the maximum style and splendor. Costs start at US$37 for a 1½-hour lunch cruise. **Victoria Falls River Safaris** (☎*213/32–1513* ✉riversafaris@zamnet.zm) operates a doubly silenced, propeller-free, water-turbine boat (from US$65), which can access areas no other boats can get to. It's excellent for game and bird spotting.

BUNGEE JUMPING Bungee jumping off the 340-foot-high Victoria Falls Bridge with **African Extreme** (☎*213/32–4231* ✉bungi@zamnet.zm) is a major adrenaline rush, with 65 feet and three seconds of free fall and a pretty spectacular view. The jump costs from US$90, but it's worth getting the US$40 video, complete with *Top Gun* music track.

CANOEING A gentle canoe trip on the upper Zambezi is a great opportunity to see birds and a variety of game. Many of the lodges upriver have canoeing as an inclusive activity, but trips are also run by a number of companies, which are all reputable and provide similar value for your money. Safari Par Excellence is the longest-running outfitter in the area and offers custom-made canoe trips that range from half-day outings to multiday excursions with costs starting at US$85.

ELEPHANT-BACK RIDING Fancy the idea of meandering through the bush courtesy of your very own ellie? Not only does **Elephant Back Safaris.** (⊕*www.elephant-back-safaris.com*) keep clients happy enough to forget their sore thighs the next day, it also has the elephants happy enough to keep having babies! Costs start at US$60 for a meet and greet to US$140 for a ride.

FLYING **Livingstone Air Safaris** (☎*213/32–3147*) will introduce you to the falls from a fixed-wing aircraft. ■ TIP→ **Consider having the right-hand door removed for excellent photographic conditions**. Twenty-minute flights start at US$76. They also provide charters and seat rates throughout Zambia and Botswana and introductory flying lessons in various small aircraft.

Batoka Sky offers weight-shift Aerotrike twin-axis microlighting (flying jargon for what resembles a motorized hang glider) and helicopter flights over the falls and through the gorges. There's a minimum of two passengers for helicopters. For microlighting you are issued a flight suit (padded in winter) and a helmet with a headset, but you may not bring a camera for safety reasons. Batoka Sky has been operating since 1992, and has a 100% microlighting safety record. Flights are booked for early morning and late afternoon, and are dependent on the weather. Prices run US$90–US$190, depending on length of flight and aircraft. Your transfer and a day visa, if you are coming from Victoria Falls, are included. The Helicopter Gorge picnic (US$265) includes lunch and drinks for a minimum of six people.

HORSEBACK RIDING You can take a placid horseback ride through the bush along the banks of the Zambezi with **Chundukwa Adventure Trails** (☎213/32–7452 ✍chundukwa@zamnet.zm). A little more adventurous? You may want to watch game from horseback or do a multiday trail ride. Costs are U$60 for 1½ hours to a full day including lunch and drinks for US$137.50

JETBOATING If you want some thrills and speed but rafting seems a bit daunting, or you can't face the walk in and out, you'll probably enjoy jetboating with **Jet Extreme** (☎213/32–1375 ✍jetextremetony@microlink.zm). A new cable-car ride, included in the cost of the jetboat ride (US$95 for 30 minutes), will mean no more strenuous walking out of the gorge. Jetboating can be combined with a rafting excursion, as the jetboat starts at the end of the rafting run, or with a helicopter trip out of the gorge. ■TIP➜ **The rafting and heli must be booked separately, although big operators like Safari Par Excellence and Livingstone's Adventure offer combinations.** Children over seven can jetboat if they are accompanied by an adult.

KAYAKING If you're feeling brave, try tandem kayaking. You do the same stretch of river as the rafting trips but in a two-seat kayak with a guide. Although you don't need previous experience, you have to be a fast study, as it entails getting a crash course in steering a kayak through serious class 5 rapids. It's not for the faint of heart or, strangely, the big and macho—there's a weight limit of 175 pounds. The trip costs US$150 and is run by Safari Par Excellence.

RAFTING & RIVER BOARDING Safari Par Excellence offers rafting excursions to Batoka Gorge that cost US$120 to US$135 for either a full- or half-day trip, including a one-day visa if you're crossing the border to do it. The new Ecolift transports rafters out of the gorge, so you only have to climb down. You can also do a combination helicopter-and-rafting trip. Bring secure shoes, dry clothes for the long drive home, a baseball cap to wear under your helmet, and plenty of sunscreen. You can also decide to try river boarding (from US$145), in which you hop off the raft onto a body board and surf suitable rapids.

RAPPELLING & SWINGING For something completely different, **Abseil Zambia** (☎213/32–1188 ✍theswing@zamnet.zm) has taken some specially designed heavy-duty steel cables, combined them with various pulleys and rigs, one dry gorge, and a 100% safety record to entertain both the fainthearted and the daring. The full day (US$115) is a great value, as it includes lunch, refreshments, and as many repeats of the activities as you like. ⚠ **Keep in mind that you will have to climb out following the gorge swing and the rappel; there's no Ecolift here. A half day (US$95) is advised during the hot months of October–December.** Work up an appetite for more daring drops by starting on the zip line (or flying fox). You run off a ramp while attached to the line, and the sensation is pure freedom and surprisingly unscary, as you are not moving up or down. Next rappel down into the 175-foot gorge, and, after you climb out, try it again facing forward. It's called a rap run. You're literally walking down the cliff face. End the day with the king of adrenaline activities, a whopping 175-foot, 3½-second vertical free-fall swing into the gorge (US$60 for one swing). Three-two-one-hoooo-ha!

SHOPPING

If you fall in love with the furniture in your lodge, visit **Kubu Crafts** (✉ *133 Mosi-oa-Tunya Rd.* ☎*213/32–0320* ⊕*www.kubucrafts.com*), a stylish home decor shop. Locally made furniture in hardwood and wrought iron is complemented by a selection of West African masks and weavings and the work of numerous local artists, including the fantastic oil paintings of Stephen Kapata. Prices can be ridiculously inflated.

> ### GOOD SOUVENIRS
>
> Shona stone carvings from Zimbabwe, woven baskets from Botswana and Zambia, and soapstone from Zambia and Zimbabwe make great souvenirs. Make sure you pack these things carefully, especially the soapstone, as it's all extremely fragile.

It's worth having a look through Mukuni Park before you buy the same article at a 500% markup. Kubu Crafts also sells tea, coffee, and cakes to enjoy in the garden.

Although the park at the entrance to the falls has stalls where you can find stone and wood carvings and simple bead and semiprecious-stone jewelry, the real gem of an African bazaar lies in the center of town, at **Mukuni Park Market** (✉*Mosi-oa-Tunya Rd. and Libala Dr.* ☎*No phone).* ■ TIP➔ **This is the place to bargain.** You'll be quoted top dollar initially, but shop around and watch the prices drop to roughly one-third of the original quote. Walk through the entire market before you commence buying. This will not only ensure that you get the best price, but will give you the opportunity to gauge the level of craftsmanship that can be expected. Look out for individual and unusual pieces, as it is occasionally possible to find valuable antiques. The market is open daily approximately 7–6.

LIVINGSTONE AND ZAMBIA ESSENTIALS

TRANSPORTATION

BY AIR

Nationwide, South African Airways and Comair/British Airways fly regularly from Johannesburg into Livingstone International Airport, 5 km (3 mi) out of town. The flight is a comfortable hop, just under two hours, and the airport is small and friendly, with helpful staff to speed you on your way. ■ TIP➔ **If at all possible, do not check your luggage through from Johannesburg International, and always lock suitcases securely, as luggage theft in South Africa is an everyday occurrence.**

Airlines Comair/British Airways (☎*01/25–4444 or 01/25–4473* ⊕ *www.british-airways.com).* **Nationwide** (☎*213/32–2251* ⊕ *www.flynationwide.co.za).* **South African Airways** (☎*01/25–4350* ⊕ *www.flysaa.com).*

BY CAR

There is a perfectly reasonable traffic code in Zambia. Unfortunately, not many people have ever heard of it. You would do well to leave the driving to your guides or negotiate an all-inclusive rate with a taxi driver recommended by your hotel or lodge for the duration of your stay. Note that taxis are generally not allowed to cross the border, so if you want to visit Zimbabwe, you will have to book a tour that includes transfers. Once at the border, it is feasible to walk into and around Victoria Falls town, or rent a bicycle.

If you insist on renting a car, you should know that some of the roads have more potholes than tar. You don't necessarily need a 4x4, but it's not a bad idea, especially if you want to off-road it a bit. Imperial Car Rental operates from the offices of Voyagers at the Day Activity Center near the Zambezi Sun lodge. Hemingways rents out Land Rovers, fully equipped with tents and other camping equipment—you can even hire a driver! Costs start from US$180 for an unequipped vehicle.

Rental Companies **Hemingways** (☎ *213/32–0996 or 097/86–6492* ⊕ *www. hemingwayszambia.com*). **Imperial Car Rental** (☎ *213/32–3454* ⊕ *www. voyagerszambia.com*).

CONTACTS & RESOURCES

CURRENCY EXCHANGE

Zambia's currency is the Zambian kwacha, which comes in denominations of ZK20, ZK50, ZK100, ZK500, ZK1,000, ZK5,000, ZK10,000, and ZK50,000 bills, necessitating carrying huge wads of notes. The kwacha is theoretically divided into 100 ngwees, but as you can buy nothing for one kwacha, an ngwee exists in name only and any bill including ngwees will simply be rounded off. At time of writing the conversion rate was ZK4,120 to the US$1.

ELECTRICITY

To use electric-powered equipment purchased in the United States or Canada, bring a converter and adapter. If your appliances are dual voltage, you'll need only an adapter. The electrical current is 220 volts, 50 cycles alternating current (AC); wall outlets in most of the region take 15-amp plugs with three straight-edge prongs. ⚠ **Power outages are a way of life in Livingstone. Do not leave anything plugged in that can be damaged by a power outage or fluctuating current.**

EMBASSIES

United States **U.S. Embassy** (✉ *United Nations Ave. and Independence Rd., Box 31617, Lusaka* ☎ *01/25–0955* ⊕ *http://zambia.usembassy.gov*).

EMERGENCIES

For minor injuries, a test for malaria, or the treatment of non-life-threatening ailments, you can go to the Rainbow or Southern medical centers or the Shafik clinic. For serious emergencies, contact SES (Specialty Air Services). Musamu Pharmacy is open weekdays 8–8, Saturday 8–6, and Sunday 8–1.

Emergency Services **General Emergency** (☎ *999*). **Police** (☎ *991*). **Fire** (☎ *993*). **SES** (☎ *213/32–2330 landline, 097/74–0307 mobile phone*).

Hospitals **Rainbow Medical Centre** (✉ *192 Kabila St.* ☎ *213/32–3519*). **Shafik clinic** (✉ *Akapelwa St.* ☎ *213/32–1130*). **Southern Medical Centre** (✉ *House 9, 1967 Makombo Rd.* ☎ *213/32–3547*).

Pharmacy **Musamu Pharmacy** (✉ *Mosi-oa-Tunya Rd.* ☎ *09/65–88219 mobile phone*).

GAY & LESBIAN TRAVELERS

Homosexuality is technically illegal in Zambia, although it is widely accepted and presents no real problem.

INTERNET

Zigzag is open from 8 to 8 and has free broadband and wireless access.

Internet Access **Zigzag** (✉ *The Warehouse, Mosi-oa-Tunya Rd.* ☎ *213/32–2814* ⊕ *www.zigzagzambia.com*).

LANGUAGE

Zambia has more than 70 dialects, but there are only four main languages: Lozi, Bemba, Nyanja, and Tonga. English is the official language and is widely spoken, read, and understood.

TAXES

Zambia has a 17.5% V.A.T. and a 10% service charge, which is included in the cost or itemized on your bill.

TELEPHONES

Livingstone telephone rates are much cheaper and more stable than the rates in Zimbabwe. Check numbers very carefully, as some are Zimbabwean mobile phones. Zambia and Zimbabwe now both have cell coverage, and there are certain areas where the networks overlap and mobile telephones work in both countries. If you have any trouble dialing a number, check with a hotel or restaurant owner, who should be able to advise you of the best and cheapest alternative. International roaming on your standard mobile phone is an option, as coverage is quite extensive.

The country code for Zambia is 260. When dialing from abroad, drop the initial 0 from local area codes. Note that all telephone numbers are listed as they are dialed from the country that they are in. Although the number for operator assistance is 100, you will be much better off asking your local lodge or restaurant manager for help. If you can't live without a telephone, get international roaming on your cell phone. Although reception is patchy, you will be surprised at how far the networks now cover this destination. Alternatively you could purchase a local Sim card with pay-as-you-go fill-ups. Pay phones are not a reliable option, and the costs of all telephone calls out of the country can be exorbitant.

TIME

Zambia operates on CAST (Central African Standard Time), which is two hours ahead of Greenwich Mean Time. That makes it seven hours ahead of North American eastern standard time (six hours ahead during eastern daylight saving time).

TIPPING

Tipping is less common in Zambia, since service charges are included, but it *is* appreciated. Small notes or 10% is appropriate. Gas-station attendants can be tipped, but you will generally tip a taxi driver only on the last day if you have used the same driver for a number of days.

TOURS

If it's serious game-viewing you desire, join a one-day excursion to Chobe National Park in Botswana with Bushtracks Africa. The trip costs US$170 and includes transfers from Livingstone, a game drive, a boat cruise, and all meals. Bushtracks is also your best bet for a visit to the Mukuni Village (US$32). Reservations must be in writing and prepaid for both.

Tour Operators Bushtracks Africa (☎ *213/32–3232* ⊕ *www.gotothevictoria falls.com*).

VICTORIA FALLS, ZIMBABWE

The town of Victoria Falls started with a little curio shop and slowly expanded until the 1970s, when it became the preferred falls destination. The political problems following independence have been well documented in the world press, and have certainly taken their toll, not the least of which is the significant poaching in the Zambezi National Park to the northwest. (If you really want to have the African game experience, take a day trip to Chobe National Park, 70 km [44 mi] away in Botswana; ⇨*Livingstone and Zambia Essentials, above.*) Regardless, the town enjoys the happy coincidence of being a shopper's paradise inside a national park. This means you can buy an elephant carving while watching the real McCoy march past the shop window. The town is extremely compact. Almost all the hotels are within walking distance, and the falls themselves are only 10 minutes away on foot. The main road that runs through town and goes to the falls in one direction and to the airport in the other is called Livingstone Way. Park Way is perpendicular. Most of the shops, banks, and booking agents can be found on these two streets, and this part of town is also where most of the hawkers operate. ■TIP➡ **Give them a clear berth, as their wares are cheap for a reason (the boat cruise is substandard, it's illegal to change money, etc.).**

WHAT TO SEE

Numbers in the margin correspond to numbers on the Victoria Falls (town) map.

❼ Falls Craft Village. The village consists of 35 life-size constructions, typical of six main ethnic groups living in Zimbabwe in the 19th century.
All artifacts are genuine. A free pamphlet and on-site guide explain the
living arrangements, various crafts, and the uses of different tools. At
the back of the village you can watch artisans carving the stone and
wood sculptures that are sold in the adjoining shop. For a small fee you
can have a *n'anga* (witch doctor) "throw the bones" to tell your fortune. There is traditional dancing every night (about US$30). ✉*Stand
206, Soper's Crescent, off Livingstone Way, behind banks* ☎*013/4–
4309* 🎟*US$20* ⊙*Daily 8:30–5.*

NEED A BREAK?

The **River Cafe** (✉*Landela Centre, off Livingstone Way* ☎*No phone*) is a
popular venue with travelers and locals in need of a fuss-free and relatively
speedy lunch. Situated inside a little shopping mall, it provides quick, easy
meals including burgers and peri-peri chicken, which is particularly good.

❾ Victoria Falls Bridge. A monument to Cecil Rhodes's dream of complet-
ing a Cape-to-Cairo rail line, this graceful structure spans the gorge
formed by the Zambezi River, 360 feet below. It would have been far
easier and less expensive to build the bridge upstream from the falls,
but Rhodes was captivated by the romance of a railway bridge passing
over this natural wonder. A net was spanned across the gorge under the

construction site, whereupon the construction workers went on strike for a couple of days. They resumed work only when it was explained that they would not have to leap into it at the end of every work-day. Although the workers did not share the current adrenaline-fueled obsession with jumping into the abyss, the net probably had a lot to do with the miraculous fact that only two people were killed during construction. The bridge was completed in only 14 months, and the last two cross-girders were defiantly joined on April 1, 1905.

To get onto the bridge, you first have to pass through Zimbabwean immigration and customs controls, so bring your passport. Unless you decide to cross into Zambia, no visa is necessary. Depending on crowds, the simple procedure can take from five minutes to a half hour. The border posts are open daily from 6 AM to 10 PM, after which the bridge is closed to all traffic. From the bridge you get a knockout view of the river raging through Batoka Gorge (the fissure containing the falls) as well as a section of the falls on the Zambian side. An added bonus is watching the bungee jumpers. ⊠ *Livingstone Way.*

⑧ Victoria Falls National Park. Plan to spend at least two hours soaking in the splendors of this park. Bring snacks and water, and supervise children extremely well, as the barriers are by no means safe. Babies and toddlers can be pushed in a stroller. If you visit the falls during the high-water peak, between April and June, you'd do well to carry a raincoat or umbrella (you can rent them at the entrance) and to bring along a waterproof, disposable camera, because you *will* be drenched in the spray from the falls, which creates a permanent downpour. Photo opportunities are very limited due to the mist. ■TIP➜ **Leave expensive cameras, cell phones, and wristwatches in your hotel or lodge safe.**

The constant drizzle has created a small rain forest that extends in a narrow band along the edge of the falls. A trail running through this dripping green world is overgrown with African ebony, Cape fig, Natal mahogany, wild date palms, ferns, and deep red flame lilies. A fence has been erected to keep non-fee-paying visitors at bay. Clearly sign-posted side trails lead to viewpoints overlooking the falls. The most spectacular is **Danger Point,** a perilous rock outcropping that overlooks the narrow gorge through which the Zambezi River funnels out of the **Boiling Pot,** but be careful, as this viewpoint is hazardously wet and precarious. In low-water months (September–November) most of the water goes over the falls through the **Devil's Cataract,** a narrow and mesmerizingly powerful section of the falls visible from **Livingstone's statue.** Around the full moon the park stays open late so you can see the lunar rainbow formed by the spray—a hauntingly beautiful sight. Early morning and late afternoon are popular visiting times, as you can see the daylight rainbows then. A booklet explaining the formation and layout of the falls is available from the Victoria Falls Publicity Association for a small fee. ⊠ *Off Livingstone Way* 🕾 *No phone* 💲 *US$20* ☉ *Daily 6–6, later around full moon.*

⑥ Zambezi Wildlife Sanctuary. Originally a crocodile farm, this place also has several wildcats in cages as well as ostriches, making it an interesting stop. During late December you can watch baby crocodiles hatch—an almost continuous process. Feeding times are 11:15 AM and 3:45 PM for the crocs and 4 PM for the lions. Drive down a short bush track about 200 feet before the entrance to the sanctuary, where you can spy large numbers of vultures preying on the leftovers from the croc feedings. The sanctuary also has a tea garden. ✉ *325 Park Way Dr.* ☎ *013/4–3576 or 013/4–4604* ⊕ *www.ilalalodge. com* 🖼 *US$5* ⊙ *Daily 8–5.*

> ## A NATURAL HIGH
>
> As the second-highest bungee jump in the world, the 340-foot leap from the Victoria Falls Bridge is a major magnet for adrenaline junkies. The view, if you can stomach it, is pretty spectacular, too. A jump with **Shearwater Adventures** (☎ 013/4–5806 ⊕ *www.shearwateradventures. com*) costs US$90, and you must produce your passport to get a bridge pass.

WHERE TO STAY & EAT

$$ ✕**Mama Africa Eating House.** Painted a wild lime green, Mama Africa wraps you in her vibrantly colored bosom and stimulates your senses. Funky sculptures abound, and a live township quartet provides toe-tickling local jazz from 7 until late. Humorously named for its size, the Elephant Turd T-Bone Steak competes with Sadza Ndiuraye ("the meal that kills you") and other dishes from all over Africa, many served in traditional black cast-iron, three-legged pots. Ground nuts, mild Mozambique peri-peri (a chili-based sauce), and slow-cooked local sadza (grain) flavors the air. Game meat is available in individual portions cooked to order. Alternatively, have a selection on a platter with the evening barbecue. Mama Africa provides a courtesy shuttle, which you can book when you make your reservation. ✉ *Back of Trading Post Shopping Centre, Livingstone Way* ☎ *013/4–1725* ✉ mamaafrica@africaonline. co.zw ⚲ *Reservations essential* ⊟ *No credit cards.*

$$$$ ✕🖼 **Victoria Falls Hotel.** Hotels come and go, but this landmark built in
Fodor'sChoice 1904 has retained its former glory as a stylish outpost in empire days,
★ while pandering to today's modern tastes, needs, and wants. Such grandeur can be a little overwhelming, and especially surprising if you've just been on safari. The hotel's manicured lawns are perched on the falls' edge, with a view of the bridge, and soothing sounds permeate the gardens (and the rooms if you leave the windows open). Cool cream walls form the backdrop for elegant mahogany and wicker furniture. In the bathroom an old-fashioned drench shower will wash away the most stubborn African dust. Halls are filled with sepia-tone photos from throughout the hotel's history and animal trophies so old they are going bald. After checking your e-mail in the E-Lounge and visiting the salon, you can dine and dance at the elegant Livingstone Room ($$$$). Two far less formal restaurants include the Terrace ($–$$$), with an à la carte menu, daily high tea, and a beautiful view of the bridge, and Jungle Junction (US$30), which has a huge barbecue buffet and traditional dancers. ✉ *Mallet Dr., Box 10* ☎ *013/4–4751 or 013/4–4760* ⊕ *www.victoriafallshotel.com* ⏎ *143 rooms, 18 suites*

8

⚐ *In-hotel: 3 restaurants, room service, bar, tennis court, pool, no elevator* ⊟V ⑩*BP*.

$$$–$$$$ ✕⊞ **Victoria Falls Safari Lodge.** Award-winning architecture, superb service, beautiful decor, and a magnificent view all set this lodge apart. About 4 km (2½ mi) outside town, it sits on a hilltop overlooking Zambezi National Park. A water hole below the lodge attracts herds of game, including buffalo and elephants. Soaring thatch roofs, huge wooden beams, and reed ceilings envelop you in a luxurious African atmosphere. The sides of the lodge are completely open to admit cooling breezes. All rooms face out, and you can fold back the glass-and-wood screens leading to your private veranda. The Makuwa-Kuwa Restaurant ($-$$$) makes full use of the view. Carnivorous options include prime Zimbabwe beef, warthog, and ostrich grilled to perfection. For dessert, dare to resist the Mosi Mousse which has a chocolate band that spans a cascade of fruit and chocolate mousse. The Boma, also on the premises, offers prix-fixe dining (US$35). There is a courtesy shuttle to and from Victoria Falls. ⊠ *Off Park Way, 4 km (2½ mi) from Victoria Falls* ✆ *Box 29* ☎*013/4–3211 or 013/4–3220* ✐saflodge@saflodge. co.zw ➲*72 rooms, 6 suites* ⚐ *In-room: no TV. In-hotel: 2 restaurants, room service, bar, pools, no elevator* ⊟*AE, MC, V* ⑩*BP*.

★ $$$ ✕⊞ **Ilala Lodge.** Near the center of town, this small gem is just 10 minutes from the falls on foot. Thatch roofs give the lodge an elegant yet African look. Dining outside under the night sky at the Palm Restaurant ($$), with the falls thundering 300 feet away, is a particularly enticing way to while away a Zimbabwean evening. The Palm also serves a great terrace lunch overlooking the bush. Guest rooms are hung with African paintings and tapestries and are filled with delicately caned chairs and tables and dressers made from old railroad sleepers. French doors open onto a narrow strip of lawn backed by thick bush. Unlike most hotels in town, Ilala Lodge has no fence around it, so at night it's not uncommon to find elephants browsing outside your window or buffalo grazing on the lawn. ⊠ *411 Livingstone Way, Box 18* ☎*013/4–4737* ⊕*www.ilalalodge.com* ➲*32 rooms, 2 suites* ⚐ *In-hotel: restaurant, room service, bar, pool, no elevator* ⊟*V* ⑩*BP*.

$$$$ ⊞ **Masuwe Lodge.** Adjacent to the Zambezi National Park and tucked away on the Masuwe estate, this tented en-suite lodge, just a 10-minute drive from Victoria Falls, is redolent of East African camps. Tents are well appointed and spacious, with private viewing decks. Game drives, elephant rides, and lion walks are all available. Transfers to and from Victoria Falls make this an appealing retreat and base to plan your safari. ☎*013/4–4424* ⊕*www.safpar.net* ➲*10 rooms* ⚐ *In-room: no a/c, no TV. In-hotel: bar, pool, no elevator* ⊟*V* ⑩*FAP*.

$$$$ ⊞ **Stanley and Livingstone at Victoria Falls.** This painstakingly composed small hotel is set on its own 6,000 acres of game reserve 10 minutes out of town. Public rooms are furnished with some spectacular antiques and have verandas overlooking a water hole where elephants and other animals come to drink. Spacious suites are decorated with dark wood, and bathrooms are a stylish study in white tile, green marble, and gold trim. All suites share the view of the water hole. The rate includes game drives and all on-site activities except elephant rides and transfers to the airport or to town. ⏰ *Box 160* ☎ *013/4–1003 or 013/4–1009* ⊕ *www. stanley-livingstone-hotel.com* ⏦ *15 suites* ♿ *In-hotel: restaurant, bar, pool, no elevator, no kids under 12* ⊟ *AE, MC, V* ⏲ *FAP.*

☪ \$ ⚏ **Jingle Bells.** A comfortable and spacious B&B that owes its name to the time of year it originally opened, Jingle Bells is a great option for a quiet stay in Victoria Falls. Decor is fresh and simple. Mariolina De Leo, the very friendly and helpful host, is fluent in Italian, English, and French. Of the rooms, two have double beds and nine have twins; all have private bathrooms. The entire house can be rented fully serviced with a cook and cleaners. ✉ *591 Manyika Rd., Box 289* ☎ *013/4–3242* ✎ marcla@mweb.co.zw ⏦ *11 rooms* ♿ *In-hotel: pool, no elevator* ⊟ *No credit cards* ⏲ *BP.*

☪ \$ ⚏ **Victoria Falls Backpackers.** Rooms at this inexpensive and jolly backpacker's lodge are named after animals, with decor to match. The owners have created a child-friendly environment (the pool has a small fence, for example), offer great booking services, and claim to get the best activity prices in town. Overland trucks are not allowed. ✉ *357 Gibson Rd., Box 151* ☎ *013/4–2209 or 013/4–2248* ⊕ *www. victoriafallsbackpackers.com* ⏦ *6 rooms* ♿ *In-hotel: bar, pool* ⊟ *No credit cards* ⏲ *CP.*

SPORTS & THE OUTDOORS

You can book all the adventures listed below (and many others) through your hotel or one of the major booking offices along Park Way:

Safari Par Excellence (☎ *013/4–4424* ⊕ *www.safpar.com*). **Shearwater Adventures** (☎ *013/4–4471* ⊕ *www.shearwateradventures.com*). **Wild Horizons** (☎ *013/4–4571* ⊕ *www.wildhorizons.co.za*).

BOATING A cruise on the Upper Zambezi is a relaxing way to take in game and scenery. Hippos, crocs, and elephants are spied fairly regularly, and your captain will stop and comment whenever something noteworthy rears its head. Shearwater Adventures has a sunset cruise (US\$35). Shearwater also offers a 30-minute white-water jetboat ride below the falls. This activity is a great adventure for the not so bold, since all you do is hang on. Children over seven can jetboat if accompanied by an adult. Beer and other cold drinks are included in the price (US\$80).

CANOEING Shearwater Adventures offers half- and full-day canoe trips and a very gentle "wine route" trip, on which you don't even paddle; you just watch the view while your guide does the work and hands you drinks and snacks (US\$70). Wild Horizons leads canoe trips on the Zambezi River above the falls. The river here is mostly wide and flat, with the occasional tiny rapid. As the river winds around islands and splits into myriad channels, you might view crocodiles, hippos, or elephants. The one-hour game drive through Zambezi National Park to reach the launch point is an added bonus. Most trips provide a bush breakfast before you start, a brief coffee or tea break, and a casual lunch on an island in the river. You can select either a half- or full-day trip or two- to three-night expeditions. No experience or physical prowess is required. Expect to pay about US\$85 for a half day and US\$105 for a full day.

8

ELEPHANT-
BACK RIDING

The Shearwater Elephant Company, part of Shearwater Adventures, has morning and evening rides accompanied by breakfast or snacks and sunset drinks (US$100). Wild Horizons offers elephant rides (US$100), including transfers and either a full breakfast or drinks and snacks. They have three baby elephants, so be prepared to fall in love.

FLYING &
PARASAILING

Shearwater Adventures runs a helicopter flight from the Elephant Hills Hotel that gets you over the falls in a couple of minutes. It costs US$95 for 12–13 minutes. **Zambezi Parasailing** (☎ *013/4–2209* ⊕ *www.victoria fallsbackpackers.com*) provides 10-minute parasails for US$50, including transfers from anywhere in town. Yes, you land in the boat.

> ## PERUSING THE MARKETS
>
> Original African art is hard to come by, and unfortunately, most of the pieces you'll come across are crude replicas. Explore with an open mind. You'll have the most luck finding something if your aim is to simply find a lovingly created piece that tickles your fancy. Do not buy anything until you have walked the entire length of the market. This will give you a sense of what is on offer and the standard of workmanship—look for objects carved entirely from one piece of wood. Pieces made from more than one piece of wood are stuck together using some very dodgy processes.

HORSEBACK
RIDING

Riding a horse through Zambezi National Park is an unforgettable experience. You get to sneak up on unsuspecting antelopes and even buffalo, giraffes, and elephants, especially during the rainy months. Safari Par Excellence is the booking agent for **Zambezi Horse Trails** (☎ *091/21–3270* ✉ zamhorse@mweb.co.zw), run by Alison Baker, a Vic Falls legend. She knows the bush like the back of her hand, rides hard, and can shoot straight. Even more important, though, she knows how to avoid having to. Experienced riders may go on game-viewing rides that range anywhere from three hours to five days. Novice riders can go for two hours but will not be allowed close to animals such as elephants and lions. Costs range from US$55 for two hours to US$100 for a full-day ride, including lunch, drinks, and park fees. Multiday trail rides are available on request.

RAFTING
& RIVER
BOARDING

Safari Par Excellence specializes in multiday trips to Batoka Gorge, as well as the standard half- and full-day adventures. Rafting starts at US$105. Shearwater Rafting, part of Shearwater Adventures, runs a full-day trip for US$110—lunch, drinks, and transfers included. Half-day trips are also available. Wild Horizons leads full- and half-day rafting trips, as well as a 2½-day trip, starting at US$95.

RAPPELLING &
SWINGING

Wild Horizons lets you swing off steel cables in the gorge. Take your pick from the flying fox, rap jump, abseil (rappel), or the big gorge swing. *For descriptions of what these crazy activities are, see Rappelling & Swinging under Livingstone, Zambia, above.* The cost is from US$30 for a single activity to US$115 for the full-day package.

SHOPPING

Several curio and crafts shops lie just beyond the Falls Craft Village, including the stylish **Elephant Walk Mall** (⊠*Sopers Crescent, behind banks and post office*). At the sprawling **Trading Post** (⊠*Livingstone Way*) you can buy a variety of crafts, from an 8-foot-tall wooden giraffe to soapstone carvings and brightly colored Zimbabwean batiks. To get your acquisitions back home, visit the international shipping agent sandwiched between the curio shops.

VICTORIA FALLS AND ZIMBABWE ESSENTIALS

TRANSPORTATION

BY AIR

Victoria Falls Airport (VFA) lies 22 km (14 mi) south of town. South African Airways, Air Zimbabwe, and British Airways all fly direct between Johannesburg and Victoria Falls daily.

Most hotels send free shuttle buses to meet incoming flights and provide free airport transfers for departing guests; arrange this in advance with your hotel. The cheapest way to get yourself to and from the airport is to book a shuttle bus with Falcon Safaris or Travel Junction in the Trading Post. These shuttles will do a one-way transfer for US$10 per person. Taxis are available and payable in local or foreign currency, but taxi fares fluctuate drastically. Be prepared for local drivers to accost you with offers of rides into town.

Airport Victoria Falls Airport (⊠*Livingstone Way* ☎*013/4-4250*).

Airlines Air Zimbabwe (☎*013/4-4316* ⊕*www.airzimbabwe.com*). **British Airways/Comair** (☎*013/4-2053 or 013/4-2388* ⊕*www.british-airways.com*). **South African Airways** (☎*04/738-922* ⊕*www.flysaa.com*).

Shuttles Falcon Safaris (☎*013/4-2695* ⊕*www.falconsafaris.com*). **Travel Junction** (☎*013/4-41480* ⊕*www.victoriafallsbackpackers.com*).

BY BUS

Most of the outlying hotels have shuttle buses that run into town hourly. Inquire at your hotel in advance.

BY CAR

The attractions in town tend to be within walking distance or just a short taxi ride away. As a result, it's probably not worth renting a car if you don't mind stretching your legs. Despite advice not to drive around Zimbabwe, it is only a two-hour drive to Hwange and is quite safe to do so if done in daylight.

BY TAXI

Taxis are a cheap and convenient way to get around town. Hotels can summon reputable taxis quickly and advise you on the cost. Tipping is not usual, but change is always appreciated.

CONTACTS & RESOURCES

CURRENCY EXCHANGE

Zimbabwe's currency is the Zimbabwe dollar. ⚠ **This currency remains particularly volatile, and although the rate of exchange at the time of writing was around Z$250 to the US$1, you can expect any number of surprises from one day to the next.** Bearer cheques, as the bills are known since they are promissory notes, not official legal tender, are in denominations that range from Z$1 to Z$100,000.

ELECTRICITY

To use electric-powered equipment purchased in the United States or Canada, bring a converter and adapter. If your appliances are dual voltage, you'll need only an adapter. The electrical current is 220 volts, 50 cycles alternating current (AC); wall outlets in most of the region take 15-amp plugs with three square prongs.

EMBASSIES

United States **U.S. Embassy** (✉ *172 Herbert Chitepo Ave., Box 4010, Harare* ☎ *04/25–0593* ⊕ *http://harare.usembassy.gov/*).

EMERGENCIES

MARS (Medical Air Rescue Services) is on standby for all emergencies. Dr. Nyoni is a trauma specialist and operates a hospital opposite the Shoestring lodge. The well-stocked Victoria Falls Pharmacy is the place to go if you need prescription medicines.

Emergency Services **Police** (☎ *013/4–4206 or 013/4–4681*). **MARS** (✉ *West Dr., opposite Shoestring* ☎ *013/4–4646*).

Hospital **Dr. Nyoni** (✉ *West Dr., opposite Shoestring* ☎ *013/4–3356*).

Pharmacy **Victoria Falls Pharmacy** (✉ *Phumula Centre, off Park Way* ☎ *013/4–4403*).

GAY & LESBIAN TRAVELERS

Homosexuality is not illegal in Zimbabwe but can be a practical problem. Although attitudes are improving, it's advisable to be extremely circumspect.

INTERNET

Internet prices can vary wildly, as the telephone rates keep climbing. The average cost at time of writing is between US$1 and US$2 for 15 minutes.

Internet Access **E-world** (✉ *Victoria Falls Hotel* ☎ *013/4–4751*). **Shearwater** (✉ *Park Way* ☎ *013/4–5806*).

LANGUAGE

Zimbabwe's official language is English. Chishona and Sindebele and their dialects are widely spoken.

TELEPHONE

The country code for Zimbabwe is 263. When dialing from abroad, drop the initial 0 from local area codes. Operator assistance is 962 for domestic and 965 for international inquiries, but it's better to ask a hotel or restaurant owner.

Zimbabwe has card-operated pay phones. Phone cards are available in several denominations, and a digital readout tells you how much credit remains while you're talking. Telephone cards are available at newsstands and convenience stores.

TIME
Zimbabwe operates on CAST (Central African Standard Time), which is two hours ahead of Greenwich Mean Time. That makes it seven hours ahead of North American eastern standard time (six hours ahead during eastern daylight saving time).

8

Botswana & Namibia's Best Safari Destinations

WORD OF MOUTH

"We cruised up the Chobe river to watch the elephants coming down to drink and bathe. There were about 100 of them in one herd and I felt quite vulnerable watching them from the water—a totally different perspective to what we had been experiencing. The elephants frolicked in the water and played together, some totally submerging themselves and using their trunks as snorkels. The babies were rolling over and over and some were wallowing in the mud nearby. We came very close to them but they were happier to play than worry about us."

—Tropical_gal

Updated by
Kate Turkington

LOOK NORTH OF SOUTH AFRICA, and you find two of Africa's most beautiful and dramatic safari destinations: Botswana and Namibia. Although both contain some of the last true wilderness areas left in the world, both *are* accessible to tourists and have excellent infrastructures. Your first night in Botswana's legendary Okavango Delta—an inland water wilderness of crystal-clear waters, perfumed water lilies, papyrus channels breaking into open stretches of sky-reflecting calm waters, hippos, crocs, elephants, and rare, shy water antelope—will linger with you forever, as will your eyeball-to-eyeball encounters with wall-to-wall big game in Moremi Wildlife Reserve. Namibia's unbelievably wide-open spaces—deserts stretching to an ever-vanishing horizon, jagged mountain peaks, flat gravel plains glistening with garnets—cannot fail to stir your soul. In the Great White Place of Etosha National Park or the Place of Mirages, your camera will click nonstop as golden lions pad over white sand, crimson-breasted shrikes flit among dry trees, and herds of black-faced impalas slake their thirst at water holes in the heat of day, watched by a crouching leopard.

BOTSWANA

In Botswana superlatives are unavoidable—and never quite adequate. A short plane ride can whisk you from scorching desert to water wonderlands, from great salt pans to fertile floodplains.

Half a century ago Botswana was a Cinderella among nations, one of the world's poorest countries. Then the Fairy Godmother visited and bestowed her gift: diamonds. The resulting economic boom transformed Botswana into one of Africa's richest countries as measured by per capita income.

The 1960s were a decade of self-determination all over Africa, led by Uganda, Ghana, and Nigeria. The British Protectorate of Bechuanaland was granted independence in 1966 and renamed Botswana. Where other nations' celebrations quickly turned sour, Botswana's independence brought an enduring tide of optimism. The country sidestepped the scourge of tribalism and factional fighting that cursed much of the continent—including bordering South Africa and Zimbabwe—and is considered one of Africa's most stable democracies. The Batswana (singular: Motswana) are renowned for their courteousness and dignity.

ORIENTATION & PLANNING

ORIENTATION

Roughly the size of France or Texas, Botswana, once relatively unknown on the tourist map, is now a popular safari destination. Nearly 18% of this very flat country's total land area is reserved for conservation and tourism. The Moremi Wildlife Reserve, the first such reserve in southern Africa to have been created by an African community (the BaTawana people) on its own tribal lands, is a major draw. Here, as in

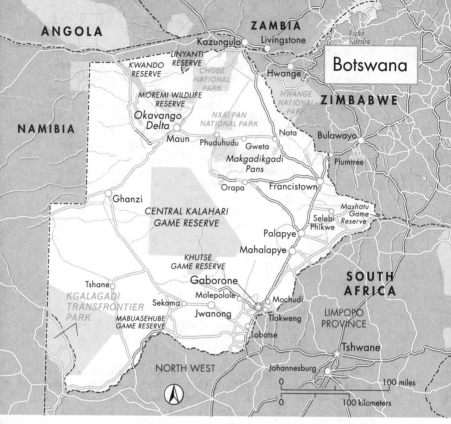

other parts of northern Botswana, you'll see elephants, lions, buffalo, wild dogs, cheetahs, leopards, giraffes, kudus, wildebeests, hippos, and hundreds of awesome birds. One hundred km (62 mi) west of Victoria Falls in Botswana's northeast corner is Chobe National Park, another of Africa's fine game sanctuaries, known for its elephants. The wide and tranquil Chobe River is surrounded by a natural wilderness of floodplain, dead lake bed, sand ridges, and forest. Downstream it joins the mighty Zambezi on its journey through Zimbabwe and Mozambique to the Indian Ocean. Upstream, where it's known as the Linyanti, it forms the border between Botswana and Namibia. In this area the Linyanti Reserve, which borders Chobe National Park, is a huge private concession, as is the Kwando Reserve, to the west, named for the river of the same name—the lifeblood of the Linyanti, Savuti, and Chobe systems.

Although cities such as Gaborone (pronounced *ha*-bo-ronee), the capital, have been modernized, Botswana has little in the way of urban excitement. Outside the cities it's a land of amazing variety: the Kalahari Desert is in stark contrast to the lush beauty of the Okavango Delta, one of Botswana's most magnificent and best-known regions. A vast area of tangled waterways and aquatic, bird, and mammal life, it's sometimes referred to as the Swamps, but this gives a false impression.

There are no murky mangroves here, no sinister everglades, just open tranquil waters of breathtaking beauty leading into narrow, papyrus-fringed channels.

THE OKAVANGO DELTA

The Okavango Delta is in Ngamiland, the tribal land of the BaTawana tribe. It's the legendary hunting area that, with the help of Dr. David Livingstone's accounts of his explorations, fueled the 19th-century European imagination. The delta is formed by the Okavango River, which descends from the Angolan highlands and then fans out over northwestern Botswana. It's made up of an intricate network of channels and crystal-pure quiet lagoons, papyrus- and reed-lined backwaters. There *is* big game, but it's more elusive and difficult to approach than in the game reserves.

MOREMI WILDLIFE RESERVE

In the northeastern sector of the Okavango lies the spectacular Moremi Wildlife Reserve. In 1963 Chief Moremi III and the local BaTawana people proclaimed 1,800 square km (about 1,100 square mi) of pristine wilderness—ancient mopane forests, lagoons, islands, seasonal floodplains, and open grassland—as a game sanctuary, a first in southern African conservation history. Here, where the life-giving waters of the Okavango meet the vast Kalahari, is one of Africa's greatest parks, teeming with game and birds and, unlike the Masai Mara or Kruger Park, with hardly any people. You'll love the Garden of Eden atmosphere even if you might encounter the odd snake or two.

CHOBE NATIONAL PARK

Huge herds of elephants and game galore roam this 11,700 square km (4,500 square mi) of pristine bush in northeast Botswana, bordering the Chobe River. Although it's one of Africa's great game reserves, its lack of roads and often almost inaccessible conditions—especially in the rainy season—mean you'll need a 4x4 to tackle it on your own. It's certainly not the most beautiful of reserves—in winter the damage inflicted by thousands of elephants gives it the appearance of a World War I battlefield with dusty plains, dead trees, and an air of desolation. But this is when game-viewing is at its best, as the lack of surface water forces the game to use the permanent water holes.

LINYANTI RESERVE

This 125,000 hectare (308,882 acres) reserve bordering Chobe's western boundary is known for the variety of its scenery and habitats, which range from waterways, marshes, and floodplains, to riverine forest and grasslands. It's the home of the legendary Savute Channel, a wide swathe of golden grasslands teeming with birdlife and game, where the river last ran over 20 years ago.

KWANDO RESERVE

Like the Okavango, the Kwando River comes down from the wet Angola highlands meandering through a few hundred kilometers of wilderness. The 2,300-square-km (900-square-mi) private Kwando concession northwest of Chobe and Linyanti has more than 80 km (50 mi) of river frontage. It stretches south from the banks of the Kwando

TOP REASONS TO VISIT BOTSWANA

The Okavango Delta Whether you are drifting dreamily in a mokoro through this water wonderland of crystal-clear, papyrus-fringed channels, or walking among ancient fig and jackalberry trees on one of the many islands, your everyday world is guaranteed to fade and disappear from your consciousness.

Big Game Although you won't find the huge herds as in Serengeti, you'll come face-to-face with more animals, birds, critters big and small, than you ever knew existed. And there won't be hordes of other visitors blocking your view or diluting the experience.

Birding Buy a bird book and marvel at more than 900 species—many

endemic—that crowd the game reserves. There's nothing quite like waking up to the joyous tumult of early-morning birdsong. A sighting of a Pel's fishing owl, one of the world's rarest birds, will have Audubon twitching in his grave.

Walking with the Bushmen Deserts get a bad rap. Far from being lifeless, they are miracles of plenty. You just have to be in the company of the right people. As the Kalahari stars begin to pulse in the blue-black dome of the sky, sit with the Bushmen outside their grass-covered, beehive huts. Watch them make a fire, listen to their dissonant music as one of them dances a dance as old as time, and then listen to the stars sing.

River, through huge open plains and mopane forests to the Okavango Delta. It's an area crisscrossed by thousands of ancient game trails traversed by wildlife that move freely between the Okavango Delta, Chobe, and the open Namibian wilderness to the north.

THE CENTRAL KALAHARI GAME RESERVE

The Central Kalahari Game reserve—the second-largest conservation area in the world (only Masai Mara is bigger)—comprises 5 million hectares (12,355,269 acres) of arid savanna. Crisscrossed by fossil rivers and covered with myriad dead lake beds, this legendary area straddles the Tropic of Capricorn. It's harsh, inhospitable, undeveloped, and largely inaccessible to humans. Although the Kalahari has the dubious distinction of being the biggest piece of sand in the world, it's not a desert like the Namib, the oldest desert in the world with the tallest dunes in the world, or the Sahara, with its shifting sands interspersed with rocky outcrops. It has scrub, thornveld, and grasses of all colors, shapes and sizes. There's grandeur and a stark, spectacular beauty to be found nowhere else, and a vastness that at first sight seems impenetrable. There's also a wealth of animal, bird, reptile, and insect life.

PLANNING

The best time to visit Botswana is in the autumn and winter months (April through September), although if you don't mind heat, then any time is a good time. In the delta during the winter months the water has come in from the Angolan highlands, and the floodplains, channels, lakes, and inland waterways are literally brimming with sparkling fresh water. Elsewhere, as it's the dry season, the grass and vegetation are sparse, and it's much easier to see game, which often have no choice but to drink at available water holes or rivers. But be warned: it can be bitterly cold, particularly early in the morning and at night. Dress in layers (including a thigh-length thick jacket, hat, scarf, and gloves), which you can discard or add to as the sun goes up or down. From October through February it gets very hot—up to 35°C (95°F)—so unless you're in a lodge with air-conditioning, can stand great heat, or are a keen bird-watcher—for it's then that the migrants return—stick with fall and winter.

ABOUT THE CAMPS & LODGES

Botswana has some of the most diverse safari accommodations in the world, where you are guaranteed exclusivity and a true wilderness experience. Whether you choose to stay in a wooden cabin, a rustic tent with an outside overhead bucket shower, a five-star, air-conditioned chalet, or safari tent with your own romantic outdoor shower and personal plunge pool, you are guaranteed some of the best game-viewing in Africa. And you won't be crowded out by other visitors. Most camps are very small, accommodating only about 12–16 people, which means that there are never more than three vehicles at that memorable leopard or cheetah sighting and the only traffic you'll encounter among the waterways of the delta are grazing hippos and dozing crocodiles. Even in the northern part of Chobe, around Chobe Game Lodge, where there are more vehicles than elsewhere, early-morning and late-afternoon rush hour usually consists of large buffalo and elephant herds trekking down to the rivers for their sundowners. Prices depend on the season and will be the highest during the high season (June-October). Always check on individual camps for special offers.

A word about terminology: "Land camps" are in a game reserve or contiguous concession and offer two daily game drives, morning and evening. If you're not in a national park, you'll be able to go out for night drives off-road with a powerful spotlight to pick out nocturnal animals. "Water camps" are deep in the Okavango Delta and often accessible only by air or water. Many camps offer both a land and a true water experience, so you get the best of both worlds.

Don't come to Botswana expecting a profound gastronomic experience. There is little or no local cuisine, so the food in the camps and lodges is designed to appeal to a wide variety of international visitors. Nevertheless, it is quite tasty—soups, roasts, pies, quiches, curries, vegetables, and lots of lovely fresh fruit. Most camps bake their own excellent bread, muffins, and cakes, and often make desserts such as meringues, éclairs, and homemade ice cream. And you'll find plenty of tasty South African wine and beer. Don't expect TVs or elevators either, even at very expensive camps, and air-conditioning is the exception rather than the rule. It's mentioned in reviews only when it is present.

Most lodging prices are quoted in U.S. dollars, and you can use dollars as tips wherever you stay. The average price per person per night at private lodges is US$500–US$1,000, which includes accommodations,

9

all meals, soft drinks, and good South African wine. Camps arrange transfers from the nearest airport or airstrip.

WHAT IT COSTS IN U.S. DOLLARS				
¢	$	$$	$$$	$$$$
SAFARI CAMPS AND LODGES	under $500	$500–$600	$600–$700	$700–$800	over $800

All prices refer to an all-inclusive per-person rate including tax, assuming double occupancy.

HEALTH & SAFETY

There are high standards of hygiene in all the private lodges, and most hotels are usually up to international health standards. But malaria is rife, so don't forget to take those antimalarials. Botswana has one of the highest AIDS rates in Africa: approximately 1 in 3 people are HIV positive. However, all the private lodges and camps have excellent staff medical programs, and you are in no danger of contacting the disease unless you have sex with a stranger. As in most cities, crime is prevalent in Gaborone, but simple safety precautions such as locking up your travel documents and valuables, and not walking alone at night, will keep you safe. On safari, there is always potential danger from wild animals, but your ranger will brief you thoroughly on the dos and don'ts of encountering big game.

IMPORTANT DETAILS

EMERGENCIES Most safari companies include medical insurance in their tariffs. **Medical Rescue International** (☎267/390–1601) has 24-hour emergency help.

LANGUAGE Although Botswana's national language is Setswana, English is the official one, and it is spoken nearly everywhere.

MONEY MATTERS The pula (the Setswana word for "rain") and the thebe constitute the Botswana currency; one pula equals 100 thebe. You will need to change your money or traveler's checks into pula, as this is the only legally accepted currency. (The currency rate fluctuates marginally.) However, you can use U.S. dollars or euros as tips at lodges and camps, and most camp prices are quoted in U.S. dollars.

There are no restrictions on foreign currency notes brought into the country as long as they are declared. Travelers can carry up to P10,000, or the equivalent in foreign currency, out of the country without declaring it. Banking hours are weekdays 9–3:30, Saturday 8:30–11. Hours at Barclays Bank at Sir Seretse Khama International Airport are Monday–Saturday 6 AM–10 PM.

PASSPORTS & VISAS All visitors, including infants, need a valid passport to enter Botswana for visits of up to 90 days.

TELEPHONE NUMBERS Both Botswana and South African telephone numbers appear in this section. Botswana numbers begin with the 267 country code, which you shouldn't dial within the country. (There are no internal area codes in Botswana.) South African numbers begin with that country code (27) followed by the area code—e.g., 11 for Johannesburg.

TIME Botswana is on CAST (Central African Standard Time), which is two hours ahead of Greenwich Mean Time. That makes it seven hours ahead of North American eastern standard time (six hours ahead during eastern daylight saving time).

VISITOR INFORMATION The main branch of Botswana's **Department of Tourism** (✉ *Private Bag 0047, Main Mall* ☎*267/395–3024* ⊕*www.botswana-tourism.gov.bw*) is located in Gaborone. The friendly and efficient staff will help with all sorts of queries and requests, from maps, accommodations, tour operators and tourist attractions, to general information about Botswana.

THE OKAVANGO DELTA

You're here for the unparalleled experience of being in one of the world's last great wilderness areas. There's no place on earth like the Okavango. It is the world's only inland delta and the only way to get around this network of waterways is by boat.

The *mokoro* boat, synonymous with the Okavango, was introduced to the delta in the mid-18th century, when the Bayei tribe (the river bushmen) moved down from the Zambezi. Previously, the nomadic Bayei, who drifted the waterways looking for food and game, used papyrus rafts, but they invented the mokoro as a more controllable craft that could be maneuvered up- or downstream. These boats were traditionally made from the trunks of the great jackalberry, morula, and sausage trees. Today, because of the need to protect the trees, you may find yourself in a fiberglass canoe. Your skilled poler is always on the alert for the ubiquitous hippos but is quite laid-back about the mighty crocs lying smiling in the sun. (In deeper waters powerboats are an option.) Bird-watching from these boats is a special thrill: the annual return of thousands of gorgeous carmine bee-eaters to the Swamps in August and September is a dazzling sight, as is a glimpse of the huge ginger-color Pel's fishing owl, the world's only fish-eating owl and one of its rarest birds. This is a water wilderness experience above all others, but don't miss the chance to go on a guided walk on one of the many islands.

You'll almost certainly see elephants, hippos, crocs, and red lechwes (a beautiful antelope endemic to the Swamps), and may catch a glimpse of the rare, aquatic sitatunga antelope. You'll almost certainly hear lions, but may not always see them; if you're very lucky, you may see a pride swimming between islands. On the other hand, you might see lots of game. Just remember that you're not in the delta for the big game—you'll see plenty of that elsewhere in Botswana. You're here for the unforgettable beauty of this amazing wilderness area.

WHERE TO STAY

$$$$ 🏠 **Jao Camp.** If you love the fanciful, then Jao (*Jow* as in "now") will delight you. This spectacular and stunning camp, a pure Hollywood-meets-Africa fantasy, is in a private concession bordering the Moremi Wildlife Reserve west of Mombo, on a densely wooded island overlooking vast plains. The landscape includes a great variety of habitats, including permanent waterways and lagoons, open floodplains,

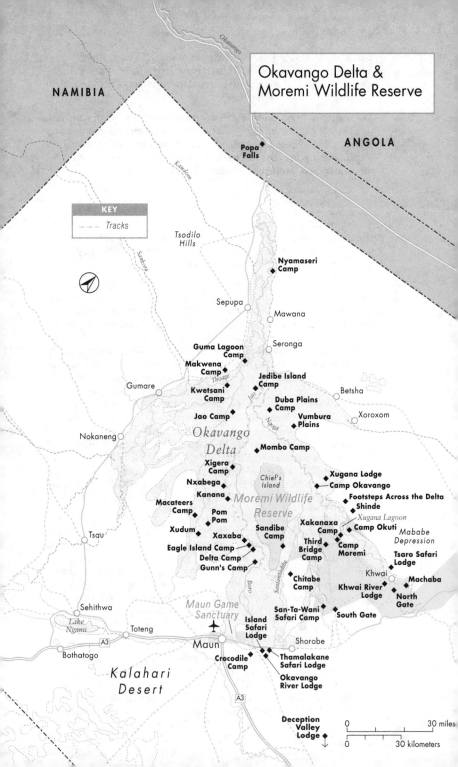

Okavango Delta & Moremi Wildlife Reserve

NAMIBIA

ANGOLA

Okavango

KEY
--- *Tracks*

Kaudom

Tsodilo Hills

Popa Falls

Nyamaseri Camp

Sepupa

Mawana

Seronga

Guma Lagoon Camp

Makwena Camp

Jedibe Island Camp

Betsha

Gumare

Kwetsani Camp

Duba Plains Camp

Xoroxom

Jao Camp

Okavango Delta

Vumbura Plains

Nokaneng

Mombo Camp

Xigera Camp

Chief's Island

Xugana Lodge

Nxabega

Camp Okavango

Kanana

Moremi Wildlife Reserve

Footsteps Across the Delta

Shinde

Xugana Lagoon

Macateers Camp

Pom Pom

Xakanaxa Camp

Camp Okuti

Mababe Depression

Xudum

Xaxaba

Sandibe Camp

Third Bridge Camp

Camp Moremi

Tsau

Eagle Island Camp

Delta Camp

Gunn's Camp

Tsaro Safari Lodge

Khwai

Machaba

Chitabe Camp

Khwai River Lodge

North Gate

Maun Game Sanctuary

San-Ta-Wani Safari Camp

South Gate

Sehithwa

Lake Ngami

Island Safari Lodge

Toteng

Shorobe

Bothatogo

A3

Maun

Crocodile Camp

Thamalakane Safari Lodge

Kalahari Desert

Okavango River Lodge

A3

Deception Valley Lodge

0   30 miles
0   30 kilometers

and thick Kalahari soils. The place is teeming with creatures of all kinds—fish, fowl, and game. Land and water activities are available, depending on the seasonal water levels, so you can take a day or night game drive in an open 4x4, glide in a mokoro through possibly the most beautiful setting in the whole of the delta, chug along hippo highways in a motorboat, or go on a guided walk. You'll see lots of predators, especially lions, who live here in the highest concentration in the country, according to a recent wildlife census. You'll be one of only 16 pampered guests when you sleep in your own spacious tree house with superb views over the vast floodplains. Lie in your canopy bed and watch the sun rise, or recline on megacushions, pasha style, and watch the translucent waters beyond the lush palms. Private bath facilities include an indoor shower, flush toilet and sink, Victorian claw-foot tub, and outdoor shower. Rare and fascinating African artifacts decorate the wood, multi-tier interior of the main building. The food is delicious, and the superb standard of service can best be appreciated as you dine in the cool thatch dining area under a canopy of trees alive with birdsong. After a night drive, eat under the night sky in the outdoor boma and watch the sparks from the roaring fire compete with the dazzling stars. ⌂ *Wilderness Safaris, Box 5219, Rivonia 2128, South Africa* ☎*27/11/807–1800* ⇆*8 chalets* ⌂*In-hotel: bar, pool* ☰*MC, V* ⎮◎⎮*FAP.*

$$$
Fodor'sChoice
★

🏠**Duba Plains.** This tiny, intimate camp deep in the delta is built on an island shaded by large ebony, fig, and garcinia trees and surrounded by seasonal (late April to early October) flood plains. It's one of the best-kept secrets in the Okavango. When the water is high in winter, the game competes with the camp for dry ground, and lions and hyenas become regular dusk-to-dawn visitors. There's wall-to-wall game, including herds of hundreds of buffalo, leopards, lions, cheetahs, elephants, hippos, lechwes, and the most beautiful of all the antelopes—the sable—all of which you can watch from one of only two 4x4 open game vehicles in the reserve. Duba Plains is also a birder's paradise, with an abundance of waterfowl. The Duba lion prides are among the few to hunt by day; they specialize in taking down buffalo. Big, cool, tented rooms are built on raised decks and have ceiling fans and gleaming furniture of Rhodesian teak that's complemented by the subtle grays and greens of the fabrics. A lattice screen divides each bedroom/sitting area from the private bathroom, which has a ceramic sink, glass shower, and plenty of storage space. The lodge's lounge and dining area is small and inviting, with comfortable chairs and couches, a bar, and a stupendous view. There's a poolside gazebo where you can relax and watch the plains after a refreshing dip, as well as a bird blind tucked behind the camp. Now rivaling its oh-so-luxurious sister camp, Mombo, for wall-to-wall game and abundant birdlife, Duba also draws guests for its remoteness, simplicity, and solitude. ⌂ *Wilderness Safaris, Box 5219, Rivonia 2128, South Africa* ☎*27/11/807–1800* ⊕*www.dubaplains.com* ⇆*6 rooms* ⌂*In-hotel: bar, pool* ☰*MC, V* ⎮◎⎮*FAP.*

$$$
🏠**Eagle Island Camp.** On Xaxaba (pronounced ka-*ka*-ba) Island, deep in the central delta, this camp is surrounded by pristine waterways, islands of tall palm trees, and vast floodplains. At dawn and dusk hip-

pos chortle, night birds call, and hyenas whoop. Activities here are water-based: gliding in a mokoro; boating on wide lagoons; and enjoying sundowners as you float on crystal-clear water (go on and drink it—it's pure) as the sun sets in a blaze of red and gold. Or have a front-row seat for the same nightly spectacle in the Fish Eagle Bar, which juts out over the water. There's plenty of animal life, too; if you're very lucky, you might even catch a glimpse of one of the world's rarest antelopes, the aquatic sitatunga. Large walk-in tents are decorated in traditional African style with cane woven headboards, lamps fashioned out of Botswana baskets, and carved African pots. The four-poster beds are carved out of Rhodesian teak, as are the bedside tables that have legs carved to look like old-fashioned sticks of barley sugar. Chill out on the huge veranda amid the *riempie* (seats of handwoven hide thongs) chairs, beautifully carved tables, and an inviting canvas hammock. Laze on the main viewing deck, which overlooks the vast expanses of lily-studded water complete with dozing hippos, before dining in style in the elegant dining room. As you walk past the huge pool that's surrounded by green lawns to the landing stage where the powerboats and mekoro are moored, the calls of the resident fish eagles pierce the wide blue sky. ⌑ *Orient-Express Safaris, Box 786432, Sandton 2146, South Africa* ☎*27/11/481–6052* ⊕*www.orient-express-safaris.com* ⇥*15 tents* ⅋*In-hotel: bar, pool, a/c* ⊟*MC, V* ⍾*FAP.*

$$$ ▦ **Shinde Camp.** Ker & Downey's oldest camp, and possibly its loveliest, lies in a vast palm-dotted area in the heart of the northern delta. Here superb guides and other friendly, well-trained staff take you under their expert wings. As you sip sundowners on a boat ride on the horseshoe-shape lagoon, cruising hippos serenade in a comic chorus, complemented by frogs, cicadas, and a myriad of other species. Your large tent, outfitted with furniture in cane and Rhodesian teak, complemented by fabrics in brown, teal, terra-cotta, and white has polished wooden floors both inside and outside on your viewing deck. Spacious bathrooms have flower-painted ceramic sinks, and a sturdy door leads to a separate outside toilet. A spiraling wooden ramp connects the dining area, built high in the trees at the top of the lodge, with a lookout deck and lounge in the middle and a boma under huge old trees at the bottom. If you want even more exclusivity and private pampering, opt for Shinde Enclave, which accommodates up to six guests with a private guide and waiter-barman. ⌑ *Ker & Downey, Box 27, Maun, Botswana* ☎*267/686–0375* ⊕*www.kerdowney.com* ⇥*9 tents* ⅋*In-hotel: bar, pool* ⊟*MC, V* ⍾*FAP.*

★ **$$** ▦ **Camp Okavango.** Most people involuntarily draw a breath when they walk from the airstrip into this sprawling campsite. On remote Nxaragha (Na-ka-ra) Island in the heart of the permanent delta, it's accessible only by plane or water. Built by an eccentric American millionaire many years ago (she used to jet off to Los Angeles to get her hair done), it combines style, comfort, and a year-round water wilderness experience. Huge old trees arch over an outdoor lounge area with sweeping lawns leading down to the water, where hippos snort all night. An electric fence around the camp keeps the elephants out but not the hippos. Don't worry though; you're quite safe within your canvas walls. In season, fishing is good and because the camp is so well established, the birdlife is prolific. Your luxury tent with private bathroom, built on a raised wooden platform overlooking the delta, is set among groves of ancient trees and is so well separated from the others that you might believe yours is the only one in camp. Cool pastel linens, handcrafted wood furniture, and colorful handwoven rugs make up the spacious interior. Common areas with worn flagstones have comfortable colonial-style furniture and carved elephant stools on which you can watch hundreds of birds feed, bathe, and drink—aided and abetted by a few cheeky squirrels. Dinners are served in the high-thatch dining area, where an original sycamore fig mokoro is suspended over the long wooden dining table. Don't miss out on a spectacular sunset view from your fiberglass mokoro as you sip chilled drinks from a bar set up in the middle of a water-lily-studded lagoon tended by a wading barman. If you're going to the sister camp, Camp Moremi, go by water transfer, a three-hour trip with an island coffee stop on the way. *Desert & Delta Safaris, Box 130555, Bryanston 2125, South Africa 27/11/706–0861 www.desertdelta.co.za 11 tents In-hotel: bar, pool MC, V FAP.*

$$ **Kanana Camp.** Set deep in the delta among grass-covered islands dotted with fig, palm, ebony, and sausage trees, Kanana is simpler and more rustic than many of the other delta camps, and its natural charm puts you in close touch with your surroundings, so you feel part of the delta, not cocooned away from it. Game drives, mokoro-ing, boating, and bush walks (there are resident Pel's fishing owls on nearby islands) are all part of the experience, but a visit to the Thapagadi Lagoon is a must. It's home to a fantastic heronry, where open-billed, maribou, and yellow-billed storks all nest, together with herons of all kinds, cormorants, pelicans, darters, and egrets. You won't forget the sounds of this avian community—squawks, squeals, honks, belches, and gargles. Safari tents (where tea and coffee are brought at dawn by a cheerful staff member) have their own wooden decks overlooking dense reed beds and a papyrus-thick floodplain; water laps almost to the front steps. Simple cane furnishings and dark-wood cabinetry are complemented by colorful rugs and a white curtain that separates the gaily decorated bathroom from the bedroom. You'll fall asleep to the sound of hippos munching, squelching, and splashing outside your tent and awake to tumultuous birdsong. Public areas are built around a massive ancient fig tree, where green pigeons feast as you enjoy imaginative food on the dining deck overlooking the delta. The emphasis is on service and comfort rather than OTT (over-the-top) clutter and style. *Ker & Downey, Box 27, Maun, Botswana 267/686–0375 www.kerdowney.com 8 tents In-hotel: bar MC, V FAP.*

$$ **Vumbura Plains.** If it's old-style African safari ambience you're looking for, then this camp is not for you. These state-of-the-art buildings are all about space, shape, light, and texture on a grand scale using pebble-and-stone motifs. Public areas of bleached untreated wood with an earth-toned decor of elephant-brown rag rugs; gray, bronze, and russet beaded beanbag chairs; fiberglass coffee tables resembling giant pebbles; hanging white cane chairs; velvet beaded cushions; and some

9

exquisite indigenous artwork overlook a superb view of the floodplains. The art-deco, carved, wooden bar, with matching stools, divides the lounge area from the dining area, which is decorated with dry, hollow palm trunks and hanging lamps that represent the local sausage trees. Sip your coffee or after-dinner drinks in deep padded armchairs by firelight on the boma deck as frogs pipe and fireflies dance. ⚠**There are many steps and long up-and-down boardwalks between the widely spaced rooms. If this seems a bit challenging, you may want to stay someplace else.** Each room has a huge wooden deck, with comfortable lie-out chairs, a sala (thatched, outdoor, daybed area) and plunge pool, and the enclosed living spaces have floor-to-ceiling windows and doors of mesh that capture every source of light, from the early rays of dawn to the blazing sunset. Softly blowing, gauzy, white curtains divide the sleeping, living, and bathroom areas, and the decor of cream, gray, soft browns, and moss green echoes the pebble-and-stone theme of the main lodge. All the classic Okavango activities are on offer—mokoro trips, picnics on nearby islands, superb game-viewing from open vehicles, evening and night drives, and guided bush walks. ∎TIP➔ **Don't miss out on the superb curio shop; it's one of the best in Botswana.** ⌂ *Wilderness Safaris, Box 5219, Rivonia 2128, South Africa* ☎*27/11/807–1800* ⊕*www.vumbura.com* ↩*2 7-room camps* ᵫ*In-hotel: bar, pool* ▭*MC, V* ⦿*FAP.*

$ ▦**Chitabe Camp.** Chitabe is in an exclusive photographic reserve bordered by the Moremi Wildlife Reserve to the north, the Gomoti Channel to the east, and the Santantadibe River in the west. It's a lovely and popular camp whose big, comfortable tents on stilts are connected by environmentally friendly raised wooden walkways that put you safely above the ground and give you a Tarzan's-eye view of the surrounding bush. Elephants, buffalo, lions, leopards, and cheetahs are among the main attractions of this area, as well as a host of small nocturnal game such as porcupines, civets, and bush babies. Chitabe lies within a study area of the Botswana Wild Dog Research Project, which has up to 160 dogs in packs of 10 to 12, so you're almost certain to see these fascinating "painted wolves." Night drives are particularly rewarding. The area has a good variety of habitats, from marshlands and riverine areas to open grasslands and seasonally flooded plains, but although it's on one of the most beautiful islands in the delta and has classic Okavango scenery, it's not a water camp as such and doesn't offer water activities. You'll sleep in a luxurious twin-bedded, East African–style tent with wooden floors, woven lala palm furniture, wrought-iron washstands, and private bath. A separate thatch dining room, bar, and lounge area, also linked by wooden walkways, looks out over a floodplain. However, the shallow water that surrounds the camp is hidden by the long grass, so it's difficult to believe that you're actually in the Okavango Delta; there are no vistas of water. For groups that would like a camp to themselves, Chitabe Trails Camp, often used by overland safaris, accommodates eight guests in similar tents built on the ground with private bathrooms, private dining room, bar, and lounge area. ⌂ *Wilderness Safaris, Box 5219, Rivonia 2128, South Africa* ☎*27/11/807–*

1800 ⊕*www.wilderness-safaris.com* ⟲8 *tents at Main Camp, 4 tents at Trails Camp* ⚲*In-hotel: bars, pool* ⊟*MC, V* ¶*FAP.*

$ ▦**Delta Camp.** This enchanting and recently refurbished traditional camp is set deep on an island in the Okavango. Reed chalets, each with private bathroom, are furnished with wood furniture and upturned mokoros; they look like something straight out of *The Swiss Family Robinson.* Each chalet faces northeast to catch the first rays of the sun as it rises above the palm trees, and below your windows are shallow, bird-filled pools, with deeper waterways only paces from your front door. Family owned for many years, the camp has an intimate, relaxed atmosphere; the goal is to experience the tranquillity of the environment. Sit under the stars at dinner, listen to the haunting calls of Okavango's birds, chill out on the extended deck with its spectacular views of the surrounding waterways, and at night sip tea or coffee around a blazing fire. Activities from the camp include guided mokoro trails into the maze of waterways and game walks on adjacent islands with a professional licensed guide. Your walks will teach you about the African environment, ranging from the habits of dung beetles and warthogs to superb bird-spotting and how to dodge a charging elephant. A major conservation plus for Delta Camp is that motorboats are not used, as the emphasis is on preserving the pristine purity of the environment. This adds immeasurably to the relaxed, peaceful atmosphere that pervades this lovely camp. Hikes on the Sitatunga Trail can be arranged for groups of at least four for six nights or more. ⌂*Lodges of Botswana, Box 39, Maun, Botswana* ☎*267/686–1154* ⊕*www.lodgesofbotswana.com* ⟲7 *chalets* ⊟*MC, V* ¶*FAP.*

$ ⚠**Footsteps Across the Delta.** This interpretive safari is the ultimate back-to-nature experience. The emphasis is on learning the secrets of the Okavango—on foot and by mokoro. Because this is a mobile camp that moves with the seasons, there is no electricity, but you'll be more than rewarded for the lack of luxury by the surrounding bird- and animal life. The night sounds are awesome, from roaring lions to the ghostly screams of Pel's fishing owl. Walking with outstanding guides is the main activity, plus game drives, night drives, boat trips, and fishing. You'll sleep in one of three tents with insect-proofing and sewn-in floors; two iron bedsteads, some wooden shelves, and a small table are the only furnishings. You'll wash in a canvas washstand outside your tent (where there are also two canvas chairs), and your bathroom consists of a bush toilet and an overhead bucket shower. ⌂*Ker & Downey, Box 27, Maun, Botswana* ☎*267/686–0375* ⊕*www.kerdowney.com* ⟲3 *tents* ⚲*In-hotel: bar* ⊟*MC, V* ¶*FAP.*

$ ▦**Kwetsani Camp.** A mere eagle's flight from its more sumptuous neighbor, Jao, Kwetsani is one of the loveliest of the delta camps. It's perched on high wooden stilts amid a forest canopy of ancient trees on Kwetsani Island, 2 km (1 mi) long by nearly 1,000 yards wide, surrounded by enormous open plains. The deck and lounge areas overlooking the floodplains are built around a massive sycamore fig and huge marula tree, and a giant jackalberry dominates the bar. The pool lies in a wooden platform below the deck, looking as if at any moment it will sail out like a raft into the surrounding water in the wet season or away into the yellow grasses in the dry season. Each spacious room, made of canvas, wood, and slatted poles, is set like a child's building block in the middle of a large wooden deck built high into the trees. Polished wooden floors; coir mats; cane armchairs; butlers' tables with tea, coffee, and biscuits; billowing mosquito nets; twinkling ostrich-egg lamps, which light up his-and-her sinks; and indoor and outdoor showers all contribute to a warm, homey atmosphere. After enjoying a game drive or mokoro trip, end your day with a sundowner (cocktail) party by the lagoon lighted by flickering lanterns, with entertainment by top local groups—hippos snorting, hyenas whooping, lions roaring, and waterbirds keening. *Wilderness Safaris, Box 5219, Rivonia 2128, South Africa* ☎*27/11/807–1800* ⊕*www.kwetsani.com* ✏*5 chalets* ⌂*In-hotel: bar, pool* ▤*MC, V* ⏹*FAP.*

$ 🏠 **Nxabega Camp.** The gorgeous Nxabega (pronounced *na*-becka) is in the very heart of the delta. Renowned for its beauty, this 17,000-acre private concession encompasses all the vegetation types of the Okavango—mopane, riverine, mixed, palm and acacia woodland, terminalia sandveld, perennial swamp, and seasonally flooded grassland. This means you can have both a water and a land experience. Because this is a private concession, you can take a night drive in an open Land Rover and by spotlight pick out not only the big predators but also some of the smaller ones: civets, bush babies, genets, or—if you get really lucky—a pale prehistoric aardvark or scaly pangolin. A special bonus is the resident naturalist on hand to complement the team of knowledgeable and friendly CC Africa–trained guides. Safari tents are on raised teak platforms, each with a private veranda overlooking idyllic water and bush views. The main lodge is of thatch and wood with dark-wood paneling inside. Animal-skin rugs, fine woven cane furniture, cushions in various ethnic designs, hand-carved wooden tables, wooden bowls full of ostrich eggs, and lamps fashioned out of guinea fowl feathers give the lounge an exotic African ambience, while the high-roofed, paneled dining room has an almost medieval banquet-hall feel. Be sure to zip up your tent at night (there's lots of game around) before you retire to your comfortable bed with its leather headboard and fresh white linen. Zip your way through to the dressing room and bathroom area with its big wooden wardrobe, glass-enclosed shower, and reed walls. Tea or coffee is brought to your tent so that you can watch the early morning delta world go by in splendid seclusion. The food is excellent, so make sure you lose some of those calories by taking a guided walk on one of the nearby islands to track game and marvel at the different varieties of birdlife. *CC Africa, Private Bag X27, Benmore 2010, South Africa* ☎*27/11/809–4300* ⊕*www.ccafrica.com* ✏*10 tents* ⌂*In-hotel: bar, pool* ▤*MC, V* ⏹*FAP.*

★ $ 🏠 **Sandibe Camp.** This sister camp to Nxabega (also run by CC Africa) is absolutely gorgeous. Both a land and a water camp, it clings to the edge of one of the delta's beautiful pristine channels. You can step into your mokoro at the campsite and switch off stress and modern-day living as you cocoon yourself in another, gentler world. Sandibe's guides are superb, thrilling you with campfire tales at night, fishing with you in the open water spaces, poling your mokoro through tunnels of interlacing feathery papyrus, walking with you on one of the many palm-studded islands, and tracking big game in an open Land Rover or on foot, depending on which you prefer. You might see hippos, lions, cheetahs, buffalo, wild dogs, leopards, elephants, and some Okavango specials: the aquatic tsessebe antelope, fastest of all antelope, and the secretive sitatunga antelope The camp has a fairy-tale feel, as if a giant had fashioned an idyllic tiny village out of adobe and thatch and set it down

> ### A HAZARDOUS HERBIVORE
>
> They may look cute and harmless, but it's been said that hippos are the cause of more human deaths than any other large animal in Africa. Though they are not threatening creatures by nature and quickly retreat to water at any sign of danger, the trouble occurs when people get between a hippo and its water.

amid an enchanted forest full of birds nestled beside a papyrus-fringed secret lagoon. Honey-colored cottages with stepped and fringed thatch roofs add to the unusual visual effect of this spectacular camp. The cottages are open and airy and decorated with a lavish use of wood; each contains a huge carved bed covered with a woven leather bedspread, colorful kilims, skillfully chosen African artifacts, and lamps fabricated of woven metal and ostrich eggs. Sit on your stone veranda or tiny personal deck that overlooks the waterways, shaded by huge old African ebony trees, or walk along the elephant dung paths to the main lodge area, where "curtains" of tattered russet bark waft in the breeze. This is a wonderful place to sit and relax or swap big-game stories with your fellow guests. Climb up to the secluded wooden decks with their comfortable sitting areas above the main sitting and dining area, and catch up on your reading or game and bird lists, or just sit and relax in the outdoor boma (hut) around a crackling fire and stargaze as you sip your after-dinner coffee or liqueur. ☐CC Africa, Private Bag X27, Benmore 2010, South Africa ☎27/11/809–4300 ⊕www.ccafrica.com ⇨8 cottages ☐In-hotel: bar, pool ☐MC, V ☐FAP.

MOREMI WILDLIFE RESERVE

Prolific wildlife and an astonishing variety of birdlife characterize this famous reserve, the first in southern Africa to be proclaimed by the local people themselves. As there are no fences, the big game—and there's lots of it—can migrate to and from the Chobe Park in the north. Sometimes it seems as if a large proportion of Botswana's 70,000 elephants have made their way here, particularly in the dry season. Be prepared to check off on your game list lions, cheetahs, leopards, hyenas, wild dogs, buffalo, hippos, dozens of different antelopes, zebras, giraffes, monkeys, baboons, and more than 400 kinds of birds. Although during the South African school vacations (around July) there are more vehicles than normal, traffic is mostly light, and at this one, unlike many of Africa's other great reserves, you'll often be the only ones watching the game.

WHERE TO STAY

★ $$$$ ⊞ **Mombo Camp and Little Mombo.** On Mombo Island, off the northwest tip of Chief's Island, this legendary camp is surrounded by wall-to-wall game, and sometimes is linked to land depending on the ebb and flow of the water. Although there is plenty of surface water in the area (marshes and floodplains), it's strictly a land-activity camp with exclusive use of a large area of the reserve, so privacy is assured. Its great wildlife, including all of the large predators, has made this area one of Botswana's top wildlife documentary locations—*National Geographic* and the BBC have both filmed here. The stunning camp has identical guest rooms divided into two distinct camps: Mombo has nine rooms, Little Mombo only three. These camps are among the best known, most expensive, and most sought-after in Botswana, so be sure to book months in advance. Each spacious room is built on a raised wooden platform with wonderful views over the open plains (you're almost guaranteed to see game as you sit there), and although rooms have a tented feel, they are luxurious, with padded chaise longues, comfortable sofas, interesting lamps, woven rugs, and polished wooden floors. You can wash off the day's dust in your private bathroom or cool off in your outdoor shower. The dining room, lounge, and bar are also built on big wooden decks overlooking the magnificent animal-dotted savanna. The atmosphere is friendly, and the personal attention, food, and guides all excellent. The camp isn't fenced, so make sure you are escorted back to your room after dinner and then just lie back in your comfortable bed and listen to the sounds of the African night, from the haunting call of the fiery-necked night jar to the dry cough of a leopard as it patrols its territory. ⌖ *Wilderness Safaris, Box 5219, Rivonia 2128, South Africa* ☎*27/11/807–1800* ⊕*www.mombo.co.za* ⤙*12 rooms* ⌂*In-hotel: bar, pool* ⊟*MC, V* ⵙ*FAP.*

$$ ⊞ **Camp Moremi.** You get the best of both water and land at Camp Moremi. Early-morning and evening game drives with excellent rangers pretty much ensure that you'll see lions, elephants, giraffes, zebras, all kinds of antelopes, and often the elusive leopard, cheetah, and wild dog. Bird-watching is excellent throughout the year, including the rare Pel's fishing owl that regularly plummets down to the shallow pool below the Tree Lodge to snag a fish; be sure to take a powerboat ride to the heronries on Gadikwe and Xakanaxa lagoons. This is the luxurious sister camp to the delta's Camp Okavango, so expect the same high level of service, food, and accommodations. Huge old African ebony trees dominate the campsite on the edge of a lovely lagoon. From the high viewing platform in the trees you can look out on a limitless horizon as the sun sets orange and gold over the smooth, calm waters. Tastefully decorated, comfortable tents are well spaced to ensure privacy. Camp Moremi's attractive timber-and-thatch tree lodge has a dining area, bar, main lounge, small library, and sundeck with great views of Xakanaxa Lagoon. ⌖*Desert & Delta Safaris, Box 130555, Bryanston 2125, South Africa* ☎*27/11/706–0861* ⊕*www.desertdelta.co.za* ⤙*11 tents* ⌂*In-hotel: bar, pool* ⊟*MC, V* ⵙ*FAP.*

$ ⊞ **Khwai River Lodge.** As you sit on the wooden deck jutting out over the clear delta waters, munching brunch or just chilling out, you may just forget the outside world. Floating water lilies, tiny bejeweled kingfishers dipping and swooping in front of you, and the sounds of gently lapping water relax even the most driven work junkie. Bigger than some of the other safari lodges and one of the oldest, Khwai is renowned for its personal attention and friendly service. The location, 8 km (5 mi) northwest of the north gate of the Moremi Wildlife Reserve, means that you will see lots of game, not only on your drives but also from the lodge itself. The excitement of seeing a hippo or elephant stroll past the viewing deck outside your deluxe tent is not something you'll easily forget. The lodge is also the stuff of bird-watchers' dreams. ⌖ *Orient-Express Safaris, Box 786432, Sandton 2146, South Africa* ☎*27/11/481–6052* ⊕*www.orient-express-safaris.com* ⇜*15 tents* ⌂*In-hotel: bar, pool* ▤*MC, V* ♨*FAP.*

$ ▦ **Xakanaxa Camp.** For a genuine bush camp experience—no bells and whistles or unnecessary frills—it would be hard to beat this old-fashioned camp (pronounced ka-kan-ah-ka). From the moment you walk through the rustic reception area, a feeling of unpretentious warmth and relaxation envelops you; it's no wonder that visitors return again and again. Each spacious tent has wooden floors, faded kilims, a huge comfy bed with down pillows, crisp white linen, handy reading lamps for making those journal notes, and a megasized bathroom under the stars (read: no roof), with shower and hand-painted washbasin. Cushioned armchairs on your deck face the never-ending horizon of reeds, water, papyrus and pampas grass. Lighting at night is au naturel (candles, hurricane lamps, and flashlights), although there's electricity during the day. The ultra-experienced staff, many with more than 10 years of experience, gets everything right from their attentive service to the superb, wholesome, home-cooked food. Even the resident croc, who sunbathes under her very own sign "BEWARE CROCODILE," has been here since she was a tiny whippersnapper. ⌖*Lodges of Botswana, Box 39, Maun, Botswana* ☎*267/686–1154* ⊕*www.lodgesofbotswana.com* ⇜*12 tents* ▤*MC, V* ♨*FAP.*

★ $ ▦ **Xigera Camp.** The cry of the fish eagle permeates this exceptionally lovely camp (pronounced *kee*-jer-ah), which is set on the aptly named Paradise Island amid thickets of old trees deep in one of the most beautiful parts of the reserve's delta. Huge airy rooms of timber and canvas are built on a high wooden platform overlooking a floodplain. Reed walls separate the sleeping area from the spacious dressing room, which in turn leads into a reed-floored shower and separate toilet. Or you can choose to shower under the stars as hippos and frogs compete in the loudest-noises-of-the-night competition. Raised wooden walkways connect the rooms to the main lodge, which sprawls beside a lagoon where a small wooden bridge joins the island to the mainland. At night this bridge becomes a thoroughfare for lions and hyenas, and it's not uncommon to see one of these nocturnal visitors walk by as you sip your postprandial coffee or liqueur by the blazing fire. This camp does not concern itself with designer ethnic chic but concentrates on old-fashioned comfort and elegance. The food is varied and excellent, and the staff all seem to be chosen for not only their superb sense of service but also for their great sense of humor. ⌖ *Wilderness Safaris,*

9

Box 5219, Rivonia 2128, South Africa ☎*27/11/807–1800* ⊕*www. xigera.com* ⌂*In-hotel: bar, pool* ⇝*5 rooms* ☰*MC, V* ⦶*FAP.*

CHOBE NATIONAL PARK

This 12,000-square-km (7,440-square-mi) reserve is home to nearly 40,000 elephants. In addition to spotting Chobe's great pachyderm herds, however, you should see lions, leopards, hyenas, possibly wild dogs, impalas, waterbucks, kudus, zebras, wildebeests (gnus), giraffes, and warthogs. Watch closely at the water holes when prey species come down to drink and are most vulnerable—they are so palpably nervous that you'll feel jumpy, too. Lions in this area are often specialized killers; one pride might target giraffes, another zebras, another buffalo, or even young elephants. But lions are opportunistic killers, and you could see them pounce on anything from a porcupine to a lowly scrub hare. Birdlife along the river is awesome: rarely seen birds include slaty egrets, rock pratincoles, pink-throated longclaws, and lesser gallinules.

The northern section of the park comprises riverine bush devastated by the hordes of elephants coming down to the perennial Chobe to drink in winter. Fortunately, the wide sweep of the Caprivi floodplains, where hundreds of buffalo and elephants graze silhouetted against almost psychedelic sunsets, softens this harsh, featureless landscape where it faces neighboring Namibia.

In the southwestern part of the park lies the fabled Savuti (also spelled Savute) area, famous for its predators. Savuti offers a sweeping expanse of savanna brooded over by seven rocky outcrops that guard a relic marsh and the dry Savuti Channel, Africa's Stolen River of myth and legend. (It's "stolen" because it mysteriously disappeared in the early 1980s and has never returned.) You may see wild dogs hunting where only a few decades ago crocodiles swam and basked on the channel banks. Savuti is dramatically different from elsewhere in Botswana; there are open spaces, limitless horizons, wide skies, and unending miles of waving tall grass punctuated by starkly beautiful dead trees—the legacy of the relentless drought. Like Chobe National Park overall, Savuti is famed for its elephants, but the female of the species is rarely seen here, for Savuti is the domain of the bull elephant: old grandfathers, middle-aged males, and feisty young teenagers. The old ones gaze at you with imperturbable dignity, but it's the youngsters who'll make your adrenaline run riot as they kick up the dust and bellow belligerently as they make a mock charge in your direction.

And while you're in the Savuti area looking for leopards and the tiny acrobatic klipspringer antelopes, be sure to pay a visit to the striking rock paintings, early humans' attempts to represent the wildlife all around. In summertime thousands of migrating zebras and wildebeests provide the equivalent of fast food for the lion prides, hungry hyenas, and cheetahs who follow the herds. The Cape buffalo herds also arrive in summer along with thousands of returning bird migrants. The

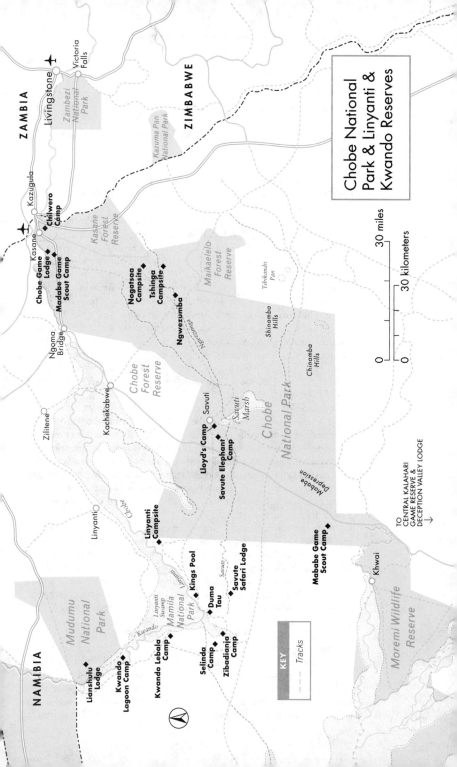

Chobe National Park & Linyanti & Kwando Reserves

30 miles
30 kilometers
0

ZAMBIA
Livingstone
Victoria Falls
Zambezi National Park
Kazugula
Kazuma Pan National Park
ZIMBABWE
Kasane
Chilwero Camp
Chobe Game Lodge
Madabe Game Scout Camp
Kasane Forest Reserve
Maikaelelo Forest Reserve
Ngoma Bridge
Nogatsaa Campsite
Tshinga Campsite
Ngwezumba
Ngwezumba
Tshikando Pan
Shinamba Hills
Chinamba Hills
Chobe Forest Reserve
Zililene
Kachikabwe
Savuti
Lloyd's Camp
Savute Elephant Camp
Savuti Marsh
Chobe National Park
Mababe Depression
Chobe
Linyanti
Linyanti Campsite
Linyanti Swamp
Mamila National Park
Kings Pool
Duma Tau
Savute
Savute Safari Lodge
Mababe Game Scout Camp
Khwai
Moremi Wildlife Reserve
TO CENTRAL KALAHARI GAME RESERVE & DECEPTION VALLEY LODGE →
NAMIBIA
Mudumu National Park
Lianshulu Lodge
Kwando Lagoon Camp
Kwando
Kwando Lebala Camp
Selinda Camp
Zibadianja Camp

KEY
--- Tracks

raptors are spectacular. You'll see falcons, eagles, kestrels, goshawks, ospreys, and sparrow hawks.

⚠ Unlike the rest of Botswana, Chobe can be crowded; there are simply too many vehicles on too few roads, particularly in season. One of the quieter parts of the park is around the Ngwezumba River, an area of forests and pans in the more remote middle of the park; the drawback here is that game is harder to find.

WHERE TO STAY

$$$$ 🏨 **Chobe Game Lodge.** The only permanent lodge set in Chobe National Park, this grand old dame—Liz Taylor and Richard Burton got married for the second time here in the '70s—still offers one of Botswana's most sophisticated stays, although the feel is more hotel-like than lodge-like. Terra-cotta tiles, Rhodesian teak furniture, African artifacts, and the ubiquitous beautiful handwoven Botswana baskets give the feel of the Dark Continent. The solid Moorish-style buildings—with their graceful high arches and barrel-vaulted ceilings—insulate the not-so-intrepid traveler from too-close encounters of the animal kind: baboon mothers have been known to teach their young how to turn a doorknob! The gorgeous gardens are a riot of color and attract lots of small fauna. There's a well-stocked curio shop with great clothes and wildlife books. Don't miss out on the well-run daily activities, from game drives to river cruises. An early-morning canoe ride is also a must. 🕿 *Desert & Delta Safaris, Box 130555, Bryanston 2125, South Africa* ☎ *27/11/706–0861* ⊕ *www.desertdelta.co.za* 🛏 *46 rooms, 4 suites* ♿ *In-hotel: bar, pool* ☰ *MC, V* � *FAP.*

$$ 🏨 **Savute Safari Lodge.** As your small plane arrives at this attractive lodge, you can see the wide swathe the dry riverbed makes through the surrounding countryside. The exterior of the main building and the safari suites are traditional thatch and timber; however, when you enter your spacious suite it's a bit like walking out of Africa into a Scandinavian design center—blond wood, dazzling white bed linens, comfortable furniture in bright primary colors, gaily colored handwoven rugs, and lots of glass. Outside on your spacious wooden deck it's back to Africa; by full moon watch the gray, ghostly shapes of elephants drinking from the water hole in front of the camp, or if the moon is not yet full, marvel at the myriad stars in the African night sky. Excellent safari guides can reveal the secrets of the African bush to you on game drives. When you're not watching the abundant game, there's a large, elegant dining room where you can enjoy scrumptious late-morning brunches and candlelit silver-service dinners, a lounge with a huge fireplace, and an upstairs viewing deck. 🕿 *Desert & Delta Safaris, Box 130555, Bryanston 2125, South Africa* ☎ *27/11/706–0861* ⊕ *www.desertdelta. co.za* 🛏 *12 suites* ♿ *In-hotel: bar, pool, a/c* ☰ *MC, V* ⊙ *FAP.*

$ 🏨 **Savute Elephant Camp.** In the semiarid Savuti region, splendid, spacious, air-conditioned, twin-bedded tents are elegantly furnished with cane and dark-wood furniture, an impressive overhead bed canopy with attendant mosquito net, woven rugs in creams and browns, white linen bedspreads, and a roomy bathroom with his-and-her sinks. For those cold winter mornings and evenings, there's even a built-in heater.

Your private viewing deck overlooking one of the busiest elephant water holes in the world has comfortable chairs and an inviting hammock. As the camp is in Chobe National Park, night drives and walking are against regulations, but you will see plenty of game and birds. If you can manage to be here at full moon, the sight of hundreds of great, gray shapes gleaming in the moonlight, jostling, rumbling, and coming and going at the water hole is truly unforgettable. ✉ *Orient-Express Safaris, Box 786432, Sandton 2146, South Africa* ☎ *27/11/481–6052* ⊕ *www.orient-express-safaris.com* 🛏 *12 tents* ♿ *In-hotel: bar, pool* 🚪 *MC, V* 🍴 *FAP.*

LINYANTI RESERVE

The Linyanti Reserve, which borders Chobe National Park, is one of the huge concession areas leased to different companies for up to 15 years by the Department of Wildlife and National Parks and the Tawana Land Board. It's a spectacular wildlife area comprising the Linyanti marshes, open floodplains, rolling savanna, and the Savuti Channel. Because it's a private concession, open vehicles can drive where and when they like, which means superb game-viewing at all hours.

Basic choices for viewing wildlife are game drives (including thrilling night drives with spotlights), boat trips, and walks with friendly and knowledgeable Motswana guides. Even in peak season there is a maximum of only six game vehicles driving around at one time, allowing you to see Africa as the early hunters and explorers might have. The Savuti Channel, once a huge river, but dry now for more than two decades, has starred in several *National Geographic* documentaries, and it's not hard to see why. Take lots of pictures, and for once you won't bore your friends with the results: hundreds of elephants drinking from pools at sunset, hippos and hyenas nonchalantly strolling past a pride of lions preparing to hunt under moonlight, and thousands of water and land birds everywhere.

WHERE TO STAY

★ $$ 🏨 **King's Pool.** The centuries-old giant leadwood tree which dominates the spacious main deck that overlooks the Linyanti River gives you a clue about your classic, yet understated, Out-of Africa-like accommodation. Everything about this camp is on a regal scale, including the tribute to the European royalty who used to hunt in this area. Old photographs of tribal leaders and Batswana maidens watch over the carved wooden furniture, comfortable wing chairs with beaded throws, inviting wooden bar with high leather-and-wood bar stools, soft furnishings in earth colors, and the open-sided dining room. There's even a small gym facing the river, where you can work off some of the yummy food before taking a river cruise (only when the water is high), a guided bush walk, a fishing trip, or a visit to the sunken blind (a must in the dry season) where you're eyeball-to-eyeball with splashing elephant feet. The massive hand-carved door of your megasized thatch-and-canvas-ceiling chalet leads into an entrance hall, bedroom with four-poster bed, a sitting area with earth-colored couches and armchairs splashed with orange and red cushions, and a huge bathroom with his-and-her basins and tiled showers. Don't miss the fascinating curio shop with classy artifacts from all over Africa. ☐ *Wilderness Safaris, Box 5219, Rivonia 2128, South Africa* ☎*27/11/807–1800* ⊕*www.wilderness-safaris.com* ↩*9 chalets* ⚒*In-hotel: bar, pool* ☰*MC, V* ⑪*FAP.*

KWANDO RESERVE

Like the Okavango, the Kwando River comes down from the wet Angola highlands and then meanders through a few hundred kilometers of wilderness. The 2,300-square-km (900-square-mi) private Kwando concession has more than 80 km (50 mi) of river frontage. It stretches south from the banks of the Kwando River, through huge open plains and mopane forests to the Okavango Delta. It's an area crisscrossed by thousands of ancient game trails traversed by wildlife that move freely between the Okavango Delta, Chobe, and the open Namibian wilderness to the north. As you fly in to the reserve, you'll see this web of thousands of interlacing natural game trails—from hippo highways to the tiny paths of smaller animals. This should clue you in to Kwando's diverse animal life: wall-to-wall elephants, crowds of buffalo, zebras, antelope of all kinds including roan and sable, wild dogs, lions, and wildebeests. Participants on one night drive came upon a running battle between a pack of 14 wild dogs and two hyenas who had stolen the dogs' fresh kill. The noisy battle ended when a loudly trumpeting elephant, fed up with the commotion, charged the wild dogs and drove them off. There's a sheer joy in knowing you are one of only four vehicles in a half-million acres of wilderness.

If you'd like to take a safari with children, there's no better place than Kwando, where under the special care of top rangers you'll not only have a truly memorable time but also learn lots about the bush. The safari starts with a safety briefing, and kids get their own tents next to Mom and Dad or you can share one. Kids learn to track and take plaster casts of spoor (to show their friends at home), sit up in the tracker's seat on the vehicle to follow game, cook marshmallows over the boma fire, tell stories, catch and release butterflies, make bush jewelry, and learn about ecology. Kids can eat on their own or with you, and if you want an afternoon snooze, they'll be supervised in the pool or at some other fun activity. This program is available at both Kwando camps; the price is the same per night as for an adult.

WHERE TO STAY

★ $$$ ⚏ **Kwando Lagoon Camp.** The camp perches on the banks of the fast-flowing Kwando River, quite literally in the middle of nowhere. Comfortable walk-through tents with private bathrooms and verandas nestle on grassy slopes under the shade of giant jackalberry trees that are hundreds of years old. After a night spent next to one of these mighty trees, a major source of natural energy, people say you wake up rejuvenated, your body buzzing with new life. From the thatch dining and bar area you can watch herds of elephants only yards away as they come to drink and bathe, or hippos snoozing in the sun. You might also spot a malachite kingfisher darting like a bejeweled minijet over the water. Go for a morning or evening game drive, drift along the river in a small boat, or go spinner- or fly-fishing for tiger fish and bream. The emphasis in the camp is on informality, simplicity, and soaking up the wilderness experience. ⌂ *Kwando Wildlife Experience, Box 550, Maun, Botswana* ☎*267/686–1449 or 267/686–4388* ⊕*www.kwando. co.za* ⇨*6 tents* ⌂*In-hotel: bar, pool* ☰*DC, MC, V* ⦿*FAP.*

☾ ★ $ 🏠 **Kwando Lebala Camp.** Lebala Camp is 30 km (18 mi) south of Lagoon Camp and looks out over the Linyanti wetlands. The secluded tents, built on raised teak decks, are magnificent. All have private bathrooms with Victorian claw-foot tubs. If you want to get even closer to nature, bathe in your own outdoor shower or just sit on your sundeck and look out at the endless vistas. On morning or evening game drives you'll see loads of game, and if you fancy a freshly caught fish supper, try your hand at spinner fishing. ⌂ *Kwando Wildlife Experience, Box 550, Maun, Botswana* ☎*267/686–1449 or 267/686–4388* ⊕*www. kwando.co.za* ⇨*8 tents* ⌂*In-hotel: pool* ☰*DC, MC, V* ⦿*FAP.*

THE CENTRAL KALAHARI GAME RESERVE

One of the biggest conservation areas in the world, this huge area has its own unique beauty, that's only enhanced by its vastness, emptiness, grandeur, and desolation. You won't see the prolific game of Chobe or Moremi, but there's unusual wildlife such as the elusive brown hyena, the stately desert oyrx, elegant kudus, African wild cats, leopards, and porcupines. And if you're very lucky, you may spot the huge, black-maned Kalahari lions, which dwarf their bush counterparts. Deception Valley—so-called because from a distance a dry riverbed appears to run deep and full—lies on the northern border of the reserve.

WHERE TO STAY

★ $$ 🏠 **Deception Valley Lodge.** This striking thatch-and-stone lodge is the only lodge in the Central Kalahari, and is worth visiting for this reason alone. Built entirely by hand by the desert-dwelling Naru people, the main lounge has deep red sofas and kilims, with wooden sliding doors leading out onto a wraparound deck which faces a busy water hole. Enjoy delicious food (try the tender oryx fillet marinated in Worcestershire sauce, olive oil, and herbs) including homemade bread and rolls, before sitting out under the blazing desert stars for a nightcap. You'll stay in a large thatch bungalow where the roomy lounge has polished wooden floors, more kilims, wrought iron and wood chairs, a deep comfy sofa, and framed genuine bushman memorabilia. Check out the quaint and original metal lamp shades. Your bedroom boasts a hand-carved headboard, crisp white linens, and plump duvets. There's a separate en-suite bathroom with a claw-foot bath and outside shower. Although you'll be taken on game drives and birding expeditions, the absolute highlight of your stay at this unique lodge will be a walk with the Bushmen themselves. Dressed in skins and thong sandals, with their bows and arrows over their shoulders, and carrying a spear and a digging stick, they'll lead you through the dry grass and bush on a three-hour walk through one of the most remote areas on earth. You'll be shown how to trap a bird or animal, how to make fire, which plants and trees will heal and sustain you, and at the end of the walk, they will dance and sing for you. This is pure magic. ☐*Islands in Africa Safaris, Box 70378, Bryanston 2021, South Africa* ☎*27/11/706–7207* ⊕*www.islandsinafrica.com* ✎*5 chalets* ♿*In-hotel: pool* ▤*DC, MC, V* ❘◎❘*FAP.*

BOTSWANA ESSENTIALS

TRANSPORTATION

BY AIR

In this huge, often inaccessible country, air travel is the easiest way to get around. Sir Seretse Khama Airport, 15 km (9½ mi) from Gaborone's city center, is Botswana's main point of entry. Kasane International Airport is 3 km (2 mi) from the entrance to Chobe National Park, and the small but very busy Maun Airport is 1 km (½ mi) from the city center of this northern safari capital. All three are gateways to the Okavango Delta and Chobe; they're easy to find your way around in and rarely crowded.

Air charter companies operate small planes from Kasane and Maun to all the camps. Flown by some of the youngest-looking pilots in the world, these flights, which your travel agent will arrange, are reliable, reasonably cheap, and average between 25 and 50 minutes. Maximum baggage allowance is 12 kilograms (26 pounds) in a soft sports/duffel bag (no hard cases allowed), excluding the weight of camera equipment (within reason). Flights can sometimes be very bumpy—take air-sickness pills if you're susceptible to motion sickness; then sit back and enjoy the fabulous bird's-eye views. You're sure to spot elephants and hippos from the air.

Air Botswana has scheduled flights from Johannesburg to Gaborone and Maun on a daily basis, and from Cape Town to Maun on Monday, Wednesday, and Friday, returning to Cape Town Tuesday, Thursday, and Sunday. The airline also flies Johannesburg to Kasane on Thursday and Sunday. SA Express Airways also has daily flights between Johannesburg and Gaborone.

Mack Air, Northern Air, Sefofane Air, Swamp Air, and Delta Air/Synergy Seating fly directly between Johannesburg's Grand Central Airport and Maun on private charters.

Airports **Kasane International Airport** (☎*267/625–0161*). **Maun Airport** (☎*267/686–0762*). **Sir Seretse Khama Airport** (☎*267/391–4518*).

Airlines **Air Botswana** (☎*267/390–5500 or 267/395–1921* ⊕*www.airbotswana.co.bw*). **Delta Air/Synergy Seating** (☎*267/686–0044*). **Mack Air** (☎*267/686–0675*). **Northern Air** (☎*267/686–0385*). **SA Express Airways** (☎*27/11/978–5577 or 267/397–2397*). **Sefofane Air** (☎*267/686–0778*). **Swamp Air** (☎*267/686–0569*).

BY CAR

All the main access roads from neighboring countries are paved, and cross-border formalities are user-friendly. Maun is easy to reach from South Africa, Namibia, and Zimbabwe, but the distances are long and not very scenic. Gaborone is 360 km (225 mi) from Johannesburg via Rustenburg, Zeerust, and the Tlokweng border post. Driving in Botswana is on the left-hand side of the road. The "Shell Tourist Map of Botswana" is the best available map. Find it at Botswana airports or in airport bookstores.

Forget about a car in the Okavango Delta unless it's amphibious. Only the western and eastern sides of the delta panhandle and the Moremi Wildlife Reserve are accessible by car; but it's wisest to always take a 4x4 vehicle. The road from Maun to Moremi North Gate is paved for the first 47 km (29 mi) up to Serobe, when it becomes gravel for 11 km (7 mi) and then a dirt road.

It's not practical to reach Chobe National Park by car. A 4x4 vehicle is essential in the park itself. The roads are sandy and/or very muddy, depending on the season.

CONTACTS & RESOURCES

ELECTRICITY

To use electric-powered equipment purchased in the United States or Canada, bring a converter and adapter. If your appliances are dual-voltage, you'll need only an adapter. The electrical current is 220 volts, 50 cycles alternating current (AC); wall outlets usually take 15-amp plugs with three round prongs, but some take the straight-edged three-prong plugs, also 15 amps. Most of the lodges and camps have their own generators, so you're able to charge your cameras and other electronic equipment. Bring a reading light if you intend to read in bed at night, as tent and chalet lights tend to be dim.

EMBASSIES

U.S. Embassy (✉ *Government Enclave, Embassy Dr., Gaborone* ☎ *267/395–3982*).

TOURS

Most operators offer ready-made safaris to many different destinations or will customize one for you. CC Africa Safaris and Tours is a highly experienced tour operator and has ready-made trips and tours to all parts of Botswana or can tailor one to your needs, from the budget-conscious to the lavish. Desert & Delta Safaris has inclusive fly-in safari packages to its own camps, as well as other destinations, such as Victoria Falls. Ker & Downey is one of the oldest and most respected safari companies in Botswana. Utilizing its exclusive camps, traditional safari experiences are offered ranging from rustic to deluxe. Orient-Express Safaris, a member of Small Luxury Hotels of the World, owns three strategically located camps in some of Botswana's most diverse ecosystems and most desirable destinations: Chobe National Park, Moremi Wildlife Reserve, and the Okavango Delta. All camps have identical thatch tented lodging with identical furnishings and plenty of bells and whistles. Watch the night sky with a state-of-the-art telescope before reading the ancient Botswana folk story placed on your bed each night. Wilderness Safaris, which owns the majority of lodges in Botswana, offers all kinds of packages, including a choice of "premier," "classic," "vintage," or "camping wild" camps in a great variety of locations and ecosystems, from the delta to the Kalahari Desert. It also offers mobile safaris and custom tours for all Botswana destinations.

Tour Operators **CC Africa Safaris and Tours** (☎ *27/11/809–4300* ⊕ *www. ccafrica.com*). **Desert & Delta Safaris** (☎ *27/11/706–0861* ⊕ *www.desertdelta. co.za*). **Islands in Africa** (☎ *27/11/706–7207* ⊕ *www.islandsinafrica.com*). **Ker & Downey** (☎ *267/686–0375* ⊕ *www.kerdowney.com*). **Orient-Express Safaris** (☎ *27/11/274–1800* ⊕ *www.orient-express-safaris.com*). **Wilderness Safaris** (☎ *27/11/257–5000* ⊕ *www.wilderness-safaris.com*).

TRAVEL AGENCIES

Visit Botswana Tourism's Web site for tour operator and travel agency information. To be listed on the Web site, these organizations must satisfy and adhere to the high standards demanded by Botswana Tourism.

Travel Agencies **Botswana Tourism** (⊕ *www.botswana-tourism.gov.bw*). **Harvey World Travel** (☎ *267/390–4360* ⊕ *www.harveyworld.co.za*). **Travel Wise** (☎ *267/390–3244*).

NAMIBIA

Many countries in Africa boast teeming wildlife and gorgeous scenery, but few, if any, can claim such limitless horizons; such huge, untamed wilderness areas; such a pleasant sunny climate; so few people (fewer than two per square mi); the oldest desert in the world; a wildly beautiful coastline; one of Africa's greatest game parks; plus—and this is a big bonus—a First World infrastructure and tourist facilities that are among the best in Africa. But you'll find all these—and more—in Namibia.

A former German colony, South West Africa, as it was then known, was a pawn in the power games of European politics. Although Portuguese navigators were the first Europeans to arrive in 1485, they quickly abandoned the desolate and dangerous Atlantic shores of the "Coast of Death," as they called it. By the late 1700s British, French, and American whalers were using the deepwater ports of Lüderitz and Walvis (Whalefish) Bay, which the Dutch, now settled in the Cape, then claimed as their own. A few years later, after France invaded Holland, England seized the opportunity to claim the territory together with the Cape Colony. Then it became Germany's turn to throw its hat into the ring. In the wake of its early missionaries and traders, it claimed the entire country as a German colony in 1884, only to surrender it to South African forces, who were fighting on the Allied side during World War I. South Africa was given a League of Nations mandate to administer the territory after the war, and despite a 1978 UN resolution to revoke the mandate, South Africa held on to Namibia for a further stormy 10 years. A bitter and bloody bush war with SWAPO (South West African People's Organization) freedom fighters raged until Namibia finally won its independence on March 21, 1990, after 106 years of foreign rule. Although most of the earlier colonial influences have now vanished, everywhere you go in Namibia today you'll find traces of the German past—forts and castles, place-names, cuisine, and German efficiency.

Often called "The Land God Made in Anger" because of its stark, surreal landscapes, untamed wilderness, harsh environment, and rare beauty, Namibia was been carved out by the forces of nature. The same savage, continuous geological movements produced not only spectacular beauty but also great mineral wealth: alluvial diamonds, uranium, platinum, lead, zinc, silver, copper, tungsten, and tin—still the cornerstone of Namibia's economy. Humans have lived here for thousands of years; the San (Bushmen) are the earliest known people, although their hunting-gathering way of life is now almost extinct. Today most Namibians are employed in the agricultural sector, from subsistence farms to huge cattle ranches and game farms. As you travel through the changing landscapes of mountains and plains, lush riverine forests, and high sand dunes, marvel at the amazing diversity of light and shade, color and contrast, and soak up the emptiness and isolation, the silence and the solitude. Far from crowded polluted cities, you could easily imagine yourself on another planet or in a land where time has stood still—a land you will never forget.

ORIENTATION & PLANNING

ORIENTATION

9

Namibia is a big country, four times as large as the United Kingdom and bigger than Texas, but its excellent road network means you can get around very easily. The country is bordered by the icy Atlantic on the west, the Kalahari Desert on the east, the Kunene River on the north, and the Orange River on the south. Although South Africa, Botswana, and Angola are its immediate neighbors, if you're traveling by road, it's easiest to access Namibia from South Africa.

NAMIB-NAUKLUFT PARK
At nearly 50,000 square km (19,000 square mi) and bigger than Switzerland, this park, which harbors the oldest desert in the world, is one of the largest national parks in Africa. Expect classic desert scenery (i.e. towering, truly awesome sand dunes), but also windswept gravel plains, rocky outcrops and inselbergs, and some of the earth's strangest living things, from plants and insects to mammals and reptiles.

THE SKELETON COAST
Named for the numerous shipwrecks that litter its treacherous Atlantic coast, as well as for the many lives lost in its perilous, icy seas, this savagely beautiful coastline with its fierce currents, swirling fogs, and unmapped sandbanks is one of the most dangerous in the world. Its

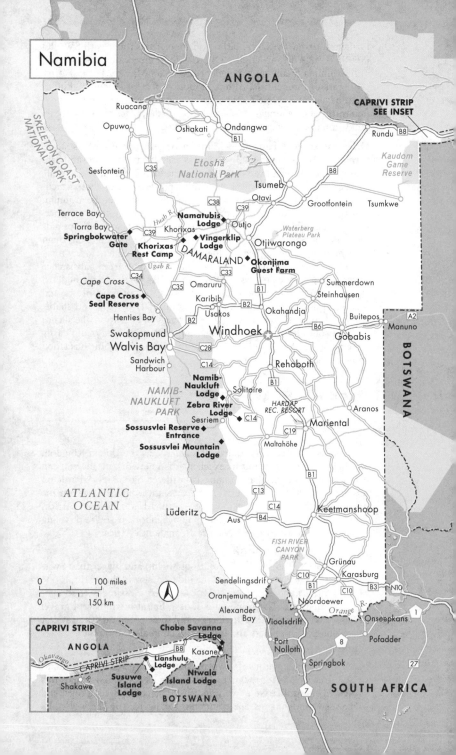

Namibia

ANGOLA

CAPRIVI STRIP SEE INSET

SKELETON COAST NATIONAL PARK

Ruacana

Opuwo
Oshakati   Ondangwa
B1
Rundu   B8

Sesfontein
C35
Etosha National Park

Kaudom Game Reserve

B8

Tsumeb   Grootfontein   Tsumkwe
Otavi

Terrace Bay
Torra Bay
Springbokwater Gate
C39   Khorixas
Namatubis Lodge
C38
C39   Outjo
Huab R.
Vingerklip Lodge
Khorixas Rest Camp
DAMARALAND
Waterberg Plateberg Park
Otjiwarongo

Ugab R.
Okonjima Guest Farm
C33

Cape Cross
C34
Omaruru
Summerdown
Steinhausen

Cape Cross Seal Reserve
C35
Karibib
B2
B1
Okahandja
B6
Buitepos   A2
Manuno

Henties Bay
Usakos
B2
Windhoek
Gobabis

Swakopmund
C28
Rehoboth
BOTSWANA

Walvis Bay
C14

Sandwich Harbour
Namib-Naukluft Lodge   Solitaire
B1

NAMIB-NAUKLUFT PARK
Zebra River Lodge
C14
HARDAP REC. RESORT
Aranos

Sesriem
Sossusvlei Reserve Entrance
C19
Mariental

Sossusvlei Mountain Lodge
Maltahöhe

ATLANTIC OCEAN
B1

C13
C14
Keetmanshoop

Lüderitz   Aus   B4

FISH RIVER CANYON PARK
Grünau   Karasburg
C10
B1
C10
B3
N10

Sendelingsdrif
Oranjemund
Orange R.
Onseepkans
1

Alexander Bay
Vioolsdrift
Pofadder

Port Nolloth
Springbok
8
27

SOUTH AFRICA

0 —— 100 miles
0 —— 150 km

CAPRIVI STRIP
ANGOLA
Okavango R.
Chobe Savanna Lodge
CAPRIVI STRIP
B8
Kasane
Lianshulu Lodge
Susuwe Island Lodge
Ntwala Island Lodge
Shakawe
BOTSWANA

dramatic scenery, towering waves, rocky beaches, and air of complete desolation highlight the insignificance of humankind when faced with the relentless forces of nature.

DAMARALAND

Situated in northwest Namibia, Damaraland is a different desert than Namib. It's a landscape of almost unsurpassed rugged beauty formed by millions of years of unending geological movement. Vivid brick-red sediments complement gray lava slopes punctuated by black fingers of "frozen" basaltic rock creeping down from the jagged rocky horizons. Millions and millions of stones, great, small, tiny, interspersed with clumps of silvery-gray shrubs and pioneer grasses litter the unending slopes, hillsides, and mountain faces. But there is life, and plenty of it, in this seemingly inhospitable landscape, including *welwitschia mirabilis* plants; colorful lichen fields; dark-green, umbrella-shaped camelthorn trees; candelabra euphorbias raising their prickly, fleshy arms to the cloudless sky; salt bushes; and the ubiquitous shepherd's tree. And of course, there are the amazing desert elephants.

ETOSHA NATIONAL PARK

Highly regarded as one of Africa's great national parks, Etosha is dominated by Etosha Pan, which was once a huge lake, but is now a landscape of white, salty plains that shimmer in the noonday sun. Other less dramatic habitats include mopane woodland, tall palm trees, and grassy savanna. The lack of surface water makes this a mecca for game-viewing, because the animals are forced to come and drink at the many water holes fed by natural springs. If you're looking to do a self-drive, this is the place to come—the roads are good, and there are plenty of affordable accommodations.

THE NORTHEAST/CAPRIVI STRIP

This area comprises a lesser-known Namibia. One where four countries meet (Namibia, Botswana, Zimbabwe, and South Africa), mighty rivers come together, tiny islands dot the rapids, myriad birds make their home in lily-studded lagoons, where one of the world's toughest fighting fish is lying in wait for a bite, and where the pristine waterways rival the Okavango Delta.

9

PLANNING

Namibia has a subtropical desert climate with nonstop sunshine throughout the year. It's classified as arid to nonarid, and, generally speaking, it gets wet only in the northwest and then only during the rainy season (October–April). The south is warm and dry, although temperatures vary dramatically between night and day, particularly in the desert.

In the Namib Naukluft the air is sparkling, and pollution practically unheard-of, and although nights always come early with dramatic suddenness, days are crystal-clear and perfect for traveling. The hottest season, the rainy season, is from December to March, but unless you're in the north you're unlikely to see much rain or experience much

TOP REASONS TO VISIT NAMIBIA

The Oldest Living Desert The Namib is everything you'd imagine a "real" desert to look like.

The Oldest Living Plant *Welwitschia mirabilis* is a fleshy green plant that spreads its long waxy stems like fat tendrils over the surrounding desert. The older the plant, the bigger and longer the leaves; many live to more than 1,000 years.

A Memorable Drive Traveling south from Swakopmund to Walvis Bay, you'll find yourself on one of the most beautiful and unusual routes in the world. The tarred coast road is dwarfed by magnificent sand dunes on one side and the wild Atlantic on the other.

Watering Hole Wonders Arm yourself with binoculars, drinks, a picnic, and patience. Open your car windows and wait for the game to come. You won't be disappointed.

Ride the Desert Express Take an overnight trip on this luxury train that operates between Windhoek and Swakopmund three times a week. You'll get the opportunity to walk in the desert, visit the biggest outdoor rock-art gallery in the world, watch lions being fed, and view a spectacular sunset or sunrise over the Namib.

humidity. Sometimes there's no rain at all in the southern Kalahari and the Namib Desert, where it can get very hot indeed, with temperatures reaching 40°C (104°F). From September through April (summer) the region's weather is clear, dry, crisp, and nearly perfect, averaging 25°C (77°F) during the day, but in the desert areas it can drop to freezing at night, especially in winter. (Bring warm clothes for after the sun goes down.) If it's game you're after, then winter (April through August) is the best because the lack of surface water ensures that animals congregate around water holes.

Along the Skeleton Coast the climate can be breathtakingly varied. Because of the pounding, fierce Atlantic and its cold Benguela Current, thick fog and mist roll over the beaches and into the nearby interior in the early morning and at night, bringing precious moisture to all the desert creatures and plants but making it chilly and damp for humans. The day that follows will be bright and sunny, and in summer, extremely hot, so dress in layers.

Etosha's best season is winter (May–September), when the weather is cooler, the grass shorter, and the game easier to see. But if you can stand the heat, summer sees the return of thousands of waterbirds to the flooded pan, as well as the great annual migration of tens of thousands of zebras, wildebeests, giraffes, and springbok and other antelopes from their winter feeding grounds on the Andoni Plains to the new, lush feeding grounds around Okuakuejo. Summer is the hottest season—40°C (104°F)—and the rainy season is from December to March, with dramatic afternoon thunderheads building up followed by heavy but short rainstorms. But almost any time is a good time to visit Etosha, because game depends on the water holes fed by natural springs which are distributed throughout the park.

ABOUT THE CAMPS & LODGES

Namibia's private camps, lodges, and other accommodations are up to high international standards. Even deep in the desert, at the tented camps, tents have en-suite bathrooms and private verandas, but don't expect TVs. Air-conditioning is the exception rather than the rule. It's mentioned in reviews only when it is present. Most prices at private lodges are all-inclusive (aka Full American Plan), including transfers, meals, activities, and usually drinks. Camps offer at least two activities a day, from morning and evening game drives to riding moon buggies over the desert dunes, or from picnics on one of the wildest coasts in the world to visiting a traditional Himba settlement.

At the national-park camps, self-catering (with cooking facilities) accommodations are basic, clean, comfortable, and much cheaper than the private lodges outside the park. They're often more fun, too. After all, you're in the very midst of the big-game action. Each camp has a restaurant with adequate, if not memorable, food; a shop selling basic foodstuffs and curios; a post office; gas station; and swimming pool. Most rooms have private toilets, baths or showers, air-conditioning, a refrigerator, and a *braai* (barbecue). Linen and towels are provided. Some of the bigger bungalows have a full kitchen with cutlery and dishes.

You won't find much truly Namibian food (although local venison, seafood, and Namibian oysters are superb); instead, cuisine is mainly European, often German. Lodges usually serve good home-style cooking—pies, pastries, fresh vegetables, lots of red meat, venison, mouth-watering desserts, and the traditional braai. Because of its past as a German colony, Namibia is known for its superb lagers, and it's well worth trying at least one. South African wine is readily available.

	¢	$	$$	$$$	$$$$
WHAT IT COSTS IN NAMIBIAN DOLLARS					
SAFARI CAMPS AND LODGES	under N$400	N$400–N$700	N$700–N$1000	N$1,000–N$1,500	over N$1,500

All prices refer to an all-inclusive per-person rate including tax, assuming double occupancy.

HEALTH & SAFETY

Malaria is endemic in the east, north, and northeast of the country, so antimalarials are essential. But elsewhere the dry, sunny climate will give you few problems. Take the African sun and the heat seriously. Always use sunscreen and a hat, and drink plenty of water to prevent dehydration. AIDS is a major problem as elsewhere in Africa; do not have sex with a stranger. In towns, don't walk alone at night, and lock your valuables, documents, and cash in the hotel or lodge safe. In game areas, never walk after dark unless accompanied by an armed guide. Because there is comparatively little traffic when self-driving, visitors are often tempted to exceed speed limits. Don't. Gravel roads, although sometimes long and straight, can be as treacherous as icy roads, and it's very easy to skid and overturn a vehicle.

IMPORTANT DETAILS

EMERGENCIES   For a general emergency, dial **International SOS** (☎*112 from mobile phone, 264/61/23–0505 Windhoek* ☎*264/64/40–0700 Swakopmund* ☎*264/81/28–5501 Tsumeb* ☎*264/64/20–0200 Walvis Bay*). Call **Netcare** (☎*264/61/22–3330*) for any medical emergency.

LANGUAGE   Namibia's official language is English, which, although widely spoken in the cities, lodges, national parks, and resorts, is usually spoken as a second language. Afrikaans is spoken by many residents of various races, and there is a large population of German-speaking people. The most widely spoken indigenous languages are Kwanyama (a dialect of Owambo), Herero, and a number of Nama (San) dialects, which are almost only spoken by native speakers.

MONEY MATTERS   Namibia's currency is the Namibian dollar, which is linked to the South African rand. (Namibia's currency is not usable in South Africa, except unofficially at border towns.) In Namibia, MasterCard and Visa are preferred by business owners to American Express. No credit cards are accepted at gas stations. Bank hours are weekdays 9–3:30 and Saturday 9–11. *Bureaux de change* at the airports often stay open late.

PASSPORTS & VISAS   All non-nationals, including infants, need a valid passport to enter Namibia for visits of up to 90 days. Business visitors to Namibia need visas.

TIME   Namibia is on CAST (Central African Standard Time), which is two hours ahead of Greenwich Mean Time. That makes it seven hours ahead of North American eastern standard time (six hours ahead during eastern daylight saving time).

VISITOR INFORMATION   The **Namibian Tourism office** (✉*Sanlam Centre, Independence Ave.* ☎*264/61/290–6000* ⊕*www.namibiatourism.com.na*), which is located in Windhoek, can provide details on camps, a free map, and a free copy of *Welcome to Namibia—Official Visitors' Guide,* which gives lots of useful information plus accommodation lists. It's open weekdays 8–1 and 2–5.

Namibia Wildlife Resorts (✉*Independence Ave., opposite Zoo Park* ☎*264/61/285–7200* ⊕*www.nwr.com.na*), also located in Windhoek, dispenses information on the national parks.

For more information on Namibia, visit the country's official tourism Web site (⊕*www.namibiatourism.com.na*).

NAMIB NAUKLUFT PARK

Namib Naukluft Park, south of Walvis Bay, is the fourth-largest national park in the world, and is renowned for its beauty, isolation, tranquillity, romantic desert landscapes, and rare desert-adapted plants and creatures. Covering an area of 12.1 million acres, it stretches 400 km (250 mi) long and 150 km (93 mi) wide, along the southern part of Namibia's coastline from Walvis Bay to Lüderitz, and accounts for a tenth of Namibia's surface area. To examine the park properly, it's best to think of it as five distinct areas: the Northern Section—between the Kuiseb and Swakops rivers—synonymous with rocky stone surfaces and granite islands (*inselbergs*) and dry riverbeds; the Middle Section, the 80-million-year-old heart of the desert and home of Sesriem Canyon and Sossusvlei, the highest sand dunes in the world; Naukluft (meaning "narrow gorge"), some 120 km (74½ mi) northwest of Sesriem, which has wall-to-wall game and birds and is the home of the Kuiseb Canyon; the Western Section, with its lichen-covered plains, prehistoric plants, and bird sanctuaries of Walvis Bay and Sandwich Harbour; and the Southern Section, where, if you're traveling up from South Africa by road, it's worth having a look at Duwisib Castle, 72 km (46 mi) southwest of Maltahöhe beside the D286—an anachronistic stone castle built in 1909 by a German army officer. The park's southern border ends at the charming little town of Lüderitz.

The kind of wildlife you'll encounter will depend on which area of the park you visit. In the north look out for the staggeringly beautiful gemsbok (oryx), believed by some to be the animal behind the unicorn myth. Also visible are springboks, spotted hyenas, black-backed jackals, and the awesome lappet-face vultures, the biggest in Africa. In Naukluft you'll see the most game, more than 50 species of mammals, including leopards, caracals, Cape and bat-eared foxes, aardwolves, and klipspringers. There are almost 200 species of birds, from the startlingly beautiful crimson-breasted boubou shrike to soaring falcons and buzzards. You'll notice huge haystacks weighing down tall trees and telephone poles. These are the condominiums of the sociable weavers, so called because they nest communally, sometimes with thousands of fellow weavers; yet each tiny bird has its own exit and entrance.

Where there are sand dunes you'll be able to observe some of the earth's strangest creatures: the dune beetle, which collects condensed fog on its back into a single droplet that it then rolls down its back into its mouth; the golden mole (thought until recently to be extinct), which spends its whole life "swimming" beneath the sand, ambushing beetles and grubs on the surface; the side-winding adder, a sand-diving lizard that raises one foot at a time above the hot sand in a strange stationary dance to nonexistent music.

Don't overlook the amazing desert-adapted plants. Ask your guide to point out a dollar bush (so called because its leaves are dollar size) or an ink bush, both of which can survive without rain for years; the gold, frankincense, and myrrh of the Commiphora plants; the Namib's magic plant, the nara melon, still harvested and eaten by the locals; and the baffling geophytes, plants that disguise themselves as stones. Watch for withered-looking desert lichens—if you pour a tiny drop of water onto one you will see it seemingly rise from the dead. Last, but by no means least, is the mind-boggling welwitschia mirabilis; the Namib's most famous, and the world's oldest, living plant.

SESRIEM & SOSSUSVLEI

Even if you're not a romantic, the Sossusvlei's huge, star-shape desert dunes, which rise dramatically 1,000 feet above the surrounding plains and sprawl like massive pieces of abstract sculpture, are guaranteed to

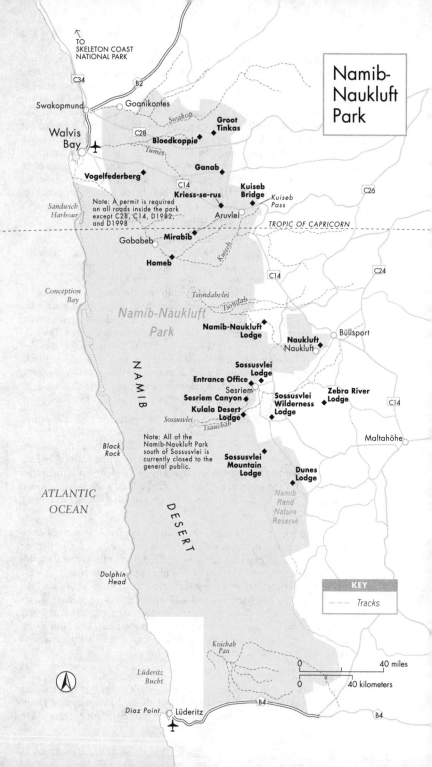

TO
SKELETON COAST
NATIONAL PARK

C34
B2

Namib-
Naukluft
Park

Swakopmund   Goanikontes

Walvis
Bay   C28   Groot
         Bloedkoppie   Tinkas

Swakop

Tumeb

Vogelfederberg   Ganab

                C14
         Kriess-se-rus   Kuiseb
                          Bridge
Sandwich   Kuiseb
Harbour   Note: A permit is required   Pass
         on all roads inside the park   C26
         except C28, C14, D1982,
         and D1998.   Aruvlei

                              TROPIC OF CAPRICORN

         Gobabeb   Mirabib

         Homeb   Kuiseb

Conception
Bay
                    Tsondabvlei

Namib-Naukluft   Tsondab
Park

         Namib-Naukluft   C14
              Lodge
                         Naukluft   Büllsport
                         Naukluft   C24

         Sossusvlei
              Lodge
    Entrance Office   Zebra River
         Sesriem   Lodge
    Sesriem Canyon   Sossusvlei
    Kulala Desert   Wilderness   C14
N   Lodge   Lodge
A   Sossusvlei
M   Maltahöhe
I   Note: All of the
B   Namib-Naukluft Park
    south of Sossusvlei is
    currently closed to the
    general public.   Sossusvlei
Black   Mountain
Rock   Lodge   Dunes
                                Lodge
ATLANTIC
OCEAN   Namib
              D   Rand
              E   Nature
              S   Reserve
              E
              R
              T
Dolphin
Head

                    KEY
                    --- Tracks

         Koichab
         Pan

              0   40 miles
              0   40 kilometers

Lüderitz
Bucht

Diaz Point Lüderitz   B4

                              B4

stir your soul and imagination. You might even dash off a sonnet or two. The landscape has continuously shifting colors—from yellow-gold and ocher to rose, purple, and deep red—which grow paler or darker according to the time of day. The dunes have their own distinctive features, ranging from the crescent-shape *barcan* dunes—which migrate up to 2 or 3 yards a year, covering and uncovering whatever crosses their path—to the spectacular, stationary star-shape dunes, formed by the multidirectional winds that tease and tumble the sands back and forth. Park gates open an hour before sunrise, so if you can, try to be among the dunes as the sun comes up—it's a spectacular sight. If you're in good shape, you can hike to the top of Big Daddy, the highest sand dune in the world. For the less active, we suggest climbing halfway up and sitting to admire the stupendous views. And if you just don't feel up to any physical exertion, simply walk up to see the stark beauty of Dead Vlei and then leisurely make your way down to sit in the shade of camel-thorn trees and watch the birdlife. Never walk in the desert without water, a sun hat, and sunblock.

About 4 km (2½ mi) from Sesriem Gate, your entry point to Sossusvlei, is Sesriem Canyon, named after the six *rieme* (thongs) that were tied to the buckets of the early Dutch settlers when they drew up water from the canyon. If you have time, cool off in the cold water and climb the towering Elim Dune, about 5 km (3 mi) away; it will take you well over an hour, but the superb views of the surrounding desert and gravel plains are worth the effort. Be warned: dune climbing is exhausting, so make discretion the better part of valor. If you're driving yourself, check with your car-rental company for distances and times, which can vary according to the state of the roads. It's more than an hour's very hot walk (4 km [2½ mi]) to climb the major route up to Dead Vlei and Big Daddy, the hub of Sossusvlei, from the parking area. With a four-wheel-drive vehicle you can park just below Dead Vlei.

9

WHERE TO STAY

$$$$ Kulala Desert Lodge. In the heart of the Namib and bordering the Namib Naukluft Park, this lodge offers magnificent views of the famous red dunes of Sossusvlei, superb mountain scenery, and vast open plains. Tented, thatch-roofed chalets (*kulala*) have a wooden platform overlooking the dry riverbed. In summer you can move your mattress onto a private star-gazing platform on your rooftop to sleep under the stars. The veranda at the main lodge overlooks a water hole and is the perfect place to observe the magnificent desert sunset. Activities include desert excursions, morning and evening game drives, trips to Sossusvlei, birding, and guided walks. You can splurge on a hot-air balloon trip over the desert (extra cost)—a once-in-a-lifetime opportunity. *Wilderness Safaris, Box 5219, Rivonia 2128, South Africa* ☎*27/11/807–1800* ⊕*www.wilderness-safaris.com* ⇨*12 chalets* ⚘*In-hotel: bar, pool* ⊟*AE, DC, MC, V* ⏃*FAP.*

$$$$ Sossusvlei Lodge. If you want to be on the spot when the park gates open at first light, then this award-winning hotel right at the Sesriem entrance is the right choice for you. Its decor in shades of terra-cotta, burnt sienna, and apricot blends perfectly with the desert surroundings.

You'll feel like an upmarket bedouin in your spacious and luxurious tented room, imaginatively constructed of concrete, ironwork, canvas, and leather. After a hot, dusty day in the desert, wallow in the swimming pool, which faces the dunes, and later gaze at the dazzling brilliance of the night skies. There's a good restaurant serving light meals. ⌂ *Box 6900, Windhoek, Namibia* ☎ *264/63/69–3223* ⊕ *www.sossus-vleilodge.com* ✍ *45 rooms* ♿ *In-room: safe. In-hotel: restaurant, bar, pool* ☰ *AE, MC, V* ◎ *MAP.*

$$$$ 🏠 **Sossusvlei Mountain Lodge.** This gorgeous lodge has a spectacular setting in the heart of the Namib Desert in the NamibRand Nature Reserve. Its ultraluxurious desert villas are built of natural rock and look out over a plain ringed by peaks. Huge desert-facing suites have private patios and sundecks and big open fireplaces to keep you warm on chilly desert nights. Shower in your megasize bathroom (even your toilet has an incomparable view) or outside in your own little walled garden. You can lie in bed and watch the stars through the skylight overhead or climb up to the observatory behind the lodge. It has its own state-of-the-art telescope through which an astronomer-ranger will guide you through the heavens. The food is as creative as the lodge itself—try tandoori-baked *kingklip* (a delicious southern African fish) served with mango salsa—and there's a super wine cellar. You can explore the area on an ecofriendly quad bike, go for guided nature walks or drives, spot some native desert birds and animals, or just sit and gaze at the incredible views. ⌂ *Africa Leisure Travel, Swakopmund, Namibia* ☎ *264/64/46–3812 or 264/64/46–3813* ⊕ *www.ccafrica.com* ✍ *10 villas* ♿ *In-hotel: pool* ☰ *AE, DC, MC, V* ◎ *FAP.*

$$$$ 🏠 **Sossusvlei Wilderness Camp.** In one of the most dramatic settings in Africa, exquisitely appointed rock, timber, and thatch bungalows cling to the side of a mountain with spectacular views of the desert as it stretches away to the horizon. You'll enjoy breakfast under spreading camel-thorn trees at the foot of Sossusvlei after the bumpy 20-km (12½-mi) drive to the dunes before returning to camp at midday via the Sesriem Canyon. Then cool off in your private plunge pool as you watch the sun set over awesome desert scenery to the calls of barking geckos. ⌂ *Wilderness Safaris, Box 5219, Rivonia 2128, South Africa* ☎ *27/11/807–1800* ⊕ *www.sossusvleicamp.com* ✍ *9 bungalows* ♿ *In-hotel: restaurant, bar, pool* ☰ *AE, DC, MC, V* ◎ *FAP.*

$$ 🏠 **Namib Naukluft Lodge.** This pinkish-brown desert-toned lodge sits in the middle of a wide plain of desert and looks like children's building blocks set down by a giant hand in the middle of nowhere. Awesome views go with the territory. You can choose to sit on your private veranda and watch the fiery desert sunset, sip a sundowner by the pool, or enjoy a meal in the open-air restaurant. The lodge will arrange outings and activities for you—don't miss out on an easy walk in the world's oldest desert. ⌂ *African Extravanganza, Box 22028, Windhoek, Namibia* ☎ *264/63/69–3381* *www.namib-naukluft-lodge.com* ✍ *16 rooms* ♿ *In-hotel: restaurant, bar, pool* ☰ *AE, DC, MC, V* ◎ *FAP.*

$ 🏠 **Zebra River Lodge.** From this delightful lodge, where personal attention and friendly service are outstanding (the lodge gets lots of repeat visitors), you can drive yourself to Sesriem and Sossusvlei (90 km [56 mi] to the gate) or to Naukluft, or take a full-day excursion with Rob Field, the friendly and knowledgeable owner (book this when you reserve your room). All activities are extra. The comfortable and unpretentious lodge has its own canyon, hiking trails, perennial springs, and superb cooking. The seven guest rooms all have views of the plunge pool and green garden. ⌂*Box 11742, Windhoek, Namibia* ☎*264/63/69–3265* ⊕*www.zebrariver.com* ↩*7 rooms, 1 cottage* ᕾ*In-hotel: bar, pool* ▭*MC, V* ⋈*FAP.*

THE SKELETON COAST

This wildly beautiful but dangerous shore, one-third of Namibia's western coastline, stretches from the Ugab River in the south to the Kunene River, the border with Angola, in the north. Its name, the Skeleton Coast, testifies to innumerable shipwrecks, to lives lost, to bleached whale bones, and to the insignificant, transient nature of puny humans in the face of the raw power of nature. Still comparatively unknown to tourists, this region has a stark beauty and an awesomely diverse landscape—gray gravel plains, rugged wilderness, rusting shipwrecks, desert wastes, meandering barcan dunes, distant mountains, towering walls of sand and granite, and crashing seas. This is not an easy ride, as distances are vast, amenities scarce or nonexistent, and the roads demanding.

Skeleton Coast National Park extends along this rugged coast and about 40 km (25 mi) inland. The southern part is open to tourists up to Terrace Bay, and the northern part is managed by the government as a wilderness area. If it's lush green pastures and abundance of game you want, then this raw, rugged, harsh, and uncompromising landscape is not for you. What you will find is dramatically different scenery, an absence of tourists (crowds around here mean one or two vehicles), and some wildlife: brown hyenas, springbok, oryx, jackals, and, if you're really lucky, a coastal lion. (The sight of a majestic oryx silhouetted against towering sand dunes or a cheeky jackal scavenging seal pups on the beaches is extremely rewarding.) The best activity, however, is just concentrating on the freedom, beauty, and strange solitude of the area. You can drive (a 4x4 gives you more flexibility) from Swakopmund north through Henties Bay via the Ugab Gate with its eerie painted skulls and crossbones on the gates or from the more northerly Springbokwater Gate. You must reach your gate of entry before 3 PM. Always stick to the marked roads and avoid driving on treacherous salt pans. Look out for an unusual wreck lying next to the road between the Ugab River

9

A VIEW FROM ABOVE

A stupendous, not-to-be-missed view of the desert can be had in a hot-air balloon piloted by the legendary Belgian Eric Hefemans of **Namib Sky Adventures** (☎*264/63/29–3233* ⊕*www.namibsky.com*). You ascend at dawn and watch the sun come up over the breathtaking, silent landscape, followed by a champagne breakfast amid the dunes. The whole event costs N$2,750.

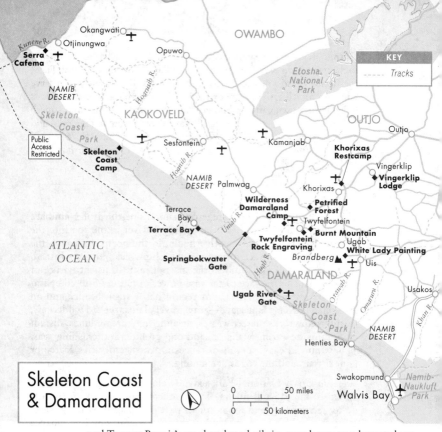

Skeleton Coast & Damaraland

KEY

---- *Tracks*

OWAMBO

Kunene R.
Okangwati
Otjinungwa
Opuwo
Serra Cafema
Etosha National Park
NAMIB DESERT
Hoarusib R.
KAOKOVELD
OUTJO
Outjo
Skeleton Coast Park
Sesfontein
Kamanjab
Khorixas Restcamp
Public Access Restricted
Skeleton Coast Camp
Hoanib R.
Vingerklip
Vingerklip Lodge
NAMIB DESERT
Palmwag
Khorixas
Wilderness Damaraland Camp
Petrified Forest
Uniab R.
Twyfelfontein
Terrace Bay
Terrace Bay
Burnt Mountain
Twyfelfontein Rock Engraving
Ugab
White Lady Painting
ATLANTIC OCEAN
Springbokwater Gate
Huab R.
Brandberg
Uis
DAMARALAND
Omaruru R.
Usakos
Ugab River Gate
Skeleton Coast Park
Ugab R.
NAMIB DESERT
Khan R.
Henties Bay

0   50 miles
0   50 kilometers

Swakopmund
Namib-Naukluft Park
Walvis Bay

and Terrace Bay; it's an abandoned oil rig, now home to a huge colony of cormorants. If you are only passing through, you can buy a permit (N\$20 per adult, N\$20 per car) at the gate. For a longer trip you must obtain a permit in advance from Namibia Wildlife Resorts.

WHERE TO STAY

\$\$\$\$

Fodor'sChoice
★

🏨 **Serra Cafema.** This astonishingly different and dramatically sited camp in the extreme northwest of Namibia, on the Angolan border, is the most remote camp in southern Africa. After a dry, dusty, but magnificently beautiful drive from the airstrip, you are guaranteed to gasp with awe as you first catch sight of the camp from a high sand dune. Built amid a grove of ancient albida trees on the banks of the wide Kunene River, it seems like a desert mirage. Only the nomadic Himba people share this area, and a visit to a local village will be an eye-opening experience and one of the highlights of your stay. Another day, ride a quad bike over the billowing sand dunes and spot the Atlantic from a high vantage point. Although tents (on raised platforms) are ultraluxurious and have private bathrooms, don't come here if you are a sissy. The flight from Windhoek is long and bumpy, and the terrain harsh and demanding, but the experience—staying by a wide river in the midst of the oldest desert in the world—is almost surreal. This is one-of-a-kind Africa. Stay for three nights to make the most of the experience: go walking, boating, birding, or quad biking; do a nature drive; or just sit by the rushing river and contemplate. ⌂ *Wilderness Safaris, Box 5219, Rivonia 2128, South Africa* ☎*27/11/807–1800* ⊕*www.serracafema. com* ⊲*8 tents* ⌂*In-hotel: bar, pool* ⊟*AE, DC, MC, V* � #*FAP.*

★ $$$$ ⛺**Skeleton Coast Camp.** If you long for a remote wilderness area, consider a three-night safari into this desolate camp in 660,000 acres of the northern part of Skeleton Coast National Park. You sleep under canvas in an elegantly furnished tent with your own small deck and awesome desert view and eat in the open-air dining room under an ancient leadwood tree. You visit an authentic Himba settlement, picnic beside the crashing Atlantic, visit the loneliest grave in the world, and drive through oryx-studded plains and shifting sand dunes with their desert birds. The days are long—you leave camp after breakfast as the morning mists drift from the coastline into the interior and don't return till after sunset—but they are packed so full of excitement and beauty that your head will still be spinning as you fall into your comfortable bed after a splendid dinner. Departures are from Windhoek every Wednesday and Saturday. ⌂ *Wilderness Safaris, Box 5219, Rivonia 2128, South Africa* ☎*27/11/807–1800* ⊕*www.skeleton-coast.com* ⊲*5 tents* ⊟*AE, DC, MC, V* ⦿*FAP.*

$$$ ⛺**Terrace Bay.** This isolated outpost and government resort is the northernmost point in the park to which you can drive. Surrounded by gravel plains, it's a popular spot for anglers and people who want to get to know the desert. Don't miss the surprising Uniab River delta—a lush green oasis in a miniature canyon a couple of miles from Terrace Bay. It's also a good stop if you're going on into Damaraland. The accommodations, once part of a diamond-mining operation, are simple and basic, though each bungalow has a refrigerator, shower, and toilet. The four-room Presidential Suite has all the modern conveniences, including air-conditioning and a fully equipped kitchen. All meals are provided, and there's a small shop that stocks basics. The resort does not accommodate day visitors. ✉*Namibia Wildlife Resorts, Independence Ave., opposite Zoo Park, Windhoek, Namibia* ☎*264/61/285–7200* ⊕*www. nwr.com.na* ⌂*In-room: no a/c (some), refrigerator. In-hotel: restaurant, bar* ⊟*MC, V* ⦿*FAP.*

DAMARALAND

Stretching 600 km (370 mi) from just south of Etosha to Usakos in the south and 200 km (127 mi) from east to west, this stark, mountainous area is just inland from Skeleton Coast National Park. You can drive into Damaraland from the park via the Springbokwater Gate, or drive from Swakopmund to Uis, where you can visit the Daureb Craft Centre and watch the craftspeople at work, or make it part of your customized safari. A good base for touring southern Damaraland is the little town of Khorixas. From here you can visit the Organ Pipes, where there are hundreds of angular rock formations, or watch the rising or setting sun bathe the slopes of Burnt Mountain in fiery splendor. You'll find yourself surrounded by a dramatic landscape of steep valleys; rugged cliffs of red, gray, black, and brown; and towering mountains, including Spitzkoppe (Namibia's Matterhorn), where Damara guides will show you the Golden Snake and the Bridge—an interesting rock formation—and the San (Bushman) paintings at Bushman's Paradise. There are more spectacular Bushman rock paintings at the Brandberg, especially the famous White Lady of Brandberg, at Tsisab Gorge, whose depiction and origin have teased the minds of scholars for decades. Other stops of interest are the Petrified Forest, 42 km (25 mi) west of Khorixas, and Twyfelfontein, 90 km (56 mi) west of Khorixas, the biggest outdoor art gallery in the world, where thousands of rock paintings and ancient rock engravings are open to the sky. It's extremely rare for this many paintings and engravings to be found at the same site. Give yourself a full day here, start early (it's hard to pick out some of the art in full sun), take binoculars, wear sturdy shoes and a hat, and bring lots of water.

Northern Damaraland consists of concession areas that have been set aside for tourism, with many tourist operators working hand in hand with the local communities. It's a mountainous landscape dotted with camel-thorn trees, candelabra euphorbias, salt bushes, and shepherd's trees. Look out for black rhinos and the first traces of the amazing desert elephants, their huge footprints trodden over by the herds of goat and sheep belonging to the local farmers. Ask your guide to point out the welwitschia (fossil plant) and the "enchanted" *moringa* tree. The Kaokoveld, north of Damaraland, although enticing because it is pristine and rarely visited, is also inhospitably rugged. If you're driving yourself, it's only for the intrepid, do-it-yourself explorer.

WHERE TO STAY

$$$$ **Wilderness Damaraland Camp.** A joint community venture with the local *riemvasmakers* (thong makers), this desolate camp is on the Huab River in central Damaraland, midway between Khorixas and the coast. From your large, comfortable walk-in tent you can look out over a landscape formed by millions of years of unending geological movement. You'll drive with an experienced ranger in an open 4x4 to see Namibia's famous fossil plant—the welwitschia—and go tracking desert elephants. After a day in the desert, cool off in the natural rock pool and watch the desert birds. *Wilderness Safaris, Box 5219, Rivonia 2128, South Africa* 27/11/807–1800 *www.damaraland.com* 8 tents *In-hotel: bar, pool* AE, DC, MC, V FAP.

$$ **Vingerklip Lodge.** In a dramatic locale in Damaraland's Valley of the Ugab Terraces, this lodge is set against the backdrop of a mighty stone finger pointing toward the sky. Take time while you're here to listen to the silence. The 360-degree views from the Sundowner Terrace are magnificent. The friendly and knowledgeable staff organizes tours to the well-known sights in the vicinity such as the petrified forest, a Himba village, and the rock engravings at Twyfelfontein. Bungalows cling to the side of a rocky hill and are clean and comfortable, but it's the remarkable views that you'll always remember. *Box 11550, Windhoek, Namibia* 264/61/25–5344 *www.vingerklip.com.na* 11 bungalows *In-hotel: restaurant, bar, pool* MC, V MAP.

¢ 🏠 **Khorixas Restcamp.** Grayish stone-and-tile bungalows, some of which face a seasonally flowing river, are scattered among trees and flowering shrubs. Although this spot is hardly the last word in luxury, it is clean, budget priced, unpretentious, and very handy for exploring the major attractions of the area. 🖉 *Box 2, Khorixas, Namibia* ☎*264/67/33–1196* 🛏*38 bungalows, campsite* 🛇*In-hotel: restaurant, bar, pool* 💳*MC, V* 🍴*BP.*

ETOSHA NATIONAL PARK

This incredibly photogenic and startlingly beautiful park takes its name—meaning "Great White Place"—from the vast, flat depression that 12 million years ago was a deep inland lake. Although the park is never crowded with visitors like some of the East African game parks, the scenery here is no less spectacular: huge herds of animals that dot the plains and accumulate at the many and varied water holes, the dust devils and mirages, terrain that changes from densely wooded thickets to wide-open spaces and from white salt-encrusted pans to blond grasslands.

The game's all here—the Big Five—large and small, fierce and gentle, beautiful and ugly. On the road from the Von Lindequist Gate to the well-restored white-wall German colonial fort that is now Namutoni rest camp, look out for the smallest of all African antelopes, the Damara dik-dik. If you see a diminutive Bambi sheltering under a roadside bush, that's it. The Namutoni area and the two Okevi water holes—Klein Namutoni and Kalkheuwel—probably provide the best chances to see leopards. Don't miss the blackface impala, native to Etosha. But the real secret of game-watching in the park is to settle in at one of the many water holes, most of which are on the southern edges of the pan and each with its own unique personality and characteristics, and wait. Repeat, wait. Even if the hole is small and deep, like Ombika, on the western side, you'll be amazed at what may arrive. Old Africa hands maintain you should be up at dawn for the best sightings, but you can see marvelous game at all times of day; one visitor was lucky enough to see a leopard and her cubs come to drink at high noon. The plains, where you should spot cheetahs, are also home to huge herds of zebras, wildebeests, and springboks, and you may see the silhouettes of giraffes as they cross the skyline in stately procession. Salvadora, a constant spring on the fringe of Etosha Pan near Halali, is a favorite watering point for some of these big herds. And where there's water, there's always game. Predators, especially lions, lurk around most of the water holes looking for a meal. Plan to spend at least half a night sitting on a bench at the floodlighted Okuakuejo water hole. You'll be amazed at the game that comes down to drink: black and white rhinos, lions, jackals, and even the occasional leopard. Don't overlook the more than 340 dazzling varieties of birds—the crimson-breasted shrike is particularly gorgeous—and watch for ostriches running over the plains or raptors hunting silently overhead.

9

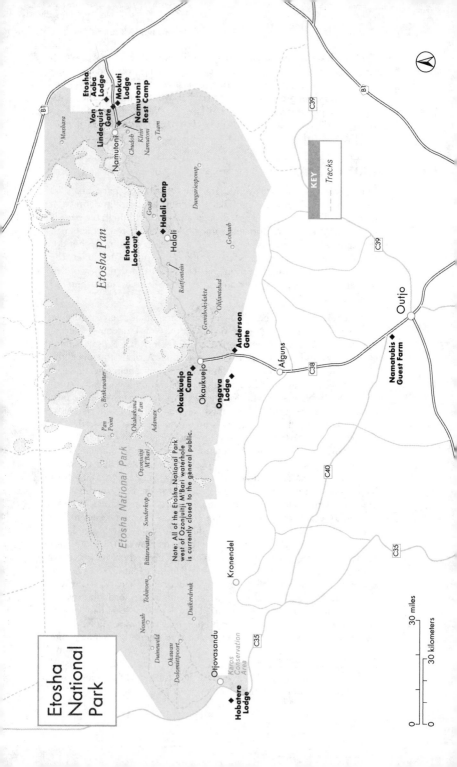

Etosha National Park

Etosha Aoba Lodge
Mokuti Lodge
Von Lindequist Gate
Namutoni Rest Camp
Namutoni

Mushara

Chudob

Klein Namutoni

Tsam

Etosha Pan

Dungariespomp

Halali Camp

Etosha Lookout

Halali

Gois

Rietfontein

Gobaub

Etosha National Park

Gemsbokvlakte

Olifantsbad

Anderson Gate

Brakwater

Pan Point

Okaukama Pan

Okakuejo

Adamax

Okaukuejo Camp
Okaukuejo
Ongava Lodge

Afguns

C38

Namutubis Guest Farm

Outjo

C39

C39

B1

B1

Ozonjuitji M'Bari

Sonderkop

Bittervater

Duikerdrink

C40

C35

Kronendel

Note: All of the Etosha National Park west of Ozonjuitji M'Bari waterhole is currently closed to the general public.

Nonab

Tobinon

Dstineveld

Okauau
Dolomietpoort

Otjovasandu

C35

*Karos
Conservation
Area*

Hobatere Lodge

KEY
--- *Tracks*

0   30 miles
0   30 kilometers

Although many tour companies offer safaris, it really is best to drive yourself, so you can stop and start at your leisure (but stick to marked roads). In addition to patience, you'll need drinks, snacks, and your camera. There are more than 40 water holes, with Rietfontein, Okaukuejo, Goas, Halali, Klein Namutoni, and Chudob regarded as the best for game-watching and taking pictures, but nothing is certain in the bush. Keep your eyes and ears open all the time, and you may come across game at any time, in any place.

The park gates are open from sunrise to sunset, and the daily entrance fee is N$80 for foreign visitors and N$10 for a passenger vehicle with fewer than ten seats.

WHERE TO STAY

The rest camps inside Etosha are all self-catering.

INSIDE
ETOSHA
$–$$$

Halali. Etosha's smallest national-park self-catering camp, roughly halfway between Okaukuejo and Namutoni, is rather barracks-like and dusty, but if you're a bird-watcher, it merits a giant check mark on your list. Rare violet woodhoopoes and bare-cheeked babblers frequent the camp, and if you walk up the rocky path to the pleasant floodlighted water hole and are prepared to sit and wait, there's a good chance you'll spot lions, elephants, and black rhinos. Halali is in the only area of the park with hills. ⊠*Namibia Wildlife Resorts, Independence Ave., opposite Zoo Park, Windhoek, Namibia* ☎*264/61/285–7200* ⊕*www. nwr.com.na* ➲*60 huts, 2 cottages* ⟋*In-room: shower, a/c. In-hotel: restaurant, pool* ▭*MC, V* ☉*Closed Nov.–mid-Mar.*

$–$$$

Namutoni. On the eastern edge of the park, this restored colonial self-catering camp is the most picturesque of the national-park camps. Hearing the bugle call from the watchtower at sunrise and sunset, you almost expect to see the French Foreign Legion come galloping over the horizon. The historic rooms are tiny—the troops didn't live all that well—so if it's comfort rather than history you're after, don't choose a fort room; opt instead for one of the fully equipped bungalows, built at a respectful distance from the fort so as not to destroy the ambience. Directly behind the fort is a floodlighted water hole for game-viewing. Meals are not included. ⊠*Namibia Wildlife Resorts, Independence Ave., opposite Zoo Park, Windhoek, Namibia* ☎*264/61/285–7200* ⊕*www.nwr.com.na* ➲*18 bungalows, 10 rooms, 1 apartment, 4 cottages, 4 dormitories* ⟋*In-room: refridgerator. In-hotel: restaurant, pool* ▭*MC, V.*

$–$$$

Okaukuejo. On the western side of Etosha, this is the biggest and noisiest national-park camp (the noise comes from the staff quarters), and the staff could certainly do with a few workshops on how to deal with the public in a pleasant way. But its floodlighted water hole—regarded as one of the finest in Africa—more than makes up for any inconvenience. Climb the spiral staircase to the top of the round tower for a good view of the surrounding countryside, and then settle down to an all-night game-watching vigil. Pleasantly furnished, spotlessly clean accommodations range from basic two-bed huts with communal facilities to large, fully equipped eight-bed cottages. Meals are not included. There are mail facilities at the camp as well as a place to fill

9

up the tank and a store to stock up on provisions. ⊠ *Namibia Wildlife Resorts, Independence Ave., opposite Zoo Park, Windhoek, Namibia* ☎ *264/61/285–7200* ⊕ *www.nwr.com.na* ➷ *70 chalets and 40 double rooms* ⌂ *In-room: kitchen (some), refridgerator. In-hotel: restaurant, pool* ▭ *MC, V.*

JUST OUTSIDE
OF ETOSHA
★ $$$$

▯ **Ongava Lodge.** Set on the southern boundary of Etosha close to the Andersson Gate, the lodge has its own surrounding game reserve as well as its own entrance into the park. It's one of Namibia's most luxurious lodges, with accommodations in private, spacious thatch chalets with handmade wood furniture—and gold faucets in the bathrooms. Chalets also have wood decks, which cling to the side of a steep, rocky outcrop overlooking a couple of busy water holes. The stunning main area has stone floors and sweeping thatch roofs, as well as myriad spots from which to gaze at the never-ending plains beyond. Take a guided walk and sneak up on some zebras and wildebeests, or sit in the bird blind just before sunset and listen to the soft twittering calls of hundreds of sand grouse as they come to drink. Lions often stray in from Etosha and join the evening party. If you want to be more on the wild side, you can stay at Ongava's Tented Camp, a small, intimate site nestled deep in the bush. You'll sleep in a walk-in tent on a slate base under a thatch awning with a private bathroom. After a day spent game-watching (tracking rhinos on foot is a highlight), it's great to cool off in the outside shower or in the plunge pool. If you want even more exclusivity and luxury, then go for Little Ongava, which has three gorgeous suites, all with their own plunge pool and *sala* (outdoor covered deck). ☞ *Wilderness Safaris, Box 519, Rivonia 2128, South Africa* ☎ *27/11/807–1800* ⊕ *www.ongavalodge.com* ➷ *10 chalets, 6 tents, 3 suites* ⌂ *In-hotel: restaurant, bar, pool* ▭ *AE, DC, MC, V* ❙○❙ *FAP.*

$$$
▯ **Etosha Aoba Lodge.** This small, family-owned and ultrafriendly lodge is 10 km (6 mi) east of the Von Lindequist Gate—about a 30-minute drive from the park; it gets lots of repeat visitors. You can slip into crisp, white bed linens in your cool, thatch chalet after a hot, dusty day in the park, or sip a cocktail on your mini-veranda while listening to the noises of the night. The owners put a lot of emphasis on excellent cuisine, which you'll enjoy under the thatch roof of the main building. Most visitors have their own vehicles, but the lodge can arrange trips into the park for you. ☞ *Box 21783, Windhoek, Namibia* ☎ *264/61/22–9106* ⊕ *www.etosha-aoba-lodge. com* ➷ *10 chalets* ⌂ *In-hotel: restaurant, bar, pool, no kids under 13* ▭ *MC, V* ❙○❙ *BP.*

$$$
▯ **Mokuti Lodge.** The close proximity of Mokuti's private park to Etosha's Von Lindequist Gate means you may wake up to find an antelope or warthog munching the grass outside your room. This was Namibia's first lodge, and it is also its largest, and the experience is obvious in the impeccable service and good food. The smallish rooms are rather sparsely furnished, but you'll be out most of the day game-spotting. You can take a walk, either guided or on your own, and be quite safe. Follow the paths, and you may come face-to-face with a giraffe or any number of gorgeous birds. Don't miss the amazing reptile park, where you can meet pythons, scorpions, tortoises, and the odd crocodile. To

catch sight of the bigger game, take an early-morning or afternoon tour into Etosha from the lodge. Air Namibia flies to and from Mokuti five days a week. ⊡*Namib Sun Hotels, Box 2862, Windhoek, Namibia* ☎*264/64/40–0315* ⊕*www.namibsunhotels.com.na* ⟿*92 rooms, 8 suites, 8 family units* ⚅*In-room: safe, refridgerator, A/C. In-hotel: restaurant, bar, tennis court, pool* ⊟*MC, V* ⊠*BP.*

$ ⊞**Namatubis Guest Farm.** Fifteen kilometers (9 mi) from Outjo on the Okuakuejo road to Etosha, Namatubis is an oasis in the surrounding dry countryside. You'll find pastel-color chalets with tile floors and Namibian rugs surrounded by green lawns and multicolor carpets of flowers and shrubs. The food is good farm-style cooking; choose either the superb steak, venison, chicken pie, or a decadent brandy pancake. You can also take day excursions from the lodge to the Vingerklip, Twyfelfontein, or the Petrified Forest and still be back in time for dinner. ⊡*Box 467, Outjo, Namibia* ☎*264/67/31–3061* ⟿*23 chalets* ⚅*In-room: refrigerator. In-hotel: restaurant, bar, pool* ⊟*AE, DC, MC, V* ⊠*MAP.*

NORTHEAST NAMIBIA

This lovely unspoiled area—one of Namibia's best-kept secrets—is as green and fertile as the Namib is golden-brown and inhospitable. It lies at the eastern end of the Caprivi Strip at the confluence of the Zambezi and Chobe rivers. Because it's relatively unknown as a tourist area, you'll get the feeling that you are truly alone with nature, unlike in Chobe where in high season you might find mini traffic jams.

WHERE TO STAY

★ $$$ ⊞**Ntwala Island Lodge.** East of Sosuwe Island Lodge, in the most pristine and secluded of all Chobe destinations, is this breathtakingly beautiful lodge. Only 80 km (50 mi) upstream from the Victoria Falls, the four art-deco-meets-Africa chalets are built on an untouched Namibian cluster of small islands linked by floating wooden walkways. You can fly in from Namibia or Botswana, but there's also a road option. Drive to Kasane in Botswana, and then board a small boat that skirts rapids and dodges hippos, as it takes you to your very own Treasure Island. A gray, mosaic-edged, kidney-shape pool surrounded by white sand shimmers outside your cream-colored, wooden, tile-roof chalet, just a couple of yards from the rushing Zambezi. Braying trumpeter hornbills, the liquid notes of the robins, and the startled call of francolins greet you. The chalets are spectacular by any standard, with huge rooms, circular wooden canopies echoing the circular bed platforms, carved half-moon chests, handwrought light fittings of metal feathers, and bathrooms big enough to host a party in. Freestanding canvas and wooden screens are topped by metal Prince-of-Wales feathers, matching the metal-curlicued towel rails and bath accessories trolley. Try your hand at tiger-fishing, marvel at the industry of the reed cormorants as they continuously crisscross the sky carrying nesting material to their heronry, or watch the sunset herds of elephants and buffalo, the unique Chobe bushbuck, a group of impala, and if you're really lucky, in the dry season, some thirsty lions. ⊡*Islands in Africa Safaris, Box 70378,*

9

Bryanston 2021, South Africa ☎*27/11/706–7207* ⊕*www.islandsinafrica.com* ✈*6 chalets* ♿*In-hotel: pool* ▤*DC, MC, V* ⦿*FAP.*

$ ▦**Chobe Savanna Lodge.** This luxury lodge lies on the banks of the Chobe River, overlooking Chobe National Park. Each North Africa–inspired stone-and-thatch cottage has a private deck, air-conditioning, and a private bathroom. Cream textured linen, vases of dried grasses, ethnic-design cushions, polished wooden floors, handcrafted furniture, and handwoven cream-and-brown rugs provide a comfortable and elegant haven. Cruise the wide river game-spotting, bird-watching, or just soaking up an awesome sunset; take a guided game walk through the unspoiled bush; or just sit out on the viewing deck with its magnificent views of the floodplains and river and watch scores of elephants and buffalos mooching about. ⌂*Desert & Delta Safaris, Box 130555, Bryanston 2125, South Africa* ☎*27/11/706–0861* ⊕*www.desertdelta.co.za* ✈*12 cottages* ♿*In-hotel: bar, pool* ▤*MC, V* ⦿*FAP.*

$ ▦**Susuwe Island Lodge.** This is classic Africa, a solid structure of wood and stone, built before the designer-chic lodge invasion. This six-chalet lodge is situated at the eastern end of the Caprivi Strip (before the Strip broadens and widens on its way to Botswana) on a small island in a teak forest. Here the deep, clear waters of the Kwando River lap the island's edges, and swamp boubous whistle their melodious calls. Take the time to climb to the highest viewing deck—up there in that bird-rich canopy your inner spirit will be restored. A brass lizard, frozen in time, scurries up a wooden stair rail, while a long-lashed giraffe with bead earrings adorns the outside of one door. Two mokoros act as bookcases; a tiny, tiled elephant watches you from a corner of the stone floor; and in your emperor-sized chalet you'll find candles in carved logs, faded kilims, and a personal plunge pool beside the rushing river. This river trip is one you won't forget, but don't expect to see big game, though elephants are around. This is not Big Five country; it's a place to totally unwind, which is perfect for the end of a safari. ⌂*Islands in Africa Safaris, Box 70378, Bryanston 2021, South Africa* ☎*27/11/706–7207* ⊕*www.islandsinafrica.com* ✈*6 chalets* ♿*In-hotel: pool* ▤*DC, MC, V* ⦿*FAP.*

NAMIBIA ESSENTIALS

TRANSPORTATION

BY AIR

Namibia's main point of entry is Hosea Kutako International Airport. It's a small, bustling, modern airport that's a splendidly scenic 45-km (27-mi) drive from Windhoek. The smaller Eros Airport handles local flights and charters. Once in the country you can make use of scheduled flights or charter flights that service all domestic destinations. Walvis Bay is the nearest airport for Namib Naukluft and the Skeleton Coast and has daily flights from Windhoek.

The national carrier is Air Namibia, which operates international flights between Windhoek and London, Frankfurt, Johannesburg, and Cape Town, and internal flights to most of Namibia's major tourist destinations. South African Airways (SAA) operates links to Johannesburg and

Cape Town. Air Botswana links Maun with Windhoek, and SA Express Airways flies between Johannesburg and Walvis Bay.

There's frequent bus service from Hosea Kutako International Airport to Windhoek's city center; the pickup and drop-off point is opposite the Kalahari Sands Hotel, on Independence Avenue. Expect to pay N$100 each way. Many larger hotels run a courtesy shuttle service to and from the airport. Taxis are available, but negotiate the price before you get in. Check on current fares at the airport information counter.

All camps in Etosha National Park have their own landing strip. Have your tour operator arrange charters or fly-in safaris for you. Air Namibia flies directly to Mokuti on the regularly scheduled flight between Windhoek and Victoria Falls. Chartered flights and fly-in safaris also use the Ongava airstrip.

Airports **Eros Airport** (☎ *264/61/23–8220*). **Hosea Kutako International Airport** (☎ *264/62/54–0271*). **Walvis Bay Airport** (☎ *264/64/20–2867*).

Airlines **Air Botswana** (☎ *27/11/390–3070 in Johannesburg* ⊕ *www.airbotswana.co.bw*). **Air Namibia** (☎ *264/61/298–2605* ⊕ *www.airnamibia.com*). **SA Express Airways** (☎ *27/11/978–5577 Johannesburg*). **South African Airways** (☎ *27/11/778–1111 Johannesburg* ⊕ *www.flysaa.com*).

BY CAR

Driving to Namibia from South Africa is possible, and there's an excellent road network for all in-country tourist attractions, but be warned that the trip is tiring and time-consuming because of the huge distances involved. The Trans-Kalahari Highway links Johannesburg to Windhoek and Gaborone. From Johannesburg to Windhoek on this road is 1,426 km (885 mi). To allow free access to game, there are no fences in the Kalahari, so don't speed, and look out for antelope as well as donkeys and cows on the road. You can also drive from Johannesburg to Windhoek (1,791 km [1,237 mi]) via Upington, going through the Narochas (Nakop) border post (open 24 hours). This is a good route if you want to visit the Augrabies Falls and Kgalagadi Transfrontier Park in South Africa first. You can also drive from Cape Town to Namibia along the N7, an excellent road that becomes the B1 as you cross into Namibia at the Noordoewer border post (open 24 hours). It's 763 km (474 mi) from Cape Town to Noordoewer, 795 km (493 mi) from Noordoewer to Windhoek. Border posts are efficient and friendly—make sure you have all your paperwork to hand over. You will need a current international driver's license.

To reach Etosha National Park you can drive from Windhoek, via Otjiwarongo and Tsumeb, and arrive at the park on its eastern side by the Von Lindequist Gate (near Namutoni rest camp), 106 km (65 mi) from Tsumeb and 550 km (330 mi) north of Windhoek. Alternatively, you can drive from Windhoek via Otjiwarongo and Outjo and come in the Andersson Gate, south of Okaukuejo, 120 km (74½ mi) from Outjo, 450 km (280 mi) north of Windhoek. The latter is the more popular route. Both drives are long, hot, and dusty, so you might want to fly if you're short on time. Travel time will depend on your driving and choice of vehicle, so check with your car-rental company. Etosha's gates open at sunrise and close just before sunset. You pay for your vehicle entry permit at the gate (N$10 for most small vehicles) and for any balance remaining on your prebooked accommodations (which include personal entry fees) at the reception area.

If you're not staying at a private lodge that provides transportation, you will need to rent your own vehicle. Air-conditioning is a must at any time of the year, as are spare tires in good condition. You can pick up rental cars at the town nearest whichever park you are visiting or at Etosha itself, but it's better to book them before you leave home. For driving on the main roads, a two-wheel-drive vehicle is fine. In some areas, though, including parts of the Namib Naukluft Park and Damaraland, four-wheel drive is essential. In Etosha a two-wheel-drive car is fine (although you get better views in a van or SUV because you sit higher up); don't exceed the speed limit of 60 kph (37 mph). Always check the state of the roads with the nearest tourist office before you set off, and never underestimate the long distances involved. Don't drive at night unless you absolutely have to. Roads are unlighted, and animals like to bed down on the warm surfaces. If you hit an animal, even a small one, it could be the end of you and your vehicle. Never speed on gravel roads (80 kph [50 mph] is reasonable), which can often be very slippery. It's very easy to skid or roll your vehicle—at least one tourist per year is killed this way. And make sure you have plenty of water and *padkos,* Afrikaans for "road food."

Automobile Associations **Automobile Association of Namibia (AAN)** (✉ *Windhoek* ☎ *264/61/22–4201*).

BY TRAIN

The Desert Express travels between Windhoek, the capital of Namibia and Swakopmund, the country's premier coastal resort. The train departs from Windhoek on Tuesday and Friday and from Swakopmund on Wednesday and Saturday. Longer journeys to Etosha and Lüderitz are available.

Trains **Desert Express** (✉ *Windhoek Railway Station, Bahnhof St., Windhoek* ☎ *264/61/298–2600* ⊕ *www.desertexpress.com.na*).

CONTACTS & RESOURCES

ELECTRICITY

To use electric-powered equipment purchased in the United States or Canada, bring a converter and adapter. If your appliances are dual-voltage, you'll need only an adapter. The electrical current is 220 volts, 50 cycles alternating current (AC); wall outlets usually take 15-amp plugs with three round prongs, but some take the straight-edged three-prong plugs, also 15 amps. The more inaccessible lodges have their own generators, but if you want to read at night in your tent, bring a good reading light.

EMBASSIES

United States **U.S. Embassy** (✉ *14 Lossen St., Box 12029, Windhoek* ☎ *264/61/22–1601*).

HOSPITALS

There's a high standard of medical care in Namibia. Consult your hotel about particular doctors or consult the white pages of the telephone directory under *M* for medical practitioners. If you get sick, go to a private clinic rather than a government one. Windhoek and Otjiwarongo both have excellent private clinics. Windhoek has the Medi-Clinic and the Catholic Mission Hospital. In Otjiwarongo there is a Medi-Clinic. Be sure you have comprehensive medical insurance before you leave.

Hospitals **Catholic Mission Hospital** (⊠ *92 Stubel St., Windhoek* ☎ *264/61/23–7237).* **Medi-Clinic** (⊠ *Heliodoor St., Eros Park, Windhoek* ☎ *264/61/22–2687* ⊠ *Son St., Otjiwarongo* ☎ *264/67/30–3734 or 264/67/30–3735).*

TOURS

African Extravaganza specializes in shuttle services, scheduled safaris, charter tours and fly-ins, self-drive options, day excursions, and transfers. For instance, it offers a three-day Windhoek/Sossusvlei shuttle for N$3,200 per person, which includes minibus transport via the scenic, serpentine Spreetshoogte Pass, accommodations at the Namib Naukluft Lodge, your own guide, all meals, and an excursion to Sesriem and Sossusvlei. African Kirikara Safaris, whose base of operations is the family-owned farm Kiripotib, 160 km (100 mi) southeast of Windhoek in the Kalahari Desert, offers small, exclusive, tailor-made safaris throughout Namibia—even for as few as two people. Dune Hopper Air Taxis, operated by NatureFriend Safaris, offers flexible fly-in packages from Windhoek or Swakopmund to the Sossusvlei area. Pasjona Safaris offers tented safaris, guided tours, accommodations in lodges or hotels, and self-drive tours. Wilderness Safaris has a seven-day fly-in safari from Windhoek, which covers most of the main tourist destinations. Elena Travel Services offers transfers to guest farms, lodges, the coast, and other towns in Namibia. Skeleton Coast Fly-In Safaris offers superb four- and six-day trips to this starkly beautiful wilderness. Included is a visit to the remarkable Himba people who with their red-ocher body coverings, elaborate plaited hair, and intricate bead necklaces and leather aprons live much as they have for centuries. You'll fly to the park from Windhoek over the impressive Kuiseb Canyon and its surrounding sea of red dunes, staying at tented camps throughout and experiencing the desert from open Land Rovers.

NACOBTA (Namibia Community Based Tourism Association) promotes community-based tourism projects throughout Namibia, benefiting both the indigenous people and the tourist. There are 45 established community-based tourism enterprises, which include campsites, crafts centers, traditional villages, indigenous tour guides, tourism information centers, and museums.

Guided rock-art safaris, including a fully inclusive six-day hike in the Brandberg (you need a doctor's certificate of fitness), are conducted by Joe Walter of Damaraland Trails and Tours. Few people know the Brandberg as intimately as Joe, who also has a wealth of knowledge on the rock art and flora of the mountain range.

Tour Operators **African Extravaganza** (☎ *264/61/37–2100* ⊕ *www.african-*

extravaganza.com). **African Kirikara Safaris** (☎ *264/62/58–1419* ⊕ *www. kiripotib.com*). **Damaraland Trails and Tours** (☎ *264/61/23–4610*). **Dune Hopper Air Taxis** (*NatureFriend Safaris* ☎ *264/61/23–4793* ⊕ *www.dunehopper.com*). **Elena Travel Services** (☎ *264/61/24–4443* info@namibweb.com). **NACOBTA** (☎ *264/61/25–0558* ⊕ *www.nacobta.com.na*). **Pasjona Safaris** (☎ *264/61/22–3421* ⊕ *www.pasjona-safaris.com*). **Skeleton Coast Fly-In Safaris** (☎ *264/61/22–4248* ⊕ *www.skeletoncoastsafaris.com*). **Wilderness Safaris** (☎ *27/11/257–5000* ⊕ *www.wilderness-safaris.com*).

Safari Primer

10

By Andrew
Barbour, Julian
Harrison, and
David Bristow

Updated by
Kate Turkington

MENTION AFRICA AND MOST OF us conjure up visions of wildlife—lions roaring as night falls, antelope cantering across the plains, a leopard dangling languidly from a tree. The images never fail to fascinate and draw us in, and once you experience them in the flesh, you're hooked. The look, the feel—the dusty smell—of the African bush seep into your soul, and long after you've gone you find yourself missing it with an almost physical longing.

Do everyone a favor, though, and pass up the impulse to rush out and buy khakis and a pith helmet. The old-time safari is dead. Hemingway and the great white hunters took it to their graves, along with thousands upon thousands of equally dead animals. Indeed, too many wildlife documentaries have conditioned foreign visitors into thinking that Africa is overrun with animals. The truth is far less romantic—and much safer—especially in South Africa, where fences or rivers enclose all major reserves. The African bush is no Disney-choreographed show, however; this wilderness is a real one.

In choosing to take a safari, you'll embark on one of the biggest travel adventures of your life. It's a big investment of both time and money—and planning well is crucial to ensure you have a good time. Even a basic question like "what should I wear?" is extremely important. In this safari section, we'll cover all the special considerations and lingo you'll need, with plenty of insider tips along the way.

GETTING STARTED

It's never too soon to start planning your safari. There are many factors to consider just regarding the destination: geography, animal migrations, weather, visa requirements, and inoculations. You must also weigh some personal factors: your budget, schedule, fitness level, and comfort requirements. Most people start planning a safari six to nine months in advance, which allows time to set a spending limit, choose an itinerary, and organize travel documents. You can wait and plan the trip over a few weeks, but doing so greatly increases your chances of being closed out of the places you really want to see. In fact, planning your trip 12 months in advance isn't unreasonable, especially if you want to travel during peak season—November through February in South Africa, July through October elsewhere—and have your heart set on a particular lodge.

Deciding where you want to go and choosing the safari operator in whose hands you'll place your trip are the most important things you need to do. Start planning for your safari the way you would any trip. Read travel books about the areas that most interest you. Talk to people who have been on a similar trip; word-of-mouth advice can be invaluable. Surf the net. Get inspired. Line up your priorities. And find someone you trust to help plan your trip.

CLOSE UP

Safari Planning Time Line

SIX MONTHS AHEAD
■ Research destinations and options, making a list of what you want to see.

■ Start a safari file to keep track of relevant information.

■ Set a budget.

■ Consult guidebooks and narrow your choices.

■ Search the Internet. Post questions on bulletin boards.

■ Contact a travel agent to start firming up details.

■ Choose your destination and make your reservations.

■ Buy travel insurance.

THREE TO SIX MONTHS AHEAD
■ Find out which travel documents you need.

■ Apply for a passport, or renew yours if it's due to expire within six months of travel time.

■ Confirm whether your destination requires visas and certified health documents.

■ Arrange vaccinations or medical clearances.

■ Research malaria precautions.

■ Book excursions, tours, etc.

ONE TO THREE MONTHS AHEAD
■ Create a packing checklist.

■ Fill prescriptions for medications; have enough for a few extra days.

■ Buy mosquito repellent.

■ Shop for safari clothing and equipment.

■ Arrange for a house sitter and a kennel for pets.

ONE MONTH AHEAD
■ Confirm flights, lodging reservations, and transfers.

■ Buy additional reading materials.

TWO WEEKS AHEAD
■ Buy traveler's checks and some local currency. Collect small U.S. bills for tips.

■ Dry-clean and wash clothes.

■ Get ready to pack; remember bag size and weight restrictions.

ONE WEEK AHEAD
■ Suspend newspaper and mail.

■ List contact numbers and other details for your house sitter.

■ Check antimalarial prescriptions to see whether you need to start taking medication now.

■ Arrange airport transport.

■ Make two copies of your passport's data page. Leave one copy, and a copy of your itinerary, with someone at home; pack the other separately from your passport.

A FEW DAYS AHEAD
■ Take pets to the kennel.

■ Pack.

■ Reconfirm flights.

■ Buy snacks and gum for the plane.

ONE DAY AHEAD
■ Enable your e-mail "out of office" message.

■ Check destination weather reports.

■ Check your house and go over your checklist one final time.

10

TRAVEL AGENTS & SAFARI OPERATORS

There's no substitute for a knowledgeable tour operator or travel agent who specializes in Africa. These specialists look out for your best interests, are aware of trends and developments, and function as indispensable backup in the rare instance when something goes wrong.

WHO'S WHO

African safari outfitter. Also referred to as a ground operator, this type of outfitter is a company in Africa that provides logistical support to a U.S.-based tour operator by seeing to the details of your safari. An outfitter might charter flights, pick you up at the airport, and take you on game-viewing trips, for example. Some outfitters own or manage safari lodges. In addition, an outfitter communicates changing trends and developments in the region to tour operators and serves as your on-site contact in cases of illness, injury, or other unexpected situations.

African-tour operator. Based in the United States, this type of company specializes in tours and safaris to Africa and works with a safari outfitter. Start dates and itineraries are set for some trips offered by the operator, but customized vacations can be arranged. Travelers usually find out about these trips through retail travel agents.

Air consolidator. A consolidator aggressively promotes and sells plane tickets to Africa, usually concentrating on a few airlines to ensure a large volume of sales with those particular carriers. The airlines provide greatly reduced airfares to the consolidator, who in turn adds a markup and resells them directly to you.

Retail travel agent. In general, a travel agent sells trip packages directly to consumers. In most cases an agent doesn't have a geographical specialty. When called on to arrange a trip to Africa, the travel agent turns to an African-tour operator for details. But before you entrust your trip to an agent, do your best to determine the extent of his or her knowledge as well as the level of enthusiasm for the destination. There are so many travel companies claiming to specialize in Africa that it's especially important to determine which operators and agents are up to the challenge.

After choosing a tour operator or travel agent, it's a good idea to discuss with him or her the logistics and details of the itinerary so you know what to expect each day. Ask questions about lodging, even if you're traveling on a group tour. A lodge that is completely open to the elements may be a highlight for some travelers and terrifying for others. Also inquire about the amount of time you'll spend with other travelers. If you're planning a safari honeymoon, find out if you can dine alone when you want to, and ask about honeymoon packages.

INTERNET CAVEAT

Although the Internet is useful for booking in Europe and other destinations with a sophisticated travel infrastructure in place, it's not an efficient option for Africa, where tangled, complicated logistics are usually the norm in trying to piece together an itinerary. The Web sites with discounted packages can be tempting, and you may be keen on

Questions to Ask a Safari Specialist

Don't forward a deposit to a safari specialist (a general term for a safari outfitter or African-tour operator) until you have considered his or her answers to these questions. Once you have paid a deposit, you're liable for a penalty if you decide to cancel the arrangements for any reason.

■ Do you handle Africa exclusively?

■ How many years have you been selling tours in Africa?

■ Are you or any of the staff native to the continent?

■ To which professional organizations do you belong? For example, the American Society of Travel Agents (ASTA) or the United States Tour Operators Association (USTOA)?

■ Has your company received any accolades or awards relating to Africa?

■ Can you provide a reference list of past clients?

■ How often do you and your staff visit Africa?

■ What sort of support do you have in Africa?

■ Do you charge a fee? (Agents and operators usually make their money through commissions.)

■ What is your cancellation policy?

■ Can you handle arrangements from start to finish, including flights?

bargain-hunting overall, but it's important to remember that a bargain price may get you a cut-rate experience.

You may manage to successfully put together a trip on your own, but you'll be just that—on your own—once in your safari destination. Faced with a challenge such as a canceled flight, or something more drastic—like the floods that swept through South Africa's Sabi Sands region a few years ago—you won't have anyone back home to help you with new arrangements. Well-established and well-connected safari specialists can take advantage of longstanding business relationships to secure the assistance their clients need, whether it be last-minute transportation or lodging or a way to communicate with family back home. Furthermore, many safari lodges, such as those run by Wilderness Safaris, require individuals to reserve through an African-tour operator or a travel agent.

10

WHAT'S YOUR BUDGET?

When setting a safari budget, you must consider how much you want to spend. You can have a low-budget self-catering trip in one of South Africa's national parks or spend a great deal of money in one of the small, pampering, exclusive camps in Botswana. Almost every market has high-priced options as well as some economical ones. When planning your safari budget, keep in mind three main factors: your flight, the actual safari costs, and extras.

LUXURY SAFARIS

The most popular safari-planning option is to book with a tour operator and stay in private lodges, which are owned and run by an individual or company rather than a government or country. Prices at these lodges include all meals and, in many cases, alcoholic beverages, as well as two three- to five-hour-long game-viewing expeditions a day. Occasionally high-end lodges offer extra services such as spa treatments, boat trips, or special-occasion meals served alfresco in the bush. Prices range from US$350 to US$1,600 per person per night sharing a double room. If you travel alone, you have to pay a single supplement because all safari-lodge rooms are doubles. Safari lodges with unique or especially extravagant facilities or options charge accordingly—up to US$1,500 per person per night. Those who can afford private lodges say they're worth every cent for the spectacular game-viewing, the knowledgeable guides, the well-prepared food, and the attention to detail.

SAFARIS ON A SHOESTRING

Don't let a tight budget deter you from a safari adventure. There are many opportunities for big-game experiences outside the luxury lodges. Your least expensive option is to choose one of the public game parks in southern Africa—Kruger National Park in South Africa, for example—where you drive yourself and self-cater (shop for and prepare all meals yourself). The price of this type of trip is approximately one-tenth of that for private, fully inclusive lodges.

Mobile safaris are another option. Travel is by 4x4 (often something that looks like a bus) and you sleep in tents at public or private camp-sites. Although self-drive safaris are popular with locals, you need to be self-sufficient and bush-savvy to travel this way.

Rates for the camps in national parks, called rest camps, start at about R235 a day for a two-bed *rondavel* and go up to R585 for a four-bed bungalow. Budget about R45 for breakfast, R55 for lunch, and R85 for dinner per person for each day on the trip. You also need to figure in the small entrance charges to the parks (usually a onetime fee of approximately R120 per person).

Booking a private lodge in the off-season also saves a bundle of money. Many lodges, in the Sabi Sands area of South Africa, for example, usually cost about US$800 per person per night during the high season but can drop to approximately US$500 a night during the slower months of July and August.

THE EXTRAS

Besides airfare and safari costs, make sure you budget for tips, medications, film, and other sundries. Plan to stay at a city hotel on your first and last nights in Africa—it'll help you adjust to jet lag and makes things altogether easier. Expect to pay from US$50 for basic accommodations to a maximum US$750 a night in the most luxurious hotels.

Plan to spend, on average, US$15 to US$25 a day (per traveler) on gratuities. In South Africa tips are on the higher end of this range and usually are paid in rand; you may also use U.S. dollars for tips, however. Elsewhere in southern Africa, U.S. currency is preferable, but tips paid in rand may also be accepted.

If you haven't yet gone digital, stock up on film before you head out into the bush; a roll of regular print film costs about US$10 in South Africa and soars to US$20 in a safari camp. And don't forget to put some money aside for souvenirs.

WHERE & WHEN TO GO

The countries covered in this book are in the southern hemisphere, and their seasons are opposite to those in the northern hemisphere. Winter runs from about June through September, spring from October through November, summer from December through March, and fall from April through May.

To make the most of your trip, plan to spend at least two nights at any one place—be it a private lodge or a rest camp. Game-viewing can't be rushed. Racing around from camp to camp is a waste of time and money—give yourself the pleasure of slowing down, appreciating your surroundings, and taking in the sights and sounds of the bush. It's also important to remember that the concept of time in Africa is different from Western time. Patience and good humor are often needed here.

South African safari destinations are covered in the pertinent regional chapters of this book. Safari destinations in neighboring Namibia and Botswana are discussed in Chapter 9, Botswana & Namibia's Best Safari Destinations.

TIMING

No two people can agree on the best time to visit the bush. Summer (December–March) is certainly hot, with afternoon rain a good possibility, but the bush is green, the animals are sleek and glossy, and the birdlife is prolific. Unfortunately, it's the worst time of year to spot game. All the foliage makes finding game harder, and animals tend to disperse over a wide area because they are no longer reliant on water holes and rivers. Winter, on the other hand, is a superb time for game-viewing because trees are bare and animals congregate around the few remaining water sources. Because the weather's cooler, you may also see lions and leopards hunting by day. Most lodges drop their rates dramatically during winter months, often lopping as much as 30%–40% off their peak-season prices. The drawbacks to a winter visit are the cold and the fact that the bush looks dead and the animals thin.

A happy compromise may be the shoulder seasons. Overall, in October and most of November the weather is pleasant, the trees have blossoms, and migrant birds are arriving—even better, the antelope herds begin to drop their young. In April the temperature is also fine, many of the migrant birds are still around, and the annual rutting season has begun, when males compete for the right to mate with females and are much more visible.

10

In **South Africa,** summer—that is, November through February—is high season because that's when South Africans take their vacations. However, the weather can be hot, with temperatures frequently reaching 100°F in January and February. There's also the rain; in Kruger, the Kalahari, and Zululand, the annual rains fall from late November through February, mostly in the form of afternoon thundershowers. In many safari locations, including Kruger, summer is the high malaria season. The remainder of the year is predominantly dry and, as there are no mass migrations, the game-viewing is good almost year-round. In winter some areas stay mild (Zululand among them), but others get very cold. For instance, in July temperatures in Kruger can dip down to the freezing point, and in the Kalahari temperatures can drop to 10°F. The winter months, July and August, are considered the low season, and therefore fewer tourists frequent the private lodges. ■TIP➡ **This is a superb time for game-viewing, and you can find some great deals.**

In **Botswana** the tourism high season corresponds to the dry season: winter, roughly July through October. Although winter days are warm— 70°F to 85°F—nights can be cold, down around 35°F. The rains arrive in late November and last through February, generally in the form of afternoon thundershowers. When these showers turn into electrical storms, the weather show can rival the most elaborate fireworks display. The threat of malaria is highest during these wet months, when mosquitoes breed. (Some 95% of malaria cases in Botswana occur December through May.) Summer days are usually in the 85°F to 100°F range. It's considered the off-season. The shoulder months of June and November are considered mostly low season, and are great times to view game at much-reduced costs.

The best time to travel to **Namibia** is winter, May through October. Winter days may be warm, but winter nights are cold to downright freezing. Rain usually falls in summer, with a short rainy season in November and the main rainy season from February to March, which is also prime malaria season. In the Namib Desert, rain sometimes doesn't fall for 10 years or more.

NATIONAL PARKS & GAME RESERVES

SOUTH AFRICA

South Africa has more than a dozen national parks and a host of provincial reserves, but only a few contain all the indigenous species that once roamed the veld in vast herds. Good roads, plentiful and cheap accommodations, and excellent facilities are what differentiate South African parks from their East African counterparts.

But if you picture yourself bouncing in an old Land Rover through an untouched golden landscape in pursuit of big game, South Africa's national parks will disappoint you. They bear less resemblance to the Serengeti than to America's national parks: they are superbly managed, sometimes overcrowded, and bear the marks of civilization.

Take Kruger National Park, for instance. It's a magnificent tract of pristine wilderness that is home to an astonishing number of animals. Like all South Africa's parks, it's completely open to the public, and you can tour and view game from the comfort of your own car. In fact, you could tour Kruger in a Porsche if you so desired. Many of the park roads are paved, and rangers even set up speed traps to nail overzealous game-watchers (take your car off-road and the dung will really hit the fan). Signposts throughout the park direct visitors to everything from scenic viewpoints to picnic sites and rest areas selling soft drinks and snacks. But this is not a petting zoo. One or two animals are killed each year to save visitors in harm's way.

The national parks look the way they do for good reason: they are the country's natural heritage, set up for the use and enjoyment of its citizens, but South Africa's game parks are becoming more attuned to foreign travelers and their expectations. Accommodations in the rest camps are cheap, comfortable, but numbingly institutional. In Kruger the South African National Parks symbol—the head of a kudu bull—is plastered over everything from your towel to the bathroom walls. All camps are fenced against the animals, and some have better facilities than small towns: gas stations, mechanics, grocery stores, laundromats, cafeterias, restaurants—even a car wash, but the restaurants' food tends to be mediocre. Not surprisingly, many foreign visitors shy away from the rest camps, dreaming instead of something more remote or more glamorous. If that's you, check out the bushveld camps in Kruger, which are more expensive than the regular camps but offer excellent accommodations, exclusivity, and, as always, great game-viewing.

Don't write off the public parks too quickly. Few people can afford to stay in the exclusive private lodges more than a few days, and the game reserves offer a chance to explore some of Africa's richest and most beautiful country at a fraction of the cost, especially if you drive yourself. Armed with a good field guide, you can learn an enormous amount about African game from the driver's seat of a rental car.

BOTSWANA AND NAMIBIA

National parks in Botswana and Namibia vary a great deal, although they're much more geared to foreign visitors than they were a few years ago. They have more facilities and a better understanding of tourists and their needs. Botswana's "low impact–high cost" tourism policy makes the national parks very pricey; park fees are more than US$30 per person *per day*. There are no permanent hutted camps, only camping sites, often in quite inaccessible places, and you will certainly need a 4×4 to get to most of them. Unless you have a lot of time and determination, stick to private lodges. Remember that the Okavango, for example, is a watery wilderness where most places are accessible only by plane or boat. Though roads between cities and towns are good (watch out for stray domestic animals and game), those in the parks are dirt roads (mud when wet) and sometimes almost impossible to drive. However, Namibia's Etosha National Park is a great place to drive yourself. There are both bush roads and paved roads between the hutted camps and excellent facilities at all the camps. And there's nothing quite like doing your own thing—stopping when you please, spending hours checking out the game at a water hole, and spotting your "very own" elephant. Namibia has an excellent tourism infrastructure, with simple but clean and comfortable accommodations in all its national parks. Road conditions vary a lot; check out conditions on a daily basis. ■TIP→ Always book national park accommodations well in advance.

PRIVATE GAME RESERVES & CONCESSIONS

In southern Africa game areas bordering national parks and other tracts of wilderness have been sectioned into private areas and leased to safari companies who then have the exclusive right to build game lodges and traverse the area for game drives or other activities. This concession system is now being extended into the national parks themselves, as government conservation authorities let private operators handle the tourism side of the business.

Staying on a private game reserve is a much more expensive option than staying in a national park, but if you can afford it, don't miss out, because private reserves offer a wildlife experience without parallel. You can get close to the animals because, after many years of exposure, they no longer see the game vehicles as a threat. That doesn't mean they don't sometimes object to your presence: an elephant charge will clear out more than your sinuses.

The rangers know the reserves intimately, and can introduce you to sights and sounds that you would have missed on your own: a medicinal shrub, a male dung beetle busily rolling its ball of dung to a suitable site, a lion ant trapping its prey. On game drives at bigger camps rangers stay in contact with one another via radio, so that if one group has a good sighting, other vehicles can come have a look, too. Most lodges coordinate this carefully, so that there's not too much traffic at any one sighting.

Although the quality of the game-viewing and the expertise of the staff are major attractions of a private game reserve, there's also the fantasy aspect. The lodges on the reserves and concessions also sell exclusivity, and many of them unite luxury and bush living. You'll get chic design, comfortable beds, flush toilets, running water, hot showers—even air-conditioning—but the bush still lies right outside your door. Nothing stops an elephant from joining you for dinner. For more details on the luxury lodge experience, *see* Types of Safaris, *below.*

TYPES OF SAFARIS

Do you picture yourself zipping from camp to camp in a tiny Cessna, getting a bird's-eye view of a water hole? Or inspecting an animal track up close while on a multiday walk through the bush? Since there are many kinds of safaris, you should think hard about what approach suits

Safari Speak

The following words and terms are used throughout the book.

Big Five: buffalos, elephants, leopards, lions, and rhinoceros, collectively

Boma: a fenced-in open-air eating area, usually circular

Braai: barbecue

Bush or bushveld: general safari area in South Africa, usually with scattered shrubs and trees and lots of game; also referred to as the bush or the veld

Camp: used interchangeably with lodge

Campground: a place used for camping that encompasses several campsites and often includes some shared facilities

Campsite: may or may not be part of a campground

Concession: game-area lease that is granted to a safari company and gives it exclusive access to the land

Game guide: used interchangeably with ranger; usually a man

Hides: small, partially camouflaged shelters from which to view game and birds; blinds

Kraal: traditional rural settlement of huts and houses

Lodge: accommodation in rustic-yet-stylish tents, rondavels, or lavish suites; prices at lodges usually include all meals and game-viewing

Mobile or overland safari: usually a self-sufficient, camping affair set up at a different location (at public or private campgrounds) each night

Mokoro: dugout canoe; plural *mekoro*

Ranger: safari guide with vast experience with and knowledge of the bush and the animals that inhabit it; used interchangeably with game guide

Rest camp: camp in a national park

Rondavel/rondawel: a traditional, round dwelling with a conical roof

Self-catering: with some kind of kitchen facilities, so you can store food and prepare meals yourself

Self-drive safari: budget-safari option in which you drive, and guide, yourself in a rented vehicle

Tracker: works in conjunction with a ranger, spotting animals from a special seat on the front of the 4×4 game-viewing vehicle

Veld: a grassland; see bushveld

Vlei: wetland or marsh

10

you best. There are high- and low-end versions of each option, and you can always mix and match options to create your ideal itinerary.

LUXURY LODGE-BASED SAFARIS

The majority of safari goers base their trips at luxury lodges, which pack the double punch of outstanding game-viewing and stylish, atmospheric accommodations. A lodge may be made up of stone chalets, thatch-roof huts, rondavels, or large suitelike tents. Mosquito nets, leather furnishings, and mounted trophies add to the ambience. Dinners are served in an open-air *boma*. All have hot-and-cold running water, flush toilets, toiletries, laundry service, electricity, and, in most cases, swimming pools. In South African lodges rooms also have air-conditioning, telephones, hair dryers, and minibars. The most lavish places also have private plunge pools.

Make no mistake—you pay for all this pampering. Expect to spend anywhere from R3,000 to R10,000 (US$400 to US$1,300) per person

> **STAR STRUCK**
>
> You'll be awed by the brilliance of the night skies on safari, especially if you live in a city. To add romance and interest to your star-gazing, study up on the southern skies and bring a star guide. Also most guides are knowledgeable about the stars, so ask questions.

per night, depending on the season. All meals, beverages, house wines, game drives, and walks are included. A three-night stay is ideal, but two nights are usually sufficient to see the big game.

The time you spend at a private lodge is tightly structured. With some exceptions, the lodges offer almost identical programs of events. There are usually two three- to four-hour game drives a day, one in the early morning and another in the evening. You spend a lot of time sitting and eating, and in the afternoon you can nap and relax. However, you can always opt for an after-breakfast bush walk, and many lodges now have spas and gyms. If you're tired after your night drive, ask for something to be sent to your room, but don't miss the bush *braai* and at least one night in the boma.

On game drives at bigger camps, rangers stay in contact with one another via radio. If one finds a rhino, for example, he relays its location to the others so they can bring their guests to have a look. It's a double-edged sword. The more vehicles you have in the field, the more wildlife everyone is likely to see. But don't worry, most lodges are very well disciplined with their vehicles and there are rarely more than three or four vehicles at a sighting. As your vehicle arrives, one already there will drive away. In choosing a game lodge, remember to check how much land a lodge can traverse and how many vehicles it uses. Try to go on a bush walk with an armed ranger—an unforgettable experience, as the ranger can point out fascinating details along the way.

All lodges arrange transfers from nearby airports, train stations, or drop-off points, as the case may be. In more remote areas most have their own private airstrips carved out of the bush and fly guests in on chartered aircraft at extra cost. If you're driving yourself, the lodge will send you detailed instructions, because many of the roads don't appear on maps and lack names.

FLY-IN SAFARIS

The mode of transportation for fly-in safaris is as central to the experience as the accommodations. In places such as northern Botswana, where few roads are paved, or northern Namibia, where distances make road transfers impractical, small bush planes take you from lodge to lodge. These planes are usually six-seat Cessna 206 craft flown by bush pilots. The planes have no air-conditioning, and in summer can be very hot indeed, especially in the afternoon. But most flights are short—approximately 30 minutes or so—so bite the bullet or you'll miss out on some of the really fabulous destinations.

However, flying from destination to destination is a special experience. The planes stay at low altitudes, allowing you to spot game along the way: you might see elephant and buffalo herds lined up drinking along the edges of remote water holes, or large numbers of zebras walking across the plains. Fly-in safaris also allow you to cover more territory than other types of safaris. In Botswana, for example, the trip between the diverse game destinations of the Moremi Wildlife Reserve in the Okavango Delta and northern Chobe National Park is 40 minutes by plane; it would take six hours by vehicle, if a road between these locations existed.

Hopping from place to place by plane is so easy and fast that many travelers make the mistake of cramming their itineraries with too many lodges. Plan your trip this way and you'll spend more time at airstrips, in planes, and shuttling to and from the airfields than tracking animals or enjoying the bush. You will glimpse animals as you travel back and forth—sometimes you'll even see them on the airstrips—but you won't have time to stop and really take in the sights. If possible, spend at least two nights at any one lodge; three nights is even better.

The best way to set up a fly-in safari is to book an all-inclusive package that includes airfare. (It's impractical to try to do it yourself.) A tour operator makes all the arrangements, and many offer standard trips that visit several of its lodges. For example, in Botswana, Orient-Express Safaris has a package that includes three camps in three very different locations.

LIGHTEN UP

The key to fly-in safaris is to pack light. In southern Africa the maximum weight allowed for luggage is 26 pounds (South Africa is the exception to this rule). Your bag should be a soft-sided duffel or something similar, so the pilot can easily fit it into the small cargo area. At most private lodges laundry is included.

△ **If your bag is over the weight limit, or if you weigh more than 220 pounds, you will be required to purchase an additional plane seat (usually about US$100).**

10

WALKING SAFARIS

Many lodges offer walks as an optional way to view game. On a walking safari, however, you spend most, if not all, of your time in the bush on foot, accompanied by an armed guide. Because you're trekking through big-game country, there's an element of danger. But it's the proximity to wilderness that makes this type of trip so enchanting—and exciting. Of course, you can't stop every step of the way or you'd never get very far, but you will stop frequently to be shown something—from a native flower to spoor to animals—or to discuss some aspect of animal behavior or of tracking.

Walking treks take place on what are known as wilderness trails, which are natural tracks made by animals and are traversed only on foot, never by vehicle, to maintain their pristine condition. These trails usually lead into remote areas that you would never see on a typical safari. In most cases porters or donkeys carry the supplies and bags. Accommodation is usually in remote camps or occasionally in tents.

The Umfolozi Wilderness Area of South Africa's Hluhluwe-Umfolozi Game Reserve, where wilderness trails were pioneered, is a popular walking safari destination. Kruger's wilderness trails, where national-park rangers guide you, are also excellent; trails need to be reserved 13 months in advance, when bookings become available.

■TIP➔ **If you consider a walking safari, you must factor in your physical condition.** You should be in good health and be able to walk between 4 and 10 mi a day, depending on the parameters of the trip. Some trips don't allow hikers under age 12 or over age 60. Also, you shouldn't scare easily. No guide has time for people who freeze up at the sight of a beetle, spider, or something more menacing up close; guides need to keep their attention on the wilds around them and on the group as a whole. The guides are armed, and they take great caution to keep you away from trouble. Your best insurance against getting in harm's way is to always listen to your guide and follow instructions.

Walking trails are usually three days, four nights. Expect to pay R2,150 for a national-parks walking trail.

MOBILE & OVERLAND SAFARIS

Most mobile-safari operations are expertly run but are aimed at budget-conscious travelers; prices are especially low if you book with a local operator after arriving in South Africa. They are mostly self-sufficient camping affairs with overnights at either public or private campgrounds, depending on the safari's itinerary and price. Sometimes you stay at basic lodges along the way. Travel is often by something that looks like a 4×4 bus.

For young people, or the young at heart, mobile safaris are a great way to see the land from ground level. You taste the dust, smell the bacon cooking, stop where and when you want (within reason), and get to see some of the best places in the region. Trips usually run 14 to 21 days, although you can find shorter ones that cover fewer destinations. Prices start at US$750 and climb to US$2,500 for all-inclusive trips. Not sure whether all-inclusive is right for you? Consider combining a mobile safari with a lodge-based one, which gives you the best of both worlds. A minimum of 10 nights is recommended for such an itinerary.

Treading Lightly

What is true ecotourism? It's difficult to say because the term is widely used but lacks a widely accepted definition. In general, however, ecotourism aims to expose travelers to natural areas, preferably those areas practicing sustainable land use while conserving these very places; to educate travelers about the physical and/or cultural environment of these areas; and to bring about positive developments for the local communities. Not every safari strives to achieve all these goals.

Definitions aside, you should, on a basic level, care and be informed about the environment and the people you visit, particularly in places where living conditions are poor. What can you do? For starters, ask your tour operator and safari outfitter for specifics about how their trips are run and what their relationship is to the local communities where the trips are held. You can also ask specific questions about ecological measures, such as whether the lodges utilize solar power and conserve water. Don't litter, pay too much or too little for services and curios or souvenirs (ask locals for advice), or feed wild animals. If you'd like to help local conservation efforts or support local communities, ask about funds and trusts set up by safari operators, and make a donation. And try to heed the ethic of taking only photographs and leaving only your footprints—but do have fun along the way.

SELF-DRIVE SAFARIS

This is a great option for budget travelers and for those who feel comfortable seeing the bush without a ranger at hand to search out game or explain what you're seeing. The two most popular and easiest-to-navigate options for this kind of trip are Kruger National Park in South Africa and Etosha National Park in Namibia. These two parks have paved, well-marked roads and a wide range of accommodations that include family-size chalets, small huts, tents, and camping sites. You may buy your own groceries and cook for yourself at all of these areas; some options, especially in Kruger, have restaurants and stores on-site.

If possible, rent a van or a 4×4, since the higher off the ground you are the better your chances of spotting game, and you can stop and start at your leisure; remember that you have to stick to marked roads. In addition to patience, you'll need drinks, snacks, and a ready camera. Keep your eyes and ears open and you may come across game at any time, in any place.

■TIP→ **Purchase a good park map that shows roads, watering holes, different ecozones, and the types of animals you can expect to find in each.** It's no good driving around open grassland searching for black rhinos when the lumbering browsers are miles away in a woodland region. You can buy these maps when you enter a park or at rest-camp shops.

When planning your day's game drive, plot your route around as many water holes and rivers as possible. Except during the height of the summer rains, most game must come to permanent water sources to drink. In winter, when the land is at its most parched, a tour of water holes is bound to reap great rewards. Even better, take a picnic lunch along and park at the same watering hole for an hour or two, especially in winter, when the car interior doesn't become too hot. Not only will you see plenty of animals, but you'll find yourself slipping into the drama of the bush.

GETTING READY TO GO

If you take the time to manage the details before you leave, the only bumps on your safari should be in your 4×4 as you traverse the African bush.

THE PAPER TRAIL

A valid passport is a must for travel to any African country. If you don't have a passport, apply immediately, because the process takes approximately five to six weeks. For a greatly increased fee, the application process can be shortened to as little as one week, but leaving this detail to the last minute can be stressful. If you have a passport, check the expiration date; if it's due to expire within six months of your return date, you need to renew your passport at once. ⚠ **Certain countries, such as South Africa, won't let you enter with a soon-to-expire passport; you also need two blank pages in your passport to enter South Africa.**

Check on what immunizations are required for the countries you're visiting. Some countries may demand an inoculation certificate if you arrive directly from a tropical area or have traveled to one prior to your safari trip.

If you're taking a self-driving safari or will be renting a car in countries other than South Africa and Namibia, you'll need an international driver's license. These licenses are valid for one year and are issued at any American Automobile Association (AAA) office in the United States; you must have a current U.S. driver's license. You need to bring two passport-type photographs with you for the license. A valid U.S. driver's license is accepted in South Africa and Namibia.

■TIP➔ **If you're planning a honeymoon safari, make sure the bride's airline ticket, passport, and visas all use the same last name.** Any discrepancies, especially between a passport and an airline ticket, will result in your trip being grounded before you ever take off. Brides may want to consider waiting to change their last name until after the honeymoon. And be sure to let the lodge know in advance that you are on your honeymoon. You'll get lots of special goodies and extra-special pampering thrown in.

TRAVEL INSURANCE

Get a comprehensive travel-insurance policy in addition to any primary insurance you already have. Travel insurance incorporates trip cancellation; trip interruption or travel delay; loss or theft of, or damage to,

CLOSE UP

Document Checklist

- Passport
- Visas, if necessary
- Airline tickets
- Proof of yellow-fever inoculation
- Accommodation and transfer vouchers
- Car-rental reservation forms
- International driver's license
- Copy of information page of your passport
- Copy of airline tickets

- Copy of medical prescriptions
- Copy of traveler's check numbers
- List of credit-card numbers and international contact information for each card issuer
- Copy of travel insurance and medical-emergency evacuation policy
- Travel agent's contact numbers
- Notarized letter of consent from one parent if the other parent is traveling alone with their children

baggage; baggage delay; medical expenses; emergency medical transportation; and collision damage waiver if renting a car. These policies are offered by most travel-insurance companies in one comprehensive policy, and vary in price based on your total trip cost and your age.

TIP→ Purchase travel insurance within seven days of paying your initial trip deposit. For most policies this will not only ensure your trip deposit, but also cover you for any preexisting medical conditions and default by most airlines and safari companies. The latter two are not covered if your policy is purchased after seven days.

Many travel agents and tour operators stipulate that travel insurance is mandatory if you book your trip through them. This coverage is not only for your financial protection in the event of a cancellation but also for coverage of medical emergencies and medical evacuations due to injury or illness, which often involve use of jet aircraft with hospital equipment and doctors on board and can amount to many thousands of dollars.

10

If you need emergency medical evacuation, most travel-insurance companies stipulate that you must obtain authorization by the company prior to the evacuation. Unfortunately, many safari camps and lodges are so remote that they don't have access to a telephone, so getting prior authorization is extremely difficult if not impossible. You should check with your insurance company before you leave to see whether it has this clause and if so, what can be done to get around it. Good travel agents and tour operators are aware of the issue and will address it.

MONEY MATTERS

Most safaris are paid for in advance, so you need money only to cover personal purchases and gratuities. (The cash you take should include small denominations, like US$1, US$5, and US$10, for tips.) If you're not on a packaged tour and are self-driving, you need to carry more money. Credit cards—MasterCard, Visa, and, to a much lesser extent, American Express and Diners Club—are accepted throughout South Africa (American Express and, for the most part, Diners Club are not accepted in Botswana) and at most group-owned lodges and hotels, but not much elsewhere. Always check in advance whether your preferred card is accepted at the lodge. If you're self-driving, note that many places prefer to be paid in the local currency, so make sure you change money where you can.

■ TIP➡ **It's a good idea to notify your credit-card company that you'll be traveling to Africa, so that unusual-looking transactions aren't denied.**

HEALTH ISSUES

If you stick to cities and safari lodges you won't be at an exaggerated health risk for most diseases. The real danger is malaria, but by taking the necessary precautions you should be well protected.

MALARIA

Malaria is the most common parasitic infection in the world. It occurs throughout the tropics and in adjacent hot and low-lying areas and infects 300 to 500 million people each year in some 90 countries, killing between 1.5 million and 3 million. Malaria infects about 10,000 returning travelers each year, killing about 1% of them. However, malaria is preventable and shouldn't prevent you from going on safari.

The disease is spread by the female Anopheles mosquito, who "feeds" between dusk and dawn, usually after midnight when you are most soundly asleep. If you have been bitten by an infected mosquito, you can expect to feel the effects anywhere from 7 to 90 days afterward. Typically you will feel like you have the flu, with worsening high fever, chills and sweats, headache, and muscle aches. In some cases this is accompanied by abdominal pain, diarrhea, and a cough. If it's not treated you could die. It's possible to treat malaria after you have contracted it, but this shouldn't be your long-term strategy for dealing with the disease.

■ TIP➡ **If you feel ill even several months after you return home, tell your doctor that you have been in a malaria-infected area.** The onset of flulike symptoms—aching joints or headache—is often the first sign that you have contracted either tick-bite fever (a bacterial infection transmitted by ticks, with symptoms including fever, severe headache, and a rash consisting of small red bumps) or malaria. Take it very seriously and go for a blood test immediately.

The first malarial protection method is to practice "safe safari"—that is, avoid getting bitten in the first place. Start your precautions by treating your clothes with a mosquito-repellent spray or laundry wash before you leave home. Most of these last approximately 14 days and through several washings and contain the active ingredient permethrin, which is sold as Permanone and Duranon. This spray is specifically for clothes and shouldn't be used on skin. You can find it at camping and outdoor stores such as Eastern Mountain Sports. Bring a mosquito-repellent spray that contains DEET and light-colored clothing, as mosquitoes (and tsetse flies) are attracted to dark surfaces, where they're hard to detect. For more tips on what to do once you're on safari, see the malaria section of Health on Safari, *below.*

There's no vaccine against malaria, but there are several medications you can use to protect yourself from getting the disease. It's vital that you take the prescribed dosage and the full course of the antimalarial medication, because the incubation period for malaria can last up to four weeks after your return. Not taking even the last tablet of a multiweek course can mask the disease for several months; when it does erupt it will be more advanced and harder to detect than if you had followed the full regimen. Medication improves all the time, so consult your doctor or travel clinic for up-to-date information.

Where children are concerned, you cannot be too safe. The CDC (Center for Disease Control and Prevention) recommends that parents of children traveling to a malarial area see a doctor four to six weeks prior to the trip. Make sure you find out which prescription antimalaria drugs are approved for use by children. Malaria's effects on young children are much worse than they are on older people, and both the effects of malaria and the side effects of malarial prophylactics put strain on young kidneys. For this and other health reasons, it's best not to visit malarial areas with children under age 10 unless you practice stringent nonchemical preventive measures. Another, easier option is to choose a nonmalarial safari destination, including the Waterberg, Pilanesberg and Sun City, or the Eastern Cape in South Africa, or Etosha National Park in Namibia.

OTHER HEALTH ISSUES
Yellow fever isn't inherent in any of the countries discussed in this book. Southern countries may, however, require you to present a valid yellow-fever inoculation certificate if prior to arrival you traveled to a region infected with yellow fever, so it's always best to carry one.

Hepatitis A can be transmitted via contaminated seafood, water, or fruits and vegetables. According to the CDC, hepatitis A is the most common vaccine-preventable disease in travelers. Immunization consists of a series of two shots received six months apart. You need have received only the first one before you travel. This should be given at least four weeks before your trip.

The CDC recommends vaccination for hepatitis B only if you might be exposed to blood (if you are a health-care worker, for example), have sexual contact with the local population, stay longer than six months, or risk exposure during medical treatment. As needed, you should receive booster shots for tetanus-diphtheria (every 10 years), measles (you're usually immunized as a child), and polio (you're usually immunized as a child).

10

WHAT TO PACK

If you're flying to safari destinations with regular airports where large airplanes are used—Hoedspruit or Nelspruit's Kruger Mpumalanga International Airport, both in South Africa—normal international airline baggage allowances apply. Otherwise, access to game-viewing areas is often by light aircraft, on short sandy landing strips; therefore, luggage weight restrictions are strictly enforced. You'll be allowed one duffel-type bag, approximately 36 inches by 18 inches, so that it can be easily packed into the baggage pods of a small plane. One small camera and personal-effects bag can go on your lap. Keep all your documents and money in this personal bag.

Do yourself a favor and leave breakables and valuables at home. If you'd be heartbroken if an item was broken or lost, it probably doesn't belong on a safari.

■TIP➔ At O.R. Tambo International Airport in Johannesburg you can check bags at Lock-Up Luggage, one level below international departures. The cost is approximately US$7 per bag per day.

CLOTHING

You should need only three changes of clothing for an entire trip; almost all safaris include laundry as part of the package. If you're self-driving you can carry more, but washing is still easy and three changes of clothes should be ample if you use drip-dry fabrics that need no ironing. On mobile safaris you can wear tops and bottoms more than once, and either bring enough underwear to last a week between lodges, or wash as you go in the bathroom sink. Unless there's continual rain (unlikely), clothes dry overnight in the hot, dry African air.

■TIP➔ In certain countries—Botswana, for example—the staff won't wash underwear because it's against cultural custom.

For game walks, pack sturdy but light walking shoes or boots—in most cases durable sneakers suffice for this option. For a walking-based safari you need sturdy, lightweight boots. Buy them well in advance of your trip so you can break them in. If possible, isolate the clothes used on your walk from the remainder of the clean garments in your bag. Bring a couple of large white plastic garbage bags for dirty laundry.

TOILETRIES & SUNDRIES

Most hotels and game lodges provide toiletries such as soap, shampoo, and insect repellent, so you don't need to overpack these items. In the larger lodges in South Africa's national parks and private game reserves, stores and gift shops are fairly well stocked with clothing, film, and guidebooks; in self-drive and self-catering areas, shops also carry food and drink. In Botswana, lodges that belong to groups such as Wilderness Safaris or Gametrackers have small shops with a limited selection of books, clothing, film, and curios. Elsewhere in Africa you're not likely to find this type of amenity on safari.

CLOSE UP

Packing Checklist

Light-, khaki-, or neutral-colored clothes are universally worn on safari and were first used in Africa as camouflage by the South African Boers, and then by the British army that fought them during the South African War. Light colors also help to deflect the harsh sun and, unlike dark colors, are less likely to attract mosquitoes. Do not wear camouflage gear. Do wear layers of clothing that you can strip off as the sun gets hotter and put back on as the sun goes down.

■ Three cotton T-shirts

■ Two long-sleeve cotton shirts

■ Two pairs shorts or two skirts in summer

■ Two pairs long pants (three pairs in winter)

■ Optional: sweatshirt and pants, which can double as sleepwear

■ Optional: a smart/casual dinner outfit

■ Underwear and socks

■ Walking shoes or sneakers

■ Sandals

■ Bathing suit

■ Warm thigh-length padded jacket, and sweater, in winter

■ Lightweight jacket in summer

■ Windbreaker or rain poncho

■ Camera equipment, plenty of film, and extra batteries

■ Contact lenses, including extras

■ Eyeglasses

■ Binoculars

■ Small flashlight

■ Personal toiletries

■ Malaria tablets

■ Sunscreen and lip balm with SPF 30 or higher, moisturizer, and hair conditioner

■ Antihistamine cream

■ Insect repellent

■ Basic first-aid kit (aspirin, bandages, antidiarrheal, antiseptic cream, etc.)

■ Tissues and/or premoistened wipes

■ Warm hat, scarf, and gloves (for winter)

■ Sun hat and sunglasses (Polaroid and UV-protected ones)

■ Documents and money (cash, traveler's checks, credit cards, etc.)

■ A notebook and pens

■ Travel and field guides

■ A couple of large, white, plastic garbage bags

■ U.S. dollars in small denominations ($1, $5, $10) for tipping

10

On a canoe safari you're in the relentless sun every day and have to protect your legs, especially the tops of your thighs and shins, from sunburn. Bring a towel or, even better, a sarong, and place it over your legs. Sunscreen of SPF 30 or higher is de rigueur.

■TIP➔**The African sun is harsh, and if you're even remotely susceptible to burning, especially coming from a northern winter, don't skimp on sunscreens and moisturizers.** Also bring conditioner for your hair, which can dry out and start breaking off.

PLUGGING IN

Most of southern Africa is on 220/240 volt alternating current (AC). The plug points are round. However, there are both large 15-amp three-prong sockets (with a ground connection) and smaller two-prong 5-amp sockets. Most lodges have adapter plugs, especially for recharging camera batteries; check before you go, or purchase a universal plug adapter before you leave home.

Safari hotels in the Serengeti, the private reserve areas outside Kruger National Park, and the less-rustic private lodges in South Africa are likely to provide you with plug points and plugs, and some offer hair dryers and electric-razor sockets as well (check this before you go). Lodges on limited generator and solar power are usually able to charge camera batteries, so long as you have the right plug.

BINOCULARS

Binoculars are essential and come in many types and sizes. You get what you pay for, so avoid buying a cheap pair—the optics will be poor and the lenses usually don't stay aligned for long, especially if they get bumped, which they will on safari. Whatever strength you choose, pick the most lightweight pair, otherwise you'll be in for neck and shoulder strain. Take them with you on a night drive; you'll get great visuals of nocturnal animals and birds by the light of the tracker's spotlight. Many people find that when they start using binoculars and stop documenting each trip detail on film, they have a much better safari experience.

CAMERA SMARTS

All the safaris included in this book are photographic (game-viewing) safaris. That said, if you spend your entire safari with one eye closed and the other peering through a camera lens, you may miss all the other sensual elements that contribute to the great show that is the African bush. And more than likely, your pictures won't look like the photos you see in books about African safaris. A professional photographer can spend a full year in the field to produce a book, so you are often better off just taking snaps of your trip and buying a book to take home.

■ TIP→ No matter what kind of camera you bring, be sure to keep it tightly sealed in plastic bags while you're traveling to protect it from dust. (Dust is especially troublesome in Namibia.) Tuck your equipment away when the wind kicks up. You should have one or more cloth covers while you're shooting, and clean your equipment every day if you can.

Learning some basics about the wildlife that you expect to see on your safari will help you capture some terrific shots of the animals. If you know something about their behavior patterns ahead of time, you'll be primed to capture action, like when the hippos start to roar. Learning from your guide and carefully observing the wildlife once you're there will also help you gauge just when to click your shutter.

PHOTOGRAPHY POINTERS

The trick to taking great pictures has three components: first is always good light. An hour after sunrise and before sunset are the magic times, because the light is softer and textures pop. For the few hours of harsh light each side of midday, you might as well put your camera away. The second component is framing. Framing a scene so that the composition is simple gives an image potency; with close-ups, fill the frame for maximum impact. Using objects of known size in the foreground or middle ground will help establish scale. The third component is capturing sharp images: use a tripod or a beanbag to rest the camera on while in a vehicle. When using a long lens (upward of 200mm), you cannot hand-hold a steady shot; you must have some support if you want your photos to be clear.

For point-and-shoot cameras, you should use a 35mm camera with at least a 300mm lens and some sort of support. No matter what camera you use, you're bound to take an embarrassing number of bum shots—animals caught fleeing—so it pays to shoot bucketloads of film. You may want to pack a couple of disposable cameras that allow you to take panoramic shots. You should also take lots of film with you because it's not always available on safaris. Also, take spare batteries—two sets of spares if you're going for longer than a week.

DIGITAL CAMERAS

Good digital cameras and their memory cards or sticks may be more expensive than basic 35mm cameras, but the benefits of being able to preview shots, select what you want and delete what you don't, store them, and then adjust them on a computer can outweigh the initial cost. The resolution of nonprofessional digital images is approaching that of good film. Cameras with eight megapixels of resolution can print high-quality, smooth A4 or letter-size prints; images with five-megapixel resolution are fine as well.

Invest in a telephoto lens to shoot wildlife, as you tend to be too far away from the animals to capture any detail with the zoom lens generally built into most point-and-shoot digital cameras. This may mean upgrading to a more robust camera. A tripod or beanbag is another must-have; it will stabilize your camera, especially when a zoom lens is extended.

Buy or borrow as many memory cards as you can—you'll use them. You may want to use multiple smaller memory cards to minimize the risk of losing an entire card's worth of images. And, as always, bring extra batteries.

10

VIDEO CAMERAS

Video cameras these days are almost universally digital. The benefits of video are threefold: it's much easier to get basically pleasing results with moving images than with still photography; video cameras are much more light-sensitive than still cameras, so you can shoot in much lower light conditions; and you can edit your tapes and show them on your VCR at home. There's also the added benefit of the zoom-lens capability on most video cameras, which can give you almost as close a look at large animals as with binoculars (the zoom doesn't work as well with smaller, far-off subjects). Video cameras are hungry for batteries, however, and you may run into recharging problems in remote safari destinations.

Another problem with video cameras (but not for the person behind the lens) is that persistent videographers can become annoying to the other people in a group, so be sensitive about this. Don't go everywhere with your camera glued to your eye while simultaneously issuing nonstop commentary. Eventually someone is going to tell you to plug it, or worse. Resist poking your lens close to strangers' faces—it looks great through the lens but these are not paid actors, and they'll appreciate being given their own space.

ON SAFARI

The pieces are falling into place, but your idea of what life is like on safari may still be a golden-tinged haze. The whos, whats, and hows still need to come into focus. If you have questions like, Where's the best place to sit in a game-drive vehicle? and Can you get near a honey badger? then read on.

GAME-VIEWING

This is the heart of a safari, and it has certain similarities regardless of the safari destination you've chosen. First, there's the overwhelming primeval atmosphere. Then there are the animals, from tiny rodents to the largest of land mammals, all going about their daily business: feeding, killing or avoiding being killed, and engaging in the never-ending territorial disputes that have evolved between species to ensure the maximum reproductive success of each animal group. The species you see are selected by time and nature; they are supremely adapted to their unforgiving habitats. You can move through the scene in dream-like wonderment, but the strong scents of the bush, the birdsong, the bellows, and the roars remind you that you are very much awake, and alive.

GAME RANGERS & TRACKERS

Game rangers (sometimes referred to as guides) tend to be of two types: those who have come to conservation by way of hunting and those who are professional conservationists. In both cases they have vast experience with and knowledge of the bush and the animals that inhabit it.

Rangers work in conjunction with trackers, who sit in a special seat on the front of the 4×4, spot animals, and advise the rangers.

For better or worse, the quality of your bush experience depends most heavily on your guide or game ranger and tracker. A ranger wears many hats while on safari: he's there to entertain you, protect you, and put you as close to the wilderness as possible while serving as bush mechanic, first-aid specialist, and host. He'll often eat meals with you, will explain animal habits and behavior while out in the bush, and, if you're on foot, will keep you alive in the presence of an excitable elephant, buffalo, hippo, or lion. This is no small feat, and each ranger has his particular strengths. Because of the intensity of the safari experience, with its exposure to potentially dangerous animals and tricky situations, your relationship with your guide or ranger is one of trust, friendliness, and respect. Misunderstandings may sometimes occur, but you're one step closer to ensuring that all goes well if you know the protocols and expectations.

■TIP→ Gratuities are a fact of life on safari. In southern Africa you may tip in U.S. currency or, when South Africa's currency is strong, in rand. Plan to give the local equivalents of about US$10 per person per day to the ranger and not much less to the tracker; an additional tip of US$25 for the general staff would be sufficient for a couple staying two days. Tips are presented as a lump sum at the end of the trip. It's a good idea to bring some thank you cards to include with the tip as a personal touch.

Wondering how to treat your ranger? Acknowledge that your guide is a professional and an expert in the field, and defer to his knowledge. Instead of trying to show how much you know, follow the example of the hunter, which is to walk quietly and take notice of all the little signs around you. Save social chatter with the guide for when you're back at camp, not out on a game drive. Rangers appreciate questions, which give them an idea of your range of knowledge and of how much detail to include in their animal descriptions. However, if you like to ask a lot of questions, save some for later, especially as several other people are likely to be in the safari vehicle with you. Carry a pocket notebook on game drives and jot down questions as they occur; you can then bring them up at dinner or around the campfire, when your ranger has more time to talk and everyone can participate in the discussion.

Wondering how your ranger will treat you? You can expect your ranger or guide to behave with respect: you are the client and he is the service provider, and you can expect delivery of that service 100% of the time. A guide should be pleasant and friendly but never too chummy or, worse, patronizing. If you believe a show-off guide or gung-ho ranger is speaking down to you, a quiet word with him should be enough to change his demeanor. (The safari world is small; a guide's reputation is built by word of mouth and can be eroded in the same fashion.)

Don't let your ranger get away with rote guiding, or "guiding by numbers"—providing only a list of an animal's attributes. Push him by politely asking questions and showing you'd like to know more. Even

10

the best guides may experience "bush burnout" by the end of a busy safari season with demanding clients, but any guide worthy of the title always goes out of his way to give you the best possible experience. If you suspect yours has a case of burnout, or just laziness, you have a right to ask for certain things. There's never any harm in asking, and you can't expect your guide to read your mind about what you like. If, for example, you have a preference for birds, insects, or whatever, ask your guide to spend time on these subjects. You may be surprised by how happy he is to oblige.

GAME-VIEWING WITH A RANGER

When you're in the care of a professional guide or ranger, you're unlikely to be placed in a dangerous situation. If you're going for a walk or ride in risky territory, your guide will first brief you about all the possible dangers and tell you how to behave in the unlikely event of an emergency. Listen to all the safety briefings and adhere to them strictly.

At most southern African camps and lodges open vehicles with raised, stepped seating—meaning the seats in back are higher than the ones in front—are used for game drives. There are usually three rows of seats after the driver's row; the norm at a luxury lodge is to have two people per row. In the front row you'll have the clearest conversations with the ranger, but farther back you'll have a clearer, elevated view over the front of the car. Try not to get stuck in the very back, though; in that row you spend a lot of time ducking thorny branches, you're exposed to the most dust, you feel the most bumps, and communicating with your ranger is difficult because of the rows between you. In closed vehicles, which are used by private touring companies operating in Kruger National Park, sit as close to the driver-guide as possible so you can get in and out of the vehicle more easily and get the best views.

The tracker will be busy searching out animal tracks, spoor, and other clues to nearby wildlife while the guide drives and discusses the animals and their environment. As described in Luxury Lodge–Based Safaris, *above,* rangers often communicate with each other via radio when someone has a good sighting.

Guided bush walks vary, but usually a maximum of eight guests walk in single file with the armed ranger up front and the tracker at the back. A bush walk is a more intimate experience than a drive. You are up close with the bush and with your fellow walkers and guides. Your guide will brief you thoroughly about where and how to walk, emergency procedures, and the like.

GAME-VIEWING ON A SELF-DRIVE SAFARI

Although most animals in popular parks are accustomed to vehicles with humans in them and will carry on unperturbed in many cases, a vehicle should still approach any animal carefully and quietly, and the driver should "feel" the response. This is for your own and the animals' safety. A delicate approach also gives you a better chance of getting as close as possible without alarming the animal. Be conservative and err on the side of caution, stopping as soon as circumstances suggest.

CLOSE UP

Game-Watching Do's & Don'ts

■ Observe animals silently and with a minimum of disturbance to their natural activities. Standing up in your vehicle and talking loudly on game drives can frighten animals away and is potentially dangerous.

■ Never attempt to attract an animal's attention. Don't imitate animal sounds, clap your hands, pound the vehicle, or throw objects.

■ Show respect for your driver and guide's judgment: don't insist that he take the vehicle closer so you can get a better photograph. Getting too close may hinder a hunt or cause animals to abandon a hard-earned meal and put you in danger. Driving off-road in certain areas can cause the guide to lose his license.

■ Don't litter—any tossed item can choke or poison animals.

■ Never attempt to feed or approach any wild animal. This is especially important to remember near lodges and in campgrounds, where animals may have become accustomed to human visitors.

■ Don't get out of the vehicle without permission for any reason, even if nature's calling.

■ Refrain from smoking on game drives. The dry African bush ignites easily.

■ Dress in neutral-toned clothes because animals pay the least attention to muted colors; if everyone in the car is wearing beige, brown, green, and tan, the animal sees one large vegetation-colored mass.

■ Forget body fragrances on game drives for the benefit of both the animals and your fellow travelers.

Human presence among wild animals never goes unnoticed. Don't get out of the vehicle, even if the animals appear friendly, and don't feed the creatures. Animals don't associate people in a vehicle with the potential food source or possible threat that they are when out of the vehicle. But for this ruse to work you must be quiet and still. The smell of the exhaust fumes and noise of a vehicle mask the presence of the human cargo, so when the engine is off you need to exercise extra caution. This is especially true when closely viewing lions and elephants—the only two animals likely to attack a vehicle or people in a vehicle. When approaching lions or elephants, never leap out of your seat or talk loudly; you want to be able to get as close as possible without scaring them off, and you want to avoid provoking an attack.

It does take time to develop your ability to find motionless game in thick bush. On the first day you're less likely to spot an animal than to run it over. All those fancy stripes and tawny colors really do work. Slowly, though, you learn to recognize the small clues that give away an animal in the bush: the flick of a tail, the toss of a horn, even fresh dung. To see any of this, you have to drive *slowly,* 15–25 kph (10–15 mph). Fight the urge to pin back your ears and tear around a park at 50 kph (30 mph) hoping to find something big. The only way to spot game at that speed is if it's standing in the road or if you come upon a number of cars already at a sighting. But remember that being the 10th car at a game sighting is less exciting than finding the animal yourself.

10

Not only do the other cars detract from the experience, but you feel like a scavenger—a sort of voyeuristic vulture.

The best time to find game is in the early morning and early evening, when the animals are most active, although old Africa hands will tell you that you can come across good game at any time of day. Stick to

---

THE LITTLE FIVE

We've all heard of the Big Five, but keep a look out for the Little Five, a term given to the animals with names that include the Big Five: the elephant shrew, lion ant, leopard tortoise, buffalo weaverbird, and rhinoceros beetle.

---

the philosophy "you never know what's around the next corner," and keep your eyes and ears wide open all the time. If your rest camp offers guided night drives on open vehicles with spotlights—go for it. You'll rarely be disappointed, seeing not only big game, but also a lot of fascinating little critters that surface only at night. Book your night drive in advance or as soon as you get to camp.

ANIMAL KINGDOM

Talk to travel agents about a safari, and sooner or later they will start babbling about the Big Five. This was originally a hunting term referring to those animals that posed the greatest risk to hunters on foot—elephants, black rhinos, leopards, lions, and buffalo—yet it has now become the single-most important criterion used in evaluating a lodge or reserve. Although the Big Five label may have helped engender tourist interest in African wildlife, it can also demean the entire bush experience, turning it into a treasure hunt. You will be amazed how many visitors ignore a gorgeous animal that doesn't "rank" in the Big Five or lose interest in a species once they've checked it off their list. After you've spent a few days in the bush, you will also recognize the idiocy of racing around in search of five animals when there are another 150 equally fascinating species all around you.

Until several decades ago, the Big Five were present in just about every game reserve. In many areas today, however, poaching and in some cases poor land management have brought about local extinction, mainly of elephants and rhinos. For instance, in the mid-1980s the Lower Zambezi Valley had 10,000 black rhinos, the highest concentration in the world. Today it has none.

■ TIP➔ **Arm yourself with specialized books on mammals and birds rather than a more general one that tries to cover too much.** Airports, lodges, and camp shops stock a good range, but try to bring one with you and do a bit of boning up in advance. Any bird guide by Ken Newman (Struik Publishers) and the *Sasol Guide to Birds* are recommended.

WILDLIFE SAFETY & RESPECT
Nature is neither kind nor sentimental. Do not be tempted to interfere with the natural processes. The animals are going about the business of survival in a harsh environment, and you can unwittingly make this business more difficult. Don't get too close to the animals; you might

cause alarm or influence a hunt by chasing away the prey or shielding a predator's approach. Don't even pick up a tortoise to help it across some perceived obstacle; you have no idea what it's really trying to do, or where it wants to go. If you're intrusive, you could drive animals away from feeding and, even worse, from drinking at water holes, where they are very skittish and vulnerable to predators. That time at the water hole may be their only opportunity to drink that day.

Never feed any wild creature—not a cute monkey, not an inquisitive baboon, not a baby tree squirrel, or a young bird out of its nest. In some camps and lodges, however, animals have gotten used to being fed or stealing food. The most common animals in this category are baboons and monkeys; in some places they sneak into huts, tents, and even occupied vehicles to snatch food. If you see primates around, keep all food out of sight, and keep your windows rolled up. (If a baboon manages to get into your vehicle, he will trash the interior as he searches for food and use it as a toilet.)

Never try to get an animal to pose with you. This is probably the biggest cause of death and injury on safaris, when visitors don't listen to or believe the warnings from their rangers or posted notices in the public parks. Regardless of how cute or harmless they may look, these animals are not tame. An herbivore impala, giraffe, or ostrich can kill you just as easily as a lion, elephant, or buffalo can.

Remember, immersion in the African safari lands is a privilege. In order to preserve this privilege for future generations, it's important to view wildlife with minimal disturbance and to avoid upsetting the delicate balance of nature at all costs. You are the visitor, so act like you would in someone else's home: respect their space. Caution is your most trusted safety measure. Keep your distance, keep quiet, and keep your hands to yourself, and you should be fine.

NIGHTTIME SAFETY

At night, never sleep out in the open in any area with wildlife. If you're sleeping in a tent make sure it's fully closed; if it's a small tent, place something between you and the side of the wall to prevent an opportunistic bite from the outside. If you're in your tent and not exposed, you should be quite safe. Few people lose their lives to lions or hyenas. Malaria is a much more potent danger, so keep your tent zipped up tight at night to keep out mosquitoes.

■TIP➜**Never walk alone after dark.** Nearly all camps and lodges insist that an armed ranger accompany you at night, and rightly so.

KIDS ON SAFARI

Many private camps now welcome children over 12 on safari, and some even younger children, but generally speaking kids under 6 may not take part in game activities, even if they are allowed in camp. Small children are potential snacks! However, certain camps offer specialized kids' programs, such as Honeyguide Khoka Moya and Ngala Main Camp, in Mpumalanga; Thanda, in KwaZulu-Natal; and the Kwando camps in Botswana. It's a good idea to check with your tour operator, because more and more camps are offering kids' programs.

In Kruger there are no age limits, but if you have small children, don't keep them locked up and bored in a car for long stretches. You'll put them off the bush forever. Instead take short drives in the early morning and late afternoon, when it's cooler. They can spend the rest of the day playing around camp, but since not all of Kruger's camps have pools, check this out in advance.

Future Nature runs a series of dedicated programs for children and young adults in Mpumalanga and central South Africa. (For more information on this program and on children in South Africa, *see* Essentials.) Specially trained educators teach small groups of kids, and there are plenty of options to choose from: tracking the Big Five in Mpumalanga; experiencing the wide-open spaces of the Karoo; canoeing South Africa's longest river, the Gariep; learning the traditional uses of plants; game drives; mammal, bird, and plant identification; hiking; and discovering South Africa's brilliant night skies. Kids get the opportunity to work with local kids of the same age on a number of community projects, giving your children the chance to leave their individual and positive mark on Africa. Programs are designed for kids 8–12 and 12–18, and can be tailored to fit in with parents' safaris. There are also programs for young adults 17 and up.

HEALTH ON SAFARI

Of all the horror stories and fantastic nightmares about meeting your end in the bush—being devoured by lions and crocodiles; succumbing to some ghastly fever like Ernest Hemingway's hero in *The Snows of Kilimanjaro*—the problem you're most likely to encounter will be of your own doing: dehydration. Also be wary of malaria, motion sickness, and intestinal problems. By taking commonsense precautions, your safari will be uneventful from a health perspective but memorable in every other way.

DEHYDRATION & OVERHEATING

The African sun is hot and the air is dry, and sweat evaporates quickly in these conditions. You might not realize how much bodily fluid you are losing as a result. Wear a hat, lightweight clothing, and sunscreen—all of which will help your body cope with high temperatures.

Drink at least two to three quarts of water a day, and in extreme heat conditions as much as three to four quarts of water or juice. Drink more if you're exerting yourself physically. If you overdo it at dinner with wine or spirits or even caffeine, you need to drink even more water to recover the fluid lost as your body processes the alcohol. Antimalarial medications are also very dehydrating, so it's important to increase your water intake while you're taking this medicine.

Don't rely on thirst to tell you when to drink; people often don't feel thirsty until they're a little dehydrated. At the first sign of dry

CLOSE UP

A Common Safari Affliction

In addition to the health hazards described in the "Health on Safari" section, there's a safari disease that's as well known as malaria: "khaki fever." Though this fever may not kill you, it can wreak havoc upon your sensibilities and your heart. In fact, it is part of the plotline in the 1953 film *Mogambo,* in which the married society girl (Grace Kelly) falls for the rugged, tanned game ranger (Clark Gable), who's already carrying on with a wild American (Ava Gardner).

When you're on safari, a magical world quite unlike the one to which you're accustomed to reveals itself. When it does, a perpetual good mood might strike and with it, a feeling of euphoria and romance. We can't

blame you. The campfire can be very seductive, and the bush is full of bewitching, sensual stimuli—a full moon hovers above the trees, a lion roars in the distance, a nightjar fills the velvety night with its trilling call. Then there's the tanned, knowledge-able ranger protecting you from the wilds of Africa, chauffeuring you around, and seemingly delivering your every wish.

Hey, heavenly things can happen…but if they do, just make sure you're pre-pared for the earthbound realities. AIDS in Africa is rife; if there's even the remotest chance of having a sexual encounter on safari, carry con-doms. Better still, abstain.

---

mouth, exhaustion, or headache, drink water, because dehydration is the likely culprit.

■ TIP → **To test for dehydration, pinch the skin on the back of your hand and see if it stays in a peak; if it does, you're dehydrated.** Drink a solution of ½ teaspoon salt and 4 tablespoons sugar dissolved in a quart of water to replace electrolytes.

Heat cramps stem from a low salt level due to excessive sweating. These muscle pains usually occur in the abdomen, arms, or legs. When a child says he can't take another step, investigate whether he has cramps. When cramps occur, stop all activity and sit quietly in a cool spot and drink. Don't do anything strenuous for a few hours after the cramps subside. If heat cramps persist for more than an hour, seek medical assistance.

MALARIA

See the malaria section under Getting Ready to Go, *above,* for details on antimalarial drugs.

If you're on safari in a malarial zone, be vigilant about protecting your-self. In the morning and evening cover exposed skin with strong insect repellent; dress in long pants, long-sleeve shirts, and shoes and socks; and wear clothes you've treated with a mosquito-repellent spray or laundry wash. Forget fashion statements and tuck your pants into your socks so your ankles aren't exposed. Spray insect repellent on your shoes, socks, and legs up to your knees, even if you're wearing pants, before you set off for a game walk or evening drive. Wear light-colored clothing, since mosquitoes (as well as tsetse flies) are attracted to dark

10

surfaces. Spray all exposed skin with an up-to-date mosquito-repellent spray or use a cream or roll-on. Most private safari lodges provide insect repellants in your room. Citronella and other natural bug repellents can be used, but don't work half as well. If you've been out on a walk it's a good idea to take a hot shower and soap your entire body when you return.

When you go to bed, make sure you turn on any fan that's over or facing your bed, since mosquitoes can't fly well in moving air; keep it on while you sleep. Use mosquito coils and sprays in your room (especially if you're traveling with children), and sleep under mosquito nets. If you are 100% vigilant, these tactics should work.

■TIP→ **Sleeping under a mosquito net or in an insect-proof tent is customary, but it can stifle airflow.** If you can't sleep, wet a sheet or towel, wring it out, and lie under it: you'll fall asleep before you know it.

MOTION SICKNESS

If you're prone to motion sickness, be sure to examine your safari itinerary closely. Though most landing strips for chartered planes are not paved but rather grass, earth, or gravel, landings are smooth most of the time. If you're going on safari to northern Botswana (the Okavango Delta, specifically), know that small planes and unpaved airstrips are the main means of transportation between camps; these trips can be very bumpy, hot, and a little dizzying even if you're not prone to motion sickness. If you're not sure how you'll react, take motion-sickness pills just in case. Most of the air transfers take an average of only 30 minutes and the rewards will be infinitely greater than the pains.

■TIP→ **When you fly in small planes take a sun hat and a pair of sunglasses.** If you sit in the front seat next to the pilot, or on the side of the sun, you will experience harsh glare that could give you a severe headache and exacerbate motion sickness.

INTESTINAL UPSET

Natural microfauna and -flora differ in every region of Africa, so if you drink local, unfiltered water, add ice to your soda in the airport, or eat a piece of fruit from a roadside stand, you may get what's commonly referred to as traveler's diarrhea. All reputable hotels and lodges have either filtered, clean tap water or provide sterilized drinking water in jugs, and nearly all camps and lodges have adequate supplies of bottled water, in some cases including it in the cost of your trip. If you're traveling outside of organized safari camps in rural Africa or are unsure of local water supplies, carry plenty of bottled water and follow the CDC's advice for fruits and vegetables: boil it, cook it, peel it, or forget it. If you're going on a mobile safari, ask your guide whether drinking water is available.

UNDERSTANDING
SOUTH AFRICA

Vocabulary

SOUTH AFRICAN GLOSSARY

South Africa has 11 official languages, including nine indigenous African languages. English is the lingua franca; in its everyday use it includes a rich assortment of terms from the other languages. Afrikaans, originally a Dutch dialect, has a shadowed history because of its role in apartheid politics, but it's still a very common language. Zulu is the most widely spoken indigenous African language; it doesn't hurt to know a few polite phrases if you're traveling to a Zulu-speaking area like KwaZulu-Natal. Below we've listed common terms, followed by some essential terms in Zulu and a menu guide. *See also* the safari-specific vocabulary list in the Safari Primer.

Ablution blocks	public bathrooms
Abseil	rappel
Backpackers	hostel
Bakkie	pickup truck (pronounced "bucky")
Banda	bungalow or hut
Berg	mountain
Boma	enclosure; dining area in lodges
Boot	trunk (of a car)
Bottle store	liquor store
Bra/bru/my bra	brother (term of affection or familiarity)
Buck	antelope
Burg	city
Bushveld	generic term for the wild indigenous vegetation of the lowveld
Cape Malay/Malay	referring to descendants of Asian, largely Muslim, slaves, brought to the Cape starting in the 1600s and erroneously lumped together under the term
Coloured	a term for people of Malay, Khoi-San, other black African, and/or European descent (⇨ *See A Note on the Term "Coloured" in Chapter 2*)
Chommie	mate, chum
Dagga	marijuana, sometimes called *zol*
Djembes	drums
Dorp	village
Fanagalo	a mix of Zulu, English, Afrikans, Sotho, and Xhosa

Fynbos	the collective name for a variety of bush plants, which can be divided into 4 basic types (proteas, ericas or heather, restios or reeds, and ground flowers)
Highveld	the country's high interior plateau, including Johannesburg
Howzit?	literally, "how are you?" but used as a general greeting
Indaba	literally, a meeting but also a problem, as in "that's your indaba."
Jol	a party or night on the town
Kloof	river gorge
Kokerbooms	quiver trees
Koppies	hills (also *kopjes*)
Kraal	traditional rural settlement of huts and houses, village
Lekker	nice
Lowveld	land at lower elevation, including Kruger National Park
Marula	tree from which amarula (the liquor) gets its name
Mokoro	dugout canoe, pluralized as *mekoro*
Mopane	nutrient-poor land
Moppies	vaudeville-style songs
More-ish	so good you will want more, mouthwatering
Muthi	traditional (non-Western) medicine
Plaas	farm
Petrol	gasoline
Robot	traffic light
Rondawel/rondavel	a traditional round dwelling with a conical roof
Sala	outdoor covered deck
Sangoma	traditional healer or mystic
Self-catering	with cooking facilities
Shebeen	a place to drink, often used in townships
Sis	gross, disgusting

Sisi or usisi	sister (term of affection or respect)
South African War	the more inclusive name for the Boer War or Anglo-Boer War and actually referring to either of two South African Wars (1880–1881 and 1899–1902)
Spaza shop	an informal shop, usually from a truck or container
Spar	name of grocery market chain in Africa
Stoep	veranda
Sundowner	cocktails at sunset
Swenka	a local term for a hard-working man characterized by his natty style of dress. Today weekly fashion contests (usually held Saturday night) for the best-dressed man in town pay homage to the fashion trend which began in the 1950s.
Takkie	(pronounced tacky) sneaker
Veld	open countryside

ZULU ESSENTIALS

Yes or hello	yebo
No	cha
Please	uxolo
Thank you	ngiyabonga
You're welcome	nami ngiyabonga
Good morning/hello	sawubona
Excuse me	uxolo
Goodbye	sala kahle
Do you speak English?	uya khuluma isingisi?

MENU GUIDE

Biltong	spiced air-dried (not smoked) meat, made of everything from beef to kudu
Bobotie	spiced minced beef or lamb topped with savory custard, a Cape Malay dish
Boerewors	Afrikaaner term for a spicy farmer's sausage, often used for a braai (pronounced "*boo*-rah-vorse")

Braai	roughly, a barbecue or grill, with sausages, fish etc.
Bredie	a casserole or stew, usually lamb with tomatoes
Bunny chow	a half loaf of bread hollowed out and filled with meat or vegetable curry
Chakalaka	a spicy relish
Gatsby	a loaf of bread cut lengthwise and filled with fish or meat, salad, and fries
Kabeljou	one of the varieties of line fish
Kingklip	a native fish
Koeksister	a deep-fried braided, sugared dough
Malva	pudding
Melktert	a sweet custard tart
Mogodu	beef or ox tripe
Moroho	mopane worms
Pap	also called *mielie pap,* a maize-based porridge
Peppadews	a patented vegetable, so you may see it under different names, usually with the word *dew* in them; it's a sort of a cross between a sweet pepper and a chili and is usually pickled.
Peri-peri	a spicy chili marinade, Portuguese in origin, based on the searing hot *piri-piri* chili; some recipes are tomato-based, while others use garlic, olive oil, and brandy
Potjie	pronounced "*poy*-key" and also called *potjiekos,* a traditional stew cooked in a three-legged pot
Rocket	arugula
Rooibos	an indigenous, earthy-tasting red-leaf tea
Samp	corn porridge
Snoek	a barracuda-like fish, often smoked, sometimes used for *smoorsnoek* (braised)
Sosaties	local version of a kebab, with spiced, grilled chunks of meat
Waterblommetjie	water lilies, sometimes used in stews
Witblitz	moonshine

South Africa Essentials

PLANNING TOOLS, EXPERT INSIGHT, GREAT CONTACTS

There are planners and there are those who, excuse the pun, fly by the seat of their pants. We happily place ourselves among the planners. Our writers and editors try to anticipate all the issues you may face before and during any journey, and then they do their research. This section is the product of their efforts. Use it to get excited about your trip to South Africa, to inform your travel planning, or to guide you on the road should the seat of your pants start to feel threadbare.

GETTING STARTED

We're really proud of our Web site: Fodors.com, which is a great place to begin any journey. Scan Travel Wire for suggested itineraries, travel deals, restaurant and hotel openings, and other up-to-the-minute info. Check out Booking to research prices and book plane tickets, hotel rooms, rental cars, and vacation packages. Head to Talk for on-the-ground pointers from travelers who frequent our message boards. You can also link to loads of other travel-related resources.

▌ RESOURCES

ONLINE TRAVEL TOOLS

The official South Africa Tourism Web site (⊕*www.southafrica.net*) is reasonable for general tourism information and pretty good on events, but you'll really struggle to find a decent hotel or other tourism product with its search engine. Another government-sponsored Web site, ⊕*www.southafrica.info*, is full of useful, but general country information and is a far better bet than the SA Tourism site. If most of your independent travel will be in and around Cape Town, visit ⊕*www.tourismcapetown.co.za* for everything from comprehensive event listings by date to accommodation links, and an e-mail newsletter that will come to your in box.

For a range of accommodation choices and links to maps by region, as well as updated traveler information, try ⊕*www.sa-venues.com*.

Getaway magazine's online portal—⊕*www.getawaytoafrica.com*—offers really good information about all of Africa as well as tours, packages, and an online booking system. For news about activities all over the region, your best bet is ⊕*www.africa-adventure.org*. The Iziko South African Museum Web site (⊕*www.iziko.org.za*) lists details for more than a dozen of Cape Town's museums. For the latest information on arts performances and exhibits, as well as a nationwide calendar of creative events, there is no better place to start than ⊕*www.artslink.co.za*. The South Africa National Parks Web site (⊕*www.sanparks.org*) outlines where the parks are, provides detailed maps, and includes information on accommodations, animals, park activities, and booking.

To stay abreast of news and events in South Africa, check out ⊕*www.iol.co.za*, the online version of Independent Newspapers, which is the biggest newspaper group in South Africa. The *Mail & Guardian* (⊕*www.mg.co.za*) provides a useful selection of South African and international news and insightful comments. All Africa (⊕*www.allafrica.com*) culls English-language news articles from regional papers.

If you feel like surfing, use ⊕*www.ananzi.com*, a local search engine, and ⊕*www.goafrica.co.za*, a comprehensive directory of Web sites pertaining to the whole of Africa. For weather information, check out ⊕*www.weathersa.co.za*.

Currency Conversion **Google** (⊕www.google.com) does currency conversion. Just type in the amount you want to convert and an explanation of how you want it converted (e.g., "14 Swiss francs in dollars"), and then voilà. **Oanda.com** (⊕www.oanda.com) also allows you to print out a handy table with the current day's conversion rates. **XE.com** (⊕www.xe.com) is a good currency conversion Web site.

INSPIRATIONS

To learn about the issues of apartheid, pick up Nelson Mandela's *Long Walk to Freedom* (1995). The book examines Mandela's life and the political road ahead. History buffs will also enjoy *A History of South Africa, Third Edition* (2001). It's a comprehensive, but interesting examination of South Africa's history.

If you're interested in learning a bit about a safari from your armchair, pick up *The Wildlife of South Africa: A Field Guide to the Animals and Plants of the Region*. If birds are more your thing, *Birds of Southern Africa* is the most comprehensive and authoritative guide.

There are also a few great movies you might want to watch before your trip. The 2006 Oscar winner for foreign film, *Tsotsi* (2005), offers insight into the harsh life of South Africa's townships. It's based on the novel by Athol Fugard. *Red Dust* (2004), based on the novel by Gillian Slovo, follows an attorney through the harrowing weeks of a Truth and Reconciliation Commission hearing in the Eastern Cape. *Catch a Fire* (2006), starring Tim Robbins, is set in the 1980s and highlights the anti-government sabotage common to that era. *Yesterday* (2004) follows one woman's struggles against HIV, and its impact on her life and on that of her young daughter. *For more suggestions see Books & Movies in Understanding South Africa.*

Safety **Transportation Security Administration** (TSA; ⊕www.tsa.gov). **South Africa Police Service** (SAPS; ⊕www.saps.gov.za).

Time Zones **Timeanddate.com** (⊕www.timeanddate.com/worldclock) can help you figure out the correct time anywhere. **WorldTimeZone.com** (⊕www.worldtimezone.com) has an Africa-specific map, as well as an interactive call planner feature to enable you to select the right time to phone Africa and other countries.

Weather **Accuweather.com** (⊕www.accuweather.com) is an independent weather-forecasting service with good coverage of hurricanes. **African Weather Forecasts** (⊕www.africanweather.net) lists weather information for the entire continent. **South Africa Weather Service** (⊕www.weathersa.co.za) forecasts weather for the whole country. **Weather.com** (⊕www.weather.com) is the Web site for the Weather Channel.

Other Resources **CIA World Factbook** (⊕www.odci.gov/cia/publications/factbook/index.html) has profiles of every country in the world. It's a good source if you need some quick facts and figures.

VISITOR INFORMATION

See the individual chapter Essentials sections for details on local visitor bureaus.

Contacts **South African Tourism** (☎800/782–9772 in U.S. or 011/895–3000 in South Africa ⊕www.southafrica.net).

▌ THINGS TO CONSIDER

GOVERNMENT ADVISORIES

As different countries have different world views, look at travel advisories from a range of governments to get more of a sense of what's going on out there. And be sure to parse the language carefully. For example, a warning to "avoid all travel" carries more weight than one urging you to "avoid nonessential travel," and both are much stronger than a plea to "exercise caution." A U.S. government travel warning is more permanent (though not necessarily more serious) than a so-called public announcement, which carries an expiration date.

■ TIP→ **Consider registering online with the State Department (https://travelregistration.state.gov/ibrs/), so the government will know to look for you should a crisis occur in the country you're visiting.**

The U.S. Department of State's Web site has more than just travel warnings and advisories. The consular information sheets issued for every country have general safety tips, entry requirements (though be sure to verify these with the country's embassy), and other useful details.

State Department warnings often do not pertain to street crime, but rather large demonstrations, or ongoing conflicts, such as wars or regional clashes. While there are warnings about crime and theft in and around Johannesburg, unless something dramatic happens to shift the general safety of a region—a sudden earthquake, a local uprising—the Travel Warning alone will not be your best resource for information about recent incidents of crime or other attacks. Check newspapers and Web sites and even travel forums for details about events on the ground.

The Web site for AllSafeTravels gathers safety information from government Web sites as well as news media and even users; sorts it; and posts it in a very searchable, user-friendly way. For a small fee they will send you customized e-mail alerts to any destination to which you're planning to travel. The upshot? You'll get a very full picture of where you'll be traveling.

General Information & Warnings U.S. Department of State (⊕ www.travel.state. gov). **AllSafeTravels** (⊕ www.allsafetravels. com).

GEAR

Goods in South Africa's pharmacies and grocery stores are very similar to those in the States. If you have a favorite brand of toiletry, bring it, otherwise expect to pay average prices for items you may have left at home. Minimarts at gas stations also stock the same range of candies and sodas you would expect of a roadside shop.

Larger markets will have a hot food section and a bakery. Film is sold at a separate register and will cost slightly more than it would at home, but is not prohibitively expensive, nor worse in quality.

Take care to bring enough prescription medicines and a copy of your prescription if you anticipate needing a refill. Ask your doctor to write down the ingredients so that a pharmacist will find a suitable substitute if necessary. Obtain your antimalarials at home.

Incidents of theft from checked baggage in Cape Town and Johannesburg airports make luggage wrapping a popular option. For a few rand, the process of wrapping a bag in impenetrable cellophane is a great deterrent against crime. Bags can be rewrapped. ⚠ **Fragile items in soft-sided bags can be crushed by the process, so remove breakable items, or place them in the center, to avoid getting squeezed.** The wrapping can be removed by hand or with a knife. Security accepts wrapped bags.

In southern Africa it's possible to experience muggy heat, bone-chilling cold, torrential thunderstorms, and scorching African sun all within a couple of days. The secret is to pack lightweight clothes that you can wear in layers, and at least one lightweight fleece pullover or sweater. Take along a warm jacket, too, especially if you're going to a private game lodge. It can get mighty cold sitting in an open Land Rover at night or on an early morning game drive. It really and truly does get very cold in almost every part of southern Africa, so don't fall into the it's-Africa-so-it-must-always-be-hot trap.

South Africans tend to dress casually. Businessmen still wear suits, but dress standards have become less rigid and more interesting since ex-president Nelson Mandela redefined the concept of sartorial elegance with his Madiba shirts. You can go almost anywhere in neat, clean, casual clothes, but you can still get dolled up to go to the theater or opera. Dinner on the *Blue Train* and in some of the smarter hotels requires a coat and tie for men. An interesting development since 1994 is that invitations to social and official events prescribe dress code as "formal or traditional," so it really is quite acceptable for men to appear at the opera or the opening of parliament in skirts made of monkey tails.

It's easy to get fried in the strong African sun, especially in mile-high Johannesburg, where the temperature can be deceptively cool. Pack plenty of sunscreen, sunglasses, and a hat. An umbrella comes in handy during those late-afternoon thunderstorms but is almost useless in Cape Town in the winter, as it will get blown inside out. But do take a waterproof coat.

If you're heading into the bush, bring binoculars, a strong insect repellent (with a good amount of DEET), and sturdy pants (preferably cotton) that can stand up to the wicked thorns that protect much of the foliage. Avoid black, white, and garish clothing, which will make you more visible to animals (and insects, which tend to mistake you for a buffalo if you wear black); medium tones will make you blend in most, but you don't have to look like an extra on the set of *Out of Africa*. Leave behind perfumes, which attract insects. Lightweight hiking boots are a good idea if you plan to set out on any of South Africa's great trails; otherwise, a sturdy pair of walking shoes should suffice. *For more details on what to pack for a safari, see the Safari Primer chapter.*

Some hotels do supply washcloths; some don't. It's always a good idea to have at least a couple of tissues in your bag, and moist towelettes as there may not be a restroom (and toilet paper) just when you need it. Even an hour in a safari vehicle

on a dry day can cover you with dust. As we're sure you already know, sanitary gels can be a lifesaver when away from soap and water, but don't fill the bottle to the top, as air pressure in the plane will cause it to expand and leak.

Make copies of all your important documents. Leave one set in one bag, another at home, and try to save them online in a PDF file, which may be the fastest way to access data if you need to replace anything. Consider carrying a small card with emergency contact numbers on it, such as the local U.S. Embassy, in case things go terribly wrong.

PASSPORTS & VISAS

American citizens only need a valid passport with two blank facing visa pages to enter South Africa for visits of up to 90 days; this includes infants. Check the expiration date. If your passport will expire within six months of your return date, you need to renew your passport in advance, as South Africa won't let you enter with a soon-to-expire passport. ⚠ **You will be denied entry to the country if you do not have two blank pages.**

Before your trip, make two copies of your passport's data page (one for someone at home and another for you to carry separately). Or scan the page and e-mail it to someone at home and/or yourself.

U.S. Passport Information U.S. Department of State (☎877/487–2778 ⊕http://travel. state.gov/passport).

U.S. Passport & Visa Expediters A. Briggs Passport & Visa Expeditors (☎800/806–0581 or 202/338–0111 ⊕www. abriggs.com). **American Passport Express** (☎800/455–5166 or 800/841–6778 ⊕www. americanpassport.com). **Passport Express** (☎800/362–8196 ⊕www.passportex-press.com). **Travel Document Systems** (☎800/874–5100 or 202/638–3800 ⊕www. traveldocs.com). **Travel the World Visas** (☎866/886–8472 or 301/495–7700 ⊕www. world-visa.com).

GENERAL REQUIREMENTS FOR SOUTH AFRICA	
Passport	Must have two blank facing pages for entry. Must be valid for 6 months after date of arrival.
Visa	Entry visa processed upon arrival for Americans. No fee.
Vaccinations	None required. If coming from a yellow fever endemic area (e.g., East Africa) be prepared to present your yellow fever certificate.
Driving	South Africa traffic moves on the left and vehicles are left steering. Most agencies will not rent to drivers under 21 years of age.
Departure Tax	Included in ticket price.

SHOTS & MEDICATIONS

South Africa does not require any inoculations for entry. Travelers entering South Africa within six days of leaving a country infected with yellow fever require a yellow-fever vaccination certificate. The South African travel clinics and the U.S.'s National Centers for Disease Control and Prevention (CDC) recommend that you be vaccinated against hepatitis A and B if you intend to travel to more isolated areas. Cholera injections are widely regarded as useless, so don't let anyone talk you into having one, but the newer oral vaccine seems to be more effective.

If you are coming to South Africa for a safari, chances are you are heading to a malarial game reserve. Only a handful of game reserves are nonmalarial. Millions of travelers take oral prophylactic drugs before, during and after their safaris. It is up to you to weigh the risks and benefits of the type of antimalarial drug you choose to take. If you are pregnant, or traveling with small children, consider a nonmalarial region for your safari.

The CDC provides up-to-date information on health risks and recommended vaccinations and medications for travelers to southern Africa. In most of South Africa you need not worry about any of the above, but if you plan to visit remote regions, check with the CDC's traveler's health line. For up-to-date, local expertise, contact SAA Netcare Travel Clinics.

■ TIP→ **If you travel a lot internationally—particularly to developing nations—refer to the CDC's** *Health Information for International Travel* **(aka Traveler's Health Yellow Book). Info from it is posted on the CDC Web site (www.cdc.gov/travel/yb), or you can buy a copy from your local bookstore for $24.95.**

The Web site Travel Health Online is a good source to check out before you travel because it compiles primarily health and some safety information from a variety of official sources, and it's done by a medical publishing company.

For more information see Health under On the Ground in South Africa, below.

Health Warnings National Centers for Disease Control & Prevention (CDC ☎877/394–8747 international travelers' health line ⊕www.cdc.gov/travel). **South African Airways Netcare Travel Clinics** (☎0800/002–609 toll-free in South Africa ⊕www.travelclinic.co.za). **Travel Health Online** (⊕www.tripprep.com). **World Health Organization** (WHO ⊕www.who.int).

Medical-Assistance Companies International SOS Assistance, South Africa (☎011/541–1216, 011/541-110 24hr emergency ⊕www.internationalsos.co.za).

TRIP INSURANCE

We believe that comprehensive trip insurance is especially valuable if you're booking a very expensive or complicated trip (particularly to an isolated region) or if you're booking far in advance. Who knows what could happen six months down the road? But whether or not you get insurance has more to do with how comfortable you are assuming all that risk yourself.

Trip Insurance Resources

INSURANCE COMPARISON SITES		
Insure My Trip.com	800/487–4722	www.insuremytrip.com.
Square Mouth.com	727/490–5803 or 800/240–0369	www.squaremouth.com.
COMPREHENSIVE TRAVEL INSURERS		
Access America	800/729–6021	www.accessamerica.com.
CSA Travel Protection	800/873–9855	www.csatravelprotection.com.
HTH Worldwide	610/254–8700 or 888/243–2358	www.hthworldwide.com.
Travelex Insurance	800/228–9792	www.travelex-insurance.com.
Travel Guard International	715/345-0505 or 800/826–4919	www.travelguard.com.
Travel Insured International	800/243-3174	www.travelinsured.com.
MEDICAL-ONLY INSURERS		
International Medical Group	800/628–4664	www.imglobal.com.
International SOS		www.internationalsos.com.
Wallach & Company	540/687–3166 or 800/237-6615	www.wallach.com.

Comprehensive travel policies typically cover trip-cancellation and interruption, letting you cancel or cut your trip short because of a personal emergency, illness, or, in some cases, acts of terrorism in your destination. Such policies also cover evacuation and medical care. Some also cover you for trip delays because of bad weather or mechanical problems as well as for lost or delayed baggage. Another type of coverage to look for is financial default—that is, when your trip is disrupted because a tour operator, airline, or cruise line goes out of business. Generally you must buy this when you book your trip or shortly thereafter, and it's only available to you if your operator isn't on a list of excluded companies.

If you're going abroad, consider buying medical-only coverage at the very least. Neither Medicare nor some private insurers cover medical expenses anywhere outside of the United States besides Mexico and Canada (including time aboard a cruise ship, even if it leaves from a U.S. port). Medical-only policies typically reimburse you for medical care (excluding that related to pre-existing conditions) and hospitalization abroad, and provide for evacuation. You still have to pay the bills and await reimbursement from the insurer, though.

Expect comprehensive travel insurance policies to cost about 4% to 7% or 8% of the total price of your trip (it's more like 8%–12% if you're over age 70). A medical-only policy may or may not be cheaper than a comprehensive policy. Always read the fine print of your policy to make sure that you are covered for the risks that are of most concern to you. Compare several policies to make sure you're getting the best price and range of coverage available.

BOOKING YOUR TRIP

Have you ever wondered just what the differences are between an online travel agent (a Web site through which you make reservations instead of going directly to the airline, hotel, or car-rental company), a discounter (a firm that does a high volume of business with a hotel chain or airline and accordingly gets good prices), a wholesaler (one that makes cheap reservations in bulk and then re-sells them to people like you), and an aggregator (one that compares all the offerings so you don't have to)?

Is it truly better to book directly on an airline or hotel Web site? And when does a real live travel agent come in handy?

▌ ONLINE

An aggregator site will search many sites and pull the best prices for airfares, hotels, and rental cars from them. Most aggregators compare the major travel-booking sites such as Expedia, Travelocity, and Orbitz; some also look at airline Web sites, though rarely the sites of smaller budget airlines. Some aggregators also compare other travel products, including complex packages—a good thing, as you can sometimes get the best overall deal by booking an air-and-hotel package.

▌ WITH A TRAVEL AGENT

If you use an agent—brick-and-mortar or virtual—you'll pay a fee for the service. A knowledgeable travel agent can be a godsend if you're booking a cruise, a package trip that's not available to you directly, an air pass, or a complicated itinerary including several overseas flights. What's more, travel agents that specialize in a destination may have exclusive access to certain deals and insider information on things such as charter flights. Agents who specialize in types of travelers (senior citizens, gays and lesbians, naturists) or types of trips (cruises, luxury travel, safaris) can also be invaluable.

▌TIP→ **Remember that Expedia, Travelocity, and Orbitz are travel agents, not just booking engines. To resolve any problems with a reservation made through these companies, contact them first.**

South African Tourism runs a training program for travel agents. Graduates are called *fundis*, which means "expert" in Zulu. A list of fundis can be found on the SA Tourism Web site.

U.S. Agent Resources American Society of Travel Agents (☎703/739-2782 ⊕www.travelsense.org).

South Africa Travel Agents SA Tourism (⊕www.southafrica.net).

▌ ACCOMMODATIONS

The Tourism Grading Council of South Africa is the official accreditation and grading body for accommodation in South Africa. However, you may still find some establishments clinging to other grading systems. Hotels, bed-and-breakfasts, guesthouses, and game lodges are graded on a star rating from one to five. Grading is not compulsory, and there are many excellent establishments that are not graded. Those that are given a grade are revisited annually. Unlike North American ratings standards, AAA or Mobil, which are based on the presence of a constellation of facilities and services, these marks are purely subjective and reflect the comfort level and quality of the surroundings. In other words, a five-star grading in a South African resort does not guarantee features or amenities as it would in North America, but chances are you'll find it very luxe, indeed.

Most hotel rooms come with private bathrooms that are usually en suite, but they may, very occasionally, be across the

Online Booking Resources

AGGREGATORS

Kayak	www.kayak.com	looks at cruises and vacation packages.
Mobissimo	www.mobissimo.com	examines airfare, hotels, cars, and tons of activities.
Sidestep	www.sidestep.com	compares vacation packages and lists travel deals and some activities.
Travelgrove	www.travelgrove.com	compares cruises and vacation packages and lets you search by themes.

BOOKING ENGINES

Cheap Tickets	www.cheaptickets.com	discounter.
E-gnu	www.e-gnu.com	books everything from safari lodges to hotels just outside Kruger's gates, often at a discount for multinight stays.
Expedia	www.expedia.com	large online agency that charges a booking fee for airline tickets.
Luxury Link	www.luxurylink.com	has auctions for high-end properties in Cape Town and Johannesburg as well coastal African beach escapes.
Mt. Beds	www.mtbeds.co.za	offers special rates at short notice for South African lodges and island escapes.
Onetravel.com	www.onetravel.com	discounter for hotels, car rentals, airfares, and packages.
Orbitz	www.orbitz.com	charges a booking fee for airline tickets, but gives a clear breakdown of fees and taxes before you book.
Priceline.com	www.priceline.com	discounter that also allows bidding.
SA-Venues	www.sa-venues.com	books lodgings in all of South Africa's major tourist destinations.
Travel.com	www.travel.com	allows you to compare its rates with those of other booking engines.
Travelocity	www.travelocity	charges a booking fee for airline tickets, but promises good problem resolution.

ONLINE ACCOMMODATIONS

All City Hotels.net	www.allcityhotels.net	is a discount booking site searchable by city or suburb.
Hotels.com	www.hotels.com	big Expedia-owned wholesaler that offers rooms in hotels all over the world.
Quikbook	www.quikbook.com	offers "pay when you stay" reservations that allow you to settle your bill when you check out, not when you book.
Rooms For Africa	www.roomsforafrica.com	clever map "drill-down" search engine makes it easy to find accommodations along your driving route.
South Africa Lodges	www.south-african-lodges. com	allows you to search for game lodges by region, and along the whale route.

corridor. You can usually choose between rooms with twin or double beds. A full English breakfast is often included in the rate, particularly in more traditional hotels. In most luxury lodges the rate usually covers the cost of dinner, bed, and breakfast, whereas in game lodges the rate includes everything but alcohol—and some include that. A self-catering room is one with kitchen facilities.

Be warned, though, that in southern Africa words do not necessarily mean what you think they do. The term *lodge* is a particularly tricky one. A guest lodge or a game lodge is almost always an upmarket, full-service facility with loads of extra attractions. But the term *lodge* when applied to city hotels often indicates a minimum-service hotel. These are usually very well appointed and comfortable but have no restaurant or room service, and thus offer very good-value bed-and-breakfast accommodations. Examples are the Protea Lodges (as opposed to Protea Hotels), City and Town Lodges, and Holiday Inn Garden Courts. A backpacker lodge, however, is essentially a hostel.

A *rondavel* can be a small cabin, often in a rounded shape, while its cousin, the *banda,* can be anything from a basic stand-alone structure to a Quonset hut. Think very rustic.

Price charts specific to each area are found in each chapter. We always list the facilities that are available—but we don't specify whether they cost extra: when pricing accommodations, always ask what's included. Price categories are based on a property's least expensive standard double room at high season (excluding holidays). Properties indicated by a ✕🏠 are lodging establishments whose restaurant warrants a special trip. Those indicated by a ⛺ are campgrounds with rustic camping accommodations. (These are different from the fairly luxurious safari tents found at many private game lodges.) Mailing addresses follow the street address or location, where appropriate.

Most hotels and other lodgings require you to give your credit-card details before they will confirm your reservation. If you don't feel comfortable e-mailing this information, ask if you can fax it (some places even prefer faxes). However you book, get written confirmation and have a copy when you check in.

Be sure you understand the hotel's cancellation policy. Some places allow you to cancel without any kind of penalty—even if you prepaid to secure a discounted rate—if you cancel at least 24 hours in advance. Others require you to cancel a week in advance or penalize you the cost of one night. Small inns and B&Bs are most likely to require you to cancel far in advance. ■TIP➔ Most hotels allow children under a certain age to stay in their parents' room at no extra charge, but others charge for them as extra adults, and some don't allow children under 12 at all. Ask about their policy on children before checking in and make sure you find out the cutoff age for discounts.

■TIP➔ Assume that hotels operate on the European Plan (EP, no meals) unless we specify that they use the Breakfast Plan (BP, with full breakfast), Continental Plan (CP, Continental breakfast), Full American Plan (FAP, all meals), Modified American Plan (MAP, breakfast and dinner) or are all-inclusive (AI, all meals and most activities). In South Africa, most accommodations from hotels to guesthouses do include breakfast in the rate. Most game lodges have FAP. All hotels listed have private bath unless otherwise noted.

Contacts Grading Council of South Africa (⊕ www.tourismgrading.co.za). Portfolio Collection (☎ 021/689–4020, 072/371–2472 after hours ⊕ www.portfoliocollection.com).

HOTELS

Your hotel in South Africa will be similar to one at home; the more you pay, the better the quality and amenities. Some

10 WAYS TO SAVE

1. Join & save. Sign up for free frequent-guest program memberships and check your property's affiliation. You may get preferential treatment (room choices, upgrades) in your favorite chains.

2. Contact & save. You can sometimes get a better price if you contact the hotel directly, rather than a central reservations number.

3. Click & save. Check hotel Web sites. Not all chains are represented on all travel sites, and many offer Internet-only rate specials.

4. Ask & save. It never hurts to ask about specials before booking, such as packages or automobile-club rates.

5. Lock in your rate. For overseas trips, look for guaranteed rates. With your rate locked in you won't pay more, even if the price goes up in the local currency. Or prepay.

6. City-hop on the weekend. High-end chains catering to business travelers are often busy only on weekdays; to fill rooms they often drop rates dramatically on weekends.

7. Check the bottom line. Verify whether local hotel taxes are included in quoted rates. In some places taxes can add 20% or more to your bill.

8. Read the fine print. Watch for add-ons, including resort fees, energy surcharges, and "convenience" fees.

9. Save by the season. Try to schedule your trip between peak seasons. Warning: if your dates straddle peak and nonpeak seasons, a property may still charge peak-season rates.

10. Consider time versus money. The money you save by staying a long way from your destination may cost you in travel time.

online booking sites have specials for more expensive properties that include a couple of extra nights at less popular locales. It's worth poking around to see if these can fit into your itinerary as they may save you some money if you're planning to visit several locations.

As at home, peak seasons mean peak prices. There are a few international chains represented in South Africa, so check with your frequent-stay program to see if you can get a better room or better rate. It might be more fun, though, to experience a local, or African establishment.

Almost every hotel stay will include breakfast in the hotel's dining room, and in South Africa that means a full array of meats, cheeses, and eggs cooked to order—a little bonus that makes it easier to ease into your touring day. If you have an early departure, be sure to have the front desk arrange a take-away bag.

Information City Lodge Hotels (☎011/557–2600 ⊕www.citylodge.co.za). **Forever Resorts South Africa** (☎012/423–5600 ⊕www.forev-ersa.co.za). **Protea Hotels** (☎021/430–5330 ⊕www.proteahotels.com). **Southern Sun** (☎011/482–3500 ⊕www.southernsun.com).

BED & BREAKFASTS

B&Bs are as ubiquitous in South Africa as they are in most other parts of the world. Many are very small and personalized, giving the visitor an insight into the lives of locals. For more information, contact the Bed and Breakfast Association of South Africa (BABASA) or the Portfolio Collection, which represents more than 700 lodging options in South Africa and publishes a respected list of South Africa's best B&Bs that may also be useful. It also offers a similar guide to small hotels and lodges.

Reservation Services BABASA (✉Box 2005, Groenkloof 0027 ☎072/947–8514 ⊕www.babasa.co.za). **Portfolio Collection** (☎021/689–4020, 072/371–2472 after hours ⊕www.portfoliocollection.com). **SA-Venues** (⊕www.sa-venues.com).

GUESTHOUSES

The term *guesthouse* may conjure up the image of a flophouse or boarding-house, but in South Africa they are a cross between an inn and a B&B. Usually located in neighborhoods, rather than downtown tourist districts, they offer an intimate experience that benefits from the proprietor's tastes and interests, often at a vast savings over hotels. A guesthouse manager might make special arrangements to drive you to an attraction, whereas a hotel might charge extra transportation fees. Often long-term visitors choose this option, as it gives people the chance to meet other like-minded travelers who are interested in experiencing the country, not just ticking off sites.

Information Guest House Accommodation of South Africa (☎021/762-0880 ⊕www.ghasa.co.za). **Sleeping Out** (☎021/762–1543 ⊕www.sleeping-out.co.za).

HOSTELS

Hostels offer bare-bones lodging at low, low prices—often in shared dorm rooms with shared baths—to people of all ages, though the primary market is young travelers, especially students. Most hostels serve breakfast; dinner and/or shared cooking facilities may also be available. In some hostels you aren't allowed to be in your room during the day, and there may be a curfew at night. Nevertheless, hostels provide a sense of community, with public rooms where travelers often gather to share stories. Many hostels are affiliated with Hostelling International (HI), an umbrella group of hostel associations with some 4,000 member properties in more than 60 countries. Other hostels are completely independent and may be nothing more than a really cheap hotel.

Membership in any HI association, open to travelers of all ages, allows you to stay in HI-affiliated hostels at member rates. One-year membership is about $28 for adults. Rates in dorm-style rooms run about $15–$25 per bed per night; private rooms are more, but are still generally well under $100 a night. Members have priority if the hostel is full; they're also eligible for discounts around the world, even on rail and bus travel in some countries.

You'll find a backpackers' hostel in almost every great destination—some are fabulous, some are a tad, well, scruffy. Most hostels are affiliated with BTSA (Backpacker Tourism South Africa). You can get a good overview of the hostel scene from "Coast to Coast" or "the Alternative Route," both of which are small, free booklets that are regularly updated. The Baz Bus (*see By Bus in the Transportation section*) offers a handy door-to-door service to backpacker lodgings all around the country.

Information Backpacking South Africa (⊕www.backpackingsouthafrica.co.za). **Coast to Coast** (⊕www.coastingafrica.com). **Hostelling International South Africa** (☎021/788-2301 ⊕www.hisa.org.za).

GAME LODGES

Game lodges in South Africa are often designed to fulfill your wildest wildlife fantasy. Top designers have created magical worlds in styles from African chic to throwback bush romance. At the highest end, you can enjoy dinner under starlight on your own deck, or swap stories around the boma at night. For some people the first glimpse of their accommodations is a thrill to rival the best game viewing.

You'll want to spend some time lingering over the photos on the Web sites to find

---

WORD OF MOUTH

Did the resort look as good in real life as it did in the photos? Did you sleep like a baby, or were the walls paper thin? Did you get your money's worth? Rate hotels and write your own reviews in Travel Ratings or start a discussion about your favorite places in Travel Talk on www.fodors.com. Your comments might even appear in our books. Yes, you, too, can be a correspondent!

your style. Many properties are listed with several booking agents, so shop around for the best price. Look for "green season" rates and other "buy three, get one free" specials on the Web sites.

Contacts Book in Africa (☎800/846–1578 or 011/833–1000 ⊕www.bookinafrica. com). **CC Africa** (☎011/809–4300 ⊕www. ccafrica.com). **Classic Safari Camps of Africa** (☎011/465–6427 ⊕www.classicsafaricamps.com). **Go2Africa** (☎021/481–4900 ⊕www.go2africa.com). **Mantis Collection** (☎021/713–2230 ⊕www.mantiscollection. com). **Portfolio Collection** (☎021/689–4020, 072/371–2472 after hours ⊕www. portfoliocollection.com). **Safarinow.com** (⊕www.safarinow.com). **South Africa Lodges** (☎021/794–9050 ⊕www.south-african-lodges.com). **Wild African Ventures** (☎800/358–8530 ⊕www.wildafricanventures. com). **Wilderness Safaris** (☎011/807–1800 ⊕www.wilderness-safaris.com).

FARM STAYS

Jacana Marketing and Reservations offers a range of farms, coastal and country cottages, and privately operated hiking, biking, and horse trails in country areas.

Contact Jacana Marketing and Reservations (☎011/656–0606 ⊕www.jacanacollection.co.za).

HOME EXCHANGES

It is really unusual for a short-term vacationer to do a home exchange, but for visiting academics or business travelers who come for a long stay and bring their families, it might be a solution. Certainly a home gives you more space and a feel for the community.

Exchange Clubs Home Base Holidays in South Africa (☎021/993–4310 ⊕www. homebase-hols.com/southafrica.shtml); the South African branch of London home-exchange alliance. **Home Exchange.com** (☎800/877–8723 ⊕www.homeexchange. com); $59.95 for a 1-year online listing. **HomeLink International** (☎800/638–3841 ⊕www.homelinksouthafrica.org); largest home-exchange network in South Africa.

Intervac U.S. (☎800/756–4663 ⊕www. intervacus.com); $90 for Web-only membership; $140 includes Web access and a catalog. **Sabbatical Homes** (⊕www.sabbaticalhomes. com); fee-based service for academics who need temporary housing in Cape Town and Johannesburg.

▌ AIRLINE TICKETS

Almost all airlines have now moved to electronic or ticketless travel. With an e-ticket the only thing you receive is an e-mailed receipt citing your itinerary and reservation and ticket numbers.

The greatest advantage of an e-ticket is that if you lose your receipt, you can simply print out another copy or ask the airline to do it for you at check-in. You usually pay a surcharge (up to $50) to get a paper ticket, if you can get one at all.

The least expensive airfares to South Africa are priced for round-trip travel and must usually be purchased in advance. Airlines generally allow you to change your return date for a fee; most low-fare tickets, however, are nonrefundable. To determine when its best to buy tickets so you can save money, check out FareCompare.com, which has historical and current airfares, and Farecast.com, which predicts fare changes based on historical data. Unlike other sites, AirfareWatchDog.com includes rates for budget airlines.

Keep abreast of fares even after buying tickets. Some airlines give you credit for the value of the price reduction if the airfare goes down later (ask about this when booking). The innovative Web site Yapta. com monitors drops in airfares for just this purpose. You'll often have to pay a fee of $75 or $100 to rebook your flight, but if the fare drops substantially, the charge may be worth it.

AIR PASS

The Star Alliance African Airpass can only be purchased by international passengers arriving to Africa on a Star Alliance carrier (United, Air Canada, US Airways, South African Airways, etc.), and is good for 4 to 10 flights. The flights are sold in segments, priced by the distance between cities. These are only economy class seats and can be expensive when compared to the discount airline pricing within South Africa, but they are a bargain for the longer routes, such as Nairobi to Johannesburg for under $300. If your itinerary includes more than two of the 25 cities served in Africa, this may be a good choice.

The Oneworld Alliance's Visit Africa Pass uses a zone system between cities in South Africa, Namibia, Zambia, and Zimbabwe that British Airways services. The minimum purchase is two segments and the maximum is 20. Prices are competitive and represent a great value when compared to regular fares. For example, Johannesburg to Windhoek is just $90 one way. The catch is that U.S. residents must fly British Airways to South Africa, and can only earn frequent-flier miles in the British Airways program, not on American Airlines, their partner carrier in the United States.

For island-hoppers, it is worth noting that Air Seychelles, Air Mauritius, and Air Austral offer an Indian Ocean Airpass that makes island-hopping easy for those with enough vacation time to wait out infrequent flights between airports in Comores, Mauritius, Madagascar, Maldives, Rodrigues, Reunion, and the Seychelles. The minimum purchase is three segments and they do represent a savings over à la carte flights. Air Mauritius usually gives the fastest response.

Air Pass Contact Info **Air Mauritius** (☎800/537–1182 or 201/871–8382 ⊕www. airmauritius.com). **Oneworld Alliance** (☎ ⊕www.oneworldalliance.com). **Star Alliance** (☎ ⊕www.staralliance.com).

10 WAYS TO SAVE

1. Commit to a date. If saving money is more important than flexibility, then nonrefundable tickets work. Just remember that you'll pay as much as $200 if you change your plans.

2. Do your homework. Web sites and travel agents can have different arrangements with the airlines and offer different prices for exactly the same flights.

3. Consolidator bargains. If you can be flexible, air consolidators can often offer better rates than Web sites or airlines.

4. Be flexible. Certain days or times of year are less expensive than others to travel. Find out when low season is and considering traveling then.

5. Fly and spend right. If you know you want to go to Africa, make sure your preferred airline flies there and that they except your credit-card miles. If you have enough time to plan, join frequent-flier clubs that will allow you to use your miles to go to Africa.

6. Early birds get worms. Look for cheap fares up to a year in advance.

7. Savings via e-mail. Sign up for newsletters from carriers that serve your destination. You might find a sale fare.

8. Check out low-cost airlines. South Africa now has several low-cost domestic carriers that offer bargain rates.

9. Airpass savings. Look for deals that you can purchase in conjunction with your international ticket to save on domestic flights or those between countries. The savings might make an expensive transAtlantic flight attractive if you save on domestic flights.

10. Fodor's talk. People who frequent online message boards (⊕ *www.fodors. com/forums*) often post when they hear of sales.

CHARTER FLIGHTS

Charter companies are a common mode of transportation when getting to safari lodges and remote destinations throughout southern Africa. These aircraft are well-maintained and are almost always booked by your lodge or travel agent. The major charter companies run daily shuttles from O.R. Tambo to popular tourism destinations, such as Kruger Park. On-demand flights, those made at times other than those scheduled, are very expensive for independent travelers, as they require minimum passenger loads. If it is just two passengers, you will be charged for the vacant seats. Keep in mind that you probably won't get to choose the charter company you fly with. The aircraft you get depends on the number of passengers flying and can vary from very small (you will sit in the co-pilot's seat) to a much more comfortable commuter plane. ■TIP→ Those with a severe fear of small planes might consider road travel instead.

Due to the limited space and size of the aircraft, charter carriers observe strict luggage regulations: luggage must be soft sided and weigh no more than 44 lbs. (20 kgs.).

Charter Companies **African Ramble** (☎044/533–9006 ⊕www.aframble.co.za) flies out of Plettenberg Bay and will take direct bookings. **Federal Air** (☎011/395–9000 ⊕www.fedair.com) is the largest charter air company in South Africa. It's based at Johannesburg Airport and has its own efficient terminal with a gift shop, refreshments, and a unique, thatched-roof outdoor lounge. They also have branches in Cape Town, Durban, and Nelspruit (near Kruger). **Nelair** (☎013/751–1870 ⊕www.nelair.co.za) is based in Mpumalanga and operates daily shuttles, some with leather seats, within Kruger Park and the Sabi Sands and Timbavati Game Reserves. **Sefofane** (☎011/701–3700 [South Africa], 267/686–0778 [Botswana], 264/61/25–5735 [Namibia] ⊕www.sefofane.com) is a Botswana-based fly-in charter company that has recently begun to operate in Kruger Park and the KwaZulu-Natal area.

▮ RENTAL CARS

The infrastructure of South Africa is so similar to that of the United States that many visitors decide to rent cars for some, if not all of their trip. Renting a car gives you the freedom to visit what you'd like and set your own timetable. Most of Cape Town's most popular destinations are an easy drive from the City Bowl. Many people enjoy the slow pace of exploring South Africa's Garden Route by car, or a few days meandering through the Winelands on their own.

Kruger Park has three distinct driving routes for self-drive trips. Many South African families make annual driving excursions to the park and create their own safari itineraries moving from camp to camp. Driving gets you close to the ground and lets you mingle with a different set of travelers than you might encounter on a fly-in safari alone. If it is your first time on safari, though, you probably want to learn about the wildlife from an experienced guide, making self-drive a less attractive option.

Rates in South Africa are similar to those in most U.S. destinations, and can vary depending on the bells and whistles and where you intend to drive. Some companies charge more on the weekend, so it's best to get a range of quotes before booking your car. Request car seats and extras such as GPS when you book, and ask for details on what to do if you have a mechanical problem or other emergency.

■TIP→ Make sure that a confirmed reservation guarantees you a car. Agencies sometimes overbook, particularly for busy weekends and holiday periods.

At the time of writing, rates on average began at about R210 per day for unlimited mileage or a slightly cheaper rate for 200 km (125 mi) per day and about R1.50 for each additional kilometer. These prices are for an economy car with a 1,300-cc engine, no air-conditioning, and a stick shift. For a car with automatic transmission and air-conditioning, you'll pay around R400 per day for unlimited kilometers and slightly less for 200 km (125 mi) per day plus about R3.50 per extra kilometer. When comparing prices, make sure you're getting the same thing. Some companies quote prices with no insurance, some include 80% or 90% coverage, and some quote with 100% protection.

The major international companies all have offices in tourist cities and at international airports, and their vehicle types are the same range you'd find at home: compacts such as VW Golfs, Toyota Corollas, and luxury BMWs and Mercedes. There is no need to rent a 4x4 vehicle as all roads are paved, including those in Kruger National Park as well as Botswana and Namibia.

Maui Motorhome Rentals offers fully equipped motor homes, camper vans, and four-wheel-drive vehicles, many of which come totally equipped for a bush sojourn. Prices start at around R1,100 per day, not including insurance. However, standard insurance coverage may be included or can be added for R140 to R230 per day.

You can often save some money by booking a car through a broker, who will access the car from one of the main agencies. Smaller, local agencies often give a much better price, but the car must be returned in the same city. This is pretty popular in Cape Town but not so much in other centers.

In order to rent a car you need to be 23 years or older and have held a driver's license for three years. Younger international drivers can rent from some companies, but will pay a penalty. You need to get special permission to take rental cars into neighboring countries, such as Lesotho, Swaziland, Namibia, or Botswana. You cannot take rental cars into Zimba-

10 WAYS TO SAVE

1. Know what you need. You can save a day's rental or more by picking up your car only when you need it and using lower-cost options for attractions in town. Plan your route ahead to see where you can use public transportation and cut days off your rental time.

2. Rent weekly. Weekly rates are usually better than daily ones. Even if you only want to rent for five or six days, ask for the weekly rate; it may very well be cheaper than the daily rate.

3. Think local. Price local companies as well as the majors.

4. Costly airport rentals. Airports often add surcharges, which you can sometimes avoid by renting from an agency whose office is just off airport property.

5. Wholesalers can help. Investigate wholesalers, which don't own fleets but rent in bulk from firms that do, and which frequently offer better rates.

6. Look for rate guarantees. With your rate locked in, you won't pay more, even if the price goes up.

7. Ask your innkeeper. Smaller inns or B&Bs sometimes have deals with local car-rental companies.

8. Pump it yourself. Don't pre-pay for rental-car gas. The saving isn't that great, and unless you coast in on empty upon return, you wind up paying for gas you don't use.

9. Get all your discounts. If you belong to an automobile club at home, such as AAA, you will often get a discount when you rent in South Africa, but you have to ask. Also, find out whether your credit card, frequent-renter program, etc. offers discounts.

10. Ask your agent. Your safari agent may be able to get you a special rate on a rental car later in your trip.

Car Rental Resources

AUTOMOBILE ASSOCIATIONS			
American Automobile Association (AAA)	315/797–5000	www.aaa.com	most contact with the organization is through state and regional members.
National Automobile Club	650/294–7000	www.thenac.com	membership is open to California residents only.
South Africa Automobile Association	083/843–22	www.aasa.co.za	
LOCAL AGENCIES			
Car Mania	021/447–3001 or 021/447–3009	www.carmania.co.za	
Imperial Car Rental	086/113–1000	www.imperialcarrental.co.za	
Maui Motorhome Rental	011/396–1445 or 021/982–5107	www.maui.co.za	
Value Car Hire	021/696–2198	www.valuecarhire.co.za	
MAJOR AGENCIES			
Alamo	800/522–9696	www.alamo.com	
Avis	800/331–1084	www.avis.com	
Budget	800/472–3325	www.budget.com	
Europcar	0860/011–344	www.europcar.co.za	
Hertz	800/654–3001	www.hertz.com	
National Car Rental	800/227–7368	www.nationalcar.com	

bwe. Most companies allow additional drivers, yet some charge. Get the terms in writing before you leave on your trip.

Leave ample time to return your car when your trip is over. You shouldn't feel rushed when settling your bill. Be sure to get copies of your receipt.

CAR-RENTAL INSURANCE

If you own a car, your personal auto insurance may cover a rental to some degree, though not all policies protect you abroad; always read your policy's fine print. If you don't have auto insurance, then seriously consider buying the collision- or loss-damage waiver (CDW or LDW) from the car-rental company, which eliminates your liability for damage to the car. Some credit cards offer CDW coverage, but it's usually supplemental to your own insurance and rarely covers SUVs, minivans, luxury models, and the like. If your coverage is secondary, you may still be liable for loss-of-use costs from the car-rental company. But no credit-card insurance is valid unless you use that card for *all* transactions, from reserving to paying the final bill. All companies exclude car rental in some countries, so be sure to find out about the destination to which you are traveling.

■TIP→ Diners Club offers primary CDW coverage on all rentals reserved and paid for with the card. This means that Diners

Club's company—not your own car insurance—pays in case of an accident. It *doesn't* mean your car-insurance company won't raise your rates once it discovers you had an accident.

Some rental agencies require you to purchase CDW coverage; many will even include it in quoted rates. All will strongly encourage you to buy CDW—possibly implying that it's required—so be sure to ask about such things before renting. In most cases it's cheaper to add a supplemental CDW plan to your comprehensive travel-insurance policy (⇨ *Trip Insurance under Things to Consider in Getting Started, above*) than to purchase it from a rental company. That said, you don't want to pay for a supplement if you're required to buy insurance from the rental company.

In South Africa it is necessary to buy special insurance if you plan on crossing borders into neighboring countries, but CDW and TDW (theft-damage waiver) are optional on domestic rentals. Vehicles entering Namibia are subject to special fees. Any time you are considering crossing a border with your rental vehicle, you must inform the rental company ahead of time to fulfill any paperwork requirements and pay additional fees.

■ VACATION PACKAGES

■TIP→Some packages are sold only through travel agents. Don't always assume that you can get the best deal by booking everything yourself.

Packages *are not* fully escorted tours. Packages combine airfare, accommodations, and perhaps a rental car or other extras (theater tickets, guided excursions, boat trips, reserved entry to popular museums, transit passes), but you travel independently between accommodations and make your own plans during the day. During busy periods packages may be your only option, as flights and rooms may be sold out otherwise. They often,

but not always, offer some degree of savings over purchasing flights and rooms separately. Be aware that prices advertised on Web sites and in newspapers rarely include service charges or taxes.

■TIP→Local tourism boards can provide information about lesser-known and small-niche operators that sell packages to only a few destinations. If you are accustomed to packaged tours, then it will be hard to break you of the habit, even in the easiest-to-navigate destination. You will certainly learn more about the sites that you are zipping past on the road from a trained tour guide, and you will not have to worry about your own vehicle, or worry needlessly about safety, as tour companies will ferry you from point to point.

Organizations United States Tour Operators Association (USTOA ☎ 212/599–6599 ⊕ www.ustoa.com).

■ GUIDED TOURS

Guided tours are a good option when you don't want to do it all yourself. You travel along with a group (sometimes large, sometimes small), stay in prebooked hotels, eat with your fellow travelers (the cost of meals sometimes included in the price of your tour, sometimes not), and follow a schedule.

But not all guided tours are an if-it's-Tuesday-this-must-be-Belgium experience. A knowledgeable guide can take you places that you might never discover on your own, provide you with specialized local knowledge as well as an understanding of seasonal peculiarities, and get you special deals. Another bonus: you may be pushed to see more than you would have otherwise. Tours aren't for everyone, but they can be just the thing for trips to places where making travel arrangements are difficult, or independent travel is discouraged. In South Africa, it is wise to go with a guide and only a guide to experience the townships on a day tour, for example.

Whenever you book a guided tour, find out what's included and what isn't. A "land-only" tour includes all your travel (by bus, in most cases) in the destination, but not necessarily your flights to and from or even within it. Also, in most cases prices in tour brochures don't include fees and taxes. Remember to tip your guide (in cash) at the end of the tour.

Recommended Companies Big Five (☎800/244–3483 in the U.S. ⊕www.bigfive.com). **Fairfield Tours** (☎021/930–3534 ⊕www.fairfieldtours.com). **Felix Unite Tourism Group** (☎021/683–6433 ⊕www.felix-unite.com). **Hylton Ross** (☎021/511–1784 ⊕www.hyltonross.co.za). **Karibu Safaris** (☎031/563-9774 ⊕www.karibu.co.za). **Premier Tours** (☎800/545–1910 in the U.S.) ⊕www.premiertours.com). **Sun Tours** (☎0861/696–059 ⊕www.suntourssa.co.za). **Thompson's South Africa** (☎031/250–3100 ⊕www.thompsonssa.com).

PHILANTHROPIC TRAVEL

Volunteering in South Africa has grown in popularity, and several international volunteer vacation organizations offer some combination of touring and service. A true volunteer experience usually requires more than providing your travel dates and sending a check, therefore it is advisable to research a range of types of commitment before picking one.

Professionals can often consult their own organizations for opportunities to transfer skills in South Africa, while students can find suitable student-oriented programs through their universities.

Fees for volunteer programs are comparable to costs for a vacation, but standards are almost always lower than those of a typical pleasure trip. Rooms are shared, meals are self-catering, and toilet facilities will not be five-star-hotel caliber. Those that look more fun than work-oriented, with smiling bikini-clad teens on their Web pages, are generally most expensive.

Contacts Aviva (☎021/557-4312 ⊕www.aviva-sa.com) is very much a vacation-oriented volunteer agency, with leisure-friendly activities to teach surfing or to help conserve penguins. Good for students with spare time, and plenty of spare cash. **Cross Cultural Solutions** (☎800/380–4777 ⊕www.crossculturalsolutions.com) organizes teams of volunteers for projects worldwide. **Global Volunteer Network** (☎800/963–1198 ⊕www.volunteer.org.nz) is a New Zealand–based volunteer placement agency with environmental projects in South Africa. **Transitions Abroad** (⊕www.transitionsabroad.com) lists dozens of South African volunteer opportunities with a range of requirements and destinations.

TRANSPORTATION

You may have a few problems trying to find your way around South Africa, but it shouldn't be insurmountable. The newest wrinkle is the renaming of place names. Countless cities, towns, streets, parks, etc. have gotten or will get new monikers, both to rid the country of names that recall the apartheid era and to honor the previously unsung.

The names in this book were accurate at time of writing, but even if names are different by the time of your trip, don't worry; all of South Africa will be coping with these large-scale changes and will undoubtedly use both names for awhile.

Another problem you may encounter while you're trying to find your way around South African cities is that geographical features, such as streets and town names, are sometimes alternately signposted in English and Afrikaans. So, for example, Wale Street and Waalst are the same road. You can be driving the N2 toward Cape Town, but find that the major road signs point to Kaapstad, the city's Afrikaans name.

Note that the first floor of a building is the one between the ground floor and the second floor. Mailing addresses are pretty straightforward. If they're not a street address, they're either a P.O. Box or a Private Bag—essentially the same, just differing in size. The only vaguely tricky variation is a postnet suite, which consists of a number, followed by a private bag and then a post office (e.g., Postnet Suite 25, Private Bag X25, name of town, postal code). Even the smallest town has its own postal code, and suburbs may have different postal codes—one for a street address and one for P.O. boxes.

■ BY AIR

When booking flights, check the routing carefully, as South Africa-bound flights from U.S. cities have refueling stops en route, and sometimes those stops can be delayed. Don't plan anything on the ground too rigidly after arriving; leave yourself a cushion for a connecting flight to a game lodge. Currently only South African Airways and Delta provide direct service from the United States to South Africa, but flights routed through Europe may be more pleasant. First, they allow you to stretch your legs and change planes, or even stop over on the way there or back. Second, most European flights bound for Africa are overnights, so you will arrive in South Africa in the morning, with plenty of time to make connections.

As a rule, you need to get to the airport an hour before a domestic flight and three hours before an international one. In peak season (midsummer and South African school vacations), it's a good idea to give yourself at least a half hour extra for domestic flights, as the check-in lines can be horrendous—particularly on flights to the coast at the start of vacations and back to Johannesburg at the end. It is not necessary to reconfirm domestic flights if you have a confirmed booking—but, hey, it's always a good idea.

If you are returning home with souvenirs, leave time for a V.A.T. inspection before you join the line for your international flight check-in. The O.R. Tambo check-in area has not yet been modernized, so it can be a jumble of people going to various destinations squeezed into a tight area at peak departure times, which can add to pre-flight stress.

The domestic terminal is far superior to the international terminal, with a large hall and plenty of room for you and your baggage trolley; baggage carts are widely available at South African airports at no charge. ■TIP➔ There are vast distances between gates, so clear security before stopping for a snack or shopping, as you don't want to scramble for your flight.

All domestic flights within South Africa are no-smoking—the longest is only two hours—and all airports are smoke-free except for designated smoking areas.

If you are visiting a game lodge deep in the bush, you will be arriving by light plane—and you really will be restricted in what you can bring. Excess luggage can usually be stored with the operator until your return. Don't just gloss over this: charter operators take weight very seriously, and some will charge you for an extra ticket if you insist on bringing excess baggage. (*See Charter Flights in Booking Your Trip*).

Airlines & Airports **Airline and Airport Links.com** (⊕ www.airlineandairportlinks.com) has links to many of the world's airlines and airports.

Airline Security Issues **Transportation Security Administration** (⊕ www.tsa.gov) has answers for almost every question that might come up.

Air Travel Resources in South Africa **Airports Company South Africa** (⊕ www.acsa. co.za) has detailed information on all of South Africa's airports, as well a form for lodging complaints.

AIRPORTS
South Africa's major airports are in Johannesburg, Cape Town, and, to a lesser extent, Durban. Most international flights arrive at and depart from Johannesburg International Airport, now called O.R. Tambo, and sometimes abbreviated O.R.T.I.A. by safari companies. It is 19 km (12 mi) from the city. The airport has a tourist information desk, a V.A.T. refund office, and a computerized accommodations service. Several international flights departing from Cape Town are also routed via Johan-

---

IS YOUR PLANE SAFE?

We all wonder this, but now you can find out for sure by searching the International Air Transport Association's Web site (⊕ www.iata.org/ps/services/iosa/registry. htm), which posts safety audits of its members. The down side? It only lists those that pass, not those that fail. Another good place to check out saftey records is the FAA's Web site (⊕ www.faa.gov/passengers/international_travel), which cites countries (not airlines) that that fail too meet FAA safety standards in their airline industry. Its downside? The site only concerns itself with countries that have airlines that fly to the U.S.

---

nesburg. Cape Town International is 20 km (12½ mi) southeast of the city, and Durban International is 16 km (10 mi) south of the city. If you are traveling to or from either Johannesburg or Cape Town airport (and, to a lesser extent, Durban) be very aware of the time of day. Traffic can be horrendous between 7 and 9 in the morning and between about 3:30 and 6 in the evening, so if you need to be, say, at Cape Town International at 5, it's better to leave at 3 and spend the extra time reading a book at the airport. It's less stressful than spending the same amount of time in traffic. The morning rush hour only affects Cape Town International if you're traveling from the city center. The Cape Town airport is much smaller than Jo'burg's and therefore much easier to get around in, although Jo'burg is quite small by international standards.

Just 40km (25 mi) outside Johannesburg, Lanseria International Airport is closer to Sandton than O.R. Tambo and handles executive jets, company jets, domestic scheduled flights to and from Cape Town, and some charter flights to safari camps. It has a 24-hour customs and immigration counter, a café, and a high-end flight store. It's a popular alternative for visiting dignitaries and other VIPs.

FLYING 101

Flying may not be as carefree as it once was, but there are some things you can do to make your trip smoother.

■ **Minimize the time spent standing line.** Buy an e-ticket, check in at an electronic kiosk, or—even better—check in on your airline's Web site before leaving home. Pack light and limit carry-on items to only the essentials.

■ **Arrive when you need to.** Research your airline's policy. It's usually at least an hour before domestic flights and two to three hours before international flights. But airlines at some busy airports have more stringent requirements. Check the TSA Web site for estimated security waiting times at major airports.

■ **Get to the gate.** If you aren't at the gate at least 10 minutes before your flight is scheduled to take off (sometimes earlier), you won't be allowed to board.

■ **Double-check your flight times.** Do this especially if you reserved far in advance. Schedules change, and alerts may not reach you.

■ **Don't go hungry.** Ask whether your airline offers anything to eat; even when it does, be prepared to pay.

■ **Get the seat you want.** Often you can pick a seat when you buy your ticket on an airline Web site. But it's not guaranteed; the airline could change the plane after you book, so double-check. You can also select a seat if you check in electronically. Avoid seats on the aisle directly across from the lavatories. Frequent fliers say those are even worse than back-row seats that don't recline.

■ **Got kids? Get info.** Ask the airline about its children's menus, activities, and fares. Sometimes infants and toddlers fly free if they sit on a parent's lap, and older children fly for half price in their own seats. Also inquire about policies involving car seats; having one may limit seating options. Also ask about seat-belt extenders for car seats. And note that you can't count on a flight attendant to produce an extender; you may have to ask for one when you board.

■ **Check your scheduling.** Don't buy a ticket if there's less than an hour between connecting flights. Although schedules are padded, if anything goes wrong you might miss your connection. If you're traveling to an important function, depart a day early.

■ **Bring paper.** Even when using an e-ticket, always carry a hard copy of your receipt; you may need it to get your boarding pass, which most airports require to get past security.

■ **Complain at the airport.** If your baggage goes astray or your flight goes awry, complain before leaving the airport. Most carriers require this.

■ **Beware of overbooked flights.** If a flight is oversold, the gate agent will usually ask for volunteers and offer some sort of compensation for taking a different flight. If you're bumped from a flight *involuntarily,* the airline must give you some kind of compensation if an alternate flight can't be found within one hour.

■ **Know your rights.** If your flight is delayed because of something within the airline's control (bad weather doesn't count), the airline must get you to your destination on the same day, even if they have to book you on another airline and in an upgraded class. Read the Contract of Carriage, which is usually buried on the airline's Web site.

■ **Be prepared.** The Boy Scout motto is especially important if you're traveling during a stormy season. To quickly adjust your plans, program a few numbers into your cell: your airline, an airport hotel or two, your destination hotel, your car service, and/or your travel agent.

The other major cities are served by small airports that are really easy to navigate. Most airports are managed by the Airports Company of South Africa.

International Airports **Airports Company of South Africa** (⊕www.acsa.co.za). **Cape Town International Airport** (CPT ☎021/937–1200). **Durban International Airport** (DUR ☎031/451–6667). **Lanseria International Airport** (HLA ☎011/659–2750). **O. R. Tambo International Airport (Formerly Johannesburg)** (JNB ORTIA ☎011/921–6262).

Domestic Airports **Bloemfontein Airport** (BFN ☎051/433–2662). **East London Airport** (ELS ☎043/706–0304). **George Airport** (GRJ ☎044/876–9310). **Kimberley Airport** (KIM ☎053/838–3216). **Pilanesberg Airport** (NTY, next to Sun City ☎014/552–1261). **Port Elizabeth Airport** (PLZ ☎041/507–7348). **Upington Airport** (UTN ☎054/332–2161).

General Information **Flight information** (☎086/727–7888).

GROUND TRANSPORTATION IN JOHANNESBURG

Most visitors arrive to Johannesburg in time to make connecting flights to other regions. If you're leaving the international terminal, the domestic terminal is to your left and is connected by a busy walkway. If you are taking a chartered safari flight and do not see your representative, stand near the information kiosk in the middle of the hall and your representative will find you. FedAir has a sign.

If you have a forced overnight in Johannesburg or are visiting for a few days, it is well worth the cost to arrange your transfer directly through your hotel or guesthouse after your long flight. Someone will greet you, and escort you to the vehicle. Get the name of the car service from the hotel concierge before leaving home and carry it in your hand baggage, as well as the phone number for where you are staying.

⚠ **Take a public bus into the city, or hop in a cab—despite its spruced-up appearance, the Metro Rail train is frequently the scene of robberies.** If your hotel or guesthouse does not have a shuttle, ask them to arrange for your transportation with a reliable company. Most lodgings have a regular service they use, so you should have no problem arranging this in advance. If it is proving difficult, that is a red flag that you might want to chose a different establishment.

Prices vary, depending on where you are staying, but plan on R350 ($50) for a ride from the airport to Sandton hotels, and about R250 or R275 ($25 or $30) for a hotel or guesthouse in Rosebank or Melrose. Most will allow you to add the charge to your bill, so you needn't worry about paying in cash.

The Magic Bus runs shuttles from the three major international airports into their respective towns and suburbs. The advantage is a saving on price, but you will lose time on a shared ride, and that may be an exhausting option if you've just gotten off a trans-Atlantic flight. The fare is R255 to Sandton or Rosebank and other Jo'burg suburbs; additional passengers pay only R30 to the same destination. Airport Link is a pre-booked private door-to-door service starting at R275 for one passenger, then an additional R50 for others going to the same destination, with slightly higher rates for Pretoria stops. Legend Tours and Transfers offers prearranged shared-ride transfers from the three international airports. Rates start at R260 from Cape Town and R355 from O. R. Tambo.

Contacts **Airport Link** (☎011/792–2017 ⊕www.airportlink.co.za). **Legend Tours and Transfers** (☎021/674–7055 ⊕www.legend-tours.co.za). **Magic Bus Airport Transfers** (☎011/394–6902 or 011/609–1662 ⊕www.magicbus.co.za).

GROUND TRANSPORTATION IN CAPE TOWN

Touch Down Taxis is the only officially authorized airport taxi. Look for the ACSA symbol on the vehicles. All major car-rental companies have counters at Cape Town International, and driving to the City Bowl or V&A Waterfront is straightforward in daylight. If your flight arrives after dark, consider pre-arranging transportation through your hotel or guesthouse. It should cost less than R200 to V&A Waterfront.

Contacts Touch Down Taxis (021/919–2834).

TRANSFERS BETWEEN AIRPORTS

The domestic and international terminals at O.R. Tambo and Cape Town are a short stroll away from each other and luggage trolleys are provided free of charge. There are many people along the walkway, which is outdoors, running along the outside of the building, so there is no need to be too worried about security, but be aware of your surroundings as you would anywhere. Don't talk to strangers. For added peace of mind, you can use a uniformed porter to transit between the two. Be sure to tip him for his services. (*See Tipping in the On the Ground section*).

FLIGHTS

South African Airways (SAA) flies from New York (JFK) and Washington Dulles (IAD) to Johannesburg and Cape Town. Delta flies from Atlanta (ATL) to Johannesburg. When booking flights, check the routing carefully, as some involve stopovers of an hour or two, which may vary from day to day.

Recent years have seen an explosion of low-cost carriers serving popular domestic routes in South Africa with regularly scheduled flights. Kulula.com, 1time, and Mango give travelers more options than ever. If you know your schedule, be sure to check their fares. The only downside is they can be hard to reach and are not always cheap.

Four major domestic airlines and two low-cost, Web-based airlines have flights connecting South Africa's principal airports. SA Airlink and SA Express are subsidiaries of SAA, and Comair is a subsidiary of British Airways. Nationwide is also giving the big guys a run for their money by accepting only online bookings.

Airline Contacts Delta (800/241–4141 www.delta.com). **South African Airways** (800/521–4845 www.flysaa.com).

Domestic Airlines British Airways (operating as Comair 011/921–0222 www.comair.co.za). **Kulula.com** (www.kulula.com). **Mango** (011/359–1222 or 027/936–1061 www.flymango.co.za). **Nationwide** (011/390–1660 www.flynationwide.co.za). **1time** (www.1time.co.za). **South African Airways/SA Airlink/South African Express** (011/978–1111 www.flysaa.com).

▌BY BUS

Greyhound, Intercape Mainliner, and Translux operate extensive bus networks that serve all major cities. The buses are comfortable, sometimes there are videos, and tea and coffee are served on board. Distances are long; for example, Cape Town to Johannesburg takes 19 hours. Johannesburg to Durban, at about seven hours, is less stressful. The Garden Route is less intense if you take it in stages, but the whole trip from Cape Town to Port Elizabeth takes 12 hours. Buses are usually pretty punctual. Greyhound and Intercape buses can be booked directly or through Computicket.

For travelers with a sense of adventure, a bit of time, and not too much money, the Baz Bus runs a daily hop-on/hop-off door-to-door service between backpackers' hostels around South Africa and other countries in the region. The rates are a bit higher than for the same distance on a standard bus, but you can break the journey up into a number of different legs, days or weeks apart, and the bus drops you off at the hostels so you don't need to find taxis, shuttles, or lifts. Tickets and reservations can be arranged directly or through almost any backpackers' hostel.

■TIP→It is illegal to smoke on buses in South Africa.

The Baz Bus offers a 7-day package for R850 and a 14-day package for R1,600. Each allows unrestricted travel; you can change direction as many times as you want and travel as far as you want. It's especially useful if you're planning a long leg followed by a few short ones before returning to your starting point.

Approximate one-way prices for all three major bus lines are R450–R500 Cape Town to Tshwane, R230–R260 Cape Town to Springbok, R120–R150 Cape Town to George, R240–R260 Cape Town to Port Elizabeth, R150–R170 Johannesburg to Durban, and R460–R500 Cape Town to Durban. Baz Bus fares are higher but include intermediate stops: R1,600 Cape Town to Durban, R320 Durban to Johannesburg via the Drakensberg or R735 via Zululand and Swaziland. A loop between Johannesburg and Durban, doing both routes, costs R1,010. Shorter distances are proportionally cheaper.

Bus Information **Baz Bus** (☎021/439–2323 ⊕www.bazbus.com). **Computicket** (☎083/909-0909 ⊕www.computicket. co.za). **Greyhound** (☎011/276-8500 or 083/915-9000 ⊕www.greyhound.co.za). **Intercape Mainliner** (☎021/380-4400 ⊕www. intercape.co.za). **Translux** (☎0861/589-282 ⊕www.translux.co.za).

■ BY CAR

The first thing you will have to remember is that South Africans drive on the left-hand side of the road. That may be confusing at first, but having the steering wheel on the right might help to remind you that the driver should be closer to

the middle of the road. You'll get used to it very quickly once you start. The most dangerous maneuver is turning onto an empty road, without oncoming traffic to orient you. Be careful not to lapse and veer to the right side.

⚠ Carjackings can and do occur with such frequency that certain high-risk areas are marked by permanent carjacking signs (⇨Safety). South Africa has a superb network of multilane roads and highways, so driving can be a pleasure. Remember, though, that distances are vast, so guard against fatigue, which is an even bigger killer than alcohol. Toll roads, scattered among the main routes, charge anything from R10 to R60.

In South African parlance, traffic lights are known as "robots," and what people refer to as the "pavement" is actually the sidewalk. Paved roads are just called roads. Gas is referred to as petrol and gas stations are petrol stations.

You can drive in South Africa for six months on any English-language license; otherwise you need an international license.

AUTO CLUBS
The Automobile Association (AA) of South Africa extends privileges to members of the American Automobile Association in the United States and the Automobile Association in Britain. Contact a local office in your home country for more information.

In South Africa **Automobile Association of South Africa** (☎011/799-1000 in Johannesburg, 021/419-6914 in Cape Town, 031/201-5244 in Durban, 0800/01-0101 24-hr toll-free emergency ⊕www.aa.co.za).

GASOLINE
■TIP→Credit cards are not accepted anywhere for fueling your tank, but nearly all gas stations are equipped with ATMs. Huge 24-hour service stations are positioned at regular intervals along all major highways in South Africa. There are no self-service

stations; attendants pump the gas, check the oil and water, and wash the windows. In return, tip the attendant R2–R3. South Africa has a choice of unleaded or leaded gasoline, and many vehicles operate on diesel—be sure you get the right fuel. Older vehicles run on leaded fuel. Check when booking a rental car as to what fuel to use. Gasoline is measured in liters, and the cost works out to about R20 a gallon. When driving long distances, check your routes carefully, as the distances between towns—and hence gas stations—can be as much as 200 km (120 mi). It's better to fill a half-full tank than to try to squeeze the last drop out of an unfamiliar rental car.

PARKING
In the countryside parking is mostly free, but you will almost certainly need to pay for parking in cities, which will probably run you less than $1 (less R7) per hour. Coin-operated parking meters are rapidly being phased out, and exist in only a few places. Cape Town was the first city to implement rechargeable smart-card parking meters. You can buy the cards from convenience stores or traffic wardens on the street, both of whom can also recharge them for you. Some towns (e.g., Grahamstown in the Eastern Cape) have "human parking meters." An attendant notes the number of your parking spot and logs it in when you park. When you return, the attendant shows you an electronic readout detailing the amount due. At Pay and Display parking lots you pay in advance. Some parking garages expect payment at the exit, whereas others require that you pay for your parking before you return to your car, and your receipt allows you to exit. Just read the signs carefully. In most cities you will find official parking guards, who usually wear brightly colored bibs or T-shirts. They do not get paid much (in fact some pay for the privilege of working a spot) so they depend on tips. You'll get the most out of these guys if you acknowledge them when you park, ask them politely to look after your car, and then pay them a couple of rand when you return and find it is safe.

ROAD CONDITIONS
South African roads are mostly excellent, but South African drivers tend to be aggressive and reckless, thinking nothing of tailgating at high speeds and passing on blind rises. During national holidays the body count from highway collisions is staggering. The problem is compounded by widespread drunk driving.

If it's safe to do so, it's courteous for slow vehicles to move over onto the shoulder, which is separated from the road by a solid yellow line. (In built-up areas, however, road shoulders are occasionally marked by red lines. This is a strict "no-stopping" zone.) The more aggressive drivers expect this and will flash their lights at you if you don't. Where there are two lanes in each direction, remember that the right-hand lane is for passing. If you're not concentrating, you might end up dawdling along in the right lane, annoying faster drivers.

It's dangerous to drive at night in some rural areas, as roads are not always fenced and animals often stray onto the road. In very remote areas only the main road might be paved, whereas many secondary roads are of high-quality gravel. Traffic is often light in these areas, so be sure to bring extra water and carry a spare, a jack, and a tire iron (your rental car should come with these).

In towns, minibus taxis can be quite unnerving, swerving in and out of traffic without warning to pick up customers. Stay alert at all times, and expect the unexpected. Many cities use mini-traffic circles in lieu of four-way stops. These can be dangerous, particularly if you're not used to them. In theory, the first vehicle to the circle has the right-of-way; otherwise yield to the right. In practice, keep your wits about you at all times. In most cities traffic lights are on poles at the side of the street. In Johannesburg the lights are only on the far side of each intersection, so don't stop in front of the light or you'll be in the middle of the intersection.

DRIVING FROM	TO	RTE./ DISTANCE
Cape Town	Port Elizabeth	769 km (478 mi)
Cape Town	Johannesburg	1402 km (871 mi)
Johannesburg	Durban	583 km (361 mi)
Johannesburg	Kruger National Park	355 km (220 mi)
Kruger National Park	Victoria Falls, Zimbabwe	You cannot take rental cars into Zimbabwe from South Africa
Johannesburg	Pretoria	58 km (36 mi)

ROADSIDE EMERGENCIES
If you have an accident or break down, call the AA and/or the car-rental agency. In the case of an accident you should also call the police and—perhaps—an ambulance. (From mobile phones you can call one number for police and ambulance.) If you are involved in a fender bender where no one is hurt, don't block traffic. Move the cars to the side of the road, and exchange contact details with the other driver. Then phone the rental company and report the accident to a police station within 24 hours. You're advised not to drive alone after dark, but if you break down at night in a scary or lonely place, call the AA, tell them you are alone in an unsafe place, and then walk away from the vehicle—not far, just a few hundred yards, preferably off into the bush on the side of the road, where you can't be seen. Wait there until the AA arrives—recognizable by the flashing orange light—and then walk back to your car. When you get your rental car, the agency will give you a detailed outline of what to do in an emergency. Read it.

Emergency Services **Automobile Association** (☎0800/01–0101). **General emergency number** (☎112 from mobile phone, 10111 from landline).

RULES OF THE ROAD
South Africa's Automobile Association publishes a range of maps, atlases and travel guides, available for purchase on their Web site (⊕*www.aashop.co.za*). Also check with your home automobile club, as many provide international maps and other resources.

The commercial Web site Drive South Africa (⊕*drivesouthafrica.co.za*) has everything you need to know about driving in the country, including road safety and driving distances in their "Travel South Africa" section.

Throughout the country, the speed limit is 100 kph (60 mph) or 120 kph (about 75 mph) on the open road and usually 60 kph (35 mph) or 80 kph (about 50 mph) in towns. Of course, many people drive far faster than that. Wearing seat belts is required by law, and the legal blood-alcohol limit is 0.08 mg/100 ml, which means about one glass of wine puts you at the limit. It is illegal to talk on a handheld mobile phone while driving.

But the most important thing for Americans and Canadians to remember is to drive left, and look right.

▌ BY TRAIN

Shosholoza Meyl, part of the rail network known as Spoornet, operates an extensive system of passenger trains along eight routes that connect all major cities and many small towns in South Africa. Departures are usually limited to one per day, although trains covering minor routes leave less frequently. Distances are vast, so many journeys require overnight travel. The service is good and the trains are safe and well maintained, but this is far from a luxury option, except in Premier Classe, the luxury service that runs between Cape Town and Tshwane (Pretoria). The old first and second classes have been replaced by referring to the cars as four-sleeper (old first class) and six-sleeper. The only difference between four- and six-sleeper is that the four-sleeper has two double bunks, whereas the six-sleeper has two triple bunks. Don't expect air-conditioning or heat in either class, and in either case you will be using a communal toilet and shower. The compartments have a sink. Bedding can be rented. The dining car serves pretty ordinary food, but it's reasonably well cooked and inexpensive. Third class is now referred to as "sitter class," because that's what you do—up to 25 hours on a hard seat with up to 71 other people in the car, sharing two toilets and no shower. You must reserve tickets in advance for four- and six-sleeper accommodations, whereas sitter-class tickets require no advance booking. You can book up to three months in advance with travel agents, reservations offices in major cities, and at railway stations. Note that though the classes have been officially renamed, most people still refer to them by their old names.

Information Premier Classe (☎086/000–8888 ⊕www.premierclasse.co.za). **Shosholoza Meyl** (☎086/000–8888 ⊕www.spoornet.co.za).

LUXURY TRAIN TRIPS

The luxurious and leisurely *Blue Train* has a couple of routes, but the main one runs from Cape Town to Tshwane (formally Pretoria). It departs once a week, takes two days, and costs around R15,000 one way during peak season, including meals and excursions. In addition to its regular run between Cape Town and Tshwane, the *Blue Train* does special packages to Durban from Tshwane (Pretoria) and can arrange chartered trips that include stays in luxury lodges. All meals and alcohol are included in the ticket price, which ranges from R17,750 for a double in low season between Cape Town and Tshwane to R30,400 for a deluxe double in high season, one way.

The Rovos Rail *Pride of Africa* runs from Cape Town to Tshwane every Monday and costs R12,195 for the two-day trip in a deluxe suite, up to R16,000 for a royal suite, including excursions, meals, and drinks. There are also biweekly overnight trips that are run between Cape Town and George. Every May a seven-day trip from Cape Town to Swakopmund (and back) is run, and in July there is a 14-day epic from Cape Town to Dar es Salaam (and, of course, back again). Prices per person sharing range from R8,160 for a deluxe suite on the Cape Town–Tshwanee run to nearly R70,000 for the Royal Suite on the six-night, seven-day trip from Cape Town to Victoria Falls. The single-occupancy supplement is 50%.

Contacts Blue Train (☎011/773–7631 ⊕www.bluetrain.co.za). **Rovos Rail** (☎012/323–6052 ⊕www.rovos.co.za).

SPECIALTY TRAIN TRIPS

A really fun way to see the country is on the Shongololo Express—a devilishly clever idea. The train is pretty basic, much like the Shosholoza Meyl trains. While you sleep at night, it heads off to a new destination. After breakfast, tour buses are loaded, and you head off to explore the surroundings. In the evening, you climb back on the train, have supper, and sleep while you head off to the next fun destination. Trips include The Dune Adventure (seeing the dunes of Namibia), The Good Hope Adventure (seeing Cape attractions), and The Southern Cross Adventure (exploring six African countries). Rates start at about R1,000 per person per night sharing. By the way, a *shongololo* is a millipede.

Contacts Shongololo Express (☎011/781–4616 ⊕www.shongololo.com).

ON THE GROUND

■ BUSINESS SERVICES & FACILITIES

If you need an office on the fly, you can, of course, use your hotel's business center. PostNet South Africa is the country's version of Kinko's, offering a range of business solutions with branches countrywide.

Contacts PostNet South Africa
(☎860/767–8638 ⊕www.postnet.co.za).

■ COMMUNICATIONS

INTERNET

Unless you have business in South Africa, leave the laptop at home and take memory cards for your vacation photos. You can check e-mail for a few rand either in the comfort of your hotel or at a public Internet café.

If you do bring your computer, you will have no problem getting service in the cities. In the smaller towns you will usually find a computer store, but it's unlikely you'll find anyone to service a Mac. It's worth bringing a long phone cord, as some hotels have only one phone jack—right next to the bed. Many Internet cafés allow you to just plug into their phone line or, in some cases, their network. Back up all your data before leaving home.

Contacts Cybercafes (⊕www.cybercafes. com) lists over 4,000 Internet cafés worldwide.

PHONES

There are toll-free numbers in South Africa. There is also something called a share-call line, for which the cost of the call is split between both parties.

The country code for South Africa is 27. When dialing from abroad, drop the initial 0 from local area codes.

CALLING WITHIN SOUTH AFRICA

Local calls are very cheap, although all calls from hotels attract a hefty premium. South Africa has two types of pay phones: coin-operated phones, which accept a variety of coins, and card-operated phones. Coin-operated phones are being phased out, and there aren't too many left in tourist destinations. Phone cards are the better option; they free you from the hassle of juggling handfuls of coins, and they're available in several denominations. In addition, a digital readout tells you how much credit remains while you're talking. Cards are available at newsstands, convenience stores, and telephone company offices. When making a phone call in South Africa, always use the full 10-digit number, including the area code, even if you're in the same area.

For directory assistance in South Africa, call 1023. For operator-assisted national long-distance calls, call 1025. For international operator assistance, dial 0903. These numbers are free if dialed from a Telkom (landline) phone but are charged at normal cell-phone rates from a mobile—and they're busy call centers. Directory inquiries numbers are different for each cell-phone network. Vodacom is 111, MTN is 200, and Cell C is 146. These calls are charged at normal rates, but the call is timed only from when it is actually answered. You can, for an extra fee, get the call connected by the operator.

CALLING OUTSIDE SOUTH AFRICA

When dialing out from South Africa, dial 09 before the international code. So, for example, you would dial 09/1 for the United States. Other country codes are 267 for Botswana, 264 for Namibia, 260 for Zambia, and 263 for Zimbabwe.

The country code for the United States is 1.

■TIP→ **If you really want to save on international phone calls, the best advice is to provide a detailed itinerary back home and agree upon a schedule for calls.** Even if they call your "free" cell phone, they'll be paying on the other end, so speak quickly or keep in touch via the Internet.

Access Codes AT&T Direct (☎0800/99–0123 from South Africa). **MCI WorldPhone** (☎0800/990–011 from South Africa). **Sprint International Access** (☎0800/990–001 from South Africa).

MOBILE PHONES

Cell phones are ubiquitous and have quite extensive coverage. There are three cell-phone service providers in South Africa—Cell C, MTN, and Vodacom—and you can buy these SIM cards, as well as air-time cards, in supermarkets. Cell phones can be rented by the day, week, or longer from the airport on your arrival, but this is an expensive option, too. If you plan on getting a cell phone while you're traveling, know that plans change frequently, so try to gather as many details before leaving to figure out which plan is right for you. Some allow free calls to your number, but charge rates close to landline calls if you call the United States. If you don't text message at home, you'll learn to in Africa, where a simple text message costs a fraction of the cost of making an actual call. This is a handy option for meeting up with friends, but for calling a hotel reservations line, it's best to make the call.

The least complicated way to make and receive phone calls is to obtain international roaming service from your cell-phone service provider before you leave home, but this can be expensive. ■TIP→ **Verizon and Sprint customers cannot use their phones in Africa.** Any phone that you take abroad must be unlocked by your company in order for you to be able to use it.

Contacts Cell C Rentals (☎021/934–1452 in Cape Town, 011/390–2922 in Johannesburg ⊕www.cellcrentals.co.za). **Cellular Abroad** (☎800/287–5072 ⊕www.cellularabroad. com) rents and sells GMS phones and sells SIM cards that work in many countries, but cost a lot more than local solutions. **Cellucity/ Vodashop** (☎021/934–0492 in Cape Town, 011/394–8834 in Johannesburg ⊕www.cellucity.co.za). **Mobal** (☎888/888–9162 ⊕www. mobalrental.com) rents mobiles and sells GSM phones (starting at $49) that will operate in 140 countries. Per-call rates vary throughout the world. **MTN** (☎119/912–3000 ⊕www. mtn.co.za). **Planet Fone** (☎888/988–4777 ⊕www.planetfone.com) rents cell phones, but the per-minute rates are expensive. **Vodacom** (☎082–111 from landline, 111 from mobile phone ⊕www.vodacom.co.za) is the country's leading cellular network.

■ CUSTOMS & DUTIES

Visitors may bring in new or used gifts and souvenirs up to a total value of R3,000 duty-free. For additional goods (new or used) up to a value of R12,000, a fee of 20% is levied. In addition, each person may bring up to 200 cigarettes, 20 cigars, 250 grams of tobacco, 2 liters of wine, 1 liter of other alcoholic beverages, 50 ml of perfume, and 250 ml of toilet water into South Africa or other Southern Africa Common Customs Union (SACU) countries (Botswana, Lesotho, Namibia, and Swaziland). The tobacco and alcohol allowance applies only to people 18 and over. If you enter a SACU country from or through another in the union, you are not liable for any duties. You will, however, need to complete a form listing items imported.

The United States is a signatory to CITES, a wildlife protection treaty, and therefore does not allow the importation of living or dead endangered animals, or their body parts, such as rhino horns or ivory. If you purchase an antique that is made partly or wholly of ivory, you must obtain a CITES pre-convention certificate that clearly states the item is at least 100 years old. The import of zebra skin or other tourist products also requires a CITES permit.

Information in South Africa **Southern Africa Customs Union** (⊕ www.dfa.gov.za/foreign/Multilateral/africa/sacu.htm).

U.S. Information **U.S. Customs and Border Protection** (⊕ www.cbp.gov). **U.S. Fish and Wildlife Service** (⊕ www.fws.gov).

∎ EATING OUT

South Africa's cities and towns are full of dining options, from chain restaurants like the popular Nando's to chic cafés. Indian food and Cape Malay dishes are regional favorites in Cape Town, while traditional smoked meats and sausages are available countrywide. Families can bring their kids anywhere, but don't expect toys and games as in American restaurants. Fortunately, restaurants open early for dinner, so you don't have to sacrifice fine dining because you've brought the kids.

The restaurants we list are the cream of the crop in each price category. Properties indicated by a ✕⚏ are lodging establishments whose restaurant warrants a special trip. Price categories are charted in each chapter and are based on the costs of main courses or a prix-fixe price, where there is no à la carte dining. If you really love seafood, you should make a point of visiting one of the very casual West Coast beach restaurants (⇨ Chapter 2), where you sit on the beach in a makeshift structure and eat course after course of seafood cooked on an open fire.

For information on food-related health issues, see Health below.

MEALS & MEALTIMES

In South Africa dinner is eaten at night and lunch at noon. Breakfast is still pretty much understood to consist of something eggy and hot, but many people are moving over to muesli and fruit. South Africans may eat muffins for breakfast but draw the line at doughnuts. Most restaurants serve breakfast until about 11:30,

but some pride themselves on serving breakfast all day.

If you are staying at a game lodge, your mealtimes will revolve around the game drives—usually coffee and rusks (similar to biscotti) early in the morning, more coffee and probably muffins on the first game drive, a huge brunch in the late morning, no lunch, tea and something sweet in the late afternoon before the evening game drive, cocktails and snacks on the drive, and a substantial supper, or dinner, about 8 or 8:30.

If you are particularly interested in food, plan your trip to include one or two of the guesthouses in the Good Cooks and Their Country Houses collection. All the establishments listed are owner managed and are noted for superior cuisine. In order for a guesthouse to qualify for inclusion, the chef must be the owner (or one of them).

Unless otherwise noted, the restaurants listed in this guide are open daily for lunch and dinner.

Contacts **Good Cooks and Their Country Houses** (⊕ www.goodcooks.co.za).

PAYING

Many restaurants accustomed to serving tourists accept credit cards, usually Visa and American Express.

For guidelines on tipping see Tipping below.

For restaurant price charts specific to each area, see the beginning of each chapter.

RESERVATIONS & DRESS

Regardless of where you are, it's a good idea to make a reservation if you can. We only mention them specifically when reservations are essential (there's no other way you'll ever get a table) or when they are not accepted. For popular restaurants, book as far ahead as you can (often 30 days), and reconfirm as soon as you arrive. (Large parties should always call ahead to check the reservations pol-

LOCAL DO'S AND TABOOS

GREETINGS

■ The first words you should say to anyone in South Africa, no matter the situation, is "Hello, how are you?" It doesn't matter if you are in a hurry, African conversations begin with a greeting. To skip this and jump to the question, as we do in the United States, is considered rude. Slow down and converse, then ask for what it is you need. After a few weeks you will get used to it and miss it when you return home to instant demands.

SIGHTSEEING

■ In general, it is odd throughout Africa, as in most places outside the United States, for a grown woman to wear shorts outside of a beach setting or safari park, and the same is true for visiting museums, houses of worship or peoples' private homes as a guest. Grown men wear pants, children wear shorts, but exceptions can be found in national parks, and while engaging in outdoor activities. Beach-town rules are certainly flexible, and many people stroll into cafés right off the beach (wearing cover-ups, of course.)

■ If you're visiting a house of worship, dress modestly. This is especially true at mosques, where women should bring scarves to cover their heads out of courtesy, wear skirts below the knees, and cover their shoulders. In fact, many mosques post signs outside advising those who may visit, and some prefer non-Muslims to remain outside.

OUT ON THE TOWN

■ If you are invited to someone's home, it is—as almost anywhere—a good idea to bring a small gift. If you know your hosts' habits, you can bring a bottle of wine, chocolates, or flowers. If you have been invited to a very humble home—as can happen in rural areas—and your hosts are struggling to feed their children, they may prefer something a bit more pragmatic than a bunch of flowers. This is delicate territory so, when in doubt, ask a trustworthy, knowledgeable third party.

■ When out at a restaurant or a club, behave as you would at home. Be polite to waitstaff and do not call out.

DOING BUSINESS

■ Arrive on time for appointments, and hand over a business card during introductions. Handshakes are the proper form of greeting in a business setting. Gifts are not part of the business culture. Address colleagues by their titles and surnames.

■ It is not uncommon for business to be conducted over a meal. You may be inclined to rush proceedings along, and force decisions, but this is not the African way. Slow down and relax.

■ Unless you are involved in a creative field, men should wear a jacket and tie to meetings, but a suit is not necessary, unless it's a really high-powered meeting. Women can get away with anything from a pretty floral dress to a severe suit, but take your cue from the general purpose of the meeting and who is going to be there. Trousers are perfectly acceptable.

LANGUAGE

⚠ **While many Americans consider the term "coloured" offensive, it's widely used in South Africa to describe South Africans who are descended from imported slaves, the San, the Khoekhoen, and European settlers. Over the years the term has lost any pejorative connotations.**

■ South Africa has 11 official languages: Afrikaans, English, Ndebele, North Sotho, South Sotho, Swati, Tsonga, Tswana (same as Setswana in Botswana), Venda, Xhosa, and Zulu. English is widely spoken, although road signs and other important markers often alternate between English and Afrikaans. *For a list of local terms and definitions, see the glossaries in Understanding South Africa.*

icy.) We mention dress only when men are required to wear a jacket or a jacket and tie.

Most restaurants welcome casual dress, including jeans and sneakers, but draw the line at shorts and a halter top at dinner, except for restaurants on the beach. Very expensive restaurants and old-fashioned hotel restaurants (where colonial traditions die hard) may welcome nicer dress, but other than the *Blue Train*, few require a jacket and tie.

WINES, BEER & SPIRITS

South African wines are excellent, and you could easily spend days or even weeks wandering around the Winelands *(⇨ Chapter 2)*.

Other than a few small microbreweries, most South African beer is made by one company, previously called SA Breweries and now called SAB-Miller, after buying a major share in Miller. There is a good selection of imported beers in most drinking holes and restaurants, but the one you really should try is made just across the Orange River. Windhoek Lager is widely acknowledged to be the best beer brewed in southern Africa.

There are also a few interesting local liqueurs to try. Van der Hum is a citrus-flavored brandy-based liqueur that appeals to a slightly more mature palette than the ubiquitous, and very popular, Amarula, which is sweet and creamy. Buchenbos is not that easy to get hold of, but it's worth it. It's also brandy based and flavored with *rooibos* tea and *buchu* (a very aromatic and therapeutic wild herb). It's made in Clanwilliam *(⇨ Chapter 2)*. Buchu brandy is becoming very popular and is also not that easy to get hold of. The Mons Ruber Estate in De Rust *(⇨ Chapter 3)* makes a good one. A number of small manufacturers are making *mampoer*—basically moonshine—in flavors ranging from the sublime (peach, rooibos, honeybush, and marula) to the, well, different (chili).

You can buy beer and wine in supermarkets and many convenience stores. Most restaurants are licensed to sell wine and beer, and many also sell spirits. In theory, on Sunday you can buy alcohol only in restaurants, and only if you're eating, but that rule is slowly being whittled away in practice. You may not take alcohol onto beaches, and it is illegal to walk down the street openly sipping from a bottle. You can, however, drink with a picnic or enjoy sundowners (cocktails at sunset) in almost any public place, such as Table Mountain or Kirstenbosch. The beach rule may be somewhat relaxed at sundowner time.

▌ ELECTRICITY

The electrical current is 220 volts, 50 cycles alternating current (AC); wall outlets in most of the region take 15-amp plugs with three round prongs (the old British system), but some take the straight-edged three-prong plugs, also 15 amps.

If your appliances are dual-voltage, you'll need only an adapter. In remote areas (and even in some lodges) power may be solar or from a generator; this means that delivery is erratic both in voltage and supply. In even the remotest places, however, lodge staff will find a way to charge video and camera batteries, but you will receive little sympathy if you insist on using a hair dryer or electric razor.

Consider making a small investment in a universal adapter, which has several types of plugs in one lightweight, compact unit. Most laptops and mobile phone chargers are dual voltage (i.e., they operate equally well on 110 and 220 volts), so require only an adapter. These days the same is true of small appliances such as hair dryers. Always check labels and manufacturer instructions to be sure. Don't use 110-volt outlets marked FOR SHAVERS ONLY for high-wattage appliances such as hair dryers.

Contacts Steve Kropla's Help for World Traveler's (⊕www.kropla.com) has information on electrical and telephone plugs around the world. **Walkabout Travel Gear** (⊕www.walkabouttravelgear.com) has a good coverage of electricity under "adapters."

▌ EMERGENCIES

If you specifically need an ambulance, you can get one by calling the special ambulance number or through the general emergency number. Europ Assistance offers professional evacuation in the event of emergency. If you intend to dive in South Africa, make sure you have DAN membership, which will be honored by Divers Alert Network South Africa (DANSA).

United States Embassies U.S. Embassy (✉877 Pretorius St., Arcadia, Tshwane ☎021/431–4000). **U.S. Consulate, Cape Town** (✉2 Reddam Ave., Westlake, Cape Town ☎021/702–7300 ⊕http://pretoria.usembassy.gov).

General Emergency Contacts Ambulance (☎10177). **DANSA** (☎0800/020–111 or 011/254–1112 ⊕www.dansa.org). **Europ Assistance** (☎0860/635–635 ⊕www.europassistance.co.za). **General emergency** (☎10111 from landline, 112 from mobile phone). **Police** (☎10111).

▌ HEALTH

The most serious health problem facing travelers is malaria, which occurs in the prime South African game-viewing areas of Mpumalanga, Limpopo Province, and northern KwaZulu-Natal and in the countries farther north. The risk is medium at the height of the summer and very low in winter. All travelers heading into malaria-endemic regions should consult a health-care professional at least one month before departure for advice. Unfortunately, the malarial agent *Plasmodium sp.* seems to be able to develop a hardy resistance to new prophylactic drugs pretty quickly, so even if you are taking the newest miracle drug, the best prevention is to avoid being bitten by mosquitoes in the first place. After sunset wear light-colored, loose, long-sleeve shirts; long pants; and shoes and socks; and apply mosquito repellent generously. Always sleep in a mosquito-proof room or tent, and if possible, keep a fan going in your room. If you are pregnant or trying to conceive, avoid malaria areas if at all possible.

Generally speaking, the risk is much lower in the dry season (May–October) and peaks immediately after the first rains, which should be in November, but *El Niño* has made that a lot less predictable.

Many lakes and streams, particularly east of the watershed divide (i.e., in rivers flowing toward the Indian Ocean), are infected with *bilharzia* (schistosomiasis), a parasite carried by a small freshwater snail. The microscopic fluke enters through the skin of swimmers or waders, attaches itself to the intestines or bladder, and lays eggs. Avoid wading in still waters or in areas close to reeds. If you have been wading or swimming in doubtful water, dry yourself off vigorously with a towel immediately upon exiting the water, as this may help to dislodge any flukes before they can burrow into your skin. Fast-moving water is considered safe. If you have been exposed, pop into a pharmacy and purchase a course of treatment and take it to be safe. If your trip is ending shortly after your exposure, take the medicine home and have a checkup once you get home. Bilharzia is easily diagnosed, and it's also easily treated in the early stages.

On hot days and days when you are on the move, especially after long flights, try to drink a few liters of water. If you're prone to low-blood sugar or have a sensitive stomach, consider bringing along rehydration salts, available at camping stores, to balance your body's fluids and keep you going when you feel listless. Alcohol is dehydrating, so try to limit consumption on hot or long travel days.

These days everyone is sun sensitive, so pack plenty of your favorite SPF product from home, and use it generously.

In South Africa, as everywhere else in the world, you need to be aware of the possibility of becoming infected with HIV (which is a big problem in Africa) or hepatitis. Make sure you use a good condom during a sexual encounter; they're for sale in supermarkets, pharmacies, and most convenience stores. If you have a favorite brand, bring your own supplies. If you feel there is a possibility you have become infected, you can get antiretroviral treatment from private hospitals. Check that your insurance covers this.

Rabies is extremely rare in domesticated animals in South Africa, but is more common in wild animals—one more reason you should not feed or tease wild animals. If you are bitten by a monkey or other wild animal, seek medical attention immediately. The chance of contracting rabies is extremely small, but the consequences are so horrible that you really don't want to gamble on this one.

As a foreigner, you will be expected to pay in full for any medical services, so check your existing health plan to see whether you're covered while abroad,

and supplement it if necessary. South African doctors are generally excellent. The equipment and training in private clinics rivals the best in the world, but public hospitals tend to suffer from overcrowding and underfunding.

On returning home, if you experience any unusual symptoms, including fever, painful eyes, backache, diarrhea, severe headache, general lassitude, or blood in urine or stool, be sure to tell your doctor where you have been. These symptoms may indicate malaria, tick-bite fever, bilharzia, or—if you've been traveling north of South Africa's borders—some other tropical malady.

The drinking water in South Africa is treated and, except in rural areas (⇨ Safari Primer), is absolutely safe to drink. Many people filter it, though, to get rid of the chlorine, as that aseptic status does not come free. You can eat fresh fruits and salads and have ice in your drinks.

■**TIP→ If on safari or camping, check your boots and shake your clothes out for spiders and other crawlies before getting dressed.**

In summer ticks may be a problem, even in open areas close to cities. If you intend to walk or hike anywhere, use a suitable insect repellent. After your walk examine your body and clothes for ticks, looking carefully for pepper ticks, which are tiny but may cause tick-bite fever. If you find a tick has bitten you, do not pull it off. If you do, you may pull the body off, and the head will remain embedded in your skin, causing an infection. Rather, smother the area with petroleum jelly, and the tick will eventually let go, as it will be unable to breathe; you can then scrape it off with a fingernail. If you are bitten, keep an eye on the bite. If the tick was infected, the bite will swell, itch, and develop a black necrotic center. This is a sure sign that you will develop tick-bite fever, which usually hits after about 8–12 days. Symptoms may be mild or severe, depending on the patient. This disease is not usually life-threatening in healthy adults, but it is horribly unpleasant. Most people who are bitten by ticks suffer no more than an itchy bump, so don't panic.

Also, obviously, keep a lookout for mosquitoes. Even in nonmalarial areas they are extremely irritating. When walking anywhere in the bush, keep a lookout for snakes. Most will slither away when they feel you coming, but just keep your eyes peeled. If you see one, give it a wide berth and you should be fine. Snakes really bite only when they are taken by surprise, so you don't want to step on a napping adder.

For information on travel insurance, shots and medications, and medical-assistance companies see Shots & Medications under Things to Consider in Before You Go, above.

OVER-THE-COUNTER REMEDIES

You can buy over-the-counter medication in pharmacies and supermarkets, and you will find the more general remedies in Clicks, a chain store selling beauty products, some OTC medication, and housewares. Your body may not react the same way to the South African version of a product, even something as simple as a headache tablet, so bring your own supply for your trip and rely on pharmacies just for emergency medication.

▌ HOURS OF OPERATION

The most surprising aspect of South Africa's business hours, especially for tourists who come to shop, is that shopping centers, including enclosed secure indoor malls, all close by 6 in the evening. It is rare for a store to remain open after dinner, just when you are ready to shop! (But cafés in malls stay open late).

Business hours in major South African cities are weekdays from about 9 to 5. Most banks close in midafternoon, usually about 3:30, but dedicated currency exchange offices usually stay open longer.

In addition, post offices and banks are open briefly on Saturday mornings from about 9, so get there early. In rural areas and small towns things are less rigid. Post offices often close for lunch, and, in very small towns and villages banks may have very abbreviated hours.

Most museums are open during usual business hours, including Saturday mornings, but some stay open longer.

Most pharmacies close about 6, but there is generally an all-night pharmacy in towns of a reasonable size. If not, look for an emergency number posted on a pharmacy.

Almost all gas stations are open 24 hours and urban gas stations have 24-hour convenience stores, some of which have an impressive range of goods.

HOLIDAYS

National holidays in South Africa are New Year's Day (January 1), Human Rights Day (March 21), Good Friday, Easter, Family Day (sometime in March or April), Freedom Day (April 27), Workers Day (May 1), Youth Day (June 16), National Women's Day (August 9), Heritage Day (September 24), Day of Reconciliation (December 16), Christmas Day (December 25), and Day of Goodwill (December 26). If a public holiday falls on a Sunday, the following Monday is also a public holiday. Election days are also public holidays, so check calendars closer to your time of travel for those, which are not on fixed dates.

In Cape Town, January 2 is also a holiday, known as *tweede nuwe jaar* (second new year). School vacations vary with the provinces, but usually comprise about 10 days over Easter, about three weeks around June or July, and then the big summer vacation from about December 10 to January 10.

MAIL

The mail service in South Africa is reasonably reliable, but mail can take weeks to arrive, and money and other valuables may be stolen from letters and packages. You can buy stamps at post offices, open weekdays 8:30–4:30 and Saturday 8–noon. Stamps for local use only, marked STANDARDISED POST, may be purchased from newsstands in booklets of 10 stamps. PostNet franchises—a combined post office, courier service, business services center, and Internet café—are in convenient places like shopping malls and are open longer hours than post offices.

All overseas mail costs the same. A postcard is about R3.50, and a letter ranges from R4 to about R15, depending on size and weight.

SHIPPING PACKAGES

If you make a purchase, try your best to take it home on the plane with you, even if it means packing your travel clothes and items into a box and shipping those to your home, or buying a cheap piece of luggage and paying the excess weight fees. If you buy something from a store accustomed to foreign visitors, they will likely already have a system for getting your items to you, often in a surprising few weeks' time.

Federal Express and DHL offer more reliable service than regular mail, as do the new Fast Mail and Speed Courier services, yet even these "overnight" services are subject to delays. PostNet also offers courier services. A parcel of up to about a pound (half a kilogram) will cost between R300 and R750 to send to the United States, and a 1-kilogram parcel (2.2 pounds) will cost anything from R550 to just over R1,000.

Express Services DHL (☎0860/345–000 ⊕www.dhl.co.za). **FedEx** (☎021/951–6660, 080/953–9599 toll-free in South Africa ⊕www.fedex.com). **PostNet** (⊕www.postnet.co.za).

MONEY

Because of inflation and currency fluctuations, it's difficult to give exact exchange rates. It's safe to say, though, that the region is a good value, with high quality accommodations and food at about two-thirds or half the cost they would be at home.

A bottle of good South African wine costs about $6 (double or triple in a restaurant), and a meal at a prestigious restaurant won't set you back more than $40 per person; an average restaurant, with wine, might be about $30 for two. Double rooms in the country's finest hotels may cost $300 a night, but $130 is more than enough to secure high-quality lodging in most cities, and charming, spotless B & B's or guesthouse with full breakfasts can be under $60 in many areas.

Not everything in South Africa is cheap. Expect to pay international rates and more to stay in one of the exclusive private game lodges in Mpumalanga, Limpopo Province, or KwaZulu-Natal—with a fly-in charter figured into the price, expect to pay between $1,500 and $2,000 per couple per night. Flights to South Africa are extremely expensive, but the rash of new low-cost carriers makes popular routes less expensive, with most trips under $100. Taxis are uncharacteristically expensive, compared to other vacation needs.

ITEM	AVERAGE COST
Cup of coffee	$1
Glass of beer	$1.50–$2
Quarter roasted chicken with salad and drink at a fast-food restaurant	$5–$7
Room-service sandwich in a hotel	$5–$7
2-km (1-mi) taxi ride	$6–$8

Prices throughout this guide are given for adults. Substantially reduced fees are almost always available for children, students, and senior citizens.

■**TIP→** Banks never have every foreign currency on hand, and it may take as long as a week to order. If you're planning to exchange funds before leaving home, don't wait till the last minute.

ATMS & BANKS
South Africa has a modern banking system, with branches throughout the country and ubiquitous ATMs, especially at tourist attractions, in gas stations, and in shopping malls. Banks open at 9 in the morning weekdays and close at 3:30 in the afternoon; on Saturday they close at 11 in the morning, and they are closed Sunday. Many banks can perform foreign-exchange services or international electronic transfers. The major South African banks are: ABSA, First National Bank, Nedbank, and Standard.

It is wise to bring two ATM cards for different accounts with you whenever traveling abroad, both in case one is stolen or "eaten" by a machine, and to give yourself an option in case a machine takes only one or the other type. Most ATMs accept Cirrus, Plus, Maestro, Visa Electron, and Visa and MasterCard.

The best place to withdraw cash is at an indoor ATM, preferably one guarded by a security officer. If you're unsure where to find a safe ATM, ask a merchant. Most machines will not let you withdraw more than the equivalent of about $150 at a time. If anyone approaches you while you're using an ATM, immediately press cancel.

CREDIT CARDS
Throughout this guide, the following abbreviations are used: **AE**, American Express; **DC**, Diners Club; **MC**, MasterCard; and **V**, Visa.

It's a good idea to inform your credit-card company before you travel, especially if you're going abroad and don't travel internationally very often. Otherwise, the credit-card company might put a hold on your card owing to unusual activity—not a good thing halfway through your trip. Record all your credit-card numbers—as well as the phone numbers to call if your cards are lost or stolen—in a safe place, so you're prepared should something go wrong. MasterCard, Visa, and American Express all have general numbers you can call collect if you're abroad.

If you plan to use your credit card for cash advances, you'll need to apply for a PIN at least two weeks before your trip. Although it's usually cheaper (and safer) to use a credit card abroad for large purchases (so you can cancel payments or be reimbursed if there's a problem), note that some credit-card companies *and* the banks that issue them add substantial percentages to all foreign transactions, whether they're in a foreign currency or not. Check on these fees before leaving home, so there won't be any surprises when you get the bill.

■**TIP→** Before you charge something, ask the merchant whether or not he or she plans to do a dynamic currency conversion (DCC). In such a transaction the credit-card *processor* (shop, restaurant, or hotel, not Visa or MasterCard) converts the currency and charges you in dollars. In most cases you'll pay the merchant a 3% fee for this service in addition to any credit-card company and issuing-bank foreign-transaction surcharges.

Dynamic currency conversion programs are becoming increasingly widespread. Merchants who participate in them are supposed to ask whether you want to be charged in dollars or the local currency, but they don't always do so. And even if they do offer you a choice, they may well avoid mentioning the additional surcharges. The good news is that you *do* have a choice. And if this practice really gets your goat, you can avoid it entirely

WORST-CASE SCENARIO

All your money and credit cards have just been stolen. In these days of real-time transactions, this isn't a predicament that should destroy your vacation. First, report the theft of the credit cards. Then get any traveler's checks you were carrying replaced. This can usually be done almost immediately, provided that you kept a record of the serial numbers separate from the checks themselves. If you bank at a large international bank like Citibank or HSBC, go to the closest branch; if you know your account number, chances are you can get a new ATM card and withdraw money right away. **Western Union** (☎ 800/325–6000 ⊕ www.westernunion. com) sends money almost anywhere. Have someone back home order a transfer online, over the phone, or at one of the company's offices, which is the cheapest option. The U.S. State Department's **Overseas Citizens Services** (☎ 202/501–4444 ⊕ www.travel.state.gov/travel) can wire money to any U.S. consulate or embassy abroad for a fee of $30. Just have someone back home wire money or send a money order or cashier's check to the State Department, which will then disburse the funds as soon as the next working day after it receives them.

thanks to American Express; with its cards, DCC simply isn't an option.

MasterCard, Visa, and American Express are accepted almost everywhere, whereas Diners Club is not quite as widely accepted. Discover is not recognized.

Reporting Lost Cards American Express (☎800/528–4800 in the U.S. or 336/393–1111 collect from abroad ⊕www.american-express.com). **Diners Club** (☎800/234–6377 in the U.S. or 303/799–1504 collect from abroad ⊕www.dinersclub.com). **MasterCard** (☎800/627–8372 in the U.S. or 636/722–7111 collect from abroad ⊕www.mastercard. com). **Visa** (☎800/847–2911 in the U.S. or

410/581–9994 collect from abroad ⊕www.visa.com).

CURRENCY & EXCHANGE

The unit of currency in South Africa is the rand (R), with 100 cents (¢) equaling R1. Bills come in R10, R20, R50, R100, and R200 denominations, which are differentiated by color. Coins are minted in R5, R2, R1, 50¢, 20¢, 10¢, 5¢, 2¢, and 1¢ denominations.

At press time, the rand was trading at about R7 to $1, a dramatic change from the days of R14 to $1, when South Africa was truly a bargain. It is still relatively inexpensive given the quality of lodgings, which cost probably two-thirds the price of comparable facilities in the United States.

To avoid administrative hassles, keep all foreign-exchange receipts until you leave the region, as you may need them as proof when changing any unspent local currency back into your own currency. You may not take more than R5,000 in cash out of South Africa. For more information you can contact the South African Reserve Bank.

■ TIP➜ Even if a currency-exchange booth has a sign promising no commission, rest assured that there's some kind of huge, hidden fee. (Oh … that's right. The sign didn't say no *fee*.) And as for rates, you're almost always better off getting foreign currency at an ATM or exchanging money at a bank.

Currency Information South African Reserve Bank (☎012/313–3911 ⊕www. reservebank.co.za).

TRAVELER'S CHECKS & CARDS

Some consider this the currency of the cave man, and it's true that fewer establishments accept traveler's checks these days. Nevertheless, they're a cheap and secure way to carry extra emergency money, particularly on trips to urban areas. Only bring American Express traveler's checks if coming from the United States, as Amex is well known and widely accepted; you can also avoid hefty surcharges by cashing Amex checks at Amex offices. Whatever you do, keep track of all the serial numbers in case the checks are lost or stolen.

Traveler's checks in either rand or other major denominations (U.S. dollars, euros, and sterling) are readily accepted by most lodgings, though most people use credit cards.

American Express now offers a stored-value card called a Travelers Cheque Card, which you can use wherever American Express credit cards are accepted, including ATMs. The card can carry a minimum of $300 and a maximum of $2,700, and it's a very safe way to carry your funds. Although you can get replacement funds in 24 hours if your card is lost or stolen, it doesn't really strike us as a very good deal. In addition to a high initial cost ($14.95 to set up the card, plus $5 each time you "reload"), you still have to pay a 2% fee for each purchase in a foreign currency (similar to that of any credit card). Further, each time you use the card in an ATM you pay a transaction fee of $2.50 on top of the 2% transaction fee for the conversion—add it all up and it can be considerably more than you would pay when simply using your own ATM card. Regular traveler's checks are just as secure and cost less.

Contacts American Express (☎888/412–6945 in the U.S., 801/945–9450 collect outside of the U.S. to add value or speak to customer service ⊕www.americanexpress.com).

▌RESTROOMS

All fuel complexes on the major roads have large, clean, well-maintained restrooms. In cities you can find restrooms in shopping malls, at some gas stations, and in restaurants—most of which are quite happy to allow you to use them.

Find a Loo The Bathroom Diaries (⊕www. thebathroomdiaries.com) is flush with unsanitized info on restrooms the world over—each one located, reviewed, and rated.

▌SAFETY

South Africa is a country in transition, and as a result experiences growing pains that reveal themselves in economic inequities, which result in high crime rates. While the majority of visitors experience a crime-free trip to South Africa, it is essential to practice vigilance and extreme care.

Crime is a major problem in the whole region, particularly in large cities, and all visitors should take precautions to protect themselves. Do not walk alone at night, and exercise caution even during the day. Avoid wearing jewelry (even costume jewelry), don't invite attention by wearing an expensive camera around your neck, and don't flash a large wad of cash. If you are toting a handbag, wear the strap across your body; even better, wear a money belt, preferably hidden from view under your clothing. When sitting at airports or at restaurants, especially outdoor cafés, make sure to keep your bag on your lap or between your legs—otherwise it may just quietly "walk off" when you're not looking. Even better, loop the strap around your leg, or clip the strap around the table or chair.

Carjacking is another problem, with armed bandits often forcing drivers out of their vehicles at traffic lights, in driveways, or during a fake accident. Always drive with your windows closed and doors locked, don't stop for hitchhikers, and park in well-lighted places. At traffic lights, leave enough space between you and the vehicle in front so you can pull into another lane if necessary. In the unlikely event you are carjacked, don't argue, and don't look at the carjacker's face. Just get out of the car, or ask to be let out of the car. Do not try to keep any of your belongings—they are all replaceable, even that laptop with all that data on it. If you are not given the opportunity to leave the car, try to stay calm, ostentatiously look away from the hijackers so they can be sure you can't identify them, and follow all instructions. Ask again, calmly, to be let out of the car.

Many places that are unsafe in South Africa will not bear obvious signs of danger. Make sure you know exactly where you're going. Purchase a good map and obtain comprehensive directions from your hotel, rental-car agent, or a trusted local. Taking the wrong exit off a highway into a township could lead you straight to disaster. Many cities are ringed by "no-go" areas. Learn from your hotel or the locals which areas to avoid. If you sense you have taken a wrong turn, drive toward a public area, such as a gas station, or building with an armed guard, before attempting to correct your mistake, which could just compound the problem. When parking, do not leave anything visible in the car; stow it all in the trunk. As an added measure, leave the glove box open, to show there is nothing of value inside (take the rental agreement with you).

Before setting out on foot, ask a local, such as your hotel concierge, or a shopkeeper, which route to take and how far you can safely go. Walk with a purposeful stride so you look like you know where you're going, and duck into a shop or café if you need to check a map, speak on your mobile phone, or recheck the directions you've been given.

Lone women travelers need to be particularly vigilant about walking alone and locking their rooms. South Africa has one of the world's highest rates of rape. If you do attract someone who won't take a firm but polite *no* for an answer, appeal immediately to the hotel manager, bartender, or someone else who seems to be in charge. If you have to walk a short distance alone at night, such as from the hotel reception to your room in a dark motel compound, or back from a café along a main street,

have a plan, carry a whistle or know what you will do if you are grabbed.

CAPE TOWN

While overall crime has declined in recent years, certain areas that are perfectly safe during the day, such as the City Bowl's side streets, are no-go at night. Again, seek the advice of locals, take taxis directly to and from your destination, and don't walk alone or even in pairs unless a resident has told you that a neighborhood is safe. Despite thousands of safe visits every year, Table Mountain, which couldn't look less threatening, has been the location of several knife-point robberies in daylight. The point is, never be completely off guard.

DURBAN

The beachfront area and downtown are frequently the scene of muggings. It is inadvisable to stroll these areas with valuables, even during the day. Seek as much information as you can from your accommodations about where you can and cannot go safely, and ask for suggested driving or touring routes if you are exploring on your own and not as part of an organized tour.

JOHANNESBURG

■ TIP→ **It is inadvisable to drive yourself in and around the city, as certain areas are known carjacking spots.** The crimes are so prevalent that there are permanent street signs marking those areas that are most dangerous. Order a car service or transportation from your hotel for trips in and around the city if you are not traveling with a local.

Never, ever visit a township or squatter camp on your own. Unemployment is rife, and obviously affluent foreigners are easy pickings. If you wish to see a township, check with reputable companies, which run excellent tours and know which areas to avoid.

THE WINELANDS

The countryside is less intense, and crime is not as common, although groups of people tend to congregate at highway exits in the Winelands, seeking rides or panhandling. Nevertheless, always remain alert, and don't let a false sense of security lead you into behaving foolishly. Avoid wandering alone in deserted areas. Most hiking trails and tourist areas are reasonably safe, but crime can and does happen anywhere.

▌TAXES

All South African hotels pay a bed tax, which is included in quoted prices.

In South Africa the value-added tax (V.A.T.), currently 14%, is included in the price of most goods and services, including hotel accommodations and food. To get a V.A.T. refund, foreign visitors must present their receipts (minimum of R250) at the airport and be carrying any purchased items with them or in their luggage. You must fill out Form V.A.T. 255, available at the airport V.A.T. refund office. Whatever you buy, make sure that your receipt is an original tax invoice, containing the vendor's name and address, V.A.T. registration number, and the words *tax invoice*. Refunds are paid by check, which can be cashed immediately at an airport bank, or refunded directly onto your credit card, with a small transaction fee. Be sure you visit the V.A.T. refund desk in the departures hall before you go through check-in procedures, and try to organize your receipts as you go, to make for easy viewing. Officials will go through your receipts and randomly ask to view your purchases.

Airport taxes and fees are included in the price of your ticket.

Contacts V.A.T. Refund Office (☎011/394–1117 ⏛www.taxrefunds.co.za).

▌TIME

South Africa operates on SAST (South African Standard Time), which is two hours ahead of Universal Time (UT). That makes it seven hours ahead of North American eastern standard time (six hours ahead during eastern daylight saving time). South Africa does not follow any daylight saving time.

▌TIPPING

Tipping is an integral part of South African life, and it's expected that you'll tip for services that you might take for granted at home. Most notable among these is getting gas, as there are no self-service stations. If the attendant simply fills your tank, tip R2–R3; if he or she offers to clean your windshield, checks your tires, oil, or water, and is generally helpful, tip R4–R5. In restaurants the size of the tip should depend on the quality of service, but 10% is standard, unless, of course, a service charge has already been added to the bill. Give the same percentage to bartenders, taxi drivers, and tour guides.

Check with management regarding tips for room service and housekeeping. Different lodgings handle it differently. In game lodges, for example, it's handled through management (which can sometimes mean someone is passed over). If you have your laundry done, leave R5-R10 for the laundress in a special envelope. Informal parking attendants operate in the major cities in South Africa and even in some tourist areas. Although they often look a bit seedy, they do provide a good service, so tip them a couple of rand if your car is still in one piece when you return to it.

At the end of your stay at a private game lodge, you're expected to tip both the ranger and the tracker. Tipping guidelines vary from lodge to lodge, but plan to give the local equivalents of about US$10 per person per day to the ranger and not much less to the tracker; an additional tip of US$25 for the general staff would be sufficient for a couple staying two days. If someone has done something special for you—a safari ranger who went all out to show you the Big Five in one game drive, or arranged a special moonlight treat— you can certainly slip him or her more. Envelopes are provided in safari rooms and tents for tipping.

TIPPING GUIDELINES FOR SOUTH AFRICA	
Bartender	10% of your bill is common
Bellhop	R5 per item
Hotel Concierge	Hotel managers say it is not necessary to tip a concierge. If one goes out of his way for you, getting tickets to a sold-out event, say, then anything from R70–R175 would be appropriate
Hotel Doorman	R5, but it is not expected
Hotel Maid	Tips are not expected for maids in South Africa, as hotels add service charges to the bill that are distributed to the staff
Hotel Room-Service Waiter	R5 per delivery is nice, but not expected
Porter at Airport or Train Station	R5 per bag
Skycap at Airport	R5 per bag checked
Taxi Driver	10%, but round up the fare to the next dollar amount
Tour Guide	10% of the cost of the tour
Valet Parking Attendant	R5 when you get your car
Waiter	10%; nothing additional if a service charge is added to the bill
Car Guards	R2–R5

INDEX

ABOUT OUR WRITERS

Brian Berkman is regularly called a legend in his own lunchtime. Although his girth is the subject of gossip columns, it is proof of an unquenchable appetite that rolls from gluttony to gastronomy. When not eating and traveling for a living, Berkman runs a PR consultancy. He is a Cape Times newspaper restaurant critic and regularly contributes to GQ and other magazines on dining and luxury travel.

Sanja Cloete-Jones started life in the Kalahari Desert and has slept under the stars in most countries of southern, eastern, and northern Africa. Travel writing her way around Australasia, she completed guides to eight countries. She has now returned to the continent that remains her first love and lives in Zambia—the heart of Africa.

Karena du Plessis is the author of two travel books: *The Overberg—Inland from the Tip of Africa* and *The West Coast—Cederberg to Sea.* She freelances for various magazines and is passionate about food, wine, and travel; she hopes to pass on this enthusiasm to her young daughter, Sofia Elena. When she's not exploring (and covering the Western Cape and Cape Town chapters of this book), she lives in the fishing village of Kalk Bay, just outside Cape Town; works in her micro vineyard; and spends time with her two horses.

Debra A. Klein caught the Africa travel bug while on assignment for Conde Nast Traveler. A year later, she returned for a long-term assignment: as a volunteer in a Ugandan HIV/AIDS NGO. She's contributed travel news and features to many publications, among them, Newsweek and The New York Times.

In the line of duty, Cape Town-based travel writer, **Jennifer Stern** has dived pristine reefs, paddled beautiful rivers, walked with wildlife, and ridden mountain bikes, horses, camels, and elephants all over southern Africa's wilder parts. She has recently pledged to do her part to go green by consolidating almost all the material that has appeared in her popular books, *Southern Africa on a Budget* and *Guide to Adventure Travel in Southern Africa* into the innovative, activity-focused ⊕*www.acesafrica.com.*

Kate Turkington is one of South Africa's best-known journalists and broadcasters. Her live Sunday night radio show on Radio 702/Cape Talk, *Believe It or Not,* is the longest-running radio show in South Africa. She started traveling in World War II, when she was evacuated from London to the fens and marshes of East Anglia, a region of Eastern England, and has not stopped traveling since. Her travel beat covers the world, but her heart and home are in Africa where she lives in Johannesburg surrounded by a very large family. She's been held up by Ethiopian tribesmen armed with Kalashnikovs in the Rift Valley, ridden astride dolphins in Cuba's Caribbean, broken bread with Buddhist monks in Tibet's oldest monastery, white-water rafted down the Ganges, and sipped coffee surrounded by a million and a half migrating wildebeest in the Serengeti.

Tara Turkington is a journalist and researcher who lives in Johannesburg. She has worked as a newspaper designer and copy editor, reporter, schoolteacher, university lecturer, heritage manager, and tourism developer. As a freelance journalist, she has written and photographed for more than 20 publications, including the *Mail & Guardian, Sowetan Sunday World,* and *True Love.*